AF693504

In Yankee Doodle's Pocket

The Myth, Magic and Politics of Money in Early America

Will Nipper

Bowmanstone Press

Copyright Notice

Copyright © 2003, 2004, 2005, 2006, 2007, 2008 William U. (Will) Nipper
All Rights Reserved

No part of this document, including text, photographs, tables, drawings and illustrations used herein, may be reproduced, stored in a retrieval system or transmitted in any form or by any means, digital, electronic, mechanical, photocopying, recording, or otherwise, (beyond that which is permitted by Sections 107 and 108 of the U.S. Copyright Law and except for reviewers for the public press,) without the prior written permission of the author.

William U. (Will) Nipper

SAN	856-1613
ISBN10	0-9816638-0-X
ISBN13	978-0-9816638-0-7

Published by:
Bowmanstone Press, LLC
1040 Autumnwood Drive
Conway, Arkansas 72034 USA

Printed in Canada by:
Friesens Corporation

Disclaimers

This book should not be used in any way to determine the value of coins, tokens, paper money or other artifacts. Neither the author nor the publisher assumes any responsibility, financial or otherwise, for consequences arising from the buying or selling of such pieces based on information in this publication. Some of the ideas expressed herein are the subjective opinions of the author and should be taken as such. Where published facts or the opinions of others are presented, the author has made a good-faith attempt to correctly relate this information and to credit the source. In the event that either has been done in error, the author welcomes corrections and will acknowledge those who make them known.

Dedication:

For Debbie, the love of my life.

For Kelsey, Shelby, Abby and little Brinley, our children.

For Mike and Sharon Lynch, their children and grandchildren.

For Louis and Minnie Poposky, their children and grandchildren.

With greatest honor and appreciation for Ted and Alice Nipper, my parents.

Acknowledgements:

Dr. Mary Moseley, for editing and translating my work into English
(from my native boorish) and for challenging me,

Jim Lovette, Roger Siboni and Ray Williams for their advice and encouragement,

Tom Rinaldo for helping me build my collection and for being my friend,

Stan Stephens for sharing his expertise on St. Patrick's coppers,

Jay Dale and Dale Photography, for assistance with the tougher photographs,

Dr. Mark Leone, Dover Publishing, the Library of Congress and Northwestern University for allowing the use of selected images,

Sylvester Crosby, Eric Newman, Michael Hodder, Dr. Louis Jordan
and other great numismatic authors, for their inspiration

and

All my family and friends who endured the better part of
a decade of yammering about "my book."

Table of Contents

Preface i

Section I: The Landscape 1

1: Mercantilism to a Tea 3
2: E Pluribus...How Many? 19

Section II: Country Money and Paper Colonies 27

3: Of Beaver, Beads and Barley 29
Country Money and Trade Goods 29
A Barter Typology 34
Trade Silver 35
Shell Games 36
4: A Necessary Evil 43
In Value Equal to Money 43
From Rags to Riches? 51
A Continental Concern 58
The Public Matter of Private Money 70
Nearly Money and Hardly Money 74

Section III: The Incidentals (1550 to 1820) 77

5: Britannia's Realm 79
Regal, Commonwealth and Patent Coinages 82
Contemporary Counterfeits and the British Evasion 102
Island Coins and Tokens 110
Privately Issued Tokens 112
6: Spain and Her New World Colonies 117
The Earliest New World Coinage 117
The Age of Cobs 120
Pistareens and Other Domestic New Plate Coinage 124
Colonial Milled Coinage 126
7: The Chorus 131
The Netherlands 131
France 136
Portugal and Brazil 144
Tools of the Trade 146

Section IV: Early American Coins and Tokens (1616 to 1840) 149

8: Colonization (1616 to 1763) 153
A Rude Beginning: Sommer Islands Coinage (Ca. 1616) 157
Massachusetts Silver Coinage (1652 to 1682) 160
Maryland's Lord Baltimore Coinage (Ca. 1659) 175
St. Patrick or Mark Newby Coppers (Ca. 1667 to 1672) 177
American Plantations Tokens (1688) 201
Elephant Tokens (Ca. 1694) 202
French Issues Used in Louisiana and Canada (1640 to 1764) 206
Oddfellows: Miscellaneous Early Tokens (Ca. 1665 to 1715) 215
William Wood's Coinages (1722 to 1724, 1727 and 1733) 218
Value Me as You Please: Dr. Higley's Copper Threepence (1737 to 1739) 224
Hibernia Voce Populi Tokens (1760) 230

Table of Contents (Continued)

9: Conflict (1764 to 1781) 233
No Stamps! William Pitt Tokens (Ca. 1766 to 1768) 234
France's Parting Shots (1760-1767) 238
Virginia's Coinage (1773 to 1774) 239
New Hampshire and Massachusetts Patterns (1776) 242
Continental Currency Coins (1776) 245
Enigmatic Rhode Island Ship Tokens or Medals (Ca. 1779) 251
10: Confederation (1781 to 1789) 255
Constellatio Nova Patterns and Private Coppers (1783 to 1786) 260
John Chalmers' Token Coinage (1783) 267
Enigmatic Confederation Era Tokens (1783 to 1785) 270
New York's Home-Grown Coinages (Ca. 1786 to 1789) 273
Vermont Coinage (1785 to 1788) 296
Connecticut State Coinage (1785 to 1788) 305
New Jersey State Coinage (1786 to Ca. 1790) 318
Massachusetts' State Coinage (1787 to 1788) 333
Confederation Coins, Patterns and Mules (1785 to 1787) 339
Finally, Fugios (1787) 349
11: Constitution (1789 to 1840) 357
Token Kings and Would Be Kings 357
Standish Barry's Silver Threepence Tokens (1790?) 359
First In the Hearts...Washington Pieces (1791 to 1820) 361
American Trade and Other Imported Tokens (1787 to 1820) 374
European Jewels in American Settings (1796 to 1798) 380
Coins and Tokens of the American West (1818 to 1820) 384
Crude and Mysterious Blacksmith Coppers (Ca. 17?? to 18??) 386
The Next Generation of Private Coinage (1828 to 1840) 390
12: Coming of Age, The U. S. Mints (1792 to 1840) 407
The Small Beginning (1792) 407
Red Cents, Yellow Fever (1793 to 1808) 414
The Origin of Specie (1794 to 1808) 420
The Rise and Fall of John Reich (1807 to 1817...1836) 430
Christian Gobrecht and the Machine Age (1835 to 1840) 435
Retrospective 441

Appendices, Etc. *445*

A: Coin-Related Processes and Terms 447
B: Continental Currency Issues (1775 to 1780) 460
B.1. Emissions by Denomination and Nominal Issue Date 460
B.2. Devices and Mottoes on Continental Currency 461
C: English/British Coinages (1558 to 1830) 462
C.1. English Hammered & Early Milled Coinages (1558 to 1685) 462
C.2. English Milled Coinages (1685 to 1714) 463
C.3. English Milled Coinages (1714 to 1830) 464
C.4. British/Irish Halfpence and Farthings (1660 to 1807) 465
D: Spanish/Spanish Colonial Coinages (1528 to 1830) 466
E: Wood's Rosa Americana Coin Types (1722 to 1733) 468
F: Attribution Guide - Privately Issued Constellatio Nova Coppers 470
G: Attribution Guide - American-Made Imitation Halfpence 473
H: Attribution Guide – Vermont Coinage (1785-1788) 480
Index and Cross Reference 489
Works and Friends, Cited and Consulted 523
Endnotes 541

Preface

Yankee Doodle didn't really have a pocket, at least not the kind *we* know. He probably just kept a cloth or leather bag tied inside his coat. Just as we do with the paper dollars and copper-clad cents that we put in them, built-in pockets are another convenience third-millennium Americans take for granted.

It was not always so. As inevitable as America's success seems to have been, the fact remains that most of our early history was spent a false step from disaster. Though it happened very quickly by history's standards, transforming a motley collection of European outposts into a wealthy and powerful young nation was quite an ordeal.

The monies of pre-1840 America were both witnesses to this remarkable change and vital instruments of it. They tell of imperial and personal triumph – and folly. They celebrate our remarkable capacity for invention and adaptation. More importantly, they speak of the great American struggle between diversity and unanimity that was and remains a defining national principle. As we evolved from *pluribus* to something approaching *unum*, so did our money.

The surprising array of monies in early America also speaks to a fundamental problem of the age: the lack of a circulating currency on which all could agree. Barter, the official system of internal commerce during the colonial era, was inadequate as the basis for a burgeoning economy. Into this commercial gap coins and tokens flowed haphazardly from many sources, foreign and domestic, and had different values depending on the locales in which they were exchanged and the degree to which their worth was compromised by debasement or counterfeiting. Paper money helped, but the usefulness of a given issue was limited in duration and by geography. It too was the target of relentless counterfeiting. All in all, the American colonial economy was cumbersome, unstable and the subject of ratcheting exploitation by colonizing powers who saw Americans not as equal partners in the enterprise, but as commercial minions.

The American Revolution only made matters worse. Fear took coins out of circulation and unbacked paper currency lost its value as inflation and British sabotage outpaced public confidence. After the war the new country was bankrupt with no mint, no power to generate revenue and no real reason to believe its great political experiment actually could work. Yet, somehow, from this paradoxical combination of exuberance and malaise, came the embodiment of the Enlightenment in the U.S. Constitution and the Bill of Rights, arguably two of humanity's greatest achievements.

It all would have been for naught, however, had the new regime failed to address its economic crises. First, in 1791, building on Alexander Hamilton's landmark report on public credit and debt assumption, Congress established the Bank of the United States as the nation's fiscal agent. Always controversial, the bank was the subject of impassioned debate when its charter came up for renewal in 1811 and again in 1836, but its existence proved vital to managing debt, enabling the Louisiana Purchase and paying for the War of 1812. The year after Congress established the First Bank of the United States, it standardized the country's monetary system and gave long-awaited approval for a federal mint. With these two developments, Americans finally had the beginnings of both a stable currency and a cohesive fiscal policy.

About This Book

On a more basic level, the maturing of America and its economy is reflected in day-to-day instruments of commerce. In the beginning, these instruments came from fields, forests and oceans. By 1840 they came from urban factories born of the Industrial Revolution. The many different types of money associated with the transition are described in the four main sections of this book.

The first two sections are foundational. Section I lays groundwork by exploring the nature of early American commerce and its close association with concurrent political and social upheavals. Section II devotes a chapter to each of two fundamental building blocks of the early American economy: barter and paper currencies. The brevity of the paper money discussion herein should not be taken as an indication of its relative importance. Its proliferation and the dramatic expansion of our early economy are, at the same time, inseparable and distinctly American.

The three chapters in Section III address foreign coins, counterfeits and tokens that circulated incidentally in the colonies and early states. These pieces entered a surprisingly cosmopolitan America a few at a time through day-to-day commerce. It was only on occasion that coins officially were brought through deliberate, *en masse* importation. By the late eighteenth century, however, counterfeit coppers could be found in quantity on almost every arriving ship. It came to a head in 1789, when merchants simply stopped accepting all coppers, bringing commerce to a standstill and inciting panic. In sheer numbers, *incidentals,* a term used by Walter Breen, dominated all other coins and tokens. English and Spanish coins dating from the mid-sixteenth century are found at the earliest American archaeological sites. In time they were joined by the issues of many other trading countries. At the other end of the timeline some of these coins were legal tender in America until 1857, the eve of the U.S. Civil War.[*]

In five chapters, Section IV presents a chronology of the early coins and tokens that, unlike incidentals, are regarded as American. Most discussions of American numismatic history begin with the 1793 opening of the first U.S. Mint in Philadelphia. While that event signals the birth of a permanent national coinage, in many ways it obscures an older and richer numismatic heritage. By 1793 coins and tokens had played an important role in the economies of the American colonies and states for nearly two centuries. Yet, these ancestral coinages often are regarded as "on the fringe" by the numismatic mainstream.

Some of these American pieces were minted in what is now the United States. Others were minted elsewhere and then deliberately brought to America. Between 1616 and 1840, the most interesting coins in our entire history emanated from both private and public sources, some legal and some not. It is these American-labeled pieces, far more than incidentals, that U.S. collectors and scholars find most compelling. After all, they are our own. Privately

---

[*] Those unfamiliar with terms used to describe coins of the period may wish to read *Appendix A., Coin-Related Processes and Terms*, before beginning Section III.

issued tokens and legitimate issues of the U.S. Mint take us to 1840 and the beginning of America's Industrial Age. Afterward, American coinage changed from being hand made craft pieces to the uniformly monotonous products of modern industrial processes. The occasion of that change is a convenient and meaningful place to stop.

Over the years a number of excellent technical works have been written on the coinages in Section IV. Examples include Edward Maris's work on New Jersey coinage and Henry Miller's on Connecticut's. Others have taken a more comprehensive view. Within this genre some have updated, but none has ever surpassed Sylvester Crosby's 1875 masterpiece, *Early Coins of America*. It is unlikely that any will in the near future. Readers are encouraged to seek out at least a reprint of Crosby's work. Collectors and non-collectors alike also are encouraged to join the Colonial Coin Collectors Club (C4) and Early American Coppers (EAC.) Both provide treasure troves of valuable information and fellowship. Another rich source of information is the *Colonial Newsletter* (CNL,) a publication of the American Numismatic Society. For those interested in paper currency, Eric Newman's comprehensive *Paper Money of Early America* is a perfect complement to "Crosby."

Except as noted, all of the photographs of coins, tokens, paper money and other artifacts herein are of selections from my personal collection. The decision to use such pieces is intended to minimize complications arising from the use of images copyrighted by others. "Under construction" and the product of a limited budget, this assemblage is far from being a truly significant collection. In some cases modern copies of coins and paper money are used as illustrations. For many rare issues these are the specimens for which we average collectors must settle. (Note: All pictured coins and tokens are shown at 1.5 times actual size, except as noted. Where possible, images of paper currency approximate actual size.)

In other cases line drawings, or rather tracings with freehand enhancements, are used. The process for producing these images is tedious, with each averaging one to three hours to complete. Even with this apparent diligence, the limits of my artistic ability insure that accuracy is relative. The reader should be careful not to assume that true specimens match the illustrations at any level other than "in essence."

Many of the men responsible for early American coins were silversmiths or goldsmiths by trade. Where this is the case and the artisan's mark is known, it is depicted at the point of his introduction. The mark at left, for example, is associated with Robert Saunderson (or Sanderson,) of Massachusetts.

In Yankee Doodle's Pocket is intended to split the difference between numismatics and history. It even might be described as a "whodunit" or, more honestly, as a love story. It gives some technical information and even attribution guidelines for selected series. However, it contains no market prices, no condition census lists, no results of particle/ray bombardment tests and only passing mention of pedigrees, all of which receive disproportionate attention in modern numismatic literature. The space that such statistics would have occupied is instead filled with context. If I have succeeded, then neither hardcore historians nor serious numismatists are likely to be fully satisfied. No matter. *In Yankee Doodle's Pocket* was written for one purpose: To further appreciation of these objects, the people and events that they represent. I hope that it does and that you enjoy it.

– Will Nipper

Section I:
The Landscape

1: MERCANTILISM TO A TEA

Early Americans were separated widely by geography, history, language and a host of other barriers, but they shared one unifying concept: The inevitable human tendency to trade. Trade occurred spontaneously in the wilderness, at street front shops, in smoky taverns and on waterfront piers. It reached down to the Caribbean, across the Atlantic and all the way to the Orient. In time, England tried to control nearly every *official* aspect of American trade.

Even a king, however, cannot watch everyone, especially when his colonies are remote and immersed in a complex socio-political landscape. When the Pilgrims arrived in Massachusetts, for example, the Spanish already had occupied Florida for over half a century and the nearby West Indies for even longer. French Huguenots had attempted settlement in what are now the Carolinas. *Coureurs de bois* ("runners of the forest") were roaming France's wilderness empire and the Dutch would soon have a foothold in what is now New York, incorporating in 1655 a 1638 settlement of Swedes and Finns. It would not be long until African traditions and slave trade economics found their way to America. Then there were the Native American populations. Each group coveted things that the others possessed. Only law and lack of currency stood between these groups and trade. Both constraints proved weak deterrents, however, as colonists circumvented the former and adapted or invented the latter. These were early signs of American independence.

Yet, until the late eighteenth century, American independence meant the separation of the colonies from each other, not as a coherent group from Mother England. Little sense of connection existed in America, let alone nationalism. By themselves and in small rural settlements colonists were scattered up and down the eastern coast, joined only by rivers and primitive dirt roads. Even in 1790, when the first U.S. Census was conducted, nearly 95 percent of the population was rural. Only twenty-four American cities had more than 2,500 people and the great cities of today were nothing more than villages. Only five of them, New York, Boston, Philadelphia, Baltimore and Charleston, had populations of more than ten thousand.[1] With its centers of learning and culture and its handful of paved, lighted streets, Philadelphia was regarded as being somewhat comparable to the sophisticated small cities of Europe. The others were thought by the world to be no more than gathering places for commercial interchange if they were known at all. In contrast, London was a crowded old metropolis of 800,000, with centuries of accumulated learning, tradition and wealth. The gap between Europe and America was much more than a mere ocean.

This gap echoes in a recurring image from the colonial era that has Adam and Eve, or Cupid and Psyche, cavorting in a paradise that is America. Looking at these images, a home-country Brit must have felt both jealousy for the Americans' freedom and a sense of superiority over the colonial simpletons. Conversely, Americans reveled in the freedom that came from being an ocean away from their king, but tried hard to emulate the culture that they so admired.

This legacy of idyllic imagery and apparently primitive culture contributed to a long held, but overstated notion that the colonial and early state economies were simple, relying almost entirely on *barter* for day-to-day commerce. What *is* true is that, throughout the colonial period, British policy sought to constrain Americans to the production of raw materials, at the bottom of the profit pyramid. In theory a simple economy kept from the manufacturing of finished goods would have little need for hard currency. After all, colonists could barter among themselves for domestic goods and, for imported goods, American merchants could rely on credit accounts established with British wholesalers. The American merchants could ship raw materials to Britain where agents sold them and used the proceeds to pay creditors. Such were the ways of mercantilism, the alchemy that colonizing powers used for changing rude colonial exports into gold and silver.

Flawed Perfection

Mercantilism's ideal machine was an empire that controlled every aspect of the value chain. Such an empire needed colonies for two reasons: 1.) to provide the parent country with monopolistic access to important raw materials and 2.) to serve as a captive market for manufactured goods. For the machine to work, the empire also had to control the movement of goods among all of its parts. This meant controlling trade routes and vital territories, to the exclusion of all competing powers. Controlling trade routes and territories sometimes meant seizing them from others. It also meant defending them against insurgents. In other words, mercantilism was a breeding ground for war. Mercantilists had to be strong militarily, and to build armies and navies, they needed gold and silver.[2]

England's entry into mercantilism began in a small way when Elizabeth I commissioned privateers, such as Sir Francis Drake, to encroach on Spanish shipping. Drake followed in the footsteps of French pirates who already had discovered that raiding a treasure galleon was a faster path to wealth than a hard honest life at sea. But fast did not always mean easy. Raiding was a risky business for the English or anyone else. Throughout most of the sixteenth century, Spain used its New World holdings to build massive military capabilities. Her "gold fleet" and the world's finest infantry made King Philip II the most powerful monarch ever to have lived. When Drake's challenge became too great to ignore, Philip sent a huge armada to restore the sanctity of his trade routes.[*] By Divine Providence, or maybe just poor meteorology and navigational ineptitude, the armada fell to a sudden storm and Elizabeth's inherited navy.[†] In the blink of a sixteenth century eye, England was transformed into a mercantile power. From that moment until the end of the colonial period, the English, and later the British, constantly were embroiled in wars with competing European powers to build and preserve economic dominance at home, in North America and elsewhere.

Their military successes notwithstanding, the true genius, and ultimately the fatal flaw of the British when it came to America, was their aptitude for codifying mercantile principles as law. It began with the [Navigation] *Act of 1651,* a law that required that any goods from Africa, Asia or America that were intended for England, Ireland or English colonies be carried exclusively aboard English, Irish or colonial ships with predominantly English, Irish or colonial crews. Furthermore, goods from other parts of Europe could only enter England, Ireland or the colonies on ships from the country of origin of the imports. This was a direct economic attack on Dutch shipping, made necessary because the Dutch were hurting British

[*] Returning Drake's treasure actually was second on Philip's list of demands, behind not defending the Dutch (Chapter 7) and ahead of restoring Catholicism in England. Elizabeth's response was the sixteenth century equivalent of "When pigs fly."

[†] The Spanish armada included about 130 ships, 2,341 cannon and 2,200 sailors and soldiers. In truth, it was less than half as large and far less formidable than the French armada that Henry VIII had defeated a half-century earlier. It was Henry's navy that started the great Royal Navy tradition, but his daughter received the credit. Taylor (65.)

interests. They simply were better businessmen. Their merchants were particularly adept at managing money, allowing them to extend more liberal credit. Moreover, their goods were of higher quality than those of the English[3] and their ships and crews were more efficient. With the Navigation Act, the threat of Dutch competition was mitigated.

The Navigation Act of 1651 was a good start, but it had a loophole that needed to be closed to ensure success of the system. It did not prevent Americans from shipping their goods to powers other than England and using the proceeds to buy products of foreign manufacture. The loophole was closed by a second navigation act in 1660 that prevented all foreign ships from trading with English colonies. Colonial goods bound for Europe effectively had to be funneled through Britain. This further benefited British shipping and cleared the path for the piling on of taxes and duties.

The *Navigation Act of 1660* also established the principle of *enumeration* wherein specific colonial products, deemed strategically important to England, could be exported *only* to the British Isles. In the seventeenth century, enumerated colonial products included sugar, tobacco, cotton, indigo and dye woods. The fact that some non-strategic colonial products such as fish, hides and flour never were enumerated provided some leeway for colonial traders. However, in the century before the Revolution, the list of enumerated goods continually was updated to optimize the positions of British producers and traders in world markets. For colonists, updating the list generally meant closing windows of opportunity. In the early eighteenth century, rice, molasses, naval stores and furs were enumerated. In 1764, a year before American calls for independence reached audible levels, Lord Grenville enumerated more products than had been listed in all the years since 1660 combined.[4]

Even in the face of the 1660 legislation, colonists found ways to circumvent the system by shipping their goods to foreign ports. To stop the leak, the *Staple Act of 1663* provided the final major statutory component of the mercantile system. It prevented practically everything except wine from the Azores and Madeira from entering the American colonies without first being shipped to England, then taxed and re-shipped. Essentially, Americans could *only* do business with British merchants and their web of intermediaries. A century later, in a 1766 issue of *The London Magazine*, an anonymous Englishman commented that, "...The American is appareled [sic] from head to foot in our manufactures...he scarsely [sic] drinks, sits, moves, labours or recreates himself without contributing to the emolument of the mother country."[5] Only the desire to be competitive prevented British merchants from gouging their American counterparts into poverty and inciting rebellion. Otherwise, England had absolute control of prices and of the market in general. In just twelve years she had built the perfect mercantilistic machine.

This brand of colonial subjugation was business as usual for most world powers. For French and Spanish colonists in the New World, the parent-child hierarchy was upheld through monarchical absolutism. Anyone who thought otherwise was quickly, often cruelly dispatched. British citizens, however, were *supposed* to be treated differently. Even with a monarch, Britain used an ostensibly republican model of government that allowed civil rights not shared by Spaniards or Frenchmen. Bostonians and New Yorkers expected treatment under the law that was equivalent to that received by Londoners. Of course, there was a catch: Equals were never truly equal, economically, culturally or otherwise. In many ways, British colonists were treated no differently than their French and Spanish brethren under the acts of 1651, 1660 and 1663. Nevertheless, the true effects of these acts went largely unnoticed because they came at a time when English royal power was being reasserted after more than a decade of absence. That absence, when the English Commonwealth ruled in place of a king, gave Americans an inkling of what self-determination might be like.

Meanwhile, the parent-child gap widened as the system steadily came to favor Britains on the European side of the Atlantic. For example, the idea that Britain deliberately would supply her colonies with specie (gold and silver coins) for commerce was completely out of the question. British mercantilism's policies restricted even the incidental exportation of gold or silver to America. This one-way flow of specie afforded British merchants a distinct advantage over their American counterparts because other forms of payment available to colonists were discounted in value in trade with the mother country.

Even had the export restrictions been absent, however, it is questionable how much specie actually would have circulated among common folk. Gold and silver denominations represented significant sums to most Americans, more than typically was expended on a day-to-day basis. By various estimates an average American worker earned about two shillings sterling per day in 1765. Using this valuation, a Guinea,[*] the primary British gold coin of the period, represented more than ten days' wages for a typical colonist.[†]

Other factors made specie scarce in colonial circulation. As the colonies grew they needed capital to finance the expansion. This often came in the form of paper currency. The presence of paper money had the effect of driving specie out of circulation. All else being equal, colonists preferred to save any hard currency they could get for a rainy day. Repeated frontier skirmishes stimulated the hoarding of specie. Hoarding, in turn, resulted in further paper issues that only compounded the trend. The so-called "Gresham's Law" (Chapter 4) was in full effect. In essence, it states that "bad money" (i.e., that with lower intrinsic value) drives "good money" (i.e., specie) from circulation.

Paper money was only truly bad when the number of issues became excessive or its redemption was delayed or pre-empted. It was a form of credit, issued on the promise of future payments; and it flourished in the conspicuous absence of specie. Without it, economic expansion and infrastructure development could not have taken place in the colonies. Both Parliament and the colonial governments fell to the allure of deferring payments, but Americans embraced paper money and other forms of credit more enthusiastically. They had to. By 1760, annual exports of British goods reached £2 million. At the same time, British merchants carried £4 million in American debts on their books.[6] The British walked a tightrope between yielding enough commercial freedom to allow the Americans to repay their debts and jeopardizing the overall profitability of the system. Colonists often used next year's production as collateral, repeating the cycle and compounding the need for paper.

Coins were not a form of credit. Instead, they represented something closer to the modern concept of cash, supply of which seemed never to match demand. At times there were

[*] One gold Guinea had a value of twenty-one shillings sterling after 1717. Guineas were named for the area in Africa from which most British gold originated.

[†] Wages are the subject of many debates among experts. It is important to remember that colonies had their own local valuations for pounds, shillings and pence. Thus, when docents at Colonial Williamsburg speak of average workers earning 4s 6d per day, for example, it should be noted that Virginia shillings were valued differently than official sterling shillings and that valuations changed over time. For these reasons comparisons must take into account differences in time and location.

shortages and, at other times, illegitimate coins proliferated. While some circulating coins originated locally in America, most actually were foreign issues. Most were incidentals that came through daily commerce, as opposed to being deliberately imported *en masse*. A few deliberately were imported and have earned the label, "American." In sheer numbers, neither deliberate imports nor the varied mix of American domestic coinages ever approached the levels of the foreign incidentals in circulation. Deliberate importations were sporadic and the fledgling mints that sprang up in America before 1800 simply were incapable of producing the volumes of coins that were needed. The other major source of coins during the period of interest, the U.S. Mint, did not exist until 1793. Aside from Congress's pre-occupation with more pressing issues of national survival, few people in America, even in the late eighteenth century, possessed the materials and skills to run a mint.

Most of the specie that did circulate in America had a Spanish connection. Between 1492 and 1825, nearly 70 percent of world gold production came from Spain's New World colonies.[7] Likewise, Spanish colonies in Mexico, Bolivia and Peru produced and traded 85 percent of the world's silver between 1500 and 1800. The first major influx of New World silver came from the Potosí District of what is now Bolivia. Between 1500 and 1800 that region produced about a billion troy ounces of the shiny white metal. During the same period, another 1.5 billion troy ounces came from Mexico, most of it after 1700. In the eighteenth century, Mexico's production averaged nine million troy ounces per year. Peru's production consistently averaged more than three million troy ounces per year during the seventeenth and eighteenth centuries.[8] New World gold production between 1500 and 1650 was about 181 tons. As early as 1585, all this bullion already amounted to a quarter of total global revenue.[9]

The global shift in power and money that accompanied Spain's apparent good fortune was monumental. It would have been even more skewed had Spain exercised more self-control. True, the windfall flipped Spain's long-standing trade imbalance with Asia. But with so much money around, sixteenth century domestic prices rose by a factor of five times. Rather than buy the expensive goods produced by their countrymen, Spaniards bought cheaper imports. Unemployment became a problem even as governmental coffers overflowed.[10] As more and more specie was drained from Spain into Europe and the colonies, Spanish hunger for it grew and the whole cycle was repeated. In the end, the English, French, Dutch and would-be Americans benefited more from Spain's windfall than did Spain.

The changes also were seen on a more basic level. Throughout the Middle Ages, European gold and silver coins grew progressively thinner and less pure as continental mines were depleted. Those who had specie were reluctant to put it into circulation for fear that they would never see its return. The trend was reversed dramatically by the tons of treasure that the Spanish transported to Europe from the New World. The influx transformed the small, paper-thin, diluted disks that were in use throughout Europe into substantial coins relatively rich in precious metal content. The patriarch of this new family of heftier coins was the Spanish dollar[*] or eight *reales* (Chapter 6.) It very quickly became the world's standard and retained that status for nearly three centuries. The dollar's dominance began not long after the establishment of the *Casa de Moneda* ("House of Money" or mint) in Mexico City in 1535.

---

[*] The word "dollar" has origins in Bohemia, where in 1516 a large silver deposit was discovered at Joachimsthal. ("Thal" means "valley," as is "Neanderthal.") Joachimsthal is now the Czech Republic town, Jáchymov. Large silver coins produced in Joachimsthal were called "Joachimsthalers." Later, the term was shortened to "thaler" or "taler." Americans corrupted "taler" to "dollar."

The proximity of all this wealth to America posed something of a dilemma for the Crown. The British wanted gold and silver from trade, but discouraged Americans from doing business directly with Spanish colonists or with southern Europeans. Direct trade made British merchants vulnerable to competition.

Given the American propensity for sailing into restricted ports, particularly in the nearby West Indies, it was natural that Spanish dollars and their fractional parts became etched indelibly on the American psyche. In the end, American acceptance of the Spanish system was so complete that it ultimately was adopted as the core of the United States' own system. Even when coins were unavailable, American paper currencies often were denominated in "Spanish milled dollars." (See Chapter 6. "Milled" is used to describe machine-made coins.) Long after British control ended and the U.S. Mint began turning out its own silver dollars, the term "dollar" still meant a *Spanish* dollar to most Americans. Moreover, Spanish silver coins remained legal tender in America until 1857, just four years before the outbreak of the U.S. Civil War!

Spanish coins were not the only specie in the colonies. British export restrictions never were easy to enforce and sometimes temporarily were relaxed, particularly during periods of acute colonial shortages. The result was an intermittent trickle of British specie. Dutch and French colonists in North America brought their native currencies as well. Specie from Portugal, the German States, the Ottoman Empire and other countries also circulated in America, in varying quantities and locations.[*]

The British did not restrict importation of base metal[†] coins. British farthings and halfpence, especially counterfeits, streamed into the country, particularly in the Northern colonies. Privately issued British pieces also made a token appearance. They were supplemented by the base metal coins of Spain, France, Portugal, the Netherlands and other countries. In fact, the coins of virtually every country that carried on international trade could be found in colonial America.

An accurate estimate of the total number of foreign coins circulating in America before 1840 is difficult to ascertain. Based on the body of information about hoards and accumulations and on contemporary writings, it is clear that base metal coins circulated in far greater quantities than silver, even considering the South where specie from the West Indian markets was available more readily. Silver coins clearly dominated over gold ones.[‡] Substantiating this, the noted archaeologist Ivor Nöel Hume wrote in 1969 that he had never even seen a gold piece from an American archaeological site, though he had seen many silver coins.[11] Of course, it is far less likely that a gold coin would have been lost without a rigorous search.

---

[*] Official New York correspondences refer to Arabian gold coins that circulated at two dollars. "Arabian" probably is a reference to "Ottoman." (O'Callaghan, various.)

[†] The term "base metal" refers to non-precious metals. Usually this meant copper and copper alloys, such as brass or bronze. Nickel, while a common base metal today, actually was considered a precious metal during the colonial era.

[‡] Nevertheless, Americans owned some gold. For example, recall William Dawes, the young shoemaker who rode an alternate route to Paul Revere's in warning the Massachusetts countryside of the regulars' advance on Lexington. Dawes moved his family to Worcester to escape the British occupation. The British would not allow anyone to leave Boston with gold. Dawes made a habit of wearing cloth-covered buttons as he walked past the guards at the edge of town. Most people of the day wore uncovered brass buttons. Dawes would often feign drunkenness to fool the guards. He eventually befriended them and became the butt of their jokes about his buttons. When they stopped harassing him, he began smuggling out his gold coins by stuffing them under the cloth of his buttons. Langguth (231.)

However, the colonial economy was not about gold. When an American purchased goods from Britain, the preferred method of payment was sterling money or sterling funds.[*] Each foreign currency (and, for that matter, each colony's currency) had its equivalent value expressed in sterling money. Payments could be accomplished by actually shipping silver coins to England. Since shipping was risky and colonists rarely had silver to send, payment more often involved using a complex system of debits and credits wherein no coins actually changed hands.

None of this is to say that Americans were poor. In 1774 the per capita income for free colonists is estimated at about £13, compared to £11 in England and £6 in France.[12†] For most colonists, the chief methods of generating wealth were agriculture and the exploitation of natural resources. Many American products directly supported British industry, as was intended. Obtaining ships masts, for example, was problematic for England, her forests having been depleted long before. Load after load of timbers were shipped from America to support the British shipbuilding industry. Early on, the fur trade fuelled American prosperity. Later rice, indigo and tobacco became chief exports. Virginia, Maryland and the Carolinas, in particular, came to rely very heavily on tobacco.

Rice took hold in the lowlands of South Carolina in the 1690's when West African slaves brought the knowledge of how to grow it. Annual rice exports ballooned from 400 thousand pounds in 1700 to 43 *million* pounds in 1740. Indigo, grown to make a beautiful blue dye used in the English textile industry,[‡] spawned an elite plantation class as South Carolina's indigo exports grew from 63 thousand pounds to half a million pounds during the 1750's. Profits from rice and indigo made South Carolina planters the richest people in the thirteen colonies, placing them only one notch below sugar planters in the West Indies. Tobacco put Chesapeake planters one notch below South Carolina's on the socio-economic scale.[13] Ironically, cotton, which became so dominant in the nineteenth century South, was not grown commercially on a large scale until its economics were made favorable by Eli Whitney's 1793 invention of the mechanized gin and the depletion of land that otherwise would have been used for growing tobacco.

Loading hogsheads of tobacco for export. Source: Montgomery (50.)[14]

Whatever crop was fuelling the economy, the downside to all this was slavery. According to the 1790 census, the United States was home to about 694 thousand slaves, nearly 18 percent of the population. Over 42 percent of them lived in Virginia. Dependence on slavery and agriculture slowed industrialization and modernization in the South, making it a region very like many Third-World countries today, with a tiny ruling class, great numbers of people on subsistence incomes and a practically non-existent middle-class.

---

[*] The term "sterling" refers to a standard of fineness, usually 92.5 percent silver with 7.5 copper and other metals, that was established in medieval England. Most English silver coins adhered to this standard.

[†] Per capita income is another controversial topic. Since a great deal of commerce revolved around bartering of goods and services, most historical economists refrain from treating per capita income as an absolute. Nevertheless, these estimates can be regarded as indications of relative wealth.

[‡] Indigo also was used to dye paper that, in turn, was used to wrap cones of West Indian sugar. The bitter taste of of indigo helped repel ants and other insects.

In contrast, New England had no great cash cows. Growing seasons there simply were too short for the big money crops. As a result, New Englanders developed commercial acumen by selling to the West Indies a diverse set of minor exports that were unneeded in England. These exports included fish, beans, naval provisions and lumber, all of which supported the West Indian sugar plantations. Sadly, the slave trade also figured into New England's economic equation. West Indians paid New Englanders with bills of exchange (Chapter 4,) cut in London for their sugar. New Englanders also helped to cut England's trade deficit by sending fish, wheat and flour to southern Europe.

Ironically, New England's greatest source of profit was the shipping of goods for others. By the 1680's, about half the ships servicing the Caribbean came from New England. By 1700, Boston ranked third in the British Empire behind London and Bristol when it came to shipping. The complex skills required to support the industry generated even more jobs and better prepared New Englanders for industrialization than did the plantation farming of the South.[15]

Out of this, America managed to develop a modest merchant fleet. It actually was easier and cheaper, by half, to build ships in America than in Europe because of the availability of raw materials. When the eighteenth century began, Boston alone claimed no fewer than fifteen shipyards. Between 1674 and 1714, New England built about 1,200 ships, second only to London in the realm.[16]

Even in New England, however, a gap separated the haves and have-nots. Three in ten of 1770 Bostonians were without *any* real assets. One tenth owned 60 percent of the total wealth, while the remaining six-tenths of the population divided the remaining 40 percent of the wealth. Still, New England's relative diversity meant that more of its people shared a stake in the economic success of the region than in the South. In many ways, New England more closely fit the profile of commercial and industrial England than did the agricultural South. This similarity effectively put New Englanders into competition with the mother country, particularly when it came to fishing, transportation and shipbuilding.[17]

Reconstructed buildings at Massachusetts' Saugus Iron Works National Historic Site. Operating from 1646 until 1668, it was one of America's first industrial sites. A – The furnace. B - The forge, which houses water-driven 500-pound hammers. C – The rolling and slitting mill. (1991 photo by this author.)

The economies of the middle colonies, such as New York and Pennsylvania, were a blend of the commercial North and the agricultural South. Growing seasons were longer, but not by enough for tobacco, rice, indigo or, later, for cotton. Small farms did manage to produce exportable products, most notably wheat. Middle colonists were spared the burdens of slavery and harsh winters. They were assured good prices because they learned the principles of commerce from their neighbors to the north.

All the while an increasing stream of finished goods to America insured that the balance of trade favored Britain. Increasing numbers of colonists gained access to the credit system because of improvements in transportation and communications. By 1770 per capita colonial imports of British goods were 50 percent higher than in 1720. Total colonial imports more than doubled between 1747 and 1765, to £2 million. In the same period, British exports to America increased from about £700,000 to about £1.5 million[18] and, in 1772, British exports to America were essentially equivalent to what all British exports had been in 1704.[19]

Part of the growth in colonial imports is attributable to the relatively cheap prices of British goods. Prices for American products increased in the late eighteenth century, while prices for British goods remained stable. In the 1740's one hundred bushels of wheat could be sold and the proceeds used to buy 150 yards of British wool cloth. In the 1760's, the same amount of wheat bought 250 yards of cloth. Brits benefited more from reselling American goods at high prices than from trying to artificially shore up prices for their own manufactured goods in the highly competitive marketplace.[20] During the same time, dramatic increases in the British population, coupled with the migration of agricultural workers toward emerging industrial centers and increasing demands in Europe and the West Indies, gave the American breadbasket added importance in the marketplace. By 1760 Britain imported more grain than it exported.[21] These trends obviously benefited the colonies, as did transportation improvements that allowed Americans freer access to domestic and imported goods.

Exports of meat, fish, flour and lumber to the West Indies, Africa and Southern Europe also helped the colonies. In addition, imports of sugar and molasses from the West Indies supported the colonial and British domestic distilling industries.[22] Along with sugar, molasses and bills of exchange, traders brought back the silver and gold coins of Spain and Portugal. To ensure that neither metal lingered in America, British trade policy discounted other forms of payment by colonists to British creditors. British businesses, on the other hand, could pay colonists by any means, *except* directly exported gold or silver, at full value.

Excessive shipping and handling charges further cut into American profits. Even with the growth of American shipping, colonists still relied on British shipping to transport goods to and from England. In the late eighteenth century, almost half of British shipping was involved in American trade.[23] Agents waiting on the British side of the Atlantic were retained to act as financial proxies for American businesses. Naturally, profits were siphoned away at every handoff. Hampered by unfair trade practices, many Americans enlisted the help of smugglers or became smugglers themselves. Some were very successful at it. John Hancock's adoptive family, for example, derived a large portion of its substantial wealth from smuggling operations. On a smaller scale and under more upright circumstances, riverboats and wagons were needed to move goods to and from the ports and to and from the American interior. The middleman already was an indispensable player.

Other problems faced American producers and merchants. Even if the weather remained favorable and spoilage was minimal, the raw materials that were being shipped back to England were plentiful in the colonies, outrunning local demand and keeping domestic prices low. At times those owing debts could not produce enough of the glutted raw materials to pay them. Moreover, American economic activities were labor intensive. Consequently, labor continually was in short supply. This meant that practically anyone could immigrate and find a job. On the downside, labor shortages fostered indentured servitude and slave labor, both of which suppressed wages.[24]

Overall, the period leading up to the Revolution was one of frenetic American growth in the face of increasingly ineffective attempts at control by the British. By the 1770's America was a commercial entity too powerful to remain a slave to the old and dying principles of mercantilism, or to British attempts at saving it.

The system was rotting from within. As a profit-building engine, it worked too well. Success induced a kind of myopia that allowed selfish commercial entities in England effectively to seize the reins of government. These entities acted not for the good of the realm, but for their own profit. Over time, lack of concern for colonial interests and the forced reliance on limited instruments of commerce tried the patience of the Americans.

Perception was everything. One cannot study the events of the colonial period without being astounded by the degree to which quarrels between entrenched European royal lineages came to affect life in America. Four wars, known collectively as the *French and Indian Wars*, were fought between 1689 and 1763. Although hostilities sometimes began on the American side, all four had roots in greed-driven struggles for mercantilist bragging rights. Sometimes these seemed to be little more than family feuds played out on a grand scale. To European monarchs, colonies served as theaters in which to wage these battles and as agents for projection of European interests. Proto-Americans, going about the business of taming the continent, usually had more immediate concerns. Yet, these quarrels became life and death struggles whenever hostilities erupted on the frontier. It was the last of these wars that put Britain and America on a collision course over who would pay £60 million of the bill.

The Tipping Point

The year 1763 found George III in the difficult position of having reached his credit limit. The British debt from the Seven Years War (or the "French and Indian War," as Americans term it,) was a staggering £137 million, with £5 million in annual interest payments against a budget that, in peace time, ran about £8 million.[25] British monarchs once had been free to wage war whenever the urge struck. Beginning with the reign of James I, however, Parliament began to question seriously the power of the monarchy. After the English Civil War, monarchical prerogatives again were sharply curtailed. Every subsequent ruler saw Parliament taking an increasingly active role in decision-making. As debts from the colonial wars mounted and British chests emptied, the Crown and Parliament began looking for other sources of funding.

In spite of its efficiency British mercantilism was not as successful as was hoped. Unlike the Spanish, the British found no cities of gold. Instead they saw only the cost of maintaining and defending far-flung settlements. To fill the gaps in funding, they expected the Americans to pay an increased share. The Seven Years War had driven the hated French from North America, but it left Britain with a vast new territory to manage and drove a fiscal wedge between her and her American colonies.

King George's answer to all this was to use bribery and coercion and surround himself with "yes men." Young, brash and intent on managing the colonies in his own way, he repeatedly chose ministers who supported his views, but lacked real influence in Parliament. Nevertheless, George III was a clever monarch who soon became a master of political manipulation. He drove out influential pro-American politicians, such as William Pitt and Edmund Burke, and paved the way for accelerated plundering of American enterprise. All the while, the royal ministries increasingly became disconnected from both Parliament and the plight of the colonists. With no moderating voice, the stage was set for new levels of

American frustration by a series of governmental blunders that made some measure of sense, but exacerbated the vulnerability of the colonists' situation and drove them closer to rebellion.

As if to prime American sensibilities, the *Proclamation Act of 1763* sought to prohibit English settlement west of the Appalachians and to have those who had already settled withdraw. The intent was to forestall any further frontier hostilities and thereby prevent additional expenditures. A seemingly logical step to those in London's ivory towers, its effect was to infuriate settlers, who largely ignored the act.

The Proclamation Act represents a turning point in colonial perceptions. Through enumeration, erosion of American privileges occurred gradually, with only temporary, regional resistance. Southerners were hit hard by duties and trade restrictions because they were the ones producing the majority of the enumerated exports. Still, they benefited from having relatively stable markets for their exports even if those markets were defined narrowly. Southerners also had the forbidden West Indian markets on which to fall back. Elite Southern planters bristled at having to make do with second-rate, out-of-fashion English goods, but they learned to live with them. Northerners and those in the middle colonies benefited from commercial shipping but were angry that they were, at least officially, denied more profitable ports. All of these impacts eventually were absorbed in the marketplace, without attention to their cumulative effects. Americans were lulled into complacency. The Proclamation Act and the legislative barrage yet to come ended that complacency.

While most of the actions of the royal ministries and Parliament were quasi-legitimate attempts to recoup expenses and re-assert control over trade, most came to be known more for their political implications than for any real economic benefit they might have provided. Even in the face of them, colonial exports and domestic consumption continued to grow at rates that were anything but constrained.[26]

Still, it was a matter of principle. The idea that taxes and fees would be imposed unilaterally was bad enough, but many Americans believed that British bureaucrats were lining their own pockets under the guise of carrying out the will of the Crown. Without oversight in Parliament, how could Americans be sure that their monies were being used for the intended purpose? Whether or not their fears were justified, propagandists were quick to spin every story to fuel unrest. Their actions insured that no royal pronouncement or act of Parliament would be seen for its true purpose.

In 1764 Parliament passed the *Sugar Act* to tax sugar, indigo, wine and other imports. It stiffened customs procedures and doubled duties on certain goods that were being re-shipped from England. Britain hoped for increased revenues. The chief benefit that an American could hope for was a less burdensome pocketbook. Another inflammatory law, the *Currency Act of 1764*, prohibited the colonies from printing paper money. Its intent was to help stabilize the colonial economy and curtail debt. Americans viewed it as an affront to free commerce and economic expansion. Acts regulating colonial currency and valuation of foreign coinage affected more people and caused more irritation than all the other regulations combined.[27]

The following year the *Stamp Act* attempted to recover French and Indian War costs by taxing paper, documents, publications and even dice. Fifty-five articles detailed specific taxes for different items. Dice were taxed at ten shillings, a pack of cards at one shilling, a college degree at £2 and a liquor license at £4. An appointment to an office was taxed at ten shillings if the office was worth less than £20 a year. For offices worth more than £20, the fee jumped to £4. Advertisements were taxed at two shillings, pamphlets at one shilling and almanacs at two pence. On top of all this, payment was required in sterling money! A whole sheet of paper for printing a newspaper was taxed at one penny, or a halfpenny for a half sheet. Anticipating that the act would pass, Ben Franklin ordered a hundred reams of large half sheets for his *Pennsylvania Gazette,* before the taxes took effect.[28]

Apart from the unprecedented and obvious invasion into American pocketbooks, the Stamp Act rightly was viewed as an attempt to rein in free expression. It spawned violent protests, mainly at the hands of Sam Adams' radical Sons of Liberty. The violence quickly was fuelled by the arrival of British troops sent to quell the unrest. Easterners could live with the Proclamation Act because it chiefly affected Westerners, but British troops on the streets of Boston were another story. In one sense, the Stamp Act merely asserted powers that the British government already had.* That those powers actually would be used was a cold and bitter slap in the face. The real start of the Revolution can be traced to these 1765 events because they were followed immediately by the first systematic refusal of colonists to cooperate.

(Left) Reproduction ca.1765 imported anti-Stamp Act English teapot.
(Right) Stamps used in 1765. Source: Mace (140.)[29]

The Stamp Act was followed closely by the expense cutting *Quartering Act*. As a result, troops were pulled from their posts in the West, leaving the frontier vulnerable to attack and adding a large measure of insult to the Stamp Act's injury. Early in 1766 the Stamp Act was repealed at the urging of Benjamin Franklin and William Pitt. The victory was hollow because, on the same day, Parliament passed the *Declaratory Act* to assert Britain's absolute power over her colonies "in all cases whatsoever."

The next year, Parliament made good on its promise by levying more import taxes under the *Townshend Acts*. Tension built as more incidents of violence erupted and the number of British troops in Boston and New York grew. When Massachusetts' legislature refused to revoke a circulating letter that declared the Townshend Acts unconstitutional, Governor Francis Bernard suspended them and, in doing so, made the protestors the *defacto* voice for the most volatile colony. As their countrymen protested, influential Americans continually pushed for reconciliation. While conciliatory messages were en route across the Atlantic to England, more violent protests occurred, straining the credibility of the peacemakers. King George and Parliament could not be sure which groups actually spoke for America. They chose to hear the raucous protestors.

* A 1724 ruling by the Solicitor General stated that taxes could be imposed on the colonies either by a representative body of their own choosing or by Parliament.

In 1773 Parliament passed the *Tea Act*. It did not add any new tax on tea, but upheld an old one. Moreover, it gave the British East India Company the right to circumvent the tax, allowing them to undersell American merchants. Could Americans really be upset at the prospect of cheaper tea? The answer came at the end of the year when Sam Adams staged his most famous protest, the Boston Tea Party.

The next attack came to be known by the Americans as the *Intolerable Acts*. Angry over the events in Massachusetts, Parliament used the first of these, the *Boston Port Bill*, to close that city's port in an attempt to starve the rebels into submission. Next, the *Massachusetts Government Act* was intended to remove any semblance of democracy from Massachusetts's government and return absolute power to the Crown. Town meetings were suspended. Another of the Intolerable Acts, the *Administration of Justice Act*, protected those who acted to suppress rebellion from trials by patriots. A second *Quartering Act* demanded that colonists provide food and board to the British occupying force. The *New England Restraining Act* required New England colonists to trade only with England and prohibited them from fishing in the North Atlantic. Clearly, the tenor of the message had shifted from cost control to vindication. If the prospect of American colonial self-rule ever existed, it was fading.

Paul Revere's 1768 view of Boston, with British ships occupying the harbor. Note that ship number five in the engraving is the Mermaid. *(See the text on Massachusetts' state coinage in Chapter 10.) Source: Library of Congress, Prints & Photographs Division, LC-USZ62-45559.*

What must have surprised the British and, for that matter, most Americans, was the degree to which the ungrateful colonies united in support of their brethren, at least in spirit. After the Stamp Act, for example, merchants in New York, Boston and Philadelphia refused to import or sell British goods. Southerners finally realized that what could be done to Massachusetts could just as easily be done to Virginia. From North to South, resistance to British taxes grew not so much because the colonists were encumbered economically, but because they refused to accept Britain's overbearing and apparently capricious right to tax.

Although in the minority, statesmen, such as Ben Franklin, Edmund Burke and William Pitt, were far-sighted enough to see that Britain's interests were best served by having a prosperous America as a trading partner. Most, however, overlooked the fact that America not only was outgrowing British policy, but also Britain herself. In 1700 the ratio of the British population to that in America was 20:1. By 1775, it was 3:1. The reasons for this trend were quite basic. Aside from the constant immigration, American women married younger, giving them a longer period in which to bear children.[30] They bore an average of eight children and had forty-two grandchildren. These children were born into a healthier environment and ate better food than did their British counterparts. Southerners moved inland, away from the malaria that long held the population (and life expectancy) in check. Moreover, the fact that Americans lived so far apart helped control the spread of epidemics, such as those that had plagued Europe for centuries.[31 *]

1779 political cartoon, "The present State of Great Britain," by J. Phillips. In it, an indolent England sleeps while the Dutch pick his pockets, America (as an Indian) tries to steal liberty in the form of a liberty cap[†] and Scotland tries to fend off an angry France. Published in London by W. Humphrey, No. 227 Strand. Source: Library of Congress, Prints & Photographs Division, LC-USZ62-45442.

Alan Taylor noted the principle that populations naturally grow to meet the supply of available food and then stabilize when equilibrium is reached. The influx of high-calorie colonial foodstuffs and advances in agriculture were accompanied by dramatic growth in what had been a relatively stable British population. Many of these people sought opportunities in America. At the same time, the food-producing potential and, hence, the potential for population growth in America, virtually was unlimited. Immigration and natural growth combined to accelerate the increase in American population.[32] Between 1650 and 1820, it grew at the incredible annual rate of about 3 percent,[33] bringing the total to 2.5 million by the outbreak of the Revolution.

Commerce followed populations. The combined gross domestic product of Britain's American colonies was 4 percent of England's in 1700. By 1770 the ratio had grown to 40 percent. Over roughly the same period, colonial consumption of British exports grew from a 10 percent to a 37 percent share of the total.[34] The net effect of all this was that Britain was fast becoming the tail and America the dog, or at least a big puppy.

By 1775 the ungrateful Americans were fed up. On the morning of April 19, after years of growing tension, war erupted at Lexington, Massachusetts. It is easy to understand why the British were unimpressed. On paper, theirs was the most formidable military force in the world. To them, the shots fired on Lexington's green were a mere pinprick, those at Concord an isolated act of mob violence. British generals had every conventional reason to believe the trouble quickly could be put to rest. They sought first to intimidate the upstarts into submission. Failing that, they sought to end the rebellion by landing a single decisive blow. But wars are not won on paper. Though it was not obvious, the Americans had the advantage of a relatively inexhaustible supply of men and materials with which to face an enemy that was supplied only by a thin line of wooden ships. The Americans had only to settle into a survival strategy, prolonging the conflict in the hope that British resolve would falter. Of course, this strategy ultimately prevailed just as it did two centuries later in Viet Nam. The Redcoats,

---

[*] According to the 1790 U.S. Census, about 63 percent of American families had five or more members and nearly a quarter of them had eight or more members. The total U.S. population was then just over 3.9 million, though it is likely that many people were missed by the census and that the true population exceeded four million.

[†] In ancient times, Phrygia, or "Asia Minor," was known for its grapes and marble quarries. During its Roman occupation, a slave was given an eggshell-shaped cap on being released. The cap symbolized freedom (i.e., as a chick emerging from its shell.) The *liberty cap*, as it came to be known, became a familiar symbol on American coins, as well as those of France, Mexico and other nations. Liberty caps often are shown atop a stick or "pole," i.e., a "liberty pole." Liberty caps were thus paraded about in celebration. The liberty pole became a symbol of the American cause during the Revolution.

along with their Hessian* and Native American allies, could make life difficult in Boston, Charleston or Philadelphia, where the heart of the rebellion appeared to beat strongest, but the American continent was simply too vast for Britain to land a decisive blow.

The Americans faced different obstacles. Congress was unable to muster the support that the fledgling army needed. It is no wonder. By John Adams' own accounting, two-thirds of the American people either opposed the war or were neutral to it. After all, most Americans *were* British and hoped desperately for reconciliation. Even had there been unwavering political support for the war, there was no available source of funding for it. Congress could only *request* the states' assistance. Consequently, General Washington fought battles on two fronts: the British in the field and Congress in its meeting halls.

As trying as the times were for American souls, defeats served as on the job training. The few battles that they were able to win kept hope alive. As the war dragged on, fence-sitting Americans warmed to the cause. With looting and pillaging, British troops managed to alienate even their Tory supporters. While American support grew, British resolve for prolonged war faded. For six and a half years, Redcoats won battle after battle and yet slowly lost the war. They took Boston, New York, Charleston and Philadelphia. In Europe, the capture of a capital city would have been decisive. Not so in America, where freedom proved a difficult idea to contain.

Though debts quickly mounted for both sides, the perceived cost of war was more painful for the British. Casting large military forces across an ocean is expensive and, given that the spoils of four prior wars were limited mainly to debt and wilderness territory, the British people tired of the exercise. For their part, the French-backed Americans were accustomed to paying for things on credit and had no illusions of financing the War by any other means. Fortunes slowly turned as Nathaniel Greene recaptured the South, ultimately driving British General Charles Cornwallis toward Yorktown, Virginia, for re-supply. Britain's fate was sealed four years earlier when Americans, under the impromptu leadership of Benedict Arnold, captured Gentlemen Johnny Burgoyne's entire army near Saratoga, New York. That victory had convinced the reticent French that the American cause was worth supporting. Combined American and French forces under General Washington forced Cornwallis' surrender at Yorktown, on October 19, 1781. Two years later, in 1783, the Treaty of Paris made official what Americans had declared in 1776. As described in the eighteenth century ditty, "...all the world...[was turned]...upside down...." America had its first real notch in the win column. Euphoria!

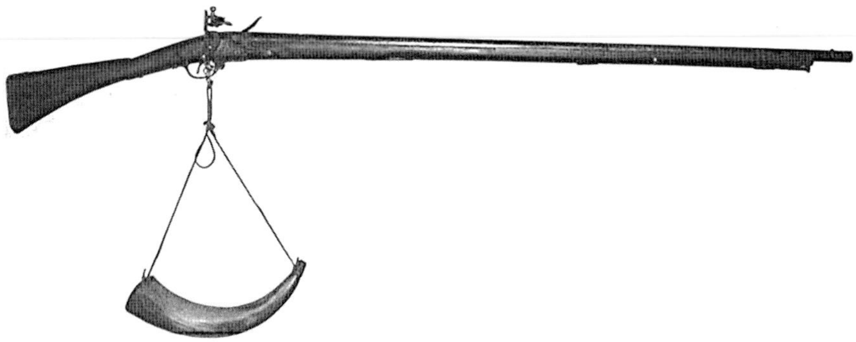

* The term "Hessian" generally is used to describe mercenary soldiers from the German states. In truth, Hessia was only one of several states that provided troops.

2: E PLURIBUS...HOW MANY?

Reality. While the Revolution solved the problem of an exploitative parent country, it brought another problem to light: The new government was bankrupt with no means to remedy the situation. The Articles of Confederation, ratified late in 1781, afforded no federal power to tax and no standard national currency. Instead, the individual states were left to their own devices. Rather than act for the good of the national economy, each state sought to protect its own interests. They were so independent that the French government hatched a plan to send thirteen different ambassadors, one to each of the new states.

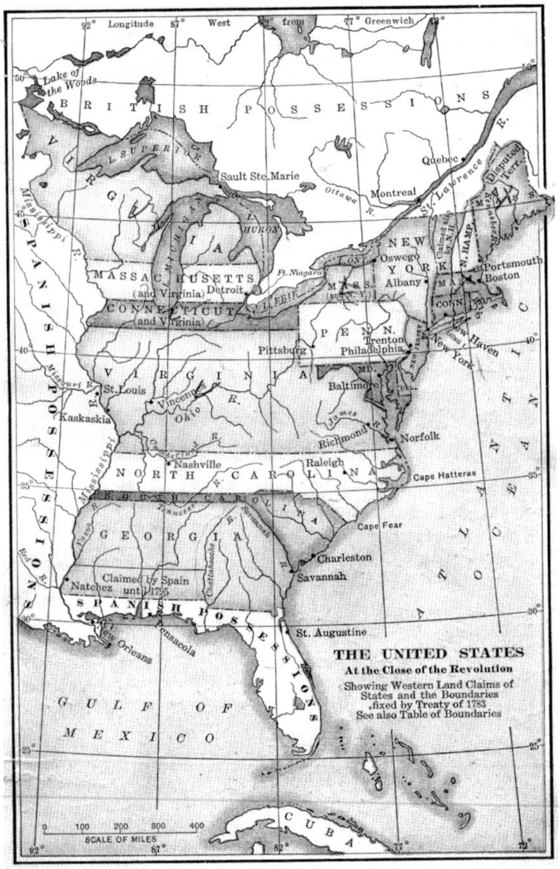

The United States at the Close of the Revolution. Source: Montgomery (opp. p.170.)

The Revolution devastated the American economy.* Coins completely disappeared from circulation because of hoarding. By 1781, the nearly $242 million in Continental Currency, authorized by Congress since 1775, was practically worthless. So were bills of credit issued by the states. At the same time, foreign and domestic debts grew daily. Without some plan, some controlling mechanism, the government was in danger of losing the lines of credit upon which it so heavily depended.

To that end the Confederation's Superintendent of Finance, Robert Morris, pushed through Congress creation of the Bank of North America. The bank was formed around a French loan and private subscriptions by American citizens. It was authorized to make short-term loans, print notes and allow depositors to have checks drawn either against their deposits or against lines of credit. The idea was to provide a stable fiscal agency to manage money and debt and thereby improve the nation's "credit rating." Because notes issued by the bank were redeemable in specie, a stockpile of silver and gold had to be maintained. To avoid over-extension, the bank kept a tight lid on its money. This need to hold on to specie was justified, but it limited the bank's ability to extend credit for support of the economic growth that was crucial to paying down debt. With growth constrained, the country's credit faltered and Morris was forced to back the bank's notes with his own personal funds. Two other large *state* banks were established in Massachusetts and New York in 1784. Both prospered, but suffered from the same limitations as their federal predecessor.[35]

* The British fared no better, ending the war owing £40 million, with two more wars having sprung from the American conflict. They also had to fear the prospect of outright invasion by the French.

Aside from devaluing currency, the war brought about the absence of imported goods, driving up prices and creating pent up demand. When foreign goods did arrive, spending frenzies further contributed to inflation. Chaotic cycles of boom and bust were the rule as territorial disputes* and financial panics followed one after another.

The states were bleeding each other and the federal government dry. Connecticut imposed greater duties on Massachusetts than it did on Great Britain. North Carolina was hit on both sides, by Virginia to the north and South Carolina to the south. New York charged a duty on New Jersey firewood entering New York City. Jealously protecting its own lucrative ports, the state of New York exercised its Confederation rights to block federal attempts at controlling customs and, hence, collecting duties.[36]

Desperation created tension between haves and have-nots. Defense of personal property rights by those who had none was central to the American cause in the Revolution. As the economic crisis worsened, debtors resented the fact that the commercial interests and moneyed classes whose property they had defended were doing nothing to return the favor. Outnumbering those to whom they owed money, debtors gained control of the elected state legislatures and passed debt-forgiving laws that trampled on the rights of creditors. This led creditors to second-guess the viability of popular government, using phrases like "tyranny of the majority." The Confederation's lack of coercive power even inspired some to call for the establishment of a limited monarchy.

The year 1786 was pivotal as the country languished in the depths of a postwar depression. Imports had fallen by almost a third in a single year and, in the previous half-decade, farm revenues had fallen by more than 20 percent. With no credit and no money to pay their rising taxes, farmers were in particularly dire straits. Seven of the states printed their own un-backed paper money. With goods in short supply and the money losing value, inflation was rampant. Creditors were forced to accept the nearly worthless state paper in payment of debts. Only Rhode Island barred such payments.[37]

The crises peaked when Daniel Shays, a Massachusetts farmer and debtor, led a rebellion that threatened to destroy the United States. The rebellion itself quickly was diffused, but in reaction to the situation the states printed even greater quantities of paper money, a move that only served to make matters worse. The Confederation was failing and it would take a different kind of revolution to save it.

In the sweltering summer of 1787 the states' delegates came to Philadelphia with the intent of revising the Articles. Amid great controversy and public suspicion they boldly scrapped the existing government and drafted the Constitution. After brilliant and heated debate, the states one-by-one accepted the new, experimental system. Approval was required by nine of the thirteen. The ninth, New Hampshire, ratified on June 21, 1788. Over the next three and a half years Congress and the states completed the reformation by adding the Bill of Rights. The sun was indeed rising on the *Federal Period*, a curious blend of patriotic optimism, governmental fine-tuning and neo-classical symbolism.

---

* Much of the ratification debate for the Articles of Confederation centered on the disposition of lands in the West. A number of states, most notably Virginia, held fast to old colonial claims. Virginia's willingness to give up its claims ultimately led to ratification of the Articles.

Still, there was this money thing. As if to underscore the lingering fragility of the economy, a 1789 copper panic caused the coins on which many Americans depended to be devalued to a fraction of their former worth. In the Confederation era, large numbers of counterfeit British halfpence circulated in the Northern states. In an attempt to drive out these lightweight impostors, three states (Connecticut, New Jersey and Massachusetts) authorized their own copper coinages, as they were allowed to do under the Articles.* The Republic of Vermont authorized its own coinage in anticipation of becoming the fourteenth state. Coinage proposals were submitted for New York as well, but state legislators turned against the idea. Instead, New York lawmakers simply looked the other way while their constituents made coppers that even included versions of counterfeit British halfpence. In 1787 the federal government's own attempt at minting coppers, the Fugio cents, succumbed to corruption and scandal. All of these coppers ultimately fell prey to the Panic of 1789. The fall of copper had little impact on the larger issue of national bankruptcy, but it ruined many individuals, played havoc with regional commerce and contributed to the Crash of 1792.

The economic issue that worried the founders most, however, was debt. After the surrender at Yorktown, Congress sent commissioners around the country to evaluate, in hard currency, claims against the army and the government. The total came to about $27 million. By 1790 the domestic debt had grown to $40.7 million, not to mention $13.2 million owed to other countries, primarily France and the Netherlands. In addition, the individual states owed more than $18 million. As the 1780's ended, the $2 million in annual interest that the government owed amounted to half of its expenditures. The debt itself amounted to 40 percent of what America's gross national product would have been, had the concept existed.[38]

Alexander Hamilton. Unsigned engraving, after John Trumbull, ca. 1870.

When Alexander Hamilton proposed that the new federal government assume the debts of the states to insure the nation's credit, Southern states, under the influence of Thomas Jefferson and James Madison, balked. They literally were in better financial waters than their Northern counterparts† and saw no reason to undertake payment of a debt that they did not, in their own opinions, create. Ironically, three men worked out the question of debt assumption over a candlelight dinner.‡ Hamilton, Jefferson and Madison struck a compromise that placed the national capital in the South, on the banks of the Potomac, in exchange for national assumption of most debts owed by the states.[39] The compromise called for the foreign debt to be paid in specie, the domestic debt through the issuance of coupon bonds. To restore faith, creditors further received bonds exchanged at the full value of securities that the market valued at only fifteen to thirty cents on the dollar. Those holding near-worthless Continental Currency were not so lucky. They received a dollar's worth of bonds for every hundred dollars in currency. As the bonds grew in value toward par, they drew foreign investors who eventually purchased 60 percent of the nation's debt. Owners could buy, sell or borrow against them, affording the

* The Confederation was a union of sovereign states. Thus, each state and the federal government had the right to coin its own money. However, the regulation of coinage was the exclusive right of the federal government.

† Besides owning a smaller share of the debt and having already repaid a large portion of what they owed, the Southern states continued their trade in the waters of the Caribbean. This brought a steady influx of specie.

‡ Ellis noted that the famous dinner likely was the culmination of a series of negotiations and not the singular historic event that Jeffersonian lore makes it out to be (Ellis, pp.72-74.)

country a long needed stable platform with which to fund expansion. Hamilton's plan for funding obligations with specie-backed long-term federal securities was right on target.[40]

Hamilton also proposed a more robust solution, the first Bank of the United States. Chartered by Congress in 1791, the new bank was to be the nation's fiscal agent, serving as a repository for government funds, making short-term loans to the government, making tax loans to individuals and issuing notes to support transactions. It was a semi-private enterprise. In exchange for depositing all its collected revenues, the federal government received one-fourth of the bank's shares. The remaining $8 million in shares could be bought by citizens at $400 each, payable partly in securities (three-fourths) and partly in specie (one-fourth.)[41]

Jefferson and his followers, even down to the time of Andrew Jackson and Martin Van Buren, bitterly opposed the existence of the bank. Part of their opposition revolved around Jefferson's argument that the $400 per share price made ownership unattainable for the average American. Jefferson also held that that centralization of assets removed control from local banks and businesses and placed it in the hands of the rich. Moreover, Americans were unaccustomed to the Bank of England model on which Hamilton based his plan.[42] That ownership of the Bank of the United States was two-thirds British did little to endear it to critics.

Thomas Jefferson. Henry Bryan Hall engraving, after Gilbert Stuart. Source: Irving (5:30.)[43]

The Jeffersonians' most enduring argument, however, was that the bank was unconstitutional. Hamilton countered with the view that the Constitution allowed for implementation of measures that were necessary but not explicitly enumerated. He also argued that central control was needed for stability and that the bank would magnify the effectiveness of the money supply by a factor of three.[44] Washington listened to both sides and ultimately agreed with Hamilton. In retrospect both Jefferson and Hamilton were right. Though it did provide a stabilizing influence, the new bank was just as conservative as its predecessor, Robert Morris's Bank of North America. At a time when the country needed credit for expansion, sitting on a pile of specie just was not a good strategy.[45] The Bank of the United States survived, but the debate over its propriety was far from over.

In a move just as important as its establishment of the bank, Congress passed the long awaited Mint Act of 1792. It established a federal mint in Philadelphia and the nation's monetary system that included gold eagles, silver dollars and copper cents. Though experimental pieces and a small issue of half dismes [sic] were produced in 1792, while the mint facility was under construction, onsite production began in 1793 with copper cents. Silver coins followed in 1794, gold in 1795. For various reasons that are explored in Chapter 12, the early U. S. Mint struggled and often fell short of expectations. As a result, foreign coins, tokens and speculative patterns continued to arrive at American ports. Nevertheless, after two centuries, America had a mint and a standard currency.

Meanwhile, to help pay off the national debt, Congress levied a series of excise taxes and tariffs. The source of most of the federal government's revenue prior to the Civil War, tariffs paid the bills, but hurt the economy because Americans paid more for imported goods and in retribution were denied access to certain export markets. Excise taxes worked no better. A

1794 attempt to tax whiskey, for example, led to an outright frontier rebellion and repeal of the tax. More than a simple dispute over taxes, the rebellion was a test of whether the new federal government in the East really controlled the independent West. Washington personally led a military campaign to end the rebellion. The 13,000 man force that he commanded in that campaign actually was larger than any with which he had fought the British.[46] Shays' Rebellion and this, the Whiskey Rebellion, revealed something about the character of the new democracy. In their aftermath there were no vindictive bloodbaths, no beheadings as there would have been in Europe – only honest debate and commitment to resolve the problems.

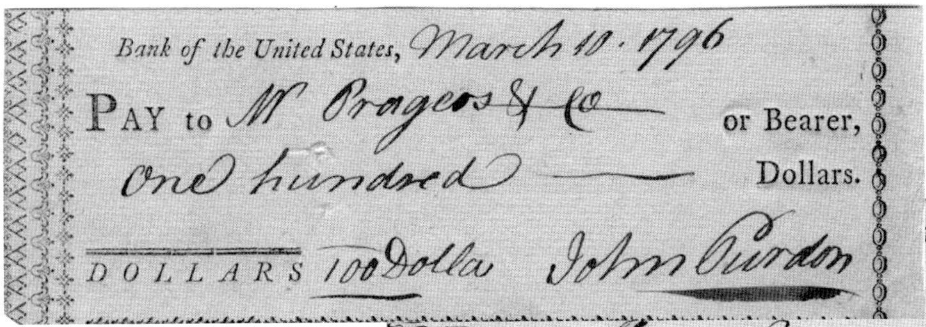

$100 checks drawn on the 1st Bank of the United States in 1793 and 1796 (shown reduced.)

Still, there were bouts of temporary insanity. In spite of Washington's 1796 farewell admonition to "...steer clear of permanent alliances with any portion of the foreign world..."[47] it remained that America was struggling to establish herself among the world powers that still claimed much of the New World. Spain, France and Britain all were waiting, like vultures, just beyond the new country's borders. Paranoia grew rampant, as evidenced by the *Alien and Sedition Acts* of 1798, under the second president, John Adams. These repressive acts primarily were a reaction to fears that foreign and seditious elements would incite rebellions within the United States. In hindsight, the Alien and Sedition Acts are seen as serious threats to civil liberties.* At the time, however, they seemed altogether appropriate.

The storm only worsened. The bitter election of 1800 that saw the birth of two-party politics nearly destroyed the nation. Three years later, Jefferson's Louisiana Purchase raised the bar of controversy even higher. It since has proved to be a stroke of pure genius. France ceded this huge territory to Spain in 1762 in the settlement of the Seven Years War. In the secret Treaty of San Ildefonso (1800,) and others that followed, Spain ceded it back to France in exchange for a snippet of Italian territory that was coveted by a Spanish princess. Some in Spain still claim that the French cheated them and that Louisiana really is theirs still. Nevertheless, Louisiana's sale to the United States was a win for both the French and the Americans. Jefferson recognized the economic potential of the West, the strategic importance of New Orleans and the danger of having the region held by the French. At the same time, a disastrous

---

* Ironically, Congressional debate over the Alien and Sedition Acts almost was identical to congressional debates following the terrorist attacks of September 11, 2001. Supporters of modern military tribunals used the same arguments that were used at the end of the eighteenth century. John Adams did not actively support the Alien and Sedition Acts, but allowed them to pass. He later viewed his inaction as a grave mistake. The modern arguments also echo those of Massachusetts' royal governor, Thomas Hutchinson, who, as the Revolution was beginning, was willing to sacrifice civil rights for security. History proved him wrong as well.

attempt at controlling rebel slaves in Haiti revealed to a cash-starved Napoleon the futility of controlling a vast trans-Atlantic territory.

The much-maligned Bank of the United States helped manage debt associated with the Purchase. The national credit rating that the bank built allowed the government to obtain more than $11 million from foreign lenders to fund the transaction. The total investment of 80 million francs (about $15 million[*]) that looked so daunting at the time has repaid itself many times over. The Louisiana Purchase mitigated foreign threats by effectively creating a buffer zone. Ultimately, it ensured the long-term economic success of the United States and, perhaps just as importantly, unleashed again the great driving force of the frontier.

Though there was turmoil, the period between 1787 and 1812 was a grand time in America. Internally, the new nation struggled to establish the viability of federal self-government. A sense of nationalism grew even as Napoleon tore Europe apart. America also struggled to define her relationship with Great Britain. To ease the settlement of new lands, Southerners and Westerners wanted to drive the British from the continent. Northerners and Easterners, on the other hand, still were heavily dependent on British trade and had little motivation to fight. Even when the British pressed captured American sailors into service, Northerners did not object because they still depended heavily on British shipping for trade. (Britain was feeling the pinch of losing its young men to Napoleon's wars and needed to supplement its merchant navy.) Southern and Western interests eventually prevailed and the War of 1812 erupted with neither side really understanding why. When it ended in 1814, there was no clear winner, but the terms of peace distinctly favored the Americans. Southerners had a door to the West and Northerners had freedom of the seas.

The charter of the Bank of the U.S. expired in 1811. By that time the number of state chartered banks had grown to 117. Most of them issued paper currencies that were supposed to be redeemable in specie. When the British burned government buildings in Washington, in 1814, state banks outside of New England suspended specie payments. Nevertheless, the federal government was required to accept notes of the state banks, many of which were discounted (i.e., inflated,) in payments of taxes and on loans. In 1816, fearful that the situation would grow out of control, Congress chartered the Second Bank of the U.S. for a twenty-year term. Part of the bank's new mission was to enforce discipline on the state chartered banks and force the resumption of specie payments. The plan, which is credited to Nicholas Biddle, head of the Bank, worked because the government deposited the state bank notes it received in the Bank of the U.S. and its branches. The Bank of the U.S. thus became a creditor to the state banks and could demand to be paid in specie. This made the state banks leery of extending themselves very far beyond what they could afford to pay in specie.[48] One more fire was under control.

All the while the population kept growing and business kept expanding. The reluctance of the chartered banks to print notes led to a proliferation of unbacked currencies by unchartered "wildcat" banks. The massive inflation that followed led to the great Panic of 1819. As the

---

[*] A century ago Charles Morris edited *The Great Republic by the Great Historians*. It was published in New York by R.S. Belcher Co. in 1901. In volume II, a section titled "What was the Louisiana Purchase?" gives a paraphrased litany of arguments that congressional opponents used to describe just how much money $15 million was. Its weight in silver would be 433 tons, enough to fill 866 wagons in a line more than five miles long. A worker loading sixteen wagons a day would be busy for more than two months and, stacked up, the dollars would reach a height of over three miles. It was far more than all the gold and silver then known to exist in all the United States.

second decade of the nineteenth century closed, opponents to the Bank of the U.S. again challenged its constitutionality. Again at issue was the right of the federal government to interpret the constitution in a way that allowed the chartering of banks. Strict constructionists argued that the Constitution was to be taken literally and that it made no provision for a central bank. On the other side, broad constructionists argued that the constitution allowed for necessary and proper interpretation. It is a debate that continues today. In the landmark 1819 Supreme Court case that every student knows as McCulloch v. Maryland, the Supreme Court affirmed the government's right to interpret the Constitution broadly. Thus, out of litigation, the modern federal government was born.[49]

The dawn of the 1820's found Americans no longer preoccupied with the affairs and threats of the European powers. Instead they turned their attention inward to the settlement of western lands. The divisive regional forces that led down the long road toward the Civil War already were well at work. As if to signal the end of one era and the beginning of another, the sixty-year reign of the unwilling arch-villain, King George III, ended with his death in 1820.

The next two decades presented a different set of political and economic difficulties that were no less challenging than the ones of the past. The *Nullification Crisis*, the discovery of gold in the Southeast, a new explosion of private paper money, the Jackson-Van Buren war against the Bank of the U.S., the corresponding era of hard times and the maturing of the U.S. Mint all shaped America's monetary and national history of the 1820 to 1840 period. All of these events are described at the end of Chapter 11 and in Chapter 12.

This was the evolutionary landscape onto which the money of early America emerged.

1840 Whig campaign print, depicting William Henry Harrison greeting a veteran at his cabin on the Ohio River. Note the hides and cider barrels outside the cabin and the liberty cap-topped flag. Source: Library of Congress, Prints and Photographs Division, LC-USZ62-5550.

Section II:
Country Money and Paper Colonies

3: OF BEAVER, BEADS AND BARLEY

COUNTRY MONEY AND TRADE GOODS

During America's early years, two domestic economies co-existed. One was centered in the thriving towns that served as terminals and distribution centers. It used the formal instruments of commerce described in the previous chapters. The other economy followed strands of civilization that branched out into the western interior and was fuelled by individuals and small communities who carried on less formal local trade. For many of these people money meant commodities and it meant bartering with Indians, as well as with fellow Europeans. Nathaniel Hawthorne described the situation perfectly:

> *...if a man wanted to buy a coat, he perhaps exchanged a bear-skin for it. If he wished for a barrel of molasses, he might purchase it with a pile of pine boards. Musket-bullets were used instead of farthings. The Indians had a sort of money, called wampum, which was made of clam-shells; and this strange sort of specie was likewise taken in payment of debts by the English settlers. Bank-bills had never been heard of. There was not money enough of any kind, in many parts of the country, to pay the salaries of the ministers; so that they sometimes had to take quintals[*] of fish, bushels of corn, or cords of wood, instead of silver or gold.*[50]

Commodities are goods that widely are recognized as useful and, consequently, have values dynamically set by the marketplace. To make them work as money, colonial authorities often found it necessary to legislate prices. In 1640, for example, Massachusetts set the value of corn at four shillings per bushel, wheat or peas at six shillings per bushel and rye or barley at five shillings per bushel. Beaver skins were valued at ten shillings per pound in Massachusetts or 160 stuivers (Chapter 7) per skin in areas controlled by the Dutch.[51] Commodities usually took the form of raw materials that could be used directly: tobacco, corn, furs, shot, powder, nails, pork, bear fat, wool, tar and pitch, indigo for dying, cheese and livestock of all sorts. Labor, too, was a commodity. In many places, for example, highway taxes could be paid by working on the roads.[52] On a more basic level, simple favors often were used to repay debts between neighbors. This was particularly true in areas settled by people with specialized skills such as woodworking, whitesmithing,[†] blacksmithing or roof thatching. In essence, anything that could be found in, produced by or imported to the colonies was recognized as money at some time, in some locales.

A halfpenny in lead musket balls, a valuable frontier commodity.

The term "country money" sometimes is used to describe agricultural commodities. Country money was inconvenient to store and transport and usually was perishable. Whenever produce had to be transported, carrying charges were added. Such fees varied, but averaged ten percent

[*] A quintal is an archaic unit of weight, usually equivalent to 100 pounds.

[†] Forging of "dark" metals, such as iron, is called "blacksmithing." One who polishes or otherwise finishes iron or steel goods is a "whitesmith." The term also is applied occasionally to those who work in lighter colored metals such as tin or silver.

of the price of the commodity for much of the colonial period. Where coinage or paper money was available in reasonable quantities, payments in country money often were discounted from the official price or refused altogether.[53] By discounting the value of payments taken in country money, the receiver simply allowed for inconvenience and risk.

Certain types of commodities more properly are called "trade goods." These generally are manufactured objects that range from trinkets, metal pots and cloth to muskets and axes. Often, the relative values of trade goods depended more on how badly an individual settler or Indian wanted or needed them than on any officially set market price. Trade goods held distinct advantages over country money. They were more durable than most agricultural commodities and could be transported, even across the Atlantic.

As money substitutes, commodities most often were traded directly for other commodities. In 1703, for example, one would expect to receive one beaver pelt in trade for six knives when dealing with the "Eastern Indians." A shirt was also worth a beaver skin, though one with ruffles fetched two skins. A trader also could exchange a beaver skin for five pecks of corn or ground meal, ten pounds of pork, six combs or a yard of broad cloth.[54]

The use of commodities as money was a natural extension of the barter system, a concept much older than the first European contact with the New World. Even before the era of colonization, for example, copper moved along routes that extended across vast distances. Copper nuggets from the Great Lakes region that are found at Virginia's ancient archaeological sites attest to this. Later, it was not unusual for Natives to tear apart copper kettles received in trade and shape them into adornments. When the first Englishmen came, sailors looted copper from their own ships to trade with the eager Indians. This created problems as most ships relied on the metal for various on-board fixtures. Copper was just the tip of a dazzling array of items on the great wooden ships. In the seventeenth century, Eastern Indians were so impressed with the objects that Europeans carried that their names for the visitors included "Metal People" and "Axe Makers."[55] The practice of trading usable goods and worthless trinkets to Indians, in exchange for America's real treasure, had begun.

Early trade items:
(Left to right) Late 18th century rose head nail; Michigan copper, a staple of pre-European trade; Copper beads on twisted cotton string (Mississippi, ca. 1730-1780.)

Even when areas became more settled, trade of commodities continued with varying degrees of acceptance and price stability. At the stable end of the spectrum, nails retained a nearly constant valuation for much of the colonial period. They were more durable than eggs or tobacco and, as such, proved to be a viable substitute for money. The idea of penny sizes for nails is a remnant of this practice. A hundred ten penny nails once together were valued at ten pence, one hundred four penny nails at four pence, etc.. This valuation changed little until mass production of nails came about in the nineteenth century. Until then, entrepreneurs such as Thomas Jefferson, literally made money by maintaining nail-making operations.

The value assigned to most commodities was less stable. Consider tobacco, a native plant that almost immediately took on monetary status. John Rolfe, husband of Pocahontas, is credited with the first European planting of it in America. Rolfe and others experimented with wild tobaccos to develop commercially viable large-leaf varieties. Sir Walter Raleigh, whose name still is linked inextricably to the plant, is credited with being the first to market it.

A pound of tobacco was valued at five shillings, about a dollar, in 1612. It officially was valued at three shillings per pound in 1619. By 1645 overproduction drove the price down to one and a half *pence* per pound. It dropped even further, to a penny a pound, in 1665. As the market fell, farmers began destroying tobacco crops in hopes of raising prices. To stop the slaughter, Virginia passed a law making it a capital crime to harm a tobacco plant.[56] Later the price of tobacco rebounded as other parts of Europe discovered its benefits...or at least its pleasures. At the wholesale level the standard unit of the tobacco trade was the hogshead, a barrel that held a whopping 550 pounds of the "In-dye-on weed" (i.e., Indian weed,) as it was called in eighteenth century anti-smoking songs. Less pious Virginians did well to keep a hogshead on hand, as the fine for failing to attend church regularly was a stiff fifty pounds of tobacco.[57]

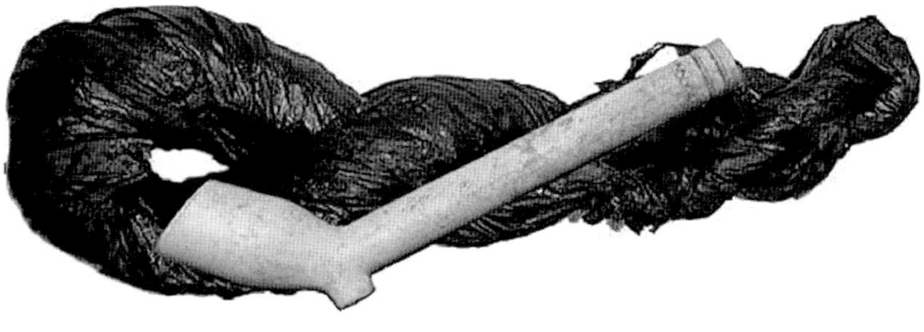

(Background) Rope tobacco (ca. 2000.) This rope was purchased recently at a local tobacco store. Ironically, it carries the brand name "Good Money." A call to the R. C. Owen Company, owners of the brand, produced no information about the origins of the name or whether it extends to colonial times.

(Foreground) Imported clay pipe (ca. 1665-1675, broken,) a common trade item.

Even in the early 1800's, Lewis and Clark carried 130 rolls of tobacco on their first expedition, to trade for passage.[58] These rolls probably were "carrots." A carrot was a cylinder-shaped bundle of tobacco, often in the form of snuff, weighing three to five pounds and wrapped in cloth. It was bound at both ends and thus resembled that for which it was named. Tobacco was used as currency in even smaller units. For this purpose, it frequently was twisted into "ropes" for convenience.

Apart from the shifting whims of the market, those who relied on agricultural produce, such as tobacco, for economic survival were subject to the risks of spoilage, unpredictable crop seasons, frontier wars and governmental restrictions. As settlements dispersed geographically, local valuations became the norm. At the same time the principle of basing an object's value on the amount of work required for its creation gradually eroded with domestic overproduction and the increased accessibility and affordability of imports. All of these factors combined to weaken the case for barter and hasten demands for coins and paper money.

The transition from commodities to money was not a singular process. It was repeated many times as settlements extended outward and westward in a pattern easily recognizable to disciples of Frederick Jackson Turner.* After a brief period of *being* the Western frontier, the

* Turner (1861-1932) was a brilliant nineteenth and early twentieth century historian who in 1893 explained the evolution of America in terms of the frontier. He painted a picture of constant re-creation of society as it moved west. This re-creation demanded innovation and adaptation that ultimately drove America's ascent. In traditional thinking, civilization was "pushed" across the continent from the East. The *Turner Thesis* turned this idea upside down. Instead, Turner argued, the frontier "pulled" dynamic elements of civilization westward. (Billington, *The Frontier Thesis*.) Turner's ideas now are mostly out of vogue among the historical community. Nevertheless, the ideas he proposed are compelling and, in this author's view, mostly correct.

earliest settlements in Virginia and Massachusetts became the settled East. As frontiersmen, settlers in these regions were forced to invent trading systems and culture in general.* When the frontier moved away from them and traditional forms of money became available, the importance of commodities diminished. Visionaries and entrepreneurs moved with the frontier, creating America as they went. Those who remained were more conservative in nature because they defined themselves in eastern or even centuries-old European terms.[59]

As towns grew their inhabitants came to view themselves as integral cogs in a large and established European system. They were concerned with establishing and maintaining a procedural fabric of laws and with prosecuting those who disrupted societal order. In contrast, those in isolated areas were preoccupied with personal struggles for survival. They cared about individual rights and violations against individuals. (It is no wonder that European wars were supported in the East, but were viewed by Westerners as little more than irritations of the Native American populations.) In areas connected to the settled East, people opposed taxes on molasses and tea without their representative consent in Parliament. Those on the frontier had neither tea nor molasses and were not even represented in the legislative bodies of their own colonies.[60] Extrapolating Turner's ideas, Easterners were tied closely to the economic order of mercantilism and favored hard currency. Westerners saw land as wealth, lacked hard capital and favored credit currency. Out of necessity, they relied on barter for commerce.

For East and West to benefit each other economically, the money of one had to be exchanged for that of the other. Somehow the produce of Western fields and forests had to be transformed into Eastern coins or bills of exchange (Chapter 4) to satisfy creditors, particularly those in Britain. This transformation was accomplished partly by traders and village merchants. These people acted as intermediaries between wholesalers (i.e., their Eastern and British creditors) and frontier citizens. At their stores or from their wagons, a basket of eggs could be traded for bullets, or butter for an axe. The merchants also could accept and spend local bills of credit, but more often the exchange was for commodities that could be re-traded.

If a commodity was perishable, then it had to be transferred quickly to another customer. Thus, perishable goods from the country tended to stay in the country. About 90 percent of economic production stayed within a given colony for home consumption and local trade.[61] Only durable commodities and those that could be dried, cured, distilled or otherwise preserved (e.g., pelts, fish or corn) could be transported effectively over long distances. Goods that could be transported eastward might be sold to the public or exported to Britain to be credited as bills of exchange. The resulting funds could be used to pay debts, import more merchandise and repeat the cycle. In any case, the transformation from raw Western products to Eastern currencies, and back again, through the trade conduit, was complete.

In some ways the commercial zone that transformed commodities to money and back again was itself something of a frontier. The real frontier usually is defined in terms of population density, typically an area beyond which the population drops below two settlers per square mile. Even in 1790, when the first U.S. Census took place, the population density of the country as a whole was a mere five persons per square mile. Many areas that officially would not have been labeled "frontier" were not far removed from it. In a sense, the "commercial frontier" was the line beyond which commodity money was preferred over coins and paper. In most cases, that line fell well east of the real frontier. Eventually, improvements in

---

* E.g., Iowa Territory's marriage fee was three goat skins or four bushels of sweet potatoes. (Crosby, p.25.)

transportation and communication extended the credit system farther into the interior and moved the commercial frontier westward.

One remarkable characteristic of both frontiers was their ability to foster free enterprise. Profit opportunities existed wherever exchanges took place. Local markets developed as the prospect of accumulating wealth brought people who could provide what today would be called value-added services. Livery service providers, woodworkers, clergymen, doctors, soldiers and even educators were needed in the West. Money also could be made by performing the difficult task of transporting goods between the frontier and the port cities. The uncertain flow of commerce from the interior to the East and across the Atlantic caused many foreign investors to pull out, leaving even more room for American entrepreneurs. As settlements in an area approached "critical mass," commerce became too complex to manage with barter alone. As settlements became more connected, commodities and trade goods yielded to more familiar currencies, usually in the form of paper and credit. Developed areas then provided bases of capital and supplies on which the expanding frontier could draw.

This all began when the fur trade brought a great wave of enthusiasm for barter and carried it to the continental interior. Early on, it was the French who dominated the fur trade, thanks to a handful of intrepid individuals. By the time Samuel de Champlain, Sieur du Pontgravé and their associates began to solidify France's hold on Canada at the dawn of the seventeenth century, their countrymen had been bartering with Native Americans for a century. Trade at easily accessible harbors and riverside settlements quickly became so competitive that entrepreneurs were forced farther and farther inland, creating both alliances and hostilities among vested parties. The noted historian, Ray Allen Billington, gave a hint of how the fur trade might have begun with the early fishermen who stopped to split, salt and dry their cod before going back across the Atlantic:

> *...The Indians who gathered to watch these strange rites were fascinated by the knives of the Frenchmen, for their own stone-age implements seemed crude by comparison. One of them, watching with covetous eyes the gleaming knife of a fisherman as he split open a fat cod, managed to signal that he would give anything he possessed for that glittering blade. The sailor, noticing the fine cloak of beaver skins worn by the Indian, indicated that he was willing to trade. Thus was born the fur trade on which the French occupation of North America rested...A knife or an axe or a few cheap trinkets worth about a livre could be bartered for a beaver robe that would fetch two hundred livres in Paris.*[62]

"Courrier du Bois" [sic,] by Frederic Remington (1891.) From "A Skin for a Skin," by Julian Ralph in Harper's New Monthly Magazine, *vol. 34, no. 501 (February, 1892,) p. 383. The article's title is from the Hudson's Bay Company motto,* Pro Pelle Cutem, *which, in turn, is from Job 2:4.*

By 1680 over eight hundred *coureurs de bois* were roaming and dealing in the French wilderness.[63] These men were a vital part of a policy that differed significantly from that of the British, who viewed native populations as inconvenient barriers to expansion of their land-consuming agricultural base. Because of fur trade, the French depended heavily on Native Americans as partners, and vice versa. While their relationship was symbiotic, it tied them to a common fate. When Indians were pushed aside, the tenuous French hold on the continent inevitably unraveled. The unraveling began quietly when two French traders, Médard Chouart (Sieur des Groseilliers) and his brother-in-law, Pierre Esprit Radisson, ran afoul of their government's bureaucratic infrastructure and turned to England's Charles II. After a 1669 expedition to Hudson's Bay that produced £19,000 in furs from a £650 investment, Chouart and Radisson were allowed to form the Hudson's Bay Company.[64] This event laid the groundwork for years of strife between England and France over dominance of the colonial West. It also marked the beginning of a transition of the fur trade from the domain of independent explorers, trappers and traders to that of major corporations and their governments. (See Chapter 7.)

A BARTER TYPOLOGY

Given that practically anything could have been used as money in the barter economy, is it realistic to think that a workable classification scheme might be devised? Maybe. One useful means of classifying goods is based on whether the item of exchange *was valuable* (i.e. useful) or merely *symbolized value*. A strand of beads symbolized value. A fur pelt, on the other hand, was valuable because it was useful. This distinction is more important than it appears. Items of symbolic value are the conceptual near-equivalents of coins. As such, their use represents a higher level of sophistication than the simple exchange of useful items. Another dimension of classification is whether the items being traded originated locally or were imported. Imported goods usually were manufactured, while goods of local origin were closer to their raw forms. There certainly were exceptions where items were manufactured locally or cultivated abroad. Moreover, most raw products needed some level of processing prior to becoming worthy of trade. Tobacco had to be cured, fish usually had to be dried, wool or cotton combed and spun, etc.. The chart below illustrates the use of these concepts in a rudimentary classification scheme.

	Generally Imported	**Generally Produced Locally**
Useful	**Manufactured** Household items (dishes, pots, pans, tin goods, needles, etc.,) steel arrowheads, woven goods, knives, axes/hatchets, tools, gun powder, smoking pipes, alcoholic beverages	**Raw (Country Money)** Agricultural food products (especially corn and wheat,) livestock, labor, wool and cotton **Processed/Manufactured** Tobacco, fur pelts, lumber, shot, nails, some alcoholic beverages, dried fish, animal fat/tallow, utilitarian ceramic and glass items [By the 1770's, many iron items (e.g., pots and pans) were being made and consumed domestically.]
Symbolic/ Decorative	**Manufactured** Trade silver and copper (effigies, trinkets, etc.,) glass trade beads (See below.)	**Raw** Copper nuggets, shells **Processed/Manufactured** Trade silver and copper, wampum, other shell beads (See below.)

TRADE SILVER

Indians and settlers alike eagerly exchanged their "hairy bank notes," as beaver pelts later were called,[65] for all manner of things. Some of the most persistent objects for which they were traded came in the form of metal trinkets, particularly those made of silver. This "trade silver" takes many forms, from simple geometric shapes in sheet metal to elaborate three-dimensional gorgets (decorative breastplates) with detailed engravings of beaver and other figures. Examples include finger rings, earrings, headbands, bracelets, armlets, brooches, buckles and pendants. Brooches were valued according to size, the monetary equivalent of the coins whose dimensions they approximated.[66] All of these forms were merely shiny extensions of bone and shell ornaments that Indians had made and traded for centuries. Some items originated in France and England, but silversmiths in Quebec, Montreal, Nova Scotia, New York and Pennsylvania made many others. Touchmarks identify specific makers. For example, an "RC" touchmark on a genuine piece is usually attributed to Montreal's Robert Cruikshank (1774 to 1808.) Likewise, "PH" may refer to Philip Huguet, who worked in Philadelphia between 1750 and 1764. "DR" is for Domonique Rousseau (1755 to 1815) and "CA" is for Charles Arnoldi (1779 to 1817,) both of whom lived in Montreal. Quebec's Guillaume Baudry (1656 to 1710) used a "B" inside a starburst. "LA" touchmarks appear on *brass* beavers thought to be the work of Louis Palin D'Abonville.[67] Aside from the many known and unidentified makers of genuine pieces, collectors should be wary of reproductions that are aged to appear genuine.

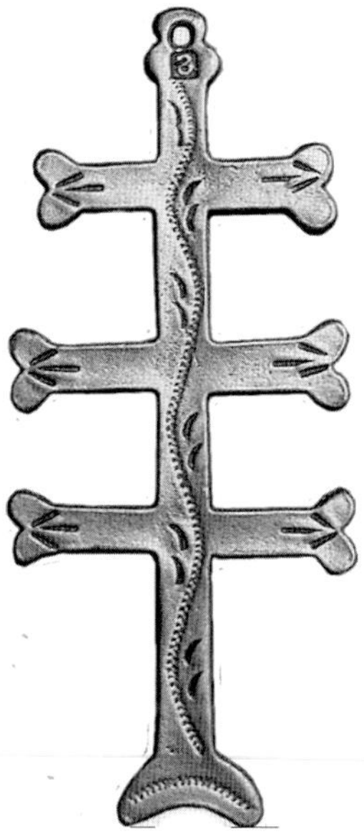

Sample trade silver forms: *(Left) Modified Cross of Lorraine. (Middle) Beaver effigy (both are modern copies.) (Right) 1768 beaver pendant. The inscription,* Paix Amitie *("Friendly Peace") suggests use as a personal peace medal. The late date of this piece raises questions about its authenticity since the French were all but gone from North America by 1768.*

Crosses were used to fulfill the dual purposes of obtaining furs and converting heathens to Christianity. One of the more commonly seen forms is a Cross of Lorraine, a Latin cross with a second, and sometimes a third, crossbar.* These were either cast or cut from a sheet.

Another common form is that of a beaver effigy. Smaller beaver-shaped pendants, a half-inch in length, were valued at one pelt. Larger ones, five or six inches long, were valued at ten pelts.[68] The Hudson's Bay Company used just such a system.

* The second crossbar symbolizes the sign that was placed over Jesus's head at his crucifixion. Traditionally, the sign is believed to have read, *Iesus Nazarenus Rex Iudaeorum*, Latin for "Jesus the Nazarean, King of the Jews." The third crossbar probably is ornamental.

Steatite (soapstone) trade silver mold with reservoirs for (left to right) a beaver, a turtle, a Cross of Lorraine and two sizes of buckles (1/2 actual size.) This inch-thick mold was found near the intersection of the Wabash River and the Ohio/Indiana border. Its back is engraved with the name "McKee." At least two McKee's played roles in early Ohio history, though no positive link between this piece and either of them exists. Captain Alexander McKee was the most notable of the Ohio McKee's. He was a trader and Deputy Agent for Indian Affairs under Sir William Johnson and helped manage relationships with various tribes of the Tuscarawas Valley in the 1760's. When the American Revolution began, McKee was suspected of siding with the Loyalists. He was paroled, but was required to remain in the vicinity of Fort Pitt. He and a handful of companions escaped the area and fled to join the British in March 1778. Another McKee, Thomas, was a Delaware who frequently was visited by officials operating in the region because he was the brother of Netawatwees, King of the Delawares. [69]

To Indians, effigies symbolized more than money. Many of them believed that all objects, including inanimate ones, were imbued with a spirit. Algonquin-related tribes called it "Manitou." Shiny objects, in particular, were conducive to Manitou.[70] One can only speculate how Indian minds reconciled this spiritual concept with the Christian symbolism of a Lorraine Cross.

At any rate, the Indians became skilled price negotiators, often going out of their way to play games and deriving great pleasure from besting Europeans in a deal. Whenever the Europeans allowed, Indians bought on credit, with or without the intent to pay. Frontier conflicts usually meant that debts were forgotten. Consequently, Indians buying large quantities of goods on credit was a good sign that unrest was brewing.[71]

SHELL GAMES

The use of *symbolic* money surrogates was not limited to trades with Indians. In areas where currency options were limited, symbolic forms emerged temporarily, until coins or paper money became available. Unlike most commodities, these symbolic forms were valued less because of their outright or perceived usefulness and more because a trading community agreed to honor them as symbols of value.

The need for such money was recognized officially in Massachusetts as early as 1637, when its governing body, the General Court, established wampum as the standard for transactions of a shilling or less. Wampum usually consists of deer hide-strung beads made from seashells. Each bead was cut skillfully and polished by hand and is generally one-eighth to one-half inch in length and one-eighth to one-fourth inch in diameter. To treat wampum as money and nothing more, as works on the early American economy are prone to do, would be to neglect the enormous cultural weight that it carried.

"THAT THIS PEACE MAY LAST FOREVER..."[72]

The history and legends of wampum are bound to the formation of the Iroquois League, around 1570. The larger-than-life founder of the Iroquois League was Hiawatha, an Onondaga who lived with the Mohawks. Late in the sixteenth century, Hiawatha formed a confederation among the Mohawk, Onondaga, Seneca, Cayuga and Oneida nations that covered a vast territory. Its governmental prerogatives fell not under a dictatorial chief, but under an unwritten democratic constitution. To govern the confederation, each nation elected three representatives to sit at a great council. Two of the representatives were there to make decisions, the third to insure that the process was carried out according to proper procedures. Mohawk and Seneca representatives would reach unanimous agreement on a governmental decision. Their decision was then passed to representatives of the Oneidas and Cayugas, who either unanimously endorsed it or modified the decision and passed it back to the Mohawk and Seneca representatives. This was repeated until agreement was unanimous among the four nations' representatives. The Onondaga representatives then acted as an executive branch. They could unanimously endorse the decision or "veto" it and pass it back to representatives of the other tribes for further consideration.[73] While few credit the Iroquois League with being the inspiration for the United States Constitution, the parallels to modern legislative, judicial and executive branches of the United States Government are astonishing.

Beads were used haphazardly as ornaments and tributes before the formation of the Iroquois League, but it was in the ceremonial rites of council that they took on real importance. Each of the Five Nations[*] was represented by beads strung in a particular pattern. Their strands were laid end-to-end in a circle to signify convening of the Great Council. Other strands were used to introduce various types of speeches and as tributary gifts. How these practices evolved is wrapped in legends that usually point back to Hiawatha, whose name means "one who seeks that which he already knows where to find" (i.e., "He who seeks peace among kindred nations.") [74]

In the most repeated legend, Hiawatha is a stranger who camps in an open field, making wampum, outside a village. Indians in the village inquire about his business, but he refuses to council with them until they present him with strands (i.e., words) like the ones he is making. He teaches them how to make the beads and together they find peace. In other words, they found the Iroquois League.[75]

Longfellow's epic *Song of Hiawatha*, written in 1854 and 1855, is based on stories such as this. One favorite of this author's tells of a great wampum bird. When struck by arrows, beads fell from its plumage, only to be replenished instantly. Contests were held to see which warrior could kill the great bird. One chief offered the hand of his daughter to the successful brave. When the warriors all failed, a young boy from an enemy tribe asked to try. Thinking that the young boy could not possibly succeed, the chief allowed him to fling an arrow. The arrow struck home and great torrents of wampum (i.e., communication) fell upon the tribes. The marriage of the boy and the princess brought lasting peace, again in the form of the Iroquois League. Strands of wampum pre-dating the League's formation are rare. Thus, it appears that the emergences of both indeed are linked.[76]

[*] The Tuscaroras joined the League in 1722. The League endured until the American Revolution when the Oneida and Tuscarora sided with the Americans and the other nations sided with the British. The official end came with the second Treaty of Fort Stanwix in 1784.

Others had their own opinions about wampum's origins. Rhode Island founder, Roger Williams, for example, credited the local Narragansett as its inventors. In describing the shell beads, Williams said, "Their white they call *Wômpam*; their black *Suckaúhock*." He added that, after eating the hen (clam,) "...they breake out of the shell, about halfe an inch of a blacken part of it, of which they make their *Suckáwhock*, or blacke money." He said that they used the *Meteaûhock*, or periwinkle (another clam species) to "...make their *Wômpam* or white money, of halfe the value of their...blacke* money" and that they "...Store up shells in Summer against Winter, whereof to make their money."[77]

The Narragansett probably got the idea from their neighbors at Gardiners Bay and eastern Long Island.[78] It appears that Long Island was the center of production and that the output was distributed inland and up and down the coast. Massachusetts' John Winthrop wrote in his journal that his bark, the *Blessing*, returned from Long Island on October 2, 1633 and that "There they had store of the best wampum peak, both white and blue." Europeans called the beads *seawant, seawan* or *zeewand,*[79] words that tie to an aboriginal name for Long Island: *Sewanhacky*, or "Land of Seawant." Another aboriginal name for the island is *Mattauwack*, from *Meht-anaw-ack* ("Land of Periwinkles.")[80]

THE DUTCH MISTAKE

Wampum got its second real boost and took on monetary status when the Dutch began settling present day New York in the 1620's. They brought metal awls called "muxes" that revolutionized how beads were made. It appears that muxes themselves even were treated as money. Long Island land deals for Huntington (1653,) Mastic Neck/Brookhaven (1657) and East Hampton (1648) all included quantities of muxes in their payment terms.[81]

Isaack de Rasiere,† Secretary of New Netherland, is credited with bringing the monetary use of wampum to the Massachusetts Bay Colony in October 1627. Seeking food and supplies for his companions, De Rasiere came to Massachusetts with trumpeters and great fanfare. After days of entertaining, he returned to his bark where he sold "sundry of his goods" to the Englishmen. In 1634 William Bradford, the second governor of the Plymouth Colony, recorded the events that followed De Rasiere's visit. First, he wrote of tobacco: "And amongst other commodities they vended much tobacco for linen cloth, stuffs, etc., which was a good benefit to the people, till the Virginians found out their Plantation [Manhattan.]"[82] Then of wampum he wrote:

> *That which turned out most to their* [i.e., the Dutchmen's] *profite, in time, was an entrance into the trade of* Wampompeake*; for now they bought aboute* 50^{li}[bra] [i.e., 50 pounds] *worth of it of them; and they told them how vendable it was at their forte Orania* [a.k.a. Aurania or Fort Orange – present-day Albany], *and did perswade them* [i.e., Massachusetts' Englishmen] *they would find it so at Kenebeck; and so it came to pass in time, though at first it stuck, & it was 2 years before they could put of this small quantity, till* y^e [the] *inland people knew of it; and afterwards they could scarcely ever gett enough for them, for many years togeather...And strange it was to see the great alteration it made in a few years amonge* y^e *Indeans themselves; for all the Indeans of these parts, &* y^e *Massachusetts, had none or very little of it; but* y^e *sachems & some spetiall persons that wore a little of it for ornaments. Only it was made & kepte amonge* y^e *Nariganssetts & Pequents, which grew*

---

* The term black is relative. The dark beads actually are violet or bluish. (See below.)

† Alternately, Isaac de Razier.

> *rich & potent by it, and these people were poore and begerly, and had no use of it. Neither did the English of this plantation* [i.e., colony], *or any other in ye land, till now that they had knowledge of it from ye Dutch, so much as know what it was, much less y^t^* [i.e., that] *it was a comoditie of that worth & valew. But after it grue thus to be a comoditie in these parts, these Indeans fell into it allso, and to learne how to make it; for ye Narigansets doe geather ye shells of which y^ey^* [i.e., they] *make it from their shors. And it hath now continued a current comoditie aboute this 20 years, and it may prove a drugg in time. In ye mean time it maks ye Indeans of these parts rich and power full, and allso prowd therby; and fills them with peeces* [guns], *powder, and shots, which no laws can restraine.*[83]

The Massachusetts standard of 1637 set the value of wampum at three dark beads or six light beads to a penny. Connecticut established its own standard of four white beads or two dark ones to the penny in 1637, but in 1641 adopted the Massachusetts standard. Wampum's use was not limited to New England and New Netherland. New York and Virginia soon passed their own versions of legislation regulating the use of wampum (or "wampumpeage," or "peage," or "peak.") Virginians knew it as "roanoke" or "roan."

The basic unit was the "fathom," a strand of 360 beads valued at 60 pence. A fathom actually is a unit of length equivalent to about six feet. However, in the wampum trade its length was allowed to vary. Where four beads were equivalent to a penny, a fathom was only 240 beads.[84]

Whatever its origins, wampum became big business. After the introduction of muxes, beads appeared in large numbers. At council, complex belts with multiple rows of beads and symbolic patterns replaced simple strands. The famous Onondaga Belt, for example, may once have been twice its current size, but still contains fifty rows of 210 beads, for a total of 10,500. In 1645 the English demanded two thousand fathoms of beads from the Narragansett in what amounted to taxes. This translates to somewhere between 560,000 and 720,000 beads. By 1650 only 1,692 fathoms had been paid and the English took vigorous measures to collect the balance.[85]

For a time, one could buy land, pay Massachusetts taxes and even attend Harvard College with wampum.[86] The price of corn, the colony's lifeblood, was set at 6s per bushel in coin or 5s 6d in wampum in 1638, indicating near parity between the two currencies.[87]

Between 1634 and 1664, Massachusetts colonists traded 21,000 fathoms (somewhere between £5 and £10 thousand – about 7 million beads) for furs. The Abenaki tribe in Maine were the willing recipients of many of these beads. Massachusetts traders sailed to Maine with loads of beads, exchanged them for skins and then headed off to ready markets in Europe. The beads cost the colonists little because they were extorted from local Indians in the form of civil fees and fines.[88]

Under the 1637 Massachusetts regulations, no one was required to accept more than a shilling's worth of beads in trade. The limitation briefly was raised to £10, but soon was lowered again to prevent anyone from having to accept too much of it.[89] In 1648 the legal tender requirement was set at £2 and the value set to four and eight beads to the penny for dark and light beads, respectively.[90] In spite of many variations in value relative to everything else, this two-to-one relationship of light to dark beads almost always held.[*]

It all was a case of mistaken identity. Europeans misinterpreted the Native American concept that they had copied. To Indians the bead strands represented something more akin to respect than to wealth. Someone held in great esteem was given strands of wampum as a symbol of respect and those who wore many beads sat in honored positions at council. The Dutch and those who followed saw the well-regarded wearing strands of beads and incorrectly associated the practice with wealth. In doing so they imposed the European concepts of possession and money on what had been purely ceremonial and tributary.[91]

A Clam by Any Other Name

Many beads were made from the homes of a particular type of shellfish that the Narragansett called *poquauhock*, or simply *quahog*. Others used the name *hens-po-qua-hock*, or *hens*. All of these terms are Native American names for clams. Linnaeus (the Swede, Carl von Linné) assigned Latin names to species in 1758, appropriately calling the wampum quahogs *Mercenaria mercenaria.*[†] (*Mercenaria* is Latin for "money.")

Initially, wampum's value was based primarily on the amount of effort required for its creation. The shells from which it was made exhibit blue-violet coloring around a white center. The thickened area where the shellfish's muscle is attached also is dark inside. This thickened area was used to make black wampum,[92] while lighter areas and the shells of other species were used to make white wampum. It is because shells with large proportions of dark coloring were more difficult to find and because the parts of the shell from which dark beads could be made were relatively small that dark beads were assigned greater value.

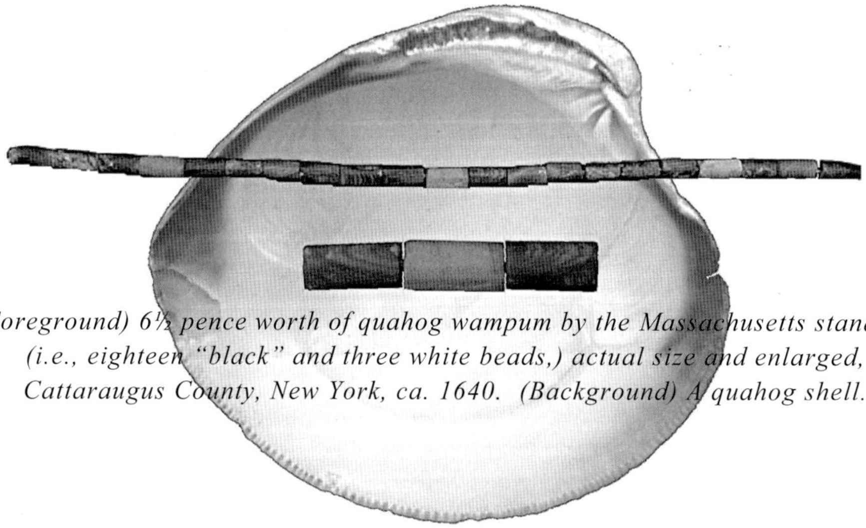

(Foreground) 6½ pence worth of quahog wampum by the Massachusetts standard (i.e., eighteen "black" and three white beads,) actual size and enlarged, Cattaraugus County, New York, ca. 1640. (Background) A quahog shell.

[*] In a sense, this valuation still applies today. A survey of companies that sell handcrafted quahog beads on the Internet reveals remarkable consistency in pricing. Beads that are entirely white generally sell for $2.50 each, while beads that are entirely purple sell for $6.00 each. Intermediate prices are charged based the degree of "purpleness" exhibited.

[†] Alternately, *Venus mercenaria.* The name Venus evidently was inspired by the Sandro Botticelli's 15th century painting, *The Birth of Venus* that shows the goddess awaiting a royal violet robe as she steps from the sea shell that has borne her from her birthplace in the sea.

By the middle of the seventeenth century, the end of wampum's use as money was near. New Netherlanders complained in 1650 that there was no consistent valuation for it. In 1648 the price of one beaver was a fathom of black wampum or two fathoms of the white. By 1660 the Seneca were charging thirty handfuls of black wampum or sixty handfuls of white wampum for a beaver.[93]

Another problem with wampum was that anyone could make it. The Dutch certainly changed the equation with the introduction of muxes. The English also learned to make the beads with more efficiency, though with less skill, than their Indian counterparts used. By the late 1640's, both Connecticut and Massachusetts already had found it necessary to pass legislation against poorly made or counterfeit wampum:[94]

> *The Commissioners were informed that the Indyans abuse the English with much badd, false and unfinished peage, and that the English Traders, after it comes to their hands, choose what fitts their marketts and occasions, and leave the refuse to pass to and fro in these Colonies, wch the Indyans, whoe best understand the qualities and defects of peage will not willingly take back.* (Connecticut Pub. Record, 1:179) [95]

Though purists vehemently disagree, quahogs were not the only shells used in wampum. It also was made from the central columns of whelk shells[*] that exhibit only white coloring. Whelk shells are softer and easier to work than those of the quahogs. In the strands observed by this author, beads made from quahog shells tend to be cylindrical in shape, while those made from whelks often take the form of holed disks.

Both strung wampum, or *peage*, and the single-bead form, *seawant*, simply outlived their usefulness. Since it was a labor-based exchange medium, the practice of counterfeiting wampum may have contributed to the decline. Obviously, beads could be made faster with muxes than with Indian drills made of bone. However, the gradual emergence of coins and paper currencies and the general inconvenience of handling the beads were the biggest reasons for the decline in its use. By the early 1660's, all of the New England colonies had stopped accepting wampum as legal currency.[96] Still, a 1671 account describes a man named John Higginson who received £160 in "country produce." He asked if, instead, he might be paid £120 in "solid cash," including beaver skins, black and white wampum, beads, and musket balls that were valued at a farthing each.[97] The last officially recorded use of wampum as money came in New York, in 1701.[98] Clearly, rude necessity in the absence of coins and paper money led these colonies to adapt a Native American custom to their own needs. That necessity made wampum the earliest form of true money used in America.

Technically, the term "wampum" implies a particular type of beads, used for a relatively short time in a relatively small area. In a more general sense, different types of trade beads actually were used throughout the continent and well into the nineteenth century. As with copper, this use actually pre-dates recognized European contact. Without more evidence, however, it cannot be concluded that the concept of money existed in North America's pre-history.

After the demise of wampum, trade beads continued to be used widely in frontier areas, in trade with Indians. Imported glass beads were introduced as early as 1633. Despite attempts by Europeans to declare them equal to wampum, however, glass beads never attained the same

---

[*] *Bucinum undatum*, *Pyrula canaliculata* or *Pyrula carica*.

levels of value in trade. In an ironic twist, they seem to have been viewed more as tributes or presents and less as money.[99]

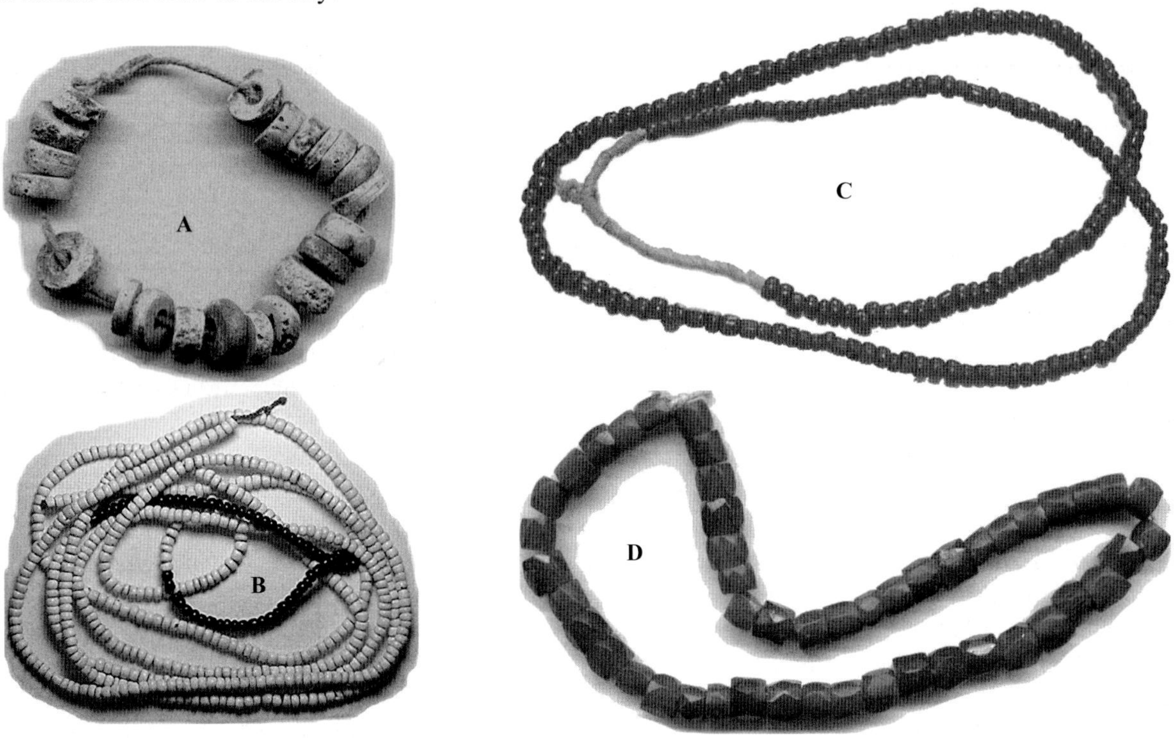

Non-wampum trade bead forms (all shown reduced): *A - Pre-European shell beads (Arkansas, ca. 1300.)* ***Glass trade beads:*** *B - White/black, original silk string, Hudson's Bay Company (ca. 1750-1800.) C – Venetian red trade beads, ca. 1650-1700. D – Blue glass trade beads (ca. 1800-1810) unearthed in Oklahoma. This style sometimes is referred to as "Russian" because the principal region where they were introduced was the American west coast, where Russian merchant ships plied their trade. Lewis and Clark carried similar beads on their journeys westward. Blue beads were especially prized. On January 9, 1806, Lewis wrote in the expedition journal, "... the blue is usually preferred [sic] to the white; these beads constitute the principal circulating medium with all the Indian tribes on this river [the Columbia;] for these beads they will dispose of any article they possess."*[100]

4: A NECESSARY EVIL

IN VALUE EQUAL TO MONEY

At least two ancient Chinese inventions were indispensable in early America – gunpowder and paper money. Gunpowder's impact was immediate and obvious. Paper money's first New World appearance came a bit later, in the mid-1680's, when a French military commander in Canada was short of hard currency. In its place he signed emergency promissory notes on the backs of playing cards. These IOUs promised that the men in his command would be paid when coins arrived from France. While the men waited, the cards took on a value of their own as they were exchanged for goods and services. Despite the French government's strong opposition to this innovative measure, it was used sporadically in Canada until 1757 and, as evidenced by examples in the Louisiana State Museum, at least until 1779 in New Orleans.

English colonists were about five years behind their French neighbors in discovering paper money, though it did not take them long to catch up. Massachusetts issued America's first paper currency in 1690.* These notes, and many that followed, were *bills of credit*, authorized authorized to meet a specific need. In this case the trigger was a military emergency. During King William's War, French Quebec turned away an invasion force of 2,200 British and colonial troops aboard thirty-two ships. To pay the failed invaders, bills of credit totaling £7,000 were printed using engraved copper plates.[101] As with the Canadian playing cards, the idea was to defer payments until hard currency became available for redemption. Both the cards and the bills were original in that the instrument of exchange was a promise and not an item with its own intrinsic value. Neither really was intended to circulate as money, but both were exchanged readily in trade and inevitably came to be viewed as such.

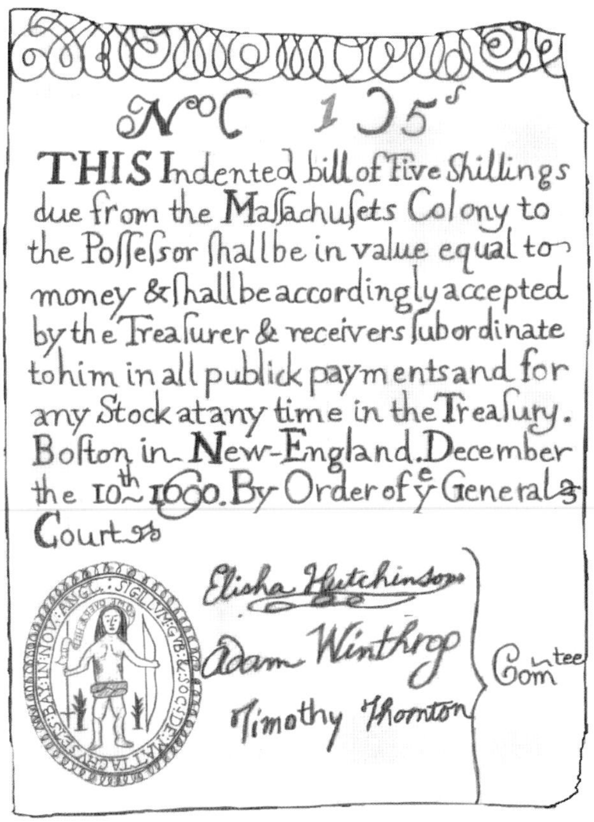
No C 135s
THIS Indented bill of Five Shillings due from the Maſſachuſets Colony to the Poſſeſſor ſhall be in value equal to money & ſhall be accordingly accepted by the Treaſurer & receivers ſubordinate to him in all publick payments and for any Stock at any time in the Treaſury. Boſton in New-England December the 10th 1690. By Order of ye General Court
Elisha Hutchinson
Adam Winthrop
Timothy Thornton
Comtee

Massachusetts five-shilling bill of credit, "...in value equal to money...," December 10, 1690. (Drawing, reduced.) The Indian in the lower left corner is surrounded by the motto SIGILLVM: GV^{R}: & SOC: DE MATTACHVSETS: BAY: IN: NOV.: ANGL.: *("Seal of the Governor and Society of Massachusetts Bay in New England.") The scroll above him reads (backwards,) "Come Over & Help Us."*

* J. W. Schuckers wrote of a bank, founded by a Boston gentleman and others, that may have printed trial notes notes as early as 1686 (Schuckers, page iii.) Newman wrote that the effort was abandoned in 1688 without notes having been issued. Newman also described unsuccessful currency proposals made as early as 1667. (*The Early Paper Money of America*, p.180.)

More Massachusetts bills were printed in 1691 and in the decades that followed. After periods of acceptance at full value, the colony's early issues routinely fluctuated in value until 1749 when British specie was used to redeem and back them. As with Massachusetts' famed silver coins of 1652 to 1682 (Chapter 8,) most or all were printed without royal approval.

In contrast, Connecticut had the Crown's blessing in financing an unsuccessful land expedition to Montreal in 1709, near the end of the colonial phase of Queen Anne's War. Boston's Jeremiah Dummer engraved the printing plates. In his younger days, Dummer apprenticed under John Hull, the man responsible for Massachusetts' silver coinage. (Dummer's silversmith mark is illustrated at left.) To retire its bills, Connecticut allowed them to be used in payment of taxes, along with silver, pork, beef, winter wheat, rye and Indian corn...That is, country money.[102]

Massachusetts 20 shilling bill of credit, May 31, 1710. (Drawing, reduced.) These were re-dated for a 1711 issue. Red under-printing served both as an ornament and to deter counterfeiters. In this case, the under-printing is a mirrored, monogrammed "AR," for ANNE REGINA *or "Queen Anne."*

By 1712 six other colonies had joined the club: South Carolina (1703,) New Hampshire (1709,) New York (1709,) New Jersey (1709,) Rhode Island (1710) and North Carolina (1712.) By the eve of the Seven Years War, the remaining colonies, Pennsylvania (1723,) Delaware (1723,) Maryland (1733,) Georgia (1735) and Virginia (1755) all were using paper currency.

Despite the Crown's misgivings about credit currency, economic expansion and repeated conflicts combined to make its use unavoidable. King William's War and Queen Anne's War were just the beginning. Between 1739 and 1742, Britain fought the War of Jenkins' Ear with Spain. A graphic event, the loss during a fight of a seaman's ear, was used to propagandize a growing trade dispute between the two countries. The dispute eventually transformed itself into a 1744 to 1748 war with France. That war, known as King George's, drew heavily on colonial resources to carry on the fight in the Canadian theater. The Seven Years War followed very shortly. After each conflict, money was owed to participating colonial governments and bills of credit, drawn against the Crown, were released into the colonies to ease temporarily the resulting deficits.

Corresponding periods of accelerated expansion followed each conflict. In funding these expansions, colonial governments supplemented the Crown's money with their own. The supplements usually were bills of credit, issued in controlled sums and denominations. They generally were accepted as legal tender within the issuing colony and in those surrounding it. That they were accepted in payment of taxes in the originating colony helped to bolster confidence. To further encourage acceptance, such tax issues typically bore interest. When a tax bill was tendered it was destroyed, a practice that helps to explain the paucity of survivors from the early eighteenth century. Ultimately these bills of credit were backed by no more than the reputation of the authorizing colonial government and, with each new issue, the Crown's discomfort grew.

French and Indian War bill of credit, New Jersey, £6, November 20, 1757. Valid for five years. Two suns at the center represent £3 each to make the denomination clearly recognizable at a glance and to foil those who would illegally "markup" the bill to a higher value. To make exchange easier, the value also is expressed as seventeen ounces and ten pennyweights of silver.

Economic expansion also was supported by *loan issues*, another form of credit currency that often was doled out by land offices set up to disperse it. Typically, these loans were secured with real estate. Benjamin Franklin aptly called them "coined land."[103] As the associated interest and principal were paid, the bills were retired.[104] Loan issues were inherently risky because they were not printed in predefined sums or denominations. Their practicality was limited because, being land-backed, they lacked an effective means of redemption.[105]

As long as currency was printed in moderation and retirement or redemption occurred quickly, the system worked and the bills retained their value. When emissions were large, as after a war, depreciation became a problem. A man might sell his farm for a £100 note and then soon find that note to be worth only £80, or less. Follow-up issues often were re-valuations, intended to redeem their devalued predecessors. As a result of the instability, British commercial interests, fearful that they were being cheated in the process, continually pressured Parliament to pass laws to restrict the colonies' ability to issue bills of credit. Such measures, passed in 1751 and 1764, rankled the colonial legislatures, but failed to stop the presses.

At the same time it was common for the Crown to extend credits to the colonies against future taxes rather than allow the direct redemption of its own paper currency. In the short term this reduced out of pocket expenses for Britain. This method of backing came to present problems, however, as the deferred debts mounted. The British simply underestimated the extent to which they would become dependent on this form of credit and the frequency with which hostilities would erupt. Likewise, interest-bearing notes with maturity dates in the distant future were especially appealing to specie-starved colonies because their initial investments were small. These colonial issues, in particular, were notorious for becoming devalued.

Paper currency became so prevalent that the German economist Johann G. Busch called the eighteenth century *das papierene jahrhundert*, or "the paper century."[106] As it applied to

America, he was correct in this assessment. Revolutionary War-era Continental Currency alone amounted to a total face value of more than $240 million. Even this figure fails to include the millions printed in the individual colonies and states during the period. Clearly coins were relatively minor players. The exception was the South, with its access to the West Indian specie and, after 1763, to Spanish Louisiana and Mississippi River trade.

In the South paper currency was less common and often took the form of warehouse receipts for tobacco or other agricultural products. John McCusker gave these the generic name, "commodity notes," or, when the commodity was tobacco,"tobacco notes." When these receipts were for storage in official warehouses, they are called "storehouse notes."[107] This practice helped to bridge the gap between barter and a fully functioning monetary system. However, commodity notes were a poor substitute for specie. Fluctuating market values and the limited shelf life of the goods on which they were based quickly made individual issues obsolete. Still, they represent a third form of paper money, after bills of credit and loan issues.

Lack of specie in the colonies usually meant that colonial notes only marginally were substantiated and, by definition, their values were inflated. Yet, even as today, increasing the supply of money was seen as a means of stimulating the economy. Gresham's Law, mistakenly named for Sir Thomas Gresham, a sixteenth century English financier, holds that coins of lesser purity will drive coins of higher purity from circulation.[108*] The same law appears to have governed the relative treatment of paper money and coins. Citizens tended to spend paper and hold fast to metal currencies, export them or melt them for their market value. Without circulating specie, familiarity with paper money begged the public's growing acceptance of it.

Printers lent their support to this logic, as statistics bear out. First, gold was not a factor in colonial trade. Gold that did enter America came in large measure from trade with the Portuguese and Spanish. Silver, or sterling money, was the real lifeblood of colonial commerce. In 1700 the amount of silver coinage circulating in New England is estimated at £200,000. In 1709 the value of paper money circulating in that part of America was £69,364. This figure rose to £219,448 by 1713. In the same year, the estimate of silver circulating in New England drops to £130,000. The amount of paper currency in circulation continued to increase until, by sometime around 1720, it is said that no silver circulated in New England.[109]

In the early eighteenth century, paper money circulated at parity with silver coins. Finished goods purchased from Great Britain had to be paid for in sterling funds. A colonial exporter of commodities engaged the services of an agent in Great Britain to sell his goods on commission. The proceeds then were added to the exporter's account. The exporter could then direct his agent to make purchases on his behalf by drawing on the deposited funds. Alternately, the colonist could ask that a *bill of exchange*, yet another form of currency, be drawn on his account. Bills of exchange essentially stated that some amount of sterling funds was available in the account. Such a bill could be sold to another person at the going rate of exchange. The buyer could then resell it or use it to pay obligations. Ultimately, the bills ended up in the hands of British creditors who then presented them to the agent of the first colonist for redemption in sterling funds.[110]

British obligations also could be paid in actual silver. However, the preference was to pay debts in bills of exchange. Holding the bills was risky because variable exchange rates caused

[*] This "law" existed long before Gresham. Both its codification into formal economic theory and its extrapolation to paper currencies occurred long after his time. Henry Dunning McLeod, a nineteenth century economist, is responsible for the mis-attribution. (Maloney, Oxford DNB.)

their values to fluctuate relative to that of silver. Insurance and handling charges associated with transporting and processing silver payments also contributed to the preference for bills. This was a complex and unwieldy system that depended heavily on the honesty of the participants.[111] By and large, it was a system for the gentry and not for the masses.

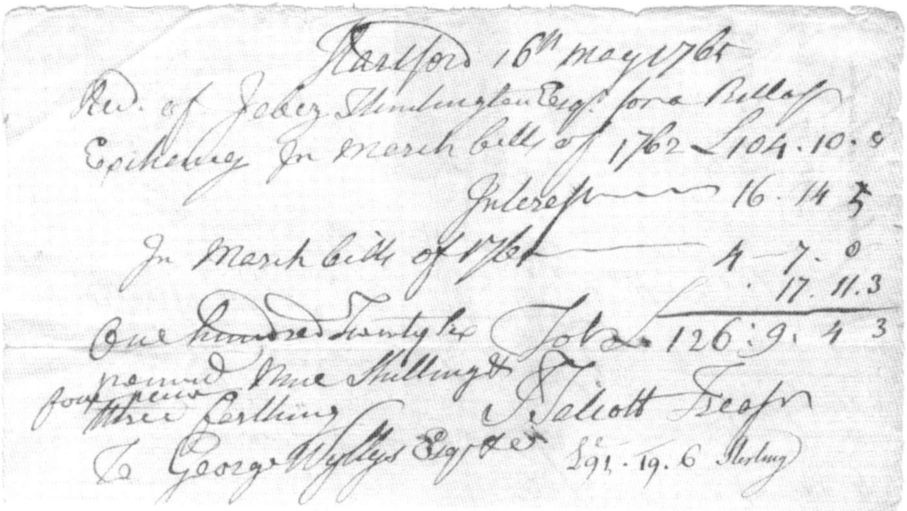

Hand written bill of exchange for George Wyllys, Esq., docketed by Jabez Huntington, Esq., in the sterling amount of £126.9.4.3. Hartford, May 16, 1765 (size reduced.) The system required that each key stakeholder maintain a copy. In 1735 Georgia issued specialized bills of exchange("sola" bills) that required only a single copy.

The paper preference effectively created a market for bills of exchange. Lulls in colonial exports (i.e., negative shifts in the balance of trade) meant that colonists accumulated debt by purchasing British goods. When colonial exports lagged Americans had little ability to generate bills of exchange with which to pay their debts. These shortages caused the price of the bills of exchange to rise, contributing both to colonial inflation and to the advantageous position that the British held over Americans in trade. Paradoxically, shortages also stimulated the American desire for and acceptance of paper since, in the absence of silver, colonists desperately needed an internal medium of exchange. The market adjusted itself whenever the price of the bills reached a level at which it became preferable to pay debts in hard currency.[112] This, too, was detrimental to the colonies as it further drained them of silver.

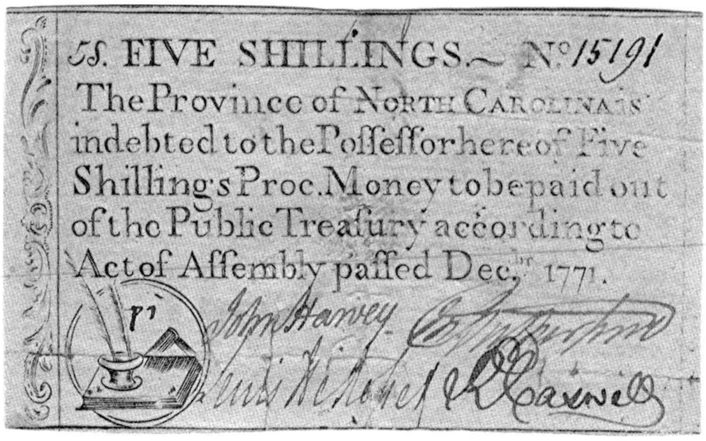

5s. FIVE SHILLINGS. No 15191
The Province of North Carolina is indebted to the Possessor hereof Five Shillings Proc. Money to be paid out of the Public Treasury according to Act of Assembly passed Dec. 1771.

North Carolina 5s., December 1771.

The colonies were not blind to the shortcomings of paper currency and, throughout the pre-Revolutionary period, attempts were made to apply reason to the process. In 1749, for example, Massachusetts successfully redeemed its extant paper money in silver, leveraging payments that it had received from the Crown for its participation in the recently concluded war with France. The colony wisely used the silver to redeem its outstanding bills of credit. An equitable exchange rate was determined and, for the year following the end of March 1750, the state redeemed its outstanding bills at one piece of eight for each £2.5.0 in *old tenor*[*] bills or 11s 3d in *middle* or *new tenor* bills. Subsequent debts were supposed to be paid in coined

[*] In the 1740s, Massachusetts made a 4:1 inflationary adjustment in its currency. Bills issued prior to the first adjustment are "old tenor." A second adjustment used re-dating. Bills issued between the first and second adjustment are "middle tenor." Bills issued after the second adjustment are "new tenor."

silver at the rate of 6s 8d per ounce.[113] An anonymously written pamphlet, published in Boston in 1749, supported the reforms, citing the "...great Mischiefs and infinite Injustice arising from a depreciating Currency...."[114] (See the Chapter 10 text on Massachusetts state coppers.)

Even with its problems, paper money met the critical needs of the rapidly growing American economy and thus was not without its proponents. Benjamin Franklin, for example, espoused the ease with which it could be managed as compared to hard currency. In 1729 he argued that having a ready supply of paper money would reduce interest rates, promote business, raise land values and encourage immigration. Franklin further proposed a labor theory that would have the value of goods based on the work required to produce them. This effectively made silver a commodity rather than the paradigm for currency valuation.[115] His thinking also was revolutionary in that it linked the supply of money to inflation.

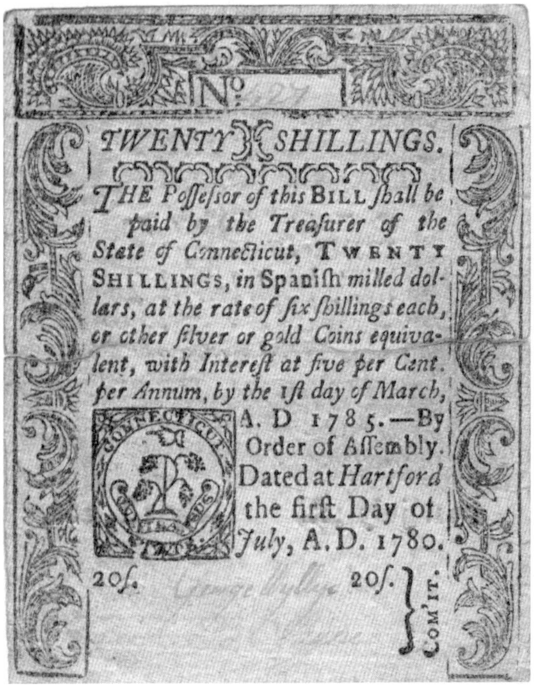

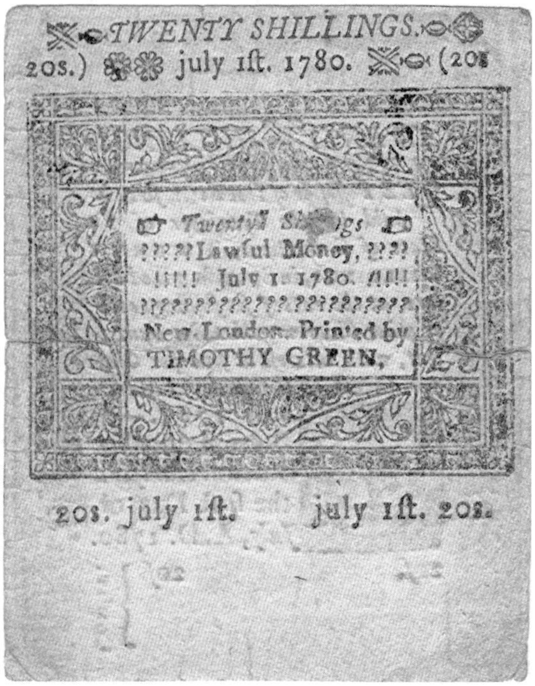

(Above) 20 shillings lawful money, Connecticut, July 1, 1780, bearing 5 pct. annual interest for 5 years. Note that the value of a Connecticut shilling was 1/6 of a Spanish milled dollar. (Left) New York, 2 shillings ($1/4, since New York valued its shillings at 8 to the dollar.) March 5, 1776.

The money supply was very serious business. British policy toward paper currency was crucial in driving the colonies toward rebellion. At times when the colonies were especially pinched, the Crown offered no recourse or relief. After 1710, for example, a law required postage to be paid in hard currency that the colonies simply did not have.[116] By the latter half of the century, bitter feelings arose out of the Crown's broader strategy to negate the rights of the American legislatures, who desperately needed the right to authorize paper currency. The *Currency Act of 1764* was a small but particularly hard-hitting component of this strategy. It was the larger overall trend, more than military occupation, taxation without representation or any other singular cause, that drove the colonies to rebellion. So says the Declaration of Independence.

The American Revolution opened the floodgates. War-induced hoarding caused the country's supply of hard currency virtually to disappear from commerce. In response the new states scurried to authorize paper money to fill the void. Some maintained the English system of pounds, shillings and pence. Others patriotically switched to Spanish milled dollars as denominations (Chapter 6.) Exchange rates were a nightmare as individual colonies had their own standards for valuing even hard currency. Evaluation of an interest-bearing bill, as it was losing value, meant doing some fairly complex calculations without the benefit of a modern calculator. Add to this mix a profusion of new denominations and one begins to understand just how dysfunctional America's Revolutionary War era monetary system really was.

The Continental Congress did little to help matters. Out of necessity any specie that it controlled was used to pay foreign powers for war supplies. If any currency were to circulate, it would have to be made of paper. The first issue of Continental Currency (i.e., currency that could circulate anywhere in America, at uniform value) was authorized on May 10, 1775. Thirty-six more authorizations followed. Before the end of the Revolution, unbacked bills were issued in such great numbers that the entire system, and the fate of the new country itself, were in peril. The same public that had embraced paper money came to abhor it.

Colonial and continental notes exist in many different denominations, reflecting: 1.) The role of small-denomination notes as surrogates for small change, 2.) inflation manifested in the issuance of large-denomination notes and 3.) the many different currency systems between which money had to be exchanged. For example, a Spanish dollar was equivalent to 4s6d in sterling funds and, thus, it was logical to produce notes of that denomination. At times New York, New Jersey and Maryland conveniently provided alternate denominations in Dutch *lion dollars* (Chapter 7) because such coins so frequently were encountered. The table below enumerates most of the many denominations that were used during the colonial and Revolutionary War period:

Denominations
British: 1d, 2d, 3d, 4d, 5d, 6d, 7d, 8d, 9d, 10d, 12d and 18d. 1s3d, 1s4d, 1s6d, 1s8d, 1s9d, 2s, 2s3d, 2s4d, 2s6d, 2s8d, 3s, 3s4d, 3s6d, 3s9d, 4s, 4s4d, 4s6d, 5s, 5s3d, 5s4d, 5s6d, 6s, 6s3d, 6s8d, 7s, 7s6d, 8s, 9s, 10s, 11s, 12s, 12s6d, 14s, 15s, 16s, 17s, 17s6d, 18s, 20s, 22s, 24s, 25s, 27s, 28s, 30s, 36s, 40s, 42s, 48s, 50s, 54s, 60s, 66s, 72s and 100s. £1, £1 10s, £1 12s, £1 15s, £2, £2 5s, £2 10 s, £3, £3 4s, £3 10s, £3 12s, £4, £5, £6, £6 5s, £8, £10, £12, £12 10s, £15, £20, £25, £30, £50 and £100
Spanish/American: \$1/36, \$1/24, \$1/18, \$1/16, \$1/15, \$1/12, \$1/10, \$1/9, \$1/8, \$1/6, \$1/5, \$2/9, \$1/4, \$1/3, \$1/2, \$2/3, \$1, \$1 1/3, \$1 2/3, \$2, \$2.50, \$2 2/3, \$3, \$3 1/3, \$4, \$5, \$6, \$6 2/3, \$7, \$7.50, \$8, \$9, \$10, \$11, \$12.50, \$13 1/3, \$15, \$16, \$17, \$20, \$25, \$30, \$35, \$40, \$45, \$50, \$55, \$60, \$65, \$70, \$75, \$80, \$90, \$100, \$150, \$200, \$250, \$300, \$400, \$500, \$600, \$750, \$1000, \$1200, \$1500 and \$2000
Spanish: 2, 4 and 8 reales. 2, 2½, 5, 10, 20, 25, 30 and 50 pesos
French: 10, 40, 50, 100, 400, 500 and 1000 ecus. 10, 100, 1000 and 10000 livres Tournois
Dutch: Lion dollar and guilder equivalents.
Other: Ounces, Pennyweights and Grains Troy

Even after ratification of the Constitution, some states insisted on their own currencies. Rhode Island, angered over the Constitution's restriction of the states' right to print paper money, delayed ratification until 1790. Furthermore, Daniel Shays' famous rebellion can be attributed, in part, to the inability of the states to produce an adequate supply of stable money for the masses. It is unsurprising that small private issues of paper currencies emerged in the 1790's.

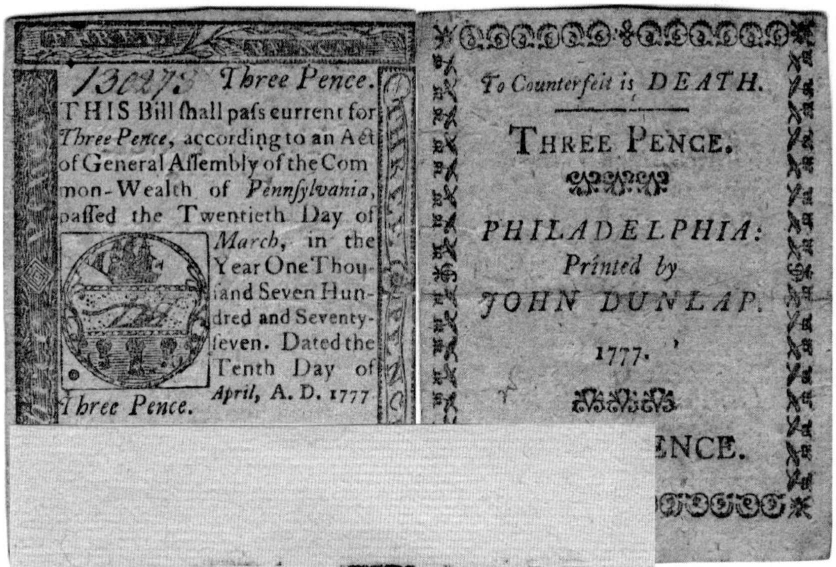

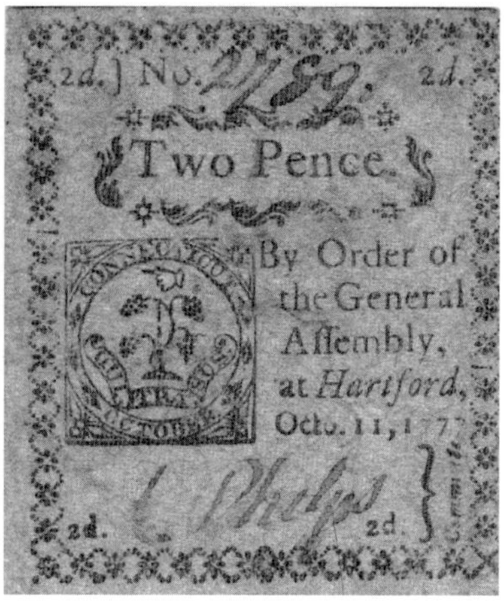

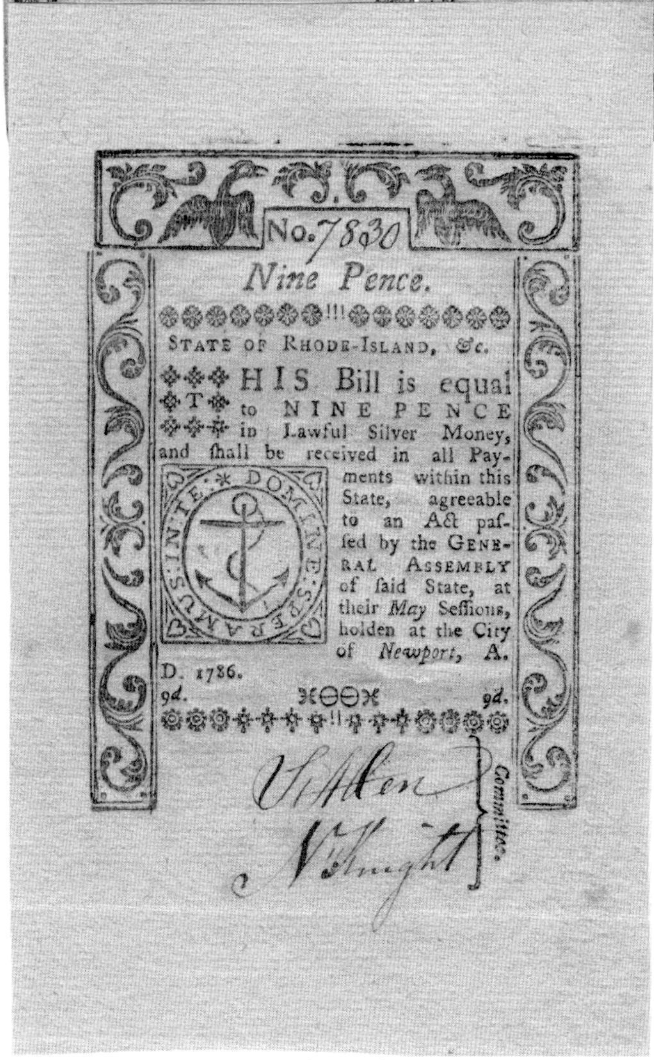

Big and Small: (Above) Small change in 1777 - 3d, Pennsylvania, and a uniface 2d note of Connecticut. (Right) Large May 1786 9d legal tender bill of credit, Rhode Island. (Reduced.) The act to authorize these notes was intended to enforce their legal tender status by making refusal to accept them a crime punishable without a jury trial. When a butcher refused to accept a bill such as this in payment, the resulting case of Trevett v. Weeden established forever every Americans' right of trial by jury.[117]

America's love-hate relationship with its paper currency did not end with the emergence of the federal government. As the nineteenth century dawned, citizens were leery of unsubstantiated currency, but still it was occasionally being issued by public and private entities. The devaluation of colonial and continental currencies left many with piles of nearly worthless rag paper. As a result Americans learned to expect very little from their governments. As they spread westward links back to those eastern governments became increasingly tenuous. Yet a ready supply of money still was needed to build infrastructure and drive commerce. That coins were yet to be produced in numbers large enough for day-to-day commerce further complicated the issue. Paper money was, indeed, a necessary evil.

FROM RAGS TO RICHES?

Most early American paper monies are made of thick, high-quality cotton or flax rag paper, like that now called card stock. For some issues Virginia and other colonies used thinner paper that today might be called onionskin, rice paper or even tissue. Prior to about 1850 paper was made by drawing a wire screen through a bin of water in which rag fibers were suspended. When the paper was intended for money, colored threads or flakes of the mineral, mica, were often added to the bin to make counterfeiting more difficult. As the screen was moved through the water it collected fibers in a thin layer on its leading side. After enough fibers collected on the screen, it was carefully inverted to allow the layer of fibers to detach and fall onto a cloth. Another cloth was laid on top, in preparation for the next layer. The process was repeated to produce a stack of fiber layers with cloths between them. When the stack reached a certain height, it was pressed between boards to eliminate excess water, and then bound. After weeks or months of drying the paper was ready for printing. This process is very different from the acid/wood pulp method used in making most modern paper. The basic process used in making rag paper for today's Federal Reserve notes, however, is not markedly different.*

Delaware, ten shillings, January 1, 1776. Printed by James Adams. Its back depicts an everyday sheaf of wheat. Also note the dark threads and the embedded mica flecks that appear as bright spots.

Benjamin Franklin brought back from his European travels a supply of attractive *marbleized*, or *polychromed*, paper that found its way into at least two issues. (See page 63.) Marbleization involves pulling paper through a bin of water on the surface of which float oil-based dyes. Since the dyes move randomly on the surface of the water, a unique swirling pattern is imparted to the paper. Marbleizing was sometimes combined with *indenting*. An indented bill was printed with a broad, patterned border, usually on the left side of its face. When it was issued, an irregular curve was cut across this border. The bill was distributed, but a stub with

* Fortunately, modern wood pulp methods were not used to make eighteenth century paper. These methods dissolve wood pulp in an acid mixture. Residual acids can destroy the paper in a few short years. The water suspension method employed before 1850 used no acids. Thus, many older notes and other documents survive. Some of them have been damaged, however, by acid-bearing inks.

the opposite side of the curve was retained. On redemption, matching the shape and pattern of the note's edge to those of the stub served to verify authenticity.

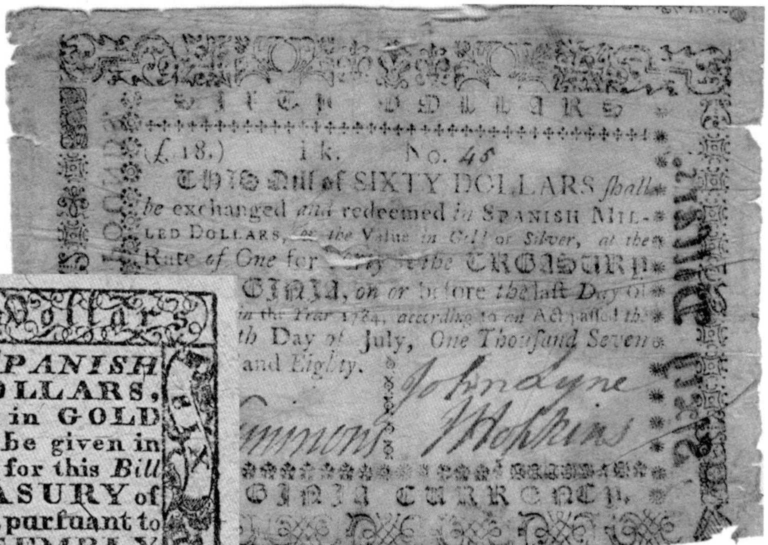

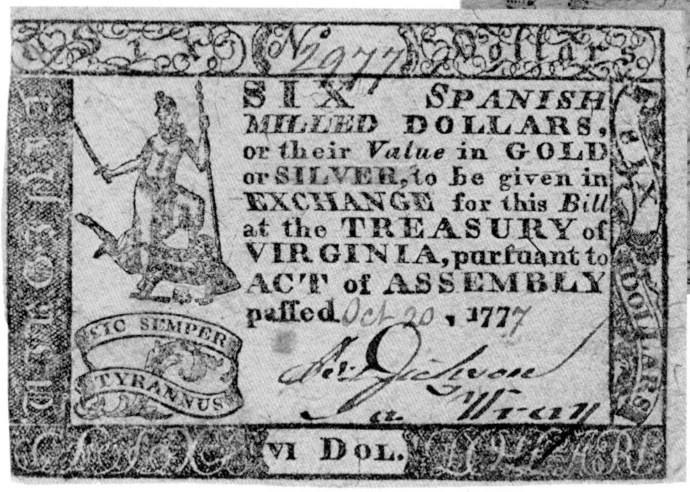

Thick and Thin:

(Top) Uniface Virginia $60 note of July 14, 1780, on very thin paper. Text from the face can easily be read when viewed from the back. (Bottom) Uniface Virginia $6 note of October 20, 1777, on very thick card stock paper. Its motto, SIC SEMPER TYRANNUS *("Thus be it always to tyrants,") would be heard again, four score and eight years later, as John Wilkes Booth made his final exit from the stage at Ford's Theater.*

Watermarks also were used to discourage counterfeiters. Watermarks were made by attaching metal shapes or wire to the screen on which the layers of fibers collected. As the fibers accumulated, fewer of them adhered to the attached shapes than to the surrounding area of the screen. In the finished paper, these areas are thinner and the design becomes visible when the paper is held before a light source.

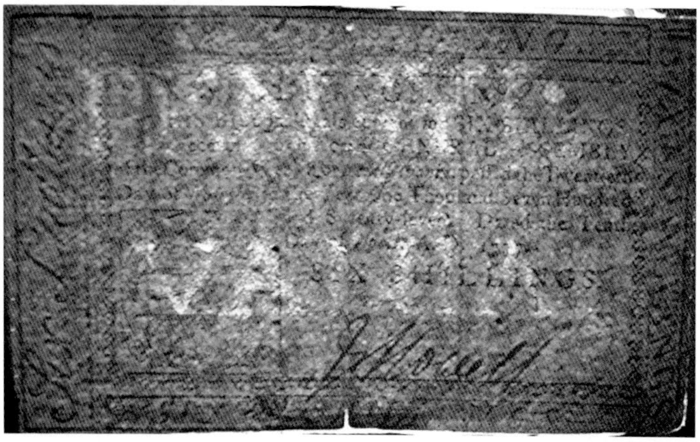

Watermarked Pennsylvania 6 s. note of April 10, 1777.

Regardless of the paper used, intaglio printing techniques typically were employed. In this process an engraved plate is covered with ink that collects in the recessed areas. The surplus is then wiped from the plate before the paper is pressed onto it from above. In many cases, the plate was made of copper. Occasionally, a cast lead plate was made from a carved mold, or cast lead type was set in a printer's chase.* After printing one side of the bills, the plate or chase was replaced with the corresponding plate or chase for the other side, the printed sheets were flipped over and the process was repeated.†

* A "chase" is an open box that tightly holds type together for printing.

† With notes, the terms "face" and "back" replace the coin-related terms "obverse" and "reverse," respectively. A note (or coin) with designs on only one side is said to be "uniface."

By the late eighteenth century, some fairly sophisticated, and some not-so-sophisticated anti-counterfeiting measures, had evolved. One of the most effective deterrents was multi-color printing. One of the least effective was the use of personal signatures that could be forged. Odd characters, broken and shifted characters, strange fonts and deliberate misspellings[*] were all tried. Most of these measures were as obvious to the counterfeiter as to the official engraver and as such were ineffective. So were inscriptions such as "To Counterfeit is Death." Even when it meant punishment by death or mutilation, counterfeiters were undeterred.

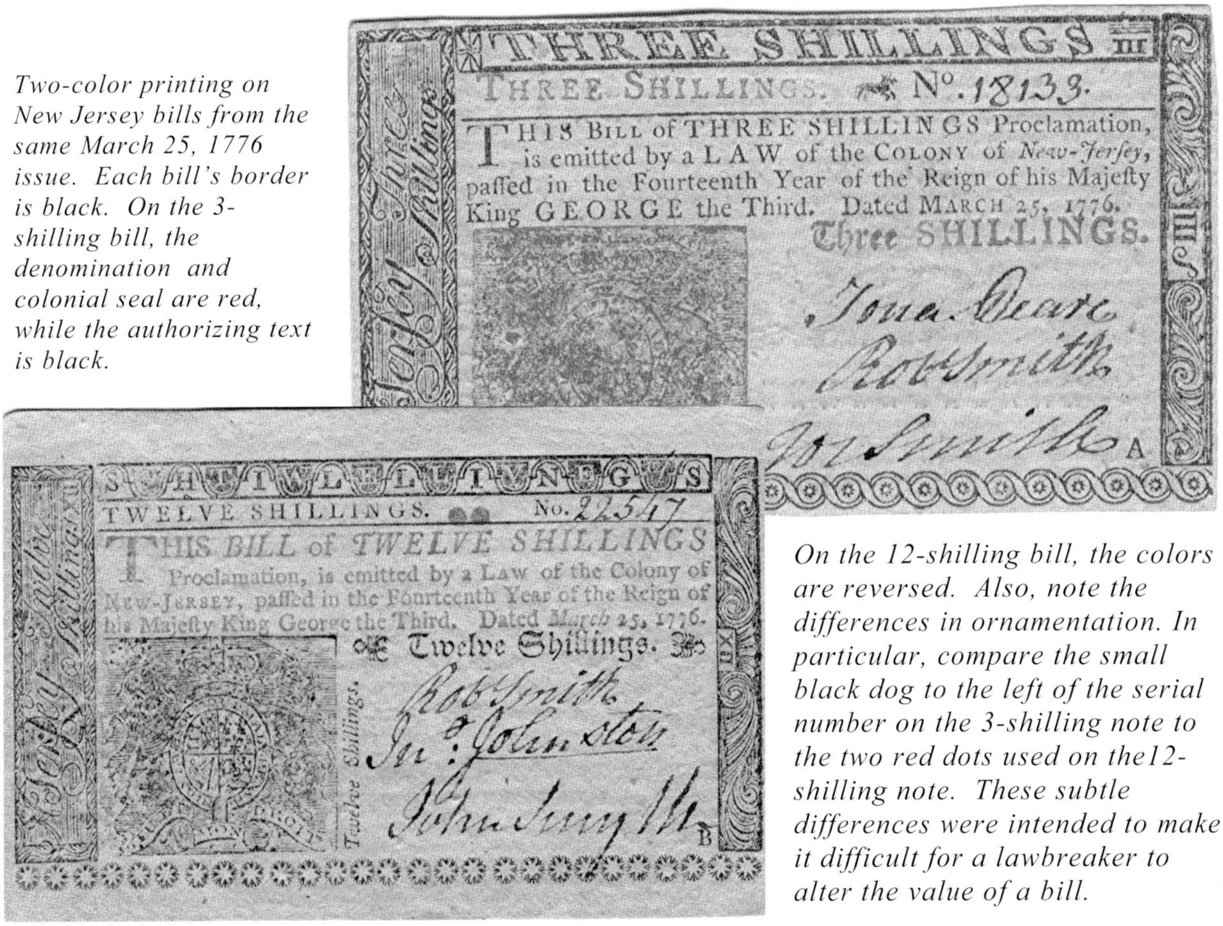

Two-color printing on New Jersey bills from the same March 25, 1776 issue. Each bill's border is black. On the 3-shilling bill, the denomination and colonial seal are red, while the authorizing text is black.

On the 12-shilling bill, the colors are reversed. Also, note the differences in ornamentation. In particular, compare the small black dog to the left of the serial number on the 3-shilling note to the two red dots used on the12-shilling note. These subtle differences were intended to make it difficult for a lawbreaker to alter the value of a bill.

Ever the innovator, Benjamin Franklin devised an ingenious, even if not-so-effective, method for using natural leaf shapes against counterfeiting. Recognizing that the patterns formed by the veins of a leaf each were unique, he created a plaster cast of the leaf, and then made a lead plate from the plaster cast. Using this lead plate the unique pattern of the leaf's veins could be replicated on a bill, creating what often is referred to as a *nature print*. Such a leaf plate is a type of *vignette*. A vignette is a component of an overall design that can be combined with type and other vignettes in a chase. Plates or vignette components of plates often were assigned to trusted third parties for safekeeping and oversight.[118]

[*] On the Virginia sixty-dollar note shown previously, "Bill" deliberately was spelled "Dill." Also, note the broken, shifted characters in "*TWENTY D*" on the left side of the face of the federally-backed 1780 New Jersey note illustrated at the end of the section on Continental Currency.

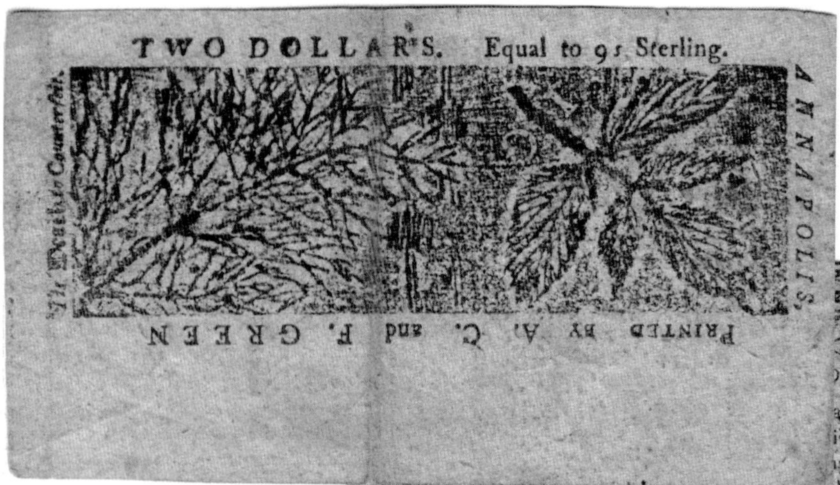

(Left) Maryland $2, April 10, 1774, illustrating the nature print technique. Note the phrase "'Tis Death to Counterfeit." *Printed at the Green Print Shop in Annapolis. Jonas and Anne Catharine Green are famous for their early protests against British policy, under the Death's head symbol of their* Maryland Gazette. *Jonas died before the Revolution, in 1767. "F. Green" refers to Frederick, a son. (Right) "Death's head" type found at Green Print Shop excavation. Photograph courtesy of Dr. Mark Leone, Archeology in Annapolis. Special thanks to Ms. Amelia Chisholm.*[119]

Bills printed before 1810 generally are square or rectangular and are roughly two-thirds the size of modern American notes. Exceptions exist on both ends of the size scale. Some early notes are four by six inches or larger, while some small change notes are as small as one-inch square. In 1722 Massachusetts was responsible for a curious issue of small-denomination coin substitutes in protest against the delivery of William Wood's Rosa Americana coins (Chapter 8.) Each denomination has a different shape – pennies are circular, two pence are rectangular and three pence are hexagonal. These diminutive notes sometimes even were cut into pieces to make change. Aside from novelty of using different shapes to indicate denominations, they also were unusual in their use of parchment (dried animal skin or tissue) for durability.

To save time, notes of several denominations often were printed simultaneously on the same sheet of paper. This meant that the printer had to be very careful to align the apparatus and the paper so that the proper designs appeared opposite each other on the finished bills. This was accomplished by using pins that punctured the paper at its corners. When the second side was to be pressed, the printer simply aligned the holes from the first pressing onto the pins. The simultaneous printing of multiple denominations also meant that the printer had to be careful to ensure that the number of notes for each denomination matched the number that he or she was authorized to print. This required a degree of arithmetic manipulation. Sometimes extra notes were printed because the combinations of plates failed to produce exactly the authorized quantities. Franklin used the term "overplus" to describe this situation.[120]

In most cases, some components (e.g., signatures or serial numbers) still had to be added manually. Sometimes every note on a sheet received the same serial number. In other cases, individual bills were numbered sequentially. Various other numbering schemes were used for tracking emissions and to make counterfeiting more difficult. Some modern reproductions of early notes are known to the collecting community by their unchanging serial numbers. Sometimes manually applied serial numbers are supplemented with printed letters or symbols that indicate a bill's physical position on the printing plate. This further helped in the accounting of quantities printed.

To further combat counterfeiting *detector* bills often were printed on colored, typically blue, paper and given to businesses. They were identical to regular bills, but could not be spent. Their purpose was to allow side-by-side comparison with suspected counterfeits. If a suspicious note was received, the spender sometimes was required to endorse it.

All thirteen American colonies/states, Vermont, the Northwest Territory and even British Florida printed paper currency in one form or another. The subjects and inscriptions used on early notes are fantastically varied, as were the colonies' motives for printing them. Some notes feature allegorical or inspirational themes, animals, buildings or tools. Some state specific reasons for existence, such as supplying the army or rebuilding the lighthouse on Georgia's Tybee Island. Lofty ideals are depicted alongside everyday items and official proclamations. Quality ranges from hand-written promissory and workman-like typeset notes to the beautiful classical engravings such as those done by Thomas Coram for South Carolina.

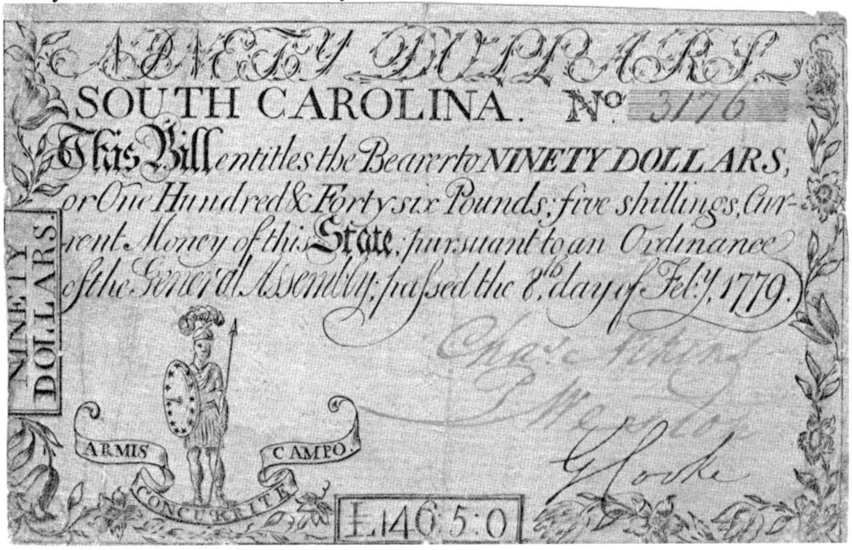

$90, or £146.5.0 in South Carolina currency. February 8, 1779. With 390 pence to the dollar, South Carolina's currency system was unique among the thirteen colonies. (See the text on Constellatio Nova pattern coins, in Chapter 10.) Engraved by Charleston's Thomas Coram, the back features Hercules or Samson strangling a lion. The face motto reads ARMIS CONCURRITE CAMPO, *or "Stay Together in Arms."*

Signatures of key figures, such as attendees of the Stamp Act Congress and signers of the Declaration of Independence or Constitution, sometimes appear on the bills. Such signatures add to collector interest and command premiums. Notable figures also were involved in actual production. Among them, Benjamin Franklin, David Rittenhouse, the U.S. Mint's first director, and Paul Revere all played direct roles in printing. Bills whose backs bear the words "Printed by B. Franklin" or "Printed by B. Franklin, and D. Hall" are especially prized.

State of Massachusetts bill of credit, one shilling, October 16, 1778. Paul Revere engraved its "codfish" face plate. Thomas Fleet engraved its "pine tree" back plate that depicts the state's most enduring symbol. (Inset) Revere's rising sun vignette from a 3-shilling note due December 1, 1779.

(Left) Drawing of a rare December 7, 1775 Massachusetts 14-shilling "Sword in Hand" note (back.) "Issued in defence [sic] of American Liberty." Engraved by Revere, these feature an American, ready to fight with a sword in his right hand and the Magna Charta in his left. The Latin part of the motto reads Ense petit placidam sub Libertate Quietem, *or "He Arms to Seek Peace with Freedom."*

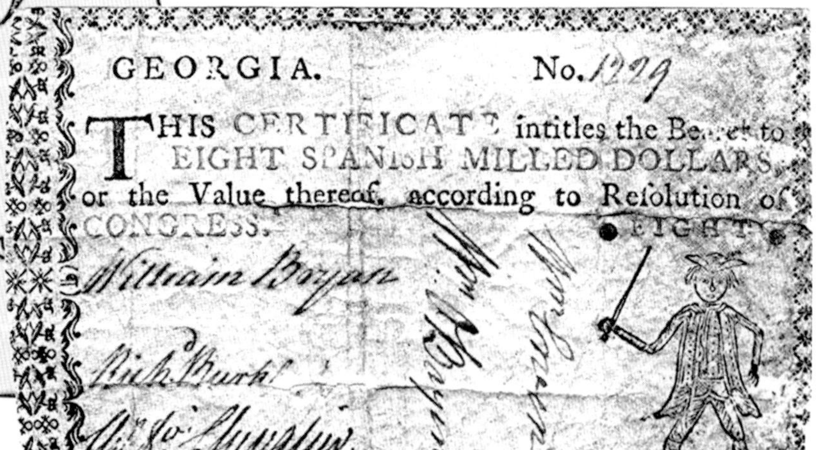

(Right) Undated [1776] Georgia $8 note depicting another defiant patriot.

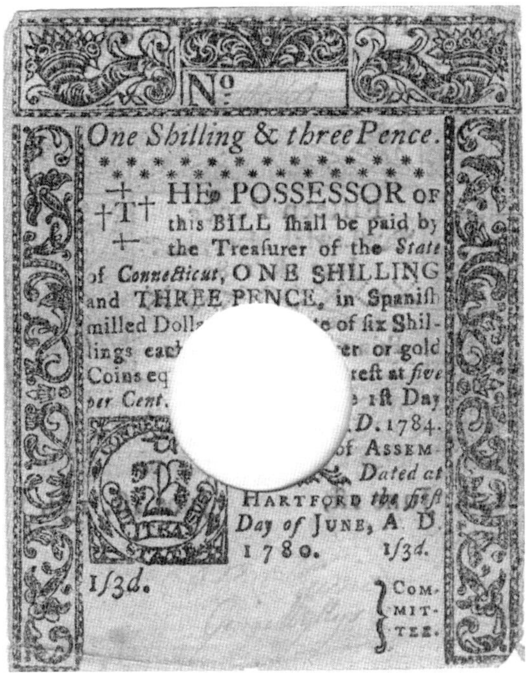

(Above) Hole-cancelled Connecticut bill, 1 shilling and 3 pence, June 1, 1780.

(Right) September 10, 1777 Georgia $4 certificate (drawing.) Issued "for the Support of the Continental Troops, and other Expenses of Government." The deer vignette is printed with a distinctive red ink. Other Georgia notes from the same period used blue vignettes and subjects ranging from beehives to battle drums to rattlesnakes.

Bills that were redeemed or otherwise removed from circulation were usually cancelled with a large "X" mark, defacing cuts or a hole. Such holes are typically round or diamond-shaped and vary in size, with most about an inch across. The method of cancellation often was prescribed in the authorizing legislation. Many cancelled notes still survive. Surviving New Hampshire pieces, for example, are far more frequently hole-cancelled than not. General issues of New Hampshire are the scarcest of those from the thirteen original American colonies, followed by Georgia. Those of New Jersey, Connecticut, Maryland, Delaware and Rhode Island are the most commonly encountered. Those of the Republic of Vermont, the Northwest Territory and British Florida are rarely seen in any condition. (Vermont made good on its redemption promises. Thus, few Vermont notes remained in circulation.)

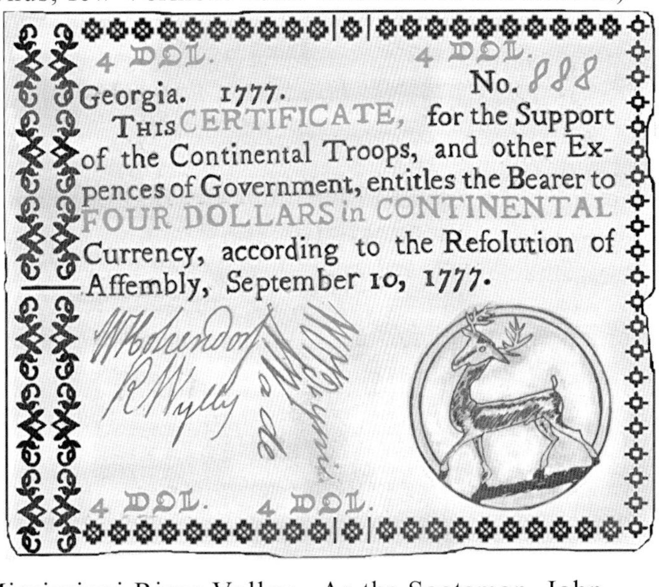

Not all American colonial notes were made for British America. A number of issues were intended for La Louisiane, the name given to French holdings in the Mississippi River Valley. As the Scotsman, John Law (Chapter 8,) began his takeover of France's finances in the 1716 to 1718 period, his La Banque Generale issued bills printed from engraved plates and denominated in ecús (Chapter 7.) Late in 1718, La Banque Generale became Banque Royale and changed its denominations to livres Tournois. From January until September, 1719, Banque Royale issued 769 million livres in engraved notes for La Lousiane. Beginning in January 1720, three new series of typeset notes with face values totaling more than two billion livres[!] were printed. They were intended to support the Compaigne des Indies, a company that Law established to facilitate the settlement of La Lousiane through his land speculation scheme. The *Mississippi Bubble*, as it was called, began to burst in May 1720. The notes quickly depreciated and France was ruined economically.[121] Several small series of notes and even playing card monies were issued in later decades, for use in La Lousiane. It is unknown whether any actually were printed in America. Some private individuals hand wrote circulating notes, a practice that continued even after the Louisiana Purchase. In contrast to Banque Royale notes that are relatively common because of large print runs, these latter issues are extremely rare or exist only as descriptions.

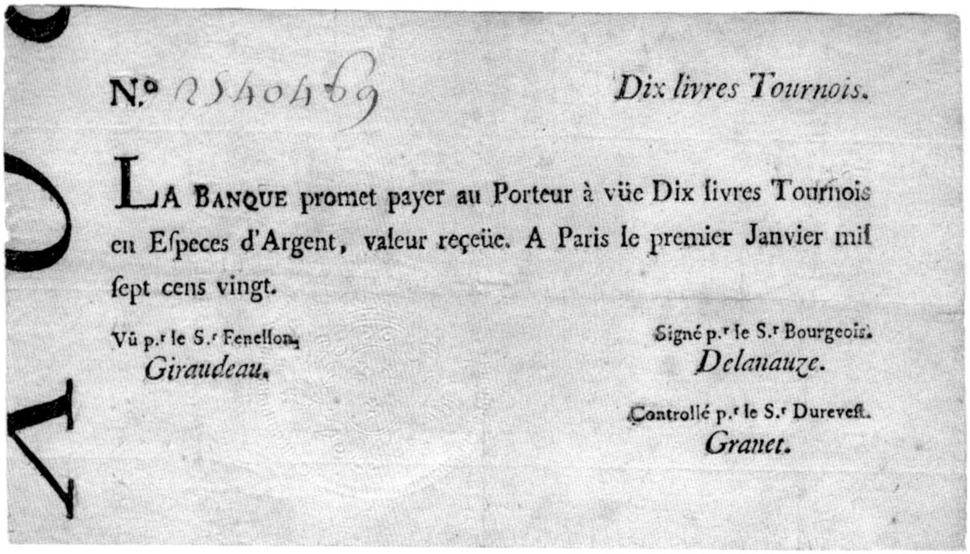

La Louisiane, dix (10) livres Tournois, January 1, 1720 (reduced.) "Banque Royal" is printed in large letters along the left edges of these uniface notes and an embossed seal was applied to the blank area in the notes' center. Signatures were printed on smaller denominations such as this.

The Spanish also got into the act, printing engraved notes that were denominated in pesos and reales (Chapter 6,) for the payment of soldiers in New Orleans in 1782. Counterfeiting was a problem there as well, as evidenced by the execution of two men in the same year. The notes were redeemed following a royal order in October 1788. These notes, Spain's first, also are extremely rare.[122]

To attempt a comprehensive study of all early American notes would be a lifelong endeavor, well beyond the scope of this work.* To own examples of all the different types is impossible, since some exist only in museums. Of some types, only single examples are known to exist. Others are not represented by surviving examples at all. Rather, they are known only by contemporary counterfeits or by descriptions or sketches that accompany their authorizing acts.

A CONTINENTAL CONCERN

Colonial and state issues notwithstanding, Continental Currency did the most to influence modern perceptions of early American paper money. As the name implies and unlike colonial currencies, it could be spent anywhere across the virtual "continent" of thirteen colonies. Its advent brought consistency of design and denominations, even if it offered little in the way of financial stability. Issued to fund the Revolution, it was backed by little more than the public's faith that the rebels might prevail. To redeem the bills, the individual states were supposed to levy taxes according to assigned quotas. True to form, they were negligent in doing so and the federal government had no means of coercing them. Nevertheless, thirty-seven different resolutions authorized the printing of these bills of credit between 1775 and 1779. Other official issues, many of which required the personal assurance of Finance Superintendent, Robert Morris, were emitted in small numbers, in 1781, 1782 and 1783. By that time his credit was better than the government's. These later notes exist in several forms, all of which are rare and seldom seen. However, the earlier, general issues are available for study. After all, more than sixteen million pieces of them, with a total face value of $241,562,775, were authorized.

* It already has been done superbly by Eric P. Newman, in *Paper Money of Early America* (4th edition, Iola, Wisconsin, Krause Publications, 1997.)

As any educated eighth-grader knows, Continental Currency ultimately collapsed into worthlessness, giving rise to the worn cliché "not worth a continental." After the war it even was used by some as wallpaper. The fall was no accident. Aside from having no real backing, the currency was the target of relentless British and Tory counterfeiting and propaganda. By early January, 1776, the forty-four gun British man-o-war, *Phoenix*, anchored in New York Harbor, already was printing counterfeits with an onboard press. Newspaper advertisements offered counterfeit currency for the price of the paper used to print it and Tory editorialists used every opportunity to undermine public confidence in the new money.[123] As if this were not enough, the Confederation continued allowing the states to issue their own currencies, further confusing the public and diluting the money supply.

Even with the difficulties, depreciation of Continental Currency was slow at first. Until September 1777, it lost scarcely any of its value. The next fifteen months, however, witnessed a precipitous fall until, by January 1779, $7.42 in continental dollars were required to equal the value of a hard silver dollar. On May 18, 1780, Congress passed a law to bring the spiral under control by authorizing the states to redeem Continental Currency at forty dollars per specie dollar. By then, Congress desperately wanted to pull the bills from circulation, but had no specie to support the redemption. What they did have was the broken promise from the states to back the bills with tax payments. So, Congress used tax credits to encourage the states to use their own issues of specie-backed currency to redeem bills at 40:1. In return, the states received credits against what they owed to the federal government. Still, depreciation continued until, by the end of 1781, continentals truly were worthless. The chart below illustrates the rapidity of the collapse.[*] It also should be noted that many state and local issues during the period suffered a similar fate. For example, it took $1,000 in Virginia currency to buy a silver dollar in December 1781.[124]

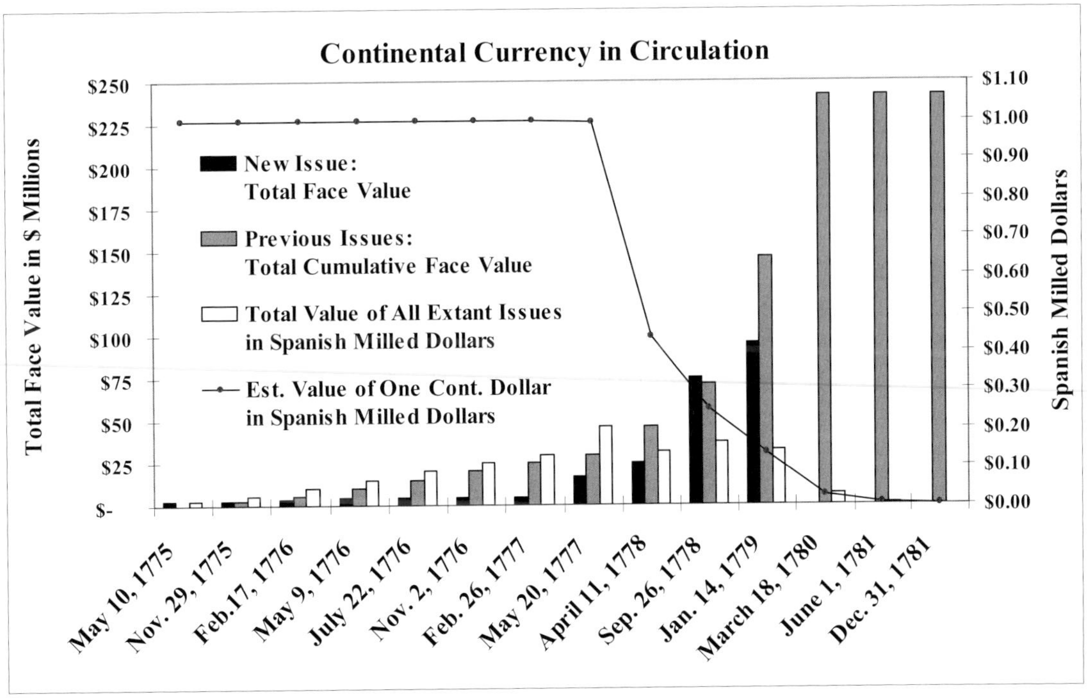

[*] In the chart, black bars represent total face value (as indicated on the left vertical axis) of the new issue whose date is indicated on the horizontal axis. Grey bars represent total accumulated face value of all prior issues. White bars represent total value of all prior *and* new issues expressed in Spanish milled dollars (SMD's.) Data points and lines refer to the right vertical axis and represent the estimated value of a single Continental Currency dollar, expressed in silver dollars (i.e., SMD's.)

It is doubtful that the currency's collapse surprised the founders. Franklin was not alone in viewing the events as a justifiable tax on the citizenry to help fund the Revolution.[125] Nor is this view without merit. Without tax revenue from the states, for the time the bills were honored, citizens and soldiers essentially loaned Congress money by accepting them in exchange for goods and services. When the government defaulted on its commitment to redeem the bills, the loans effectively became a form of tax. Without tangible backing for Continental Currency, inflation was a natural trend that simply accelerated too far, too fast to be reversed by military successes at Saratoga, or even Yorktown. Congress had no war chest and the public knew it. As confidence waned, so did the value of Continental Currency.

To simplify the task for printers, the thirty-seven authorizing acts were condensed into eleven distinct runs. (See Appendix B.1 for details.) The run authorized on February 17, 1776, included small-denomination fractional currency. These feature a distinctive motif that is attributed to Franklin. Higher-denomination issues feature face vignettes framed by Latin mottoes that vary by denomination. They stress inspirational themes such as persistence and harmony. Most of them came from books owned by or known to Franklin.* (See Appendix B.2 for a full listing.) When forty-dollar bills were introduced, Congress opted for a Francis Hopkinson design that uses *CONFEDERATION* in place of a Latin phrase. With few exceptions, backs of bills from this group feature nature prints. The first issue of twenty-dollar bills are printed on Franklin's thin marbleized paper. Otherwise, thicker mica-flecked rag paper with embedded color fibers is the norm. The young nation apparently was going through an identity crisis. Earlier issues bear the phrase, "The United Colonies" or "United States of North America," in their face borders, while later ones proclaim "United States." In this and many other ways the story of Continental Currency is the story of the Revolution itself....

The Second Continental Congress convened in Philadelphia at the Pennsylvania State House, known later as Independence Hall, on Wednesday, May 10, 1775. No one really had been surprised by the events at Lexington and Concord three weeks before, but the delegates were in a tizzy over what to do next. The session had just begun when Sam Adams's emissary brought news of a daring raid on Fort Ti[conderoga] by the unlikely team of Benedict Arnold and Ethan Allen with his Green Mountain Boys. The bloodless night raid gave the rebels badly needed cannon and other military supplies. It also should have given Congress a boost in confidence.

However, on hearing the news, many of delegates were more concerned with returning the stolen cannon and asking for forgiveness than with using them to American advantage. They debated the wording of an apology to be handed to the British when they inevitably took back their cannon. Franklin apparently was in denial. His only suggestion was a resolution thanking William Pitt, Edmund Burke and others in Parliament for their support of American interests.[126] The Adams boys, Sam and his cousin, John, could hardly believe what they were hearing from Pennsylvania's John Dickinson. Dickinson was the chief proponent of reconciliation. His *Olive Branch Petition* to achieve reconciliation was later approved, but George III refused even to read it and declared the Americans to be in rebellion. Congress was sending two conflicting messages: "Reconcile" and "Prepare for war!" To the latter end, the delegates allocated some provisions for the war effort and, on June 17, finalized a fateful letter, the subject of which had been the topic of debate for the previous week:

---

* Emblems and mottoes for denominations of less than eight dollars and thirty-dollars were taken from a 1702 edition of *Symbolorum ac Emblematum Ethico-Politicorum*, by Joachim Camerarius, that Franklin owned. The eight-dollar design came from *Idea Principis Christiano-Politici Symbolis* (Diego Saavedra, 1660,) the $55 design from *Emblematum Repositorum* (J. C. Weigels,) etc.. Francis Hopkinson was responsible for designs of several of the larger denominations. (Newman, *The Early Paper Money of America*, p.75.)

To George Washington, Esq... We, reposing special trust and confidence in your patriotism, valor, conduct, and fidelity, do, by these presents, constitute and appoint you to be General and Commander in chief, of the army of the United Colonies, and of all the forces now raised, or to be raised, by them, and of all others who shall voluntarily offer their service, and join the said Army for the Defence of American liberty, and for repelling every hostile invasion thereof: And you are hereby vested with full power and authority to act as you shall think for the good and welfare of the service... This commission to continue in force, until revoked by this, or a future Congress... By order of the Congress. Dated, Philada. June 17, 1775.[127]

Six days later, to fund the war effort, the delegates authorized a $2 million issue of Continental Currency, to be denominated in Spanish milled dollars or "the value thereof in gold or silver." There were to be 49,000 of each denomination from one to eight dollars and 11,800 twenty-dollar bills. John Adams, John Rutledge, James Duane, Benjamin Franklin and James Wilson were named as a committee to "get proper plates engraved, to provide paper, and to agree with printers...."[128]

1st Issue, May 10, 1775, $30. The face vignette shows a wreath on a tomb in the mountains. The motto SI RECTE FACIES *("If You Act Righteously") implies an honorable end for those who do right. The back bears two vignettes. The left vignette shows waves blown by a strong wind. Its motto reads* VI CONCITATE *("Driven by Force.") The right vignette shows the sun shining on a calm sea, with the motto* CESSANTE VENTO COQUIESCEMUS *("When the Storm Ceases We Will Rest.")*

The Philadelphia printing firm chosen to produce the new currency was Hall and Sellers. David Hall had learned the printing trade in Edinburgh. He worked at Watt's Printing Works in London, where he met William Strahan. Strahan corresponded with a former Watt's employee who lived in America, Benjamin Franklin. In 1743 Franklin invited Hall to come to America. Hall immediately impressed Franklin and became a trusted foreman and partner. In 1748 Franklin turned operation of the business over to Hall and thus was able to pursue his own intellectual curiosities. For the next eighteen years the firm still was known as Franklin and Hall. They printed *Poor Richard's Almanac* and the immensely successful newspaper, the *Pennsylvania Gazette*. The firm also printed government documents. Even in retirement Franklin earned nearly £500 a year from the partnership.[129] In 1766 he sold his share to Hall, who also ran a large stationery store. Franklin had been wise to keep Hall as a partner. Otherwise, he might have been a serious competitor.[130]

Another player, William Sellers, came to Philadelphia from London around 1764 and opened a stationery store of his own on Arch Street, between Second and Third. After the Franklin-Hall partnership dissolved, Hall sold half of his firm to Sellers, creating Hall and Sellers. When Hall died in 1772 his sons, William and David, continued the partnership on Market Street.[131] In 1775 the firm was well qualified, well connected and ready to print money.

It was a good thing because America had an army to pay. On July 23, 1775, Congress passed a resolution that set monthly pay scales for military personnel. The schedule below gives an indication of how at least some of the new money was intended to be used.[132]

Monthly Pay Scale for Military Personnel

Post	Regiment	Light Infantry	Artillery
Commissary general of musters, deputy muster master general and lieutenant colonel	$40	-	-
Deputy commissary genl. of stores/provisions	$60	-	-
Deputy adjutant general and colonel	$50	-	-
Brigade major	$33	-	-
Commissary of artillery	$30	-	-
Judge advocate and chaplain	$20	-	-
Major	$33 1/3	-	-
Captain	$20	$20	$26 2/3
Captain Lieutenant	-	-	$20
Lieutenant	$13 1/3	$13 1/3	$18 2/3
Lieutenant fire worker	-	-	$13 1/3
Ensign	$10	$10	-
Serjeant [sic]	$8	$8	$8 1/3
Corporal, drummer, or fifer	$7 1/3	$7 1/3	$7 ½
Private	$6 2/3	$6 2/3	-
Adjutant or quarter master	$18 1/3	-	-
Bombardier	-	-	$7
Matross (i.e., gunner's assistant)	-	-	$6 5/6

All but the twenty-dollar bills were printed on thick, mica-flecked rag paper with what would become the usual dimensions: about $2^7/_8$ by $3^5/_8$ inches. Twenties were longer, not as tall and were printed on Franklin's thin white paper with a marbleized edge. Their dimensions, about $4^7/_8$ by $2^3/_8$ inches, and marbleization are unique among the continental issues. All of these bills bear the date May 10, 1775, for the day that the congressional session began. However, none entered circulation until August. [133] In late July, Congress authorized another $1 million in thirty-dollar bills. The addition actually totaled $999,990 because of the way that bills were arranged on the sheets.[134]

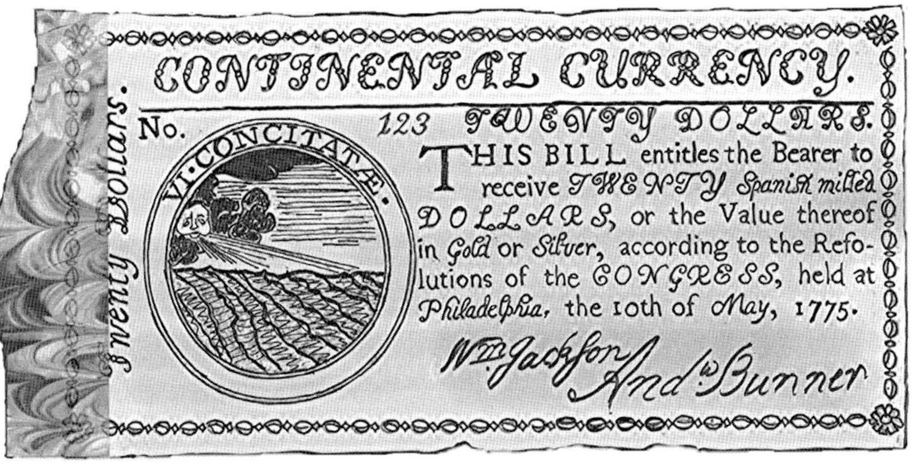

First issue, May 10, 1775, $20, indented. (Drawing, on paper marbleized by this author.) Originals are printed on Franklin's paper. Face and back vignettes are as on the back of the $30 note above. The same polychrome paper was used by the Bank of North America to print small change notes in 1789.

Congress reconvened in Philadelphia on November 29, 1775. A week later they authorized a second issue of $3 million, in denominations of one through eight dollars, and 83,611 of each. Already nervous about counterfeiting, the delegates were careful to stipulate that the new bills should be numbered differently from the May 10 issue and that the ink used to do so should be of a different color, bright red.[135]

By the end of 1775 the rebels had proven their resolve on the hills above Boston, Washington was struggling to forge a rag-tag mass into an Army and the construction of a *four-ship* navy had been authorized. Both the war effort and the new currency appeared to be gaining ground. In January 1776 an additional $10,000 was authorized for the redemption of worn bills. As the new issue was being printed, Washington's critics began to question Congress's choice for general. He silenced them with a stroke of pure genius, sending Henry Knox, a Boston bookseller who resembled a mountain, to Fort Ti to retrieve its cannon. Knox had his men build forty-two sleds and used teams of oxen to drag the cannon through deep winter snow to the outskirts of Boston. The monumental effort is remembered as a defining event in American history. On the night of March 4, 1776, Washington's men quietly built breastworks on Dorchester Heights, overlooking Boston from the one piece of high ground that the British had neglected to fortify. When General William Howe awoke the next morning, he was staring up at an American force ready to turn him and his men to cannon fodder. The British retreated and the wisdom of Congress's choice was, at least temporarily, affirmed.

By then it was obvious that notes of smaller denominations were needed as coin surrogates. When a third Continental Currency issue was authorized in Philadelphia, it included the fractional denominations $1/6, $1/3, $1/2 and $2/3, and used a new design. The new style is attributed to Benjamin Franklin and is referred to as the Fugio motif. The accompanying one- through eight-dollar notes are similar to the 1775 issues of May 10 and November 29. The total amount authorized was $4 million, $1 million of which was made up of fractionals. Both fractionals and higher denomination notes from this issue bear the date February 17, 1776. Each fractional denomination was to number 600,000 bills. Each denomination of one- through four-dollars was authorized for 130,436 bills, give or take one because of printing considerations. Denominations of five through eight dollars were to have 65,217 bills each.[136]

The fractional bills are smaller than the norm, measuring about 3¼ by 2½ inches. Their central devices are described in detail in the discussion of the 1776 Continental Currency coins and 1787 Fugio cents (Chapters 9 and 10.) Aside from obvious similarities in design to the Continental Currency coins, the $1/6 notes share a curious misspelling with a rare variety of the 1776 coins. The word "currency" appears as *CURRENCEY* on both. Edges of the 1776 coins also mimic the notes' borders.

The face vignettes of the fractionals feature a sundial outlined by a square frame. In the corners of the frame are dots. The $1/6 notes have only one dot, in the upper-left corner. The $1/3 note has two dots, one in each of the two top corners. The $1/2 notes have three dots, leaving only the lower-left corner blank. The $2/3 note has every corner filled. A letter below the face vignette gives the position of the note on the plate.

Fractional note, Fugio motif, February 17, 1776, $1/2. FUGIO *is short for* TEMPUS FUGIT *("Time is Fleeing.") Note the dots in corners of the sundial's frame and the "C" plate position on the face. (Inset) Sundial vignettes from the $1/6, $1/2 and $2/3 denominations, respectively.*

The choice of fractional denominations based on $1/6 seems odd at first. However, at 4½ shillings, or fifty-four pence to the dollar, division into six equal parts is logical because six divides evenly into fifty-four. That is, $1/6 was equivalent to nine pence, 3/4 shilling or a sixpence and a three pence. The $1/3 fractional was equivalent to eighteen pence (1½ shillings,) $1/2 to twenty-seven pence (2¼ shillings) and $2/3 to thirty-six pence (three shillings,) all perfectly reasonable sums of money to eighteenth century Americans in desperate need of small change.

On May 9 and May 27, 1776, Congress authorized the printing of $5 million in denominations of one to eight dollars (138,889 of each.) Congress still was meeting in Philadelphia when they authorized another $5 million in paper on July 22 and August 13, 1776. In this issue, the one-dollar denomination was omitted, suggesting that the Continental Currency coins were anticipated. Thirty-dollar bills, missing since the first issue, were resumed. Together, the July and August resolutions called for 76,923 bills of each denomination. Another $5 million authorization on November 2, 1776 used the same denominations and counts, and included a provision for more fractional notes. The new fractional notes never were printed, however, because those from the February 17 issue still were being signed.[137] The summer, 1776, issues came on the heals of the Declaration and the exuberance it inspired. Excitement was short-lived, however, as New York fell in a rout, Washington retreated across New Jersey and Congress fled Philadelphia ahead of the invasion that seemed inevitable. Congress and the public also fled from the illusion that the war was going well. Washington's army was dwindling away to nothing as enlistments expired. No one wanted to fight for a loser.

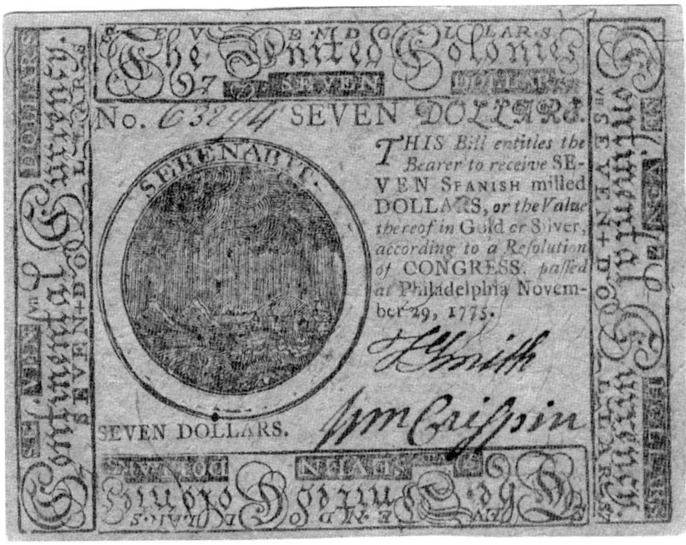

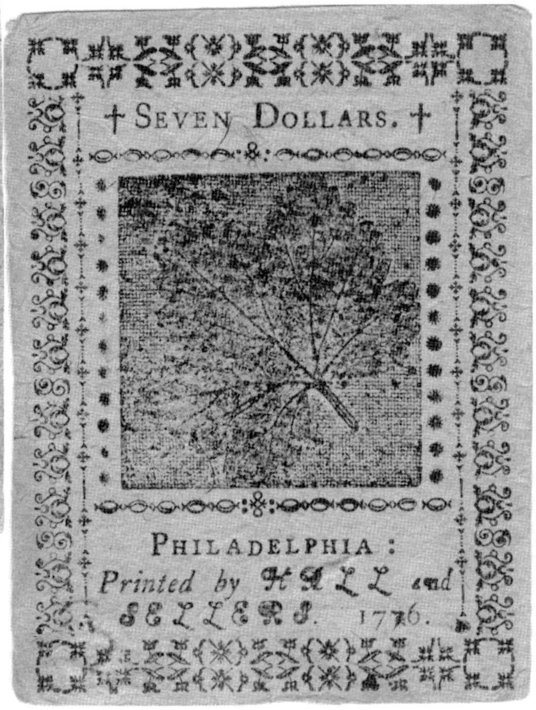

July 22, 1776, $7. The face shows a storm at sea. Its motto is SERENABIT *("It Will Be Calm.") The back features a maple nature print. Note the low serial number, 49, indicating an early printing.*

From December 20, 1776, until February 27, 1777, the displaced Congress met in Baltimore. On February 26, a day before moving back to Philadelphia, the delegates authorized another $5 million in denominations of one through eight dollars and thirty dollars, in the same quantities as the previous issue. These are known collectively as the "Baltimore issue."

Baltimore issue, February 26, 1777, $5. It features a face vignette with a bloody, skeletal hand picking food from a thorny bush. The motto is SUSTINE VEL ABSTINE *("Survive or Give Up.")*

During this time, the cause received an essential boost. Washington crossed the ice-bound Delaware River on Christmas Eve, 1776, and beat a passel of surprised Hessians at Trenton before marching on to a small but moral victory at Princeton. With the added inspiration of Thomas Paine's *The American Crisis* and its delineation of "...the summer soldier and sunshine patriot..." from those that stand their ground, the cause found new life in the form of new recruits. In October 1777 the patriots dealt a stunning blow by defeating "Gentleman Johnny" Burgoyne's army on a farm near Saratoga, New York. The following month Congress submitted the Articles of Confederation to the states for ratification. Hopes seemed to be on the rise.

Between May 20, 1777, and April 18, 1778, Congress authorized $16.5 million in bills, most all of which read "Philadelphia." From late October 1777 until June 18, 1778, however, Congress again was in temporary exile while General William Howe and Philadelphia mutually occupied each other. Fleeing ahead of Howe, the delegates had met for a single day (September 27, 1777) in Lancaster and then moved on to York. They were in York when they passed an April 11, 1778, resolution authorizing more bills, another $25 million.

As a small agricultural community on the Susquehanna River, York, Pennsylvania, was an unlikely national capital. But with Howe in Philadelphia, Congress could not be choosy. It was in York that Congress adopted the Articles of Confederation. Bills authorized at York bear the phrase "at York Town" and have come to be known collectively as the "Yorktown issue." They are very scarce because subversive British counterfeiting practices caused them to be recalled very quickly. A few escaped because the deadline for the recall was extended until after the time when Continental Currency became worthless.

$8 bill from the April 11, 1778 Yorktown issue. The message on the harp reads MAJORA MINORIBUS CONSONANT *("The Large [states] and the Small [states] in Harmony.")*

With the Yorktown issue, a forty-dollar bill was added and denominations under four dollars were discontinued, strong hints that devaluation was taking hold, in spite of the success at Saratoga. For the forty-dollar bills, Philadelphia's Francis Hopkinson contributed a patriotic face vignette that features a Divine Eye looking down on the new constellation of thirteen stars. The stars are arranged in a circle as on another Hopkinson-connected design, the American flag. Rather than a Latin saying, the motto on the new forty-dollar bills reads simply, *CONFEDERATION.* (Also, see Chapter 10.) Another subtle but meaningful design change is noted: The phrase "The United States" replaced "The United Colonies," for good.

(Left) *January 14, 1779, $40, with Hopkinson's CONFEDERATION motif in red and black. (Right) Francis Hopkinson. By James B. Longacre, after Robert Edge Pine.*[138]

A

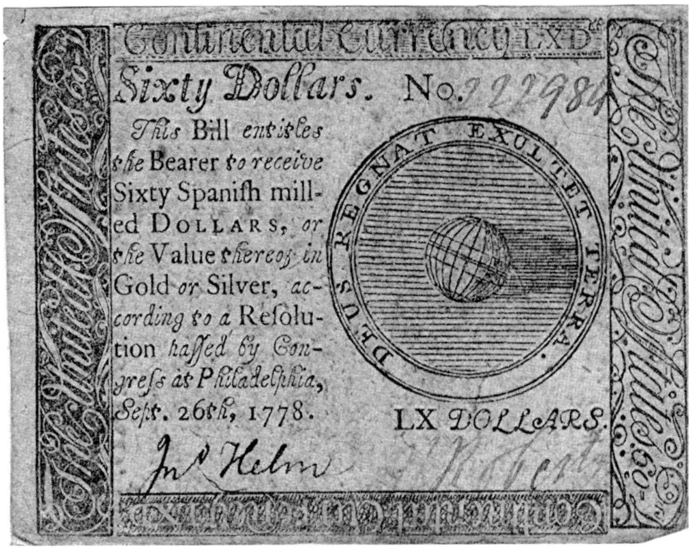

B

C

(Below) A - $60, September 26, 1778. The face device is a globe, floating in space, with the motto: DEUS REGNAT EXULTET TERRA *("God Reigns, Let the Earth Rejoice.") In place of a nature print, its back features a bow. B – Companion $50 bills feature a 13-step pyramid with the backs depicting arrows. The arrows and bow were replaced in 1779 by nature prints: parsley on the $50, willow with hemlock on the $60. The motto on the $50 bills is* PERENNIS *("It Will Last.") C – Reverse of the Great Seal of the United States, featuring the Divine Eye atop a pyramid. Both sides of the seal can be found on the backs of today's one-dollar Federal Reserve notes.* *

---

* After several failed attempts beginning in 1776, the Great Seal emerged close to its current form in 1782. One side of it features the familiar eagle and shield that usually are traced to a sketch by Charles Thomson, Secretary of Congress. The *E PLURIBUS UNUM* motto is credited to the Swiss-American artist and coin collector, Pierre Eugene Du Simitiere. The seal's other side is relatively obscure and seldom was seen before 1935, when Franklin Roosevelt resurrected it. On it a Divine Eye, in a golden glory, looks down on an unfinished pyramid that awaits a new generation of architects. Above the eye are the words *ANNUIT COEPTIS* ("*Providence has Favored Our Undertakings.*") At the base of the pyramid is the date *MDCCLXXVI* (*1776.*)

By the summer of 1778 inflation was more than a hint. Congress returned to Philadelphia and resolved to create a new issue dated September 26, 1778. This time, 340,914 notes were printed for each denomination, almost seven times the volume of the May 1775 emissions. Fifty- and sixty-dollar denominations were added and again Hopkinson was called upon for the new designs. All told, the September 26 issue called for more than $75 million in new bills. There was no new specie, only renewed promises.

A final issue of January 14, 1779 included more than $95 million in new currency. Denominations of one to five dollars were reinstated alongside new denominations of thirty-five, forty-five, fifty-five, sixty-five, seventy and eighty dollars. Again Hopkinson contributed new designs, this time for the thirty-five-, forty-five-, seventy- and eighty-dollar denominations. The January 14, 1779, issue marked the end of regular-issue Continental Currency.

Continental Currency, January 14, 1779, $55. The red and black face vignette has storm clouds fading before the sun and the motto POST NUBILA PHOEBUS *("After the Dark Clouds Comes the Sun.") The back features willow leaves.*

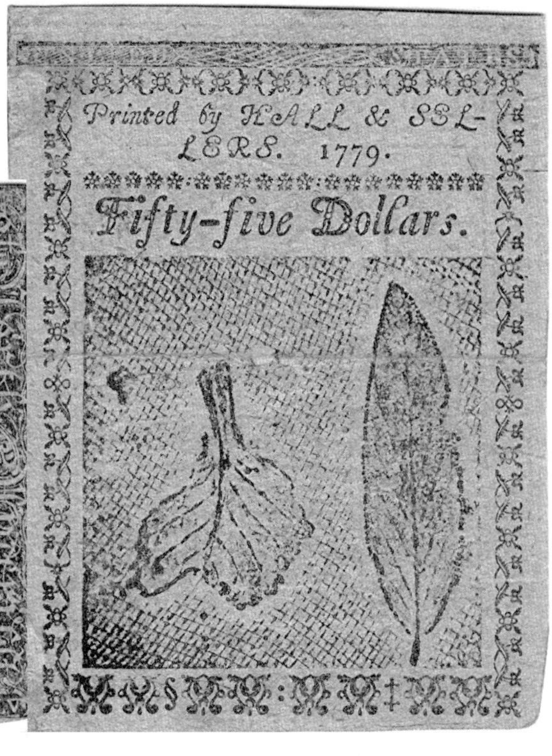

In spite of advancing American fortunes and French assistance, public confidence in Continental Currency continued to fade. Recognizing this, Congress knew it had to remove the bills from circulation and sought to have the states pay for their redemption. On March 18, 1780, a resolution was passed to encourage the states to print their own monies, with federal backing, to redeem continentals at the 40:1 ratio. The rules governing redemption were complicated, but the initiative resulted in the removal from circulation of 46 percent of the outstanding Continental Currency, totaling more than $111 million.[139]

Below it are the words *NOVUS ORDO SECLORUM* ("*A New Order for the Ages.*") William Barton, who was, among other things, a heraldry expert, may have suggested the design, after Hopkinson.

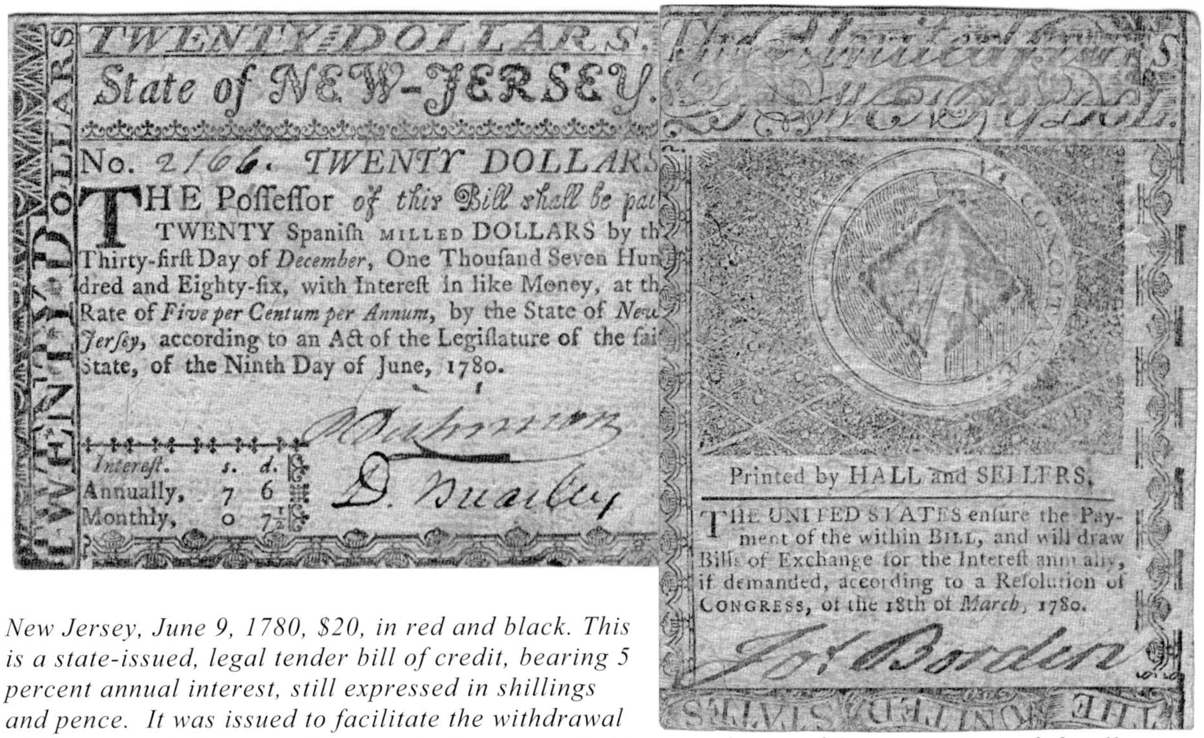

New Jersey, June 9, 1780, $20, in red and black. This is a state-issued, legal tender bill of credit, bearing 5 percent annual interest, still expressed in shillings and pence. It was issued to facilitate the withdrawal of Continental Currency. Because the issue was tied to a resolution of Congress, it was federally backed. On the back of the note, authority is given as The United States, rather than New Jersey. David Brearly and Philemon Dickinson signed the face. Brearly was a signer of the U.S. Constitution. Dickinson was a Revolutionary War general and brother of John Dickinson. Joseph Borden, who provided the signature of federal backing, was a New Jersey representative to the 1765 Stamp Act Congress. Note the shifted characters in "TWENTY D," on the left edge of the face.

By August 1781, with the war still not over, Continental Currency essentially was worthless. To preserve some measure of credibility for the new government, Robert Morris began issuing notes in his own name, on behalf of the United States. Then, after the cessation of hostilities, Congress authorized indented bills for the payment of taxes. Nearly $8 million in these bills was authorized between 1782 and 1787. Many actually were used for the intended purpose. Others never were printed. Consequently, very few survive. A small issue of $160,000 in *Subsistence Notes* was printed in 1783 to pay army officers' benefits. The same year, Robert Morris, through the Office of Finance, authorized another $500,000 in *U.S. National Debt Notes* to pay soldiers furloughed after the Revolution. After the Office of Finance was eliminated, the Board of Treasury continued to print money to meet the army's pay requirements. Rather than print new notes for these 1785 issues, the Board simply chose to trim references to the Office of Finance from the 1783 versions. All of these 1780's issues are very rare.[140] Most resemble checks, yet all are regarded as Continental Currency. New types, including notes signed by U.S. Treasurer, Michael Hillegas, under Morris's authority, recently have been discovered and are being researched.[141]

As the 1790's neared, two chapters of the American paper money saga had been written: *colonials* and *continentals*. Americans invested their hopes in these currencies, only to have them devalued to the point that they were used for wallpaper and as chamber pot conveniences. While the Constitution later did provide a limited means of recovery to those who converted their Continental Currency to bonds, many felt betrayed.

THE PUBLIC MATTER OF PRIVATE MONEY

Given that the next few decades brought an unprecedented explosion of private currencies, it is understatement to say that American frustration only was just beginning. The exclusivity of the coining right and the complexity of the minting process ensured that no more than a select handful of men understood and were capable of making coins. In contrast the printing press was fast becoming an instrument familiar to many Americans. It was, after all, the first medium of true mass communication. That the technology would be applied to the mass production of private paper money was inevitable. Congress made this possible by neglecting to make any provision for preventing private entities from issuing their own notes.

The 1790 to 1840 period witnessed major change in America, with dramatic population shifts and accelerating technological development. As the country grew and extended westward, the establishment of branch and standalone frontier banks closely followed. Early on these branch banks began issuing privately their own paper money to satisfy local demands. By 1800 about twenty banks were operating in this way. In several cases they began issuing notes in areas that were not yet states. Not to be outdone, firms other than banks joined in. Unbacked currency proliferated and with it came more cycles of boom and bust. Until the federal government called private paper to a halt in 1861, Americans were on a very rough ride. How that came to be is at least partly bound to the growth printing technology. Early private notes usually were hand-written on partially printed forms resembling checks. Aside from being easy to counterfeit, notes produced in this way could not easily be rendered in significant quantities. Quantities were further limited by the use of soft copper plates that tended to wear quickly. When a new plate was engraved, or an old one re-engraved, the design inevitably changed slightly because the work was done by hand. Because the public had no fixed standard with which to compare, variation was the counterfeiters' friend.

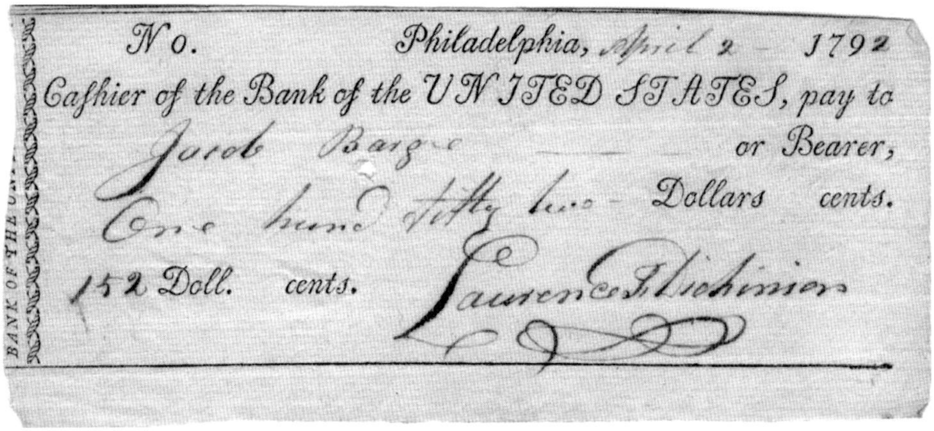

Bank of the U.S. check, $152, 1792 (coincidentally written on the day the Mint Act of 1792 passed.) This check mimics the form of early private-issue paper currencies (i.e., handwritten additions to pre-printed forms.)

Enter Jacob Perkins. Perkins was an inventor with an over-active mind. He was born in Newburyport, Massachusetts, as the son of a tailor. When just fifteen years old, in 1781, he became the operator of a goldsmith shop on the death of Edward Davis, the man to whom he had been apprenticed. Perkins quickly learned to delegate menial tasks to family and friends so that he could pursue his creative calling.[142]

That calling led him to a seemingly endless string of inventions that began early and kept coming. At twenty-one he invented a nail-making machine. He later added locks for banks, new types of valves and a screw propeller to his list of patents. An advocate of high-pressure steam technology, he invented a steam-powered rocket and a steam powered gun capable of firing 1,200 rounds per minute. This early machine gun evidently did not work particularly well. It was demonstrated to the Duke of Wellington, who passed on the opportunity, and to the French, who ordered a single example. (Perhaps the French might have fared better against Wellington had they purchased more of them.)[143]

Perkins was the die maker for some of the 1787 to 1788 Massachusetts cents and half cents, and for gold, silver and white metal funeral medals worn in memory of George Washington. He also may have been associated with certain other Washington pieces of the 1790's (Chapters 10 and 11.) It was reported in area newspapers that he was being considered when the new U.S. Mint needed a superintendent. The same newspapers reported that Perkins had invented devices that cut round planchets, imparted edge devices and detected counterfeits.[144]

Jacob Perkins, ca. 1826 Pendleton lithograph, after a painting by Chester Harding Source: Library of Congress, Prints and Photographs Division, LC-USZ62-47792.

He made a number of trips to England and actually lived there for most of his later life. Perkins' London home was on Fleet Street, above his business. He took his technology and a son, Ebenezer, to London in 1819. There, with the help of a wealthy American who acted as a patent agent and as a £12,500 investor, he formed a company and landed a banknote contract with the Bank of England. The new enterprise was successful and, in 1821, other family members were brought over. In 1834 he invented the first practical refrigerator and, two years later, air conditioning. Five years later he made the first postage stamp, the famed "Penny Black." Jacob Perkins died in 1849.[145]

This unassuming, genial man completely revolutionized paper currency. In 1804 he cracked the code for alternately hardening and softening steel, making it possible to create steel plates that greatly outlasted softer ones made of copper. He also devised a method of mounting dies together, so that small design elements could be combined to produce very complex compositions. Since each design element could be produced by a different engraver, the composite design proved very difficult to counterfeit. The use of these dies brought unprecedented consistency to the printing process. Changing a note's denomination was as simple as changing a number die. He also invented a technique for micro-printing a denomination many times in the background of a note, a feature still used today.[146] In 1815 Perkins joined the Philadelphia printing firm of Murray, Draper and Fairman.[147*]

Soon after, Asa Spencer joined the company. Spencer invented a geometric lathe that made possible the creation of dies with ornate geometric designs like those seen on present day notes and postage stamps. Without the proper equipment, these designs are very difficult to replicate.[148] The duo of Perkins and Spencer created modern paper currency. Yet, they often are forgotten. Perkins, in particular, remains an under-celebrated genius.

The federal government was an early adopter of the new technology. The new processes, and the Murray, Draper and Fairman label, were used on *U.S. Treasury Notes* authorized in 1815. Skittish over the failure of Continental Currency, the federal government had been reluctant to

---

[*] One of the partners in the firm, Gideon Fairman, engraved the reproduction of Gilbert Stuart's portrait of Washington that is so familiar to anyone who has handled a modern dollar bill. (Goodwin, p.141.)

print paper money. The financial crisis surrounding the War of 1812, however, forced the issue. With the country once again in dire financial straits, the Treasury printed more than $36 million in notes between 1812 and 1815. Denominations ranged from three to one thousand dollars. Until 1815 these were issued for one year at 5.4 percent interest. Some 1815 notes bore the 5.4 percent rate, but for an indefinite period. *Small Treasury Notes*, (three-, five-, ten-, twenty- and fifty-dollars) of 1815 bore no interest.[149] In general, these U.S. Treasury Notes of 1812 to 1815 did not circulate. They were not legal tender. Those bearing interest were redeemed and, as a result, only a handful survive from the entire series. Some varieties are known only from *specimens* (unsigned trial printings) or descriptions. Others are known only by their legislation and lack even descriptions.

With no federal notes in true circulation and the new printing technology in place, the stage was set for the explosive growth of privately issued paper currency. As the number of banks and bank failures grew, economic emergencies became commonplace. Many banks existed for no other purpose than to print money. Unscrupulous individuals operated in droves, printing millions in speculative paper. In 1819 and again in 1837, the country fell into panic, in part because of the proliferation of unsubstantiated banknotes. Each panic was followed by expansion that required more paper money. Thus, as in colonial times, the cycle continued.

Local issuers catered to their constituents. Texas notes, for example, were printed in English and Spanish. In many other locales, small denomination "scrip" notes reflected the familiarity of the populace with Spanish denominations. One of the notes pictured below, for example, has a face value of 12½ cents (one reale or *bit,* as described in Chapter 6.) Pennsylvania notes often were denominated in German thalers, Louisiana notes in French livres. In the 1830's one Louisiana bank printed on its ten-dollar notes both the English word, "ten," and the French version, "dix." The popularity of these notes among riverboat travelers gave the South the nickname "Dixie."

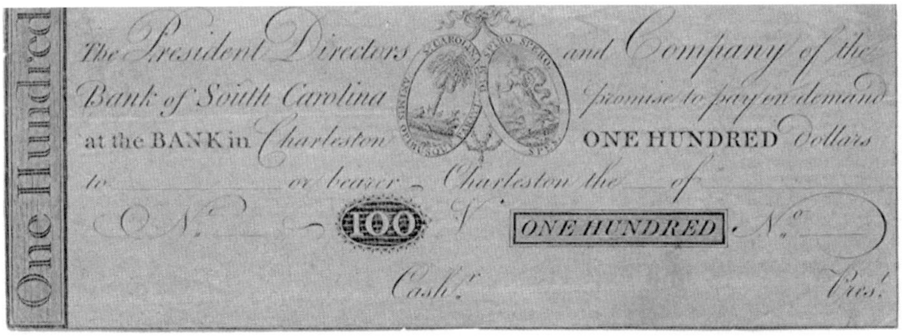

Engraved private notes from the early 19th century:

(Top) Unissued Bank of South Carolina note, $100, ca.1815. This note combines engraved-plate printing with hand-written text.

(Bottom) X-cancelled 1812 $5 note; Union Bank of New London, Connecticut. It apparently was redeemed by Normand Smith, who signed the back.

From 1837 until 1843, another large group of U.S. Treasury Notes was issued in response to the financial crisis of the period. As were their 1812 to 1815 predecessors, these were interest bearing. Only a handful circulated and even fewer survive. By 1887, of nearly $80 million in U.S. Treasury Notes with issue dates of 1843 or before, only $83,425 had escaped redemption.[150] Other U.S. Treasury Notes were issued in 1846 and 1847, in support of the War with Mexico, and in the 1857 to 1861 period, to combat the third major economic crisis of the nineteenth century.

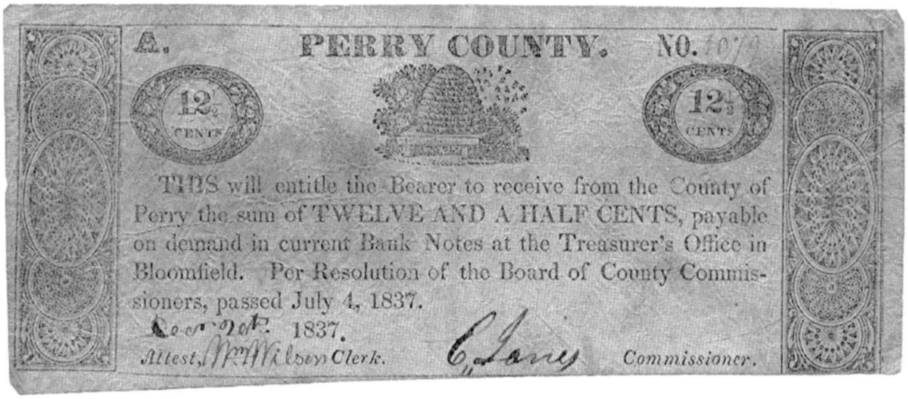

New technology:

(Top) Unissued Ohio scrip, $1, ca.1820. By Murray, Draper and Fairman. Its design is simple but uses Spencer's lathe-cut dies for the location and denomination. It also has embedded fibers to thwart counterfeiters. As most notes of the period, it is uniface. Its backing was "current Bank Notes," giving its issuer control over the method of redemption.

(Bottom) 12½ Cents, County of Perry (Penn.) 1837. Low-denomination notes were issued during economic emergencies and sometimes are referred to as "scrip."

Over time designs became increasingly complex. In the 1830's patriotic symbols and portraits co-existed with stock commercial images of sailing ships, railroads, steamboats, factories and even slaves. The Towanda Bank note below, for example, features portraits of Lafayette and Franklin juxtaposed with Liberty and Commerce. Even with the complexity of the notes, counterfeiting continued to be a monumental problem. Books that described counterfeits were printed to help merchants avoid loss. An 1839 publication, for example, listed 254 banks whose notes had been counterfeited or altered, along with nearly fourteen hundred fake banknotes.[151] Most notes of the period were printed entirely with black ink. That changed in the 1840's when photographic reproduction became possible. Since early photographic processes created images only in black and white, adding green, red or blue inks discouraged counterfeiters with access to the new technology. Thus, "greenbacks" were born.

In the end privately issued notes played a vital, if often destabilizing, role in cultivating the growth of the new nation. They became a ubiquitous fixture in American culture and helped the nation's fiscal policy to mature. The golden age of private notes ended just as Confederate currency burst onto the scene. Sweeping 1860's reforms produced the nation's first legal tender paper currency. By that time important lessons had been learned.

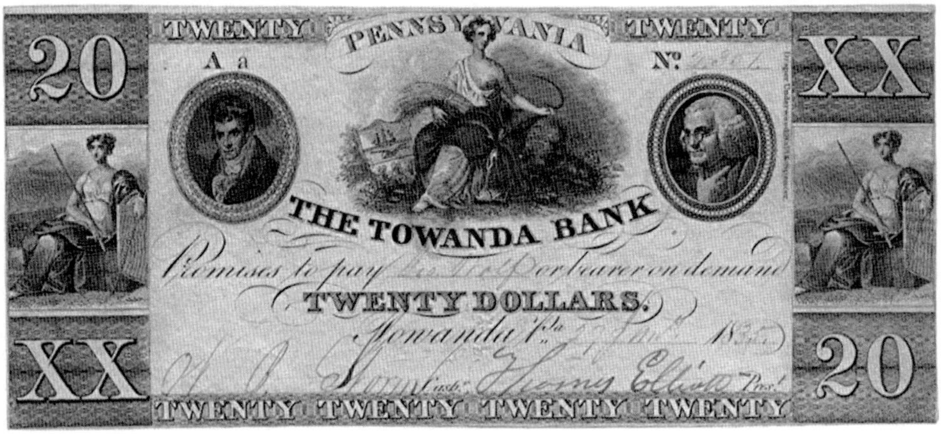

$20, 1835, Towanda Bank (Pennsylvania, reduced.)
In complexity, this note is a far cry from the earlier hand-engraved pieces shown above.

NEARLY MONEY AND HARDLY MONEY

The body of surviving documents from the Colonial, Confederation and early Constitutional periods encompasses many other types of official and semi-official fiscal paper. Land documents, for example, are among the most numerous of the surviving artifacts from the era. Certificates of indebtedness, vouchers, checks and indentures also are common. Outstanding loans were exchanged among lenders just as they are today. As land routinely was traded, documents were used to convey titles. In this sense they helped commoditize land and were an integral part of the economic system. While none of these documents truly are money, all were part of the overall system and, therefore, deserve at least passing consideration. For example, during and after the Revolution the states found it difficult to pay soldiers who fought for the cause. By paying them with interest-bearing certificates, debts were deferred until revenues could be collected. As the Crown had done with its emergency paper money, the states underestimated the associated costs and often found themselves unable to pay.

£7 10 9 Numb. 8898

STATE of CONNECTICUT.

Treasury-Office, June 1, A. D. 1780

THE State of Connecticut doth owe unto Mr. Timo. Lockwood who hath served in the Connecticut Line of the Continental Army, the Sum of Seven pounds ten Shill [illegible] being one fourth Part of the Balance found due to him, which Sum shall be paid to him or his Order at this Office, in Gold [illegible] Bills of Credit equivalent thereto in Value, on or before the first Day of Ju[illegible] Thousand Seven Hundred and Eighty Five with Lawful Interest thereof from th[illegible] anuary last until paid, which Interest shall be paid unto him or his Order [illegible] same Place, on the first Day of June, if demanded, pursuant to an Act of the [illegible] held at Hartford, the second Thursday of May last.

J. Lawrence Treasurer.

Certificate of indebtedness issued in 1780 by the State of Connecticut to Tymothy Lockwood, for £7 10s 9p. Lockwood could withdraw annual interest payments on the note for ten years, at which time the voucher was retired. The back of the voucher bears Lockwood's signature for each of the years between 1780 and 1789, indicating his receipts of payments. A one-inch circular hole in the document signifies final cancellation. (Shown greatly reduced.)

Late in 1776 the federal government tried to raise money by holding a national lottery. The effort failed miserably but did not stop other authorities from holding their own lotteries. Nor did it stop citizens from trading lottery tickets as securities, a practice no more risky than accepting bills of credit.[152] Celebrities often were asked to sign the tickets to lend legitimacy to the process. Washington-signed tickets, for example, now are highly sought collectables that fetch thousands of dollars.

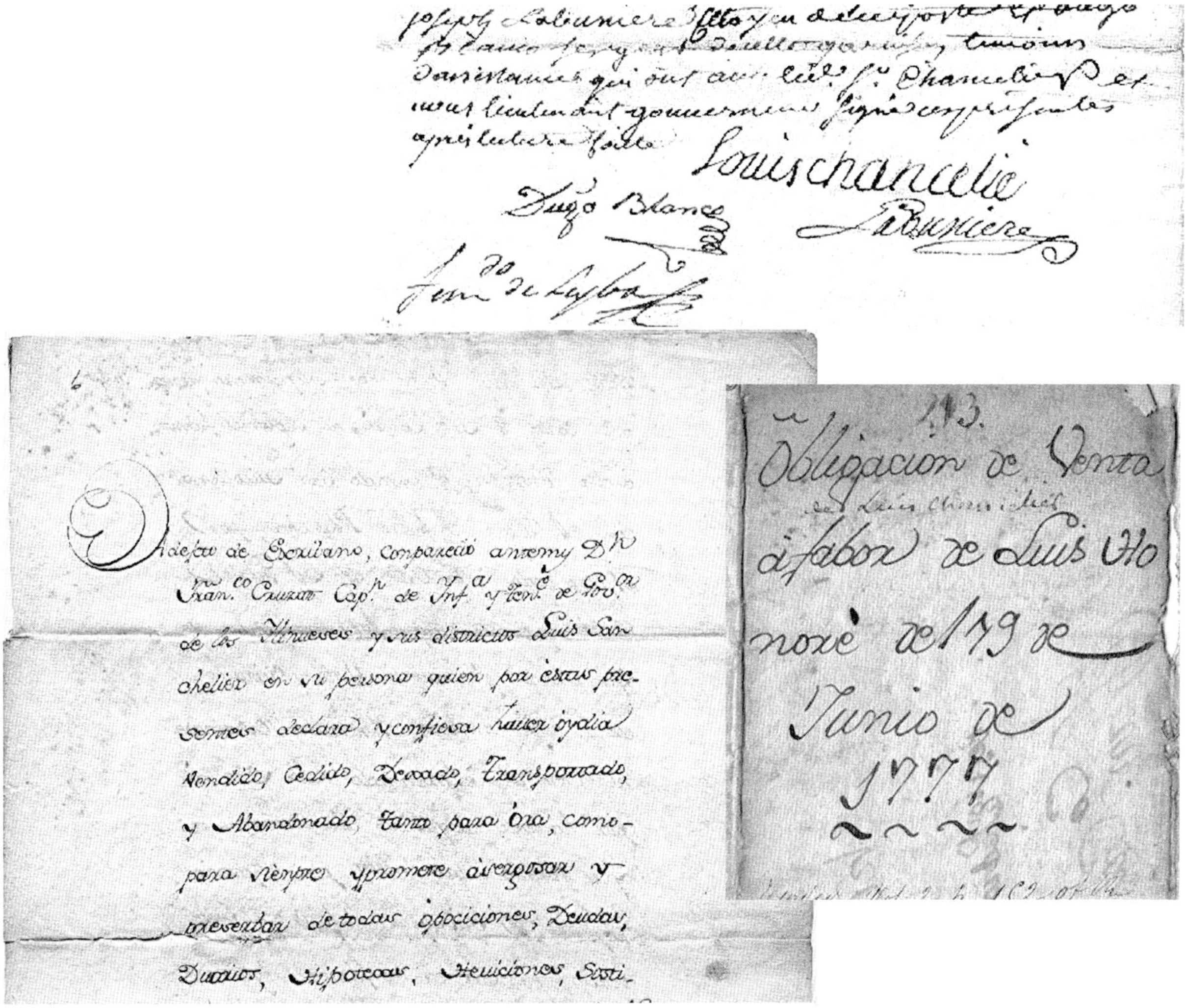

Land document, St. Louis, June 1777, issued while Spain still controlled much of Louisiana. Written in an old Spanish style, it bears the signatures of two colonial lieutenant governors of Upper Louisiana, Fernando de Leyba and Francisco Cruzat. The document describes the purchase of a house and land for 500 pounds of peltorie (skins.) Both Cruzat and De Leyba were players in the American Revolution. Cruzat became Lieutenant Governor on August 23, 1775, the day England's George III issued a "Proclamation for Suppressing Rebellion and Sedition." De Leyba replaced Cruzat three years later and was seriously ill on May 26, 1780, when Captain Emanuel Hess attacked St. Louis and Cahokia, Illinois with 950 British and Native American troops. St. Louis, then a town of seven hundred people, lost seventy-nine in the battle but managed to repel the attack with cannon fire. De Leyba died of his illness two days later. Ironically, his re-replacement was Francisco Cruzat. In January 1780, Cruzat sent troops under Captain Eugene Pourre on a long wilderness march to capture the British fort at St. Joseph, Michigan. Pourre returned triumphantly on March 6 – five days after America's Articles of Confederation were ratified. Cruzat remained at his post until his replacement in the autumn of 1786.[153] The lives of Cruzat and De Leyba are reminders that the Revolution was played out in places other than the thirteen British colonies and was in fact part of a larger, global war.

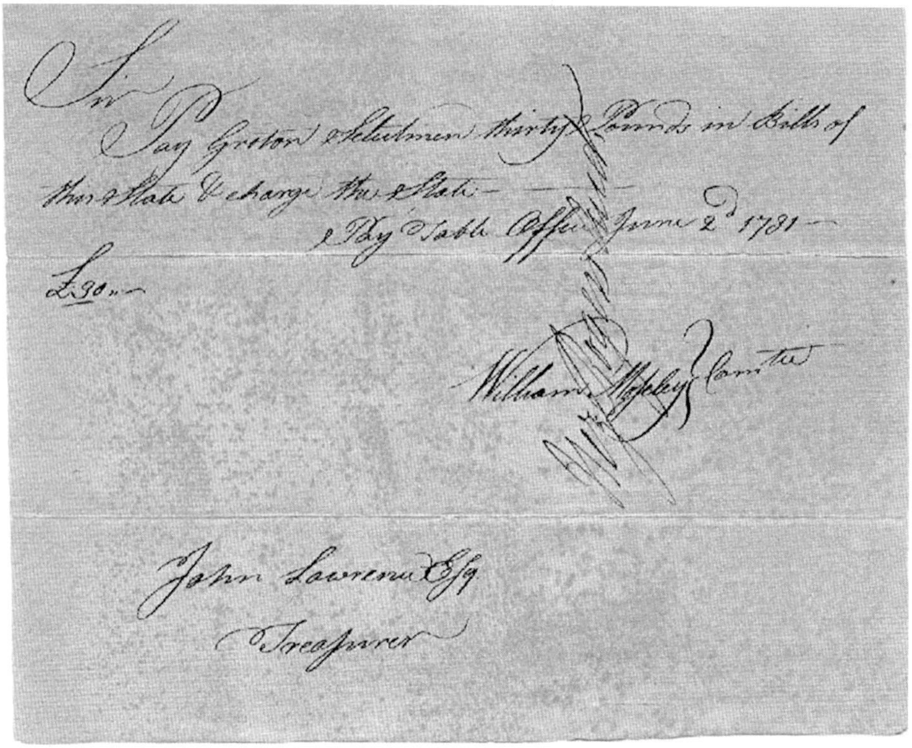

Sir
Pay Groton Selectmen thirty Pounds in Bills of
this State & charge the State —
Pay Table Office June 2d 1781 —
£30..
William Moseley Comtee
John Lawrence Esq
Treasurer

Voucher, Groton, Connecticut selectmen, June 2, 1781, £30 (reduced.) Other types of vouchers were used, as well. This is a simple note voucher authorizing payment of £30 in "Bills of this State to the Groton Selectmen, to cover their expenses."

Clearly, these types of fiscal documents and many others like them were all part of a burgeoning economic system that was far more complex than the simple barter system, which tradition holds to have been pervasive in early America. They offer the collector diversions from pure numismatics and enrich modern understanding of early American life.

(Left) Benjamin Franklin. Unsigned 1873 engraving after Alonzo Chappel.[154]
(Right) U.S. dollar, issued in 2006 to commemorate the 300th anniversary of Franklin's birth and his many contributions, particularly in the field of early American currency.
(The Continental Currency coin featured on its reverse is discussed in Chapter 9.)

Section III:
The Incidentals
(1550 to 1820)

5: BRITANNIA'S REALM

Next to the gold and silver coins of Spain and her colonies, those of Britain circulated in early America more frequently than any other nation's, despite official attempts to forestall their coming. Moreover, British and Irish base metal coins and counterfeits outnumbered *any* specie in America, including Spain's, even though their circulation essentially was limited to the northern colonies.

The numismatic heritage that Great Britain bestowed on America is ancient and complex. Between 1560 and 1820, dozens of types and denominations were issued through a host of different mints, designers and engravers.[*] Any of these coins might have been found in America as evidenced by contemporary documentation and finds at archaeological sites. Such finds trace the storied lineage of English and British monarchs from Elizabeth I through the Stuarts to George III, as well as the decade-long interruption of the English Commonwealth. When it comes to specie, the English numismatic family tree has relatively few branches. Base metal coinages, however, tell a different story. A list of British base metal coin and token classes that circulated in America includes:

- *Regal* halfpence and farthings, including those issued for Ireland, the Isle of Man, Virginia[†] and British holdings in the West Indies
- Early *patent* halfpence and farthings intended for Ireland and England[‡]
- *Gunmoney* coinages associated with James II. (American usage questioned.)
- *Imitation* British and Irish halfpennies and farthings that either were cast or struck, particularly in the late eighteenth century
- *Evasion* halfpennies with devices or legends modified to avoid counterfeiting laws. In contrast, imitations were intended to appear as similar as possible to regal issues.
- Privately-issued tokens, some of which fall under the heading "*Conder tokens,*" for reasons described below

Of course the monetary unit that the thirteen American colonies knew by heart and by law was Britain's "pound sterling." Originally "pound sterling" meant just that, a troy pound of silver at the 92.5% purity level that emerged as a standard in medieval England. Origins of the term "sterling" are unclear. However, the Latin name for a Roman pound of 12 ounces is *libra.* Alternately, libra means "a pair of scales," as in the astrological symbol of the same name. "Libra" is the reason for the use of the £ symbol to express quantities of pounds sterling. As the price of silver rose, the pound denomination shrank to a more manageable size, but the name and the symbol remained.

One twentieth of an English pound was termed a "shilling," from the Old English *scilling,* and was abbreviated with a small "s." Authorities disagree as to the original meaning of "scilling." It probably comes from an old Scandinavian word, *skille* (or *scyll,)* meaning "to divide." [155] In

---

[*] A chart of English and British denominations, by monarch and metal, is given in Appendix C.

[†] Virginia halfpence, pennies and shillings are discussed as American issues in Chapter 8.

[‡] Technically, American plantation tokens, William Wood's Hibernia and Rosa Americana coinages also fit within the category (Chapter 8.) These, however, generally are given American rather than foreign incidental status.

this sense it could refer to the division of a pound into multiple parts. Before "shilling" came into wide use, however, an "s" was used to abbreviate *solidus,* meaning "solid." A solidus, or more properly a *numus solidus* ("solid [gold] coin,") was a coin type that originated in Rome and continued to be made in Europe into the 1500's. Troops being paid in solidi gave rise to the word "soldier," but no one is quite sure how "solidus" might have evolved into "shilling." Officially, English shillings fluctuated between 87.96 and 94.14 grains in weight, but remained at sterling fineness throughout the early American period.

A twelfth of a shilling was called a *denarius* and was abbreviated with a small "d." The word "denarius" is from the same Latin root as "denary," meaning "made of ten parts." A denarius originally was a Roman silver coin valued at ten of another denomination called an *ass* (pronounced "az".) By about 300 B.C.E., a denarius was equivalent to a day's wages, as in the Biblical parable of the vineyard owner, from the twentieth chapter of Matthew.[*] Because of this *per diem* connotation, a denarius sometimes is used as a metaphor for a day.

The more common word for a denarius is "penny," a term whose etymology rivals that of "shilling" for murkiness. It probably comes from the Anglo Saxon word, *penig*, and may be related to the Old High German word, *pending* that evolved into *pfennig*. All of these terms are merely words for "a coin."[156] Eventually, a troy pound was divided into 240 pennyweights, each at 24 grains.[†] A penny (or "pence") was then a silver coin of one pennyweight.

Familiar denominations that appear in contemporary literature are derivatives of pounds, shillings and pence. For example, a crown is a gold or silver coin of five shillings. A florin is valued at two shillings, a groat at four pence.[‡] One-half of a penny obviously is a halfpenny, in slang a "haypenny" or "hapny." A half of a halfpenny is a fourthling, in slang a "farthing."

Large silver pounds and half pounds were issued briefly in the 1640's. However, most pound coins were made of gold and are known as sovereigns, unites or laurels. Ryals, half-sovereigns, double-crowns, half-pounds, half-laurels and angels are all names for various types of ten-shilling gold coins. Though crowns generally are large silver coins, gold double-crowns, crowns and half crowns were minted sporadically. Valued at sixty shillings, the largest denomination of British hammered (hand struck) coinage is the triple-unite. All of these larger denominations and types certainly were rare in the colonies if they appeared at all.

When introduced in 1663 as Britain's first entirely milled (machine made) coin, the Guinea, was intended to be valued at twenty shillings. Inflation in the price of gold quickly drove up the exchange rate so that, even after a weight reduction in 1670, the Guinea's value increased relative to sterling money. In the 1680's they circulated at twenty-two shillings and by 1695 were valued at nearly thirty shillings. At that point Parliament set the limit at twenty-five shillings. It was lowered to twenty-two shillings before settling at the final value of twenty-one shillings, by proclamation in 1717.[157] Guineas and half-guineas were minted in most years

[*] The parable tells of a vineyard owner who hires workers in the morning for a day's work. The workers agree to the customary wage of a denarius. The owner hires additional workers at various hours of the day, right up until sunset. At the end of the day, the owner pays all of the workers equally. When the workers who had been at work the longest protest, the owner reminds them that they were paid according to their agreement and that it is his prerogative to reward each as he sees fit.

[†] A grain was equivalent in weight to dried grain of wheat, from the center of a seed head (Webster, p.1208.)

[‡] "Florin" derives from the Old Italian "fiore," for flower. At times, English florins used flowers in their designs. "Florin" also refers to a family of European gold coins that emulate those of Florence. "Groat" is from the Old Dutch "groot," meaning "a thick coin." Most English groats, however, actually are quite thin.

until 1813. Guineas remained fairly consistent at 128.09 to 131.18 grains in weight and 22 carat (0.917) fineness. Third-guinea gold pieces were issued only during the reign of George III and then only between 1797 and 1813. Particularly impressive, but not greatly relevant to America, are two- and five-Guinea coins that were issued at various times until 1753.

The antecedent to modern Guineas and sovereigns is a twenty-shilling coin called a broad. Broads and fifty-shilling gold coins, designed by Thomas Simon for the English Commonwealth, were issued in very small numbers. Few if any ever reached American shores, though silver Commonwealth denominations almost certainly did.

In 1600 and 1601, London's Tower Mint issued silver bullion coins for the Company of Merchants in denominations of eight-, four-, two- and one-testern. The intent was to create a trade coinage equivalent to Spanish dollars and their fractional parts.[158] These now rare pieces sometimes are called "portcullis coins" because their reverses depict the famed portcullis* that controls the Thames River entry to the Tower of London and thus to the kingdom. It seems likely that these coins might have entered the colonies indirectly through trade, though no known hard evidence supports this notion.

Scottish coinage barely survived the seventeenth century, but managed to add some colorful names to the mix, including the bodle (a billon twopence,) turner (a later copper twopence) bawbee (sixpence) and merk (or "mark," at thirteen shillings, fourpence.) In the sixteenth century an English pound was worth five debased Scottish pounds. When Scotland's James VI became England's James I in 1603, the ratio was twelve to one in favor of the English pound. Scottish shillings thus were equivalent to English pennies. A gold *unit* of Scotland was equivalent to four English crowns or twelve Scottish pounds. Mercifully, Scottish coinage ended in 1707 with the Act of Union that formally made Scotland part of Great Britain, thereby eliminating the need for a separate coinage.

(Right) Ca.1694 William and Mary bodle, found in Nova Scotia. Note the monogrammed "WM" and Scottish thistle.

(Left) 1673 Scottish merk of Charles II, 13s.4d (Scots,) a little more than a shilling (English.) Note the monogrammed pairs of C's (for Charles II.)

At times halfpence and farthings were minted for Irish circulation. They were lighter in weight than their English counterparts, a characteristic that only added to Irish frustration. On these coins Ireland is referenced by its Latin name, *Hibernia*, which means "a cold place."† Even these lightweights were welcome arrivals in America.

* A portcullis is a wooden gate of horizontal and vertical bars. The vertical bars form spikes at the base of the gate. The gate itself is raised and lowered to control entrance. The portcullis that controls entry to the Tower of London from the Thames River became symbolic of security and power. It still is depicted on British pennies and occasionally on other coins.

† Compare to "hibernate." In contrast, the Latin name for Scotland is Caledonia ("a warm place.") Compare to "calorie," a unit of heat. In many ways, Ireland still is a cold place for Englishmen.

This basic grounding in the British monetary system is a necessary framework for examining official issues. That system, familiar to the first Jamestown colonists, survived until 1971, when a decimal-based scheme replaced it. (See Appendix C for a full listing of denominations.)

REGAL, COMMONWEALTH AND PATENT COINAGES

Until 1561 all English coins were made by hand using the ancient method of hammering. That year Eloye Mestrelle, a Frenchman, demonstrated to the Royal Mint a new milling process that used a horse-powered screw press to produce coins of high quality. Unfortunately, his end-to-end process took longer than simple hammering and, though milled coinage was attempted intermittently over the next eleven years, after all the experimentation, Royal Mint employees reverted to the old technology. They also managed to have Mestrelle hanged on trumped-up charges. His only real crime had been threatening mint employee's jobs with technological change. A century later, in 1662, progress won out as the last hammered English coin tumbled down the side of the coiner's anvil.[159]

Mestrelle's demonstrations came early in the long reign of Elizabeth I, last of the direct Tudor line and mother to the age of English colonialism. This bastard daughter of Henry VIII and Ann Boleyn ascended to the thrown in 1558, on the death of her Catholic half-sister, Mary. A staunch but tolerant Protestant, she survived smallpox and conspiracies to become one of the greatest English monarchs. While domestic welfare ultimately suffered because of the debts she accumulated, she was chiefly responsible for England's emergence as a true world power. In many ways the defeat of the Spanish Armada in 1588 signaled a passing of the baton after which the fortunes of Spain faded and those of England soared. The navy that her explosive, enigmatic father had built gave England the ability to project its culture to unexplored areas, most notably Virginia, the colony named for her, the so-called "Virgin Queen."

1564 sixpence of Elizabeth I, a product of Eloye Mestrelle's milling process. Most hammered sixpence coins have her bust surrounded by a beaded circle.*

Small denomination silver pieces and a lead token with her visage have been found in and around Jamestown and on Roanoke Island. In particular, a 1563 sixpence was found on the north end of Roanoke Island. That piece is holed, suggesting that it may have been a gift to an Indian friend of Sir Walter Raleigh's "Lost Colony."[160] These Tudor silver coins represent the earliest English type likely to be found at an American archaeological site. The copper halfpence and farthings that dominated the late colonial era still were the better part of a century away from their first appearance.

---

* Elizabeth wears a high collar and faces left. A Tudor rose is behind her. The obverse legend reads *ELIZABETH · D[EI] · G[RATIA] · ANG[LAND] · FRA[NCIAE] · ET HIB[ERNIAE] · REGINA* ("Elizabeth, by the Grace of God, of England, France and Ireland, Queen.") The text on French coinage in Chapter 7 contains an explanation of why Elizabeth believed that her dominion included France. The reverse depicts a cross pattee over the royal shield, with the date, a star mintmark and the legend *POSVI DEVM ADIVITOREM MEVM* ("I Have Made God My Helper,") at once a symbol of her religious devotion and of her arrogance.

When Elizabeth died in 1603 without heirs, attention turned to Scotland and James, the son of her cousin, Mary Queen of Scots. Although his father was Henry Stuart, Lord Darnley, both of James's parents were descendants of England's Henry VII (Tudor.) In 1567, at the tender age of thirteen months, James became king of Scotland as James VI. The Protestant reformer John Knox preached the sermon at his coronation. At about the same time, Elizabeth I imprisoned James's mother for her suspected involvement in a plot to take the English crown. She was held for nineteen years before Elizabeth finally had her beheaded in 1587. Thus, James never knew his mother. On Elizabeth's death, he became James I of England.

Under strict Calvinist tutelage in Scotland, James grew into a very learned man. He ultimately mastered seven languages and became a fine author, a skill that proved to be both a blessing and a curse. He was a patron of William Shakespeare who wrote *Macbeth* for his king.[161] James also commissioned a common language translation of the Bible. Known as the *King James Translation,* it became the greatest selling book of all time.

Undated (ca. 1604) James I shillings.[*]

Not everything ran smoothly during James's reign. His firm belief in the *Divine Right of Kings* strained relations with an emerging Parliament and fit closer to the Catholicism that he despised than to his own Protestant faith. Public opinion of him suffered when a booklet of his Divine Right beliefs, written for his eldest son Henry, and titled *Basilicon Doron* ("The Kingly Gift,") somehow found its way into the streets. Unfamiliar with time-honored English legal customs, James made a habit of using his prerogative to step on the rights of his subjects. That disregard sometimes took the form of religious intolerance. In reaction, a 1605 Papist coup led by Guy Fawkes attempted to kill James by using gunpowder to blow up Parliament. The plot was foiled and the perpetrators executed.[†] As if religious prejudices were not enough, James's Scottish heritage engendered English hatred, approaching racism, against him.[162]

Still, he understood the potential of the Virginia Company and Jamestown, the settlement named in his honor. His reign also saw the establishment of Nova Scotia, or "New Scotland," and the flight of the so called Pilgrims to Massachusetts. His political skill and a relative lack of foreign entanglements enabled him to ride out the storms. James I died peacefully in 1625 at the age of fifty-nine. Though formal recognition of Great Britain came in the next century, England, Scotland and Ireland first were brought together when James assumed England's throne. This is made evident by a comparison of the arms on his coins to those of his

[*] The obverse legend reads *IACOBUS D[EI] G[RATIA] ANG[LAND] SCO[TLAND] FRA[NCIAE] ET HIB[ERNIA] REX* ("James, by the Grace of God, of England, Scotland, France and Ireland, King.") Note the use of the Latin *I* in place of *J* in *IACOBVS* and the addition of James's Scotland to the legend. The denomination is given as *XII* [pence]. The reverse depicts the royal arms, with the surrounding legend *EXURGAT DEVS DISSIPENTVR INIMICI* ("Let God Arise and His Enemies be Scattered.") The beaded circle that surrounds both obverse and reverse vignettes identifies this as a hammered, rather than a milled, coin. The combined arms inspired the creation of a one pound gold coin optimistically called a unite.

[†] Some Britains still celebrate Guy Fawkes Day on the November 5 anniversary of the "Gunpowder Plot."

predecessor. Elizabeth's shield features only English leopards and French fleurs de lis, each occupying two quarters. (Again, see the text on French coinage in Chapter 7 for an explanation of the French symbol's presence on English coins.) James's shield has Elizabeth's entire arms in each of the first and fourth quarters. In the second quarter is the Scottish lion within an elaborate frame. In the third quarter the Irish harp made its English numismatic debut. The harp had been used before to symbolize Ireland, but not on English coins. Its appearance had been overdue since Henry VIII made Ireland a kingship.[163]

In addition to English coins, a surprising number of coins with Irish associations have been found at Jamestown. Those who settled Virginia came from areas where Irish coins would not have circulated, begging the question of why such a large portion of these early finds are Irish.

The answer may lie in the business and political ties that linked Virginia Company investors with Irish lands and affairs. Many of these investors were involved in the Elizabeth's bloody colonization of Ireland. In the late sixteenth century the quest for commercial wealth and royal favor drove the attention of a few well-to-do gentlemen from southwestern England toward the Emerald Isle and points west (i.e., Roanoke's "Lost Colony.") These ambitious, decidedly Protestant promoters, known as the West Country Men, included Sir Francis Drake and Sir Walter Raleigh. While the Roanoke opportunity ultimately passed them by, the wealth that they had garnered for their investors was redirected into the Virginia Company and the Jamestown enterprise.[164] It is entirely possible that some of that wealth took the form of "liberated" Irish coins and that some of them made it to Virginia.

Undated (ca. 1605) James I Irish Sixpence.

The Stuart line took a detour when Prince Henry died in 1612 without ever having had the chance to rule. In his place James's second son ascended as Charles I, in 1625. James's rocky relationship with his subjects was a cakewalk compared to that of his successor. Though raised as a strict Protestant, Charles alarmed his subjects by marrying a Catholic, Henrietta Maria, sister of France's Louis XIII. Then, under the guidance of his advisors, Charles allowed several disastrous foreign ventures, prompting Parliament to stop granting him money for such campaigns. The growing tension between the Royals and Parliament surfaced in the very first year of Charles's reign when he dissolved the legislative body. The following year Parliament sought to impeach a close advisor to the king. Desperate for money to finance his ventures and eager to quell unrest, Charles initiated the unpopular practice of quartering troops among the people under forced loan arrangements. Charles and Parliament reached an agreement in 1628, but it lasted only until the following year. The break-up occurred over the collection of taxes and duties and Charles's meddling with accepted church procedures. He waged a harsh campaign against both Catholics and non-conforming Protestants, driving many of them to America, particularly during the 1630's. A conflict known as the Bishops' Wars erupted in 1637 when Charles tried to force Scots to become Episcopalians. Having ruled without Parliament since 1629, he finally had to call a session in 1640 to ask for war money. When Parliament refused, he suspended them again. Enough was enough. Parliament reconvened and asserted its power, denying Charles the ability to suspend them and taking control of the right to tax.[165]

On the surface Charles accepted their terms. However, his belief in the Divine Right simply was too strong to engender trust. His cause was hurt further when Henrietta Maria was implicated as a supporter of a 1641 rebellion in Ireland.* Outright civil war erupted that same year when Charles attempted to seize those in the Commons who opposed him.

Charles I coinage: *(Left) Ca. 1644 half-crown, with Charles on horseback, sword in hand. (Right) Ca. 1633-1634 shilling.*†

After defeats in 1644 and 1645, Charles surrendered to the Scots, who handed him over to the English army. He escaped and aligned himself with dissenting Scots, but again was defeated and captured in 1648. By then militant extremists under Oliver Cromwell had taken control of Parliament. Charles's son, who eventually became Charles II, begged for leniency on behalf of his father, even presenting Parliament with a signed, blank sheet of paper on which they were to write their own terms. It was to no avail. On January 30, 1649, Charles I was beheaded on charges of treason. Aside from the political and social upheavals that ensued, the event had numismatic repercussions both in Britain and America.

1653 Commonwealth shilling. Note that its legends are in English rather than Latin and read GOD WITH US 1653 *(obverse) and* THE COMMONWEALTH OF ENGLAND *(reverse.) Presumably, this was done to appear less royal and more egalitarian. The obverse shields symbolize Great Britain and Ireland.*

Cromwell established the harsh, repressive Commonwealth government that ruled until 1660. Lacking the heritage of a legitimate king, Cromwell took the title "Protector." To a great extent the Commonwealth was self-absorbed in its own affairs, leaving the colonies to test the waters of self-government. It was during this time and partly because of these events that the first coins were minted in America. (See the text on Massachusetts silver coinage in Chapter 8.) Nevertheless, the Commonwealth government resisted the exportation of specie to America, just as the Crown had done. Overall, mintages of the Commonwealth era were relatively small and it is questionable whether many of them arrived on American shores.

---

* See the St. Patrick/Mark Newby coppers text in Chapter 8 for more information on the 1641 Irish Rebellion.

† Obverse legends for both coins are the same as on the previous piece, with the name *CAROLVS* (*Charles*) in place of *IACOBVS*. The reverses of both coins feature the legend *CHRISTO AUSPICE REGNO* ("I Reign Under the Auspices of Christ") around an ornamented, oval shield.

Thomas Simon's 1658 half crown depicting Cromwell as an emperor. The regime had become more fascist by 165, adopting Cromwell's portrait. The obverselegend reads OLIVAR D[EI] G[RATIA] R[E]P[UBLIC] ANG[LAND] SCO[TLAND] ET HIB[ERNIA] &c PRO[TECTOR] *("Oliver, by the Grace of God, Protector of the Republic of England, Scotland, and Ireland, etc.." The reverse features a crowned[!] shield, with St. Andrew's cross, the Irish harp and the English crosses. Around it is the paradoxical legend* PAX QVEAERITVR BELLO 1658 *("Peace is Sought Through War [in] 1658.")*

The Stuarts were anything but idle during the Commonwealth era. Charles, the eldest son of Charles I, assumed the rule of Scotland after agreeing to proclaim Presbyterianism there and in England. When he attacked England, Cromwell's forces drove him back. He fled to France, then to Germany and finally to the Spanish Netherlands (Belgium.)[166]

"Oh, Prodigious Change!"[167]

Then the winds of fortune changed. The Commonwealth weakened after Cromwell's death in 1658[*] and collapsed two years later. *Carolus a Carolo* ("Charles from Charles," or Charles II) ascended to the English throne amid the huge celebration known as the Restoration. He promised amnesty and religious toleration, policies that were welcomed after years of repression. However, they proved very difficult to carry out. Debts from an old war with the Dutch, a plague outbreak in 1665 (killing 100,000 in London alone) and the great London fire of 1666 further undermined Charles's efforts. He negotiated alliances with the Dutch, Swedes and French, promising Louis XIV that he would adopt Catholicism. The French connection collapsed when Charles's Protestant nephew, William of Orange, married his Catholic niece, Mary. William and the French king were bitter enemies and anti-Catholic sentiment exploded in England, leading to another dissolution of Parliament in 1681. It remained dissolved for the four remaining years of Charles's reign.

The Restoration era produced important numismatic innovations in the forms of copper halfpence and farthings. Of all English or British coins, the lowly halfpence had the greatest effect on American numismatics. Understanding their ascent requires a look at the demise of the penny. Understanding their designs requires a trip into antiquity.

The penny denomination is very old, dating to the eighth century. For centuries pennies were made of silver. By the seventeenth century, however, inflationary erosion of value had reduced the size of silver pennies, halfpence and farthings so much that they no longer were practical to carry. Pennies then weighed a scant eight grains each, about $1/55^{th}$ of an ounce, and soon would be relegated to service as keepsakes, token gifts from the Crown to the poor on

[*] John Evelyn, a Royalist who witnessed Cromwell's funeral procession, wrote of it in his diary, "...there was none that cried but dogs, which the soldiers hooted away with a barbarous noise, drinking and taking tobacco in the streets as they went." (Rhys, I., p.334.)

Maundy Thursdays. Other minor coins were hoarded rather than spent. Though tried more than a century later, a copper penny was too large to be a viable substitute.

The rather brilliant solution was a copper halfpenny, production of which began in 1672. When it came to a design for the new halfpence England turned to ancient Rome and one of its coins, a *sestertius*. These substantial copper and brass pieces were made from the time Caesar Augustus became emperor in 27 B.C.E. until the middle of the third century A.D.. Their obverses almost always feature a bust of the day's ruler, whose name appears in the legend. Reverses usually depict allegorical figures or goddesses. The piece above features a laureate bust of Severus Alexander opposite Roma, the city goddess, seated on a globe and facing left. She holds a spear of war in her left hand and an olive branch of peace in her right. This sestertius is similar to rare pieces that depict Antoninus Pius, who ruled from 138 to 161 A.D., on their obverses and Britannia on their reverses, commemorating Rome's occupation of Britain. The Dutchman, John Roettier, adapted the design for an English medal, using Charles II's mistress, Frances, Duchess of Richmond, as his model for Britannia, in 1667.[168]

In 1672 when Britain began making its own coppers, it was the Antoninus Pius design that again they chose to emulate. In modified form, the same concepts were used later on William Wood's Hibernia coinage, Voce Populi coppers, Vermont coinage, Connecticut state coinage, New York's Nova Eboracs, counterfeit halfpence, Auctori Plebis tokens and blacksmith tokens, all of which have American ties. The seated figure (i.e., as Liberty instead of Roma or Britannia) appears again on the obverses of many nineteenth century U.S. Mint issues (Chapter 12.) Thus, in an indirect way, these nearly two-millennia-old sestertia circulated in America.

A – An almost paper-thin James I silver penny (1.5x and at actual size.) The obverse depicts a rose, with the legend ROSA SINE SPINA ("A Rose without Thorns.") The reverse bears a thistle, with DEI TUETA UNITA ("God Unites Us.") B – 1673 Charles II twopence. C – Ca. 235 A.D. Roman sestertius. sestertius.* D – 1768 engraving of Britannia. Note that her staff is topped by a liberty cap, later an later an American symbol. (See p.16n.) By Francesco Bartolozzi after Giovanni Battista Cipriani. Source: Library of Congress, Prints & Photographs Division, LC-USZ62-45529.*

Immediately after production of halfpence and farthings began, two major problems became evident. The first was the difficulty of producing copper blanks of adequate quality and legal weight. With the English copper industry struggling, the solution was to import blanks from Sweden. To make this viable, import duties on copper conveniently were suspended.[169]

---

* This piece dates from about 235 A.D. It depicts Severus Alexander, who ruled from 222 A.D. until a Thracian Thracian army officer's bloody coup ended his life in 235 A.D. The young man had been a gentle, civil ruler, but, he also was a "momma's boy" and never was liked by the legions. The word "sestertius" effectively means "semi-tertius," or "two and a half." Thus, it was denominated at two and a half asses. Before the second Punic War (218 B.C.E.,) when a denarius was worth ten asses, a sestertius was worth one-fourth of a denarius.

The second problem, that of counterfeit coppers, never was solved. It remained an issue as long as lightweight counterfeits could be produced for less than the coins' nominal value. In a proclamation of December 15, 1674, can be found the first in a long series of attempts to curtail base metal counterfeits. The proclamation describes legal actions to be taken against any who "...make and utter forgeries, halfpence or pieces of brass, or other base metals, with private stamps."[170] None of the legislation worked. In one mid-eighteenth century period of seven years, the Solicitor of the Tower Mint reported 650 various counterfeiting prosecutions.[171] By the end of the century, counterfeiting of halfpence reached a fever pitch.

Charles II coppers: *(Left) Halfpenny of the type minted between 1672 and 1675. (Right) 1675 farthing, excavated in Maryland. Farthings of this type were minted between 1672 and 1675, in 1679, 1684 and 1685. Issues of 1684 and 1685 are rare.*

Difficulties notwithstanding, the new coppers quickly became a commercial fixture on both sides of the Atlantic. They were just the right size for day-to-day business. According to the royal standard, an avoirdupois pound of copper was to make forty-six halfpence or ninety-wo farthings. Thus, with 7,000 grains to the pound, the standard weights of halfpence and farthings were 152.17 and 76.09 grains, respectively.

In addition to the new coppers and the usual cast of specie, near the end of Charles's reign an effort was made to jumpstart the ailing Cornish tin industry by introducing farthings in that metal. To increase their value and fight counterfeiting, a square plug of copper was inserted through a hole in each coin's center. The date was moved from beneath the exergue line at Britannia's feet to the edges of the coins. The full edge lettering thus read *NVMMORVM + FAMVLVS + 1684* [or 1685]. The meaning is "Familiar Coinage [of] 1684."[172] Softness and the tendency of these bi-metallic issues to corrode limited their longevity and explain why few of them survive. Though experiments with tin coinage continued for a few years even after Charles's death in 1685, it is questionable whether many of them, of any variety, actually made it to America. The Thames River, on the other hand, has given up many to dredging.

Ca. 1685 Copper-plugged tin halfpenny of James II, Charles II's successor.

Charles II also revived a practice that his grandfather had begun in 1613. At that time small change was in short supply, particularly in Ireland. James I sought to resolve the problem by selling a royal patent to mint farthings to one of his favorites, John Harrington, Lord of Exton. Harrington's paper-thin farthings were made of copper with a thin coating of tin to give the appearance of silver. This was necessary to reassure Englishmen and Irishmen still skittish about base metal coinage. The coins were supposed to weigh at least six grains. When it was discovered that most weighed only five grains, they were recalled and replaced with a slightly heavier un-silvered issue. Given that examples of these farthings have been found in America, including one of the recalled pieces found at the site of a 1620's Virginia settlement, Wolstenholme,[173] it is clear that they are relevant to American numismatics.

The years that followed saw the patent change hands several times. After Harrington died in 1614 it passed to his son. It passed back to Harrington's widow, Lady Anne, when their son died a few months later. Lady Anne gave or sold it to Lodewicke, Duke of Lennox, who also became the Duke of Richmond. On Lodewicke's death, in 1624, it passed jointly to his Duchess and to Sir Francis Crane. James I "Lennox" farthings may have been issued for another year afterward, until the death of James I and the advent of Charles I "Richmond" issues by the duchess. Charles issued a second patent to Crane and Henry Howard, Lord Maltravers, in 1634.[174]

Patent farthings: *A – 1613, James I, "Harrington" issue. B – 1614 to ca. 1625, James I, "Lennox" issue. C – 1625 to 1634, Charles I, "Richmond" issue. D – 1634 to 1636, Charles I, "Maltravers" issue. James I obverse legends are minor variations of* IACO[BUS] D[EI] G[RATIA] MAG[NAE] BRI[TANNIAE,] *or "James I, by the Grace of God, of Great Britain, …." The legend is continued on the reverse, with* FRA[NCIAE] ET HIB[ERNIAE] REX *("…France and Ireland, King.") Charles I pieces replace IACO with* CARO[LUS] *or* CAROLUS. *E – 1636 to 1644 Charles I, Maltravers "rose style" patent farthing.*

Attribution of these farthings requires a keen eye because, until 1636, all of them featured a crown and crossed scepters on the obverse and a crowned harp on the reverse. Beyond the James v. Charles distinction, differences are quite subtle.

By the 1630's patent farthings were being counterfeited extensively. Consequently, Lord Maltravers introduced smaller diameter, but thicker, "rose" farthings in 1636. These kept the crown and scepters, but replaced the harp with a crowned Tudor rose. They

also incorporated innovative wedge-shaped brass inserts to thwart counterfeiters. On a cleaned piece, these resemble a bright wedge in a round pie.

Public and parliamentary pressure brought a hiatus in the light patent coinage beginning in 1644. Then, after the Restoration, Charles II revived the practice by issuing a patent to Thomas Armstrong, Sr., who made farthings in 1660 and 1661, mainly for use in Ireland.[175] Even with small change in very short supply, Armstrong's tiny farthings met with strong opposition and never were accepted. When the effort failed, underweight private merchant tokens emerged to take their place.

In the later years of Charles II's reign, from 1680 to 1684, a new patent allowed Thomas Armstrong, Jr., and George Legg to mint halfpence bearing Charles's bust opposite a reverse that features a crowned Irish harp. Judging from the relative lack of recorded complaints, patent halfpence were better received than the diminutive farthings. A 1681 halfpenny from this series was found in 1975, along with contemporary pieces, at a Philadelphia road construction site. When Charles II died the Armstrong-Legg patent passed to Sir John Knox,

Lord Mayor of Dublin, who continued to produce similar halfpence, bearing the bust of James II, until 1688.[176]

1683 Charles II, Thomas Armstrong (Jr.) and George Legg patent halfpence. Issued from 1680 to 1684.

American circulation of patent coppers is supported well beyond occasional archaeological finds. Patent farthings were so pervasive that a 1635 Massachusetts law forbade their use. At about the same time Virginia's Governor, Sir John Harvey, asked the Crown for relief of his colony's small change shortage.[177] The response *may* have come in the form of patent farthing shipments. Decades ago a farmer near Yorktown found a group of them in clay pots. The group also contained a 1663 Scottish twopence,[178] indicating that patent farthings continued to circulate in some areas well after 1635. Their use, however, probably peaked under Charles I.

The political and numismatic landscape became more complicated with the death of the second Charles in 1685. He left many heirs, all of them illegitimate. The absence of rightful descendants meant that the crown fell to James, Duke of York, Charles's brother of dubious abilities. Back in 1646 when Charles I was captured by Cromwell's forces, the young James had been seized as well. After escaping, he served in the armies of France and Spain before returning to England during the Restoration. When New Amsterdam was captured in 1664, it was renamed New York after the young duke. In 1685 it was his turn to rule as James II.

James was neither popular nor effective. A Catholic who favored absolute rule, he was a lightning rod for anti-Papist sentiment. The situation came to a boil in the summer of 1688 when the Archbishop of Canterbury and six bishops were tried for challenging James's right to suspend laws that he had found inconvenient. The defendants were acquitted, the public was delighted and James was furious. At the same time his wife was birthing a son, giving rise to fears that the Catholic regime would continue. The Bishop of London, along with other bishops and Whig and Tory leaders, persuaded James's daughter, Mary, and son-in-law, William of Orange, to come to England and rule jointly as William III and Mary II. In an almost bloodless coup called the *Glorious Revolution*, James II was forced out late in 1688. He fled to Ireland in March 1689 and there raised an army bent on returning.[179]

1689 gunmoney half-crown. Note the month (September) and the denomination "XXX" (thirty pence) on the reverse.

In Ireland his Jacobite* Jacobite* supporters melted melted bronze cannon to produce coins bearing James's likeness. These generally well-made coins are called *gunmoney* and were issued in denominations of sixpence,

* The term "Jacobite" derives from "Jacobus," Latin for "James."

shilling, half-crown and, later, a crown. The premise was that those who accepted the bronze coins would be repaid in silver, with interest, when James returned to power.

To facilitate the calculation of interest most of these 1689 and 1690 coins also were dated with their month of issue. The first of two gunmoney series includes sixpence, shillings and half crowns whose obverses feature a left-facing bust of James II. Their reverses bear a crown atop crossed scepters, along with the ornate initials *J R,* for *Jacobus Rex*, ("James, King.") The second issue added a crown denomination with James on horseback and a sword of vengeance in his hand.

Despite many efforts spanning decades and monarchs, the Jacobites never returned to power. Any real chance of their return ended when William defeated his inept father-in-law at Boyne (Ireland) in July 1690. While pre-revolution standard issues from James's reign were honored because of their precious metal content, later regimes afforded gunmoney only insulting, trivial value. Gunmoney coins probably circulated sparingly as pennies and halfpence in the colonies even though their face values were considerably higher. The presence of gunmoney in early America was established more than thirty years ago when a laborer unearthed a sixpence while working on the construction site of a hotel in Williamsburg, Virginia.[180]

A group of tin pennies and halfpence also belongs with the gunmoney series. These small denomination coins feature the Irish harp on their reverses. They essentially were a continuation of issues made before the Glorious Revolution, under James and his predecessor. As did the earlier tin coinages, these tin and copper-plugged issues had dates on their edges. Those bearing James's bust were issued between 1685 and 1687. Even his successors issued edge-dated tin pieces in 1689 and 1690.

Afforded no more respect than his gunmoney, James ended up in France where he died in 1701. His replacements, William III and Mary II, were an odd couple. William was both the nephew of Charles II and the great-grandson of William the Silent, "the Dutch Washington" (Chapter 7.) When France's Louis XIV used aggression and connivance in an attempt to take the Spanish Netherlands, the Dutch worried that they might be next. The Spanish Netherlands were all that stood between them and Catholic France. The Dutch called on William, the twenty-year old Prince of Orange and Count of Nassau. The young prince beat back the French and, when peace finally was made in 1678, he emerged as the hero of the Netherlands and the defender of Protestants. A year earlier, on his twenty-sixth birthday, an arranged marriage brought the quiet, asthmatic, slightly hunchbacked and very Protestant prince together with the Catholic elder daughter of Anne Hyde and the future James II.

Even with all the stars aligned against them, the intelligent young couple actually managed to forge a congenial marriage. Mary acknowledged that her role was secondary to William's in matters of state, as her position on their coins indicates. She assumed the full responsibilities of the monarchy only in his absence. Public acceptance of their joint rule was hedged by a series of laws made to limit the abuse of royal prerogatives and insure Protestant succession. Future monarchs were required to belong to the Church of England.[181]

William and France's Louis XIV hated each other. When Louis challenged William's right to the throne in 1689, the War of the Palatinate erupted and quickly evolved into King William's War (1689 to 1697,) the first of the four French and Indian wars. In America it took the form of frontier skirmishes, a British victory at Port Royal and their failed attempt to take Quebec.

Its eventual peace left the French threat considerably weaker, but William's image suffered and the peace was shaky at best.

William persuaded his people to accept the first Grand Alliance, an agreement between the Holy Roman Empire and the Dutch, to limit the expansion of France. He warded off the War of Spanish Succession (Chapter 6) until the end of his reign, but was blamed for it when diplomatic efforts eventually failed.[182]

Still, the time of William and Mary was not without peaceful accomplishments. The Bank of England was founded in 1694, giving the government an all-important means of dealing with debt and later serving as a model for the Bank of the United States. On the American side, the College of William and Mary was named in honor of the royal couple. It became the alma mater of Thomas Jefferson, Patrick Henry and other American icons.

William & Mary: *A – 1694 halfpenny. B –1689 Guinea, a modern copy. C – 1692 Irish halfpenny. Royal halfpence of 1689-1692 were made of tin with a copper plug. They have the relief edge lettering* NVMMORVM FAMVLVS *and are edge-dated, like the James II plugged halfpence of 1685-1687 and edge-dated plugged farthings of 1684-1687. Some rare 1689 halfpence feature small busts of William and Mary and a 1689 halfpenny type places the date in the obverse legend rather than in exergue on the reverse. No 1693 halfpence were made. 1694 halfpence are copper and have plain edges. William and Mary farthings followed a similar pattern, but copper issues began in 1693. D – 1689 half-crown. Legends of the halfcrown and Guinea begin on the obverse and read* GVIELMVS ET MARIA DEI GRATIA MAG[NAE] BR[TANNIAE] FRA[CIAE] ET HIB[ERNIA] REX ET REGINA, *or "William and Mary, by the Grace of God, of Great Britain, France and Ireland, King and Queen."*

William's public image continued to suffer after his thirty-three year old queen died of smallpox in 1694. It seems she provided much of the positive public relations for the pair. William, on the other hand, was more serious and withdrawn.[183] He was left to grace Great Britain's coins alone until his death in 1702.

(Left) 1699 William III copper halfpenny. With minor variations, this type was minted between 1695 and 1701. Some 1698 and 1699 issues have the date in the reverse legend, rather than in exergue. Farthings are similar. Their production ended in 1700.

(Right) 1701 William III twopence at twice actual size

William and Mary were childless. However, the order of succession was set under the 1689 Settlement Act. Mary's sister, Anne, the younger by two years, was the successor to the throne. She ascended over the claims of her Jacobite half-brother, James Francis Edward, the "Old Pretender," who had been the baby born during the bishops' trials of 1688. Anne was uneducated, chronically obese, frequently ill and totally unprepared to rule.

Anne's ties to the Marlboroughs through her best friend, Sarah Jennings, had caused friction with William and Mary during their reign. Jennings was married to John Churchill, the Duke of Marlborough and ancestor of Sir Winston. John Churchill served the Crown well, but was involved in political intrigues against William, apparently out of a belief that his contributions were not being fully recognized by the king. After Mary's death William assuaged his sister-in-law's anger by appointing Churchill to a high government position.[184] Churchill led the formation of the second Grand Alliance against a France that had grown powerful in the brief peace that followed King William's War. And, in those days, a strong France was a harbinger of more hostilities.

Sure enough, the War of Spanish Succession that William had tried to avoid erupted in 1702, under Anne. Again the hostilities manifested themselves in American frontier conflicts, this time along two fronts: the New England-Canada border and the amorphous borderland between the Carolinas, Louisiana and Florida. As the war progressed Britain quickly dominated the Southern theater. Before long the fort at St. Augustine was Spain's last stronghold in Florida and by 1706 the Choctaws were the only Southeastern tribe still loyal to France. In preparation for a western campaign British settlers were ordered to move into the region and win over Indian tribes with great bargains in trade. However, the western campaign never materialized because continued threats against Charles Town (i.e., Charleston) kept the Carolina forces close to home. In retrospect, the British failure to act amounted to forfeiture of the chance to control the lower Mississippi Valley.[185]

In the Northern theater French and Indian marauders destroyed Wells, Maine, in the summer of 1703. By 1709 intensifying frontier raids eventually goaded New England into sending 1,900 troops to Port Royal in Acadia. They wrested the post from the French and renamed it Annapolis after their queen. In 1710 a large British naval assault on Quebec ended when ten ships and nine hundred men were lost on the rocky shoals of the St. Lawrence, the victims of blinding fog and faulty navigation. Nevertheless, the peace terms, agreed upon in 1711 and formally ratified in the 1713 Treaty of Utrecht, gave Britain a great deal of new territory, including Gibraltar, Newfoundland, Acadia and the basin around Hudson's Bay. Furthermore, the Iroquois at last were under unchallenged British control.[186] British ownership of the continental interior and the area around the Gulf of Mexico would have to wait for the next war, but after the second French and Indian war (a.k.a. Queen Anne's War,) Britain had two wins and France again was left to sulk.

Examples of Anne's coinage:
(Left) Obverse of a 1707-E half-crown.[*] *(Right) 1711 shilling.*

The gains in territory and the formal Union with Scotland that occurred during Anne's reign were the beginnings of the British Empire, but the prolonged period of war had been costly in monetary and political terms. Parliament continued to consolidate its power as an unhappy electorate steadily forced Anne's allies from office. Weary from years of political and personal struggles, Anne died on August 1, 1714.[187]

During her reign she had supported the production of specie, but opposed the minting of base metal coinage by the government. Base metal coins were not as profitable as specie and relatively large quantities of them still were in circulation from the times of her predecessors. Consequently, no Anne halfpence or farthings were issued for general circulation. Even so, patterns of both denominations exist. Halfpenny patterns bearing Anne's portrait are many times as rare as their smaller companions.

Hanovers at the Helm

Anne was the last of the Stuart line as none of her seventeen children survived to adulthood. When she died the Settlement Act of 1701 ensured that the throne passed to Sophia, granddaughter of Charles I, and her (Sophia's) heirs. Sophia was married to Ernest Augustus, Elector of Hanover and Duke of Brunswick-Lunenburg. Since Sophia also died in 1714, but before Anne, the crown fell to her son, George Louis, or George I. With him began the century-plus reign of the Hanover line.

---

[*] The "E" that appears below Anne's bust is the mintmark for a short-lived Edinburgh issue from melted Scottish coinage. The coin's edge lettering reads *DECVS ET TVTAMEN REGNI V. DECVS ET TVTAMEN* means "An ornament and a safeguard." This refers to the use of edge lettering to deter those who would clip silver from the coins' edges. This practice would be used on many British coins and still is used out of tradition, though no current British circulating coinage contains gold or silver. *REGNI* refers to the date of the monarch's reign. On this coin, the complete phrase is *REGNI V*, indicating the fifth year of Anne's reign (1707.)

England's new king was born in Germany and spoke little or no English. He spent most of his time focused on Hanoverian and extra-marital affairs and never was popular. Still, if and when Jacobites reasserted royal claims, Britains knew that George I stood as a barrier to the return of the Catholic Stuarts. George had a mean streak, divorcing his young wife and sending her to prison for the last thirty-two years of her life for an act of marital infidelity. He was known more as a laughing stock than as a noble leader. At one point, for example, the bug-eyed king's love of agriculture prompted him to inquire about the viability of closing one of London's great parks, St. James's, so that he could plant turnips on the land.[188]

George's awkwardness led to an inordinate reliance on Sir Robert Walpole, said to be Britain's first true prime minister. The king needed strong allies to navigate through the challenges of the Jacobites. Jacobite trouble began again in 1715 when Scottish noblemen rebelled and proclaimed that one of their number should be recognized as James III. The rebellion was squelched and the guilty parties beheaded, but George's public image continued its decline.

Obverse of a 1725 George I Guinea.

It suffered a second blow when the South Sea Company, a finance group contracted to manage Britain's national debt, collapsed in a 1720's debacle similar to that of John Law's concurrent regime in France. (See Chapter 8.) The value of South Sea shares ascended to irrational heights before the inevitable collapse ruined many prominent investors. George had made a point of appointing his German favorites to high positions in the company. When several of them were implicated in the "South Sea Bubble," any perceived integrity that the royal entourage might have held was in serious question.[189] The public constantly was reminded of the debacle thanks to the "SSC," [Silver from the] *S*[outh] *S*[ea] *C*[ompany], markings that appeared on 1723 silver coinage.

1723 South Sea Company shilling. Note the draped bust and the "SS C" reverse markings.

But for his portrait and the direction it faces, George I gold and silver coins resemble those of Anne. His coppers are referred to as "dump issues" because they were made thicker and with smaller than usual diameters. The standard weights for the new coppers, however, remained the same as before.

George I: *1718 dump halfpenny and 1719 dump farthing. Dump farthings and halfpence were issued from 1717 to 1724. No farthings were issued in 1718.*

George I kept a number of mistresses, the most notable being Ehrengharde Melusina, Gräfin von der Schulenburg, who later figured prominently in William Wood's coinage efforts for Ireland and America. (Chapter 8.) George died of a massive cerebral hemorrhage while traveling with her in 1727. Very few in Britain mourned his death. No state funeral was held and his body was shipped back to Hanover for burial. His son, George Augustus, who became George II, never forgave the cruel treatment of his mother and openly welcomed his father's death. Sir Robert Walpole openly welcomed the transition as well. The British people seemed eager to forget their fallen king and embrace the new generation.[190]

At first their optimism seemed misplaced. George II was an intelligent and learned man, but he had been given no preparation for bearing the crown. As Prince of Wales, George Augustus lived a life of parties and games and was afforded only token responsibility in his father's government. When told of the king's death and the imminence of his own coronation, he suspected that a practical joke was being perpetrated against him. Fortunately, his charming and flirtatious wife, Caroline, was there to help George's public image. Her influence over him was well known and often used by Walpole and other ministers. [191]

1733 George II halfpenny, young head style, depicting George II as a relatively young man. He was 44 years old when he assumed the throne. Young head halfpence were minted between 1729 and 1739. Young head farthings were minted from 1730 to 1739, excluding 1738. Similar young head halfpence with Irish harp reverses were minted in 1736-1738, 1741-1755, except for 1745, and 1754. Irish young head farthings were minted in 1737, 1738 and 1744. Irish coppers are lighter, at 135 and 67.5 grains, respectively. Since regal halfpence rarely deviate from the standards by more than a few grains, weight is a strong factor in establishing authenticity.

Not so helpful was George II's only son, Frederick. The king and his prince absolutely hated each other. The hatred was fuelled by Frederick's constant siding with opposition elements in the government. As George II had done, Frederick openly longed for the death of the sitting monarch, describing his father as "...an obstinate self-indulgent miserly martinet with an insatiable sexual appetite." As Frederick, or "Poor Fred," as George and Caroline called him, grew in popularity, so did the king's anger toward him.[192]

In 1731 Robert Jenkins, a British sea captain, had his ear cut off by Spanish coast guards. When Jenkins showed his preserved ear to Parliament, the incident galvanized anti-Spanish sentiment and prompted the War of Jenkins' Ear. Eventually, this war merged with another. In 1739 Britain was pulled into the War of Austrian Succession against Spain and France. Four years into the conflict, at the age of sixty, George II successfully led an army of allied British, Hanoverian, Hessian, Austrian and Dutch troops against the French at Dettingen (Bavaria.) In doing so, he became the last English monarch to fight alongside his troops.

In America the conflict erupted in 1744 and became the third French and Indian war, or King George's War. In it the French launched numerous frontier attacks and an unsuccessful assault on Port Royal. The British took the French settlement at Louisburg, but returned it when peace came in 1748. All in all King George's War served only to solidify Britain's holdings in North America and to give the king's public opinion a needed boost through his battlefield exploits in Europe.

1745 George II half crown, LIMA issue. Beneath George's bust is the word "LIMA," indicating that the silver used in its manufacture came from a captured shipment of Spanish silver that was bound from Lima, Peru. This was clearly a wartime slap in the face of the Spanish.

Old head coppers: *1753 halfpenny and 1754 farthing. Old head halfpence were minted from 1740 to 1754, except 1741. Old head farthings were minted in 1741, 1744, 1746, 1749, 1750 and 1754. Some 1754 farthings were minted after George's death, perhaps as late as 1763. The series also includes halfpence and farthings bearing Irish harp reverses. Old head Irish halfpence were minted in 1736-1738, 1741-1744, 1746-1753 and 1755. Old head Irish farthings were minted in 1737, 1738 and 1760.*

He needed the boost because, during the war, the Jacobites mounted another challenge. This time the threat came from Charles Edward, "the Young Pretender," son of the Old Pretender. While Jacobites managed to take control of several Scottish cities, the rebellion ultimately failed and, for a few short years, peace prevailed.

Like a smoldering ember, however, the 1748 settlement ending King George's War left so many unanswered questions that yet another war erupted in the mid-1750's. Known in Europe as the Seven Years War, Americans simply call it the French and Indian War. In it Britain aligned with Prussia rather than Austria, her traditional partner, because the Prussian monarch was Frederick the Great, nephew of George II. George underestimated just how aggressive his nephew might be and again found himself pitted against the hated French, along with their Austrian, Russian and Polish allies.

Before the war, the French began building a string of forts with the intent of closing the American West to the English. Finding this utterly unacceptable, Virginia's Governor Robert Dinwiddie sent young George Washington to warn the French. Washington was well received, but the warning was ignored. Early in 1754 Dinwiddie sent Washington back with a small force to expel the French and their Indian allies. Through his own military blunders, Washington was forced to withdraw and build Fort Necessity, where he briefly held ground before surrendering. These events marked the unofficial start of the fourth French and Indian war. Several other disastrous expeditions followed, but Britain and France remained officially at peace until war was declared in Europe in 1756. For the next two years French and Indian combatants swooped down on English frontier settlements at will. The French were entrenched firmly in the St. Lawrence Valley and none of the British campaigns seemed capable of dislodging them.

Then, in the fall of 1757, William Pitt took charge of the war effort. By the next year the momentum began to turn in Britain's favor. Pitt long had been associated with Poor Fred and the entourage of young opposition politicians known sarcastically as the Patriot Boys. As such, Pitt's ascent rankled the king. Nevertheless, George II needed leadership that only a man such as Pitt could provide.

The war also produced legendary English officers, most notably Colonel Jeffrey Amherst and General James Wolfe. Wolfe died in a pivotal battle on the Plains of Abraham that led to the British capture of Quebec. A year later, when British forces took Montreal, the cumulative successes were enough to persuade the Indians to turn on their French friends. For all intents and purposes the North American war was over by 1759, but it took the 1763 Treaty of Paris to formally end hostilities. The European side of the war already had ended with a treaty at Hubertusburg. With the peace, Britain firmly was in charge of America east of the Mississippi River, Canada, the West Indies and even India. Spain held the vast Louisiana Territory west of the Mississippi, leaving France with two islands in the St. Lawrence River and the city of New Orleans, which they held only by duping the English negotiators.

The wars fought under George II overshadow the genius of his ministers, such as Walpole and Pitt, and the fact that he was a brilliant politician. George died in 1760 while sitting on a different type of "throne." He suffered a massive heart attack while trying to overcome one of his frequent bouts of constipation. The successful outcome of the war was his swan song. It allowed him to exit on a wave of popularity, a privilege granted few monarchs. George also had the satisfaction of outliving Frederick, the son he so had despised, by nine years.[193]

The crown fell to Frederick's son, George William Frederick, George III. George III would rule for six decades, though he was reduced in latter years to a figurehead by blindness and insanity. George was in his early twenties when he ascended to the throne and had just turned thirty-eight when the American colonies declared independence. Early on he was a popular king who enjoyed traveling among his subjects, though he never ventured to America. History might have turned out very differently had he come.

1766 George III Irish halfpenny. A similar portrait of the young king appeared on Irish halfpence of 1769. In looking at these coins, one cannot escape the impression that George III was weak-chinned and soft. These physical traits belie the fact that he was a very formidable king.

As it happened, the Seven Years War left Great Britain at the top of the heap politically and militarily, but badly bruised from an economic perspective. George III also inherited a monarchy that had been severely drained of its power by Parliament and tarnished by the personal flaws of his predecessors. The new king sought to reverse this trend. He was honest, hard working and bound by duty to God and country. This is a very different image from that of the tyrant described in the Declaration of Independence. He lost his naivety in 1760's and, by the 1770's, was systematically manipulating the government through bribes and the placement of yes men in key Cabinet positions. His dealings were so distasteful to many that a faction grew to advocate the idea that Great Britain be made a republic. Some of them apparently even desired an American victory in the Revolution, in the hope that that George's regime would topple. [194] Of course, it never did, even with the loss of the colonies.

1781 Irish halfpenny. Irish halfpence briefly returned in 1775 and 1776 and again in 1781-1782. No more Irish halfpence were minted in the 18th century. The 1760 George II farthings were the last official Irish coins of their denomination in the century. Irish George III halfpence retained the same lighter weights as George II Irish issues.

In spite of that loss, both George III and Britain found their groove in the 1780's. In some ways, it was if the burden of foreign intrigue had been lifted and the country left to mend. The end of the decade, however, foreshadowed trouble to come. George began to suffer from fits of delusion, at one point speaking to a tree as though it were the King of Prussia. He recovered for a time and, through personal integrity, preserved the British monarchy through the turbulent years of the French Revolution, when every world ruler was in peril from within.[195]

The first decade of the new century found George III again occasionally facing his personal nemesis. By 1810 the nemesis had won. The king was blind and solidly locked in the prison of his mind, conditions now believed to have been the result of a debilitating physical disease called porphyria. When he died in 1820, at the age of eighty-two, he still was very much revered by his countrymen who knew that he had served them well.

The George III portrait most familiar to American numismatists appears on British halfpence of 1770 to 1775. The same portrait appears on farthings of 1771 to 1775. No farthings were minted in 1772. With the exception of these issues and coppers of 1799 and 1806-1807, coins generally were in short supply during George III's reign. As will be seen in the sections that follow, counterfeiting reached epidemic proportions during this period. Most counterfeiters sought to emulate the coppers shown above. Irish halfpence of 1781 and 1782 also were prime targets. Irish counterfeits even show up occasionally as undertypes on American issues.

Similar portraits appear on the gold and silver coins of the period. The year 1787 is the only one during George III's reign in which meaningful numbers of shillings and sixpence coins were issued. Even then they may have been hoarded, based on contemporary writings that tell of widespread shortages.[196] Gold Guineas were issued for most years between 1761 and 1799, and in 1813. Except for a handful of years, half Guineas were produced continuously between 1762 and 1813. Commensurate with the status of specie, the legends on these coins give a considerably more ostentatious version of George's title than do coppers. The legend on a Guinea of the period reads *GEORGIVS III DEI GRATIA M B F ET H REX F D B ET L D S R I A T ET E*, or "George III, by the Grace of God, of Great Britain, France and Hibernia, King; Defender of the Faith; Duke of Brunswick and of Lunenburg; and Arch-Treasurer and Elector [of the Holy Roman Empire.]"

18th century numismatic portraits of George III: *A – 1786 Guinea by Thomas Pingo. This bust of George III is the same as that used on the pattern Virginia shillings of 1774. (Chapter 9.) The reverse quartered shield is also similar to that used on Virginia's coinage. The reverse shield evolved from the ornate form on the Guinea above to a spade-shaped shield and finally to an oval, military-style shield. B – 1787 Shilling by Lewis Pingo (Thomas's son). C – 1771 halfpence. D – 1774/3 farthing. Numismatists disagree on whether Richard Yeo or Thomas Pingo made the dies for C and D.*

(Left) 1797 George III cartwheel penny. (See below.) (Right) Actual size comparison of the relative diameters of an 1884 U.S. small cent, an 1845 U.S. large cent, the 1797 cartwheel penny at left and a 1797 cartwheel twopence. The twopence is 1/5 inch thick and weighs a whopping two avoirdupois ounces, more than twice the weight of a later U.S. silver dollar. Even these may have circulated sparingly in the former colonies, though the role that they might have played is unclear.

In 1797 the British government made a bizarre attempt at producing counterfeit-proof copper pennies and twopence. Matthew Boulton who, with James Watt, often dubiously is credited with inventing the steam engine, developed a steam-powered minting process that could produce these coins with their broad flat rims. Boulton's numerous attempts to persuade the government that he should be allowed to mint coins failed, but rampant counterfeiting finally convinced them. Boulton promoted the idea that the intrinsic value of a copper should closely approximate its face value. Accordingly, one of his pennies weighs a full avoirdupois ounce, the twopence twice as much. Their immense sizes earned them the nickname "cartwheels." Conrad Heinrich Küechler's innovative design for the cartwheels includes incuse lettering on the flat rims. All are dated 1797. To produce them, Boulton built a state of the art mint at Soho, near Birmingham. By 1800, the price of copper rose to the point that many of them were melted.[197] Ironically, cartwheels were not entirely successful in preventing counterfeiters as a cast lead counterfeit recently was found.[198]

In 1789 Boulton observed that two-thirds of the halfpence at tollgates and other venues were counterfeit and that the problem was growing worse. Yet, neither halfpence nor farthings was mentioned in the 1797 contract for the cartwheels. Boulton's team prepared halfpence patterns, but the government held to the ridiculous notion that so many counterfeits and trade tokens would be driven from circulation that the demands on Boulton would be too great. On this groundless premise, Boulton was denied the business.[199]

Küechler's 1799 halfpenny.

By 1799, however, public demand for small change convinced the government to reverse its decision. The 1797 pattern halfpence were overlooked in favor of a more conventional Küechler design. Because the price of copper had risen by about five percent, the new halfpence and farthings were made lighter than their proportional weights would have been as cartwheels.[200] As a result, they were unpopular even though they were larger and heavier than halfpence of the 1770's. In 1806 and 1807, another series of halfpence and farthings was made. The new issues were close to the original standard in weight. Again, a Küechler design was used and the Soho Mint did the work. Similar, but still lighter (by denomination) Irish pennies and halfpence were issued in 1805, with farthings following in 1806. Thus, after the American Revolution, 1799 and 1805 through 1807 were the only years in which George III appeared on regal coppers.

Later numismatic portraits of George III: *(Left) 1806 halfpenny. Similar, but lighter Irish halfpence were issued in 1805 and 1806. (Right) 1819 "bull head" sixpence.*

Queen Charlotte bore George III fifteen children. Their eldest son, George, ruled as prince regent from 1810 to 1820 and then as King George IV until his death in 1830. As prince regent, he was in charge during the War of 1812 and for Wellington's glorious triumph over

Napoleon. Flamboyant and given to excesses of food and drink, George IV punctuated the changing of the guard.

1822 George IV farthing

These later issues are included because British numismatic influence on America did not end with independence. Some of the 1700's-dated counterfeit coppers that are described in the next sub-chapter actually may have been made and circulated on both sides of the Atlantic well into the nineteenth century. Moreover, nineteenth century quasi-British tokens filtered down into the northern states from Canada at least until 1840. Nevertheless, coins of George IV and post-Revolution George III issues clearly circulated in America far less often than before. Pounds and pence grudgingly gave way to dollars and cents. Images of cuirassed* monarchs and Britannia seated lost their lost their places in American consciousness. In their place came familiar depictions of Liberty.

Examination of the coins made for Elizabeth I through George IV reveals some interesting patterns. First, the basic halfpence and farthing designs begun with Charles II persisted throughout the early American period and, for that matter, throughout most of the nineteenth and part of the twentieth century. Second, except for halfpence issued during the joint rule of William III and Mary II (1688 to 1694,) when both monarchs were featured, and during Anne's reign (1702 to 1714) when no coppers were issued for circulation, obverses of circulating coppers depict the laureate bust of the king within a circumscribed Latinate variation of his name, accompanied by the word *REX* ("King.") Even when a copper is too worn to determine its exact date, a reasonable estimate can be inferred simply by determining the direction in which the obverse portrait faces. Charles II faces to the left. His successor, James II, generally faces to the right, though a few issues have him facing to the left. William and Mary also face right because they considered themselves the rightful heirs to the throne of Charles II. The halfpenny and farthing patterns made during Anne's reign have her facing left. The alternating pattern continues on Georgian coppers and is mirrored on specie.

CONTEMPORARY COUNTERFEITS AND THE BRITISH EVASION

CONTEMPORARY COUNTERFEITS

The regal issues above tell only part of the story. Imposters, tokens and island coinages filled the voids left by chronic shortfalls in official production. In the absence of specie, the most widely used coin form in eighteenth century America, by a significant margin, was the British halfpenny. Farthings circulated in the colonies as well, but to a lesser extent. Ironically, as many as two-thirds of the coppers in America actually may have been counterfeits. This is evidenced by American non-collector accumulations that contain large proportions of them. Moreover, eighteenth century newspapers, American and British, routinely carried editorials lamenting the abundance of lightweight imitation coppers. For years the commercial role of imitation coppers was underestimated, perhaps because the coins themselves attracted little attention. Today, however, counterfeit British coppers are among the hottest topics in early

* A cuirass is a piece of armor that covers the upper body. It typically is made up of individual plates that are that are bound together to provide flexibility. The plates often are made of thick leather.

American numismatics. Understanding of various groups of them is still evolving. Except for a few halfpence that are linked to unauthorized Confederation era American mints, no absolute place of origin ever has been established for the various groups of imitations.

Collectively, American imitations, British counterfeits and halfpence of uncertain origin are referred to as "Tory coppers." All circulated in America, but Tory coppers by American makers are prized most by collectors. The Holy Grail lies in determining which are American. The primary tools for this determination are the coins themselves since, for obvious reasons, little or no documentation about them exists. Consequently, the field is not without subjectivity as numismatists' interpretations greatly differ.

It long has been held that primitiveness and poor planchet quality correlate directly to the likelihood of American origin, though no real evidence exists for such a conclusion. Similarities exist between unattributed imitations and known American pieces, yet solid evidence for definitive attribution seems always to fall short. Some are beginning to explore quantities of signature trace elements present in the alloys that make up borderline pieces on the assumption that knowing the metal's source might suggest the place of minting. However, raw copper routinely was exported from the colonies, and finished copper was even more routinely imported from Europe. Copper from two or more sources easily could have been mixed, particularly since available metal often came from the recycling of broken fixtures, old buttons, flawed castings, etc.. As a result, the origin of the copper reveals little about the locations of mints. Even with their questionable heritage and contrary to traditional wisdom, counterfeits contain relatively pure copper. The metallurgical properties of copper make the substitution of lesser metals impractical because the resulting alloys are impossibly brittle. Counterfeiters could not afford protracted refinement. When a choice existed they evidently preferred lighter coins to impure ones. The lighter the coin, the greater the profit.
Given the large number of varieties and die-linked "families" of varieties, it is likely that many pieces forever will retain the status of "possibly American." Further, since these counterfeits may have circulated well into the nineteenth century, it is just as likely that many will retain the status of "possibly colonial."

Except for those bearing ludicrous combinations of monarch and date (e.g., George III pieces with 1740's dates or George II pieces with 1770's dates,) no proven alternative to honoring their asserted dates exists. This may not be far from the truth since the greatest numbers of them are struck George III counterfeits, whose populations appear to track the production of regal halfpence in the 1770's. Until contrary evidence is found, it also seems reasonable to assume that most counterfeits, except for known New York-made pieces, originated abroad. The fact that many dates and varieties are found in quantity, in non-collector accumulations on both sides of the Atlantic, speaks against their American origin since it is unlikely that counterfeits made in the colonies would have been exported.

More problematic are rare examples dated 1781 and 1785. These dates seldom are seen on imitation halfpence from purely European accumulations. While the obverses of some 1781 and 1785 pieces resemble those on halfpence made for Ireland in 1781 and 1782, no corresponding issues of regal British coppers appeared in the 1780's. Were these imitations made in America? Were they made *specifically for export* to America? These unanswered questions only add interest to the topic.

Though it peaked during his reign, the counterfeiting problem is much older than George III. By the 1750's it was already too serious to ignore. In 1753 it was estimated that 40 percent of the coppers circulating in England were illegitimate. The infection was particularly acute around Birmingham. In 1754 Parliament threw in the proverbial towel and called an end to regal production. When official production resumed in 1771, the counterfeiters were ready. Regal coppers were produced in significant numbers in the years 1771 to 1775. In spite of a new, tougher law passed in 1771,[201] counterfeit coppers dated 1770 to 1777 are found in significant numbers, in America, Great Britain and Canada. Those dated 1775 are the most commonly encountered, while 1770 and 1777 pieces are quite scarce. Always popular with American collectors, 1776 halfpence exist only in the form of counterfeits.

Counterfeits come both in struck and cast forms and both in lead and tin compositions, but most are made of copper. George III counterfeits, in particular, almost always are made of copper. Early counterfeit halfpence (i.e., before the 1770's) tend to be cast, while later ones usually are struck. Cast pieces are particularly difficult to attribute since making them required little equipment and could be done by anyone, anywhere. Counterfeit coppers almost always are lighter than their regal counterparts, sometimes weighing less than half of the official standard.

Cast counterfeit halfpence: *(Top) 1700 William III, copper. (Middle) 1729 George II, copper. (Bottom) 1738 George II, tin.*

Their devices and legends are direct imitations of those on regal coppers. Even so, crudeness of the devices used on counterfeits sometimes gives them a comical appearance, with swollen lips, retrograde dates and other distortions. Well-reasoned typologies exist and are being refined. However, as a relatively new area of study, classification requires nearly as much art as science and will not be attempted here. Varieties for all years combined number in the thousands. This partly is a consequence of the use of directly engraved devices, rather than device punches. Members of at least one family of varieties exhibit outlines around major devices, a telltale sign that the die maker began by engraving an outline in the die, then added details within.[202] In the context of directly-engraved devices, executed in the negative on their dies, some varieties loose their "primitive" stigma. Even with the use of these older methods, some varieties exist in such numbers that they must have originated at larger, established mints rather than from small "barn" operations. Perhaps a bit of moonlighting occurred.

Counterfeiters risked imprisonment, or worse, for one very simple reason: greed. At 2,240 pounds, a ton of copper could produce 103,040 full-weight halfpence (at 152.17 grains or 46 to the pound,) with a total face value of about £214 13s 5d. At 105 grains, a very respectable weight in the counterfeit world, nearly 66.7 halfpence could be made from a pound of copper and a ton of it could yield £311 in face value. Counterfeiters are thought to have sold their wares at significant discounts, perhaps 25 to 30 percent under face value. At a 30 percent discount, the price for £311 face value in counterfeits would have been about £217 15s 7d.

Obviously, this is not all profit because production costs must be considered. In 1797 Matthew Boulton was allowed 4d per pound to make legal coppers. Using this as an estimate, production costs for minting a ton of copper would have been about £37 6s 8d. Since a counterfeiter actually made more coins per ton, his (or her) costs may have been somewhat higher. If the difference is proportional to the number of coins made, then £47 per ton might be a reasonable estimate of operating expenses. Then there is the copper itself. Copper in the 1780 to 1790 period fluctuated between £80 and £90 per ton. Over the next decade, it fluctuated between £90 and £120 per ton.[203] Adding these costs to that of production yields total expenses in the range of £127 to £167 per ton and profits in the range of £50 to £90 per ton of copper, even after the discount. In short, the gains appear to have been worth the risk. The chart below illustrates some estimates of the returns that counterfeiters could expect for their illicit investments. The pages that follow also illustrate a few of the many varieties of counterfeits.

Other key differences between unattributed halfpence and those ascribed to American mints are discussed in Chapter 10. Since all counterfeits thought to be of American origin were made in the 1780's, they technically are *imitations* and not counterfeits. By that time, there were no American laws against counterfeiting British coins and no British laws that applied in America. Imitations and counterfeits are two types of less-than-legitimate coins. Members of a third type, evasion coppers, are discussed below.

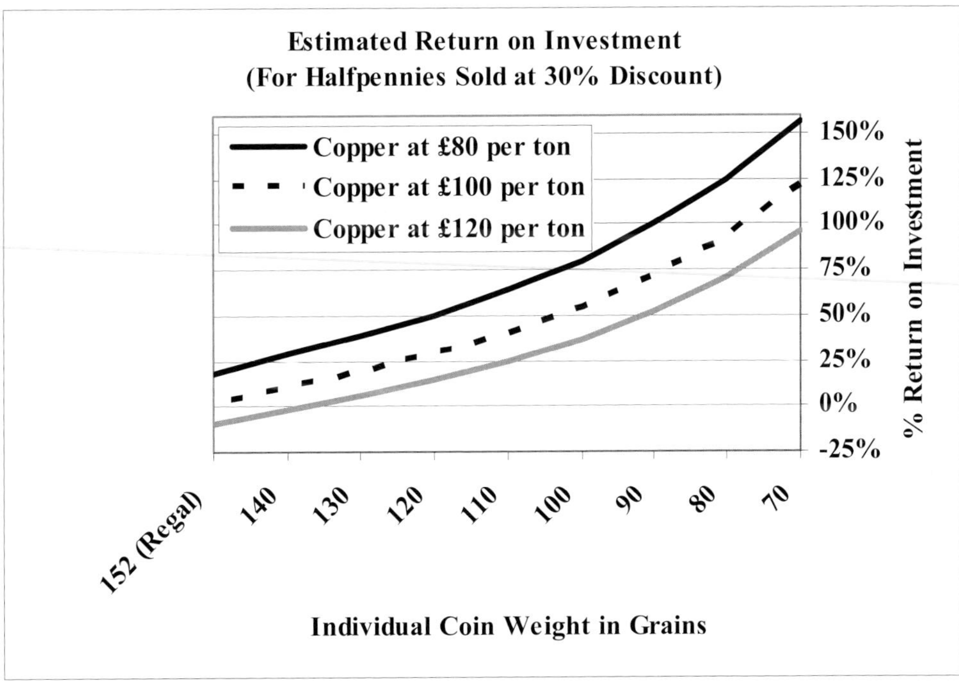

Assorted Contemporary Counterfeit Coppers (At slightly less than 1.5x)

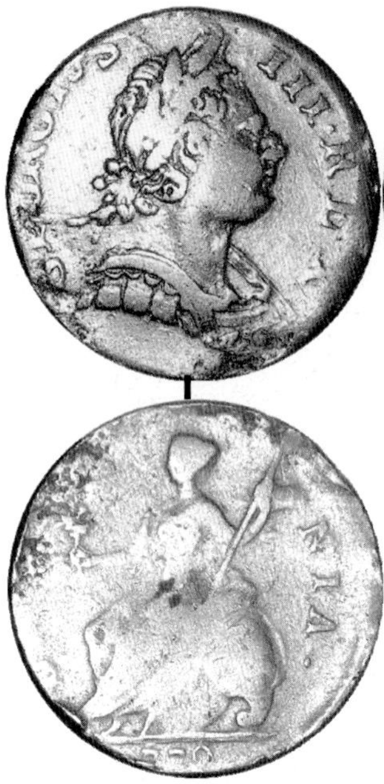

1770

1772

1773

1773

1773

1774

1774

1774

Assorted Contemporary Counterfeit Coppers (continued)

1775

1775

1775

1775

1775

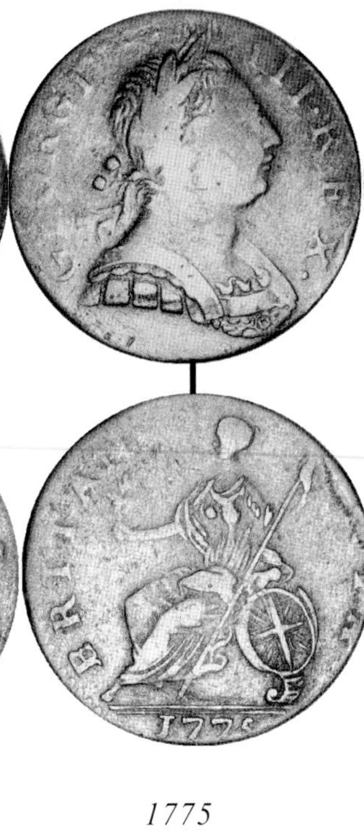

1775

1775

1776

Assorted Contemporary Counterfeit Coppers (continued)

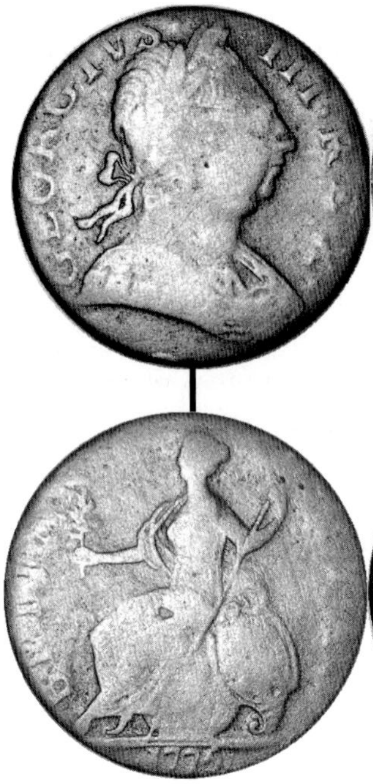

1776

1777
(Technically an evasion. Note DO REX in legend. See below.)

177?

1794
(A scarce date)

1773 (Irish)

1775 (Farthing)

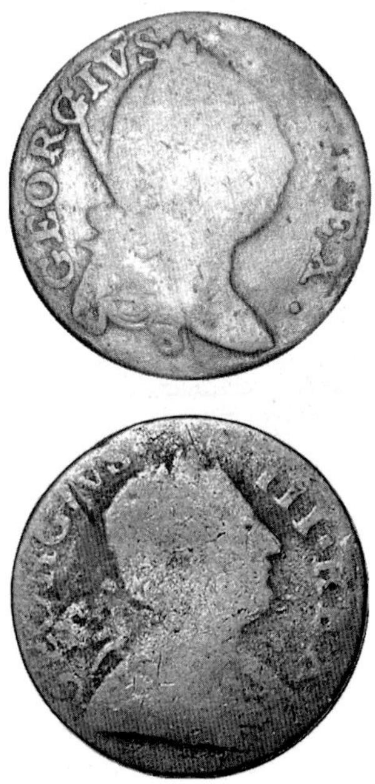

(Top) 1781(Irish)
(Bottom) 17??

EVASION COPPERS

The terms "counterfeit" and "imitation" imply efforts toward exact replication. The end products sometimes were crude, but devices and legends were intended to be reasonably exact copies of regal coins. Since true counterfeits were illegal or of questionable legality, it follows that the success of a counterfeiter depended on his or her ability to avoid being caught. Another approach used the coins themselves to evade the law. In 1742 Parliament passed an act that made counterfeiting coppers punishable by imprisonment. No one took it seriously until eleven years later when a follow-up act called for enforcement. After the passage of the 1753 act, unauthorized coiners took advantage of a loophole. That loophole allowed inexact copies of regal coppers (i.e., those with legends or devices that differ from official versions) to be made without penalty.[204] Collectively, such pieces are known as *evasion coppers* or simply as *evasions*.* Both farthings and halfpence evasions are known, but most are halfpence. After halfpence. After all, halfpence offered a greater return on investment.

On an evasion, *BRUTUS SEX, GULIELMUS SHAKESPEAR* or *GOD SAVE THE KING* might be used in place of *GEORGIVS III REX*. In place of *BRITANNIA*, one might find *BRITAIN RULES, BATER SEA* or even *BONNEY GERL*. To an illiterate public, it is doubtful that the differences were noticed.

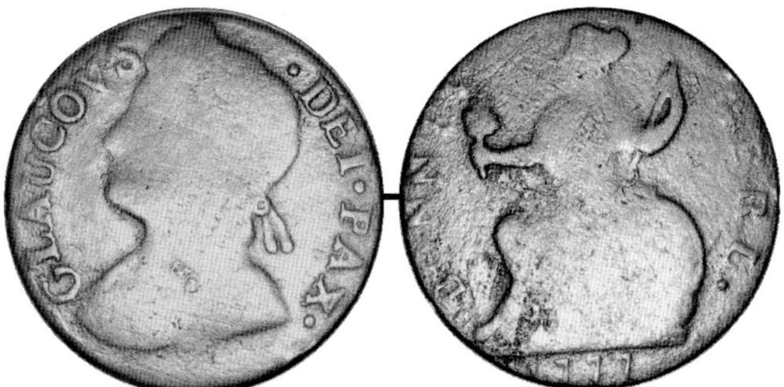

1777-dated George II style *evasion halfpenny. GLAUCOVS DEI PAX / BONNEY GERL*

While it is not known for certain that counterfeiting peaked in the 1770's, the general belief is that it did. On the other hand, evasions traditionally are regarded as somewhat later issues that are backdated. This conclusion is supported indirectly by the fact that few if any evasions are found in early American hoards and accumulations. The same hoards and accumulations often contain large proportions of counterfeits.

One of the more unusual evasions: ROMULUS / VIRTVS NVNQDEFICIT ICXXX, Cobwright R.0010 V.0020 (Atkins-429.)

The possible implication is that the absence of evasions is due to their emergence after formal colonial ties with England were severed. On the other hand, it may have been perceived as unnecessary to go to the extra trouble of producing evasive coinage for America when crude counterfeits worked perfectly well. Several evasions actually bear 1790's dates, as late as 1796. At least one early American coin, the Washington North Wales halfpenny (ca. 1795,

---

* Evasion coppers are better-documented cousins of the counterfeits. The best reference for evasions is *A journey* is *A journey through the Monkalokian rain forests in search of the Spiney Fubbaduck* [sic] by Malachy Greensword (A pseudonym for Mullhulland Ignatious Cobwright, which also may be a pseudonym,) second ed. in 1993. Before "Cobwright", a section of James Atkins' *The Tradesman's Tokens of the Eighteenth Century* (1892) was the primary reference for evasions. Atkins' numbers still frequently are used both for counterfeits and evasions.

Chapter 11,) actually is an evasion copper. As is the case with many other evasions, Washington North Wales tokens probably came from the mint of Birmingham token maker William Lutwyche.

Evasion halfpence: *(Left) 1779 GEORGE SUSSEX / BATER SEA, Cobwright G.0460 B.0020 (Atkins-203.) Battersea is a London neighborhood. (Middle) 1760 (ca. 1790?) GEORGE [II] RULES / NORTH WALES evasion Halfpenny, Cobwright G.0305 N0030 (Atkins-173.) No legal coinage was made for North Wales. Compare its reverse to that of the Washington/North Wales token in Chapter 11. (Right) GULIELMUS SHAKESPEAR / STRATFOR DIENSIS 1781, Cobwright G.1280 S.0050 (Atkins-388,) calling to mind William Shakespeare and his Stratford on Avon home.*

ISLAND COINS AND TOKENS

Commerce brought other kinds of British coppers to America. At the end of the eighteenth century and the beginning of the nineteenth, copper coins and tokens were produced for use in the British holdings of Barbados, Bermuda and the Bahamas. They were made to supplement the island currencies of barter, cut Spanish silver pieces, and the assorted coins, tokens and counterstamps of many nations. Early Americans knew all of these.

Though Britains began colonizing the eastern Caribbean island of Barbados* in 1627, it had no coins until a token penny issue of 1788. The pennies' sponsor is believed to have been Phillip Gibbs, a local plantation proprietor. Their designer was the Royal Mint's John Milton.[205] On their obverses is a depiction of an African, emblematic of the thousands of slaves who were brought to work in the dismal conditions of the island's sugar plantations. The African wears a plumed crown and beneath him is the legend *I SERVE*. The demeaning message is that the kings of Africa serve the plantations of Barbados. Conditions there were so bad that banishing a slave from America to the "sugar islands" was considered the equivalent of a death sentence.

* The word "barbados" is Spanish for "bearded ones," a likely reference to indigenous bearded figs.

1788 penny, Pineapple reverse

The reverse of the 1788 penny tokens depicts a pineapple, which became a national symbol of Barbados's agricultural prowess. In the eighteenth century, as now, pineapples also symbolized hospitality. For example, it was common for a New England sailor, returning home from trips to the West Indies, to place a pineapple on his doorstep to let friends know of his safe return and to welcome their visits. The date *1788* appears below the pineapple, with the circumscribed legend • *BARBADOES* [sic] • *PENNY* • above.

1792 halfpenny, Neptune reverse, proof restrike

A second reverse type and halfpence were added in 1792. Both feature an ornate and rather George III-looking rendition of Neptune, the Roman version of the Greek sea god, Poseidon, driving his shell chariot. Circumscribed above him is the legend *BARBADOES* • *HALFPENNY* (or *PENNY*.) The date *1792* appears beneath the waves.

1793 Bermuda penny

Bermuda followed with handsome pennies that were issued based on George III's 1793 authorization of at least £200. (Actual mintage estimates range up to 83,539 coins.) Bermuda had not enjoyed its own coinage since the 1616 *hogge money,* made for what were then called the Somer Islands (Chapter 8.) The 1793-dated pennies are linked to the creation of a new capital in Hamilton, named for Governor Henry Hamilton. Produced by Matthew Boulton in the latter half of 1793, they entered circulation in April 1794.[206] They feature Jean Peter Droz's rendition of George III. Droz's name appears in tiny letters on the King's shoulder, as *DROZ F*[*ECIT*], i.e., "[Jean Peter] Droz made it." The obverse legend is the traditional *GEORGIVS III D*[*EI*] *G*[*RATIA*] *REX*. The reverse features a ship, sailing westward, with the simple legend *BERMUDA* and the date *1793*. Some have suggested that the ship represents Captain George Somers' vessel, the *Sea Venture*, that he crash-landed on the islands in 1609. However, the ship on Bermuda pennies has the appearance of being from the eighteenth rather than the seventeenth century.

Bermudans expanded and began colonizing the Bahamas in 1656. For years the Bahamas served as headquarters for various pirate groups. In 1717 George I commissioned Captain Woodes Rogers to drive out the pirates and take control of the islands, inspiring by 1728 the motto *EXPULSIS PIRATIS RESTITUTA COMMERCIA* ("The Pirates Expelled, Commerce Restored.") In 1806, when the Bahamas Assembly ordered £500 in pennies from Boulton's

Soho Mint, they chose this motto for the coins' reverses. It appears in exergue below an east-sailing ship, with island mountains in the background. Above the ship is the simple legend *BAHAMA (*from the Spanish *baja mar,* or "shallow sea.") The artisan was Conrad Heinrich Küechler.[207] The obverses used Küechler's design for 1806 British halfpence.

1806 Bahamas halfpenny

The coinage of one other British-held island has American relevance. The Isle of Man is a tiny island in the Irish Sea, equidistant from England, Scotland and Ireland. Its history dates to the Iron Age and is flavored with Celtic, Viking and Christian influences. Vikings occupied the island from the ninth century until their ejection by the Scots in 1266. The English took over in 1288 and, in 1406 granted possession to the Earls of Derby. In 1765 the Crown bought the island from the Duke of Athol to stop its use as a rendezvous point for smugglers. The House of Keys that still governs the Isle of Man is one of the world's oldest legislative bodies.

1786 Isle of Man halfpenny. Fourteen Manx pence equaled one British shilling. As a result, Manx halfpence are lighter than British regal halfpence.

The Manx symbol, three joined legs, probably originated in Viking times and may have evolved from the ancient swastika. The legend *QUOCUNQUE JECERIS STABIT* ("Which ever way you throw, its stands") first appeared numismatically with the three legs in 1668. The phrase may be an allusion to the passing of the island back and forth between Scotland and England. Manx coppers, particularly those dated 1709, 1733 and 1786, almost certainly were used incidentally in America.

PRIVATELY ISSUED TOKENS

Even with regal, counterfeit, evasion and island coinages, shortages still plagued both the colonies and the home country. Many niceties that a prosperous government could provide its citizenry came to be viewed by Parliament and the Crown as luxuries when budgetary belts tightened. Among these luxuries were minor circulating coins. Powerful factions in Parliament perennially argued that such coins should be the enterprise of the private sector and that government should produce only specie. Rather than securing profit, base metal coinages were viewed as an expense. The labor needed to produce a gold or silver coin essentially was the same as that required for a base metal coin, but the profit in specie was many times greater. Another view leading to the same conclusion was the idea that base metal coinage simply was beneath the dignity of the Crown to produce. Either way, the obvious result was a paucity of small change. When small change was hard to come by in Britain, it was nearly non-existent in America and Ireland. Clearly, merchants and common folk needed something. That need did not go unnoticed by entrepreneurs and employers who fired up the presses (or hammers, or melting pots) whenever small change shortages became particularly acute.

Tokens were a less than ideal solution to the problem. Their light weights meant that anyone accepting them at face value risked their devaluation. This was particularly hard on the poorer classes, who had no other options. While these pieces were not major players in American commerce, they came as castaways and entered circulation alongside other incidentals. Shortages of proper coinage and, hence, token mintages, were greatest during three periods:

- The reigns of Elizabeth I and James I (1558-1625.)
- The English Civil War and the decades that followed (1642-1700.)
- The late eighteenth and early nineteenth centuries (1787-1820.)

The Reigns of Elizabeth I and James I (1558-1625)

During this period shortages triggered the minting of copper, copper-tin alloy and lead tokens. The patent farthings issued under James I and Charles I were intended to replace these tokens in circulation. At least one lead token was found at the Jamestown excavations and primitive lead tokens from this period regularly are recovered from the Thames River. They typically bear very simple line-drawing devices (e.g. hearts, geometric designs, religious symbols, ships, chalices, etc.) and rarely are dated. Little is known about their issuers or how the tokens actually were used. It is known that some were cast because a mold was found under a contemporary English house. It is also known that the practice continued well beyond Elizabethan times because a specimen was found at the site of Thomas Jefferson's birthplace in Shadwell, Virginia.[208] These also may have been analogous to the pieces described in a 1701 Massachusetts law that prohibited the use of "lead pennies."[209]

The English Civil War and the Decades That Followed (1642-1700)

The second major period of token production occurred after the 1642 outbreak of the English Civil War caused hoarding of coins. Token issues appeared before the end of the decade and then proliferated throughout the 1650 to 1674 period. Laws that accompanied the introduction of regal farthings and halfpence in 1672 and 1673 drastically curtailed, but did not stop token production. In addition to those of municipalities, tokens bearing the names of inns, taverns, grocers, tobacconists and practically every other kind of commercial entity were common. Most of them are farthing tokens in copper or brass, though a few halfpenny tokens, a few lead farthings and at least one bi-metallic plugged issue exist. Odd shapes exist as well: hearts, squares, diamonds, etc.. Sizes also vary. This hardly is surprising since no standard with which to compare existed prior to the regal farthings of 1672.

(Left) 1667 Norwich farthing with that city's arms.

(Right) Will Wellard's token, ca. 1660. His establishment was AT THE [SIGN OF] *THE COCK IN DOVER* [Kent]. *The rose device calls to mind the rose patent farthings issued earlier in the 17th century.*

So called Raleigh Plantation Token, ca. 1635-1660. These tokens depict a cherubic figure reclining against a skull and surrounded by the Ourobouros, a serpent that swallows its own tail. The Ourobouros is an ancient Greek symbol for the eternal cycles of time. The reverse legend spells out this thought: ★ *AS· SOONE· AS· WEE· TO· BEE· BEGVNN :* ★*WE DID BEGIN TO BE VNDONN:. In other words, the cycle of life and death begins as soon as we are born. Attempts have been made to associate this symbolism with Sir Walter Raleigh's failed Roanoke Colony and to claim that the plants depicted on the tokens represent tobacco. However, the symbols depicted on these tokens were well known in England and there is no real evidence for an American association. A vignette almost identical to the obverse appears with the same caption in George Wither's 1634 work,* A Collection of Emblemes Ancient and Modern: Quickened With Metricall Illvstrations, both Morall and Divine... *(Title page reads:* Printed in London, by A.M. for sale in the book store of Henry Taunton.*) Another illustration in Wither's book depicts time as a flower, almost identical to the one on the reverse of the tokens, within the circle of the Ourobouros. Its caption reads "Time, is a Fading-flowre, that's found Within Eternities wide round." It is likely that the design for the tokens was taken from the book and that these actually are English domestic trade tokens from the mid-seventeenth century.*

The industrial city of Birmingham was a likely source for many of these pieces, as was London and the maritime city of Bristol. Bristol was no doubt the point of departure for many that came to America. Yet, the towns and commercial entities that the tokens represent are scattered across the English and Irish countrysides. Given the tokens' usually diminutive sizes, it is possible that they could have been made on small presses carried by itinerate minters who peddled their services from town to town. The fact that some devices are shared by different tokens suggests that punches were used over and again. The number of different varieties is at least a thousand, some of which have been found at Jamestown and other American sites.[210]

THE LATE EIGHTEENTH AND EARLY NINETEENTH CENTURIES

A third family of British and Irish tokens emerged after 1787 when four major trends converged: 1.) Treasury deficits fed the reluctance of the government to provide its citizens with base metal coinage, 2.) the natural depletion of the supply of coins in circulation was accelerated because few new coins were produced, 3.) the application by private companies of emerging industrial technologies to the minting process enabled mass production and 4.) the rapid transition of Britain from an agricultural to a commercial and industrial economy and the associated population shift away from rural areas to urban ones increased the need for circulating coinage.[211] As in America, urbanization meant a shift from barter to money.

Given that production of regal coppers ceased in 1775, it is not surprising that shortages became acute by 1787 or that tokens made to relieve the shortages primarily were halfpence. Employees of large industrial concerns, in particular, needed to be paid. It is for this reason that private halfpenny tokens initially emerged in 1787. The concept worked so well that other types of commercial entities joined in the fray. When, in the mid-1790's, the tokens attracted the attention of collectors, a whole new set of subjects and devices were added specifically for them.

The period spawned large token making enterprises. The government even encouraged the growth of private token making as a substitute for regal coinage. Mints such as those owned by Obadiah Westwood, Peter Kempson and Matthew Boulton, grew large, their outputs rivaling the capabilities of the Royal Mint in quantity and at least equaling them in quality. Some, such as Boulton's, attained semi-public status, like that of modern American defense contractors. Private tokens went into hiatus when Boulton was contracted to make the 1797 cartwheels, the 1799 coppers and the issues of 1805 to 1807. They re-emerged in the 1810 to 1820 period. Finally, in 1821, under new management, the Crown at last responded with massive copper issues. By then the token makers were focused on pennies, silver issues and even gold. Parliament might have tolerated copper, but specie clearly crossed the line of acceptability.

In 1798 an Englishman, James Conder,* identified the different varieties of these tokens issued to that time. As a result, these coppers widely are known as *Conder tokens*. Ironically, Conder tokens became the targets of counterfeiters in the same manner as their regal cousins.

Conder token examples:

(Top) 1791 Liverpool halfpenny. The obverse bears the arms of Liverpool and its motto DEUS NOBIS HÆC OTIA FECIT *("God has made us this leisure/rest.") The reverse is similar to the Washington Liverpool halfpence (Ch. 11.) John Gregory Hancock, Sr. made both sets of dies. The edge of this token reads PAYABLE AT THE WAREHOUSE OF THOMAS CLARKE. xx. Clarke was a grocer who lived at 12 Cable Street in Liverpool. His warehouse was at 4 Marshall Street. Peter Kempson extensively counterfeited these tokens.*

(Bottom) Ca. 1795 satire of Thomas Paine made for collectors. Paine, of course, was the Irish immigrant whose pamphlet Common Sense *helped to ignite and sustain the Revolution. When things looked darkest, after a disastrous string of lost battles, his essay,* The American Crisis, *brought Americans together and gave them hope. What is not well known is that Paine gave the considerable proceeds from his publications to the cause. To Americans, he was a true hero. But the British held him in much lower regard, as evidenced by this token. It shows Paine hanging from gallows in front of a church with the legend THE END OF PAIN[E.] The church may be a deliberate contrast to Paine's atheism, about which he kept quiet, revealing it only after the War in his classic work,* The Age of Reason. *On the reverse, pandemonium erupts from a pair of breeches. Below them, a severed head (Paine's) lies next to the body of a snake. The reverse legend reads PANDORAS BREECHES, an allusion to the story of Pandora's box. An ornate border surrounds the scene. In this case, the released evils clearly represent the American Revolution. On this specimen, a die break extends diagonally across the reverse's right side.*

---

* James Conder's 1798 work is called *An Arrangement of Provincial Coins, Tokens, and Medalets Issued in Great Britain, Ireland and the Colonies Within the Last Twenty Years; from the Farthing to the Penny Size.* A 1910 work by Richard Dalton and S.H. Hamer, titled *The Provincial Token-Coinage of the 18th Century,* now generally is used as the chief reference (re: "D & H" numbers.)

1795 Coventry halfpenny. On its obverse is the figure of the legendary (or mythical) Lady Godiva. The obverse legend reads PRO BONO PUBLICO *(For the Public Good,) an allusion to Lady Godiva's selfless service to Coventry. In the year 1040 the Saxon, Lady Godiva, supposedly struck a deal with the militant lord of the area. He was heavily taxing the local serfs to finance his campaigns. To prove their honor and in exchange for lower taxes, Lady Godiva proposed to ride nude through Coventry. If no one peeked, the lord was to grant her request. Legend says that none did. Later, however, a peeper named Tom (i.e., Peeping Tom) was added to the story. The reverse depicts a local landmark, the Coventry market cross. The reverse legend simply reads COVENTRY HALFPENNY. William Lutwyche of Birmingham made these for Reynolds & Company (merchants.)*

1795 John Kilvington halfpenny. Kilvington was a merchant and tea trader at 153 Drury Lane in London. The obverse figure probably honors Queen Charlotte's father, the Duke of Brunswick.

1797 Mail Coach token. It was issued as a tribute to mail coaches. It is sometimes seen as an undertype for backdated counterfeit halfpence. Its obverse shows a mail coach en route. The legend reads MAILCOACH HALFPENNY / PAYABLE IN LONDON / TO TRADE EXPEDITION AND TO PROPERTY PROTECTION. The reverse legend, within a wreath, reads TO J PALMER E[SQUIRE] THIS IS INSCRIBED AS A TOKEN OF GRATITUDE FOR BENEFITS RECE[IVE]D FROM THE ESTABLISHMENT OF MAIL COACHES. Beneath the legend are the script initials, JF, believed to be those of the issuer, who may have been John Fittler.

Some Conder tokens were made for export and have come to be regarded as American (Chapter 11.) Such tokens inspired American Hard Times tokens of the 1830's and 1840's, as well as Civil War tokens of the 1860's. As likely did the evasions, however, most Conder tokens emerged too late to have circulated in America in large numbers. Even so, they round out a remarkably diverse numismatic heritage that Britain incidentally conveyed to her colonies and former colonies. British insistence on retaining her specie and her indifference to the need for circulating base metal coinage made this diversity possible. These factors also forced Americans to look elsewhere for coinage. When they did, Spain's New World colonies provided an obvious and convenient alternative.

6: SPAIN AND HER NEW WORLD COLONIES

THE EARLIEST NEW WORLD COINAGE

As the centuries rolled by, through the Middle Ages, Europe's meager supplies of precious metals dwindled and, across the continent, coins steadily became lighter and less pure. Then, with a sudden jolt, centuries-old trends were reversed completely as ton after ton of gold and silver was shipped from Mexico, Peru and Colombia, back to Spain. The almost unfathomable amounts of gold and silver from her New World colonies changed everything numismatic. Spanish coins flowed over all the world, generally setting the standard for purity and consistency for nearly three centuries. Many of these coins came to British America from southern Europe. Even more came directly from the Spanish colonies.

It all was dirty money. When the conquistadors arrived in Mexico, they found a society ripe for conquest, enslavement and economic exploitation. Even so, Indians in Mexico were more advanced than their northern cousins in many ways, and especially when it came to trade and money. The Aztecs, for example, used an array of useful and symbolic trade goods including gemstones, colored feathers, amber, woven materials, stone beads, red seashells, live eagles and skins. High-value transactions sometimes were accomplished using quills filled with gold dust. The conquistador, Hernando Cortés, wrote of very thin, coin-like tin disks used in trade, while the Aztec ruler, Montezuma, is known to have paid his gambling debts with coin-like golden "quoits." Other debts may have been paid with T-shaped copper plates known as "hoe" or "axe" money. Long after the Spanish conquest, cocoa beans still were used as money at 140 beans to the reale, Spain's unit of silver currency. Vestiges of this practice, tiny forty-bean coins, were used in remote areas of Mexico and Guatemala even into the twentieth century.[212]

Spanish settlers very quickly became dissatisfied with native currencies and wanted their own. By the 1520's there were enough merchants and tradesmen in Mexico that weight-stamped gold pieces began to circulate as money. Almost immediately, unscrupulous individuals began making golden objects that were so debased that they came to be known as *tepuzque*, an Indian word for copper.[213] Scholars disagree on whether tepuzque actually were coins and whether any survive. Presumably, most were re-melted to recover whatever gold they contained.

Five-sided, gold alloy, stamped object. One of several recovered in 1992 from the ca. 1528 wreck of the Tumbaga off Grand Bahamas Island. It features a crowned "C" (for King Carlos I) and the fineness "XV⁝" (15.75 karats, or 0.656.) If it is an example of tepuzque then it may represent the very first coinage made in the New World. [214]

Tepuzque was just the beginning. During the sixteenth century about 250,000 Spaniards settled in the Americas.[215] Given the size of this migration, it is not surprising that petitions for a New World mint began as early as 1528. Nor is it surprising, given the flood of specie that was exported over the decades that followed, that the very basic need for coinage to support local commerce has been forgotten as the true reason for the New World's first coinage.

In 1535 Charles I (a.k.a. Carlos I, a.k.a. Holy Roman Emperor, Charles V,) ruling in the name of his mentally challenged mother, Johanna the Mad (a.k.a. Jahanna la Loca,) ordered that a mint be built in Mexico City, which Cortés founded in 1523 on the ruins of Tenochtitlán, the razed Aztec capital. The idea for a mint grew out of Charles's keen interest in building up New Spain and improving relationships with the harshly treated Indians. Funding for the it came from revenue generated by a tax known as the "King's Fifth." Three decades earlier Charles's grandparents, Ferdinand and Isabella, had mandated that one-fifth of all silver and gold mined in Spanish colonies be paid into the Royal Treasury. Using revenue from this tax as funding, Charles sent a viceroy, Antonio de Mendoza, to confiscate Cortés's Mexican palace and build a mint within it. There the mint operation remained until around 1562, when the government purchased a larger building that still is known as the National Palace. (Cortés probably did not miss his old home since he was Spain's richest man at the time of his death in 1547.)[216]

Once the mint was established, citizens could buy bulk silver onsite or bring their own and have it rolled into sheets, cut into planchets and minted into coins. If silver was brought from outside the mint, a fee of about three percent was charged for assay. Another fee of about three percent was charged for the actual coining. Minting fees were divided among the assayers, coiners, die makers, guards, magistrates, etc., who ran the mint. After minting and payment of fees, the coins were handed back to the original supplier of the silver. As for base metal coinage, the Spanish government supplied copper, dispensing coined pieces in exchange for silver brought to the mint.[217]

The silver unit of Spain's realm was the *reale*' (often Anglicized to "reale" or "royal.") A reale originally was a gold coin of medieval Italy. Reales took on Castilian relevance when the charmingly named monarch of that Spanish territory, Don Pedro the Cruel, issued a fourteenth century regulation referring to *numus regalis*, or "royal coin." Then, the 1497 *Ordenanza* of Ferdinand and Isabella put the reale on firm footing by making it officially equivalent to 52.99 grains of 0.9306 fine silver,[*218] just a shade better than the 0.925 fineness of sterling.

The Mexico City Mint was allowed to make silver coins in denominations of one-fourth, one-half, one-, two- and three-reales, beginning in 1536. The four-reale denomination was authorized a year later to replace three-reale coins that often were mistaken for two-reale pieces. Few three-reale coins survive. The one-fourth-reale denomination also is rare because it was minted from only 1552 to 1555, before going into a siesta that lasted until 1794.
The bureaucratic door was left open for eight-reale pieces (or *ocho de a reale*s, "dollars") to be made at the mint, but until recently the existence of very early examples only was theorized. Production of New World eight-reale coins was thought to have been delayed by the Spanish domestic introduction of the gold escudo,[†] or sixteen-reale piece, in 1536, and the fact that minting large coins simply was beyond the capabilities of the colonial mint. However, a 1538[‡] eight-reale coin of Mexico City mintage was discovered in 2002. That single specimen is the oldest known New World dollar. Whether the piece was an experiment or part of a full production run is a matter of speculation still. Circumstantial evidence suggests that the Mexico City mint also produced gold coins, but the practice officially was forbidden.

---

[*] The ordinance set the reale at 1/67th of a mark. A mark, or marco, was a commonly used weight of German origin that was equivalent to one half of a Cologne pound. In modern terms, a mark weighed 230.047 grams, or 3,550.16 grains. Dividing 3,550.16 grains by sixty-seven yields 52.99. The fineness was set at eleven dineros and four grains. A dinero was equivalent to twenty-four grains, with twelve dinero considered pure. Thus, the fineness was $11^1/_6$ divided by 12, or 93.06%.

[†] "Escudo" is from the Latin *scutum*, or "shield." The name derives from the use of a shield device on the coins.

[‡] New World coins were undated until 1580. "1538" was discerned by analyzing devices and the assayer's initial.

Carlos and Johanna silver coins fall into two groups. The first is known as the "early series" and is believed to have been minted until 1542, when new device punches arrived from Spain.* The second group, the "later series," is attributed to the years 1542 through 1572. Early series coins generally are much rarer and less likely to have been found in the English colonies. Coins of both series were struck by hand hammering. The hammering process and deviations in the placement of letters punched into the dies resulted in many varieties.

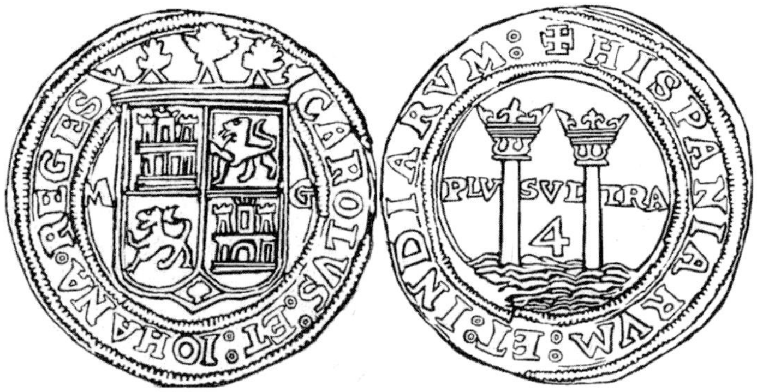

Later series four- and one-reale coins, Mexico City, 1542-1572.

Carlos and Johanna silver coins from both series feature a crowned, quartered obverse shield, with the symbols of the Castile and Leon territories (castles and lions, respectively.) A diamond shaped insertion at the shield's base holds a pomegranate, symbol of Granada and of fertility. The shield usually is flanked by an "M," for Mexico, and the initial of the assayer. Severe punishments for improper assays insured that coins were, on average, of proper weight and fineness, before the assayer's initial was applied. On the early series, the circumscribed obverse legend begins with a Jerusalem cross, symbol of the crusades, and reads *KAROLUS: ET: IOHANA: REGES*: ("Charles and Johanna Regents....") The legend is completed on the reverse with *HISPANIARVM: ET: INDIARVM:* ("...[of] the Spains and the Indies.") Smaller denominations abbreviate the same legends and, on later issues, *KAROLUS* is replaced with *CAROLUS*. On their reverses, the one-, two-, three-, four- and eight-reale silver coins feature the crowned Pillars of Hercules, symbolizing the giant rocks that flank the Straits of Gibraltar, rising from the sea. Since ancient times, these great rocks were thought to mark the edge of the world. Columbus transformed them from harbingers of the abyss to a gateway for the New World, as emphasized by the words *PLVS VLTRA* – "[There is] More Beyond [the Pillars of Hercules.]" On early issues, *PLVS* VLTRA appears within a panel midway up on the pillars and either in the foreground or background. Later the panel was removed and different abbreviated versions of *PLVS VLTRA* were used. On one-, two- and three-reale coins, the denomination is indicated by dots, one per reale, between the Pillars of Hercules. Four- and eight-reale pieces use numerals in place of dots. One-fourth reale coins feature a crowned obverse "K" and reverse "I" (for Karolus and Iohanna) as devices. The half-reale silver pieces present a crowned obverse "KI" or "KJ," opposite the pillars.

Coppers were denominated in *maravedi*, each of which was equivalent to 1/34th reale. Never popular with the Indians, they were issued in denominations of two- and four-maravedis between 1536 and 1538 and for about a decade beginning in 1542. (One-maravedis coins were added in 1542.) Not until 1814 did Mexico again produce coppers. Four-maravedis coppers are similar to the one-fourth reale silver coins, but add a castle and lion flanking the initial on each side. Two-maravedis pieces use a crowned "I," with *PLVS VLTRA,* opposite a crowned castle.

---

* Early references place the end of the early series at 1555, when Johanna died.

These were the first copper coins made in the New World, though Spain had provided coppers for Santo Domingo as early as 1505 and fifteenth century billon "blancas"* have been found at a La Isabel, a settlement that Columbus founded and visited several times before 1500.

Later two-maravedis copper of Carlos and Johanna, roughly similar in style to those sent to Santo Domingo early in the sixteenth century.

That coins continued to bear the names of Carlos and Johanna until 1572 is remarkable, given Johanna's 1555 death and Charles's 1556 abdication. The new ruler, Charles's son by Princess Isabella of Portugal, ascended to the throne as Philip II. In 1568 a new mint opened in Lima, Peru, and began hammering coins identical to the Mexican pieces, but bearing Philip's name. Most of these early coins were well made, resembling their European contemporaries.

THE AGE OF COBS

When Philip II issued a 1570 decree for new designs, it appeared that the practice would continue. In the early 1570's, however, the aesthetics of New World coinage took a turn for the worse. As Spain's hunger for silver grew, it became apparent that precious metals were more easily tracked and shipped if they first were coined or cast into small ingots. Making the coins look good became a secondary objective behind making them transportable. They could be made much more quickly and with less effort if they took the form of *macuquinas* or, as the English called them, "cobs."

At least two possible origins exist for the word "cob," both of which allude to the method of their manufacture. "Cob" probably is short for the Spanish *cabo de barra* or "end of the bar." The other possible origin is Middle English, in which "cob" refers to a lump, loaf or piece. To make a cob, the end first was cut from a bar of silver or gold. This small piece then was pounded flat and weighed. If it was too heavy, a portion was clipped away and the piece re-weighed. The process was repeated until the proper weight was attained and the insignia legally could be applied. The result was often an oddly shaped piece that scarcely resembled a coin at all, but was of the correct weight and fineness. Because these "planchets" had uneven surfaces, the design imparted by the dies is rarely ever even close to being complete.

Silver cobs were produced in denominations of one-, two-, four- and eight-reales from about 1572 to 1773, even though more attractive colonial milled coins were introduced in 1732. A half-reale denomination was added in 1621. When the eight-reale denomination entered full production in the 1570's, the flow of silver back to Spain dramatically increased.

The Mexico City and Lima mints began turning out silver cobs around 1572. With several interruptions, minting continued in Peru until 1752. The most notable interruption came after the 1660 discovery of fraud at the Lima mint. As a result, it closed until 1684. Cob production began in San Luis de Potosí and La Plata in 1574. Both mints are in present day Bolivia. In 1620 a mint was added in Santa Fe de Bogata, Colombia. The Potosí and Santa Fe de Bogotá mints had their own bouts with fraud in the mid-seventeenth century. Even so, the eighteenth century saw new mints spring up in Guatemala City (1733,) Santiago, Chile (1750) and Popayan, Colombia (1758.) Other, smaller ones also were opened along the way.[219]

* Billon appears whitish (in Spanish, *blanco*,) like silver. Billon is, in fact, a lower-grade mixture of silver, tin and copper.

*1736 Philip V gold doubloon, Lima, pillars and waves, Jerusalem cross, modern copy. Note that 1736 appears twice on the obverse: once in the bottom row as [1]736 and again in the legend (*PHILLIPUS V D[EI] G[RATIA] HISPAN[IARVM] ET INDIARVM REX.ANO 1736, *or "Philip V, by the Grace of God, of Spain and the Indies King, in the Year 1736.") In the cells formed by the pillars, L is the Lima mintmark, 8 is the denomination (in escudos) and the top A is the assayer's initial. In the middle row, P V and A are from* P[LVS] V[LTR]A. *The date is given a second time, as* [1]736, *in the bottom row of cells. (See text below.)*

Extraordinarily detailed Charles II cob 8 reales, Mexico City, 1733. Note the elaborate shield, the circular pellets at the ends of the cross's arms and the spread ends of the arms. Some Bolivian cobs feature the circular ornaments with a Jerusalem cross, but only Mexican cobs have them with this cross shape.

Typical Philip V cob 8 reales, Mexico City, ca. 1707-1723. This example was found washed ashore on a Florida beach. Note its odd shape and irregular thickness.

Ca. 1595 Philip II cob 4 reales, Segovia (Spain) Mint. Note the complete absence of cross arm ornaments. This piece serves as a reminder that cobs also were minted domestically in Spain.

The first gold cobs emerged from the Bogotá mint in 1622, the last from the same mint in 1756. They are similar to the silver pieces and were issued intermittently in denominations of one-, two-, four- and eight-escudos. Spain's flagship gold coin was the *doubloon*, or eight-escudos. Its value was sixteen Spanish dollars, or 128 reales. Two-escudo coins were known as *pistoles*, a name sometimes shared by gold coins of similar size from other countries.

Mexican gold cobs, displaying the more elaborate Hapsburg shield opposite a Jerusalem cross, appeared in 1690 and were produced until 1732. Peruvian gold cobs originated in the late 1690's, long after the debasements, and except for the one-escudo denomination, use the pillars and waves motif described below. The mints in Bolivia, Chile and Guatemala never produced gold cobs, though milled gold coinage emerged later from Chile and Guatemala.

Typically, obverses of silver cobs display the crowned shield of the Hapsburgs, surrounded by the assayer's initial, the denomination and symbols for the mintmark. The obverse legend is rarely visible, but bears the name of the sitting king with the phrase *DEI GRATIA.* The reverse legend, when present, completes the sentence: *REX HISPANIARUM ET INDIARUM.* The reverse design is arrayed around a central cross. On most gold and some silver cobs, this device is a Jerusalem cross, again symbolizing the Crusades. Each arm of a Jerusalem cross, or *cross potent,* has a straight cross member across its end. On some silver cobs, the cross is simple (i.e., without cross members.) On Mexican silver cobs the cross ends are spread and usually end with a ball or pellet. Regardless of the cross type used, the quadrants it forms almost always contain castles and lions.

In the two decades leading up to 1651, the mints at Potosí, Lima and Santa Fe de Bogotá had produced cobs that were fraudulently debased and miserably formed. A 1652 survey in Ireland revealed them to be short of the standard by a startling 37 percent.[220] The infractions were so severe that fifty death sentences were handed out and world confidence in Spanish silver waned. To differentiate the debased cobs and thereby restore confidence, the shield was dropped in 1652, in favor of the Pillars of Hercules, on issues from the offending mints. The new style sometimes is referred to as the "pillars and waves" motif.

B

A

C

8 reale Potosi cobs: *A – Ca. 1621, Philip III (made prior to the 1652 design change). B – 1682, Charles II. Note the pillars and waves. C – Ca. 1667, Charles II. From the wreck of the* Senorita de Santa Christina *that sank in the Bay of Cadiz in 1672. It was a "black" ship, rigged with dark sails to make it less visible to pirates.*

On it the two vertical pillars and two horizontal lines effectively divide the reverse into six cells as on a tic-tac-toe board. The top row of cells typically contains the mintmark, the denomination in reales and the assayer's initial(s.) The second row contains some variation of *PLVS VLTRA*. The bottom row contains the assayer's initial, a two- or three-digit date (e.g., [16]52 or [1]652) and the mintmark. In the early 1650's, some debased cobs were counterstamped to indicate a lower value, creating six- and three-reale denominations from eight- and four-reale pieces, respectively.

Cob designs appear simple, but can be extremely difficult to decipher. Aside from the complex array of symbols, strikes rarely are centered, insignia rarely complete. Legend variations, assayer initials, mintmarks, etc., aid in attribution, which can be very challenging. Even though cobs were not truly coins, they played a vital role in world, Spanish and American history and economics. They transcended a period of great strife that saw Spain take and then loose its preeminence on the world's stage. Unlike Britain, whose fortunes rested on its system of laws and the tenacity of its people, Spain's fate as a colonial power was shaped by unbridled greed and by the idiosyncratic personalities of its kings.

Early in this turbulent era, Philip II emerged as a pivotal figure. He is famous for marrying England's Queen Mary, the Catholic daughter of Henry VIII. He is infamous for enslaving the Dutch and then losing his armada at the hands of Mary's Protestant half-sister. The Dutch and English were not Philip's only enemies. His Spain fought with virtually every other European country at one time or another. He managed to conquer and become king of Portugal and more remote conquests, the Philippine Islands, were named in his honor.

Philip III succeeded his father in 1598. His reign was more peaceful, mainly because of his disinterest in government. Philip III's Spain produced Cervantes and El Greco and, at the end of his reign, the Pilgrims departed England for the New World. He died in 1621.

(Left) 1604 Philip III Spanish domestic 4 maravedis, hammered. These may have circulated in British America as farthings.

(Right) 1662 Philip IV Spanish domestic 8 maravedis, hammered. Eight and sixteen maravedis coins sometimes circulated in British America as farthings or halfpence.

His son came to power as Philip IV and ruled until his own death in 1665. It was during his reign that the great scandal broke at the Potosí mint. Perhaps he was too busy conceiving his thirty-two children to notice. Like his father, Philip IV had little interest in government and, accordingly, Spain's influence as a world power declined.[221] He was a great art collector and patron of Velazquez and Rubens. His collection formed the foundation of the Prado, one of the world's great art museums.

Charles II, Philip's frail, possibly retarded, son and the last of the Spanish Hapsburg rulers, became king at the age of four, in 1665. Ruled by Charles's Austrian mother until 1675, Spain continued its decline. Before his death, Charles II, who had no children, named Philip of Anjou as his heir under pressure from Spanish officials. France's Louis XIII, Philip IV's son-in-law, laid claim to the Spanish throne for his own son. The Bavarian, Joseph Ferdinand, also laid claim, as did Archduke Charles, son of Leopold I, the Holy Roman Emperor. Fearing the rise of France, the British and Dutch opposed the French claim. Under William III, the English struck a deal with the French, allowing Joseph Ferdinand to rule, but splitting Spain. France would receive Naples, Sicily and other territories, while Archduke Charles was to receive Milan. In an attempt to preserve Spanish unity, Charles II insisted that Joseph Ferdinand be the sole heir. The parties agreed and all of the claims appeared to have been settled. Complications arose, however, when Joseph Ferdinand died in 1699. This led to a second agreement that was accepted by Britain, France and the Netherlands, but not by Leopold I. Tensions rose further after Louis XIV deferred to Charles II's wishes and broke the treaty.

Charles died in 1700 and England's William III succumbed two years later, just before war erupted with England, the Dutch and several German states on one side, and France, Spain, Portugal and others on the opposite side. The war lasted until 1709 and was known in most of Europe as the War of Spanish Succession. It was the first ever world war. In the British colonies, it was Queen Anne's War, the second of the French and Indian wars. When the hostilities ended Philip Anjou was left to rule Spain as Philip V, the first of Spain's Bourbon kings, until his death in 1746, with a brief interruption in 1724. That year, Philip abdicated so that his son, Louis-Phillipe could rule as Luis I. However, the childless Luis was dead of smallpox within months. All but a few colonial pieces bearing his name are believed to have been lost at sea. Most, if not all, of the surviving examples are from Bolivian mints. Cobs lingered on through the 1746 to 1759 reign of Philip V's second son, Ferdinand VI. Their time ended in 1773, under Ferdinand's half-brother, Charles III. The reigns of Ferdinand VI and Charles III are discussed below.

It is important to remember that the cob's crudeness was deliberate and that they co-existed with other hammered pieces and with the fine milled coinages that Spain had been making since 1586. Cobs were melted to make the silver coins of Massachusetts, Maryland and the United States and were familiar to all Americans well into the nineteenth century. After the illegal debasements, fraudulent cobs were viewed poorly in America. Debased specimens were contemptuously called "Peruvians." Even legitimate cobs were susceptible to clipping and sweating[*] to knock off small slivers of metal. Wyman Parker estimated that, by the end of the seventeenth century, most Spanish pieces circulating in New England were reduced by one-fourth of their official weights.[222] Such problems, along with counterfeiting, helped to justify America's first silver coinage.

PISTAREENS AND OTHER DOMESTIC NEW PLATE COINAGE

During and after Queen Anne's War, Spanish pretenders issued coins, just as supporters of England's James II had done earlier. The 1711 piece below is an example of such coinage, probably attributable to supporters of Archduke Charles, given the monogrammed *CAROLUS III* device. This coin is a *pistareen,* a two-reale coin of lower than normal weight and fineness. Official pistareens effectively were tax-paid, having had the King's Fifth removed at the time of minting to pay war or other debts. Philip III re-implemented the tax in 1642 to pay debts that had arisen from internal rebellions and the Thirty Years War. The resulting debased coins

[*] Sweating involves shaking or beating a bag of coins to dislodge small pieces of metal. The metal is retrieved by burning the bag. If done repeatedly, one could accumulate enough metal to sell while the sweated coins retained the appearance of being full size and weight.

came to be known as "new plate" or *plata provincial*, meaning "[silver] plate of the [Spanish] provinces."

(Top) 1711 pistareen of a pretender to the title Carlos III, not to be confused with the actual King Charles III who ruled later in the eighteenth century. (See below.)
(Middle) 1721 cross pistareen of Philip V, Madrid.
(Bottom) A silvered brass counterfeit version of the same coin, with a Seville mintmark.

The intent was to retain new plate pieces as domestic coins. Predictably, however, Spanish merchants preferred the heavier colonial issues. Against their government's wishes, they held colonial issues and exported pistareens. As a result, through West Indian trade, pistareens were relatively common in British America. Britain even repaid a debt to Massachusetts in 1750 with chests of pistareens and heavier colonial two-reales coins aboard the *Mermaid*.[223]

Although nominally valued at two reales or a quarter of a dollar, the light weight of pistareens caused them to be valued at one-fifth of a Spanish dollar. When periods of inflation hit the American colonies, the values of the various colonial monies varied wildly relative to that of Spanish dollars. Spanish dollars were always more stable than the colonial currencies and circulated at higher values, even though the sterling money valuation of a Spanish dollar officially was set at 4s 6d. To bring some sanity to the situation, Britain's Queen Anne issued a 1704 proclamation limiting the value of a Spanish dollar to no more than six shillings in sterling money. Currency values still fluctuated, but not as greatly because the American colonies gradually accepted the new standard.

At the rate of six shillings to a dollar, a colonial two-reale coin was equivalent to 1s 6d. In contrast, a pistareen generally was valued at 1s 3d. In areas where a Spanish dollar was considered equal to five shillings, pistareens and shillings were equivalent. Even though minting of pistareens ceased in 1771, they continued to be used in America until 1825, first as twenty-cent pieces (called, "double-dimes") before being devalued to seventeen cents and then demonetized altogether.[224]

The most commonly encountered new plate design is that of a "cross pistareen." The term "cross" refers to the reverse figure formed by lines that partition the four quadrants of the central reverse device. During the early eighteenth century, most one-, four- and eight-reale new plate coins appeared similar to cross pistareens, differing only in size.

Cross pistareens and Spanish silver coins in general were the subject of much counterfeiting. As with contemporary counterfeit British halfpence, additional study is needed to identify who made them, where and when. Some are made of silver or silver alloys, others are silvered base metal. A great many simply are made of copper. Real or counterfeit, early Americans knew well pistareens and their new plate siblings.

COLONIAL MILLED COINAGE

By 1600 Spanish domestic mints already were making milled coinage and doing it very well. It took until 1732, however, for the practice to extend to the Spanish colonies. New debasements at some of the mints and the generally poor quality of the cobs are likely to have precipitated the change. The new process came first to Mexico. The new coins were made on screw presses and were stunning contrasts to the primitive cobs. The eight-reale coin, in particular, represents one of numismatics' greatest designs. Known as "pillar dollars," or as *dos mundos* ("two worlds,") and issued from 1732 to 1772, they solidified the dollar as the world's standard currency.

That pillar dollars were used and accepted so widely is reflected in their multi-lingual names. The Spanish also referred to them as *columnario pesos*. ("Column pesos." *Peso* means "weight.") Similarly, the Italians called them *colonnato*. The Egyptians, evidently confusing the columns for cannon, called them *abu-mafta,* or "two cannon." Germans called them *sauelen piasters* ("pillar pieces of eight,") the Dutch simply *reaal von achten,* or "eight reales."[225]

(Right) 1763/2 pillar eight reales of Charles III, Mexico City, assayed by M[anuel] and F[rancisco] de la Pena. On eight-reale coins the crown atop the left pillar was changed from the royal crown to the crown of the empire in 1754. Before, both crowns were identical representations of the royal crown. (Jordan.) The change may seem minor, but well could have represented something of an effort to re-assert the fading eminence of the Spanish Empire. (Compare the crowns on the two examples.) The date on the 1763/2 piece uses a "3" punched over a "2." This technique was used to extend the life of a die for another year, a practice employed later by the U.S. Mint. (e.g., 1942/1 Liberty dimes.) Also note that the mintmark for Mexico City appears as an "M" with a tiny "o" above it. (Left) Reverse of a 1741 pillar eight reales of Philip V, Mexico City, cast counterfeit.

Examination of the classic devices on these coins helps in understanding their popularity. On the reverse are the two worlds, old and new, under the Spanish crown, hence the name *dos mundos*. On either side of the two worlds are the Pillars of Hercules. Each pillar, or column, is crowned and wrapped with a scroll. The scroll on the left reads *PLVS*, the one on the right

VLTRA, continuing the "more beyond" theme begun under Charles and Johanna. The remainder of the legend reads *VTRAQUE VNVM* – "One on Both Sides [of the Atlantic.]"

The new silver coins were debased slightly relative to pre-1728 Mexican issues, at 91.66% fineness, with weight at 52.2 grains per reale. The 1728 order to reduce fineness came four years before the new designs actually were put into production. In the interim, Mexican cobs adhered to the new weight standards. The difference in silver content presumably was used to upgrade mint technology. Even with the reduction, these coins held or even gained value relative to the coins of other nations.[226]

Minor pillar coinage: *A – 1751 two-reales, Ferdinand VI, Mexico City. B – 1744 one-reale, Philip V, Mexico City. C – 1762 half-reale or medio, Carlos III, Guatemala. The design was also used on four-reale coins. In time, all of Spain's New World mints were brought into compliance with the standard. Potosí was the last to transition, in 1767.*

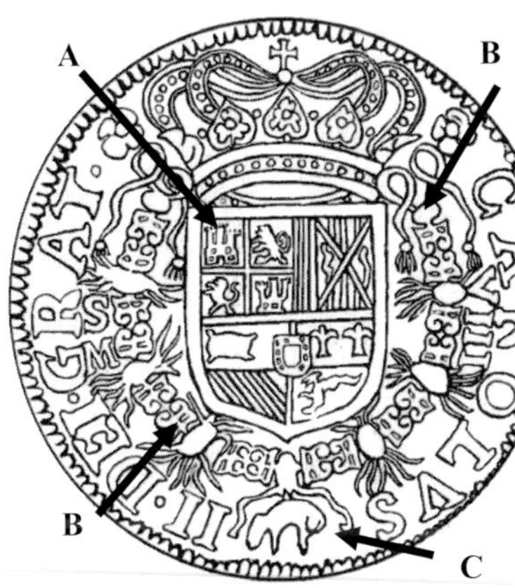

Colonial gold coins were unaffected by the debasement, but their designs were modified to closely resemble coins minted in Spain. The new gold coins were issued in denominations of one-, two-, four- and eight-escudos. Their obverses feature a right-facing bust of the current monarch, with the traditional legend containing his name, ...*D*[EI] · *G*[RATIA] · *HISPAN*[IARUM] · *ET* · *IND*[IARUM] · *REX,* and the date.

Obverse of a 1700 eight-escudos coin of Charles II. Devices from these Spanish domestic issues were combined on the new colonial gold issues. Devices common to coins made on both sides of the Atlantic include: A – *The complex Hapsburg shield,* B – *the collar of the Order of the Golden Fleece, and* C – *the Golden Fleece.*

Gold coin reverses feature a crowned Hapsburg shield. Sometimes it is surrounded by the ceremonial chivalric collar of the Order of the Golden Fleece, the Hapsburg/Bourbon version of Britain's Order of the Garter. The symbol of the Order of the Golden Fleece, a gold-covered sheep's fleece, alludes to the mythical quest of Jason and the Argonauts. The collar is composed of alternating strikers and bursts of flame. Strikers are steel tools that were used in conjunction with flints to generate sparks. The fleece hangs from an ornamental knot at the bottom of the collar. The obverse bust wears a similar collar on many gold coin varieties. Reverse legends vary. The most frequently encountered is *IN UTROQ FELIX AUSPICE DEO* ("Happy in the favor of the Lord, on Both Sides [of the Atlantic.]") In addition, *INITIUM SAPIENTIAE TIMOR DOMINI* ("Fear of the Lord is the Beginning of Wisdom," from Proverbs 9:10) and *NOMINA MAGNA SEQUOR* ("Following in the Great Name") are used.

When Philip V died in 1746, he was succeeded by Ferdinand VI. Ministers in Ferdinand's court were divided between those who were pro-British and those who were pro-French. When the European powers began fighting the Seven Years War in 1756, Ferdinand managed to steer clear of the hostilities. That changed when his half-brother, Charles III, came to the throne in 1759 and sided with France. At the time the choice seemed ill-advised. Charles III, however, proved his detractors wrong in the latter years of his reign.

1732 four escudos of Philip V, Madrid Mint, a later gold issue whose devices are shared with contemporary Mexican pieces, carrying forward the utraque unum *theme. The obverse bears Philip V's profile. The reverse depicts the crowned shield of Castile and Leon, On both Spanish colonial and domestic gold coins, the assayers' initials and the mintmark generally appear in the reverse legend.*

His regime brought changes to Spanish silver coins. In 1772 the elegant pillars by which dollars and their fractional parts were known were shrunk and placed beside a crowned shield of Castile and Leon. The waves on which they rested and the two worlds were removed. Obverses were given portraits of the less than handsome king with legends that remained essentially the same. The new coins were and still often are referred to as "portrait coinage."

A

B

C

Portrait coinage of Charles III, Mexico City mint:
A – 1778 two-reales.
B – 1779 one-reale. Many of these are found holed. Circumstantial evidence suggests that they were strung or wired together and worn inside the coats of travelers for security.
C – 1779 8 reales. "Chop" marks indicate that it traveled to the Orient and there met the approval of a merchant.

In spite of his homeliness, Charles III is viewed by many as the greatest of the Bourbon kings of Spain. He was an intelligent and popular reformer who sided with America and France during the Revolution and, as a result, was able to reclaim Florida under the 1783 Treaty of Paris. He ruled until his death in 1788, when his son Charles IV ascended to the throne. Charles IV allowed his chief minister to rule the affairs of state. His reign was marked by defeats, first as an ally of the French against the British and then at the hands of Napoleon. In 1808 a coup forced Charles to abdicate in favor of his son, Ferdinand VII. Napoleon tricked Charles and Ferdinand into surrendering the crown before awarding it to his own older brother, Joseph Bonaparte. A disastrous series of uprisings and invasions followed. These are the bloody incidents immortalized in paintings by Francisco Goya. In 1814 Ferdinand returned to power. The next year Joseph Bonaparte fled to New Jersey[!,] where he spent most of the next seventeen years. Ferdinand ruled until his death in 1833. His portrait coins and those of Charles III and Charles IV all were as well known to early Americans as their predecessors.

***Obverses of Charles IV and Ferdinand VII portrait conage**: (Left) 1792 Peruvian mint rendition of a Charles IV eight-reales. (Middle) Obverse of an 1807 Charles IV eight-escudos. Note that Charles wears the Golden Fleece collar. (Right) 1817 Ferdinand VII portrait eight-reales, Potosí mint.*

The Spanish Legacy

With small change eternally in short supply in America, a common practice was to cut larger coins in halves, fourths, eighths and even sixteenths. This could be accomplished with a hammer and chisel or with a large pair of shears. An eighth of a Spanish dollar, a reale, was called a "bit" in slang. Later Americans equated a bit with 12½ cents. (Cents did not exist until the late 1780's.) If a bit was cut smaller than a full eighth, it was called a "short bit," the later equivalent of a dime. The corresponding larger piece was a "long bit." A half-bit was called a *medio,* meaning "between," or a *picayune.*[*]

***An eight-reales coin, with simulated cut fractions:** A – four-bits. B – short bit. C – long bit. D – two-bits.*

Eight-reale coins last were minted in 1825, but continued to have legal tender status in the United States until 1857. As evidence of this, an 1852 issue of the *New York Herald* advertised goods priced in bits and even in shillings.[227] Moreover, echoes of the cut pieces live on in American culture, from the nostalgic two-bit price of a shave and a haircut to commodities markets that, until recently, used eighths of a dollar as their bidding increment.

[*] "Picayune" was a slang term that has come to mean anything small or petty. In its early days, the newspaper, the *New Orleans Times Picayune* literally cost one picayune, hence its name.

Pillar dollars also may be the source of an even more pervasive American tradition. Bookkeepers are thought to have abbreviated Spanish milled dollars by drawing the right pillar ("|") and overlaying it with an "S" to represent a scroll wrapped around it. The result was the dollar sign ("$.") Others attribute the dollar sign to a similar abbreviation for "peso." In this theory, peso was abbreviated with a "P" in which the curved stoke is extended to wrap around the down stroke, or, in a third theory, by a monogrammed representation of "P" and "S," as in "P[eso]S." A fourth theory says that the dollar sign came from the "8" that appears on the pillar dollar. Whether any of these theories is true, the earliest known use of a dollar sign-like symbol, in 1768, came from an obscure Irish-born trader, John Fitzpatrick, who operated a store near the Gulf of Mexico, at Manchac, Louisiana.[228]

The emerging numismatic picture of early America is one of several regions, each dominated by a particular type of coinage. The South, with its proximity to the West Indies, was most familiar with Spanish and Portuguese coinage. Its large scale agricultural economy meant that goods were traded in bulk in an international marketplace, a practice for which specie was well suited. New England, with its active retail economy, thrived on small change. For this kind of commerce, British halfpence were ideal. The Middle Colonies were a blend of the two and relied on both coin types. The Middle Colonies also were subject to Dutch influence and, hence, were familiar with Dutch coinage of the period. Louisiana and Canada were likely to see French coinage at least until the mid-1760's. Then, Spanish Louisiana and the Mississippi River brought Spanish coinage even closer to the South and West.

Central vignette from a Corporation of Richmond, Virginia, one-dollar note of 1861, greatly reduced. As on many notes of the period, Spanish milled dollars, not their U.S. cousins, were used to visually convey the concept of "dollar" to Americans.

Even with these regional differences, Spanish colonial coins were a kind of continental currency that was universally accepted. As the direct ancestor of the U.S. dollar, it can be argued that the Spanish dollar still is the world's standard nearly a half-millennium after it first appeared. This longevity is apparent even more when the silver content of the Spanish colonial dollar and its relationship to the U.S. silver dollar are examined, as in the table below.

Relative Weights (in Grains) of Spanish and American Silver Dollars (1536-1935)	**Total Weight**	**Fineness**	**Silver (Ag) Weight**	**Ag Wt. Relative to 1536-1572 Coinage**	**Ag Wt. Relative to U.S. Silver Dollars (After 1840)**
Charles and Johanna (1536-1572)	423.90	93.05	394.44	100.00%	106.24%
Early cobs (1572-1732)	417.76	93.05	388.72	98.55%	104.71%
Late cobs and pillar dollars (1732-1773)	417.60	91.66	382.77	97.04%	103.10%
Portrait dollars (1773-1820)	417.60	90.28	377.00	95.58%	101.55%
U.S. silver dollars (1794-1803)	416.06	89.24	371.29	94.13%	100.01%
U.S. silver dollars (after 1840, excluding trade dollars)	412.51	90.00	371.26	94.12%	100.00%

7: THE CHORUS

Though British, Irish and Spanish pieces dominated the American coin scene, any piece of reasonable weight and fineness was accepted. Coins of virtually every nation that traded beyond its borders were likely to have been used in America. Dutch, French and Portuguese coins all achieved notable levels of circulation and are discussed in this chapter. A comprehensive list would have to include Sweden, China, the Ottoman Empire, various German states and a host of others.

THE NETHERLANDS

For much of its history, the people of the Netherlands were minions, first of Charlemagne, then Burgundy, then the Hapsburgs and finally Spain. In the sixteenth century they were at the forefront of the Protestant Reformation, not a favorable place to be when dominated by Catholic Spain. The Inquisition under Charles V was devastating. Philip II was even worse. He tried fanatically to root out Protestants, taking away freedoms and fortunes and allowing Spanish soldiers to rape and pillage the Dutch at will. Finally, Protestants and Catholics joined to protest these atrocities. When the stern Spanish general, Alva, formed the Council of Blood and sentenced nearly the whole country to death, enough finally was enough.

In 1568 Louis of Nassau led an attack on the oppressors at the northern Dutch city of Groningen. The attack eventually failed and Louis was killed. The rebellion might have died with him. It had no galvanizing leader or theme, save a shared hatred for the Spanish. Louis' death, however, brought a real hero to the front. His brother, William the Silent, Prince of Orange,* assumed leadership of the movement. William was a wise and resourceful leader who many times fought back from the brink of defeat. Many now refer to him as the "Dutch Washington." When the besieged city of Leyden literally was on the brink of annihilation from starvation in 1574, William cut the famous dikes, flooding the Spanish camps. He bought flat-bottom barges and scows, filled them with arms and food and manned them with grizzled seamen. In a heroic struggle, the men rowed, pulled and carried the barges across shallow lakes and mudflats to the gates of Leyden, all the while dodging Spanish gunfire. Leyden was saved and the event proved to be the turning point of the *eighty-year* rebellion. In their honor, William offered the citizens of Leyden the choice of temporary tax amnesty or a new university.[229] Choosing the latter was a wise decision. Their university remains as one of the world's great centers of learning.

The rebellion was far from over, but profound and lasting world events were unfolding. For years the Dutch effectively protected the English from invasion by the Spanish. Englishmen even volunteered for service in the Dutch military. Elizabeth I feared that the protection would end in 1584 after an assassin, seeking Philip's 75,000-guilder bounty, ended William's life. The disarrayed Dutch went so far as to offer Elizabeth their crown, an honor she refused in part because she was having her own problems with Catholics. Sir Francis Drake and the Seadogs urged full-scale war with Spain. Instead, Elizabeth sent a small army to aid the Dutch cause. Delayed by a Drake-led raid on Cadiz, Philip II responded by sending his Armada against

* Orange was a small French principality to which William, as Count of Nassau, held a claim.

England in 1588. The outcome and its effects are well known. Philip lived another ten years and managed to garner some revenge, including the infamous sacking of Antwerp, but Spain never was the same. It took another sixty years, until 1648, for the long struggle of the Dutch to be over. Many factors, not the least of which was the military genius of Prince Maurice, the son of the slain William the Silent, contributed to the Dutch victory. In the end, however, there was no decisive battle. The Dutch simply outlasted the Spanish.

Having won independence, seven northern provinces combined to form the United Provinces, or the Dutch Republic. Holland was the most influential of the seven and often gives its name to the group. The ten southern provinces were populated mostly by French Catholics who had given up the rebellion and settled with Spain. This area became the Spanish Netherlands and, eventually, Belgium.

The rebellion had some unexpected results. In the midst of wartime devastation, the Dutch grew rich by looting Spanish possessions in the East Indies. The end of the Armada left them with a near monopoly on Asiatic trade.

The skills that enabled Dutch success did not come easily or overnight. Rather, they were earned the hard way. Engineering expertise came from years of winning back land from the sea. When the economics of fighting hydraulic battles were unfavorable, the Dutch learned to trade for what they needed. They soon discovered that trips to the East Indies could be very profitable, even with the dangers that accompanied such journeys. When one particular trip involving sixty-five ships was being planned, fears of competitive rivalries among the crews lead to the formation of the Dutch East India Company to ensure that all would be seeking the same goals. The Englishman Henry Hudson, sailing for the company, discovered America's Hudson River in 1609.[230]

The Bank of Amsterdam was founded the same year. Modern banking and investment concepts such as checking, credit, stock markets and coinage regulation followed soon after. In 1626 the Dutch bought Manhattan from which they built New Amsterdam. In 1634 they gained footholds in the Caribbean. There they became wealthy from producing sugar and, when locals proved too fragile to work the cane, the Dutch developed the slave trade to supply labor.[231]

The genius of their brand of mercantilism was its efficiency. They could trade in far-flung markets with much less expense than their English, French and Spanish competitors who were all bent on absolute control of those with whom they traded. That control that came at a huge price. Rather than pouring profits into maintaining colonies and armies, the Dutch wisely invested in their own commercial infrastructure. They became experts at building and navigating ships. Their's used simplified rigging that cut by half the number of crewmen required for operation of an English vessel of the same size. Their ships could be built cheaper because they used wood from the Baltic region, gained through the trade of grain. These ships had greater hauling capacity than English ships of the same size, in part because they carried no guns. Their officers achieved command positions by demonstrating naval excellence, unlike those of England who were rewarded because they were titled gentlemen.[232] In the 1609 to 1621 period, the Netherlands operated 16,000 ships, crewed by 160,000 men and averaging fifty-seven tons. The small Dutch country of three million people then had more men and ships on the water than did Spain, England and France combined.[233]

Freedom brought with it an explosion of literary, scientific and artistic thought and expression. In the seventeenth century more books were printed in Holland alone than in the rest of Europe combined. Holland also led Europe in science, horticulture and navigation,[234] to say nothing of the parade of great artists such as Johannes Vermeer (born in Delft) and Rembrandt van Rijn (born in Leyden.)

(Left to right) 1750 Holland 2 stuivers. 1754 Dutch East India Company duit and 1769 Overyessel duit. Duits produced by the Dutch East India Company usually bear the company's monogrammed initials VOC, *for* Vereenigde Oostindische Compaigne.

The Dutch understood and used money, credit and banking principles better than any other power. Yet, their monetary system was complex and unwieldy, reflecting the factional confederation of provinces that made up the Dutch Republic. Near the lower end of their monetary system was the *stuiver* or *stiver*, manifested as a small silver or billon coin. A stuiver was divided into eight *duits*. Duits are roughly farthing-sized copper coins that saw use in the American colonies, particularly those with Dutch populations. Many were produced by provinces, such as Friesland or Overyessel,* and by the Dutch East India Company. Most are dated and bear the name of the issuing authority on their obverses. Reverses feature variations of provincial or company arms that usually include one or more rampant lions.

1734 Silver Rider. (See below.) Obverse legends carry a theme of "New silver money of ...[province name.]" Reverse legends are variations of CONCORDIA RES PARVÆ CRESCUNT *("Through concord, small things increase.")*

* Overyessel means "Over (beyond) the Issel." The Issel is a tributary to the Rhine River that served as a provincial boundary.

Circulating alongside stuivers and duits were several large silver coins whose values were continually (and confusingly) adjusted to account for inflation and to suit export purposes. An intermediate denomination, a *gulden* or *guilder*, was equivalent to twenty stuivers. A *ducaton* was a three-guilder or sixty-stuiver coin that is crown-sized and passed at six shillings in Massachusetts and at 7s 6d in Maryland. A very similar but slightly larger coin called a "silver rider," because its obverse depicts a knight on a charging horse, was originally valued at sixty-three stuivers. Ducatons and riders were so similar that the two coins' names and usage ultimately converged. Hence, a silver rider came to be valued at sixty stuivers.

Leg dollar obverse. The legend reads MO[NETA] : NO[VA] : ARG[ENTEA] : PRO : CONFŒDERATIO : BELG[EI] : TRAI. *("New silver money for [the] Utrecht [Province] of the Belgian Confederation.")*

The Dutch also produced fifty- (sometimes forty-eight-) stuiver pieces called *Rijksdaalders* or, in English, "rix dollars." Rix dollars passed at five shillings in Massachusetts and at six shillings in Maryland. As such, they were equivalent to Spanish dollars and French ecus. (See below.) A comparable coin was called a "leg dollar" because its obverse features a knight who appeared one-legged due to the placement of his shield. These coins contained substantial amounts of silver and, whenever possible, merchants chose to keep them, sending export coinages to the colonies in their place.

Dutch traders routinely carried riders, ducatons, rix dollars and leg dollars to the American colonies. When a young Ben Franklin reached Philadelphia after returning to America from England in 1726, his fortune consisted of a single "Dutch dollar" that he had received when the ship stopped in New York.[235]

1625 Rijksdaalder or, as Americans called it, a rix dollar.

The Dutch provinces produced *Leeuwendaalders*, or "lion dollars," as an export coinage between 1575 and 1713. They were lighter than rijksdaalders and ducatons and were officially valued at between thirty-six and forty-two stuivers. They were used routinely in the New Netherlands (New York,) and were also a leading currency in Maryland, Pennsylvania, New Jersey and Virginia. Along with rix dollars and pieces of eight, they were current in Carolina in 1700.[236] Lion dollars were found in the coins recovered from the 1711 sinking of the H.M.S. Feversham, off Nova Scotia, and in a hoard discovered at a Castine, Maine, road cut.[237] The coins were named for the rampant lion on their reverses. English colonists derisively called them "dog dollars" because of the ragged appearance of the lion.

1589 Leeuwendaalder, also known as a lion dollar or dog dollar.

Much less common in the American colonies was a fourteen-guilder gold coin called a "golden rider" and a smaller gold trade piece called a "gold ducat" or "trade ducat." Trade ducats contained less than forty percent of the gold of the golden riders, but were of higher fineness (0.986, as compared to 0.917.)

Dutch gold coins that circulated in America:
(Left)1751 golden rider and (Right) 1777 gold or trade ducat

In 1614, five years after Henry Hudson's discovery of the river that bears his name, Dutch merchants formed the New Netherlands Company and obtained a temporary fur trade monopoly in what are now known as New York and New Jersey. Based on the promise of further economic development in the area, the Dutch West India Company was founded in 1621 and was given a twenty-year trade monopoly in America and Africa.* To encourage settlement, the company sought and obtained formal status for the area that they called New Netherlands, in 1623.

Settlers recruited by the company began to spread out around the newly established Fort Orange (now Albany) and the Delaware and Connecticut River valleys. When the threat of attack by Indians became too much, Director General Peter Minuit purchased Manhattan for about sixty guilders worth of trinkets. Dutch settlement continued to expand, particularly after the *patroon* system was started in 1628. Patrooning was similar to the English land grant system. A merchant was given a large tract of land and, in return, managed its commercial development and paid fees to the company.

* Between 1624 and 1654, the Dutch also held a small region of Brazil. The Dutch West India Company set up shop in Recife, the region's capital. Though Dutch Brazil issued its own coins, it is unlikely that many of them made the journey to British America.

New Netherlands boasted only five thousand colonists in 1660, two thousand more than New France,[238] but its success caught the eye of the English. When at war with the Dutch from 1652 to 1654, Oliver Cromwell even planned an attack on the colony, but never carried it out. English claims were based on the discovery of the region by John Cabot in 1498. As if he needed them, Charles II used these claims in the 1664 wresting of the colony from Dutch Governor, Peter Stuyvesant. This action precipitated another war that lasted until 1667. One of the terms of peace was that the Dutch abandoned their claims in America. Ironically, they briefly recaptured New York in 1673, during another war with Britain and France. After 1674, however, the region was firmly in British hands.

This is not to say that the Dutch were done. In the seventeenth century they had established numerous footholds in the Caribbean and South America. During the American Revolution, their traders in the West Indies helped supply Americans with arms. When inhabitants of the tiny Dutch-held island of St. Eustatius fired a cannon salute to a ship carrying an American flag in 1776, the Netherlands became the first nation in the world to recognize formally the sovereignty of the United States of America.[239]

Today, Aruba and the Netherlands Antilles are all that remain of the Netherlands' New World empire. Still, driving through New York and New Jersey, one is constantly reminded of Dutch presence and culture. Place names such as Wall Street (named for "de wal," Peter Stuyvesant's palisade to guard New Amsterdam's north end,) Tappan Zee and Fishkill ("kill" is Dutch for "creek") echo the language. American tales such as Washington Irving's *Rip Van Winkle* and The *Legend of Sleepy Hollow* are deeply rooted in Dutch heritage. Dutch coins also serve to connect moderns to a forgotten part of American history.

FRANCE

Likewise, the overshadowing of Franco-American culture by the English belies the economic role that France played in the colonization of North America. French coins are not as well known or studied as Anglo-American pieces. Perhaps the fact that none actually were made in North America fuels a reluctance to embrace them. Only a handful of issues can be labeled exclusively as American colonial. Moreover, several colonial issues were intended for use in *any* French colony, in North America or elsewhere. American numismatics might have developed differently had there been technology for making coins out of beaver pelts.

Politics and Religion

When New World colonization began, France was a country torn apart by internal and external power struggles extending back hundreds of years. That the French became a colonizing power at all was something of a miracle. That they would later lose their North American colonies seems almost to have been pre-ordained.

In spite of their control of vast territories, few Frenchmen actually lived in North America. By 1760 their numbers were estimated at only 85,000. These colonists were as prolific as their English counterparts. Only about 12,000 of them were immigrants.[240] Nevertheless, that so few could hold such a vast territory permanently was never really a strong possibility.

French woes began very early. When Charles IV died without a male heir in 1328, Philip VI, of the House of Valois, ascended to the throne. His distant cousin, Edward III of England, protested and declared himself King of France. The 116-year long Hundred Years War, a series of feudal battles and wars-within-wars, began in 1337.[241] In 1415 England's Henry V defeated the squabbling French at Agincourt to take control of Paris and most other French territory. The French King, Charles VI, declared Henry his heir, leaving the dauphin (rightful heir,) Charles VII, with only a token kingdom.[242] Then, when it appeared the English would complete their conquest by taking Orléans, Joan of Arc emerged from nowhere to redeem the dauphin and make him king. After two dozen more years of strife, the English finally were expelled, the last battle taking place at Castillon in 1453.[243] Even so, the old English claims to France persisted for years, with fleurs de lis and the abbreviation *FR*[ANCORIVM] gracing British coins as late as the time of George III.

For the next two centuries French kings struggled to consolidate old feudal territories, wage war with Spanish Hapsburgs, deal with the spread of the Italian Renaissance and fend off the Protestant Reformation, particularly as French Calvinists, known as Huguenots, practiced it.

In 1562 twelve hundred Huguenots were massacred by edict, igniting the three-decade-long War of Religion. Ten years later, the massacre of thousands of Huguenots coincided with the marriage of another Huguenot, Henry of Navarre, of the House of Bourbon, to Marguerite de Valois to become the rightful heir to the crown of Henry III. Jubilant at news of the carnage, Pope Gregory XIII ordered celebrations in Rome and a Vatican medal was struck to commemorate the occasion.

The celebrations were premature. Henry of Navarre rallied Protestants and moderate Catholics to defeat the Catholic League opposition. In 1593 he became Henry IV, the first of France's Bourbon kings. Though the terms of ascendancy required that he adopt Catholicism, Henry IV signed the 1598 Edict of Nantes that ended the War of Religion and designated free cities within which Huguenots could practice their faith. The nightmare resumed, however, when Huguenots again came under fire after Henry's assassination by a Catholic fanatic in 1610.[244]

After Henry's assassination the crown fell to his nine-year-old son, Louis XIII, by Marie de Medici. The domineering De Medici ruled France until Louis' murderous intrigues forced her retirement and exile. In 1624 Louis XIII entrusted the reins of government to his mother's former protégé, the brilliant ecclesiastic, Cardinal Richelieu. Richelieu was instrumental in subduing rebellious nobles and consolidating Louis' power. All the while he relentlessly persecuted Huguenots. Louis' entire reign was spent trying to return all of France to Catholicism. He did, however, ally with Protestants to defeat the Spanish and Austrians in the Thirty Years War, the final victory coming in 1648, five years after Louis' death and six years after Richelieu's. Moody, enigmatic and a generally weak ruler, Louis never lived up to the image of his father. Only through Richelieu's skill and the influence of the Duke de Luynes did Louis achieve any real claims of success.[245] The Thirty Years War and internal bickering that characterized Louis' rule effectively prevented meaningful settlement in North America.

At age fourteen Louis married Anne of Austria, daughter of Spain's Philip IV, through an arrangement. The two disliked each so much that everyone was shocked at the birth of Louis XIV. As his father had been, Louis XIV was a child king. He was only four when Louis XIII died in 1643. France was then ruled by another powerful statesman, Cardinal Mazarin, who carried Richelieu's initiatives into the reign of the new king. On Mazarin's death in 1661, however, Louis XIV declared that absolute power was his. He perceived himself as God's one representative on earth, worthy of all praise and adoration.[246] He is rumored to have remarked *L'état, c'est moi* ("The state, it is I," or "I AM the state,") a claim also said to have been repeated by Napoleon. All of this attention on Louis reduced nobles and important government officials to minor players, free to engage in petty intrigues. Louis XIV may have been king, but corruption reigned.

Still, the period was marked by extensive improvements in France's economic infrastructure. Cities and roads were built and canals were dug. The navy and merchant marine were enhanced. Tariffs kept out foreign goods and the future looked bright as exports increased. Louis kept abreast of every detail.[247] Again, however, war blocked French expansion. Squabbles with Spain periodically flared throughout the late seventeenth century and England's William III reinvigorated the Grand Alliance against France just before the War of Spanish Succession. Under William's successor, Anne, the war went very badly for the French. When formal peace finally came in 1714, France effectively had been removed from the role of superpowers. Even so, she retained control of her territories...for the time being.

Louis XIV died a year later, at age seventy-seven, having outlived two generations of male heirs. His great-grandson, Louis XV, was a sickly five-year old. The dying king willed that the government be handed to the Duc du Maine. The French Parliament, however, insisted that Philippe, Duc d' Orléans, Louis XIV's nephew of dubious character, be named regent. It was the Duc d'Orleans who presided over the John Law debacle (Chapter 8.) When Philippe died in 1723, André Hercule de Fleury succeeded him, effectively acting as Prime Minister after 1726.[248] When De Fleury died in 1743, Louis XV decided to go it alone. This was a mistake, given that he had little experience at and even less interest in government. His tendency to turn power over to less than honorable friends and the near bankruptcy of the government prepared the way for the French Revolution and the ultimate demise of his successor.

Though he had nothing to gain, Louis XV entered War of Austrian Succession in 1740. He sided with the winners, headed by Prussia's Frederick II, but his diplomats botched the peace negotiations, making France the war's only loser. Worse still, shifting post-war alliances put France on the wrong side during the Seven Years War as Prussia turned against her. By the end of that conflict, France's ephemeral American empire effectively had vanished. As Sanche de Gramont observed, the sixteenth century belonged to Richelieus and Mazarins, the eighteenth to Walpoles and Pitts.[249]

When Louis XV died of smallpox in 1774, the crown fell to his twenty year old grandson, the ill-equipped and ill-fated Louis XVI. Four years earlier Louis XVI had married Archduchess Marie Antoinette of Austria. Early on, the new king made meager attempts at reform, but soon found his locksmithing hobby and hunting adventures more interesting. Likewise, his queen became obsessed with fantasies and elaborate parties. Louis' support of American independence at Benjamin Franklin's urging threw his country into dire financial straits and sealed his personal fate. As the welfare of his people declined, Louis resisted efforts to give them, as the "third estate,"[*] more political power. The people reacted by forming the National Assembly. In 1789 open rebellion erupted. Louis' failed attempts at repression and Marie Antoinette's treasonous plotting eventually led to their imprisonment and public beheadings in 1793.

[*] The people were called the "third estate." The nobles and clergy made up the first and second estates, respectively.

Louis' immediate successor was chaos. The two years after the royal couple's beheadings are known as the Reign of Terror. During that time thousands were executed, including those who presided over the executions themselves. The Jacquard loom became the symbol of British industrialism. For France it was the Guillotine.

The resulting power vacuum left open the door for a coup led by Napoleon Bonaparte. In 1804 Napoleon's first conquest was complete, and he declared himself Emperor. Bent on restoring French prestige, he soon launched the Napoleonic Wars. The brilliant general rode roughshod over Europe until an even greater general, Britain's Duke of Wellington, and the Russian winter finally stopped his advance. After Napoleon's defeat by Wellington at Waterloo in 1815, France settled into becoming the nation that the world knows today.

Exploration and Colonization

The tumultuous sixteenth and seventeenth centuries left France unprepared to enter the age of colonialism. She was united, but poor both financially and in terms of the will to colonize. Rather than coming from a great national mandate, impetus to explore and colonize emanated from individuals and small groups who sought commercial success for themselves.

The early French navigators and explorers were an impressive lot. The first of them came for fish, oil and whalebone. Fishermen from Breton and Normandy may have fished the Grand Banks even before Columbus' famous voyage. They certainly were doing it by 1504. In 1508, Thomas Aubert sailed up the northern coast of America and brought back Indians to Rouen, where they were baptized in a great celebration. Giovanni da Verazzano (as in New York's Verazzano Narrows,) sailing for King Francis I, mapped the American coast all the way from Florida to Cape Breton in 1524.[250] Three years later an explorer at St. Johns reported that eleven Norman, one British and two Portuguese ships all were fishing actively in the harbor.[251]

In 1534 Francis I sent Jacques Cartier. Francis had an affinity for gold and diamonds and believed that Cartier could find them, along with a passage to the Orient and its riches. After landing in Newfoundland, Cartier explored the Gulf of the St. Lawrence. Believing that the St. Lawrence might lead to the Pacific, he returned the following year and began explorations that led to the place he called Montreal. After spending the winter of 1535 to 1536 with friendly Indians near what is now Quebec, he returned to France with stories of a fertile land, but no gold. Further exploration was delayed by war, but in 1541 Cartier returned on behalf of the Huguenot, Sieur de Roberval. Roberval was an ambitious man who envisioned starting his own colony. In 1542 he came with a crew of would be colonists recruited from the dregs of French society.[252] After a hard winter near present day Quebec and attacks by hostile Indians, Roberval and his crew returned to their homeland.[253] By then, France was so weary from religious strife and civil war that there was little motivation to continue exploration.

Huguenots made two other ill-fated attempts at North American settlement. Jean Ribaut's circa 1558 settlement in what is now South Carolina and a 1564 settlement at Fort Caroline in Florida both were too close to the trade routes of Spain's Philip II. Consequently, both were annihilated.

It was up to fishermen and a few traders to maintain a North American presence as they carried on in the names of their sponsors. Trade and settlements generally hugged the coastline and riverbanks. Only when forced by game shortages, competition or Indian hostilities did traders venture inland.[254] Of these reasons, competition was the greatest motivator. By 1580 over four hundred ships and twelve thousand men from several countries competed for fish, whales and seals in the Newfoundland-St. Lawrence region.[255] At trade, the only way to win was to venture up the rivers into the perilous wilderness. It was hardly an enticing recipe for settlement.

A hint of permanence was achieved in the form of a 1605 settlement at Port Royal, in Nova Scotia. Discovery of the fur trade finally made settlement viable, but it took the navigator, Sieur du Pontgravé, and the explorer, Samuel de Champlain, to make it happen. Champlain had been in the service of Sieur de Monts, the man who backed the 1605 settlement based on a fur trade monopoly awarded by King Henry. Jealous merchants challenged the monopoly in the king's court and forced De Monts to abandon his enterprise. Reluctantly, Champlain returned to France. However, he had learned from his wilderness experiences and in 1608, with Pontgravé, led the establishment of a new trading settlement at Quebec. The new enterprise enjoyed early success, but created jealous rivalries among the Indian tribes. When Champlain sided with the Huron against a branch of the Iroquois and was soundly defeated in 1615, the expansion of the French in North America again was thwarted.[256]

The government of New France (Canada) was run by these sorts of chartered companies and associations until 1663, when the royal government stepped in. Suddenly, there was even less incentive for immigration.

The French lost out again in 1669 when Médard Chouart (Sieur des Groseilliers) and his brother-in-law, Pierre Esprit Radisson, founded the Hudson's Bay Company. They did so not under their own King Louis XIV, but for England's Charles II. French bureaucracy simply had made starting the new company too difficult.[257]

"The Courrier Du Bois [sic] and the Savage" by Frederic Remington (ca.1891.) Source: "A Skin for a Skin," by Julian Ralph in Harper's New Monthly Magazine*, vol. 34, no. 501 (February, 1892.)*

If anything the French were resilient and, by 1689, they again were ready to tangle with their cross-channel rival. The ensuing war, King William's, was an English victory, but it raised French awareness of the strategic importance of settlements in Canada, the Illinois Country and Louisiana. At the same time, competition with the Hudson's Bay Company drove French traders ever westward, past the Great Lakes to the Rocky Mountains. Their countrymen once again were ready to fight in 1702, with Queen Anne's War. Both conflicts resulted in treasury deficits and territorial losses for France, but still they came back for more.

Recovery from Queen Anne's War occurred just in time for a ruinous 1720's financial scandal at the hands of Scottish financier John Law. The combination of outrageous investor speculation and poor turnout of potential colonists underscored the difficulties of settling Canada and Louisiana. Juxtaposed against France's more profitable Caribbean holdings in Martinique, Guadeloupe and Saint Dominique (now Haiti,) the continent just was not much of a draw.

By 1744 it was time for yet another North American conflict with the British. The result by then was familiar. King George's War ended in 1748 with the British in firm control of disputed territory. For their part, the French were left seething for revenge and still holding much of North America, albeit by a thread.

George Washington, at 25. Source: Irving (I, frontispiece.)

Skirmishes erupted again when British settlement expanded into French-held territory. The events triggered an eighteenth century arms race wherein both powers feverishly built wilderness forts to forestall the advance of the other. Much of the unrest revolved around the issuance of Ohio Valley land grants by Virginia's Governor Dinwiddie. Dinwiddie sent Virginia militia under a naïve, young and then very foolish George Washington to protect British settlers. The mission was a failure, but in the years that followed British troops methodically captured French forts and towns. By 1760 all of North America east of the Mississippi, except New Orleans, was in British hands. In the 1763 Treaty of Paris, the British demanded Florida, which was then in the possession of Spain. France ceded New Orleans and her vast holdings west of the Mississippi, the Louisiana Territory, to Spain to compensate for the loss. Thus, by the end of 1763, the French were gone from North America. In their absence, for a while, peace ruled the frontier.

Ultimately, the greatest obstacle to French colonial ambitions was France itself. There was no systematic approach to mercantilism comparable to Britain's. No sustaining riches came from French colonies. After Henry IV, no great monarch, such as Elizabeth I, provided vision. In vision's place was only political infighting, religious strife and profound class inequity. Of course, France was able to exact *some* measure of revenge against their nemesis during the American Revolution. It was a small comfort after centuries of finishing second.

French Domestic Coinage

In the middle ages the French monetary system paralleled that of the English. The French *livre* was equivalent to the English *libra*, or pound. The *sol,* short for *solides*, the French version of *solidus,* was equivalent to the English shilling. Likewise, the French *denier* was equivalent to the English *denarius*. As did the English, the French had derivatives such as the *douzain* and *sixain* (dozen and six deniers, respectively.) Over time the French system proved less stable than that of the English and their coins became debased, triggering the introduction of new denominations. To stabilize the livre, the *ecu* ("shield" – from the presence of a shield in the ruling Bourbon family's coat of arms) was introduced in 1640, with a value of three livres. Ecus fluctuated constantly in value, peaking at nine livres in 1720, during John Law's regime.

French minor coins also found their way to the colonies. By the time they reached America, they usually were quite worn, as are the examples shown below. The relationship of French base metal denominations, such as the sol (or sou,) denier and Liard, to the livre were:

1 livre = 20 sols or sous = 80 Liards = 240 deniers.
Alternately, 1 denier = 1/3 Liard = 1/12 sol or sou = 1/240 livre.

After the French Revolution, the *franc* replaced the livre. Francs were divided into twenty sols, each of which was equivalent to one hundred *centimes*. Thus,

1 sou or sol = 5 centimes = 1/20 franc.
And, 1 franc = 100 centimes = 20 sols or sous = 1 livre.

In 1760, when Britain's George III came to power, the value of an ecu was about that of six livres. At that time, an ecu was the rough equivalent of an English crown or a Spanish dollar. The principal French gold coin was the *Louis d'or* ("gold Louis".) Its value was four ecus. Its actual gold content was about eighty percent of that of a British Guinea, yet it sometimes is referred to as a "French guinea" in contemporary valuation tables. Gold Louis were accompanied by *demi-Louis* ("half Louis") and double Louis. Four-, eight- and ten-Louis gold coins also were issued briefly in the seventeenth century.

French domestic coins from the early colonial era: *(Left) 1550 douzain that corresponds to an English shilling. This style was used through the reign of Louis XIII. Sixteenth century Huguenots may have brought these to America. Host pieces counterstamped for French America in the late 17th century approach it in age. Its obverse features a royal shield with three fleur de lis. The obverse legend reads HENRICVS 2ND FRANCORIVM RE[X], or* "Henry II, King of France." *The reverse legend reads SIT NOMEN D[OMI]NI BENEDICTVM* – "Blessed be the Name of the Lord." *The central reverse device is an ornament surrounded by four fleur de lis, two crowns and two H's (for Henry II.)*
(Right) Ca. 1604 double Tournois (two deniers) of the French state, Chateau-Renaud. The obverse features a bust of Francois de Bourbon, Prince Conti (The legend reads F· DE· BOVRBON· P· CONTI.)

Very small, short lived base metal denominations such as *Lorrains* and *Vacquettes* complete the list. The table below summarizes the astonishing array of denominations of French domestic coins issued between 1600 and 1800. Any of them might have been found in French or even British America.

Copper, bronze or billon	Denier Tournois, Double Lorrain, Vacquette, Double Vacquette, Sixain, 6 Blans, Douzain, Liard, 5 Liards, 2 Deniers, 3 Deniers, 4 Deniers, 12 Deniers, 15 Deniers, 16 Deniers, 30 Deniers, 1/2 Sol, Decime, 2 Decimes
Generally silver	Quarter Franc, Demi-Franc, Sol, 2 Sols, 4 Sols, 4 Sols 2 Deniers, 10 Sols, 15 Sols, 20 Sols, 30 Sols, 33 Sols, 60 Sols, 1/48 Ecu, 1/24 Ecu, 1/20 Ecu=6 Sols, 1/16 Ecu=5 Sols, 1/12 Ecu, 1/10 Ecu=12 Sols, 1/8 Ecu, 1/5 Ecu=24 Sols, 1/4 Ecu, 1/2 Ecu, Ecu, 6 Livres, 5 Francs
Gold	1/2 Ecu d'or, Ecu d'or, Lis D'or, 1/2 Louis d'or, 24 Livres, Louis d'or, Double Louis d'or, 4 Louis d'or, 8 Louis d'or, 10 Louis d'or

Domestic coinage of Louis XIV: *A – 1662-I (Limoges) 1/12 ecu. Obverse legend:* LVD[OVICVS] ·XIIII · D[EI] · G[RATIA] FR[ANCIAE] ·ET· NAV[ARRE]· REX *("Louis XIV, by the Grace of God, of France and Navarre, King.") Reverse legend: SIT· NOMEN ·DOMINI · BENEDICTUM. ("Blessed be the name of the Lord.") B and C – Liards of France, 1699-D & 1657-D. Worn as typical of French domestics that circulated in the colonies. Note the large "D" mintmark, for Lyon. D – 1694-B (Rouen) gold double Louis. Reverse legend:* CHR[ISTV]S REGN[AT] [CHRISTVS] VINC[IT] [CHRISTVS] IMP[ERAT] *("Christ Reigns, Christ Conquers, Christ Rules.") Louis XIV's sagging mouth was caused by a broken jaw from the botched extraction of his last rotten teeth at age forty.*[258] *Note the sun above the "Sun King." E – 1709-9 (Rennes) ecu.*

Faces of Louis XV: *F – 1721-A (Paris,) demi sol au bust enfantin (6 deniers.) G – 1759-AA (Metz,) ecu. Note the file marks, used to adjust weight prior to striking. H – 1774-A (Paris) double Louis.*

Later French issues: *(Left) 1792 France, Louis XVI bronze two sols, Paris Mint ("A" mintmark.) Large numbers of these hefty coins were issued during Louis XVI's last days. They so closely matched the size of early U.S. large cents that they almost certainly passed as such. (Center) Undated (1796) REPUBLIQUE FRANCAISE ("Republic of France") cinque (five) centimes. This is a post-revolutionary copper issued in the fifth year of the Republic. It has the "A" mintmark. The obverse portrait is of France, wearing a liberty cap (page 16n,) a radical departure from the regal portraits. Since a franc was valued at about nineteen cents and this coin equates to 1/20 franc, it too would have passed freely alongside early U.S. cents.*
(Right) 1812, demi-franc of the French Empire and Napoleon, "A" mintmark. The obverse bears his portrait and title as emperor. A franc was equivalent to about nineteen U.S. cents. Thus, in size and weight, this demi franc was almost indistinguishable from a U.S. dime.

PORTUGAL AND BRAZIL

The coins of at least one other colonial power figured significantly in the history of early America. Until Christopher Columbus upstaged them, the Portuguese led the world at exploration. In the 15th century, under Prince Henry the Navigator, they built an empire in Africa and the Azores, and Cape Verde in the Atlantic. They became obsessed with the idea of reaching India by sailing around the southern tip of Africa, the Cape of Good Hope. In 1486 Bartholomew Diaz rounded the Cape for the first time, but turned back before reaching India. Bartholomew Columbus, Christopher's brother, was with Diaz on that voyage and Christopher himself sailed on other Portuguese voyages. Diaz's countryman, Vasco da Gama, completed the route to India a few years later.[259]

By 1494 the territorial claims of Spain and Portugal were sufficiently in collision that Pope Alexander VI found it necessary to impose an imaginary north-south line, 100 leagues (about 340 miles) west of the Azores and Cape Verde. Spain could claim lands west of the line, Portugal points east. The line barely touched the eastern edge of South America that had not yet been discovered. When the line was moved by treaty to 370 leagues (about 1,250 miles) west of Cape Verde, Portugal gained the eastern part of Brazil, a land that their Admiral Cabral discovered in 1500. Extending the line around the earth gave the Portuguese the Philippines, a claim that they abandoned in the 1529 Treaty of Saragossa, in exchange for the rest of Brazil. Brazil aside, Portugal lagged behind Spain in extending its New World empire. It did not help that Spain's Philip II seized his rival and its small empire when the Portuguese royal line petered out in 1580. It was not until sixty years later that a revolt restored independence.

Afterward, Portuguese domestic coins and those minted in Brazil regularly appeared in America through trade. The Portuguese began minting coins in the New World in 1695. Their most important contribution to American circulating coinage was the gold *Johanne* or *Joe*, named for its obverse visage of Johanne (John) V, who ruled from 1706 to 1750. The term was also applied to coins of his successor, Jose (Joseph) I, who ruled from 1750 to 1777. A Joe was denominated at eight escudos. A Portuguese escudo was equivalent to those of Spain. Thus, one Portuguese gold escudo was equivalent to two Spanish dollars or sixteen reales. One escudo also was equivalent to 1,600 *reis,* a tiny unit that inspired a monetary system proposed for the American Confederation. A Joe (or, more properly, a *dobra*) was equivalent to 12,800 reis. Smaller gold coins called *half-Joes* (or *pecas*) and *moidores* were denominated at 6,400 and 4,000 reis, respectively. Joes and moidores particularly were well known in America.

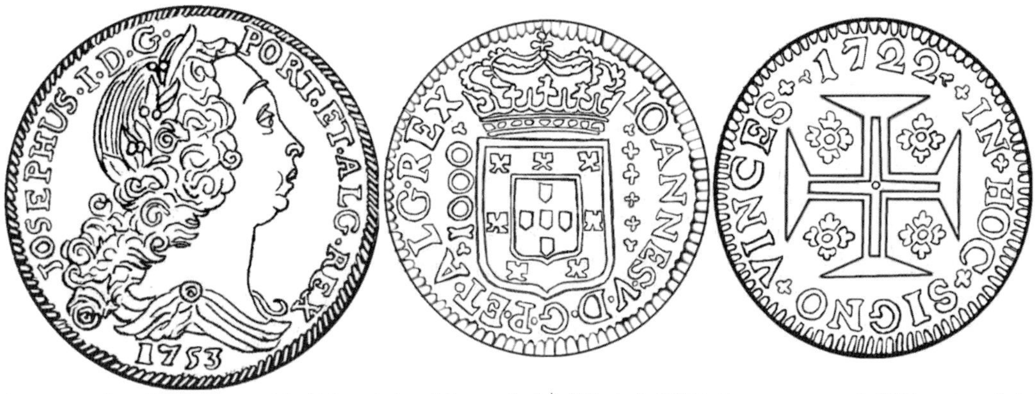

(Left) Obverse of a 1753 peca (6,400 reis) of Joseph I.[*] *(Right) 1722 Portuguese 1,000 reis of John V.*

Other denominations were expressed directly in reis. Generally, coins of less than twenty reis were copper, while those valued between twenty and 640 reis were silver. Coins valued at a half escudo (800 reis) or greater were gold. Combined, Portugal and Brazil produced the following denominations: 1½, 3, 5, 10, 20, 40, 60, 75, 80, 120, 150, 160, 200, 300, 320, 400, 600, 640, 800, 1,000, 1,600, 2,000, 3,200, 4,000, 6,400, 10,000, 12,800 and 20,000 reis.

Designs on Brazilian issues usually celebrate Portugal's navigational leadership and religious devotion, often featuring an amilas[†] overlaying a Jerusalem cross. The spaces between the cross's arms usually contain the abbreviated legend *STAB. SUBQ. SIGN. NATA* ("It was Born Under this Sign and It Will Remain.") This is a variation on the theme *IN HOC SIGNO VINCES* ("Under this Sign You Shall Conquer,") the message allegedly given by Christ to Constantine in a vision on the night before the fateful 320 A.D. Battle of Milvian Bridge. Constantine used the cross on his banners and, by winning the epic battle, built his empire.

1783 Brazilian silver 160 Reis (1/10 Escudo) The reverse legend reads MARIA ·I · E[T] · PETRUS · III · D[EI] · G[RATIA] · PORT[UGALIÆ] · REGES · E[T]· BRAS[ILIA]· D[OMINUS], *or "Mary I and Peter III, by the Grace of God, Regents of Portugal and Lords of Brazil." They ruled jointly from 1777 until Peter's (Pedro's) death in 1786. Mary (Maria) ruled until 1799. Note the reverse cross and amilas.*

[*] This coin's legend reads *JOSEPHUS·I·D[EI]·G[RATIA]·PORT[UGALIÆ]·ET·ALG[OBIORUM]· REX* or "Joseph I, By the Grace of God, of Portugal and Algarve [southern Portugal], King."

[†] An amilas is a globe-like navigational device, replicas of which now serve as den and courtyard ornaments.

Portuguese coppers: *(Left) 1699 Peter II 20 reis. (Center) 1734 Johanne V 10 reis. (Right) 1775 Josephus 10 reis. Reverses usually featured variations of Portugal's arms. These likely were accepted as pennies and halfpence in America. (Shown at 125%.)*

Collectively, Dutch, French and Portuguese coins played a supportive role in American commerce. They circulated behind Spanish silver and British copper and provided a backdrop for the various early American coins and tokens described in the following chapters.

TOOLS OF THE TRADE

With English, Irish, Spanish, French, Dutch, Portuguese, American and other coins all in circulation, the ability to convert readily from one system to another was an absolute necessity. To ease conversions, colonial governments, almanac publishers and others frequently printed equivalence tables. These sheets were indispensable to merchants because they listed commonly encountered denominations with their respective values in pounds, shillings and pence. In addition to sterling money conversions, the tables usually listed local money equivalents. Early tables even rated various commodities and trade goods against more proper currencies.

Guinea coin weight of William III (ca. 1700.)

Gold and silver coins usually were weighed prior to conversion to ensure against clipping, shaving or sweating. Weighing also helped to guard against counterfeits and provided a means of discounting greatly worn coins. Colonial merchants almost always owned hand-held balance scales and sets of standard *coin weights* for this purpose. These coin weights frequently are made of brass and resemble coins. Most, however, are thicker than coins and some take other shapes, such as squares or diamonds.

Unless groups of them were weighed together, considerably less effort was expended to handle conversions of base metal coinages. The gain in accuracy rarely was worth the effort for a single coin. A copper either approximated the size and weight of a regal halfpenny or farthing, or it did not. With lightweight imitations, privately issued tokens and patent coinages of questionable weight and legality came the minor coins of Spain, France, the Netherlands, Portugal and their colonies. Britains on both sides of the Atlantic constantly complained, called for regulation and petitioned their legislative bodies for provision of standard small-denomination coins. In the end, however, very little was or could be done to fix the problem.

Other exonumia (non-coins) came with the foreign incidentals. The earliest American sites yield sixteenth century German and Dutch *jetons*, or counting pieces, more frequently than actual coins. Similar coin-like jetons were in wide use throughout Europe. They come in various sizes and feature hundreds of different devices and legends. Most convey religious or political messages. One variety, for example, features the German equivalent of "God is Watching" as an admonition to accountants to be honest. Jamestown had jetons and one was found at the site of Augustine Heermans' 1640's warehouse, in what was then New Amsterdam. The latter piece commemorates Prince Maurice of Nassau becoming the Stadholder of Utrecht, in 1590.[260] Maurice, whose military genius helped his country win independence, benefited greatly from his teacher, the Dutch mathematician, Simon Stevin van Brugge.[261] This coincidence bears a subtle irony, as explained below.

Since they are not coins, jetons rarely are dated and almost never display a denomination. Most are of copper or brass, though a few silver and a very few gold pieces exist. Those in gold and silver have little, if any, American relevance. Many of the jetons found at American sites originated in Nurnberg, Germany, a late-1500's center for their manufacture. While the Romans are known to have used rounded pebbles, flat die-struck jetons appear to have originated in thirteenth century France. By 1400, German makers gained a virtual monopoly on the jeton market with their *Reichenpfenniges*. Eventually, a handful of families became dominant in the industry: the Krauwinckels, the Laufers and the Schultes.[262]

German jeton (Nurnberg Reichenpfennige) by Hans Schultes I, ca. 1553-1584, brass, edge-clipped planchet. Typical of jetons found at American sites.

Jetons were important because they worked in conjunction with a counting board to perform business calculations, in a manner similar to that used with an abacus. A counting board or cloth usually was laid out in three columns marked by vertical lines. Horizontal lines marked rows. The board was thus divided into squares or cells as on a checkerboard. Calculations were performed by laying out jetons (or reckoning counters) to represent the operands, systematically moving them from one cell to another and then interpreting the resulting configuration. A single calculation might involve several steps.

The word "jeton" actually derives from the French *jeter*, meaning "to push," a reference to the act of moving the counters. The use of these chequered (i.e., checkered) boards by accountants and government officials gave rise to the term "exchequer" to describe the British Treasury. Even the word "calculate" derives from *calx*, meaning "pebble."[263] Such aids were in great demand because medieval arithmetic relied on Roman numerals, a system clearly not designed for commercial use. Addition and subtraction were difficult enough, but multiplication and division were a nightmare. Initially, each row on a counting board corresponded to a Roman "digit" (i.e., I, V, X, L, C, etc..) Over time, Roman numerals gave way to Arabic conventions and the concept of zero was introduced. Still counting boards endured, with zero simply expressed as a cell devoid of counters.

Decimal arithmetic made jetons and counting boards German jeton, Hans Krauwinckel, ca. 1605, brass. The obverse depicts a counting board and jetons in use by a businessman. The reverse features the letters of the alphabet. Such pieces may have doubled as educational tools.

Then came Simon Stevin van Brugge or, in Latin, *Stevinus*. Stevinus began as a bookkeeper, but became a physicist, mathematician and inventor. His theoretical contributions are legion, but in life his recognition was limited. He *was* heralded for inventing a wind-driven carriage and for his theories on warfare. His smallest "invention," however, revolutionized mathematics and commerce. In 1585 he re-discovered the decimal point.[264] Stevinus also is credited with adding the word *disme* (later anglicized to "dime") to the English language. *Disme* means "tenth" and is a consequence of his use of decimal places.

No longer needed as computing aids, jetons continued to be made for use in games, gambling and as play money. In these capacities, they are called *spielmarkes* (in German, a piece marked for *spiel, or* "play.") A common early nineteenth century British type, for example, is made of brass and is backdated to resemble a 1791 *spade Guinea*. These undoubtedly were passed off on the ignorant as gold pieces. Other pieces do not imitate coins and thus should be regarded more as medalets. Whether any jetons saw use as halfpence or farthings is debatable. Sizes, appearance and metallic compositions suggest that they might occasionally have been accepted as such and Jamestown colonists did trade them to the Indians for food.[265] What *is* certain is that their presence in numbers implies that significant commerce was taking place even among America's earliest colonists. Moreover, the trade was global, as evidenced by the artifacts that were left behind. These artifacts originated in a varied mix of actively trading countries and reflect many different cultures. Jamestown's jetons, for example, could have been brought by German craftsmen – glassmakers and carpenters – who arrived in 1608.[266]

Later (1790-dated) jetons: (Left) Louis XVI. (Right) George III, resembles a contemporary "spade Guinea." Compare both to the Washington large success tokens in Chapter 11.

With the emphasis on the relative weights of coins, it is doubtful that early Americans really paid much attention to the societies they represented. Still, it took the interplay of many world cultures, in trade and war, to give America the tools of commerce that it needed. To fully explore the myriad foreign coins and tokens that early Americans encountered is well beyond the scope of this work. Nevertheless, a survey of more commonly encountered forms from a few key countries can help moderns to understand both the mechanics of day-to-day colonial commerce and the larger strategies that were projected from Europe onto the New World.

Section IV:
Early American Coins and Tokens
(1616 to 1840)

House Rules: A General Introduction

As it happens, no clear boundaries define the category "early American coins and tokens." In many cases no one knows when, where, why or by whom particular pieces were made. Many issues lie between American and foreign, between early and later, or even between coin or token, and something else. Nonetheless, meaningful study requires categorization, even if the categories are subjective.

The year 1840 was a watershed for American numismatics. By then the U.S. Mint had gained sufficient momentum to become the country's primary source of coinage. Foreign and private issues continued to be used for many years afterward. However, they generally circulated in the background and to a lesser extent than before. Shortages still occurred, but they were more acute and event- or policy-driven than chronic. The Jackson-Van Buren era, in which northern businessmen made private coppers, and the period leading up to the U.S. Civil War, in which foreign coins, fractional currency, encased postage stamps and private "copperhead" tokens filled the need for small change, are notable examples. Just as printing technology made possible the proliferation of paper currency, new minting technology changed the landscape of American coinage. The 1836 introduction of steam powered presses at U.S. Mint made standardization possible. The change mirrored a larger societal transition from primitive to industrial, after which hand-crafted variation gave way to machine-made uniformity. The coins that circulated in America before 1840 were not necessarily more primitive than later issues, but they were made by different means and came from a wider variety of sources. Thus, those made before 1840 legitimately can be called "early."

What, then, does it mean to say that a piece is American? Any of them made in what is now the United States certainly is American. Those made elsewhere, but *officially* earmarked for American use also are American. A third qualifying group contains pieces of foreign origin that were intended to circulate elsewhere, but instead purposely were introduced "wholesale" into American circulation. In comparison, foreign incidentals entered American circulation through "retail" channels, almost always circulating elsewhere first, before coming to America. Using this distinction, at least three originally Irish issues qualify as American, as do certain French coins. As more information comes to light, some varieties of foreign-made counterfeit halfpence even may join the ranks of American coins.

Finally, the term "coin" implies official valuation and use in a general monetary context, to the exclusion of special-purpose medals, jetons, coin weights, receipts and many tokens. The definition omits, for example, tokens used only for specific purposes, such as for tithing or theater admission. What, then, can be said of a token or medal that is pressed into service as a coin? The rule should be, "Actual use trumps intended use." That is, if a piece is used as a coin and accepted generally in exchange for goods and services, then it becomes a coin, or at least a token. In early America, with legal coins in short supply, the distinction between coins and tokens almost was irrelevant.

This rather broad definition of early American coins and tokens notwithstanding, some pieces are called early American more out of tradition than substantiated fact. The recent trend has been to exclude anything marginal from the category. Here, however, tradition receives the benefit of the doubt on the chance that absence of evidence might not be evidence of absence.

One tradition that deserves *not* to be preserved is the use of the word "colonial" to describe early American issues made outside the U.S. Mint. The American colonial period ended in 1776 from one perspective and in 1783 from another. Yet, the golden age for so-called colonials was the late 1780's and the most prolific year was 1787. The term "colonial" also obscures the fact that there were several more or less distinct early numismatic periods in America, each with its own coins and tokens. These periods are treated in the chapters of this section:

- Chapter 8: Colonization (1616 to 1763)
- Chapter 9: Conflict (1764 to 1780)
- Chapter 10: Confederation (1781 to 1788)
- Chapters 11 and 12: Constitution (1789 to 1840)

Most early American coins and tokens have characteristics that distinguish them from milled foreign issues and from those made later at the U.S. Mint. Early coins and tokens often are crudely designed and poorly manufactured, with many resembling folk-art pieces. While significant knowledge of minting technology available before 1840 exits, little is known about the actual machinery and techniques that were used at specific mints. Often only the coins themselves bear witness to their origins.

Nuances in style and striking from the hands of the craftsmen who made them give these pieces charms not found among others that circulated in America. Locating a particular variety can take years, a circumstance that only adds to the thrill of the hunt for collectors. Even if early American coins and tokens were not so historic, they still would be objects of endless fascination.

1790 Albany church penny from the First Presbyterian Church of Albany, New York. On January 4, 1790, the church authorized one thousand of these uniface coppers to be sold to parishioners at twelve to the shilling. The parishioners then were expected to return them, over time, in collection plates.[267] *It was a win-win situation. The church profited from the exchange of silver for nearly worthless coppers and parishioners were able to contribute regularly, even when small change was in short supply. The legend on these tokens simply reads either* D CHURCH Penny *or* CHURCH Penny *(without the "D.") "D" may signify that the token is a denarium (penny,) or it may be the initial of a church pastor. Other churches sold paper versions or tokens made of lead. Metal or paper, these amounted to prepaid coupons and were not truly money. Hence, they are excluded from the census of early American coins and tokens. This usage also differs from the older traditional purpose of communion tokens, which was to prove membership in a persecuted church. Communion tokens continued to be used for various purposes well into the 19th century.*

8: COLONIZATION (1616 TO 1763)

On June 27, 1763, with the French finally ousted from any meaningful presence in North America, Benjamin Franklin wrote to John Whitehurst, "Here in America she [Britain] has laid a broad and strong foundation on which to erect the most beneficial and certain commerce, with the greatness and stability of her empire."[268] Franklin had no reason to believe otherwise. For the preceding century and a half, the thirteen American colonies had not always been happy, but they still were proud and content to be British. Likewise, Canada and Louisiana struggled to remain French. Both powers took this devotion for granted. Accordingly, neither went to great effort to provide its colonists with proper coinage. Given the sovereignty of the colonizing powers, the ability of the colonies to make their own coins was limited severely. While a few domestically made pieces did materialize, most American coins from this period are a varied mix of imported patent issues, second-hand castoffs and generics. All of the imports reinforced the message that the interests of the colonies were secondary.

In the unlikely event that their importation was planned, the last of the deliberate imports to enter America before 1763 were the Hibernia Voce Populi coppers of 1760. These halfpenny- and farthing-sized tokens are believed to have been minted after the death of George II by Irish supporters of various claimants to the vacant throne. Their obverses seem to portray the different pretenders, though the exact identities of the portraits are unknown. With the coronation of George III, the tokens became obsolete and candidates for export. In spite of their early date, the obverse legend *VOCE POPULI* ("Voice of the People") might well have resonated with restless colonists in the years leading up to the Revolution.

1749 British halfpenny. An American coin?

A long dry spell preceded the coming of the Voce Populi tokens. The only coins officially entering British America between 1739 and 1760 were shipments of regal coppers, the most notable being one of more than ten long tons sent to Massachusetts in 1750 aboard the *Mermaid.* These coins were used to repay the colony for its military participation in King George's War. Because the shipment was so large, some even regard 1749 British halfpence as American coins.

A local Connecticut issue of 1737 to 1739 indisputably is American. These are the copper threepence tokens believed to have been made in Simsbury, Connecticut, by the multi-talented Dr. Samuel Higley. Higley's tokens already were considered rare by 1800, suggesting a small issue and local circulation. Some of the copper used in their production might have come from Simsbury mines that Higley owned and that later saw use as Newgate Prison, the nation's first state penitentiary.

A few years earlier, under George I, William Wood, of Wolverhampton, petitioned for and received the right to mint coins made of a bizarre copper-based alloy called Bath metal.

Wood's coins were minted primarily between 1722 and 1724, and are known as the Rosa Americanas, the first circulating coins to bear the word "America." They supposedly were rejected in the northern colonies and then subsequently shipped to the South. During the same period Wood produced similar coins for use in Ireland, or "Hibernia." His Hibernia coins eventually were rejected by the Irish, and it is believed that many of them were shipped to the American colonies. Archaeological evidence suggests that Wood's Hibernia coins were relatively rare in early America. It is ironic, then, that worn examples of these coins are among the most numerous American pieces of the period available to modern numismatists and collectors.

Until 1763 shipments of French domestic and colonial issues were regular arrivals in Louisiana and Canada. Eighteenth century imports joined older counterstamped issues and a 1670 series of Louis XIV silver coins that were made for French America. The 1670 issue was small and examples are rare today. However, most of the eighteenth century issues were produced in greater numbers. Some of them were by-products of John Law's ruinous fiscal regime of 1719 to 1721. Other French copper imports of 1717 to 1723 were not associated with Law. Accompanying them during the 1709 to 1764 period were large numbers of imported French billon coins. All of these pieces circulated alongside British coins in North America and have varying claims to American status.

Some of the rarest and most mysterious pieces of the American colonial period are associated with Gloucester County, Virginia. Only one example of these 1714 brass tokens [?] was known until 1981, when a second was found. Because the legends on both examples are incomplete, it was only with the discovery of the second specimen that numismatists were able to decipher their wording. The obverse legend alludes to the Gloucester County courthouse. The names of two men, Righault and Dawson, whom history has all but forgotten, appear on the reverses, around a hollow star. A smaller-diameter, apparently uniface example, was found in 1982 and bears the date 1715.

A unique piece, known as the New England stuiver, appears to be Dutch and seventeenth century in origin, but now is suspected of being a nineteenth century fabrication. Its current location is unknown, though a photograph of it appeared in popular numismatic references for many years.

Another very rare token issue, long suspected of being Dutch, features Cupid and Psyche cavorting in a wooded paradise that serves as a metaphor for colonial life. Their reverses feature an eagle as part of a crest. Around the eagle are the words *NEW YORKE* [sic] *IN AMERICA*. The old Dutch spelling, "Yorke," and the fact that a specimen was found at the Hague led scholars to assume for decades that the brass and lead tokens were indeed Dutch. However, new findings suggest that the reverses of these tokens represent the family crest of Francis Lovelace, the second English governor of New York after the Dutch relinquished control of the area.[269]

Some issues had origins and reasons for existence that are unknown today. For example, in the 1690's there appeared a group of tokens whose obverses feature an inaccurate depiction of an elephant. Of three major types of these tokens, two bear American reverse legends. Reverses of the third type have the arms of London and appeal for divine preservation of that city. The exact origin and intended usage of elephant tokens remain mysteries and little more than tradition actually binds them to the colonies. Nevertheless, all of them, including the London pieces, long have been associated with America.

Some saw the need for coinage in the American colonies as a business opportunity. For example, Richard Holt, a tin mine owner and friend of James II, was hurt financially when the market value of tin plummeted in 1687. Holt represented a group of fellow mine owners whose solution was to solicit a patent from James II to mint tin tokens for the "American plantations," as the colonies then were known. Unfortunately, however, tin is very active chemically. Its degradation is rapid, particularly when exposed to cold weather, making the tokens unsuitable for use in New England. The apparent solution was to give them a Spanish denomination, 1/24th-reale, and send them to the warmer southern colonies, where the inhabitants were familiar with Spanish trade and denominations. Whether they ever actually arrived in America is an unsettled question.

Other coins originally intended for circulation elsewhere found their way to American shores. In 1681, for example, Mark Newby brought St. Patrick coppers to New Jersey. These coins had the official approval of New Jersey's governing body, but originally may have been minted in the 1660's for use in Ireland. No other American coin series is as vexing as the Newby's coppers. Both their origins and the paths that they traveled are tantalizing mysteries.

Such imports helped stem the tide of small change shortages that continually plagued the colonies from the North to the South. Alongside them, at the turn of the eighteenth century, contemporary legislation describes private lead tokens that appeared in Philadelphia and Massachusetts to offset local shortages. To this author's knowledge, no confirmed examples survive. Elsewhere, tobacco drove the economies of areas in which it was grown. Even where a single commodity dominated, growth, diversification and fluctuating market conditions eventually led to calls for hard currency. Maryland found the need for coinage during the tobacco glut of the late 1650's. In desperation, planters petitioned Cecil Calvert, their Lord Proprietor, for relief in the form of hard coinage. Virginia, another tobacco colony, had been given the right to have coinage by its charter. (See Chapter 9.) Calvert must have assumed that Maryland had the same right of coinage when he ordered a series of silver pieces for his beleaguered tenants. He was wrong. The Commonwealth did not approve of his exporting silver to America. In the waning days of Cromwell's regime, the Catholic Calvert was lucky to escape with no more than an order to cease producing the coins. That he escaped so lightly probably reflects on the Commonwealth's political need to appease moderate Catholics.

Just before, in Massachusetts, the demand for hard currency reached a peak at a time when world confidence in its monetary system, that of Spain, was at low ebb. Recall that, in the mid-1600's, the huge Spanish mint in Potosí, Bolivia was found to be producing coins at less than the authorized level of fineness. These events created a worldwide panic that gave people in far away little Massachusetts one more reason to demand a reliable currency. The colony had the opportunity to produce its own, thanks to Oliver Cromwell, whose rise had left Britain temporarily without a true monarch. In 1652 Massachusetts saw the void as a chance to declare itself a commonwealth and stake claim to one of the tenets of sovereignty, the right of making coins. The quaint NE and tree coins that Massachusetts produced between 1652 and 1682 have been sought eagerly by numismatists for more than three centuries. In minting them, the Commonwealth of Massachusetts not only produced the first domestic American coinage, but also committed one of the first acts of rebellion by an American colony against the Crown.

Traditionally, the first coins to be treated as early American were the silver-washed "hogge money" coppers minted in England for the Sommer Islands,* in 1616. Since these islands, now known as Bermuda, were once part of the territory claimed by the Virginia Company, most regard the coins as American. In truth, the Virginia Company connection had been severed by the time the coins were made and no evidence is known to prove that they ever circulated in what is now the United States.

While Massachusetts' famed silver coinage was the first that English colonists made in America, tokens newly discovered in Newfoundland may prove to be the first made in the broader North American context. These lead tokens were excavated by archaeologists at Ferryland, a seventeenth century fishing village. Dr. Louis Jordan described them in a presentation to the annual convention of the Colonial Coin Collectors Club (C4) in 2006. [270]

In 1621 Sir George Calvert, soon to be the first Lord Baltimore, purchased a proprietary patent for a tract of land and established a fishing-based colony that he called Avalon, in Newfoundland. He was granted formal claim to the area in 1623, by James I. In Calvert's name, Captain Edward Wynne and twelve intrepid settlers came to establish a permanent settlement at Ferryland. Wynne and his men prepared the way for Calvert's coming by building facilities that included a large "mansion house." They achieved some measure of success, for, by the middle of the decade, the settlement was home to about a hundred settlers. In 1627 Calvert came to Avalon and, the following year, he returned with his wife and about forty members of his extended household. Calvert soon grew tired of the cool climate, however, and left in 1629, turning his attention to a warmer region around the Chesapeake.[271] That region became Maryland.

In Calvert's absence came Sir David Kirke, with whom the newly found tokens are believed to be associated. Kirke had won fame by helping take Nova Scotia and Quebec from the French. Along with Marquis Hamilton and the earls of Pembroke and Holland, Kirke was given the "Grant of Newfoundland" by Charles I, in 1637.[272] Sir David's knighthood, and probably the grant itself, came as a reward for Kirke's military actions on behalf of the Crown. Kirke arrived in 1638, evicted Calvert's left-behind representative from the mansion house and quickly took charge, both as governor and as a monopolistic merchant. There he ran things as he pleased until the Commonwealth clipped his wings. In 1651 Kirke was recalled to England to answer for his controversial business practices. In the process, Cecil Calvert, Sir George's son and the second Lord Baltimore, filed one of several suits to win back control of the area. Calvert won and Kirke died in prison, in 1654. Even so, Kirke's widow, Lady Sara, and sons ignored the ruling and continued to build their commercial empire. Kirke descendants remained a formidable commercial family for most of the remainder of the seventeenth century. The Kirke family was involved in the three major commercial undertakings that made Canada: the St. Lawrence fur trade, the fisheries and the Hudson's Bay fur trade.[273]

Ferryland's planters and fishermen were a hearty lot. They had to be, given hard work, tough climate and relentless mosquitoes that they were forced to endure. Not surprisingly, they often turned to alcohol and tobacco for release. For this purpose, Kirke ran a "common tavern" in his own house.[274] It seems likely that the lead tokens were used as small change in the tavern. Based on the sizes of the recovered pieces, units of one, two and three were used, though just what the unit was is in question. The "DK tokens" differ from most Elizabethan lead tokens in

* Alternately, Somer Islands. Seventeenth century spellings are phonetic and vary accordingly.

that they are struck rather than cast. Based on research done by Ray Williams and presented at the 2006 C4 convention, it appears that the weights of the tokens correspond to musket balls of known calibers.[275] Since musket balls were accepted in their most useful (spherical) form as half-farthings, the reason for pounding them flat and stamping them with David Kirke's monogram is a mystery. Perhaps they were not made from musket balls, but from fishing weights that were common in Ferryland. And, perhaps they served another purpose. As jetons? Struck brass and handmade slate jetons have been found at Ferryland, including at least one of the types produced by Hans Krauwinckel (Chapter 7.)[276]

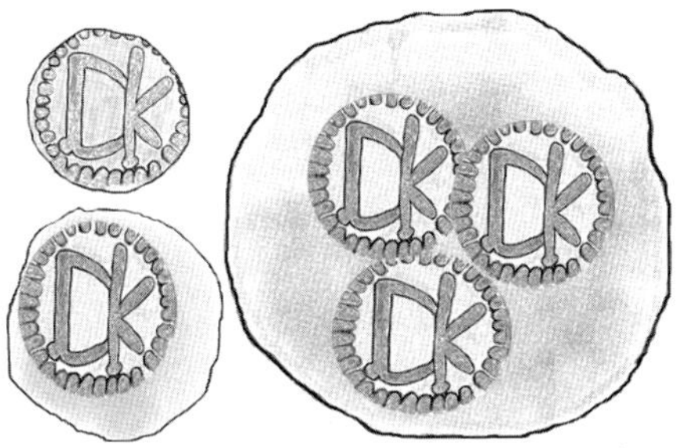

Ferryland's lead "DK tokens," approximately actual size.

Of all these early series, only the Massachusetts silver issues and Dr. Higley's copper threepence can be assumed to have been made in America. Yet all, except the DK tokens, are regarded as American and each has its own part to play in the narrative of American history. This narrative is not a single epic story. Rather, it is the collection of many smaller, often personal threads that together weave a very complex and interesting fabric.

A RUDE BEGINNING: SOMMER ISLANDS COINAGE (CA. 1616)

The first of these threads began in June 1609 when Admiral Sir George Somers (or Sommers) departed Plymouth, England, for Jamestown. With him aboard a nine-ship fleet were Sir Thomas Gates, John Rolfe, Rolfe's pregnant wife and five to six hundred others. Their mission was to provide relief and reorganization for the beleaguered colonists in Virginia. However, fate, disguised as nature, intervened. Soon after departing, the fleet was scattered by a sudden violent storm that raged for three days. Somers and 150 people aboard the flagship, *Sea Venture,* were separated from the others and blown far off course. To their pleasant surprise, they wrecked without casualty on the rocks of a beautiful island inhabited only by hogs and other wildlife. Over the next several months, the men reincarnated the *Sea Venture* in the form of two new cedar ships, *Patience* and *Deliverance.* In May 1610 they made the two-week journey to Jamestown and reunion with their companions. Left behind were Mrs. Rolfe and her baby girl, Bermuda, both of whom died on the islands.[277] Mrs. Rolfe's death paved the way for her husband's famous marriage to the Indian princess, Pocahontas.

Somers, a man of about fifty-six years, returned a few months later aboard a thirty-ton ship in search of food for Virginia. Luck was not with him this time. He soon died of exhaustion on what came to be named after him as St. George's Island.[278] Somers' body was returned to England for burial, but his heart literally remains on St. George's. (It is buried on the island.)[279] The English memorialized him by calling the area the Sommer Islands. Shakespeare further insured Somers' immortality by telling of his adventure in *The Tempest.*[280] The Bard drew from the accounts of Sylvester Jourdain and William Strachey. Strachey, whose signet ring recently was found on St. George's, survived the shipwreck to become a key figure in Jamestown's survival.

That the Sommer Islands now are called Bermuda is an obvious clue that Somers was not their true discoverer. That honor probably goes to the Spaniard, Juan de Bermudez, Captain of the ship, *La Garza* ("The Heron.") In 1505 Bermudez found the islands while he was transporting hogs to the West Indies.[281] He even may have visited two years earlier. Bermuda also appears on a Spanish map published by Peter Martyr in 1511 and on Sebastian Cabot's 1544 *Mappa Mundi* ("map of the world.") The Spaniard, Hernando Camero, filed an application to settle the islands in 1527, but nothing came of it. Over the next few decades, many ships fell victim to the region's unpredictable weather and wrecked in Bermuda, but no one settled permanently.[282]

Somers was not even the first Englishman to see the islands. In 1593 Captain James Lancaster left Plymouth, England, bound for the East Indies. One of his English seaman, Henry May, transferred to a French vessel under the command of a Captain De la Barbotiere. About half of the men aboard the French ship survived its wreck on Bermuda's rocks, an event now depicted on the country's seal. Over the next few months, May, De la Barbotiere and the other survivors lived off local wildlife and built a cedar ship that they sailed to Nova Scotia, before hitching a ride to France.[283]

In any case, it did not take the Virginia Company of London long to conclude that the islands represented a commercial opportunity. In 1612 a group of company affiliates obtained a royal patent that gave them control over the area. That year the first governor, Richard Moore, brought a group of sixty settlers aboard the *Plough.* They set about building forts in strategic locations. The following year, Spaniards sailed into Castle Harbor to investigate the King's Castle fortifications. The Spanish retreated after two cannonballs were fired from the fort, unaware that the English had only one more ball in their arsenal.[284]

By 1614 it became clear to the Virginia Company that the islands were not as well suited for agriculture as originally thought. To cut their losses, the company returned control to the Crown. The next year the Bermuda Company was chartered by Virginia Company shareholders. They purchased rights to the islands for the sum of £2,000, calling the new venture the Somers Isles Company. With the Virginia Company out of the picture, the *formal* American connection was severed.

Richard Moore was replaced in 1615 by a series of men who took turns governing for a month at a time. In May 1616 Daniel Tuckar, a Virginia planter, arrived to take his turn. He found the colony in disarray, but quickly began putting settlers back on the straight and narrow path.[285] Tuckar has the reputation of a tyrant, but one suspects he was merely a stern disciplinarian. At one point, five men grew so disgruntled with his ways that they built a boat and *rowed* to Ireland.[286]

Tuckar secured authorization for coinage in denominations of two-, three-, six- and twelve-pence for use in the islands. The coins were hand struck in England and were composed of copper, with a light coating of silver. They were short-lived because, in the salt mist of Bermuda, this combination of metals is extremely prone to electrolytic corrosion. By 1624 Captain John Smith, of Jamestown fame, already was writing of them as relics of the past.[287] In 1875 Sylvester Crosby knew of only four examples.[288] Today, something over a hundred specimens of all denominations combined are thought to survive. Most are shillings. That more examples have surfaced primarily is due to the advent of metal detectors.[289] A group of fifteen hogge money coins were found in a garbage pit near King's Castle, in 1993 and 1994.[290]

The coins' obverse designs feature a hog that Captain Smith claimed was a descendant of the animals that escaped Juan de Bermudez's crew. Smith wrote that the hogs were very black and mean, giving rise to the place name, Isle of Devils.[291*] The coins themselves very often are called "hogge money." Denominations are given, above the hog, in Roman numerals (i.e., *II*, *III*, *VI* or *XII* pence.) Around the obverse perimeter of the two largest coins are the words *SOMMER* ★ *I*[S]*LANDS* [sic] ★ (on shillings) or, on the sixpence coins, ✠ *SO*[or U]*MMER* ✠ *I*[S]*LANDS*. The two smallest coins have only their denominations as obverse legends. Reverses of all the coins feature an image of a fully rigged ship that presumably is the *Sea Venture,* and are without legends. Varieties include twopence coins with small or large stars beneath the hog's belly, sixpence coins that have large or small portals and shillings with large or small sails. The extremely rare threepence coins are known in only one variety.

Ca. 1616 Sommer Islands sixpence.

Trade between Bermuda and Virginia was common and one would expect that they circulated, however briefly, in America. Perhaps owing to their tendency to corrode, none have ever been found at archaeological sites in the area now occupied by Virginia[292] or in any other part of the United States. Of course, an example could be found on American soil at any time. Because the coins' minting occurred after the formal Virginia connection was severed, they technically are not American. Nevertheless, they almost universally are treated as the first American coinage.

Since many of the key figures in Bermuda's early history had strong Virginia connections, including hogge money as American is not entirely inappropriate. Moreover, throughout the eighteenth century, the relationship between America and Bermuda grew closer. Bermuda became a trading and whaling center and was a favorite mooring for both American and pirate ships. During the Revolution, the American need for powder and other war supplies and Bermuda's need for food made the two natural allies, even though islanders remained loyal to the Crown.

Most of the many extant hogge money copies are electrotypes or thicker, struck specimens that weigh considerably more than genuine coins. They also exhibit styles that clearly are from a later period. Hogge money weight standards never have been accurately determined. Crosby detailed only a shilling at 177 grains and a sixpence of unspecified weight.[293] Walter Breen gave the weight range of shillings as 63.5 to 177 grains, sixpence at 36 to 63.1 grains, threepence at 21.6 grains (he provided only one weight) and twopence at 19.5 to 26.9 grains.[294] The wide variations in weight may be due more to corrosion than to poor quality control at the mint. All genuine specimens seen by this author exhibit some measure of corrosion. Sommer Islands coins are relatively large in diameter, but very thin, a feature that further promotes corrosion. They were indeed a rude beginning.

History repeats on a 20th century Bermuda cent

[*] Another theory attributes the "Isle of Devils" reference to demonic-sounding cries of local wildlife.

MASSACHUSETTS SILVER COINAGE (1652 TO 1682)

In 1602, a half-decade before Jamestown's settlement and a half-century before the first domestically made American coins, the English explorer Bartholomew Gosnold discovered an area that he called Northern Virginia. There he named Cape Cod for its indigenous fish and Martha's Vineyard for his infant daughter. A dozen years later, fellow Jamestowner, Captain John Smith, explored and mapped Northern Virginia's coast. Smith later claimed to be the first to rename the region New England.[295] New England included the areas known today as Massachusetts, Connecticut, Rhode Island, New Hampshire, Maine and Vermont, but it took first root in Massachusetts. Compared to Virginia, New England's settlement was slow in coming. When settlers finally arrived, however, they did so in great waves. Their numbers, their commercial lifestyles and a paucity of good circulating money drove the need for local coins. An unlikely convergence of events in Massachusetts, England and, oddly enough, South America made that coinage possible.

In 1606, when James I chartered The Virginia Company of London, he also chartered The Virginia Company of Plymouth. The two companies generally were referred to as the London Company and the Plymouth Company, respectively. The London Company's allotted territory was to the south (i.e., Virginia,) the Plymouth Company's to the north (i.e., New England.) The territories overlapped by three degrees of latitude.[296] In addition to claiming the Sommer Islands, the London Company founded Jamestown and began the settlement of Virginia. The Plymouth Company, on the other hand, essentially was inactive by 1609, having done nothing.

Meanwhile, back in old England, Puritans sought to reform, or purify, the Anglican Church from within. There the Protestant Reformation had not achieved all that was hoped. Much of its momentum had been absorbed in the entrenched hierarchy of the Church of England. Puritans wanted to put parishioners more directly in touch with God's laws by eliminating bishops and simplifying church procedures. However, the reformers met with great persecution from the Crown for their attempts at change.

In 1608 a left-wing extremist group, ill-content to work within the Church, fled first to Amsterdam, then to Leyden, where they lived peacefully among Dutch Calvinists. Though the extremists escaped persecution, they were uncomfortable with Dutch society and were denied access to the better paying jobs. So, after twelve years, about half of them returned briefly to England. There they obtained permission from the London Company to settle in Virginia. Joining other separatists who had remained in England, the combined group of just over a hundred set sail from Plymouth aboard the *Mayflower*. Sixty-five days later, on November 19, they arrived in the New World, but far to the north of where they intended to be. It took until December 26 to find a suitable harbor and move the group to land, where they founded the Plymoth [sic] Colony on the mainland side of Cape Cod Bay.[*] Of course, these were the "Pilgrims."[†]

---

[*] The Mayflower group's spiritual leader was William Brewster, an educated man whose descendant, Dr. Samuel Higley, later played a role in the coinage of Connecticut. See the section on Dr. Higley's threepence tokens of 1737-1739, below, in this chapter.

[†] The group's elected leader, John Carver, died in April 1621. William Bradford was unanimously elected as his successor. Bradford, who would be elected for thirty consecutive annual terms as governor, referred to the separatists who returned from Leyden as "Pilgrims." Those who came aboard the Mayflower were called the

A City on the Hill

Their tiny colony soon was swallowed by the tide of a larger immigration. In 1620 the Plymouth Company was re-chartered as The Council for New England. The council began making land grants and otherwise encouraging migration. In 1628 a land grant was given to John Endecott and five other men. Within a year Endecott brought a group of sixty settlers to Salem to join the remnants of a fishing colony that had been formed on Cape Ann in 1623. In the spring of 1629 Endecott secured a new charter under the name, "The Governor and Council of London's Plantation in the Massachusetts Bay, in New England." This Massachusetts Bay *Company*, as it was called, became synonymous with the Bay *Colony* and eventually assimilated the old Plymoth Colony. [297]

The Bay Colony's charter is famous not for what it contained, but for what it omitted. Virginia then was operating under a similar charter, its third, that required its board of directors to meet *in England*. Massachusetts Bay's charter held no such provision. John Winthrop, an influential Puritan, immediately recognized the omission as an opportunity to build a new society, his famous "city on the hill," in America. He envisioned an autonomous religious state, free to operate as it pleased. This concept was very different from the commercial puppet for which Charles I had hoped when he approved the charter.[298]

John Winthrop. After John Singleton Copley. Source: Mace (58.)

Ultimately, Winthrop's lure of freedom proved to be a far better incentive for settlement than the limited possibility of commercial success. Intensifying religious persecution and Charles's 1630 suspension of Parliament in favor of despotic rule drove educated and powerful men toward Winthrop's vision. He secured Bay Company approval and began bringing colonists by the shipload. They founded a town near a clear-running stream on the Shawmut Peninsula, calling it Boston after the town from which many of them came.[299] By the time immigration slowed to a trickle around 1640, by most estimates, about twenty thousand people had moved to New England.

A few of these colonists were stockholders in the corporation. Stockholders who agreed to abide strictly by Winthrop's version of the Puritan faith were called "freemen." These freemen made up a governing body called the General Court. This system insured that the Puritans retained control, even though freemen were a small, elite minority class within the colony. Over time, the General Court evolved to include representation by other classes and, when it came to self-government and the minting of coins, Massachusetts' ruling body took some very bold initiatives.

Settlers quickly began to spread outward from Boston, founding an expanding circle of small towns and moving into other regions of New England. The General Court tried to make sure that whole towns were transplanted at once and in close proximity to existing villages. The leaders frowned on individuals who struck out on their own, some of whom did so to escape Winthrop's autocracy.[300] Contrary to popular belief, the immigrants were not society's

---

"Old Comers." Only later was the term "Pilgrim" applied to the entire group who came to America. (Samuel Eliot Morison, intro to Bradford, pp.xxiii-xxv.)

outcasts. Rather, they were honest, educated, business-savvy and sometimes wealthy citizens who were accustomed to life in a commercial society. As a result, the Massachusetts economy was already in need of a standard currency less than two decades after the Pilgrims arrived.

The first attempt at such a standard was made in 1637, when the General Court assigned wampum its official valuation. Wampum worked as money for a time, but in the end was no more than a necessity money that served as a placeholder until something better came along. In addition to trading with local Dutch and Indian populations, New England colonists regularly dealt with merchants in the West Indies. When they did, they encountered Spain's New World currency that consisted primarily of irregular silver cobs. Recall that cobs were not originally meant to be coins. They were flattened lumps of metal that were assayed, weighed and stamped to facilitate the accounting of gold and silver being shipped back to Spain. Many of them never made it to Spain and instead entered the West Indian trade. There, some of them were exchanged for the fruits of New England's labors.

These crude quasi-coins had irregular protrusions that easily were removed by the unscrupulous. If done carefully, the lightened cob still could be passed at full face value. Moreover, simple legends and devices made them easy prey for counterfeiters who used sub-standard alloys in their fabrications. Dutch coins also were counterfeited extensively. With so many lightweight and dubious coins in circulation and good ones so scarce, something had to be done.

Seeds of Independence

During the 1640's Massachusetts petitioned an unsympathetic Charles I for a standard currency, only to have their requests ignored. After all, it was Charles and his father from whom the Puritans had fled in the first place. Already by 1635, a year before the founding of Harvard College, Charles had become so annoyed at New England's success that he hatched a plan to annul its charter and place his own man, Sir Ferdinando Gorges, in charge. The plan never was carried out because Charles had on his hands a festering civil war. Throughout the 1640's he fought to retain his crown and, by 1643, was so preoccupied with the rebellion that New England essentially was left on its own. During this time, New England grew ever more autonomous and even formed an independent confederation called The United Colonies of New England. In essence, it was a precursor to the American Confederation.[301]

As the decade progressed, Oliver Cromwell emerged as the military leader of the religious and political rebellion. Charles and his Catholic supporters adhered to the principle of the Divine Right of Kings. Protestants, on the other hand, tended to side with powerful Parliamentary factions that pushed for more republican control. Early battles were indecisive, but Cromwell's forces eventually gained the upper hand. The Stuart king was captured, convicted of treason and beheaded in 1649. The rebels, of course, established the English Commonwealth. New England's Protestants might have had cause for optimism, but as it happened, the Commonwealth government paid only sparing attention to them and had no more interest in supplying them with coinage than did the royals.

In spite of New England's relative isolation, other unfolding world events came to greatly affect it. In 1648 the huge Spanish mint in Potosí was found to be producing coins of less than the legally prescribed purity. The perpetrators, who had been in business since 1640, were caught and executed. Since the entire world depended on Spanish coins, a global panic ensued.[302] To some in Massachusetts, the logical solution to this world problem was a local coinage. However, coinage was the right of sovereignties, not colonies. Emboldened by the absence of a true king, Massachusetts declared itself a commonwealth and authorized coinage. Whether or not they realized it, these 1652 events were bold steps toward independence, more than a century before the American Revolution.

The Players and Their Stage

John Hull, an up-and-coming citizen of the colony, was appointed mint master, with Robert Sanderson (or Saunderson) as his assistant. In a phrase, Hull was a "pillar of society." The son of a blacksmith, he came with his parents, a younger brother and a stepbrother to Massachusetts in 1635, at the age of eleven. The family[*] built a home near what is now the intersection of Washington and Summer Streets in downtown Boston. In 1647, at the age of twenty-two years, John married Judith Quincy and the couple settled into an addition built on to the Hull family home.[303]

John and Judith Hull continued to expand the home site, building numerous extensions and outbuildings. One such building was a silversmith's shop. It is not clear when Hull actually entered business as a silversmith, but he certainly had some protagonists. His father, Robert, appears to have encouraged the endeavor and other men in the area might have served as mentors. For example, John's stepbrother, Richard Storer, had been apprenticed to a goldsmith in England, but moved to Braintree, Massachusetts, three years after the Hulls' arrival in America. Given the duration of a typical apprenticeship, Hull's would have ended when he was about twenty-six, which came to pass in 1650.[304] Surviving bills of exchange from 1650 and 1651 are believed to have been payments for his work.[305]

Robert Sanderson was older and more formally trained in the craft. Born in 1608, he had already served a nine-year goldsmithing apprenticeship, under London's William Rawlins, by the time the Hulls arrived in Boston. In 1639 Sanderson and his wife, Mary, immigrated to New Hampshire where Mary bore a daughter. From there, they moved to Watertown, Massachusetts, where their son was born. By 1652 the Sandersons lived in Boston and Robert was partnered with his friend, John Hull.[306]

In the partnership, it appears that Hull may have handled the business affairs and that Sanderson was the real artisan.[†] Of the thirty-four known pieces bearing Hull's mark, all but one also bear Sanderson's mark. The sole item bearing only Hull's mark is a plain cup, probably made around 1650, prior to the partnership.[307‡]

---

[*] The Hull family was apparently not without its black sheep. At about the same time that John was being made mintmaster, his younger brother, Edward, was accused of piracy for raiding French ships. Edward had been granted permission by Rhode Island's Assembly to raid Dutch ships during a period of hostilities with that country, but the license did not extend to French ships. The entire Hull family was sued. John and his father were acquitted, but Edward skipped the trial and fled to England. Subsequent letters suggest that Edward continued to act on the family's behalf in England. (Jordan, *John Hull, The Mint and the Economics of Massachusetts Coinage*, p.5 and Clarke, pp.73-75.)

[†] In November, 2002, this author had the privilege of seeing one of Hull's original business journals at the New England Historical and Genealogical Society facility in Boston. Viewing was facilitated by Dr. Louis Jordan, Director of Special Collections at the University of Notre Dame, and author of the book, *John Hull, The Mint and the Economics of Massachusetts Coinage.*

[‡] The Henry Needham Flynt Silver and Metalware Collection at Historic Deerfield, Massachusetts contains notable examples of the firm's work. A few miles away, in Salem, Nathaniel Hawthorne's House of Seven Gables displays a Massachusetts shilling (below,) found during restoration.

When the General Court decided to establish a mint, Hull was an obvious choice to run it. Hull asked for and received approval for Sanderson to be his assistant.[308] The facility itself appears to have been set up on the original Hull homestead.[*] Perhaps owing to fear of retribution, the colony's records of expenditures for establishing the "Mint House" were cut from treasurer's account book.[309] Still, the records show that the mint building was to be ten by sixteen feet and that Isack Cullimore was assigned to supervise its construction.[310] In addition to a small allowance for waste, Hull was to be paid a sum equivalent to 5 percent of his production, one shilling for every twenty produced. This figure quickly was raised to 6¼ percent.[311] The requisite silver was to come from re-processed Spanish coins and other silver items brought to the mint by the citizenry.[312] While not everything that Nathaniel Hawthorne[†] wrote qualifies as history, he generally was on target in describing Hull's sources. (The part about English buccaneers is a bit of hyperbole.):

> *Hereupon all the old silver in the colony was handed over to Captain John Hull. The battered silver cans and tankards, I suppose, and silver buckles, and broken spoons, and silver buttons of worn-out coats, and silver hilts of swords that had figured at court, - all such curious old articles were doubtless thrown into the melting-pot together. But by far the greater part of the silver consisted of bullion from the mines of South America, which the English buccaneers – who were little better than pirates – had taken from the Spaniards and brought to Massachusetts.*[313]

As long as silver poured in, Hull's fortune was assured. Still, from Hull's journal, Louis Jordan noted that the mint operated not on a continuous daily basis, but sporadically whenever the citizens provided meaningful quantities of silver. Such events apparently dictated the creation of dies. The resulting gaps between flurries of activity undoubtedly explain many of the variations that are observed in Hull's coins.[314]

Steel for dies is believed to have come from the Hammersmith Iron Works, an early bog-iron smelting works to the northeast of Boston. It is now designated as a National Historic Site (the Saugus Iron Works in Saugus[‡].) Traditionally, execution of the dies is attributed to Joseph Jenks (or Jenckes,) a principal figure at the iron works.[315] This seems plausible, given the proximity of the works to Boston, the otherwise limited availability of iron and steel and Jenks's celebrated steel-making skills. However, no documented evidence of a strong working relationship between the mint and the Hammersmith Iron Works is known. Jenks unsuccessfully applied for a coining franchise of his own in 1672, suggesting that he was experienced in making dies and mint equipment. Jenks's petition came at a time when business at the iron works was slack and he was looking for other work. It also came at a time when little silver was being brought to Hull's operation. Thus, Jenks's real chances of solo success may not have been great.[316]

---

[*] John Hull and his extended family acquired numerous properties around Boston and New England. However, most of the properties were acquired considerably later than 1652 when General Court authorized the mint to be built on property owned by John Hull. In 1652 the only property that can be established as "owned" by John Hull is his part of the original homestead near Washington and Summer Streets. (Jordan, *John Hull, The Mint and the Economics of Massachusetts Coinage*, Chapter 1.)

[†] Hawthorne's great grandfather was John Hathorne [sic], a judge at the 1690s Salem witch trials. Hawthorne added a "w" to distinguish himself from his infamous ancestor.

[‡] Saugus is the original name of a very nearby Indian village. English settlers renamed it Lynn and then later changed it back to Saugus. Hammersmith was a village populated by the iron workers. Regardless of its name, the worksite provides an interesting window into the workings of a seventeenth century American industry. One of its chief lines of business was that of making iron fireplace backs, a few of which still survive. A friend of this author owns an original Hammersmith fireback, bearing the date 1663.

A Good Run

Times had been better when Hull's first production began two decades earlier, in 1652. That initial output consists of very simply designed pieces known as *NE* or *New England* coins. Their official production lasted less than half a year for reasons described below. However, beginning in 1653, Hull was given four successive seven-year minting contracts. Already an important man, the contracts made him rich.

It has long been assumed that the four contracts correspond to four distinct sub-series of "tree" coins depicting willows, oaks, pines (first issue) and pines again (second issue,) in that order. Mounting circumstantial evidence and recent re-interpretations suggest that the arboreal design themes do not all fit neatly within the seven-year contract periods. These interpretations are based on minor variations in legends, the use of particular design elements, apparent emission sequences and the subtle marks left by specific minting technologies.[317]

In the latest and best of these analyses, Michael Hodder constructed die families that appear to correlate with specific patterns of business. The willow tree shillings, for example, fall into to die families that may indicate two separate issues, separated by some length of time. Oak and early pine tree shillings, on the other hand, appear to have been made in several distinct issues that reflect sporadic activity spanning a considerable period. Generally, each of the smaller denomination issues (six-, three- and twopence) exhibits few die variations, implying short and probably very concentrated periods of production. All in all, these series reflect the kind of on-demand, shop-owner business model that one might expect from a silversmith.[318]

Die families for the later pine tree shillings are complex and heavily interrelated, suggesting continuity of issue and a business approach more akin to that of modern mints than the craftsman's shop model of the earlier pieces.[319]

Though appealing in its simplicity, the traditional, discreetly compartmentalized willow-oak-pine-pine sequence clearly is too simple to explain the complexity of this marvelous group of coins. Nevertheless, the sequence does provide an approximate chronology and basic road map that that are supported by the tell-tale signs of technological advances over the three-decade period of their issue.

In 1658, two years before the end of the first contract, Oliver Cromwell died and the English Commonwealth began to crumble. After the monarchy was restored by the 1660 ascent of Charles II, Massachusetts' coins and its attitude in general became sources of royal consternation. In spite of numerous conciliatory letters, bribes paid to authorities and offers to place a suitable royal image on the coins, official pressure to halt the enterprise increased.[320] By the end of Hull's fourth contract in 1682, the Crown had lost its patience. In 1684, partly in reprisal for having minted coinage, Charles II revoked Massachusetts' charter. By that time, Hull had been dead for a little more than a year and silver had long since stopped flowing.

Hull's life had been rich in many ways.* A year after marrying Judith Quincy, he joined the militia as a corporal and eventually rose to the rank of captain. He also participated in a

---

* Hermann Clarke related Captain Hull's story in a 1932 biography, *John Hull: A Builder of the Bay Colony*. The classic work on Massachusetts silver coins is Sydney P. Noe's 1943 book, *The Silver Coinage of Massachusetts*. Noe duly credited Sylvester Crosby with the first comprehensive work on the subject, *The Early Coins of America*, published in 1875. Noe numbered the die varieties of the oak and pine *sub-series*

number of business ventures and held several political offices. In 1658 he became city treasurer for Boston. In addition to his many real estate investments, Hull became active in shipping, warehousing, importing, mining and even horse-raising operations. He was a member of the General Court's lower house, representing several different constituencies, and served from 1676 to 1680 as treasurer of the Bay Colony, whose interests he represented on trips to London. To a great extent, Hull's involvement in coinage served to fund his ventures and gave him influential contacts who benefited his career.[321]

Charles II died not long after Hull. His incompetent brother, James II, assumed the throne and sent Edmund Andros to govern Massachusetts. Andros would have imposed discipline, but soon was distracted by an order to re-seize New York from the Dutch. Andros was recalled, along with James II, in 1688 and 1689. Sanderson out-lived both Hull and Charles II, dying a wealthy man in 1693. Subsequent attempts to rekindle interest in the mint never proved economically viable or politically palatable.

Massachusetts' silver coins continued to circulate for many years after Hull's time. About two hundred pieces, representing all of the major types, were found aboard the wreck of *H.M.S. Feversham*, a ship bound from New York that sank off Nova Scotia in 1711. The recovered coins had circulated for three to nearly six decades. Several are cut into fractional pieces to make change, as were Spanish silver coins.[322]

As with other early American coins, it often is difficult to separate fact from fiction when studying these pieces. They long have been revered for their place in history, literature and folklore. Many of the survivors were bent and later straightened, leaving a line of extra wear where the bend occurred. Legend says that they were bent as charms against the power of witches, though no contemporary supporting evidence seems to exist for this notion. Sydney Noe suggested that this practice might have inspired the nursery rhyme about a "crooked man who walked a crooked mile and found a crooked sixpence, against a crooked stile."[323]

Weighty Matters

The standard weights for all Massachusetts silver coins were 72 grains for shillings, 36 grains for sixpence, 18 grains for threepence and 12 grains for twopence. Except for pine tree sixpence coins, actual specimens approximate these weights, though slightly lighter pieces of all denominations are far more common than slightly heavier ones. Delinquents often ignored stiff penalties and clipped silver from the coins' edges just as they did with cobs. By repeating this crime several times, one could accumulate enough silver to re-sell.

A shilling weighing less than 65 grains is likely to have been clipped. At least one surviving NE shilling is so severely clipped that only the outlined letters "NE" remain. Some pieces appear clipped even when they are whole. Pine tree sixpence coins, for example, are almost always struck on light planchets. The example shown later in this section is unclipped but weighs only 31.5 grains, less than 88 percent of the standard. Sterling fineness (0.925) is typical for all of Massachusetts' silver coins. The Spanish coins used to make many of them

---

1,2,3,..., respectively. For the NE and willow sub-series, he used numbers to designate obverses and letters to denote reverses. These conventions, updated for varieties discovered since Noe's time, still are the most widely used. More recently Michael Hodder's narration of Stacks' 2002 sale of the Hain family collection and the 2005 sale of the John J. Ford collection have become standard references. Dr. Jordan's work also has provided understanding far beyond that which existed even in the late twentieth century.

were very near sterling fineness and required little or no additional refinement. For silver from other sources, Hull's operation maintained assaying capabilities to insure purity. Massachusetts' choice of standard weights was no accident. The intent was to keep the coins in the colony and encourage coining. They were 22½ percent lighter than their English counterparts and were thus worth 22½ percent less in England than in Massachusetts. In actual trade the difference often was 25 percent.[324] By converting regal coins to lighter provincial pieces, one stood to profit since coins having a greater total face value could be made from the same amount of silver.

In 1642, a decade before the mint was established, the colony attempted to keep silver within its borders by raising the value of a Spanish dollar to 56d, two pence higher than in England. The difference was not enough and, three months later, the dollar was raised again, to 60d. When the value was raised to 66d in 1652, the offer to turn dollars into provincial shillings was too good to refuse, even after paying Hull's minting fee. Still, North America's lack of good silver drew the coins out of Massachusetts. They soon could be found from Barbados to Canada and were being exported to England for melting.[325] To slow the drain, Massachusetts implemented border search laws in 1654 and strengthened them in 1669.[326] Both efforts failed. As Massachusetts' silver stores dwindled, the colony, almost in desperation, raised the value of a dollar to 72d in 1672. This was too much. A dollar was then worth more than its equivalent in coined shillings, and no one brought silver to Hull's mint. As another incentive that proved ineffective, Hull's fee was reduced to five percent plus wastage in 1675.[327] None of these measures saved the era of the "Boston shillings" from its end by 1683.

NE or New England Coinage (1652)

The first Massachusetts coins and, for that matter, the first coins made in America, bear the initials *NE* (for *N*[ew] *E*[ngland]) on their obverses, Roman numeral denominations, in pence, on their reverses – and nothing else. The simple devices appear as little more than a silversmith's marks. NE coins were produced in denominations of shilling (*XII*,) sixpence (*VI*) and threepence (*III*.)

According to tradition, all of the NE coins were made in the summer and early fall of 1652. Their authorizing act, passed in May of that year, demanded that coins be in circulation by September. Production supposedly started in June when the *design* was authorized.[328] For minting to begin so quickly suggests that the punches (The term "die" is an overstatement.) were prepared beforehand and that the choice of Hull and Sanderson as coiners had been a foregone conclusion.

The NE coins were made the old fashioned way, by placing a blank or strip on an anvil or stump, positioning a punch over it and then striking the punch with a hammer. If struck on a strip, then the finished coins would still have to be cut away from the surrounding metal with a punch or shears. Using shears, variances in strip thickness could be overcome by adjusting the diameter of finished coins. The authorizing act called for the coins to be "...flatt and *square* on the sides...,"[329] implying that either planchets or finished coins indeed were cut from strips. Presumably because square coins were impractical, the order was quickly changed to say that the coins should be made in "...a Round forme...."[330]

Only about seventy original examples of all NE denominations combined are known to exist. Less than ten of them are sixpence coins and only one of them is a threepence. Though six punch combinations (i.e., die varieties) are known for shillings, from three obverse and four reverse punches, the rarity of the NE sub-series makes varietal attribution irrelevant, except to establish authenticity. Modern copies abound and a very few pieces, such as the example at left, may be contemporary counterfeits. Unfortunately, without solid provenance, proving that a suspect piece is a contemporary counterfeit, or a new variety, is at best difficult.

NE shilling, not a known variety. Possibly a contemporary counterfeit.[*]

By late 1652 it was recognized that the NE coins had problems that limited their practicality. They were too easily counterfeited and silver could be clipped or shaved from their edges, leaving a coin too light, but still relatively coin-shaped and apparently legitimate. In October 1652, just four months after their authorization, an order to cease production of the NE coins was recorded.[331]

Then, in exchange for a seven-year contract, Hull agreed to a new design that would, at least theoretically, make clipping and counterfeiting difficult. Even so, he may have continued producing NE coinage for some time, an idea supported by the existence of multiple shilling varieties. Moreover, a 1654 attempt to hire a die maker may have coincided with the arrival a coining press. This could mean that production of the next sub-series, the die-struck willow tree coins, was delayed until 1654. It could also mean that NE coinage continued to be produced in the interim.[332]

Willow Tree Coinage (ca. 1653 to 1660?)

Though Hull's second design theme is known as a willow tree, no contemporary evidence exists for the convention. The authorizing act demands only that "a tree" be used. W. Elliot Woodward, a nineteenth century numismatist, used the term "palmetto," an ironic choice given that palmettos cannot survive Massachusetts' long winters. The trees actually may be tamaracks (evergreens native to Massachusetts) or locusts. In any case, a series of 1860's sales saw the name quickly evolve to "willow tree."[333] The new motif was more complex and thus more difficult to imitate than that of the NE coins. It also extended closer to the coins' edges, making undetected clipping or shaving less likely.

These new coins might have been struck by hammering, as were the NE pieces, or possibly with a drop, roller or rocker press. A drop press uses pulleys to lift a heavy weight within a vertical frame, like that on a Guillotine. The raised weight is released and allowed to fall onto the top die. Thus, in essence, a drop press is little more than a mechanized hammer.

---

[*] This example allegedly was found with a metal detector in a plowed field near the old Connecticut River Valley town of Windsor, Connecticut. It does not match exactly any of the known dies used on NE coinage and it is light at 56.7 grains, but is believed to be "from the period." The immediate area where it was found has yielded a number of early Massachusetts silver pieces. This example is holed, presumably to be worn as a pendant by its owner, who might well have been a Native American.

Rocker and roller press work altogether differently. Both effectively rotate two opposed gear-driven shafts, or rollers, over a strip of metal passed between them. On a rocker press a lever attached to the back of a top gear is moved back and forth (or up and down) in a rocking motion. The lever is pulled in one direction to press the design. The gears are then released, the lever pulled back and the strip pushed forward into position for the next coin. Rather than rocking back, a roller press simply continues the motion through the full 360 degrees. With small coins, multiple die images can fully encircle the rollers.* The coin designs are cut either directly into the rollers or into curved dies that are mounted so that their faces are flush with the rollers' surfaces. In either case the die faces are convex rather than flat, which means that the designs must be oval, elongated in the direction of rotation, to produce circular coins. Elongation also helps to even the force across the die surfaces.[334] However, cutting oval images into convex surfaces, in the negative, to make circular coins must have presented a challenge of counter-intuition to the die makers.

Hodder suggested that the learning curve associated with a new technology, such as a rocker press, might help explain the crudeness of the willow tree issues, which appear to have been struck multiple times on each side, resulting in blurred devices. Even the best-preserved pieces lack clear details. With hammered coins or those made with a drop press, this can be explained by shifting of the blank or strip between blows. If a rocker press was used, lateral die movement, rather than multiple hammer blows, might have produced the erratic images.[335]

By whatever means willow tree coins were made, they are nearly as crude, at least as rare, and exist in the same denominations as their forebears. About seventy specimens of all denominations combined are known, and again most of them are shillings. Only about fifteen are sixpence coins and but a trio are threepence. Whether more shillings were made, relative to the other denominations, is not known. However, Hull's profits clearly were greater with the larger coins.

Willow tree devices vary from multiple-struck amorphous masses of curved lines, to fairly well formed trees. When well struck, the trees on Noe obverses 1 and 2 are roughly conical. On obverse 3, the tree is broader, vaguely resembling, in outline, the oak trees that were to come. Noe recognized five die combinations for shillings, along with one variety each for sixpence and threepence coins. Numerous re-cuttings expand the list of apparent varieties. As are their predecessors, these coins are so rare that varietal attribution is irrelevant for all but the very wealthy. The number of variations does, however, raise some important questions: Were willow tree coins produced in greater numbers than the surviving population suggests, or are they merely experimental relics of a transition period? Were they re-melted to produce later issues? Made at a second mint? Was the die steel simply too poor to produce more than a handful of each variety? To date, no research has come close to finding the answers to these questions.

Willow tree shilling species: *Noe 1, 2 and 3, respectively.*

All willow tree coins and all Massachusetts silver types that followed them, with one exception, share the date 1652. The exception occurred in 1662 and is described below. An

* Richmond farthings (Chapter 5,) for example, were made with rollers that produced nine impressions per complete rotation. (Jordan, *John Hull, The Mint and the Economics of Massachusetts Coinage,* p.87.)

oft-repeated fallacy claims that this obsessive dating was an evasive maneuver, intended to give the impression of the coins having been made during Cromwell's rule. As the theory goes, when the Royalists returned to power in England during the Restoration, Massachusetts' leaders planned to avoid charges of treason by claiming that their coining indiscretions occurred at a time when English sovereignty did not exist. Actually, it is almost certain that 1652 was chosen to commemorate the year in which Massachusetts declared itself a commonwealth and authorized coinage. Contemporary writings by Edward Randolph, an English informant who reconnoitered Boston, and others all but prove this scenario to be the correct interpretation of the 1652 dating.[336]

Willow tree shilling legends begin on the obverse with *MASATHVSETS : IN :* and finish on the reverse with *NEWENGLAND : ANDOM : 1652* ("Massachusetts, in New England, in the Year of Our Lord, 1652.") For shillings, Noe identified three obverses (1, 2 and 3) and five reverses (A through E.) Reverse variations in punctuation include the absence of the second colon on reverse C, replacement of one colon with a stop on reverse D and the use of a stop in both places on reverse E. The smaller sixpence coins shorten *AN DOM* to *A DOM,* while threepence have it abbreviated it even further, to *A·D*.

(Right) Willow tree shilling, Noe 3-D. Other shilling varieties are Noe 1-A, 2-B, 3-C and 3-E. (Left) Willow tree threepence. (Both modern copies.)

Genuine examples are not so clearly struck.

Newly proposed chronologies notwithstanding, it still is believed that willow tree coins immediately followed the NE coinage and that most or all of them were made at some point within the 1653 to 1660 timeframe of Hull's first seven-year contract.

OAK TREE COINAGE (CA. 1660 TO 1667)

The year 1660 was an eventful one. Charles II re-established the monarchy and John Hull received a new contract. The new contract may have occasioned the design change from willows to oaks. According to an apocryphal (and probably contrived) story, Sir Thomas Temple showed the new king an example of Hull's latest coinage, explaining that its design recalled an oak tree at Boscobel in which, as prince, Charles had hidden to avoid Cromwell's troops. Charles II is said to have replied, laughing, that the Massachusetts colonists were "...a parcel of honest dogs."[337]

If a rocker press was not in use earlier, Hull's mint almost certainly was in possession of one by 1660. Its gears and shafts were much easier and, consequently, cheaper to manufacture, than the mechanism of a screw press. Even more economy could be achieved by using hemispherical gears rather than circular ones, a feature made possible by the fact that a rocker press's range of motion is limited to 180 degrees, at most. Upgrading to a rocker press would have been a logical early step into mechanization. Much of the evidence for Hull's having done so centers on a characteristic "S" bend exhibited by many of his coins when viewed edge-on. This phenomenon is seen on European pieces known to have been produced on rocker presses. A rocker press also tends to elongate dentils on the leading edge of the coin being struck, another characteristic shared by many oak tree coins.

Unlike the simple up-and-down motion of drop and screw presses, dies in rocker or roller presses move in curved orbits, ideally passing face-to-face in perfect opposition. In practice, the dies often are misaligned. One side appears centered because, unlike a planchet with its rim, a strip has no practical boundaries for the strike to overlap. However, the other side of a coin struck with the misaligned dies appears off-center. Such is the case with many oak and pine tree coins, especially the smaller denomination pieces.

1662 oak tree twopence. Note the misalignment of the two dies. Jordan observed that a roller press with multiple dies on its shafts would have been the most efficient means of producing large numbers of small-denomination coins. However, all oak tree twopence coins are from a single set of dies, suggesting that a rocker press was used.[338]

Originally, oak tree coins were produced in denominations of three-, six- and twelve- pence, as had been the case with NE and willow coinage. In 1662 an oak tree twopence denomination was authorized. All of the resulting twopence coins bear the actual date of the authorization. That "1662" was used when a new denomination was authorized further confirms the theory that obsessive use of the 1652 date on other denominations and styles commemorates declaration of the Massachusetts Commonwealth and the original authorization of coinage.

In general, oak tree coins bear the same legends as the willows. However, two rare early shilling varieties, Noe-2 and Noe-3, use *ANDO*, in place of *ANDOM*. The example below is a Noe-2, differentiated from Noe-3 by a rosette (⁙) following *ANDO*. The rosette probably was intended to conceal a die maker's spacing error.

Ca. 1660-1667 oak tree shilling, Noe-2 variety. The lack of detail on the obverse right side of this example is due to the imminent collapse of the reverse die, which was used with no other obverse. As the reverse die broke apart, metal flowed into its recesses rather than into obverse details. The collapse must have occurred quickly, given Noe-2's rarity. Note the rosette at 11:30, on the reverse, amid signs of the collapse.

Shilling varieties Noe-1, 2 and 3 are particularly interesting. Though better made than the willow tree shillings, they exhibit some characteristics of their ancestors and probably were the first of the oak tree shillings to be made. All three share a common obverse die whose legend begins at 11 o'clock, as on the willow tree shillings. Several wide-planchet Noe-3 oak tree shillings and a recently discovered example of Noe-2 show traces of the outer edges of a *prism-shaped* obverse die.[339] Certain willow tree examples exhibit similar traces of die edges that are circular arcs, suggesting the use of cylindrical dies. Unlike a cylindrical die, a prism-shaped die easily can be held firm in a vise or within a roller. This apparent change and the experience gained in several years of minting may help to explain why oak tree coins generally lack the blurring observed on the willows. It could also be that the transition from willows to oaks was due to a technological advance that may or may not have coincided with the start of the 1660 contract. Thus, the oaks may have begun earlier than the assumed 1660 to 1667 contract period and endured for some time after its end.

In general, oak trees differ little on Noe shilling varieties one through nine, but take on a different look with Noe varieties ten through fourteen. First, the shrubs or shoots that appear at the sides of the trees become larger and more distinct. The tree's trunk changes from parallel vertical lines to a single, thick vertical line on Noe-13. At the same time, curving oak branches become straight and spiny. The tree on Noe-14, actually a re-cut version of the one on Noe-13, has a decidedly thickened tree trunk and branches. This *spiny oak* may have been a transitional pre-cursor to the pine tree issues that followed.

Oaks on shillings: *Noe 2-3, 11 and 14.*

Oak tree sixpence coins (Noe 15 through 22) exhibit an apparent degree of experimentation among varieties. At least one known sixpence is struck over a shilling and some sixpence varieties omit *IN* from the obverse or use *ANO* rather than *AN DOM.* On Noe-21, a re-cut version of Noe-20, one of the S's is reversed. Probably a simple mistake, this feature recurs on oak tree threepence coins. Threepence coins (Noe 23 through 28) and the 1662 twopence issues (Noe 29 and 30) use the simplified obverse legend *MASATHVSETS* and reverse legend *NEWENGLAND.*

Pine Tree Coinage: First (ca. 1667 to 1675) and Second (ca. 1675 to 1682)

Hull's third contract was in effect from 1667 until 1675. It appears that it was during this time that a pine tree theme was adopted. Except for the appearance of the trees themselves, these coins are refined versions of their oak tree predecessors.

On pine tree coins, symmetrical, gently curved branches radiating from a central trunk replaced the twisted boughs of the oaks. The degree of curvature of the pine branches varies from none, on Noe-2 shillings, to considerable, on Noe-8 and Noe-11 shillings. Two rare shilling varieties, Noe-13 and Noe-14, now thought to be contemporary counterfeits, have branches that resemble nested bowls.

First issue pine tree species: *Noe 1, 2, 8 and 13. Noe-13 is a contemporary counterfeit.*

Overall, design variations on pine tree coins are minor compared to earlier issues, indicating a more consistent manufacturing process. Even so, plenty of interesting variations exist (e.g., an inverted "N" on Noe-11 shillings.) First issue pine tree pieces apparently were produced in numbers roughly comparable to oak tree coins, in denominations of three-, six- and twelve-pence, over a considerable period of time. The twopence denomination was dropped, presumably because it was deemed unnecessary. It certainly was less profitable for Hull.

The example below is a Noe-2 pine tree shilling. It is one of the more common varieties of shilling from this sub-series and is characterized by very straight tree branches. At the obverse five o'clock position, this piece exhibits a split. Numismatists disagree as to the cause of such features that often appear more than once on a given coin. They may have been caused by the act of cutting the planchet from a sheet, by expansion during striking or, more likely, by irregularities in the silver itself. Sometimes, the splits appear to be intentional cuts, perhaps done later to verify genuineness. Shillings from this sub-series are large in diameter and thin. They often exhibit the "S" curves seen on oak tree issues, suggesting continued use of a rocker, or similar press. A few examples of Noe-1 pine tree shillings appear on oversized planchets that are nearly square. Some of them are essentially uncirculated and may have been produced as presentation pieces. The square shapes suggest that the designs still were being impressed into strips of silver, and then cut to their final shapes.

Ca. 1667-1675 pine tree shilling, first issue, large planchet, Noe-2 variety[*]

Pine tree sixpence coins are known in three varieties: Noe-32, Noe-33 and Noe-33a. Most of them are struck on planchets that are too small. Noe-33a differs from Noe-33 in that its dies were correctly aligned, resulting in more centered striking. Noe-33 and Noe-33a sixpence and Noe 34 and 35 threepence coins exhibit "berries" at the base of the tree. The Noe-32 variety, which is represented by only twelve to fifteen known examples, lacks berries. Noe-33 and Noe-33a together account for the remainder of the few dozen known pine tree sixpence coins, the rarest combination of design and denomination in the oak and pine sub-series.

Ca. 1667-1675 pine tree sixpence, Noe-33 variety. Note the misalignment of the dies, resulting in an off-centered strike that is skewed upward on the obverse. Also, note the "berries."

The smaller denominations evidently were made in substantial numbers, though it is not clear just how their mintages relate to those of the shillings. The one known surviving volume of Hull's personal ledger is from the later fourth contract period (1675 to 1682,) when only shillings were authorized. It describes the business in great detail, but says nothing about mintages of the earlier, smaller denominations.

The term "small planchet," by which the later shillings universally are known, is a misnomer. The diameter was reduced, however, the thickness was increased to maintain the same weight. This brought their dimensions more in line with regal shillings and made clipping more difficult. Thicker planchets also were more compatible with screw press technology and, from all indications, these coins were made on just such a device. They are rounder, more uniform

[*] Enlarged photographs of this variety seem to show an "S" embedded in the branches of the pine tree. While this probably is pure coincidence resulting from the positioning of the branches, one might speculate that it is a secret mark, placed by Sanderson. The original authorizing act called for a secret mark to be placed on the coins and periodically changed to prevent counterfeiting. Though a tiny cross is observed on one willow tree shilling variety, it appears that the secret marks never were actually used. Such marks would have provided little deterrent to counterfeiters who simply would have reproduced them.

and apparently produced in significantly greater numbers than any of their predecessors. Hence, they generally are less rare as a type.

The pine trees used on this sub-series generally resemble the form used on the sixpence, above, and the shillings, below. Legends are analogous to those used on the "large planchet" sub-series. To compensate for the smaller planchet diameter, however, *AN DO* is used in place of *AN DOM* on fourth contract shillings.

Small planchet shillings: *(Left) Noe-16, modern copy. (Middle) Noe 17. (Right) Tree from Noe-28.*

In Noe's attribution system, varieties one through eleven are large diameter shillings, ostensibly from the third contract. Varieties twelve through fourteen are counterfeits, generally ascribed to the same period (ca. 1667 to 1675.) Varieties 32, 33 and 33a are sixpence coins and varieties 34 through 37 are threepence coins, also from the third contract period. Noe varieties 15 through 31 all are smaller diameter, thicker shillings from the fourth contract period (1675-1682.) Noe-31 pieces are contemporary counterfeits.

Hull's personal journal and anecdotal evidence both attest to the relatively large mintages. After the death of his wife, Samuel Sewall, a judge in the infamous Salem witch trials, married John Hull's plump daughter, Hanna. Nathaniel Hawthorne invented a legend that her dowry consisted of her weight in pine tree coinage. According to Hawthorne, as the older, portly Sewall, watched, in a suit with pine tree coins as buttons, his young bride sat in one bucket of a balance scale while coins were poured into the other![340] Nineteenth century illustrations and lore transformed Hawthorne's fiction into accepted fact. The story is pure fancy, but Hull undoubtedly possessed the wealth to fill Hannah's bucket had he been so inclined.

Aside from counterfeits, many reproductions of these pieces were (and are) made. Unfortunately, a large proportion of them are deceptive copies. Such copies proliferated in the nineteenth century and continue to fool the unwary. Most, such as those struck by Thomas Wyatt, are relatively easy to identify when compared to genuine varieties, as are those made by historical and numismatic societies for use in commemorative celebrations. Still, only through familiarity and careful analysis can one be sure that a given piece is genuine.

Other pieces, such the 1657 Hingham, Massachusetts shilling shown in Appendix A, are pure fantasies. More famously, Charles Bushnell's nineteenth century *Good Samaritan* "discoveries" caused quite a stir. On them, a vignette of the Biblical Good Samaritan helping a victim replaces the usual tree. Eric Newman was instrumental in laying to rest any claims to legitimacy that these pieces might have had.[341]

Of far greater interest is the possible existence of a 1652 pine tree silver penny. Sir Martin Fowlkes illustrated such a piece in 1763. Crosby included the Fowlkes illustration, but noted that he knew of no surviving example or contemporary reference. Crosby also described two

1662 oak tree pennies that he believed were altered from twopence coins.[342] Whether a Massachusetts silver penny ever really existed remains a mystery.

Massachusetts made other attempts at coinage: patterns in 1776 and the world's first cents and half cents in 1787. Neither of these later series approaches the 1652 to 1682 silver issues with regard to economic impact, historic relevance or enduring popularity. These are more than seventeenth century relics. They are the essence of New England and of early America. On a more personal level, they are tangible reminders of the ingenuity and independence of the people who made them.

MARYLAND'S LORD BALTIMORE COINAGE (CA. 1659)

Maryland's first foray into coinage also was shaped by Commonwealth Era politics, with religious differences in a supporting role. Recall from the chapter introduction that George Calvert had tried in the early 1620's to establish a colony called Avalon, in Newfoundland. The northern climate there proved a deterrent both to settlement and to Calvert's continued interest in the area. As a result, the effort ultimately failed. However, a visit to Virginia convinced him that the more southern region was ripe for colonization. In 1632, as the first Lord Baltimore, he secured proprietorship over a large grant of land in what he called Maryland, after Henrietta Maria, the wife of Charles I, his benefactor. A colonial charter was drafted, but Calvert died in 1632, before its final provisions were executed. On his death, the proprietorship passed to his son, Cecil, the second Lord Baltimore.

The younger Calvert proved to be a skilled and resourceful politician. He needed these talents to navigate Maryland's turbulent early history. Calvert's first two hundred, predominantly Catholic, colonists founded the city of St. Mary's in 1634. His brother, Leonard, was made the colony's first governor. With the Catholic-leaning Charles I on the throne, Calvert operated as he pleased until the start of the English Civil War turned the situation sour.[343]

As Virginia had done, Maryland very quickly became economically dependent on tobacco. It was not long until Protestant planters in Virginia saw the Civil War as an opportunity to assert old claims on Calvert's land. Richard Ingle, a tobacco trader, looted St. Mary's and took control of the colony in 1645. Only Cecil Calvert's skilful maneuvers in London prevented Ingle from having the Maryland charter revoked. In 1647 Virginia's governor, William Berkley, re-established Calvert's authority. Calvert's position again grew tenuous after Charles I was beheaded in 1649. Another Catholic, Maryland's new governor, Thomas Greene, brazenly recognized Charles II as the true king in 1651. In response, Cromwell's agents ousted Greene and outlawed Catholicism in Maryland. A *colonial* civil war followed, with Protestants taking control in 1655. Two years later, Cromwell acquiesced to the rule of law and once again established Calvert's authority.[344] At about the same time, a glut of tobacco caused prices to plummet and Maryland colonists suddenly found that they could not grow enough of it to pay their rent or buy musket balls. They complained to Cecil Calvert for remedy.[345]
Calvert's answer was a risky one. He may have assumed incorrectly that, as did Virginia's charter, Maryland's included the right to produce coinage.[346] Or, he may have based his assumption of the right of coinage on a 1544 law that gave the Bishops of Durham the right to strike coins. At any rate, in 1659, to assuage the anger of his tenants, Calvert authorized silver shilling, sixpence and four pence (groat) coins.[347] Copper pennies also were produced. It long was assumed that the few surviving pennies were no more than patterns. However,

recent discoveries in America, by metal detectorists, seem to confirm that they saw use. That they circulated simply may have been deemed un-newsworthy by contemporary writers.
All of this took place in the last days of the Commonwealth, as Cromwell's regime lingered on after its leader's death. Richard Pight, a mint clerk in charge of dies, informed on Calvert and an arrest warrant was issued in early October 1659. The dies and remaining coins were seized. Calvert won his case in a hearing before the Council on Plantations (i.e., colonies,) but it is unclear whether he was allowed to continue making the coins or sending them to Maryland.[348]

Some evidence suggests that Calvert's plans were carried out. Philip Calvert became governor of Maryland in November 1660 and, following a letter from his brother, Cecil, began securing legislation to push the coins into circulation. An act of April 12, 1662 specified that Maryland householders and freemen were to exchange casks of tobacco for coins at the rate of two pence per pound. Each taxable person in a household was to accept the equivalent of ten shillings over a period of three years. The colony was then home to about 5,500 taxable persons.[349] Thus, a reasonable estimate for the total value of the allocated coinage is 55,000 shillings or £2,750. [350] The actual numbers produced are not known, but one speculative scenario that is consistent with the relative numbers of surviving specimens places the authorized mintage at 20,000 shillings, 45,000 sixpence coins and 37,500 groats.

Whatever their mintages, the coins quickly disappeared and Maryland reverted to a barter economy, authorizing a number of commodities as media of exchange. That hemp was included in the list of acceptable items of exchange led Walter Breen to conclude that Maryland was the first legal entity in America to sanction the exchange of marijuana.[351]

Cecil Calvert received little more than a slap on the wrist for his transgression. Apparently the need for the support of moderate Catholics drove Commonwealth ministers to be lenient. The popular belief is that his offence was putting his own portrait on a coin. In reality, the charges revolved around his unauthorized exportation of silver to the colonies. [352]

In a bit of irony, the artisan for all of Calvert's coins probably was Thomas Simon, Cromwell's own coin designer. The silver denominations all bear similar designs and likely were struck at the Tower Mint in London. Obverses depict a bust of Cecil Calvert, along with the legend ✠ *CAECILIVS* : *D*[OMI]*N*[V]*S* : *TERRAE-MARIA* : *&TC.*, or "Cecil, Lord of Maryland and Other Lands." Reverses bear the Calvert coat of arms and the legend *CRESCITE ET MVLTIPLICAMINI*, or "Grow and Multiply." The penny's obverse is similar to that of the silver coins, but its reverse features a crown and pennants, circumscribed by the legend ✠ *DENARIUS* : *TERRAE-MARIA* ("Maryland Penny.")

1659 Lord Baltimore sixpence and a penny's reverse, This sixpence is holed/repaired, at 12 o'clock on the obverse. The high percentage of survivors that are holed may indicate use as medals, suspended for wearing around the neck.

By 1700 none of Lord Baltimore's coins could be found in Maryland. Today the number of surviving specimens is estimated at thirty-five to forty shillings, thirty-five to forty-five groats and seventy to eighty sixpence coins.* Only eight to twelve pennies are known[353] (seven confirmed plus word from a reliable source of a small group having been found recently in an archaeological context.) Thus, all denominations and varieties are considered rare.

Shilling varieties include a unique "small head" piece, another unique example with Lady Baltimore's quartered arms (as on Maryland's current state flag) and a few pieces struck in copper. Sixpence coins have their rarities as well: A misspelling (*MVLTILICAMINI,*) a "large head" variety, punctuation variations and copper strikings. The groats also include a very rare small head variety.

Calvert's coins were made slightly lighter than the Massachusetts series to discourage circulation outside of Maryland. Elsewhere, they would not have been honored at their declared value. Standard weights for shillings, sixpence and groats were 69.8, 34.9 and 23.3 grains, respectively. The intended fineness is thought to have been 0.925 (sterling fineness.) The copper pennies are small, the intended weight probably being 58.33 grains.[354] By comparison, a U.S. cent of 1909 to 1942 weighs about 48 grains.

Almost all of the direct copies of Calvert's coins are crude electrotypes or secondhand casts made from other copies. None of the copies known to this author is deceptive. In 1860 a Philadelphia coin dealer, William Idler, used the Maryland penny design on a token that advertised his shop. Idler struck these *storecards* in several metals and used legends that describe his business. While his devices are faithful reproductions, the extra legends render them non-deceptive. Calvert's coins were as close as Maryland ever came to having an official coinage of its own, though Maryland silversmiths John Chalmers and Standish Barry each privately minted coins after the Revolution (Chapters 10 and 11.)

ST. PATRICK OR MARK NEWBY COPPERS (CA. 1667 TO 1672)

New Jersey was the next colony to have its own coinage, thanks in some part to Mark Newby (or Newbie,) a man born in Earsdon, Northumberland, England. Newby's story is one of new beginnings. The first came in 1662 when, at about twenty-four years of age, he moved to Dublin with his parents. The Newbies were members of the Society of Friends, or Quakers, and their move was intended to escape religious persecution in their native England.[355]

Within a year, Mark Newby had married Elizabeth Bridge Wilbre, a widow, in County Kilkenny. By 1672 she, her three children by her first marriage and two by Newby, all were dead. Newby waited two years, and then married Hannah Holmes, who bore him four children.[356] The new family settled first in Dublin, then in nearby County Wicklow, an area known for its beautiful hills and valleys. Despite an old tradition that he was a tallow chandler,† Newby more likely was a retailer of general merchandise. His decision to leave what appears to have been a successful business in Dublin, for the country, may have been spurred by acts of religious intolerance against his family or his establishment.[357]

---

* In 2002 a silver canister containing nineteen of Lord Baltimore's sixpence coins was found in England. The coins had been in the possession of the same family since the seventeenth century. The modern owners had assumed them to be gaming tokens of little value. When the canister was submitted to an English auction house, the welcome truth about their treasure was discovered.

† A chandler is candle maker or seller. A tallow chandler also can refer to one who trades in tallow.

On September 19, 1681, Mark, Hannah and their children left the Wicklow hills for America's West Jersey aboard a pink (a narrow-sterned sailing ship,) called the *Owners Adventure.* With them were a number of Quaker Friends, including William Bates, Thomas Thackara, George Goldsmith and Thomas Sharp. Newby and his companions arrived at the Capes of Delaware two months later, on November 18. They landed at Elsinburg and there waited out the winter. When the weather eased, they bought a boat and used it to search the Third Tenth, an area that had been reserved by West Jersey's commissioners for proprietors coming from Ireland, for a favorable place to settle. They found and purchased a tract on Newton Creek, near what is now Camden, New Jersey. In time, the settlement grew to become the town of Newton as birds of Newby's feather, merchant-craftsmen and shopkeepers, flocked to the area.[358]

Newby quickly became an influential citizen of West Jersey. Early in 1682 he was chosen to serve in the General Assembly. However, his roles as pioneer and civic leader are not nearly as interesting as the cargo that he carried on the *Owners Adventure.* A May 8, 1682, act of the West Jersey General Assembly reveals the contents of his stash:

> *...That Mark Newby's halfpence, called Patrick's halfpence, shall from and after the said eighteenth instant pass for halfpence current pay of this province, provided he the said Mark give sufficient security to the speaker of this house, for the use of the General Assembly, from time to time being that he the said Mark, his executors and administrators, shall and will change the said halfpence for pay equivalent upon demand and provided also that no person or persons be hereby obligated to take more than five shillings in one payment.*[359]

The legislation established several firsts: It gave New Jersey its first coinage, gave America its first *official* copper coinage, and allegedly made Mark Newby one of the first bankers in the region.[360] To ensure that he lived up to his end of the bargain, Newby was required to post three hundred acres of land as security.[361]

The word "security" is important. Walter Breen and others have written that Newby brought roughly a cask of coins, estimated to contain £30 or 14,400 coppers.[362] Other numismatists have estimated the number as either higher or lower. Dr. Philip Mossman, for example, used New Jersey's standard of eighteen halfpence per shilling to arrive at an estimate of 10,800.[363] Roger Siboni and Vicken Yegparian, however, building on earlier work by David Gladfelter, have presented convincing evidence that the number of coins brought by Newby was much smaller. Their case revolves around the value of the three hundred acres held as security or collateral. At the going rate, three hundred acres would have been valued at about £3 11s 5d, or a little more than 1,700 halfpence. As a merchant in coin-starved Ireland, Newby would have had far less difficulty obtaining 1,700, or even 2,500 coins, than a cask containing many thousands of them.[364] Had "security" been "surety," the argument would be unviable. In this new light and with his ingenuity notwithstanding, describing Newby as a banker seems generous.

In any case, Newby's coins are known as St. Patrick coppers because that iconic figure graces their reverses. Their obverses feature a kneeling, harp-playing king, gazing up at a golden crown. There the certainty ends. What is known about the actual origins of the coppers can only be extrapolated from isolated fragments of evidence. Seventeenth century violence *may* have destroyed any Irish records that explained who made them, when, where and why. Even the unlikely circumstances by which an English Quaker might have obtained a small hoard of them are shrouded in mystery. Clues litter the British Isles as do the stones of broken castles. The paths that they form are wide at first, but quickly narrow and vanish into the Irish mist.

The coppers come in two sizes, traditionally said to be halfpence and farthings (A convention is used here, for convenience.) Weights of the halfpenny-sized pieces are roughly consistent with Irish halfpence that came later. However, the average weight of the smaller coins is considerably greater than half the average weight of the larger ones. In fact, the farthings typically weigh about two-thirds as much as the halfpence. This odd ratio led J. Earl Massey to call the halfpence three-farthings pieces[365] and Sylvester Crosby to suggest a use other than as coinage.[366] Mossman noted that, since profit was an ever-present concern and heavier coins meant less profit, it is unlikely that deliberately overweight farthings were produced. [367] So, was a relationship other than halfpenny to farthing intended? West Jersey's authorizing act offers no clarification since it names the coins as halfpence, but fails to say which of the two sizes was to be used. Since any coins were welcome in America, Newby's cache might have contained both sizes and any distinction between them might have been an irrelevant omission.

St. Patrick halfpence are six to eight times as rare as the farthings. Accordingly, halfpence die varieties number about thirty, while farthing varieties exceed two-hundred and fifty, from more than four hundred dies.[368] Oddly, many farthing varieties are known by only one or two survivors. Why so many varieties exist and why many of them are so rare are unknown. Farthing mintages must have been much greater than those of the halfpence. Why? Were the halfpence part of a small, early production run made before their weights were reduced, when it became clear that profits were too low? If this were true, then both sizes of coins should be regarded as halfpence.[369] Even the smaller St. Patrick coppers are at least ten times as heavy as patent farthings of the 1613 to 1644 period and Sir Thomas Armstrong's farthings of 1660 and 1661. At 80 to 112.8 grains,[370] St. Patrick farthings are even heavier than regal farthings that debuted in 1672. St. Patrick halfpence weights vary between 120 and 176½ grains.[371] Most fall within the 130 to 140 grain range, not out of line with what one would expect from a later Irish halfpenny. Such heft suggests an official coinage rather than a token issue, but the weight variances seem great for coins produced under any sort of royal auspices and could imply that a degree of experimentation took place. The variances might also imply limited official sanction and, hence, no hard and fast weight standards.

Given that the farthings generally are made from poorer quality planchets, two completely different copper sources might have been used. In 2006 Mossman presented an analysis showing that the smaller St. Patrick coins are much more susceptible to weight loss from wear than the larger pieces, implying that they are made of something other than pure copper. (He explained that raised details on pure copper coins become flattened into the surface. In contrast, less pure alloys are less malleable. Consequently, metal is eroded away during wear.)[372] Sweden supplied much of the copper used in Europe during the latter part of the seventeenth century, while the English copper industry struggled. If high-quality Swedish copper was used for some of the St. Patrick coins, then the differences in size and composition may be due to a change in the availability of planchets or raw copper. That is, it might be that halfpence were made from Swedish or other high grade copper while farthings were from domestic sources of lesser quality. The existence of two coin sizes might also imply two entirely different production dates since Sweden's dominance of the European copper industry came after 1670. Though an untested idea, small amounts of a more valuable metal, such as silver, might have been added to the smaller coins to increase their value to a halfpence each. It is worth noting that, in 1722, William Wood added traces of silver to his coins, forming the brittle alloy that he called "Bath metal." (See below, in this chapter.) Though unlikely, it also might be that analysis of signature trace elements present in the St. Patricks' metal could reveal its sources.

A fair number of farthings are struck in silver and at least one is known in gold. The purpose of these off-metal strikings is unknown. Their use as presentation pieces seems more likely than any intent to mint circulating coins of higher denominations. Still, they exist in numbers just large enough to hint at an issue for circulation. Over the last few decades, modern forgeries of the silver and gold pieces have surfaced. Even specialists were fooled by these for a time and, hence, one should be skeptical of any off-metal specimen offered.

The mysteries deepen. While the time of American introduction of St. Patrick coins is known to be 1681 or 1682, the actual date of their creation is uncertain. This is hardly surprising since, for decades, seventeenth century Ireland had been a very troubled land. Its conquest by Elizabeth I, at the turn of the turn of the seventeenth century, left scars that have not healed, even to the present day. Under James I, large numbers of Englishmen and Scots began emigrating to Ireland, to seek a better life. Many of them settled around Ulster. The English Crown made it easy for the colonists to displace Irish landholders, in much the same way that American Indians later were removed from their ancestral lands. Discrimination against the native Irish increased as the colonial government in Dublin gained power. As the old traditions and powerful clans lost their influence, Ireland increasingly became divided along ethnic and religious lines.

In the 1630's Presbyterians in Scotland rejected royal attempts to enforce loyalty to the Anglican Church. A mercenary army, composed primarily of Irish Catholics, was assembled to invade Scotland and force compliance. The invasion never occurred, but elements of the army regrouped with the aim of eliminating the "Ulster Scots" from Ireland. When the reconstituted army joined Catholic peasants who already were committing atrocities against their Protestant neighbors, a reactionary Scottish army, under Robert Monroe, sailed to Ireland to intervene.*

The situation exploded with the Ulster Rebellion of 1641. The rebellion began as a populist uprising by Irish Catholic peasants, spurred by the local aristocracy. It was met with harsh reprisals from the colonial government in Dublin. To regain control, in 1642, the Catholic aristocracy formed an alternative confederation government that existed for six years. This Catholic Confederation held Kilkenny as its seat of government.

Charles I then was embroiled in the English Civil Wars and was forced to soften his anti-Catholic views. He began courting the Confederation for its military resources. Throughout the 1640's, Ireland was a seething, violent mix of discontented factions: Royalists, rebelling Puritans, Catholics and the old Irish who clung to their traditions and wanted to rid the country of all foreign interlopers. During this period, the Vatican supported its Irish flock, periodically sending emissaries and aid in various forms.

Finally, in 1650, the year after Charles I's beheading, Oliver Cromwell pacified Ireland with a crushing invasion. Before the long conflict, two-thirds of good Irish land was owned by Catholics. By 1660 and the Restoration of Charles II, ownership was two-thirds Protestant.[373] Charles II knew that the ruinous state of Ireland presented an untenable situation and, in the decade that followed his return, began half-hearted efforts to rebuild the country. Somewhere, sometime, between the rending asunder and the attempts at rebuilding, amid the turmoil of Charles I and the tense calm of Charles II, came the St. Patrick coppers.

* The bloodthirsty Scottish interveners, known as Covenanters, agreed in 1638 to oppose Charles's requirement that they become Episcopalians. During the English Civil War, they aligned themselves with Parliament.

The Charles I and Charles II Camps

In the nineteenth century Sylvester Crosby, Dr. Edward Maris and Dr. Aquilla Smith, the dean of Irish numismatists, all offered similar litanies of early sources that assign St. Patrick coins to various periods. Apparently, he earliest source known to them was John Evelyn's 1697 work, *Numismata.*[*] Evelyn categorized the silver pieces as medals and associated them with the reign of Charles II (1660 to 1685.)[374] Another 1697 reference, of which Crosby, Maris and Smith probably were unaware, came from John Sharp, the Archbishop of York. Sharp described the St. Patrick coins as money rather than as medals, but expressed uncertainty as to the time of their issue.[375] Ralph Thoresby, an antiquarian who inherited a substantial coin cabinet and then built it up even more, may have been the first writer to assume original circulation as halfpence and farthings when he described the St. Patrick coinage in 1715. Thoresby also concurred with the Charles II dating.[376]

Walter Harris, in his 1745 publication of James Ware's works, also assigned the St. Patrick coins to the Charles II period. He may have been the first to call out the fact that the arms of Dublin appear on the halfpence. He agreed with Evelyn that the silver pieces are medals, aided in his conviction by the observation that two silver examples he had seen, from the same dies as the copper pieces, were milled. Since copper coins were never milled, he concluded that all must represent medals.[377]

Other circumstances point to 1670's circulation and, in some cases, to 1670's origins. Michael Dolley concluded that St. Patrick coppers were minted in Dublin as part of a 1670's movement away from underweight tokens and toward larger coins with metal content that approximated their respective face values.[378]

Similarly, Michael Hodder cited the arms of Dublin on halfpence reverses as an indication of co-existence with tokens issued around 1675. Moreover, at least one St. Patrick farthing was found in the ruins of the sunken yacht, *Mary,* that sank in March 1675, confirming existence of the coppers by the mid-1670's.[379] By then, early regal halfpence and farthings were circulating in England and could have provided a basic weight model for St. Patrick coinage.

St. Patrick coins circulated on the Isle of Man at least until 1679 when the Manx legislature demonetized them. Dr. Brian J. Danforth provided a possible explanation for Manx circulation by noting the connection between James Butler, Lord Ormond, who served as Lord Lieutenant of Ireland, and the Earls of Derby, who controlled the Isle of Man. (See below.)[380]

Dr. Aquilla Smith also was in the Charles II camp. He examined the relative weights of the copper specimens and noted that the weights specified by the Kilkenny government for its copper coinage do not line up with those of the St. Patrick coppers. By Smith's calculations, a Confederation halfpenny was to be minted at ninety grains, or sixty-four to the Troy pound.[†] Ninety grains fits within the ninety to ninety-six grain range that William Martin Leake observed for St. Patrick farthings, but is outside the 130 to 135 grain range that he cited for the

---

[*] The full title is *Numismata: A Discourse of Medals, Antient [sic, "archaic form of ancient'] and Modern. Together with some Account of Heads and Effigies of Illustrious, and Famous Persons, in Sculps, and Taille-Douce, of Whom we have no Medals extant and Of the Use to be derived from them. To which is added A Digression concerning Physiognomy.* Printed in London, for Benjamin Tooke, in 1697.

[†] A Troy pound equates to 5,760 grains. It is not clear to this author whether the 7,000 grain avoirdupois standard should have been used. In that case, a Confederation halfpenny would have weighed 109.375 grains. In either case, Smith's argument holds.

halfpence. Smith used these findings, the pronounced style differences between the St. Patrick coppers and those known to have been made by the Confederation and the apparent suspension of private tokens in Dublin between 1659 and 1663 as evidence to conclude that the St. Patrick coppers are private tokens, minted at some time between 1660 and 1680.[381]

The Confederation called only for halfpence and farthings. If J. Earl Massey was correct in calling the larger coppers three-farthing pieces, then Smith's argument is strengthened and direct production of St. Patrick coins by the Confederation is all the more unlikely.

St. Patrick coppers exhibit some unusual physical features. Their edges are reeded, a bit like modern half dollars, quarters and dimes. On specie, this practice is used to thwart those who would shave metal from the edges of coins. On the St. Patrick coins, it is probably an anti-counterfeiting measure since shaving copper would not have been profitable. Today, edge reeding is accomplished by striking coins within a collar. The blank expands during striking, pressing against the collar to impart an edge design. In the seventeenth century, reeding and edge lettering *generally* were done with a machine that applied pressure as the blank was rolled across a flat edge die.

Denis Diderot's 18th century illustration of an edging device called a Castaigne machine.[382] (Image used through the courtesy of Dover Publishing.)

As were the rose farthings and later plugged tin issues, most St. Patrick coins are bi-metallic in that brass *splashers* were applied to both denominations, presumably to further combat counterfeiting. As the coins were being struck, a molten drop or a flake of brass was applied where the crown appears above the king. After striking, this gave the appearance of a golden crown. The molten drop method seems to have been used on St. Patrick coins since some splashers appear to have, for lack of a better term, splashed. (See the halfpenny below.) Some specimens have gouges in the crown area, probably from attempts to remove what was perceived to be gold. A few specimens are without any evidence of splashers. Apparently these were either simple errors of omission or the result of production shortcuts. These features are further evidence against the involvement of the Catholic Confederation. Neither brass "splashers" nor edge markings are found on their specie. Why would they go to the trouble of making a predominantly copper issue difficult to counterfeit and not do so for more valuable coins?

Other early writers subscribed to the theory that the St. Patrick coins should be associated with the time of Charles I rather than Charles II. In 1724, for example, Bishop Nicholson assigned them to the time of Charles I (overall, 1625 to 1649) and noted that the coins were "still common in Copper and Brass." He also recognized the coppers as halfpence and farthings. By his reckoning, the time of issue was around 1641 and they were struck by "...Papists, when they rebelled in Ireland and massacred the Protestants, pretending to act under the King's authority."[383]

Leake may have been the first to note the odd relative weights of the two sizes of coppers as well as the first to suggest that they were coins authorized by the Catholic Confederation.[384]

Little analogy to the St. Patrick coins may be seen in the Confederation's seal that depicts a crown, a harp and a dove. The seal's dominant features, a cross and a flaming heart, are missing from known coins of the Irish Confederation.

Maris noted that other writers, such as [J.] Simon and [?] Humphrey, joined Leake and Nicholson in asserting a 1641 or 1642 date and Catholic mint origins.[385] For his part, Simon referred to a contemporary plan, which the Earl of Castlehaven was asked to submit, for founding an order of knights to honor St. Patrick. Simon asserted that the coins were made in conjunction with the founding of the order. He also took the view that the silver pieces were intended by the Kilkenny government to pass as shillings. Smith refuted Simon's knighthood theory on the grounds that no evidence exists that such an order was formed until years later.[386]

In his 1881 work, The Coins of New Jersey, Maris sided with the Charles I camp. Maris apparently became convinced of this dating when he viewed uncirculated specimens whose kings, in his opinion, indisputably depict Charles I. He further argued that, being unauthorized, the coins would have been slow to enter circulation. Consequently, large numbers of them could have survived for the four decades between the 1641 rebellion and Newby's coming to America.[387] Always the diplomat, Sylvester Crosby chose to give his opinion indirectly, rather than, in his words, "decide where doctors disagree," by saying that the quantities that Newby brought with him were sufficiently large to imply that St. Patrick coppers were minted not long before he brought them to America. Thus, Crosby used some of Maris's evidence, but to support an opposing view.[388]

Over a century later, Walter Breen followed Maris's lead in associating the coins with Charles I, but added the nuance that the coins were made at the Tower Mint, at the hands of Nicholas Briot, an engraver most active in the 1640's. This attribution was based on stylistic similarities and punch links between the St. Patrick coppers and other Briot efforts. Breen associated the coins with the courting of Irish Confederation mercenaries from the Ulster Rebellion to fight against Cromwell and his Parliamentary allies. Charles needed a way to pay his hired troops. If this were the case, then possession of such coins would have been an act of treason during the Commonwealth period and they almost certainly would have disappeared from circulation, at least until 1660 and the Restoration.[389]

The Other Camps

Still more theories exist. Crosby related one by Dr. Robert Cane that offers an altogether different version of the origin of the St. Patrick coppers. This theory has received considerable attention in recent discussion groups. Cane concluded that the St. Patrick coinage was minted on the continent of Europe and then shipped to Kilkenny for use by the Confederation. He proposed to call the coins "Rinuccini Confederate money," after Giovanni Battista Rinuccini, the former Archbishop of Fermo, who was sent as papal nuncio to Ireland in 1645. It is known that Rinuccini brought arms, ammunition and money in support of the Catholic cause. Though the money needed most was specie, Cane believed that Rinuccini brought the St. Patrick coppers for use by the Confederation's army.[390]

A number of research avenues have opened based on the ideas that Cane espoused. Among these are the possibilities that the St. Patrick coins were minted at the Vatican or in a country sympathetic to the Catholic cause and the possibility that skilled coiners could have been brought to Kilkenny. These theories beg an explanation for St. Patrick's Episcopalian robes, which suggest an attempt to usurp St. Patrick as an Irish, rather than a Catholic, symbol.

The obverse legend *FLOREAT*: *REX*: ("Flower the King" or "May the King Prosper") is shared by both St. Patrick coin types and is somewhat ambiguous as to its subject. If the coins were sent from the Vatican or made by the Irish Catholic Confederation government, then the meanings of the devices and legend might be somewhat different from the obvious. That is, they could mean "The king may prosper [only if he submits to the authority of the church in Rome.]"

St. Patrick's farthings depict him in the foreground, driving out a small dragon* and a host of "serpents" (pronounced "Protestants" by seventeenth century Irish Catholics.) It long has been thought possible that clues might be hidden in the assortment of symbols that appear before the saint. These include serpents, lizards, a winged beast, flying four-winged birds, a two-winged bird or bee, what may be toads, etc.. The origin of the scene may be a 1619 Leonard Gaultier engraving with many analogous symbols. A version of it appears in Thomas Messingham's 1624 work, *Florilegium Insulae Sanctorum.*† (See illustration, below.)

Though neither of the coppers is exactly like the engraving, only one other known, contemporary depiction of St. Patrick is as similar. That reference appears on merchant tokens made for Richard Grenwood, of Dublin, around 1660. Such tokens usually were denominated as farthings and were in common use between 1653 and 1672. The devices on one side of Grenwood's token depict the saint almost exactly as he appears on the St. Patrick farthings, raising the question of which came first. If Grenwood's token imitated circulating St. Patrick coins in the manner that hard times and Civil War tokens imitated U.S. cents in the nineteenth century, then St. Patrick coppers clearly existed prior to the Restoration. In the other scenario Grenwood's tokens were made first, then St. Patrick coppers were made after the Restoration. In either case, it is likely that the Gaultier engraving either was influential in the design of both St. Patrick coppers and Grenwood tokens, or that all three shared a common inspiration.

On St. Patrick farthings, the church appears to the saint's *left* and his right hand is extended outward, palm-up. The church is absent from the halfpence, having been replaced by a shield that bears the arms of Dublin. Behind the shield is a group of followers, segregated by gender. Other followers watch St. Patrick from his right side. Their numbers vary, with six to eight men and three or four women. The legend above St. Patrick and his followers reads *ECCE GREX* ("Behold the Flock.") The followers are missing from the farthings and the legend is changed to *QUIESCAT PLEBS* ("Let the People be at Peace,") an appropriate mantra for the besieged Charles I, but one that could also refer to Restoration era attempts to pacify and rebuild Ireland.

---

* Breen saw instead a Pegasus, or winged horse, in Gaultier's engraving, an observation that eludes this author. A Pegasus usually is interpreted as the muse of poets. Breen thought that it symbolized satirical or seditious poetry of the type that a ruling regime would seek to drive from the country. (Breen, Encyclopedia, p.34.) Dragons symbolized, in European medieval lore, the personal evils that challenge the character of every mortal. Tales of virtuous knights slaying dragons generally are allegories for men overcoming their personal flaws.

† *Florilegium Insulae Sanctorum* (Paris, 1624) means "Anthology of Island Holies." Messingham's book is very rare. However, reproductions of Gaultier's engraving are accessible in other texts.

Leonard Gaultier's engraving. A church appears in the distance, behind St. Patrick and to his right. He is surrounded by a flock of lesser followers, all in prayer. The eight followers to the saint's right are men, while the five to his left are women.[391] *They appear not as peasants, but as well-dressed citizens. The robed and haloed saint raises his right hand in an expression of blessing. He wears a double-peaked bishop's mitre* and carries a staff that is topped with a double-beamed, metropolitan or Lorraine cross. An angel flies above, wielding a scroll that proclaims in Latin that "Here [in St. Patrick] is the voice of Ireland," (*Haec est vox Hibernigenarium.*) Another scroll, above, reads* Veni adiuua nos, *or "Come [and] be with us." Source: Harry Ransom Humanities Research Center. The University of Texas at Austin.*

(Top) St. Patrick "farthing," Breen-208 variety family. The obverse depicts a kneeling, harp-playing king. The reverse features an image of St. Patrick with symbols before him and a church in the background.
(Bottom) Halfpenny, Vlack 3-C variety. Note the arms of Dublin and the "flock."

On the farthings, the saint's staff is topped by a double-beamed cross, as in the engraving. On halfpence, however, the staff ends in a shepherd's crook and the saint's right hand holds a trefoil such as that with which St. Patrick allegedly taught his subjects about the Trinity.† On some rare farthing varieties, St. Patrick is depicted with a nimbus, or halo, as in the engraving. Forms of the churches depicted on St. Patrick farthings vary. The church depicted on the engraving and on some farthings may be one that stood at Armagh, built on or near the site of Patrick's original church. St. Patrick is said to have been given the crozier of Christ and to have kept it in the church at Armagh. Even earlier, Armagh was an important regional capital for Celtic Ireland. Given that Armagh's church building was burned in 1642, it is conceivable that the farthings could commemorate its memory. The church in Gaultier's engraving is surrounded by a wall and has in front of it a bell- or watchtower. Its surroundings are rural,

* A mitre is a decorated cloth cap. By the seventeenth century, mitres had evolved into a form with twin peaks as seen on the coins.

† Despite St. Patrick lore, snakes never have inhabited Ireland and there is no real evidence that he used a trefoil to represent the Trinity. One school of thought questions whether St. Patrick even represents a single, actual person. Central to this argument is the variety of dialects used in writings attributed to him.

the landscape rolling and wooded. Whether these features were literal or merely intended to convey pastoral calm is a question to be answered. Contemporary images of Irish churches might help reveal the identity of the structure depicted by Gaultier. That halfpence refer to Dublin and farthings to a possible other location could support the theory of distinct issues.

A booklet published in 1832 by Henry William Talbot, first proprietor of the Leinster Express, gives yet another view. The article that the booklet contains allegedly was copied from an old manuscript in the possession of a gentleman from Portarlington, though it is not clear just whose manuscript is referenced. The text unambiguously describes St. Patrick coppers and asserts that some were coined in the Castle of Lea, by order of the Catholic Confederation, after Lord Castlehaven briefly captured several Queens County castles. The nominal value of the coppers is said to have been discounted by the fact that prices became inflated, negatively impacting those who had accepted them. The article then takes an odd turn by asserting that the coppers struck at Lea are scarce and were marked with an "L," under St. Patrick and under King David. [392] No examples known to this author exhibit this characteristic.

Even if the serpents, lizards and dragons on the farthings can be explained away as beasts being driven from Ireland, two creatures remain to vex. The first is a four-winged bird that flies ahead of the saint. In spite of recent claims that a four-winged bird existed in prehistoric China, such a creature appears to have been rare or non-existent in Irish lore. Curiously, however, the *Book of Armagh*, a very early illuminated version of the gospels, depicts St. Mark as a four-winged eagle. Another farthing denizen, variously described as a pig, a rabbit or a toad, actually resembles a small bush in the Gaultier engraving.

For centuries Dublin was represented by three flaming watch towers that punctuated its city wall. The flames symbolized zeal for defense of the city, not its burning. In time, the three towers evolved into three full castles, with watch towers at each of their ends. These symbols appear in an oval shield on St. Patrick halfpence. On many halfpence specimens, the six towers are clear, but the castle walls between them are poorly struck and cannot easily be discerned. Consequently, the watchtowers can sometimes resemble six sheaves of wheat.

The king depicted as both coins' central obverse device is by most accounts, the Biblical King David, kneeling while he plays a very Irish looking harp and gazes up at the golden crown that floats in the heavens. On some halfpence varieties, the king kneels on a tiled or checkerboard floor. When this feature is represented on farthings, the coins' reduced size causes the tiles' shapes to be distended. Breen mistook these odd shapes for creatures, calling them "sea beasts."[393] Tiled floors graced many royal, parliamentary and lesser halls of the seventeenth century and also appear in a David-with-harp woodcut from the 1516 *De Bibel Int Carte*, commonly called "The Antwerp Bible." [394] Alternately, the tiles might have been inspired by a 1641 Nuremburg Portugaloser, a thaler-size silver coin whose depiction of David is almost identical to the king on the St. Patrick halfpence.[395] David also appears with his harp, but without the tiled floor, on a Bern psalmenfennig of 1659 to 1680 and on a gold coin of Pope Clement X, issued by the Vatican during his 1670 to 1676 papacy.[396]

A figure very like the obverse king appears in a booklet associated with Charles I. *Eikon Basilike* ("The King's Image") apparently is a combination of Charles's own attempts to justify his actions and efforts by others to pay tribute to him. Its frontispiece depicts a kneeling king, sans harp, gazing upward at a glowing heavenly crown. His earthly crown lays forsaken on the floor beside him. The engraving was done by William Marshal, an artisan to the court of

Charles I, and is believed to have been inspired by Titian's painting of St. Catherine in prayer before a crucified Christ. Titian's painting was part of Charles I's personal collection. If Marshal's engraving were the only image of a kneeling king from the period, one might conclude, as did Maris and others, that the St. Patrick coppers depict Charles I.[397]

However, the truth may be more complex. The floating heavenly crown in the *Eikon Basilike* frontispiece is an eastern, or Jerusalem crown that has at each of its points a Star of David. The cast-aside crown is the that of an earthly king. On the St. Patrick coppers, however, the crown types are reversed. This led researcher Oliver Hoover to conclude that the St. Patrick coppers depict David and that their association with Charles I is at best unsupported and at worst simply a wrong conclusion.[398] Still, an Irish medal of the period depicts Charles I opposite a glowing earthly crown held over a shepherdless flock by a divine hand that extends from the clouds. Thus, the question of crowns, in this author's opinion, remains open. The real death knell for the Catholic Confederation theory of origin seems to ring from the robes of St. Patrick on the coins. They are Episcopalian, not Catholic.[399]

The Old Testament King David is depicted playing his harp on countless images that date back many centuries (e.g., in the ninth century *Utrecht Psalter*.) In George Wither's 1635 book of emblems, and elsewhere, David plays a harp and gazes at God's glory from the same position as the king on the St. Patrick coins. The text below Wither's emblem describes the Lord's love for music and harmony.[400]

At the very least Charles I identified closely with King David and with music, a fact that was well-known and celebrated in the seventeenth century. Favorites of Charles I included the poet Henry Lawes and his musically ingenious brother, William. William Lawes was so dear to Charles that he was appointed Composer to the King. When William died in battle, fighting for Charles, the King grieved more than he did for his own relatives. In 1648, after William's death, a collection of his music was published. Its dedication is written to Charles I and compares Lawes' work to a psalmist bringing work to King David for approval. It also compares the difficulties facing Charles I with those faced by David.[401] After the Restoration, Charles II continued the tradition of having court composers and musicians and might well have viewed them in the same way that his father did.

Two farthing varieties: *(Inside) Breen-213 and (Outside) Breen-212. Note: A – Splasher. B - Symbols (serpents, dragons and others.) C - Tiled floor under the king. D - Three diminishing stars in the legend. E – Breen's "Masonic" punctuation.*

Legend punctuation varies significantly on the farthings. In some cases, nothing or a simple colon follows *REX*. On other varieties, the end punctuation is a group of three periods arranged in a triangular pattern ("∴") that Breen called "Masonic."[402] Other varieties have as their end punctuation a string of four stars (two large, then two small) or three or more stars in order of descending size. Interesting reverse features are not limited to punctuation. One rare variety omits the "C" in *QVIESCAT* and is probably a simple mistake.

Nor is the obverse or "king" side without interesting symbols. On many farthing varieties, nothing appears below the King, but at least three have what looks to be an "8" or a coupled pair of annulets in that position.* Others depict a small bird or martlet below the king. A rare variety even places a bird *above* the king. These mysterious symbols may be akin to mintmarks or *differents,*† suggesting multiple mints or die makers. The large number of farthing die varieties certainly supports this idea. The multitude of varieties even might be the result of local mintages for use as communion tokens or parish membership "cards."

Halfpence varieties are differentiated not on the presence of symbols, but on punctuation, positioning of legend components, presence of the tiled floor and letter sizes. At least five halfpenny varieties separate *FLOREAT* into two parts around the crown (i.e., the legend reads *FLORE* [crown] *AT REX*..) The other halfpenny varieties use variations of *FLOREAT.* [crown]. *REX.* None of the roughly thirty halfpenny varieties is common.

A New Theory

Until December 2002, the foregoing described most of what was known about the St. Patrick coppers. Then Dr. Brian J. Danforth introduced a significant body of new research that, while not universally accepted, dramatically challenged the numismatic world's view of these pieces. A paraphrasing of Danforth's work follows, along with some editorial comments.[403]

Danforth places the probable time of issue as the 1667 to 1669 period, when Ireland was being rebuilt after the ravages of the Commonwealth era. In 1662, James Butler, Lord Ormond was appointed Lord-Lieutenant over the Dublin government. No stranger to Ireland, he found a devastated country and an unpaid army with seditious elements still loyal to the Commonwealth. He sought to help stabilize both the Irish economy and the unruly army by introducing a legitimate coinage. Charles II, to whom Ormond had remained loyal, supported him in this endeavor.

After the 1660 Restoration, Charles sought to re-establish royal coinage and to drive Commonwealth issues from circulation. To this end, the Royal Mint turned to producing silver and gold coins for England. Economic reality and production difficulties slowed their progress and led to a neglect of small copper coinage. In the absence of small change, private merchant tokens, counterfeits and cut pieces were used to fill the void. Often, the private tokens were produced by Royal Mint employees who supplemented their incomes "on the side." These tradesmen and city tokens were lightweight and were typically devalued when the time came to redeem them. Many people, especially the poor, were badly shorted in these exchanges. Moreover, the tokens' acceptance was limited to the specific area in which it was produced or introduced and they were, therefore, a poor surrogate for coinage.

If the problem was serious in England, it was catastrophic in Ireland, where many of the tokens in circulation were English rejects. The proposed solution for Ireland was another round of patent farthings such as those introduced under James I and Charles I. This time the patent was given to Sir Thomas Armstrong in 1660. (Chapter 5.) Lord Ormond and others were very much opposed to this approach and ultimately succeeded in bringing about its demise. Ormond

* An annulet is a heraldic symbol thought to derive from a chain mail link. In the usual context, it symbolizes one who defends something.

† A mintmark identifies a mint, while a different identifies the die maker or other craftsman.

knew that something better was needed to reduce Irish dependency on light weight tokens and English whims.

In 1667 he petitioned the Crown for £30,000 in farthings for Ireland. His request came in the context of the English pre-occupation with restoring regal specie coinage and on the heels of the 1665 outbreak of the plague and the 1666 fire that devastated London. As a result, the Royal Mint was not well positioned to meet the request for Irish coins. Danforth asserts that Ormond may have turned to an innovative Royal Mint engineer, Peter (or Pierre) Blondeau for help. Blondeau, a Frenchman, followed in the footsteps of his countryman, Eloye Mestrelle. (Recall that Mestrelle had tried unsuccessfully to convert the Royal Mint from hammering to milling in the 1560's.) Blondeau came to England a century after Mestrelle with a new anti-counterfeiting technology of which only he had knowledge. Blondeau found that he could use an oversized screw press to impart reeding or other edge designs in one step, a dramatic improvement over competing methods. To do this, he used a one-piece collar lined with a strip into which the edge design was engraved.

This general concept was not new. Leonardo da Vinci experimented with collars as early as 1614. However, collar-based edging devices were problematic. The collars were segmented into multiple parts and were expensive to make and use. As illustrated above, the other common edging technology rolled a coin between two parallel strips, under pressure. This process was labor-intensive and expensive since it required a second step, after the coin was struck. The coin often slipped, causing the edge design to overlap itself. The process may have been suitable for thick specie coins, but not for thin minor coinage. Blondeau's process, on the other hand, was viable both economically and technically, for all coins sizes and types.

As had been the case with Mestrelle, however, mint employees opposed the new technology and succeeded in thwarting Blondeau's attempts at modernization. In spite of successful trials in which Blondeau demonstrated the superiority of his method, the technology was rejected. The opposition even accused Blondeau of counterfeiting since his trial pieces resembled regal coinage. Following the rejection, Blondeau was paid to go to Ireland during 1654 and 1655 to investigate the possibility of implementing an Irish mint. To preserve the secrecy of his technology, he worked at his own Drury House mint in London on the Strand. At about the same time, he was allowed to make a small quantity of bullion coins for English circulation. This small role was not enough to keep Blondeau from being discouraged and returning to France in 1659.

When England's coinage problems accelerated after the Restoration, a Royal Mint official, Henry Slingsby, suggested that Blondeau be invited to return. Working with his influential ally, Blondeau laid out a plan for modernizing the mint. He also was given a patent that protected his technology. With this legal protection, Blondeau was free to implement his vision. He also secured permission to participate in outside projects, a significant step toward the minting of tokens.

To facilitate modernization, the mint house that had been set aside for the Armstrong patent was appropriated, remodeled and stocked with modern equipment. Under pressure to produce, the mint used Blondeau's edging method alongside older techniques. The updated mint produced shillings through Guineas from 1662 to 1664 and later added very large and beautiful five Guinea coins. Regal copper farthings, proposed in 1665 to mitigate the token problem, were not minted until 1672. The delay was due partly to the collapse of the English copper industry and the fact that the mint still was recovering from the plague and great fire of 1665 and 1666. The attention to specie and the corresponding delay in producing coppers were particularly hard on Ireland since England's cries always were heard first.

Danforth asserts that this period would have been the logical time for Blondeau to make the St. Patrick coppers. Blondeau *may* have been the only person who possessed the technology economically to place reeded edges on small denomination coinage. Furthermore, he was familiar with the Irish situation because of his 1654 to 1655 investigations. He also owned at least five coining presses and the license to use them. Moreover, Blondeau's desire to keep his technique secret could help to account for the lack of documentation about the St. Patricks.

The timing of Lord Ormond's petition also fits this scenario. Near the end of his tenure as Dublin's Lord Lieutenant, he was silent about coinage. Reading between the lines, he may have gotten that for which he had asked. When Ormond stepped down in 1669, his successor, Lord Roberts, made no effort to propose Irish coinage. Roberts' own successor, Lord Berkeley, requested permission to stop token production in Ireland. By that time, private tokens were already on their way out because of the regulations associated with the beginning of regal copper production in 1672. Thus, Berkeley's attacks might have been aimed at the St. Patrick coppers. As if all this were not enough, Ormond was the guardian of William, Earl of Derby, between 1672 and 1676. Since the Derbies held title to the Isle of Man, this could explain the brief circulation of St. Patrick coppers there.

Some of the St. Patrick coins also seem to bear witness to Blondeau's methods: 1.) They show no sign of the edge device overlaps that characterize their contemporaries; 2.) Blondeau's large presses caused dies to fail quickly, possibly explaining the large number of farthing varieties; 3.) He is known to have had problems obtaining centered strikes and many of the surviving farthings have centering anomalies; 4.) Others exhibit what appears to be metal flow outside a broken collar. A large press striking off-center could very well have caused collar damage and collapse; and, 5.) In Paris, Blondeau studied under Nicholas Briot, who pioneered the use of oversized presses. Blondeau may well have ended up with some of Briot's puncheons. This could explain the links to other Briot products to which Walter Breen alluded. As for the weight ratio of halfpence and farthings, Slingsby is known to have advocated denominations of 3/2d, 7/4d and 5/4d as supplements to the small silver coins that were in short supply for making change. The 3/2d denomination fits well with the larger St. Patrick coins if the farthings are treated as halfpence.

Danforth makes the point that coins such as the St. Patrick's issues were possible only because of the convergence of highly skilled engineers and politicians. That these types of men were associated closely is borne out in Blondeau's 1672 will that names Slingsby, Isaac de Caux and John Colborne as the heirs to his secret process. His five screw presses went to Slingsby. The combined value of the hard assets and the potential value of the process were considerable. Colburne's will names his own brother and Slingsby and says that if Slingsby fails to perform, a hint at continuance of the operation, Peter Johnson would receive his share. Johnson was the man who developed the die hardening process that enabled Blondeau's technology. Peter la Castill, the technician who made the collars for applying edge designs, also received a bequest. Next to Blondeau, the most important player may have been Lord Ormond, who provided the need for coinage. It appears that Dr. Danforth has provided a well-reasoned and possible, if not likely, solution to the mystery of St. Patrick coppers. Nevertheless, doubts remain and his theory is far from universal acceptance.

Another (Remote) Possibility

Many of the details of the theory "fit" remarkably well. However, in the natural course of critical review, others began to raise doubts about some of Danforth's findings. In a search for further evidence to either support or refute his theory, this author found an often overlooked knight-engineer who, during the same rough time period, sought to create for Ireland a counterfeit-resistant copper coinage. Information about the knight, Sir Edward Ford, is, at best, far from conclusive. Nevertheless, his story deserves further research even if it fails to offer the "smoking gun" for the St. Patrick coppers.

Though many entries in the journals of Parliament refer to the affairs of the Royal Mint and Ireland, mentions of St. Patrick coins are conspicuously absent. Samuel Pepys, a prominent civil servant under Charles II, was associated with Henry Slingsby, Pierre Blondeau and the machinations of the Royal Mint. Pepys kept a very detailed diary that dwells at length on money and mints. Yet, he made no note of St. Patrick coinage. It is unlikely that an operation capable of producing large numbers of dies and coins, using a revolutionary new process, would have escaped Pepys's curiosity and pen.

For this author, a new adventure began innocently with Thomas Coonan's 1954 work, *The Irish Catholic Confederacy and the Puritan Revolution.* Coonan wrote that the Confederation government, to relieve the scarcity of coin and as a show of "...concord between Charles I and the Irish people," established a mint for half-crowns and coppers, specifically the St. Patrick coppers.[404]

At first glance, Coonan appears to confirm the 1641 to 1642 mintage period and the Catholic Confederation as the origin for the St. Patrick coppers, though the subject does not seem to be mentioned elsewhere in his book. It might be easier to accept Coonan's "obvious" conclusion were it not for the fact that coins known to have been made by the Kilkenny government are so different from the St. Patricks. Moreover, as noted by Smith, the weights of the St. Patrick coins do not match up with those authorized by the Kilkenny government.[405] Could Coonan have seen references to the Catholic Confederation's mint, examined examples of St. Patrick coppers and, possessing no other information, erroneously assumed that the two were the same?

As contemporary sources, Coonan quotes Thomas Carte[406] and Richard Bellings.[407] This author obtained an electronic copy of one Coonan source, Carte's *History of the Life of James, Duke of Ormonde; containing an account of the most remarkable affairs of his time, and particularly of Ireland under his government: With an appendix and a Collection of Letters*, in which the St. Patrick coins receive no mention. The Carte papers, which Coonan also quotes, are accessible electronically, in calendar form, at the website for the Access to Archives (A2A) program and Oxford University's Bodleian Library, Special Collections and Western Manuscripts department.[408] So far, no undeniable reference to the St. Patrick coppers has been found in the Carte papers. If Coonan's conclusions about St. Patrick coins actually were based on early source material then that material must be contained in Bellings' work, which is itself rare and has thus far eluded this author.

Perhaps another explanation for the St. Patrick coins exists. The Carte Papers contain a very interesting 1664 petition by Sir Edward Ford (or Forde, or fforde,) complete with odd spellings common to the period:

To the Kings most Excellent Majestie etc.[? script unclear]

The humble petition of Sir Edward Ford

Shewith **:.** [Note the similarity to Breen's "Masonic" punctuation.]
That in the December 1660 your Majestie granted Sir Thomas Armstrong a pattent heere of 21 years for the sole making of Farthings in Ireland at the yearly rent of 16l:13s:4d

That his farthings being ordonary ones & easily counterfeited and nothing offered for the retaking them, hee could never doo any good in it, your Majesties rent lost and hee dead,

That your petitioner hath a new Invented way of making brass or copper Tokens of 1: 2: & 3: farthings which prevents counterfeits wherein my Lord Liutenat is satisfied and yet your petitioner with all will take order that his Agents who vent [? script unclear] *his shall retake them,*

Which will give your people there extraordinary content: very many of them not being able to live without them, and so necessitated to take unlycensed Tokens which every pety tradesman make & yet refuseth to retake, as he pleaseth, to the extream losse to all, the meaner Sort:

Prayeth **:.**

Your Majesties gracious letter for the passing to[? script unclear] *your petitioner: a grant in Ireland for his new invented Tokens & though most chargaboll yet for the Same rent & Time Sir Thomas had for his comon farthings, with such clauses as have been formerly*

And hee Shall [the] *Ques*[tion] *pray* [symbol, possibly a question mark][409]

Several aspects of Ford's petition are worth noting:

- His tokens are differentiated from Armstrong's "comon" or "ordonary" farthings in three ways: 1.) They are made through a newly invented process. Might the new process refer to the use of splashers or to the edge-reeding of base metal coinage? 2.) The new method prevents counterfeiting. 3.) The new proposal has a formal mechanism for redeeming the tokens, thereby making them superior both to Armstrong's farthings and to "unlycensed" tradesmen tokens.

- His tokens are to include both three- and two-farthing denominations. Given that the relative weights of the two sizes of St. Patrick copper coins hover around the ratio of 3:2, it is conceivable that they could represent the three- and two-farthing denominations that are mentioned in Ford's proposal. Even if not, the proposal clearly establishes that a three-farthing piece was being considered at the time.

- His tokens are made of copper "or" brass. Unfortunately, the petition does not say "copper with a brass splasher." Nor does it say "copper and brass." Both terms were used to describe copper and copper alloys of the period.

- The "*Lord Liutenat,*" presumably referring to Ormond, is satisfied with at least the anti-counterfeiting qualities of Ford's proposal.

- Ford asks for the same terms as were given to Sir Thomas Armstrong in 1660. Though Armstrong's patent was supposed to have a term of twenty years, his farthings, which were similar in form to earlier Harrington, Lennox, Richmond, Maltravers and "rose" pieces, apparently were never minted in large quantities. Their light weights, alone, bred rejection and could have opened the door for a new, more substantial issue.

- Ford's proposal promises to give the Irish "extraordinary content." Could this be the peace alluded to by St. Patrick farthings, with the motto "QUIESCAT PLEBS"?

Who was Sir Edward Ford?

He was born around 1605 at Up Park, Harting Parish, West Sussex, the first son of Sir William and Anna Ford. The Fords were an old Devonshire family that had grown prosperous in the wool trade and, by 1546, had begun building their estate at Up Park.[410 *] For the next century and a half, they were involved in countless real estate transactions in and around Harting.

Sir William Ford was known as "the soape projector."[411] That is, he promoted soap. Mark Newby, the tallow chandler who brought St. Patrick coins to America, was only about eight years old when Sir William died in 1646. Nevertheless, the tallow and soap trades might have afforded them shared acquaintances.

Sir Edward's mother was the daughter of Sir Edward Caryll, of West Harting. The Carylls were an old Catholic family who retained their faith throughout the tumultuous Commonwealth period. Later, members of the Caryll family took the side of the Jacobites.[412]

No evidence confirming Sir Edward as a Catholic has been found. Nevertheless, both the Carylls and the Fords, including Sir Edward, were heavily involved in business of Harting's once Catholic church, the Church of St. Mary the Virgin. Memorials and monuments to members of both families occupied various spots throughout the building. For example, a silver paten, given to the church in 1671 by Ford's daughter, bears the family arms. Beside an old ruined chancel from the early seventeenth century sits a tomb house, reserved for Caryll family monuments.[413] The church later became known as the Church of St. Mary's and St. Gabriel's and is now Anglican. It dates to the fourteenth century and, as do many churches from that period, resembles some of the ones depicted on St. Patrick farthings.

A search for Ford family symbols that might tie to the St. Patrick coppers produced only disappointment. The Ford escutcheon is described as "azure three crowned lions or." Its three crowned golden lions on a blue background appear to have no parallel to the coppers. However, the Caryll escutcheon, described as "argent three bars and in chief three martlets sable" ("three silver/white bars topped by three black martlets,") does share its footless birds with some St. Patrick farthings. Probably by coincidence, the escutcheon of the Husses,

---

[*] Up Park took on much of its current grandeur at the hands of Ford Grey, the grandson of Sir Edward, who became the Earl of Tankerville. In the nineteenth century it was, for a time, the home to the author, H.G. Wells, who was the son of an Up Park maid and of one of its groundskeepers. (Meade-Fetherstonhaugh and Martin, pp.102-103.)

another prominent Harting family bears ermine that, as depicted, closely resemble "creatures" observed on some St. Patrick farthings.

After entering Oxford's Trinity College in 1621 as a gentleman commoner, Edward Ford left without achieving a degree. Even so, by 1629 he was named a "virtuoso" student of Oxford's "Inner Temple." Engineering appears to have been Ford's first love. In 1641, at his own expense, he attempted to build a navigable canal to alleviate London's water shortage. When civil war erupted, Ford remained fiercely loyal to Charles I. He was an officer in the kings army from the beginning of the first civil war and in 1642, Charles made him High Sheriff of Sussex. Ford was captured after the siege of Chichester and was sent to London, where his release probably was secured by his brother-in-law, Henry Ireton, a Cromwell stalwart and future commissary-general of the New Model Army. By June 1643 Ford was at it again, threatening Southampton with an army of Royalists. On October 4, he was knighted at Oxford and two months later, he captured Arundel and its castle. He was made governor, but could not hold the town. The remainder of his military career saw him twice being held as a hostage and then as a prisoner in the Tower, after which he retired to the continent.[414]

In 1647, the Queen solicited his aid in preparing the way for Lord Berkeley's ill-fated negotiations with the army. For several years afterward, Ford was looked upon with great suspicion. In 1649, just after Charles I lost his head, Ford was listed by parliament as delinquent. In 1656, however, Oliver Cromwell spared Ford the indignity of the decimation tax that was levied against Royalists. Cromwell also encouraged Ford in a successful project in which water from the Thames was raised ninety-three feet to London's highest streets. The same technology was used elsewhere in the country to drain mines and flooded lands. [415]

Though he never quite rose to the level of the Royal Society, Ford was a philosopher and economist. In 1666, he wrote the pamphlet, *Experimental Proposals how the King may have Money to pay and maintain his Fleets, with Ease to the People; London may be rebuilt, and all Proprietors satisfied; Money may be lent at 61. per cent. On Pawns, and the fishing trade set up, and all without Straining or Thwarting any of our Laws and Customs.* At the end of it, he penned *Defence of Bill-credit.*[416]

This pamphlet came just after London's great fire and offered a way to rebuild the city, while lowering taxes by providing an alternate source of government income. In it, Ford proposed paper money on the security of taxation and a place for "Banks of Loan upon Pawns, truly called Mounts of Piety." He also claimed to have invented a means of protecting "Bill-Money" from counterfeiting.[417]

Pepys and Others on Ford

Ford's exploits did not escape the pen of Samuel Pepys. Pepys was little more than a clerk with delusions of grandeur. Yet, he floated among the most influential denizens of Restoration England. Among the many famous diaries that survive from the period, his stands alone for its flighty, moody, self-aggrandizing style and the sheer breadth of its subjects. Pepys' incessant upsucking acquainted him with mints and minters, subjects about which he often wrote. Henry Slingsby, Master or Co-Master of the Mint from 1662 to 1680, for example, appears many times in Pepys' diary. Pepys' first reference to Sir Edward Ford appears in an entry of September 13, 1664:

...after dinner at the Fishmongers hall, where we met the first time upon the Fishery committee – and many good things discoursed of concerning making of Farthings, which was proposed as a way of raising money for this business;[418]

A second, non-numismatic reference comes eight days later in connection with an invention for curing smoky chimneys:

This day my wife showed me bills printed, wherein her father, with Sir John Collidon and Sir Edward Ford, have got a patent for curing of smoky chimneys.[419]

The next reference by Pepys, recorded on November 6, 1663, alludes again to Ford's desire to make farthings and have them be used to help fund the Committee of the Fisheries:

And then, Sir G[eorge] Carteret being gone, I took my Lord aside, who doth give me the best advice he can; and telling me how there are some projectors, by name Sir Edwd Ford, who would have the making of Farthings, and out of that give so much to the King for the maintenance of the Fishery; but my Lord doth not like that, but would have it go as they offered the last year; and so upon my desire, he promises me when it is seasonable to bring me into the commission with others, if any *of them take. And I perceive he and Mr. [William] Coventry*[420] *are resolved to follow it hard.*[421]

The footnote to Pepys' diary entry states that Ford proposed to make his farthings from Swedish copper. The footnote goes on to say that the Fishery Company, Under James, Duke of York and later King James II, supported the proposal, as did the Queen mother. The footnote also says that the proposal was once more approved in a 1664 meeting [of the Fishery Company?][422] This author is presently searching for documents that support these details.

Ford's proposal was ultimately rejected on the protests of Prince Rupert, the well-liked cousin of Charles II who wanted his own coinage patent. (Prince Rupert is better known for inventing the mezzo tint method of printing, for his military career and for being a competent artist.)[423] Dispute also arose about payments to the king. Ford offered 6s 8d in the pound, a plan to which the officials of the mint were hostile. The plan was revived in 1667 and 1668, apparently without effect. Evidently, officials at the mint were still opposed to it. Instead, according to Pepys' editors, Ford was allowed to make farthings for Ireland.[424]

On January 4, 1667, the following entry is recorded in the *Calendar of State Papers Domestic* for Charles II:

Order at a general meeting of the Fishing Company, approving the proposal of Sir Edw. Ford and the petition grounded thereon, and appointing a committee to present the same to the King, and to prepare arguments in its favour, and attend the Council to speak in its defence. Annexing,

I. Petition of the Governor and Company of the Royal Fishing to the King, for a grant of the sole power of coining and issuing farthings, not to be counterfeited, according to a proposition made by Sir Edw. Ford, he giving security to prevent the export of gold and silver, by importation of counterfeit farthings; to hinder prejudice to the people by taking back farthings at the same rate; to give 21s. worth of farthings for 20s. silver, and 5s. out of every 20s. to the fishing company.

II. Statement of the inconveniences and losses resulting from the issue of tradesmen's tokens, especially in the late contagion and fire, and yet that the profits of them are such that they are made, in spite of an order to the contrary.[425]

Pepys' next reference to Ford came on December 3, 1664. In it, Pepys displays a quaint bit of either genuine excitement or sarcastic displeasure at seeing the proposal again:

Up, and at the office all the morning, and at noon to Mr. Cutler's, and there dined with Sir W. Rider and him, and thence Sir W. Rider and I by coach to White Hall to a Committee of the Fishery; there only to hear Sir Edward Ford's proposal about farthings, wherein, O God! to see almost every body interested for him; only my Lord Annesly, who is a grave, serious man. My Lord Berkeley was there, but is the most hot, fiery man in discourse, without any cause, that ever I saw, even to breach of civility to my Lord Anglesey, in his discourse opposing to my Lord's. At last, though without much satisfaction to me, it was voted that it should be requested of the King, and that Sir Edward Ford's proposal is the best yet made. Thence by coach home....[426]

It is worth noting that both John Berkeley and George Carteret were present for different airings of Ford's proposal. Both men were key figures in the founding of New Jersey and Berkeley eventually replaced Ormond as Ireland's Lord Lieutenant.

Of Sir Edward Ford, the Oxford alumni chronicler, Anthony Wood (b.1632, d.1695,) wrote:

Some time after his majesty's restoration he invented a new way of farthings , of which he made demonstration to the king and council so plainly, that they were satisfied that they could not possibly be counterfeited, and that one farthing could not be like another, but that they should differ in some little thing. *And having then a design to get a patent for the making of them for England, was put aside by prince Rupert, and at length was content with one only for Ireland: To which place taking journey soon after, he died there before he could effect his design.*[427]

Might the "little" differences between Ford's farthings correspond with the many varieties of St. Patrick farthings?

Sir Edward Ford died in Ireland on September 3, 1670. His remains are interred in the family burial area at Harting's principal church, the Church of St. Mary and St. Gabriel.[428] The burial took place on October 15, 1670. His wife had died earlier. Their only surviving daughter, Catherine, had married Ralph Lord Grey of Warke. By his will, through Grey, Ford's home, Up Park, became the property of the Earls of Tankerville until its sale in 1745.[429] Given that the Up Park estate sits atop a high hill, one can imagine that for his entire life at home, Ford had looked out at a view very like that on the St. Patrick farthings.

It is written that Ford's death came before his plan could be carried out. However, one source indicated that Ford had been in Ireland for some time before his death, preparing for the operation.[430] Unfortunately, Ford's will makes no mention of coinage or mint equipment.[431] What, then, became of the work that he had done over the six years between his 1664 proposal and his death? Might the Irish have made use of it?

Clearly, it cannot be said with certainty that Sir Edward Ford made or provided the means for making the St. Patrick coppers. But, neither can it be said with certainty that he did not. Two other documents are currently being researched for information about Sir Edward: *The Calendar of State Papers Domestic of Charles II*, a chronological summary of Restoration era state documents and *The Harleian Miscellany*, John Harley's eclectic multi-volume collection of seventeenth century essays and reports.

With so much uncertainty, any new bit of information, however unlikely it is to contain the absolute answers, is worthy of exploration. Such is the case with information surrounding Sir Edward Ford, whose attempts to gain the coining privilege at the very least present a curious set of circumstances.

Oddball Heresies and Speculations

Recall that some St. Patrick farthings appear to feature martlets, which are small footless birds. In heraldry, martlets symbolize a fourth son. Traditionally, the fourth son received no property in the disposition of his father's estate. Recall too that, by 1660 and the Restoration, ownership of viable Irish land was two-thirds Protestant whereas before 1640, it had been two-thirds Catholic. Given the shift, Irish Catholics might well have viewed themselves as "fourth sons." Under Charles II, reforms allowed limited reclamation of Catholic lands. If the birds that appear on some St. Patrick farthings are indeed martlets, then perhaps they were intended as symbols of empathy and as reminders of the land reforms.

Even more speculatively, popular books, both fictional and non-fictional, assert the existence of a strong Anglo-Judaic link. Whether such a link exists, whether anyone recognized it in the seventeenth century and whether the Stuarts believed or even pretended to believe it are fringe ideas to consider. To explore these questions requires flirting with ideas that lie outside the body of accepted scholarship about events in early church history. Nevertheless, "A little folly, now and then, is relished by the wisest men." – Willy Wonka.[432]

Though modern scholars question the very existence of King David, the Bible recognizes him as the direct ancestor of Jesus Christ. Great controversy arises from the idea that the Stuarts are from Christ's bloodline and that the secrets of how the lineage was transferred to Europe were preserved by secret societies. The bloodline is asserted by some to be the true meaning of the *Holy Grail* (that is, the "San Gréal," a corruption of "Sangréal," or "Holy Blood.")[433] As the theory goes, Joseph of Arimethea (a.k.a., James, the Brother of Jesus) brought the Gospel and Jesus's family to France and Britannia in the first century. Joseph of Arimethea is mentioned in texts as a merchant of metals, particularly tin, who traveled to Western Europe after the Crucifixion. He supposedly was given a considerable amount of land in Somerset and there, in Glastonbury, in 63 A.D., built a small church to the scale of a Hebrew temple. This was a year after James supposedly was excommunicated in Jerusalem and is the assumed year of Mary Magdalene's death. Part of the theory holds that Mary Magdalene was, in fact, the wife of Jesus and that it was in her memory that the church at Glastonbury was dedicated. Whether these events are true or mere legend, in time and through apostolic missions, the tiny church grew.[434]

The next chapter in this theory revolves around the children of Jesus and Mary Magdalene. Their eldest son is known as Galains (or Alain) in Grail lore. Galains was celibate and, thus, the order of dynastic succession fell to the second son, Josephes. Josephes's bloodline supposedly produced the lineage that includes the seventeenth century Stuarts. According to the theory, as the Roman church matured, it sought to hide the existence of Jesus's bloodline in Britannia. The Nazarenes, the true followers of Jesus and James, along with their doctrine that Jesus was mortal, survived generations of persecution. In Ireland, the Celtic Church developed in relative isolation, with traditions that were aligned closer to the Nazarenes than to Rome.[435] The Glastonbury church also continued to grow and, by sometime in the fifth century, St. Patrick was, by some accounts, its abbot. Afterward, he moved to Ireland, where he supposedly found the tradition of Messianic lineage alive and well.[436]

As the power of the Roman Church grew, it was up to secret societies to protect the lineage tradition. In the seventeenth century, various related groups bore the responsibility. These groups were forced underground by the Puritanical repression of the Commonwealth. However, with the Restoration and a new sponsor in Charles II, they re-emerged, still clinging to Judaic precepts. If these antithetical ideas genuinely were believed by the regime of Charles II or even just used as instruments of propaganda, then it is possible that the symbolism of the St. Patrick tokens was intended to appeal to Irishmen who might believe the story of Messianic lineage. If this were the case, then they might accept the Stuarts as their true monarchs.

In this context, the image of King David and the martlet of the fourth son take on added meaning. David and, hence, Jesus and the Stuarts, descended from Judah, the fourth son of Jacob. Thus, the martlet might be taken as a symbol of the scattering of landless Jews and the settlement of certain of them in the British Isles.

Masonic Ties?

Could Breen have been correct in his use of "Masonic" to describe the triangular punctuation ("∴") on some farthings? Could the coins really be linked to Freemasonry? The checkered floor that sometimes appears beneath the King could be taken as a Masonic mark. Likewise, the "8" that appears on some farthing varieties could represent an hourglass (mortality) or the joined globes of Heaven and earth, both of which are Masonic symbols.

Though it is not clear whether any of the key players in the St. Patrick coinage were Freemasons, Henry Slingsby is known to have been an associate of Sir Robert Moray, the Restoration-era statesman, mathematician and philosopher who wrote a history of Masonry and always attached symbols of Freemasonry to his signature.[437] Moreover, John Evelyn, diarist and prominent member of the Royal Society, was an associate of Moray, Slingsby and Lord Ormond.[438]

It was under Charles II that the Royal Society emerged. This was a group of brilliant men who studied mathematics and the sciences. Famous members included Robert Boyle (alchemist, philosopher, discoverer of Boyle's Law and authority on the lore of the Holy Grail,) Robert Hooke (inventor, discoverer of micro-biology and Hooke's Law, architect and re-builder of London after the great fire of 1666,) astronomer Edmund Halley (chronicler of Halley's comet,) architect Christopher Wren, philosopher Francis Bacon and scientist/mathematician, Isaac Newton. Though his time of greatest influence came later, Newton, in particular, embraced Judaic heritage as the source of scientific knowledge. Royal Society members who were active during the time of the Commonwealth were forced underground and became known as the Invisible College.[439]

Many of these men also were Rosicrucians,* another secret society with strong ties to various shadowy groups. Rosicrucians especially were concerned with preserving and using ancient mathematics and science.[440] One of the principles that held great fascination for them was that of the *Golden Mean*, a mathematical relationship that occurs frequently in nature. The basis of the Golden Mean is an irrational number,† $f = (1+\sqrt{5})/2 = 1.61803....$ It has been asserted that, when art, architecture and music incorporate the Golden Mean in their proportions, the result is pleasing to the senses. It has also been asserted that some natural spirals and even the height of an average person divided by the distance from his or her navel to the floor approximate the Golden Mean. The Fibonacci Sequence is also an object of Rosicrucian fancy. This is an integer sequence where any given term is the sum of the previous two (i.e., 0, 1, 1=0+1, 2=1+1, 3=1+2, 5=2+3, 8=3+5,....)‡ As the sequence increases toward infinity, the ratio of a given term to the one before it approaches the Golden Mean. In a recent experiment, median weights for thirty St. Patrick halfpence and sixty farthings that appeared in recent auctions were compared. The ratio of the two median weights is about 1.62:1, very close to the Golden Mean. Could the makers of St. Patrick coins have intended to produce a naturally pleasing and harmonious coinage by incorporating the Golden Mean in the relative weights of coins?

The lineage theory also may be hidden in other symbols found on St. Patrick coins. Trinity College in Dublin holds a great Irish treasure known as *The Book of Kells*, a magnificently illuminated version of the four gospels based largely on the 384 A.D. Latin Vulgate text of St. Jerome. No one knows exactly where or when *The Book of Kells* was created, though it almost certainly originated at some time between the seventh and tenth centuries.[441] On its folios 129v and 290v, Saints Matthew, Mark, Luke and John are depicted symbolically. The symbol for St. Luke is a winged calf,[442] looking vaguely like the dragon (or Pegasus) on St. Patrick farthings. St. Luke is known both as a healer, what Ireland needed in the late seventeenth century, and as the apostle who related Jesus's genealogy. Moreover, the figures who populate the reverses of St. Patrick halfpence look very much like the men who appear on folio 7v of *The Book of Kells*. Some scholars believe that, in *The Book of Kells*, these men represent the ancestors of Jesus.[443]

The Messianic lineage theory is not without a hint of official sanction. The so-called *Stone of Destiny* or *Stone of Scone* is a flat rock that was used at the coronations of Scottish kings, stolen by the English, used in the coronations of English kings and queens and then just recently returned to Scotland. The stone's legend is that it is the pillow on which the biblical Jacob laid his head when he dreamed of a ladder to Heaven. Its existence in the British Isles is thought by some to be symbolic of the transfer of the Messianic bloodline to Europe. Though scholars now believe the Stone of Destiny to be a block of Scottish sandstone, the legend endures. Some Scots believe that the English were duped into taking a false stone and that the real one never left Scotland. These theories are entertaining to ponder, but are they true or merely recent fabrications?

Equally remote is the possibility that St. Patrick coins are artifacts of the *sixteenth* century. Yet, numismatic researcher, Stan Stephens, possesses a St. Patrick farthing apparently bearing the engraved date 1553 in Roman numerals. The numerals probably commemorate the brief reign of Queen Mary (1553 to 1558,) the staunchly Catholic daughter of Henry VIII and wife

---

* The origins of the group are unclear. The word itself comes from "Rose Cross," or from the group's alleged 15th century founder, Christian Rosenkreuz. Benjamin Franklin and Thomas Jefferson also were Rosicrucians.

† An irrational number is one that cannot be expressed as a ratio of integers (...,-3,-2,-1,0,1,2,3,....) Unlike repeating decimals such as one-third (1/3 = 0.3333...,) an irrational number never repeats. Commonly used examples include pi (3.14159...) and the square root of two (1.41421....)

‡ Among Leonardo Fibonacci's uses for this sequence was the prediction of rabbit reproduction rates.

of Spain's Philip II. Her reign gave hope to Catholics, who thought she would restore the church that her father sought to expunge and that her sister, Elizabeth I, shunned.

Finally, what is Mark Newby's story? He was selected to serve a second term on the General Assembly in May 1683. However, Thomas Thackara replaced him on September 8, apparently because Newby had died. An inventory of Newby's estate is dated September 4, 1684. In all likelihood, a period of one year from the day of Newby's death was allowed for redemption of any remaining coins from circulation.[444]

Among other articles, Newby's estate contained a small iron furnace, some brass and pewter, a pair of scales with weights, three sieves and some silver plate. These all were instruments that could have been part of a mint operation.[445] The sheer numbers of farthing dies, however, point to a substantial enterprise. Newby's small accumulation of hardware and supplies would have constituted only a small portion of the required equipment. Thus, it is unlikely that Newby actually was running a mint in West Jersey. Even so, he could have been associated in some way with a mint in Ireland. Indeed, such a direct association is one possible explanation for Newby's acquisition of the coppers.

John Lorenzo has proposed that Anthony Sharp, the prominent Dublin wool merchant and Quaker, helped engineer the *Owners Adventure* journey and that Newby was only a pawn. Sharp had access to highly-placed men whom Newby would not have known. These men might have given him opportunities to acquire the coppers.[446] Sharp also made numerous attempts at programs to help Dublin's poor.[447] Could the coppers have been part of one of his plans? Sharp was a shareholder in the New Jersey colony, but never made the journey to America. Instead, he sent his nephew, Thomas Sharp, who came with Newby, to attend to his affairs. It also appears that Newby's appointment to the General Assembly might have been as Anthony Sharp's personal representative. Barring some new revelation, however, no real reason to doubt Newby's having acted on his own is known.

Some of Newby's descendants are alive and well in America. Perhaps some long forgotten family papers will someday be discovered and the puzzle of his involvement will be solved. Records of Quaker meetings held in Newby's home or at those of his neighbors also might hold clues.

In conclusion, there are no conclusions. The excitement of the hunt for facts must go on, unabated, in the hope that the answer will one day be found. After the patent farthings, the St. Patricks were the second of four issues of early American relevance that originally were intended for Ireland. They were followed by William Wood's 1720's coinage and the Hibernia Voce Populi coppers of 1760. Both are discussed in this chapter. Neither were the St. Patrick coppers the last coins to be associated with New Jersey. Over a century after the St. Patrick coppers were introduced, the *state* of New Jersey made its own coinage that, in turn, has its own mysteries. (Chapter 10.)

AMERICAN PLANTATIONS TOKENS (1688)

After Charles II died in 1685, without legitimate heirs, the crown fell to his less kingly brother, James, Duke of York. As James II, he too added to the Stuart numismatic legacy. His 1688 American plantations tokens are unusual in several respects, not the least of which is that they are made of tin (97.5 percent.)[448] The denomination used is Spanish, not English (1/24th reale.) And their triumphant portrayal of James II on a rearing steed is laughable, given his fading fortunes and outright fear of horses.

Several of James's influential friends who owned tin mines were hurt by the 1680's collapse of the market for that metal. Thinking that new uses for tin would breathe life into the market, they persuaded James to allow its use in domestic coinage. The results are the tin farthings and halfpence, some with copper plugs to increase their value, that were minted for domestic use during the same period. (Chapter 5.)

The mine owners, known as "tin farmers," also approached James about making token coins for the colonies, or "plantations," as they were called. However, using nearly pure tin to make coins presents significant technical challenges. Oxidation, or *tin pest*, plays havoc with tin coins, often leaving their surfaces riddled with a black, rust-like corrosion.

Aside from being very soft and chemically active, tin turns to powder when subjected to prolonged cold temperatures.[*] Consequently, the tin coins were unsuitable for use in New England. They could, however, be used in the South, where the weather was warmer and trade with Spanish neighbors was common. For this reason, the tokens were denominated at 1/24th of a Spanish reale. This Spanish reference no doubt led to their being called "Florida plantation tokens." Since a Spanish dollar was valued at 54 pence, or thereabouts, depending on location, the value of the tokens was about 0.271 pence, or roughly a farthing. Their standard weight was 140 grains.[449]

The Tower Mint struck them for Richard Holt, who represented his fellow tin farmers, just weeks before James II was removed from the throne in the essentially bloodless coup known as the Glorious Revolution. Though James's supporters, or Jacobites, hoped for a return to power and even minted promissory gunmoney coinage, James never regained the throne. (Chapter 5.)

American plantation tokens' obverses depict the short-timer king on a rearing horse, with the legend, *JACOBVS II D*[EI] *G*[RATIA] *MAG*[NAE] *BRI*[TANNIAE] *FRAN*[CIAE] *ET HIB*[ERNIAE] *REX*, or "James II, by the Grace of God, of Great Britain, France and Ireland, King." Reverses feature the combined arms of England, Scotland, Ireland and France, with the legend *VAL*[EO] *24 PART*[EM] *REAL*[E] *HISPAN*[IAE], or "Value of 1/24th Spanish Reale."

Four rare error varieties are differentiated from the several more common, normal ones. Of the error varieties, the most elusive is one on which the arms of Scotland and Ireland are transposed. Eric Newman designated it variety 2-G. Another error has the "4" in "24" laying on its side. Two die varieties, Newman 3-C and 6-C, share this characteristic and are known as the "Sideways-4" varieties. The fourth error variety omits the "I" in *HIB* and is called the "HB REX" variety, Newman 1-A.

[*] True in theory. However, a sample of pure tin in this author's freezer shows no degradation after twelve years.

In 1828 Matthew Young, a London coin dealer, located two pairs of the original dies and produced a few hundred restrikes. These are the obverse dies Newman designated 4 and 5 and the reverse dies he called D and E. The combinations 4-E and 5-D are used on both originals and restrikes, complicating attribution. On both of these obverse dies, the top of James's head fits between the "G" in *MAG* and the "B" in *BRIT*. Thus, if James's head falls elsewhere on a given piece, then the piece is an original. The Newman 5 die eventually developed a vertical die crack beginning at the 2 o'clock position on the rim. Newman 5-D examples with this die crack are assumed to be restrikes, however the crack could have occurred during Holt's time.

(Left) Newman 3-C, a sideways-4 variety.

(Right) Obverse of the HB REX, Newman 1-A variety

Young also obtained a beaded edge die that apparently had suffered some degree of damage. The presence of an unbroken ring of edge beads or the absence of die rust can help bolster the case for a coin alleged to be original. In general, restrikes fall within the weight range of 120 to 138.3 grains. Originals are slightly heavier, at 134.5 to 154 grains,[450] and are more likely to exhibit tin pest. Exceptions to both rules exist. Today, even Young's restrikes are scarce and originals are at least twice so.

Eric Newman questioned whether the coins actually circulated in America, on the basis of his knowing of none having been found on this side of the Atlantic.[451] Dr. Louis Jordan buttressed this argument by noting that James II fled to France in December 1688, before abdicating in late January 1689. Presumably, these events dissolved any rights of coinage the tin miners held, including the ability to use the Royal Mint's facilities.[452] Nevertheless, samples were prepared as early as mid-August 1688,[453] and some early run pieces could have been exported to America. At least one has been found at Jamestown and others have shown up at Billingsgate Dock in London, where ocean-crossing ships were moored.[454] The fragility of tin easily could explain the scarcity of examples found in the field. That specimens are dredged up from the depths of the Thames River also suggests some degree of English circulation. In the end the American plantations tokens had little affect on the colonial economy. They were merely tin tokens for a tin king.

ELEPHANT TOKENS (CA. 1694)

One of the most ironic design elements to emerge from the American colonial period is that of an elephant. Inaccurate depictions of a well-fed pachyderm grace the obverses of a series of halfpenny-sized tokens that appeared in the late seventeenth century. These tokens fall into three major types, based on the respective locations to which they refer. Of seven varieties, one refers to New England, two to Carolina and four to London. With the exception of one London variety, their reverses are linked by a common appeal to God for preservation.

Exactly who made them, when, where and for what purpose are stories waiting to be written. The Carolina and New England varieties are dated 1694. The London pieces are undated, but a persistent theory suggests that they were originally minted in the late 1660's to show support in the face of plague and fire.[455] This is unlikely since at least two of them are struck over 1672 halfpence.[456] It is more likely that the London pieces were issued at about the same time as the Carolina and New England types. One of two obverse dies is used on all three types. It seems odd that an obverse die would be used before 1670, put away for a quarter of a century, and then resurrected. Still, in the right care, dies or device punches can survive for long periods (e.g., the American plantations tokens, re-struck after 140 years.) That no pre-1690 references to elephant tokens are known also hints at a later mintage for the London pieces. If the 1690's attribution is correct, then the appeal to providence may simply be a blessing and not tied to any specific time or event.[457]

One theory holds that the Royal Company of Adventurers commissioned the tokens, an attribution that originated with Robert Vlack in the mid 1960's.[458] The company was reorganized as the Royal Africa Company in 1697, with an *African* elephant as its symbol. Part of the support for this theory hinges on the founding of the company by the Duke of York and his subsequent attempt to consolidate power over New England, as James II. James and his supporters formed a sham conglomeration of colonies called the Grand Dominion of New England for this purpose. Since James II was deposed in 1688 and the Grand Dominion ceased to be a viable entity by 1689, it is questionable whether the connection is valid.[459] Moreover, the elephant on the tokens cannot definitively be identified as either African or Asian. It has characteristics of both and neither. Still, the elephant is almost identical to illustrations that appear on maps of West Africa that were engraved by Dutch map makers, Joan Blaue (in 1635 and 1662,) Jan Jansson (in 1654) and others.[460] Thus, the elephant may well be African, after all.

An Elephant from Jan Jansson's 1654 map of West Africa. Image used through the courtesy of the Melville J. Herskovits Library of African Studies, Northwestern University.

The two Carolina varieties' legends mention *Lord Proprietors*, presumably the eight men rewarded in 1663 by Charles II for their support during the rule of the Commonwealth. Prior to that time, several other men were given chances at turning a profit in what are now the Carolinas. For example, Elizabeth I gave Sir Humphrey Gilbert a license to take the West Indies from Spain in 1578. In return, he was to receive what became North Carolina. Gilbert failed on his first expedition and died on his second. His half-brother, Sir Walter Raleigh, took over the grant in 1584, only to fail with Roanoke Island's "Lost Colony." Different members of the Virginia Company, including Captain John Smith, wanted the area. However, when the Virginia Company's charter was revoked in 1624, the title reverted to the Crown. Charles I conveyed the title to Sir Robert Heath in 1629. What was then called Carolana, after Charles (i.e., *Carolus*,) was re-assigned to Lord Maltravers. It changed hands several more times, but no one was very successful at colonizing the region. Consequently, in 1663, Charles II revoked the old Heath claim and gave it over to eight of his influential friends, the proprietors.[461] Three of the proprietors were members of the Royal Africa Company, suggesting a connection between Carolina and company members, if not with the company itself.[462] More solid evidence of a connection between the tokens and the company may yet emerge, but for now none is known.

Adding to the mystery, none of the elephant tokens has obverse legends or explicit denominations. They are known on both thin and thick planchets. Even small differences in thickness translate to wide variances in weight for all three types. Thin planchets may weigh as little as 140 grains, thick planchets as much as 233 grains.[463] This could imply that different individuals, mints, or planchet sources were involved in their production or that production occurred over a relatively long period of time.

The elephant tokens may have an official connection. After an initial run of regal copper halfpence between 1672 and 1675, tin and copper-plugged tin pieces followed in the 1680's. Copper issues were resumed in 1694, bearing the juxtaposed busts of William III and Mary II. Mary's death of smallpox came the same year, prompting a redesign of regal coinage. In England, New designs are usually accompanied by undated patterns. Could pattern issues for the *colonies* also have been considered? A number of petitions to mint coins for the colonies were received in 1694.[464] Perhaps the Carolina and New England pieces were patterns of limited mintage, while the London pieces were made in numbers and distributed to build "brand recognition" for a mint seeking competitive advantage. Coincidentally, the Bank of England was established in 1694. Could the elephant tokens have been associated somehow with it?

Crosby quoted Thomas Snelling who, in 1769, wrote that the Carolina and London pieces were not intended as money, but rather might have been made for a "London Workhouse." Snelling had also heard that they might have been intended for monetary use in Tangier, in Africa, but never made it there. He also noted that an elephant die remained in the Tower Mint and that it appeared to be the work of the die engraver, Rotiers[sic.] He made no mention of the New England pieces.[465] Snelling probably was referring to James or Norbert Roettier, who used an elephant or an elephant with a castle on gold coins of Charles II, James II and William and Mary to indicate the African Company and Guinea as the source of their gold.[466]

The usual London variety: plain cross, thick planchet and tusks close to the rim

Tradition regards all of the elephant tokens as American, though supportive evidence for this is sparse at best. It is possible that New England and Carolina tokens were given to colonists as mementos or to prospective colonists as advertising or recruiting pieces. Walter Breen alluded to excavated pieces and to old, non-collector American accumulations from New York and New Jersey that contain London pieces. He also raised the possibility that elephant tokens could have been among £300 in halfpence and farthings brought from Bristol to Pennsylvania in 1682 by a group of Quaker refugees.[467] (Could these be related to Newby's coppers?) If this deliberate importation could be documented, it would certainly lend credence to the idea that the elephant tokens are American. It is more likely, however, that the Quakers simply brought tokens of the types that were minted during the decade prior to their coming to America.

All three major types of elephant tokens are scarce or rare. Most of the survivors are of the type referring to London, although three of the four London varieties are very rare. These three varieties may have been prototypes. The fourth, more common, London variety exists in numbers large enough to infer a production run. A few hundred of them are known on both thick and thin planchets, with the thick planchet pieces accounting for the great majority of survivors. The reverses of these pieces bear the city arms of London, a plain or hollow cross on a shield, with a dagger in the upper left quadrant. The legend reads *GOD : PRESERVE :* ✱ *: LONDON :*.

Two of the three rare London varieties present a saltire cross, on which two diagonal lines mark the center. On the first of the two saltire cross varieties, the dagger appears incorrectly in the cross's upper *right* quadrant. On the second variety, the dagger position is corrected. The third rare London variety has a hollow cross, with the simple legend *LON* ✱ *DON* ✱. With no reference to the Deity, it sometimes is called the “Godless” variety. On it, the dagger appears in the correct position.

The three rare London varieties are known only on thin planchets. The two saltire cross varieties and the New England type use the same obverse die, with the elephant's tusks distant from the rim. The more common London variety, the *Lon Don* variety, and both Carolina varieties use the only other obverse die. On it, the elephant's tusks are close to the rim. The two obverse dies apparently shared a common punch, as the elephants themselves are identical.

The three rare London reverses: *(Left) Saltire cross, incorrect dagger placement, (Middle) Saltire cross, correct dagger placement. (Right) Lon Don or “Godless” reverse.*

Two reverse die varieties are recognized for the Carolina type, though the same reverse die was actually used for both. The original reverse die simply was repunched to correct a misspelling. It first read *GOD: / PRESERVE: / CAROLINA AND: / THE LORDS: PROPRIETERS:* [sic] / *1694*. About eight examples with this errant spelling are known. On the corrected version, an "O" is punched over the last "E" to correct the error. About thirty examples of the corrected version are known. On the example below, an "E" can be clearly seen within the second "O" of *PROPRIETORS*. The reverse center is almost always weakly struck on Carolina tokens, as in the example below. The Carolina pieces all are struck on thin planchets, though some variation in thickness has been observed. The rarest elephant type has the reverse legend GOD: / PRESERVE: / NEW: / ENGLAND: / 1694, in five lines. Only three examples are known to exist, on both thick and thin planchets.

(Left) 1694 Carolina O/E variety.

(Right) Reverse of a 1694 New England elephant token.

In researching the elephant tokens, two other remotely possible explanations for their inspiration have surfaced. The first is a ship called the *Elephant* that was captained by Robert Kingsland. It was known to have carried official documents to Bermuda in the 1670's for Perient Trott, a director of the Somer Islands Company. His son, Nicholas, was a political figure in Carolina after 1690, while other Trott descendants rose to prominence in New England.[468] A second coincidental, but probably unrelated event, is the signing of statutes for Denmark's orders of chivalry by their king, Christian V, in December 1693. A foreigner who was deemed worthy could be admitted to the exclusive order, whose symbol was and is still an elephant. Perhaps an English dignitary earned this honor and commemorated the event with an issue of tokens or medalets. Neither of these ideas is anything more than conjecture. Still, the elephant tokens have held their secrets for more than three centuries and, therefore, any new lead is worthy of at least passing consideration.

FRENCH ISSUES USED IN LOUISIANA AND CANADA (1640 TO 1764)

Not all imported American coins have English or Irish origins. For well over a century, France sent coins of various types and denominations to its huge territories in Canada, or New France, and what was then called Louisiana. Numismatists long have argued about which of these pieces are truly American. The controversy exists in part because France issued, re-issued and exported coins for *general* use in any of its New World holdings. Rather than enter headlong into the debate, a survey of types is presented with only scattered inflammatory comments about American relevance.

Using this approach, the following groups of French-American colonials emerge: [469]

- Early countermarked issues [old billon sols marqués (1640) and milled sols (1658)] and officially imported French domestic coins
- 1670 issues for French America
- Later countermarked issues: Spanish silver (1683) and old sols (1692 to 1700)
- 1709 to 1713 billon mousquetaires
- 1719 to 1722 John Law-associated issues
- 1721 to 1722 copper sols
- Ca. 1725 gold mirlitons and silver pieces from the wreck of the ship Le Chameau
- 1738 to 1764 billon sous marques
- Late 1700's coppers for Guadeloupe, Cayenne and other holdings (Chapter 9)

EARLY BILLON COUNTERSTAMPS AND OFFICIALLY IMPORTED DOMESTICS

By the mid-1600's, there were enough soldiers, traders and other colonists in French America to need coinage. At the same time, old worn billon sols were everywhere in French domestic circulation. Believing that a single solution would solve both problems, Louis XIII issued a 1640 edict requiring that the old sols be recalled for counter-stamping and exportation to New France. The edict stipulated that the old billon sols be marked with a fleur de lis inside an oval of beads and given a colonial value of fifteen deniers. With the counterstamp, the old hammered sols, many of them dated 1618, became *sols marqués*, or *marked sols*.[470] These hand-me-downs were less than ideal. Their weights were as varied as their worn undertypes.

(Left) Old counterstamped sol from the 1640 re-issue.

(Right) A 1550 example, showing how some appeared prior to re-issue.

Then, in 1658, milled billon douzains and sixains that recently had been made for French domestic use were dealt a similar fate. They were recalled, given the same counterstamp and shipped to New France.

After several re-valuations, both sets of counterstamped coins themselves were recalled in 1692 and, as did the odd handful of official billon imports that accompanied them, they disappeared into the French wilderness. Nevertheless, these re-issued culls are the first French coins to be called American. Many others followed.

1670 Louis XIV Issues

The *crème de la crème* of French American coins is a three-denomination series authorized in 1670. A royal edict from Louis XIV for the *Compaigne des Indes Occidentales* ("Company of the West Indies") called for coins to be minted in two silver denominations, five and fifteen sols, and one copper denomination, a double denier. Today, the five sols coins are rare, the fifteen sols are seen once or twice in a lifetime and only a few copper "doubles" are known.

1670-A (Paris) French American five sols.

The obverses of both silver coins feature long-haired busts of Louis XIV with the legend *LVD*[OVICUS] *XIIII D*[EI] *G*[RATIA] [sun device] *FR*[ANCIAE] *ET NAV*[ARRE] *REX*, or "Louis XIV, by the Grace of God, of France and Navarre, King." Aside from being the different or hallmark of mint master Pierre Cheval, the sun in the legend alludes to Louis XIV as the "Sun King." The reverses of these coins bear a central crowned shield with three fleurs de lis and the words *GLORIAM RENI TVI DICENT 1670* ("They Shall Speak of the Glory of Thy Kingdom 1670.") This was a double reference to the Deity and to the arrogant King![471]

1670-A double denier for French America

The copper doubles survive as reminders of an issue that apparently never was, even though 2.4 million pieces were authorized.[472] Their obverses feature the same legend as the silver coins, but surrounding a crowned "L." The "L," of course, represents Louis XIV. It splits the 1670 date and floats above an "A" mintmark, for Paris. The reverse legend, in four lines, reads *DOVBLE / DE LA / MERIQVE / FRANCOISE* ("Double of French America.")

The intended weight of the fifteen sols pieces, of which only twelve to fourteen are thought to survive, was 107.9 grains. The five sol pieces were to weigh a third as much, at 35.97 grains. The authorized mintage for the smaller coins was 200,000, five times that of the fifteen sols. Both were minted in 0.917 fine silver. The copper double deniers are believed to weigh about 105 grains.[473]

In Quebec the silver coins circulated at one and a third times their nominal values to restrict them to local circulation. This gave the larger coins the value of twenty sols, or one livre, and the five sols the value of six sols, eight deniers.[474] All from this three-denomination series stand out in part because of their unquestionable association with New France.

1683 and 1692 to 1700 Overstrikings

A 1683 edict resulted in the counterstamping of Spanish and Mexican silver coins with a fleur de lis, accompanied by Roman numerals to indicate weight. A Spanish dollar of full weight received no Roman numerals, but lighter ones received numerals that increased from I to IIII as their weights decreased. These all are very rare and only their Caribbean presence actually links them to Louisiana or New France.

1593 douzain, counterstamped ca. 1692-1700 and bearing the "H" mintmark of La Rochelle.

In 1692, however, another edict of Louis XIV called for the overstriking of all old billon coins with new designs and a colonial valuation of fifteen deniers. The chosen counterstamp consists of four crowned pairs of back-to-back L's (i.e., " ⅃L," for "Louis,") set in the form of a cross, with fleurs de lis in the angles between its arms. The obverse legend is similar to that of the 1670 issues. Some of the under types of these coins date to the Middle Ages.[475] The example above was a century old when the counterstamp was applied. As did the weights of the earlier overstrikes, weights of the 1692 to 1700 overstrikes vary greatly by undertype.

As described in Chapter 4, resourceful French military officers in Canada circumvented coin shortages by paying their men in playing card money, beginning in the 1680's. For obvious reasons, the French government looked unfavorably on this practice. Undoubtedly, the counterstamped coins were an attempt to bring an end to New France's unconventional paper currency. It did not work, at least not entirely and not immediately.

1709 to 1713 Billon Mousquetaires

However, more successful efforts were afoot. A 1709 edict authorized the issue of fifteen- and thirty-denier billon coins. Sometimes these were silvered to enhance the illusion of their being solid specie. Though only minted until 1713, demand for them continued for more than two decades. They were called "mousquetaires," with varying opinions as to why. Walter Breen speculated that the name was adopted because the intended users were habitants (colonists) who relied on muskets.[476] Robert Vlack instead pointed to the outlined, hollow cross reverse design that is similar to emblems worn by elite Mousequetaires in France, such as the three characters whom Alexandre Dumas and the Mars candy company made famous.[477]

In French America, the need for coinage particularly was acute in port towns and cities. Barter carried furs and other goods from the forests to the ports, but those who lived in the cities needed a regular medium of exchange. Larger ports such as Quebec, the capital of New France, and New Orleans, the capital of Louisiana, had particular needs that only could be met by coins. "Larger" is a relative term since, aside from wilderness traders, all of Louisiana boasted only 122 soldiers, seventy-seven settlers and eighty slaves in 1708.[478] Because the billon mousquetaires had a lower intrinsic value than their silver domestic cousins, they circulated in the colonies and not in France proper.[479]

Both the fifteen- and the thirty-denier pieces feature a pair of crowned back-to-back L's, surrounded by three fleurs de lis, the usual obverse legend (*LVD*[OVICUS] *XIIII D*[EI] *G*[RATIA] [sun device] *FR*[ANCIAE] *ET NAV*[ARRE] *REX*) and the date. Reverses present a hollow Greek cross, with fleurs de lis filling the angles between its arms. At the end of each arm is a triangular group of three pellets. The reverse legend gives the denomination – *PIECE DE XXX* [or XV] *DENIERS* – and the mintmark, which was always "D," for Lyon.

1711-D billon mousquetaire, 30 deniers, silvered.

That these coins were successful is evidenced by the continued demand for them through the 1730's. In 1738, a new, but very similar coin took the stage. (See the 1738 to 1764 billon sous marques described below.)

1717 Perpignan Copper Issues

Other coins were issued in the interim. In 1716, Louis XV had been king for a year, yet he was only six years old. Acting in his name, the Duc d'Orléans authorized colonial coppers of six and twelve deniers and bearing the date 1717. The coppers were made at the Perpignan mint. Obverses bear the young bust of Louis XV and assert his kingship over France and Navarre. Reverses have the denomination, *XII* [or *VI*] *DENIERS,* and the word *COLONIES*, centered above the date. Perpignan's "Q" mintmark appears below the date. The different of mint master Christophe Bordeau, a cockleshell, appears to the left of the mintmark. Very few of these pieces survive. The attempted coinage is believed to have been aborted because of poor quality, as noted at the time. On the other hand, their rarity simply may be the result of their dispersal through normal circulation.[480] Either way, this issue clearly had little or no impact on the economy of North America.

1719 to 1721 John Law-Associated Issues

Several French coins are associated with John Law, the convicted killer, gambler, son of an Edinburgh goldsmith and financial wizard, whose ideas found such favor in France that he essentially gained control of the country's treasury. Under Law, the Compaigne des Indes Occidentales grew so powerful that it was given the rights to collect taxes, control foreign colonies and produce coins.[481] It is the question of which of the coins produced during his tenure are truly American and colonial that elicits the greatest controversy among numismatists who study the coinages for France's colonies.

Law spearheaded a ruinous investment scheme aimed at colonizing the lower Mississippi River region. Its hopes of success were based on the value that *potentially* could come from land. That is, the plan called for land to be used to back currency and generate wealth. After the King of Sardinia wisely declined to participate in his scheme, Law found a backer in the Duc d'Orléans.[482] The Compaigne des Indes Occidentales was supposed to recruit large numbers of European settlers to Louisiana. Investors willing to establish plantations were given land grants, or concessions, mostly along the Mississippi River. Law, himself, received a large concession in what is now Arkansas.[483] In retrospect, the whole affair seems ridiculous. By 1719 the *paper* value of the company's stock was about eighty times the combined value of all the legitimate currency in France![484]

In 1720 reality set in and the house of cards began to tumble. Though the enterprise received a great deal of attention, only relative handfuls of settlers actually came. For example, a 1721 visitor recorded a population of only forty-seven on Law's huge Arkansas concessions, considerably fewer than the exaggerated claim of nine thousand Germans who supposedly had been recruited from the Palatinate.[485]

Many of those who did immigrate performed ancillary support services, such as keeping shops, acting as surgeons, etc., and did not actively produce wealth from the land. To make the situation look better, *engages* (those paid to facilitate settlement) were converted to *habitants* (colonists) on paper.[486] It was not enough. As a result of the meager settlement and limited productivity, the anticipated wealth never materialized. Investors panicked as their money frittered away and Law's name became a mockery. Banished, Law died a pauper in Venice nine years later.[487] The debacle that he precipitated came to be known as "The Mississippi Bubble."[*]

(Left) 1720-S (Reims) sol de 12 deniers. (Right) 1720-K (Bordeaux) 20 sols, Note the Engravers General privy marks: (obverse) fleur de lis for Jacque Petit and (reverse) button for Jean Moulinier.

Between July 25, 1719 and January 5, 1721, Law's company held the right to mint coins. According to Michael Hodder, all coins issued under the control of the company can be called "John Law coins," but only those that specifically were earmarked for the colonies can legitimately be called "French colonial coins." Other writers have indicated that only certain coins dated 1719 or 1720 fit this description. As Hodder pointed out, Law was reluctant to export coins. Colonies were supposed to produce wealth from raw materials, not require its importation. Thus, the term "colonial relevance" is reserved only for those coins for which an official letter of authorization exists.[488] This is a valid and technically correct interpretation, but one with which this author differs slightly. Law's enterprise was all about colonization.

[*] Emerson Hough offered a semi-factual account in a 1902 book of the same name. A more factual account can be found in Judge Morris Arnold's 1991 work *Colonial Arkansas 1686-1804: A Social and Cultural History.*

The monies that the company minted (and printed) could not have been more closely tied to the colonies. By Law's definition, colonial lands essentially *were* currency. Therefore, any Law-associated piece legitimately can be called colonial. Moreover, the scheme's collapse was not immediate. Those who settled the concessions remained for some years after 1720. Law's own concession still was inhabited as late as July 1723.[489] The settlers still needed Law's coins, even the ones dated 1721. As Willy Wonka, the fictional candy magnate, admonished, "Oh, you should never, never doubt what nobody is sure about."[490]

Designs of the 1719 to 1721 coppers vary. Most depict a right-facing obverse portrait of Louis XV, with the legend, *LUDOVICUS XV DEI GRATIA,* that is continued on the reverse with *FRANCIAE ET NAVARRE REX.* The meaning is "Louis XV, by the Grace of God, of France and Navarre, King." Reverse devices also vary, with most presenting a crowned shield adorned with three fleurs de lis, as shown above. Twelve-denier coppers weigh 181 to 185 grains, six-denier pieces around eighty-eight grains and three-denier pieces around forty-six grains.[491] Weights of the two larger coins compare favorably with contemporary halfpence and farthings. As such, they almost certainly trickled into British America.

(Right) 1720-A Compaigne des Indies demi-livre or 1/6 ecu. Gadoury-296.

LUD[OVICUS] *XV D*[EI] *G*[GRATIA] *FR*[ANCIAE] *ET NAV*[ARRE] *REX* appears entirely on the obverses of silver coins issued between 1719 and 1721. These pieces bear either a crowned coat-of-arms or variations of crowned, back-to-back L's. Silver demi- (half-) livres weigh about fifty-seven grains.[492]

(Left) 1720-A Livre de Huit L, petit Louis d'argent or 1/3 ecu. Gadoury-305.

Reverse legends of some period silver coins read *SIT NOMEN DOMINI BENEDICTUM*, or "Blessed be the Name of the Lord." The 1720 silver livre de huit L (livre of eight L's) piece, at left, features a reverse design with four pairs of crowned, back-to-back L's and four fleurs de lis. Its legend is *CHR*[ISTV]*S REGN*[AT] [CHRISTVS] *VINC*[IT] [CHRISTVS] *IMP*[ERAT], or "Christ Reigns, Christ Conquers, Christ Rules." Its weight is twice that of the demi-livre above.

Law-associated gold coins also exist, though all now are rare. Their designs combine the legends of the silver livre, immediately above, with the devices of the demi-livre above it. Louis d'ors of twenty livres weigh 150.5 grains. Petit Louis d'ors had a value of ten livres and were intended to weigh 75.2 grains.[493]

Either the number of Law-associated coins actually reaching New France and Louisiana was small, or else they disappeared fairly quickly in circulation, as archaeological evidence of their use is lacking. Ample archaeological evidence for circulation of the next issue, however, has been found, even in British America.

1721 to 1722 Copper Sols

Requests for coinage by French colonists continued after the fall of the Law regime. In response, a 1721 edict ordered coppers to be issued in two denominations, one to pass at eighteen to twenty deniers, and a smaller coin to pass at nine deniers. Only the nine-denier coins actually were minted. Dated 1721 and 1722, they bear either the mintmark "B" for Rouen or "H" for La Rochelle. While originally intended for New France, they actually were general issues for use in all French colonies. Presumably to employ better copper than that used for the 1717 Perpignan issues, Swedish blanks were purchased.[494]

1722-H (La Rochelle) sol de 9 Deniers

In Canada, merchants preferred silver or billon pieces over the new light coppers. Even after devaluation to six deniers and attempts to force acceptance, most of them were returned to France. In 1731 the unwanted coppers were shipped to Louisiana where, by some accounts, confusion over their official status bred a reluctance to use them.[495] Speculators exploited them into worthlessness.[496] As unpopular as they were, they have been excavated at many early French American sites, sometimes together in significant numbers. Mobile's Dauphin Island, for example, has yielded at least eight of them.[497]

The obverse design of these coppers features crowned, crossed L's with the legend *SIT NOMEN DOMINI BENEDICTUM.* Reverses simply read *COLONIES FRANCOISES*, or "French Colonies," above the date and mintmark. Reverse differents identify the engravers and ringmasters. Minor varieties include a "1722/1" overdate and double-punched dates. The intended weight for these pieces was 94.43 grains,[498] making them suitable for acceptance as farthings or even light halfpence in British America.

Coins from Le Chameau (1725)

Other French coins intended for North America never quite made the full journey. For exampled, the transport ship *Le Chameau* was dispatched to carry supplies to New France in August 1725. In addition to livestock, poultry and ammunition, she carried one hundred troops, forty-eight cannon and 82,010 livres in gold and silver. She sank in a sudden storm, on the reefs of Nova Scotia. There were no survivors, at least no animate ones.[499]

In the 1960's about nine thousand silver ecus and six hundred gold twenty-livre coins, called "mirlitons," were recovered from the wreck. The gold coins bear 1720's dates and an obverse bust of a young Louis XV with the usual legends. Reverses display two intertwined, script L's within a wreath. Above them floats a crown. Their reverse legends are identical to the livre de huit L shown above. One mystery, the use of the term "mirliton" ("a reed flute") to describe these 100.6-grain pieces, has never been explained.[500]

The silver ecus essentially are larger versions of the livre de huit Ls on which the eight reverse L's are exploded to make room for a central cross of fleurs de lis. The reverse legends read *SIT NOMEN DOMINI BENEDICTUM,* as on other pieces in this section, and edges read *DOMINE*

SALVUM FAC REGEM ("God Save the King.") The intended weight of these large silver coins was 364.06 grains (0.917 fine,) only slightly lighter than contemporary Spanish dollars. Most recovered examples exhibit corrosion commensurate with many years on the sea floor. The salvage efforts also produced various smaller, fractional silver pieces.[501]

(Left) 1725-H ecu, recovered from the wreck of Le Chameau.
(Right) Reverse of a mirliton, again with the "H" mintmark of La Rochelle.

1738 to 1764 Billon Sous Marqués

In the late 1730's new requests for monies arrived from the North American colonies, possibly because of the lingering need to redeem emergency-issue card money from Canadian circulation. Louisiana's Governor Bienville and New France's Governor Hocquart both ordered coins. The response was a billon issue of twelve- and twenty-four denier coins.[502] In size and fabric these coins are very similar to the 1709 to 1713 billon issues that long had circulated.

In New France, the new thirty-denier coins were called *sous*, in Louisiana *sols marques*, leading to the amalgam *sous marques*.[503] The smaller coins were referred to as *half sous*. Reverse designs of both denominations feature a single crowned "L" with three fleurs de lis and the same legend as found on the 1709 to 1713 issues, but with *XV* replacing *XIIII* as the king's ordinal number. Obverses feature two very ornate L's, their tops intertwined, with a crown above. The obverse legend is an abbreviated version of *SIT NOMEN DOMINI BENEDICTUM*, with the date. The mintmark appears at the base of the reverse.

After 1763, when these coins were returned to France for "recycling," they were counterstamped with a crowned "C" and sent to the Caribbean. They could not be used in France because of their light weight and low fineness. Names for the counterstamped pieces include *sols estampés*, *sols tampees* and *stampees* ("stamped sols.") In the West Indies, they joined several types of old worn coins that, in the salt air of the islands, had turned dark, inspiring the nickname "black dogges."[504] (See Chapter 9 for more details.)

1741-A sous marqués Target weights of these pieces were 33.72 (30 deniers) and 16.86 grains (15 deniers.) Breen observed a range of 28 to 41 grains for the larger coins.[505]

Over time, the proportion of silver used in *sous marqués* declined in favor of cheaper copper. Doubtless this also contributed to their tendency to discolor. Yet, like the 1709 to 1713 pieces, these coins only can be viewed as successful. They were issued until 1764 and Robert Vlack identified 248 different date/mintmark combinations from twenty-nine different mints, for sous marques alone. The number of combinations is even greater if the half sous are included. Counting both denominations, over eight million of these pieces were struck. Vlack also describes many counterfeits, both contemporary and possibly modern.[506]

On taking possession of New France in 1764, the British devalued *sous marqués* to farthings by ordinance. Those already in circulation migrated to newly Spanish Louisiana where they retained their original value. Those that had remained in the treasury were returned for counterstamping and reissue.[507] Along with a nine-deniers copper issue of 1767, the counterstamped reissues are among the last French colonial coins with credible ties to British America. (See Chapter 9.) Perhaps because no mints sprang up in New France or Louisiana to create a local legacy, or because French territory was so quickly Anglicized, the field is among the least understood in American numismatics. The overview of types presented here fails in many ways to provide the coverage it deserves and, though literature on the subject is limited, further investigation is strongly recommended.[*]

Investigations need not be restricted to coins. Great cities such as Quebec, Montreal, St. Louis, Mobile and New Orleans proudly wear their French heritage. The best understanding of French colonial life that moderns can attain, however, exists in much smaller places, such as Natchitoches, Louisiana, and Ste. Genevieve, Missouri. Among many other historic gems, Natchitoches boasts a reconstructed early seventeenth century stronghold, Fort St. Jean Baptiste, to serve as a reminder that wilderness colonization was always a fragile undertaking.

Ste. Genevieve is quaint Mississippi River town that lies about an hour's drive south from St. Louis. The town dates to the mid-eighteenth century and still retains much of the culture and some of the architecture of its French colonial beginnings. Of the five early *poteaux en terre* ("posts in the ground") houses remaining in the United States, three are in Ste. Genevieve. The most notable is the Bolduc House that dates to the post-colonial, 1788 to 1793, period. It represents the style of earlier French houses, as well as that of houses in the West Indies. A tour reveals much about the lifestyle of Louis Bolduc, an upper middle-class merchant, and his family. It also reveals the cosmopolitan nature of trade along the river. Bolduc faired well with Indians, the Spanish, the British and the Americans, all of whom had their time in Ste. Genevieve. Given the pervasively Anglo view of history that most Americans share, a walk on the other side can be quite enlightening.

[*] Robert Vlack's new book, *An Illustrated Catalogue of the French Billon Coinage in the Americas* (Colonial Coin Collectors Club, 2005,) a decades-long labor of love, is an excellent reference for this series.

ODDFELLOWS: MISCELLANEOUS EARLY TOKENS (CA. 1665 TO 1715)

Back on the English side and around the turn of the eighteenth century, small change shortages wreaked havoc in commercial centers such as Boston and Philadelphia. It appears that, in response, some Philadelphians produced or imported brass and lead tokens. Massachusetts even went so far as to authorize privately issued lead pennies in 1701 and to set procedures for their redemption. Apparently, none of them has survived the three centuries since their issue, as none has ever surfaced. They bore the marks of their makers, but neither the marks nor the makers are known today. It also is likely that other forgotten token types existed.

The late seventeenth century and early eighteenth century also may have seen the issuance of three other unusual and mysterious types, all with American associations: 1.) the New Yorke [sic] in America tokens of 1668 to 1673, 2.) a unique piece traditionally known as the New England stuiver; and, 3.) Gloucester, Virginia tokens of 1714 to 1715. All three were known in Crosby's time. Breen called them "apocryphal farthings," implicitly downplaying their importance.[508] Others have labeled the New England stuiver and, erroneously, the New Yorke in America tokens, as later fabrications. The New England stuiver is ostensibly of Dutch origin. Until about a decade ago, the same could be said of the New Yorke in America tokens.

New Yorke in America Tokens (Ca. 1668 to 1673)

The assumption that the New Yorke in America tokens are Dutch originated with the mid-nineteenth century discovery of the first specimen at the Hague. The reverse spelling *NEW YORKE* lent weight to the idea that they were Dutch and of early mintage. The theory that Crosby offered in 1875 seemed entirely reasonable: that an inhabitant of New Netherland requested them during the small change shortages of 1701 to 1706. By Crosby's time, three examples in lead, including the specimen from the Hague, and one in brass were known.[509] The first brass example was discovered in a lot of jetons imported from Europe. Since then, the ratio of brass to lead specimens has been reversed. Only one additional lead specimen has surfaced, bringing the total to four. During the same period, the number of known brass specimens has grown to about twenty.[510] In the 1950's the age of these tokens briefly was questioned because examples were found in accumulations of American private tokens of the 1861 to 1865 period.[511] In 1992, however, John Kleeberg found strong evidence that the tokens are of English origin and are from the 1668 to 1675 period.[512]

During the 1630's the Dutch were very successful at building trade with the Indian populations in and around present-day New York. As their commercial empire grew, it collided with expanding English interests. Both nations plotted to move into the Hudson River Valley. When Englishmen moved into the area in 1646, the seasoned Old Dutch governor, Peter Stuyvesant (at left,[513]) protested. Stuyvesant negotiated a boundary that lasted until 1659, when English representatives were sent to spy on their neighbors under the cover of a cattle-farming enterprise. Stuyvesant was not fooled. Tension grew until excitement over the 1660 restoration of the English monarchy turned attentions elsewhere. The situation simmered on a back burner until 1664, when Charles II rewarded those who had aided the Restoration by ordering the seizure of all Dutch holdings in America.[514] Taken by political intrigue and the threat, rather than the use of force, New

Netherland became New York. Its southern province became New Jersey. Peter Stuyvesant, who for years had warned of an English takeover, sailed away in disgrace.[515]

Richard Nicolls directed much of the takeover and was New York's first English governor. He was recalled and replaced by Francis Lovelace in May 1668. At the same time, English merchants, particularly those in Bristol, issued private tokens for use as small change. Kleeberg hypothesized that Lovelace intended to provide similar tokens for New York. In England, it was common practice to "test market" undated patterns in advance of dated general issues. The use of an arabesque design in place of an actual date on the New Yorke tokens may indicate that they were intended for this purpose. The existence of the tokens in both lead and brass might also suggest a degree of experimentation. On the other hand, the trade tokens that New Yorke pieces appear to emulate also come in different metals, including lead. On a New Yorke tokens, the reverse legend is circumscribed around an eagle and reads ❀ *NEW - YORKE · IN - AMERICA* ⁜ ∽. The *cinquefoil* (❀,) a five-petaled flower, is another feature common to Bristol tokens of 1662 to 1670.[516]

After Edmund Andros replaced Lovelace, Sir John Werden, Secretary to the Duke of York, wrote to the new governor "I'me told that noe law prohibitts [sic] y[e] [the] sending our brass farthings thither if it be worth y[e] while to carry y[m] [i.e., them] thither."[517] Werden might have been referring to the new regal *copper* farthings that entered circulation in 1672 or his statement might have been a reference to the precedent that Lovelace had set.

The New Yorke tokens' central reverse device is a screaming eagle, perched on a ragulated staff (a branch with angular protrusions,) at each end of which appears to be attached oak leaves. Kleeberg showed that this design mimics the Lovelace family crest. In the absence of an official New York seal, Lovelace apparently used his family's symbol on the tokens. The obverse motif also echoes the Lovelace name, even though no legend is present. It depicts the eternal lovers, Cupid (in Greek, Eros) and Psyche, in a grove of palms. Cupid, at left, holds a bow. At right, Psyche, identified by a butterfly on her shoulder, has Cupid's arrow of love embedded in her breast. Popular sixteenth century prose referred to love as a snare or net. The notion of a net was also interpreted as "lace." Thus, the vignette is likely a rebus, or picture puzzle, meaning "love's lace" – Lovelace.[518]

Perhaps the tokens were for use in Manhattan's King's House tavern. Lovelace had it built next door to the old Dutch Stadt Huys (state house) in 1670. The tavern served as New York's city hall from 1697 to 1703. As an archeological site, it has produced smoking pipes, ceramic and glass bottles, marbles and other items.[519] To this author's knowledge, however, no New Yorke in America tokens have surfaced there.

New Yorke in America tokens vary greatly in weight. They likely were intended either as light farthing tokens or as "calling cards." Most brass examples fall between 36 and 54 grains. A single worn brass example is extremely light at 20.8 grains. Lead examples naturally are heavier. The three examples for which weights are recorded are at 61.99, 66.51 and 72.2 grains.[520] Pending dating of the New England stuiver and the St. Patrick coppers, the New Yorke in America tokens are the oldest known American base metal issues, the first issues for New York and the first of billions of American pieces to feature an eagle.

The New England Stuiver (ca. 16???)

In contrast, the New England stuiver is mystery yet to be solved. Recall from Chapter 7 that stuivers are small Dutch coins that are believed to have circulated as farthings in the American colonies. It was assumed for years that this is the denomination represented by the unique New England stuiver. The reverse legend of this piece is split into four lines and reads *ИEW EИGLAИD* W. The N's are reversed and the "M" is inverted. The obverse features two emaciated lions, one at the top and facing to the viewer's left. The other is inverted below, its head facing to the viewer's right. On the left side of the obverse, the head of the top lion faces the letter "I." Beneath "I" and adjacent to the rear of the bottom lion is the letter "V." On the right side of the obverse, in similar positions, are the letters "S" and "C." If the letters are read top-to-bottom, then left-to-right, the legend is *I.SVC.*

The undated "New England stuiver."

Crosby proposed two theories for the meaning of *I.SVC.* The first, less likely, explanation is *I Stuiver Von Connecticut.* ("One Stuiver of Connecticut.") His other interpretation is that they are the initials of a Dutch merchant, as *I... S... Van C....*[521] Around 1970, the New England stuiver disappeared from popular numismatic discourse and many now believe it to be a nineteenth century fabrication.[522] Its weight, composition and current location are unknown.

Gloucester, Virginia Tokens (1714 to 1715)

The third oddfellow is associated with Gloucester (pronounced "Gloster") County in southeastern Virginia. Until 1981 only one genuine example was known to exist. It is so worn that the legends only partially are decipherable. Only when a second example was discovered in an old Gloucester, Virginia, collection were numismatists able to discern the full legends. Both of these specimens are dated 1714.* A much smaller, 1715-dated specimen, was discovered in an area around the old Gloucester County Courthouse in 1979, using a metal detector. It too is dilapidated, its obverse either completely worn away or never struck.

Obverses of the two larger specimens feature a frontal view of a building presumed to be the old Gloucester County courthouse. In its dimensions and symmetry, the tokens' building appears similar to the courthouse at Colonial Williamsburg. The building has a central door, flanked by two windows and a chimney at each end. Below it are the Roman numerals *XII.* This suggests an intended denomination of twelve pence. However, all three specimens are made of brass and would have achieved only limited acceptance as shillings.

The circumscribed obverse legend of the two larger pieces appears inside a beaded border and reads *GLOVCESTER • COVRT • HOVSE • VIRGINIA •*. The reverses present a geometric star, with the legend *RIGHAVLT • DAWSON • ANNO • DOM • 1714,* also inside a beaded border. The star may be a Masonic symbol. Only a hint of the star is visible on the smaller token. Its legend reads [RIGA]*VLT* [A]*N*[NO] *DO*[M] [1]*715*. From the spacing of the legends and the

* In 1875, Crosby actually wrote of two examples (*Early Coins of America*, p.323,) one of which later (after 1976!) was revealed to be a cast copy of the other.

token's size, it is clear that some words present on the larger tokens deliberately were omitted from the smaller piece.

1714 Gloucester token

Who were Righault and Dawson and what was the nature of their business? No one knows, but men with these names are known to have settled in Gloucester County. Several Virginia courthouses were built using donated land and materials. Often, the donations came in return for token considerations such as a pound of tobacco. Perhaps Righault and Dawson helped to build Gloucester County's courthouse and wished to make their contributions known. Their tokens probably were made locally, given the simple design and variation in weight.* Gloucester tokens well may be America's first domestically made base metal coins or tokens. On the other hand, they may be patterns, store cards (metallic business cards,) tax receipts, warehouse receipts for tobacco or even markers associated somehow with day-to-day court business. Regardless of their intended uses, mintages of the Gloucester tokens and the two other apocryphal farthings must have been very small.

WILLIAM WOOD'S COINAGES (1722 TO 1724, 1727 AND 1733)

The opposite is true of the next issue that is of interest to American numismatics. Born in 1671, William Wood was a successful British metallurgist and ironmaster who lived in Wolverhampton, in the county of Stafford. It is not known when coinage first interested him, but a series of 1717 patterns† share some characteristics with coins that Wood later produced for America and Ireland. These early patterns probably are his doing.

Wood developed an alloy that he believed ideal for coining, calling it "Bath metal." Bath metal is 75 percent copper, 24.7 percent zinc and 0.3 percent silver,[523] a combination that, in spite of Wood's claims, has few redeeming qualities. It is brittle and must be heated before striking into coins. Nevertheless, armed with his new wonder metal, Wood set about devising a way to convince the Crown to give him a patent to make coins for America and Ireland.

He needed a lobbyist, whom he found in Ehrengarde Melusina, a frail but beautiful German baroness who was in great favor with George I. Melusina accompanied the would-be king as he traveled from Hamburg to England prior to his coronation. She so captivated him that he raised her to the level of peerage and gave her the title "Duchess of Kendal."[524] The English people awarded her less flattering titles such as "the King's whore" and "the Maypole." [525] As George's mistress, she held great influence over him. Her services were effective, but not cheap. On Wood's behalf, she obtained two very similar patents, one for American coinage,

* Hodder ("The Gloucester County, Virginia Courthouse Tokens," p.1679-1682) gives the weight of the larger (24 mm) tokens as 61.1 and 43.44 grains. He gives the smaller token's metrics at 18.2 mm and 25.3 grains.

† The patterns are in denominations of twopence, penny, and halfpence. All three obverses depict a right-facing George I. Reverses have as their central devices crowned denominations ("1/2," "I" and "II.") Only the twopence is dated. Their legends give George's title in detail commensurate with the relative sizes of the coins. None of them mentions America or Ireland.

the other for Irish, and sold them to him for £10,000 each.[526] Both were recorded on July 12, 1722.[527] The justification for Wood's enterprise is found in the American patent*:

> ...*Within his Majesties Islands Dominions and Territories in America there is a great Want of small money for making small payments to such as would voluntarily accept the same and that Retailers and others do suffer by reason of such Want and Whereas the said William Wood hath humbly represented to his Majestie that he the said William Wood hath Invented a certain Composic[i]on or mixture consisting partly of fine virgin Silver partly of superfine Brass made of pure Copper and partly of double refined linck otherwise known as Tutanaigne or Spelter* [both terms for zinc]....*to be made for coynage of such moneys herinafter prescribed and the small moneys to be made with the same metal...for the Service of his Majesties Subjects in America who will voluntarily accept the same...*[528]

Rosa Americana Coinage (1722 to 1724, and 1733)

Coins made under Wood's patent were the first ever to bear the word "America," albeit in the Latin form, "Americana." Because their central reverse device is the double rose of the Tudor and Plantagenet families, these coins are known as "Rosa Americana" coinage, as "Rosa Americanas" or simply as "Rosas." Rosa Americanas were made in twopence, penny and halfpenny denominations. Similarly, the coins Wood made for Ireland are collectively referred to as "Hibernia coinage," or as "Hibernias." Hibernias were made in halfpenny and farthing denominations.

Apparently, Wood's initial focus was on the Rosa Americanas. For unknown reasons, the American patent was recorded first in the Roll of Patents.[529] Though both Rosas and Hibernias were issued in the 1722 to 1724 period, the bulk of surviving Rosa Americanas are dated 1722. In contrast, most surviving Hibernias are dated 1723.

The prescribed term of the American patent was fourteen years. Over the first four years, it allowed Wood to produce two hundred "tunns" of coins. Then, for the remaining decade, his allotment dropped to ten tons per year. To discourage British domestic circulation, both Rosas and Hibernias were made lighter than regal issues of the same denominations. Accordingly, standard weights for Rosa Americana twopence, pennies and halfpence coins were set at 233.83 grains, 116.67 grains and 58.33 grains, respectively.[530]

Assuming that Wood produced the allotted one hundred tons of Rosa Americanas in 1722 to 1723, his output would have had a face value of about £56,000, at the standard weights. The mix of denominations is unknown, but pennies appear to have been produced in greater numbers than either twopence or halfpenny coins. If the proportions were 50 percent twopence, 40 percent pennies and 10 percent halfpence, as surviving populations suggest, then a speculative estimate of respective mintages is 3.360 million, 5.376 million and 2.688 million. Actual mintages probably were much smaller.

For the privilege of making coins, Wood was to pay a comptroller an annual salary of £200 to oversee operations. He also was required to pay an annual processing fee of £100. Initially, Sir

* Crosby included the entire text of the patent. As was the custom of the eighteenth century, in more than eight pages of laborious "legalese," no punctuation is present to make reading easier.

Isaac Newton was appointed as the comptroller. Newton's knowledge of the physical sciences was needed to make sure that Wood and his Bath metal met expectations. Newton soon requested that his nephew, a Mr. Barton, be given the position with respect to Wood's Irish coinage. Crosby noted that Barton probably was given responsibility for the American operation as well.[531]

Others are associated with the enterprise. Michael Hooder wrote that the dies may have been designed by John Croker, of the Royal Mint, given their similarity to Croker-designed royal coinage. Hodder also quoted Dr. Harry Nelson in attributing the engraving to Messrs. Lammas, Harold and Standbroke.[532] Crosby quoted Thomas Snelling, who wrote that dies were engraved by Messrs. Lammas, Standbroke and Harold. Snelling also wrote of the involvement of a Cornhill "hardwareman" named Marsland, another man named Kingsmill Eyres and others. The Rosa Americana coins "were struck at the French Change, in Hogge Lane, Seven Dials, by an engine that raised and let fall a heavy weight upon them when made hot, which is the most expeditious way of striking Bath metal, which was the sort of metal they were made of."[533] In other words, a drop press was used. It was undoubtedly the ability to *anneal*, or soften, the copper-based planchets with heat, that allowed the minters to avoid multiple strikes and the inevitable chatter and shifting of dies between blows. Thus, Wood's coins are free from the telltale anomalies that typically characterize coins made on drop presses.

***"Rosa" coinage:** A and B – 1722 twopence and halfpenny.* ***Pennies:** C – 1722, small uncrowned rose and thin letters, Thin. D – 1722,uncrowned rose, VTILE DVLCI. Note the V's in place of U's on the reverse. E – 1723, crowned rose.*

The standard weight of a Hibernia farthing is the same as that of a Rosa Americana halfpenny. Likewise, a Hibernia halfpenny is equivalent in weight to a Rosa Americana penny. The Hibernias were too light, but the Rosa Americanas were a joke at their respective face values.

Factors other than weight also limited the Rosa Americanas' acceptance. For starters, the twopence coins were confusing to Americans because no other circulating base metal coin was close in size and because no one informed local colonial officials that the coins were coming.[534] As a result, New York merchants refused to accept them. In their second act of monetary defiance (after the silver issues of 1652 to 1682,) Massachusetts issued £500 in small-denomination "coins" made of parchment for use in place of Wood's pieces. (Chapter 4.) After their rejection in New England, Rosa Americanas allegedly found a home in the southern colonies, though Ivor Nöel Hume wrote in 1998 that he knew of none ever having been found in Virginia.[535] Though examples have been found in other American locations, it is doubtful that many Rosa Americanas actually circulated in the colonies.

The obverses of regular issue twopence coins feature a bust of George I, surrounded by minor variations of the legend *GEORGIUS* · *D*[EI] **:** *G*[RATIA] : *MAG*[NAE] **:** *BRI*[TANNIAE]**.** *FRA*[NCIAE]**.** *ET* · *HIB*[ERNIAE]**.** *REX* ·, or "George, by the Grace of God, of Great Britain, France and Ireland, King." Halfpenny and penny legends generally are simplified to *GEORGIUS* · DEI · GRATIA · *REX* ·. The central reverse device is a double rose symbolizing the royal families. The reverse legend reads · *ROSA* · *AMERICANA* · *UTILE* · *DULCI.* The full meaning, "The Rose of America is Useful and Sweet," is taken from a classical poem by Horace. Translated, the poem reads "He took all the applause who blended sweet and useful" (i.e., .".mixed business and pleasure.")[536] The implication was that America was both conducive to business and a pleasurable place to visit.

On regular issue twopence coins, *UTILE* · *DULCI* appears on a banner. The other denominations and certain rare prototypical 1722 twopence coins have the phrase alone, without the banner. The prototypical 1722 twopence dies and an undated regular issue 1722 variety use the spelling *GEORGIVS.* Except for the undated 1722 twopence variety, the date follows *AMERICANA.* A distinction sometimes is made based on whether a period (or *stop*) follows *REX* or the date on twopence coins, on both 1722 and 1723 issues. One of the chief attribution points for pennies is the use of V's in place of U's in *UTILE DULCI.* Another point is the use of rosettes and stops in the legends. For halfpence, the degree to which the legends are spelled out, the use of stops and the presence of overdates are key points of attribution.

On 1723 and 1724 issues, a crown tops the double rose. The exception is a rare 1723 halfpenny variety with an uncrowned rose. Prototypical twopence and pennies of 1724 feature a large bust with a bulging collar bone. No 1724 halfpence are known. Pennies of 1724 use overpunched 1723 reverses and are very rare. A number of other prototypes and off-metal strikings complete the list. (Appendix F. contains additional information about ways to distinguish rare prototypical issues from more common regular issue Rosa Americanas.) Wood made no more coins for America after 1724, though the Duke of Newcastle wrote an October 1725 letter on Wood's behalf reminding the Governors of Massachusetts and New Hampshire of their obligation to assist in making sure that the coins circulated.[537] In addition, rare 1733 George II pattern twopence coins exist in several metals, including steel. They are seldom seen, except as modern electrotypes, and feature a rose at the end of a full, leaved stem. Since Wood died in 1730, genuine specimens probably were made by surviving relatives seeking to revive his enterprise under the new regime of George II. If so, they were unsuccessful. Similar 1724 pattern pence, some bearing George I's right-facing bust and others Queen Wilhelmina's left-facing bust, use the reverse legend *ROSA : SINE : SPINA*, or, "A Rose without Thorns." The same theme was used on George II halfpence patterns in 1727.

(Left) 1733 Rosa Americana twopence pattern, George II. (Right) Its possible inspiration: A ca. 1690 token (or medalet) featuring Mary II and a rose. The legend reads MARIA II DEI GRA[TIA] EX CANDORE DECVS *("Mary II, by the Grace of God, a Beautiful Ornament.")*

Hibernia Halfpence and Farthings (1722 to 1724)

Wood's Irish patent allowed him to make £108,000 in Hibernia coins.[538] The anticipated profits evidently justified paying Ehrengharde Melusina's £10,000 fee for delivering the patent. The situation quickly deteriorated, however, as the coins were introduced into Ireland at a very turbulent time. In 1720 Parliament passed an act to limit the power of Ireland's government. The following year, a plan to establish an Irish national bank with English directors widely was decried as an attempt to control Irish financial affairs.[539]

Foolishly and in keeping with British tradition, Wood had not consulted with Irish authorities to gain acceptance of his coins. The Irish Parliament was enraged and petitioned for the patent to be revoked. When their petitions were denied, Wood's coins became a target for those who long had opposed *any* meddling by the British. Wood did little to help the situation, promising to cram his coins down the throats of the Irish.[540] Jonathan Swift (of *Gulliver's Travels* fame) got into the act, using the pseudonym M. B. Drapier to write satirical letters protesting Wood's coins. Even though Swift's most virulent letters came after the issue was settled and the coins were no longer being minted, English authorities tried to identify and silence the author. They never succeeded and, all the while, other accusations of bribery and corruptions incited ever more contempt for Wood and his coins.[541]

1723 Hibernia farthing, harp right

The heating required for striking probably led to the discoloration exhibited by many surviving specimens. Others have rough surfaces and filed edges, suggesting the possibility of cast planchets. Propagandists used every flaw or perceived flaw to lambaste the coins.

To counter criticism and encourage acceptance, Wood offered a discount: £116 in his coins for £100 pounds sterling. Still, resistance grew, with more attacks aimed at the coins' quality and weight. Wood's image was burned in effigy in the streets of Dublin. Opponents were temporarily quieted when the King agreed to have the Privy Council, his powerful circle of advisors, review the matter. When the Privy Council reported that the coins should continue, the protests resumed. Eventually, Wood gave up on his coins being used in Ireland. However, a compromise was struck in early 1725 wherein Wood resigned his patent and limited the amount of imported coins to £40,000.[542] Of this total, £17,000, over 9 million coins, were dated 1722. Another £23,000, over 12 million coins, were dated 1723 or 1724.[543] Based on the number of survivors of each date, 1723 issues were in the vast majority.

In return for the surrender of his patent, Wood was to receive an annual pension of £3,000 for a period of eight years, more than he realistically could have hoped to receive in profits from coining.[544] Authorization of the pension was one of George I's last royal acts. In a day when a person could live fairly well on £20 a year, £3,000 was a fortune. Wood even asked to have the pension split into three equal parts so that he could manage the large sum more easily. He died in London in 1730, three years before his pension expired, and was buried in Wolverhampton, not quite a week after his fifty-ninth birthday.[545]

On the surface, Irish opposition to Wood's coins was bitter. However, to the extent that they were allowed to enter circulation in Ireland, they were accepted. Whereas £20,000 pounds in copper coins circulated in Ireland in 1722, the number rose to £50,000 by 1728, with Wood's coins being the only significant influx.[546]

Speculators evidently bought some of the coppers at their melt value and shipped them to America, where they appear to have been accepted. Hibernias have been found in numerous American non-collector accumulations, suggesting widespread circulation. Also, assuming legitimate provenance, a group of Hibernias that recently were offered through a popular online auction service were found in South Carolina, using a metal detector. Nevertheless, the general belief is that the main influx of Wood's Hibernia coinage in America came later than the 1722 to 1723 period. As of 1998, Hume was unable to cite any examples that had been found at Virginia archaeological sites.[547] Yet, some evidence exits for American circulation right up until the outbreak of the U.S. Civil War. Dr. Danforth suggested that the coins' partial demonetization in 1737 and the subsequent importation of fifty tons of new royal halfpence and farthings into Ireland brought an end to use of Wood's coins there.[548]

As with the Rosa Americanas, the most desirable Hibernia specimens are those that employ pattern or prototype dies and those struck in metals other than Bath metal. The obverses of regular issue Hibernias essentially are identical to the Rosa Americanas. They feature a bust of George I, surrounded by the legend *GEORGIUS · DEI · GRATIA · REX ·*. The reverse device is a seated rendition of Hibernia, playing or leaning on a harp. On several 1722 halfpence varieties, the harp is to the viewer's left and Hibernia is poised to play it. On other varieties, the harp is to the viewer's right and Hibernia's left elbow rests on it as she waves a sheaf in her right hand. On all but one rare prototype variety, Hibernia actually faces to the left.

The piece at right, below, is a 1723/2 harp right halfpenny. In the die used to strike this coin, the last "3" was punched over a "2" to prolong use. This overdate is relatively common and is known in "3 over small 3" and "3 over large 3" varieties. On the other hand, a 1723 halfpenny variety with a beaded cincture, or waistband, is considered rare. All varieties have the simple reverse legend *HIBERNIA* and the date, but with differences in punctuation and placement. Ignoring varieties, the 1722 and 1723 issues are very common relative to most early American coins, 1724 issues less so. Harp left issues are scarcer than their harp right counterparts.

***Halfpence:** (L to R) 1722 rocks reverse, 1722 harp left reverse and 1723/2 harp right.*

A number of rare prototype varieties also exist, including 1722 harp left farthings and a 1722 halfpence type that depicts the harp to the viewer's left and Hibernia looking back over her left shoulder at an odd rock formation that rises above and behind her. As might a modern numismatist, she appears to be puzzled about why the rock formation appears behind her. The obverse of this "rocks variety" features a very long-necked George I and the abbreviated legend *GEORGIVS D G REX*. (Note the use of a "V" in *GEORGIVS*.) Another extremely rare 1723 prototype halfpence variety has a star between *HIBERNIA* and *1723*, while an additional 1723 prototype features a larger than normal bust of George I. A handful of strikings from various prototype and regular issue dies are known in silver. They are coveted, but the "rocks" and "star" varieties are legendary, standing far above them in the eyes of collectors. Rare or common, in this sense, Wood's troubled coins have won redemption. Though he neither foresaw nor intended it, however, the most lasting legacy of his efforts may be that they cultivated the independence of both Americans and Irishmen.

VALUE ME AS YOU PLEASE: DR. HIGLEY'S COPPER THREEPENCE (1737 TO 1739)

With a little imagination, every old coin has a story to tell. Holding a Higley copper, one might envision traveling through Simsbury, Connecticut, on a snowy evening. Digress for a moment and picture the window of a local tavern glowing warmly from the four candles of a special lantern. A welcome sight, the four rayed, flickering lights proclaim from behind frosted glass that this is a "four-star" establishment. That is, for a fee, the tavern-keeper provides the four essentials: beds, victuals, drinks and livery services. To beat back the chill, you stop in and order a tankard of hot flip, a tasty blend of beer, raw eggs and molasses, heated to odd perfection with an iron rod* from the fireplace. You sit down at a small table, its top made from a single, wide plank. The tree from which it came must have been huge, a reminder of the country's great natural wealth. England had no such treasure and, hence by law a tree so large could only be harvested for the King's use, that is, unless it blew down in a storm. In that case, the fortunate landowner could keep his "windfall." What other king is so generous?

The door opens and a local doctor, Samuel Higley, comes in from the cold to order a drink of his own. He stands by the fireplace and, as is the custom in taverns of the day, pulls a long clay pipe from the several stashed in a hole above the mantel.† He breaks off the end mouthed

* The rods are called loggerheads. Tavern patrons who consumed too much flip and fought with them were said to be "at loggerheads."

† Stowing pipes in the fireplace helped tavern-keepers reduce the chance of fire.

by the previous smoker and tosses it in the fire. Stuffing his pipe with fine Virginia tobacco and lighting it with a burning twig, Higley ambles over to take a seat.

Conversation reveals that he is something of a renaissance man: a Yale graduate who has studied medicine, the trades and, oddly, metallurgy. He even owns a local copper mine and, perhaps most surprisingly, makes his own coins. What would His Majesty, George II, think? After all, only sovereign nations can make coins. Individuals or even colonies who do so are traitors to the Crown.

The hour grows late. Dr. Higley graciously thanks you for your company and offers to pay the bill – it comes to six pence. From a small bag, he pulls a few coppers, each the size of a common hapny, and gives the tavern-keeper two of them. She smiles knowingly and gestures "more." In a time when the value of a coin depends on its weight, no right-minded merchant will accept the two halfpence for a debt six times as great. Dr. Higley insists that his home-made coins are made of good copper and are worth threepence each. After some good-natured negotiation, he reluctantly throws a few more on the table, binds his coat and leaves. The bright coppers appear golden in the candlelight. Each one bears the simple image of a deer and the words *VALUE ME AS YOU PLEASE*, a cynical testament to Higley's difficulty in passing his "threepence."

The story is fanciful, but the doctor and the coppers are very real. Higley, or Granby, coppers from the 1730's are among the most popular and highly sought early American pieces. Combining known specimens from all fifteen recognized die varieties, only about seventy examples exist. Even in the 1770's, the noted Swiss-American collector, Pierre Eugene du Simitiere, was unable to locate decent examples of all of the major varieties.[549] Fourteen decades later, the situation had not changed. John Mitchelson, speaking to the New York Numismatic Club in 1910, said that even though he knew most everyone in Simsbury, (now Granby,) Connecticut, where he lived and the tokens are believed to have originated, only one person whom he met had actually heard of Higley's coppers.[550]

What is known about these tokens comes mainly from Higley family tradition and from local history of the area around Granby. The story began in 1666 when Connecticut was just three decades old[*] and John Higley, Samuel's father, had just arrived in Windsor. Five years later John married his employer's daughter, Hannah Drake. Hannah is believed to have been related both to Sir Francis Drake and to Sir Walter Raleigh. John Higley's mother, Katherine Brewster Higley, also had a famous relative in Elder William Brewster, the spiritual leader of those who came to America aboard the Mayflower.[551]

In Windsor, John Higley became a wealthy importer of Barbados rum and other goods. With his father-in-law's help, he became a landowner. In 1684 John and Hannah moved their family to Simsbury and three years later they had their ninth child, Samuel. In 1705, when Samuel was eighteen years old, copper ore was discovered in Simsbury.[552] That event would figure heavily in Samuel Higley's life, but first he attended Yale and learned to be a schoolmaster, then a surgeon. He also studied metallurgy and became an expert at making and working

[*] Connecticut was founded in 1636 when Thomas Hooker and about a hundred of his compatriots grew tired of Massachusetts' strict rules and struck out on their own. Hooker's belief that "...the foundation of authority is laid...in the free consent of the people..." (Bennett, p.68) is the Declaration's central idea.

steel.[553*] When John Higley died in 1714 Samuel inherited land. When the estate was dispersed, Samuel faired comparatively well as a middle child among fifteen siblings. He even was named one of the co-executors of his father's will.[554] In 1719, Samuel Higley married and built a home.[555]

In 1727 he patented a new method for making steel, and the following year the General Court of Connecticut granted him the exclusive right to manufacture it in the colony.[556] At about the same time Higley purchased additional land near Copper Hill and began mining copper.[557] These activities add up to strong circumstantial evidence that Simsbury had a mint. Though no contemporary documents proving that Samuel Higley began producing tokens in 1737 are known, the persistence of his association with them and his unusual combination of knowledge and skills (i.e., working copper and steel, the latter required for making dies) all but confirm that at least the 1737-dated coppers are by his hand.

Coppers dated 1739 and undated pieces, generally attributed to 1738, are another story. Samuel Higley is thought to have died in 1737 aboard an England-bound ore ship. Thus, the identities of the individuals responsible for later issues are unknown. Walter Breen credited Samuel's older brother, John, with the later pieces,[558] but this is an idea that remains more conjecture than substantiated fact.

Higley's threepence coppers clearly achieved some level of local circulation. All are worn. However, they did little if anything to retire the large issues of paper money that Connecticut had printed since 1709. In hopes of alleviating the problems associated with depreciating currency, John Read of Boston solicited Connecticut's help in obtaining a royal patent to mint coins. He was ignored. Based on the 1739 date of Read's petitions, which seemingly overlaps the tokens' production, Sylvester Crosby suggested that Read might have been in cahoots with Higley's operation.[559] In one of Read's letters to the General Court of Connecticut concerning his proposal, he asked that "...[Rev. Timothy] Woodbridge of Simsbury..." be allowed to serve as an intermediary. Read also indicated that "...mine adventurers Mr. [William] Cradock & others..." were linked to the proposal.[560] Breen noted that both Woodbridge and Cradock were friends of the Higley brothers.[561] Thus, Read might have taken over the operation and minted the 1738 and 1739 tokens after Samuel Higley's demise.

Was Simsbury copper used in the tokens? Probably, though the area's mines never were very productive. Jonathan Belcher corroborates this in contemporary letters. Belcher, who later became Governor of Massachusetts and New Hampshire, then of New Jersey, partnered with a handful of men in signing a thirty year lease of the mines beginning in 1712. Belcher's[†] letters lament the questionable quality of ore from the mines and his resulting losses. He claims to have invested £15,000 over the three decades during which he leased the mines. At times, his complaints led to open disputes, at least one of which was with Samuel Higley.[562]
It also is possible that Samuel Higley refined copper himself, though much of the Copper Hill ore was shipped to England. Several years ago, Dr. Dan Freidus performed neutron activation analyses on Higley coppers to determine their metallic composition. His study showed them to

[*] Higley family genealogy asserts that John Higley's descendants include John Brown, the abolitionist fanatic who conducted a violent antebellum raid at Harper's Ferry, Brewster Higley VI, who wrote *Home on the Range*, Governors Jonathan Trumbull, Sr. and Jonathan Trumbull, Jr. and artist Col. John Trumbull.

[†] The Belcher Foundation credits Belcher with founding Princeton University, as well as establishing the scheduling of Thanksgiving Day as the fourth Thursday in November. The foundation also draws links between the layout of the Belcher's family/gubernatorial seals and the Great Seal of the United States. (Belcher Foundation website.)

be of no more pure copper than other contemporary pieces.[563] This contradicts a traditional belief that the rarity of Higley tokens is due to their having been used by goldsmiths who sought very pure copper to make alloys. On the other hand, eighteenth century *perception* of purity was based on far less precise analytical methods than those employed by Freidus.

In addition to his metallurgical analysis, Freidus developed an attribution scheme for describing die combinations seen on the surviving pieces. In 1875, when he wrote his monumental work, *Early Coins of America*, Sylvester Crosby knew of eleven different die combinations. Freidus and others have added four, bringing the total to fifteen.* Using Freidus's taxonomy, obverse and reverse dies each are divided into four major styles. Qualifiers provide further discrimination based on minor variations. Freidus uses numbers to identify obverse dies and letters to identify reverse dies. Using his system, major die combinations are 1-A, 1-B, 2-B, 3-B, 3-C, 3-D and 4-C. The order of die pairings supports the idea that the undated varieties may be 1738 issues. A chart of the major styles follows, with secondary qualifiers omitted for brevity.

Higley Threepence Dies, Using Dan Freidus's Taxonomy[564]

	Desig-nation	Distinguishing Characteristics
Obverses	**1**	A stylized deer is the central design feature. The index finger of a left hand points to the legend, as ☛*THE·VALVE·OF·THREE·PENCE*☆. Used with reverses A and B.
	2	As on the obverse 1, a stylized deer is the central design feature. The legend reads ☛*VALVE.ME.AS.YOU.PLEASE*☆. A small, ornamented Roman numeral *III* follows. Used only with reverse B.
	3	The third obverse type is essentially the same as the second, except that *VALUE* replaces *VALVE*. Used with reverses B, C and D.
	4	The fourth obverse type is completely different and was unknown to Crosby. Its central device is a wheel rather than a deer. Its legend's meaning is unknown: ☛*THE.WHEELE*[sic].*GOES.ROUND.* Only one specimen with this obverse is known. Howland Wood discovered it in 1913.[565] This obverse is only paired with the undated (1738?) reverse C.
Reverses	**A**	Three hammers, each crowned, with one above and two below, make up the central device. The legend on this reverse type is preceded by a star and simply reads ☆*CONNECTICVT 1737·*. Used only with obverse 1.
	B	The second reverse differs from the first in its legend, which reads: ☛*I.AM.GOOD.COPPER.* ❧✿❧ *.1737*. Used with obverses 1, 2 and 3.
	C	The third reverse has a broadaxe as its central device, circumscribed by the legend: ☛ *J.*[i.e., I]*CUT.MY.WAY.THROUGH.* Unlike reverses A and B, it bears no date. Used with obverses 3 and 4.
	D	The fourth reverse is similar to the third, except the broadaxe's orientation varies slightly and the date, *1739*, is added. Used only with obverse 3.

The devices and legends pose intriguing riddles about their intended meanings. The deer probably is symbolic of Connecticut's natural wealth. The star and pointing hand seen on some varieties may be Masonic, though Higley's membership never has been established. It is more likely that the star is a symbol for copper. The symbol, ♀, long has been used to symbolize

* Freidus detailed these varieties in *The History and Die Varieties of the Higley Coppers* for the American Numismatic Society's Coinage of the Americas Conference in New York, Oct. 29, 1994.

copper. It also is the symbol for the planet Venus. Venus, as the Morning Star and Evening Star, also long has been symbolized by a hollow, five-pointed star, as ☆. Venus's star commonly is seen in conjunction with a waning moon, ☾.[566] Higley obverse 3 sometimes exhibits what looks to be such a moon, beneath the "O" in *YOU,* though it is not clear whether this feature was intentional or the product of a die anomaly.

When the copper ran out, the Simsbury mines lived on in another capacity. Beginning in 1773, some of them were used as a prison – or dungeon. Captured British soldiers were held there, as were debtors and those who had committed more serious offences. The mine tunnels were a Hellish place to be interred. Their incessant cold and dampness make them unpleasant even for short visits during warmer months. "Bowls" carved into the rock at points where water seeps into the mines were used by prisoners to capture and hold drinking water. The only quality making the place tolerable was the ease with which an escape could be made. Eventually known as Old Newgate Prison, after the infamous English facility, the mines were used in that capacity until 1827 and thus constituted the nation's first state penitentiary.

Lore has it that local merchants, especially tavern keepers, refused to honor the halfpenny-sized coppers at six times their intrinsic value, leading Higley to adopt the more flexible legend, *VALUE ME AS YOU PLEASE.* In the early 18th century, the purity of copper was measured by its malleability and symbolized by hammers. Three hammers indicated that the copper was very pure. As with *VALUE ME AS YOU PLEASE*, the legends, *I AM GOOD COPPER* and *I CUT MY WAY THROUGH*, as in "A coin of good copper cuts through doubt," may have been attempts to convince merchants that the tokens were of sound value. The meaning of *THE WHEELE GOES ROUNDE* is unknown. It could allude to fortune's wheel and changing fates. More likely, the twelve spokes of the wheel represent months or signs of the zodiac and the wheel's turning represents the march of time.

1738(?) Freidus 4-C (modern copy)

The piece above and the three below are commonly seen reproductions of Higley coppers. Such reproductions are worthy of study because most genuine examples are very worn and because obtaining a specimen with full details is cost prohibitive for most people. The leftmost example below may be a cast from one of the struck copies made by John Bolen in 1864, though it lacks Bolen's identifying dot within the "C" in *PENCE*. Were it genuine, its variety would be Freidus 1-A. Copies such as this are quite similar to the originals and, consequently, should be regarded as potentially deceptive. The second piece is a modern (2005) reproduction of the genuine Freidus 3.3-B.a variety shown below. The third piece is a potentially deceptive copy of Freidus variety 3-C, made in the early 1960's. The reproduction of the unique Freidus 4-C, the "Wheele Goes Round" variety, that appears above, was also made in 2005.

1737 Freidus 1-A (Older Copy) *1737 Freidus 3.3-B.a (Modern Copy)* *1738(?) Freidus 3-C (1960's copy)*

The piece below represents one of the four varieties discovered after Crosby's time. Note that the deer on the obverse exhibits double striking, a feature common to many specimens. The recurrence of this characteristic led Breen to suggest that the tokens were struck by hand, and that the extra strikes were needed to strengthen weak impressions.[567] A drop press also could produce this effect and is a possibility. The reverse of this piece exhibits an interesting tapering of the planchet that results in preservation of greater detail in some areas than in others. This feature and the token's slightly oval shape at least suggest that a rolling process or rocker press might instead have been used.

1737 Higley threepence, VALUE ME AS YOU PLEASE / I AM GOOD COPPER, Three hammers reverse; Freidus 3.3-B.a variety.*

Perhaps owing to the primitive conditions under which they were made, Higley coppers vary considerably in weight, from 119 to 178 grains.[568] The poor, often corroded state of many known survivors makes exact determination of their original weights difficult.

Higley's coppers represent several firsts. They are the first wholly private issues and the first coppers made in America.† Of course, they were Connecticut's first coins. Just as in

* Thus, its variety designation is obverse die 3, qualified as sub-variety 3. Its reverse is die B, sub-variety a. Even in its worn state, this coin is the centerpiece of this author's collection. It was part of the Waldo Newcomer collection before passing to Colonel Green and then to Burdette Johnson, of St. Louis.

† Barring discovery of new information about the brass New Yorke in America and Gloucester tokens.

Massachusetts, Maryland and New Jersey, Connecticut's numismatic legacy did not end with its first issue. As a state under the Articles of Confederation, Connecticut again had an indigenous coinage. Above all, Higley's coppers epitomize early American culture: simple, folksy, original, entrepreneurial and independent. They are as ghosts from that time.

Non-deceptive copy of Freidus variety 2-B. The Connecticut Historical Commission now operates the site of Higley's mines and the Old Newgate Prison site as a museum, offering these copies of Higley coppers as souvenirs. Even copies as crude and as clearly marked as this occasionally are offered as genuine.

A long drought followed Higley's coppers, with no domestic American coins or tokens produced for nearly three or, possibly, four decades. Aside from occasional shipments of British halfpence, no coins intentionally were imported until after 1760.

HIBERNIA VOCE POPULI TOKENS (1760)

When George II died in that year, several pretenders vied to be his successor. It is believed that proponents authorized tokens to gain public support for their respective candidates. These tokens, known by their legends as Voce Populis, generally are attributed to John V. Roche, of South King Street in Dublin. In addition to making Irish army buttons, Roche made some of the many medals that commemorate Admiral Edward Vernon's New World victories over the Spanish during the War of Jenkins' Ear. [569*]

Most Voce Populis approximate the weight of light Irish halfpence. However, rare, smaller examples are considered to be farthings. The intended weight for the Voce Populi halfpence appears to have been 116.67 grains. For farthings, it probably was 58.33 grains (i.e., sixty and 120 to a pound, respectively.)

Farthing, large letters obverse.

All Voce Populis bear right-facing busts of men whose exact identities never have been established. Clearly, several different individuals are represented. Except for an error variety[†]

---

[*] Vernon led several successful attacks on Spanish strongholds in the New World in 1739-1741, most notably at Portobello (now in Panama.) His exploits are celebrated on nearly three hundred different medals. One of the men with him was Colonel Lawrence Washington, George's father. In honor of the admiral, Lawrence Washington named his home Mt. Vernon.

[†] Dr. Phillip Nelson, a medical doctor, wrote the original defining work on varieties of Voce Populi coinage in 1905. Nelson knew of twelve halfpence varieties. That number was expanded to sixteen by Robert Vlack. Nelson's nomenclature, as extended by Robert Vlack and others, still is used today. In 1976, Jerry Zelinka authored an expanded and much clearer classification scheme for halfpence using integers to denote obverse dies and letters to denote reverse dies. He skipped obverse designators 9 through 12 and reverse designators G through J to allow for future discoveries. Zelinka also documented five different border types. Zelinka's work

that reads *VOOE POPULI*, the obverse legends all read *VOCE POPULI* ("Voice of the People.") Reverses feature a left-facing, seated rendition of Hibernia, with her name as the sole legend. The proper date is 1760, but two reverse dies were made with the errant date 1700. Both dies were corrected, but a few examples of the tokens with the incorrect date are known.*

Sixteen halfpenny varieties with nine different portrait types and five different border types are recognized. These variations occur on twelve obverse and eleven reverse dies. Portraits on the two farthing varieties are similar to each other and are differentiated by either *small* or *large letters*.

On four halfpenny varieties, a "P" appears on the obverse, either below the bust (on Nelson 11, 13 and 14) or in front of the bust (on Nelson 12.) It could mean *prince* or *princeps*. Alternately, it might signify "pretender," though no one seeking the throne would want to be so described. The pretenders included Jacobites James Francis Edward "James III" Stuart (a.k.a. the *Old Pretender*) and Charles Edward "Bonnie Prince Charlie" Stuart. Also included in the list is Irish Parliamentarian John Hely-Hutchinson.[570] Obviously, none of them had names that began with "P" and, thus, the true meaning of the letter is unknown. The Jacobite claim to the throne that had been asserted periodically since the Glorious Revolution never again was taken seriously after 1760.

(Left) Nelson 12 (Zelinka 15-N,) "P before face" variety. Nelson varieties 10 through 14 have similar portraits. On Nelson varieties 11, 13 and [the very rare] Nelson 14 variety, "P" appears below the bust. Nelson variety 10 does not have a "P." (Right) The obverse of Nelson 14 (Zelinka 16-O.) Zelinka called this the "peculiar long-headed bust."

Other Voce Populi halfpence portraits:
(Left) The young bust from Nelson 1 (Zelinka 1-A, the "boyish head.) (Right) The stern bust from Nelson 9 (Zelinka 6-C.) Portraits similar to that on Nelson 9 appear on Nelson varieties 2, 6, 7 and 16.

Traditional wisdom holds that, after the coronation of George III, the obsolete tokens were shipped en masse to America, where the "Voice of the People" message would have been well received. However, American resistance to British rule did not begin in earnest until 1765.

---

appears as an article in *The Colonial Newsletter* ("The Enigmatic Voce Populi Halpenny of 1760," v.15, no.3., October 1976, pp.555-565.)

* Nelson 2 and Nelson 6 have a line added to the first "0" to form a "6." "6A" denotes the rare uncorrected version of Nelson 6. Many Nelson 6 examples have been altered to resemble the much rarer Nelson 6A.

Voce Populi tokens do occasionally surface in American finds and long have been accepted as American, although solid evidence of their systematic importation is lacking.

All of the Voce Populis share a kind of primitive style that is faintly reminiscent of classical Greek and Roman coins. Assuming that they deliberately were imported, they represent the fourth and final group of deliberate Irish imports to enter America in significant numbers, behind patent farthings, St. Patrick coppers and William Wood's Hibernia pieces. Of course, genuine and counterfeit Irish halfpence circulated incidentally in America, sometimes appearing as undertypes for other coins. *Éireann go Brách.*

Nelson 4, the "tall head" variety. Zelinka designated it 2-A, the "older head." Compare to the "young head" or "boyish head" on Zelinka obverse 1, with which reverse A is shared.

*Nelson 8 (Zelinka 3-C.)** *Note the use of diagonal lines as dentils. This portrait type also appears on Nelson varieties 5 and 15. A similar portrait appears on Nelson variety 3, the VOOE POPULI variety.*

The Voce Populis marked the end of the purely colonial phase of American numismatic history. Gone was the innocence, the absolute and unwavering faith that the American plantations would always march in lock-step with the Crown. In its place came the budding realization that, not only could the colonies go it alone, it was their moral imperative to do so.

* Nelson 8 (Zelinka 3-C) often is confused with the more common Nelson 15 (Zelinka 3-A.) The rosette near the base of the harp and the wideness of the "N" in HIBERNIA identify the example below as Nelson 8. Nelson 15 has a circle in place of the rosette and the "N" is narrow.

9: CONFLICT (1764 TO 1781)

THE TUG OF WAR

> *But what do we mean by the American Revolution? Do we mean the American War? The Revolution was effected before the war commenced. The Revolution was in the minds and hearts of the people.* – John Adams, in a letter to Hezekiah Niles, February 13, 1818.[571]

The coins, tokens and medals of the turbulent period that followed are few in number, but full of meaning. They occupy a spot very near the Revolution's ground zero. They carry new themes and were minted for new purposes. Some promote unifying ideas and claim continental scope. Others are more provincial. While coins occasionally had been used to make political statements during the colonial period, early issues were viewed almost exclusively as instruments of commerce and not as means of advancing political ideas. That changed for both sides in the 1760's as the American colonies slipped ever closer to open rebellion.

The first such piece appeared in the late 1760's, to celebrate repeal of the Stamp Act. Pitt tokens, or perhaps medalets, probably were sponsored by New York's Friends of Liberty and Trade. True or not, tradition says that they were designed by Boston's Paul Revere and minted by the Philadelphia gunsmith, William Smithers. Following closely the 1765 Stamp Act Congress, these tokens may represent one of the earliest cooperative protests against British rule. Both halfpence and rare farthings honor William Pitt, the English master statesman who, along with Benjamin Franklin, primarily was responsible for ending the despised act.

Only one other series debuted in America before the Revolution began. In 1769 Virginia's economy was large, diverse and badly in need of circulating coinage. To meet this need the colony petitioned for relief in the form of the coins that its charter had promised more than a century and a half earlier. Anxious to keep its greatest colony from joining the fray, the Crown finally granted Virginia's request for halfpence in 1773. George III no doubt was keen on the idea of putting his crest and smug profile before Virginians to remind them of their place. However, by the time the new coins arrived in America, war was at hand and the colonial treasurer was afraid to release them without explicit royal orders to do so. The orders came too late and the new halfpence quickly disappeared into hoards. Others apparently were held from release until late in the war, when coin shortages were particularly acute. By then, even blatant Loyalist symbolism was not enough to keep Virginia's halfpence from circulating. Technically, the term "colonial" is used to describe coins that a parent country makes for its colonies. In this sense, Virginia halfpence are the *only* British coins to earn the proper title "American colonial" since they are the only ones produced officially by the Crown for one of the thirteen colonies.

When it erupted in 1775, the Revolution put any real hopes of American domestic coinage on hold. Even so, citizens of two states, Massachusetts and New Hampshire, took steps toward producing coins. Three pieces, each unique and all dated 1776, are thought to have been patterns for Massachusetts. Rare 1776 New Hampshire patterns, if they are not circulating issues, also exist in three styles. Two of the three styles may be later fabrications, though the third probably is from the period.

The only pieces minted in significant numbers in America during the Revolution are the famous 1776 Continental Currency coins. These dollar-sized icons were Congress's first attempt at national coinage. With devices that reprise the fractional currency authorized on February 17, 1776, no other coins are as close to the essence of the Revolution. Their Fugio obverse vignettes almost scream "Franklin!" Their *WE ARE ONE* motto and chain of thirteen links are the distinctive marks of nation in the making. These symbols simultaneously convey unity *with* and independence *from* each other. Yet, for all that is known of the fateful year in which they originated, surprisingly little is understood about the coins or the people who made them. A few pieces were minted in silver, a few in brass and a significant number in pewter. Though not the rarest of early American coins, all of them are historical treasures.

The last issue associated with the Revolutionary period is that of 1779 Rhode Island ship tokens, or medals. Minted either in pewter or brass, these ambiguous pieces almost certainly were intended as propaganda, but for whom? On one side, they portray Americans retreating as Admiral Richard Howe's forces approach a tiny island off Newport, in 1778. The tables were turned the following year, when Howe was forced to flee the island ahead of the French. Accordingly, the tokens' opposite sides appear to depict Howe's flight. The legends apparently were directed at the Dutch, who unofficially were helping the American cause through trade in military provisions. The intent may have been to convince them that Britain would prevail and that aiding the Americans was folly. Since the date of Howe's flight appears opposite that of his triumph, however, the meaning is clouded. No one has proven that these pieces circulated as coins in America, though many examples exhibit wear and, as do no other types, they clearly depict specific events in the Revolution.

The exceptions in this group of revolutionary coins are counterstamped and recycled French colonies' pieces and a 1767 issue of copper sols that carry a generic "French Colonies" label. By 1764, the French had ceded their North American wilderness empire to England and Spain. Consequently, these coins actually circulated more in the Caribbean than elsewhere. Still, they often are treated as American. Most of the 1767-dated sols were held until after the French Revolution when, beginning in 1793, they were counterstamped *RF*, for *Republique Francaise* – "French Republic."

NO STAMPS! WILLIAM PITT TOKENS (CA. 1766 TO 1768)

These coins, medals, tokens and, indeed, the Revolution itself, sprang from events that began in 1764. That year a mentally unstable Boston lawyer, James Otis, published a remarkable pamphlet called *Rights of the Colonies Asserted and Proved.* It argued the radical idea that Britain had no right to tax the colonies at all. With his quill and the help of mass communication, Otis lit a wildfire that could not be extinguished. Discourse quickly mobilized sentiment against the Sugar Act and its taxes on imports such as sugar, wine and indigo.

James Otis, Jacques Reich engraving after a J. D. Blackburn painting. Source: Mace (142.)

Then, in 1765, with its fervor for taxes still building, Parliament made its most serious pre-Revolution error in judgment with Lord Grenville's Stamp Act. Under this act taxes were levied on all paper, printed documents and even dice. Distributing a document publicly meant that a fee had to first be collected by a representative of the Crown. In exchange a stamp was applied to signify approval. It was an affront to commerce that would cost the colonies an estimated £100,000, almost three times the impact of the Sugar Act. In passing the Stamp Act, Parliament ignored Benjamin Franklin's more reasonable revenue proposals, such as creation of a central paper money-issuing bank in Philadelphia and letting the colonies themselves decide how to raise funds.[572] Beyond its economic impact, the Stamp Act threatened free expression and, in taxing dice, angered the rough and ready dock workers and seamen whom Samuel Adams, legendary rebel, maltster and cousin of John Adams, molded into revolutionary mobs.

Within months the Stamp Act spawned a gathering, in New York, of delegates from nine of the thirteen colonies. This *Stamp Act Congress* represents one of the earliest acts of unity among colonies that had always and adamantly regarded themselves as separate from one another. It was only the second time that anything close to a truly *continental* congress had convened. The first was a 1754 conference in Albany that was limited to talk about plans for protecting the frontier from Indian attacks.

American resistance to the Stamp Act coalesced around Samuel Adams, who helped found the radical Sons of Liberty, the group responsible for the Boston Tea Party and other pre-war acts of protest against British authority. The protests were not always dignified. For example, a tax official died after being tarred and feathered by an angry mob and the home of Thomas Hutchinson, the royal governor of Massachusetts, was ransacked violently. Hutchinson and his family barely escaped. In April 1775 the British were in pursuit of Adams and his financial supporter, John Hancock, when they encountered the first armed resistance at Lexington.

Samuel Adams. Ca. 1870 engraving. Henry B. Hall, after Copley.[573]

In 1765 and 1766, however, the issue was the Stamp Act and its most effective opponent was not even an American. William Pitt was Parliament's greatest orator and the man whose management skills had saved Britain from defeat in the Seven Years War. Pitt skillfully built the case against the Stamp Act. As he neared the end of the climactic speech of the debate over its repeal, Pitt issued a prophetic warning for Parliament:

> *I have been charged with giving birth to sedition in America. I rejoice that America has resisted...The gentleman asks, When were the colonies emancipated? But I desire to know when they were made slaves...America, if she fell, would fall like a strong man. She would embrace the pillars of the state, and pull down the constitution along with her. Is this your boasted peace? Not to sheathe the sword in its scabbard, but to sheathe it in the bowels of your countrymen? Will you quarrel with yourselves...now* [that] *the whole House of Bourbon is united against you...?*[574]

William Pitt, 1778.
Source: Library of Congress, Prints & Photographs Division, LC-USZ62-45223.

Pitt's compelling words foretold the world war that the American Revolution became. Parliament listened and, on February 22, 1766, at 2:30 in the morning, the House of Commons voted for repeal of the Stamp Act. About a month later, King George III made it official and,[575] when word of the repeal reached America two months later, Pitt, "The Great Commoner," was an instant hero.

In retrospect, it should be noted that Pitt's motives actually fall under the heading of enlightened self-interest. Though he supported colonial interests and clearly opposed undue taxation, Pitt never abandoned the idea that the colonies existed for the benefit of Great Britain. As did Franklin, he realized that a few American representatives in Parliament could never garner enough support to adequately represent the colonies. Pitt simply was smart enough to realize that keeping the colonies happy was just good business. As a contemporary Englishman said of the Americans, "If we allow France and Holland to supply them with fabric, we may just as well give up all ideas of having colonies at all."[576]

Stamp Act stamp, two shillings and six pence. The stamps arrived in America, but the refusal of the colonists to cooperate resulted in very few stamps actually entering the public arena. Consequently, few surviving examples are known to exist outside museums and even those are generally from specimen printings. Even so, other contemporary official stamps are relatively common and bear a strong resemblance to those that were intended for America under the Stamp Act.

It appears that the New York's Friends of Liberty and Trade, a related but less drastic group than the Sons of Liberty, chose to honor Pitt and commemorate the 1766 repeal with tokens or medalets. If the tradition that the tokens were designed by Boston's Paul Revere and manufactured by the Philadelphia gunsmith, William Smithers, is true, then these pieces mirror the Stamp Act Congress as an early act of unity among the colonies.

While best known for their activities in Boston, the Sons of Liberty also were active in New York. In the years following the Stamp Act's repeal, merchants in Boston, New York and Philadelphia continued their protests by refusing to import British goods. In theory British pocketbooks would be hit so hard that Parliament would be forced to yield relief. Overall, American imports fell by about a million pounds during this period. For New York, whose imports fell from nearly half a million pounds to only about £74,000 in 1769, the boycott was an especially bitter pill. At the same time, the last New York bills of credit were retired and hard currency disappeared from circulation. Leaders of Boston's Sons of Liberty advocated continuing the policy of non-importation. Others, however, thought that non-importation helped only smugglers and wealthy merchants, with whom Boston was rife. The Friends of Liberty and Trade were among those who celebrated the Stamp Act's repeal, but favored an end to the policy of non-importation. They drank to "trade and navigation and a speedy removal of their embarrassments."[*577] In all likelihood, a member of the Friends chose to convey this view with tokens. If so, then the actual minting may have occurred as late as 1770.

Pitt tokens come in two sizes that are called halfpence and farthings. The halfpence are scarce, with survivors numbering a few hundred. Farthings are very rare, with only a handful of survivors, almost all holed, presumably for use as pendants. Contrary to tradition and based on appearance, Pitt tokens may be of English manufacture.[578] Obverses of the smaller pieces closely resemble those from a group of English medals made in Pitt's honor. Moreover, no *hard* evidence tying either denomination of Pitt tokens to an American maker is known.

---

[*] In the eighteenth century, "embarrassment" referred to a barrier rather than an awkward social situation.

English manufacturers made teapots and other goods bearing anti-Stamp Act messages for the American market. Why not tokens?

Obverses of both Pitt tokens feature his profile facing left, perhaps in deliberate opposition to the right-facing portrait on George III's halfpence. The style of Pitt's portrait is reminiscent of colonial-era folk paintings and drawings. Similar figures may be seen in the propagandist engraving that Paul Revere later created to publicize the Boston Massacre. The legend that surrounds each of the Pitt token portraits reads **:***NO · STAMPS***:** *THE · RESTORER · OF · COMMERCE · 1766***.** On the halfpence, the last "R" in *RESTORER* is much smaller than the other letters, perhaps implying a spacing miscalculation by the die maker. The farthings have a similar design with the portrait slightly modified. On both, the central reverse device is a three-masted ship with the word *AMERICA* appearing diagonally beneath its bow. The circumscribed legend reads *THANKS TO · THE · FRIENDS · OF · LIBERTY · AND · TRADE***.**

Pitt pieces: *A – 1766-dated Pitt halfpenny. B – Obverse of a holed farthing. C – A later medalet depicting Pitt as Lord Chatham in 1773. The halfpenny exhibits a straight planchet clip (edge clip) at 2 o'clock on its obverse, indicative of its maker trying to obtain as many planchets as possible from a strip of copper. In this case, the planchet was at the very edge of its strip. The first "6" in the date shows the mark of shears used to remove the planchet from its place in the rolled strip.*

The standard weight for the halfpence of this issue appears to have been in the range of 84 to 89 grains, considerably less than a standard British halfpenny that weighed 152.17 grains. The farthings weigh between 51 and 65 grains. As with St. Patrick coins, the ratio of halfpence to farthing weights is approximately 3:2, suggesting a relationship other than halfpenny to farthing and lending credence to the idea that the original intent may have been to create medalets rather than coins or tokens. Even so, both sizes appear to have circulated. Pitt halfpence sometimes retain traces of silvering. Rarely is the silvering intact over the entire surface. Any trace of it is considered desirable by collectors.

The subject of these pieces and their close proximity to the Revolution have long given them exalted status among those who see history in coins. As a footnote, not everyone associated with this episode became an iconic patriot. For example, William Smithers was accused in 1778 of high treason, by the Pennsylvania Supreme Executive Council, for counterfeiting Continental Currency notes.[579] Nor were all of the founders steadfast in their opposition to the Stamp Act or in the conviction that it would be repealed. Richard Henry Lee, the Virginian who later proposed independence to Congress, hedged his bet by applying to be a stamp distributor. His actions later proved to be a source of personal embarrassment.[580] Finally, James Otis, the man whose lightning pen arguably started the Revolution in 1764, was killed in his farmhouse doorway by real lightning, in the spring of 1783. By then lucid thought had been, for many years, an infrequent visitor to this overlooked and underrated patriot.[581]

FRANCE'S PARTING SHOTS (1760-1767)

The 1760 fall of Montreal marked the practical end of New France. After the 1763 treaty made it official, some French coins that were devalued by the British in Canada found their way to newly-Spanish Louisiana. In addition, the unrelenting need for small change in France's Caribbean holdings meant that worn, discolored sous marqués, fifteen deniers coins of 1692-1705, mousquetaires, billon double sols of 1738 to 1764 and even 1782 Cayenne two sous all continued to circulate there as "black doggs" or *noirs*. Passing at 1½d in the British West Indies, they were joined in 1765 by shipments of sous marques and mousquetaires that had been sent from the French treasury back to the mint to be re-issued with a crowned "C"counterstamp. Brits in the West Indies valued the reissues at 2¼d. As demand increased, these *sols estampés* or "stampees" were supplemented with new pieces, on billon and copper blanks, bearing *only* the counterstamp. English coiners in Birmingham even made phonies, incorporating the full sou marqué design *and* its counterstamp in a single die, for use by their countrymen.[582]

Crowned "C" stamp on a copper blank.

In 1766 Louis XV signed an edict authorizing the last French issue commonly associated, rightly or wrongly, with America. Old billon coins again were recalled and, to replace them, 1.6 million copper twelve-denier coins were minted, each of them bearing the generic "French Colonies" designation and the date *1767.*[583] If contemporary documentation is to be believed, only a small percentage of these coins actually entered circulation in 1767. The remainder inexplicably were held until 1793, just after the birth of the French Republic. Their release finally came when they were ordered by Georges Henri Victor Collot, governor of the ultra-valuable Caribbean sugar colony of Guadeloupe. To signify that France was under new management, these later releases received the obverse countermark *RF,* for *Republique Francaise.*[584] Countermarked examples certainly are more common than unmarked examples, though the difference in numbers of survivors is not as great as one might expect. Thus, the 1793 release also could have included unmarked pieces.

These coins may have served as large cent substitutes in America after the U.S. Mint exhausted its planchet supply in 1815. The intended weight of the French coppers, 188.89 grains, about thirty-seven to a pound,[585] loosely equates to the 168-grain standard weight for U.S. cents from the 1795 to 1816 period. (Chapter 12.)

Reverses of these twelve-denier coins feature the French royal scepter and the scepter of justice,[586] with the legend *COLONIES FRANCOISES L*[UDOVICUS] *XV*, or "French Colonies of Louis XV." Obverses display a crowned wreath surrounding three fleurs de lis. The legend reads *SIT NOMEN DOMINI BENEDICTUM* ✠ *1767* ("Blessed be the Name of the Lord.")

Both countermarked and unmarked pieces frequently are referred to as "Collots," after Guadeloupe's governor who, as a French officer, fought beside Washington's men in the American Revolution. Collot was appointed governor of Guadeloupe in 1793, just in time to authorize release of the coins before the colony was captured by the British, who turned him over to the Americans. In 1796 the French minister to the United States offered Collot a chance to explore the American interior for the purpose of gathering intelligence to use should America join forces with the British. Starting in Pennsylvania with a French cartographer,

Joseph Warin, along with two Canadians and three Americans, the expedition found and descended the Ohio to the Mississippi. The group then ventured upriver to St. Louis, briefly exploring the Illinois and Missouri Rivers, before heading south to New Orleans. There they were captured and held by the Spanish for nearly two months. During this time Warin died of injuries he had received during the expedition.[587]

1767-A French Colonies copper sols de 12 deniers: *(L to R) Obverse without RF counterstamp. Reverse. Obverse with the RF counterstamp*

After being released Collot returned to France to finalize his notes and maps from the expedition. When Spain traded Louisiana back to Napoleon in 1800, Collot was named one of the commissioners who would administer the re-acquired territory. However, the new post never materialized because Napoleon sold the territory to the Americans. Though Collot died in 1805, in Paris, his notes finally were published in both French and English, in 1826.[*588]

Circulation of Collots in Louisiana or British America almost certainly was incidental and any continued association of the coins with Collot, the explorer, is purely speculative. Even so, Collot was a well known figure, with ties to Guadeloupe, Louisiana and the Republic of France, who literally might be the "missing link" for tying these coins to America.

VIRGINIA'S COINAGE (1773 TO 1774)

Jamestown's 2007 quadricentennial is a reminder of Virginia's pivotal role in the Revolution. That role deliberately was minimized by northern publishers in the decades after Appomattox. However, it was a Virginian who proposed independence, a Virginian who justified it and a Virginian who, with French help, eventually won it, the decisive battle coming but a few miles from Jamestown. It would have been a shame had the era ended without a numismatic memento of the state's unique history.

In its 1606 charter, Virginia was given the right to its own coinage, a privilege no other American colony ever enjoyed. However, the right went unexercised because tobacco so quickly became Virginia's dominant medium of exchange. Virginia's early survival was inseparable from tobacco's success. Tobacco-based currency, however, was inherently problematic. Seasonality of production, spoilage, climatic variation and the whims of the marketplace all made for more instability than a proper monetary system could stand.

Several official attempts were made to discourage the use of tobacco in trade. In 1633, for example, Virginia removed its monetary status because of the tendency to fluctuate in value. Three years later Virginia Governor, Sir John Harvey, petitioned the Crown for small change

[*] The English version of Collot's work is titled *Journey in North America, Containing a Survey of the Countries Watered by the Mississippi, Ohio, Missouri and Other Affluing Rivers.*

with which to pay workers in the time between when harvested tobacco was shipped and when payment for it arrived.[589] The response *may* have been a shipment of patent farthings such as those described in Chapter 5. In the 1640's overproduction caused tobacco prices to drop precipitously. However, it appears that nothing actually was done to help the situation until 1645, when an attempt was made to legislate coinage. As no coins associated with this legislation ever have surfaced, it seems unlikely that any were produced. By the 1680's angry farmers burned tobacco plants in an effort to raise prices. To stop the practice, laws were passed making the harming of a tobacco plant a crime punishable by death.[590] Other, more reasonable legislation was intended to stabilize the situation by expanding the list of commodities that were legal in trade.

Virginia laws passed in 1714 and 1727 set the values of world gold and silver coins according to their respective weights. The legislation did nothing to relieve the scarcity of small change that, for the vast majority of people and businesses in Virginia, was a far greater concern. The situation continued to worsen until just before the outbreak of the Revolution. By then and by all measures, Virginia was the largest of the thirteen colonies, with nearly a third of America's population and accounting for about 60 percent of her total exports to Britain.[591] Clearly, Virginia's economy had long since outgrown tobacco as a day-to-day medium of exchange.

Beginning in 1769 the Virginia General Assembly petitioned the Crown to allow the purchase of £2,500 in copper halfpence. The Crown was anxious to appease its largest colony to keep her out of the growing tension. Moreover, the coins offered an opportunity to remind Virginians of their colonial status by putting before them the king's portrait and royal arms, just as swords and firearms were arranged decoratively on the walls and ceilings of Williamsburg's capitol, a clear sign to visitors that British authority resided within. After long negotiations, five tons of coppers from the Tower Mint finally arrived in Richmond late in 1773. Their arrival was reported in the February 23, 1774, issue of the *Virginia Gazette*.[592]

The plan hit a snag when Virginia's treasurer and one of the richest men in America, Robert Carter Nicholas, refused to release the halfpence into circulation without royal authorization. Governor Dunmore complained to London about the lack of authority, prompting a royal proclamation that was published in the *Virginia Gazette* on February 23, 1775. The proclamation said that five tons of coppers were ready to be shipped to Virginia. By then, however, the coins already were in circulation, as evidenced by another article in the same issue. The second article stated that embargoed goods from the ship *Thomas*, seized by the Surry County Committee of Safety, had been sold for £138 11s 9d in Virginia halfpence.[593] The proclamation authorizing the coins' release had come when war was less than two months away. Consequently, many halfpence were hoarded and disappeared from circulation. Others probably were held in storage until late in the war when someone remembered their whereabouts and released them. Even though their legends are distinctly loyalist, they readily were accepted because of shortages created by the war.

Ironically, Thomas Jefferson wrote that coppers *never* circulated in Virginia. Sylvester Crosby evidently took his word for it and, in a rare miscalculation, treated the halfpence as unauthorized tokens.[594] Nevertheless, several have been found at archaeological digs at Colonial Williamsburg and other Virginia sites. As part of Jefferson's 250th birthday celebration, for example, a special exhibit of items found on the grounds of Monticello was put on display. Among the items were what appeared to be two mislabeled examples of Virginia halfpence! Ivor Nöel Hume also cited a particularly well-preserved example found under the

Peter Scott House on Duke of Gloucester Street in Williamsburg. Soldiers quartered there in January 1776 accidentally burned the Scott house and, in doing so, unwittingly marked the latest date of that coin's circulation.[595]

Halfpenny obverses depict a right facing bust of George III by Richard Yeo, accompanied by the legend *GEORGIVS • III • REX •*. The majority of surviving specimens have a period or "stop" after *GEORGIVS*. Reverses bear the crowned shield of the Hanovers with a legend that simply reads *VIRGI NIA 1773 •*. The number of strings on Ireland's harp, in the lower left quadrant of the arms, further helps to differentiate the forty or so known die combinations. Few collectors, however, discriminate beyond "stop" and "no stop." Varieties with stops have either seven or eight harp strings, while "no stop" varieties also include reverses with six harp strings. A few presentation pieces were minted on heavier planchets and have fully denticulated (tooth-like) borders. These sometimes erroneously are referred to as "pennies."

A

B
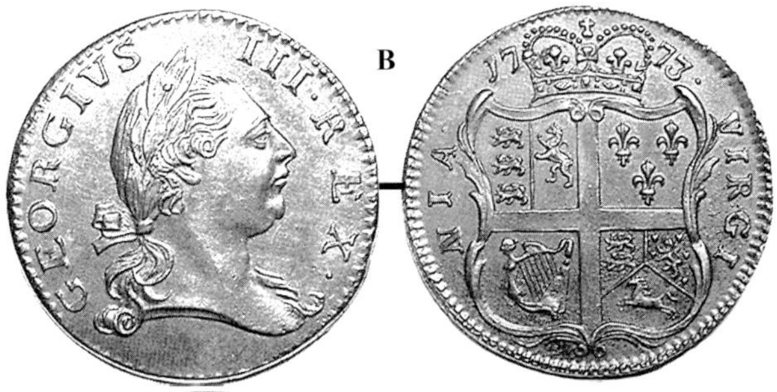
C

D
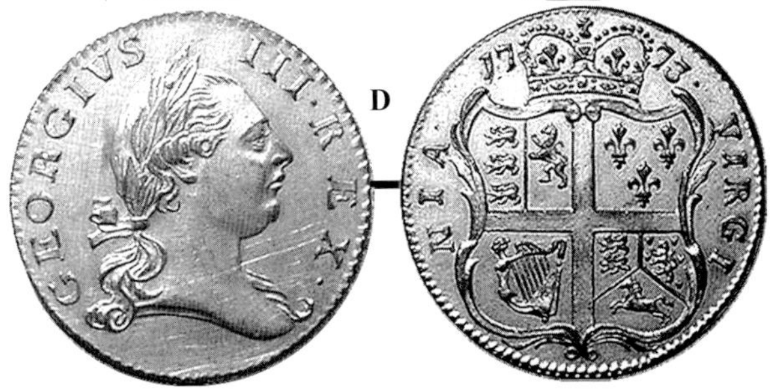
E

F

G

1773 Virginia and similar coinage: *A – A "stop" variety halfpenny. B – "No stop" variety, seven harp strings. C – Obverse of a 1774 Virginia shilling by Thomas Pingo. Silver shillings were minted to a standard of 83.3 grains, at sterling fineness. D – Halfpenny, no stop, seven harp strings. This halfpenny was silvered, either to pass as a shilling in the eighteenth century or later to fool collectors. Given the period's scarcity of specie, design similarities between Virginia halfpence and contemporary British specie and that neither explicitly states a denomination, it is easy to understand how a silvered or gilded Virginia halfpence might have passed for a higher denomination. E – 1786 Guinea, by Pingo (Compare to Virginia shilling.) F – 1787 regal shilling by Richard Yeo. G – Modern souvenir copy of a Virginia halfpenny made for the Colonial Williamsburg Foundation (CWF.) Even such non-deceptive copies occasionally are offered to the unwary as genuine in the marketplace.*

Very rare pieces were struck in silver and feature a slightly different obverse portrait by Thomas Pingo. Their reverses virtually are identical to those of the halfpence, but bear the date *1774*. Since British patterns rarely are dated, the silver specimens probably were intended as presentation pieces. They are referred to as shillings, or occasionally as Guineas.

Regular Virginia halfpence were minted to a standard of 116.67 grains (sixty to the pound,) the so-called pennies to a standard of 134.6 grains. At sixty to the pound, the five tons of halfpence that Virginia requested would have contained about 672,000 coins.

A keg of uncirculated halfpence was found in Richmond just before the Civil War. Many of the specimens known today can be traced back to this find. These hoard pieces typically display some mint red, interrupted by spots of very dark coloration. Most of the hoard coins are of the more common stop or period die varieties. The find is referred to as the Cohen Hoard, after Mendes Cohen, the dealer who initially purchased and distributed the coins.

NEW HAMPSHIRE AND MASSACHUSETTS PATTERNS (1776)

NEW HAMPSHIRE PATTERNS (1776)

New Hampshire was much less in the limelight. For years its farmers had been concerned more with fighting New Yorkers over property rights than with fighting the Crown over tyranny. Its government was based entirely on custom and rule by governors. Fearful that this arrangement would be insufficient to preserve order, New Hampshire adopted an emergency constitution on January 5, 1776. The soon-to-be state experimented with pattern coppers in June 1776, a month before the country declared independence. New Hampshire's legislature authorized acceptance of any coins made in the colony on par with its paper money and gave pewterer/silversmith, William Moulton, responsibility for turning a scant hundred pounds of copper into coins. At the 152.17-grain halfpenny standard, about 4,600 coppers *could* have been minted.[596] However, opinions differ as to whether the project ever progressed beyond the pattern stage. Only a handful, perhaps twenty, genuine, crude pieces survive from the effort. More pieces exist, but many of them are of questionable authenticity.

New Hampshire copper pattern, type one.

New Hampshire coppers take two basic forms or types. The first depicts an obverse pine tree with the legend *AMERICAN LIBERTY*. The reverses simply feature a harp, the date *1776* and no legend. The harp is similar to one appearing on contemporary seven-dollar Continental Currency notes. The intended meaning, as given on the notes, probably was *Majora Minoribus Consonant,* or "The Large [states] and the Small [states,] Together in Harmony." Both struck and engraved specimens exist, but those given the best chance of being authentic are cast. These cast pieces range in weight from 145 to 155 grains,[597] bracketing the halfpence standard and accounting for most of the survivors.

The other New Hampshire type has a very stylized tree, flanked by *17* and *76*, on the obverse. On one variety of this type, the line of a rounded hill intersects the tree trunk. On the one other variety, the line is flat, as seen on the modern copy above. Type two reverses feature the large initials *WM*, presumably William Moulton's, in the center. The circumscribed legend reads *AMERICAN*: *LIBERTY-*. Second-type pieces generally are not regarded as genuine, partly because it is very doubtful that New Hampshire would have allowed Moulton's, or anyone else's, initials to appear so prominently on official issues. Also, second type pieces are light, in the vicinity of 80 grains and all of them are cast. Nevertheless, they were known in Crosby's time and somehow could be related to the genuine examples. Perhaps Moulton made them as advertising pieces to pave the way for his involvement in the issue that New Hampshire sought to authorize, or as a private venture, when the official coining operation failed to materialize.

(Left) 1776 New Hampshire copper pattern, type 2, style 1. (Right) Type 2, style 2, modern copy. (Below) Moulton's mark.

New Hampshire patterns are so rare that the probability of encountering a genuine specimen is almost zero. Yet, copies number in the millions. Anyone claiming to have an authentic New Hampshire copper should be treated with a polite, but healthy measure of skepticism. Farmers of "The Live Free or Die!" state fought honorably in the Revolution, but left precious little in the way of a tangible numismatic legacy.

Massachusetts Patterns (1776)

Their New England neighbors, in Massachusetts, had been practicing for independence since 1652. The decade leading up to 1776 is remembered primarily for events that transpired within her borders: Stamp Act protests, the Boston Tea Party, the Boston Massacre, Lexington and Concord, Bunker Hill and Breed's Hill. Massachusetts also is remembered for iconic individuals such as the Adams cousins, James Otis, John Hancock and Paul Revere. Massachusetts led the way, but paid the price of freedom by enduring blockades, occupation, siege and scathing warfare. It is hardly surprising that, near the onset of the Revolution, someone in Massachusetts saw fit to experiment with copper coinage. That person might have been Paul Revere. The coinage experiments apparently took place just before and just after July 4, 1776. All that remain from them are three coins that generally are considered to be patterns. Three types and precisely one known example of each type exist. Two are now in institutional collections, those of the Massachusetts Historical Society and the American Numismatic Society. The third is private hands.

Later portrait of Paul Revere. After Charles Saint Memin (Original, early 19th century. Reproduction pub. ca. 1887.) Source: Library of Congress, Prints & Photographs Division, LC-USZ62-7407.

Judging from legends, the oldest of the three is the so-called "Province Halfpenny." Its obverse displays the commonwealth's symbol, an Indian, standing with bow and arrow. The obverse legend reads *PROVIN*[CE] *OF MASSA*[CHUSETTS]:. That it is dated 1776 and refers to the *province*, rather than the *state,* indicates a time of issue just prior to the Declaration of Independence. It is struck over a 1747 Irish halfpenny, is holed and weighs 127 grains.[598]

The reverse of the Province Halfpenny bears a figure of Liberty, seated on a globe and facing left. This single crude rendition may be the first of Liberty's many personifications on American coins. A watchdog sits at her feet to warn of approaching redcoats. The reverse legend partially is obscured, but probably reads something like *D*[EFENSOR LIB]*ERTATIS*[599] or "Defend Liberty." The date is in exergue, below Liberty. The Province Halfpenny surfaced early in the twentieth century and now belongs to the American Numismatic Society.

The 1776 Massachusetts "State Penny."

The second 1776 Massachusetts copper depicts a stylized, conical pine tree on its obverse. The tree is similar to that represented on the Sons of Liberty flag and recalls John Hull's seventeenth century Boston shillings. The circumscribed obverse legend reads *MASSACHUSETTS STATE*, placing its date of issue after July 4, 1776. The symbols *1d* and *LM* flank the tree's trunk. The meaning of *1d* clearly is "one penny." The phrase "Lawful Money" was in common use and refers to the Massachusetts valuation of six shillings to a Spanish dollar. Thus, *1d LM* equates to 1/72 of a Spanish dollar, the value of a penny. As such, this unique specimen is called the "State Penny." It weighs 198 grains.[600] Its reverse depicts Liberty seated on a globe, with the legend *LIBERTY AND VIRTUE.* Again, the date 1776 appears in exergue, beneath Liberty and, as on the Province Halfpenny, a watchdog sits at her feet. The object in her extended right hand may either be a warning bell or a liberty cap.

Massachusetts' State Penny was found by a grocer as he was excavating to expand his home in the northern part of Boston, near Hull or Charter Street. The site is not far from the small house-turned-museum where Revere reared his seventeen children. Around 1852 the grocer sold the State Penny to a young boy who collected coins.[601] After changing hands several times, it now belongs to the Massachusetts Historical Society.

The third Massachusetts type, sometimes called the "Janus Copper," has three rather theatrical-looking faces on its obverse and a seated Liberty reverse. The three faces look to the right, left and three-quarter center. Breen observed that this is reminiscent of the Hindu God, Brahma, who saw the past, present and future.[602] The Roman goddess, Janus, had just two faces and saw only the past and the future.* It is likely that the faces are anonymous, that they simply are keeping watch in all directions and thus that the Janus Copper's name is a misnomer. The obverse legend reads *STATE OF MASSA*[CHUSETTS] *½ D* or "State of Massachusetts Halfpenny." Again, the word "state" is telling because Massachusetts was not known as a state until after the events of July 4, 1776.

* Janus gave her name to the month January, the boundary between the past and future years.

The reverse of the Janus Copper presents a figure of Liberty seated on globe and facing right. She holds a staff in her right hand and what may be an alarm bell in her left, though Crosby wrote that her left hand holds a liberty cap.[603] Again, a dog sits at her feet, ears peaked. The circumscribed reverse legend reads *GODDESS LIBERTY*. As on the other 1776 Massachusetts pieces, the date appears beneath an exergue line.

The 1776 "Janus Copper."

The lone Janus copper was found among currency proofs printed by Paul Revere. This circumstance and similarities to his other work led to the attribution of the Janus Copper to him[*].[604] All three types are similar enough to conclude that the same person made them, whether or not that person was Revere. Perhaps in his role as courier for the Sons of Liberty, Revere was an intermediary between the maker and John Hancock or Samuel Adams. Perhaps he intended to copy the designs, as he is known to have done with engravings of the period.

With only three 1776 Massachusetts coppers known and all accounted for, the odds against locating another specimen are great. Yet practically every online coin auction, many gun shows and some flea markets offer copies in great numbers. Most of these copies of copies are lead-filled electrotypes that actually are heavier than the originals. In addition to building on Massachusetts' seventeenth century heritage of coinage, the patterns represent America's first numismatic personifications of Liberty. Their symbols echo the spirit of rebellion voiced by Hull's silver coinage. Eleven years later the "Pine Tree State" again would add to this heritage by producing coins in the Confederation Era. (Chapter 9.)

CONTINENTAL CURRENCY COINS (1776)

No early American coins are more famous than the so-called Continental "Dollars" of 1776. These were, in fact, the only coins produced in significant numbers in America during the entire Revolution. They clearly represent the first attempt by the fledgling U.S. government to create national coinage. Yet, the circumstances of their creation and reasons for their existence are long forgotten secrets. They may have been intended as patterns or they may have been intended for circulation. The truth probably lies somewhere between. That they are at the same time so historic and so mysterious only adds to their appeal.

Continental Currency coins *must* be linked in some way to the bills of the same name. Recall that Congress began issuing bills of various denominations in 1775 and that the fractionals authorized on February 17, 1776, used a sundial vignette on their faces. That device is part of a rebus. The mottoes in the vignette read *FUGIO* (short for *TEMPUS FUGIT,* or "Time is Fleeting") and *MIND YOUR BUSINESS*. Long attributed to Benjamin Franklin, the meaning to an eighteenth century citizen likely would have been, "Time is wasting, so get to work [building American business.]"

[*] A mysterious engraved copper bearing an eagle and other symbols also was found in Revere's stash. Neither its creator nor the meaning of its symbolism is known.

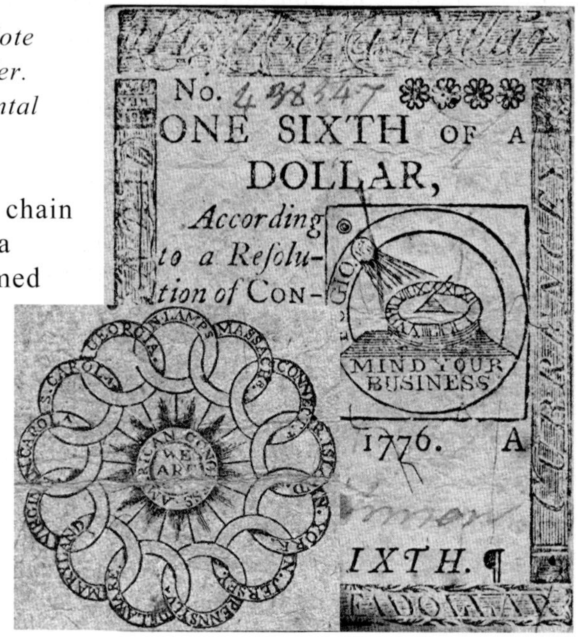

February 17, 1776 Continental Currency \$1/6, face. Note the misspelling "CURRENCEY" in the right-side border. (Inset) "Chain" vignette used on the backs of Continental Currency fractional notes.

The backs of the fractional bills present a circular chain of thirteen joined links, each bearing the name of a newborn state. In the center, on a rayed band formed by two concentric circles, are the words *AMERICAN CONGRESS,* along with the unifying and, at the time, wishful message WE *ARE ONE*. Continental Currency coins use the same devices and themes, and share the 1776 date. In July 1776 Congress suspended production of the one dollar bills. The next month, the state of New York followed suit and discontinued its own dollar notes. It is conceivable that these steps were taken because there were too many dollar notes in circulation or because the notes had depreciated. However, one dollar notes were produced in no greater numbers than other denominations and would not likely have been singled out. Moreover, even at the end of 1776, Continental Currency bills were devalued by only 1¼ percent of their corresponding value in specie.[605] Thus, it seems likely that the suspension of dollar notes came in anticipation of their outright replacement by coins. Other than their size, this is the most compelling argument for calling the Continental Currency coins "dollars." Both Eric Newman and Walter Breen wrote that they were intended to back the redemption of the one-dollar bills.[606] This is entirely logical, since foreign governments were reluctant to accept un-backed paper currency from a not-yet-recognized nation. The coins are known in silver, brass and pewter. The pewter pieces may have been intended as substitutes until silver was available, in the manner that supporters of James II issued gunmoney in the seventeenth century (Chapter 5.)[607] A concurrent attempt to acquire a large quantity of silver from France failed[608] and the expectation of its arrival doubtless affected Congress's plans for coinage. Still, any connections between the shipment and the 1776 coinage are tenuous.

Suggesting another possible scenario, a 1776 New York newspaper article described a rumored copper coinage that ultimately would have been denominated as pennies. However, Congress had little justification for producing minor coinage in light of the critical need for silver to support the war effort.[609] In addition, a February 20, 1777, mint proposal, for which the coins might have been patterns, never was acted upon.[610] Some in Congress may have pondered a tri-metallic system, with brass pieces representing something akin to pennies and silver pieces emulating Spanish dollars. If so, then what was the intended role of the pewter specimens?

Details about the circumstances under which the coins were minted are equally sketchy. Congressional committees were formed to write the Declaration of Independence, formulate a foreign policy, raise an army and perform myriad other tasks associated with founding a nation, including the creation of coinage. While history immortalized the men who drafted the Declaration and performed other vital duties, the coinage committee's membership roster is forgotten. Intuition suggests that Franklin or even Jefferson might have been members of it. If so then why was neither man's participation recorded then or later? Could it be that neither wanted to be associated with an effort that ultimately failed? Or is it that the committees were so numerous, their activities so frenetic and the record-keeping so inconsistent that documents simply were lost? Or were the creation of coinage and the implication of sovereignty that it carried so indefensibly treasonous that contemporary records never existed or were purposely destroyed? It is entirely possible that the answers never will be found.

More than a thousand combined specimens of all varieties and metals survive. Most are worn, suggesting some level of general circulation. Even so, they have been collected since the beginning. British officers occupying New York in the summer of 1776 saved them.[611] Their appeal to collectors may explain the fact that a relatively large proportion of surviving specimens are uncirculated or nearly so.

One die variety holds an important clue in the phrase *EG FECIT*, which long has been interpreted to mean "Elisha Galludet made it." Galludet was the New Jersey engraver responsible for the 1776 Fugio fractional bills and for ornamental devices used on other notes. Thus, he is the most likely candidate for the die maker. It was common practice for an engraver to sign his work with initials followed by the word *FECIT* ("made it.") Newman strengthened the case for Galludet by observing that the coins' designs are two-dimensional, as one would expect from an engraver of plates for documents.[612]

A less accepted theory suggests that *EG* refers to Elbridge Gerry, who chaired a committee of the Treasury.[613] (Gerry also was associated with the practice of defining political boundaries to serve particular interests, hence the term "Gerrymandering.") Another idea, unlikely and founded on no more than this author's hunch, is that *EG* might have a second meaning. As it does in other contexts, *EG* might stand for *exempli gratis*, or "for the sake of example." Thus, the second meaning of *EG FECIT*, in less than proper Latin, might have been something like, "made for the sake of example." In this scenario, the variety with *EG FECIT* could represent a pattern and, contrary to general belief, might have been made early in the series.

In all, six different dies were used, nine if re-cuttings are counted. With these re-cuttings, five known obverses and four reverses combine to produce seven varieties. Either Eric Newman's classification scheme or a more recent one devised by Michael Hodder generally is used to describe varieties. Hodder's taxonomy recognizes the fact that some dies are simply re-cuttings and not entirely different dies.[614] The most obvious differences among known dies and re-cuttings are noted below. More subtle differences are found in the sundial numerals, the names/positions of the states in the reverse links and in the position of the gnomon (the part of the sundial that casts a shadow.) All seven die combinations are rare in the relative context of collector demand, even if not in the context of early American coinage.

Varieties fall into two distinct groups, understanding of which might be the key to the history of the series. The groups are distinct because dies used to produce varieties in either are unused on any of the varieties from the other. Based on his analysis of the series' probable emission sequence, Hodder speculated that the first group might have been made in New York before the British occupation that began in September 1776. He further speculated that the second group might have been made in Lancaster or Philadelphia after the government fled New York in advance of invading redcoats. This is a plausible scenario, but one that, by Hodder's own account, lacks conclusive evidence.[615] The tables below and the chart on the next page describe the varieties in each group.

	Newman Variety	Hodder Variety	Known Specimens
Group I	1-A	1-A.1	Known only in brass. Very rare.
	1-B	1-A.2	Known in both brass and pewter. Very rare.
	1-C	1-A.3	Most common variety in pewter. Very rare in silver.
	2-C	2-A.3	Known only in pewter. Third most common variety.
Group II	3-D	3-B	Second most common variety in pewter. Very rare in silver.
	4-D	4.1-B	Known only in pewter. Very rare.
	5-D	4.2-B	Known only in pewter. Very rare.

In both groups, edges generally exhibit a twin olive leaf design that is analogous to ornamentation on the fractional notes and is later repeated on the edges of the larger denomination 1783 Constellatio Nova patterns. (Chapter 10.)

	Newman Die	Hodder Die	Distinguishing Characteristics
Obverses	1	1	*CURENCY* spelling.
	2	2	*CURRENCY* spelling, without *EG FECIT*.
	3	3	*CURRENCY* spelling, with *EG FECIT*.
	4	4.1	*CURRENCEY* spelling as on $1/6 Continental Currency notes.
	5	4.2	To conceal the misspelling, *CURRENCEY's* "Y" is overcut with a "*snowflake*" and the second "E" is overcut with "Y."
Reverses	A	A.1	Reverse rings composed of dots. The "N" in *AMERICA*^{N} is very small, probably indicating a spacing miscalculation.
	B	A.2	Same die, with the dots overcut by lines. Re-cut from A.1.
	C	A.3	Same die, with lines fully replacing dots. Re-cut from A.2.
	D	B	Lines used. The "N" in *AMERICAN* is normal size.

The primary difference between the two groups is the exclusive use of a single reverse die within each (Hodder reverse A for Group I and reverse B for Group II.) Group II also contains Hodder/Newman obverse 3, the *EG FECIT* die. Differences in Group I spellings of "currency," differences in the makeup of the rings on Group I reverses and the absence of brass examples from Group II all suggest that the Group I pieces were made first and that the rare varieties and metals were intended as patterns. When taken together, the differences in the two groups may point to different die makers and possibly even to different mints.

If there was a second mint and whether or not the off-the-wall speculation that *EG FECIT* has a second meaning is true, then perhaps the Group II pieces were made first as patterns in New York. It seems likely that Galludet would have added his initials to the first die of the series rather than the third. The Group I pieces could have been made for circulation after the evacuation, at a hastily assembled mint and by another die maker. This could explain the evolution of the reverse rings from dots to solid lines. The brass Group I pieces may represent a desperate attempt to use whatever metal was available, as opposed to the planned use of a third metal. James Spilman has suggested an alternate theory in which the differences in the two groups might be the result of a competition aimed at selecting a die maker.[616]

Varieties of 1776 Continental Currency Coins

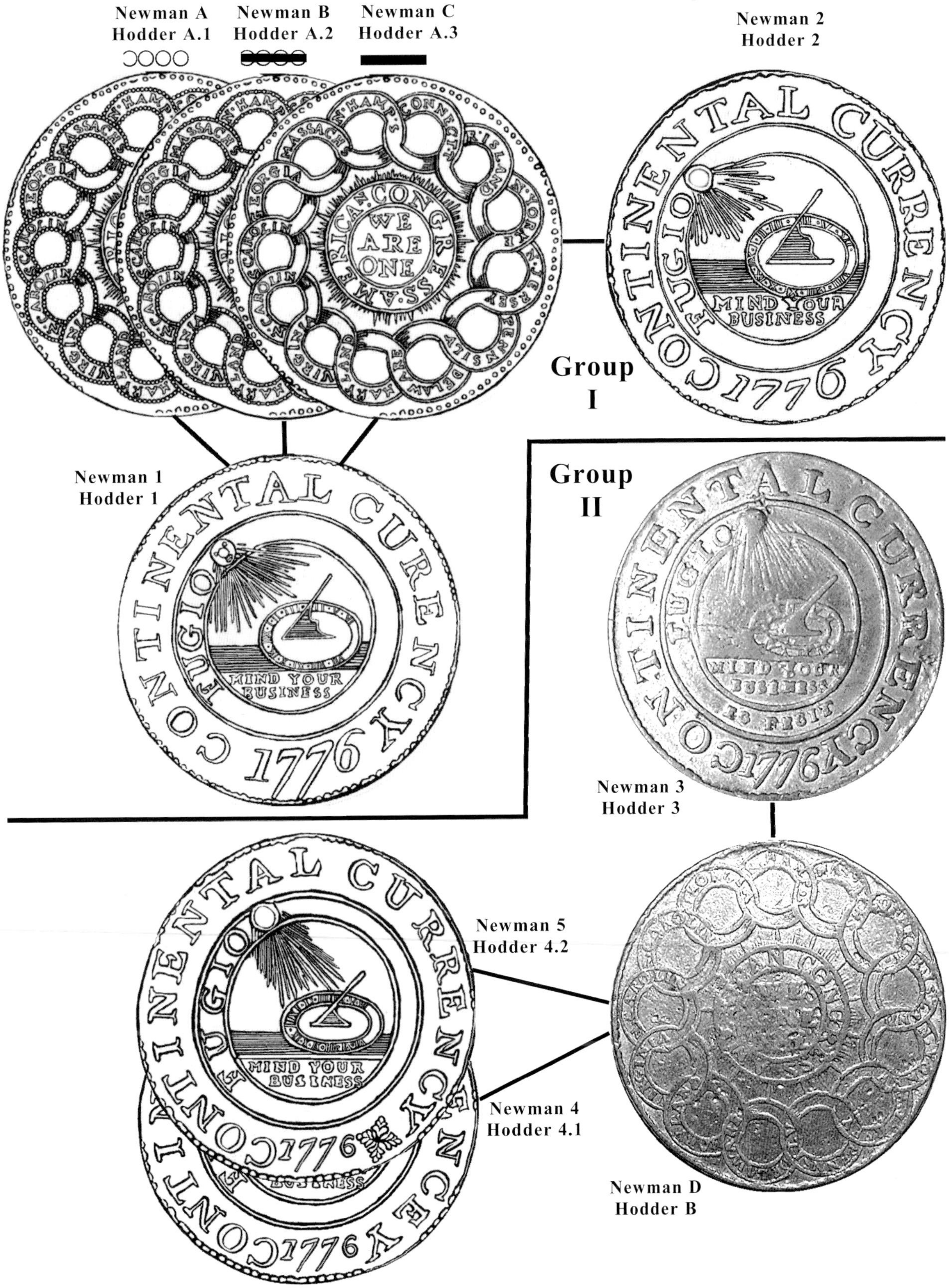

Continental Currency coins are placed close to 1776 by roughly contemporary documents. Breen, for example, gave a 1789 reference and Crosby cited Watson's Chemical Essays, a work published in Dublin, Ireland, in 1791.[617] Moreover, Lester C. Olson cited a 1784 illustration of a Continental Currency coin that is taken from a German work describing American medals. In the illustration, *CONTINENTAL CURRENCY* is translated to *AMERICANISCHE LANDES MUNTZE* and *WE ARE ONE* becomes *WIR SIND EINS*.[618] Olson also presented the idea that the use of iconography symbolic of the number thirteen (e.g., the links on the reverses of Continental Currency coins) in a national context represents a compromise between those who favored unity and those who preferred autonomy of the states.[619] (Almost every Confederation Era American coin echoes this duality.)

1783 Felicitas Britannia et America medal obverse.

A contemporary medalic reference to Continental Currency coins also exists. The reverse of the very rare 1783 *Felicitas Britannia et America* ("Peace [Between] Britain and America") medal is almost identical to Newman reverse C. Its obverse crudely depicts America as an Indian princess making peace with Britannia in front of St. Paul's Cathedral and various other London landmarks. The scene calls to mind a Queen Anne-era fountain at St. Paul's that depicts America and Britannia with Caledonia and Hibernia. The pewter medals commemorate the Treaty of Paris, but incorrectly give the signing date as September 4, 1783, the day after the actual signing. September 4 was the day that news of it reached London, suggesting a British origin for the medals. Nevertheless, the American reverse, the overall crudeness and the choice of metal all argue for American origin. As with the 1776 state patterns in the previous section, Continental Currency coins were and are frequently copied. *Most* copies are not deceptive to anyone accustomed to viewing the genuine article. Restrikes of Dr. Montroville Dickeson's 1876 copies, made before World War I by Thomas Elder and again in the early 1960's by Q. David Bowers,[620] are among the most frequently encountered. These exhibit proof-like characteristics and lettering wholly unlike the originals. Other copies are electrotypes. Still others deceptively are struck in lead or other soft metals.

(Left) Bowers' ca. 1960 restrike of Dickeson's copy, "aged."

(Right) Newman 3-D. Correct weight (254 grains) and specific gravity (7.36.) Is it a deceptive copy or a genuine example?

Known genuine examples of Continental Currency coins in pewter weigh between 232 and 286 grains. The specific gravity of genuine pewter examples ranges between 7.15 and 7.45.[621]

Copper/brass specimens weigh 199 to 314 grains, averaging 241 grains. The four known silver pieces average 374 grains,[622] close to the weight of a Spanish eight-reale coin, which was set at slightly over 385 grains in 1776.

Technical measurements aside, after more than a century of serious study, the Continental Currency issue of 1776 remains one of the most intriguing topics in American numismatics.

ENIGMATIC RHODE ISLAND SHIP TOKENS OR MEDALS (CA. 1779)

Equally mysterious are the Rhode Island ship tokens, if they are tokens at all. Are they medals as is more likely? Who made them? Where were they made? Why? Where did they circulate? Because of their Dutch legends, they long were believed to have originated in the Netherlands. Most numismatists now believe that they were made in England, probably for Dutch circulation. Part of this theory is based on the availability of metallurgic technology to the minters. Most examples of these tokens are made of brass; however, certain rare pieces are known in pewter. English manufacturers, such as Matthew Boulton, had access to brass-making technology that probably was unavailable to the Dutch.[623] One popular theory says that the medals were created to convince the Dutch that the British were winning the American Revolution. Another, Walter Breen's, suggests that they actually were done to satirize the British. Whatever the case, these pieces did circulate somewhere, as many are found worn. This circulation is the only real basis for calling them tokens rather than medals.

To be sure, the British had reason to be concerned about their continental neighbors. In 1779, the Revolution was well on its way to becoming a world war. The Dutch, always masters of commerce, actively were engaged in selling war materials to the Americans. Much of the dealing took place on the tiny Caribbean island of St. Eustatius. There, in 1776, the Netherlands became the first world power formally to recognize American independence by firing a military salute to a ship, the *Andrew Doria*, that was flying the American flag.[624]

Admiral Earl Richard Howe. Reproduced 1794 engraving by R. Dunkarton, after John Singleton Copley. Source: Mace (161.)

Whereas other coins and tokens of the period refer to broad ideas or issuing authorities, Rhode Island ship tokens refer to specific events that took place in August 1778 and in October 1779. On orders from General William Howe, General Henry Clinton took control of Newport, Rhode Island, for the British in December 1777. The following August, Major General John Sullivan's ten thousand American militiamen and four thousand French troops, under Admiral Comte d'Estaing, gathered to reclaim the strategic town. Admiral Richard Howe, William Howe's brother, stood ready to defend the British position. The battle was to take place on tiny Conanicut Island, west of Newport. As D'Estaing's ships moved into position, a three-day storm scattered both his fleet and Admiral Howe's, and devastated Sullivan's troops. The French ships were forced to return to Boston for repairs. The Americans, vulnerable in their exposed position facing Howe's fleet and Clinton's advance, abandoned the island.[625] It is this retreat to which the reverses of the tokens refer. They depict American troops fleeing Conanicut Island toward a flotilla of small evacuation boats, with Richard Howe's ships bearing down from the west. The circumscribed legend reads *D'vlugtende AMERICAANE*^{N} *van ROHDE YLAND Aug*^{t}, *1778*, meaning "The Fleeing Americans of Rhode Island, August 1778."

(Note the unusual use of lower case letters, suggesting medalic intent.) "Fleeing Americans" is political "spin." In truth, the Americans fought admirably to shield the evacuation.

The obverses are the real subjects of controversy. They depict Richard Howe's flagship, with the circumscribed legend *DE ADMIRAALS FLAG van ADMIRAAL HOWE 1779*, or "The Admiral's Flag[ship] of Admiral Howe, 1779." Howe's flagship was the 64-gun *H.M.S. Eagle.*[*] It is thought that the Eagle was the first ship ever to be attacked by a submarine. In September 1776, Ezra Lee, aboard the tiny one-man American submarine, Turtle, tried to screw a mine into the hull of a British warship (believed to have been the *Eagle*) anchored near where the Statue of Liberty now stands. The attack failed because the Turtle's screw hit metal rigging rather than the wooden hull. Lee escaped in David Bushnell's invention by exploding the bomb as a diversion.

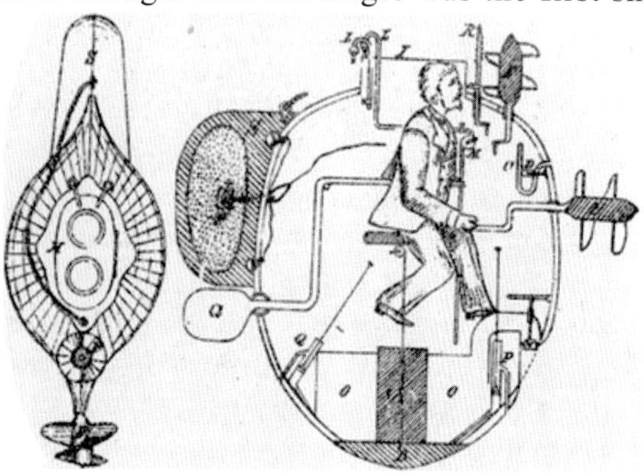

Bushnell's Turtle. *Source: Library of Congress, Prints & Photographs Division, LC-USZ62-110384.*

One of the three known medal varieties has the word "*vlugtende*" beneath his ship. It actually should read "*vluchtende*," Dutch for "fleeing." Howe was forced to abandon Rhode Island in late October 1779. Apparently, *vlugtende* refers to his retreat.

Breen noted that the ship's sails are furled, indicating that it is not moving and, therefore, not in retreat.[626] On the other hand, furled sails could imply that the ship was not ready for battle. With a strong French presence in the area, the threat of conflict always was close at hand. The British fleet never was more than an alarm away from full sail. Moreover, what may have seemed to be a retreat by Howe actually was part of a shift in British strategy to the southern theater. Thus, the furled sails may satirize the reticence of the British command to engage the French while they had the chance. Why they did not engage is open for debate. William Howe respected the Americans, having fought beside them in the last French and Indian War. Moreover, both Howes favored a more liberal approach to colonial affairs than the Crown's. Was their decision to avoid a fight an extension of their political views?

On some specimens *vlugtende* has been scraped away. At some point, it was removed from the die itself, creating a second variety. An ornament replaces it on the third variety. Was the use of *vlugtende* a simple mistake, intended for the reverse, and not as a reference to Richard Howe? Was it an act of satire or subversion? No one can say for sure, but the fact that the word is misspelled suggests that the designer or engraver was not intimately familiar with the Dutch language. This clearly buttresses the theory that the tokens are of English origin.

The reverse of a Rhode Island ship token also is ambiguous. Its design might be seen by an Englishman as symbolizing American cowardice and retreat in the face of overwhelming force. On the other hand, it might be seen as a celebration of the Americans' well known ability to retreat and fight another day.

---

[*] It is thought that the Eagle was the first ship ever to be attacked by a submarine. In September 1776, Ezra Lee, aboard the tiny one-man American submarine, *Turtle*, tried to screw a mine into the hull of a British warship (probably the *Eagle*) anchored near where the Statue of Liberty now stands. The attack failed because the *Turtle's* screw hit metal rigging rather than the wooden hull. Lee escaped in David Bushnell's invention by exploding the bomb as a diversion.

1779 Rhode Island ship tokens/medals: *(Left) In brass, vlugtende removed from die. (Right) A 1930's copy with an ornament and Horace M. Grant's initials (HMG. See below.)*

The first known appearance of ship tokens in numismatic literature came in 1785, in a Japanese guidebook of European coins.[627] Thus, it is at least certain that the tokens were issued sometime between 1779 and 1785, that they were perceived by some as European and that they describe a very real series of events in the midst of the Revolution.

A 1778 political cartoon depicting America, cutting off the horns of the cow of British commerce, while a Dutchman milks it and Spain and France watch with bowls of milk. A troubled Englishman watches while the British lion sleeps and dog urinates on its back. In the background, the Howe's sit drunk in Philadelphia and the Eagle has run aground. Source: Library of Congress, Prints and Photographs Division, LC-USZ62-15755.

Rhode Island ship tokens/medals usually are found made of brass and weighing 130 to 160 grains. Recorded weights of the rare pewter pieces range from 129 to 170 grains. Electrotype copies and 1930's struck copies by Providence coin dealer, Horace M. Grant, abound. Unaltered Grant copies bear his initials in the waves beneath the Eagle.

By the 1779 date that ship tokens commemorate, the tide of the war had begun to turn. Two more years of fighting, mostly in the South, culminated at Yorktown, Virginia. Even after hostilities ceased, however, the question of what Americans would use for money was no closer to being answered than when the Revolution began. That question was a microcosm of the universe of problems that remained to be solved before enlightened self-government could expect to survive. All the world’s eyes were on America, which in the late 1780's was consumed by an outpouring of legislative and public discourse over government and the rights of man. That discourse had no precedent and has had no sequel in world history. Out of it emerged the definition of America. Ideas that today seem so profound and so much a part of democracy's secular religion were, in the 1780's, very real and pragmatic answers to the basic question on the minds of all Americans: “Now what?”

10: CONFEDERATION (1781 TO 1789)

The Matter of States

The American victory in the Revolution was hardly the long shot it is made out to have been. With a vast continent, an even greater ocean, the French and debt all allied against them, the British advantage was more fragile than it appeared. For the Americans, the real gamble came after the war. That the prodigals' little experiment in democracy would fail and that they would return to the stifling constancy of the Crown seemed sure bets. It was painfully obvious to the Founders that their hypothesis needed proof, and quickly, in the form of a real, working and sustainable central government.

From Franklin's Pennsylvania Gazette, May 9, 1754. Source: LOC, Prints and Photographs Division, LC-USZ62-9701.

.

Proposals for such things were nothing new in America. Benjamin Franklin devised a plan for confederation as early as the 1754 conference in Albany and re-circulated a modified version of it in the summer of 1775. Obviously, neither version came to fruition. Immediately after declaring independence, Congress frantically tried to establish an acceptable contract among the former colonies. However, consensus proved elusive because most delegates feared strong central authority. Southern delegates particularly were sensitive to the handling of slavery issues. Then there were questions of whether poor and middle-class citizens even were qualified to govern and whether large, populated colonies should have greater influence than their small-state brethren. In spite of myriad proposals and offered compromises, six weeks passed after independence was declared and the supposedly united states had no workable plan for government.

Nor was one in offing as the war forced Congress to suspend deliberations. When debate finally resumed, it was around John Dickinson's plan that, as written, proved too controversial because it was perceived as trampling on the rights of individual states. Only after the delegates bled Dickinson's plan of all real authority did it become tolerable. With many interruptions, debate continued until November 1777, when the Articles of Confederation at last were delivered to the states for ratification.

The battle was just beginning. Diluted as they were, the Articles remained full of contentious provisions. At the heart of the new debate was the manner in which the West would be settled. Several states held old claims to western territories and were reluctant to cede them to any federal government. Virginians, for example, citing their original charter, still dreamed of a commonwealth that stretched far into the continental interior. "Landless" states, those without formal claims to western lands, believed that they were being shorted. One of them, Maryland, wanted its citizens to have the right to settle the same lands that Virginia claimed and used that desire as an excuse to oppose the new government. In time, the disputes of the landless states were resolved, with the exception of Maryland's. The twelve states that did ratify the Articles of Confederation considered letting Maryland be a separate country before wiser heads and compromise prevailed.[628] On March 1, 1781, five years after debate began and just seven and a half months before the British surrender at Yorktown, the Confederation was born.

Shortly thereafter Congress took up the issues of coinage and creation of a federal mint. Robert Morris, the era's Alan Greenspan, recognized the need for a single monetary system to replace the several that the states were using. In 1782 Gouverneur Morris, Assistant Financier to the Confederation and no relation to Robert Morris, proposed just such a scheme. It was based on a quantity of silver small enough that the currency of almost every state, as well as Spanish dollars, could be expressed in whole multiples of it. Robert Morris quickly became the champion of the proposed system and ordered pattern coins to be made in various denominations. These patterns portray the thirteen states as stars in a new constellation, a *Constellatio Nova*,* with the eye of God at its center, watching over them. The scheme was brilliant, but was, as Thomas Jefferson successfully argued, far too complicated for the average, uneducated American. He held that a simpler system, based on multiples of two and ten, would be much easier to use and administer. By mid-1784 the Morrises' plan was comatose and a year later it was officially dead, leaving the country still without a mint or federal coinage. To fill the void, a chaotic mix of state and private issues emerged.

Ironically, the man who most vigorously promoted a unified system was a willing contributor to the chaos. After the proposal that he championed failed, Robert Morris ordered the private minting of roughly halfpenny-sized tokens that closely resemble the official patterns. All but a few of these coppers are dated 1783 or 1785, though all probably were made in 1785 and 1786.

Morris's venture was not the first private coinage of the era. An Annapolis silversmith, John Chalmers, produced silver shillings, sixpence and threepence tokens in 1783. The most common varieties of his shillings feature two birds fighting over a worm. Above them is a "hedge," beyond which is a wriggling snake. This symbolism has several possible interpretations, all of which seem to point either to Chalmers' views on federalism or to Maryland's ill-fated western intentions.

Almost comical Georgivs Triumpho coppers also appeared at about the same time, either as an early attempt to honor George Washington or as a satirical reference to George III. If the figure on these tokens is George III and they were minted in 1783 as their dates assert, their legend, *GEORGIVS TRIUMPHO* ("George Triumphant,") is laughable. King George was hardly triumphant at that moment. Different questions surround the 1784-dated "ugly head" tokens that clearly depict Washington. Their primitive style gives these rare and mysterious tokens the appearance of folk art pieces.

Questions also haunt the *USA* or "bar" coppers that appeared in New York City late in 1785. They seemingly appeared out of thin air, but almost certainly are of English origin. Obviously inspired by the buttons of American soldiers, these coppers are simple reminders of the price of independence. Perhaps a proud former soldier commissioned them.

Not all Confederation Era coinage came from private sources. Under the Articles, the federal government held the power to coin and regulate money. The states could coin money as well, as long as they followed federal regulations. By the time Congress decided on the basic ground rules for coinage in July 1785 and set standard weights in August 1786, some states had

* The correct representation is "Constellatio Nova." However, numismatists disagree on whether the coins, which are described below, read "Constellatio Nova" or "Nova Constellatio." The latter is more commonly used.

grown tired of waiting. South Carolina received a coinage proposal in 1785 from Charles Borrell, though no coins seem to have resulted.[629] Vermont, which was not even yet a state, Connecticut and New Jersey began producing coins under their own standards. Each of them hosted its own little "soap opera," usually stemming from efforts to have private entities manage all or part of the coining business. New York considered several proposals and patterns, but ultimately decided not to sponsor an official state coinage. Steering an altogether different course, the Commonwealth of Massachusetts built its own mint and became the first state to follow the new federal standards.

The party ended quickly as, after ratification of the U.S. Constitution, the state mints operated on borrowed time. With its new-found power, the federal government took back the right of coinage. However, still-active state contracts were allowed to run their courses and some mints continued even after their legal authorization ended. At least one of them lingered after the Copper Panic of 1789 decimated the value of most coppers. Collectively, the state issues provide the bulk of early American examples and varieties studied today. For this reason, the period between 1785 and 1790 often is called the "era of the states' coppers."

The future state of Vermont was the first to make its own coinage, contracting out mint operations to a group of private citizens who produced coins that are among the crudest of all early American issues. Still, their earliest efforts are charmingly symbolic. Between 1785 and 1788, Vermont themes evolved from wooded landscape scenes and new constellations to baby heads and then, ultimately, to pieces that resemble British halfpence. Lack of a steady die source eventually drove Vermont coiners to rely on Machin's Mills, an unauthorized Newburgh, New York mint run by Revolutionary War hero, Thomas Machin, and his partners.

Machin and his associates eventually became key players in many Confederation Era coinages, including those of Connecticut, the first *bona fide* state to issue its own coins. Connecticut also was the most prolific of the states when it came to coinage, producing over 350 different varieties between 1785 and 1788, or a little later. Connecticut's inventive die maker, Abel Buell, used methods that were years ahead of his time. Unfortunately, however, scandal overtook the operation after its principal owner tried to obtain the contract for the 1787 Fugio cents, the first federal coinage fully authorized by Congress. When the scandal broke, the main conspirators skipped town and, as in Vermont, those who remained with the operation turned to Machin's Mills. Just as with royal halfpence, Connecticut's coins were subject to imitation by unauthorized mints. Some of these imposters were produced by Machin's Mills, others by mints whose identities never have been established. Imitations combined with legitimate coins to yield African heads, Hercules heads, small heads, laughing heads, muttonheads and many other fascinating types, all of which loosely resemble British halfpence.

New Jersey followed in 1786 when it granted the right of coinage to three recent immigrants and their war hero benefactor, Matthias Ogden. The effort was rife with tribulation as the partners proved inept at cooperatively running a business. Still, over 140 New Jersey die varieties are known, all with a horse's head and plow on their obverses and a shield on their reverses. Memorable varieties include early date-under-beam prototypes, coulterless[*] examples, deer heads, "running fox" varieties, camel heads, serpent heads, those with horse heads facing left, etc.. The coppers were made by various combinations of the three partners, by Ogden and his friends and by contemporary counterfeiters. Not surprisingly, some varieties

[*] A *coulter* is a bar or blade attached to a plow's beam to break dirt clods and push them aside.

may have been made at Machin's Mills. The latest date on a New Jersey copper is 1788, though one or more of the operations continued at least until 1790.

Massachusetts labored under a different set of problems, one of which was the misconception that a state-owned facility could be run as profitably as a private mint. Cost overruns and an apparent tendency toward legislative micro-management ultimately placed the state's mint in little better position than those of its neighbors. Even so, Massachusetts' coins are of higher quality and enjoyed more public acceptance than most states' coppers. Massachusetts' cents and half cents all share an obverse figure of the standing Indian that symbolized freedom for the Commonwealth. Reverses feature a heraldic eagle, a device that was, and still is, used on many later varieties of federal coins. On the eagle's breast is a shield, in the center of which are the incuse words *CENT* or *HALF CENT*. These coins, dated 1787 and 1788, are the first ever to bear explicitly the new decimal denominations created by Congress.

To the south, New York sought to avoid complications by declining both private coinage proposals and construction of a state mint. Before that position was adopted, however, several individuals submitted coinage proposals, some of which were accompanied by patterns. James Atlee, the son of a brewer, apparently was involved in two separate proposals to mint New York coppers, once on his own and again in conjunction with Thomas Machin. John Bailey and Ephraim Brasher also were among those who petitioned unsuccessfully for private contracts. It is not known whether the two men acted together or separately. It appears that, in the process, Bailey, with or without Brasher's help, submitted pattern *Excelsior* ("Most Excellent") coppers. It also appears that Bailey made 1787 *Nova Eborac* ("New York") coppers without any state contract. As do Connecticut and later Vermont coppers, the Nova Eboracs loosely resemble British halfpence that still were very much in circulation.

Ephraim Brasher was an associate of Alexander Hamilton through mutual ties to the Bank of New York. When New York City was the nation's capital, he was George Washington's neighbor. In 1787 Brasher made what *may*[*] be the only American gold coins prior to the 1795 U.S. Mint issues. Intrinsically, Brasher's coins roughly are equivalent to Spanish doubloons. He made them in two styles, one of which directly resembles a Spanish doubloon. The other combines the sun rising over a mountain on its obverse with a reverse eagle that calls to mind the Great Seal of the United States. A unique half-doubloon also exists in the same style. Presumably to indicate his backing, Brasher counterstamped "EB" on each of his coins, and on some foreign gold coins. For all the fame that his doubloons share, they actually had negligible effect on the overall New York and U.S. economies. Most now reside in museums and, when one enters the market, the asking price is usually in the millions of dollars!

Brasher's golden gems aside, the real workhorses of early American coinage remained British halfpence and their contemporary counterfeits. Despite numerous lamentations and attempts at controlling them, counterfeits and imitations[†] were ubiquitous in the Confederation. Most such Tory coppers are believed to be of British or Irish origin, though American-made pieces exist. Many of those known to be of American origin were made at Machin's Mills. During the Revolution, Machin had been instrumental in building and deploying a great chain across the

[*] Pending confirmation of a piece recently discovered in the Louis Eliasburg collection, Baltimore's Standish Barry also may have produced his own gold coins in the 1780's. (See below.)

[†] After the 1783 Treaty of Paris, British halfpence no longer were an official coinage in America. Producing unauthorized British halfpence in the United States technically could not be called counterfeiting. Thus, halfpence of American origin more properly are called imitations.

Hudson River at West Point. The chain helped to foil the early British strategy of controlling the river and thus splitting America into two easily conquerable regions. By the mid-1780's Machin's glory days were behind him and he had turned to coinage as a source of income. All of the known Machin's Mills-associated products are coppers, but there exists a tantalizing hint that a few silver pieces also might have been made. While Machin's Mills produced state-specific coins, the firm is best known for its imitation British halfpence. Other American-made imitation halfpence are linked variously to Walter Mould, James Atlee, Albion Cox, John Bailey and, possibly, Ephraim Brasher. All of these men operated in and around New York City at roughly the same time. Other very crude imitations suspected to be of American origin usually are attributed to an unidentified mint in "Bungtown," the slang name for North Swansea, Massachusetts. The area is thought to have been a relative hotbed of illicit coiners.

Ironically, Thomas Machin, who apparently had no legal authority to coin, succeeded beyond anyone who did obtain state authority. He accomplished this not by acting against the law, but beyond its reach. His risk was minimal since British counterfeiting laws did not apply in America and neither Congress nor the state legislatures could exercise enough control to stop the practice. In the 1780's a skilled American worker could earn about two shillings Sterling for a day's work. No easy way exists to compare this figure to modern wages because of changes in buying power, work hours, etc., brought about by the Industrial and Information Revolutions. Nevertheless, a halfpenny represented about a fourth to a sixth of an hour in late eighteenth century wages. This was hardly a fortune, but it was a meaningful sum.

Imitations and states' coins notwithstanding, between 1785 and 1787, a number of individuals submitted ambitious proposals to mint coins for the Confederation itself. Patterns that emerged during this period are ascribed with widely varying degrees of certainty to the Wyons of Birmingham, England, Walter Mould, Matthias Ogden, James Atlee and others. Through transactions that are only partially understood, some of the dies used to produce these pieces were exchanged between mints, resulting in unlikely mulings and clouding the issue of who coined what. With the exception of scarce Ogden/Atlee-associated pieces known as the Immunis Columbia coppers, all of these patterns are extremely rare.

The race for a contract to make America's first federal coinage ultimately was won by a less than forthright competitor, James Jarvis. In 1787 Congress still was reluctant to build a mint and attempted instead to contract with private individuals for copper cents. Jarvis, who then controlled the mint producing Connecticut's state coinage, captured the federal prize by bribing a corrupt federal official. Jarvis was to produce coins of the Fugio motif, similar to that of the 1776 Continental Currency pieces. These became known as Fugio or Franklin cents, after their supposed designer. Jarvis's proposal was chosen over Ogden's even though Ogden was a man of considerable resources and integrity. Had the outcome been different, private production of America's coins might have become the norm and the U.S. Mint might never have been built. As it happened, when word of Jarvis' bribe leaked out, the affair ended in scandal and America remained a country without a coinage.

The Copper Panic of 1789, the Constitution's consolidation of federal power and the Mint Act of 1792 all combined to bring down the final curtain on Confederation coinage. For about a decade, however, entrepreneurs and new states had presided over one of the most interesting periods in American numismatics. That the era ended without realizing the dream of a federal mint must have disappointed the Founders profoundly, especially when they looked back on the hopeful spring of 1781.

CONSTELLATIO NOVA PATTERNS AND PRIVATE COPPERS (1783 TO 1786)

THE 1783 PATTERNS

At that time a few visionaries recognized the inherent weaknesses of their new government. Six months before the surrender at Yorktown, Superintendent of Finance Robert Morris already had conceived a plan to put the Confederation's finances in order by enforcing a single national currency. He knew that America and its economy never would flourish as long as the states held to their own currency standards. Morris was not alone in this thinking. Alexander Hamilton, another strong proponent of centralized government, prepared a similar plan only to discover that Morris had beaten him to the punch.[630]

Robert Morris. Engraving by James B. Longacre and Henry B. Hall. Source: Irving (4:342.)

Morris's plan was based on an idea conceived by an associate who shared his surname, but not his bloodline. Gouverneur Morris, the Confederation's Assistant Financier and later author of the Constitution's famed preamble, proposed an ingenious but very complicated scheme for coinage. It was based on the concept of a least common multiple (LCM*) that mathematically linked all but one of the different valuations of the Spanish dollar used by the states. That number is 1,440 and, for his *unit* that he called a *mill*, Morris chose a quarter grain of silver. The idea for such a small unit was based on the Portuguese *reis*. (Chapter 7.)[631]

Gouverneur Morris. Engraving by Henry B. Hall. Source: Irving (3:146.)

In 1782 the thirteen states used five different currency standards. In their local monies, for example, a Spanish dollar was equivalent to eight North Carolina shillings, seven and a half Maryland shillings, six Virginia shillings or five Georgia shillings. To understand how Morris' unit connected these systems, the states' dollar valuations first are converted from shillings to pence (Columns A and B, in the table below.) Then, as shown in column C, each number from column B is broken down into its unique combination of prime number factors. For example, 96 = 3 x 2 x 2 x 2 x 2 x 2 and 90 = 5 x 3 x 3 x 2. The LCM of a group of numbers is the product of the *shortest* list of primes that can be used to factor completely all of the numbers in the group. For the column B numbers other than South Carolina's, this list of prime factors includes five, three (used twice) and two (used five times.) By multiplying combinations of factors from this list, any column B number, except 390, can be obtained. The product of the necessary prime factors is 1,440 = 5 x 3 x 3 x 2 x 2 x 2 x 2 x 2. At 390 pence to the dollar, South Carolina's system contained the prime factor, thirteen, and thus was too cumbersome to include.[632] With South Carolina's valuation, the LCM would have been 18,720 = 1,440 x 13!

* The LCM of a group of integers is the smallest number evenly divisible by all of them. For example, 12 and 6 are common multiples of 2 and 3, but 6 is their LCM. At the British standard of 54d per dollar, a shilling equaled 320 mills and a penny equaled 26 $^2/_3$ mills. Perhaps it is no accident that conversion of Britain's denominations required the use of fractional arithmetic, making their use more difficult.

Local Currency Standard	(A) Local Shillings Per Dollar	(B) Pence Per Dollar (A x 12)	(C) Prime Factors	(D) Units Per Local Shilling (1,440 ÷ A)	(E) Units Per Local Penny (D ÷ 12)
NY, NC	8	96	$96 = 3 \times 2^5$	180	15
MD, PA, NJ, DE	7½	90	$90 = 5 \times 3^2 \times 2$	192	16
VA, MA, CT, RI, NH	6	72	$72 = 3^2 \times 2^3$	240	20
GA	5	60	$60 = 5 \times 3 \times 2^2$	288	24
LCM (States ex. SC)			$\mathbf{1{,}440 = 5 \times 3^2 \times 2^5}$		
SC	32½	390	$390=13 \times 5 \times 3 \times 2$	$44\ ^4/_{13}$	$3\ ^9/_{13}$

By definition of an LCM and excepting South Carolina, all of the states' shilling valuations, expressed in pence, divide evenly into 1,440. Moreover, though a Spanish dollar officially contained 377 grains of pure silver, Congress believed that its content was only *about* 360 grains, or 360 x 4 = 1,440 quarter grains.[633] Thus, twelve of the states' currencies and Spanish dollars all were related by whole quantities of Gouverneur Morris's 1/1,440 unit. It was a thinking man's solution, with a mathematical elegance befitting the Age of Reason.

Pattern denominations of 1,000 mills (one *mark,*) 500 mills (one *quint,*) 100 mills (one *cent* or *bit*) and 5 mills (one *five*) were called for. Eight-mill copper pieces and ten thousand-mill gold pieces were discussed but apparently never produced, not even as patterns.[634] Referring to column E in the table above, three "eights" would have equaled a penny in North Carolina and New York. Two eights would have equaled a penny in Maryland, Pennsylvania, New Jersey and Delaware. In Georgia, three fives would have equaled one penny. Elsewhere, four fives were required to change a penny. The proposed system appeared to be the right medicine.

Robert Morris asked handyman, craftsman and tinkerer, Benjamin Dudley, to prepare plans for a mint. It took Dudley only a week to draft a schematic diagram. The whole plan was submitted to Congress in January 1782 and a proof-of-concept project was approved five weeks later. Dudley was to assemble a mint in an abandoned building at Fourth and Vine Streets in Philadelphia. Consulting with David Rittenhouse, the noted Philadelphia mathematician and astronomer, Dudley proceeded to build a coining press. Samuel Wheeler assisted in its actual construction. Even though momentum appeared to be growing, the process dragged on for the rest of the year. Predictably, Robert Morris was beside himself.[635]

In January 1783 the anxious Superintendent of Finance directed Dudley to prepare pattern dies for the new denominations. A blacksmith, John Jacob Eckfeldt, forged five pairs of dies that Adam DuBois finished. DuBois's fee was $72.00 for finishing four die pairs, while Eckfeldt received only $5.18. Dudley was paid a modest $75.24 and living expenses for his preparatory work. He was later paid another $77.60. Another $22.42 was paid to John Swanwick for dies.[636] Since Swanwick was not known as a die maker, he likely was being reimbursed for bills drawn against his business partner, Robert Morris, or used as an intermediary to convey the money to the real die maker, who may have been either Dudley or DuBois.[637]

The patterns themselves are simple, yet stunningly symbolic. Their shared reverse theme consists of a central, very Masonic-looking Divine Eye, surrounded by thirteen stars and a burst of rays. A similar design occupied the faces of forty-dollar Continental Currency notes that first appeared in an issue authorized on April 11, 1778. Francis Hopkinson, the

Philadelphia-born patriot who signed the Declaration of Independence for New Jersey, is credited with the design. Either Dudley or Du Bois likely adapted it for use on the coins.

Francis Hopkinson's face vignette design from a Jan. 14, 1779, forty-dollar Continental Currency note.

The device and *CONSTELLATIO* ❁ *NOVA* legend represent the thirteen new states as stars in a new constellation, under God's watchful eye. Obverses present the denomination, in units (*1.000*, *500*, *100* or *...5*,) underneath *U*[nited].*S*[tates]. Both appear within a circular wreath and the circumscribed *French* legend *·LIBERTAS ·JUSTITIA·1783* ("Liberty [and] Justice [in] 1783.") The edges of the mark, quint and at least one of the cents share a leaf pattern. The others have plain edges. All of the silver patterns are approximately 0.926 fine. The official weights were 270 grains for the mark, 135 grains for the quint, 27 grains for the cent and 75 grains for the fives. (Note: 0.926 x 270 = 250.02 grains of pure silver, or 1,000 units, etc..)

Mark or 1,000 units (modern copy.)

The patterns were not finished until late April, 1783, when they were shown to the President of Congress and future U.S. Mint Director, Elias Boudinot. Soon after, Robert Morris had a promising meeting with the coinage committee, headed by Thomas Fitzsimons, and responded to various committees' requests for information. Just when the project appeared again to be gaining ground, Congress adjourned. When they returned in July, the mint proposal was ignored. It was dying in committee, having fallen to Congress' higher priorities and the shortage of metal available for coins. By mid-August, 1783, the effort essentially was dead.[638] Robert Morris wrote in his diary on August 19, "I sent for Mr. Benjamin Dudley, and informed him of my doubts about the establishment of a Mint and desired him to think of some employment in private service, in which I am willing to assist him in all my power."[639]

Silver quint or 500 units (modern copy.)

Then, early in 1784, Charles Thomson, Secretary to Congress, prodded the coinage committee for its report. Fitzsimons sent Robert Morris's plans and the patterns to Thomson. After a time the patterns were returned to Morris, who forwarded the silver pieces to Thomas Jefferson. On May 11 Jefferson returned the silver patterns to Charles Thomson. A receipt in Jefferson's handwriting, for 1.8 marks (one mark, one quint and three cents,) confirms this transaction. With the mark and quint no longer in the limelight, Thomson hid them in a secret compartment of his desk where they remained and were forgotten for many years.[640]

Jefferson proved a worthy opponent to the Morrises' scheme, arguing that it was far too complicated for the average, uneducated American. In Jefferson's view, the familiar Spanish system, enhanced with decimal denominations, was much easier to use and administer. The issue was very much on the minds of congressmen in the spring of 1785. On May 13, with Jefferson in Paris, they heard a "Grand Committee" report on *Propositions Respecting the Coinage of Gold, Silver and Copper*. The report took into account earlier documents by Robert and Gouverneur Morris, as well as Jefferson's paper, *Notes on the Establishment of a Money Mint, and of a Coinage for the United States*. The Committee favored a silver-based coinage. They noted that silver ruled in France, where a grain of gold was worth fifteen in silver. Gold was favored in Spain where the ratio was 16:1 and in England, where it was a fraction higher than 15:1. The Committee reasoned that neighboring North American countries, who placed less of a premium on silver, would allow it to flow into the United States. They cited Robert Morris's recommendation of a ratio *less than* 15:1, based on the large quantities of gold expected to flow into the world economy from Portugal after recent discoveries there.[641]

The committee considered Gouverneur Morris's unit, but clearly preferred the convenience of decimal arithmetic. They also noted that Morris's plan would introduce new and unfamiliar calculations that would compromise the nation's ability to achieve uniform accounting. They cited an alternative plan, Jefferson's, that called for a silver dollar and a copper coin valued at $0.005, or $1/200, between which would be decimal denominations. The committee also viewed as crucial that gold and silver coins be valued sufficiently above the price of bullion to make minting profitable, but not so high as to invite counterfeiting. They reasoned that a 2 to 2¼ percent margin was reasonable.[642]

Then, recognizing the detrimental effects of counterfeit halfpence, they turned to copper. At best, false Birmingham halfpence weighed 1/72 pound. With copper selling at about $1/8 per pound, each bogus coin *actually* was worth about $1/576 against a face value of roughly $1/100. Thus, the committee concluded that the American economy was spending nearly six times what it should on "vile Coin." They noted thousand-Guinea orders for Birmingham coppers and that no packet arrived from England without "some hundred Weight of base Half Pence [sic]." By what they called a modest estimate, the previous twelve months' imports had cost the newly united states thirty thousand dollars, more than twice the cost of a mint.[643]

As for weights, the Committee proposed that America's dollar approximate the new Spanish dollars that they believed to contain 365 grains of silver. For the unnamed 1/100 coppers, they favored a standard of forty-four to the pound, nearly seven grains heavier than Britain's halfpence. The report concluded with an analysis of the cost of maintaining a mint with its requisite eight artists and laborers. The committee reasoned that one hundred pounds of copper a day could be transformed into forty-four dollars in coins. Finally, they gave the 1/100 coins the decimal name "decads," a term invented by Jefferson.[644]

On July 6, 1785, nearly two months after the report of the Grand Committee, the following appeared in the Journal of Congress:

> *Resolved, That the money unit of the United States of America be one dollar.*
> *Resolved, That the smallest coin be of copper, of which 200 shall pass for one dollar.*
> *Resolved, That the several pieces shall increase in a decimal ratio.*[645]

The resulting Coinage Act of 1785 made Jefferson's idea the law of the land. The fact that Washington supported the decimal plan could not have hurt its chances.[646] The author of the Declaration of Independence won the argument not with rousing speeches, of which he was incapable, but with subtle, behind-the-scenes lobbying. He circulated notes and working papers among influential delegates who grew to oppose the Morris plan. Even Gouverneur Morris agreed with Jefferson on the need for simplicity.[647] It can be argued that Jefferson's scheme partly has been responsible for the economic success of the United States because it allows ordinary citizens to participate in commerce. However, Americans had to wait another seven years for a federal mint. Congress simply lacked the will and resources to support one in 1785. All that remained from four years of effort was a literal handful of patterns.

The mark and quint pieces in Charles Thomson's desk might have been lost forever had they not accidentally been discovered a century later, by a descendant. Afterward the patterns were bought and sold by a series of noted collectors and, to this author's knowledge, remain in private hands today. Ironically, no one ever has seriously challenged the claims of the Thomson family, or any of the subsequent owners, to what actually are national treasures. These coins belong in public institutions for all Americans to see and appreciate. Perhaps they someday will be returned.

Charles Thomson. After a ca. 1783 drawing by Pierre Eugene du Simitiere. Source: Library of Congress, Prints and Photographs Division, LC-USZ62-44786.

The smaller-denomination patterns traveled more extensively than the Thomson mark and quint. The cents (or bits) drifted to Europe, with one surfacing in a London pawn shop between 1882 and 1884. Another was found in England, a third in Italy. Only one five is known. It once was in the unlikely hands of Joseph Bartlett, a young, Harvard-graduated eccentric who traveled to London in 1784. There he visited Samuel Curwen, an old Salem Loyalist and coin collector who had taken up residence in England after the Revolution. Curwen's diary records that Bartlett presented a five to him as a gift. The coin itself was unknown until it surfaced in a Paris collection of English colonial coins nearly two centuries later. As described below, these emigrant pieces may have played a role in the creation of Robert Morris-associated private coppers in 1785.[648] It seems reasonable to assume that more cents and fives were made. If so, then additional survivors may be waiting discovery.

Two other mysterious pieces have surfaced. The first is a quint that shares its obverse and leaved edge with the Thomson quint, but has a different reverse and is lightweight. On it, the central device fills the entire reverse and there is no reverse legend. The second piece is a struck, plain-edged mark of lesser fineness.[649] The role that they played is unknown.

Robert Morris' Privately-Issued Coppers (Dated 1783, 1785 and 1786)

Robert Morris eventually fell on hard times. His 1790's enthusiasm for private land speculation notes landed him a spot in debtors' prison.[650] For most of his life, however, a shrewd business sense was his ally. Not surprisingly, he saw the coinage vacuum left by Congress as an opportunity for privately issued tokens. It appears that, working through business associates, he ordered coppers similar in design to the Constellatio Nova patterns.

These coppers are dated 1783, 1785 and 1786. In 1785 both Morrises owned interests in the firm of Constable, Rucker and Company, a firm with merchandising operations in England and America. If the tokens were made in England as thought, then it is likely that Constable, Rucker and Company played a pivotal role in procuring and transporting them to America.[651]

Indeed, evidence suggests that the tokens came from England and that they were minted in 1785. In mid-March 1786 at least three London newspapers ran articles describing the 1785-dated pieces, claiming that Congress recently had made them and that they were in general circulation in America. A few days later *The Morning Chronicle and London Advertiser* corrected the report, saying that the coppers were made in Birmingham at the request of a New York merchant. The merchant probably was William Constable. The following October, London's *Gentleman's Magazine* ran a drawing of a 1785 piece. Almost exactly two years later, the same magazine featured a *1783-dated* specimen and described it as a *new* issue. In March 1786 an article in John Mycall's *Worchester Gazette* (Massachusetts) referred to high quality coppers that were circulating in New York. The article may be the first known American mention of the coppers. Had they entered circulation in 1783, it is unlikely that they would have escaped news coverage until 1786. Rather, the 1783-dated pieces probably are backdated to imitate the patterns or to commemorate the Treaty of Paris.[652]

Still, doubts still linger about where and when the private tokens were made, leaving open the possibility of mintage as early as 1783, and maybe even in America. The case for American origin is based partly on the unknown disposition of the equipment that Benjamin Dudley built for minting the patterns. Robert Morris surely had access to it and could have purchased it once the pattern issues had been rejected. The argument for earlier mintage is based partly on the fact that Constellatio Nova design reappeared on Vermont coinage in mid-1785. How could the Constellatio Nova tokens have been new in 1785 if identical design elements were used in remote Vermont only months later? The unexplained dispositions of certain caches of public copper further complicate the issue,[653] though it now appears that the copper in question was turned over to James Jarvis.[654] *

Reverse of a Vermont "landscape" copper, Ryder-7 variety.

The more likely scenario is that Samuel Curwen's "five" served as a model for English token makers who were acting on Robert Morris's request, via Constable, Rucker and Company. Several of the private-issue Constellatio Novas dies and their siblings were used in conjunction with 1785 Immune Columbia patterns (below, this chapter.) Since Birmingham's Wyon family is believed to have made the Immune Columbias, it is likely that they also made the private Constellatio Nova coppers. It even is possible that the Immune Columbias simply were alternatives that Morris rejected in favor of the private Nova Constellatio coppers. As for Vermont coinage, the 1783 federal patterns or sketches of them could have provided inspiration. Even if inspiration did not arrive until 1785, trade often carried the newest, most stylish ideas and goods to the interior surprisingly quickly, often in a matter of days. Thus, the Constellatio Nova private coppers cannot be eliminated as a possible source of the Vermont designs.

* Vermont coppers, the Immune Columbia patterns and James Jarvis are all discussed later in this chapter.

Selected Varieties of Constellatio Nova Private Coppers (Also see Appendix F.)

1-A
1783
Large US
Less
Common

2-B
1783
Small US
Common

3-C
1783
Small US
Less Common

1-B
1785
Scarce

3-B
1785
Common

4-D
1785
Scarce

4-C
1785
Rare

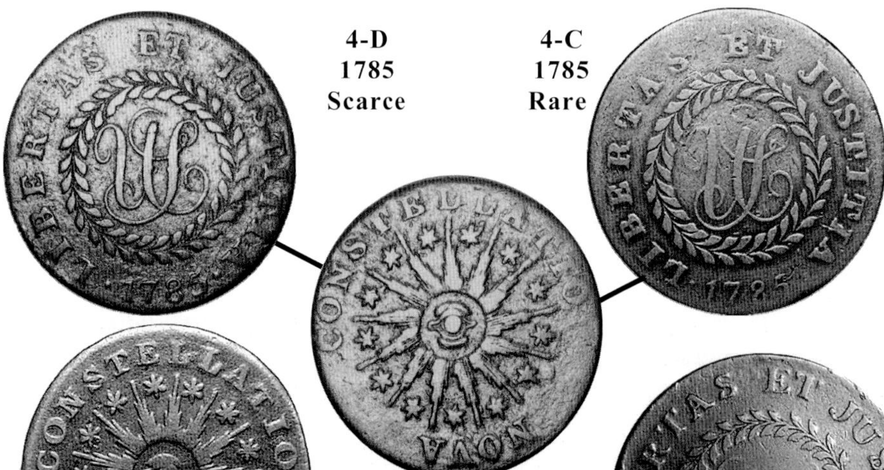

5-E
1785
Scarce

2-A
1785
Small
Date
Rare

Rev. A
1786 (1-A)
Very Rare
(~20 known)

Private Constellatio Nova issues mimic the 1783 patterns, but do not bear denominations. The 1783- and rare 1786-dated coppers feature a Roman-font version of *U·S* on their reverses. Reverses of the 1785-dated pieces replace Roman letters with a well executed, monogrammed script *US*. On obverses of the coppers, differences in the thirteen rays that extend outward from the Divine Eye distinguish varieties. These rays either are pointed (lines) or blunt (club-like, with incised ends.) The two blunt rays varieties, Crosby 3-C[*] (1783) and 1-B (1785,) share the same obverse die. The one 1786-dated variety features pointed rays and has very small digits in its date. Its relatively crude style suggests the work of an apprentice engraver. One 1785 variety, Crosby 2-A, also exhibits a small date. An extremely rare counterfeit 1785 variety is especially crude and has only twelve stars. It may well be a Bungtown product.

Reverse wreaths also exhibit variations, including differences in the numbers of leaves and their angles relative to the wreath's central stem. Counting the rare 1786-dated pieces and excluding the 1785 counterfeits, ten varieties are known from eight obverse and nine reverse dies. The 1783-dated issues include one "large US" and two "small US" varieties. The large US die variety, Crosby 1-A, is believed to have been made by a different artisan than all of the others. It is punch-linked to the 1783 Georgivs Triumpho coppers that are discussed below.[655] This connection and recent discoveries regarding the Georgivs Triumphos further support the case for English origin of the Constellatio Nova private coppers.

Constellatio Nova coppers are seen as undertypes for Connecticut, Vermont and other coppers because they provided a ready source of cheaply available planchets. Occasionally the undertype shows through in a spectacular fashion. The intended weight of the Constellatio Nova coppers probably began at fifty to the pound (140 grains,) but seems to have evolved downward to sixty to the pound (116.67 grains.)[656] Whatever the circumstances of their issue, this underrated series gives the average collector a unique opportunity to appreciate the essence of the Confederation through its symbolism.

JOHN CHALMERS' TOKEN COINAGE (1783)

John Chalmers, a prominent citizen of Annapolis, Maryland,[†] was responsible for another series of Confederation Era private tokens. By 1783 Annapolis was a bustling town full of elegant brick mansions that were made possible by tobacco. Because it was a major port, rum, coffee, tea, sugar, trade goods and slaves always were available. It also was a town full of merchants and artisans who catered to the upper crust of society. In 1770 Reverend Jonathan Boucher called Annapolis the "...genteelest town in North America," while an official of the Crown described its "polished society" and large concentration of "fashionable women." The Washingtons attended plays and balls in Annapolis, and the general enjoyed betting on the horses at the racetrack. A century earlier, in 1694, the royal governor, Francis Nicholson, had seen to the town's elegance when he laid out its design.[657]

However, Annapolis was not all cotillions and Madeira. It also was a political town. Governor Nicholson's design was based on two great circles from which every major street radiated. One of the circles was intended for a church. The other, on the town's highest hill, was set aside for a state house. There, work on Maryland's current state house, America's oldest that is still in

[*] Sylvester Crosby's 1875 work *Coins of Early America* still is regarded as the authority for this and several other series. It is Crosby's die variety numbering system that still is used almost universally.

[†] Annapolis was called Arundel Towne for much of its early history, but was renamed for Queen Anne.

use, began in 1772. Eight years later and just in time for the furor over ratification of the Articles of Confederation, it was complete enough for the state legislature to occupy.[*]

Between November 1783 and August 1784, its Old Senate Chamber was home to the U.S. Congress. As such, Annapolis was the first post-war U.S. capital and a candidate for the permanent seat of the new government. It witnessed both the dramatic resignation of Washington's commission and ratification of the Treaty of Paris.

In this political crucible John Chalmers held several minor offices. He even served for a time as sheriff of Baltimore. In fulfilling his civic duties, he undoubtedly rubbed shoulders with many powerful men. As the proprietor of a silversmith shop, Chalmers provided a valuable service to Annapolis's moneyed classes and held a vested interest in the politics and economics of the new nation.

Thus, it is not surprising that Chalmers privately minted shilling, sixpence and threepence tokens in 1783. They may have been advertising pieces, political statements or simply a means of satisfying his customers' need for coinage. The exact reason for their existence is unknown. Chalmers' note engraving friend, Thomas Sparrow, is believed to have been the die maker for the tokens. The initials *TS* appear on the rare sixpence tokens.

Chalmers' 1783 rings shilling

Chalmers' shillings exist in three varieties. Ultra-rare rings shillings, of which four are known, exhibit a reverse design similar to that of the 1776 Continental Currency coins and to backs of the fractional notes of February 17, 1776. The shillings' reverses feature a circle of twelve rings, eleven of which have stars at their centers. A thirteenth ring, presumably representing Maryland, appears inside the circle at the bottom. Through it rises a liberty pole (Page 16n.) A Divine Eye gazes down on the liberty pole, which is flanked by a twelfth and a thirteenth star. An ornate border surrounds the scene. On the obverses of rings shillings, three script lines read *Equal to One Shi*[lling.] Below are two clasped hands and, surrounding the assemblage, are the words ❁ *I. CHALMERS* ❁ *ANAPOLIS* ❁ *1783*. Note that the Latin "I" is used in place of "J" as Chalmers' initial. It is conceivable that Chalmers offered the rings shillings to Congress as patterns for consideration by the Confederation.[658]

Two less rare shilling varieties are available to collectors. They are known respectively as "long worm" and "short worm" varieties. No more than three hundred examples of both varieties combined are thought to exist. Though surviving short worm shillings outnumber long worm shillings by a ratio of about five to one, the market values them similarly.

The "worm" shilling varieties share a central obverse motif within a beaded circle: Two birds sharing or fighting over a worm. Above the birds is a wriggling snake, crawling to the viewer's right. A "hedge" separates the snake from the birds and around the periphery is the legend 8 *ONE* ❁ *SHILLING* 8 *1783*. To the viewer, the date appears upside down, at the base of the vignette.

[*] The familiar dome and cupola that occupy the reverse of Maryland's state quarters were added in 1788. The legislature now meets in a turn of the (twentieth) century addition to the original building.

1783 Chalmers' shillings: *(left and center) long worm. (center and right) short worm.*

(Note the relative length of the worm and relative positions of the obverse legends.)

The meaning of all this symbolism is uncertain. The leading theory is that the hedge represents a land border and that the birds represent states disputing territorial ownership, as Maryland did in trying to preserve its western claims. Chalmers is thought to have opposed a strong federal government and may have used the snake to represent the threat of it devouring the states.[659] Though the notion is speculative, the worm varieties might have been a satirical, sour grapes reprisal against the federalist view, after rejection of the rings shillings by representatives of the new government.

Alternate theories may merit consideration. For example, the snake could represent Great Britain waiting for the former colonies to fall into disarray. If this is the case, then the hedge might represent the Atlantic Ocean. On the other hand, the snake might represent a larger feast being ignored by the quibbling birds. In this context, the feast could be representative of Canada or perhaps Maryland's lost lands beyond the Appalachians (the hedge.) Or, the birds could be a simple play on Thomas Sparrow's name.

Aside from the length of the worm, the worm or "bird" varieties are differentiated by the position of the legend relative to the hedge. On the short worm variety, the "N" in *ONE* and the "N" in *SHILLING* are directly across from each other, at opposite ends of the hedge. On the long worm variety, the second "I" in *SHILLING* is opposite the "N" in *ONE*. The same reverse is common to both varieties and features a central wreath surrounding two clasped hands. The apparent connotation is that cooperation represents the other side of strife. The reverse legend reads ✤ *I. CHALMERS. ANNAPOLIS.*

(Left) Chalmers' sixpence (large letters) and (right) threepence.

Chalmers' sixpence and threepence issues are quite rare. Sixpence obverses feature a cross and are known with either small or large letters. At the cross's center are the same clasped hands that appear on the shillings. At the ends of the horizontal cross arms are two tiny initials, "T" and "S," presumably Thomas Sparrow's. The cross's vertical arms end in stars. Leaf-like ornaments fill each quadrant and the obverse legend reads *I*[OHN]. *C*[HALMERS]. *SIXPENCE 1783*. The reverse is as on the shillings, except that a star replaces the clasped hands and the ornament is omitted. Threepence obverses feature an indiscriminate plant, or small bouquet, within a wreath, and a legend that simply reads · *THREE* ✤ *PENCE* · *1783*. Reverses are similar to those on the shillings, but without the wreath and with a star in the legend. In addition, *ANNAPOLIS* is abbreviated by *ANNAP*^{S}.

To keep them local, Chalmers' tokens were made lighter than British pieces of the same denomination. They also are lighter than Cecil Calvert's seventeenth century issues. Outside of Maryland, Chalmers' tokens would have been discounted. This argues against the "pattern" theory for the rings shillings. The shillings apparently were made to a standard of 55.7 grains, sixpence to 27.85 grains and threepence to 13.925 grains, all at sterling fineness.[660] Chalmers probably used Spanish coins as his source of silver, since their fineness approximates sterling.

Maryland is unique among the states in having three distinct early silver issues of its own. Chalmers' tokens were second, behind the 1659 Lord Baltimore series. In 1790, Standish Barry, another Maryland silversmith, produced the third. (See Chapter 11.)

ENIGMATIC CONFEDERATION ERA TOKENS (1783 TO 1785)

Georgivs Triumpho Coppers (1783)

The origins of the curious tokens known as Georgivs Triumpho coppers are less certain, though recent developments may be closing gaps in understanding. For example, Mike Ringo established punch links between them and 1783-dated "large U.S." Constellatio Nova coppers. He also described a 1775 counterfeit British halfpenny that shares its reverse device punch with the Georgivs Triumphos. These findings tell of British origins.[661] Most examples weigh about 116 grains, consistent with the lightweight counterfeit halfpence, from Birmingham, then in circulation.

1783 Georgivs Triumpho copper, named for its ambiguous "George triumphant" obverse legend. Note that the "H" is formed from two I's.

In the early 1960's Robert Vlack alluded to the initial circulation of Georgivs Triumpho coppers in Georgia and Virginia, then in Jamaica and Florida.[662] More recently Michael Hodder raised the possibility that the obverse dies could have been prepared in England, the crude reverse dies in America.[663] However, neither idea is substantiated by solid evidence and similarities in lettering and denticulation discount the dual die maker theory. In 2002 two examples of a very interesting counterfeit surfaced. Both mule a die-worn Georgivs Triumpho obverse with an imitation of the reverse from a 1767 twenty-four skilling piece of the Danish West Indies (the Virgin Islands.) Genuine six, twelve and twenty-four skilling pieces are fifty percent silver. The newly discovered mules, however, are coppers.[664] Intuitively, the mules must have had at least a passing connection with the West Indies. Perhaps the maker was counterfeiting both types for American circulation. Where, then, was his (or her) mint?

*Reverse of a genuine 1757 Danish West Indies, Frederick V 12 skillings. This piece is similar to a counterfeit 24-skilling reverse that is muled with a Georgivs Triumpho obverse. Genuine Danish West Indian coins from this period are as legitimately American as Oregon beaver tokens and Texas jolas. (Chapter 11.)**

* These Danish West Indies coins from the mid-eighteenth century defy classification. After being discovered by Columbus, the Virgin Islands (St. Croix, St. Thomas, St. John and several dozen smaller islands) were passed between powers like a political football. By 1740 they were controlled by Denmark and were known as Danske

The *GEORGIVS TRIUMPHO* ("George, Triumphant") legend suggests a tribute to George Washington rather than homage to the vanquished George III. Accordingly, one numismatic camp long has regarded the tokens to be early representations of the general, predating a flurry of Washington pieces minted in the 1790's and later. Many such pieces were made in the early nineteenth century and backdated 1783, either to commemorate the Treaty of Paris or to evade counterfeiting statutes. The Georgivs Triumphos, however, are definitely from the Confederation period. Dennis Wierzba, an authority on New Jersey state coppers, recently discovered a 1787-dated Maris 73-aa* variety New Jersey copper struck over a Georgivs Triumpho.[665] The existence of such overstrikes long had been reported, but never substantiated. They are important since they effectively prove that Georgivs Triumpho coppers were struck in the 1780's.

Only one die variety exists for genuine Georgivs Triumphos and on almost all examples a vertical die break bisects the reverse. The reverse devices clearly are satirical, featuring a seated Britannia imprisoned in a waist-high cage or, possibly, a loom. The cage has thirteen vertical bars or stripes and is held together at its corners by fleurs de lis, symbolizing France's support of America during the Revolution. The reverse legend *VOCE POPOLI*, the Italian version of the Latin *VOCE POPULI* ("Voice of the People,") again hints that the obverse portrait is Washington's. This legend offers an ideological, even if unintended, link to the Irish Voce Populi series and the somewhat "goofy" obverse portrait is very similar to one of George III used on genuine and many counterfeit 1776 Irish halfpence. Were it not for the punch links to the "large U.S." Constellatio Novas, an Irish origin for the Georgivs Triumphos might seem likely. The Irish always have had a penchant for satirizing English monarchs. Or, perhaps all of this ambiguity is deliberate and these are simply evasion coppers. (Chapter 5.)

WASHINGTON "UGLY HEADS" (1784)

If Georgivs Triumphos were not the first tokens to depict Washington, the 1784 "ugly heads" probably were, even if that depiction is a bizarre caricature. These strange and very rare pieces feature a bald, right-facing head of Washington on their obverses and rings similar to those of the Continental Currency coins, with a slightly altered sequence of states, on their reverses. The obverse legend reads *WASHINGTON THE GREAT D*[EI] *G*[RATIA]. Whether the wording is a genuine but naïve tribute to Washington or pure satire is anyone's guess. Their reverses have no legends, save the abbreviated names of the states within the rings and the date, *1784*, which is split into two lines.

Amercansk, or Danish America. The Danish government produced one- and two-skilling copper coins for use by the islanders in 1740. In the Danish system, twelve skillings equaled a mark, six marks equaled a daler and two dalers equaled a ducat. In 1767 Denmark made six-skilling coins out of 50 percent silver. In 1740, 1748, 1757, 1763 to 1765 and 1767, twelve skilling coins were made in the same alloy. Twenty-four skilling pieces were minted in 1763 to 1767, except 1766. Gold one-ducat gold trade coins also were made n 1749 and two-ducat gold trade coins were produced in 1708 and 1749. The obverse of the coin above features a rigged ship with the legend *DANSKE AMERCANSK XII SKILL*[ING] or *Danish America 12 Skillings*. The central reverse device is a crowned monogrammed "FV" for Frederick V. The reverse legend reads [Frederick V] *D*[E] *G*[RATIA] *DAN NOR VAN GOT REX* (*Frederick V of Denmark, Norway, Vendalia and Gothland, King.*)

* See the section on New Jersey state coppers (1786-1788,) in this chapter.

By 1995 four copper examples and a fifth in white metal were known. At least one more unverified copper example has been found since then. The first ugly head was discovered before the Civil War and is now in the Smithsonian Institution. At least two were found in Maryland, suggesting local origin, despite the fact that one bears the Royal Navy Arrow and Cross as a countermark.[666] Stylistically, the "ugly heads" resemble nineteenth century fantasy pieces (See Appendix A and the text on Fugio cents,) fueling speculation that they may be later issues. This author, however, sees no real reason to believe that they are not from the 1780's.

Bar or USA Coppers (1785)

Almost as mysterious, bar coppers are thought to have been minted in England, probably in Birmingham, and probably at the request of an American. Their minimalist designs, reminiscent of the twentieth century rather than the eighteenth, long have been considered classic. The side generally regarded as the obverse bears simply a monogrammed Roman *USA,* without date or legend. That the "S" is larger than the "U" and the "A" probably is another reminder that the states were not ready to submit entirely to the federal control. The other side has thirteen horizontal, raised bars (or stripes,) again without date or legend. Devices for both sides are taken from American military buttons. Only one die variety is known, though a very few examples are struck on oval planchets. Even the standard round specimens are scarce, with fewer than two hundred believed survivors.

Ironically, when their first known circulation was recorded in a *New Jersey Gazette* article of November 12, 1785, bar coppers were said, tongue in cheek, to have been more common than the buttons they imitated.[667] The article described their abundance in New York City, which was then a teeming port city of about 40,000 people. Since January 1785 it had been the seat of Congress. Perhaps a patriotic businessman wanted to commemorate the city's becoming the national capital by ordering tokens.

New York's old city hall / federal hall as it appeared in June, 1789, with Trinity Church in the background. The hall was the U.S. Capitol (1785-1789) and the site of Washington's first inauguration. Robert Hinshelwood after Diedrich Knickerbocker. Source: Irving (4:512.)

Bar coppers are among the most frequently copied of all early American issues because they have always been in great demand among collectors. Fortunately most copies are non-deceptive. On all genuine examples the left down stroke of the "A" passes over, not under, the loop of the "S" in *USA*. Wear or weak striking, however, often obscures this feature, as seen below. Fortunately, two other features distinguish genuine pieces. On the bar side, the second bar (or the twelfth, depending on the viewer's interpretation of "up") has a small downward-pointing spur, likely the product of a slip by the die engraver. Also, a die crack links the sixth and seventh bars (or seventh and eighth, again depending on orientation.) The die crack appears as a faint, raised line that joins the two bars.

The same *New Jersey Gazette* article that announced the bar coppers opined that if Congress did not establish a mint, the next new coin might be the soldiers' buttons themselves.[668] Given the date of their first known appearance, the minting of bar coppers probably occurred at about the same time that the Coinage Act of 1785 was being passed (i.e., July 6.) Since it was not until August 8, 1786, that new regulations created and named cents and half cents, the old custom of calling bar coppers "cents" clearly is inaccurate. The 1786 regulations set the weight of a cent at one hundred coins to 2¼ pounds of copper, or 157½ grains each. This was about five conspicuous grains heavier than standard British halfpence and nearly double the weight of the bar coppers. At an apparent weight standard of 83.3 grains, or 84 to the pound, the bar coppers still are just heavier than either farthings or half cents.

A – 1785 Bar or USA copper. B – Military button, USA, ca. 1775, found at Fort Johnston, South Carolina. C – Military button, bars, ca. 1780, found near Yorktown, Virginia.

The 1786 regulations also set the fineness of gold and silver coins at 11/12 and defined the dollar at 375.64 grains of pure silver. The half dollar and dime were created at the same time, as was the double-dime (pistareen.) Gold eagles (ten dollars) and half eagles (five dollars) were set to contain 246.268 grains and 123.134 grains of fine gold, respectively, (a value ratio of 15.25:1.) On the day that Congress defined a monetary system for the United States of America, it first set the pay scale for district Superintendents for Indian Affairs.[669] Priorities are priorities.

NEW YORK'S HOME-GROWN COINAGES (CA. 1786 TO 1789)

By the time the federal standards were set, Vermont, Connecticut and New Jersey had grown tired of waiting and had begun cooking with their own recipes. New York lagged behind them until a small, diverse group of men sought the state's attention. Their names: Atlee, Bailey, Brasher, Cox, Mould, Machin and others, eventually became synonymous with American Confederation Era coinage. By the time each of them became active in New York, most were or soon would be involved in the coinage for other states or for the Confederation itself. These men are mentioned many times in the sections that follow, but their brief convergence in New York, in the mid-1780's, offers the best opportunity for introductions.

Ephraim Brasher's Gold Coinage (1786 to 1787)

One of them, Ephraim Brasher, made some very special gold coins. The U.S. Mint began minting gold in 1795, but only Brasher, and possibly Standish Barry (below,) are believed to have done so privately in America prior to the 1830's. Brasher's gems are legendary for their great rarity and for the astronomical prices they command in the marketplace. They first were recognized numismatically in 1838, when the U.S. Mint's aging Chief Coiner, Adam Eckfeldt, rescued an example from the melting pot and added it to the institution's adolescent coin cabinet.[670] In real life they have been the objects of famous heists, first from Yale University and then from the DuPont family. In both cases the treasures eventually were recovered. In fiction, Raymond Chandler's novel, *The High Window,* a detective story about the recovery of a stolen Brasher doubloon, was adapted for the 1947 movie *The Brasher Doubloon.* For all their fame, however, Brasher's coins made little impact on the New York economy and apparently received little notice. Why he made them and exactly how and where they were intended to be used are still unknown. Was he acting on his own or on behalf of a sponsor? Were the coins to circulate locally or in international trade?

Born in 1744 of Dutch ancestry, Brasher became involved in precious metals at a young age. He and his brother, Abraham, each were apprenticed to either silver- or goldsmiths whose identities are lost in time. In addition, William Gilbert, the brother of Ephraim's first wife, Ann, was a well-known silversmith. Ephraim served briefly during the Revolution as a grenadier and afterward remained in the state militia, attaining the rank of first major. He belonged to a prestigious veteran's organization called the Columbian Order and held many civic offices, including that of coroner. He was shrewd. As Tories evacuated New York after the war, he profited greatly from buying their confiscated properties at rock-bottom prices and then re-selling to them to patriots.[671] He was connected. In 1789, when New York was the nation's capital, Brasher lived on Cherry Street, next to one of his customers, President Washington. Brasher's place of business was nearby at 77 Queen Street.[672] Five years earlier, when Alexander Hamilton and friends founded the Bank of New York, they chose a site a stone's throw from Brasher's home. Through family and social ties, Brasher was "in" with key people at the bank and, when someone was needed to *regulate* gold coins, he was a shoe-in. The few foreign gold coins that circulated in America varied greatly in weight and fineness, and thus needed regulation.[*] Brasher provided this service, counterstamping regulated pieces with "EB" to show his approval. Even these marked foreign gold coins are highly sought collectibles, along with spoons, cups, trays and any other objects that bear his mark.

The real prizes, however, are Brasher's own coins. With a unique exception, all known examples of them are of the dimensions of Spanish doubloons. The exception is a half-doubloon. Recall that "doubloon" is another word for an eight-escudos coin and that an escudo was equivalent to two Spanish dollars or sixteen reales. A Spanish dollar was fractionally larger than the new American dollars, giving a doubloon the value of about $16.20.[†]

Brasher made his coins in two styles. For the supposed first he chose to emulate a 1742 doubloon of a type minted in Lima, Peru. The rationale behind this choice is unknown, though it is likely that he simply chose a familiar form that would be unquestioned by local businesses. Both Brasher's version and the Lima originals feature the Pillars of Hercules on their obverses. Recall from Chapter 6 that these columns represent the great rocks that flank the Straits of Gibraltar at the western entrance to the Mediterranean Sea. The Spanish doubloons feature the columns surrounded by waves, while Brasher's have the columns floating above the waves. Beneath the waters, in tiny letters, Brasher inserted his surname. An ornament that may represent either a cross or the sun floats above the columns and the columns themselves are topped by ornaments reminiscent of fleurs de lis. The columns on Lima

[*] Regulation refers to the practice of diminishing the weight of specie (through shaving, filing or clipping,) or making them heavier or more pure (with inserted plugs of higher fineness) to meet established standards.

[†] William Swoger postulated that Brasher's doubloons instead might have been valued at $15. If Brasher used the 1786 standard of 375.64 grains of silver to the dollar and a gold to silver ratio of 15:1, the value is indeed about $15. (Swoger, "Brasher's Gold," in *Coin World*, June 1, 1992, p.23 and following. Also, see "Brasher Doubloons Labeled $15 Coins," in *The Numismatist*, vol. 118, no. 12, December, 2005, pp.28-29.)

doubloons are slightly convex at their centers, in the Athenian style.* Brasher's, on the other hand, are straight-sided. As on the Lima pieces, two horizontal lines cross behind Brasher's columns, dividing the central text into three lines. His text is identical to that on the Lima pieces. The top line reads *L*[IMA] · *8* · [ESCUDOS] *V,* where "L" names Lima as the mint and "V" denotes a minter/assayer whose name is forgotten. Why Brasher did not use *N*[EW YORK] and *B*[RASHER] in place of "L" and "V" is a mystery. The middle line of text reads *P*[LUS] · *V*[LTR] · *A* · ("More Beyond.") The third line contains the obsessive date [1]*7·4·2*, again imitating the Lima doubloons. A beaded circle surrounds the entire vignette.

(Left) Brasher's 1786 Lima style doubloon; (right) Copy of a 1736 Lima doubloon

Only two Lima-style Brasher doubloons are known and only one of them retains enough of its outer legend for reasonable interpretation. Even then, only the bottom portions of the letters and numbers are visible. Still, it is relatively certain that the legend reads *PHILIP · V ·D*[EI] · *G*[RATIA] *H*[ISPANARIUM] *REX AN*[N]*O · 1786 ·*. ("Philip V, by the Grace of God, of Spain, King, in the year 1786,") as if it were from the Spain of Philip V. Between the "G" and "H," just outside the beaded circle and again in tiny letters, is the abbreviation *NY*. The die engraver, presumably Brasher himself, also inscribed circular lines to aid in the alignment of the outer legends. Vestiges of these lines appear along the baselines of the larger letters.

The reverses of Brasher's Lima style pieces also emulate Spanish doubloons, though not as well as the obverses. On Brasher's version the reverse is makeshift, suggesting that a second, less skilled hand might have been involved. The central reverse device of a true Lima doubloon is a Jerusalem cross, with castles and rampant lions in its quarters. Brasher's doubloons imitate this form, but the arms of his cross end in trapezoids rather than rectangles. Slips by the die engraver show behind the lion in the upper right quadrant, below the castle in the lower right quadrant and at the base of the legend's ornament. The castles themselves are crude compared to the stone fortifications on Lima doubloons. As on the obverses, a beaded circle encloses the central vignette and the outer legend is only partly legible: [ornament] *I HISPAN* [letter] [letter] *D*[?] [letter] [date] *IND REX*. The full legend, beginning on the obverse, properly would have read *PHILIP V DEI GRATIA HISPANARIVM ET INDIARVM REX* ("Philip V, by the Grace of God, of Spain and the Indies, King.") A third date, after 1742 and 1786, is practically off the flan and is unreadable. Nevertheless, a case can be made for *1776*. As on all Brasher-associated coins, the Lima style pieces bear his counterstamped initials within an oval. On both Lima style specimens, the counterstamp appears at the center of the reverse cross. However, on one of them, the initials are inverted relative to the coin's

---

* Ancient Greeks observed an optical illusion that occurs when the parallel sides of a column are viewed at a distance. That is, columns with straight sides appear thinner in the middle. To correct this, they made columns whose centers bulged. From a distance, these columns appear straight-sided.

devices and legends. This suggests that the counterstamp was intended as a stamp of approval, as on regulated foreign coin, rather than a post-striking design element.

The Lima style doubloons took on added interest in 2005 when a very similar piece was found in a forgotten corner of the legendary Louis Eliasburg collection. Unlike Brasher's doubloons, that piece is cast, has a reeded edge and, in place of the "EB" countermark, bears the mark *SB*. *SB* may be the mark of Baltimore silversmith, Standish Barry (Chapter 11.)[673] Whether the two issues somehow are related is a wholly new question that deserves research.

(Left) New York style half-doubloon, 1960's brass copy. (Right) Doubloon, Gallery Mint copy, gold.

Brasher's other, New York style, doubloons are far better known. After all, they are four times as common with eight known examples. A ninth piece, the unique half-doubloon, shares the same dies. The New York obverses feature a landscape of mountains behind still waters, with the rayed sun rising over the tallest peak. At the base of the scene is the word *BRASHER* in small letters. A beaded circle surrounds the vista. Outside the circle, the legend reads *NOVA* ✤ *EBORACA* ✤ *COLUMBIA* ✤ *EXCELSIOR* ✤, or "New York in Columbus' Land, Most Excellent." On the reverse a heraldic eagle rises within a full circle wreath. As on later federal issues, the eagle grasps an olive branch and a bundle of arrows and, as on the Great Seal of the United States, it has a shield on its breast. On seven of the eight known New York style specimens and on the half-doubloon, the *EB* counterstamp, in an oval cartouche, appears on the eagle's wing. On one doubloon it is centered on the eagle's breast, partially covering the shield.

Brasher's New York style doubloons always have been in the limelight. However, his Lima style pieces have been denied the levels of respect that they deserve. Some even have questioned their eighteenth century provenance. A hybrid theory suggests that their obverse die might have been made in the eighteenth century and that the crude reverse die was made later. At times the Lima style pieces have been removed from popular price guides based on such doubts. The keys to unraveling the arguments of detractors lie in the metallic composition of the pieces relative to the New York style pieces and in the *EB* counterstamp itself. Using the results of a study by Johns Hopkins University, Michael Hodder showed that the Lima and New York style pieces are made of the same alloy and that their composition is unlike that used in contemporary Spanish colonial gold coins. The alloy also differs from that used for nineteenth century U.S. Mint issues. These facts help to invalidate claims that the Brasher coins were struck later, over planed-down Spanish or U.S. gold pieces.[674]

The 1786 date of the Lima style pieces suggests that they were made before the New York style doubloons. Though eighteenth dates are not always what they seem, Hodder's analyses showed that the same punch was used to impart counterstamps on both styles and that rust spots that emerged on the "EB" punch were in an earlier stage of development on the Lima style pieces. The latest state of the rusting is found on the half-doubloon. Thus, the Lima style reverses were counterstamped before any of the 1787 New York style pieces, and the half-doubloon was counterstamped after all of the known doubloons. It follows that if the New York-style coins are from the eighteenth century, then the Lima-style pieces are as well.[675]

Brasher's doubloons were minted to apparent standards of 411.42 grains and 22 karat fine gold, or 0.917, the federal standard. The lone half doubloon weighs 204 grains. These were probably Brasher's best guesses at the actual Spanish standard weights. Even more detailed analysis of the rust progression on the EB punch on the foreign coins that Brasher regulated could reveal much more about his efforts.[676] No measure of scientific precision, however, diminishes the status of Brasher's doubloons as the crown jewels of early American coinage.

James F. Atlee's (?) Non Vi Virtute Vici Coppers (1786)

James Falconer Atlee's name is linked with many varieties of state, pattern and other coppers, maybe too many for the scant body of hard evidence that exists. Punch linkages that once unequivocally tied Atlee to a diverse set of copper varieties bearing Confederation, New Jersey, Connecticut, Vermont and even British legends, are being re-evaluated. Even so it is clear that Atlee was a key player on his own and in association with his father, Samuel Atlee, and with others, such as Walter Mould, Matthias Ogden and Thomas Machin. In addition to involving him in the production of official and quasi-official coppers, these associations gave James Atlee the opportunity to produce imitation British halfpence and to become a partner in Machin's Mills, perhaps the most prolific mint of the period, public or private.

Thanks to numismatic researcher, Gary Trudgen, quite a lot is known about the Atlees. James was born to Samuel and Ann Atlee in Bristol, England, in 1762. The couple had another son, John, who was two years older. Samuel Atlee had been a confectioner, but by the time of the Revolution he ran a brewing and distilling business near Bath. The distilling business went bankrupt in 1782 and Samuel and Ann divorced. Samuel immigrated to New York, arriving in October 1783. The move was timed auspiciously because New York was then a city full of opportunities as its Tory inhabitants evacuated their homes and businesses. Samuel soon remarried, rented a brew house and, in the spring of 1784, began advertising porter beer from Greenwich Street near the Hudson and North Rivers.[677]

The facilities actually belonged to relatives of George Harrison. With two partners, Harrison had operated the well-equipped brewery until his death in 1773. Family plans to sell the property were interrupted by the outbreak of war and instead it served as an American guardhouse, as a British convalescent hospital and as the target of looting by both sides. After the British evacuation in 1783, Richard Harrison, George's son, restored the equipment to working order and found a willing tenant in Samuel Atlee. Close to both a foundry and river transportation, the brew house and associated buildings were logical places to house mint facilities. For a time, however, Samuel operated his brewery there, under the name Samuel Atlee and Company. The name soon was changed to Atlee and Company, presumably to signify James's arrival in America. An advertisement bearing the new name appeared in November 1784. James's older brother, John, remained in England, with his mother.[678]

The brewery struggled. Legal problems arose with its customers and, by the end of 1784, the Atlees advertised heavily discounted prices. In January 1785, Samuel and his immigrant partner, William Alexander, made an unsuccessful plea for tax relief. Alexander left the company, but the business continued on with Samuel Atlee, John Perkins and James F. Atlee.

Even price cuts from the original £3.4.0 per barrel of porter to £1.2.6, by the end of April 1785, did not help. As the year dragged on, there were further price cuts and the court appointed a man to oversee the company's books. By January 1786 the brewery business was history and in mid-1787 James Atlee left New York City to join Thomas Machin in Newburgh. Even so, Samuel Atlee continued to pay rent on the large brewery building until December.[679]

How the Atlees used the building after the demise of the brewery and, for that matter, how they paid the rent given their business's failure, are the subjects of great curiosity. So too is the question of how they might have become involved in coining enterprises. In particular, how did the younger Atlee learn to make dies as he is alleged to have done?[680]

The knowledge might have come from Albion Cox, an assayer and recent immigrant with whom the Atlees formed a mysterious partnership in 1786. The partnership was involved in court cases in October 1786 and September 1787. With Simeon Bayley, Daniel Van Voorhis and William Coley, Cox had been a partner in a New York City silversmith firm at 27 Hanover Square. He left the firm in April 1786, and two months later was involved with Walter Mould and Thomas Goadsby in a New Jersey coining enterprise (below.) Goadsby was a New York dry goods merchant who knew the ways of business, but probably did not have knowledge of mint processes. On the other hand, Walter Mould seems to have possessed considerable die engraving skills and may have learned the trade in England. (On August 18, 1785, he asked Congress to allow him to "conduct a mint.")[681] Cox's other partners, Bayley, Van Voorhis and Coley, were involved in Vermont's coinage venture with Coley as the supposed die maker. Any or all of these men might have educated James Atlee.[682] It also is conceivable that one of them could have made some of the device punches long attributed to Atlee and that Atlee merely added lettering to the dies while he learned the trade.

At any rate, James Atlee made two unsuccessful attempts to obtain legal coining franchises in New York. The first probably began in 1786, while he still lived in New York City. Rare 1786-dated coppers, known by their obverse legends and, for lack of a better name, as the *Non Vi Virtute Vici* coppers, *may* have been part of this proposal. This Latin phrase means "Not by Force, but by Virtue, have I Conquered." Walter Breen ascribed to it a dual meaning, writing that it could refer to Washington's victory in the Revolution or, given the difficulty New York and other states were having with lightweight imitation halfpence, it could mean "Not by Force [of law], but by Virtue [of being full weight and good copper], have I conquered [public acceptance]."[683] The two varieties of Non Vi Virtute Vici coppers are known as "large heads" and "small heads." Their obverse portraits are different. However both depict simple, well-executed, right-facing profiles of a uniformed officer who *must* be George Washington.

Reverses feature Liberty or Justice holding a liberty cap-topped staff, or liberty pole, with her right hand. On the large head pieces, the liberty pole doubles as a flagpole. The figure sits on a crate that symbolizes commerce. On the small head pieces she also sits on a globe. On both reverses, the legends read *NEO-EBORACENSIS 1786*, or "At New York, 1786." The figure extends the scales of justice in her left hand. Similar devices appear on the circa 1785 Immune [sic] Columbia coppers and the 1786 and 1787 Immunis Columbia pieces (below.)

The issue of Non Vi Virtute Vicis must have been small, as one would expect of proposal patterns. However, some of them circulated since most of the twenty-five to thirty-five small head survivors and one of the two known large head pieces are worn. It is possible that both were patterns and that the small head pieces were distributed as handouts to encourage acceptance rather than as a true circulating coinage. At sixty to the pound, however, both would have been accepted alongside other coppers. The late-March 1786 article in John Mycall's Worchester, Massachusetts newspaper, alluding to the high quality of New York's circulating coinage, may refer to these pieces rather than Robert Morris's Constellatio Nova tokens. New York never authorized an official coinage and other unofficial coins bearing New York legends were still a year in the future. If Mycall's article refers to the Non Vi Virtute Vicis, then they were made prior to Walter Mould's involvement with the New Jersey mint at Rahway (below) and Atlee's involvement with Thomas Machin's operation in Newburgh.[684]

1786 Non Vi Virtute Vici patterns: *(Left) small head and (Right) large head varieties*

The Non Vi Virtute Vici coppers also appear to pre-date the flurry of New York coinage proposals and legislative activity that occurred early in 1787. One possible implication of all this is that James Atlee was running his own mint in New York City, with Walter Mould's assistance. Aside from his key role in New Jersey's coinage, Mould apparently was involved in proposed coinages for the Confederation and appears to have teamed with Atlee in the production of imitation British halfpence. If it existed, this New York City mint might have served as a proving ground for Atlee's skills, under Mould's tutelage.

A unique pairing of the large head obverse with an otherwise unknown shield reverse, of the style used on New Jersey state coppers (below,) further hints at Mould's involvement. Because its reverse legend, *E PLURIBUS UNUM,* is nationally-oriented as opposed to being New York-specific, the muling usually is grouped with the Confederation patterns (below.)

In January 1787 New York let it be known that state coinage proposals would be accepted. James Atlee's was the first to be received, on Groundhog Day, February 2, just two days after he had petitioned to become a citizen. Whether or not the Non Vi Virtute Vici coppers were submitted at the same time, Atlee's proposal would soon have company.

1787 Pattern & Circulating Issues (Possibly) by John Bailey

Another player, John Bailey, was born in 1755 and thus was a young man when the Revolution began. Yet, he made the battle sword that George Washington carried throughout the war.* In time Bailey made quite a name in New York as a worker of iron and maker of fine cutlery. On February 11, 1787, Bailey and Ephraim Brasher submitted coinage proposals to the New York legislature. The two men could have been working together, or not. The records are unclear,

* Washington's battle sword and scabbard can be seen at the Smithsonian's Museum of American History in Washington, D.C.. Its silver and green ivory handle speaks of Bailey's artistic skill. Its blade is beautifully engraved and grooved for lightness and speed. On the General's death, the sword passed to his nephew, Captain Samuel T. Washington, along with the admonition to "...[use it only in] self-defense or in the defense of [the] country and its rights." (America's Smithsonian: Celebrating 150 Years, p.138.)

referring only to "the several proposals." The only real evidence of collaboration between Bailey and Brasher comes from the linking of punches and styles on coins and the circumstance that Brasher's business was at 77 Queen Street while Bailey lived at 22 Queen Street.[685] Nova Eborac coppers and New Jersey copper varieties known as the "running foxes" (both below) generally are attributed to Bailey, but share punches with Brasher's doubloons. The bottom line is that someone, presumably Bailey or Brasher in support of a coinage proposal, produced coppers known as the New York Excelsiors. Quatrefoils (✤) appear on Brasher's doubloons, on the running foxes and on the Excelsiors, suggesting that all of them somehow are related. However, Bailey was a supplier of punches and other tools and thus could have sold or loaned Brasher equipment without the two being partners.

1787 Excelsior copper (old electrotype from a worn original,) obverse eagle facing right, small reverse eagle. Compare the eagle and quatrefoils to those on Brasher's doubloons.

The Seal of the State of New York occupies the obverses of the Excelsior coppers. Two figures, Liberty and Industry, stand beside an oval vignette of the sun rising over a mountain, as on Brasher's New York style doubloons. Atop the vignette is an eagle on the demi-globe of the Western Hemisphere, its head turned to the right on some issues, to the left on others. Under the vignette is the motto, *EXCELSIOR* ("Most Excellent,") for which the coins are named. On Excelsior reverses a spread eagle flies in a field of thirteen stars, as on the Great Seal of the United States and on Brasher's New York style doubloons. The legend reads *E PLURIBUS UNUM.* The date, *1787,* appears in small font, below the eagle.

1787 New York Excelsior pattern varieties: *A - Large eagle reverse, transposed arrows with Excelsior eagle-right obverse. B – Excelsior, eagle-right obverse with small eagle reverse (proper arrow placement.) C – Excelsior, eagle-left obverse with small eagle reverse.*

Reverses of most of the rare surviving examples depict a small eagle with arrows in its left talon and an olive branch in its right. This configuration sometimes is interpreted to imply a preference for peace over war since left is considered inferior in heraldry. Reminiscent of similar arrow and branch placements on prototypical Massachusetts state coppers, two rare Confederation pattern dies and on some early U.S. Mint issues, a second reverse depicts a large eagle grasping arrows in its *right* talon. This transposed arrangement sometimes is said to express a preference for war.*

That several apparently unrelated types exhibit transposed arrows suggests that placing arrows in the eagle's right talon may have been an acceptable variation on the theme and not a deliberate signal. Even so, the "correct" placement appears always to have replaced the transposed placement on series in which both configurations were used. On the Excelsiors, both reverses are paired with an obverse whose demi-globe-sitting eagle faces to the viewer's right, while the eagle-facing-left obverse is paired only with the correct, small eagle reverse.

Whether working alone or as partners and whether either of them was involved in producing the Excelsiors, Bailey and Brasher were denied the state's official business. New York had grown increasingly reluctant to venture into private contracts or to build a state mint. Yet the legislature left open the door for those who wanted to coin coppers on their own, as long as standards were upheld. It appears that Bailey seized this opportunity to begin making other coppers, possibly with Brasher's assistance. Some Bailey-attributed pieces are outright imitations of British halfpence, complete with Georgian legends (below.) Others present a distinctly New York design and are called the *Nova Eboracs*. Nova Eborac obverses present a mailed bust facing to the viewer's right. The figure has a laurel wreath around his head and a legend that reads *NOVA EBORAC,* meaning simply "New York." Nova Eboracs feature three different obverses, respectively known as "small," "medium" and "large" heads.

The three obverses are paired with four different reverses to create four varieties, all dated 1787. All four reverses feature a seated Liberty, pole and cap in hand and leaning on a shield with the New York arms at its center. On one variety, Liberty faces to the viewer's right. On all the others, she faces to the viewer's left. The reverse legends all read *VIRT ET LIB* 1787 ("Virtue and Liberty,") with variations in placement and punctuation. This general form imitates a British halfpenny, and, by implication, Connecticut and some Vermont coppers.

The size of the obverse bust, the orientation of the reverse figure and differences in punctuation all are used to differentiate the four Nova Eborac varieties. Examples of the very scarce large head variety, particularly those with heavier weights that range upward to nearly 157 grains, close to the federal standard, may be prototypes. They even may have been submitted as part of a coinage proposal. Lighter versions of the large head variety, those weighing around 120 grains, may have been later issues made for circulation.

The small heads are very rare and also may have been associated with a coinage proposal, though they differ stylistically from the other varieties. On the other hand, they simply might be contemporary counterfeits. Breen believed them to be linked to the New Jersey "deer head" coppers that generally are ascribed to Gilbert Rindell (see below.)[686] The other three Nova Eborac varieties all have quatrefoils in both legends, while the small heads feature six-pointed stars on their obverses, as on the deer heads.

---

* Later, the "eagle-left" obverse gained new life when it was paired with a pattern die believed to have been submitted for consideration by the Confederation. This "late-life marriage" probably occurred after both dies fell into the hands of others who sought to produce as many coppers as possible from any available dies.

Nova Eborac Varieties	Reverse	Obverse
Large Head ✤ ✤*NOVA* *EBORAC*✤ ✤*VIRT.ET* [head & staff] *LIB.* ✤		
Medium Head (Rev. Fig. Left) ✤*NOVA* ✤ *EBORAC*✤ ✤*VIRT.ET* [head & staff] *LIB* ✤		
Medium Head (Rev. Fig. Right) ✤*NOVA* ✤ *EBORAC*✤ ✤*VIRT* [staff & head] *ET.LIB* ✤		
Small Head ✶ *NOVA* ✶ *EBORAC*✶ ✤*VIRT. ET.* [staff] *LIB*✤		

The two medium head varieties were minted in numbers large enough to have circulated. On most examples, either the obverse or the reverse is weakly struck. It appears that, in an attempt to achieve high relief, their dies were punched very deeply. Under eighteenth century presses, metal could not be made to flow properly into the dies' deeper recesses. The usual result is a lack of detail, the exact opposite of the desired high-relief effect. Some "reverse figure facing left" pieces have partial or even missing dates.

All four Nova Eborac reverses depict a figure that is, in appearance, very similar to that on the unattributed Connecticut "muttonhead" varieties (below.) The quatrefoils on Nova Eboracs also are similar or identical to those on the Excelsiors, on New Jersey running fox varieties and on Brasher's doubloons, further suggesting some level of collaboration.

The Excelsior coppers range in weight from 123 to 165 grains. The intended weight for the more common Nova Eboracs varieties is unknown, but probably was the Birmingham standard of 116.67 grains. At this weight, sixty pieces can be made from a pound of copper.

Thomas Machin's Proposed New York Coppers (1787)

James Atlee's second attempt at a New York coining franchise came in conjunction with a proposal submitted by Thomas Machin on March 3, 1787. It joined Atlee's first proposal, tendered on February 2, and one or more Bailey and Brasher proposals that had been on the table since February 11. Silversmithing and Vermont coinage partners, Daniel Van Voorhis and William Coley, submitted another proposal on February 16, apparently without accompanying patterns. Machin's proposal may have been accompanied as many as three different patterns. It also appears that James Atlee might have made them.

One pattern type reflects Machin's personal history. A true hero of the Revolution, he had been wounded at Bunker Hill (June 17, 1775) and afterward recuperated in the home of his politically-minded friend, George Clinton. Machin returned in 1778 to play a supervisory role in building and deploying a huge chain across the Hudson River near West Point. The chain was over 500 yards long, weighed 65 tons and was floated across the river on twelve- by sixteen-foot rafts. At its ends artillery posts stood ready to pulverize any enemy ship forced by the river's sharp turn to slow or stop. Concentric rings of fortified positions protected the artillery posts. The chain was removed in the winter, when ice prevented shipping on the river. The British had planned to split New England away from the other colonies by taking control of the Hudson. However, the American defenses so completely thwarted their strategy that no ship ever even tried to get through. Remnants of the Great Chain, a major and under-appreciated accomplishment of eighteenth century American engineering, still are revered fixtures at West Point. The importance of the chain was not lost on General Washington, who greatly appreciated it and sent Machin a personal letter commending his efforts.

After the war Machin built his home on land that was owned by Clinton, who by then was New York's governor. The place was near Great Pond, which now is called Orange Lake. Because the area frequently flooded, Machin built a drainage canal leading into the lake. On the canal he built a sawmill and a gristmill. The mills were not yet the site of a mint. Thus, any patterns made for the March 3 proposal likely would have been minted in New York City.

Numismatic discovery of the first pattern type came in 1859. Not surprisingly, it features George Clinton. For his part, Clinton vehemently opposed ratification of the Constitution and probably was supportive of an independent New York state coinage. A series of anti-ratification letters written under the pseudonym, Cato, long were attributed to him. It was partly in response to these letters that Alexander Hamilton, John Jay and James Madison penned the iconic *Federalist Papers*. Recent scholars have determined that Clinton probably was not Cato. After all, Clinton's views were well known and having his name publicly associated with the opposition carried more weight than any series of anonymous letters ever could.[687] Despite Clinton's opposition to Washington's federalism, the two were old friends and the President never forgot Clinton's staunch support of the Revolution. While New York was the U.S. capital, the two men frequently took tea at Clinton's Queen Street home. They shared a love for agriculture, Washington as a plantation owner and Clinton as an amateur botanist. Linden trees that grew at Mount Vernon were gifts from the Governor, who later served as Vice-President under presidents Jefferson and Madison.[688]

George Clinton as governor. Source: Irving (2:224.)

Atlee's medalic portrait of Machin's friend is stylized rather than realistic and shares few similarities with contemporary depictions of Clinton. Its obverse legend reads simply *GEORGE ✱ CLINTON ✱*. Some examples of these pieces, including the first three found, were overstruck on 1787 Immunis Columbia coppers (below.) Evidence suggests that the Immunis Columbia coppers actually were made somewhat later than Machin's March 3 proposal. If this is true, then the coppers bearing Clinton's portrait also might have been made later and not as part of the Machin/Atlee proposal for New York coinage.

Machin/Atlee New York pieces: *A – George Clinton obverse with the Machin/Atlee Excelsior reverse. B – Excelsior reverse with the standing Indian obverse. C – Standing Indian obverse with the eagle on demi-globe reverse. (Modern copy.) The similarity of Machin's Excelsior die to Bailey's probably is due to convergent interpretations of the same theme and not to plagiarism or die sharing.*

In any case, reverses of the Clinton pieces are very similar to Bailey's Excelsior reverses and also imitate the New York seal as it appeared on the state's paper money. It appears that New York allowed flexibility in determining which direction the eagle atop the seal faced and in the relative positions of Liberty and Justice. On the Machin/Atlee Excelsiors, Justice stands to the viewer's left, Liberty to the right. This configuration is opposite to that of Bailey's Excelsiors. Other differences are manifested in the Machin/Atlee central vignette, which features cliffs rather than rounded mountains of Bailey's Excelsiors and Brasher's doubloons. Moreover, Bailey's seal-top eagle faces either right or left, while the eagle on the Machin/Atlee pieces always faces to the viewer's right. The similarity of Atlee's Excelsior reverse to Bailey's likely reflects their differing interpretations of the same theme. They certainly are not from the same punches. Nor is it likely that one man sought to imitate the other's work.

The second Machin/Atlee pattern style pairs the same Excelsior reverse with a standing Indian, another device taken from New York's paper currency. Its legend reads *LIBERNATUS LIBERTATEM DEFENDO* ✱ ("[I am] Born Free [and Therefore] I Defend Liberty.")

The third Machin/Atlee pattern style pairs the standing Indian with an eagle, similar to the one at the top of New York's state seal. The eagle stands on a demi-globe, wings spread, foretelling America's dominance in the Western Hemisphere. The eagle faces to the viewer's right and its circumscribed legend reads *·NEO-EBORACUS 1787 EXCELSIOR·* ("New York, Most Excellent, 1787.")

The probable intended weight for all of these ill-fated issues was either 152.17 grains, that of British halfpence, or the yet-to-be-used federal standard of 157½ grains. All are very rare with ten to fifteen known examples of each style. In the late 1860's, John Bolen struck accurate copies of all three in small numbers. Today, Bolen's copies command prices in the hundreds of dollars. Genuine examples, on the other hand, often sell for more than twice the four- and five-figure estimates given in price guides.

Machin's proposal of March 3, 1787 coincided with a report to the legislature that all but condemned the practice of awarding coinage contracts to private individuals or companies. On April 18, New York abruptly ended all consideration of private or state coinage. Two days later, the lawmakers followed with an act banning the circulation of lightweight coppers. At almost exactly the same time, Machin, Atlee and others formed the partnership that established Machin's Mills as a mint. Though their attempts at becoming New York's official coiners had failed, Brasher, Bailey, Machin, the Atlees and their supporting casts soon would be engaged in a successful and altogether different kind of coinage...

American-Made Imitation British Halfpence (Ca. 1786 to 1789)

Numismatists acknowledged the existence of American-made imitation British halfpence more than a century ago. Until about three decades ago, however, the numismatic community afforded them little respect. Perhaps the stigma of "imitation" or "counterfeit," their apparent Britishness or the crudeness of their execution engendered this attitude. It took Robert Vlack's studies of 1963 and 1974 to bring these fascinating pieces to light.[*] Today no collection of early American coins is nearly complete without at least a smattering of them.

American imitations fall into a kind of grey area between counterfeiting and legitimacy. They held no official blessing from any American authority. At the same time, imitating a foreign coin technically could not be called counterfeiting. By the mid-1780's they were well beyond the reach of British anti-counterfeiting measures. Yet, something was not quite proper about the practice of making them. Coppers were important to the American economy and those who coined falsely profited at the expense of fellow citizens and of their new government.

[*] Eric Newman pioneered work in the field. In 1963 Vlack published the first edition of the book *Early American Coins*. It positioned these coppers alongside coins traditionally called "colonials." In 1974 Vlack followed up with a series of plates detailing the varieties of imitation halfpence then thought to be of American origin. The varieties themselves are designated using Vlack's notation, which has been extended for recent discoveries. Vlack's system assigns sequential integers to obverse dies. Reverses are denoted by the last two date digits and a letter to differentiate dies of the same year. Mules are indicated by a two-character suffix for the state whose die is muled. Thus, "Vlack 9-76B" denotes obverse "9" paired with the second ("B") 1776-dated reverse. "Vlack 15-85NY" denotes obverse "15" muled with a 1785 New York-associated die. Die states sometimes are indicated for the 21-87D pair using Roman numerals: "21.I-87D.I" and "21.II-87D.II."

Still, imitations were, in some sense, better than nothing and American imitations may have been tolerated because they were no worse than the British-made counterfeits that poured into the country. The Confederation government avoided the complicated issue by relegating creation and enforcement of anti-counterfeiting laws to the states. New York inadvertently furthered the confusion by abstaining from the legal authorization of coinage. It was in New York that most of the American imitations are believed to have originated. Those who had tried unsuccessfully for a New York coinage contract were, in effect, all dressed up with no place to go. They had the skills and equipment to coin halfpence. Lacking official authorization was a mere technicality. Ironically, absence of governmental oversight is what ultimately made at least one group of them profitable even as the sanctioned mints struggled.

Imitation halfpence often are struck crudely on lightweight, poor quality planchets. Some of this was intentional since less copper and lower refinement costs meant higher profits. The intended weight of most New York imitation halfpence probably was 116.67 grains, sixty to the pound, though most are somewhat lighter, ranging from 80 to 117 grains. It also is generally held that the coins were struck weakly from shallow-relief dies to simulate wear and foster acceptability. Wear, after all, implies a history of repeated acceptance in circulation.

While many imitation farthings exist, none ever has been proven to be of American origin. This is hardly surprising since the cost of producing halfpence was only marginally greater than the cost of producing less valuable farthings. Moreover, farthings never were popular in America and would have seen limited acceptance. Years after the fact, it was suggested that Machin's Mills coined a few *silver* pieces as well,[689] but none has been positively identified. They likely would have imitated British or Spanish coins then in circulation. Establishing the authenticity of an American-made silver imitation would be a major numismatic coup. (The American Numismatic Society collection includes imitations of Spanish coins that some believe to be candidates for this honor.)

American-made imitation halfpence presently are differentiated from their foreign-made cousins by their unfimbriated shield lines. That is, on the reverses of all known American pieces, the bands that form crosses on Britannia's shield lack outlines. Foreign-made pieces generally have fimbriated, or outlined, crosses. This feature is not an absolute criterion because some foreign-made pieces exhibit unfimbriated bands and some pieces with fimbriated shield lines may yet prove to be of American origin. Therefore, a lack of outlines suggests, but does not prove, American origin. Additional evidence of American manufacture usually can be found through comparison of letter punches. This cannot be regarded as absolute proof either, since punches sometimes were shared among coiners. Moreover, multiple punches apparently were produced from the same matrix or template, meaning that different coiners could have used identical punches. An old assumption that crudeness of design implies American origin also has fallen by the wayside as very crude British-made imitations have surfaced.

Other characteristics hint at American origin. For example, all of the known American pieces use "1" or "I" as the first digit in the date. In contrast, regal halfpence and many supposed British counterfeits use a "J." American-made pieces, particularly those from Machin's Mills, typically exhibit triangular dentils and the globe on which Britannia sits lacks detail compared to British pieces that sometimes show lines of latitude and longitude. However, exceptions exist and, thus, these characteristics again suggest but do not prove American origin.

For years, *all* American-made imitation halfpence were attributed to Machin's Mills by default. Sometimes the Machin umbrella even deliberately is spread over foreign counterfeits and evasions out of ignorance or the desire to inflate the value of a given piece. The truth is far more complex and is believed to have involved several different die makers and mints.
In the 1980's Gary Trudgen built on previous findings by Newman and Breen to reveal much about the circumstances behind the American imitations. That landmark work continues to be refined as information emerges. Trudgen identified three, then four groups of American imitations.[690] The following discussion generally follows his taxonomy, but adds a fifth group. It also differs slightly in assigning muled and controversial varieties to particular groups. Using this modified approach, five possible groups of American imitation halfpence are:

- **Group I**: Pieces believed to have been made by James F. Atlee in New York City between early 1786 and mid-1787. Dates: 1771, 1772, 1774, 1775 and 1776.
- **Group II**: Pieces believed to have been made by John Bailey and (possibly) Ephraim Brasher in New York City around 1787, or possibly 1788. Dates: 1747 and 1787.
- **Group III**: Pieces made at Machin's Mills in 1787, 1788 and possibly later, with James Atlee's likely involvement. Dates: 1778, 1787 and 1788.
- **Group IV**: Two rare mulings of imitation halfpence dies with Confederation and New York pattern dies. Dates: 1776 and undated (1787 inferred.)
- **Group V**: A catchall group of six rare varieties, with claims to American origin, that do not clearly fit with any of the other groups. Dates: 1772, 1777, 1783, 1784 and 1786.

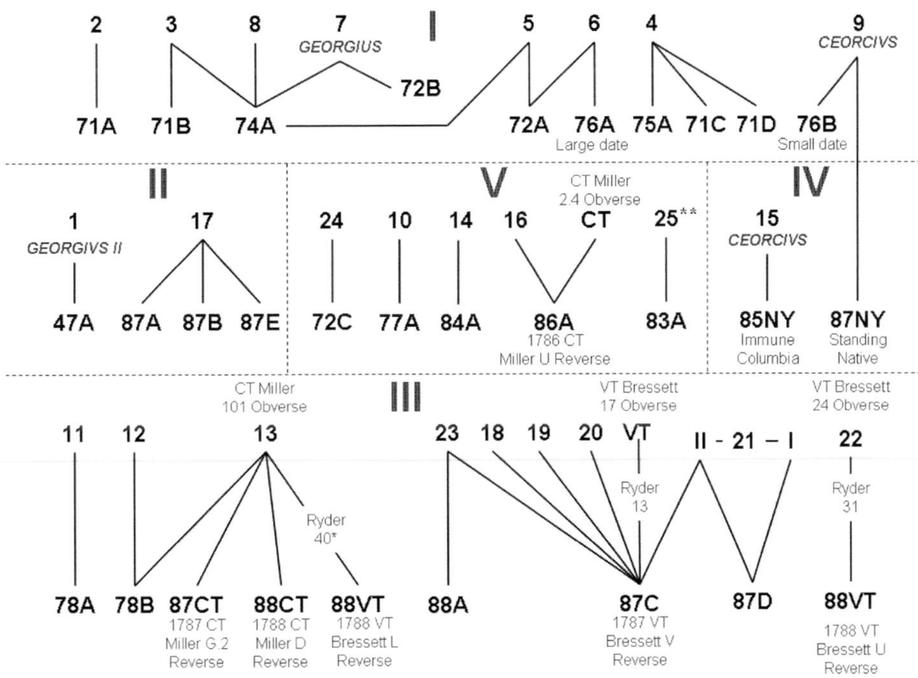

Five Groups Of American Imitation Halfpence By Vlack Varieties

These groups are charted at left and discussed below. In addition, a detailed attribution guide is presented in Appendix G. Presently forty-one varieties, from twenty-seven obverse and thirty reverse dies, are recognized.*

*Thought to be a modern fabrication. See below. ** Named "Ringo 25-83A" in honor of Mike Ringo.

* The exact numbers depend on whether the die states of obverse 21 and reverse 87D are counted separately and whether Vlack obverses 5 and 8 are counted as different dies. (See below.)

GROUP I: MOULD-ATLEE-COX IMITATION HALFPENCE

Group I imitation halfpence probably were made in New York City between early 1786 and mid-1787 by James Atlee and his associates. This was after the failure of Samuel Atlee's brewery, but before James departed for Newburgh and Machin's Mills. It was during this time that the Atlees formed their partnership with Albion Cox and that Cox's involvement with Walter Mould began. Given his metallurgical expertise, it is very likely that Cox played a role in the Group I coppers. Mould's association with the Group I pieces is inferred from: 1.) his contemporary presence in the New York City area, 2.) his association with Cox and, by implication, with James Atlee, 3.) the fact that some letter punches apparently were shared between Group I halfpence and coins that Mould produced in New Jersey.[691] These associations are the reasons that Group I imitation halfpence sometimes are called Mould-Atlee-Cox or Mould-Atlee Tory coppers.

Group I halfpence are characterized by thinner, weak-chinned portraits of George III. The group includes fourteen varieties from eight obverse and ten reverse dies. All are backdated, presumably to further the illusion of long time circulation. Recently, a 1771 Group I copper that was overstruck on a 1774 Group I piece sold at auction[692] and, more recently, a 1774 Vlack 7-74A was found overstruck on a rare 1785 Confederatio pattern. (See below, in this chapter.) These finds confirm that the nominal dates are meaningless. One Group I obverse die was re-used with a Confederation pattern die to create a rare Group IV mule (Vlack 9-87NY, below) and with a Vermont-associated reverse device punch on Vlack 9-76B. Vlack varieties 2-71A, 3-71B, 4-71C, 4-71D, 5-72A, 6-72A, 3-74A, 5-74A, 8-74A, 4-75A and 6-76A are all roughly similar in style. Vlack 4-75A is the only Group I variety that can be called "common." At the other end of the spectrum, Vlack 4-71C, 4-71D and 9-76B are all very rare.* Jack Howes recently discovered Vlack 5-74A, then showed that obverse 8 actually is reworked from the obverse 5 die and that the die received minor reworking even between 5-72A and 5-74.[693]

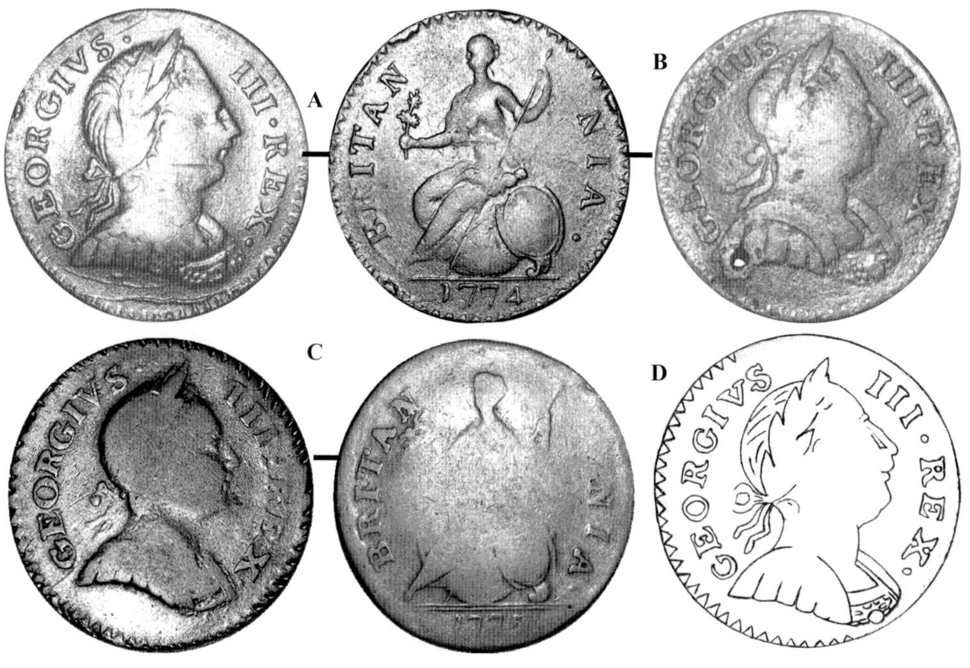

Selected Group I varieties:

A – Vlack 3-74A. (Note the under-bust die cracks.)

B – Vlack 7-74A. (Holed. Note GEORGIUS spelling).

C – Vlack 4-75A. (Dentils added later.)

D – Vlack 2-71A. (Note it distinctive profile.)

* If counted in Group I as it generally is, the list of very rare varieties also includes Vlack 24-72C. (See Group V, below.)

All Group I varieties, save three, have the familiar legends *GEORGIVS III REX* (obverse) and *BRITANNIA* (reverse.) Vlack obverse 7, from Vlack 7-72B and 7-74A, features a bust slightly more similar to regal halfpence of 1771 to 1775 and uses the spelling *GEORGIUS*. Both of these "U" varieties are scarce. Always crudely made, Vlack 9-76B has a very small date and uses the spelling *CEORCIVS* rather than *GEORGIVS*. The bust on Vlack obverse 9 is from the same punch as that on obverse 2, used on Vlack 2-71A. In a very worn state, obverse 9 also is paired with the undated and equally worn Atlee/Machin standing Indian New York pattern die as Vlack 9-87NY (Group IV.) This pairing is undated, but 1787 is inferred from the date of Machin's New York coinage proposal. Only three examples of this muling are known. Given the errant use of C's in place of G's and the absence of corrective over-punching, obverse 9 may have been an error die that saw no use until the coiners exhausted their supply of good dies. Alternately, the C's may have resulted from deliberate substitution for a missing "G" punch.

(Top) Vlack 6-76A, large date.
(Bottom) Vlack 9-76B, small date.
Compare to the inset date from 6-76A.

Vlack 9-76B and 9-87NY actually may be Group III varieties made at Machin's Mills, but James Atlee evidently made the device punch for Vlack obverse 9 in New York City. Presumably the standing Indian reverse became available after the April 18, 1787 rejection of Machin's New York proposal and the coincidental formation of the Machin's Mills enterprise. However, the device punch for Vlack reverse 76B could have been created *after* Atlee's mid-1787 departure for Newburgh. Eric Newman showed that this device punch is the same as that used on the bulk of the Vermont "standard heads" (below) and that the small date numerals on Vlack reverse 76B are identical to those on certain Connecticut reverses (e.g., 1786 Miller reverse A. See below.)[694] The Machin's Mills principals formed a partnership with the group responsible for Vermont coinage on June 7, 1787. If the device punch for reverse 76B was prepared under the terms of the Vermont partnership, then Vlack 9-76B probably was made at Machin's Mills and thus belongs in Group III. It also seems logical that Machin, rather than Atlee, might have retained the standing Indian die after April 18 and that Vlack 9-87NY could have been created after Machin and Atlee joined forces in Newburgh.

Group II: Bailey/Brasher Halfpence

Group II pieces tentatively are attributed to John Bailey and Ephraim Brasher and are believed to have been made during 1787, in New York City. Trudgen found several characteristics that Group II coppers share with Brasher- and Bailey-associated pieces, such as Brasher's doubloons, Bailey's Excelsior patterns, Nova Eboracs and New Jersey "running fox" coppers. These similarities are most apparent on "E" and "X" letter punches.[695] Group II pieces are characterized by portraits with long, pointed noses that appear as extensions of the King's forehead. The portraits are dissimilar from any known Atlee products.

Group II boasts only four varieties, all dated either 1747 or 1787. The 1747-dated variety, Vlack 1-47A, is the only one from any of the five groups that features George II, the only one whose obverse bust faces left and the only one with a date not in the 1770's or 1780's. The three 1787-dated Group II varieties, Vlack 17-87A, 17-87B and 17-87E, all share the same obverse and similar reverses. Vlack 17-87E is very rare, the other two relatively common. (See Appendix G for information on telling them apart.)

(Right) Vlack 17-87A. One of only two Group II obverses. Note the shape of George III's forehead and nose.

(Left) Vlack 1-47A, the other Group II obverse. Note that George II faces to the viewers left, as on genuine halfpence during his reign.

Group III: Machin's Mills Halfpence

Group III pieces generally are attributed to Machin's Mills, with dies probably by James Atlee. They likely were made in late 1787 and into 1788, or later. Their dates are 1778, 1787 and 1788, all years in which no regal British halfpence were minted. The backdated 1778 pieces may commemorate Thomas Machin's critical role in deploying the Great Chain.

On April 18, 1787, the very day that New York decided to reject his and all other coinage petitions, Machin formed a partnership with five other men, David Brooks, James Grier, James Jiles and the father-son team of Samuel and James Atlee. Of the five, Brooks was the best connected, serving on the state monetary commission. Crosby printed the entire text of the articles of agreement that formed the partnership. The agreement is detailed, yet cunningly evasive. Without the context of what is known about the business, one might conclude that the partners were engaged in a kind of general manufacturing operation. In context, however, phrases such as "...Samuel Atlee, and James F. Atlee being possessed of certain implements for carrying on said trade...," "...Thomas Machin being possessed of certain mills, doth hereby agree to let the parties...have the free use of them..." and "James F. Atlee and Thomas Machin shall equally manage, act and perform that part of the trade that concerns the manufactury [sic] of hard-ware..." all make perfect sense. "Hardware" was the eighteenth century euphemism for imitation and counterfeit coppers. To fund their venture, the partners each contributed £50. Since the Atlees were to provide equipment and Machin was to provide the site, the others were given the responsibility of providing certain legal and administrative services and each was required to pay an additional £10.[696] Coining operations must have begun immediately.

Machin's son, Thomas, Jr., was an eyewitness to the goings on at the mint. His account was given many years later, in a letter first published by E. M. Ruttenber in 1875. The younger Machin was a child when the mint was in operation, but his letter contains a detailed description of the two-story facility. According to the letter, the wooden, thirty-by-forty foot mill was set beside a dug canal. There men melted old cannon, pouring the copper into molds and removing the zinc. When the copper cooled they rolled it into strips of coin thickness and one to two feet width. A screw-driven punch was used to cut planchets that were then turned overnight in vessels to smooth their edges.* The coining press was also screw-driven. A ten-foot horizontal lever at the top of the screw had 500-pound lead weights mounted at each end. Four men used ropes to pull the weights back and forth, a half-turn, alternately raising and lowering the upper die.† A fifth man sat in a pit that was dug next to the press. His job was to extract a finished coin and replace it with the next blank. Using these methods, a team could coin about sixty coppers in a minute. Machin added that the operation continued for four or five years until around 1790 and, curiously, that small quantities of silver pieces also were coined. He wrote that the men wore masks and spoke of the devil to frighten the curious. (The masks probably were for protection.) [James] Atlee, whom Machin called "the engraver," wore a particularly hideous mask that scared away some boys who came to fish around the mill. At some time after 1790, the equipment was removed to New York City[697] and the mill was converted to process grain. In a letter to Crosby, Charles Ira Bushnell claimed that the mint operation had continued into 1791, that the bulk of the equipment was removed in 1792 and that, for some years afterward, the ship, *Newburgh,* carried the press as ballast.[698]

Coining press, from Denis Diderot's L'Encylopedie, *an amazing 18th century compendium of industry and technology. (Illustration used through the courtesy of Dover Publishing.)* [699]

Machin's Mills, or Group III, coppers comprise fifteen varieties from ten obverse and nine reverse dies. The obverses are characterized by King George's pursed lips, the general plumpness of his portrait and sharply triangular dentils. One pairing, Vlack 21-87D, sometimes is split into two separate varieties based on the existence of two states for each of its dies. One of the ten obverses is muled with two different Connecticut reverses. The Connecticut pairings are known to collectors of that series as Miller 101-D and Miller 101-G.2. (below, in this chapter.) Two other obverses are muled with Vermont reverses, though one of the pairings is thought to be a modern fabrication. One Vermont obverse is paired with a Machin's Mills reverse. The mulings are known to Vermont collectors as Ryder-13, Ryder-31 and Ryder-40.‡ Only the mules depart from the *GEORGIVS III REX* and *BRITANNIA* legends. The muled Vermont and Connecticut reverses read *INDE ET LIB* ("Independence and Liberty.") The muled Vermont obverse reads *VERMON AUCTORI* ("[By] Authority of Vermont.")

* Charles Ira Bushnell added that the vessels also contained sand, sawdust and water (Crosby, p.191.)

† Used in this manner, the balls and lever function as a flywheel. Once set in motion, the momentum of the balls continues to cause the screw to turn, raising or lowering the upper die and allowing the workers a short breath-catching respite.

‡ Ryder-40 is believed to be a modern fabrication. See the text on Vermont coinage.

Incredibly, Vlack reverse 87C is known to be used opposite six different obverses. It usually is seen with Vlack obverses 18, 19 or, in a much worn state, with the Vermont obverse Bressett 17, which Vlack simply called “VT.” The ubiquitous VT-87C muling also is known as Vermont Ryder-13, the "Britannia" variety. It may represent an attempt by Atlee at copying the Vermont mint's work prior to the Machin-Vermont agreement. Reverse 87C also is used on two extremely rare varieties, 20-87C and 23-87C, and with the early state of obverse 21 that is known as 21.II. Obverse 23, which closely resembles that of the 1788 Connecticut variety, Miller 2.D, another Machin's Mills product, is paired with reverse 88A.

Selected Group III coppers:

A – Vlack 12-78B. Vlack 12-78B is similar to 11-78A.

B – Vlack 19-87C.

C – Vlack 23-88A.

D – Vlack 23-87C.

E – Vlack VT-87C (a.k.a. Vermont Ryder-13.) Note its late reverse die state compared to Vlack 19-87C.

F – Vlack 22-88VT or Ryder-31. The reverse is very near collapse.

G – The same reverse, slightly earlier state, used on a Vermont Ryder-25 (See below.)

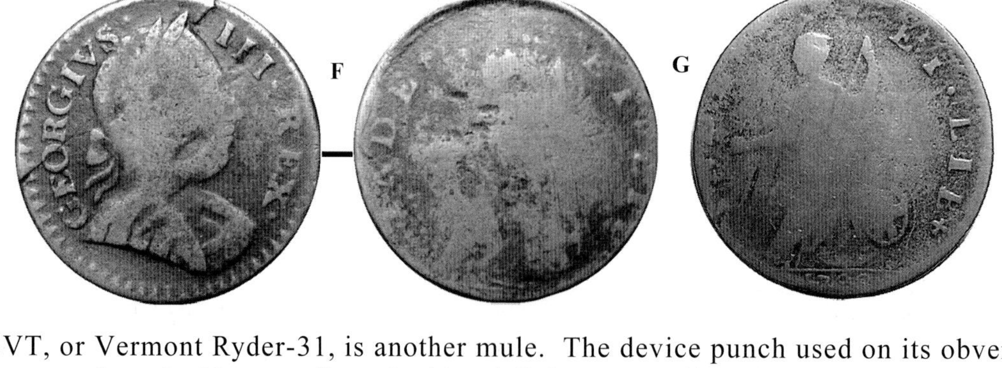

Vlack 22-88VT, or Vermont Ryder-31, is another mule. The device punch used on its obverse is the same one used on the Vermont “standard heads” that are attributed to James Atlee. Its reverse is the same as that used on Vermont Ryder varieties 25, 28, 29 and 39. Vlack 22-88VT has a Connecticut connection as well. Its reverse is used on the 1788 Connecticut variety 1-I. Hence, Vlack 22-88VT is also known as the Connecticut variety, Miller 100-I. Given the worn die states seen on the mules, it seems likely that they came late in the life of Machin's mint.

A – Vlack 13-78B. B – Vlack 13-88CT (illustration made from two different coins.) C – Vlack 13-88VT (again from different coins.) Vlack obverse 13 is paired with four reverses: Vlack 78B, 87CT (The pairing known as Connecticut Miller 101-G.2,) 88CT (a.k.a. Connecticut Miller 101-D) and 88VT (a.k.a., Vermont Ryder-40, using Bressett reverse L.) The pairing of Vlack 13 with the Vermont reverse, Bressett L, is thought to be a modern fabrication because its die states are inconsistent with other occurrences of the same dies. The 1787 Connecticut Miller reverse G.2 is paired with Miller obverse 52, an extremely rare muling. The 1788 Connecticut Miller D reverse also appears on Miller 2-D and 16.1-D, both common Machin's Mills products. Vermont reverse Bressett L is also used on Vermont varieties, Ryder-19 and 20. Note the roundness of George II's head and his pursed lips on all but Vlack 22-88VT.

Obverse 21 is particularly interesting because of its two distinct states of die wear. In addition to being paired with reverse 87C, the early state, 21.II, is paired with the early state of reverse 87D as Vlack 21.II-87D.II. The later states of both dies are paired as Vlack 21.I-87D.I. Most, if not all Vlack 21.I-87D.I pieces are struck on broad planchets, apparently without the use of a collar. Neither they nor any of their Group III companions look the part of having originated at the Confederation's most successful mint. They are masterpieces, however, compared to Group IV and Group V coppers.

Vlack 21.I-87D.I. Note the broad planchet, resulting from being struck without a collar, and the late, worn die states.

Group IV: Rare Mules with Known Dies, but Uncertain Mints

Group IV boasts but two varieties: Vlack 15-85NY and 9-87NY. Here they are placed in a separate group because, while numismatists may be relatively certain of the origin of their dies, it is not clear where or when the coins actually were made. Both varieties are probably late life marriages of convenience rather than deliberate attempts to create new designs. That is, both were created in an environment where the coiners were content to use any available dies.

The reverse of Vlack 15-85NY is from a 1785 Immune Columbia pattern that may have been submitted for consideration as a Confederation pattern by the Wyons. Or, the Immune Columbias might have been presented to Robert Morris as alternatives to the Constellatio Nova tokens. However, Vlack obverse 15 is crude and clearly not a Wyon product. It uses a Vermont device punch and the spelling *CEORCIVS*. As such, it may have been a spoiled die that was retained for use in a pinch. The path by which the two dies came together is a mystery. Regardless, Vlack 15-85NY is an extremely rare variety that is struck on small crude planchets. Vlack 9-87NY is even rarer, with only three known examples. It reuses Group I obverse 9 and the standing Indian from Machin's New York coinage proposal. Neither of the dies used on Vlack 9-87NY bears a date, but 1787 is inferred from the use of the standing Indian die.

(Top) Vlack 15-85NY. Immune Columbia refers to "Columbus' land, immune from tyranny." (Bottom) Vlack 9-87NY.

Group V: The Unclassified

Group V contains six varieties that exhibit intriguing similarities to the coppers in Groups I through III. They continue to defy attribution, sometimes appearing to straddle the boundary between domestic and imported. One of them, Vlack 24-72C, probably belongs with Group I. Its 1772 date suggests that it belongs with Group I pieces that likely were made in New York City. On the other hand, its style is slightly more similar to Machin's Mills Group III pieces. Vlack 24-72C is very rare, though at least two examples appeared in the Beach-Grünthal Hoard.[*] Its peripheral obverse legends are always very weak, the reverse usually stronger.

As for the other five varieties in the group, one theory has their place of manufacture as Bungtown, the nickname given to the area around North Swansea, Massachusetts. As with the term "Machin," "Bungtown" has been used as a catchall for crude, un-attributed imitations. By this definition, Bungtowns include coppers that are ostensibly from the Connecticut, New Jersey, Massachusetts and Constellatio Nova series. Why not imitation halfpence as well?

---

[*] Workers in Montclair, New Jersey, found the Beach-Grünthal hoard in 1922. It was beneath a boulder near the site of a mansion that had been Washington's military headquarters. Among a 1722 Rosa Americana penny, a handful of New Jersey state coppers, and cast and counterfeit halfpence, were about two dozen coppers from Groups I, II, III and V. The hoard passed to Harry Prescott Clark Beach, then to dealer Henry Grünthal, then to the American Numismatic Society. (John Kleeberg, *Reconstructing the Beach-Grünthal Hoard*, *American Journal of Numismatics*, Vol.7-8, New York, The American Numismatic Society, 1997, pp.187-208.)

The 1784 variety, Vlack 14.84A, differs radically from the others. It depicts both George III and Britannia as emaciated figures that may have been intended as satirical metaphors for a defeated Britain. Most now concede Vlack 14.84A to be of American origin, though the debate is still open. An example in New Jersey's Beach-Grünthal Hoard proves American circulation, if not American origin.

Vlack 14.84A

Obverses of (L to R:) *Vlack 24-72C, Vlack 10-77A (Compare to Group II's Vlack 17-87A) and Vlack 16-86A.*

Another group V variety may be a contemporary counterfeit of a 1787 Group II copper. Vlack 10-77A is both excessively rare and excessively crude. The shape of its obverse figure's profile is reminiscent of Bailey's obverse 17 from Group II. The excessively rare variety, Vlack 16-86A, would be relegated to the bin of crude British-made imitations if it did not share its reverse with a Connecticut obverse to create the Group V rarity, Vlack CT-86A that is known to Connecticut aficionados as Miller 2.4-U. Another variety, named Ringo 25-83A, in honor of the late collector and authority on imitation halfpence, Mike Ringo, has only its resemblance to Vlack 16.86A to support its claim to American status. That general consensus does not exist on the American-made status of Ringo 25-83A is the reason why it is not generally referred to as Vlack 25-83A.

With the exception of Vlack 24-72C, it is doubtful that Ephraim Brasher, James Atlee, Samuel Atlee, Walter Mould, Albion Cox, Thomas Machin, John Bailey or their immediate circles of friends had anything to do with the Group V pieces. It also is uncertain that the Group V coppers originated in New York. In this age of scientific accuracy, about all that can be said of the Group V imitations is that it somehow *feels* as if they should be included with the New York issues. With far greater certainty, it can be said that, from the crudest imitations to Brasher's doubloons, New York's indigenous coins are a very interesting lot.

VERMONT COINAGE (1785 TO 1788)

Without stopping to think, most regard Vermont as one of the original thirteen colonies or states. It was, in fact, the fourteenth state to enter the Union, joining in 1791. Even so, the citizens of Vermont supported and participated in the fight for independence. Made up of settlers spilling over from surrounding colonies and claimed by both New York and New Hampshire, Vermont was a natural to be the fourteenth state. However, between 1777 and 1791, Vermont was a free and independent republic, in its own right.

As they had in Massachusetts, settlers of this beautiful wilderness came slowly at first, then in ever widening streams. Samuel de Champlain found the area and claimed it for France in 1609. Of course the Abenaki, Iroquois and Algonquin tribes already knew where it was. A few British families from Massachusetts began moving into the southeastern part of Vermont, around Fort Dummer, on the Connecticut River, by 1725. At the same time a wave of land speculation swept New England. By 1749 New Hampshire's governor, Benning Wentworth, was eager to reap his share of financial benefits. Over the next fifteen years Wentworth granted 129 different townships to speculators. With each grant, he held out five hundred acres for himself. For the most part the speculators who received these "New Hampshire Grants" were absentee owners who never lived on their lands. Rather than providing an orderly framework for the development of communities, as had been the case in Winthrop's Massachusetts, the speculators sold the land and left the settlers to fend for themselves. This hands-off approach had a profound effect on the development of Vermont. The speculators unwittingly nurtured a strong spirit of independence.[700]

Another important dynamic unfolded to the south as settlers filled central and western Massachusetts and Connecticut. After years of speculative land auctions, the last available real estate in the area sold in 1762. Overflow settlers streamed into New York's Hudson River Valley where tenant farmers already occupying the region hoped for annexation by Massachusetts. Unhappy with the rising tide of new neighbors, the tenant farmers rebelled against their landlords. The Crown settled the matter by setting the border between Massachusetts and New York at a line twenty miles east of the Hudson. With the west closed by the new boundary and no more real estate in Connecticut, settlers turned north into Vermont where more land and more unrest awaited them.[701]

Bickering was nothing new to these people. As early as 1754 New York speculators complained to the Crown that they were losing out in Vermont land deals. After being put on the back burner while the French and Indian War ran its course, the issue resurfaced when the Crown ruled in 1764 that New York had rights to everything up to the Connecticut River, Vermont's *eastern* border. By then, however, Vermont already was settled, mainly by New Hampshirites. The New York speculators, including Cadwallader Colder, made sure that the old New Hampshire claims were invalidated and demanded either payment or eviction. In response, brothers Ethan and Ira Allen organized resistance against the New York sheriffs and other officials who tried to enforce the law. This movement was the origin of the Green Mountain Boys and of Vermont's move toward its own independence.

At a January 1777 conference in Westminster, representatives from towns in Vermont and New Hampshire declared independence as New Connecticut. Something about the name or the continued exertion of claims by New York caused the initiative to languish. Consequently, two months after the Westminster meeting, delegates met again in Windsor to re-declare independence under the name "Vermont" that they took from the old French name *Verde Mont*, or "Green Mountain." The new name stuck.

The freedom that the Republic of Vermont offered appealed greatly to Americans in New Hampshire border towns. As a result, many of these towns attempted to secede from the United States and join the new republic in 1778. Their defection lasted only until the Continental Congress forced them back into the fold the following year. Congress's anxiety increased even more as the Allens began negotiations with the Crown. More American towns attempted defection in 1781 and Vermont expanded its claims to include territory that belonged to New York. Both New York and New Hampshire pulled soldiers away from the Revolution to defend their lands against possible encroachment by the Republic of Vermont.

To stop the bleeding, Congress offered Vermont a place in the United States if it would give up claims to territories in New York and New Hampshire. Vermont agreed early in 1782, just in time for Congress to lose interest in the deal. By then the threat of British invasion from Canada had subsided. Moreover, the southern states resisted Vermont's admission because another northern state entering the union would change the balance of power. Not surprisingly, Vermont returned to Britain's negotiating table.

Finally, on March 4, 1791, President Washington met with Vermont officials in Bennington to secure statehood. The deal they struck included a payment of $30,000 to New York to silence its longstanding claims. After birthing a state, Ethan Allen, whom many regarded as a thug, was not among the Vermont delegation. He had died the previous year.

The Men, Their Mints and Their Coins

As a republic in the late 1780's, Vermont produced coins that run the gamut from pitiful to quaintly original. Of the coppers produced by states, or would-be states, under the Confederation, Vermont's are the scarcest overall. About forty different die combinations are known. "About" is used because at least two varieties are controversial as they are suspected of being newer fabrications. The thirty-eight non-controversial varieties were produced from twenty-six obverse and twenty-six reverse dies. Of the forty varieties, five are dated 1785, six are dated 1786, four are dated 1787 and the remaining twenty-five are dated 1788.[*] The small number of known varieties for each of the first three years reflects the difficulty the mint experienced in finding and keeping a reliable die maker. That the final legal production year yielded the most varieties is indicative of an alliance that developed with Machin's Mills.

Reuben Harmon, Jr., the man chiefly responsible for Vermont's coinage, came to the republic from Suffield, Connecticut, with his father around 1768. In 1785, while living in Rue Port (now Rupert,) the younger Harmon formed a vision of making coins for his future state. Already a successful businessman, he began

[*] In the 1920s, Hillyer Ryder built on earlier work by Rev. Edmund Slafter to write the defining work on these varieties, *The Colonial Coins of Vermont*. Ryder's work has been expanded by John Richardson, Ken Bressett, Tony Carlotto and others. Still, Ryder's system, as expanded by Richardson, is the most widely used method of classifying Vermont varieties. Ryder and Richardson used single integers to designate varieties. Their designations usually are prefixed by "RR." Bressett used integers to denote obverses and letters to denote reverses. "KB" usually prefaces Bressett's designations. Thus, Ryder-Richardson variety "RR-12" is equivalent to Ken Bressett's variety "KB 11-K." The best attribution and general reference for Vermont coppers is *The Copper Coins of Vermont and Those Bearing the Vermont Name* by Tony Carlotto (The Colonial Coin Collector's Club; Printed by Bookcrafters, Chelsea Michigan, 1998.)

assembling the necessary copper and equipment and located a mint site on land that he owned. He recruited skilled partners, William Coley and Daniel Van Voorhis, from their silversmithing firm in New York City. Elias Jackson, of Litchfield, Connecticut, also joined Harmon as a partner, though his role is unclear.[702]

Harmon approached "the Representatives of the Freemen of the State of Vermont in General assembly" in June 1785 and gained approval for minting coins. The authorizing act was proposed and passed on the same day, the fifteenth. Harmon apparently had connections, having been a representative to the legislature and a justice of the peace. Clearly, the legislature held high hopes for the endeavor as the act itself reads "...this assembly being willing to encourage an undertaking that promises so much public utility...." The act also regulated the new coinage:

> *...granted to the said Reuben Harmon Junior Esq. the exclusive right of coining Copper within this State for the term of two years from the first day of July...and all Coppers by him coined, shall be in pieces of one third of an ounce, Troy weight each, with such Devices and Mottos as shall be agreed upon by the Committee appointed for that purpose...before he enter on the business of coining shall enter into a bond of five thousand pounds...shall be of full weight...shall be made of good and genuine Metal.*[703]

David Sheldon, Abraham Underhill and Benjamin Baldwin acted as sureties in the payment of Harmon's bond to Vermont's treasurer, Ira Allen.[704]

In exchange for an exclusive two-year minting privilege, Harmon and his partners were obligated to surrender one percent of their production to the Vermont treasury. The specified weight standard for the new coppers equates to 160 grains, about eight grains heavier than British halfpence. On October 27, 1785, at the request of the partners, the standard was lowered to 111 grains, that is, "four pennyweight, fifteen grains," a weight more consistent with contemporary counterfeit halfpence than with full-weight coppers.[705] Actual weights of Vermont coppers vary from 77½ to 185 grains, with earlier die varieties tending toward the higher end of the scale.[706] The wide ranges may be due to the multiple planchet sources, inconsistent quality of the metal used, primitive planchet making equipment or simply the lack of skilled, attentive labor.

William Coley, who had moved to Vermont at the onset of operations, was Harmon's initial die maker. The mint building was a crude structure built near Rue Port on the banks of Millbrook Stream, a tributary to the Pawlette River. The coins' obverse design was set by the legislature and was to be a landscape view of the tree-covered Green Mountains, with a rayed, smiling sun rising over them. A plow in the foreground would symbolize agricultural strength. Perhaps not by coincidence, the scene resembles the view from the original mint site.[707] The obverse legend was to read *VERMONT*[EN]*S*[IUM]. *RES* **.** *PUBLICA*., or "By the Authority of the People who Live in the Green Mountains." Coppers of 1785 use the word *VERMONTS.* or *VERMONTIS.*, while in 1786 the more formal *VERMONTENSIUM* is used. Vermont coppers of this basic design have become known popularly as "landscapes."

The 1785 Ryder varieties, two through five, and 1786 varieties, six through eight, all are landscapes. Their central reverse design is shared with Constellatio Nova coinages: an all-seeing Divine Eye surrounded by the thirteen groups of rays and stars of a new constellation. The 1786 landscapes bear pointed rays, while most 1785 Vermont landscapes feature blunt or club rays that have incised ends. Ryder-5's are the only 1785 landscapes with pointed reverse rays. Their rays actually are more similar to those on Constellatio Nova obverses Crosby-2 (1783) and Crosby-3 (1785) than to the rays on the 1786 landscapes. The circumscribed reverse legends of the landscapes all read *STELLA. QUARTA. DECIMA·*, or prophetically, "The Fourteenth Star."

Obverse of the struck version of 1785 Ryder-5. The lines that make up Ryder-5's reverse rays are in groups of seven as on 1783 Constellatio Nova obverses 2 (1783) and 3 (1785.) Also note the density of the forest relative to the other landscapes.

Examples of Ryder-5 are very rare and are either prototypes, contemporary counterfeits or later fabrications. The possibility that they are later fabrications earns Ryder-5 the label "controversial." In 1875 Sylvester Crosby knew of a single struck example and two cast pieces that he deemed counterfeits.[708] Today a few more are known in both struck and cast forms. The two forms are very similar but not identical. For example, struck examples have an exergue line under the plow, while the cast versions do not. Assuming that both forms are contemporary to the 1780's, they should actually be treated as distinct varieties. Unlike the other landscapes, the sun on Ryder-5 pieces rises to the viewer's left and over a *dense* forest of small trees.

Selected landscape varieties:

A – 1785 Ryder-3 (Bressett 2-B.)

B – Obverse of 1785 Ryder 4 (Bressett 3-C.)

C – 1786 Ryder-7 (Bressett 5-E.)

D – 1786 Ryder-8 (Bressett 6-E.)

As does Ryder-3,Ryder-2 (Bressett 1-A) has VERMONTS. in its obverse legend and incised club rays on its reverse. On Ryder-2's obverse, a die break developed through the "8" and plow. In time it broadened into the mountains and came to resemble a tornado. (See Appendix H for more notes on attributing Vermont coppers.)

In February 1787, a few months before his coining privilege was set to expire, Harmon realized that he was not going to be able to cover expenses without an extension. He petitioned for ten more years and was given eight, until July 15, 1795. To further help the firm recover its expenses, fees due the republic were suspended for three years, after which they were to be reinstated at the rate of 2½ percent. Again Harmon was required to post a £5,000 bond. This time, Nathaniel and Lemuel Chipman stood surety.[709]

The extension coincided with a major change in the design of the coppers. The landscapes may have faced difficulties in gaining acceptance. Their designs, at least on their obverses, were very different in appearance than any other coins then in circulation. By the time of the extension and design change, another shift already was underway as the business relationship between Coley and Harmon was ending. Coley may have decided that wealth was not coming to him as quickly as he had hoped or he may have seen greater opportunity in other coinage initiatives that were emerging in New York. Regardless, Coley's departure meant that Harmon soon would be forced to seek new dies and die makers.

In place of the landscape motif, Harmon was directed, with no further specification, to use an obverse "head," [710] a form that more closely resembled British halfpence and the new cents of Connecticut. Both ultimately imitated ancient Roman sestertia. On the Connecticut coins the obverse legend reads *AUCTORI CONNEC*, or "By the Authority of Connecticut." On 1786 varieties with the new motif, Vermont copied the idea with *AUCTORI VERMON.* Beginning in 1787 the legend was altered to read *VERMON AUCTORI,* with the same meaning.

On halfpenny reverses, the British replaced the sestertias' Roma with Britannia. Vermont and Connecticut employed a similar reverse figure that most likely represents Liberty. However, Vermont's authorizing act is again non-specific, referring only to "a woman." [711] Connecticut and Vermont both used the phrase *INDE*[PENDENCE] *ET LIB*[ERTY,] or "Independence and Liberty." With only four exceptions,* all non-landscape Vermont copper reverses share a form of the legend *INDE ET LIB* with differences in word position (e.g., the errant form, *ET LIB INDE*,) placement, spacing and punctuation.

An early attempt at the new design, probably the first, is wholly unlike any other variety. Its obverse profile very much resembles an infant's and thus has become known popularly as the "baby head" variety of 1786.

1786 Vermont "baby head" copper, Ryder-9. Breen suggested that the 1786 Connecticut variety, Miller 3-D.1, the "scholar's head," might have been the "baby head's" inspiration. (Breen, Encyclopedia, *p.62. See below.)*

Tradition says that Coley produced the dies for the baby head variety and then, in disgust over the crudeness of his effort, left to rejoin his old partners. Tony Carlotto suggested that, instead of being a failure, the resemblance of the variety to a baby was intentional and that it might commemorate the 1785 births of Clara Harmon, Richard Van Voorhis or both. The figure's clothing and bow do more closely resemble a baby's gown than a cuirass or toga.[712] The image even could represent the young republic or commemorate the anticipated birth of Vermont as a new state.

* The exceptions are: 1.) the Ryder-13 *BRITANNIA* reverse, 2.) ET LIB INDE on Ryder-18, 3.) the same legend on Ryder-35 and 4.) Ryder-1, the *IMMUNE COLUMBIA* muling. (All described below.)

Given that the skill employed in producing the landscapes is greater than that exhibited on the baby heads, is it likely that Coley made the dies for both? It can be argued that the baby head obverse is executed adequately, but most examples lack the details that would result from an understanding of metal flow during striking. The reverse is indisputably crude. Thus, Harmon or someone else may have made the baby heads' dies after Coley's departure. Even if this were the case, Coley's letter punches could have been used. Another possible scenario is that William Buell (below) may have been the die maker. Regardless of who made the baby head dies, Coley's 1786 departure to rejoin his old partners left Harmon without a proper die maker.

One other feature that was introduced on the baby heads is a grouping of four wheat sheaves that appear on the reverse shield. Except for rare occurrences on Bressett reverse G (on Bressett 8-G, Ryder-10,) the sheaves appear on no other Vermont varieties. They may have been added to reverse G after the main device punch was applied.[713]

A remarkable twist of fate may link three Vermont varieties to Connecticut's state coinage and its chief die maker, Abel Buell. The tale of it was told to Charles Ira Bushnell in 1855 by Buell's grandson, Abel Buell Moore. In it, the elder Buell sent his fourteen-year-old son, William, to the apothecary to buy a jug of *aqua fortius* ("strong water," known lately as nitric acid.) Presumably, the acid would have been used to bring up the shine of planchets. As young William returned, he was accosted by a small band of Indians who, in a tragic lapse of judgment, became convinced that the jug held rum. Whether William helped them to their conclusion is unknown, but one of the Indians grabbed the jug, drank its contents and immediately died. William escaped, but the dead man's incensed tribesmen issued the modern equivalent of a mob contract on his head. He supposedly fled to Vermont under the cover of darkness, taking with him some of his father's worn dies or device punches.[714] The story contains inaccuracies since Moore heard it second- or third-hand. Yet, it also may contain some elements of truth. And, even if it is no more than family lore, Harmon may have solicited Abel Buell's die making services through other channels.

If true, this story explains why the two 1786 varieties and one 1787 variety of Vermont, mailed bust left coppers have an obverse figure that is identical to 1785 mailed bust left Connecticut coppers described below.[*] Ryder-10 (1786,) Ryder-11 (1786) and the very rare Ryder-15 (1787) exhibit this obverse figure. All three of these varieties were struck on very poor quality planchets and, since the punches were worn, even coins with little wear are lacking in detail. On Ryder-15 the date is always obscured by a major die break, perhaps explaining the rarity of the variety.

1786 draped bust left, Ryder-11.

When Buell's punches or dies became too worn for use, Harmon again was without the tools he needed. Consequently, he approached the proprietors of Machin's Mills and struck a deal wherein their die maker would create Vermont dies in exchange for a 60 percent share of the Harmon's company. Harmon also would receive 40 percent of Machin's non-Vermont profits

[*] Compare Ryder-11 to Connecticut variety Miller 7-D.1, in the text on Connecticut state coppers.

and £600.[715] The terms of the deal are remarkable, given that Machin held no state charter. They reflect both the strength of his position in the marketplace and Harmon's frustration. After the deal was struck, the Vermont mint was moved to the banks of the Pawlette River and the coppers took on a more consistent appearance. It is probable that all twenty-five 1788-dated varieties and three of the four 1787-dated varieties of Vermont coppers were made using Machin's Mills dies that supposedly were created by James Falconer Atlee. Two 1787 varieties and twenty-two of the 1788 varieties share the same right-facing mailed bust and seated female figure from the same pair of device punches. These often are called the "standard head" varieties. They are differentiated by variances in lettering, punctuation, die breaks, etc.. Even though the dies took on a more consistent appearance, planchet quality and striking improved little. Vermont coppers made from Machin's Mills dies typically are struck softly and are missing central details.

1788 standard heads: *(Left) Ryder-16 / Bressett 15-S. (Middle) Ryder-20 / Bressett 10-L. (Right) Ryder-25 / Bressett 16-U. The standard heads include 1787 Ryder varieties 12 and 14, as well as 1788 Ryder varieties 16-26 and 28-38. Note the weakness of central detail inherent to all of them.*

The first 1787-dated variety made with Machin's Mills dies may have been Ryder-14, the second Ryder-12. Both are standard heads. The one other bust right variety of the year, Ryder-13, may be dated 1787 by circumstance. Its reverse (Bressett reverse V) is from a worn state of the 1787 Machin's Mills *BRITANNIA* die, Vlack 87C, that was used in conjunction with at least five different Machin imitation halfpence obverses (Vlack obverses 18 through 21 and 23.) Ryder-13's could have been made even before the two mints joined forces or later when using an old worn die was more convenient than making a new one. Ryder-13's obverse (Bressett obverse 17) stylistically is similar to that of the 1788 variety Ryder-27 (Bressett 18-W.) However, Ryder-27 is the only variety exhibiting "domed" hair.* Because the two busts differ so markedly from the standard heads and because the word "Britannia" appears on the reverse of Ryder 13, these two varieties sometimes are known as the "bastard heads."

Decades ago, Eric Newman noticed similarities between Ryder-27 and known Group III imitation halfpence from Machin's Mills, including imitations of Connecticut coppers (Vlack 13-87CT/CT Miller 101-G.2 and Vlack 13-88CT/CT Miller 101-D.) He also found that the

* On Ryder-27's obverse, hair radiates downward and outward from a central crown point as seen on some Machin's Mills, Connecticut and Nova Eborac varieties.

device punches used on Group I imitation variety Vlack 9-78B are the same as those used on Vermont standard heads. In doing so, Newman effectively showed that the standard punches originally were made to produce imitation British halfpence. Among other important implications, this finding laid to rest an old and contentious accusation that the shields on Vermont copper reverses bear crosses because the Republic of Vermont anticipated successful negotiations with the British.[716]

Bastard heads: *(Left) 1787 Britannia reverse, Ryder-13 / Bressett 17-V. Recall that the reverse from this coin, in an earlier die state, is Vlack reverse 87C from the Group III American-made counterfeit halfpence. (Right) Obverse of 1788 Ryder 27/Bressett 18-W. Note the figure's "domed" hair.*

Two 1788 varieties also are mulings. The first, Ryder 39 (Bressett 25-U,) is associated with a small family of Connecticut coppers that almost certainly were made at Machin's Mills. These Connecticut coppers are the "small head" varieties Miller 1-I (1788,) 1.1-A and 1.1-VV (both 1787.) Bressett obverse 25 is from the same die as the Connecticut obverse, Miller 1.1. Bressett's reverse U, from Ryder-39's flipside, is used on four other Vermont varieties, Ryder-25, 28, 29 and 31, all of which are standard heads.

(Top) Mock-up of Ryder-39, using the Bressett obverse 25 from a Connecticut Miller 1.1-A and the Bressett reverse U, from Ryder-25.

(Bottom) Mock-up of Ryder-40 using the obverse of Machin's Mills imitation halfpenny Vlack 13.78B and Vermont reverse Bressett L, from Ryder-20.

The second 1788 muling is the controversial Ryder-40 variety. It is controversial because the three or four known Ryder-40's, including one at the Smithsonian, possibly are modern fabrications. Ostensibly, they are mulings of Machin's Mills obverse Vlack 13 with Bressett's Vermont reverse L, both of which are in advanced states of wear. The controversy exists because Ryder-40's die states seem to contradict those of the same dies on other coins.[717]

Numerous other punch links and first cousin, once removed relationships tie Vermont coppers to those from Machin's Mills and Connecticut. As shown earlier, for example, Ryder-31 (Bressett 24-U) is also known as Machin's Mills variety Vlack 22-88VT and as Connecticut variety Miller 100-I.

(Right) Ryder-31, a.k.a., Machin's Mills Vlack 22-88VT and as Connecticut Miller 100-I.

(Left) Ryder-1, the Immune Columbia muling.

Another variety, Ryder-1 (Bressett 26-Z,) has a crude obverse paired with a worn 1785 Immune Columbia die (below, this chapter.) This muling probably was made long after its date suggests, when the Immune Columbia die had outlived its original purpose and was floating between mints. The crudeness of Ryder-1's obverse lettering suggests the work of a less skilled engraver. Recall that the Immune Columbia die also is paired with a similar imitation halfpenny obverse that has the errant legend *CEORCIUS III REX.* That pairing is known as Group IV imitation halfpence variety Vlack 15-85NY. Yet another Vermont obverse, Bressett 23 (used on Bressett variety 23-S, or Ryder-30,) is strikingly similar to both in crudeness, exhibiting the same poor letter alignment. Vermont obverse 23 is unique in its use of an inverted, backward "C" in its obverse legend, *VERMON ✱ AUↃTORI.* Ryder-1, Ryder-30 and the imitation variety, Vlack 15-85Y, are so similar that the circumstances surrounding their creation *must* be similar.

A number of different host coins were used as undertypes for Vermont coppers. Some of the most spectacular overstrikings occur when the host is a Constellatio Nova copper. A 1787 New York law forbade lightweight coppers from circulating. This gave Thomas Machin and others a ready source of coins that were illegal in New York, but acceptable in Vermont.

The Vermont mint closed in 1789, though Vermont coppers continued to be produced at Machin's Mills. Harmon is thought to have moved to Ohio around 1790, where he lived out his days making salt.[718] All of his Vermont varieties are collected avidly and even common ones demand premium prices, particularly when they occur on unblemished planchets. In a sense it is surprising that such crude coins would now be so highly prized. Part of the attraction may stem from the desire to return to the simplicity that was early Vermont. Even today, much of the state is like its coins – rustic, charming, historic – a pleasant, rural escape from New England's crowded cities.

(Note: Appendix H contains notes on varietal rarity and a detailed attribution guide for Vermont coinage.)

CONNECTICUT STATE COINAGE (1785 TO 1788)

In the autumn of 1785, as it did in most of the other states, commerce in Connecticut stood on very wobbly legs. There, counterfeit halfpence circulated in epidemic proportions alongside the credit currency that had been a local staple since early in the century. In the 1730's Samuel Higley and John Read had tried with little success to find an answer. Nearly a half-century later, a handful of influential men were ready to try their hand by giving their new state a second chance at copper coinage.

Among this new generation were two state assemblymen, Joseph Hopkins and Samuel Bishop. With John Goodrich and James Hilhouse, a former assemblyman and future U.S. Congressman and Senator, they formed a partnership called the Company for Coining Coppers. The partners submitted a coinage proposal to Connecticut's bi-cameral General Assembly on October 18, 1785. Two days later, after deliberations that saw the associated memorial (bill) bounce back and forth between the upper and lower houses, narrowly avoiding being tabled until the next session, the "C.C.C." was granted most of what the partners had requested. They would be allowed to mint up to £10,000 in coppers, about three million pieces, at six penny weight, or 144 grains, each.[719] The act allowed them up to five years to complete their assignment. In exchange for the coining privilege, the partners were to pay Connecticut five percent in royalties and allow state oversight. A provision to give the coins very limited legal tender status, "...for the purpose of making even Change [sic], for any sum not exceeding three Shillings," was removed before final passage.[720] Four days after passage of the original act, a law prohibiting unauthorized minting of coppers in Connecticut was added as an afterthought.[721] Of course such a law carried no weight in New Jersey, New York or anywhere else outside of the state.

Between passage of the coinage bill and November 12, 1785, when the organization of the C.C.C. became official, four new partners were added, bringing the total to eight. Each of them held an equal 12½ percent share of the company.[722]

Among the eight was the silversmith, die maker and very talented fellow, Abel Buell. A mint was constructed around him in New Haven and, for several months, the operation ran very smoothly. Buell proved to be skilful and innovative, making extensive use of *hubbing*[*] techniques and apparently inventing an automatic planchet-feeding device.[723] It is because of him that, in spite of the planchet irregularities exhibited by many of their coppers, the coins produced by the C.C.C. are of significantly higher quality than those made in or for Vermont.

Even with the new coins, the unchecked importation of counterfeit coppers continued to be a problem in Connecticut. In May 1786 the state legislature made an unsuccessful attempt to pass a law that would have levied a substantial fine against anyone importing more that fifty unauthorized coins. Only coins authorized by Congress or any one of the states and having value equal to legal Connecticut issues were to be exempt.[724] The text of the bill is not specific, but it is likely that some of the targeted coppers were counterfeits of Connecticut coins and not simply counterfeit or imitation British halfpence.

---

[*] Hubbing refers to the practice of combining various design elements, such as major devices, letters, dates, dentils, etc., into a single punch. In theory, hubbing allows replacement dies to be made very quickly and very similar to other dies made with the same complex punch. Differences still occurred, however, because presses used to create hubs were weak and finer details still had to be added to the die by hand.

Other problems arose. By the summer of 1786 the C.C.C.'s supply of copper was depleted and the partners were forced to suspend operations. In September, however, Mark Leavenworth, William Leavenworth and Isaac Baldwin were allowed to use the mint facilities, presumably because they owned a supply of copper.[725]

By the first of November the partners were forced to make improvements in the mint's failing equipment. These improvements required capital, prompting a shift in ownership of the C.C.C.. By June 1787 Baldwin and the Leavenworths, together, emerged with a 12½ percent, or one-eighth, share. James Hilhouse and Abel Buell each had the one-eighth share with which they had begun. Joseph Hopkins was out altogether and John Goodrich was down to a one-sixteenth share. A new partner, James Jarvis, steadily had been buying interest in the company for over a year and by then owned a controlling share at nine sixteenths, or 56¼ percent.[726] At that point the company was re-chartered as James Jarvis and Company. Trouble was afoot.

A Corporation Corrupted

Jarvis was unsatisfied with merely controlling the company. His eye was on a much greater prize and he would do whatever was necessary to get it, legal or otherwise. The Confederation was on the verge of awarding what would be a very lucrative contract to mint hundreds of tons of *federal,* Fugio cents. Jarvis had submitted a proposal for federal coinage to Congress seven months earlier. In exchange for a $10,000 bribe, an influential official on the Treasury Board used his influence to award the contract to Jarvis's company and insure its cheap access to federal copper. Tradition says that at least part of this copper came from rings that held together barrels of ammunition sent by the Marquis de Lafayette during the Revolution.

It should have been obvious that something was amiss. Jarvis had taken possession of 12,809 pounds of federal copper in January 1787, five months before the C.C.C. was re-chartered and four months before the awarding of the contract was official.[727]

Jarvis directed Abel Buell to begin making dies for the 157½-grain Fugio cents, even as the New Haven mint continued to produce lighter and, therefore, more profitable Connecticut coppers. It is likely that at least some of the federal copper illegally found its way into the state coins of Connecticut. As if this were not enough to signal a problem, the mere reorganization of the C.C.C. as Jarvis and Company *may* have resulted in the loss of the company's legal right to make Connecticut coinage.[728]

Turning copper into planchets was labor intensive and Jarvis soon realized that meeting the increased production demands would require new sources of ready-made blanks. He traveled to Europe in an attempt to buy planchets on credit, leaving his merchant father-in-law, Samuel Broome, to run the mint. The plan met with problems, however, as no one in Europe would honor Jarvis's credit. On May 21, 1788, Broome turned over to the federal treasury 398,577 Fugio cents, 8,968 pounds of them, a small fraction of the expected total. The shortfall triggered a committee investigation that resulted in the voiding of Jarvis's federal contract and a failed attempt by the government to recover the remaining copper.[729]

As the truth about their dealings became known, Jarvis and Broome sold the remaining copper and much of the mint equipment to Machin's Mills and by early 1789 were on their way to Paris. Left behind, Abel Buell justifiably was afraid. As a teenager he had been convicted of counterfeiting Massachusetts paper money and, as a result, had lost an ear to the justice system. The punishment would have been much greater were it not for Buell's youth at the time of the infraction. Fearing that his punishment would this time be much greater, Buell fled to England. He left the mint in the hands of his young son, Benjamin, who continued to operate on his own and with the supposed help of Machin's Mills.[730] The surrender of Abel Buell's interest in the company to Benjamin may have been based on the premise that youth would preserve the boy from wrath as it had saved the father. Abel Buell apparently joined Jarvis in proposing a Paris-based subsidiary to Matthew Boulton's English operations.[731] Boulton, however, showed characteristic good judgment in rejecting the offer.

The State of Connecticut held its own investigation in 1789. The investigators found that the original C.C.C. was innocent of wrongdoing, but rescinded its right of coinage and determined that Benjamin Buell's continued operation of the mint was illegal. The New Haven mint was done.[732]

In the time that it legally existed, the C.C.C. minted about 1.5 million coins. Jarvis's subsequent New Haven operations, which presumably used the same facilities, produced 3 to 3.5 million Connecticut coppers, many of which were made in 1788 and 1789, but were back-dated "1787" to give the illusion of legitimacy.[733]

Sylvester Crosby related a second-hand 1854 account of the mint from the notes of Charles Ira Bushnell. The witness whose account Bushnell transcribed was Henry Meigs of New York City. Meigs was a very young child when the mint was working, but he claimed to remember a red frame house near the center of the north shore in New Haven. There he was given coppers by the men who ran the mint. Meigs also associated two merchants, Jeremiah Platt and Samuel Broome, with the operation and suggested that Broome might have been a sub-contractor. A source other than Meigs related that a second building, two miles inland from the first, also was used and that it still contained an old coining press and some copper.[734] This may have been either a counterfeiting operation not associated with the C.C.C. or a building for ancillary processes, such as the manufacturing of planchets.

Similar Differences

Of the coins produced by the states under the Articles of Confederation, Connecticut coppers are by far the most numerous,* both in population and in number of die varieties. Given that approximately 354 different varieties are recognized,† the primary mints must have been

* Though the estimate of 5 million coins truly was significant for the period, it is important to remember that production was spread over a period of at least four years.

† Henry Clay Miller's 1920 book, *The State Coinage of Connecticut,* is the standard reference for Connecticut coppers. Within a given year (1785-1788,) Miller used integers to index obverse die families (that he called "types") and letters to index reverse die families. Owing to the sheer numbers of dies, reverse designations include upper case letters, lower case letters, double lower case letters and double upper case letters. With the exception of 1787 reverse "WW," on which the reverse figure faces right rather than left, reverse die families are differentiated by date and legend punctuation. Obverse die families are differentiated by the dates of the reverses with which they are paired, the style of the bust and by legend punctuation. Miller used qualifying numbers to describe individual dies within a family. Among other minor differences, these individual dies exhibit variations in the placement of legend letters/symbols. For example, the variety "6.4-F.5" is from obverse die family "6," die "4," reverse die family "F," die "5." All dies in family "6" share the same legend punctuation with obverse families "2" through "5." Obverse family "6," however, has a different bust than that on families "2" through "5." Obverse die "6.4" is unique among family "6" dies in the exact positions of its legend letters/symbols. Reverse family "F" is unique in its combination of date and legend punctuation. The placement of the legend and punctuation make die "F.5" unique within the "F" family. Some dies were used in two different years and hence are known as "biennial" dies. The obverse die "5.3" from 1786, for example, is

substantial operations. Thirty of these varieties are dated 1785, forty-two are dated 1786, a whopping 245 varieties are dated 1787 and thirty-seven are dated 1788. Obverse dies number approximately 207, while about 183 reverse dies are known. Even so, all Connecticut coppers share the same fundamental design: Obverses display a cuirassed or toga-draped bust figure, wearing a wreath on his head and facing either right or left. The circumscribed legend is always a version of *AUCTORI CONNEC*[TICUT,] meaning "[By] Authority of Connecticut." Broken punches, errant phrasing or intentional punch substitution resulted in variations such as *AUCTOPI*, *AUCTOBI* and *CONNFC,* In form the obverse figures resemble those of British monarchs on official and counterfeit British halfpence. On British coins the image symbolizes authority. The use of armor implies that the monarch has the means to protect his people. The wreath on his head symbolizes honor. Though Connecticut had no monarch, it is reasonable to assume that the symbols were intended to convey similar meanings for the state.

Connecticut reverses present a seated female figure, with a form of the legend *INDE* [PENDENCE] *ET LIB*[ERTY,] or "Independence and Liberty." Misspellings, such as *ET IIB* and *ETLIB INDE*, occur. On all varieties the date appears on the reverse, at the base and in exergue. As are the obverses, the reverses are imitations of British halfpence. On the British versions, Britannia sits atop the globe, staff in hand and shield at her side. She faces to the viewer's left, her right hand reaching out to offer the olive branch of peace. On the Connecticut versions, the figure is Liberty and a liberty cap tops her staff. With one exception, the contemporary counterfeit 1787 Miller variety, 1.4-WW, she also faces to the viewer's left. By depicting Liberty in the same fashion as British halfpence feature Britannia, Connecticut displayed a subtle form of support for a unified national view. The three grape vines that grace the shield on Connecticut's state seal appeared on Liberty's shield in 1785, disappeared in 1786 in favor of a blank shield, and then reappeared in 1787. These vines helped to balance the national view, represented by the seated Liberty, with a symbol of Connecticut statehood.

The collective varieties of Connecticut coppers came from the authorized mint in New Haven and several other, unauthorized mints. Machin's Mills is believed to have been responsible for many varieties, particularly those of 1788. Walter Mould often is credited with making the "laughing head" and "horned bust" varieties of 1787, either in New York or New Jersey. Unidentified mints or forgotten die makers at the known mints produced the varieties known as "African heads" and "muttonheads," as well as some of the "small heads." An unidentified mint (Bungtown?) apparently produced a pair of very rare and primitive counterfeit varieties.

Obverses of Abel Buell's earliest 1785-dated pieces depict a mailed bust, facing to the viewer's right. The first varieties were produced with hand-cut dies. However, Buell quickly transitioned to complex die punches that imparted multiple letters or symbols. He combined the major devices with lesser elements into a single punch, or hub. These hubs bore a positive image. When the design was pressed into a *working die,* the image became negative. When the working die was used to strike a coin, the coin's image again was made positive and in relief. In addition to the convenience of being able to quickly replace worn dies, this process also made die engraving easier since it could be done in the positive, which is more intuitive.

The hubbing process involves successively softening and then hardening steel for the working dies. This is accomplished by heating the steel to a precise temperature, as determined by

---

the same as obverse die "7," for 1787. No qualifying numbers were assigned in die families consisting of a single die. Obverse "2" and reverse "D," which are used on the 1788 variety Miller 2-D, for example, are unique within their respective families and thus require no further qualification.

observing its color, and then cooling it at a prescribed rate. Doing so correctly represents a significant technological achievement for the eighteenth century and is further evidence of Buell's abilities.

1785 coppers: *A – Mailed bust right, Miller 1-E. In contrast to the other 1785 varieties here, dies for Miller 1-E were hand cut. Some believe Miller 1-E to be a contemporary counterfeit. Note the "1/E" painted label, an old collecting practice. B – Obverse of mailed bust left, Miller 7-D.1. The die is near collapse, with prominent bulges on either side of the bust. Compare to the example of Vermont Ryder-11 shown previously. C – Miller 5.1-F.5. D – Miller 6.4-F.5.*

Late in 1785, for unknown reasons, Buell began creating dies whose mailed obverse figures face left (refer to varieties Miller 7-D.1, 7-D.2 and 8-D.) This may have been an attempt to differentiate Connecticut coppers from the ubiquitous counterfeit George III halfpence.[735] Dies for the 1785-dated mailed bust, head-left pieces apparently failed very quickly. Consequently, they are scarce and generally exhibit significant die buckling, as on the Miller 7-D.1 example, above. They share device punches with Vermont varieties Ryder-10, 11 and 15, possibly for the reasons discussed in the Vermont text. The mailed bust left obverse style endured as, except for two rare varieties, all of the *legal* 1786 Connecticut coppers share a version of it. In contrast, only four varieties of the C.C.C.'s 1787 issues share a similar mailed bust left obverse style. However, another mailed bust left style was used on the 1787 varieties known as "triple leaves" (below.) Variations of the mailed bust left style also appear on the coins of other, illegal mints through 1788, even on pieces made after the demise of Jarvis's company. Several of these variations are described below.

This is not to say that all 1786 mailed bust left pieces made by the C.C.C. are identical. For example, Miller 5.3-N is one of four varieties known as "Hercules heads" because of the odd appearance of their obverse busts.* Obverse die 5.3 originally looked very much like others in the same die family. Early on, however, the die began to collapse and had to be re-engraved, resulting in the distorted portrait shown below. The companion die, reverse N, was used until it literally fell apart. Consequently, most or all examples of 5.3-N lack significant reverse detail.

* The other Hercules head varieties are 5.3-G, 5.3-B.2 (both 1786) and 7-I (1787.) The obverse die is the same on all four varieties.

(Top) 1786 mailed bust left copper, Miller 5.7-H.1, a typical 1786 variety. Note the large die break across the obverse figure's neck. (Bottom) 1786 mailed bust left, Miller 5.3-N, Hercules head.

Two very rare 1786 C.C.C. varieties, Miller 6-K and 7-K, probably were made late in the year. They mark a change in the clothing of the obverse bust from a leather cuirass to a draped toga. Though the draped bust, head left style was pervasive in 1787, it appears only on these two varieties from 1786. Moreover, the earliest 1787 draped bust left varieties share the large letter punches used by the C.C.C. in 1786 and appear to be the logical successors to Miller 6-K and 7-K. Thus, Miller 6-K and 7-K likely are the first of many draped busts.

Walter Breen speculated that Miller 6-K and 7-K signify the use of the mint by Baldwin and the Leavenworths in the fall of 1786.[736] On the other hand, Dr. Philip Mossman found that specimens from these two varieties are close in weight to the official, 144-grain standard. Most 1786 pieces made earlier by the C.C.C. are slightly lighter than the standard, while early 1787 C.C.C. draped bust varieties also approximate the official weight. Thus, given their weights, it is likely that the two 1786 draped bust varieties correspond to the upgrade of mint equipment that occurred in November 1786. The upgrade would have allowed more precise rolling of the planchet stock and, hence, more standard weights.[737]

Legion other 1787 draped bust left varieties used small letter punches. That the small letters varieties share letter and other punches (e.g., cinquefoils: ✿, and fleurons: ➔ or ⬅) with the Fugio cents is strong evidence that the change in letter size corresponds to the change in management at the New Haven mint. Both large and small letter varieties exhibit apparent errors in spelling, such as *AUCTOPI*, *AUCTOBI*, *IIB* (for *LIB*) and *CONNFC*. Though some of these errors undoubtedly are the result of broken punches, others may have been the result of die maker carelessness or substitution when the proper punch was unavailable.

Obverses of 1787 draped bust left varieties 46-BB, large letters, and 43.1-Y, small letters. Note the difference in letter sizes between the two varieties and the apparent misspelling, CONNFC, on Miller 43.1-Y. Also note that crosses punctuate the legend on Miller 46-BB, while cinquefoils are used on Miller 43.1-Y.

Buell briefly reverted to cutting mailed bust left dies by hand in 1787, presumably because so much time was being spent finishing the details on hubbed dies.[738] Only four 1787 mailed bust left varieties resemble the C.C.C.'s 1786 mailed busts. Three of them, 8-N, 8-O and 8-a.1, are from a single hand-cut obverse die. The bust on obverse 8 is large, earning it the nickname "tallest head." The fourth 1787 mailed bust left variety, 7-I, reused the Miller 5.3 Hercules head obverse die and is quite rare. Examples of all four varieties approximate the official standard weight. It is plausible, therefore, that the old Hercules die and the hand-cut obverse 8 die were used temporarily in service with the new equipment that was installed late in 1786, while 1787 draped bust hubs were being prepared. [739]

1787 Miller 8-O, the "tallest head" obverse. Note the crude hand engraving in the shoulder area. Varieties 8-N and 8-a.1 are rare.

A second mailed bust left style also appeared on 1787-dated pieces and is represented by fourteen known varieties. This style depicts a markedly different, more delicate and apparently younger obverse figure. These are called "triple leaves" varieties because of the clusters of three leaves that appear in the wreath worn by the obverse bust. Mossman found two groups of triple leaves varieties. Coins from the first group comprise six varieties (2-B, 9-E, 10-E, 11.1-E, 11.2-K and 11.3-K) that closely approximate the approved legal weight for Connecticut coppers. They have large or medium letters and thus are associated with the 1787 large letters varieties, and possibly with Benjamin Buell. The eight varieties that make up the second group (5-P, 9-R, 9-D, 12-Q, 14-H, 15-F, 15-R and 15-S) are far lighter and may have been produced after Jarvis's mint ceased operations. All eight have medium or small letters and the sprig held by liberty appears to consist of wheat ears.[740] Note that obverse 9 is shared by both groups, hinting that the triple leaves varieties may have bridged mint administrations.

***"Triple leaves" varieties:** (Left) 1787 Connecticut mailed bust left, Miller 14-H, medium letters, wheat ear reverse. Note the two-toned appearance of its obverse, triple leaves in the wreath, the use of fleurons in the legends and the pheons (arrowheads: ➤ and ◄) that flank its very small date. This piece is light, suggesting that it may have been made at Machin's Mills. (Right) Miller 15-F. Note Connecticut's trio of grapevines that appear on the reverse shield and the spelling CONNECT.*

The average weight of the lighter triple leaves group approximates that of Machin's Mill issues, suggesting that they may have been made at Machin's Mills or at least on Machin's planchets. On the example above, the alloy appears to be improperly mixed, imparting a two-toned appearance to the obverse. Machin's Mill issues are notorious for such poor planchet quality. In addition, the date on this variety is very small, as on some Machin's Mill issues.

The vast majority of 1787 varieties, about 175 of them, are of the draped bust left, small letters style. They fall into three groups, based on punctuation and planchet weight: 1.) those with crosses in the legends and that approximate 144 grains as a standard, 2.) those with fleurons in the legends and that generally are a few grains lighter than the 144-grain standard, and 3.) those with cinquefoils in the legends and that typically are lighter than the cross or fleuron varieties. One theory holds that, over time, weight was reduced to shore up profitability and the reductions were indicated by changes in punctuation.[741] It is not clear, however, why anyone at the mint would want to call attention to illegal weight reductions.

Changes in punctuation on 1787 draped bust left coppers: *(Left) Miller obverse 25, crosses. (Center) Miller obverse 37, fleurons. Note the AUCTOBI misspelling. (Right) Miller 33.25-Z.24. Note the small letters and cinquefoils. This variety has a diagnostic die break at 11:30 o'clock on its reverse.*

Using Miller's method of classification, more than a hundred of the known varieties are from 1787 obverse die family 33, corroborating Buell's advanced use of hubbing techniques. The piece above, at right, illustrates this form. Such 1787 draped bust left, small letters pieces with cinquefoils in their legends probably are the last issues of the New Haven mint under Jarvis's control. The small letter and cinquefoil punches are shared with the Fugio cents and likely were made in the summer or fall of 1788, though they are dated 1787. Since the legality of Jarvis's operation was questionable, backdating must have helped the coppers to blend with earlier, legal C.C.C. issues.

THE OTHERS

Other mints made unauthorized counterfeits of Connecticut coppers. The example below comes from an unknown mint, if not from an unidentified C.C.C. die maker. It is dated 1785 and probably was made in that year or early in 1786, given Buell's early transition to mailed bust left figures. This variety is designated Miller 4.1-F.4. Its obverse bust exhibits coarse hair and exaggerated lips and has become known as the "African head" style. The reverse figure on this variety is bare-breasted. The one other African head variety, Miller 4.2-F.6, is extremely rare. Official or counterfeit, the inspiration for both varieties probably was Miller 6.5-M.

1785 African head, Miller 4.1-F.4

Another contemporary counterfeit, 1786 variety 2.1-A, has a mailed obverse bust that faces right and is smaller than usual. Its reverse legend erroneously reads ETLIB INDE. For years, the group of six varieties to which this piece belongs was associated with James Atlee, either at his alleged New York mint or at Machin's Mills, through linking of a broken "A" punch that appears on other Atlee-attributed coins. The style of the reverse figures on these coins undeniably mimics that of Atlee-attributed Vermont coppers. Recently, however, the broken "A" theory has lost favor and some have questioned whether Atlee ever was a die maker. These 1786 pieces might be attributed to Machin Mill's anyway, were it not for the fact that the mailed bust right style was long gone by the time Machin began his operation. Instead, members of this group now are considered unattributed as to their origins.

Distinctive profiles from a related group of unattributed 1786 mailed bust right coppers: *(Left) Miller*

2.1-A, "small head." (Center) Miller obverse 3, the "scholar's head," from variety 3-D.1. (Right) Obverse of Miller 1-A, the "double chin" variety, whose odd appearance is due to a damaged die.

The 1787 "muttonheads" are an odd pair of varieties that, likewise, are presently unattributed. Both of them, Miller 1.2-C and the very rare 1.2-mm, have reverse figures that long have been compared to those on John Bailey's Nova Eborac coppers. Further, Gary Trudgen found evidence of punch linking to Bailey-attributed coins.[742] Thus, Bailey seems to be the prime suspect for having made them.

1787 muttonhead, Miller 1.2-C.

Nineteenth century numismatists thought that the muttonheads' obverse bust bears resemblance to old Plymoth's Governor, William Bradford. Consequently, they called the Miller 1.2 obverse the "Bradford head." Other early nicknames include "bull head," "porcine head" and "fat head." If the muttonheads indeed were made in New York, then they provide a humorous and ironic comment on the sanctity of statehood under the Confederation.

The muttonheads' creators evidently believed that making coins appear as if they had been circulated improved their chances of being accepted. To create this illusion, they purposely ground details from the dies and may even have struck them with a hammer to flatten some parts of the design.* As a result, even nearly uncirculated muttonhead examples can exhibit limited detail. The piece above, for example, has experienced little actual wear. Though all such pieces exhibit some lack of detail, some die states are missing legends or facial features almost completely. At some point the dies were re-engraved to strengthen these details. Some such specimens from reworked dies depict Liberty with exaggerated, bare breasts.

* Grinding down of die fields to raise details is called "lapping." Missing details associated with muttonheads are thought to be the result of intentional, excessive lapping of their dies.

Two extremely rare 1786-dated varieties (Miller 2.3-T and 2.4-U) are attributed to Bungtown, or North Swansea, Massachusetts, by default. Both are pathetically crude imitations of mailed bust right pieces. One of them, Miller 2.3-T, even may be an imitation of the African head varieties (An imitation of an imitation?) or perhaps a nineteenth century hoax.

Only two examples of Miller 2.3-T are known.

1787 laughing head, Miller 6.2-M. Note the star on the obverse figure's breastplate, a Mould diagnostic.

A group of four mailed bust left varieties now are believed to be the work of Walter Mould, but the specifics of his involvement beg explaination. This group includes the comical 1787 "laughing heads" (Miller 6.1-M and 6.2-M) and the 1787 Miller 4-L variety, called the "horned bust" variety because of a horn-shaped die break protruding from the chest of the obverse figure. Miller variety 4-L is relatively common, suggesting that a large mint operation was involved in its manufacture. If Mould was the maker, then these coins probably originated at the Morristown, New Jersey mint that he established (below, in this chapter.) The group also includes a crude mailed bust right variety, 1.3-L. All varieties from the group share a horseshoe-shaped "U," for which Mould is known.

(Right) 1787 "hornless" horned bust, Miller 4-L The "hornless" horned bust variety is so named because it was minted before the horned-shaped die break developed.

(Left) 1787 Mailed Bust Left, Miller 13-D. Note the wheatear sheaf in Liberty's hand.

Some 1787 Connecticut coppers *are* attributed to Machin's Mills. The 1787 Miller variety 13-D above, for example, is believed to have been produced either at Machin's Mills or at the New Haven mint, under Benjamin Buell, with the collaboration of Machin's Mills. Note the stylistic similarity of this piece to the Miller 14-H, triple leaves variety, above. This piece exhibits the wheat ears style reverse seen on some triple leaves varieties. Miller 13.D is associated with two other mailed bust left varieties, 3-G.1 and 3-G.2, which have Atlee-associated, Machin

Mills reverses. Wheat ears are found on seven rare 1787 draped bust varieties: 32.4-F, 32.4-X.5, 32.4-Z.3, 32.4-Z.20, 37.6-B, 37.6-k.4 and 50-F. These too are believed to be Machin's Mills products.

(Left) 1787 small head, Miller 1.1-A.

(Right) Obverse of the 1787 Machin's Mills variety Miller 3-G.1.

Machin's Mills-attributed pieces also include three 1787 mailed bust right varieties on which the obverse figures' heads are small. Two of these "small head" varieties, Miller 1.1-A and the ultra-rare Miller 1.4-WW, use the errant reverse legend *ETLIB INDE*. The third, 1.1-VV, has the correct legend. As mentioned before, Miller 1.4-WW is the only Connecticut variety on which the seated reverse figure faces to the viewer's right. The only other Confederation Era copper to share this characteristic is previously described Nova Eborac variety. Extremely rare varieties, Miller 52-G.1 and 52-G.2, are similar to the "small heads" and generally are associated with them and, by implication, with Machin's Mills.

Most or all of the thirty-seven 1788-dated Connecticut varieties are attributed to Machin's Mills. These pieces are variations of styles used previously, including a small head variety (Miller 1-I,) eight mailed bust right varieties (2-D, 3-B.1, 3-B.2, 4.1-B.1, 4.1-K and 4.2-R, 5-B.2 and 6-H,) twelve triple leaves varieties (7-E, 7-F.2, 7-K, 8-K, 9-E, 10-C, 11-G, 12.1-E, 12.1-F.1, 12.2-C, 12.2-E and 13-A.1,) and sixteen draped bust left varieties (14.1-L.2, 14.1-S, 14.2-A.2, 15.1-L.1, 15.2-P, 16.1-D, 16.1-H, 16.2-O, 16.3-N, 16.4-A.2, 16.4-L.2, 16.5-H, 16.6-H, 16.7-P, 17-O and 17-Q.) Miller 6-H has a slightly bloated obverse figure known as the "boxer head." Other 1788 mailed bust right varieties are known as "round heads."

(Left and center) 1788 Mailed bust right, Miller 2-D, struck on a flawed planchet. (Right) 1788 draped bust left, Miller 16.1-D. Weight: 65 grains, less than half the standard. This example is weakly struck because it simply did not contain enough metal to fill the recesses of the dies. The Miller D reverse is paired with the Group III New York imitation halfpence obverse Vlack 13, as variety 13-88CT.

The 1788 wheat ear reverses, Atlee-associated reverses, light planchets and cinquefoils all point to Machin's Mills. Cinquefoils on the draped bust left varieties betray a need to present an image of continuity. In nearly all cases, 1788-dated pieces are much lighter than the 144-

grain standard, further implicating Machin's Mills. Though the official standard weight for all Connecticut coppers was 144 grains, specimens vary from 37 to 241 grains, an incredible range. As seen above, within this range, pieces believed attributable to specific mints exhibit clustering around certain weight ranges.

While many varieties immediately are recognizable, the sheer numbers of them usually drive even seasoned specialists back to "Miller" or, more recently, to Stack's January 2000 sale of the George C. Perkins collection. These two sources remain the best guides for attribution. Connecticut coppers appear both with undertypes and as undertypes for other series, offering the added challenge of attributing the undertypes. Occasional multiple- and off-center strikes add even more interest to the series.

Acquiring an unattributed Connecticut copper is similar to buying a lottery ticket. Varieties run the gamut from relatively common to unique. Accordingly, the value of two almost identical varieties can vary by thousands of dollars in the marketplace. New varieties still are being discovered, making the Connecticut series one of the most interesting and challenging in early American numismatics.

Approaches to their attribution are almost as varied as their attributors. After narrowing by date and major group, many choose to start with the reverse. Miller listed the reverses of each year by the punctuation used. Using his tables it usually is possible to narrow the field of candidates. Then, using his detailed descriptions of each reverse, the exact die can be identified. Since Miller also listed all of the obverses then known to be paired with a given reverse, it is also possible to narrow the field of candidate obverses. His detailed obverse die descriptions then can be used to eliminate all but the correct obverse die. This process may take an hour or more to complete and, though challenging, usually is well worth the effort, even if the piece is determined to be a relatively common variety. Miller also estimated the rarity of each variety. However, many of his estimates since have been revised. Thus, current auction records are the most accurate sources of rarity information. Since few dealers can afford to invest the time to properly attribute Connecticut coppers, the series offers diligent collectors the chance of discovering an unknown variety or, at the very least, the possibility of "cherry picking" a rare variety at the cost of one more common.

$10.00 Connecticut tribute token, issued by McCawley-Grellman Auctions for the 2006 C4 Convention and sale in Boston.

The intrigue of the Jarvis scandal makes the Connecticut story all the more fascinating. More about the incident may be found in the text on Fugio cents, below. Well-connected contractors paying kickbacks to federal officials are as much in the news in 2007 as they were in 1787. It seems the old lessons were never truly learned. Finally, while a full accounting of all Connecticut copper varieties is well beyond the scope of this work, the table below summarizes the apparent chronology of the mint operations that produced them.

Major Groups of Connecticut State Coppers (1785 to 1788)

Date	Style	Characteristic Weight	Probable Time of Minting	Known Varieties	Probable Mint
1785	Mailed bust right (MBR.)	Slightly light	Oct-Nov 1785	25	C.C.C.
	Mailed bust left (MBL,) 7.1-D, 7.2-D and 8-D.	Slightly light	Nov-Dec 1785	3	C.C.C.
	African heads, MBR, 4.1-F.4 and 4.2-F.6.	Slightly light	Early 1786	2	Unknown
1786	MBL	Nearly full weight	Jan-Nov 1786	32	C.C.C.
	Draped bust left, (DBL,) 6-K and 7-K.	Nearly full weight	Nov-Dec 1786	2	C.C.C
	MBR. "Double chin," 1-A. "Scholar heads," 3-D.1 and 3-D.4. Also, smaller heads, 2.1-A, 2.1-D.3 and 2.2-D.2.	Very light	Early 1786	6	Unknown Perhaps James Atlee, and others, in NYC
	Extremely rare, crude imitations with right-facing busts, 2.3-T and 2.4-U.	Unknown	Unknown	2	Unknown. Possibly Bungtown
1787	MBL, triple leaves, large or medium letters, includes 9-E, which has the wheat ear reverse.	Nearly full weight	Jan-May 1787	6	C.C.C.
	DBL, large letters.	Nearly full weight	Jan-May 1787	29	C.C.C.
	MBL, hand cut dies (8-N, 8-O, 8-a.1) and the reused Hercules head obverse (7-I.)	Nearly full weight	Jan-June 1787	4	Jarvis & Co.
	DBL, small letters, crosses in legends. Includes obverse 16.3, which has only colons and obverse 29.2, which has five-pointed stars.	Nearly full weight	Summer-Fall 1787	17	Jarvis & Co.
	DBL, small letters, fleurons in legends.	Somewhat light	After draped bust left, small letters, crosses in legends.	32	Jarvis & Co.
	DBL, small letters, cinquefoils in legends.	Somewhat lighter than the above	After draped bust left, small letters, crosses in legends. Until Sept 1788.	129	Jarvis & Co.
	MBL, triple leaves, medium or small letters, wheat ear reverses.	Very light to somewhat light	After June 1, 1787. Into 1789?	8	Jarvis & Co., Benjamin Buell or Machin's Mills

Date	Style	Characteristic Weight	Probable Time of Minting	Known Varieties	Probable Mint
1787 Cont.	Small heads: MBR (1.1-A, 1.1-VV and 1.4-WW.) Miller 1.4-WW (~2 known) has rev. fig. right. Round heads: MBR (52-G.1 and 52-G.2, both very rare.) Also, two MBL varieties, 3-G.1 and 13-D. 13-D has a wheat ear reverse.	Very light	After April 18, 1787. Into 1789?	7	Machin's Mills
	DBL, small letters, wheat ear reverse.	Very light	After April, 1787. Into 1789?	7	Machin's Mills
	Laughing heads & horned busts, MBL, 6.1-M, 6.2-M and 4-L. One very rare MBR variety, 1.3-L.	Very light to somewhat light	1787-1788	4	Walter Mould and others, in Morristown, NJ
	MBR muttonheads, Miller 1.2-C and the very rare 1.2-mm.	Somewhat light	Unknown	2	John Bailey in NYC
1788	MBL, triple leaves in wreath.	Very light	1788-1789?	12	Machin's Mills, Jarvis & Co or Benjamin Buell
	DBL.	Very light	1788-1789?	16	Machin's Mills, Jarvis & Co or Benjamin Buell
	MBR. Includes small head 1-I, "boxer head," 6-H and wheat ears.	Very light	1788-1789?	9	Machin's Mills

NEW JERSEY STATE COINAGE (1786 TO CA. 1790)

The story of New Jersey state coinage is equally well suited for tabloid journalism. By its omissions, the weak Confederation government afforded the states a great deal of leeway in regulating mints, a task for which they obviously were ill prepared. Accordingly, both authorized and unauthorized mint operations produced New Jersey-style coppers. At least two mints of the latter persuasion emerged, though little or nothing is known of either. The legal New Jersey mint operations themselves teetered between success and failure. However, by one reliable estimate, their combined casts of characters made at least four million coppers between 1786 and 1788, or 1789, or 1790.[743] Of course St. Patrick coppers, imported over a century earlier, actually were New Jersey's first coins. Dr. Edward Maris included them in his defining 1881 work, *A Historic Sketch of the Coins of New Jersey.*[*] By 1786, however, Newby's coins must have been viewed as little more than quaint old curiosities.

[*] "Maris" remains the standard reference for New Jersey coppers, though several varieties subsequently have been added and others have been de-listed. Maris used integers to describe obverse dies and letters to describe reverses. Thus, variety "8-F" describes the pairing of obverse die "8" with reverse die "F." Maris lumped all of the St. Patrick's halfpence and farthings into varieties 1-A and 2-B, respectively. He also included three Confederation pattern mulings that share reverse die C with the New Jersey coppers (later in this chapter.) He designated the 1786 Immunis Columbia, Washington and large eagle mulings as 3-C, 4-C and 5-C,

Recorded die combinations of New Jersey's state coppers number about 140, second only to those of Connecticut among the states' coinages. Eighty-nine obverse dies and sixty-five reverse dies are known, and the numbers slowly are growing. How their many combinations came to exist still is a mystery full of twists and turns. On one side are the fragmented records of the lives of the men involved. On the other side are the coins themselves, with all their peculiar traits. Sometimes the two seem to contradict each other.

The idea of coining New Jersey's coppers appears to have originated with General Matthias Ogden, a hero of the Revolution and member of the state's assembly. In the spring of 1786 he found willing partners in three English immigrants, Albion Cox, Thomas Goadsby and Walter Mould. As seen earlier, Mould and Cox may have been involved in a New York City mint a few months earlier. Mould was in America by the winter of 1783[744] and, given the attributes of a unique New Jersey copper that bears his initials, was a skilled engraver. Thus, it likely is he who made the rare New Jersey pieces that are considered prototypes. These may have been used during the proposal process to demonstrate his engraving prowess. They are tied, through a common reverse, to patterns that Mould may have made for a proposal to the Confederation itself (later, in this chapter.)

The other partners, Cox and Goadsby, were charter shareholders in the Bank of New York.[745] Both had come to New York City and were active in local politics at a time when patriots were taking back properties that had been in Tory hands during the British occupation. An importer of dry goods, Goadsby was involved in a 1785 court case stemming from his outspoken opinions about taxes and the treatment of Tories. Cox testified for the prosecution, against Goadsby. In another case, Alexander Hamilton, as Goadsby's attorney, opposed Aaron Burr. Both attorneys achieved power and fame – Burr as Vice President and Hamilton as Secretary of the Treasury. Burr eventually killed Hamilton in a legendary 1804 pistol duel, but the 1780's legal battles ended peacefully and Cox and Goadsby became friends, or at least business associates.[746] The disputes foreshadowed the litigious environment in which New Jersey coppers were issued. Given the events that transpired, it is remarkable that coins were produced at all, let alone in significant numbers. Nonetheless, the key players, who included a number of Confederation era numismatic notables, somehow muddled through.

Ogden provided Mould, Goadsby and Cox with both investor backing and the clout to gain legislative approval for the project. The Cox-Goadsby-Mould petition was presented to the New Jersey legislature on May 23, 1786.[747] It was well received because the state was beset with lightweight counterfeit coppers and because it carried the weight of Ogden's name and reputation.

Ogden and his new friends were not without competition. William Leddel submitted another proposal just two days later. Leddel claimed to have a ready supply of copper and the necessary "...sundry Iron Factories, in which the Coinage of Coppers would be, by him, easily performed." Though Leddel offered to pay the state the equivalent of one ninth of his production, more than Ogden's offer of one-tenth, his proposal was summarily dismissed.[748] As some New Jersey varieties never have been attributed definitively to a specific mint, it is at least possible that Leddel produced coppers on his own, without legal authority. However, the legislative deck had been stacked against him. In addition to considerable other assets, Ogden held the lucrative mail-carrying rights between New York and Philadelphia, which he exchanged for a favorable vote on the coinage measure by Assemblyman Daniel Marsh. It was at the Elizabethtown sites of Marsh's grist and saw mills, a mile from each other, on the

Rahway River, that Ogden's mint facilities initially were located. Today both sites lie within Rahway. Marsh leased the sites for seven years, far longer than actually was needed.[749]

After Ogden paid a required £10,000 surety bond and bought necessary supplies, Goadsby, Cox and Mould appeared ready to coin. The partners were authorized to mint three million coppers, that is, £10,000, at fifteen per shilling and 150 grains. For this privilege they were required to pay 300,000 coppers, or the equivalent in New Jersey paper currency, to the state via its treasurer, James Mott. They would have two years from June 1, 1786, to complete their work.[750] It ultimately would take a tad longer and it did not happen as Ogden planned.

The Split

An argument flared almost immediately over an unrecorded cause. The disgruntled group petitioned for and received the right to split the partnership in November 1786. After the split Cox and Goadsby could legally produce two million coppers, while Mould was allowed to produce one million, provided he could meet his own surety bond. He did so in January 1787, and elected to move his operation to a spot near Morristown, a village blessed with local copper mines and rich history.[751] Washington's men camped there in the early months of 1777 and the general used it as his headquarters during the terrible winter of 1779 to 1780. Morristown also had witnessed the trial in absentia of Benedict Arnold and the courtship and marriage of Alexander Hamilton to Betsy Schuyler. John Cleve Symmes, Chief Justice of the New Jersey Supreme Court, actually owned the Morristown mint house. Symmes was the father-in-law of William Henry Harrison, who would be elected President in 1840. Ironically, Symmes's name for the mint property was *Solitude*.[752*]

The coins generally attributed to Morristown are of good workmanship. They typically are found on broad planchets that are slightly thinner than other legal New Jersey issues. This planchet type sometimes is referred to as "Morristown stock." Mould also *may* have used the mint's resources to supplement his income by producing coppers for which he owed nothing to New Jersey, namely, the Connecticut laughing head and horned bust coppers.

For their part, Cox and Goadsby began producing coppers at the Rahway mint in late 1786 or early 1787. A 1787 start date is likely since the team was working without Mould's talents. In general, varieties thought to have been made at Rahway appear on planchets that are smaller in diameter and slightly thicker than those from Morristown stock. These planchets occasionally appear brassy and sometimes are referred to as "Rahway stock." Additional characteristics that *appear* to be indicative of either Morristown or Rahway manufacture are discussed below.

Trouble re-surfaced in the fall of 1787 when Cox fell behind on debts to his creditors, who included Goadsby and an English relative, William Cox. Goadsby had loaned Albion Cox £1,200 for which Samuel Atlee co-signed. Both Goadsby and William Cox filed suits and, by the end of the year, Albion Cox was in debtors' prison. Goadsby shipped the Rahway minting equipment and planchet supply to Walter Mould at Morristown to protect them from seizure by Cox's creditors. When Cox was freed in January 1788, he sought to have the supplies returned. By early February, the press was back at Rahway. A series of court battles ended in June with

[*] Symmes also wrote *The Hole at the North Pole*, which gave rise to a theory that the earth is hollow and made up of concentric shells. As the theory goes, there literally exists a hole at the North Pole that leads to the center of the earth. In 2007, a small, vocal group of people still subscribe to this ridiculous notion. Some of them further espouse that "Symmes's Hole" is a saucer port for extra-terrestrials.

the bondholder, Ogden, taking control and bringing the equipment to his Water Street home in Elizabethtown.[753] Albion Cox soon left for England. In 1792 Thomas Pinckney, the U.S. minister to Great Britain, persuaded him to return as assayer of the embryonic U.S. Mint.[754] There Cox spent a short but distinguished career, having overcome the burden of indebtedness.

After Ogden moved the Rahway equipment and supplies to Elizabethtown, he and his friend, Gilbert Rindell, resumed producing coppers and paying off the commitment to the state. Rindell made the last payment on July 3, 1788, thus enabling Ogden to reclaim at least part of his investment. The payment was made under the name "Cox and Goadsby." Mould's part of the obligation was paid the following month. In the meantime, Goadsby moved to Vermont.[755]

As Cox had done, Mould fell behind on debts to creditors. It was a creditor's lawsuit that brought Mould's troubles to Ogden's attention. Before a court order that awarded the goods to Ogden could be served, however, Mould appears to have sold everything at Morristown to Machin's Mills. He fled to Ohio, where he died in 1789 of unknown causes.[756]

It appears that Ogden continued to produce backdated coppers after the operations were supposed to have ended. He undoubtedly paid the state obligation first to recover his bond, and then continued mint operations to milk whatever profits remained. The state may have looked the other way in deference to Ogden. Many of the pieces believed to have been struck by Ogden at Elizabethtown are overstruck on other coins using dies that are ostensibly of Cox-Goadsby making, apparently after the supply of virgin planchets was exhausted.

Seven decades later, Mary Barber Chetwood recalled one of the mints to her son, Francis Chetwood. The daughter of Revolutionary War colonel, Francis Barber, and possibly of Matthias Ogden's sister, Mrs. Chetwood had lived next to the mint as a child of seven or eight. Though not specified in her son's 1858 letter describing the recollection, it has been assumed that she referred to Ogden's Elizabethtown mint. She remembered that her mother had purchased New Jersey coppers a "...bureau drawer nearly full at a time...." (One can only speculate what treasures those drawers held.) She also remembered that men named Rindle [sic] and Cox operating the machinery.[757] This seemingly legitimate recollection is interesting because it has Rindell and Cox working together at Elizabethtown, or perhaps at Rahway.

Mrs. Chetwood further remembered that a horizontal lever nine or ten feet long was set atop the press and that the apparatus was positioned beside a lined pit. One man sat with his legs in the pit. As men turning the lever minted a new copper, the pitman brushed it off the press and into the pit for collection. She also recalled that the planchets were made elsewhere and brought to the site, and that finished coins were taken away in kegs.[758] (To where? Is this a clue to the long-standing mystery of how the coins were distributed publicly?) That planchets were brought to the mint suggests that one of the sites specialized in producing them.

Other individuals and mints contributed to New Jersey's state coinage, though the circumstances of their participation are not fully understood. For instance, it is inferred from his own testimony that John Bailey made some of the coppers, probably the series of varieties known as the "running foxes." These were likely made at Bailey's New York City mint. It also is possible that James Atlee or others at Machin's Mills had a hand in some varieties. It is further possible that the Rahway, Morristown and Elizabethtown mints shared the services of itinerate craftsmen. Likely counterfeiters further complicate the picture. A mysterious Mr. Hatfield, for example, is rumored to have produced unauthorized New Coppers in his barn.

In 1789 and 1790 the whole episode drew to a close. With the 1789 panic, the intrinsic values of most circulating coppers plummeted to a fraction of what they had been. However, state law still required that New Jersey coppers be accepted at full value. This was a boon for Ogden since devalued coppers from other sources, which otherwise were of little worth, gave him a ready supply of cheap planchets. This sudden availability of planchets may explain an apparent late spike in production and could be the reason for the reuse of some dies after their intended retirement. New Jersey clearly was in a bind and the only obvious answer was to demonetize its coppers. The state assembly did just that in June 1790.

The Copper Conundrum

When it comes to the coppers themselves, things are not always as they seem. It long has been recognized that some dies were used intermittently over a long period. Consequently, a coin bearing the date *1786* could have been made in 1788 or even later. That fifty-three varieties are dated *1786* and minting did not begin until late 1786 or early 1787 is an obvious clue that something was out of kilter, as is the fact that only twelve varieties bear the date *1788*, when much of the actual production likely occurred. Seventy-five varieties are dated *1787*. The 1787 Maris J reverse, in particular, seems to have been used and retired several times in succession and possibly by different mints. Reverse J appears on what are believed to be Rahway mint varieties from late 1786 or early 1787 (e.g., 13-J and 14-J) and on other varieties believed to have been minted in Elizabethtown as late as 1790 (e.g., 34-J and 35-J.)[759] The J reverse die appears so frequently that some method of hubbing must have been used. The same can be said of reverse L.

Maris 56-n is equally perplexing. Maris reverse n also occurs on two rare varieties, 57-n and 58-n, but specimens of Maris 56-n are so plentiful that they suggest a mintage far beyond what a pair eighteenth century die reasonably could produce. Again, the implication is that hubbing may have been used. If complex hubbing was used frequently, then the chance of building a complete and accurate New Jersey die chronology is slight. The discounting of punch-links as attribution criteria presents another obstacle to understanding the series since a single template could have been used to produce nearly identical punches. Even so, device forms, ornamentation, letter shapes and punctuation choices join the planchet types as important source clues, if not definitive indicators.

The obverse legends of all New Jersey coppers read *NOVA CÆSAREA,* Latin for "New Jersey." The Bailiwick of Jersey is the name of the tiny English Channel island for which the American colony was named. The island's Latin name, *Caesarea,* recalls its having once belonged to the Roman Caesars. *Nova Caesarea* on coins also may be an oblique reference to "new money." In Rome the ascent of a new Caesar sometimes caused money bearing the image of his predecessor to be considered obsolete in favor of the money of the "new Caesar."

All New Jersey obverses feature a horse's head, above a torse, above a plow. A torse is a wreath that is wrapped in and thus bound by a cord. On New Jersey coppers, the torse lays horizontally and is seen edge-on. When displayed in this fashion, it is customary in heraldry to show the wrapped cord as dividing the wreath into six sections. On New Jersey coppers, these sections resemble beads beneath the horse, which, except for three scarce 1788 varieties, always faces to the viewer's right. The horse symbolizes strength, the plow agricultural wealth and the torse honor. The same icons appear on the New Jersey state seal designed by the Swiss-American artist/coin collector, Pierre Eugiene du Simitiere. Though most renditions of the seal show the horse facing to the viewer's right, the law establishing its design failed to explicitly state a direction for the horse to face. Thus, the vagueness of the seal's official definition may be the simplest explanation for the existence of the three "head left" varieties.

The obverse plows vary remarkably and have their own descriptive terminology, as shown here. Most of these terms were familiar to rural Americans until the middle of the twentieth century.

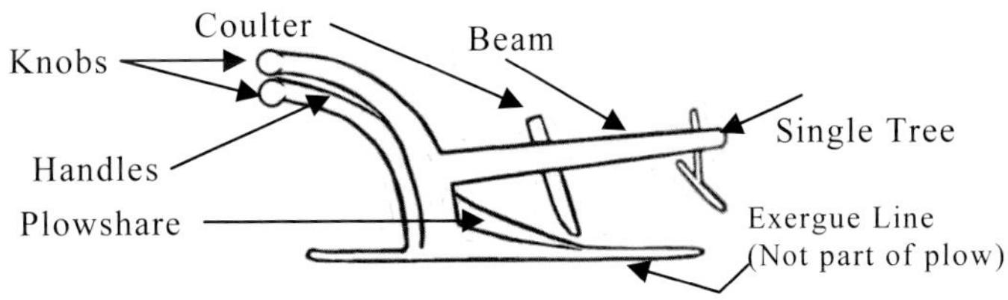

To further complicate the task of attribution, planchets of the type used at Morristown are found struck with dies that may be from the Rahway operation and vice versa. Ogden's apparent use of various undertypes after his takeover of the Rahway operation, where blank planchets had been used before, is a source both of comfort and consternation. Undertypes sometimes can be used to establish an earliest possible minting date for a coin, but they often raise questions about the business practices and relationships that caused specific undertypes to be used. Except for a handful of varieties that are accepted as Morristown products, attributing New Jersey coppers to specific mints without a crystal ball is speculative at best. For this reason, any attributions used here should be regarded only as "best guesses." At the very least, variations in style can be used to break the 140 New Jersey varieties into meaningful study groups, even if few of these groups can be associated definitively with die makers, mints or even the dates that they bear. One such breakdown, based primarily on obverse characteristics, is:

1. Coulterless prototype dies with dates under their plow beams
2. Coulterless dies with dates at the base, in exergue
3. (Believed) Rahway dies
    a. On Rahway planchets
    b. On Morristown planchets
4. (Believed) Morristown dies
    a. On Morristown planchets
    b. On Rahway planchets
5. "Head left" dies (Those on which the horse faces to the viewer's left)
6. (Believed) Elizabethtown issues
    a. On virgin planchets
    b. Overstruck on other coin types
7. "Deer head" or "plaited mane" dies
8. "Camel head" dies
9. "Running fox" dies
10. "Serpent head" dies
11. Crude imitations or counterfeits from one or more unknown mints

Prototypes and Other Coulterless Varieties

Aside from the Confederation patterns, New Jersey's state coinage probably began with three prototypical varieties that probably were made by Walter Mould in mid- to late-1786. Their plows have no coulters. Recall that a *coulter* is a bar or blade attached to a plow's beam to break clods of dirt and push them to either side. The three prototypes, which are designated Maris 7-C, 7-E and 8-F, have their dates beneath the plow beams. On all other New Jersey varieties, the date appears below the entire plow and beneath the exergue line.

1786 date-under-beam prototypes: *(Left) Maris 7-C. Reverse C is shared with the Confederation patterns discussed later in this chapter and with Mould's less rare 6-C variety. Obverse 7 is also used with reverse E. (Right) Obverse of Maris 8-F. Apparently the date-under-beam motif was not accepted. Only six or seven examples of all three prototype varieties, combined, are known to exist.*

Reverses of all New Jersey coppers feature a large central shield with thirteen alternating red and white vertical stripes, crowned by a blue field.[*] At the top of the shield are three crests or points. The positions and relative heights of these points, most notably the central or *chief* point, can be a significant aid to attribution. The reverse legend portends later U.S. issues: *E PLURIBUS UNUM*, or "Out of Many, One." New Jersey state coppers are the first general issue coins to bear this now familiar phrase.[†] As on most Confederation Era coins, the combination of a state obverse with a federal reverse represents a compromise between those who wished for unity and those who would preserve the independence of the states.

Coulterless obverses 8½ and 10½.

A group of fourteen date-in-exergue varieties *without* coulters once were thought to be very early issues, maybe even Mould prototypes. These are Maris varieties 8½-C, 9-G, 10-G, 10-gg, 10-h, 10-oo, 10½-C, 11-G, 11-H, 11-hh, 11½-G, 12-G, 12-I and 22-P. All except 10-G, 11-H, 12-G and 12-I are very rare and seldom encountered. The coulterless varieties now are believed to have been made at various times and perhaps at both Rahway and Morristown. The reason is that the C and I reverses also are used outside the coulterless group (e.g., on varieties

---

[*] Except for reverse c that has fourteen stripes, presumably in error. In heraldry, blue is shown by using horizontal hatching, red by vertical hatching and white by the absence of hatching. A blue field at the top is called a "chief azure" and the red stripes are "pales gules."

[†] Confederation copper patterns that used Maris reverse C (below, in this chapter) probably came first, but never achieved "general issue" status. These patterns comprise Maris obverses 3, 4 and 5. Maris used obverse numbers 1 and 2 to designate the St. Patrick coppers.

6-C and 24-I) and in less worn die states than on the coulterless varieties. Thus, some varieties that lack coulters were made after other varieties with coulters. This author owns a worn example of Maris 12-I that appears to be an overstrike. (From Elizabethtown?)

(Left) Maris obverse 12 (from varieties 12-I and 12-G.) Its horse has a particularly detailed mane and looks downright angry compared to the carousel pony on obverse 7. (Right) Reverse H (from variety 11-H.) Note the narrowness of its shield.

"Standard" Dies

Varieties *with* coulters are far more numerous. In all, with the "head left" dies included and the "plaited manes" (below) excluded, obverse dies suspected to have originated at Rahway or Elizabethtown may account for as many as eighty-one of the 140 total varieties. Their shields typically are well proportioned and feature an outline that ranges from faint to well defined. On most but not all of these reverses, the chief point is considerably higher than the other two points. Twelve different reverses, J, L, T, U, Y, a, c, d, e, i, l and m, share this basic form. They are paired with twenty-eight different obverses, 13 through 16, 18, 26, 28, 29, 29½, 30 through 33, 36 through 39, 41, 42, 42½, 43 through 47, 47½, 52 and 55, to account for forty-two varieties. The L reverse alone is paired with nine different obverses, the J reverse with seven. Notable variations include the shield on reverse c, the only one in the entire series with seven "red" stripes rather than six, and the asymmetrical shield on reverse l.[*] In contrast to the "standard" shields, those on reverses M, N and O, used on varieties 18-M, 19-M, 24-M, 18-N, 19-N and 21-N and 21-O, are *extremely* wide.

(Left to Right) Rahway reverses R, U and N, in order of increasing shield width. Note the extreme width of the shield on reverse N.

The almond-shaped Shields on reverses P, Q and R lie near the other end of the width spectrum. They are reminiscent of, but slightly wider than those on reverses H and I. Narrow-shield reverses I, P, Q, R, and the wide-shield reverse M, all share obverse 24. Likewise, obverse 21 is seen opposite wide-shield reverses N and O, as well as narrow-shield reverses P and R. Reverse P is also paired with coulterless obverse 22, whose style closely resembles obverses 10 and 23½. Reverse R is paired with obverses 21, 21½, 23, 23½ and 24. By now, the "mix-and-match" qualities of the series should be obvious.

Three reverses, f, g and Z, have similar outlined shields, but with *low* chief points. All three are paired with typical 1787 obverses on varieties 37-f, 38-Z, 48-f and 48-g. However,

---

[*] Varieties with the "standard" shield: 13-J, 14-J, 15-J, 15-L, 15-T, 15-U, 16-d, 16-J, 16-L, 18-J, 18-L, 26-d, 28-L, 29-L, 29.5-L, 30-L, 31-L, 32-T, 33-U, 36-J, 37-J, 37-Y, 38-a, 38-c, 38-L, 38-Y, 39-a, 41-c, 42-c, 42.5-c, 43-d, 43-Y, 44-c, 44-d, 45-d, 45-e, 46-e, 47-e, 47.5-e, 52-i, 55-l and 55-m.

reverses f and g also are shared with the only three head left varieties in the series, Maris 49-f, 50-f and 51-g. Reverse dies f and g are from this “standard” group, but the engraver's identity and, prior discussion notwithstanding, the reasons for having the horse's head face left, are unknown. These also are the only three varieties whose plows lack a singletree, the device to which a horse is hitched. They traditionally were assumed to be Goadsby efforts from late 1787 or early 1788, while Cox was in debtors' prison. However, Goadsby’s seizure and shipment of the Rahway equipment and supplies to Morristown roughly coincides with Cox’s imprisonment. Thus, it is unlikely that Goadsby had access to a press during the time that Cox was away.[760] None of the head-left varieties is common, the rarest by far being 51-g. Maris 51-g also boasts the largest obverse horse of the three head left varieties. Varieties 37-f, 48-f, 48-g and 50-f are among those known on both Rahway and Morristown planchet stock. Obverses 37 and 48 also share reverse X, whose shield is similar to others in the group, but is more bullet-shaped and nearly flat across the top.

(Left) The complex plow and low-chief-point shield from head-left varieties. The absence of a singletree on the plow may indicate that it is built for a two-horse team, in which case a doubletree is needed. The complex plow could also be an attempt to showcase new technology. (Center) 1788 Maris 50-f. (Right) 1788 Maris 51-g obverse. In contrast to the plows, the head left horses are relatively simple.

Within this broad die group, obverse variations give rise to colorful names. For example, obverse 16 is called the "protruding tongue" obverse because it has a horizontal die anomaly extending outward from beneath the horse's snout. Obverse 18 has a similar, but vertical die break that gives its varieties the nickname "bridle." A dramatic die anomaly under the horse's jaw on obverse 37 gives its varieties the nickname "goiter."

1786 variety 16-L, the protruding tongue obverse and the horse from 1787 obverse 37, with its "goiter." Obverse 16 is paired with reverses J, L, S and d. Obverse 37 is paired with reverses J, X, Y and f. The 1786 obverse 18, the bridle obverse, is paired with Rahway-shield reverses J and L, and with wide-shield reverses M and N.

Obverse 26 is found opposite reverse d, an ostensibly Rahway combination. Yet, obverses 16 and 25 through 28 are also known opposite reverse S whose shield lacks a clear outline, is slightly asymmetrical and has a nearly even chief point. The possible implication is that varieties using reverse S are Elizabethtown products. Horses on obverses 13 through 16 and 18 through 26 have manes that trail behind as if blown by the wind. Obverses 28 through 33, 36 through 48 and 55, on the other hand, feature horses with “combed” manes. Horses from this die group usually are compact and have thick necks, but on obverses 41 through 46 and others, they have thinner, hooked necks and slightly bulbous snouts.

(L to R) 1786 obverses 15 and 21; 1787 obverses 43 and 55. Note the differences in neck shape, manes and plow beam / handle curvature. Also note the slightly bulbous snout on obverses 43 and 55, as well as obverse 55's prominent knobs .

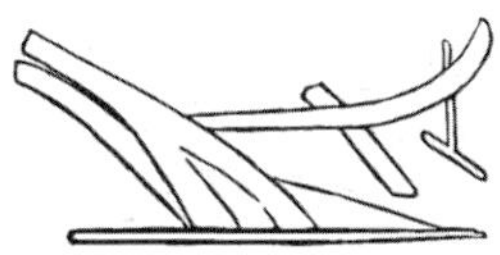

The plow from obverse 44, the "sleigh runner" plow.

Within the group, plows vary significantly. Those on 1786 obverses 13 through 16, 25 and 26 have straight beams, as do those on 1787 obverses 27 through 30, 32, 33, 52 and 55. Otherwise, the beam is curved or slightly curved. Plows on obverses 27 through 30 and 32 exhibit small knobs on their handles. Both the handle curvature and the knobs are exaggerated on obverse 55, while the nearly straight plow handles on obverse 44 resemble those of a sled, hence the nickname "sleigh runner."

1787 Maris variety 34-J, the most common plaited mane or deer head variety.

A group of varieties known as "plaited manes," "braided manes" or "deer heads" sometimes are ascribed to Gilbert Rindell, though no hard evidence exists for this attribution. Obverses 34 and 35 from this group share the ubiquitous reverse J. Rare varieties 34-V and 35-W have small shields with ornaments below them, similar to the Morristown varieties described below. Overstrikes suggest that some of these 1787-dated pieces may have been made as late as 1790, a contributing factor in the Rindell attribution.

The horse from obverse 72, a crudely executed die that resembles the plaited manes.

Varieties 70-x, 71-y, 72-z, 72½-aa, 73-aa and 73½-aa appear to be crudely executed plaited mane types. They possibly are counterfeits, produced by an unnamed source. All are scarce or rare and frequently come overstruck on Connecticut or other coppers. At least one Maris 73-aa example is struck over a 1783 Georgivs Triumpho. Whether these crude pieces are Rindell's is debatable. Their reverse shields are somewhat similar to those Mould made at Morristown. Varieties 69-w and 40-b sometimes are grouped with the plaited manes. The w reverse appears to bear a crude imitation of more typical shields. Only two or three 69-w variety coppers are known.

Their obverse legends feature a star between *NOVA* and *CÆSAREA,* suggesting something other than a legal issue. The w reverse is used with 1787 obverse 68, whose horse resembles that on 1788 Morristown obverse 67 (below.) Obverse 40 has a more legitimate claim to being a plaited mane variety. Its horse is very similar to the one on obverses 34 and 35. The only reverse with which obverse 40 is known to be paired is Maris b, which itself is ambiguous.

(Top) Varieties 17-b and 17-K (1786.) (Bottom) 1787 variety 53-j. Note the shield size on reverse b and the ornaments on reverses b and j.

Reverse b's shield is similar to those believed to be from Rahway or Elizabethtown, but has ornaments beneath it, apparently a Morristown mark. In addition to being paired with obverse 40, it appears opposite obverse 38, as well as a third obverse, 17, that also has elements of the Morristown style. Moreover, Maris variety 17-b is known on Rahway, Morristown and overstruck planchets. Its obverse has a straight plow beam and a hint of knobs on its handles. It also is used opposite reverses J and K. Reverse K's shield has a slightly lowered chief point, as on some believed Morristown varieties. Because it represents an intersection of styles and planchet types, a hunch suggests that Maris 17-b is a variety that ultimately may hold the key to many of the series' mysteries. Similarly, Variety 53-j is ambiguous, with its tall horse and ornamented shield. Though varieties 17-J, 17-K, 17-b and 53-j usually are attributed to Rahway or Elizabethtown, they may be the result of collaboration between Morristown and the other mints. Perhaps this collaboration occurred when workers traveled between jobsites.

MORRISTOWN DIES

Meanwhile, in Morristown...Maris obverses 6 and 59 through 67, including 62½ and 64½, likely are Walter Mould's creations. A piece presently thought to be unique and designated as Maris variety 62½-r all but confirms this attribution. The lone example of 62½-r only recently was discovered in an old collection and once may have been Walter Mould's own "pocket piece." Obverses 60, 61, 62 and 63 have a grouping of three sprigs beneath the torse. In place of the sprigs, obverse 62½ has the initials "WM." Otherwise, Maris 62½-r is similar to the more common Morristown issues. It subsequently was discovered by Roger Siboni that traces of the initials also appear beneath the sprigs on obverse 62, prompting speculation that Mould was asked to remove them and that he did so simply by lapping them away and covering the remaining traces with ornamental sprigs.[761]

As does the 62½ obverse, obverses 6 and 60 through 63 present tall, erect horses with long snouts. Obverses 59 and 65 through 67 exhibit compact horses, more like those on dies from the other mints. The 64 obverse has the same compact horse, but with a swollen snout.

Mould dies: *A – Maris 6-C. B – Maris 6-D. (Both dated 1787.) Note the die break that formed on reverse D. 6-D is more common than 6-C, which is avidly collected because its reverse is shared with New Jersey prototypes and with rare Confederation patterns (below.) C – 1787 variety 64-t. Note the broad horseshoe-shaped U's, indicative of Morristown origin.*

Variety 64-t sometimes is found on Rahway stock, the inverse of Rahway dies found on Morristown stock. The t reverse further is associated with obverse 64½ and mimics the "standard" shield, or vice versa. Variety 59-o also resembles the "standard"issues with its compact horse, lack of sprigs and un-ornamented shield. It sometimes is called the "saw tooth variety" because both sides exhibit triangular dentils not unlike those on Machin's Mills halfpence.

The under-shield ornaments that characterize Morristown reverses p through s are missing from reverses t and u, but reappear on reverse v, whose shield points are roughly even. Reverse u has a wide shield reminiscent of that on reverse C. Other recognizable Morristown characteristics include the wide, horseshoe-shaped U's and a telling base-of-shield die crack on reverse D, the straight plow beam on obverse 64, the only straight-beam Morristown obverse, and small die breaks that appear in the horse's mane on obverse 61. These die breaks often are obscured by weak striking.

Maris variety 63-s best represents Morristown. Like most other Morristown varieties, examples of Maris 63-s typically are struck on broad planchets and highlight Mould's engraving skills. They also show his trademarks, the sprigs that sometimes appear between the torse and the plow on obverses and the ornaments that appear beneath the reverse shields.

Two other 1787 Morristown varieties, Maris 60-p and 61-p, both scarce, exhibit the blundered reverse spelling *PLURIBS,* a mistake likely made in haste or by an apprentice or helper. Both "pluribs" varieties are known for central weakness of detail. A comparison of their obverses illustrates the fact that die differences can be minor. Note, for example, the respective positions of the horses' ears relative to *CÆ*, the shape of the horses' snouts and the relative positions of the plow beams on the examples below. All told, believed Morristown varieties number eighteen: 6-C, 6-D, 59-o, 60-p, 61-p, 62-q, 62-r, 62½-r, 63-q, 63-r, 63-s, 64-t, 64-u, 64½-r, 65-u, 66-u, 66-v, 67-v, from twelve obverse and ten reverse dies.

Morristown dies: A – Obverse 62½. B – Maris 63-s. C – Maris 60-p. D – Maris 61-p. E – The horse from 1788 Morristown obverse 67. Note that its torse has eight divisions, two more than the traditional six. Note: 1 – Mould's initials. 2 – Under-shield ornaments (compare to 53-j, above.) 3 – Sprigs. 4 – The PLURIBS spelling error.

THE OTHERS

Other varietal groups are distinctively different from those discussed above. One such group comprises the "running foxes," named for a tiny animal that appears on their reverses. Breen argued that the animal actually is a horse, a device sometimes used by John Bailey in his non-numismatic work.[762] Close examination, however, shows the figure to be much nearer in appearance to a fox than a horse. These are indeed the likely work of John Bailey, from his assistance of Ogden. Aside from Bailey's own testimony, the most compelling evidence of his involvement is the use of quatrefoils like those on New York's Nova Eborac coppers and on Brasher's New York style doubloons.

1788 running fox variety 75-bb. Note the fox, quatrefoils and under-shield ornaments. Also note the obverse's stylized horse and plow and the developing rim die break, or "cud."

The running fox varieties, in order of rarest to most common, are: 77-cc, 76-cc, 74-bb, 75-bb and 77-dd. Maris also listed 78-dd and numismatists subsequently recognized 77½-dd.

However, neither obverse 77½ nor obverse 78 is anything more than a later die state of obverse 77. All running fox reverses share a broad shield with vine-like under-shield ornaments. On reverse cc, the fox follows *UNUM*. On reverses aa, bb and dd, the fox precedes the legend. Running fox obverses all are dated 1788 and feature stylized horses and plows that differ markedly from those found on Rahway and Morristown issues. Their plows have straight beams. On obverse 76, the coulter and singletree often are weakly struck, giving the illusion of being coulterless. Though it is unclear when Bailey's assistance of Ogden began, his affidavit stated that he made no New Jersey coppers after April 15, 1788, and that the ones he made prior to that date were legal.[763] Assuming that Bailey was truthful in statements about his activities, his support may have come during the time that Ogden was battling in court for the Rahway equipment.

Other hands probably made the three 1787-dated dies known as the "camel heads." Designated Maris 56-n, 57-n and 58-n, camel heads nearly always are found overstruck on other coin types, some of which are very rare. For example, a Maris 56-n is known overstruck on a New York George Clinton copper. That the Clinton coppers may have been made well after Machin's 1787 New York coinage proposal seems to indicate that the camel head varieties were produced near the end of production of New Jersey coppers. Camel heads are so named because of their horses' bulbous noses. Their horses, plows and shields stylistically are just different enough from the Rahway, Morristown, Elizabethtown and running fox varieties to suggest an altogether different artisan. Maris 56-n examples survive in large numbers, while 57-n and 58-n are rare. The camel heads long have been suspected to be products of Machin's Mill's and its supposed die maker, James Atlee. The use of many different undertypes, including Machin's Mills imitation halfpence, seems to fit a scenario wherein devalued coppers were being re-coined into New Jersey coppers that still were accepted. Machin may have done so in the brief window of time that may have existed after the 1789 panic and before his operation was dismantled, around 1790. Alternately, Ogden simply may have borrowed the services of James Atlee or others from Machin.

1787 camel head, Maris 56-n, the most common of the three camel head varieties. Ironically, this piece is not an overstrike.

Ogden also might have purchased planchets from Machin's operation. Camel heads on virgin planchets typically are thin and light, characteristics of Machin's products. The obviously large mintage of the Maris 56-n variety hints at die hubbing and could mean that a different mint was involved. This author once thought that Abel or Benjamin Buell might have been involved in their manufacture. The elder Buell clearly knew something of hubbing technology. This is very unlikely given the apparent late emergence of the camel heads. Only Machin's mint and Ogden's are thought to have then been active and Abel Buell had left the country.

Yet another mysterious variety, Maris 54-k, is known as the "serpent head" because of its horse's oddly curved neck. Maris 54-k long has been regarded as a contemporary counterfeit and dubiously attributed to a mint run by a man named Hatfield, though no real evidence of Hatfield's mint has ever been discovered. The idea seems to have arisen from a statement made to Charles Bushnell by a Mr. J. R. Halsted that appears in Crosby's 1875 *Early Coins of America*. Halsted supposedly had an acquaintance who knew Hatfield. Hatfield told the acquaintance that he, with the help of a Negro, made coins in a barn near Elizabethtown.[764] This bit of hearsay apparently is all that links Hatfield to the serpent heads. Could Maris 54-k's instead have been made at Machin's Mills? By William Leddel? A speculative theory suggests that Hatfield actually produced the running fox varieties. This theory is based on the notion that a man named Hatfield ran a horseracing track in the area and used a horse as his symbol.[765] In a personal conversation, Ray Williams proposed that Hatfield simply was employed at Rahway and that the Rahway mint was forgotten for a time. If Hatfield (or Leddel) independently produced any New Jersey coppers, they likely are included in the handful of crude, lightweight counterfeits that complete the list of New Jersey varieties.

(Top) 1787 serpent head, Maris 54-k. (Bottom) 1787 variety 46-e, a common variety that very often is confused with 54-k. Note the clashed, failing die state of obverse 46. Clashing occurs when the two dies are brought together without a planchet between them, resulting in the transfer of part of the design from one die to the other.

That final group of varieties consists of rare and primitive emissions that border on the bizarre. They often are assigned to Bungtown, the catchall attribution for all such ruffians, and include varieties 79-ee, 80-ff, 81-ll, 83-ii and 84-kk. It is reasonable to conclude that all of these are imitations. Whether all of them actually date to the eighteenth century is, however, an unsettled issue.

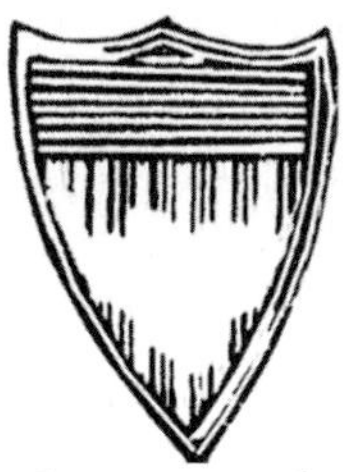

(Left) The crude shield from reverse ii. (Right) obverses from varieties 79-ee (1788) and 80-ff (1786,) respectively (each unique or nearly so.) Note the pitiful lettering on both obverses and catastrophic die break on 80-ff. Maris also listed a unique example that he called 82-hh. It was subsequently discovered to be a worn specimen of the rare Rahway variety, 36-J. Maris variety 79-ee has the "look" of a 19th century fantasy piece.

Not surprisingly, this rich and nuanced series has many devotees. More than two centuries after New Jersey's state coppers so chaotically came into being, "Jersey" specialists are perhaps the most numerous and avid group among those who pursue early American coins. Given that rare and better-preserved New Jersey coppers literally now are worth many times their weights in gold, only the most persistent collectors have topped the "100 variety" mark. Even so, "common" varieties, such as 6-D, 34-J, 46-e, 48-g, 56-n, 63-s, 67-v, etc., offer anyone so inclined the opportunity to appreciate these vestiges of New Jersey's early statehood.

MASSACHUSETTS' STATE COINAGE (1787 TO 1788)

By late 1786 more than a century had passed since the striking of John Hull's last pine tree shilling. During that time Massachusetts' General Court received and denied several petitions by private parties to supply coins. For example, a proposal from William Chalkhill was received in March 1702 or 1703, depending on one's choice of calendar. Chalkhill had been a moneyer at the Tower of London and offered to bring over to Massachusetts £10,000 in coppers. A legislative committee reviewed the offer, concluding that £5,000 would be sufficient and that the money should be in pennies. However, the measure was tabled and apparently never acted upon.[766]

Then, with the eighteenth century half gone, Massachusetts received that huge shipment of coins from Britain aboard *H.M.S. Mermaid* for having sent troops to Cape Breton during King George's War. The debt came to £183,649.2.7½. Payment arrived on September 18, 1749, in the forms of Spanish silver and British copper. There were 206 chests, each with 3,000 ounces of milled eight reale coins, and another containing 2,000 ounces. In addition there were eight 3,000-ounce chests of pillar dollars and another 6,000 ounces of mixed silver. The total came to 650,000 ounces, enough to cause a great deal of concern while Massachusetts' treasurer looked for a suitably secure place to store it all. More concerns arose when it was found that some of the chests held debased new plate coinage. The shipment also included £1,699.10.8 in halfpence and £441.14.0 in farthings, more than 1.2 million coppers, weighing ten tons and filling a hundred casks.[767] All told, it was more treasure than anyone in America ever had seen. Massachusetts wisely used the silver to redeem its outstanding bills of credit. (See Chapter 4.)

Parliament paid £173,129.5.11¾, just under 5s 4d per ounce, for the silver on the open market, through the Bank of England. This figure plus the £2,111.4.8 in copper and £8,408.11.11¾ in fees, commissions, shipping and handling charges, etc., made up the full sum owed to the colony.[768] There, at the stipulated rate of exchange, the total value of thc 650,000 ounces was about £216,667. By weight, an ounce was equivalent to about 1.05 Spanish dollars. Thus, the 644,000 ounces of silver eight reales contained an estimated 675,000 coins, enough to redeem more than £1.5 million in old tenor bills. The shipment allowed Massachusetts to stay on the firm ground of the silver standard until wartime inflation forced its abandonment in 1775. The new coppers also helped for a time, but the small change shortages that plagued the colony and its neighbors for decades simply would not go away.

Massachusetts' next flirtation with coinage was the 1776 patterns that apparently never were produced in numbers. Then, a decade later, with coins in particularly short supply, Seth Reed and James Swan each submitted proposals. Both efforts came in the spring of 1786. Reed's proposal was tabled until the next session of the General Court to give him an opportunity to produce more credible samples of the ores that he claimed to possess. His proposal appears to have gone no further. Swan's proposal fared even worse. It was ignored.[769] There may have been others. A day before Reed's proposal was deferred, a three-man committee was appointed to perform a comprehensive study on the best ways for the Commonwealth to arrive at coinage. One version of the resolution that established the committee includes the words "...application hath been made to this Court by *divers[e] Persons* praying for a Right of coining Copper in this Commonwealth...."[770]

The committee reported on June 7, 1786, offering opinions that silver coins should be the same alloy and value in all states and that for Massachusetts to mint its own would be counter-productive. With regard to copper coinage, the committee referred to Reed's proposals and estimates. In one offer, he had agreed to pay £1,100 lawful money for the right to coin £20,000 in copper. He also offered to double his remittance if the sheeting of copper was practicable in the state.* The committee estimated that the state could purchase the facilities, equipment and materials and pay workmen's wages to produce £20,000 at a cost of £10,200, leaving £9,800 as profit. They recommended that the denominations be penny, halfpenny and farthing and, to protect the interests of the public, that the *state itself* should build a mint.

Despite further offers from James Swan and an admonition from Governor James Bowdoin to delay action until Congress provided a national coinage, the General Court appointed a second committee to study the matter. The new committee favored the expedited creation of a federal mint over the creation of one by the state. Nevertheless, after much discussion and pronouncements by numerous other individuals and committees, a coinage bill passed on October 17, 1786. It called for a commonwealth mint to be erected for the production of gold, silver and copper coins. The mint was authorized to produce $70,000 in copper cents and half cents, the designs of which were to be at the governor's discretion. While there were subsequent discussions about buying silver and the capability of the mint to produce coins of various sizes, it appears that only coppers actually ever were struck.[771]

It sometimes is asserted that doubts resulting from ineffective private coinage efforts in Vermont, Connecticut and New Jersey influenced Massachusetts' decision to build a state mint. However, Massachusetts came to its decision before efforts at the official mints of the other states ran into trouble. Massachusetts’ decision to move forward seems instead to have been based on simple cost/benefit analyses. Perhaps the other states and the federal government would have done well to follow Massachusetts' diligence, if not her execution.

At any rate, the new state mint was located at 910 Washington Street in Boston,[772] not far from John Hull's seventeenth century facilities. The General Court appointed Captain Joshua Wetherle, a local goldsmith, as mintmaster. Wetherle's appointment came early in May 1787 and a short time later he was assessing available copper and equipment. He also hired as die maker Joseph Callender, an engraver who had studied under Paul Revere.[773]

By the end of May the new governor, John Hancock, had taken office. Designs were finalized in June, with the same motif chosen for both cents and half cents. Obverses of both denominations feature a standing Indian with a bow in his right hand and an arrow in his left. Similar figures were used elsewhere to represent freedom as the Commonwealth's symbol. The divided, circumscribed obverse legend reads *COMMON ★ WEALTH* [OF].

The reverse design is a spread eagle with the olive branch of peace in its right talon and a cluster of war arrows in its left. Covering the eagle's breast is a shield, like that used on the New Jersey state coppers. The denomination, *CENT* or *HALF CENT,* appears incuse on the shield. The date, *1787* or *1788*, appears in exergue beneath the eagle. Above the eagle is the remainder of the legend, *MASSACHUSETTS.*

Since the new coins conformed to the federal system of one hundred cents to the dollar and bore explicit denominations, they represent the world’s first true cents and half cents. However, the coppers were decimal in name only. They actually circulated at 108 and 216 to

* It was not until Paul Revere established a rolling mill at Canton in 1801 that sheet copper actually was produced in bulk in Massachusetts or any other former colony.

the dollar, respectively, as if they were halfpence and farthings.[774] Given that so much about the series was explicitly defined, it is ironic that official weight standards were not specified. Cents appear to cluster around 155 grains in a relatively narrow range. The variance is small for the period and the average is close enough to the cent standard of 157½ grains to assume that parity with the federal benchmark was intended. Even so, a case can be made for the British halfpenny standard of 152.17 grains. Massachusetts half cents, particularly those dated 1788, cluster around 76 grains, the ideal weight for farthings.[775]

1788 half cent, Ryder[*] 1-B, dies by Jacob Perkins, Callender's successor. As on coppers of Connecticut and New Jersey, a national symbol (the eagle) balances symbols of statehood (the Indian and legend.)

Always stingy and oscillating between responsible oversight and micro-management, the General Court complained that Callender's dies wore too quickly and that he charged too much for them. His fee was £1.4.0, more than four dollars, per die.[776] In the summer of 1788, the legislators demanded that Jacob Perkins, of Newburyport, replace Callender. Perkins, then a man in his early twenties, had agreed to work for one percent of the value of the coins made from his dies. His tenure began on August 30, 1788.[777]

The products of the two die makers easily are differentiated. Cents made with Perkins' dies have *closed* S's that resemble 8's and all are dated 1788. Cents made with Callender's dies have *open* S's and are dated either 1787 or 1788. Callender made dies for all of the 1787 half cents, while Perkins made dies for all of the 1788 half cents.

On November 5, 1788, Governor John Hancock reported that £939 in coppers had been coined at a staggering cost of £2,136.5.7, far from the ratio the coinage committee had predicted. Part of the cost overrun was due to the impurity of the scrap copper that was used. The copper came from stocks of old mortars, brass cannon, sprues[†] and the like that had been held by Hugh Orr on behalf of the state. These rough sources required extensive refining that escalated operational costs. Even with the extra effort some coins still exhibit evidence of impurities. Realizing that the mint was costing far more than expected, the General Court directed Wetherle to coin any remaining copper and then shut down the operation. On December 29, 1788, Wetherle reported that about 900 pounds of copper remained.[778] On January 22 his accounting showed that the remaining stock had been used to produce an additional £109.2.7 in coins.[779] Added to previous production, this brought the total to £1,048.2.7 or about $3,494. Perkins was paid the measly sum of £3.18.10[780] for work that apparently produced sixteen dies. This equates to about 59 pence, a little more than a dollar per die.

---

[*] The chief references for this series are Crosby's 1875 *Early Coins of America,* Hillyer Ryder's 1919 article "The Copper Coins of Massachusetts" (*American Journal of Numismatics*, vol. LIII, pp. 69-76) and Ryder's 1920 ANS publication *The State Coinages of Massachusetts.* Crosby's work is particularly useful for understanding the legislative measures that governed the coins. Ryder used Crosby's system of qualified integers to indicate obverse dies and letters for reverse dies. Ryder obverse 2 received qualifiers to indicate that a re-cutting occurred. For example, Ryder variety 2a-F has the original obverse 2, while variety 2b-A has the re-cut obverse 2. Some authors ignore this distinction, referring only to variety 2-F.

[†] A "sprue" (in older texts, "sprewe") is the scrap left in the channel where molten metal is poured into a mold during casting.

Assuming that this represents one percent of production, per the terms of his contract, Perkins' dies were used to make £394.3.4 or $1,313.89 in coins. None of the recorded deliberations says how much of this total was accounted for by half cents. However, it is possible to make educated guesses about the relative proportions of the two denominations. Suppose that surviving examples exist in proportions roughly equivalent to the original mintages, a notion that is at least intuitive, even if potentially inaccurate. Numismatists use a scale of one to nine to estimate the rarity of early American coins within ranges and sub-ranges. In his booklet, *Variety Checklist and Rarity Ratings for American Colonial Issues and States Coinages*, the late Thomas Madigan listed rarity ratings for Massachusetts coppers by leading experts in the field.[781] By combining the midpoints of the ranges assigned for varieties made by Perkins, the ratio of surviving cents to half cents can be estimated at 2.5:1. If this proportion also holds for the original mintage, then an estimated 43,796 1788 half cents and 109,491 1788 cents are needed to arrive at Perkins' total of $1,313.89.

(Top) 1787 cent, Crosby 3-G, Callender's dies. Note the open S's and compare to the next example. Also, note the small period before COMMON.
*(Middle) 1788 cent, Cros*by 1-C, Perkins' dies. Note the close*d S's.*
(Bottom) 1788 cent, Crosby 10-L, Perkins' dies. Note the "wood grain" effect and other planchet flaws, indicative of impure alloys

However, this calculation has a problem since the 1788 half cents all came from a single obverse die. Smaller diameter dies are capable of producing more impressions than their larger counterparts and it is, therefore, possible, but unlikely, that an eighteenth century die produced 43,796 half cents. Most numismatists place a cap of 30,000 to 35,000 on halfpenny-sized dies. Thus 35,000 might be a reasonable cap for 1788 half cent production. If this were the case, then the estimate of Perkins' 1788 cent output adjusts to 113,889 to complete the $1,313.89. Applying similar logic to the approximately $2,180 in remaining coppers yields estimates of 92,994 1787 cents, 93,644 1788 cents and 62,724 1787 half cents from Callender's dies.

Beyond the Callender/Perkins distinction, differences between most varieties are subtle. Their attributions hinge on such factors as the position of the bow tip relative to the Indian's right foot, the number and relative lengths of pleats in his tunic, the orientation of the obverse star relative to horizontal, the number and positions of the reverse olive branch leaves, the splaying of the arrows, their positions relative to wingtips, etc.. Attribution generally requires consulting with old friends Crosby and Ryder, neither of whom provided truly usable guides.

Nevertheless, a few varieties immediately are recognizable. For example, Ryder reverse F, used only on the rare 1787 cent variety 2a-F, has arrows in the eagle's *right* talon and the olive branch in its *left*. Variety 2a-F is believed to be a prototype, since the few surviving examples tend to be heavier than the assumed standard. Another easily recognizable feature appears on 1787 cent reverse A, used with the 1787 re-cut obverse, Ryder 2b. This relatively common variety exhibits a die irregularity extending upward from the eagle's head and, consequently, is known as the "horned eagle." Yet another distinguishing characteristic is the small period that appears before *COMMON* on cent obverse 3, from 1787 Ryder variety 3-G. Cent obverse 4 from 1787 is the same as 1788 obverse 17. It is recognizable by a missing line between the Indian's shoulder and neck that gives the impression that his head is floating above his body on cent varieties 4-C, 4-D, 4-J and 17-I.

A handful of cent varieties are believed to be contemporary counterfeits,[*] possibly of Bungtown origin.[†] All of these are very rare. One of them, Ryder 1-B, depicts a stooped Indian with a jutting jaw. The eagle on reverse B holds a branch with four leaves. This suggests that Ryder 1-B was made to imitate the horned eagle reverse, the only legitimate issue with four, rather than five leaves, on the eagle's branch. The imitations occasionally are found as undertypes on the late Connecticut issue from Machin's Mills, Miller 16.3-D. Others in this group of contemporary counterfeits, 1787 varieties 7-H and 5-I and 1788 variety 14-J, are characterized by very plump Indians and small eagles.

Half cents exhibit some distinguishing characteristics as well. The 1787 half cent reverse D (from varieties 1-D, 4-D and 6-D,) for example, is characterized by very thin letters. 1787 half cent reverse A has a space of about a half a digit's width between *17* and *87*. In addition, the 8's on Perkins' 1788 half cent reverse A are uneven when compared to those on the more common reverse B (i.e., *178*^{8} on reverse A, *1788* on reverse B.)

Overall, the Massachusetts' state mint and the supposed counterfeiters produced fourteen 1787 cent varieties, twenty-four 1788 cent varieties, nine 1787 half cent varieties and two 1788 half cent varieties. Even with the relatively small number of varieties, completing the series is challenging because of the rarity of the four contemporary counterfeits and the subtleties between legal varieties, particularly those of 1788 cents.

The decision to close the state mint was followed by another flurry of private coinage proposals, the most notable being two from John May of Boston. Jonathan Peirce of Salem also submitted a proposal, as did another man whose identity is lost. May's proposals entered the negotiation phase, but the General Court wisely decided to wait for federal direction once they realized that the U.S. Constitution prohibited coinage by the states. The authority of the new federal government took effect on March 8, 1789.[782]

By then, or shortly thereafter, Callender was engaged in private business at Half-Square, State Street in Boston.[783] As described in Chapter 4, Perkins went on to revolutionize the process for printing paper currency and, in doing so, changed the course of America's economic history. He also produced medals that commemorated the 1799 death of Washington and may have

[*] Massachusetts coin dealer, Henry Evans, made potentially deceptive copies in the 1930's. Fortunately, Evans placed a small E by the obverse star to set them apart from genuine pieces.

[†] Also see the discussion of the W. Woart Jus Pacis token in Chapter 11. Only two or three Woart pieces are known. They are uniface and in white metal. Their obverse design mimics the Massachusetts coppers and their letter punches match those on the private Constellatio Novas. Moreover, a William Woart appears to have lived in Boston in the 1790s. Even so, no proven connections to Confederation coppers or to the period exist.

played a collaborative role in producing rare 1792 patterns that bear the first president's likeness (Chapter 11.)

Massachusetts Copper Varieties

Cents Die Maker	Date	Est. Mintage	Obverses - Reverses - Varieties	Obverses (Ryder)	Reverses (Ryder)	Varieties (Bold letters indicate rare varieties.)
Callender	1787	~92,994	5-7-11	2a/2b, 3, $4_{87}/17_{88}$, 6, 8	A, C, D, E, F, G, J	**2a-F**, 2b-A, 2b-C, 2b-E, **2b-G**, 3-G, 4-C, 4-D, **4-J**, 6-G, **8-G**
	1788	~93,644	10-7-14	5, 6, 7, 9, 10, 12, 13, 15, 16, $17_{88}/4_{87}$	H, I, K, L, M, N, O	6-N, 7-M, **9-M**, 10-L, **12-H**, 12-I, **12-K**, 12-M, **12-O**, **13-I**, 13-N, 15-M, 16-M, **17-I**
Perkins	1788	~113,889	6-7-9	1, 2, 3, 4, 8, 11	A, B, C, D, E, F, G	1-D, 2-B, 3-A, 3-E, 4-G, 8-C, 11-C, 11-E, 11-F
Other (Ctft.)	1787	Small	3-3-3	$5_{87}/14_{88}$, 1, 7	B, H, I	**1-B**, **5-I**, **7-H**
	1788	Small	1-1-1	$14_{88}/5_{87}$	J	**14-J**
Callender		~186,638	15-14-25	12,443	13,331	The two columns at the immediate left contain the estimated <u>average</u> number of coins from obv. and rev. dies, respectively.
Perkins		~113,889	6-7-9	18,982	16,270	
1787		~92,944	8-10-14	11,618	9,294	
1788		~207,533	17-15-24	12,208	13,836	
Totals:		~300,477	23-25-38[*]	13,064	12,019	

Half Cents Die Maker	Date	Est. Mintage	Obverses - Reverses - Varieties	Obv. (Ryder)	Reverses (Ryder)	Varieties (Bold letters indicate rare varieties.)
Callender	**1787**	~62,724	6-4-9	1, 2, 3, 4, 5, 6 Avg. 10,454	A, B, C, D Avg. 15,681	1-D, 2-A, 3-A, 4-B, 4-C, **4-D**, 5-A, **6-A**, **6-D**
Perkins	**1788**	~35,000	1-2-2	1 Avg. 35,000	A, B Avg. 17,500	**1-A**, 1-B
Totals		~97,724	7-6-11	Avg. 13,961	Avg. 16,287	Again, averages reflect coins per obv. or rev. die.

[*] On cents, 1787 obverse 5 and 1788 obverse 14 are from the same die. Likewise, 1787 obverse 4 and 1788 obverse 17 are from the same die. These are "biennial" dies (i.e., used on coins of two different years.) Thus, the obverse die count is 23 rather than 25.

As for its 1787 and 1788 coppers, Massachusetts produced coins of far higher quality than those of its neighbors. Quality helped the coins gain acceptance. Unfortunately, however, the endeavor was too costly to sustain and, in the end, Massachusetts' coppers cannot be said to have been any more successful than those of Vermont, Connecticut or New Jersey. Nor did the Massachusetts cents and half cents achieve the historical and numismatic notoriety of their seventeenth century silver predecessors.

CONFEDERATION COINS, PATTERNS AND MULES (1785 TO 1787)

The individual states were not the only public bodies that considered issuing coinage contracts to private firms. In the late 1780's America's numismatic future literally was up for grabs. The alluring prospect of a huge federal contract brought out the best and the worst in entrepreneurial spirit. During this time at least eight individuals submitted competing proposals in the hope of becoming the official coiner for the Confederation:

- Peter Allaire
- Joseph Hopkins
- James Jarvis
- General Matthias Ogden
- Soloman Simson
- Daniel Van Voorhis
- Captain Frederick H. Walden
- An anonymous proposer

James Jarvis eventually won the battle, if not the war, on the strength of his conniving and bribery. By the time that affair ended, Jarvis' company had minted only a fraction of the Fugio cents that Congress intended. Of the seven losing proposals it appears that only Ogden's resulted in a significant number of coins. Even that assumption represents a leap of faith since the coins in question, the Immunis Columbia coppers, and their supposed die maker, James Atlee, never have been tied definitely to Ogden's proposal. The Simson, Walden, Allaire, Van Voorhis and anonymous proposals are documented in the Journals of the Continental Congress and associated records, but seem not to have resulted in tangible patterns.

Several other pieces with Confederation themes exist, presumably having been made for consideration by Congress. Some of their dies are brought together in logical combinations. Other pairings clearly are less deliberate mules, apparently the coincidental result of dies and equipment being passed between coiners. While the circumstances surrounding these mulings never have been explained, the dies used to make them often and generally are attributed to various combinations of six people:

- **George Wyon III (1,)** with or without the help of his twin sons, **Thomas (2)** and **Peter George (3.)**

- Thomas Wyon, with or without the help of his brother, Peter George Wyon.

- **Walter Mould (4,)** with or without the help of **John Bailey (5)**.

- John Bailey, with or without the help of Walter Mould.

- **James F. Atlee (6.)**

It is possible that other, still unidentified, individuals on either side of the Atlantic might have been involved. Excluding Jarvis' Fugio cents and including pieces with multiple "degrees of separation," the known Confederation pattern dies touch thirty-four different varieties in several different series. If varieties that are assigned to other series are removed from consideration, the number of apparent Confederation patterns drops to eighteen. Of these eighteen, all but small planchet Immunis Columbia coppers are prohibitively rare. Thus, it is not surprising that many copies exist. In the nineteenth century, for example, John Bolen struck very realistic copies of several of the patterns that now themselves are highly prized.*

The eighteen "pure" varieties appear to separate into three groups based on probable die sources. Each of the groups seems to revolve around a central theme or set of dies. For the first group, the main dies carry the message that the American Confederation was hostile to tyrants. These patterns are accompanied by a group of dies whose designs present various national themes. The second group features a imperfect allusion to a paradise, free from tyranny and under the watchful eye of God. Members of the third group carry a more proper expression of the same theme, together with an eagle and national motto that survive even in the twenty-first century.

In one sense, all eighteen coins are evolutionary dead ends. Still, their symbols: a circle of thirteen stars, heraldic eagles, *E Pluribus Unum*, a crested shield and others, endure in American mythology. Aside from their classical metaphors, this assemblage offers two of the earliest portraits of George Washington to appear on coins. Overall, the designs range from the run-of-the-mill to the sublime.

Group I: The Confederatio Decads and Related Pieces (1785 to 1787)

First, the sublime, the famed Confederatio decads (more properly, "Inimica Tyrannis America[na] Confederatio" decads.) Recall that May 13, 1785, found Thomas Jefferson in Paris recording his thoughts on the kinds of coins befitting America. His recommendations included a decad, a copper coin equivalent to one hundredth of a Spanish dollar.[784] At about the same time, Gouverneur Morris proposed a crown-sized coin that used the symbol of an Indian, trampling on a monarch's crown, with the legend *MANUS INIMICA TYRANNIS* ("This Hand is Hostile to Tyrants.")[785]

Another design, then under consideration by Congress, was a large gloried circle containing thirteen stars in a cross pattern and surrounded by the word *CONFEDERATIO* ("Union.") That design, which Jefferson may have conceived, appears as a sketch in the Papers of the Continental Congress, in 1785.[786] It also appears as the reverse for about eight surviving specimens known as the "Confederatio, large stars decads." A second version with a smaller circle of stars that appears on at least two surviving decads, but not in official records, is called the "Confederatio, small stars reverse."

How these decads came to exist is a subject of at least two different theories. Crosby perpetuated an unsubstantiated claim that has them coming from Birmingham, England, and

* Bolen's copies also are rare. Fortunately, on one group of them, he left a mark, a small "dot," within the "Y" of *TYRANNIS* to foil those who would deceive. In addition to realistic copper strikings, Bolen made some pieces in brass and silver, metals that generally were not used for the originals. He made at least one example that muled two reverses known as the Confederatio "large" and "small" stars designs (See below.) Crosby described such a muling as genuine, but this piece is unknown today, suggesting that even the master might have been fooled.

Thomas Wyon. Breen added to the tale by implicating Walter Mould as a student of the Wyons.[787] If this were true, it would make sense that the Wyons made these pieces and passed them to Mould, who conveyed them to Congress. It also seems logical that Jefferson took the design concepts to the Wyons in the first place, since he was already in Europe. However, on August 18, 1785, Walter Mould submitted a request to Congress that he be allowed to "conduct a mint." By then he had been in America for nearly two years, since the winter of 1783, and thus would not likely have been the intermediary between the Wyons and Congress. So, how did the Wyons or anyone else in Europe become aware of the designs, produce patterns and transport them to America in the three months between May and August 1785? The answer may be that Jefferson already had knowledge of the designs before he left for Europe and that only later did they show up in the records of Congress.

The two types of Confederatio decads take forms very near but not identical to the ones that Jefferson and Congress contemplated. The engraver chose, or was directed, to use a female figure who may be either an Indian princess, the Roman hunting goddess, Diana, or Artemis, her Greek counterpart. The figure stands, bow in one hand, readied arrow in the other, beside a pedestal on which sets a liberty cap. Her right foot rests on a tyrant's crown and her defiant gaze is to the right, to the east, to Europe and its bloated, inbred sovereigns.

(Left) 1785 Confederatio America Inimica Tyrannis pattern, large stars.

(Right) 1785 Confederatio Americana Inimica Tyrannis Pattern, small stars.

The large stars reverse most closely resembles Congress's recorded sketch. Since no renderings of the small stars motif appear in the congressional records, the reason for its existence is unknown. Perhaps the die maker, someone in Congress or Jefferson simply wanted to model variations of the design. On the decads, the obverse legend that most closely fits the classical form of "America," *AMERICANA,* is known only with the small stars reverse. The obverse legend on the Confederatio large stars decads reads *INIMICA TYRANNIS AMERICA*. In either case, the meaning is "The American Union is Hostile to Tyrants."

Breen's interpretations notwithstanding, it appears likely that the coins were in America from the beginning and that Walter Mould was their maker. Aside from doubts about Mould being in Europe at the right time, the patterns' obverse legends can be traced back at least to July 1778, when *MANUS HAEC INIMICA TYRANNIS* ("This hand is raised against tyrants") was used on regimental flags in Philadelphia. The same words appear on the flag that Colonel Alexander Hamilton raised to start the hostilities at Yorktown in 1781. Furthermore, the same phrase appears, with the symbol of an armed Indian treading on a crown, in Robert Morris's 1782 papers.[788] These circumstances all point to the possibility, if not the likelihood, of

American manufacture. In asserting George Wyon's involvement, Breen noted punch links with the Constellatio Novas and Immune Columbias. (See below.) If he actually was the Wyons' student, Mould might have acquired punches identical to those of his mentors. Even if he was not, he might have acquire punches made from the same template while still in England. Only eight to ten examples of these two great treasures are known, in copper. In 1995, a silver, reeded-edge, small stars piece came to light, opening the exciting possibility of an intended companion denomination in that metal. This seems logical since Jefferson and the Grand Committee favored silver.

The Confederatio decads are afforded a claim to official sanction because they appear in congressional records. However, four undocumented dies also are used in pairings with the Confederatio dies and with each other. Some of these pairings may have been presented as alternative suggestions, on equal footing with the Confederatio patterns. Others, particularly those that are obvious mules, probably were experiments. The four secondary dies feature:

1.) A shield with the circumscribed legend ∗ *E* ∗ *PLURIBUS* ∗ *UNUM* ∗. This die saw use as the reverse for New Jersey state coppers, opposite Maris obverses 6, 7, 8½ and 10½, bolstering the case for Mould as its die maker. In the New Jersey series, this "shield die" is known as Maris reverse C. The shield die is also paired with each of the other secondary dies. Those pairings, too, are recognized in the New Jersey series.

2.) A right-facing bust of Washington with the legend *GEN. WASHINGTON*. In addition to being paired with the shield die, this "Washington die" is paired with the Confederatio large stars reverse and with a "large eagle" secondary die. (See below.) The pairing of the Washington and shield dies is known to New Jersey aficionados as Maris 4-C. A newly discovered variety, designated as Maris 4½ - p, is thought to be a contemporary counterfeit of Maris 4-C.

3.) A rendition of Liberty or Justice, seated on a globe. She is wrapped in a flag and faces to the viewer's right. The flag is anchored to a pole atop of which sets a liberty cap. The figure holds the pole in her right hand and the scales of justice in her left. The date, in exergue, is *1786*. The legend reads *IMMUNIS COLUMBIA* · ("Columbus' Land, Immune from Tyranny.") The design is similar to that of the 1785 Immune Columbias pieces, in Group II, and is even more similar to 1786- and 1787-dated Immunis Columbia pieces in Group III. The pairing of this Group I Immunis Columbia die with the shield die, above, is known to students of the New Jersey series as Maris 3-C. The Group I Immunis Columbia die also is paired with the Confederatio large stars reverse to create an apparent mule that bears two dates, 1785 and 1786.

4.) A 1786-dated heraldic eagle motif similar to that on the 1787 New York Excelsiors, but with a wide shield and transposed arrows.

The wide shield gives rise to the name "large eagle." Pairings with this die appear to have been made later, perhaps by another coiner. The die appears opposite the 1785 Confederatio large stars die to create another dual-date variety. It also appears opposite the shield die on a variety known in the New Jersey series as Maris 5-C.

1785 small stars paired with a 1787 New York Excelsior reverse.

In two cases Group I dies are paired with dies from outside the group. The first such pairing mates the worn 1785 Confederatio small stars die with the 1787 New York Excelsior small eagle reverse to create a third dual-date piece of which there are at least two known examples. The second pairing is unique and has the Confederatio large stars die opposite an otherwise unused 1785 Constellatio Nova reverse from Group II.

Group II: The 1785 Immune Columbias and Related Pairings

The second group of Confederation patterns probably represents the origin of the Immunis Columbia theme. The group's two nearly identical obverse dies resemble the other Immunis Columbia pieces, except that Liberty (or Justice) sits on a crate rather than a globe. Used in this way, the crate symbolizes commerce. The group is tied intimately to the Constellatio Nova private coppers, sharing three dies with that series: Crosby's obverse die 2 (from Crosby 1783 variety 2-B in the Constellatio Nova series) and $3_{1783}/1_{1785}$ (from Crosby 1783 variety 3-C and 1785 variety 1-B in the Nova Constellatio series,) and obverse 3 (from Crosby 1785 variety 3-B in the Nova Constellatio series.) (Note that Crosby's obverse 3 of 1783 is the same as the die he designated as number 1 for 1785 issues.) Another Constellatio Nova obverse die, not used on Morris's tokens, is used opposite Immune Columbia obverses, while an otherwise unused 1785 Constellatio Nova reverse is paired uniquely with the Confederatio large stars die. For this group, the Wyons probably *are* the prime suspects. That is, if the Wyons were r esponsible for Constellatio Novas, then they probably made the Immune Columbias as well. The Immune Columbias may even have been alternative designs for Robert Morris's private tokens rather than standalone patterns for consideration by Congress. George Wyon operated at 2 Temple Street in Birmingham between 1784 and 1789. Apparently without supportive evidence, Breen speculated that the business burned before 1790 and that any records that might have clarified the situation thus were destroyed.[789]

Part of this whodunit revolves around the Wyon twins, Thomas and Peter George. They were born in 1767, making them seventeen or eighteen years old in 1785 when the Immune Columbias were made. Were the twins old enough to assist? Both certainly were well known engravers by the 1790's and the family did have its prodigies. Thomas Wyon's son, Thomas Jr., for example, later was made the Royal Mint's *Chief* Engraver at the unprecedented early age of twenty-three![790] Breen asserted that Walter Mould lettered the 1785 Immune Columbia dies on the premise that George Wyon would have used the correct Latin phrase *Immunis Columbia*.[791] Given that Mould probably was not involved, could one of the Wyon twins, instead, have committed the so-called error?

Obverses of Robert Morris's Constellatio Nova private coppers paired with a 1785 Immune Columbia die:
A – 1783 Crosby obverse 2.
B – 1783 Crosby obverse 3,
a.k.a. 1785 Crosby obverse 1.
C – 1785 Crosby obverse 3.

The 1785 Immune Columbia pieces are known in copper, silver and gold, possibly indicating a desire for a tri-metallic system.[*] About twenty of these pieces are known in copper with pointed rays, two in copper with blunt rays, five in silver with pointed rays and a single pointed-rays example in gold. The gold specimen resides in the Smithsonian Institution. In 1843 Matthew Stickney traded it to the U.S. Mint for a specimen of the rare 1804-dated U.S. dollar. (Chapter 12.) Market value aside, the U.S. Mint received the better end of the deal.

In what must have been late life marriages of convenience, an Immune Columbia die is paired with a crude Vermont die on Ryder 1 and an equally crude imitation halfpence obverse on Vlack 15-85NY. Vlack 15-85NY uses the blundered spelling *CEORCIVS,* most likely the result of not having a "G" punch at hand. These two rare mulings almost certainly are by the same coiners, who probably operated at Machin's Mills. The unanswered question of how Immune Columbia dies were conveyed to America serves to convolute the history of this rare series.

Group III: Immunis Columbia Coppers & A Related (?) Mule (1786 to 1787)

At least one other *Immunis* Columbia variety probably *was* a pattern intended for viewing by Congressional decision makers. General Matthias Ogden, the Revolutionary War hero and New Jersey assemblyman who minted coins for his state, corresponded with Congress about coinage as early as January 1786, nearly a year before his quarrelsome partners began minting New Jersey state coppers.

Ogden probably asked James Atlee to make pattern dies to support his Confederation proposal. Ogden submitted his plan on March 23, 1787, offering to pay 15 percent of the gross production to the Treasury.[792] This was a better offer than the one made by his chief competitor, James Jarvis. Ogden had the resources, equipment and integrity to make good on the contract. Jarvis' only advantage was his skullduggery.

The 1786-dated pieces from Group III probably were patterns made for Ogden's proposal. It does, however, seem odd that "1786" appeared on coins used for a proposal submitted in the spring of 1787. Perhaps a call for proposals was anticipated in 1786. Obverses of the 1786

---

[*] The term "tri-metallic" refers to the eighteenth century idea of having coins of multiple denominations that are identical in design, but different in composition and, consequently, in value.

pieces are similar to, maybe even copied from, the Group I Immunis Columbia pieces and Group II Immune Columbia pieces described above. The 1786 Group III reverse features a crude eagle that actually resembles a pterodactyl, a prehistoric flying reptile. The arrows and branch are transposed, indicating an apparent preference for war over peace as on some New York patterns and Massachusetts coppers. Only two examples of this 1786 version are known to have survived.

The 1787 version is more common and is found on two planchet types. Those of the first type are thin and have a diameter large enough to accommodate the entire design, including the dentils that encircle the coins' rims. Only four Immunis Columbia coppers with this planchet type are known. At least one of them is known to be free of the reverse die cracks that characterize every other 1787 Immunis Columbia copper, implying that it was struck very early in the series. All four examples are overstruck on New Jersey state coppers. Three of these undertypes are of the variety Maris 26-s that have die cracks of their own. The fourth specimen is simply too worn to identify the variety of its undertype.[793]

Planchets of the second type are thicker and smaller in diameter, so small that some portions of the date or legends are always struck off the planchets. None of the known small-planchet examples is an overstrike. The fact that all of the known smaller diameter pieces exhibit die cracks suggests a time of minting later than that of the larger diameter, thinner specimens. Today even the smaller diameter Immunis Columbia coppers are scarce, though an exact count of survivors is unknown. Breen stated simply that "...over 100 survive..."[794] and most numismatists believe that they number fewer than two hundred.

(Top) 1786 Immunis Columbia, pterodactyl reverse. (Bottom) 1787 Immunis Columbia, small planchet.

Immunis Columbia obverses from both years depict Justice or Liberty seated on a globe, holding a pole and liberty cap in her right hand and scales of justice in her extended left hand. The obverse legend reads *IMMUNIS COLUMBIA*, or, again, "Columbus's Land, Immune [From Tyranny]." The 1787 reverses feature an eagle with an olive branch in its right talon and thirteen arrows in its left. The reverse legend is the familiar ∗ *E* ∗ *PLURIBUS* ∗ *UNUM* ∗.

Paradoxically, the overstruck Maris 26-s New Jersey state coppers are believed to have been made at Rahway or Elizabethtown, after March 23, 1787, the date of Ogden's Confederation proposal. Moreover, another New Jersey state copper variety, Maris 17-b, is known on two planchet sizes whose measurements very closely parallel the Immunis Columbia coppers. This suggests that the planchet stock used for Maris 17-b might have been the same as that used for the Immunis Columbia coppers and circumstantially strengthens the links between Ogden, New Jersey and the Immunis Columbias.[795]

However, Maris 17-b coppers also are believed to be *later* Rahway products. Were the Immunis Columbia coppers made in time for Ogden's proposal? The larger diameter pieces possibly were made as follow-up patterns for Ogden's proposal, while the smaller diameter pieces probably were made in anticipation of receiving the contract, using stock that may have been on order at the time of the proposal. As seen above, the history of the New Jersey operation is quite complex, causing old assumptions about when and where particular varieties were struck to be challenged. Dies appear to have been used, retired and then used again. The theory that Immunis Columbia coppers were made too late for inclusion in the proposal hinges on Maris 26-s and 17-b varieties having been made later, but perhaps some were made sooner. Since 1787 Immunis Columbia coppers are known to be overtypes for *particular* die states of 1786 New Jersey Maris 26-s coppers, accurate dating of the New Jersey pieces may be the key to solving the Immunis Columbia mysteries.[796]

Some of the rare 1787 New York pattern coppers bearing the likeness of Governor George Clinton and generally attributed to Thomas Machin and/or James Atlee are overstruck on Immunis Columbia pieces. This raises questions about the chronology of the George Clinton pieces.

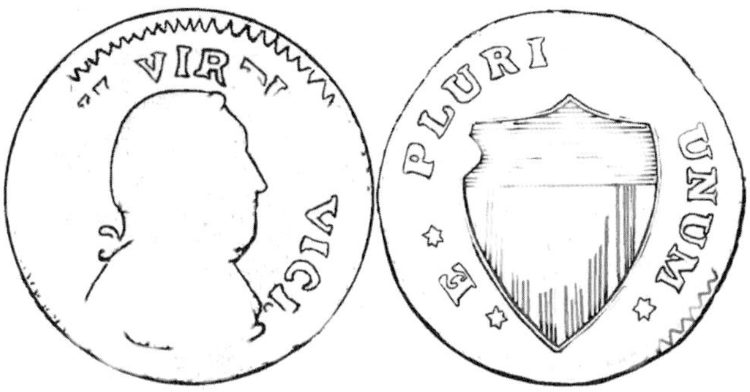

[1787] large head Non Vi Virtute Vici die muled with an otherwise unused shield reverse.

One more pairing completes Group III. It is a unique piece that pairs a large head Non Vi Virtute Vici obverse with a reverse similar to the shield designs above. Though its reverse die is not known to be paired with any other obverse, it bears some similarity to New Jersey Maris reverse K. Atlee's alleged association with the Non Vi Virtute Vicis is the basis for grouping the muling with the Immunis Columbias, but it is equally likely that a contemporary counterfeiter, or at least an inexperienced die maker, was at work. Unfortunately, the Non Vi Virtute Vici/shield mule itself is too worn to reveal much about its origins.

The charts on the two following pages summarize the three groups of Confederation patterns and mulings. As did the Articles themselves, these pieces failed to capture the imaginations of Americans and ultimately were rejected. In a sense, however, both the coins and the Articles were rough drafts that influenced their successors and were necessary steps toward unity. Unfortunately, the next step turned out to be a false one.

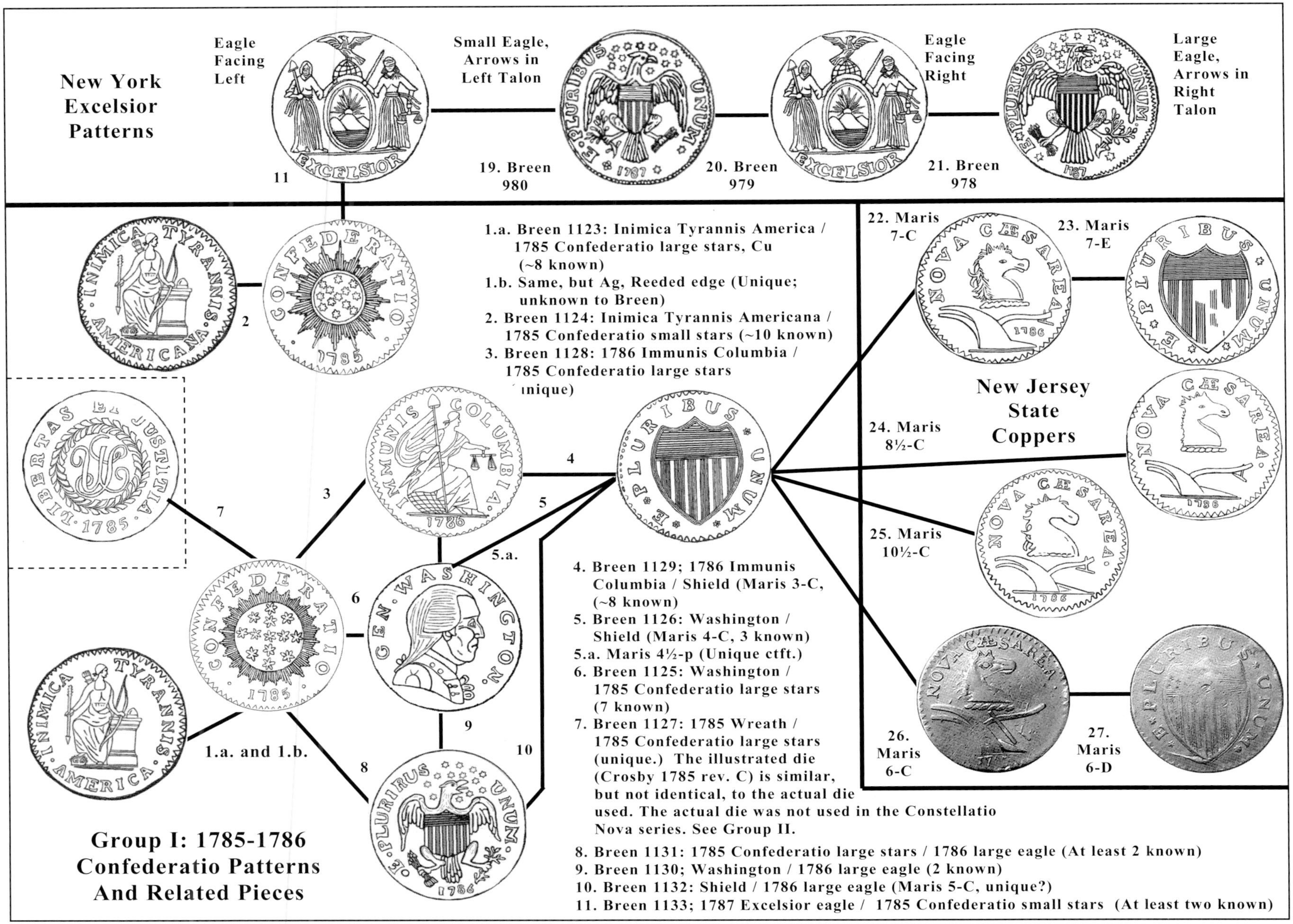
New York
Excelsior
Patterns
Eagle
Facing
Left
11
Small Eagle,
Arrows in
Left Talon
19. Breen
980
20. Breen
979
Eagle
Facing
Right
21. Breen
978
Large
Eagle,
Arrows in
Right
Talon
1.a. Breen 1123: Inimica Tyrannis America / 1785 Confederatio large stars, Cu (~8 known)
1.b. Same, but Ag, Reeded edge (Unique; unknown to Breen)
2. Breen 1124: Inimica Tyrannis Americana / 1785 Confederatio small stars (~10 known)
3. Breen 1128: 1786 Immunis Columbia / 1785 Confederatio large stars
(unique)
22. Maris
7-C
23. Maris
7-E
New Jersey
State
Coppers
24. Maris
8½-C
25. Maris
10½-C
26.
Maris
6-C
27.
Maris
6-D
2
3
4
5
5.a.
6
7
8
9
10
1.a. and 1.b.
4. Breen 1129; 1786 Immunis Columbia / Shield (Maris 3-C, (~8 known)
5. Breen 1126: Washington / Shield (Maris 4-C, 3 known)
5.a. Maris 4½-p (Unique ctft.)
6. Breen 1125: Washington / 1785 Confederatio large stars (7 known)
7. Breen 1127: 1785 Wreath / 1785 Confederatio large stars (unique.) The illustrated die (Crosby 1785 rev. C) is similar, but not identical, to the actual die used. The actual die was not used in the Constellatio Nova series. See Group II.
8. Breen 1131: 1785 Confederatio large stars / 1786 large eagle (At least 2 known)
9. Breen 1130; Washington / 1786 large eagle (2 known)
10. Breen 1132: Shield / 1786 large eagle (Maris 5-C, unique?)
11. Breen 1133; 1787 Excelsior eagle / 1785 Confederatio small stars (At least two known)
Group I: 1785-1786
Confederatio Patterns
And Related Pieces

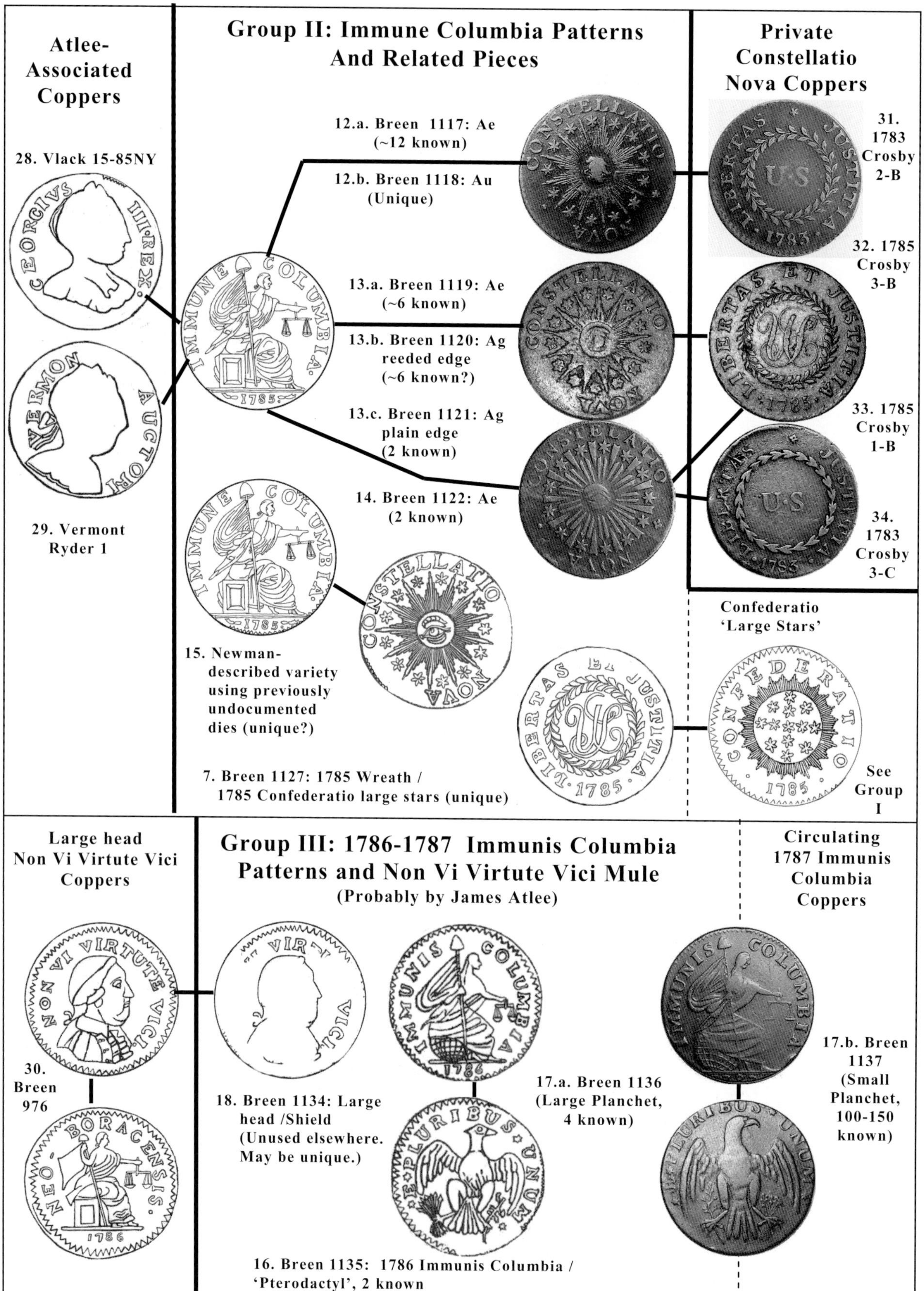
Atlee-
Associated
Coppers
28. Vlack 15-85NY
29. Vermont
Ryder 1
Group II: Immune Columbia Patterns
And Related Pieces
12.a. Breen 1117: Ae
(~12 known)
12.b. Breen 1118: Au
(Unique)
13.a. Breen 1119: Ae
(~6 known)
13.b. Breen 1120: Ag
reeded edge
(~6 known?)
13.c. Breen 1121: Ag
plain edge
(2 known)
14. Breen 1122: Ae
(2 known)
15. Newman-
described variety
using previously
undocumented
dies (unique?)
7. Breen 1127: 1785 Wreath /
1785 Confederatio large stars (unique)
Private
Constellatio
Nova Coppers
31.
1783
Crosby
2-B
32. 1785
Crosby
3-B
33. 1785
Crosby
1-B
34.
1783
Crosby
3-C
Confederatio
'Large Stars'
See
Group
I
Large head
Non Vi Virtute Vici
Coppers
30.
Breen
976
Group III: 1786-1787 Immunis Columbia
Patterns and Non Vi Virtute Vici Mule
(Probably by James Atlee)
18. Breen 1134: Large
head /Shield
(Unused elsewhere.
May be unique.)
17.a. Breen 1136
(Large Planchet,
4 known)
16. Breen 1135: 1786 Immunis Columbia /
'Pterodactyl', 2 known
Circulating
1787 Immunis
Columbia
Coppers
17.b. Breen
1137
(Small
Planchet,
100-150
known)

FINALLY, FUGIOS (1787)

How Much Land Does One Man Need?

With its logical grid of townships and sections and its allowances for the needs of Everyman, the [Land] Ordinance of 1785 made possible the orderly settlement of the American West. Though its importance rarely is acknowledged, it was for decades the world's envy because it was as radical as the notion of self-government itself. For the first time in history, a government *wanted* its citizens to own land and to prosper from it.[797]

For many veterans of the Revolution, the ordinance offered a chance at the dream that they won but had been denied by a Congress strapped for money. At the end of the war, Congress gave the veterans certificates of indebtedness in lieu of the bounties that they deserved. By 1786 the certificates were worth about twelve cents on the dollar in the marketplace. Only the federal government still honored them at full value. Given the country's dire financial situation on one hand and its abundance of land on the other, the benefits of exchanging certificates for real estate were obvious.

A few months after passage of the land ordinance, a handful of veterans gathered in Boston's Bunch of Grapes Tavern to hear Brigadier General Benjamin Tupper tell of endless fields of rich black soil in Ohio. Under the Ordinance of 1785, 640-acre tracts there could be had for as little as a dollar an acre.

A year later Reverend Manasseh Cutler, representing the veterans under the name Ohio Company of Associates, was on his way to New York with a $250,000 down payment and instructions to negotiate with the government for a million acres. There, in the city, Cutler found William Duer, secretary of the Confederation's powerful Treasury Board. Duer had been appointed to the board by his friend, Alexander Hamilton, whom he had assisted in founding the Bank of New York.

Over a fine oyster supper, Reverend Cutler told Duer of the veterans' plan. Then Duer informed the preacher that he himself represented a group of well-connected officials who were interested in a cut of the deal. In exchange for shepherding the proposal through Congress and arranging finances, Duer and his connections asked only that they be given a *small* plot of land on the Ohio and Scioto Rivers. Thus, on July 27, 1787, Cutler's Ohio Company of Associates was given nearly 1.8 million acres for $1 million face value in securities and, at the same time, *five million* acres were set aside for Duer and friends, who would operate as the Scioto Company.

Even though the Scioto Company had not yet paid for its land, they began selling it to French immigrants. Then a land agent, ironically named William Playfair, embezzled the company's funds. When the French immigrants arrived, they found that the Scioto Company's unpaid claim on the land had expired and that the Ohio Company was its new owner. Some of the immigrants returned to the East, some purchased plots from the Ohio Company and some settled on the French Grant, a tract set aside by Congress for their relief.

By 1792 this and other escapades had earned William Duer a bevy of lawsuits, a spot in debtors' prison and the utter disgust of Alexander Hamilton. Duer is even blamed by some for a severe financial crash that shook the country in 1792.

In sharp contrast to the Scioto Company, the Ohio Company was very successful at attracting orderly settlement. Reverend Cutler had feared that no one would come to the new territory if it lacked a legal framework. In response to this concern, Congress passed the Ordinance of 1787, also known as the Northwest Ordinance. The new ordinance worked so well that it soon became America's standard formula for turning unsettled lands into territories and territories into states.[798]

These events are linked to Confederation Era coinage through William Duer, the same official who accepted from Connecticut's James Jarvis a $10,000 bribe in exchange for a federal coinage contract and the right to buy the public's copper at a rock bottom price.

The New Federal Cents

On Saturday, April 21, 1787, Congress approved the minting of three hundred tons of copper according to the federal standard, "...agreeably to the proposition of Mr. Jarvis," provided that a 15 percent premium be paid to the treasury for the coining privilege. After James Madison naively inserted "twenty" as the maximum number of years for the term of the contract, the measure was approved. The plan appeared to be falling into place as seventeen days later the Board of the Treasury was authorized to use the public supply of copper for the purpose and on July 6 a cent design was approved. A federal employee was to oversee the operation and all of the profits were to be paid against the domestic debt.[799] By the time the measure was approved, Jarvis already was in possession of some of the copper.

At the authorized weight of 157½ grains per coin and without accounting for waste, a pound of copper produces $44^4/_9$ coins. At this rate the 300 tons of it could produce almost 30 million cents, worth about $300,000. Initially the Board of Treasury sold Jarvis 71,174 pounds, nearly 32 tons (at 2,240 pounds per ton,) of the public's copper at the discounted rate of 11¼ pence per pound.[800] Even after accounting for a 15 percent royalty that Jarvis was to pay to the treasury in coin, the deal was quite a bargain.

The obverse design of the new cents was to feature a sundial at its center, with the sun above at twelve o'clock. Beneath the sundial the motto *MIND YOUR BUSINESS* would admonish citizens to "Get to Work" and "Take Care of Business." To the left of the sundial the word *FUGIO*, short for *Tempus Fugit*, or "Time is Fleeing," was to imply urgency of action. The date 1787 was to appear to the right of the sundial.

This Fugio cent design, of course, mimics that of the 1776 Continental Currency coins and February 17, 1776, Continental Currency fractional notes. As discussed earlier, the sundial theme is associated with Benjamin Franklin and the coppers even sometimes are called "Franklin cents." One can easily imagine the legends appearing in the pages of *Poor Richard's Almanac*, Franklin's enormously successful periodical of wit and wisdom.

Fugio cent reverses also have a familiar design. Within a ring of thirteen round chain links on a raised circle are the words *UNITED STATES* or, sometimes, *STATES UNITED*. In the center of the circle is the message *WE ARE ONE*. Unlike the Continental Currency coins, whose rings bear the names of individual states, the rings on Fugio cents are plain on all but a single pattern reverse. Several variations of the design exist, resulting from the use of about sixty different die combinations, some of which have been discovered only recently. Currently, twenty-five obverse dies and thirty-seven reverse dies are recognized. On the obverses, variations are manifested in the choice of punctuation (e.g., crosses versus cinquefoils,) a punch substitution ("C" in place of "G" in *FUGIO*,) the exact positioning of legends and mottoes, die breaks and, particularly, in the shape of the rays that extend out from the sun.

A typical Fugio cent, Newman 17-S (Kessler 17-S.1.)[*] On the obverse, note that the rays around the sun are composed of thin lines that are described as "pointed." Also note that the obverse legend is punctuated with cinquefoils. The reverse motto has STATES on the left and UNITED on the right and, thus, it is said to be a "States United" reverse. This reverse is recognizable by its die cracks, one of which enters the ring at 10 o'clock, near the edge.

Except for an extremely rare "American Congress" prototype, whose reverse is radically more ornate than the other varieties, reverses are differentiated by the makeup of the *label* (the flat, circular device at the center,) the relative positions of *UNITED* and *STATES*, the letter positioning of *WE ARE ONE* and the presence of eight-pointed stars on the label. Regularly seen die breaks and die clashes also help with attribution.

The American Congress prototype reverse from Newman variety 1-CC

The reverse of the rare American Congress prototype replaces *UNITED STATES* with *AMERICAN CONGRESS,* has rays from the label to the chain and bears the name of a state on each of its thirteen rings. This reverse and the obverse master hub are stunning masterpieces, both testifying to Abel Buell's consummate skills as an engraver. Yet, Buell must have known that this very complex reverse die would be difficult to replicate in production. All other varieties have plain links and lack the central rays.

Newman reverse Z, the raised rim reverse

On three scarce varieties (Newman 1-Z, 12-Z and 19-Z) from a single reverse die, the label actually is made from two raised, concentric rings. Hence, these are called "raised rim" varieties. Because reverse Z is paired with obverse die 1, which is used with the American Congress pattern reverse and is the only die to use crosses in its punctuation, the raised rim reverse is considered to be prototypical.

---

[*] Eric Newman is credited with the classification system most commonly used for Fugio cents. (*The 1776 Continental Currency Coinage / Varieties of the Fugio Cent*; originally printed by Wayte Raymond in 1952; Reprinted by Sanford J. Durst; New York; 1982.) That system assigns numbers to obverse dies and letters to reverse dies. Thus, a coin of die variety "21-I" has obverse die "21" and reverse die "I." For reverses beyond "Z," a double letter is used. The double letter designations are based on the similarity of dies. For example, the SS reverse designation was chosen to represent a die with similarities to the S reverse. In Robert Kessler's taxonomy, the related dies are given integer designations. Thus, Newman reverses S and SS are equivalent to Kessler reverses S.1 and S.2, respectively. Kessler's work, which has become something of a collectors' item in its own right, is *The FUGIO Cents* (Colony Coin Company; Newtonville, Massachusetts; 1976.)

On the Newman Y reverse, used only on variety 15-Y, distinctive eight-pointed stars separate *STATES* and *UNITED* at the six and twelve o'clock positions. Rarely is more than one star actually visible, even on well preserved pieces.

Newman reverse Y, the eight-pointed stars reverse

While the reverses above are recognizable immediately, for the majority of dies the differences are subtle and require the aid of a detailed attribution guide, such as Newman's or Kessler's, to discern. At a minimum, it is easy to divide the Fugio cents into three major groups of varieties based on the appearance of the sun's rays:

Group I: Pointed-rays varieties that use simple lines as rays. These are found on both prototype and production pieces, representing the bulk of surviving specimens and all but a handful of known varieties. Those with crosses as punctuation are considered prototypes. Regular issue pieces feature cinquefoils and periods. Including the American Congress prototype, this group presently contains fifty-three varieties from eighteen obverse and thirty reverse dies.

Newman 21-I, a Group I Fugio cent. "United States" reverse. Note the extreme die-clashing that is particularly evident on the reverse, where the sun appears to be peeking out from behind one of the rings.

Group II: *Club* rays with *convex* ends. On these pieces some of the rays resemble clubs with rounded ends. Two such varieties, Newman 3-D (ten club rays) and Newman 4-E (fifteen club rays) are known. These are thought to have been made after Benjamin Buell assumed control of the Connecticut mint and possibly with help from Machin's Mills. The copper used in these pieces is different from that used in the pointed rays varieties, suggesting the possibility of a second planchet source, such as Machin's Mills. However, Group II specimens are approximately equivalent in weight to the pointed rays varieties, if not slightly heavier, and Machin's Mills was not given to making coins heavier than they had to be. Thus, the true source of these varieties is still in question.

Newman 4-E, a Group II Fugio cent. United States. Note the convex club rays and the boldness of the WE ARE ONE motto.

Group III: Club rays varieties with *concave* ends. That is, the rays' ends curve inward. The rays often are compared to "musket butts," because they resemble the part of a musket's stock that fits against one's shoulder. Group III consists of six such varieties, all rare to extremely rare, from five obverse and five reverse dies. They are somewhat crude and on average are even heavier than coins from either of the other groups, again raising questions about when and where they were minted. Newman obverse 2, which is used with reverse C, features the

spelling "FUCIO." This often is called a blundered die, but may be the result of not having an available "G" punch. Even the G's on many, if not all Group I pieces are made by punching a "C" and then adding a crossbar. The existence of any real connection between Newman 2-C and New York's imitation halfpence that bear the "CEORCIVS" spelling is doubtful.

Group III, Newman obverse 2, concave club rays, "FUCIO" spelling.

Most regular issue Fugio cents range in weight from 122 to 165 grains. Prototypes and some club rays examples average slightly more than "regular" issues, tending toward the high end of the range. Those whose rays have concave ends have the highest average weight among the three groups, but only by a small measure. The number of Group III specimens available for study may be too small to draw meaningful statistical conclusions about their relative weights.

Though Jarvis had instructed Abel Buell to stop working on Connecticut dies and begin making dies for Fugio cents, Connecticut production continued because, at 144 grains, the lighter state coppers were more profitable to manufacture. This probably is why Samuel Broome produced only about 400,000 Fugio cents from 8,968 pounds of copper while Jarvis was in Europe, failing in his attempt to buy planchets on credit. Broome delivered the meager fruits of his labors to the federal treasury on May 21, 1788.[801]

Four months later, on September 30, a committee of inquiry reported that the Board of Treasury actually had established two contracts with Jarvis. The first governed the sale of the copper to his mint. The second, which was executed by the Board of Treasury *without* authorization, added forty-five tons, the 15 percent that was to be paid by Jarvis, to the original 300 tons. Apparently, Congress had intended the authorized 300 tons to include the 15 percent premium. The committee of inquiry noted that Jarvis had paid for only a small portion of the copper that he had received, that production levels were disappointing and, therefore, that immediate steps should be taken to recover the remaining copper.[802] It was too late. As news of the bribery scandal leaked, Broome sold the remaining copper and equipment to Machin's Mills and left the country to join Jarvis in Europe. The government voided Jarvis's main contract and fined him $10,842. No money or copper ever was recovered.[803]

It was Abel Buell's subsequent departure that left the Connecticut mint in the hands of his son, Benjamin, who may have sought the assistance of Machin's Mills in carrying on. It is doubtful that many more Fugio cents were made after the departure of the elder Buell and, thus, the total mintage is believed to have remained at about 400,000.

In a case of horrible timing, William Duer's friend, Royal Flynt, bought the leftover coppers on credit for one-third of their face value, on July 7, 1789. Less than two weeks later, the Panic of 1789 drove down the value of the coppers to below twenty-five cents on the dollar. As the price plummeted, Flynt was hauled away to debtors' prison.[804]

The chicanery did not even end with the eighteenth century. Around 1860 lawyer and collector, Charles Ira Bushnell, was involved in a curious hoax, in which he claimed that a group of dies had been found at the site of Samuel Broome's store in New Haven. Major Horatio N. Rust acquired these dies and directed that they be used to produce what long have been called "New Haven restrikes." The story evolved to include a teenager, C. Wyllys Betts, of New Haven, who allegedly found the dies and made the restrikes. This myth has survived in part because, at about the same time, Betts did make fantasy pieces, coins that never existed, such as 1660's Connecticut shillings.

Actually, Betts, who grew to become a well-respected numismatic author, had nothing to do with producing the "restrikes." Instead, the minting was engineered by Bushnell in Waterbury, Connecticut.[805] Bushnell's "restrikes" occasionally are confused with genuine Fugio cents. The perpetrators even copied the American Congress pattern and made fantasy pieces that have no genuine counterparts. Fortunately, easily identifiable differences clearly mark them as having used later technology than that available in 1787. The reverse rings are always thinner than on genuine examples, the legends "cleaner" and more consistently positioned. On the other hand, the New Haven restrikes fall within the same general weight ranges as the genuine articles and thus can be deceptive.

1787 Fugio cent, pointed rays. Modern copy by the Gallery Mint. Such modern imitations have little numismatic value. New Haven "restrikes," on the other hand, are often valued at hundreds of dollars. In fact, few differences separate older "restrikes" from those made today.

The Bank of New York acquired a keg of uncirculated Fugio cents in 1788. The keg remained forgotten in the bank's vault until just before the Civil War, when it was discovered and its contents put into cloth bags before being forgotten for another seventy odd years. In the twentieth century, the coppers were discovered once again and, over time, were distributed to valued customers and friends of the bank. Though the numbers have dwindled, a few hundred specimens remain in the bank's vaults even today.

Fugio cents have a legitimate claim to being the United States' first official coinage. After all, they had the full backing of Congress. Unlike the 1776 Continental Currency coins and the 1783 Nova Constellatio patterns, Fugio cents unequivocally were intended for general circulation. Charts below list recognized varieties of Fugio cents. For attribution guides, see the works by Newman and Kessler cited earlier.

Had the government's first attempt at contracting coinage to private enterprise been more successful, the U.S. Mint might never have been established. And, the private effort might have succeeded had Matthias Ogden won the contract over Jarvis. Ogden had the resources and integrity to deliver results. Clearly, Jarvis did not. Still, it is unfair to place all the blame on Jarvis. In comparison to William Duer, he is almost "small time." The Fugio affair was just one of Duer's diversions.

The 1781 to 1789 period began and ended with unsuccessful coinage attempts by the new federal government. Even with the failures, this easily was the most prolific period for new issues in America's numismatic history. If Americans gained nothing else from the experience, at least they learned what not to do. Early in 1789 the Constitution that had been ratified in 1787 took effect, as did Washington's tenure as president. Whether the changes meant a better outlook for America's coinage remained to be seen.

Fugio Cent Obverses

Group	Newman Obverse	Ornaments	Rays	Fugio Spelling	Pairings
I Prototype	1	Cross after date	Pointed	FUGIO	1-CC (American Congress prototype)
					1-B, 1-L, 1-Z
I	6-22	Cinquefoils; On obverse 10, the "1" in the date is re-punched over a horizontal "1"	Pointed	*FUGIO*	6-W, 7-T, 8-B, 8-X ,9-P, 9-Q, 9-S, 9-T, 10-G, 10-T, 10-OO, 11-A, 11-B, 11-X, 12-M, 12-S, 12-U, 12-X, 12-Z, 12-KK, 12-LL, 13-N, 13-R, 13-X, 13-JJ, 13-KK, 14-H, 14-O, 14-X, 15-H,15-K, 15-V, 15-Y, 16-H, 16-N, 17-I, 17-S, 17-T, 17-WW, 18-H, 18-U,18-X, 19-M, 19-Z, 19-SS, 20-R, 20-X, 21-I, 22-M
II	3, 4	Cinquefoils	Convex	*FUGIO*	3-D(15 club rays,) 4-E(10 club rays)
III	2, 23	Cinquefoils	Concave	*FUCIO*	2-C, 23-ZZ
	5, 24,25	Cinquefoils	Concave	*FUGIO*	5-F, 5-HH, 24-MM, 25-PP

Fugio Cent Reverses

Group	Newman Reverse	Label Characteristics	Pairings
I Prototype	CC	American Congress; States' names on rings	1-CC
I	A	UNITED at top, STATES at bottom	11-A
	B, H, I, JJ	UNITED left, STATES right	1-B, 8-B, 11-B, 13-JJ, 14-H, 15-H, 16-H, 17-I, 18-H, 21-I
	C,G, J-X, KK, LL, OO, SS, WW	UNITED right, STATES left	1-L, 6-W, 7-T, 8-X ,9-P, 9-Q, 9-S, 9-T, 10-G, 10-T, 10-OO, 11-X, 12-M, 12-S, 12-U, 12-X, 12-KK, 12-LL, 13-N, 13-R, 13-X, 13-KK, 14-O, 14-X, 15-K, 15-V, 16-N, 17-S, 17-T, 17-WW, 18-U, 18-X, 19-M, 19-SS, 20-R, 20-X, 22-M
	Y	UNITED left, STATES right; 8-Pointed stars on label	15-Y
	Z	UNITED left, STATES right; Label rims are raised concentric circles	1-Z, 12-Z, 19-Z
II	D, E	UNITED left, STATES right	3-D, 4-E
III	F, HH, JJ, PP, ZZ	UNITED left, STATES right	2-C, 5-F, 5-HH, 13-JJ, 23-ZZ, 25-PP
	MM	UNITED right, STATES left	24-MM

Relative Rarity of Fugio Cent Varieties:

Relative Rarity[806]	Varieties
"Common"	12-X, 13-X
Less Common	4-E, 8-B, 8-X, 11-X, 12-M, 15-Y
Scarce	3-D, 6-W, 9-P, 11-B, 13-R, 16-N
Rare	7-T, 12-U, 14-O, 15-H, 15-V, 16-H, 17-S, 18-H, 18-U, 19-Z, 1-B, 21-I, 22-M
Very Rare	1-L, 2-C, 9-Q, 9-S, 9-T, 10-G, 10-T, 11-A, 12-S, 12-Z, 13-N, 19-M, 19-SS, 20-R, 20-X
Extremely Rare	1-CC, 1-Z, 5-F, 12-KK, 12-LL, 13-KK, 14-H, 15-K, 17-I, 17-WW, 18-X
Excessively Rare	5-HH, 10-OO, 13-JJ, 14-X, 17-T, 23-ZZ, 24-MM, 25-PP

11: CONSTITUTION (1789 TO 1840)

TOKEN KINGS AND WOULD BE KINGS

When Congress finally passed the Mint Act in April 1792, it was as much as anything an experiment whose benefits took many years to become evident. While the U.S. Mint was striving toward mediocrity, foreign and private coinages continued to supplement American commerce. Some of the privately made pieces came from kings of the thriving British token industry who hoped that Americans would abandon efforts to build a public mint in favor of private contracts. To make their respective cases, some of them produced samples for consideration by Congress. Others were more subtle in soliciting Yankee acceptance, routing American-themed tokens indirectly through the marketplace. Often the token kings used George Washington's familiar image to capitalize on his great fame.

Obadiah Westwood was a token king. In 1791 his mint supplied a load of attractive cents that bear Washington's profile opposite a heraldic eagle. Their dies were executed by Westwood's prodigious teenage employee, John Gregory Hancock, Sr.. Tradition holds that Washington rejected Hancock's cents as too monarchical. However, the obverse portrait did not go to waste as it appeared on 1791 Liverpool and 1793 "ship" halfpence, both of which are Westwood products that blend English and American themes. Hancock reprised his patterns with another Washington series in 1792. These include pieces known as "American Armies" patterns, "large eagle with stars" patterns and the derogatory, sour grapes-laden "Roman head" coppers.

Peter Kempson and Sons were undeterred by the rejection of Hancock's patterns and in 1795 sent their own versions of Washington tributes in the forms of the "Liberty and Security" pennies and halfpence. Kempson's mint also produced London advertising pieces that bear Washington's likeness opposite a fireplace grate.

Unrelated Washington pieces, known as success tokens, "double heads" and North Wales tokens emanated from unidentified mints. The brass, sometimes silvered, success tokens feature *fifteen-starred* Constellatio Nova reverses, placing their apparent date of issue at about 1792. This was after Vermont and Kentucky joined the original thirteen states and before Tennessee was admitted in 1796. This iconography may be a false lead, however, as some or all of the success tokens actually may have been made as much as a half-century later. The double heads probably are later issues as well, while the 1795 North Wales tokens are almost certainly from the 1790's, but are more properly called evasion halfpence (Chapter 5,) rather than tokens or samples. As such, they could be from the mint of William Lutwyche, another token king.

At least one group of 1790's Washington pieces is of American origin. In 1792 a young Pennsylvanian, Peter Getz, made silver half dollar and copper cent samples similar to Hancock's 1791 cents, copying the Englishman's style with a far less skilled hand. Getz's pieces also were rejected by Congress and the President and may even have been the true object of Washington's opposition to monarchical coinage. Given their time and place of manufacture, Getz's samples could just as easily be numbered among the more official 1792 patterns that were made in anticipation of the U.S. Mint's opening (Chapter 12.)

Standish Barry, a Baltimore merchant and silversmith, issued a very small number of 1790-dated silver threepence tokens that also may depict Washington, though it is possible that they actually bear Barry's own portrait or that of another man, as hypothesized below.

Most of the remaining tokens from the eighteenth century's last decade are candidates for inclusion as Conder tokens (Chapter 5.) For example, 1787-dated *Auctori Plebis* ("Authority of the People") tokens mimic Connecticut state coppers and convey a patriotic message, but clearly have British ties. They are included in this chapter, rather than the prior one, based on a hunch that their American usage came slightly later than 1787. In the same genre, undated, British-made Kentucky or "starry pyramid" tokens (ca. 1792) feature a Masonic triangle of fifteen stars. On their reverses a hand presents a scroll that reads *OUR CAUSE IS JUST*. Of similar style, Talbot, Allum and Lee cents from 1794 and 1795 are advertising pieces made in Britain for a New York business. The 1789-dated Mott tokens also could have been made in Britain for another New York business, though some evidence suggests that they may be later issues and that their place of origin might even have been in America. Finally, the 1794 Franklin Press tokens are collected as American, but actually allude to a London print shop where the legend for which they are named worked as a young man.

An altogether different group consists of three well-executed types, all made to celebrate new beginnings. All three probably were intended as medals. The first of them, the Castorland demi ecus of 1796, were made in Paris for a colony of French aristocrats who escaped the revolution in their country to find a new home in New York State. Myddleton tokens of the same year depict a similar English attempt at settlement in Kentucky. Theater at New York pennies, of circa 1798, are the third member of this trio. Of the three, only the demi ecus achieved any notable levels of monetary circulation.

After Washington's untimely death in 1799, coiners on both sides of the Atlantic again produced commemorative medals and quasi-coins in his honor. With few exceptions, these generally are omitted from discussions of early American coins. Valued as memorials and souvenirs, they never were meant as money. Afterward, in the beginning years of the nineteenth century, production of circulating private coinages for America waned.

Imports enjoyed a brief revival from about 1815 to 1820, a period when the U.S. Mint and the U.S. economy itself again struggled in the wake of war and its debt. At that time Birmingham token kings, most notably partners, Matthew Boulton and James Watt, sent a variety of Washington pieces such as the Unity [sic] States cents, with their evasive legends. Most of these later issues were backdated "1783" to nostalgically recall the Revolution, to avoid anti-counterfeiting laws and to capitalize on the growing sense of nationalism in America.

Elsewhere, two rare token issues from what was then the remote West qualify as early American. In 1818 the postmaster at a fort in what is now San Antonio, Texas, was given a patent to mint coins. The postmaster, Jose Antonio de la Garza, produced copper half-reales that were known in Texas as *jolas*. The second western issue was minted in England for the North West Company to support the beaver fur trade in Oregon, an area that was then in British hands. These 1820 tokens are the only American-associated pieces of the period to unambiguously depict George IV.

By then private tokens and British influence on American coinage clearly were in the midst of decline. Nevertheless, the possibility that counterfeit British halfpence continued to be imported well into the nineteenth century cannot be ignored. To an American who rarely saw an official United States coin, any piece of reasonable size and weight still was very welcome. In addition to outright counterfeits, pieces resembling British halfpence and known as "blacksmith tokens" are believed to have made their way into America from Canada. These mysterious pieces always are very crudely made and usually are without legends. Blacksmith tokens are difficult to place chronologically because their creation and use seem to have spanned several decades. They may or may not truly belong in a discussion of the early American monies, but their proximity of time and place merits at least some consideration. The same can be said of the 1781-dated North American tokens that are collected as American, but which probably fit with a large group of Canadian tokens from the 1810 to 1840 period.

The final days of early American coinage saw a brief renaissance of private domestic issues in reaction to acute economic and political situations. The first wave came when a gold rush in the southern Appalachians created a regional specie shortage. In response, talented individuals in Georgia and North Carolina began making gold coins from the output of local mines. These coins bear the last names of their respective makers, Bechtler and Reid.

A few domestic tokens circulated between 1793 and 1833, before a second great wave of them, principally in the form of one-cent copper tokens, appeared during Andrew Jackson's turbulent administration. They emerged in response to the country's self-inflicted economic difficulties. This era of "hard times" began in 1833 and lasted through the Van Buren administration, until 1844. By the time the hard times ended, so had the era of early American coinage.

Foreign coins still circulated and private tokens still were made as the middle of the nineteenth century approached. However, with the ascent of the U.S. Mint (Chapter 12,) massive westward migrations and the Industrial Revolution, Americans slowly turned from the old coins and tokens they had used. This period of great change began inauspiciously with a tiny silver issue by a Baltimore silversmith.

STANDISH BARRY'S SILVER THREEPENCE TOKENS (1790?)

Or did it? The silversmith was Standish Barry. This former colonel in the First Rifle Regiment was born in 1763, at the end of the Seven Years War, and lived until 1844. His shop was on Baltimore's Market Street in 1784 and 1785. Between 1785 and 1787 he and Joseph Rice were in business as Rice and Barry. Barry later operated alone on Baltimore Street and, between 1796 and 1808, kept a shop on North Gay Street.[807] Barry's silversmithing activities seem to have tapered after 1808.

Even so, he produced tiny silver threepence tokens that are the same size and weight as those by made by John Chalmers. Barry's mintage must have been very small because few, perhaps twenty, of his tokens survive and all exhibit die damage. They may have been hand struck since it unlikely that such a small effort would justify investment in complex mint apparatuses.

Standish Barry's threepence (at twice actual size.)

Reverses give the denomination, *THREE PENCE,* in two lines and within an ornamented circular border. *STANDISH BARRY* is entwined in the border. Either Barry's left-facing bust, or that of George Washington, appears on the obverses of these tiny coins, within a circle and sporting a rather large nose. The obverse legend, circumscribed outside the border, reads

BALTIMORE TOWN JULY 4 90. The July 4, 1790, date may celebrate some event relevant to Barry's business, such as his opening on Baltimore Street. This is speculation, however, since no one knows for certain what Colonel Barry actually commemorated and since the Baltimore Street site was not his first business location.

Independence Day celebrations received only standard mention in area newspapers from 1790, an odd indifference, given that Baltimore had served briefly as the nation's capital from December 1776 to February 1777. Celebrations likely occurred on July 3 or July 5, 1790, given that the fourth fell on Sunday. Though early references to Barry's threepence probably exist, they have eluded this author. The scarce publicity further suggests a small mintage and possibly even another issue date.

A huge July 4 celebration *was* held in Baltimore, in 1828. Aside from celebrating national independence, the event marked the laying of the first stone of the Baltimore and Ohio Railroad by Masons. An estimated crowd of fifty-thousand, including Charles Carroll, the last surviving signer of the Declaration, were on hand. Festivities included a grand procession in which men representing various trades marched together, carrying banners and exemplary samples of their respective wares. The "principal marshal" for the group of "Watch-Makers, Jewellers [sic,] Silver-Smiths and Engravers" was Standish Barry. The group placed special emphasis on the fact that their banner had been carried in the "Procession of 1809." Ironically, the banner carried a depiction of time, with the message "I transmit thee to the future."[808]

Is it possible that Barry first introduced his tokens at the 1828 celebration and that 1790 refers to the date that his then current business was established? Or, might the tokens have been made for the 1809 celebration? In this case, could "90" be a transposition of "09," made carelessly by an engraver working in the negative to create dies? Of course, any pre-1828 reference to Barry's coins would invalidate these hypotheses. However, none has been seen by this author. (In June 1862, *The Merchants' Magazine and Commercial Review* described the sale of one of them, "...very rare, and the history quite undecided, brought \$22.)[809]

Charles Carroll, of Carrollton. Charles Willson Peale after Rembrandt Peale, ca 1823. Both the artist and the subject were in their 80's when this painting was done. Source: Independence National Historic Park.

Two apparently nude boys in flesh-colored suits and winged hats, portraying Mercury, almost stole the show, but ninety-one year old Charles Carroll was the main attraction at the 1828 celebration. At the time Carroll noted that, in his experience, laying the railroad's cornerstone was second only to signing the Declaration, if not first.[810] Portraits on the threepence resemble Charles Willson Peale's painting of Carroll, nose and all. Could they depict the "Old Signer" rather than Barry or Washington? In these unlikely scenarios, threepence coins could have been an appeal to nostalgia, made for ceremonial use, rather than as practical circulating tokens. On the other hand, threepence still would have been money in 1790.

Regardless of when he made them, how and why, Barry's tiny tokens added to the Maryland silver tradition that began with Lord Baltimore's coinage of 1659 and continued with John Chalmers' 1783 tokens. Barry also might have made the Brasher-like doubloon described in Chapter 10. If so, then the truth about Colonel Barry is just beginning to unfold.

FIRST IN THE HEARTS...WASHINGTON PIECES (1791 TO 1820)

Washington as a civilian. Source: Irving (5:348.)

In the 1790's, however, the first President occupied center stage. No figure had personified the Revolution more than George Washington and no American in the two centuries since his death has engendered even remotely comparable levels of admiration. By 1790 Washington was thought, by common folk, without the opiate of a king, to be as close to deity as a human possibly could be. Around him developed a uniquely American blend of secular religion and hero worship that simply has no parallel in modern times. As with all significant religious movements, Washington's legacy incorporates the notion of voluntary self-sacrifice in exchange for rebirth to a higher form. In his case, the voluntary self-sacrifice was his surrender of military command two days before Christmas, in 1783. That a victorious general would willingly hand over his sword to civilians was absolutely unheard of. Conquering generals always wanted absolute power and never simply walked away from it. Nevertheless, to the world's astonishment, Washington did just that. Whether his was a calculated political move or one based on a legitimate desire to break the mold of monarchical tradition, in sacrificing power and self-glory, Washington raised greatness to a new level. He had, in the hearts of many, transcended mortal flaws and was reborn to a higher existence. It is little wonder that his image was considered first when America's coinage was being designed. His name and visage brought instant credibility to anything they adorned.

On the surface, the President decried all of this attention. Yet, in the spring of 1791 he embarked on a third grand tour of the colonies, knowing full well that there would be banquets, parades and toasts in his honor. The trips were not all pomp and circumstance. At times they were even life threatening, such as when his ferry ran aground at the mouth of a flood-swollen Maryland river. Nor were they mere feeding frenzies for his ego. Profound issues of national significance hung in the balance and could only be resolved at the grassroots level. Not the least of these was the need to win genuine state and local support for the federal Constitution. The pre-eminence of federal government was threatened as the states bickered over land, Indian affairs and trade.[811] Even the fundamental character of the nation was at stake. Would regionalism and states' rights carry the day? Would America be a nation of industry, as Hamilton proposed, or an agrarian democracy as Jefferson wanted? The only thing that almost all Americans agreed upon was their reverence for President George Washington.

The 1791 tour preceded Congressional debate over establishing a U.S. Mint and coincided with the explosive growth of the English token industry. Years of accumulated war debt had left the British government reluctant to provide its citizens with luxuries, such as circulating coppers, and opened the door for private mints to produce tokens. Hundreds of different types were issued and some of them ended up in America.

It was Congress's less than stellar track record in establishing a mint that led the token kings to pin their hopes on private contracts and to seek popular support for their own products by shipping Washington-adorned patterns and samples to America. For half a decade these pieces trickled into American ports. The flow stopped after 1796 when it became clear that the U.S. Mint had at least a fighting chance and that John Adams, a pro-mint Federalist, would be the new president.

Then, after Washington's unexpected death in 1799, a number of tributary medals emerged to keep his memory alive. For the most part, these medals easily are differentiated from contemporary tokens and patterns. Because they are not truly coins or tokens, medals frequently are omitted from discussions such as this. Nevertheless, one group of "funeral medals" are included in collections of early American numismatic material. Jacob Perkins of Newburyport, Massachusetts, made and sold them as mementos of Washington's passing. Recall that Perkins was a die-maker for some of the Massachusetts coppers of 1787 to 1788 and that, among many other innovations, he played a pivotal role in the development of printing technology for paper money (Chapter 4.)

On January 10, 1800, the following advertisement appeared in *The Essex Journal* newspaper, from Newburyport:

> *Jacob Perkins*
>
> *Takes leave to inform the public that he will now be able to answer orders for the Medals in memory of the late illustrious Gen. WASHINGTON, from any part of the continent, and to any amount, executed on Gold, Silver, or White Metal, with punctuality and dispatch – from 3 to 5 thousand can be made daily.*
>
> *A liberal discount will be made to those who purchase quantities to sell again.*[812]

Obverses of Perkins' funeral medals depict a small bust of Washington within a wreath. The circumscribed epitaph reads *HE IS IN GLORY, THE WORLD IN TEARS.* Reverses feature either "GW" monogrammed on a funeral urn or a macabre skull and crossbones motif. The two reverse legends are variations of a biographical theme: *B*[ORN] *F*[EBRUARY] *11.1732.* *G*[ENERAL of the] *A*[MERICAN] *A*[RMIES] [17]*75.* *R*[ESIGNED 17]*83.* *P*[RESIDENT of the] *U*[NITED] *S*[TATES of] *A*[MERICA 17]*89.* *R*[ESIGNED 17]*96.* *G*[ENERAL of the] *A*[RMY of the] *U*[NITED] *S*[TATES 17]*98.* *OB*[ITUARY] *D*[ECEMBER] *14*[or 15].*1799.*[*]

Jacob Perkins' 1799-1800 funeral medals: (Left) Skull and crossbones reverse. (Middle) Obverse. (Right) Funeral urn reverse.

Perkins failed to mention in his advertisement that he also made a few funeral medals in copper. Regardless of their metal, they are almost always holed for suspension as pendants. They also exist in oval forms, though only round medals merit discussion as coins or tokens. Round examples almost always exhibit wear, suggesting some circulation as money.

Perkins might also have been involved in the creation of a mysterious 1792 Washington issue that is die-connected to patterns produced by John Gregory Hancock, Sr.. Fortunately, a

[*] Though seldom discussed, Washington was offered and reluctantly accepted command of the Army in 1798 when it appeared that the U.S. would be at war with France. He was not an active commander, but his position at the head of the Army gave credibility to the officers under him.

number of research projects are currently underway to comprehend the full range of Perkins' activities and bring to light the many contributions of this under-appreciated and talented man. For his part, Hancock created a number of different Washington types and mulings between 1791 and 1793.

Hancock's Homages (1791 to 1793)

Born in 1775, John Gregory Hancock, Sr. was unrelated to Boston's famous John Hancock. He was, however, a brilliant young engraver for Westwood's Birmingham mint. In 1791, as a mere teenager, Hancock prepared several different patterns, including those known as "small eagle" and "large eagle" cents. Both varieties feature a left-facing, uniformed bust of Washington, with the obverse legend *WASHINGTON PRESIDENT.* The bust is modeled after an engraving made from a drawing by Pierre Eugene du Simitiere.[813]

The small eagle reverse features a thin bird, as on the Great Seal of the United States, with eight stars, overhead bunting, an olive branch and arrows. The legend reads simply *ONE CENT,* with the date *1791*. The large eagle variety has a more robust bird, sans date, stars, and bunting, but with a ribbon in its mouth. On the ribbon are the words *UNUM E PLURIBUS* [sic.] The small eagle's shield has a narrow chief azure, while the large eagle's shield has only vertical stripes and no chief azure. The large eagle variety is obverse-dated. Most large and small eagle cents have the edge lettering *UNITED STATES OF AMERICA*. However, a number of mulings and rare edge letterings, such as *BERSHAM BRADLEY WILLEY SNEDSHILL, PAYABLE AT MACCLESFIELD LIVERPOOL OR CONGLESTON* and *PAYABLE AT SHREWSBURY,* clearly connect these patterns to the Conder tokens. One unique muling, whose purpose is unknown, pairs the large eagle reverse with an ornate George III obverse.

W[illiam?] and Alexander Walker of Birmingham actually ordered the Washington patterns, shipping a cask that contained about four thousand of them to the associated Philadelphia firm of Thomas Ketland and Sons, to be shown to dignitaries. Breen speculated that the cask held about 2,500 large eagle and 1,500 small eagle pieces.[814] At the time Congress was considering a coinage bill by Robert Morris, a draft of which called for Washington's portrait on a new federal coinage. Though Washington rejected as too monarchial the idea that his image be placed on the nation's coins, it is not clear whether his objections came after being shown Hancock's patterns or after his simply having read the bill. Breen presented as hearsay the idea that Washington also was opposed to the whole idea of having contractors mint the coins of the United States. In any case, Westwood's opportunity had passed and Hancock's patterns were relegated to service as improvised American cents.[815]

Rejection did not stop Hancock from reusing his obverse dies. The large eagle variety's obverse is paired with a ship motif on rare 1791 Liverpool halfpence. With edge lettering that reads *PAYABLE IN ANGLESEY, LONDON OR LIVERPOOL* and reverse devices that are shared with several different Conder tokens, the Liverpool halfpence clearly belong to that series. Beneath the reverse ship are two oak branches that symbolize strength. On a unique white metal specimen that is probably a die trial, the oak branches are replaced with laurel branches, symbolizing honor. The laurel branch reverse is also borrowed from Conder tokens. The Washington obverse would have had limited acceptance in Liverpool, just as British reverse and edge letterings would have limited their use in America. Thus, the pairing of dies and the rarity of these pieces point to an issue for collectors. Even so, almost all of the survivors are worn, indicating that they circulated.

Hancock's small eagle obverse also was reused on a similar token that may have seen wider America circulation. As implied by its name, the reverse of the "Washington ship" halfpence features a three-masted, square-sailed ship, moving to the viewer's right. Its legend reads simply *HALFPENNY 1793*. The framed date is inserted beneath the ship and actually is an overdate, "1793/2." The ship die developed a central bulge that obscures some of the details on all but the earliest strikes. Except for a few plain-edged specimens that probably are errors and a few overstrikes on other tokens, edge letterings are as on the Liverpool halfpence.

Hancock cents and halfpence: *A – 1791 small eagle cent. B – 1793/2 ship halfpenny. C – Large eagle cent, gilded. As with several pieces of this variety, this specimen has gold applied to its surface. Given the prominent denomination on the coin's reverse, it is unlikely that the gilding was done to deceive. Rather, it is likely that the gold was applied to create a memento of Washington's second inauguration. D – Liverpool halfpenny. Liverpool halfpence always are found on cut-down planchets. Note the reverse's oak branches. E – The laurel leaf Liverpool reverse that is used on a number of British Conder tokens and on a unique white metal Washington Liverpool halfpenny.*

Perhaps because debate over Morris's bill had slipped into 1792, to improve the 1791 designs or to serve as a backup plan in the event of their rejection, Hancock apparently prepared a much smaller issue of 1792 patterns. There might actually have been two separate, but die-linked 1792 issues, one of which may have involved a die maker other than Hancock. If so, that other die maker could have been Massachusetts' Jacob Perkins.

The first type from the 1792 series exists in copper, silver and gold, some with plain edges and others with edges that read *UNITED STATES OF AMERICA ·*. The purpose of the silver and gold specimens never has been fully explained, though Eric Newman offered a plausible argument that the single known gold example was Washington's pocket piece.[816] The competing theory, Breen's, is that three different metals were intended to be used in a tri-metallic currency system with copper cents, silver half dollars and gold ten-dollar coins. This is unlikely because the weights simply do not correspond to those then being considered.[817] Two almost identical 1792 obverses from this ultra-rare type are known. They are similar, but not identical to the 1791 large and small eagle pieces. The 1792 Washington bust and its obverse lettering exhibit very subtle differences when compared to the 1791 pieces. The 1792 reverse eagle resembles that on the 1791 large eagle pieces, but its shield adds a wide chief azure and *ONE CENT* is replaced with an arc of twelve stars above a single star. (See illustration A, below.) The edge lettering generally is the same as on the 1791 pieces, but the other differences are sufficient to raise suspicion about the identity of the die maker.

The 1792 patterns and Mulings: *A – 1792 large eagle with stars pattern. B – The Large eagle's obverse with the first "American Armies" (AA) reverse (below.) C – Hancock's "Washington born Virginia" (WBV) obverse with the first AA reverse. D – The WBV obverse with the second AA reverse. E – The WBV obverse with the 1792 eagle reverse (about 3 known.) F – Albert Collis's 1959 uniface restrike of the WBV obverse. Note the relative positions of the legends on the two AA reverses.*

The 1792 Washington obverse also is muled with a biographical reverse that was, in turn, paired with a different, undated Hancock-attributed obverse. This undated obverse is further paired with a second biographical reverse that is nearly identical to the first. These two pairings are the "Washington Born Virginia" or "American Armies" patterns that constitute the second major 1792 type (illustrations C and D, above.) The undated obverse features Hancock's 1791 Washington device punch with the legend *GEO*[RGE]. *WASHINGTON BORN VIRGINIA FEB.11,1732.*[*] Both biographical reverses give a litany of Washington facts: ✸ *GENERAL OF THE AMERICAN ARMIES 1775. RESIGNED 1783. PRESIDENT OF THE UNITED STATES 1789.* That Washington's resignation is so prominently featured is a clue to how important the event was. Though examples exist in silver, most are copper and almost all of the survivors are worn, suggesting that they entered circulation. A very few copper examples have the

[*] Washington was born under the "Old Style" calendar. The calendar was adjusted forward 11 days in 1755/6.

"Washington Born Virginia" obverse muled with the 1792 "large eagle with stars" reverse. The mulings (illustrations B and E, above,) link the two types.

The copper Washington Born Virginia/American Armies pieces are the only members of the 1792 series that exist in numbers large enough for the wealth-challenged to collect. Even they are quite scarce. The pairing of the undated Washington Born Virginia obverse with the first biographical reverse is extremely rare. However, its pairing with the second reverse, which differs from the first only in the placement of its text, is represented by fifty to sixty survivors.

Jacob Perkins appears to have acquired the WBV obverse die from Hancock's widow around 1819. The possibility exists that Perkins might actually have played a role in the producing the original patterns, but this is conjecture. In 1959 Albert Collis purchased the obverse die for $5,000, from a Perkins descendant. Collis used this original die to create a transfer die with which he minted uniface "restrikes" in a number of metals, including platinum. Collis then donated the original die to the American Numismatic Association, where it still resides.[818] So called "Collis restrikes," in copper, appear regularly in Internet auctions and at coin shows.

1792 Washington Roman head

Hancock was not yet finished. After Washington and Congress rejected his patterns, he created a rare satirical piece that depicts a distinctly effeminate, Roman emperor-looking Washington, opposite a scrawny eagle. The traditional olive branch and arrows that the eagle carries appear almost too heavy for sustained flight. These pieces sometimes are referred to as "Roman heads" or as "Hancock's revenge." The existence of these proofs was kept secret for four decades for fear of inflaming tensions between Great Britain and the United States.[819] Hancock died in 1815, while a relatively young man and long before the world knew of his sour-grapes creations.

Neither Hancock's 1791 pieces nor those of 1792 conformed to the standards that were being debated by Congress under Robert Morris's bill that was introduced on December 21, 1791. Hancock possibly was unaware of the standards under consideration. However, he apparently had knowledge of the *designs* originally specified in the Morris bill. Thus, his reasons for departing from the specified weights are not fully understood.

Peter Getz's 1792 Patterns

Having rejected the Hancock-Westwood patterns, Washington and Congress began to solicit proposals. It was Robert Morris's job to hire potential coiners to produce trial strikings. One of the men whom he hired was twenty-three year old Peter Getz of Lancaster, Pennsylvania.[820] For unknown reasons Getz chose to emulate Hancock's cents that already may have been rejected, a lapse in judgment that apparently ended his chances of employment.

Getz produced 1792-dated pattern copper cents and silver half dollars between December 1791, and April 1792. Early strikings likely were done in the cellar of a home/saw factory at Sixth and Cherry Streets in Philadelphia. The site was owned by John Harper, a Trenton saw maker and tinkerer whose skills later proved valuable on the eve of the U.S. Mint's construction.

Robert Birch may have supervised the creation of dies and the sinking of date and letter punches for Getz's patterns,[821] though the details of Birch's involvement are uncertain. Later strikings were made in a Sixth Street coach house on a press made by Adam Eckfeldt (Chapter 12.)[822] Getz's copper cents probably were distributed to representatives, the silver half dollars to senators. Breen hypothesized that the original authorized 1791 mintage in silver was about three dozen, one for each of twenty-six Senators, plus extras for Vice President John Adams, who presided over the Senate, and other dignitaries. Breen further speculated that the authorized mintage in copper was eighty to a hundred, one for each of sixty-six representatives, plus extras for dignitaries.[823] It is intriguing to speculate that, as suspected of Hancock's 1792 patterns, a gold specimen might have been struck for Washington himself.

1792 Getz copper cent pattern, William Idler copy, ca. 1858 (below.)

Getz appears to have experimented with different edge devices. Most of his edges are plain, but about a half-dozen of the fifty odd copper survivors and about a fourth of the approximately twenty known silver examples have alternating circles and squares as their edge devices, as on some U.S. dollars of 1794 to 1803. Two silver examples of Getz's patterns have twin olive leaf edge devices, reminiscent of the 1776 Continental Currency coins. At least three silver undertypes are known: a 1679 English halfcrown, a Spanish colonial four reales and a French half ecu. One or two coppers are struck over 1794 or 1795 U.S. cents, with another rumored to be overstruck on a 1795 or 1796 plain-edged U.S. cent or cent planchet. These overstrikes on U.S. Mint products, together with die rust progressions, indicate that Getz continued to produce examples after his design was rejected and at least until 1796.[824]

Specimens of each denomination are known on two different planchet types. One type has a larger diameter, but is relatively thin. The other is thicker, but has a smaller diameter. Unlike the 1791 and 1792 Hancock pieces, Getz's patterns generally do conform to the Morris bill's weight standards. As such, they might fit just as well with the 1792 U.S. Mint-associated patterns described in Chapter 12.

A unique silver example of a completely different variety features a very large eagle and shield. Its reverse die apparently was cancelled with a chisel, as it exhibits a raised line connecting the eight o'clock and two o'clock obverse positions. Whether the large eagle specimen is a legitimate strike or a later re-tooling long has been debated, but its provenance extends to 1831[825] and most now accept it as genuine. Getz's hand also is seen in Masonic medals of the era, indicating that he was active in creating designs other than his submitted patterns.

Around 1860 the Philadelphia coin dealer, William Idler, had very accurate reproductions of Getz's patterns struck. As minted, Idler's reproductions could be differentiated from originals by the tiny word "COPY" near the tip of Washington's bust. However, many of these now very collectable reproductions have had "COPY" removed to deceive, as on the example above. Idler's run also included storecards with his business information and address on their reverses, in place of Getz's eagle. For most collectors, Idler's copies are viable alternatives since much-worn copper originals exceed ten thousand dollars in the marketplace and the best preserved silver originals now command prices in the hundreds of thousands of dollars.

SUCCESS TOKENS (CA. 1792?)

One of the most enigmatic series (possibly) to emerge from this is the Washington success tokens. These pieces are found in two sizes: 1.) large, about the diameter of a modern quarter dollar, but thinner; and 2.) small, about the diameter of a modern dime and, again, thinner. Both have similar designs and are made of brass, although examples of the smaller type occasionally are found silvered.

Success Tokens: *A - Large success token, brass. Note the die break running through Washington's head and nose. Two examples of small success tokens, B - Silvered brass and C - Brass, with a reeded edge. Note the test cuts in the silvered specimen. These likely were done to ascertain whether the piece was solid silver. A silvered piece such as this could easily be mistaken for a dime.*

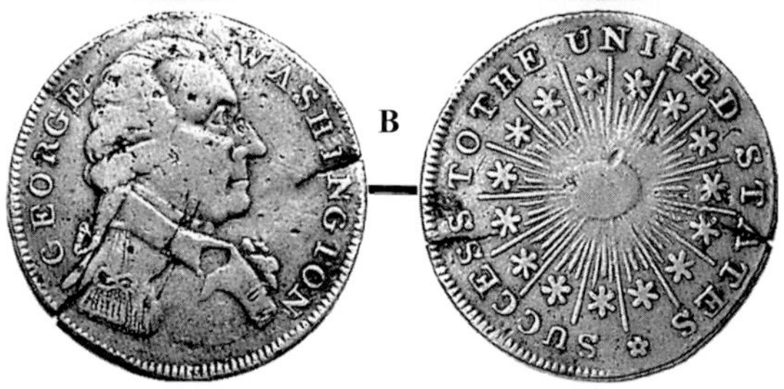

Their reverse designs mimic those of the Constellatio Novas and the Vermont landscape issues in that they feature the new constellation and its ever watchful eye. Success tokens, however, have *fifteen* stars, evidently dating them to a time after the admission of Vermont and Kentucky as states and before Tennessee was admitted. Thus the issue date is ostensibly between 1792 and 1796. Indeed, the reverse legend, *SUCCESS TO THE UNITED STATES*, is consistent with the historical context of Washington's second inauguration, when many glasses were raised to the country's success.*

On both types, Washington's obverse portrait is tall, relatively thin and has a slightly exaggerated nose. Some large token variations are referred to as "Roman nose" or "Bob Hope nose" styles. The obverse legends on all success tokens simply read *GEORGE WASHINGTON*.

The success tokens may well be of domestic origin and from the early 1790's. If so and if he is not a legitimate suspect, then Jacob Perkins should at least be brought in for questioning. Some pieces of the puzzle, however, still seem not to fit. The smaller token's obverse die was reused on a British temperance token of the 1840's, a possible indication that Washington success tokens were minted in England and in the mid-nineteenth century. In style, metallic composition and size, the larger pieces are very similar to 1790's-dated jetons produced in the nineteenth century and bearing images of France's Louis XVI and Britain's George III. (See

* Celebrations for Washington's second inauguration were far less elaborate than those of his first. His second inaugural address, which was given on March 4, 1793, in Philadelphia, was only 133 words in length.

"Tools of the Trade," in Chapter 7.) The similarities are further evidence that success tokens may be from a later date than they appear. Nevertheless, they remain part of the genre.

Kempson & Sons' Tokens (1795, 1796 and Ca. 1800)

Between 1791 and 1801, Britain's third most prolific token king was Peter Kempson of Little Charles Street, in Birmingham. Kempson and Sons continued to make buttons, medals and pocket calendars at the same address until 1823. At one time or another, the firm employed each of the Wyon twins.[826] With the U.S. Mint was still struggling, in 1795, Peter Kempson threw his hat into the ring with penny and halfpence offerings.

Breen credited the penny dies to Thomas Wyon and the halfpenny dies to some combination of three men named Arnold, Dixon and Mainwaring.[827] The reverse legend shared by both denominations, *LIBERTY AND SECURITY*, gives the pieces the name "Liberty and Security coppers."

Kempson's penny is a large coin made at the Tower penny standard of 304.3 grains. It features a left-facing military bust of Washington, with the simple legend, *GEORGE WASHINGTON.* The general flashes a subtle, Mona Lisa-like smile. The halfpenny's bust is slightly different, more formal and tight-lipped, and faces to the viewer's right. Halfpence vary between 140 and 160 grains, bracketing the Tower's halfpenny standard.

Both denominations' reverses feature a spade-like shield over which hovers a spread eagle, with arrows and an olive branch in its talons. The shield is divided in half, vertically. Its left side has fifteen vertical stripes, the right an arrangement of fifteen stars, again accounting for the addition of Vermont and Kentucky to the original thirteen states. On the halfpence, the stars' field is horizontally striped to indicate heraldic blue. On the pennies, the field is plain, indicating white. Except for a few 1795-dated examples, Kempson's pennies are undated, but the halfpence bear the split reverse date *17 95*. Even fewer pennies have ornamented engine-turned rims. Two undated pennies, struck in pewter, present Washington's head facing right, looking stern and rather like an Indian. On these unusual patterns, thin rays radiate out from the head.

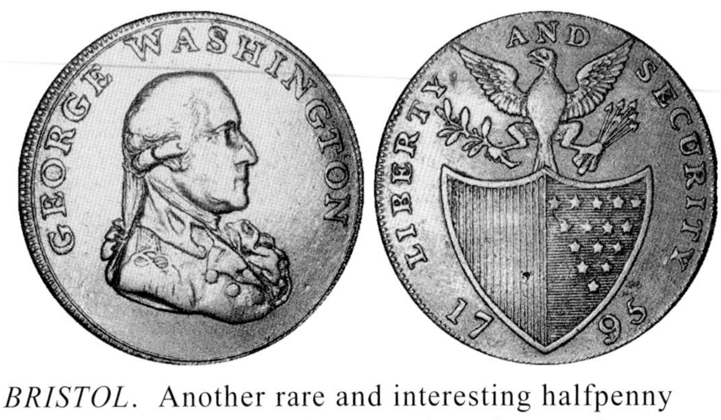

(Above) Undated (1795) Liberty & Security penny. (Below) 1795 halfpenny. Both of these specimens have the "asylum" edge.

The typical edge lettering for pennies is *AN ASSYLUM FOR THE OPPRESS'D OF ALL NATIONS,* but only a few halfpence with this wording are known. The usual edge lettering for halfpence is *PAYABLE IN LONDON LIVERPOOL OR BRISTOL.* Another rare and interesting halfpenny edge reads *BIRMINGHAM REDRUTH AND SWANSEA,* followed by a series of mysterious astrological symbols. A few specimens of both denominations are known with plain edges and the halfpence are known with edge letterings *LIVERPOOL OR LONDON* or *LONDON· LIVERPOOL*. Rare white metal halfpence and mulings of the liberty and security dies with contemporary tokens also are known. Presumably these were struck for Conder token collectors in Britain. One of them mules the penny reverse with an *AM I NOT A MAN AND A BROTHER* anti-slavery obverse, a British anti-slavery theme that was repeated on 1830's American hard times tokens (below, in this chapter.) Other halfpence mulings associate the liberty and security reverse with obverses that refer to Ireland and Cork.

The halfpence hub was reused on a trade token of the same year. On it, Washington's portrait is surrounded by the legend *G*[EORGE] *WASHINGTON THE FIRM FRIEND TO PEACE & HUMANITY*. Made for the American market, these "grate tokens" are advertising pieces for a London company that made fireplace grates. Their reverses feature such a grate, surrounded by the legend, *PAYABLE BY CLARK & HARRIS · 13 WORMWOOD S*^{T}. *BISHOPSGATE*. Under the grate appears *LONDON 1795*. The edges of these pieces feature diagonal reeding rather than lettering, though a handful are known with edges referring to London. A scarcer variety features buttons on Washington's coat that are much smaller than those usually seen.

1795 grate token, diagonally reeded, or "engrailed," edge, large buttons.

The Kempsons' mint probably also was responsible for a later series of copper and tin pieces known as the "Republic America" and "funeral" pennies. The only real difference between the two is found in their obverse legends. Both legends read *GEORGE WASHINGTON*, but the Republic America pennies have the date, *1796*, whereas the funeral pennies use *BORN FEB*[RUARY] *11·1732 DIED D*[E]^{C}[EMBER] *·21·1799*. Little is documented about these pieces and they probably never circulated. The penny denomination is inferred from their diameters, which are the same as that of the Liberty and Security pennies. The surname of the engraver, Thomas Wyon, appears at the base of Washington's bust.

Ca. 1800 funeral penny in tin.

The shared reverse has a center vignette that features a crossed cannon and faces, symbolizing Washington's military and political successes, respectively. A caduceus passes through the center, symbolizing science. In the foreground is a scroll bearing the words *REPUB*[LIC]. [of] *AMER*[ICA]. The circumscribed legend appears within a beaded border and reads *GEN*[ERA]^{L} *OF THE AMERICAN ARMIES 1775 RESIGN[E]*^{D} *THE COMM*[AN]^{D} *1783 : ELEC*[TE]^{D} *PRESIDENT OF THE UNITED STATES 1789* ✚ *RESIGNED THE PRESIDENCY 1796* ✚. The funeral pennies, if not the Republic America pennies as well, clearly were minted after the turn of the nineteenth century since they reference Washington's death in December 1799. Some edges are plain and some read [PAYABLE] *IN LONDON & ANGLESEY*, another link to British trade tokens of the era.

North Wales Tokens (ca. 1795)

Members of another series, the North Wales tokens, always have been dubbed mysterious. It is not known exactly when, where or by whom they were made. This is hardly surprising since nearly two dozen identified and many more unidentified private mints operated in England in the last decade of the eighteenth century. North Wales tokens apparently were made to look worn. Their dies were ground so that, even on less-circulated specimens, details are lacking. No uncirculated specimens are known.

But are they really mysterious? In style and form they clearly fit with the evasion halfpence (Chapter 5.) Evasions generally are regarded as having been issued in the 1780 to 1820 period and are believed to have circulated sparingly in America. If William Shakespeare, Sir Isaac Newton, Romulus and Colonel Kirk appear on evasions, why not George Washington?

North Wales token obverses feature a portrait of Washington somewhat resembling Hancock's. The obverse legend reads *GEOGEIVS* [sic] *WASHINGTON,* the misspelling again suggesting an evasion issue. The reverse displays a crowned harp, with two stars at its base and the legend *NORTH WALES.* A very rare variety has two pairs of stars at the base of the harp.

(Left) North Wales token. Note the reverse die break. (Right) Reverse of a backdated 1760 evasion copper.

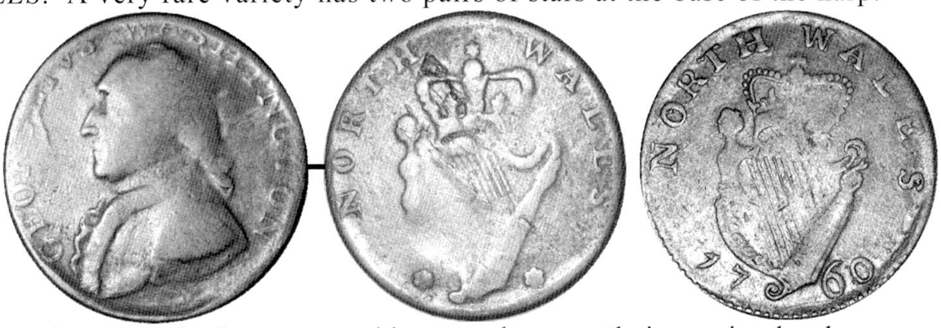

North Wales tokens are known in both copper and brass and, as are their evasion brethren, are light, ranging downward to about ninety grains. William Lutwyche's mint is known both for producing evasions and for copying others' token designs, making it the probable source for these pieces.

Later Washington Pieces (1815 to 1820)

When the War of 1812 ended in 1815, a groundswell of patriotism brought widespread remembrances of the Revolution and its greatest hero. At the same time war-induced hoarding and production shortfalls at the U.S. Mint brought coin shortages. Predictably, it would not be long before at least one other British token maker began producing Washington coppers, probably at the request of an American merchant.

These later issues came primarily from the Soho Mint in Birmingham. Matthew Boulton and James Watt, the man credited with making the steam engine practical,* were behind their creation. Boulton's mint was the second largest English token source, behind the Parys Mine operation, which is best known for its contributions to the Conder series.[828]

* Watt usually is given credit for inventing the steam engine. As often happens, the true inventors are overlooked. Thomas Newcomen and John Calley invented a steam engine in 1705. However, the Newcomen Engine was very inefficient and it took Watt's refinements and those of others to make it a viable engine for the Industrial Revolution.

Sometime around 1820 Boulton and Watt's Soho Mint and die makers, Thomas Wells Ingram and Edward Savage, began turning out Washington coppers.[829] These "small military," "large military" and "draped bust" types were backdated 1783 not to deceive, but to commemorate the Treaty of Paris that consummated the Revolution. All three types allude to the victory with the obverse legend *WASHINGTON & INDEPENDENCE.* All three feature seated Liberty reverses reminiscent of Britannia on 1797, 1799 and 1806 to 1807 British regal coppers. After all, Boulton and Watt produced the cartwheel twopence and pennies of 1797 and the halfpence of 1799.

About ten minor variations of the large military bust pieces exist, all of them plain-edged. Two minor variations of the small military bust obverse, one of which has a center-grained beaded edge, also are known.

1783 backdated Washington coppers:
A – (Ca. 1815) Type 1, large military bust.
B – (Ca. 1815) Type 2, small military bust, center-grained edge. Note the initials "T.W.I." and "E.S." for Thomas Wells Ingram and Edward Savage, respectively. Also, compare the relative distances between "W" and Washington's bust on A and B.
C – Type 3, draped bust, no button, original. On the originals, a tiny "I" (probably for Ingram) appears in the folds of the toga.
D – (1980's) Type 3, draped bust. Stack's advertising piece (See below.)

The draped bust type exhibits the most significant variations. The scarcer of two draped bust sub-types has a button tying Washington's toga at the shoulder. Four legitimate "with button" varieties and a unique contemporary counterfeit are known. The counterfeit depicts a brooding, thick-necked Washington with a large head, along with the misspelling, *INDEPEDENCE.* The more common "no button" sub-type has three original die varieties. It also appears that a few legitimate early restrikes in brass were made using original, rusted dies.

Other draped bust varieties erroneously are called restrikes. Coin dealer, W. J. Taylor, made one set of them in 1850. His pieces are not true restrikes since they were from new dies. Taylor acquired the original hubs in scrap from the then defunct Soho Mint. His pieces feature slightly different lettering and larger dates than the originals. They also are heavier, at around 150 grains. The originals were made to a light standard of 116.67 grains, or sixty to the pound.

Taylor's variations include a corded edge variety, as well as bronzed and rare silver pieces. Ironically, Taylor also muled the UNITED STATES reverse with a die featuring a kangaroo. Above the kangaroo is the word *MELBOURNE*[, AUSTRALIA,] below it, in exergue, *W.J.TAYLOR MEDALLIST TO THE GREAT EXHIBITION 1851*. W.S. Lincoln made more "restrikes" in 1860. Lincoln bronzed a few pieces, in addition to striking fifty to a hundred pieces in silver and two in gold.[830]

An unused pair of draped bust dies surfaced in the mid-twentieth century. In the 1980's, the New York coin dealership, Stack's, created transfer dies from which advertising tokens were struck.[831] Stack's restrikes are not deceptive since the company's logo always occupies one of the two sides.

Type 4, "1783" Unity States cent and reverse of an 1805 draped bust U.S. cent.

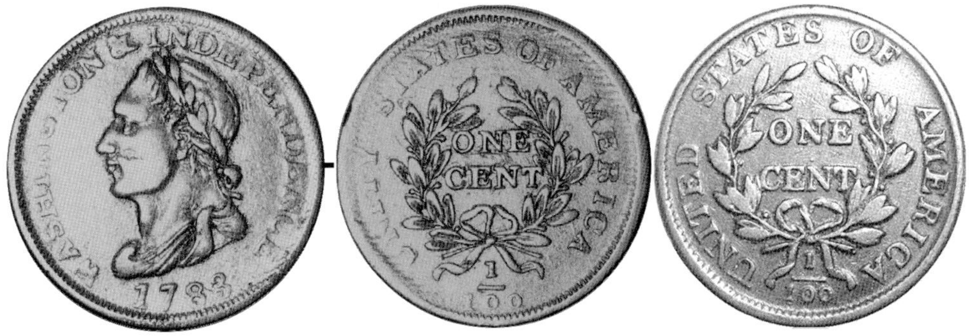

The obverse of a fourth type is very similar to that of the draped busts. Known as "Unity [sic] States cents," these most likely are a related Birmingham product from the same 1815 to 1820 period, though the exact mint and engraver never have been established definitively. The name Unity States is derived from the evasive reverse legend, *UNITY STATES OF AMERICA*. These tokens use the wreath and 1/100 fraction from U.S. draped bust cents of the 1796 to 1807 period, precluding 1780's mintage. A very rare variety has three leaves on the reverse wreath node, near the "F" in *OF*. As on the official U.S. cents, the denomination *ONE CENT* appears within the wreath. Parallel marks filed or pressed into the Unity States reverse die further obscure the true legend to a casual observer. Without these evasive measures, these tokens might have been viewed as counterfeits. Obverses of the Unity States tokens, which are not evasive, present Washington with a laurel wreath, toga and legend similar to those on the draped bust type.

A curious token with double heads makes up a fifth type. These resemble post-1810 tokens struck to honor Wellington, Napoleon's nemesis. As are the four types above, they probably are circa 1820 Birmingham pieces made for the American market, though they are sufficiently different from the others that an earlier date of issue might be possible.

Type 5, Undated double head cent

These undated one cent tokens feature identical, left-facing portraits of Washington on both sides. The portraits depict Washington in uniform, with a laurel wreath around his head and looking very much as he does on the small military bust pieces. An elongated eight-pointed star appears beneath him on each side of the tokens. The legend on one side reads *WASHINGTON*, while the other side simply reads *ONE CENT*. A few "double heads" have engrailed edges, but most are plain-edged. All are from a single set of dies, though there exists at least one variation in rim treatment (flat with a beaded border as opposed to raised.)

None of these five later Washington types is rare, though certain *varieties* are unobtainable. Collectively, these pieces represent the last of the early American Washington series.

AMERICAN TRADE AND OTHER IMPORTED TOKENS (1787 TO 1820)

None of the pieces in this section was a major contributor to American commerce and again, none is of great rarity as a type. Most belong with the Conder tokens. Just as British merchants asked the private mints to supply them with usable small change, a few American merchants followed suit, probably using their British agents and contacts to place the orders. One included piece, the Franklin Press token, is clearly not American and any circulation of it here was incidental. Nevertheless, because of its link to Benjamin Franklin, it always has been included in lists of early American coins and tokens. Another token, immediately below, might more properly be grouped with later Canadian pieces.

1781 (Ca. 1792 to 1820) North American Token

North American tokens were made later than their 1781 dates imply, but how much later is an open question. Broad agreement exists that William Mossop made them in Dublin, but was it William, Jr. or William, Sr.? Punch link evidence implies that the younger Mossop made them in the 1815 to 1820 timeframe, when American coppers were in very short supply. North American tokens certainly resemble many Irish and Canadian tokens of 1810 to 1840. On the other hand, their obverse device appeared on an Irish token made by the elder Mossop in 1792.[832] Thus, while the later period seems a likely scenario, the basic design elements were in use for many years. What seems clear is that the North American tokens were made for the American or the Canadian market and that they circulated in the early part of the nineteenth century.

Obverses of North American tokens feature a seated figure leaning on an Irish harp, with the date below. Above the figure is the legend, *NORTH AMERICAN TOKEN*. On the reverse is a two-masted ship, sailing to the left, with the simple legend, *COMMERCE*. On most examples, the details are "mushy," the likely result of a deliberate attempt to make the coins appear circulated. North American tokens seem to have been minted to a standard of sixty to the pound, though a few much heavier examples exist. The weightier specimens presumably were made for presentation or for the collector market.

1787 Auctori Plebis Tokens

Given that they were pictured in a 1795 book of English tokens, Auctori Plebis tokens are definitely from the eighteenth century.[833] They generally are associated with Peter Kempson's Birmingham mint because of similarities to Hampshire and Norfolk Conder tokens that are known Kempson products. Their obverse legend recurs on a motley crew of evasions, suggesting the possible secondary involvement of William Lutwyche.

(Left) 1787 Auctori Plebis token, apparently minted to a standard of 116.67 grains, sixty to the pound. (Right) 1794 halfpenny Conder token (D&H 21,) Robert Campin, Haberdasher, Goat Lane in Norwich.

The central obverse device on an Auctori Plebis token is a draped bust figure so similar to 1787 Connecticut coppers that one of them must have been used as a model. Auctori Plebis's busts always are weakly struck and can be almost invisible, even on little-worn pieces. The obverse legend, ❀*AUCTORI*: ❀ ❀*PLEBIS*: ❀, or "By Authority of the People," is a generalization of *AUCTORI CONNEC*. Neither this legend nor that of the reverse, ○ *INDEP: ET· LIBER* ○, or "Independence and Liberty," makes sense in a scenario of purely English circulation. Thus, it is likely that American merchants ordered these pieces.

Reverses depict a seated figure, probably Britannia or Hope, leaning on an anchor, with her right arm draped over a globe. The figure sits on a commercial crate and is looking down at the globe. At her feet and to her right reclines a crowned British lion. The anchor sometimes symbolizes Ireland and may do so here. Alternately, all of the reverse devices could be symbols of peace and reconciliation. That is, the reverse symbolism could represent a melancholy Britannia, who lost America, but still has the Royal Navy, commerce and the homeland as blessings. In this context, the obverse could depict a laurelled, victorious America, where the people rule, though the Conder token connection makes this interpretation questionable.

A curious series of evasion coppers are related tenuously to the Auctori Plebis tokens by their obverse legends. Their busts face right rather than left and two varieties of them resemble 1766 Irish halfpence. They bear the dates *1736*, *1756* and even *17336* [sic.] Each evasion's reverse features an Irish harp rather than the reclining figure of the Auctori Plebis tokens. Their reverse legends typically are evasive: *HISPANOLA* (Haiti,) *NORTH WALES* or *BRITISH ISLES*. The two varieties whose obverse busts most closely resemble that of the Auctori Plebis's are uniface. One variety bears the initials *IC,* as on certain other evasions. That the identity of "IC" is unknown only makes them more interesting.

1789 Mott Tokens

On the obverse of a 1789-dated Mott token is an enigma, on its reverse, a paradox. The reverse bears a rendition of a regulator pendulum clock with a tiny eagle finial. The legend reads *MOTTS, N.Y., IMPORTERS, DEALERS, MANUFACTURERS OF GOLD & SILVER WARES*. The obverse features a defiant eagle with a shield on its breast, the olive branch of peace in its right talon and the arrows of war in its left. The date above it boldly reads *1789* and the legend, in an endless circle, reads *CHRONOMETERS, CLOCKS, WATCHES, JEWELRY, SILVER WARE,*. It is obvious that the Mott pieces are New York advertising tokens from the late 1780's.

Perhaps. William and John Mott operated a *grocery store* at 240 Water Street in New York by 1789. The nineteenth century numismatist, Charles Ira Bushnell, associated the tokens with their firm because of the coincident date.[834] However, the tokens make no mention of groceries.

They could refer to a different Mott. For example, Jordan Mott is listed in New York business directories, with various partners, for four decades. In 1810 he advertised that he "Has on hand an extensive assortment of CLOCKS, GOLD and SILVER WATCHES, JEWELRY and SILVER WARE."[835] Thus, Jordan Mott appears to be a likely candidate for the maker or importer of the tokens. However, this scenario is also problematic since Jordan Mott's name did not appear on business listings until 1796. He was born in 1768 to Isaac and Anne Coles Mott. Whether Isaac, a distiller, had any connection to William and John Mott is unknown.[836] Nor is it known whether 1789 was a significant date with respect to either Mott family.

The eagle on the Mott tokens is very similar to those used on U.S. gold and silver coins of 1807 to 1908. The original concept for that eagle generally is credited to John Reich, a German immigrant who worked as engraver for the U.S. Mint (Chapter 12.) The similarity of the two birds suggests that Reich might have taken his design from the Mott tokens, or vice versa.

1789 Mott token, thin planchet and Reich's eagle from an 1807 U.S. gold coin.

The tokens conceivably could have been issued in 1839 for the fiftieth anniversary of a Mott enterprise. The fact that the term "chronometer" was not in wide use until well into the nineteenth century supports this theory. The year 1839 could have been the fiftieth anniversary of the grocery store, but probably not the clock firm.[837] That eagle figures similar to Reich's existed prior to 1800 complicates the picture even further.[*]

Another clue to the time of mintage *may* be found in the planchets themselves, which are known in two thicknesses. Thin planchets are much scarcer than thick ones and range in weight from 163 to 171 grains. Thick planchets range up to 208 grains. U.S. large cents of 1793, 1794 and part of 1795 were minted to a standard of 208 grains. During 1795 the cent standard was reduced to 168 grains, near the center of the weight range for thin-planchet Mott tokens.[838] Could Mott tokens have straddled the time of the change, thus explaining the two planchet sizes? It is also worth noting that some Mott tokens exhibit a diamond edge pattern remotely similar to that on some of Peter Getz's 1792 Washington patterns.

---

[*] A ca.1797 to 1800 political cartoon called *Providential Detection* features an eagle that closely resembles Reich's. The lower edges of its wings are smooth, unlike those on Reich's eagle, but similar to the one on the Mott tokens. Moreover, the obverse of the Great Seal of the U.S. features an eagle that has in its talons an olive branch and arrows. (Olson, figure 10.)

At some point a die break developed near the upper left corner of the clock. If this break were limited only to thick or only to thin planchet pieces, the order of minting would be evident. Instead, both thicknesses appear with and without the break, suggesting that pieces of the two thicknesses were contemporaries.

Reports of a Mott token struck over an 1830's U.S. large cent have surfaced and, if legitimate, would prove that Mott dies were in use after 1830.[839] It would not, however, prove that all of the Mott tokens are of later issue unless the overstruck piece lacks the die break. Existence of such a specimen also would point to the tokens having been struck in America.

Another report, dating to the 1920's, tells of a piece with the edge lettering, *PAYABLE IN LONDON OR BRISTOL*. If this piece could be located, it would suggest that the Mott tokens were 1790's merchant tokens minted in England on behalf of the Motts and perhaps struck on planchets intended for British Conder tokens.[840]

Without hard facts, intuition speaks loudly. It says that Mott tokens probably were first minted in England around 1796, when the weight change in U.S. cents occurred. Jordan Mott was then starting his business and the British token industry was alive and well. The tokens might then have been minted sporadically over a period of several years, using dies that were at some point shipped to America. The 1789 date may even commemorate the first inauguration of George Washington in New York on April 30, 1789. If there is a tie between the tokens and the Mott business at 240 Water Street, then the Talbot, Allum and Lee cents of 1794 and 1795 (below) might have served as inspiration. That firm operated within spitting distance of the Motts' Water Street address.

Kentucky or Starry Pyramid Tokens (ca. 1792 to 1794)

Kentucky or "starry pyramid" tokens probably appeared in America between 1792, when Kentucky joined the union, and 1796, when Tennessee came aboard. Their reverses are Masonic, featuring a rayed pyramid of fifteen stars or suns. Each star has the initial(s) of a state, with Kentucky at the top. Reading from left to right and bottom to top, the states are in the order of their formal admissions to the union. Thus, Kentucky's position is a consequence of its being the newest state. If the tokens circulated in America, it is probably because they were ordered by a merchant in New York or Philadelphia and not out of any intended use in then backwoods Kentucky. Their *E PLURIBUS UNUM* legend even implies a national scope.

Obverses feature a right forearm, with a rolled-up sleeve, whose hand holds a paper on which is written *OUR CAUSE IS JUST*. The nature of the cause is undocumented and the remainder of the obverse legend, *UNANIMITY IS THE STRENGTH OF SOCIETY*, also is something of a mystery. Both phrases appear frequently in political and religious rhetoric of the era, often as encouragement to support the new government.

Most Kentucky tokens have plain edges. Those with lettered edges, such as *PAYABLE IN LANCASTER LONDON OR BRISTOL*, *AN ASSYLUM FOR THE OPPRESS'D OF ALL NATIONS* and *PAYABLE AT I. FIELDINGS MANCHESTER*, were made for eighteenth century collectors. The same can be said of the few surviving examples with diagonally reeded edges, a unique silver specimen, etc.. The intended weight of the Kentucky tokens is unknown. Actual weights vary widely between 132 and 192 grains. The dies probably were made by John Gregory Hancock, Sr. and the tokens minted at Obadiah Westwood's mint in Birmingham. Don Taxay, however, asserted in 1976 that they were made in Lancaster (England.)[841]

Talbot, Allum & Lee Cents (1794 and 1795)

In 1794 the fledgling U.S. Mint was nowhere close to keeping up with the public's demand for coinage. To meet local needs, the New York City importing firm of Talbot, Allum and Lee, doing business at 241 Water Street, contracted with Kempson and Sons to produce substitute cents.

On their obverses, these tokens feature a standing Liberty, pole in hand, in front of a bale of cotton. Their obverse legend reads *LIBERTY & COMMERCE,* while the date, *1794* or *1795*, appears beneath Liberty, in exergue.

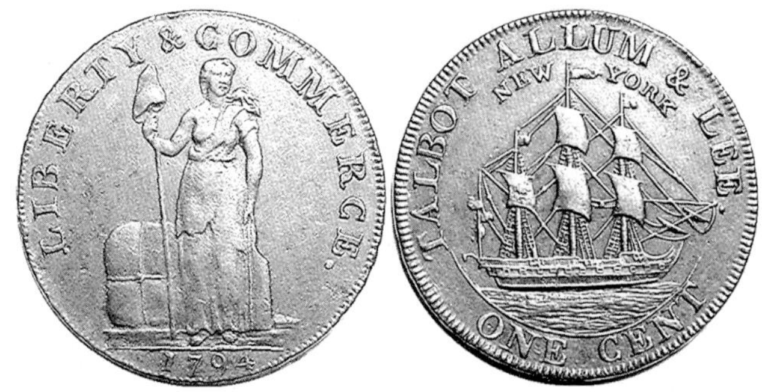

1794 T.A. & L. cent, with NEW YORK

The central reverse design is a three-masted ship sailing to the viewer's right. Above it the legend reads *TALBOT ALLUM & LEE ONE CENT.* With the exception of a rare 1794 variety on which it was omitted, *NEW YORK* appears over the ship.

The 1794 issues have edge lettering, *PAYABLE AT THE STORE OF* [TALBOT, ALLUM & LEE.] The 1795 issues use the edge lettering, *WE PROMISE TO PAY THE BEARER ONE CENT.* Other edge letterings exist, but are rare. The obverse also is muled with various British trade tokens (e.g., with a Birmingham halfpenny, a stork or Promissory halfpenny, Earl Howe, John Howard, Blofield Cavalry and City of York tokens.) Some of these mulings are rare, others relatively common. As with Kentucky tokens, these unusual mules and edge letterings probably were made for British collectors. Three normal strikings in silver are probably presentation pieces. The tokens' usefulness faded after James Lee's 1796 retirement dissolved the original partnership. The business continued on until 1798, as Talbot and Allum.[842] Once thought very scarce, hoard discoveries have made them available to collectors.

These cents may have been minted to the British halfpenny standard of 152.17 grains (46 to the pound.) They are too light to pass for the 208-grain U.S. cents that were then in production. Most of the tokens weigh about 140 grains, or fifty to the pound. They were produced in relatively large numbers for a private issue, so large that the firm had more than it could use. The U.S. Mint purchased 1,076 pounds of extra coppers (between 49,000 and 54,000 pieces) from William Talbot in 1795. Later, the Mint purchased another 1,914 pounds, 88,000 to 96,000 pieces, the remaining stock at that time.[843] These were cut down in size and used as half-cent planchets. Talbot, Allum and Lee designs can be seen as undertypes on some varieties of 1795 and 1797 U.S. half cents (Chapter 12.)

1794 Franklin Press Tokens

Born in Boston and having learned the printing trade from his brother, Benjamin Franklin went to London late in 1724 to further his career. Thanks to Franklin's writings, quite a bit is known about his time there. After a stint at Palmer's Print Shop, the thirty-year-old Franklin moved to Watt's Printing Works on Wyld Street. He started as one of about fifty lowly printers, but quickly was moved to a better job composing type. His strength and speed impressed those with whom he worked. It seems that he made a habit of carrying two heavy type forms while his compatriots could handle only one.[844]

Perhaps their performance was hurt by the services of the local alehouse that sent over a young boy bearing libation at regular intervals during the day, starting before and continuing through breakfast. Franklin, on the other hand, was called the "water American" because he drank only water. It seems that he also made an impression with his skill at swimming, by displaying various feats of surface and submarine skill and by teaching many to swim.[845]

Many of the ideas that Franklin espoused later in life already were with him in London. The entire time he was saving his money and waiting for a chance to return to America. To that end he negotiated a rent reduction, from 3s 8d to 1s 8d a week, from his elderly landlady. She acquiesced because she enjoyed his company. The feeling was mutual, but still he longed for home. The chance came when an associate opened a store in Philadelphia, employing Franklin as a clerk. It was then July, 1726.[846]

Years later a very successful Franklin returned to London. In 1768, while living there, he revisited the site of Watt's Printing Works. By then Watt had been dead for five years and the shop was operating under the name Bayliss and Cox. It probably was this firm (actually Bayliss and Son, as it had become) that had Franklin Press tokens minted in 1794. Perhaps they were done as advertising pieces or to commemorate a special event. No one knows for certain. The fact that the tokens were "payable" implies that they were more than simply commemorative pieces and not really intended for export to the American market.[847]

1794 Franklin press token.

In 1958 Raymond Williamson attributed them to William Lutwyche, but this is unconfirmed. The existence of an example with the edge lettering *AN ASSYLUM FOR THE OPPRESSED OF ALL NATIONS* suggests some kinship with the Washington pieces produced by Kempson and Sons and is another allusion to America. A unique piece with diagonal edge reeding exists, as does an odd muling of the Franklin Press obverse with a Dutch East India reverse.[848]

The tokens' obverses display Franklin's press, with the date underneath and the circumscribed legend *SIC ORITUR DOCTRINA SURGETQUE LIBERTAS* ("Thus, learning is disseminated and liberty shall spring forth,") a reference to Franklin's unprecedented understanding of the power of printing in mass communication. The reverse legend reads *PAYABLE AT FRANKLIN PRESS LONDON.* Most examples show a die break in the interior of the press, though the example above does not. The weight standard for these tokens appears to have been sixty to the pound.

As Franklin's fame soared, "his" press became famous in its own right. In 1842 it was brought to Washington, D.C. and exhibited in the U.S. Patent Office. It later was put on display at the 1876 U.S. Centennial celebration and today resides in the Smithsonian Institution.[849]

EUROPEAN JEWELS IN AMERICAN SETTINGS (1796 TO 1798)

Another group of three types with American relevance are more medals than tokens. As such, they are of high quality. They probably were used as honoraria and circulated only sparingly when lesser coins and tokens were unavailable. All three are rare in their original forms.

1796 Castorland Demi Ecus

At the end of the eighteenth century, aristocratic families fleeing the French Revolution settled in the Beaver River region of New York, in what are now Lewis and Jefferson Counties. Land for the settlement was purchased from William Constable, Robert Morris' business partner. The families formed a company and chose as its symbol a beaver nibbling on a maple tree. The French word for beaver is "castor," as in the infamous castor oil. Hence, the settlement was called Castorland. The company's representative, Pierre Chassanis, divided the land into 100 acre tracts, selling shares at $152.88 each. Even though they received a chilly welcome from their ex-English neighbors, the Frenchmen managed to start a living tapping maple trees, building a forge, trapping beaver and doing the things that settlers generally do.[850]

Trouble started when Chassanis was restrained from leaving France during the French Revolution and a trustee, Rudolph Tillier, was appointed to manage the colony. After the hard winters of 1794 to 1795 and 1795 to 1796, deaths of their cattle, several epidemics and the revelation that Tillier was a crook, the colonists dispersed. Tillier managed to pilfer the company's finances. Robert Morris filed suit against him for Chassanis, but Tillier fled to Louisiana before any money could be recovered. Many of the former Castorland colonists also fled to Louisiana. Their land holdings were absorbed by the New York locals. Chassanis died in 1803, but the company lingered on until 1814.[851]

Not much remains from the endeavor. Tillier had persuaded the Paris Mint to strike silver demi ecus for the colony's use. However, it is a matter of speculation whether the pieces were used as coins or as medals. They might have been commemorative tokens or premiums for those who bought land. Most originals, however, are well worn, suggesting circulation.

Their attractive design was conceived and executed by Benjamin DuVivier. The obverse features a female crowned figure that represents either France or Castorland. The legend reads *FRANCO-AMERICANA COLONIA* ("French-American Colony") and *CASTORLAND 1796.* The reverse depicts Ceres, goddess of agriculture, surrounded by symbols of plenty: a tapped maple tree with sap flowing, a wheat sheaf and sickle and, on her right arm, a cornucopia, the emblem of abundance. Below her is a beaver. The legend reads *SALVE MAGNA PARENS FRUGUM,* or "Hail the Great Parent of Crops."

These pieces were made of 11/12 (or 0.917) fine silver to a probable standard weight of 227.53 grains,[852] though most originals are slightly heavier. They have crudely reeded edges and are quite rare. Even rarer are original copper pieces that also have reeded edges and approximate the silver versions in weight. A gold example also is rumored to exist.

Two sets of restrikes were made from the original dies and also are rare, though not as highly valued as the originals. They can be differentiated from the originals by a reverse die bulge that developed near *PARENS* and by die breaks around the sap bucket and the "S" in *PARENS*. The deterioration is notably worse on the second restrikes. In most cases, the edge reeding is more uniform on the restrikes than on the originals and the restrikes are slightly lighter, under 200 grains. The second restrikes added edge lettering: *CUIVRE* ("copper") or *ARGENT* ("silver.") In some cases edges are reeded over the lettering.

1796 Castorland demi ecu, "restrike," ca. 1846-1860. Note the abbreviations DUV and DV, both for DuVivier.

By the time a third series of restrikes was made the original reverse was kaput and had to be replaced with a copy die.[853] The new reverse has vertical serifs on letters and edge devices, like those on the second restrikes. Third restrikes, too, are scarce.

Edge Symbol	Period Used[854]
Rooster	Before 1821
Anchor	1822-1842
Ship's prow	1843-1845
Hand	1846-1860
Bee	1860-1879
Cornucopia	1880 and After
None	Some 1897-1920.

The table at left enumerates edge symbols that can be used to date the endless parade of later so called restrikes made from copy dies over the last two centuries. The reeded edges are gone, but the lettering continues. Bronze and gold strikings with *BRONZE* and *OR*, respectively, were added. A tiny edge symbol added to the lettering helps to date these later creations. Most pieces seen today have a matte finish, indicating twentieth century origins. Nineteenth century versions typically are mirrored proofs.

MYDDLETON TOKENS (1796)

In much the same vein as John Law's debacle, Castorland and William Duer's speculative land dealings in Ohio, Philip Parry Price acquired a huge tract of land in what was about to become the state of Kentucky. He began recruiting English workers to come and settle in the new land. As with the other speculations, Price's endeavor eventually failed. If the tokens (or, actually, medals) that commemorate the settlement are any indication, Price's failure may have been due more to the manner in which he recruited workers than to any flaw in the business model that he pursued. The entire project ended when Price was sent to London's infamous Newgate Prison for enticing Britain's best and brightest to leave the country.[855]

Price's tokens are among the most beautiful numismatic items to emerge from the eighteenth century. Unfortunately, their message was deeply insulting to his countrymen. Their reverses depict a seated Britannia, dejected, with the fasces, the Roman symbol of governmental power, and the broken scales of justice at her feet. The spear in her right hand is pointed downward, symbolizing surrender or defeat. The reverse legend reads *PAYABLE BY P*[HILIP] · *P*[ARRY] · *P*[RICE] · *MYDDELTON.*

Obverses depict the flipside, that is, Hope presenting her children, Science and Industry, to Liberty, who stands with a capped liberty pole. At her feet, a liberty tree, or a metaphor for the settlement itself, sprouts through a laurel wreath (honor,) amid an anchor and cornucopia, symbolizing commerce and abundance, respectively. The obverse legend reads *BRITISH SETTLEMENT KENTUCKY 1796.*

The Soho Mint of Boulton and Watt, struck them in both copper and silver. The German immigrant, Conrad H. Küechler, engraved the dies.[856] Since all of the two dozen or so survivors in both metals are proofs, it is virtually certain that they never circulated and instead were intended as presentation pieces or medals. They are plain-edged but sometimes are encased in a tight-fitting holder that is sometimes referred to as a bezel.

1796 Myddleton token.

A few copper examples are known on which the obverse is muled with a reverse that simply reads *COPPER COMPANY OF UPPER CANADA* in the center of a circle. Circumscribed outside the circle are the words *ONE HALF PENNY·*. These mulings were done around 1810 for collectors or for use as samples. They were unseen on the American side of the Atlantic until around 1870 and, therefore, are excluded from the ranks of early American coins.[857]

THEATER AT NEW YORK PENNIES (CA.1798)

The rare Theater at New York coppers would be regarded as medals were it not for their edge inscription, *I PROMISE TO PAY ON DEMAND THE BEARER ONE PENNY X.* These large, well-made pieces probably never circulated as they are always proofs and in pristine condition.

Their obverses depict the Park Theater that opened in January of 1798 to Shakespeare's *As You Like It.*[858] The theater was on Chatham Street, now 23 Park Row, and was managed by William Dunlap (b.1766, d.1839.)[859] New Jersey-born, Dunlap was a playwright, author and pioneer in the arts. His 1798 play *André* is considered to be the first notable American play to use local material. It is a tragedy based on the demise of Major John Andre, the brave and popular young British officer whom Washington hanged as a spy in 1780. Dunlap also was a founder of the National Academy of Design and, in the 1830's wrote *History of the American Theater* and *History of the Rise and Progress of the Arts of Design in the United States.*[860]

c.1798 Theatre at New Yorke penny.

In the early nineteenth century the Park Theater hosted noted actors, such as Junius *Brutus* Booth, father of Lincoln assassin John Wilkes Booth, and Tyrone Power, great-grandfather of the twentieth century movie star. For years the London-style theater drew crowds to a playbill that was heavily laden with Shakespearean material. Admission was expensive, at fifty cents for seats in the pit and one dollar for box seats. Even so, the narrow streets around the theater were the scenes of the New York's first traffic jams as patrons arrived by carriage, spawning the designation of the city's first one-way street.[861] The theater burned to the ground in 1820 but was rebuilt by owners John Jacob Astor and John Beekman. In 1821 another fire delayed the re-opening and, on December 16, 1848, the theater again burned to the ground. It never was rebuilt.[862] The last play known to have been performed there was another Shakespearean piece, *Anthony and Cleopatra*.[863]

Dies for the Theater at New York pennies are believed to have been made by Benjamin Jacob, of Birmingham, England. Jacob worked for the stove grate makers, turned token manufacturers, Peter Skidmore and Sons, of Clerkenwell (with a store in London.) On the Theater at New York pennies, the name *JACOBS* appears at the base of the building. It is thought that the "S" is possessive, as in "Jacob's [work]." Jacob is also known to have produced similar tokens with architectural themes, using hand cut letters as on the Theater tokens.[864] The theater tokens probably were issued to commemorate the opening of the facility, dating them to around 1798.

The obverse legend of the Theater pennies reads *THE· THEATER· AT· NEW· YORK. AMERICA*. Their reverses feature a bay front scene, with two ships in the background. The foreground depicts a keg, a shipping crate, a cornucopia, a bale of cotton and an anchor. In the upper right-hand corner of the bale is a triangle. The meaning of the triangle is unknown, but it probably is a Masonic symbol. The reverse legend reads *MAY·COMMERCE·FLOURISH.*

A unique tin example mules the theater obverse with a comical scene that features a thistle-framed view of a girl standing in a washtub. She holds up her skirt to keep it dry. Around her is the legend ✱ *ANTIENT SCOTTISH WASHING* ✱ *HONI. SOIT. QUI. MAL .Y. PENSE* ("Ancient Scottish Washing - Shame on he who thinks evil of it,") alluding to Henry VIII's Order of the Blue Garter. The true meaning and purpose of this odd muling are lost.

The theater tokens and the theater itself also may be linked to a more common and physically smaller issue of admission tokens, bearing on one side the word *ADMIT* or *PAID,* and on the other the date, *1817*. Because their use was specific and non-monetary, the smaller pieces are typically excluded from the list of early American coins and tokens.

1817 theater admission token.

COINS AND TOKENS OF THE AMERICAN WEST (1818 TO 1820)

Not all early American pieces were confined to the East. Texas briefly produced its own indigenous coinage and, even farther west, the fur trade necessitated tokens in the Columbia and Umpqua River valleys of Oregon.

THE TEXAS JOLAS (1818)

Meaningful exploration of Texas began in the early seventeenth century when Spanish Franciscans ventured into the area in search of souls and buffalo hides. Spanish officials were conspiring to establish a permanent presence in Texas when they heard that France also planned to occupy the area. Spanish fears were realized when La Salle (Robert Cavelier, Sieur de La Salle) and his band of followers built Fort St. Louis on Matagorda Bay in 1685.[*] The French effort foundered, however, when part of the group mutinied and murdered their leader, then set off on foot toward Canada. Those who remained at the fort were killed or enslaved by the Indians. On finding the fort's charred remains, the Spanish were delighted. The euphoria was short-lived, however, as Spanish settlers also found the Indians too hostile for co-existence. As a result, Texas remained free of European occupation until 1714, when the French established a post at Natchitoches (Louisiana) on the Red River. When the leader of that expedition, Louis de St. Denis, crossed southern Texas and showed up at the Spanish presidio at San Juan Bautista in Mexico, his band immediately was imprisoned. Ironically, St. Denis had been invited by the Franciscan, Fray Hidalgo, who hoped to use the tiny French presence to spur his Spanish countrymen into action.[865]

Hidalgo's ruse worked. The Spanish quickly built a series of outposts, including what now is called San Antonio, to prevent the Indians from becoming too friendly with the French. Their concerns were justified since the Indians adored French trade goods and disdained the regimented culture that the Spanish demanded. Frontier skirmishes erupted frequently. Nevertheless, by 1750 Spain populated and controlled southeast Texas, effectively creating a buffer to keep out Frenchmen. In 1763 ownership of Louisiana was transferred to Spain, temporarily ending any remaining French threat. Texas remained a vast, sparsely populated Spanish province until the infusion of Americans and Mexicans that occurred after 1825.[866]

In the years before these new settlers arrived, the presidio at San Fernando de Bexar suffered a shortage of small change. The local governor, a man named Martínez, commissioned local merchant/jeweler Manual Barrera to mint 8,000 half reale coins, called *jolas,* in 1817. Barrera's jolas were withdrawn the following year, presumably because they were unacceptable to the public.[867]

No surviving examples of this tiny issue are known to exist. However, late in 1818, Martínez gave a second commission for 8,000 jolas to the local postmaster, José de la Garza. These, too, were virtually unknown to numismatists until a cache of about sixty, found on the banks of the San Antonio River in 1959, joined the few recognized examples.[868]

---

[*] La Salle's sunken ship, *The Belle*, was found beneath the waters of Matagorda Bay in 1995 by then Texas State Marine Archeologist, J. Barto Arnold. Using a special retaining structure, Texas Historical Commission archeologists were able to excavate the ship as if it were on dry land. The artifacts that were discovered include everything needed to establish a colony in the New World. Currently, the wreck and its contents reside at Texas A&M University, awaiting full preservation and public display.

Garza's 1818 Texas jola

The surviving copper jolas are crude, bearing Garza's initials (*JAG*,) the denomination (½ [reale],) and the date (*1818*,) on their obverses. Reverses feature only an incuse five-pointed star, an early, perhaps the earliest, version of the Texas "lone star." Except for a dubious series of *proclamation* or commemorative four reale silver medals issued by or for provincial officials in Florida in 1760 and 1789, Texas jolas represent the only known American indigenous coinage produced by Spanish colonists.

North West Company Tokens (1820)

The other western issue of the period is associated with Oregon. Early on, the Spanish wanted to leverage their missioning of southern California to buttress claims to its northern coast. Spain could have colonized the entire Pacific Northwest, but backed away when they realized that the continental interior held less promise of finding gold than did the southern regions. Later Russian traders made contacts in the area, but failed to establish a large and permanent presence. Meaningful settlement of Oregon began only after Lewis and Clark explored the region. Even then, civilization came slowly. The fur-reaching potential of the area was obvious, but early entrepreneurial efforts failed to capitalize on it. It took German immigrant, John Jacob Astor, to get the ball rolling.[*]

Astor wanted to challenge the pre-eminence of the great Canadian fur enterprises, the Hudson's Bay Company and the North West Company, by shipping furs from the Rockies to the Orient. In 1808 he organized the American Fur Company. In 1810 and 1811, he began a two-pronged commercial assault, sending both ships and an overland expedition to the mouth of the Columbia River. Early in 1812 they met in Astoria, which now is in the state of Washington. Profitable trade began immediately. More importantly, in bringing hopeful news back to St. Louis, a group of Astorians blazed what would become the famous Oregon Trail.[869]

Then came the War of 1812. Fearing attack by the British, Astor's investors sold the enterprise to the North West Company for $58,000. The North West Company was so successful that the Hudson's Bay Company feared development of a regional monopoly in the Northwest. To forestall the monopoly, the Hudson's Bay Company built a string of posts to control the flow of supplies into the region, sparking a trade war between the Canadian giants. When the North West Company became unprofitable in 1821, it was absorbed into the Hudson's Bay Company and the expanded company received a twenty-one year monopoly from the Crown.[870]

A year before the merger the North West company issued a brass token coinage, presumably to be used in exchange for pelts. This assumption is based on the fact that many examples have been found in Indian burial grounds in the valleys of the Columbia and Umpqua Rivers.[871] All but one surviving specimen are holed, as for suspension from the neck or from garments. Most are corroded from their having been buried.

It is thought that these brass tokens originated in Birmingham, England, that they were made by or at the request of John Walker & Company[872] and that they carried a value of one pelt each. In this sense, they are comparable to the trade silver items described in Chapter 3. It

[*] Recall that Astor was also part owner of the Theatre at New York.

also seems likely that the natives used them to buy goods from company posts. A competing theory holds that they were issued simply to commemorate the impending merger.[873]

North West tokens are the only early American pieces to clearly bear the likeness of George IV. Their obverse legends read simply *TOKEN 1820*. Reverses depict a realistic right-facing beaver within the circumscribed legend *NORTH WEST COMPANY*.

These sometimes have been associated with contemporary Canadian tokens. The area where they were used falls between the forty-second parallel of latitude, established by the 1819 Adams-Onis Treaty as the northern border of Spanish California, and the 54° 40′ latitude, the territory south of which was treatied to Britain and America by the Russian Czar in 1824 and 1825. Britain and the U.S. agreed to jointly occupy the territory in 1818 and the U.S. accepted the forty-ninth parallel as the southern border of British Canada. British claims to the intermediate territory were strong, based on the eighteenth century explorations of Captains James Cook and George Vancouver and the commercial presence of the Hudson's Bay Company. The flow of Americans along the Oregon Trail, however, was both overwhelming and irreversible. By the 1840's, enthusiastic Americans were crying, "Fifty-four forty or fight!" Ultimately, the dispute was settled by treaty and the boundary stayed at the original forty-ninth parallel. There it remains today.[874]

CRUDE AND MYSTERIOUS BLACKSMITH COPPERS (CA. 17?? TO 18??)

North West tokens were not alone in having a Canadian connection. Of all the early issues that are afforded some measure of American relevance, wafer thin blacksmith coppers are the crudest and most enigmatic. Numismatists cannot agree on their place of origin, time of issue, where they circulated or even which pieces belong to the group. Blacksmith coppers are more often associated with Canada than America, but the line is blurred. Several theories about the origins of the term "blacksmith" have been proposed. At least three of them point to individual smiths. Modern use of the term is tied to works by Canadian numismatic contemporaries, R.W. McLachlan and Howland Wood. In a 1910 article for *The Numismatist*, Wood[*] quoted McLachlan, who had written of a Montreal blacksmith minting coppers when he needed cash.

Evidence discovered by Gary Trudgen offers a second possible explanation. In 1774 there was an official inquiry into a disastrous fire that destroyed a New York fort on Lake Champlain. Located at Crown Point, the fort was built in the latter half of the French and Indian War. There, a decade after the official peace, pitch in the chimney of a Mrs. Ross caught fire while she was baking beans. The fire spread to the fort's powder magazine and caused a massive explosion. In the subsequent inquiry, testimony revealed that 26th Regiment Private, William Gilfoil, working as a blacksmith in and around the fort, made his own coppers.[875] Still, no copper ever has been identified as coming from his anvil (or molds,) and, thus, any connection

[*] Howland Wood's article, "The Canadian Blacksmith Coppers," first appeared in *The Numismatist* (Vol. 23, April 1910, Philadelphia. Various reprints.) Wood's numbers (1-46) are the basis for most attributions. The list of blacksmiths is expanded in *Canadian Colonial Tokens, A Charlton Standard* Catalogue (5th edition; By W.K. Cross; North York, Ontario; Charlton Press, 2003.)

between Gilfoil's coppers and the blacksmith coppers remains unproven. Wood apparently was unaware of Gilfoil's exploits and, as have most who followed, treated blacksmith coppers as nineteenth century products, made too late for Private Gilfoil to be the culprit.

No such documentation accompanies a third story that tells of an unnamed American soldier-blacksmith who served under Benedict Arnold's command during the 1775 winter march on Quebec. Cold and starving, the blacksmith allegedly hand made coins with which to buy goods from the locals in the Maine wilderness. Had he taken time to strike all of the blacksmith tokens, there would have been little time for soldiering.* Nevertheless, this story and the two before it are bolstered by the fact that many pieces come from non-collector accumulations in the northernmost reaches of New York, near the Canadian border. A more generic version of the tale has the blacksmith coppers being made by village craftsmen, including blacksmiths. Because of limited access to steel and other materials, their dies would have been inferior, their issues crude.[876]

Still another theory holds that English button makers made and exported the blacksmith coppers in the early nineteenth century and that the blacksmith stories either were evasive or invented to give the tokens North American relevance.[877] This theory has its problems as well. Eight of Wood's forty-six varieties and another unknown to him are linked through shared dies to certain American-made hard times tokens of the mid-1830's (below.) If blacksmiths were imported, how and why were the dies brought together with those of the later tokens?

Blacksmith tokens also are similar to real and counterfeit Canadian tokens of the 1810 to 1840 period. Two of Wood's blacksmith varieties have the reverse legend *SHIPS COLONIES & COMMERCE*, as do imported 1830's tokens associated with Prince Edward Island. One of them, Wood 9, has a ship obverse, similar to the P.E.I. tokens. Wood 10 has the same reverse motif with a harp obverse. Other dubious additions made since Wood's time appear to emulate Nova Scotia tokens. In addition, in 1832 a Montreal grocer, Joseph Tiffin, ordered tokens that were dated "1812" to avoid import restrictions. These "Tiffin tokens" were extensively counterfeited, leading some to include the counterfeits in the blacksmith series.

Lower Canada issues that appear to satirize the rule of Governor James Craig sometimes are included as well. Their obverses bear a crude left-facing caricature, probably Craigs' or that of George IV, with the legend *VEXATOR CANADIENSIS*, or "The Tormentor of Canada." Reverses present a seated Britannia-like character with jumbled legends that seem to taunt "Don't you wish you could catch them?" with "them" presumably referring to those who produced the tokens. The date on most such varieties is 1811, a year framed by Craig's 1807 to 1812 tenure.[878] Given that it faces left, the obverse portrait might represent George IV. In that case, however, these pieces would be backdated, a scenario that seems unlikely. On the other hand, George IV ruled as Prince Regent during his father's last troubled decade of life (1810 to 1820) and could well be the target of the tokens' attack.

Most of the forty-six core Wood varieties are without legends or dates. Most bear a cuirassed male bust. In some cases the man faces left as if he were George II or George IV. On others he faces right as if he were George III. The bust left pieces usually are paired with reverses that feature a Britannia-like figure facing right. Thus, the figures on both sides are in reverse orientation from their positions on George III coppers. They are, however, consistent with

---

* A precedent for this can be found in the actions of medieval crusaders who minted coins from looted gold and silver as they marched through the Middle East.

early-run George IV farthings. Since George IV became king in 1820, could this be a clue to when at least one group of blacksmith's were made? Since both George III and George IV orientations exist, could the blacksmiths have bridged the transition of power? On some blacksmiths, the obverse figure faces right, the reverse figure left, as on George III coppers. Might this indicate a pre-1820 origin for these varieties? On these, the reverse figure usually holds a pair of scales as on Tiffin and some 1820 Nova Scotia tokens.

A set of varieties, Wood 23 through 29 and another added since his time, are die-linked with U.S. hard times tokens of the mid-1830's. Around 1835 Benjamin and Daniel True made dies for tokens that advertise J[ohn]. & C. Peck's patent tin machine, and others that tout the plow factory/machine shop/air furnace of Nathanial Starbuck & Sons. Ironically, the Peck obverse is paired with a very crude eagle reverse from the blacksmith series. The eagle itself may be an imitation of the 1813 to 1815-dated Britannia/eagle tokens made on behalf of a Boston merchant who had moved to Montreal. The Peck obverse is also paired with a right-facing Britannia reverse from the blacksmith series. Both the Britannia and the eagle reverses have triangular dentils reminiscent of those on American-made imitation George III halfpence. The eagle and a right-facing bust obverse from the blacksmith series are paired with a Starbuck reverse. The Pecks, Starbucks and the Trues all were located in Troy, New York. How, when and where dies from the two series were brought together are mysteries. The Peck and Starbuck dies existed in 1835 or thereabout. Were the blacksmith dies made after, before or at about the same time? Did blacksmith dies fall into the hands of the Trues, or vice versa, or were both sets of dies somehow transferred to a third party? It seems unlikely that the Trues made blacksmith dies.

Reverses of (Left) an 1813 Montreal token made for an expatriated Boston merchant and (right) of an a extremely crude die shared by Peck hard times tokens and the blacksmith series.

Three of Wood's varieties are dismissed as counterfeit George III halfpence. Others, Wood 33, 34 and 35, are suspected of being evasions rather than blacksmiths. Wood 33, in particular, has come under fire. It features a crude right-facing bust within the legend *GEORIUVS · III · VIS* (or *VTS*.) The reverse features a right-facing Britannia (?) with the apparent legend *BRITI*. *VTS* long has given rise to speculation about a Vermont association, but this seems unlikely. Both legends are as one might expect on an evasion and Wood 33 planchets are thicker and heavier than those of true blacksmiths. Yet, most Wood 33 specimens come from American and Canadian accumulations, meaning that the issue is far from settled.

All blacksmith coppers are very lightweight. All are pathetically crude and weakly struck. The examples on the following page are typical. Though weight standards are unknown or non-existent, a number of pieces that weigh in the range of 60 to 80 grains have been observed. In the end it seems all that can be said with certainty is that many of the pieces Wood described *are* nineteenth century products and that the remainder *may be*. It also seems likely that, as a whole, local imitations were minted over a fairly long period of time by more than one person or groups of people, that there is little reason to regard the blacksmiths as separate from other crude local issues and that, whatever the facts might be, blacksmith coppers make for some good stories.

Blacksmith coppers and similar pieces: *A – Wood 11. B – Wood 14. C – Wood 33. The much rarer Wood 34 shares the BITIT reverse legend, but its obverse and reverse figures face in directions opposite to those on Wood 33. Wood 34 also is more crude and may be an imitation of Wood 33. D_1 – Wood 23, one of a small group of blacksmiths whose dies are paired with hard times token dies by Daniel and Benjamin True of Troy, NY. D_2 – A mockup of one such pairing, known to hard times token collectors as Rulau HT-370 (below.) Here, the obverse of Wood 23 is paired with a Nathaniel Starbuck & Sons hard times token reverse from the 1830's. E – A Ships Colonies & Commerce token from Prince Edward Island, ca. 1830. Though these tokens are not blacksmiths, the ship and/or reverse legend are repeated on several blacksmith varieties that were added since Wood's time. F –1794 contemporary counterfeit halfpenny from Chapter 5. This is not a blacksmith token, but note its rough similarity to Wood 33. G_1 – An 1812-dated copper Tiffin token, ca. 1832. Compare its reverse to the obverse of 1781-dated North American tokens. G_2 – A very thin local counterfeit Tiffin token in brass. This piece is not regarded as a blacksmith token.*

THE NEXT GENERATION OF PRIVATE COINAGE (1828 TO 1840)

PRIVATELY-ISSUED GOLD OF THE AMERICAN SOUTHEAST (1828 TO 1840)

By 1820 private coin production waned and by 1845 it might have died altogether had the intervening period between not been another of boom and bust in America. The stage for one group of private issues had been set years earlier when, nearly a half-century before the discovery of gold at Sutter's Mill, the nation's *first* gold rush came to North Carolina. Over the next three decades, the small amounts of gold that trickled from North Carolina and Georgia were the country's chief source of the metal. When large deposits were found in the region in 1828, another gold rush immediately followed as thousands of the want-to-be-wealthy streamed into the southern Appalachians. To make room for them, America perpetrated one of her most heinous national crimes by moving advanced southeastern Indian populations hundreds of miles along the infamous Trail of Tears, to Oklahoma reservations.[*]

Shipping gold from Georgia to Philadelphia for coining was no less perilous. The vast untamed territory between mine and mint was fraught with many dangers. As a result much of the new-found gold remained local or was shipped directly to Europe.[879] With the sudden influx of people developed an acute, regional shortages of circulating specie. A southeastern branch of the U.S. Mint would have relieved the problem, but repeated requests for one in the southern Appalachians all were denied.

In the absence of a federal mint, two private mints emerged to stem the tide. One was operated by jeweler, gunsmith and watchmaker, Templeton Reid, the other by a family of German immigrants with the surname Bechtler. Neither mint held any official sanction, yet neither broke the law. Federal statutes prohibited the states from minting coins, but said nothing about individuals doing it privately. Together the Reid and Bechtler issues form one of the two principal groups of American private issues during the 1830 to 1845 period, *regional* gold coins.

Reid's eagle and quarter eagle

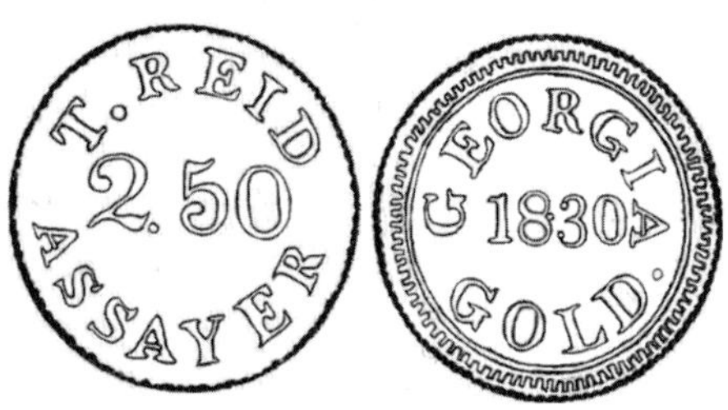

Reid's production began in 1830 and declined rapidly after the public lost confidence in the purity of his gold. The Bechtlers' production peaked in the 1830's and declined with the 1838 opening of federal mint branches in Dahlonega, Georgia, and Charlotte, North Carolina. Even so, Bechtler gold continued to command great respect in the South for many years.[880] The two private mints set a

---

[*] The pain inflicted by this death march and river boat journey became evident to this author with a visit to one of its stops, the site of Cadron Blockhouse, near Conway, Arkansas. The site, once a gathering spot on the Arkansas River, dates to the late eighteenth century. A stone's throw away is a cemetery where fifty-four Indian men, women and children are buried, the victims of fevers, exhaustion and ill treatment by the U.S. government's representatives.

precedent for the celebrated territorial gold coinages that emerged after the California gold rush began in 1849.

Templeton Reid was a Jack-of-all-trades metalworker, jeweler and gunsmith. In July 1830, he began making \$2.50, \$5 and \$10 gold coins in Milledgeville, Georgia. The next month he moved his operation to Gainesville to be closer to the gold mines. By October detractors succeeded in raising doubts about the value of his coins. Walter Breen, however, suggested that, while Reid's coins were lighter than the federal standard, their higher fineness (0.942 v. 0.917) made them worth more, not less, than their federal counterparts.[881] Ken Bressett took another view, writing that the weights of Reid's coins were tolerable, but the assay was incorrect.[882]

Either way, Reid's coins are more notable for their history than for their designs, which trend toward utilitarian. Obverses share the legend *T. REID ASSAYER* (or *TEMPLETON REID ASSAYER*) encircling the denomination: *2.50, \$5,* or TEN *DOLLARS.* Reverses of his \$2.50 and some ten-dollar coins have the date, *1830*, surrounded by the legend *GEORGIA GOLD.* Reverses of the five-dollar coins have *\$5* in the center, surrounded by *GEORGIA GOLD 1830.*

After his brief foray into coinage, Reid moved to Columbus, Georgia, where he spent his last days designing cotton gins. In 1849 he produced a few ten and twenty-five dollar coins that replaced *GEORGIA* with *CALIFORNIA.* All genuine Reid coins are very rare, since the original mintages totaled only about 1,600 pieces and many of them later were melted at the Philadelphia mint.[883]

August Bechtler's 141-grain, 20 carat half eagle.

Bechtler pieces also are rare, but considerably less so, as a group, than Reid's. Immigrant German metallurgist, Alt Christoph Bechtler first arrived in New York on Columbus Day, 1829. After a short stint as a clock and watch repairman in Philadelphia, Bechtler, two sons, Karl and August, and a nephew, Christopher, moved to Rutherfordton, North Carolina. Local citizens soon began bringing gold to the family for assaying and stamping. After making his own mint equipment, the elder Christoph Bechtler took the next step, minting \$2.50 and five-dollar gold coins. Coins from his first series, beginning in mid-1831, bear the obverse legend *C. BECHTLER, ASSAYER,* inside a beaded circle. Within the circle is the word *RUTHERFORD*[TON]. On the reverse is another circumscribed legend, *NORTH CAROLINA GOLD.* At the center is the denomination, *250.* [sic], or *5 DOLLARS* and, on both denominations, the fineness, *20 C*[ARATS].. The same year, Bechtler produced another series on which the coins' weights, *75 G*[RAINS] and *150 G*[RAINS]., respectively, were added.[884]

Around the end of the year 1831, a gold dollar bearing the denomination *ONE* and weight *30 G*[RAINS,] became the nation's first gold dollar and, as such, fulfilled Alexander Hamilton's 1791 wish. Another version, made slightly later, bears the weight, *28 G*[RAINS.] Within the \$1.00, \$2.50 and \$5.00 denominations, Bechtler created several variations of weight and fineness. In addition to 20 carat/150 grain five-dollar coins, he produced five-dollar coins at 20 carats/140 grains, 21 carats/134 grains and 22 carats/128 grains. Similarly, \$2.50 coins were produced at 20 carat/70 grains, 21 carat/67 grains and 22 carat/64 grains. The lighter weight 20 carat pieces were made in anticipation of the Mint Act of 1834, which set lower weight standards for federal gold coins.[885] To indicate the change, Bechtler added the date of the bill, *AUGUST 1, 1834*, to some of his five-dollar coins. For a series of 22 carat issues, Georgia gold was used and noted in the legends. Other minor variations, including a one-dollar coin with *ONE* oddly reversed, also exist.

Bechtler gold dollar, reversed ONE.

In 1840 the business passed from Christoph to his son, August. From then until 1850, when the operation ceased, the coins bear the names *BECHTLER* (without an initial,) *A. BECHTLER* (August) or *C. BECHTLER* (Christopher, Jr., Christoph's nephew.) Except for a numeric "1" that was used in place of *ONE* on one-dollar coins and other weight/fineness variations, the basic designs remained the same. Because of the accuracy and consistency with which the Bechtlers worked, their coins readily were accepted by those loyal to the South until well after the Civil War.[886]

Hard Times Tokens (1833 to 1844) and Their Antecedents

A number of different tokens and quasi-tokens emerged in the late eighteenth and early nineteenth centuries. Most are very rare and seldom encountered. Some of them, such as an 1821 issue for the Philadelphia art and natural phenomena museum founded by celebrated artist Charles Willson Peale, are advertising pieces. The same is true of a 1793 to 1795 issue that apparently was struck at the new U.S. Mint for John Bill Rickett's Circus. Rickett's marketing ploy evidently worked as George Washington and other notables attended his shows. In June 1793 Rickett staged the first *successful* parachute jump in North America when a man whom he sponsored dropped a cat, a dog and a squirrel from a balloon at an altitude of one mile.[887]

The numismatic jury still is out on the origins of a very rare uniface token struck in white metal, whose obverse device is as that on Massachusetts coppers of 1787 to 1788. Its letter punches appear identical to some of those on the Constellatio Nova private coppers. The tokens' legend reads *W. WOART JUS PACIS* (possibly "William Woart Justice and Peace.") Dennis Wierzba noted that a William Woart lived in Boston, on Cornhill Street, in the 1790 census. Woart is believed to have been a carpenter. Another William Woart, or perhaps the same man, married Mary Loring in 1798. At about the same time a John Woart operated an inn in Boston, "At the Sign of the Dragon."[888] Thus, the Woart pieces may be Massachusetts' first merchant tokens and, thereby, deserving of more attention.

Other tokens emerged from the early nineteenth century and are accepted as having been merchant tokens. Among these are the 1828 to 1832 (?) issue for Hugh and John Kirkman (?) of Nashville, Tennessee, early 1820's issues for New York merchants Seabury Tredwell and Joseph Kissam and rare 1823 to 1824 brass tokens of Richard Trested. Trested's tokens advertise his New York engraving business. Their obverses bear a John Reich-style eagle (Chapter 12) under a gloried liberty cap and are reminiscent of the Mott tokens.[889] Other tokens signify memberships in clubs, societies or churches. Still others are canal tokens, turnpike tokens or counterstamped American, British or Spanish coins. Political election medalets debuted with 1824 Andrew Jackson pieces, made for his unsuccessful bid at the presidency. Moderns can only speculate how many other early tokens and types may have been forgotten.

All of these early pieces soon were overtaken by a tide of more than four hundred token varieties that account for the bulk of privately issued American pieces in the years leading up to the 1840's. Their emergence is tied closely to Andrew Jackson's quarrels with the Bank of the United States and associated upheavals in the national economy. It was an old and deeply-rooted argument. When the Bank's charter came up for renewal in 1811, the Constitutional debate about its propriety resumed. New debts accompanied the War of 1812 and, in the end, the stability that the Bank provided in managing them was enough to sway opponents toward approving its re-charter for a second, twenty-year term. By then it was 1816.

However, controversy would not have a long sleep. In 1819, acting as policy watchdog, the Bank declared the myriad privately issued notes then circulating in the country to be worthless. It was a necessary pronouncement, but one that spawned a panic that threw the nation into financial chaos. Businesses went bankrupt and some Americans literally starved to death. Both the "common man" and the American experiment needed a savior.

Andrew Jackson.
Source: Library of Congress, Prints & Photographs Div., LC-USZ62-117120.

Redemption appeared to be on the way when a paper money-hating people's candidate out of frontier Tennessee, Andrew Jackson, won both the popular and the electoral votes with a plurality in the presidential election of 1824. With no candidate owning a clear majority, however, the decision fell to the House of Representatives, who awarded the office to John Quincy Adams under the influence of its speaker, Henry Clay, of Kentucky. When Adams named Clay Secretary of State, Jackson was livid, denouncing the whole affair as corrupt. The widespread perception that he deserved the presidency made him all the more popular and, by the election of 1828, Jackson would not be denied. In his first term, he vowed to rid democracy of the electoral college and return control to the people. When it became clear that he could not, Jackson turned to another of his goals, eliminating the Bank of the United States.

As the election of 1832 neared, Clay and the Bank's head, Nicholas Biddle, saw the chance to set a trap for Jackson that would spoil his hopes of re-election. They crafted a proposal to renew the Bank's charter early, four years ahead of its 1836 expiration. Jackson either would have to allow the re-charter or veto it just before the election. However, Clay and Biddle badly misjudged both Jackson's resolve and the way the veto would be perceived by the electorate. Jackson killed the early re-charter and handily won a second term.

Believing that he still was in the driver's seat, Biddle foolishly sought retribution by raising interest rates and foreclosing business loans. This only fuelled mistrust of Biddle and his bank. Jackson turned up the heat in 1833 when he removed federal specie deposits from the Bank and transferred them to state banks. Stripped of specie backing, the high-and-mighty Biddle had been bested by the backwoods president. The Bank of the United States never recovered and its charter expired in 1836.

Another of Jackson's initiatives was the repayment of the national debt. He was, in fact, the only president ever to achieve that elusive goal. He did so primarily through the sale of public lands, some of which were made available by his ruthless evacuation of Indians via the Trail of Tears. Still averse to paper money, Jackson issued an 1836 "specie circular" in which he declared that payments for federal lands could only be made in specie. Lacking specie with which to make payments, many banks collapsed, leading to the infamous Panic of 1837.

All told, Jackson's fiscal policies and those of his aristocratic hand-picked successor, Martin Van Buren, were no better than the Bank's. In fact, the economy of the Jackson-Van Buren years was so bad that the period of 1833 to 1844 became known as the era of *hard times*. During this time small change-starved merchants and those wishing to make political statements coined their own tokens that were reminiscent of and inspired by the Conder tokens. This new generation of "hard times tokens" provides a unique and fascinating view into the business, political and social environments of the era. Their legends include phrases such as "I Follow in the Footsteps of My Illustrious Predecessor," "Locofoco," "Substitute for Shinplasters" and "A Plain System, Void of Pomp." All of these are political jibes at Jackson, Van Buren and their Democratic supporters, whose constituency mostly was made up of the common people of the rural South and West. It was no accident that most of the hard times tokens were made and used by business folk in the North.

1837 half cent token, Low 49/Rulau 73.[*] *Obverse: [eagle] U.S. STANDARD WEIGHT AND VALUE 1837. Reverse: [wreath and stars] HALF CENT WORTH OF PURE COPPER, by Edward Hulseman, an engraver of button dies. No official half cents were made in 1837, but 1930's dealer, Wayte Raymond, sold albums that included a slot for this token. Thus, it is treated by some as official, even though it had no government sanction. Hulseman also designed the 1847 cents made privately for Hawaii.*[890]

Another common theme, "Millions for Defence [sic], Not One Cent for Tribute," alludes to Jefferson's turn-of-the-century refusal to pay tribute monies to Barbary pirates off the coast of Tripoli. With subtle irony, these almost appear to support the Jackson regime, which claimed Jeffersonian ideals. Other tokens, however, regale Jackson's opponents, such as Henry Clay and Daniel Webster. All but a few varieties emulate contemporary large cents in size and nominal value. As were their counterfeit predecessors, the tokens filled a gap and were profitable to their sponsors because they could be manufactured for a fraction of a cent.

One notable non-large cent exception is the 1837 half cent token, above. Another is the 1837 Feuchtwanger cent. German-born New Yorker, Dr. Lewis Feuchtwanger, proposed an alternative alloy that might have resulted in an early appearance of small cents. The alloy that he introduced was "German silver," a combination of copper, nickel and zinc. He petitioned Congress and won the support of a powerful senator, Thomas Hart Benton, of Missouri (see below.) Even so, Feuchtwanger's petition ultimately was denied and the nation was forced to wait another two decades for small cents. Feuchtwanger minted a half-million samples of his proposed cents and a much smaller quantity of three-cent pieces.[†] Feuchtwanger's cents apparently circulated, as most survivors are worn. He went on to write books on gems and lived until 1876. Had his proposal been accepted, the U.S. Mint would have saved the public

---

[*] Lyman H. Low described 183 varieties of hard times tokens in *Hard Times Tokens* (Originally published in New York, 1899; Supplemented in 1906; Reprinted in 1955 and 1977.) In recent years, Russell Rulau extended Low's work in his *Standard Catalog of United States Tokens, 1700-1900* (Iola Wisconsin; Krause Publications; 1994.) Both systems are used to describe these token. Rulau's work is among the best numismatic books.

[†] An extremely rare 1837 twenty-five cent token in German silver also is known. It is controversial and may be a later fabrication, perhaps by nineteenth century dealer Charles Ira Bushnell. (Rulau, p.81.)

39

millions and he would have gone down in history as a hero.[891] In 1856 Congress and the U.S. Mint reduced the size of the cent. For the new small cents, Mint Director James Ross Snowden chose a pinkish alloy of 88% copper/12% nickel and a flying eagle motif by Chief Engraver, Christian Gobrecht. The new cents, though made from an alloy inferior to Feuchtwanger's, were very similar in appearance. It seems the good doctor had been right all along.

(Left) 1837 Feuchtwanger cent, variety Rulau 5-H.1. (Right) 1857 U.S. flying eagle cent.

Still other exceptions include a series of holed election medalets that honor Martin Van Buren and William Harrison. These are excluded from the list of true hard times tokens. Nonetheless, they are contemporaries that appear to have circulated in some quarters.

Brass 1840 election medalet. Obverse: [military bust of William Henry Harrison] MAJ: GEN^L. W. H. HARRISON / BORN FEB. 9. 1773. Reverse: [log cabin, with whiskey barrel] THE PEOPLES CHOICE IN THE YEAR 1840. This humble relic opens a window into the culture and politics of an earlier, simpler time.

Two 1838 designs are exceptional for their use of kneeling slaves to make anti-slavery statements. The New York-based American Anti-Slavery Society issued these pieces late in 1837. On the more common variety, the slave is a woman. A male version was planned but never advanced beyond the pattern stage. The questions, "Am I not a woman & a sister?" and "Am I not a Man & a brother?," both common in anti-slavery rhetoric of the era, originated in England and had appeared on an earlier series of British tokens. The issuance of the American versions coincided with the abolition of slavery by a number of Caribbean entities.

1838 Low 54, Rulau HT-81. Obverse: [Kneeling Female Slave] AM I NOT A WOMAN & A SISTER 1838; Reverse: [Wreath] UNITED STATES OF AMERICA / LIBERTY 1838. In this piece can be seen the growing social consciousness that would be mobilized in the latter half of the Civil War.

At the time, however, Andrew Jackson's desire to abolish the Bank of the United States was as polarizing as anyone else's attempts at abolishing slavery. The 1834, Low 8/ Rulau HT-9, token is representative of the anti-Jackson sentiment. It links the demise of the Bank (*PERISH CREDIT*) with economic downfall (*PERISH COMMERCE*) and touts these events as *MY* [i.e., Jackson's] *VICTORY*. It also adds *DOWN WITH THE BANK* as Jackson's battle cry. Its obverse depicts Jackson as a running boar to symbolize his rural background. On the boar's side are the words *MY THIRD HEAT*, alluding to an anticipated third presidential term. The reverse features Old Hickory's bust and refers to the tokens as *MY* [Jackson's] *SUBSTITUTE*

FOR THE U. S. BANK. It adds *MY EXPERIMENT, MY CURRENCY* and *MY GLORY.* To Jackson's friends, victory and glory referred to his military successes. Referring to his economic policies in the same terms is blatant sarcasm.

1834 Low 8/Rulau HT-9

Other tokens offered similar digs at Jackson. The obverse of the 1834 token, Low 12/Rulau HT-25, features a blind Jackson walking awkwardly with a sword and moneybags. It played on the fears of those who saw danger in his control of both military and fiscal policy. On Low 51/Rulau HT-70, *I TAKE THE RESPONSIBILITY* and the image of Jackson sitting in a treasury chest with sword and moneybag in hand convey the same message. The circumscribed words *THE CONSTITUTION AS I UNDERSTAND IT* came from Jackson's second inaugural address. Critics used the phrase to cynically imply that he held no regard for the Constitution. Elsewhere, the use of *VETO* further reinforced the perception of over-used executive power,[892] particularly as it referred to his 1832 veto of the Bank's re-charter.

In speeches, Jackson often referred to Jefferson, who called for smaller government that served the common man (i.e., *A PLAIN SYSTEM VOID OF POMP.*) The balking donkey that became the symbol of the Democratic Party and the phrase *ROMAN FIRMNESS* allude to Jackson's legendary stubbornness. A Jackson nickname, "Jack," also may have been inspirational in the donkey's conception. The donkey also represents Jackson's balking at a proposal to print paper money. At the time, the Bank of the United States followed policies that supported paper or credit currency. Another dig, *L.L.D.* on the donkey's side, sarcastically refers to the honorary law degree bestowed on Jackson by Harvard College in 1832.[893]

The Democratic donkey is born:

(Left) 1834 Low 12 /Rulau HT-25.

(Middle) 1833 Low 51 /Rulau HT-70.

(Bottom) 1837 Low 19 /Rulau HT-33.

As Jackson's successor, Martin Van Buren's polices also were attacked fiercely. On Low 19/Rulau HT-33, for example, the legend *I FOLLOW IN THE STEPS OF MY ILLUSTRIOUS PREDECESSOR* is from Van Buren's inaugural address. The tortoise on its obverse carries a chest labeled *U. S. TREASURY*. Under the tortoise are the words *FISCAL AGENT*, referring to the slowness of Van Buren's sub-treasury system that used banks to transfer funds to the states. This practice often was referred to as Van Buren's *EXECUTIVE EXPERIMENT*.[894]

Martin Van Buren. Ca. 1844 unsigned lithograph after D. Dickinson. Source: Library of Congress, Prints & Photographs Division, LC-USZ62-95455.

Other tokens refer to specific policy events. One such group features the mythical Phoenix, rising from the flames, with the legend *SUBSTITUTE FOR SHIN PLASTERS*. This stems from Jackson's 1836 ordering of agents who handled public money to stop accepting paper currency in payment of public debts such as for the purchase of land. The move caused a draining of specie from the East to satisfy needs in the West. A panic ensued in the East, coinciding with one in England. Loans were called, businesses failed and a bank run began in May 1837. On May 10, to slow the collapse, Jackson ordered the suspension of government payments in specie (*SPECIE PAYMENTS SUSPENDED*.) The result was disastrous. In November a convention was held to discuss resumption of specie payments. This is indicated by *NOV*$^{\underline{R}}$ on the obverse of Low 47A/Rulau HT-66A. The re-emergence of prosperity is depicted as a Phoenix (specie payments) rising from the ashes of burning "shinplasters," a slang term for the worthless paper money that Jackson sought to eliminate.[895]

(Left) 1837 Low 47A/Rulau HT-66A.
(Right) Mock shinplaster, published in 1837 by Henry R. Robinson, 52 Courtlandt Street, New York. He promises to redeem the note by paying Thomas Hart Benton, or the bearer, fifty cents in "Counterfeit Caricatures." Dated May 10, the day Jackson suspended specie payments. On it, Jackson rides a pig that is galloping toward the edge of a cliff. He is chasing the "gold humbug" butterfly that represents his attempts to curtail the amount of circulating paper money relative to specie. He thinks he is close ("By the Eternal!! I'll have it, Benton!") Benton, on a jackass, rides behind, cheering him on ("Go it thou Roman!! A greater man ne'er lived in the tide of times!!") His whip is a quill, called "Expunger," alluding to an attempt by Benton to expunge records of an 1834 censure against Jackson. Van Buren, riding a fox and dropping his crown, has cunningly parted ways with Jackson, taking a downward path toward the Bank ("Although I follow in the footsteps of Jackson it is expedient, at this time, to deviate a little!!") Nicholas Biddle stands atop the Bank, watching the scene. Source: Library of Congress, Prints and Photographs Division, LC-USZ62-1582. (Shown greatly reduced.)

1838 Low 55/Rulau HT-63; Note LOCOFOCO on the obverse figure's headband. The figure bears a subtle resemblance to the one on 1839 booby head large cents. (Chapter 12.)

A comical 1838 token, Low 55/Rulau HT-63, recalls an October 29, 1835, Democratic caucus at Tammany Hall in New York. That night, two factions packed the house with supporters who argued over a Congressional nominee. To end the meeting at a time advantageous to their side, one group caused the gas that lit the room to be turned off. The other faction rose to the occasion, producing candles and strike-anywhere matches called "Locofocos."* Newspapers reported the triumph of the Locofocos and the name became associated with the entire Democratic Party.[896] It was not long until it appeared on a token whose obverse depicts a head that could only be described as "goofy," surrounded by stars and the date *1838*. On a U.S. large cent of the period, Liberty wears a headband emblazoned with her name. On the token, the headband reads *LOCOFOCO*. Its reverse features a circular wreath with a circumscribed legend that refers to soldier, turned Missouri Congressman, turned Senator, Thomas Hart Benton. Benton had served under Jackson in the War of 1812. The two did not get along and, in a Nashville hotel brawl, in 1813, Benton's brother, Jesse, twice shot Jackson. One bullet could not be removed until 1832, and then without anesthetic, but the 1813 wounds had healed without serious effect.[897] In politics, Benton and Old Hickory became allies, with Benton as the country's most powerful and outspoken proponent of Jackson's fiscal policy. The token's reverse legend, *BENTON EXPERIMENT,* alludes to his role in supporting Jackson's policies. *MINT DROP* could refer directly to a batch run at the mint, or it may be using mint candy as a metaphor for money.†

The "ship of state" metaphor also is frequently used on period political tokens. One such piece, Low 62/Rulau HT-20, depicts a doomed ship with *EXPERIMENT* on its side crashing into rocks. The legend reads *VAN BUREN METALLIC CURRENT 1837*. The opposite side depicts a ship labeled *CONSTITUTION* sailing smoothly within the legend *WEBSTER CREDIT CURRENT* [sic] *1841*.

As a U.S. Senator from Massachusetts, Daniel Webster strongly supported the Bank of the United States and credit currency. He opposed Jackson on many issues, but the two worked together in diffusing the *Nullification Crisis*. Roots of that crisis ran deep. After the War of 1812 the industrial North had sought to implement protectionist policies. Southerners knew that such measures would hurt their positions in the marketplace and opposed tariffs in favor of free trade. In 1816 the protectionists had enough influence to insure passage of a minor revenue-raising tariff. As the post-war economy cooled, protectionist enthusiasm and influence increased. In 1820 a much stronger measure passed the House, but failed in the Senate. By 1828 the two sides were clearly divided, with protectionists holding a majority. John C. Calhoun and Robert Hayne, both of South Carolina, led the free-traders. Unable to win with a majority, they asserted the old, controversial doctrine of nullification wherein a state could render null and void any federal law that it deemed unconstitutional or unjust.

---

* Locofoco is concocted from the notion of "loco" meaning "location" (or "here") and "foco," alluding to "light." The implication is "light where you are" or "strike anywhere."

† A "drop" is a small hard candy, of mint, fruit or other flavor, that is made by pouring a hot mixture into a mold that has recesses for multiple pieces. The mixture flows through channels that connect the recesses. When the candy cools, it is removed from the mold and literally dropped, to separate individual pieces – Hence, the name.

Webster used James Madison's reasoning to set a rhetorical trap and logically dismantle the doctrine, in a historic 1830 debate against Hayne.[898] Nevertheless, South Carolina formally adopted the nullification doctrine in 1832 and, in doing so, moved to the very brink of secession. It was states' rights late, Civil War early.

(Top) Low 62/Rulau HT-20.
(Middle) Low 44/Rulau HT-69. Note the reappearance of Jackson in a money chest.
(Bottom) 1841 Low 69/HT-58. On some 1841 varieties, the Webster ship appears opposite an elaborate NOT ONE CENT reverse (see below,) as on Low 58/HT-16.

Webster had used powerful words to win the nullification debate, but the real deterrent to secession was Jackson's threat to use any force necessary to insure preservation of the Union. In the end, South Carolina backed down and a compromise reduced the tariff over time. The settlement temporarily saved both the Union and face for all involved. For all his fiscal, political and social warts, Jackson's stand against nullification is worthy of a Lincoln or a Washington. As much for his legendary military performances at New Orleans and in Florida, it is why his image still occupies American twenty-dollar bills.

During this period two new political parties replaced the old Federalists and Republicans: Jacksonian Democrats and the National Republicans. The latter became the Whig Party. As a Whig, Webster held presidential aspirations in 1836 but garnered little support. When fellow Whig, William Henry Harrison, was elected in 1840, Webster became Secretary of State. Harrison died a month after his inauguration and John Tyler assumed the presidency. Tyler parted ways with the Whig leadership and the Harrison cabinet abandoned ship, but Webster remained until 1843. He returned to the Senate and served until 1850, without ever realizing his executive ambition.

"Plain Sewing Done Here," a ca. 1834 political cartoon depicting Henry Clay attempting to pacify Jackson by sewing shut his mouth. Source: Library of Congress, Prints and Photographs Division, LC-USZ62-92612.

The architect of the tariff compromise was Kentuckian, Henry Clay, who was then a senator. His work in ending the Nullification Crisis and in the Compromises of 1820 and 1850 earned him the title "The Great Pacificator." Aside from presiding over the "bargain" that gave John Quincy Adams the presidency, Clay ran unsuccessfully for President himself as a National Democrat or a Whig six times between 1824 and 1848.

1840 Low 193 / Rulau HT-79B (silvered. HT-79A is unsilvered.) The obverse features a draped bust of Henry Clay with legend: HENRY CLAY AND THE AMERICAN SYSTEM. The reverse simply reads UNITED WE STAND.

Similar tokens tout the virtues of Jackson, Van Buren, William Henry Harrison, William H. Seward and Gulian C. Verplanck. The Seward and Verplanck tokens replace the wreath with an eagle and are believed to date from around 1834. On the tokens both men are referred to as *OUR* [i.e., New York's] *NEXT GOV*^{NR} and A *FAITHFUL FRIEND TO OUR COUNTRY*. One Seward variety calls its subject *THE GLORY AND PRIDE OF OUR NATION*.

Many varieties of hard times tokens directly imitate U.S. large cents. Their obverse figures resemble the head of Liberty on official cents, with only minor differences. Their reverses have wreaths as on their official counterparts, but with altered legends. One such alteration reads *MILLIONS FOR DEFENCE* [sic] *NOT ONE CENT FOR TRIBUTE,* with *NOT ONE CENT* prominently featured where one would expect to find *ONE CENT*. The full phrase again refers to Jefferson's refusal to pay protection money to the Barbary Coast pirates. It was a cry heard first during the 1790's XYZ affair, wherein French officials attempted to extort bribes from American envoys.* On the tokens, *NOT ONE CENT* simply was intended to evade legal entanglements.

Use of the Liberty obverse theme was not limited to patriotic tokens. It also was used opposite several commercial or *store card* reverses. Likewise, the *MILLIONS FOR DEFENCE* reverse theme appears opposite several commercial obverses.

Faces of Liberty: *(Top) 1837 Low 33/HT-48. (Middle) Liberty is combined with the suspension of specie payments on (Bottom) Low 67/HT-68.*

* In the late 1790s Franco-American relations soured after Jay's Treaty of 1795 brought England and the U.S. closer. President Washington sent Charles Pinckney to smooth things out. As the new President, John Adams sent Elbridge Gerry and John Marshall to join Pinckney. In exchange for seeing the American envoys, the French foreign minister Charles Maurice de Talleyrand tried to extort bribes through intermediaries known only as X, Y and Z. The popular myth is that Pinckney's answer was "Millions for defense, sir, but not one cent for tribute." When news of the "XYZ Affair" reached the U.S., pro-British/anti-French factions were outraged. However, Adams eventually sent another peace party and the tension was diffused.

In another marriage of patriotism and commercialism, the Richards token below pays tribute to the Marquis de Lafayette, Washington's idealistic and naively ambitious French protégé. Americans remember his youthful enthusiasm for their revolution and, later, for that of France. In 1824, however, it was an aging, nearly penniless Lafayette who returned to America for a final triumphant tour. Huge crowds welcomed him wherever he went. His visit re-kindled sweet memories of Washington and the struggle for independence. In gratitude Congress voted to give Lafayette money, $200,000 in 6 percent bonds, and a whole township, thirty-six square miles, in Florida. He was embarrassed, but accepted the gifts to avoid offending his adoring hosts. Not even death could mute Lafayette's infatuation with America. When the end came in 1834, as he had requested, his French grave was covered with American soil. He and his son, George Washington Lafayette, had returned from the 1824 tour, to France, with a canvas bag full of hallowed ground from Bunker Hill. The Richards's token commemorates his death by featuring a standing Lafayette, with cane and top hat, as portrayed in a popular contemporary painting by Art Sheffer.[899]

(Left) An older Lafayette. Jacques Reich after Samuel F.B. Morse (inventor of the telegraph.) Source: Mace (170.) (Center) 1834 Low 83/Rulau HT-150. The obverse hails Lafayette as A FRIEND TO AMERICAN FREEDOM who DIED MAR[CH] 20, 1834. The reverse is a pure store card, advertising H. M. & E. I. RICHARDS, MANUFACTURERS OF JEWELRY NEAR THE UNION HOUSE in ATTLEBORO, MASS. The Richards' firm also made hard times tokens, including their own. Edward Hulseman made dies for the Richards. (Right) The same token counterstamped four times and made into a "humdinger." The counterstamp reads WM. HOWE. Howe may have been the Detroit bookseller who had his own tokens made during the Civil War. Humdingers were toys made by passing a string through holes in a button or holed coin. By pulling the string, the coin was made to spin, producing a humming sound. Many early coppers met ends as humdingers, buttons, gears, fence post markers or wheels for pie crimpers.

With liberty and commerce for all:

(Left) 1837 Low 114/Rulau HT-249 is a store card for J. H. DAYTON UNION STEAM WASHING EST. at 17TH ST. NEAR 5TH AVENUE in N.Y.. Dayton offered WASHING DONE FOR SHIPS, ST[EAM]BOATS, HOTELS & PRIVATE FAMILIES.

(Right) 1837 Rulau HT-284 is a store card for GEORGE A JARVIS, WINE & TEA DEALER at 142 GRAND at the CORNER OF ELM STREET in NEW YORK.

(Left) 1837 Low 247A /Rulau HT-240 advertises ACCOMMODATION at CENTRE MARKET in N. YORK's 14TH WARD. The building is reminiscent of Boston's Quincy Market, where customers still walk through rows of merchants and cart vendors who vie for accommodations. (Right) The obverse of Low 97/Rulau HT-293 remembers the MERCHANT'S EXCHANGE OF WALL ST. in N. YORK. BUILT 1827 BURNT [sic] 1835. The reverse carries the familiar NOT ONE CENT legend.

In making tokens for different merchants, coiners often re-used the same or related dies to create new varieties. For example, the striking federal eagle used on Samuel Maycock's store card also was paired with an advertisement for umbrella vendor, Henry Crossman. Other store cards for Maycock and Crossman feature crude versions of a Liberty obverse.

A – 1837 Low 125/Rulau HT-289 advertises S. MAYCOCK & CO. at 36 CITY HALL PLACE in N-Y. SAML. MAYCOCK and JOHN HAGUE manufactured EVERPOINTED PENCIL CASE[S].

B – 1837 Low 126/Rulau HT-290 also advertises Maycock's business, but uses a federal eagle to do so.

C – 1837 Low 113/Rulau HT-244 is the eagle version of Henry Crossman's store card.

D – 1837 Low 112/Rulau HT-243 advertises H[ENRY] CROSSMAN MANUFACTURER [OF UMBRELLAS] at 92½ CHATHAM ST. [in] N.Y.

(Right) W. A. Handy's store card used another version of the federal eagle to advertise his Providence, Rhode Island business. 1834 Low 78/Rulau HT-427 advertises his WHOLESALE & RETAIL MERCHANT [and] *TAILOR business at NO. 1 WASHINGTON ROW.*

Patriotism and nostalgia aside, in a group of purely commercial tokens can be seen the burgeoning availability of consumer goods and the relentless overtaking of Jefferson's agrarian democracy by industrial capitalism. In some cases the two sides of these commercial tokens even represent two different merchants. The double advertising piece below, for example, was made by H. M. and E. I. Richards for Nathaniel March (obverse) and William Simes (reverse.)

1837 Low 124/Rulau HT-194. One side features NATH^{L}. MARCH BOOKSELLER & STATIONER at N^{O}. 7 EXCHANGE BUILDINGS in PORTSMOUTH, N.H. The other side advertises WILLIAM SIMES & C^{O}., DEALERS IN TEAS, WINES & GROCERIES at N^{O}. 1 PEIRCE'S BUILDINGS in Portsmouth.

One of the most complex commercial hard times tokens touts the prowess of an Attleboro, Massachusetts, button making establishment. Its obverse copies a trade award presented to the firm by the American Institute. It shows Liberty or Commerce seated among symbols of patriotism, science, shipping, agriculture and industry.

1833 Low 75/Rulau 152 copies a medal given by the AMERICAN INSTITUTE in NEW YORK. Below NEW YORK is Edward Hulseman's "H" mark. The reverse reads COPY OF A MEDAL AWARDED TO ROBINSON 'S JONES & C^{O} FOR THE BEST MILITARY, NAVAL, SPORTING & PLAIN FLAT BUTTONS. The company was reorganized as R. W. Robinson and Co. in 1836. 1836 Low 103/Rulau HT-154 reflects the change and adds GOLD in front of MEDAL.[900]

Purely commercial tokens:

1835 Low 92 / Rulau HT-353 is for a TROY [,NY] provider of bookkeeping services such as the calculation of interest tables. Its legends read BUCKLIN'S INTEREST TABLES and BUCKLIN's BOOK KEEPING. Bucklin's tokens often are poorly executed.

1837 Low 107 / Rulau HT-219 tells of HENRY ANDERSON['S] MAMMOTH BOOT, a CHEAP BOOT & SHOE STORE at CHATHAM SQUARE in NEW YORK. The Mammoth Boot was advertised heavily in period newspapers.

A

A – 1835 Low 273 / Rulau HT-307 was made for ROBERT B. RUGGLES, GOLD BEATER, 225 CANAL ST^{T}., NEW YORK.

B

B – 1833 Low 74/Rulau HT-428 is EPHRAIM A. HATHAWAY['S] store card for the CITY COAL YARD in PROVIDENCE, R.I. There, one could buy ANTHRACITE and BITUMINOUS COAL, both vital commodities for an industrial economy. The firm is rumored to have covertly supported the Confederate cause during the Civil War.

C

C – Boston merchant Alfred Willard used 1835 Low 328/Rulau HT-171 to advertise his business. Its obverse features an elaborate comb around which are the words ALFRED WILLARD, 149 WASHINGTON S^{T}., BOSTON. Its reverse lists Willard's product lines: IMPORTER OF JEWELRY, FANCY GOODS, CUTLERY &^{CT} BRUSHES, PERFUMERY, COMBS &^{CT}. WHOLESALE OR RETAIL.

D

D – Taunton, Mass. was home to another brush company. The obverse of 1835 Low 300, Rulau HT-181 features a boar, a prime source of brush bristles. On its side, in script, are the words CASH FOR BRISTLES. The obverse legend reads ALL KINDS OF BRUSHES MADE TO ORDER. OFFICE IN BOSTON, NO. 12 ELM ST. The Boston office presumably was a marketing outlet. The reverse gives the factory's location: JOHN J. ADAMS NO. 11 MAIN ST., TAUNTON MASS. MANUFACTURER OF EVERY DESCRIPTION OF BRUSHES WHOLESALE & RETAIL.

The two pieces below are representative of tokens that are harbingers of the new industrial era in America. One of them refers to the multi-functional machine shop run by Nathaniel Starbuck and Son in Troy, New York. The products and industrial processes listed on Starbuck's tokens are more worthy of a modern factory than a craftsman's shop. Likewise, the complex woodworking machine invented by S. B. Schenk is indicative of technological change. The machine allegedly could plane and shape eighteen feet of board per minute, an impressive feat to anyone who has hand planed rough wood.

The tokens of Starbuck and Schenk are altogether appropriate subjects with which to end discussion of American private coinage. They are separated by a great cultural schism from the earliest American coins and tokens and from the old frontier barter economy. Great changes were afoot and neither America nor its spending money ever would be quite the same. In time, millions upon millions of monotonously uniform metal disks were spat from steam powered industrial presses to be used by Americans, a growing number of whom worked in factories themselves.

(Top) 1835 Low 284 / Rulau HT-368 features N. STARBUCK & SON [in] TROY [NY] AIR FURNACE, PLOUGHS, PLOUGH CASTING AND SLEIGH SHOES. MILL CEARING. POTASH KETTLES. CAULDRONS. The reverse features an industrial screw, a Starbuck's specialty that was a very difficult item to manufacture until the mid-19th century. The token reads MACHINE SHOP. TURNING. BORING. SCREWS FOR PAPER, OIL & CIDER MILLS, &C. (Bottom) 1834 Low 84 / Rulau HT-158 pictures and describes the WOODWORKING PATENT PLANING MACHINE MADE BY S. B. SCHENK [of] ATTLEBORO, MASS. The reverse says THIS MACHINE IS CAPABLE OF PLANING, TOUNGING & GROOVING, OR JOINTING, OR RABBITING [sic] 18 FEET OF BOARDS OR PLANK IN A MINUTE.

By 1844 the hard times had abated. Stephen C. Foster probably was referring more to general melancholy than to Jackson-Van Buren fiscal policies when he later penned the song "Hard Times." Nonetheless, his lyrics are an appropriate epitaph for the 1833 to 1844 period:

> *Let us pause in life's pleasures and count its many tears,*
> *While we all sup sorrow with the poor;*
> *There's a song that will linger forever in our ears;*
> *Oh Hard times come again no more.*
>
> *Tis the song, the sigh of the weary,*
> *Hard times, hard times, come again no more*
> *Many days you have lingered around my cabin door;*
> *Oh hard times come again no more...* [Foster, c.1855.]

Manifest Destiny's collision with Mexico, California's gold rush, the Compromise of 1850, *Uncle Tom's Cabin*, the Mississippi's first bridge, Harper's Ferry and Fort Sumter all quickly followed. In these tumultuous years leading up to and including the Civil War, hard times tokens and the South's regional gold coins inspired other private issues: merchant tokens, western territorial gold coins, small "copperhead" tokens and metal-encased postage stamps, to name a few. Copperheads, in particular, mirror hard times tokens in that they were produced when small change was in very short supply and were used primarily in the North. Whereas war between Jacksonians and the Bank spawned their predecessors, it was war between South and North that inspired the copperheads. As emergency issues, even the federal government's fractional notes of the 1860's shared their purpose with the hard times tokens.

The private issues of 1789 to 1844 hid a quiet revolution in America's coinage. As tokens, shinplasters and foreign incidental coins filled the new republic's commercial shortfalls, the U.S. Mint slowly and painfully evolved from a beleaguered colony of craftsmen into a major industrial operation. The first shots of the half-century-long revolution were fired in 1791.

12: COMING OF AGE, THE U. S. MINTS (1792 TO 1840)

THE SMALL BEGINNING (1792)

Resolved by the Senate and House of Representatives of the United States of America in Congress assembled, That a mint shall be established under such regulations as shall be directed by law.

Resolved, That the President of the United States be, and is hereby authorized to cause to be engaged, such principal artists as shall be necessary to carry the preceding resolution into effect, and to stipulate the terms and conditions of their service, and also to cause to be procured such apparatus as shall be requisite for the same purpose.

...Approved, March 3, 1791 by George Washington, President of the United States....[901]

The time had come. The catalyst was the January 1791 submission to Congress of a very thorough examination of the country's hard money by the Secretary of the Treasury, Alexander Hamilton. He had been directed to do so eight months earlier by the House of Representatives. The lengthy report, simply called *Report of the Secretary of the Treasury on the Subject of a Mint*, reviewed the existing coinage situation and then very clearly and logically framed the central issues for the coming debate: What should be the nature of the country's monetary standards? Assuming that both gold and silver are to be used, what should be the ratio between them? What alloys should be used and in what proportions? How to pay for the coinage? What denominations and sizes of coins should be minted? In what numbers and what devices should each bear? Should the acceptance of foreign coins continue to be allowed? At what rate and for how long?[902]

The British token kings, such as Boulton and Watt and Obadiah Westwood, were in the running for contracts that would have made an American mint unnecessary. Boulton and Watt even entered formal discussions to that end and, at one point, their huge Soho-based firm was asked to consider establishing a branch in America. For his part, Thomas Jefferson vehemently opposed the use of private contractors, attempting instead to hire the talented Swiss engraver, Jean Peter Droz (or Drost, as it sometimes appears,) away from his Paris home and his job with Boulton.[903] Jefferson's views on the subject had been greatly influenced by the essays of Thomas Paine,[904] who argued for a full separation from European dependencies. Contract coinage proponents eventually came around to the idea of a government-run mint, even if only for a short time. They were doubtless helped in their decision by the Fugio debacle. The man whose opinion mattered most also recognized the need for a transfusion of circulating coins and longed for the mint to become reality. In an address to Congress on October 25, 1791, the first President made clear his views:

...The disorders in the existing currency, and especially the scarcity of small change, a scarcity so peculiarly distressing to the poorer classes, [I] *strongly recommend the carrying into immediate effect the resolution already entered into concerning the establishment of a mint. Measures have been taken pursuant to that resolution for procuring some of the most necessary artists, together with the requisite apparatus....*[905]

Washington's admonition touched off a flurry of Congressional activity in late 1791 and early 1792. More than a decade after he first championed his own plan, Robert Morris hastily prepared a coinage bill, introducing it on December 21, 1791. In the debate that followed, Hancock's Washington cents were considered and rejected on the strength of anti-monarchical sentiment. Getz's patterns met a similar fate. In the end, Morris's coinage bill was modified to require:

> *...That, upon the said coins* [see below] *respectively, there shall be the following devices and legends, namely: Upon one side of each of the said coins there shall be* an impression emblematic of liberty, *with an inscription of the word Liberty, and the year of the coinage; and upon the reverse of each of the gold and silver coins there shall be the figure or representation of an eagle, with this inscription, "United States of America" and upon the reverse of each of the copper coins, there shall be an inscription which shall express the denomination of the piece....*[Section 10, Mint Act of April 2, 1792.]

On April 2, 1792, the final bill became law as the Mint Act [of 1792.] It was part Hamilton, part Jefferson and part wishful thinking. In twenty sections, it established both the United States' system of money and the U.S. Mint, with all its officers, rules and procedures.* Some sections would have unexpected and lasting repercussions. Section eleven, for example, resolved the question of how gold should be valued relative to silver. However, the ratio that it inflexibly set at 15:1 soon would become an issue as the world's relative valuation of the two metals shifted. Section fifteen forced the Mint to return on demand a depositor's own metal in coined form, a requirement that proved very costly and inefficient. Section sixteen made the Mint's gold and silver coins "lawful tender," but afforded no such status to copper coins, a situation that continued until 1965. Consequently, no one was required to accept them and few did. The act was far from perfect. Still it was firm commitment to federal coinage that never before had existed. The long-awaited money that it defined consisted of:

- **Gold "eagles,"** each equivalent to ten dollars. Eagle coins were to weigh 270 grains at 11/12 (0.917) fineness, containing 247.5 grains of pure gold. The remaining 1/12 was to be mostly copper with small amounts of silver. Fractional issues included a half eagle ($5) and a quarter eagle ($2.50) that were to be proportioned accordingly. Hamilton had argued for a gold dollar but no provision was made for it.[906] Note that a dollar would have contained 24.75 grains, a fraction more than a pennyweight, of gold.

- **Silver "dollars,"** equivalent to eight-reales. Fractional parts were established as half dollars, quarter dollars, tenth dollars (dismes) and twentieth dollars (half-dismes.) The law dictated that a dollar should weigh 416 grains at 1,485/1,664 (about 0.892) fineness, with the remainder in copper. A dollar thus contained 371.25 grains of pure silver. The fractional denominations were to be proportioned accordingly. Also, note that 371.25 ÷ 24.75 = 15, conforming to the 15:1 ratio of gold's value to silver's.

- **Coppers "cents"*** based on British halfpence, but made deliberately heavier at 264 grains,† (note on next page) twice as much as the half cents that were also authorized. Both denominations were to be made of pure copper.

---

* For the full text of the Mint Act of 1792, see *The United States Statues at Large*, the Second Congress, Session I, Acts of April 2, 1792, Statute I, Chapter XVI, volume 1, pages 246-251.

* Some early prices are written in British form (i.e., [pounds].[shillings].[pence,]) In the new system, this became [eagles].[dollars].[cents].[mills] For example, "$123.45½" might be written as "12.3.455" or even "12.3.45.5."

David Rittenhouse. After Charles Willson Peale. Image ©iStockphoto.com/HultonArchive.

An ailing, sixty-year-old David Rittenhouse was appointed the first Mint Director, at a salary of $2,000 a year. He was Robert Morris's second choice, behind Francis Hopkinson,[907] who recently had died of a seizure, at fifty-three years of age. Rittenhouse was an accomplished scientist whose talents often are overlooked in the shadow of Franklin. He was born near Germantown, Pennsylvania and there showed an early aptitude for mathematics. As a surveyor he extended the Mason-Dixon Line and helped establish several major geo-political boundaries. He built clocks, advanced surveying instruments and very intricate astronomical devices, called orreries, that precisely imitated the movements of heavenly bodies. His surveying instruments were in constant demand because of their unparalleled quality. He mastered Sir Isaac Newton's *Principia* early in life, made detailed and very useful astronomical observations and may have built the first telescope assembled in America.[908] His understandings of mathematics, mechanics, philosophy and physics all were essential to the early U. S. Mint. Perhaps just as importantly, he was a man of great commitment, integrity and experience, having served in wartime on Congress's Committee of Safety and more recently as Pennsylvania's treasurer. He also had been a consultant to Benjamin Dudley on minting the 1783 patterns. In many ways Rittenhouse was like the legendary mathematician and scientist, Sir Isaac Newton, who had filled the mint director's role in England decades earlier.

That was London. This was Philadelphia. In mid-July, 1792, Rittenhouse obtained permission to begin minting minor coins,[909] even though the facility that the Mint eventually would occupy remained an old distillery. Several workers were hired in advance, including Henry Voigt and Adam Eckfeldt. The Mint and the country were fortunate to have these two men of great ingenuity and talent. Voigt, a Dutchman, was a watchmaker who had a reputation for invention. Before his tenure with the Mint, he made America's first steamboat, John Fitch's, possible by inventing a special condenser and other components. He also assisted Rittenhouse in the construction of his orreries.[910] With Droz unavailable, Voigt tentatively was made Chief Coiner a salary of $1,500 per year. He was expected to serve part-time as engraver as well.[911]

Adam Eckfeldt was the son of John Jacob Eckfeldt, who had helped with Robert Morris's 1783 patterns. The younger Eckfeldt learned the blacksmith and machinist trades and had built a foundry to make nails. These skills brought him to the attention of Mint officials. He built much of the Mint's early coining equipment, including the first of its five screw presses and an automatic planchet feeder that he had invented.[912] He received a $500 annual salary. Eckfeldt succeeded Voigt as Chief Coiner in 1814 and remained in that post until his resignation in 1839. However, his most enduring legacy was the long line of Mint employees who were his kin. His son, Jacob, for example, served for forty years as Assayer beginning in 1832.

---

* Gold dollars (1849-1889) and double eagles ($20, 1849-1916 and 1920-1933) were added when gold was discovered in California. Bronze two cent pieces (1864-1873,) silver trimes (three cent pieces, 1851-1873,) cupro-nickel trimes (1865-1889,) nickels (1866-,) double-dimes (twenty-cent pieces, 1875-1878,) three-dollar gold coins (1854-1873) and four-dollar "stellas" (1879-1880) were added still later. Some of the new denominations were responses to regional shortages, others to spurious political arguments.

In an odd move, Washington assigned the Mint to Jefferson's Department of State rather than Hamilton's Department of the Treasury.[913] As a result, or perhaps as the cause, Jefferson remained extraordinarily intimate with the nation's mint and money. He had invested considerable influence and intellectual capital in their creation and naturally wanted to see the experiment succeed. It was his monetary system that Congress adopted. It was he who most wanted a federal mint and he who sought to lure Droz. It was his friend, Rittenhouse, whom he wanted and received as Mint Director. It was another of his friends, Dr. Benjamin Rush, the nation's premier doctor and chemist, whom he helped place in the Mint Treasurer's role (in 1797.) It would come as no surprise when Jefferson and Hamilton later clashed over control of the Mint.[914] For the time being, however, the nation's coinage was Jefferson's baby.

On July 11, 1792, Jefferson recorded in his account book that seventy-five dollars in silver had been delivered to be coined. Just two days later, another entry records that fifteen hundred half dismes had been received from "the Mint," even though it did not physically exist. The work took place in John Harper's cellar. (Recall from the discussion of Peter Getz's patterns, that Harper was a saw maker from Trenton, whose home/saw factory was at Sixth and Cherry Streets in Philadelphia.) In 1844 Philadelphia numismatist and antiquarian, James McAllister, having interviewed Adam Eckfeldt, wrote a memorandum that confirms the mint location as Harper's cellar.[915] The question of how raw silver so quickly could be transformed into coins, particularly by an interim operation in a saw maker's cellar, remains unanswered. One theory is that the silver delivered to be coined had already been processed into planchets with reeded edges and that the planchets were held until needed.[916] At any rate, it likely was on a single day, July 13, that fifteen hundred tiny silver half dismes, the first of many billions of United States coins, were made.[*917] Either Adam Eckfeldt or Henry Voigt probably struck them.

The identity of the half dismes' die maker is an old riddle that revolves around a Mr. Birch. No one ever has produced definitive proof of Birch's identity, but on cent patterns made in 1792, the Birch name appears in tiny letters at the base of the obverse bust. The style of the half dismes is similar enough to the cents that the same artist is likely behind both coins.

For decades, the prime suspect was Robert "Bob" Birch, a London-born New Yorker who advertised his painted portraits, engraving, hair lockets, etc., as well as "...Any curious Punch or Instrument made in steel, iron brass, &c."[918] All are items that fit a die maker's skills. Of late, however, attention has shifted to William Russell Birch, a successful British engraver, miniaturist and maker of cameos.[919] The catch is that he did not actually immigrate to Philadelphia until 1794, following the death of a wealthy patron. If William Birch was the engraver, how did the cent and half disme dies arrive in Philadelphia in 1792? Were they engraved in England and sent to America in 1792? Were they engraved in America, based on an imported example of William Birch's work? William Birch seems never to have landed a prominent position at the U.S. Mint. However, he was famous for making miniature copies of Washington portraits by Gilbert Stuart, another well-known artist who also would have a brush with coinage. Crosby cited references that Massachusetts' Jacob Perkins, whose name seems to touch ever more areas of early American history and numismatics, might have made some of the 1792 dies and even might have been considered for the Mint's top position.[920]

A controversial tradition holds that the silver used for the 1792 half dismes once graced Martha Washington's dinner table. Breen lent credence to this notion by observing that the

[*] See the end of Chapter 7 for a discussion of Simon Stevin von Brugge (Stevinus) and the word "disme." "Disme," which may have rhymed with "steam," was anglicized to "dime." (See page 441.)

surviving Mt. Vernon tableware all is Sheffield *plate,*[921] implying that the good stuff was taken for use elsewhere. Washington depositing silver and receiving it back as half dismes fits the intent of section fifteen and if anyone received expedited service, it would have been the President. Nevertheless, other evidence suggests that the silver was the government's.[922] The single known copper half disme is a *die trial*, struck as a test in softer metal to avoid damage that silver might have caused if the dies were inadequate or improperly mounted in the press.[*] In any case, President Washington evidently was proud of the tiny half dismes and took care to acknowledge them in his 1792 State of the Union Address, which he delivered in November:

> *...In execution of the authority given by the Legislature measures have been taken for engaging some artists from abroad to aid in the establishment of our mint. Others have been employed at home. Provision has been made of the requisite buildings, and these are now putting into proper condition for the purposes of the establishment. There has also been a small beginning in the coinage of half dismes, the want of small coins in circulation calling the first attention to them.*[923]

Obverses of these diminutive coins feature a left-facing bust of Liberty with the legend, *LIB*[ERTY] *PAR*[ENT] *of SCIENCE & INDUSTRY.* These encouraging words were used in some form on all subsequent 1792 pattern issues except those for the quarter dollar. The half dismes' reverses depict an eagle, wings spread in flight, with legend *UNI*[TED] *STATES OF AMERICA.* Below the eagle is the denomination, *HALF DISME* ★. As such, these are the world's first true decimal coins and, perhaps more so than the Continental Currency coins or the Fugio cents, they have a claim to being the first official coins of the United States. The 1844 McAllister memorandum relates Adam Eckfeldt's opinion that the half dismes were requested by the President for use as gifts and not as currency.[924] Eckfeldt's view notwithstanding, Washington's address makes it clear that they were much more than gifts or patterns. They were made to circulate. That they came into existence before the official mint facility was complete is inconsequential.

As for the Mint, Rittenhouse estimated on July 10, 1792, that the immediate cost would be \$10,000, including \$4,266.67 for the property, \$933.33 for repairs, wages and the like, and \$4,800 for fifteen tons of copper. Before the day was out Washington issued a warrant for the entire amount.[925] It was a strong vote of confidence for David Rittenhouse, who purchased lots and, on July 31, at ten in the morning, laid the foundation stone. During the summer and fall of 1792, buildings and equipment were made ready under the gaze of the President, a frequent visitor to the site. The main structure, the first of all U.S. Government-owned buildings, was completed, save internal accoutrements, on September 7.[926] Six pounds of copper was purchased on September 11 and, ten days later, two more coin presses arrived from Boulton and Watt. They had been ordered by Droz, on America's behalf. With the one made by Adam Eckfeldt, this brought the total to three.[*927] On October 6, fifteen gallons of rum were purchased and, on October 17, fifteen-and-a-half gallons more were added, hopefully for use in celebration of some milestone having been reached. On November 10 a pair of rollers was purchased for seventy dollars.[928] The buildup continued until, in time for Christmas, 1792, the property that had been the old Shubert Distillery at Seventh Street and Sugar Alley, between Market and Arch Streets, was transformed into the first United States Mint.

---

[*] A rumored example in tin or white metal has not been seen since the 1880's.

[*] The fourth press was purchased in 1794 from Hannah Ogden, the widow of General Matthias Ogden. Its was the press used by Ogden at Rahway and Elizabethtown. A fifth press was purchased in 1795. (Sheldon, pp.14-15.)

There, using an obverse die allegedly prepared by Adam Eckfeldt and a reverse die in the style of the mysterious Mr. Birch's, a handful of dismes were made. These attributions are based primarily on a letter by B. L. C. Wailes, of Natchez, Mississippi, who visited the Mint in 1829. The letter indirectly credits Eckfeldt with the dismes' obverse by saying that he made the first die used at the Mint.[929] The 1792 disme obverse, however, was executed by an artisan of considerable skill, perhaps more skill than would be expected of Adam Eckfeldt, a blacksmith himself and the son of another. Though no evidence for the claim can here be presented, this author believes that the disme obverse may be the work of Perkins, Wright (below,) Rittenhouse or even Droz. The reverse is indeed very much like that on the celebrated little "half sisters" (half dismes) and is likely part of the "Birch connection." Most surviving examples of these disme rarities are of copper, though a few exist in silver. Unlike the half dismes, all indisputably are patterns.

(Above) Facade of the first U.S. Mint. Source: Evans (13.)[930]

(Left) 1792 Eckfeldt/Birch(?) dime pattern. An unknown number were minted in silver at 41.6 grains. At least two silver examples with reeded edges, a few more than a dozen copper examples with reeded edges and two copper plain-edged examples are known to exist.

(Right) Wright's 1792 quarter dollar trial. Two are known in copper and four in white metal, all with reeded edges. (The third and fourth white metal specimens were discovered in 2002 [!,] in the holdings of the New York Historical Society.) White metal uniface strikings from each die also exist.

Pattern or trial status also befits the 1792 quarter dollars that used dies prepared by Joseph Wright, yet another well-known portrait artist. George and Martha sat for him and he was much in favor with the President. The elegance and simplicity of his quarter place it at the pinnacle of American coin design. His delicate obverse rendition of Liberty is absolutely timeless. For the reverse, Wright depicted an equally elegant eagle, prophetically perched atop the Western Hemisphere. Unfortunately, the issue never was to be as the dies broke during hardening, after initial die trials were completed.

Cent patterns also were made during this time. As authorized, cents were nearly 112 grains heavier than British halfpence and thus required a good deal of copper, a commodity that was becoming expensive. To remedy the problem, Henry Voigt suggested that cents could be made with small silver plugs embedded in their centers. By using silver valued at three-fourths of a cent and one-fourth of a cent worth of copper, the coins could be made physically smaller.

Using dies that he prepared, Voigt struck a handful of *silver-centered cents*, as well as some in billon and a few in copper. Jefferson supported the idea and sent the patterns, along with an explanatory letter, to Washington, a week before Christmas Day, 1792.[931]

1792 silver-centered cent. About a dozen genuine pieces with reeded edges exist, as do a small number of billon and solid copper pieces. At least one copper "doughnut" (i.e., struck without a silver plug) exists. Weights: Billon – 78.2 grains. Copper with silver plug – 69.12 grains. Copper without plugs – 63.1 grains.[932]

The reception was less than enthusiastic. It was not that bi-metallic coins were new. The proposed cents reprised 1680's halfpence of James II that used a copper plug inserted in tin. The memory of James's unpopular coins even may have played a role in the silver-centered cents' rejection. More likely, the cause of their rejection was the trouble and expense of making them. The experimental cents offered no real advantage over the large ones that Congress actually had approved and were noticeably smaller than the halfpence to which people were accustomed. Jefferson's letter also stated that Rittenhouse planned to make a few of the smaller pieces in pure copper and a few in a mixed alloy of silver and copper.[933] The existence of at least two reeded edge billon pieces indicates that other ways of incorporating silver were considered, though none was adopted. When a Mint building was demolished in 1911 to make way for the Frank H. Stewart Electric Company, workmen found two of the planchets for the silver-center cents in the area of what would have been the smelting room. The unlikely discovery suggests that Voigt's experimental patterns were made at the Mint and not in Harper's cellar or some other pre-Mint location.[934]

Birch's 1792 large cent pattern, first style, with curly hair.

Jefferson's December 18 letter to Washington also indicated that "...he [Rittenhouse] will make the real cent authorized by Congress, 4 times as big [at 264 grains.]"[935] These undoubtedly are the large coppers known as "Birch cents." Though they were as Congress demanded, they faired no better than the silver-centered cents. As did the Washington patterns by Hancock and Getz, Birch's cents had a perception problem. At the base of the reverse is the abbreviation *G*[EORGE] * *W*[ASHINGTON]. *P*[RESIDEN]^{T}., a reference no less monarchical than the President's image itself. Breen observed that the obverse portrait of Liberty has a hairstyle reminiscent of an Afro-American slave girl, but whether this feature actually figured in the deliberations is unknown.[936] Given that only one survivor is known from these dies and that it is made of white metal, the effort seems never to have progressed beyond the die trial stage. A second set of dies features a wavy-haired Liberty and replaces *G** *W.P*^{T}. with the fraction, *1/100*. While neither of the Birch cent designs ever was used to produce circulating coinage, the fraction survived until 1808 and similar wreaths graced American cents until 1909.

Birch cent, second style, with wavy hair. Second-style pieces are extremely rare and are made of copper (209 to 286 grains.)[937] *Some have plain edges, others are lettered: TO BE ESTEEMED * BE USEFUL * (or with one star, as in: TO BE ESTEEMED BE USEFUL *.)*

With these tiny handfuls of patterns and coins ended a very eventful year.

RED CENTS, YELLOW FEVER (1793 TO 1808)

As the curtain rose on 1793, the absence of a Chief Engraver meant that the die making job fell to the Chief Coiner, Henry Voigt. In all likelihood, it was Voigt, the inventor-mechanic, who made the dies for the "chain cents," the first *circulating* coins made *at the Mint.*[*]

The cents are named for their reverses that, once again, depict the thirteen original states as links of a chain. The chain recalls earlier devices from the Continental Currency coins and notes, and the Fugio cents. Once a symbol of solidarity, by 1793 a chain was perceived as "...a bad omen for liberty..."[938] Other objections to chain cents arose. Because their rims were only slightly upset, they wore quickly and did not stack well. The obverse bust of Liberty also was much ridiculed. Some thought she looked frightened, disheveled or even insane.[939] A 1796 letter by Carlisle Pollack, presumably referring to the chain cents, uses the phrase "...fool's head with flowing hair..." and compares Liberty to an "...Indian squaw,"[940] a most derogatory term in the day's parlance. Much of the die finishing work for both Liberty's bust and the chain was done by hand, creating subtle variations that modern specialists crave. Four obverse and two reverse dies were used on six varieties of chain cents, five of which exist today in numbers large enough to be collectible.

Because the presses then in use were limited in the amount of pressure that they could exert, successful coin devices had to be simple and set within blank fields. The reverse of a chain cent is perfect for such technology. When all else is worn away, the links usually still can be seen. Only 36,103 chain cents were made, all between March 1 and March 12, 1793, when the planchet supply was exhausted. An estimated five percent of them, about eighteen hundred,

[*] A later Mint Director, Elias Boudinot, reported in 1795 that the Chief Coiner made dies until a permanent engraver could be found (Taxay, *The U. S. Mint and Coinage*, p.104.) Dr. William Sheldon wrote that Droz created the dies for the chain cents, echoing Crosby's view as expressed in "The Cents of 1793" in *The American Journal of Numismatics*, January, 1897 (Sheldon, p.12.) Sheldon wrote the definitive work on 1793-1814 large cents in 1949. The first edition was *Early American Cents*, with later editions taking the name *Penny Whimsy*. Sheldon numbered each die combination, beginning with the first chain cent dies, in two lists. The first list includes "collectible" varieties (i.e., those that exist in sufficient numbers to collect.) The second list contains varieties that are so rare as to be "non-collectible." These he designated NC-1, NC-2, etc.. Sheldon also was the author of *The Varieties of Human Physique*, a bizarre attempt to scientifically link body types to intelligence. Part of his work involved taking legitimate nude photographs of Ivy League students. One of his subjects was Hillary Clinton. In the end, no correlation was found.

survive.[941] (Even a piece in a basal state of preservation commands a four-digit price in today's market.)

1793 large cent, chain style, Sheldon 4 variety, 208 grains, the standard established by an amendment of January 14, 1793.[942]

Around the obverse bust of Liberty, a chain cent's legend reads simply *LIBERTY 1793*. On their reverses, the circular chain is surrounded by the words *UNITED STATES OF AMERICA*. On the earliest variety, America is abbreviated as *AMERI.*. On all varieties, within the chain are the denomination *ONE CENT* and the fraction *1/100,* an aid for the illiterate public. The edge device is an alternating series of vines and reeding, commonly known as "vine and bars." (See the illustration in Appendix A.)

Responding to public outcries over the chain design, David Rittenhouse collaborated with Adam Eckfeldt, or someone under Eckfeldt, to produce new cents that are today among the most popular of all American coins. They are known as "wreath cents" and between April 9 and July 17, 1793, 65,353 of them were made. An estimated 4,000 to 4,500, six to seven percent, survive.[943] Aside from the change in Liberty's portrait, a beaded border and a leafy sprig were added to the obverse. On the reverse, a delicate wreath replaced the chain. The identity of the plant represented by the wreath has been debated for decades. The unusual arrangement of berries in linear sprays only helps to fuel controversy since no commonly encountered species shares the same leaf/berry configuration.[944]

Legends are the same as those found on chain cents. Early varieties use the old vine and bars edge, though some feature a newer lettered edge that reads *ONE HUNDRED FOR A DOLLAR*. On the last 12,001 wreath cents, those minted after July 5, the leaves beneath Liberty's bust are narrow and lean to the right. On those made before, the leaves are more symmetrical, with a central leaf that is nearer to vertical. (Compare the illustrations below.) Wreath cents with right-leaning sprigs are from the die combination that Dr. Sheldon designated as 11. Sheldon 11 pieces with vine and bars edges are designated as Sheldon 11a while Sheldon 11b and 11c have variations of the lettered edge.[945]

Two odd wreath cent varieties, of which a total of only four or five examples together are known, differ chiefly in the type of plant used in the sprig beneath Liberty's head. The two varieties share a common obverse on which triple leaves replace single leaves in the sprig. Traditionally, these non-collectible varieties have been called "strawberry leaf" cents. Some now believe them to be contemporary counterfeits, based on 1996 findings by John Kleeberg. Central to Kleeberg's argument is the observation that the letters in the coins' legends are hand-cut rather than punched. Another numismatist has suggested that, rather than being counterfeits, these pieces might represent patterns submitted by a private coiner as a proposal.[946] Including the strawberry leaf cents, wreath cent varieties number eleven, from seven obverses and eight reverses. Seven of these varieties are collectible.

1793 wreath cents: *(Top) Sheldon 11a. (Bottom) Sheldon 6. (Center inset – see below) "Strawberry" leaves. Compare Sheldon 6's sprig, typical of Sheldon varieties 5 through 10, to Sheldon 11a's. Examination of surviving Sheldon 11 examples yields some interesting results. Assuming the survival rate for the 12,001 Sheldon 11 pieces is the same as for the other varieties, approximately 800 Sheldon 11's survive. Of these, 50-65 have the vine and bars edge (Sheldon 11a,) while the remaining pieces have the lettered edge (Sheldon 11b and 11c.) Again assuming a similar survival rate, Sheldon 11a pieces would have accounted for perhaps 750-1,000 of the 12,001 pieces made with the Sheldon 11 die combination. From mint records it is known that those with the vine and bars edge were made first. Assuming that about the same number were made for each of the ten days of production (July 6-17, less Sundays,) about 1,200, all of the Sheldon 11a pieces, could have been made on July 6, 1793. What were the lives of the coiners like on that day? What was for dinner? What was in their thoughts as they struck the piece above?*

Because of the need for circulating small change, half cents were next to be minted, beginning on July 20, 1793. Half cents were thought necessary because Americans still relied on bits, eighth-reale Spanish coins, that were valued at 12½ cents. Making change required the ability to "break a cent." The initial half cent issues of 1793 numbered only about 35,334,[947] of which a few hundred survive.

Half cent, 1793 liberty cap style, facing left. The legends on the first half cents are identical to the chain cents except for the denomination and the fraction (1/200 [Dollar].) The reverse features a wreath that surrounds the denomination and the edge reads, TWO HUNDRED FOR A DOLLAR.

No one knows who actually made the dies for them. The better of the two obverses may be the work of Joseph Wright, who died of yellow fever in mid-September 1793, a few days before the first half cents were delivered. A second, cruder obverse may be Adam Eckfeldt's. The reverses also are thought to be Eckfeldt's work, though the fineness of the wreath is reminiscent of Wright's style. Roger Cohen suggested that Wright might have assisted.[948]

Within an unusual beaded obverse border, the central figure on a 1793 half cent is a left-facing bust of Liberty, hair flowing. On her right shoulder is a pole, at its end a liberty cap or pilleus. American versions of the liberty cap surely were inspired by the *Libertas Americana* medals that Benjamin Franklin commissioned Parisian sculptor Augustin Dupré to create in 1782. The medals celebrate the American victory at Saratoga that paved the way for French entry into the War and the final joint victory at Yorktown. Given Franklin's diplomatic style, it is safe to assume that the medals also were intended to further America's relationship with France.

Augustin Dupré's Libertas Americana medal, (actual size.) The medal's symbolism is credited to Franklin, its legends to Robert Livingston. Dupré struck at least two gold examples (for Louis XVI and Marie Antoinette.) He also struck a few silver specimens and many in copper. Each member of Congress received a copper striking.[949] *LIBERTAS AMERICANA means simply "American Liberty." The commemorative date is given as 4 JUIL.[July] 1776. The reverse depicts Minerva (God) in arms, defending a young Hercules (America) from a British lion whose tail is tucked. Minerva's shield bears three fleurs de lis. Thus, the image is of God using France to defend America from Britain. Hercules is doing well on his own. He is strangling serpents that represent the armies of Generals Burgoyne and Cornwallis at Saratoga and Yorktown, respectively. The reverse legend reads NON SINE DIIS ANIMOSUS INFANS ("The Infant is Not Bold Without Divine Aid.") The reverse also gives the surrender dates for the two battles: 17 OCT. 1777 (Saratoga) and 19 OCT. 1781 (Yorktown.)*

Wright's 1793 liberty cap cent, Sheldon 13, head of '93. Note the beaded border and Liberty's high rounded cheek. The reverse wreath is more delicate even than that on the 1793 half cents.

In September 1793, just before his death, Joseph Wright modified the liberty cap design to produce a beautiful, high relief, right-facing bust of Liberty for a new cent. These 1793 pieces have become the most desirable of all U.S. cent types. Of the scant 11,056 minted, perhaps two hundred survive. Wright probably never even saw the fruits of his labors. As did the chain and wreath styles, these early liberty cap cents targeted the 208 grain standard, though variations in planchet thickness bred inconsistency. And, as do the last group of wreath cents, they have lettered edges. Five varieties, Sheldon 12 through 16, are known. Of them, Sheldon 14 is the most easily recognizable variety because of a vertical die crack that bisects its obverse.

Two months after Wright's death, English-born Robert Scot was hired as Chief Engraver. Scot had been an engraver of watchcases and bank note plates and had little knowledge of die making techniques.[950] He was both inept and petty, and his professional jealously outweighed his talents. The existence of Wright's "head of '93" punch allowed the production of 1794 cents to begin while Scot got his bearings. Scot's own 1794 liberty cap cents are less striking than Wright's. Scot did, however, add a serrated rim (i.e., raised and with dentils) that facilitates better stacking. On what must be considered the most curious example of his work, the rare 1794 Sheldon 48 cent variety features ninety-four tiny stars embedded in the reverse dentils. Perhaps the odd little stars were an experimental anti-counterfeiting device.

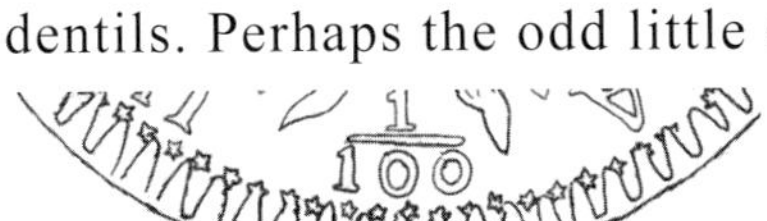

Detail of Sheldon 48 reverse. Note the tiny stars in the dentils.

The 1794 cents have become a magnet for collector attention, at least in part because five different heads were used. Wright's head of '93 is used with edge variations on 1794 Sheldon varieties 17 through 20 (the first head.) The punch used on 1794 Sheldon varieties 21 through 40 generally is attributed to Robert Scot (the second head.) A very similar punch, also thought to be Scot's, was used on 1794 Sheldon varieties 41 through 66 (the third head.)[951]

In November 1794 Rittenhouse hired John Smith Gardner as Acting Assistant Engraver, at a salary of $2.25 per day. The device punch used on 1794 varieties 67 through 71 probably is Gardner's work (the fourth head,) as is the punch for 1795 Sheldon varieties 74 through 79. The final 1794 cent variety, Sheldon 72, uses Gardner's "head of '95" (the fifth head.) [952*]

John Smith Gardner's 1794 liberty cap cent variety, Sheldon 69. Note its serrated border for stacking and the circular bottom curl.

The number of cent varieties dropped in 1795 because the need for silver half dollars and dollars pre-empted copper production for most of the year. The 1795 Sheldon 76 variety marks a transition to thinner 168-grain planchets with plain edges. Sheldon varieties 74, 75 and 76a appear on thick, lettered edge planchets, while varieties 76b through 79 use the thinner planchets.[†] The shift came in December 1795 when the price of copper rose to $0.36 per pound. At $0.36 per pound, 208 grains of copper was worth nearly 0.94 cent. With production costs added, the expense of making a cent was greater than its value, an obviously unsustainable situation that prompted Congress to consider dissolution of the U.S. Mint. To save the institution, Washington gave verbal approval for the weight reduction.[953]

1795 "Jefferson head" cent, Sheldon 80. Note the "crab claw" leaves in the wreath.

A curious 1795 cent die combination may be one consequence of Congress's deliberations. These odd pieces could be contemporary counterfeits or perhaps patterns that accompanied a private proposal. No real evidence exists for linking them to John Harper or his cellar, but numismatists long have speculated that Harper responded to criticism of the Mint by submitting samples along with his own proposal of November 4, 1795.[954] If so, Harper clearly was less skilled as an engraver than Wright, Gardner or even Scot. These so-called "Harper cents" depict a bust of Liberty that bears a remote resemblance to Thomas Jefferson. Thus, they also commonly are called "Jefferson heads" (Sheldon 80, plain edge and NC-1, lettered edge.) Harper's motives and opportunities notwithstanding, the simplest explanation for the Jefferson heads may be that their dies were executed by an inexperienced mint employee.

Despite receiving a raise to $3.00 per day, Gardner left the Mint at the end of March 1796. Liberty cap cents were produced for another two months using an obverse device punch

[*] Gardner's other claim to fame is his invention of something called a "stenographic telegraphic" to record the words of a speaker in characters. (Stewart, p.93.) Moderns are left to guess how it worked.

[†] A few 1795 Sheldon 79 cents have reeded edges. This probably was an experiment as only a handful survive.

generally attributed to Scot. This device punch is used on 1796 liberty cap varieties 81 through 87.[955]

In these early years epidemics of yellow fever and other diseases created an air of desperation, particularly in the late summer months when Philadelphia's mosquitoes were at their worst. In 1793 the epidemics killed the U.S. Mint's most talented engraver, John Wright, and its assayer, Joseph Whitehead. Mint treasurer, Dr. Nicholas Way, succumbed in 1797. When the epidemics were particularly bad, extra employees were brought in to watch over the bullion reserves and dies were carted off to the vaults at the Bank of the United States for security. During the summers and falls of 1797 through 1799 and 1802 through 1804, the Mint closed altogether and the horses that provided a primary source of power were turned out to pasture. Mint employees were asked to sign a promise to return, or face fines.[956]

It comes as no surprise that cents from this period are noted for unusual varieties. The epidemics meant die shortages that caused old ones to be pressed into service, creating odd combinations such as one year's obverse with another's reverse. Sickness also meant that apprentices did the work of experienced men, a scenario that may explain errors such as *1/000* fractions. At least one example of Sheldon 75 is struck over a Talbot Allum and Lee Cent, signaling the Mint's continual struggle to find planchet sources. Boulton and Watt's firm was the preferred source of planchets, based on both quality and price. Sometimes, however, the Mint was forced to look elsewhere and, when it did, to settle for lesser quality.

Even with all the attention paid to cents, half cents were not forgotten. Those of 1794 represent the U.S. Mint's first attempt at hubbing. As with the 1794 cents, the 1794 half cents are an aesthetic step backward from the 1793 liberty caps. Starting with 1794 half cents, Liberty faced to the viewer's right rather than to the left. This feature, along with their serrated rims, identifies the 1794's as coming from Scot's hand. Nine die combinations and numerous variations in edge lettering combine to add interest to the 1794 half cents, of which 81,500 were minted, per the official report.

Scot's 1794 Liberty cap half cent, Cohen 4a, Breen 6b. *

Gardner's designs were used on half cents between 1795 and 1797. They are less distinctive than his cents and Liberty's head is smaller and in lower relief than on the half cents of 1793 and 1794. On some 1795 half cents and on the rare 1796 variety, Breen 1/Cohen 1, the pole to Liberty's cap is omitted. Only about two dozen 1796 "no pole" half cents are known, most with a bisecting horizontal obverse die break. With or without poles, 1796 half cents are rare because a total of only 1,390 pieces were struck. However, mintages totaled 267,530 for 1795 and 1797 combined.

* With Paul Munson, Jr., and Ray Munde, Roger S. Cohen, Jr. built on Crosby's *United States Coinage of 1793, Cents and Half Cents,* to write *American Half Cents, the Little Half Sisters* (Self-published in Bethesda, Maryland, 1971, Also, Arlington, Virginia; Wigglesworth and Ghatt, 1982.) Cohen's variety designations are as Sheldon's, with sequential numbers and letters for edge variations. Walter Breen's designations from his *Encyclopedia of United States Half Cents* (South Gate, California; American Institute of Numismatic Research, 1984) also are frequently encountered.

1795-1797 liberty cap half cents: *(Left) Gardner's 1795 liberty cap half cent, no pole. (Right) 1797 half cent with pole to cap, Cohen 2, overstruck on a cut down Talbot, Allum and Lee cent. Another 1797 obverse is known for a second, misplaced "1" that floats above the "1" in the date.*

The transition of half cents from plain to lettered edges occurred during this time and both edge types are known, even on 1797 pieces. An experimental third and rare edge type that appeared in 1797 is called the "gripped" edge. Gripped edges have irregularly spaced incuse lines running perpendicular to the coins' surfaces. Most or all of the gripped edge specimens feature a bust that is positioned very low on the obverse, practically resting on the date.

Resourcefulness is evident in the manufacture of Gardner's half cents. They exist on normal planchet stock, on thick stock from spoiled, cut-down cents and on cut-down tokens (typically Talbot, Allum and Lee cents,) even further emphasizing the difficulty of maintaining a steady planchet supply. From the beginning, the Mint's cantankerous rolling equipment primarily had been devoted to the production of specie. Cents and half cents were, after all, not legal tender. For them, Mint Directors preferred to import sheet copper from which strips and blanks could be cut. The sheets varied in thickness and quality, resulting in waste and what can generously be called less-than-perfect coins. This was seized upon by wealthy, well-connected, importers who wanted to negotiate with the token kings for rights to import ready-made coppers. Swayed by their wealthy friends, factions in the House and Senate repeatedly sought to abolish the U.S. Mint outright.[957] Though they never succeeded, they created well-publicized hostility toward the Mint that persisted for many years.

THE ORIGIN OF SPECIE (1794 TO 1808)

The nation's silver and gold coinage lagged behind its coppers. One reason for the delay was Congress's insistence that mint officials post hefty bonds before being allowed to mint specie. Neither Chief Coiner Henry Voigt nor Connecticut coinage veteran, Albion Cox, who was then Assayer, could afford the requisite $10,000. Once Jefferson convinced Congress to lower Voigt's bond to $5,000 and Cox's to $1,000, however, the barrier was removed.[958]

The need for small change aside, it was decided in 1794 that hefty dollars would make a stronger political statement than any fractional denomination. In preparing for the new dollars, Cox complained that the legislated 1,485/1,664 fineness (about 0.8924) was too difficult to produce accurately. He also argued, erroneously, that alloys with less than ninety percent silver blackened with use. Incredibly, without any legal authorization, the U.S. Mint switched to 0.900 fineness.[959]

1794-1795 flowing hair dollar, Bolender 5 variety. The number of leaves under the eagle's wing (in this case, three, otherwise, two) and the faint die cut behind Liberty's top curl identify the variety.[*]

In time the unannounced change proved regrettable. By law citizens could deposit silver and gold and, in return, receive coins in the denominations that they specified. Higher fineness meant that depositors had to supply extra silver to receive back the same amount in coins. Infuriated depositors complained to Congress for settlement, eroding the Mint's already fragile public image. The Mint's business model had another basic flaw in that deposits included everything from foreign coins to chains and ingots, in all states of purity. The Mint bore all the costs of assaying, refining and re-coining the deposits, a liability that further threatened its continued existence.[960] A modest fee was added in 1795, for sub-standard deposits.[961]

Silver for the first American dollars is believed to have come from a large supply of French coins that were deposited by the Bank of Maryland in July 1794. On October 15 of that year, the first two thousand silver dollars were made on a press far too weak to adequately strike coins so large. Accordingly, only 1,758 of them passed muster, while the rest probably were relegated to the planchet bin for recycling. As evidence of this, at least one 1795 dollar is known with a 1794 dollar as its undertype.

The design for the first American dollars is Robert Scot's. Their obverses feature a young head of Liberty with flowing hair and facing to the right. She is surrounded by stars, eight on the left, seven on the right, to account for the original thirteen states, plus Vermont and Kentucky. The reverse surrounds a scrawny eagle with an olive wreath. The bird stands on a simple rock or ledge. Only the coins' third sides (i.e., their edges) bear the denomination: *HUNDRED CENTS ONE DOLLAR OR UNIT.* True to their purpose, the 1794 dollars were valued more as demonstrations of American minting prowess than as circulating coinage. They are impressive for their size alone, even if not for their workmanship. Though most eventually did circulate, many were distributed to influential people and possibly even to foreign dignitaries. Perhaps a few more than a hundred 1794 U.S. silver dollars survive.

Using Scot's smaller but practically identical dies, Voigt supervised the first run of 1794 half dollars. The first shipment of them, consisting of 5,300 pieces, was delivered on October 15, 1794. More 1794-dated pieces were delivered early in 1795.[962] As on the dollars, these coins have lettered edges: *FIFTY CENTS OR HALF A DOLLAR.*

By March 1795 the continuing need for small change brought half dismes back to the stage and, beginning a tradition that lasted for more than a century, the Mint settled into the artistic

[*] Milford H. Bolender wrote the defining work on this and the next dollar series. It is called *The United States Early Silver Dollars from 1794 to 1803* (Self-published in Freeport, Illinois, 1950.)

rut of producing all denominations with essentially the same design. It was an old British custom, alive and well in America.

1795 flowing hair half disme, the 18th century equivalent of "Mini Me."

The flowing hair designs on silver coins were no better received than the cents had been. The 1796 Pollack letter continues, "Nothing could be more wretched; an unmeaning fool's head on one side and something that resembles a turkey cock on the other. Oh, shame, shame, shame."[963]

Some specie coins from this period exhibit "adjustment marks." These show as fine parallel lines beneath the coins' designs and are the result of filing done to reduce planchet weights prior to striking. Adjustors, who most frequently were women, wore leather aprons that were dusted periodically to return filings to the melting pot. In the case of some early dollars, plugs were inserted prior to striking to adjust fineness or weight. The extent of this practice is only beginning to be revealed, as new plugged examples have surfaced.

Scot adapted the flowing hair design of the dollars and half dollars for the much smaller half dismes. At 20.8 grains, half dismes were so small that edge lettering was impractical and was replaced by reeding. The nearly eight thousand half dismes produced in the spring of 1795 were backdated 1794, their dies having been prepared the year before.[964]

As 1795's spring faded into summer, a new press capable of exerting the pressure needed to mint large diameter coins arrived.[965] As a result, production of 1795 dollars topped 160,000 pieces and 1795 half dollar mintage was even greater at nearly 300,000 pieces. Production of half dismes increased more than ten fold, to almost eighty thousand. These were sizeable gains to be sure, but still not enough for a country of more than four million people.

Other changes were in the works as both Scot's flowing hair designs and David Rittenhouse's tenure as Mint Director ended in June, 1795. Rittenhouse was replaced by a reluctant South Carolinian, Henry William de Saussure. De Saussure came from an old and distinguished French (Lorraine) family. His Huguenot grandparents immigrated to America in 1730 and both he and his father served in the Revolution. Henry William was born in 1763 and, as a teenager, had volunteered and fought in the 1780 siege of Charleston. He survived capture and incarceration on a disease-ridden prison ship. After the War he studied law in Philadelphia and, in July 1795, was appointed Mint Director by President Washington.[966]

As the President and the new Director shared a meal, Washington expressed a desire to begin the minting of gold coins. He also revealed his frustration over Rittenhouse's inability or unwillingness to do so. The President may have been unaware that Robert Scot and others already were working on half eagle dies at Rittenhouse's request. De Saussure must have been very proud when, on July 31, he signed for the 744 1795-dated half eagles that had been coined. The minting of half eagles continued into September before being interrupted in favor of eagles, America's flagship coins. Coining of 1795 eagles began on September 22 and continued into 1796.[967]

(Left) Capped bust obverse of the style used on eagles between 1795 and 1804, on half eagles of 1795-1800 and 1802-1807, and on quarter eagles of 1796-1798, 1802 and 1804-1807.
(Right) The small eagle reverse from a 1795-1797 eagle. The same motif was used on half eagles of 1795-1798. In the years 1795-1797 combined, only 18,512 half eagles and 13,244 eagles were coined.

On the obverses of eagles and half eagles, Liberty wears a tall hat that long was mistaken for a liberty cap or even a turban, hence the occasional use of the name "turban head." It is, in fact, a style of cap that was fashionable for the 1790's. Liberty's long hair curls around and over her cap in an odd way not seen before or since. Were it not for the earlier date of the half eagles' introduction, the head might be associated with bare-headed draped busts that Scott crafted for silver and copper denominations a few months later, from a different muse. (See below.)

The reverse that eagles and half eagles share is copied from a first century Roman cameo.[968] Commonly known as the "small eagle" reverse, it depicts a scrawny bird, perched on a palm frond and holding a wreath in its mouth. With the exception of one very rare 1795 eagle variety, the palm frond has thirteen leaves. The unexplained exception has only nine. Both the eagle and the head of Liberty always have been held as testaments to Scot's ineptitude. Neither eagles nor half eagles bear explicit denominations, not even on their edges, which are reeded.

On both, the head of Liberty is surrounded by a partial circle of stars. Before De Saussure's successor realized the impracticality of doing so, a star was added for each new state in the Union. Thus, for 1795-dated half eagles, the border contains fifteen stars, ten on the left and five on the right. When Tennessee joined the Union in 1796, eagles took on a sixteenth star, first in an eight left/eight right configuration, then twelve left/four right in 1797, the final year for eagles with small eagle reverses.

Eagle and half eagle designs are almost identical, but the evolution of half eagles was more complex. The five dollar denomination was much more in demand and was, over time, minted in far greater numbers than the eagles. This meant that more dies were required. When the yellow fever epidemics struck, every die, regardless of its condition, was pressed into service. The small eagle reverse persisted on half eagles until 1798, though fewer than ten 1798 half eagles of this type are known. Rare pieces dated 1795 and 1797 exist opposite a later reverse. They almost certainly are the result of old obverse dies being used in emergencies.

All 1795, all 1796 and some 1797-dated half eagles with small eagle reverses have fifteen stars in the ten left/five right configuration. Other 1797 half eagles have sixteen stars in the eleven left/five right configuration. The 1797 half eagles with fifteen stars must have been made using dies that were prepared before news of Tennessee's admission to the Union. Very rare 1798 half eagles with small eagle reverses have thirteen obverse stars arranged eight left/five right. The same obverse die is seen again opposite the "large eagle" or "heraldic eagle" reverse that is described below.

The nation's silver coins evolved as well. De Saussure brought in the respected Philadelphia portrait artist, Gilbert Stuart, to draw a new rendition of Liberty. Stuart's model was a buxom young lady, Anne Willing Bingham. Once called "the most beautiful woman in Philadelphia," she came from a wealthy and historic family. When Stuart's drawings were made she was twenty-one years of age. From John Eckstein's "models" of Stuart's drawings, Scot created the draped bust obverses. For his role Eckstein was paid thirty dollars on September 9, 1795. He also may have had a hand in creating a new reverse.[969] On it the small eagle survived, but was positioned on billowing clouds rather than on a flat rock. The wreath was modified to consist of two halves, an olive branch on the left and a palm frond on the right. Breen suggested that the palm frond was intended to symbolize De Saussure's southern heritage, while the olive branch symbolized the North.[970] What irony it is if the symbolism actually places the South and North on opposite sides and, by so doing, foreshadows the conflicts that were to come.

As did the eagles and half eagles, the new dollars differed in their numbers of obverse stars. The 1795 and 1796 issues feature fifteen stars in an eight left/seven right configuration. The 1797 issues have sixteen stars either in a nine left/seven right or a ten left/six right pattern. A rare 1798 variety has fifteen stars (eight left/seven right,) but most of that year reflect the settling on thirteen stars (seven left/six right.)

Constant criticism of the Mint so frustrated De Saussure that he resigned in October 1795, after only three months in office. He became a judge, a role that better suited his personality and talents.[971] Most of the variations in coinage that are described above actually occurred under his successor, Elias Boudinot. Born in Philadelphia, in 1740 and from Hugenot stock, Boudinot was the son of a silversmith and postmaster. He fought briefly in the War, then served as New Jersey's delegate to Congress between 1777 and 1778, and again between 1781 and 1784. In 1783 he was its President and, in that ceremonial role, signed the provisional treaty with Britain.[972] Along with the other Confederation era Presidents of Congress, he became the subject of trivia questions such as "Who was *really* the first U.S. President?"

When Boudinot assumed leadership of the Mint, its relationship with Congress already was hostile and it grew even worse during his tenure. He faced a litany of challenges. An outspoken Federalist, his goal of buying ready-made planchets for cents and half cents flew in the face of Republican factions who sought to dissolve the Mint in favor of private contracts.[973] To complicate matters, Albion Cox died on November 27, 1795, forcing the suspension of specie production until another assayer could be found.[974] Then, in January 1796, the House debated withholding Mint appropriations based on its poor performance. The attack was narrowed to address the Mint's methods of acquiring copper and eventually was defeated. Ill feelings, however, remained. Renewed interest in having Boulton outfit an American mint surfaced in 1799 and Boudinot sent an inquiry to him, but nothing came of it.[975] In 1800 Senator James Hilhouse, of Connecticut state coppers fame, proposed abolition of the Mint on the grounds that it was costing too much relative the benefits it was providing. Hilhouse wanted the Secretary of the Treasury to report on alternatives for supplying the nation with coinage. Another attempt at abolition was made in 1802. Yet another centered on the 1792 Act's binding of the Mint to the seat of government. This prompted debate over whether the operation should be moved to Washington, D.C., the new capital. Only a series of short-term extensions kept the Mint in Philadelphia. These political machinations, of which the foregoing are a mere sample, were distracting and further served to degrade the Mint's reputation.[976]

Boudinot's relationship with Congress was amicable, however, compared to his feud with the Mint Treasurer, Dr. Benjamin Rush. Boudinot had reluctantly appointed Rush on the death by yellow fever, in 1797, of Dr. Nicholas Way. Rush's wife, Julia (Stockton,) was Boudinot's niece by marriage. The Rush-Boudinot acrimony started when the former Attorney General, William Bradford, destroyed a will that would have given his estate to his wife, who was Boudinot's sister. Instead, he gave over his wealth to his physician, Dr. Rush, and died penniless. Boudinot and other family members took Rush to court, but the doctor won out in the settlement. The family and professional quarrels intensified until 1802, when Boudinot accused Rush, a signer of the Declaration and respected former diplomat,[*] of having given false testimony in the Bradford case. Rush countered that Boudinot had been using mint resources, including the dung of the Mint's horses, for his own personal benefit.[977] With each charge and counter-charge, the Mint's efficiency and its employees' morale incrementally declined.

In another controversy, Henry Voigt was accused in 1803 of using Mint tools and facilities to the profit of his own business. Testimonials by other mint employees showed that, not only were the charges baseless, but Voigt actually had used his own resources to help the Mint.[978] The Voigt scandal quickly fizzled, but the Rush-Boudinot bickering ended only when Boudinot resigned in 1805.

A decade earlier, when he assumed the Mint Director's role, dismes, quarters and quarter eagles had yet to make appearances. Denominations that were in production betrayed an air of haste with their spacing errors, repunched letters, overdates, reuse of worn dies, etc.. Still, the madness held some method. Half dismes, for example, took on the new small eagle reverse, with the expected progression of obverse star configurations: fifteen (eight left/seven right) then sixteen (nine left/seven right,) before finally settling on thirteen (seven left/six right.)

In 1796 the nation's first quarters were struck using the new modified small eagle reverse. The first run came in April, nearly two months before Tennessee's admission to the Union and, hence, a fifteen star pattern (eight left/seven right) was used. Subsequent batches of 1796 quarters were made into the early part of 1797, [979] but the fifteen star configuration remained. After this brief run of only 6,146 pieces, quarters disappeared again until 1804. No bother. Americans actually preferred the two reale coins of Spain and her colonies. The draped bust, small eagle half dollars of 1796 and 1797 were produced in even smaller numbers, less than four thousand for both years combined. On them, '½' appears below the eagle, the first non-edge appearance of a denomination on a U.S. Mint-made silver coin. No more half dollars were made until 1801.

1796 draped bust quarter, small eagle reverse.

For the first quarter eagles, those of 1796, Scot redesigned the small eagle reverse to emulate the obverse of the Great Seal of the United States. The result became known as the "large eagle" or "heraldic eagle" reverse. On it a spread eagle has covering its breast a large shield of thirteen heraldic red and white stripes with a heraldic blue chief azure. In the eagle's mouth is a scroll, bearing the words *E PLURIBUS UNUM.* Though it had appeared earlier on

* Rush, the "father of American psychiatry," was a lifelong crusader against slavery and capital punishment, To his discredit, he was wrong in his fervor for bloodletting as a cure for diseases and he had a penchant for criticism. His military career ended abruptly when his supposedly anonymous letter to Patrick Henry, that was critical of Washington's performance as Commander, was shown to the General, who recognized its author. (Sullivan, Robert B.. "Benjamin Rush." *American National Biography Online.* See bibliography.)

Confederation era patterns and coppers (Chapters 10 and 11,) this was the first appearance of the motto on a U.S. Mint-made coin.

The heraldic eagle reverse from an 1806 half dollar.

Above the eagle are billowing clouds and a field of stars. On the Great Seal the eagle carries an olive branch in its right talon and arrows in its left. On Scot's new reverse, the positions of the arrows and olive branch are reversed as they are on Massachusetts prototype cents and some of the rare Confederation patterns. No satisfactory explanation ever has been found for this apparent statement of belligerence. Was it Scot's error or was it intended as a message to foreign powers, particularly France, with whom war then loomed? The latter seems likely since the "error" was repeated several times and on other denominations. Perhaps the choice of talons was used as an unspoken signal, in the same manner as the captains of warships changed figureheads to signal their intent. The *U.S.S. Constitution*, which was commissioned in 1797, for example, displayed a dragon figurehead when the nation was at war and another, non-specific figurehead in times of peace.

The first appearance of quarter eagles may have been connected to Tennessee's joining the Union, and they may have been made to serve as presentation pieces or for inclusion in sets. The first 963 quarter eagles made bear no obverse stars; however, the field of stars above the reverse eagle contains sixteen stars and the shield has sixteen stripes. The other 432, 1796-dated quarter eagles have sixteen obverse stars in an eight left/eight right configuration. The 427 quarter eagles of 1797 were made after Boudinot fixed the number of obverse stars at thirteen (seven left/six right.) Even then, the reverse retained its sixteen stars and sixteen shield stripes. The same reverse die even was used on 1798/7 dismes, since quarter eagles and dismes were exactly the same diameter. Thirteen obverse stars were used in 1798, in configurations of six left/seven right and eight left/five right. Seven left/six right and eight left/five right obverse star configurations were used for the remainder of the series. No quarter eagles dated 1799, 1800 or 1801 were minted; however, the design and the denomination returned in 1802 and again between 1804 and 1807. The greatest mintage of the draped bust quarter eagle series came in 1807, a whopping 6,812 pieces, perhaps a shoe-box full.

Rare 1795, 1797 and 1797/5 half eagles with heraldic reverses actually were minted later, perhaps as late as 1799.[980] Except for a single known 1797 coin with sixteen stars, these pieces have fifteen obverse stars (ten left/five right.) Heraldic reverse half eagles that are not backdated (i.e., beginning with the 1798's,) feature thirteen obverse stars (eight left/five right.) The heraldic style continued on half eagles until 1807 with various punch blunders, overdates and other anomalies.

On eagles, Scot's heraldic reverse first appeared in 1797, with sixteen obverse stars (ten left/six right.) In 1798 the transition was made to thirteen stars (nine left/four right, then seven left/six right.) The stripes on the reverse shield changed as well. Through 1798 there had been seven red and six white stripes. In 1799 the design flipped to six red and seven white stripes, accompanied by variations in the shield stripes on other denominations. Some half eagles, for example, have red stripes composed of five vertical lines. On others, the stripes have only three lines. Expediency and experimentation trumped consistency as design requirements.

President Jefferson suspended the eagle denomination in 1804. The move was necessary because the United States officially had set the value ratio of gold to silver at 15:1. The world's markets valued silver less highly at 16:1. This meant that a foreign investor could exchange fifteen units of silver for one unit of gold in the United States, and then sell the unit of gold for sixteen units of silver on the market, a profit of 6.67%. The nation's gold reserves were being sucked dry. A corresponding glut of silver was expected at the U.S. Mint. However, depositors did not want to wait for their silver to be coined on the Mint's slow presses. Instead they held fast to their bullion and precious little of it flowed into the Mint.

A similar fate befell silver dollars. The heraldic eagle design had been adopted for them in 1798, at a time when U.S. dollars were equivalent to Spanish dollars in trade. A Spanish dollar contained slightly more silver, about 5.7 grains more, so it was advantageous to export U.S. dollars and trade them for pieces of eight. As a result, silver dollars left American shores almost as readily as their gold counterparts. Thus, dollars, too, had to be suspended in 1804, making 1803 the last year for which draped bust dollars were made for circulation.

1798 draped bust dollar, heraldic eagle reverse.

The rare 1804 dollars that make numismatic headlines and sell for millions of dollars actually were minted decades later. The first group of them was made in 1834 to fill presentation sets for VIP's. Since no dollars then were being issued for circulation, Mint officials concocted 1804 proof dollars from draped bust dies to complete denomination sets. These are the so called "Class I"* proofs. The most famous of them is from a set that was given to the King of Siam. Twice in the late 1850's, more 1804 dollars were made from different dies for prominent collectors ("Class II" and "Class III" proofs.) The same period even produced proof "restrikes" of 1801 to 1803 dollars that actually were made from muled and concocted dies.

Smaller denominations fared little better than eagles and dollars. For example, draped bust half dollars with heraldic reverses were minted in every year from 1801 to 1807, except 1804, and draped bust quarters reappeared in 1804 with a heraldic reverse and the denomination, in the form *25 C.*, below the eagle. The 1804 quarter mintage was a scant 6,738 pieces, about that of the 1796 run, but higher mintages were seen in 1805 through 1807. Then the denomination disappeared again, until 1815, while Americans again returned to their two-reale coins.

As quarters had done, dismes made their first appearance in 1796. They bore Scot's draped bust obverse and the small eagle reverse common to other U.S. silver coins of the day. Disme obverses of 1796 have the fifteen star (eight left/seven right) configuration. By 1797 dismes

* A poorly struck, over-graded (author's opinion) specimen sold in 1999 for more than four million dollars! Many copies exist. This author viewed a twenty-piece roll of counterfeit 1804 dollars, made recently in Indonesia.

were modified to display first sixteen, then thirteen obverse stars. In 1798 their reverses took on the heraldic eagle motif. Except for the years 1799 and 1806, when no dismes were produced, the design endured with the expected variations until 1807. Dismes, particularly those of 1796 and 1797, were produced in small quantities. The public preferred bits and bullion depositors preferred larger coins that also meant less work for the Mint.

One characteristic used to differentiate heraldic reverses is the pattern of stars above the eagle. For unknown reasons, Scot oscillated between two configurations known as "arc" and "cross" patterns. Stars in the former pattern are arrayed in two concentric arcs, with extra stars beside the eagle to complete the prescribed number: thirteen, fifteen or sixteen. The cross pattern has stars arranged in straight lines that intersect. Again, the number of stars varies. One quarter eagle (and disme) reverse from 1804 [!] displays fourteen stars arranged in the cross pattern.

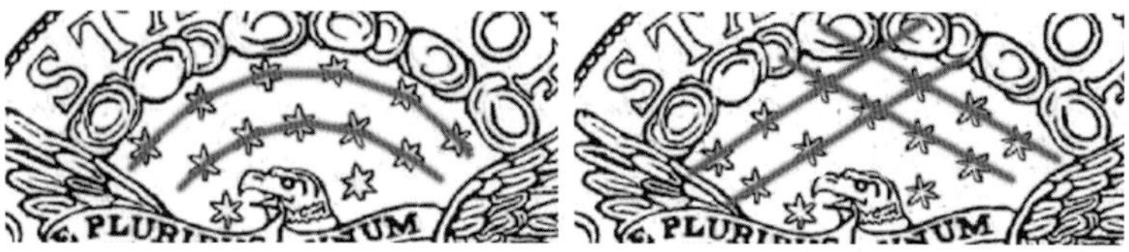

Thirteen stars in (left) the arc pattern and (right) in the cross pattern.

Not even lowly coppers escaped Scot's draped bust motif. Years later, in recounting U.S. Mint history, Adam Eckfeldt testified that draped bust cents entered production in July 1796, replacing the liberty caps that Scot had created in the two months after Gardner's departure.[981] When half cent production resumed in 1800, after a two-year hiatus, draped busts replaced Gardner's 1795 to 1797 liberty caps. Even so, Gardner's old reverse, identified by the use of single leaves at the top of the wreath, appears on some 1802 half cents.

Scot's draped bust on an 1804 half cent; Cohen 10/Breen 9, crosslet 4/stems. (Compare to plain 4, stemless insets.) The length and presence or absence of stems, length of the ribbon ends and the presence of "crosslets" or serifs on date numerals all are used to distinguish varieties. One famous 1804 variety is made from a damaged obverse die. It has what appears to be a spike extending from Liberty's chin and, hence, is called the "spiked chin" variety.

The more things changed, the more they remained the same. The coppers' designs were unpopular, fever outbreaks continued and good die steel and planchets remained elusive. Even so, Scot was able to create a cent obverse device punch from which he made nearly twenty dies, all bearing the first three digits of the date (i.e., *179.*) In 1798 the obverse punch had deteriorated too much for use and had to be replaced.[982] The result was a minor change in Liberty's hairstyle. The last die from the old punch made its appearance on overdated cents from 1800 (i.e., *1800/1798.*) Cents from the two obverses punches are called Type 1 and Type 2, respectively. Minor reverse variations were tried as well. Three different reverses are used on 1796 draped bust cents alone. The third, the "reverse of '97," was used for the duration of the draped bust style cents. All in all, reverse die variations are relatively minor and are primarily based on the numbers and placement of leaves and berries.

Cents of 1799 and 1800 come on particularly wretched blanks that even then were referred to as "black copper." The half cents of 1800 and 1802 are no better since they often were struck on copper from cents that failed inspection and were recycled. There were no 1801 half cents, but those of 1803 to 1808 were struck on better, imported blanks.[983]

(Top) 1797 cent, type 1, Sheldon 135.

(Bottom) 1805 cent, type 2, Sheldon 269. Note the differences in the lower hair curls. Both examples share the reverse of 1797.

Draped bust cents, particularly those before 1802, are replete with interesting varieties. Many variations revolve around the *1/100* fraction. There exist large and small fractions, several *1/000* fractions and even one with *100/000*. The 1796 Sheldon variety 104 appears to have the legend *LIHERTY* because of a broken "B" punch, while 1807 Sheldon variety 271 has a dramatic die flaw extending from the back of Liberty's head to the rim, earning it the name "comet head."

The Mint report for 1799, the key date of the draped bust cent series, shows a mintage of more than 900,000 cents, but most of them actually were dated *1798*. The rarity of genuine 1799's tempts some to deception as there are countless re-engraved 1798's in the marketplace. Genuine 1799's are known with normal dates (i.e., *1799* on Sheldon 189) and overdates (i.e., *1799/8* on Sheldon 188 and NC-1.) The handful of less rare 1800/179 overdate varieties sometimes are referred to as "poor man's 1799's."

A large mintage, more than 750,000 cents, also was reported for 1804, but most of these coins actually are dated 1803. Just before the Civil War someone obtained, in scrap metal from the U.S. Mint, a broken, rusted 1803 obverse die and an anachronistic 1820 reverse die. The 1803 obverse was altered and used to create 1804 "restrikes" for sale to collectors who could not afford the genuine article. Most genuine 1804 cents feature a cud die break along the top of *RTY* in *LIBERTY* and all are from a single die combination, Sheldon 266. As a date, 1804 is the second rarest of the draped bust cent series, behind the 1799's, and also is the subject of many deceptions.

The last of the draped bust cents are dated *1807*. By then Elias Boudinot had been gone from the U.S. Mint for two years. Though in his late sixties, he did not take retirement sitting down. In 1805, the year of his resignation, he founded the Natural History Department at what would become Princeton University and, eleven years later, he was a central figure in the founding of the American Bible Society. The man whom Benjamin Rush described as having a "canine appetite for wealth" became famous for his philanthropy and religious conviction. He wrote against slavery and left 13,000 acres wooded for Philadelphia's poor to use as fuel. An ahead-of-his-time advocate of liberal treatment of Native Americans, Boudinot wrote about and promoted the idea that they were descended from the so called "Lost Tribes of Israel."[984]

An Irish-born Pennsylvania educator, Robert Patterson, assumed the Mint Director's post in January 1806. During the Revolution, he had been a military instructor and assistant surgeon, rising to the rank of brigade-major. At the time of his appointment as Mint Director by his friend, President Jefferson, Patterson was a professor of mathematics at the University of Pennsylvania. Patterson was only three years younger than Boudinot. Yet, he served as Mint Director until his death in 1824, at the age of eighty-one. Mirroring Boudinot, Patterson lived a full life, contributing to literary and scientific journals and, at the time of his death, had been president of the American Philosophical Society for five years.[985]

THE RISE AND FALL OF JOHN REICH (1807 TO 1817...1836)

Patterson's tenure is marked by sweeping changes in the nation's coinage, most of them at the hands of John Reich, a German who had become an indentured servant to escape the Napoleonic Wars. Recognizing Scot's shortcomings and Reich's talents, Jefferson requested Reich's appointment by Elias Boudinot as Assistant Engraver in 1801. Internal U.S. Mint politics, however, kept the appointment from materializing. Through Henry Voigt's efforts, Reich eventually gained his freedom from indenture and, over Robert Scot's jealous objections, Reich was hired in 1807 at a salary of $600 per year. His assignment was to improve the designs that had been created by the aging Scot.[986]

The old man did not take the presence of a more talented assistant lightly and he never treated Reich fairly. After ten years without a pay raise, Reich had enough and left the U.S. Mint. It was then March 1817. In the decade of his tenure Reich updated every denomination of U.S. coinage except dollars and eagles, neither of which resumed production until two decades after his leaving. In the late twentieth century it was discovered that Reich had a signature: The thirteenth obverse star (i.e., the lowest star on the right) of every denomination, always has a notch on one of its points.[987]

Reich's initial focus was on the denominations most in demand, half eagles and half dollars. For the 1807 half dollars, he created a capped bust figure of Liberty. Debate over whether the lady's cap is a true liberty cap still rages. Jefferson later argued that it was a cap fashionable for the day and not a slave's pilleus. Echoing the words of William Pitt in squashing the Stamp Act, Jefferson reminded an inquirer that Americans had never been slaves.[988] The cap question exists because the Mint Act's provision for devices "emblematic of liberty" defined no universally accepted symbol. Reich's interpretation depicts a substantial lady whom contemporary writers called his "fat mistress." She may well have been. As on Scot's draped bust half dollars, Reich's obverses surround Liberty with a partial circle of stars. By this time the seven left/six right configuration had become the norm.

Reich's reverses feature an eagle more lifelike and more provoked than Scot's, clutching arrows and olive branches in the "correct" talons. The motto scroll appears above the eagle rather than in its mouth and the denomination appears on the reverse, in the form *50 C.*.

Even though different device punches were used over time, the same basic half dollar style changed very little and was minted in every year from 1807 to 1836, except 1816.[*] Those of 1807 and 1808 have the largest head and eagle. Those of 1809 to 1811 feature a smaller head and eagle. A less detailed, but higher relief head was used during the war years of 1812 to 1815 and on the first 1817's. After Reich's departure, or perhaps precipitating it, Scot made a

[*] Al C. Overton published *Early Half Dollar Varieties 1794-1836* in Colorado Springs in 1967. An expansion of his earlier work, it remains widely used and respected.

handful of dies dated 1817 and 1818. At least one of them has what appears to be a period in the date, as in *181.7*. One last Reich obverse half dollar die is dated 1818/7. At least two more heads complete the series. In the last year of the type, 1836, mintage of half dollars topped six and a half million. High mintages and the fact that banks retained many of them mean that plenty of well-preserved specimens of the type are available to modern collectors.

Reich's slowly evolving capped busts and eagles on half dollars of 1808 and 1830.

The higher mintages were no accident. Reich made improvements in the ways that dies were produced that carried on well beyond his tenure. His punches were closer to complete designs than Scot's and, therefore, required less hand finishing. This meant fewer mistakes and longer die life, since dies did not have to be re-softened for hand engraving. It also meant that the coins were more difficult to counterfeit since the genuine articles were more uniform in appearance. Lettered edges were retained throughout the period, but some varieties have what are called "experimental edges." Some 1809 varieties, for example, have either *XXXX* or *IIII* separating the words. Some 1830 and 1831 varieties have what have been called "plaques" that frame small groups of diagonal lines between the words. As were all before 1836, these edges laboriously were applied after striking through the use of a milling machine.

On September 30, 1807, Reich's new half eagle design entered production.[989] Its style is very much like that of his half dollars, but Liberty's cap is more elaborate and her bust more completely fills the obverse. On their reverses, the denomination appears as *5 D.*. This design was used until 1812.

One of the true rarities in American numismatics is Reich's 1808 capped bust quarter eagle of a design similar to his half eagles. Only 2,710 of this one year type were made and only a tiny fraction of them survive. They are miniature versions of the 1807 to 1812 half eagles with *2½ D.* as the denomination. No one knows why they were even made since, after 1808, quarter eagles disappeared again until 1821.

(Left) Reich's capped bust half eagle of 1812.

(Right) Obverse of an 1821 half eagle, Scot's modification of Reich's capped head.

A new capped *head*, by Reich, was introduced on half eagles of 1813 to 1815. After Reich's 1817 departure, Scot made minor modifications for the half eagles of 1818 to 1829. When quarter eagles were made in 1821 and 1824 to 1827, they used Scot's version. Quarter eagles underwent a diameter reduction in 1821, but diameter reduction of half eagles did not come until later.

Reich adapted his capped bust designs for dismes in 1809. No 1810-dated dismes were made, but 65,180 were minted as 1811/9 overdates. Dismes made another brief appearance in 1814, and then disappeared until 1820. The die anomalies continued. For example, one reverse die that was used both in 1814 and 1820 lacked spaces in its reverse legend, resulting in what are called the *STATESOFAMERICA* [sic] varieties. After this rocky start, Reich's dismes were made in every year from 1821 to 1837. New equipment brought a slight diameter reduction, planchet standardization and minor design changes in 1828.

When quarters returned in 1815, they too bore Reich's capped bust. After another gap in 1816 and 1817, the denomination resumed in 1818 and was minted until 1828, missing only 1826.

Changes had come earlier to coppers. In 1808 the nation was gripped with nostalgia for the days of the Revolution. This sentiment is reflected in Reich's "classic head" cents of 1808 to 1814 and half cents starting in 1809. Both depict Liberty with an eighteenth century hairstyle. In her hair she wears a fillet, or headband. The use of a fillet technically was wrong since, in classical depictions, fillets were reserved for winning *male* athletes. Though maligned by later numismatists based on this arcane argument, the classic head cents are among the favorites of collectors. The quality of the die steel supplied by Boulton apparently was good during this period, based on the high mintages from relatively few dies.[990] However, many of the early classic head cents come on poor quality planchets. Well struck, less worn examples on smooth planchets are especially desirable (and expensive.)

During the War of 1812 an embargo prevented the Mint from importing English planchets, forcing reliance on lower quality, locally produced blanks. Despite public outcries over hoarding-induced coin shortages, the government was reluctant to authorize minting of coins or even to pay mint employees. In 1814, out of desperation, Mint Director Patterson illegally ordered all remaining copper coined into cents to pay his workers.[991] All of this fed a cycle of smaller mintages, lower morale and poorer quality. The pre-war supply of half cent planchets from Boulton and Watt was exhausted in 1811, halting production. No matter, the banks did not want them anyway.[992] Half cents did not return until 1826. The same problem killed cent production in 1815, the only date of the past 215 that fails to grace an American cent.

Reich's classic head on an 1812 large cent, Sheldon 289 variety. Note the disappearance of the fraction and the introduction of an unbroken circular wreath. The first 1808's had only twelve stars (hopefully by mistake.) The series features an overdate (1811/0) and rare 1810 "restrikes" in white metal.

A fire at the U.S. Mint on January 10, 1816 has been blamed for the interruption of coinage, but its effects were in fact minimal. On the day after the fire occurred, Mint Director Patterson wrote to then President Madison that only the wooden mill house, an adjoining building containing rolling and drawing machines, and the melt house had burned. The coining presses themselves were undamaged. Moreover, the damaged equipment was old and in need of replacement. When new rolling equipment was ordered, in a first for the Mint, steam replaced horses as its source of power. By May 1817 the repairs were complete.[993]

With the war over and planchets again available for the 1816 mintage, Robert Scot took back the engraving reins and created what became known the "matron head" cents, allegedly using Patterson's wife as the model.[994] The new design and his treatment under Scot were so insulting to Reich that they must have contributed greatly to his resignation in the following year. In spite of his having revised the designs of almost every denomination of U.S. coinage, Reich received no credit from his titular superior. Instead Scot routinely belittled him and copied his work. The year 1818 brought the need for a new device punch.[995] On it Scot made slight changes to the matron's face and hair. It was to no avail as Ms. Liberty retained every measure of her homeliness.

First and second matron heads on 1816 (N-4[*]) and 1833 (N-5) cents, respectively.

Note the differences in hair curls and the die break on the 1833 specimen.

The matron head cents boast several interesting nuances, such as an 1817 variety, Newcomb 16, that has fifteen stars rather than the standard thirteen. Also of interest are the overdates (e.g., *1819/1818*, *1820/181*, *1823/22* and *1824/22*) that probably reflect Scot's failing eyesight. The old man died in 1823, at the age of seventy-nine.[996]

The U.S. Mint reported no 1823 cents and 1,262,000 from 1824. Yet, there exist a reasonable number of 1823 cents. Thus, it is likely that Scot's death delayed delivery of the 1823's until the following year. As a date, 1823 is the scarcest of the matron heads. A broken 1823 obverse and an 1813-vintage reverse that escaped from the Mint in scrap were used to create 1823 "restrikes" for collectors as late as the 1870's.

By the 1820's, the Mint's penchant for nepotism fast was becoming an established tradition. James Rush, Benjamin's son and also a medical doctor, became Mint Treasurer in 1813. Another doctor, Samuel Moore, became Mint Director in July 1824. He was Robert Patterson's son-in-law. Patterson's son, Robert Maskell Patterson had wanted the job, but had to wait to get it.[997] In 1832 Jacob Eckfeldt, Adam's son, became Assayer. He followed John Richardson, the son of Joseph Richardson, who had succeeded Albion Cox.

Reich's classic head half cent design was resurrected on the strength of a large order by a Baltimore firm, in 1825. No half cents were minted in 1827 or 1830, but production in 1826,

[*] Howard Newcomb wrote *United States Copper Cents 1816-1857* (Lawrence, Massachusetts, Quarterman Publications, 1991,) the definitive work on the "matron heads" and the designs that ultimately replaced them. Newcomb sequentially numbered the varieties for each year. Thus, "1816 N-4" denotes the fourth 1816 variety.

1828 and 1829, together, topped a million pieces. When another merchant ordered 400 thousand half cents in 1831, William Kneass, a Philadelphia born banknote and bookplate engraver hired after Scot's death, updated Reich's original design.[998] Kneass's modified classic head was used on half cents until 1836, though mintage figures for both proofs and circulating issues are clouded by poor record keeping.

(Left) Reich's classic head half cent of 1808-1814, 1826, 1828 and 1829.

(Right) Kneass's modified version of 1831-1836. Note its smaller date numerals.

In addition, Kneass modified the designs of half dismes, dismes and quarters. For them he retained Reich's capped bust motif, apparently content to make minor modifications to existing designs rather than face the slings and arrows associated with introducing new ones. Kneass's half dismes were minted continuously from 1829 to 1837, dismes from 1828 to 1837 and quarters from 1831 to 1838. Diameter reductions that occurred during the period are particularly evident in the quarters.

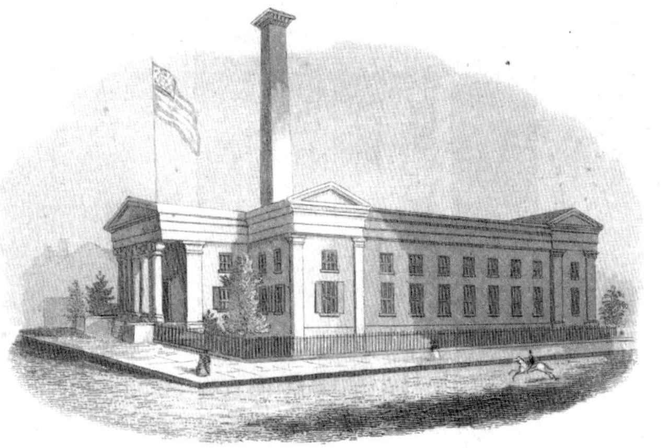

In 1829 Congress saw fit to build a new mint facility on Juniper Street in Philadelphia. The architect, William Strickland, designed a $120,000 building in marble, in the style of a Greek temple. The cornerstone was laid on July 4, 1829, with a targeted completion date three years out. Construction took nearly a year longer than expected and cost more than $209,000 to finish. The old facility sold at auction in April 1833, for $10,100.[999]

The second U.S. Mint, as it appeared in 1889. Source: Evans (opp. p. 13.)

Even as the new facility was being built, the exportation and melting of U.S. gold coins reached intolerable levels. A single 1831 melting in Paris eliminated 40,000 half eagles.[1000] To stop this trend, both the weight and fineness of American gold coins had to be reduced. This was accomplished by the Mint Act of 1834. It reduced the eagle from 270 grains at 11/12 fineness (roughly 0.917) to 258 grains at 232/258 fineness (about 0.899.) The reduction fuelled the expectation that gold would flow into the mint for re-coining. To be ready for the effort, Moore asked Kneass to prepare new quarter eagle and half eagle dies.

True to form, Kneass essentially replicated John Reich's classic head. As if the new smaller sizes would not immediately be recognizable, Kneass was instructed to omit the reverse motto that characterized the older, heavier coins, as a visual aid. Quarter eagles and half eagles of 1834 were the first to bear the new designs.

Kneass's 1838 quarter 1831 and half disme (2x actual size.) Note the half disme's motto.

In the meantime, Christian Gobrecht was hired as assistant engraver. Gobrecht, who was born in Hanover, Pennsylvania, in 1785, was the son of a German Reformed Church minister. He apprenticed as a clock-maker, but his engraving skills became known soon after he moved to Philadelphia in 1811. He invented a type of melodeon, a talking doll and the *camera lucida*, a device that projects the image of an object onto paper for tracing. In 1817 he invented a device for transcribing the image of a three-dimensional medal onto a two-dimensional medium. The same year Robert Patterson had offered him a job as Scot's assistant, but Gobrecht wisely declined. When Scot died in 1823, Gobrecht unsuccessfully sought the endorsement of then President James Monroe. The request initially was denied. Monroe later reconsidered and offered him $600 a year, but Gobrecht was making more money doing ad hoc project work for the Mint. With the support of then Chief Coiner, Adam Eckfeldt, the affable, but less talented Kneass received the job and Christian Gobrecht was left waiting in the wings.[1001]

Twelve years later, in July 1835, the Mint's pot again received a stirring when Robert *Maskell* Patterson followed in his father's (and his brother-in-law's) footsteps as Mint Director. The younger Patterson was born in the year that the Constitution was ratified. He was educated in medicine at the University of Pennsylvania and in chemistry in London. At Penn he taught mathematics, chemistry and natural philosophy as well as holding administrative positions. Later he held similar positions at the University of Virginia. As his father had done, he also became president of the American Philosophical Society.[1002]

CHRISTIAN GOBRECHT AND THE MACHINE AGE (1835 TO 1840)

At about the same time as Patterson's appointment, probably in August 1835, Kneass suffered a debilitating stroke. Though he stayed on until his death in 1840, his work was finished. As if fate were intervening, Robert Maskell Patterson had offered Gobrecht the job of assisting Kneass. On Kneass's death in 1840, Gobrecht was named Chief Engraver, a position that he held until his own death in 1844.[1003] In time, Gobrecht completely redesigned every denomination of American coinage. Between 1836 and 1838 he experimented with modifications to Kneass's classic head quarter eagles and half eagles. The result was a series of transitional varieties that differ only subtly from Kneass's 1834 to 1835 designs. Gobrecht continued to experiment with half eagles through 1838 and quarter eagles through 1839, but his classic heads never strayed far from Kneass's examples.

Gobrecht's 1836 transitional half eagle.

Ironically metal for the new classic heads did not come from the anticipated re-coining of old gold. Instead, it came from wholly new sources in Georgia and North Carolina (Chapter 11,) from debt payments by the French government and from the 1838 arrival of James Smithson's bequest of 104,960 gold sovereigns to the American government. The latter, of course, was used to establish the Smithsonian Institution.[1004] As a result of the southeastern gold discoveries, two new branch mints were established and, for the first time, mintmarks were seen on U.S. gold coins: "C" for Charlotte, North Carolina, and "D" for Dahlonega, Georgia. The 1838 quarter eagles, with mintmark "O," were made at another new branch mint in New Orleans. Out of arrogance, coins made in Philadelphia bore no mintmarks. Mintmarks were used only to denote coins made by the "lesser" branch mints.

In July 1838 Patterson received permission to resume production of eagles after a three-and-a-half-decade break. Rather than enlarging the classic head dies from half eagles, Gobrecht prepared entirely new ones. After much experimentation he finally saw what he wanted in a painting by Benjamin West that was exhibited in Philadelphia. Gobrecht evidently was impressed by West's depiction of Venus in the painting *Omnia Vincit Amor* (or "Love Conquers All.") From it he created the braided hair coronet eagles, half eagles and quarter eagles.[1005] Except for adding a reverse motto in 1866 and minor adjustments along the way, Gobrecht's coronets survived with very little change until 1907 on quarter eagles and eagles, and until 1908 on half eagles. At seventy years, the "Liberty with coronet" is one of America's longest-lived coin designs.

Gobrecht's coronet in 1901, at age sixty-three.

In 1835, before his stroke and with the probable help of Gobrecht, Kneass had begun transforming the designs of cents as part of the overall update effort. The last varieties of 1835 cents employed one of these new device punches, known as the "head of '36." The same head was used on all 1836 cents, the first 1837's and even on an 1839/6 overdate. It is characterized by plain cords in Liberty's hair. Gobrecht made a slightly modified version with a less-pointed end to the bust that was used on some 1837's, before he replaced it with the "head of '38." On the new head, the cord that binds Liberty's hair appears as a beaded or twisted cord. The head of '38 was used into 1839.

Gobrecht experimented with two other transitional heads during 1839. The names by which collectors know them, "booby heads" and "silly heads," give an indication of how they have been perceived. Both depict Liberty with silly expressions. The silly heads' have a misplaced lock of hair that hangs ridiculously over the forehead. The booby heads are best understood by viewing an example. The transition was nearly complete with Gobrecht's "coronet" cents of 1839 and half cents of 1840.

Half cents and large cents continued to evolve until 1857, when inflationary pressures associated with the Civil War rendered both impractical. By then they were worth more in the melting pot than in the purse. A foolish rumor that the recesses of the dark coppers harbored disease hastened their demise. Of course, cents live on in diminished size, the direct descendants of the halfpence that circulated in America since the time of Charles II.

Transitions:
A – 1835 cent obverse, Scot's head of '34.
B – 1837 obverse, Gobrecht's head of '36. Note the plain cords in Liberty's hair.
C – 1838, head of '38. Note the beaded cords.
D – 1839 "booby head." The booby head was named for its comical expression and the fact that hair curls wrap completely around Liberty's shoulder, a physical impossibility everywhere except in an M. C. Escher drawing.

America's last "halfpence" and "farthings":
E – Gobrecht's "coronet," petite, forward leaning head of '40 (Used 1839-1843.)
F – 1845 "standard coronet." With lettering variations, this basic style was used until 1857.
G – The same form on an 1851 half cent. Half cents of 1840-1850 are rare proofs and restrikes. Only coronet half cents of 1851-1857 truly are collectable.

From the beginning, coppers had been the focus of much of the Mint's attention. Between 1793 and 1836, 39.2 percent of all coins produced there were either cents or half cents. In all, these coppers numbered more than 77.6 million. About 90.6 percent of them, some 70.3 million pieces, were cents. Cents amounted to 35.6 percent of all coins produced by the Mint during the 1793 to 1836 period, leaving 3.6 percent for half cents. More than 71 million additional cents and half a million more "little sisters" were minted in the two decades leading up to 1857, but the age of innocence was over. With their heavy rims and complex die hubs, the coronets of 1839 to 1857 were less the products of men than machines.

As much attention as the cents received in pre-industrial America, they accounted for a scant one percent of the total face value of coins produced by the Mint between 1793 and 1836. Their use primarily was a Northeastern phenomenon. Half cents were used and appreciated even less. Still coppers were the first-born of the Mint in 1793. They are a tie to America's colonial past and, a century and a half after the last warm, red large cent fell from its press in 1857, they are again first in the hearts of many who collect early American coins.

Numismatically speaking, America's Industrial Age began on March 23, 1836. On that day a commemorative medalet, bearing the words *FIRST STEAM COINAGE* was struck on the Mint's new steam press. The original plan probably called for the medalets to be produced on

February 22, the anniversary of George Washington's birth, but the apparatus was not ready. The significance of these medalets, which have been restruck many times, is obvious.

Liberty cap medalet, issued to commemorate the striking of the first coin on a steam-powered press at the U. S. Mint on March 23, 1836. Dies bearing the February 22 date were modified to account for the postponement. Yet a few February-dated examples exist. Original copper versions of the medalets were struck on large cent planchets. Restrikes were sold at U.S. Mint gift shops as late as the 1960's.

Several technological advances came to the mint in 1836, but it was the steam press that provided the most immediate impact, both figuratively and literally. Robert Maskell Patterson's Chief Coiner, Franklin Peale,* had seen steam-powered presses in France and Germany. They used a rotary motion to drive a knee joint and linkages, thus abandoning one Archimedean machine, the screw, for another, the lever. In 1835 Patterson asked Peale to create a model based on what he had seen. The following year the Philadelphia firm of Merrick, Agnew and Tyler delivered the first working model.† The complex motion of the press loaded a planchet with finger-like devices, then, in subsequent movements, quickly struck and ejected a finished coin. The striking occurred within a reeded collar, eliminating the need for a second milling process to impart edge devices. Still, there were limitations. Until modified in 1874, for example, such machines were unable to replicate with quick blows the relief that a screw press produced through steadily increasing pressure, or "squeeze."[1006] Nevertheless, the new presses meant that from March 23, 1836 onward, the process of making American coins, and the coins themselves, would be changed forever.

Along with the new press, a new milling machine made the task of upsetting rims easier. More importantly, a new French reducing lathe revolutionized the way that dies were made. Several years of experimentation were needed, however, before the new device reached its full potential. It worked on the principal of a pantograph. A six-inch model of a coin's major devices first was crafted in wax or clay. The model then was used to create a plaster cast, which, in turn, was used to create a metal version. The metal form was then mounted on the lathe. As it turned, a spring-tensioned pointer traced the model's contours. At the other end, a graver precisely imitated the pointer's movements in miniature, cutting the design into the end of a metal cylinder that became a hub. The result still required hand-finishing, but the process was a dramatic improvement and still is used.[1007]

The following November a new type of half dollar became the first circulating coinage to be made on the new machinery. The first design step was a small one as Gobrecht essentially copied Reich's old form. Edge reeding replaced lettering, Ms. Liberty lost weight and the denomination was spelled out as *50 CENTS* rather than *50 C.*.

---

* (Benjamin) Franklin Peale was one of seventeen children of the artist and natural phenomena museum proprietor, Charles Willson Peale. Charles Willson was but one of a pack of famously artistic Peales, that included his brother, James Peale, and sons Raphaelle, Rembrandt, Rubens and Titian Peale.

† The original 1836 steam press can be seen at the American Numismatic Association headquarters in Colorado Springs, Colorado. It was restored to working order by the late Joe Rust, of the Gallery Mint Museum.

That these are transitional coins is reflected in their weight standards. The 1836's were made to the old standards of 208 grains and 0.8924 fineness. The Mint Act of 1837 reduced the weight to 206¼ grains, but raised the fineness to 0.900, making for smaller diameter coins. For the 1838 and 1839 half dollars, the denomination was altered to read *HALF DOL*. A small batch of 1838's, probably comprising fewer than two dozen pieces, was struck in New Orleans, ostensibly to test new equipment. Aside from being a legendary rarity, the 1838-O half dollar is the first U.S. coin to bear a mintmark.

Gobrecht's 1837 reeded-edge half dollar.

Patterson envisioned something more for the dollar. The ban on silver dollars was lifted in 1831, but no action was taken until 1835. Soon after his appointment, Patterson hired the artists, Thomas Sully and Titian Peale, to assist in redesigning the nation's silver coinage. Sully had been a student of Gilbert Stuart and of Benjamin West. Peale was a painter and naturalist from a family of notables. Concurrently, or possibly even before Peale and Sully were hired, Gobrecht made sketches that depicted Liberty in new ways.[1008]

Patterson conceived, from Britannia's example, a seated figure of Liberty for the new dollars. To bring this concept to fruition, Gobrecht went back and forth between the renderings by Peale and Sully and his own drawings. He eventually settled on a depiction of Liberty seated on a rocky ledge and holding a liberty pole and cap.[1009] At her side is a shield across which is a scroll that reads LIBERTY to satisfy the requirement that designs be emblematic of liberty. The seated figure wears a classical, diaphanous and somewhat revealing gown. No pedestrian ring of stars distracts the eye from her classical lines. However, on the first working die, Gobrecht included his signature beneath the ledge. In small letters, it reads *C*[HRISTIAN]. *GOBRECHT F*[ECIT], or "Christian Gobrecht Made It."

Gobrecht, Peale and Sully also collaborated on an eagle design for the reverse. The Mint kept around a pet eagle to serve as a model. Though "Old Pete" met an accidental death in 1836, either he or his stuffed carcass, which still resides at the current Philadelphia mint, helped to inspire a view of the national bird in flight.[1010] On the first of the new reverses, Old Pete flies upward through a field of twenty-six stars, thirteen small and thirteen large. The large stars symbolize the original states. The smaller ones symbolize the twelve states that joined the Union in the years since, plus Michigan that was soon to join.

Eighteen plain-edged proofs were made late in 1836 at the old 416 grain, 0.8924 standard. They were made *coin turn*. That is, a hypothetical hole drilled above Liberty's head would pass through the reverse *below* the eagle. This configuration often is denoted by the symbol "↑↓" to indicate orientation of the dies.

Gobrecht's prominent signature was an immediate lightning rod for criticism. Yet, on a second set of dies, the signature simply was moved upward and onto the rocky base. On the final day of 1836, a thousand pieces were authorized for delivery by two warrants. These dollars, too, were plain-edged and in coin turn alignment. They were sent to the Bank of the United States and entered circulation. Three months later, another six hundred coins were made from the same 1836 dies, but at the new 412.5 grain, 0.900 standard established by the Mint Act of 1837. This time the dies were made *medal turn* as denoted by the symbol, "↑↑." In contrast to coin turn pieces a hypothetical hole drilled above Liberty's head would pass through the reverse *above* the eagle.

No more dollars were issued until July 5, 1838, when twenty-five reeded-edge proofs were delivered. Their central devices are like those of 1836, but thirteen stars were added to the obverse and all the stars were removed from the reverse. These dollars were made coin turn and probably did not enter circulation. Three hundred 1839-dated pieces were delivered on December 31, 1839, using similar dies and the same orientation as the 1838's.

They were proofs or proof-like, but still entered circulation. [1011] The total output of "Gobrecht dollars" for the years 1836 to 1839 was less than two thousand pieces. Though some technically qualify as coins for circulation and actually did circulate, it is counter-intuitive to regard them as anything but patterns. Restrikes made in the late 1850's clouded the issue with mules and by using die alignments that portray the eagle flying on a level plane.

In 1840, when silver dollars finally were issued in significant numbers, the sensuality of Gobrecht's seated Liberty was muted at the hands of the miniaturist, Robert Ball Hughes. Hughes's Liberty is fatter and more heavily clad. The most obvious clothing addition is a piece of drapery between Liberty's left elbow and knee. The dramatic flying eagle was replaced by a stocky bird that might just as well have borne John Reich's signature.

Hughes's 1843 seated Liberty dollar (1840-1873,) no motto. A motto banner was added above the eagle, in 1866, as part of the religious awakening of the Civil War. Half dollars and quarters of the period essentially are smaller versions of the dollar.

Gobrecht's original seated Liberty did appear in a circle of stars on quarters of 1838, 1839 and 1840, and on half dollars of 1839. For the average collector, however, the best way to appreciate the elegance of Gobrecht's design is to view a "no stars" dime or half dime from 1837 or 1838. This short-lived type depicts a Liberty unencumbered by the stars, extra drapery or the hefty arms that soon were added. The seated Liberty and reverse devices underwent changes, but survived until 1891. As with coppers and gold coins, the Machine Age had begun for silver.

(Left) 1837 half dime, no stars. For the first time, the word "dime" appears in its anglicized form on a coin. It appeared earlier, at least by 1786, in print (Re: The Massachusetts Centinel, *October 18, 1786, page 3, "[News from] Boston.")*

Note that a wreath replaces Reich's eagle. Compare its spatial composition to that of a dime of 1853 (right.) Both are shown at 2x actual size. The dime features arrows flanking its date to signify a weight change that occurred in 1853.

RETROSPECTIVE

Early products of the U.S. Mint merely complemented the mix of coins, tokens and small change notes in circulation. In those days, a typical American might go for months or even years between sightings of federal coins. Most sooner would recognize a Spanish or British coin than an American one. That it took half a century to change this situation can be attributed to politics, greed, geography, disease, poor funding and very real technological and logistical limitations. Yet, even with these challenges and despite horrible public relations, the U.S. Mint succeeded. Between 1793 and 1840, its average annual output topped five million coins, several times the greatest annual production of any other pre-1840 American mint.

During this period the U.S. Mint operated in a reactive, on-demand mode in which mintages of individual denominations were tied closely to and always lagged somewhat behind public needs. One such need was the ability of banks to transfer large amounts of capital to and from each other. In the absence of gold eagles and silver dollars, half eagles and half dollars played this role and, consequently, were minted in greater numbers than other denominations. Before 1840 nearly two-thirds of silver coins and more than three-fourths of gold coins from the Mint were half dollars and half eagles, respectively. Half dollars accounted for an amazing 39.1 percent of *all* coins made at the Mint prior to 1840. On the strength of half dollar mintages, silver coins accounted for 59.3 percent of total output. Gold coins, on the other hand, accounted for less than 2.4 percent of the coins produced. Almost four-fifths of them were half eagles. When eagles and dollars returned, the importance and relative mintages of both half eagles and half dollars declined, at least until discoveries of gold and silver in the West brought them back later in the nineteenth century.

These discoveries and the rapid expansion of settlements across the continent spurred the creation of new branch mints. The branch mints helped to alleviate localized shortages and allowed the supply of denominations to vary somewhat, according to regional needs.

U.S. Mint Branches

City and Mintmark	Years of Operation	Principal Product(s)	Reason for Founding
Charlotte, NC – 'C'	1838-1861	Gold coins	North Carolina gold discovery
Dahlonega, GA – 'D'	1838-1861	Gold coins	Georgia gold discovery
New Orleans, LA – 'O'	1838-1909	Silver and gold coins	Improved distribution
San Francisco, CA – 'S'	1854-	Circulating coins; Modern proofs	California gold discovery
Carson City, NV – 'CC'	1870-1893	Silver and gold coins	Comstock Lode discovery
Denver, CO – 'D'	1906-	Circulating coins	Improved western distribution
West Point, NY – 'W'	1984-	Proofs; bullion issues	Overflow; special issues

Until their 1820's devaluation, pistareens were surrogates for quarter dollars. Consequently, only about one in twenty U.S. silver coins in the 1793 to 1840 period was an American quarter. However, the need for small change was such that dimes, even though partially supplanted by one-reale coins, were minted in greater quantities. Dimes and half dimes each accounted for about one-fifth of total silver coin production. In contrast, because of their long hiatus, only about one in a hundred silver coins produced at the Mint before 1840 was a dollar.

Estimated U.S. Mint-Issued Coins per Person in Circulation (1793 to 1840)*

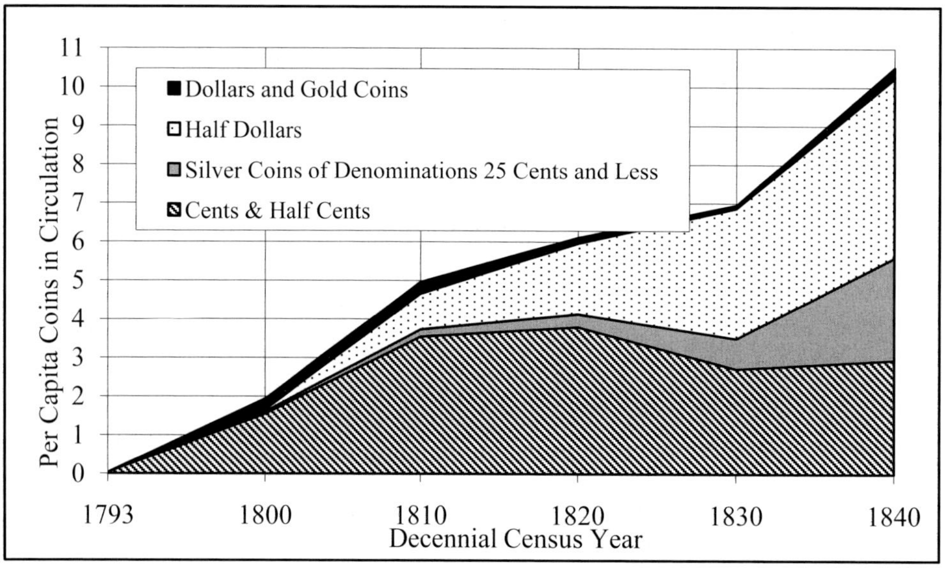

Copper coins accounted for the remaining 38.3 percent of production. Cents dominated, accounting for 92.3 percent of these coppers, whose use was greatest in the commercial Northeast. As were their farthing predecessors, half cents never were popular and public demand for them was sporadic at best.

* These rough estimates reflect the annual mintage figures given in *A Guide Book of United States Coins* (by R.S. Yeoman; edited by Ken Bressett; Racine, Wisconsin; Western Publishing Company; fifty-third edition, 2002.) The estimates assume (with tolerable inaccuracy) that all coins minted, including proofs, entered circulation and remained in circulation for twenty years. It should be noted that U.S. Mint figures for any given year do not always correspond to mintages for that calendar year. Moreover, some reported coins never entered circulation, some were bought back to be melted and twenty years probably is not an accurate estimate of average coin survival "in the wild." Except for 1793, U.S. population figures are from the decennial U.S. Census and reflect total U.S. population. The figure used for the 1793 total U.S. population is estimated from the 1790 population by applying a 3 percent annual growth rate.

U.S. Mint Production, 1793 to 1840

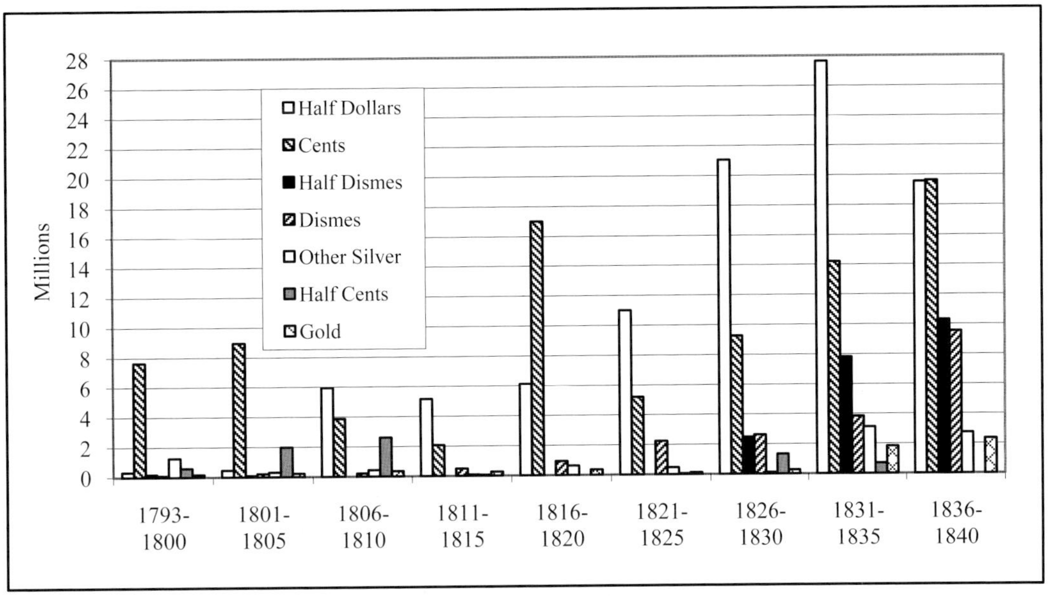

After 1840 American coins took on a more uniform appearance and were produced in numbers that could, at last, support commerce. The watershed event that made both changes possible was, of course, the introduction of steam-powered presses. The steam press had been invented just a few years earlier. That the dramatic gains in production coincided with the equally dramatic growth in U.S. population is just another in the long series of events that enabled America to be the economic power that it has become.

Though coin shortages still occurred in the nineteenth and twentieth centuries, they were more the result of politics, bureaucracy, temporary wartime emergencies and poor strategic planning than technological shortcomings or yellow fever. Today, using advanced electric presses, the U.S. Mint's operations are capable of producing more coins in a couple of days than the early Mint did in its first half century.

Indeed, the contrasts between David Rittenhouse's start-up colony of eighteenth century Philadelphia craftsmen and today's large multi-site manufacturing operations are startling. The evolution is bound to the explosive industrialization of the nineteenth century American economy, punctuated with remote discoveries of precious metals. The early Mint relied on the sweat of men and animals, and the monotonous toil of women. Employees labored in cramped rooms that were lit by tallow candles and whale oil lamps. First a pair of oxen, then horses provided power for rolling and hauling.[1012] The Mint's early history is the accumulated tale of these small groups of skilled men and women who dutifully assayed, melted, refined, weighed, filed, engraved and performed other difficult tasks, for low pay and even less respect.*

Today most Americans view their coins indifferently, as utilitarian necessities. They came by this view honestly. In the nineteenth century, nepotism flavored the doings of the Mint Director, Chief Engraver and Chief Coiner. Bursts of artistic and mechanical brilliance came from Wright, Reich, Gobrecht and others. Often, however, the most gifted artisans and

* The U.S. Mint's early work week ran from Monday through Saturday, eleven hours per day. Sheldon states that all workers were paid $1.25 per day (Sheldon, p.10.) Bowers gives a range of fifty cents per day for female planchet adjusters to $1.80 per day for the chief pressman. (Bowers, *The History of U.S. Coinage*, p.183.)

technicians were held back in favor of less talented men who simply had connections. Talented outsiders either were offered positions as assistant engravers or given menial tasks that they performed on commission.

For unknown reasons, it became tradition that all denominations of the United States' circulating coins have similar designs, according to the British model. As a result, the mint's first 114 years of production are marked by broad generational themes with names and symbols familiar to American collectors: flowing hair, draped bust, capped bust, seated Liberty, Barber/Morgan, etc.. A seated Liberty dollar looks very like an oversized seated Liberty half dime, or dime, or quarter, or half dollar. Later, a Barber half dollar looks almost exactly like a Barber quarter, shares its obverse with contemporary dimes and is a mirror image of then-circulating Morgan dollars and Liberty nickels. Likewise, gold denominations of the 1840 to 1907 period are monotonously similar.

Not until Teddy Roosevelt ushered American coin design into its golden age by calling on the greatest artists of the early twentieth century did the situation improve. Roosevelt also saw to it that civil servants were rewarded on merit rather than bloodline. While nepotism is held in check at the modern Mint, the problem of mediocre design inexplicably has returned. Where is T.R. when he is needed? Consider the equally uninteresting Federal Reserve Notes and the nation's trend toward becoming a "cashless society" and it is easy to understand why modern Americans have little appreciation for their four-centuries-old monetary heritage. At the same time the political and physical boundaries that once defined nations are besieged by multi-national corporations, the Internet and alliances, such as the European Union, all rushing toward globalization. Once symbolized by flags and coins, global empires now are known by their corporate brands.

At risk is something far greater than the appreciation of a few old relics. America is less a place than a concept, less a finished product than a work in progress, an eclectic accumulation of myth, mystery, magic and politics that, between the late sixteenth and mid-nineteenth centuries, coalesced to form a glorious vision of new beginning. That vision did not appear overnight. Rather, it was developed painfully from and is deeply rooted in America's colonial and early national history. Without an understanding of that history, the vision is in danger of forever being lost. Nowhere is history more evident than in the coins, paper money and trade practices used by early Americans. It is this simple reality, much more than the arguably trivial rewards of collecting, that make them relevant today.

Q.E.D.

One of the U.S. Mint's first steam coining presses. Source: Evans (34.)

Appendices, Etc.

Appendix A: Coin-Related Processes and Terms

Appendix B: Continental Currency Issues (1775 to 1780)

Appendix C: English/British Coinages (1558 to 1830)

Appendix D: Spanish and Spanish Colonial Coinages (1558 to 1830)

Appendix E: Wood's Rosa Americana Coin Types (1722 to 1733)

Appendix F: Attribution Guide - Privately Issued Constellatio Nova Coppers

Appendix G: Attribution Guide - American-Made Imitation Halfpence

Appendix H: Attribution Guide – Vermont Coinage (1785 to 1788)

Index and Cross References

Works Cited and Consulted

Endnotes

A: COIN-RELATED PROCESSES AND TERMS

Many of the facts that experts proclaim as truths about early coins actually are inferences regressed from evidence that the coins themselves display. A coin can tell a great deal about the process that brought it into being. On the surface the art of coining appears simple, but it actually demands expertise spanning a number of different technologies. In many cases that expertise was rare or non-existent in the American colonies.

One of these technologies was the refining of metal from ores, the starting point for coinage. The process for refining copper was very different from that needed for silver, which, in turn, was very different from that needed for gold. Refining copper involved a carefully choreographed series of heatings and coolings that resulted in ever more pure lumps of metal. Silver refining, on the other hand, involved forcing oxygen through molten ore to combine with any lead that was present. The resulting lead oxide floated to the top and could be skinned off for use as a pigment in white paint, while silver remained. Gold was far more dangerous than either to extract because the ore had to be crushed and mixed with poisonous mercury. Mercury combined, or amalgamated, with the gold to form an amalgam that could be separated from the waste material. The amalgam then was heated to vaporize the mercury, leaving behind gold. The mercury vapors then were condensed and reused. Those who ran the distilling apparatus very often were afflicted with debilitating mental and physical ailments that today are associated with mercury poisoning.

American colonists generally were spared the tribulations of ore refinement because the Crown greatly restricted the degree of it that could take place outside of Britain. Instead, the Americans usually relied on recycled metal from other coins, broken fixtures and the like, that required considerably less refinement. Spanish silver coins, for example, were often "re-cycled" because their purity, or ***fineness***, was very near that of sterling silver.* Nevertheless, some refinement occasionally was required.

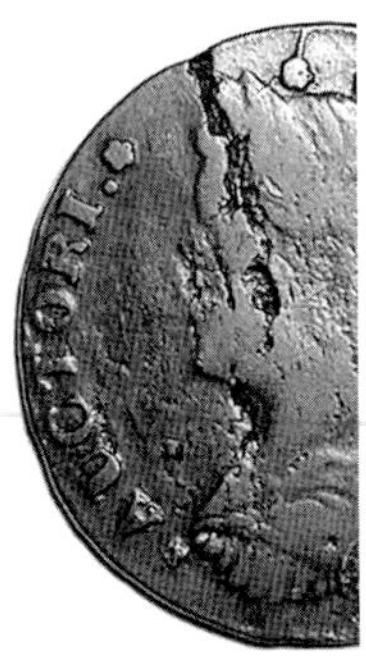

Voids on a 1787 Connecticut copper (Chapter 10.)

The relative purity of the metal was critical for two main reasons. First, the value of a finished coin depended on the amount of pure metal it contained. Second, even similar alloys can behave very differently when worked. Mixing alloys was a precise and complicated business and failure to do it properly produced metal that was too soft or too brittle. Failure to remove impurities also can result in surface irregularities on the finished coins. Such coins may exhibit ***voids*** where impure metal has fallen away from the surface.

The purity of precious metals was determined through the use of various ***assaying*** methods. These methods usually involved mixing a weighed sample of the material being assayed with substances that were known to combine with impurities. Heating the mixture caused most of the impurities to react with the added substances either to vaporize or to produce a slag that

* Fineness is usually expressed in thousandths, as a decimal fraction. For example, sterling silver, at 92.5% purity, is said to be 0.925 fine. Likewise 22 karat gold is said to be 11/12 pure or 0.917 fine.

could be separated from the pure metal. The weight of pure metal that remained, when compared to the original weight of the sample, revealed the purity of the sample. Assaying required skill and those who did it well always were in demand.

The basic process for imparting a coin's design has changed very little since ancient times: The design is stamped on both sides of a round, flat metal ***blank*** (or ***planchet***, or ***flan***.) In the seventeenth and eighteenth centuries, producing planchets of uniform size, weight and thickness also was a formidable task. Sometimes, as is the practice today, metal was passed between rollers several times with the rollers drawn progressively closer each time, until a sheet or strip of metal with the desired thickness was obtained. Even slight differences in planchet thicknesses meant significant variations in the weights of individual coins.

The equipment required for this rolling process was expensive and not widely available in America until the nineteenth century. Paul Revere, for example, opened the first large-scale copper-sheeting mill in the former colonies in 1801.[1013] Smaller operations produced narrow rolled strips, but even small rolling equipment required a substantial investment.

Once a strip was made, planchets could be punched from it. One method for doing this involved laying the strip over a round hole in an anvil and then striking a solid punch aligned over the hole. The sides of the hole combined with the punch to form a shearing mechanism. For this purpose the more sophisticated operations used a small press that drove the punch against a fixed anvil. The "break" was cleaner if the planchets first were hardened.

A second planchet cutting method also involved shearing, but used two hollow punches resembling segments of pipe. One of the punches was smaller in diameter and could slide inside the other. By laying a strip over one of the punches and then driving the other punch through the strip and into or around the other punch, the two punches were made to act as shears. This method could also be executed using a press. Some planchets produced in this fashion exhibit evidence of misalignment of the two punches. Even when the punches were aligned the shearing sometimes was incomplete and had to be finished with a pair of nippers.

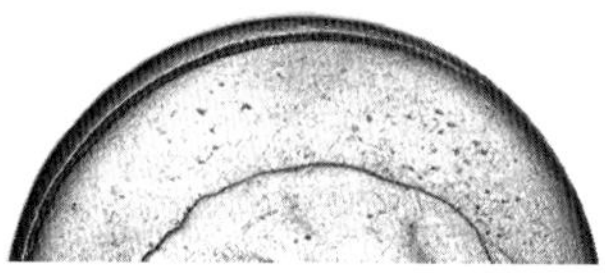

Planchet cutter mark resulting from misaligned punches on a 1694 Carolina elephant token (Chapter 8.)

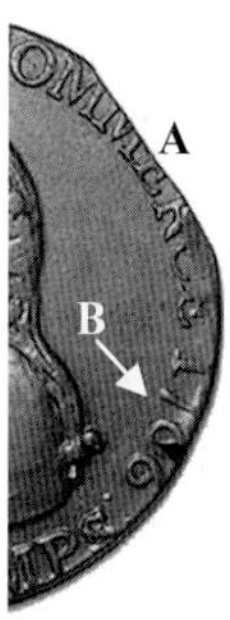

To save money and labor, the workers tried to punch as many planchets from a sheet or strip as possible. Sometimes a punch overlapped the hole left by a previously punched planchet. The result was a planchet that had a rounded piece missing from its edge. Such a planchet is said to be ***clipped*** or to ***have a clip***. If the punch overlapped the edge of the sheet or strip, the resulting clip had a straight, rather than a curved, edge. This type of clip is called an ***edge clip***.

A – *Edge clip on a 1766 William Pitt halfpenny (Chapter 9.)* **B** – *Marks left by nippers or shears that were used to complete the cut.*

A more basic planchet making technique began with rolling or casting metal into a bar, the end of which was sheared off with a chisel or other tool, in the way that one cuts a patty of sausage, and then flattened. In some cases planchets even were cast in molds. In whatever manner they were made, it was not uncommon for planchets to be tumbled in a sand-filled drum to smooth out rough spots.

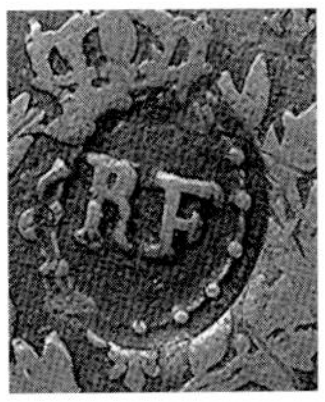

By far the most efficient means of obtaining planchets was to recycle old devalued coins. A coin struck on top of another is called an ***overstrike***. The first coin is called the ***host*** or ***undertype*** and the coin struck on top of it is the ***overtype.***. In some cases, a stamp was applied to an existing coin so that it could be reused or re-valued. This practice is referred to as ***counterstamping***.

"RF" counterstamp on a 1767 copper sol de 12 deniers (Chapter 8.)

Apart from the technologies used in obtaining planchets, coiners had to know how to make steel implements. Under mercantilism, the American colonies were restricted from even making steel. The British instead wanted them to ship raw iron back to England, where it could be refined and sold at a substantial profit. As a result, steel was rare and expensive in America, and few Americans developed the expertise to work it. Steel was needed to make ***dies,*** tools that bore the reverse image of the design that ultimately appeared on the coins.

British Royal Mint medal depicting the ancient hammering method of striking coins

To impart a coin's design, two dies are brought together, under great pressure, with the planchet between them. In early times, one die was held over the planchet and struck with a hammer, giving rise to the terms ***hammered coinage***, ***striking*** and ***struck coinage***. Die-stamped coins, in general, are also said to have been struck. The lower die was mounted in an anvil or stump and thus sometimes is referred to as the ***anvil die***. Multiple hammer blows usually were necessary to fully impress the design. The force of each blow often caused the planchet to move, or the die to ***chatter*** (vibrate,) resulting in blurred images on the finished coins.

From an anonymous print (ca. 1840?.)
Also see the illustration on page 291.

Later the ***obverse*** ("heads") and ***reverse*** ("tails") dies were mounted in a ***screw press***. As with the hammering method the lower anvil die was stationary. The upper die was mounted in a way that it could move up and down with the turning of the screw. No rule seems to have governed which of the two dies was the anvil die. A long, horizontal lever at the top of the press was used to turn the screw, alternately raising and lowering the upper die. Heavy weights on either end of the lever enabled it to act as a flywheel. This feature allowed workers to use momentum to turn the screw more quickly. When the press was raised, a worker, usually sitting in a pit to place the striking point at eye level, removed the finished coin and placed another blank planchet on the lower die. The workers moved very fast, producing as many as a hundred coins per minute. As a result, many "pitmen" lost fingers in the process. The diagram at left depicts a screw press. It was not unusual for the weights at either end of the top lever of a large press to tip the scales at several hundred pounds each.

Large screws were very expensive in colonial times. A lower-cost alternative was the ***rocker press*** in which hemispherical gears were used to roll one die over the other. This was a scaled down version of a European approach that called for embedding the dies in rollers. A rocker press could be used to impart the design on a planchet, strip or sheet. If the impressions were made on a strip or sheet, the finished coins then were punched or cut from it without blank planchets ever having been made. The dies for a rocker press had rounded surfaces to accommodate the curvature of the gears. The faces of the dies also had to be oval to produce round coins. The term ***milled*** sometimes is used to describe coins made with rollers. More often, however, the term is used to describe any coin made with machines rather than by hand.

Another type of apparatus used to strike coins was a ***drop press***. A drop press employed pulleys to lift a heavy weight which, when released, fell against the upper die and drove it into the planchet. This method was analogous to and only slightly more advanced than hammering.

Die making was, in itself, an ordeal. Dies had to be harder than the planchets, yet soft enough to be engraved. The usual method for achieving this was to ***anneal*** the die, that is, to heat it to a specific temperature. When the steel cooled naturally, it became soft enough to ***engrave*** or ***punch*** the design into its surface. Planchets often were annealed for the same reason. The molecular structure of copper, for example, causes it to harden when it is worked or struck. Annealing restores its softness and makes striking easier.

When the design was complete, the die was reheated and then cooled at a specific rate for re-hardening. The temperature ranges within which this can be done are relatively narrow and American coiners seldom knew the proper temperatures to use. Even when they did, there existed no more accurate measure of temperature than observing the color with which the steel glowed. Even so, years of experience taught skilled workers how to discern the various states of hot steel.

It was known that quickly submerging a hot die in cold water hardens it, but this practice caused the outer surface to cool faster than the interior. Consequently, the very outer layer of the die, its sides and design-bearing surface, hardened, while the interior remained soft. With use this softness caused the center of the die's surface to ***buckle*** or ***collapse*** inward, while the harder perimeter remained intact. Over time the design surface developed a cupped appearance and ultimately broke apart. Coins struck with a buckled die typically have clear details near their edges, but very weak detail at their centers where the die surface receded and failed to make solid contact with the planchets. Techniques such as misting and submersion in oil or sand evolved to provide more uniform cooling and hardening, but dies still failed.

1785 Connecticut copper (Chapter 10) from a buckled obverse die.

Even if a die did not collapse, it eventually showed the signs of wear. At times wear took the form of ***die cracks*** or ***die breaks*** that show as raised lines on the finished coins. The lines are caused by the flow of planchet metal into the die's cracks during striking. Sometimes the cracks met each other, causing an entire piece of the die to fall away. As the planchet's metal filled the hole left by the missing piece, a blank area called a ***cud*** formed at the corresponding location on the finished coin.

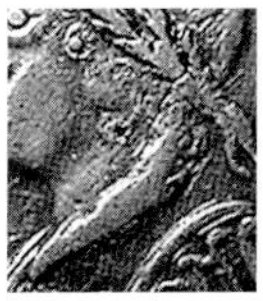

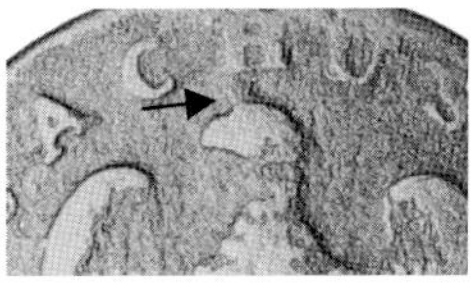

Die cracks and breaks: (L to R) *Die crack on a Washington success token (Chapter 11.) Die break on a 1786 Connecticut copper (Chapter 10.) "Horned eagle" die crack on a 1787 Massachusetts cent (Chapter 10.) Rim cud on a 1775 contemporary counterfeit British halfpence (Chapter 5.)*

Early and later die states of a 1787 Machin's Mills reverse die (Chapter 10.)

Some dies deteriorated in discrete, traceable phases that collectors know as ***die states***. A coin made from dies that were without deterioration is said to have been made from ***perfect dies***. A die progresses through ***early***, ***middle*** and ***late die states***. The final state before total collapse is called the ***terminal die state***. Coins that may be relatively common in one die state may be rare in another. For obvious reasons, coins with terminal die states usually are quite rare. Worn dies could be ***re-cut*** or ***re-engraved*** to strengthen particular details. They might also be ***lapped***. In lapping, the ***fields*** of the die (i.e., areas that do not bear design elements) are ground or polished away to effectively raise the relief or to remove surface irregularities. If the lapping was done carelessly or excessively, details might be lost. It also appears that details sometimes deliberately were removed to simulate wear and thus imply long time acceptance in trade.

Early die makers simply engraved or scratched their designs into the surfaces of the dies, a difficult task since it meant working freehand in the negative. However, they soon learned to appreciate the simplicity and consistency of using ***punches*** – for letters, dates and even major ***devices*** (design elements such as portraits or animals.) When multiple letters, numerals or other symbols are included on the same punch, that punch is said to be ***complex***.

Ornamentation sometimes included what appear as small round beads or regular tooth-like rim elements call ***dentils***.[*] It was not unusual for a punch to have several dentils arranged in an arc. The die maker would work his way around the die, punching a few beads or dentils at a time. Even when a die's primary device was applied with a punch, details still had to be added by hand. Hence, those who made dies are sometimes still referred to as engravers.

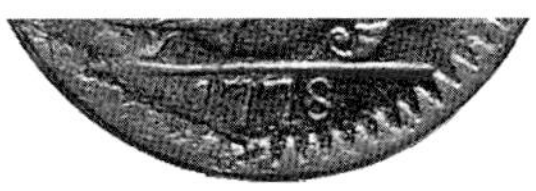

Dentils on a 1778-dated Machin's Mills halfpence (Chapter 10.)

Dates often were ***re-punched*** or re-cut to extend the life of a die into the next year. Coins produced with such a die are called ***overdates***. If, for example, a "3" is punched over a "2" to make a 1723-dated die from one dated 1722, then traces of the underlying "2" still may be

[*]"Dentil" literally refers to "tooth." Sometimes the term is expressed as "denticle," with the same meaning.

present on the coins from that die, whose date would be described as "1723/2." Re-punching also was used to simply strengthen details or to correct errors in placement.

(Left) Repunched "1" on a 1786 Vermont copper (Chapter 10.) (Middle) 1763/2 overdate on a Spanish pillar 8 reales (Chapter 6.) (Right) "O" over "E" error correction, 1694 Carolina elephant token (Chapter 8.)

In some cases dies accidentally were brought together without a planchet between them, resulting in the transfer of some design elements from the obverse to the reverse die, and vice versa. This phenomenon, known as ***die clashing***, ultimately was destructive because die steel is much harder than the planchets.

Results of die clashing on a 1787 Fugio cent (Chapter 10.) Traces of the reverse rings are evident in the obverse fields. The sun from the obverse peeks out from behind a reverse ring. Also note the obverse lettering and symbols that appear beneath the rings on the reverse. Die clashing sometimes is mistaken for overstriking.

Early American coins are classified by ***series***, then by ***type*** and then by ***die variety***, or simply, ***variety***. Sometimes varieties are further differentiated by die state. A series can represent a wide range of coin types that are related in some way. For example, the Connecticut state copper *series* contains numerous coin types made by a number of different mints, both legal and illegal, in the late 1780's. Yet, all are related to the attempt by Connecticut to produce its own state coinage. Coins belonging to the same *type* generally are related by appearance, weight or metallic composition. A Massachusetts oak tree shilling, a "small" planchet pine tree shilling and a "large" planchet pine tree shillings might be regarded as belonging to different types. Oak tree shillings with curved branches might be viewed as a different ***sub-type*** from those with spiny branches. While tradition usually dictates the coins that make up a particular "series" or "type," no hard and fast definitions for the terms actually exist.

A variety represents a unique combination of an obverse and a reverse die. For example, between 1785 and 1788, over 140 different combinations of dies were used to make New Jersey state coppers. Each combination determines a variety. Two varieties may appear very similar and yet differ greatly with regard to rarity and market value. Re-cuttings, differences in edge ornamentation, planchet sizes or other characteristics effectively create ***sub-varieties***. Technically, these are not separate varieties because they are not the result of dies having been replaced, only modified.

One of the two dies, generally the anvil die because it was supported, almost always lasted longer than the other. For example, suppose obverse die "1" was used with reverse die "A." If die "A" wore out first then die "1" might have been paired with a new reverse die, "B." Thus, the combinations "1-A" and "1-B" constitute two different varieties. From the relative condition of die "1" on each of the two varieties, it might be possible to determine that the "1-A" variety coins were made before the "1-B" variety coins. In practice, this order or ***emission sequence*** seldom is easy to determine because dies seem to have been used for a while, changed out and then used again later, sometimes in different years.

Since very few colonial era mint records survive, or ever existed, estimates of total mintages frequently are guesses made from extrapolations of die life expectancy, numbers of surviving specimens and information in the legislative acts that authorized the coins. Large issues rarely were counted individually. Rather, quantities of metal were specified by weight, in pounds or tons. Standard weights for individual coins typically were given on a "per pound" basis (e.g., forty-six to the pound, sixty to the pound, etc..) This provides a means of estimating mintages without actually counting and, with the knowledge that seven thousand grains constitute a pound, standard weights can be expressed in grains.

In coin making, aesthetic and technical challenges go hand in hand. Crafting a die in a way that allows metal to flow into its recesses during striking is no mean achievement. Eighteenth century human-powered presses, with their relatively weak and inconsistent pressures, made the task even more challenging. Having high-relief designs on opposite sides of a coin meant that details would be missing from one or both sides because metal could not be made to flow into the die's deepest recesses. The most successful designs were simple and in low relief and smaller coins were easier to mint than large ones, since the pressure was more concentrated.

The late eighteenth century marked the first uses of ***hubbing*** in America. A positive-image master die or ***hub*** was made bearing the coin's major devices and some minor elements. The hub was used to impress this main design into a ***working die***. Punches then were used to add other details that might have been missing from the hub. Use of hubbing techniques meant that dies could be produced more quickly and uniformly, though hand finishing slowed the process.

In the past, precise comparisons of lettering were used as a means of identifying or ***punch linking*** varieties and types. The assumption was that the die maker made his own punches and, therefore, that the punches were each unique, like fingerprints. If one variety could be tied to its maker, then all other varieties that share the same letter characteristics were assumed to be made by the same hand. In practice, however, different die makers could have obtained punches from the same source. Since a common template (or ***matrix***) sometimes was used, multiple, nearly identical copies of the same punches could be produced. Moreover, one die maker could give, loan, sell or bequeath his punches to another. As a result, punch linking is no longer widely considered to be a reliable means of identifying die makers.

In some cases coins were given a finishing treatment prior to release. The French, for example, were fond of soaking finished coins in an acid solution to brighten them. ***Silvering***, the chemical deposition of a thin layer of silver or tin on a coin's surface, sometimes was used to give base metal the appearance of more valuable silver. Pewter, tin and ***billon***, a diluted silver alloy, were sometimes used to achieve a similar effect. In at least one case, that of the St. Patrick coppers (Chapter 8,) ***splashers*** were used as an anti-counterfeiting measure. A splasher is a small flake or molten drop of a second metal that is applied to a blank just before striking. On most St. Patrick coppers, a brass splasher was applied to the spot where a crown appears on the finished coins, giving the crown the look of gold. The presence of a second metal or alloy in the form of a splasher or inserted plug makes a coin ***bi-metallic.***

Edge devices also were used against counterfeiting and, for specie, to protect them from ***clipping*** and ***shaving***. By clipping or shaving metal from several coins' edges, one could accumulate enough to sell. If this were done carefully, the lightened coins retained their basic shape and, thus, could be returned to circulation. ***Sweating***, a more insidious method of removing precious metal, involved vigorously shaking a cloth bag full of coins and rocks to break off tiny slivers. After a time the bag could be burned and the metal recovered.

In most cases, edge designs were applied by a different method than that used today. Presently, a ***collar*** surrounds the planchet during striking. Under pressure, the planchet expands against the collar. Designs or letters on ring-shaped dies placed in the collar are transferred to the expanding planchet. In colonial times, however, the typical method involved a specialized machine that effectively treated the planchet as a wheel, rolling it, under pressure, across a long strip-shaped die that imparted the edge design. The apparatus often slipped, causing the design to skip or overlap. (See the illustration on page 182.)

Several different types of edge ornamentation were used. Unornamented edges are called simply ***plain***. Edges with raised lines that run perpendicular to a coin's surface are said to be ***reeded*** or ***grained***. If the reeding is confined to the very center of the edge, then it is said to be ***center-grained***. If the lines are slanted with respect to the coins' surface, the term ***engrailed edge*** is used. An edge that is marked by irregularly spaced incuse lines or arcs is said to be ***gripped***. Edges also may bear symbols or words. In this case the edge is said to be ***lettered*** or ***ornamented***. If the ornamentation consists of a series of leaves or double leaves, the edge is said to be ***leaved*** or ***double-leaved***, respectively. ***Rope*** edges resemble a length of twisted rope. Regardless of the device, the edge of a given coin should be viewed as its ***third side***.

Sample edge types:
A – Plain.
B – Reeded or grained.
C – Engrailed.
D – Gripped.
E – Center-grained.
F – Lettered.
G – Vine and bars.
H – Rope.

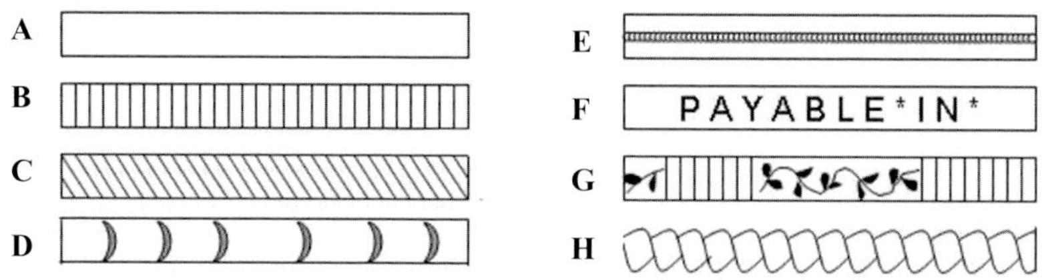

In some cases coins were minted for presentation or examination rather than for circulation. The designs on such pieces were considered drafts, pending approval, and may differ markedly from the final versions that actually entered circulation. These coins are referred to as ***patterns***. Traditionally, British patterns were undated. However, dates do appear on patterns made under the auspices of the early U.S. Mint. Several American-made colonial and Confederation Era pieces are assumed to be patterns but are without supporting documentation to prove their status.

Coins made for circulation are called ***business strikes***. Others are designated as ***proofs*** because of the special processes by which they are made. The term "proof," in fact, refers to these processes and not, as in common usage, to the coin's state of preservation. Various methods have been employed to create proof coins over the last four centuries. In modern times a proof coin usually is one that has been made using special dies and polished planchets that yield a mirrored finish and cameo devices. Proofs usually are struck multiple times under higher than normal pressure to achieve the maximum possible amount of detail. Some elements of these modern proofing processes were in place in Britain in the seventeenth and eighteenth centuries. Evidence of the practice can be found in a few eighteenth century, British-made American coin types such as 1774 Virginia "pennies" (Chapter 9,) 1796 Myddleton tokens (Chapter 11) and certain of William Wood's pieces (Chapter 8.) Others fall short but have sufficient characteristics of a proof to merit the adjective ***proof-like***. Proofing processes took until the 1830's to genuinely flourish in America and, with the exception of certain British domestic pieces, most early proofs are beyond the reach of average collectors.

The term ***specimen striking*** or ***presentation piece*** is more appropriate for most of the surviving "special" pieces. Specimen strikes differ from regular or business strikes only in the amount of care and precision that are used in their making. Clean, sometimes oversized planchets and multiple blows were used in creating specimens, but they technically are not proofs in the pure sense. Large diameter planchets insured a full ring of dentils, or other rim devices, and complete legends. Some specimens are struck in different metals or on unusually thick planchets called ***pieforts***. Those struck in different metals are called ***off metal strikings***.

Dies occasionally were used in ways that never were intended. The combination of an obverse and a reverse that never were meant to be used together on an original coin is called a ***mule*** and its dies are said to be ***muled***. A coin made after its official production ended, but with *original dies,* is called a ***restrike***, a term that often mistakenly is applied to *any* later struck imitation. To preserve the original dies, some of these quasi-restrikes are made with ***copy*** or ***transfer dies***, made from the originals.

Copies of early coins are made in other ways and, while this work is not intended as a collector's guide, so many copies of early American coins exist that familiarity with them is essential. Copies were produced for many different reasons, some legitimate and some not so legitimate. Since the mid-nineteenth century, coins have been copied to provide collectors with examples of pieces that they might not otherwise be able to afford.

Unfortunately, copies have also been used fraudulently. One need only browse the "colonial" sections of most online auctions to find examples being used for less than honorable purposes. Sellers frequently lead with a non-committal statement akin to "...very rare...from an old estate...I am a bumpkin and don't know whether this coin is genuine. If it is, it could be worth thousands...." These pieces frequently are accompanied by a high opening bid price to imply authenticity. In one such auction a two-dollar flea market copy recently appeared with a similar statement of *potential* authenticity and an opening bid of $15,000!

Legal copies made since 1973, that is, after passage of the Hobby Protection Act, must bear the clearly rendered, incuse* word "COPY" on either the obverse or reverse. However, older copies may not be so clearly marked and "COPY" may have been omitted deliberately or removed from newer pieces. A copy may also have been made deliberately to look worn or artificially colored to appear older.

Several terms apply to coins that are not quite what they purport to be. Legally, the words ***copy***, ***replica***, ***reproduction*** and ***facsimile*** all have slightly different meanings. For the purposes of this book, however, they are considered to be analogous. All imply a piece made some time after the original coin was in use and not for the purpose of circulation as money. In contrast, the word ***counterfeit*** or the phrase ***contemporary counterfeit*** usually applies to a piece made for circulation while the genuine article was still in use. Sometimes counterfeits are rarer and more prized by collectors than the official issues that they emulate.

---

* ***Incuse*** refers to designs that descend into the coins surface, as opposed to rising above it. When a design rises above the coins surface, it is said to be ***in relief***.

The term ***fantasy piece*** or ***fabrication*** applies to a piece whose design existed only in the imagination of its maker. That is, no original coin like the one in question actually existed. The piece below is just such a fantasy. No known coins originated in 1657, from Hingham, Massachusetts, as the piece claims. Its maker and age are unknown, but it is thought to have originated about three centuries after its date proclaims.

"1657 Hingham Shilling," a fantasy piece

The term ***fake*** sometimes is applied to all less than authentic pieces, though its meaning actually is too vague to be useful. Another vague adjective, ***authentic***, usually refers to a genuine article unless it is accompanied by a qualifier (e.g., ***authentic reproduction***.) Even the term ***genuine*** can be qualified into uselessness as illustrated by a well-known mass-produced copy whose accompanying documentation reads, "Genuine Facsimile Edition." A copy that presents a danger of being confused with the genuine article is said to be ***deceptive***. Otherwise, it is said to be ***non-deceptive***. Fortunately, the vast majority of copies are non-deceptive.

Copies generally are made in one of three ways: striking, casting or ***electrotyping***. The process of striking copies is identical to that of making genuine coins and, when done "properly," the result can be quite deceptive. This author recently purchased a very well made struck copy of an early nineteenth century U.S. Mint-made half dollar. Its appearance is practically indistinguishable from an original. Unlike the silver originals, however, the struck copy is readily attracted to a magnet! In the mid-nineteenth century, several famous numismatists engaged in making struck copies of very rare coins. Even their copies now are highly sought collectibles that can fetch hundreds or even thousands of dollars. Some of them were hoaxes, such as the so called "New Haven restrikes" of 1787 Fugio cents (Chapter 10,) instigated by Charles Ira Bushnell to fool the numismatic community.

Less deceptive examples from the nineteenth century are John Bolen's copies of 1737 Higley coppers, Thomas Wyatt's copies of Massachusetts silver coinage, Montroville Dickison's 1876 copies of 1776 Continental Currency coins and John Warren/William Idler copies of Peter Getz's 1792 Washington patterns. Idler also made non-deceptive copies of Maryland's Lord Baltimore coinage for use as advertising pieces. Idler's contemporary, C. Wyllys Betts, struck crude fantasy pieces that, for a time, stood the numismatic community on its head.

Unlike some copy types, struck copies usually pass the ***ring test***. That is, when lightly dropped on a tabletop, a procedure not recommended for rare pieces, they emit a ringing sound very much like that made by originals. Most non-struck copies, on the other hand, sound dull on impact. A safer method of performing the ring test is to balance the coin on one's finger tip and tap its edge with another coin.

Many makers of struck copies alter the design slightly or leave a secret mark to betray their handiwork. Also, copies made in the nineteenth century, or later, are usually too perfect. Their lettering is too crisp and their planchets are too clean to have been made in early America.

Recently, unscrupulous individuals have been producing struck copies of later U.S. coins from dies created by ***spark erosion***. In this method, a guide makes hundreds of passes over the surface of a genuine coin. As the guide rises and falls to the coin's contours, it controls a pointer that blasts away a tiny amount of metal from the surface of a die using an electric spark. The result is a die that can be used to produce nearly identical copies of the original coin. Only under high magnification can the tell-tale marks left by this process be seen.

Cast copies can be just as deceptive as their struck counterparts. As the name implies, molten metal is poured into a mold, which may have been engraved, impressed or itself cast from a genuine coin. Cast copies usually exhibit surface irregularities from bubbles, impurities in the molten metal or from the mold itself (e.g., when sand or plaster molds are used.) The ***lost wax*** technique sometimes is used. Using this method, a plaster mold is made directly from the coin. Wax is poured into the mold and allowed to harden. The wax coin is then embedded in plaster or sand and hot metal is poured in. The wax vaporizes and is displaced by the metal.

In any casting scenario where many pieces are made from the same mold, the mold may be deformed by the heat, producing uneven surface characteristics. If the mold is two-piece, a seam may be produced around the edge of the copy. Copies sometimes exhibit signs of filing or buffing where a seam or burr has been removed. Cast copies may or may not pass the ring test. To complicate the task of authentication, a few apparently genuine pieces, such as certain 1776 New Hampshire patterns (Chapter 9,) were cast.

Edge of an electrotype copy of an ancient Roman coin.

Electrotypes usually are the least deceptive of the copies. In this process, a plaster cast is made from an original coin or from a copy. The cast is then electroplated with a thin layer of metal. The metal is removed from the cast, yielding a thin shell. This is repeated for the other side of the coin being copied. The two shells then are glued around a metal disk. Unless removed, a seam usually appears around the edge where the shells are joined. Typically, the interior blank is made of lead, resulting in copies that are heavier than the originals. Copies made in this way produce a dull thud when subjected to the ring test. Moreover, though not an advisable test, scratching the edge of a copper electrotype usually reveals a bright, silver-colored interior. Most extant copies are electrotypes.

Accurate weighing, determination of specific gravity and bombardment/diffraction studies are excellent ways to tell copies from originals, but each requires specialized equipment. Weighing has its limitations as the weights of early coins varied significantly. However, for most issues, weight ranges have been established and published. Specific gravity, a property discovered by the Greek mathematician, Archimedes, compares an object's weight in water to its weight in air to give an indication of the material of which the object is made.

Bombardment/diffraction tests are more accurate and use controlled bursts of radiation to detect trace elements, but generally require expensive equipment that is of limited availability. Another authentication technique involves the photographic or digital enlargement of genuine coins to produce transparencies. Overlaying a transparency of a genuine coin onto an image of a suspected copy, or vice versa, can reveal minor differences. Caution must be used, however, because differences can be caused by simple wear.

A Few Drops from the Ocean of Reproductions

Third-party grading services can help to authenticate questionable pieces, but the best way to identify copies "on the spot" is to know exactly how originals look under magnification. To gain the knowledge needed to dismiss *most* copies, one simply needs to examine as many known originals as possible.

Many copies available today originated during the U.S. bicentennial celebration of 1976. No statistically reliable studies on copy populations is recognized, but experience suggests that the following may be the ten most frequently copied early American coins:

- 1776 Continental Currency coins
- 1652-1682 Massachusetts silver issues
- 1776 Massachusetts state patterns
- 1776 New Hampshire state patterns
- 1783 Constellatio Nova patterns
- 1737-1739 Higley coppers
- 1616 Sommer Islands coins
- 1785 Bar or 'USA' cent
- 1790's Washington pieces
- 1787 Brasher gold doubloons

It should be noted that arly paper money also is copied frequently. Stiff, yellowish-brown paper imprinted with all black ink is a sure sign of a copy. To thwart counterfeiters, early printers used multiple colors of ink and high-quality, non-yellowing rag paper. Not surprisingly, eighteenth century anti-counterfeiting measures, such as embedded mica flakes, watermarks and serial numbering, also can be used to detect copies (See Chapter 4.)

In the end, knowledge is the key. Copies can add to a numismatist's knowledge and fill holes in collections. Nevertheless, it is critical that copies be recognized for what they are and nothing more. If, when buying a coin or note, the deal seems too good to be true, then it probably is.

The bulk of this appendix is devoted to the processes used to manufacture early American coins and copies of them. As difficult as minting coins and printing notes were, the more difficult task actually may have been distributing them. Imagine the challenge of finding people to accept, in exchange for their labors, thousands of coins of a type that they had never seen or notes that had no real backing. Banks of the day would have been of little assistance. Merchants could not have distributed coins in the volumes that they were produced. Connecticut coppers, for example, numbered in the millions. How were these coins distributed? This question, the subject of ongoing research, is yet to be fully answered. Add to the lack of distribution channels the fact that many early coins were produced without official sanction, and, hence, clandestinely, and one begins to appreciate the full plight of those attempting to profit from making coins.

B: CONTINENTAL CURRENCY ISSUES (1775 TO 1780)

B.1. EMISSIONS BY DENOMINATION AND NOMINAL ISSUE DATE

	1775[1014]		1776				1777		1778		1779	Totals
	May 10	Nov. 29*	Feb. 17	May 9	July 22	Nov. 2	Feb. 26	May 20	April 11	Sep. 26	Jan. 14	
$1/6	-	-	600,000	-	-	-	-	-	-	-	-	$100,000
$1/3	-	-	600,000	-	-	-	-	-	-	-	-	$200,000
$1/2	-	-	600,000	-	-	-	-	-	-	-	-	$300,000
$2/3	-	-	600,000	-	-	-	-	-	-	-	-	$400,000
$1	49,000	83,611	130,436	138,889	-	-	-	-	-	-	139,811	$541,747
$2	49,000	83,611	130,437	138,889	76,923	76,923	76,923	253,850	-	-	139,811	$2,052,734
$3	49,000	83,611	130,436	138,889	76,923	76,923	76,923	253,839	-	-	139,811	$3,079,065
$4	49,000	83,611	130,435	138,889	76,923	76,923	76,923	253,839	208,335	-	139,811	$4,938,756
$5	49,000	83,611	65,217	138,889	76,923	76,923	76,923	253,840	208,330	340,914	139,811	$7,551,905
$6	49,000	83,611	65,217	138,889	76,923	76,923	76,923	253,839	208,335	-	-	$6,177,960
$7	49,000	83,611	65,217	138,889	76,923	76,923	76,923	253,840	208,330	340,914	-	$9,593,990
$8	49,000	83,611	65,217	138,889	76,923	76,923	76,923	253,851	208,330	340,914	-	$10,964,648
$20	11,800	-	-	-	-	-	-	-	208,330	340,914	139,811	$14,017,100
$30	33,333	-	-	-	76,923	76,923	76,923	253,850	208,335	340,914	182,070	$37,478,130
$35	-	-	-	-	-	-	-	-	-	-	182,070	$6,372,450
$40	-	-	-	-	-	-	-	-	208,335	340,914	182,070	$29,252,760
$45	-	-	-	-	-	-	-	-	-	-	182,070	$8,193,150
$50	-	-	-	-	-	-	-	-	-	340,914	182,070	$26,149,200
$55	-	-	-	-	-	-	-	-	-	-	182,070	$10,013,850
$60	-	-	-	-	-	-	-	-	-	340,914	182,071	$31,379,100
$65	-	-	-	-	-	-	-	-	-	-	182,070	$11,834,550
$70	-	-	-	-	-	-	-	-	-	-	139,811	$9,786,770
$80	-	-	-	-	-	-	-	-	-	-	139,811	$11,184,880
A†/B	$2,999,990 $3,000,000	$3,009,996 $3,010,000	$4,000,000 $4,000,000	$5,000,004 $5,000,000	$4,999,995 $5,000,000	$4,999,995 $5,000,000	$4,999,995 $5,000,000	$16,499,995 $16,500,000	$25,000,000 $25,000,000	$75,001,080 $75,001,080	$95,051,695 $95,051,695	$241,562,745 $241,562,775

* Figures for the November 29, 1775, issue include $10,000 authorized for the replacement of worn bills.
† Counterfeit detection notes and counterfeits are known for most issues. These are not counted. Neither are any trial printings. "A" totals reflect actual notes printed. "B" totals reflect notes authorized.

B.2. DEVICES AND MOTTOES ON CONTINENTAL CURRENCY

Denom.	Face Devices and Mottoes	Back Devices
Fract-ionals	**Device:** The sun peering down on a sundial **Motto:** *FUGIO* (*TEMPUS FUGIT, I* [Time] *am Fleeting*)	1776: A circular chain of 13 links
$1	**Device:** An acanthus plant crushed by a weighted bowl **Motto:** *DEPRESSA RESURGIT* (*Though Crushed it Recovers*)	1775-1777: Ragweed and Willows; 1779: Tansy
$2	**Device:** Grain being threshed **Motto:** *TRIBULATIO DITAT* (*Affliction Improves It*)	1775-1779: Raspberry and 2 Filberts; 1779: Mulberry
$3	**Device:** An eagle fighting with a heron **Motto:** *EXITUS IN DUBIO EST* (*The Outcome is in Doubt*)	1775-1777: Skeletonized Elm and Maple Fruit; 1779: Rose
$4	**Device:** A wild boar charging a spear **Motto:** *AUT MORS AUT VITA DECORA* (*Either Death or an Honorable Life*)	1775-1777: Skeletonized Maple Fruit; 1778: Buttercup; 1779: Mulberry
$5	**Device:** A hand, gathering food, being pricked by thorns, bleeding **Motto:** *SUSTINE VEL ABSTINE* (*Survive or Give Up*)	1775-1777: Betony and Sage; 1778: Willow; 1779: Feverfew
$6	**Device:** A beaver gnawing a tree **Motto:** *PERERVERANDO* (*By Perseverance*)	1775-1777: Buttercup; 1778: Sage
$7	**Device:** A severe storm at sea **Motto:** *SERENABIT* (*It will be Calm*)	1775-1777: Buttercup; 1778: Grape and Sage
$8	**Device:** A 13-stringed harp **Motto:** *MAJORA MINORIBUS CONSONANT* (*The Large* [Colonies] *in Harmony with the Small* [Colonies])	1775-1777: Henebit and 2 Buttercups; 1778: 3 Sages
$20 and $30*	**Devices:** 1. A strong wind blowing up waves 2. The sun shining on a calm sea 3. A wreath on a tomb in the mountains **Mottoes:** 1. *VI CONCITATE* (*Driven by Force*) 2. *CESSANTE VENTO CONQUIESCEMUS* (*When the Storm Ceases, We Will Rest*) 3. *SI RECTE FACIES* (*If You Act Righteously*)	**$20:** 1775-1777: Vignette, 1778: 3 Willows, 1779: Grape. **$30:** 1775-1777: 2 Vignettes, 1778: 3 Willows 1779: Climbing Fumitory
$35	**Device:** A plow in a field **Motto:** *HINC OPES* (*Hence Our Wealth*)	1779: 2 Willows
$40	**Device:** An all-seeing divine eye looking down on 13 stars **Motto:** *CONFEDERATION*	1778: Carrot; 1779: Poterium
$45	**Device:** Beehives under a shelter **Motto:** *SIC FLOREAT REPUBLICA* (*May the Nation Flourish*)	1779: Ground Ivy
$50	**Device:** A stepped pyramid with 13 levels **Motto:** *PERENNIS* (*Everlasting*)	1778: Arrows 1779: Parsley
$55	**Device:** The sun coming out after a storm **Motto:** *POST NUBILA PHOEBUS* (*After Dark Clouds Comes the Sun*)	1779: Willow
$60	**Device:** A globe **Motto:** *DEUS REGNAT EXULTET TERRA* (*God Reigns, Let the Earth Rejoice*)	1778: Bow 1779: Willow and Hemlock
$65	**Device:** A hand holding a balance scale **Motto:** *FIAT JUSTITIA* (*Let Justice be Done*)	1779: Parsley
$70	**Device:** A lone tree **Motto:** *VIM PROCELLERUM QUADRENNIUM USTINUIT* (*For Four Years it Has Withstood the Force of the Storm*)	1779: Maple
$80	**Device:** A large tree **Motto:** *ET IN SECULA SECULORUM FLORESCEBIT* (*...And it Will Flourish for Ages and Ages*)	1779: Strawberry

* Faces of Some, Backs of Others

C: ENGLISH/BRITISH COINAGES (1558 TO 1830)

Tables C.1.-C.3. use the following symbols to denote primary metals used in coinage alloys: Au for gold, Ag for silver, and Cu for copper and Sn for tin. Patent coinages are omitted.

C.1. ENGLISH HAMMERED & EARLY MILLED COINAGES (1558 TO 1685)

Coin	Value	Eliz. I (1558-1603)	James I (1603-1625)	Charles I (1625-1649)	Common-wealth (1649-1660)	Charles II (1660-1685)
Triple Unite	£3	-	-	Au		
50 Shillings	£2 10s	-	-	-		Au†
2 Guineas	£2	-	-	-		Au†
Fine Sovereign	£1 10s	Au	-	-		
Rose Ryal		-	Au	-		
Sovereign	£1 2s	-	Au	-		
Pound	£1	Au	-	-		
Sovereign	£1	-	Au	Au, Ag		
Unite	£1	-	Au	-		Au
Laurel	£1	-	Au	-		
Broad	£1	-	-	-	Au	Au†
Guinea	£1	-	-	-		Au†
Guinea	£1 2s	-	-	-		Au†
Ryal	15s	Au	-	-	-	-
Spur Ryal	15s	-	Au	-	-	-
Spur Ryal	16s 6d	-	Au	-	-	-
Half Pound	10s	Au	-	Ag	-	-
Half Sovereign	10s	-	Au	-	-	-
Double Crown	10s	-	Au	Au	Au	Au
Half Laurel	10s	-	Au	-	-	-
Half Unite	10s	-	-	Au	-	-
Angel	10s	Au	Au	Au	-	Au
Half Guinea	10s	-	-	-	-	Au†
Half Guinea	10s 6d	-	-	-	-	Au†
Angel	11s	-	Au	-	-	-
Double Crown	11s	-	Au	-	-	-
Crown	5s	Au*, Ag	Au, Ag	Au, Ag	Au, Ag*	Au, Ag*
Half Angel		Au	Au	-	-	-
8 Testern	8 Reales	Ag	-	-	-	-
Halfcrown	2s 6d	Au*, Ag	Au, Ag	Ag	Ag	Ag*
Quarter Angel		Au	-	-	-	-
4 Testern	4 Reales	Ag	-	-	-	-
2 Testern	2 Reales	Ag	-	-	-	-
Shilling	12d	Ag*	Ag§	Ag	Ag	Ag*
Testern	1 Reale	Ag	-	-	-	-
Sixpence	6d	Ag*§	Ag§	Ag	Ag	Ag*
Groat	4d	Ag	-	Ag	-	Ag
Fourpence		-	-	-	-	Ag†
Threepence	3d	Ag*§	Ag	Ag	-	Ag*
Half Groat	2d	Ag	Ag	Ag	Ag	Ag
Twopence		-	-	-	-	Ag†
3 halfpence	1½ d	Ag	-	-	-	-
			-	-	-	-
Penny	1d	Ag, Cu‡	Ag	Ag	Ag	Ag*
3 farthings	¾ d	Ag	-	-	-	-
Halfpenny	½ d	Ag, Cu‡	Ag	Ag	Ag	Cu
Farthing	¼ d	-	-	-	-	Cu, Sn & Cu

Notes:

None - Hammered types only
* - Both hammered and milled types exist
† - Milled types only
‡ - Issues exclusively for Ireland
§ - Irish and English types exist.

C.2. ENGLISH MILLED COINAGES (1685 TO 1714)

Coin	Value	James II (1685-1688)	James II Gunmoney (1689-1690)	Wm & Mary (1688-1694)	William III (1695-1702)	Anne (1702-1714)
5 Guineas	£5 to £5 5s	Au	-	Au	Au	Au
2 Guineas	£2 2s	Au	-	Au	Au	-
Half Guinea	Guinea	£1 1s	Au	Au	Au	Au
Crown	5s	Ag	Brass*, Pewter & Brass	Ag	Ag	Ag
Halfcrown	2s 6d	Ag	Brass*, Pewter	Ag	Ag	Ag
Shilling	12d	Ag	Brass*	Ag	Ag	Ag
Sixpence	6d	Ag	Brass*	Ag	Ag	Ag
Fourpence	4d	Ag	Pewter	Ag	Ag	Ag
Threepence	3d	Ag	-	Ag	Ag	Ag
Twopence	2d	Ag	-	Ag	Ag	Ag
Penny	1d	Ag	Pewter*	Ag	Ag	Ag
Halfpenny	½ d	Sn & Cu	Pewter*	Cu, Sn & Cu	Cu	Cu (Patterns only)
Farthing	¼ d	Sn & Cu	-	Cu, Sn & Cu	Cu	Cu (Patterns only)

Notes:

* - Rare examples exist in other metals

C.3. ENGLISH MILLED COINAGES (1714 TO 1830)

Coin	Value	George I (1714-1727)	George II (1727-1760)	George III (1760-1820)	George IV (1820-1830)
5 Guineas	£5 5s	Au	Au	-	-
5 Pounds	£5	-	-	-	Au
2 Guineas	£2 2s	Au	Au	-	-
2 pounds	£2	-	-	-	Au
Guinea	£1 1s	Au	Au	Au	-
Sovereign	£1	-	-	Au	Au
Half Guinea	10s 6d	Au	Au	Au	-
Half Sovereign	10s	-	-	Au	Au
Third Guinea	7s	-	-	Au	-
Quarter Guinea	5s 3d	Au	-	Au	-
Crown	5s	Ag	Ag	Ag	Ag
3 Shillings (Bank Token)	3s	-	-	Ag	-
Halfcrown	2s 6d	Ag	Ag	Ag	Ag
18 Pence (Bank Token)	1s 6d	-	-	Ag	-
Shilling	12d	Ag	Ag	Ag	Ag
Sixpence	6d	Ag	Ag	Ag	Ag
Fourpence	4d	Ag	Ag	Ag	Ag
Threepence	3d	Ag	Ag	Ag	Ag
Twopence	2d	Ag	Ag	Ag, Cu	Ag
Penny	1d	Ag	Ag	Ag, Cu	Ag, Cu
Halfpenny	½ d	Cu	Cu	Cu	Cu
Farthing	¼ d	Cu	Cu	Cu	Cu
Half Farthing	$^{1}/_{8}$ d	-	-	-	Cu
Third Farthing	$^{1}/_{12}$ d	-	-	-	Cu

C.4. BRITISH/IRISH HALFPENCE AND FARTHINGS (1660 TO 1807)

	English/British Halfpence	English/British Farthings	Irish Halfpence	Irish Farthings
Charles II 1660-85	1672-1673,1675	1671(patterns only) 1672-1676,1679, 1684-1685 (tin)	Ca.1670 (St. Patrick's) 1680-1684 (Armstrong / Legg)	1660-1661 (Armstrong) Ca.1670 (St. Patrick's)
James II 1685-1688	1685-1687 (tin)	1684-1687 (tin)	1685-1688 (Knox) 1689-1690 (pewter, gun money) 1691 (brass, Limerick siege)	1691 (brass, Limerick siege)
William III and Mary II 1688-1694	1689-1692 (tin,) 1694	1689-1692 (tin,) 1694	1692-1694	None
William III 1695-1702	1695-1700,1701	1695-1700	1696	None
Anne 1702-1714	patterns only	1714 (patterns only)	None	None
George I 1714-1728	1717-1724 (dump)	1717,1719-1724 (dump)	1722-1724 (Wood)	1722-1724 (Wood)
George II 1728-1760	1729-1739 (young head) 1740,1742-1744, 1746,1749,1750, 1754 (old head)	1730-1737,1739 (young head) 1741,1744,1746, 1749,1750,1754 (old head)	1736-1738, 1741-1744, 1746-1753, 1755 (young head) 1760 (old head)	1737, 1738,1744 (young head) 1760 (old head)
George III 1760-1820	1770-1775 1797 (cartwheels,) 1799 (Soho 1st type) 1806,1807 (Soho 2nd type)	1771,1773-1775, 1799 (Soho 1st type) 1806,1807 (Soho 2nd type)	1766,1769 (London, 1st type) 1769,1775,1776, 1781, 1782 (London, 2nd type) 1805 (Soho)	1806 (Soho)

D: SPANISH/SPANISH COLONIAL COINAGES (1528 TO 1830)

Notes:

S	=	Minted in Spain	M	=	Minted in Mexico
B	=	Minted in Bolivia	Pe	=	Minted in Peru
Ch	=	Minted in Chile	Ph	=	Minted in the Philippines
Co	=	Minted in Colombia	G	=	Minted in Guatemala

Regular text denotes milled coinage.
Italic text denotes cob coinage.
Underlined text denotes that both types were produced.

Metal	Denomination	Charles I & Johanna 1516-1556	Philip II 1556-1598	Philip III 1598-1621	Philip IV 1621-1665	Charles II 1665-1700
Cu unless otherwise noted	Dinero			S	S	
	Ardite			S	S	
	½ Maravedi				S	
	1 Maravedi			S	S	
	2 Maravedis			S	S	S
	3 Maravedis			S		
	4 Maravedis			S	S	S
	8 Maravedis			S	S	S
	16 Maravedis				S	
Ag	¼ Real	M		S,B	Co$_{\text{Billon, Ag}}$	
	½ Real	M	M	S,B,M	S,B, Co,M	S,B,Co, M,Pe
	1 Real	M	M	S,B,M	S,B,Co, M,Pe	S,B,Co, M,Pe
	2 Reales	M	M	S,B,M	S,B,Co, M,Pe	S,B,Co, M,Pe
	3 Reales	M				
	4 Reales	M	M	S,B,M	S,B,Co, M,Pe	S,B,Co, M,Pe
	8 Reales		M	S,B,M	S,B,Co, M,Pe	S,B,Co, M,Pe
	50 Reales			S	S	S
	100 Reales				S	
Au	1 Escudo			S	S	S,Co, M,Pe
	2 Escudos			S	S,Co	S,Co, M,Pe
	4 Escudos			S	S	S,M,Pe
	8 Escudos			S	S	S,M,Pe
	100 Escudos			S	S	

Metal	Denomination	Philip V 1700-1746	Luis I 1724	Ferdinand VI 1746-1759	Charles III 1759-1788	Charles IV 1788-1808	Ferdinand VII 1808-1833
Cu Unless otherwise specified	Barilla (1/16 Real)				Ph		
	Octavo (1/8 Real)				Ph	Ph	
	Quarto (1/4 Real)				Ph	Ph	
	1 Maravedi	S		S	S		S
	2 Maravedis	S		S	S	S	S
	3 Maravedis			S			
	4 Maravedis	S		S	S	S	S
	8 Maravedis Treseta Seiseno Dieciocheno Croat	S,S_{Ag} S S S_{Ag} S_{Ag}		S	S	S	S
	16 Maravedis				S		
Ag	¼ Real		B,M	S		B,Ch,Co, G,M, Pe,Ph	Ch,Co,G
	½ Real	S,M,B, Co,G, Pe		B,*Ch*,Co, *G,M,Pe*	S,B,Ch, Co,G,M, Pe	S,B,Ch, Co,G,M, Pe	S,B,Ch,Co, G
	1 Real	S,M,B, Co,G, Pe		S,B,Ch, G,M,Pe	S,B,Ch, Co,G, M,Pe	S,B,Ch, Co,G, M,Pe	S,B,Ch,Co, G
	2 Reales	S,M,B, Co,G, Pe		S,B,Ch, G,M,Pe	S,B,Ch, Co,G,M, Pe	S,B,Ch, Co,G,M, Pe	S,B,Ch,Co, G
	4 Reales	S,M,B, Co,G, Pe		S,B,Ch, G,M,Pe	S,B,Ch, G,M,Pe	S,B,Ch, G,M,Pe	S,B,Ch,G
	8 Reales	S,M,B, Co,G, Pe	B,M	S,B,Ch, G,M,Pe	S,B,Ch, Co,G,M, Pe	S,B,Ch, Co,G,M, Pe	S,B,Ch,Co, G
	50 Reales			S	S	S	
	100 Reales				S		
Au	½ Escudo	S					S
	1 Escudo	S,Co, M,Pe		S,*Ch,Co, G,M,Pe*	S,*B,Ch, Co,G,M, Pe*	S,*B,Ch, Co, G,M,Pe*	S,B,Ch,Co
	2 Escudos	S,Co, M,Pe		S,*Ch,Co, G,M,Pe*	S,*B,Ch, Co,G,M, Pe*	S,*B,Ch, Co, G,M,Pe*	S,B,Ch,Co
	4 Escudos	S,Co, M,Pe		S,*Ch,Co, G,M,Pe*	S,*B,Ch, Co,G,M, Pe*	S,*B,Ch, Co, G,M,Pe*	S,B,Ch,Co
	8 Escudos	S,Co, G,M, Pe		S,*Ch,Co, G,M,Pe*	S,*B,Ch, Co,G,M, Pe*	S,*B,Ch, Co, G,M,Pe*	S,B,Ch,Co
	100 Escudos			S	S		

E: WOOD'S ROSA AMERICANA COIN TYPES (1722 TO 1733)

	Description
2d	Undated 1722 prototype. Plump bust. GEORGIVS. Uncrowned rose. UTILE DULCI without banner.
	Undated 1722 prototype. Thin bust. GEORGIVS. Uncrowned rose. UTILE DULCI without banner.
	Undated 1722 regular issue. Thin bust. GEORGIVS. Stop after REX. Uncrowned rose. UTILE DULCI on banner, as on all twopence varieties that follow.
	1722 regular issue. Thin bust. GEORGIUS. Uncrowned rose. Variations: 1.) Stop after REX, 2.) No stop after REX.
	1723 prototype. Drooping bust. Small letters. GEORGIUS, as on all 1723-1724 twopence that follow. Small crowned rose. Small letters. Crown top splits AME and RICANA.
	1723 regular issue. Jowled bust. Medium letters. Crown centered on 'I' in AMERICANA, as on all 1723-1724 twopence that follow. Variations: 1.) No stop after REX/no stop after 1723, 2.) Stop after REX/no stop after 1723, 3.) No stop after REX/stop after 1723, 4.) Stops after REX and 1723, 5.) UTILE DULCI.
	1724 prototypes. Bust with bulging collar bone. Variations: 1.) MA B FRA, 2.) M A B FRA, 3.) Metals – silver, copper, Bath metal, silvered, 4.) With 1723 reverse.
	1733 prototype. Bust of George II, facing left. GEORGIVS II. Stemmed rose, with leaves. Variations: 1.) Metals – steel, copper, lead, Bath metal, 2.) Uniface strikings. Many electrotypes and cast copies.
1d	1722 prototypes. Tall bust (hair rises to midpoint of 'I' in DEI, stop before GRATIA is above forehead and not above hair..) GEORGIVS and VTILE DVLCI. Large uncrowned rose. Rosettes before and after ROSA AMERICANA.
	1722 regular issues. Shorter bust (hair rises to midpoint of 'I' in DEI, stop after DEI is above hair.) GEORGIUS and VTILE DVLCI. Large uncrowned rose. Variations: 1.) Long hair ribbons (prototype?,) 2.) Short hair ribbons.
	1722 regular issues. As above, but UTILE DULCI and slightly smaller uncrowned rose. Variations: 1.) No rosettes, 2.) Rosette before ROSA, stop after DULCI, 3.) Rosettes Before ROSA and after DULCI, 4.) Stop placement after REX, 5.) No stop after REX, 6.) 1722/1722.
	1723 regular issues. Crowned rose. Variations: 1.a.) Numerous small pellets at center of rose (prototype?,) 1.b.) Larger, less numerous pellets, 2.) Size and shape of '3' in 1723, 4.) Stop after 1723, 5.) No stop after 1723, 6.) Placement of stop after REX.
	1724/3 prototype. Long-nosed bust. D GRATIA. Re-punched 1723 reverse.
	1724/3 prototypes. Bust of 1722-1723. DEI GRATIA. Re-punched 1723 reverse. Variations: 1.) Metals – copper, silver, Bath metal, 2.) No stop after REX.
	Undated (1724) patterns. ROSA : SINE : SPINA reverse. Variations: 1.) George I and 2.) Queen Wilhelmina Charlotta.

	Description
1/2d	1722 prototype. GEORGIUS DEI GRATIA, ROSA.AMERI. and VTILE DVLCI. Uncrowned rose.
	1722 prototype. GEORGIUS D : G :, ROSA.AMERI. and UTILE DULCI. Uncrowned rose.
	1722 regular issue. GEORGIUS DEI GRATIA, ROSA AMERICANA and UTILE DULCI. Uncrowned rose.
	1723 regular issue. Uncrowned rose. Same legends as 1722 regular issue. Variations: 1.) Overdate, 1723/2, 2.) Copper
	1723 regular issue. Crowned rose. Variations: 1.) Stop after date, 2.) No stop after date, 3.) Silver.
	1723 presentation issue in silver. Small crowned rose.
	Undated (1727) pattern, George II obverse, ROSA : SINE : SPINA reverse.

F: ATTRIBUTION GUIDE - PRIVATELY ISSUED CONSTELLATIO NOVA COPPERS

(Note: O_1 represents the first "O" in CONSTELLATIO, O_2 represents the second "O" in CONSTELLATIO and O_3 represents the "O" in NOVA.)

Obverses:

Date	Die	Distinguishing Characteristics
1783	Obv. 1 1-A Less Common	Legend: CONSTELLATIO ★ NOVA• Devices: Large eyeball, coarse pointed rays in groups of 5. Long rays are extended past the stars by short fine lines. A diagnostic mark, with upward-pointing protrusions resembling denticles, starts at the middle of the long ray that points to the "A" in CONSTELLATIO and passes through O_2. Unlike all other obverses, no long ray points to any part of the "A" in NOVA. The period after NOVA is large and a long ray points to its left side.
	Obv. 2 2-B Common	Legend: CONSTELLATIO ★ NOVA• Devices: Small eyeball, fine pointed rays in groups of 7. The legend's star has rounded points. Long rays are extended past the glory's stars by short fine lines. The period after NOVA is normal size and not pointed to by a long ray. Long rays point to near the centers of the bases of "A" and "I" in CONSTELLATIO.
	Obv. 3 3-C Less Common	Legend: CONSTELATIO ◇ NOVA• (Note change in spelling and punctuation) Devices: Small eyeball, 13 cuneiform rays with incised ends. Between each pair of large rays are pairs of shorter rays resembling tongs.
1785	Obv. 1 1-B Scarce	Same die as 1783, number 3.
	Obv. 2 2-A Rare	Legend: CONSTELLATIO NOVA (Note the return of the 1783 spelling and absence of punctuation) Devices: Same. Fine rays in groups of 7. The longest rays are not extended past the stars, giving the appearance of a small central device. The only letter with a long ray pointing at the center of its base is the first "L." Long rays point at the left side of "S," the downstroke of the "N" in NOVA and just right of O_1's center.
	Obv. 3 3-B Common	Legend: CONSTELLATIO NOVA Devices: Same. Fine rays in groups of 7. Long rays are extended past the stars by short fine lines. Long rays point to center of O_1, completely miss O_2 and O_3 and point to the center of the base of the first "L."
	Obv. 4 4-C Rare, 4-D Very Scarce	Legend: CONSTELLATIO NOVA Devices: Same. Fine rays in groups of 7. The longest rays are not extended. Long rays point to left side of O_1, the right side of O_2, right of O_3's center and just right of A's center.
	Obv. 5 5-E Scarce	Legend: CONSTELLATIO NOVA Devices: Same. Fine rays in groups of 7. The longest rays are not extended. Long rays miss O_1, point to the right side of O_2 and to the center of O_3.
	Obv. _ Unique (?)	Legend: CONSTELLATIO • NOVA(?) Devices: Same, but with only twelve stars and deeply indented pupil.
1786	Obv. 1 1-A Very Rare	Legend: CONSTELLATIO NOVA Devices: Same. Fine rays in groups of 7. The longest rays are not extended. Long rays point to the left side of O_1, completely miss O_2 and to the right of O_3 and to the center of "i."

Reverses:

Date	Die	Distinguishing Characteristics
1783	Rev. A 1-A Less Common	Legend: LIBERTAS ★ JUSTITIA•1783• Devices: Large Roman US, with U's right side leaning slightly outward. 24 leaf-pairs, angled outward from the central stem. The leaf tips point outward toward the legend and would intersect a circle drawn around them. If extended, the downstroke of the "J" would intersect the tip of the leaf below it. The "J" curls tightly inward, its end pointing at its downstroke, and might be described as "closed." The leaf directly below the star points directly at it.
	Rev. B 2-B Common	Legend: LIBERTAS ★ JUSTITIA •1783• Devices: Small Roman US, with U's sides parallel. 24 leaf-pairs, angled outward from the central stem. The leaf tips point outward toward the legend and would intersect a circle drawn around them. If extended, the downstroke of the "J" would intersect the stem of the leaf below it. The "J" curls gently and, at its base, resembles a "U." That is, it is "open" compared to reverse A. The leaf directly beneath the star does not point at the star, missing it to the left.
	Rev. C. 3-C Less Common	Legend: LIBERTAS ✪ JUSTITIA•1783• Devices: Small Roman US, with U's sides parallel. 23 leaf-pairs, folded very close to the stem. The leaf tips are slightly rounded, point along the line of the central stem and would not intersect a circle drawn around them. The leaf pairs resemble hearts. Note the use of a quatrefoil rather than a star.
1785 Reverses	Rev. A 2-A Rare	Legend: LIBERTAS ET JUSTITIA 1785 Devices: Monogrammed script US. 30 leaf-pairs, angled outward from the central stem. The leaf tips point outward toward the legend and would intersect a circle drawn around them. Small date, low and very distant from the "L" in LIBERTAS, the "A" in JUSTITIA and the wreath. This, the tightness of the wreath and its distance from the legends, give the appearance of a small wreath. The leaves are distinct from each other. The "7" is tall. The top serif of the "1" points slightly upward. 5's top line is short, its curl thick at its center and oddly formed. The centers of both sides of 2-A are often weakly struck.
	Rev. B 1-B Scarce 3-B Common	Legend: LIBERTAS ET JUSTITIA •1785• Devices: Monogrammed script US. 30 leaf-pairs, angled outward from the central stem. The leaf tips point outward toward the legend and would intersect a circle drawn around them. A die break usually joins 4 to 6 of the bottom wreath pairs, between "L" and "5," and is thickest above the "L."
	Rev. C 4-C Rare	Legend: LIBERTAS ET JUSTITIA •1785• Devices: Monogrammed script US. 30 leaf-pairs, angled outward from the central stem. Yet the leaf tips are squared and would not intersect a circle drawn around them. The curl of the "5" is open and its lower part is exaggerated and downward-pointing. Two leaves above the script "U" touch but do not strongly overlap. Compare to reverse D.
	Rev. D 4-D Very Scarce	Legend: LIBERTAS ET JUSTITIA •1785 • Devices: Monogrammed script US. 29 leaf-pairs, angled outward from the central stem. Yet the leaf tips are squared and would not intersect a circle drawn around them. The date numerals are large and round. The "5" is very round and its lower part is on the same line as the other digits. Its top line curves upward. Two leaves above the script "U" overlap each other by 50%+, a key diagnostic.

Date	Die	Distinguishing Characteristics
	Rev. E 5-E Scarce	Legend: LIBERTAS ET JUSTITIA •1785• Devices: Monogrammed script US. 26 leaf-pairs, angled outward from the central stem. Medium date numerals. The "5" well proportioned and its lower part is on the same line as the other digits. Its top line is flat. The downstroke of the "J" and other letters are thick. The "L" and "J" are slightly low relative to other letters in the legend. The top serif of the "1" is long. Leaf pairs on the left side are very close, those on the right farther apart.
	Rev. _ Unique (?)	Unique counterfeit. Legend: LIBERTAS ET JUSTITIA • 1785 • Devices: Monogrammed script US, crude and misshapen. 23 leaf-pairs, angled outward from the central stem. Wreath is out of round, flattened at top. The S's are crudely formed from two punches. Crossbars of the T's are very long.
1786 Reverse	Rev. A 1-A Very Rare	Legend: LIBERTAS ET JUSTITIA •1786• Devices: Small Roman US. 23 leaf-pairs, angled outward from the central stem. The "1" is a "J." The "6" is small and high relative to the other numerals. The "S" and "T" touch. TAS and JU are low.

G: ATTRIBUTION GUIDE - AMERICAN-MADE IMITATION HALFPENCE

Varieties:

Date	Group	Variety	Rarity	Also Known As
1747	**II**	1-47A	Rare	
1771	**I**	2-71A	Scarce	
		3-71B	Rare	
		4-71C	Extremely Rare	
		4-71D	Extremely Rare	
1772	**I**	5-72A	Very Rare	
		6-72A	Very Rare	
		7-72B	Very Rare	
	V	24-72C	Extremely Rare	
1774	**I**	3-74A	Rare	
		5-74A	Presently Unique	Discovered in 2006 by Jack Howes
		7-74A	Very Rare	
		8-74A	Scarce	
1775	**I**	4-75A	Relatively Common	
1776	**I**	6-76A	Scarce	
		9-76B	Extremely Rare	
1777	**V**	10-77A	Extremely Rare	
1778	**III**	11-78A	Relatively Common	
		12-78B	Relatively Common	
		13-78B	Rare	
1783	**V**	25-83A	Extremely Rare	
1784	**V**	14-84A	Very Rare	
1785	**IV**	15-85NY	Extremely Rare	
1786	**V**	16-86A	Extremely Rare	
		CT-86A	Extremely Rare	CT Miller 2.4-U
1787	**III**	18-87C	Scarce	
		19-87C	Relatively Common	
		20-87C	Extremely Rare	
		21.II-87C	Extremely Rare	
		23-87C	Extremely Rare	
		21.I-87D.I	Very Rare	
		21.II-87D.II	Scarce	
		13-87CT	Extremely Rare	CT Miller 101-G.2
		VT-87C	Very Common	VT Ryder-13
	II	17-87A	Relatively Common	
		17-87B	Relatively Common	
		17-87E	Extremely Rare	
	IV	9-87NY	Extremely Rare	
1788	**III**	23-88A	Relatively Common	
		13-88CT	Scarce	CT Miller 101.D
		13-88VT_2	Extremely Rare	VT Ryder-40/Bressett 17-L
		22-88VT_1	Scarce	VT Ryder-31/Bressett 24-U, CT Miller 100-I

Obverses:

Vlack Obverse	Pairings	Distinguishing Characteristics
1	**1-47A**	GEORGIVS • II • REX • Tall, thin left-facing bust of George II. Very large stops. Used only with reverse 47A. (See example in Chapter 10.)
2	**2-71A**	GEORGIVS III • REX• Device punch same as on V.9. Similar to V.3, V.5 and V.8 obverses, but chin is stronger and more clearly doubled. Nose points between stop and REX. Medium width head. "X" ends just below the point where the front neckline intersects the cuirass.
3	**3-71B** **3-74A**	GEORGIVS. III•REX• Bust as on V.5 and V.8. Nose points to just left of "R" in REX. Usually exhibits three horizontal die cracks below bust: 1. 5:00 to 7:00 at bottom, 2. 6:00 to 7:30 just above it, and 3. a short crack at 6:30, just below bust. Wide head. (See example in Chapter 10.)
4	**4-71C** **4-71D** **4-75A**	GEORGIVS• III : REX• Small head, high cheekbone. Top leaves of wreath extend well above head. Nose points to colon. (See example.)
5	**5-72A** **5-74A**	GEORGIVS . III•REX• Bust as on V.3 and V.8. Nose points at very right side of the base of "I" in III.
6	**6-72A** **6-76A**	GEORGIVS• III•REX . Tall thin head. Nose points between stop and REX. Front of bust is rounded. (See example in Chapter 10.)
7	**7-72B** **7-74A**	GEORGIUS• III•REX• (i.e., "U" instead of "V") Small head with rounded features and clear double chin. Small stops. Legend uses GEORGIUS spelling. Nose points to left base of "R" in REX. (See illustration in Chapter 10.)
8	**8-74A**	GEORGIVS . III REX• Bust as on V.3 and V.5. No punctuation between III and REX. Nose points between III and REX, nearly to last "I".
9	**9-76B** **9-87NY**	CEORCIVS III REX (i.e., "C" instead of "G") Bust as on V.2. III and REX widely separated. Nose points to very right side of "R" in REX. (See illustrations in Chapter 10.)
10	**10-77A**	GEORGIVS III REX (?) Vaguely similar to Group II obverse 17, but very crude. Possibly a contemporary counterfeit. Probably hand-engraved rather than punched device. (See illustration in Chapter 10.)
11	**11-78A**	GEORGIVS III .REX . Small head on thick neck, as on V.12. Nose points at middle of "R" in REX. Stop between III and REX closer to REX. "Puckered" lips. GEORGIVS starts away from shoulder and finishes close to head.
12	**12-78B**	GEORGIVS III .REX . Similar to V.11. Nose points to a point below stop between III and REX. The stop is nearer to III than to REX. Faint smile. GEORGIVS starts near shoulder and finishes close to head. On some specimens, a die irregularity makes the final stop appear to be a colon. (See example in Chapter 10.)
13	**13-78B** **13-87CT** **13-88CT** **13-88VT$_2$**	GEORGIVS III .REX . Head is more oval and smaller than on V.11 and V.12. GEORGIVS starts away from shoulder and finishes away from head. Nose points between stop after III and REX. A bulge that obscured III developed in later die states. 13-87CT is a.k.a., CT Miller 101-G.2. 13-88CT is a.k.a. CT Miller 101-D. 13-88VT is a.k.a. VT Ryder 40. Thought to be a modern fabrication. (See examples and illustrations in Chapter 10.)

Vlack Obverse	Pairings	Distinguishing Characteristics
14	14-84A	GEORGIVS . III .REX Completely different from all other American-attributed obverses. Emaciated bust of George III, pronounced necklines. On higher-grade examples, depressions from sides of punches evident around letters. "G" and "I" in GEORGIVS widely spaced. REX ends opposite chin. (See illustration in Chapter 10.)
15	15-85NY	CEORCIVS ✸ III • REX• Device punch as used on Vermont "standard heads." Very crude letter placement. The first "C" rests on the bust, the "S" on the hair. "VS" and III are low. (See illustration in Chapter 10.)
16	16-86A	GEORGIVS III REX (?) <u>Very</u> crude bust. See comments on next obverse and on reverse 86A. (See illustration.)
17	17-87A 17-87B 17-87E	GEORGIVS . III .REX . Tall, thin bust. The nose is pointed and is nearly in line with the forehead. Sharp, angular bow and round knot. (See example in Chapter 10.)
18	18-87C	GEORGIVS• III .REX . Similar to V.19. Round head with pursed lips. First "G", "S" and stop after GEORGIVS all close to bust. First "I" in III close to forehead. "R" and "E" in REX touch. III.REX is tightly grouped. Jaw line forms a nearly circular arc. Nose points at right side of the upright of "R". The line that forms the top of the nose is nearly straight from bridge to point. First "G" nearly touches shoulder.
19	19-87C	GEORGIVS• III .REX• Round head with pursed lips, similar to V.18. Legend is distant from bust. Stop after GEORGIVS high and distant from head. "R" and "E" in REX do not touch. Jaw line forms a nearly circular arc. Nose points at upright on "R". Last stop is larger than the first two. (See example in Chapter 10.)
20	20-87C	GEORGIVS III .REX . Head as on V.19. (Round with pursed lips.) First "G" and "S" are both close to bust. III is not close to forehead. "R" and "E" in REX touch. Nose points at right edge of "R".
21.I (Late die state, large planchet) & 21.II (Early die state, small planchet)	21.I-87D.I 21.II-87C 21.II-87D.II	GEORGIVS III .REX . Round head with pursed lips, as on V.19 and V.20. GEORGIVS starts slightly away from shoulder and ends on head. III and REX are distinct from face. Nose points at stop after III. The first "I" in III is low. Double chin. On the later die state (21.I,) peripheral lettering is very weak or missing, particularly between "IVS" and "R". The crown of the head and base of the bust are often missing on the late state; and a bulge may be evident in front of the neck and chin. On the earlier die state (21.II,) the lettering is generally intact. 21.I is used with reverse 87D.I. 21.II is used with reverse 87C and 87D.II. The combination 21.I-87D.I is struck on wide planchets, apparently without the use of a collar. The other combinations use normal planchets. (See example in Chapter 10.)
22	22-88VT$_1$	GEORGIVS• III .REX . Known to collectors of Vermont coppers as Bressett obverse 24. It is paired with Vermont reverse U to produce 22-VT88 (or, in Vermont terminology: Ryder-31 or Bressett 24-U.) The bust is a Vermont "standard head". The nose points to the upright of the "R". The "S" sits on the head. The stop after it is high. The second "I" in III is low and leans to the right. (See example in Chapter 10.)

Vlack Obverse	Pairings	Distinguishing Characteristics
23	23-87C 23-88A	GEORGIVS .III .REX Similar to 1788 Connecticut variety Miller 2-D (Another Machin's Mills product – See below.) Thick neck and pursed lips. Nose is slightly hooked, almost parrot like. The nose points at the right side of the last "I" in III. "S" is close to the head. First "I" in III is low. "X" is close to the chest. (See illustration in Chapter 10.)
24	24-72C	GEORGIVS III REX .(?) Very elegant round upward-peering head. Well-shaped nose points between widely spaced III and REX. Reminiscent of Group III obverses, but clearly different. Peripheral lettering always weak or missing. (See illustration in Chapter 10.)
25	25-83A	Extremely rare obverse. Similar to obverses 16 and CT and hence sometimes included with this series.
CT	CT-86A	Similar to obverse 16, but with AUCTORI CONNEC in legend. Used with reverse 86A (extremely rare.) This pairing is the basis for treating Vlack 16-86A as American.
VT	VT-87C	VERMON AUCTORI. Known to collectors of Vermont coppers as Bressett obverse 17. It is paired with a worn reverse 87C to produce VT-87C (or, in Vermont terminology: Ryder-13 or Bressett 17-V – See below..) The figure bears a silly expression. The nose points to the base of the "T." The "N" is near the head. The left edge of the "A" just grazes the forehead. The bust itself is somewhat similar to that on Vermont Ryder-27 (the other "bastard head".) That it differs from all other Vermonts "may indicate that it was Atlee's attempt at imitating the Vermonts prior to the deal that brought together the Vermont and Machin's Mills operations. (See example.)

Reverses:

Vlack Reverse	Pairings	Distinguishing Characteristics
47A	1-47A	1747 BRITAN NIA• Pole points well to left of date. Both feet rest squarely on the double exergue line. Branch top near left side of the base of "N." NIA begins high. The date is evenly spaced, with 7's slanting to the right. Double exergue line. (See example in Chapter 10.)
71A	2-71A	1771 BRITAN NIA • Pole points at left edge of first "7" in date. Small date. Left foot rests over single exergue line. NIA starts at a point nearly even with wrist.
71B	3-71B	1771 BRITAN NIA . Pole points at first "1" in date. NIA starts at a point even with forearm. Left foot rests on single exergue line.
71C	4-71C	1771 BRITAN NIA . Pole points to left of date. Both feet far to left of date. Branch hand points to left down stroke of "A." On 71A and 71B, the branch hand points at "T." A die break from Britannia's neck and chest may explain the rarity of this reverse.
71D	4-71D	1771 BRITAN NIA .(?) Used only with obverse 4. Excessively rare.
72A	5-72A 6-72A	1772 BRITAN NIA. Pole points just to left of date. "B" is close to foot. Small date. A vertical die crack developed from the right wrist upward and through the branch.

Vlack Reverse	Pairings	Distinguishing Characteristics
72B	7-72B	1772 BRITAN NIA Pole points well to left of date. Britannia's right hand points at left edge of "A" in BRITAN. Double exergue line.
72C	24-72C	1772 BRITAN NIA• Extended pole would point just to left of date. Date weak and rises slightly from left to right. Left foot rests on single exergue line. Die break from base of branch to knee. Top of branch ends under middle of "A." (See obverse illustration in Chapter 10.)
74A	3-74A 5-74A 7-74A 8-74A	1774 BRITAN NIA . Pole points at "1" in date. Die crack extends from a point between foot and exergue line through tops of BRI. Single exergue line. (See Vlack 3-74A example in Chapter 10.)
75A	4-75A	1775 BRITAN NIA• Pole points well to left of date. NIA begins low, just above waist. Left foot very lightly touches double exergue line. The die developed a central bulge that often obscures details. Double exergue line. (See example in Chapter 10.)
76A	6-76A	1776 BRITAN NIA• Large date. Extended pole passes just to the left of the "1" in date. Die cracks developed near Britannia's left elbow, running to the "I" in NIA and vertically from the base of the branch. Single thick exergue line. (See example in Chapter 10.)
76B	9-76B	1776 BRITAN NIA Small date. Vermont device punch. Extended pole just strikes top left of the "1" in date. Right arm points directly at the base of "T." Top of branch below "N." Single exergue line. (See illustration in Chapter 10.)
77A	10-77A	1777 BRITAN NIA Extended pole would point at left side of the first "7" in the date. "Banana" shaped left leg. Foot rests on double exergue line. Date numerals widely spaced, their tops aligned. Used only with obverse 10.
78A	11-78A	1778 BRITAN NIA . Extended pole would nearly overlap the down stroke of the first "7" in the date. The "8" is large and just touches the bottom of the double exergue line. Right foot rests on top exergue line. The two exergue lines are close and sometimes appear to be a single line. Top of the branch just misses the right edge of "A" in BRITAN. Bulbous "beehive" hair as on reverse 78B.
78B	12-78B 13-78B	1778 BRITAN NIA . Extended pole would strike the right edge of the "1" near the top. "8" is small and does not touch the exergue line. Single exergue line. Right foot rests above the exergue line. Top of the branch is under the center of the "A" in BRITAN. "I" is closer to "A" than to "N" in NIA. Bulbous "beehive" hair. (See Vlack 13-78B example in Chapter 10.)
83A	25-83A	Similar to 86A, but dated 1783. used only with obverse 25 (excessively rare) and not universally accepted as part of the series.
84A	14-84A	1784 BRITAN NIA• Scrawny Britannia. Tightly spaced lettering. "AN" lower than "BRIT." Small date. "17" is low, "8" lower, 4 still lower. The "1" is actually a "J." Double exergue line. Top of branch completely misses "N." As on obverse 14, letter punch edges sometimes evident. (See illustration in Chapter 10.)
85NY	15-85NY	The 1785 Immune Columbia from the Wyons" Confederation pattern submission. (See illustration in Chapter 10.)
86A	16-86A	1786 BRITAN NNIA• [sic] Very crude, wildly contorted Britannia. "BRI" not aligned with "TAN." Shield rests on its side. Long thin left arm almost forms a right angle.

Vlack Reverse	Pairings	Distinguishing Characteristics
87A	17-87A	1787 BRITAN NIA • BRITAN begins just below the point where Britannia's shins cross. Extended pole would pass between "1" and "7." The "1" is high (i.e., 1787) and close to the exergue line, which is doubled. "787" is lower, slanting away from the horizontal. Britannia's right hand points to the "A" in "BRITAN" and the branch points past the "N." Large, low stop. (See example in Chapter 10.)
87B	17-87B	1787 BRITAN NIA • BRITAN begins just below the point where Britannia's shins cross. Extended pole would nearly overlap the down stroke of the "7." Tops of date numerals nearly aligned. All are close to the doubled exergue line. Britannia's right hand points to the "T" in "BRITAN" and the branch points to the base of "N." Later die states have weak lower exergue line, giving the appearance of a single line. The branch itself nearly disappeared as the die bulged.
87E	17-87E	1787 BRITAN NIA • BRITAN begins just above the point where Britannia's shins cross. Extended pole would just graze the left side of "8." The "1" is slightly high, but not as much as on rev. 87A. Double exergue line. Britannia's right hand points to the "A" in "BRITAN" and the branch points past the "N." Used only with obverse 17. The likely reason for reverse 87E's rarity is the major die break that it suffered from the shield through a point between "T" and "A."
87C	18-87C 19-87C 20-87C 21.II-87C 23-87C VT-87C	1787 BRITAN NIA • Extended pole would closely parallel, but not overlap the down stroke of the first "7" in the date. Very large date numerals. Single exergue line. Right foot rests on the exergue line. Top of the branch is under the down stroke of the "N" in BRITAN. BRITAN begins close to the right leg. "Bubble and bun" hair. (See examples in Chapter 10.)
87D.I (Late die state, large planchet) & 87D.II (Early die state, mall planchet)	21.I-87D.I 21.II-87D.II	1787 BRITAN NIA • Extended pole would closely parallel, but not overlap the "1", which slants to the right. Very large date numerals. Double exergue line. Lines are thick and widely separated. The right foot rests on the exergue line. Top of the branch is completely to the right of the "N" in BRITAN. BRITAN begins close to the right leg. Stop after NIA rests on shield. The earlier die state (87D.II) is used with obverse 21.II on normal-sized planchets. The later die state (87D.I) is used with the later die state of obverse 21 (21.I) on rare large planchet pieces. (See example in Chapter 10.)
87CT	13-87CT	1787 INDE ✱ ET LIB ✱ Connecticut reverse Miller G.2 (Also used with the extremely rare Connecticut variety Miller 52-G.2..) Similar to reverse 88CT. Top of branch points to "E" in ET. Grapevines rather than crosses on shield. Heavy double exergue line. Used only with obverse 13 (extremely rare.) V.13 is known in the Connecticut series as obverse 101. Hence, Vlack 13-87CT is equivalent to Miller 101-G.2. Miller 52-G.2 is believed to be another Machin's Mills product.
87NY	9	Atlee's standing Indian from Machin's 1787 New York proposal. Used with obverse 9. Example shown is a modern copy. The three known genuine examples of Vlack 9-87NY are from a later die state and are struck on small, crude planchets. (See illustration.)

Vlack Reverse	Pairings	Distinguishing Characteristics
88A	**23-88A**	1788 BRITAN NIA. Extended pole would pass between the "1" and the first "7" in the date, striking the "1" at its base. Double exergue line. The top of the branch points to the left side of the "N" in BRITAN.
88CT	**13-88CT**	1788 INDE ✱ ET ✱ LIB ✱ Connecticut reverse Miller D (Also used with Connecticut varieties Miller 2-D and 16.1-D.) Similar to reverse 87CT. Top of branch points to "T" in ET. Heavy double exergue line. Used only with obverse 13 (not rare.) Vlack 13-88CT is equivalent to Miller 101-D. Miller 2-D and 16.1-D are also believed to be Machin's Mills products. (See composite example in Chapter 10.)
88VT$_1$	**22-88VT$_1$**	1788 INDE+ ET•LIB+ Vermont Bressett reverse U. As on the example, the reverse is often obscured by the bulging die. The reverse device punch is that used on most Vermont "standard" heads. (See 88VT$_2$ below.) The extended pole passes well to the left of the date. is known in the Vermont series as Ryder-31. The reverse is used with four other Vermont obverses on Ryder-16, -21, -22 and -25 . In the Connecticut series, the reverse is shared with the rare small head variety Miller 1-I. Hence, 22-88VT$_1$ is also known as CT Miller 101-I.
88VT$_2$	**13-88VT$_2$**	1788 INDE ETLIB Vermont Bressett reverse L. The reverse device punch is that used on most Vermont "standard" heads. (See 88VT$_1$ above.) Vlack 13-88VT$_2$ is also known in the Vermont series as Ryder-40 and is believed to be a modern fabrication rather than a legitimate variety. The same reverse is used on Vermont Ryder-19 and -20.

H: ATTRIBUTION GUIDE – VERMONT COINAGE (1785-1788)

Note: Since beginning this appendix, a superior guide has been published (in *The Copper Coins of Vermont and Those Bearing the Vermont Name* by Tony Carlotto. The Colonial Coin Collector's Club; Printed by Bookcrafters, Chelsea Michigan, 1998.) Rather than abandoning the appendix, this author elected to complete and include it for the benefit of more casual students of Vermont's copper coinage and those who do not have access to Carlotto's work.

Relative Rarity by Ryder-Richardson Variety:

Relative Rarity	Ryder-Richardson Variety (RR)
Common	13
Somewhat Scarce	6, 16, 25, 27
Scarce	2, 7, 9, 10, 11, 12, 14, 20, 23, 24
Very Scarce	4, 8
Rare	3, 17, 29, 31
Very Rare	18, 19, 21, 22, 28, 36, 39
Extremely Rare	1, 5, 15, 26, 30, 32, 35, 38
Excessively Rare	33, 34, 37, 40

Obverses, by Bressett die designations:

KB	Legend	Distinguishing Characteristics	Varieties
1	VERMONTS • RES • PUBLICA• 1785 •	Landscape. A sun ray points directly at the period after RES. Another sun ray points to the right side of the "P." The top of the second tree from the left points toward the base of "S." A tornado-like die crack over the "8" eventually obscured the plow's center. Compare to obverse 2.	1-A = 1785 Ryder 2
2	VERMONTS• RES• PUBLICA • 1785 •	Landscape. A sun ray points well to the right of period after RES. The top of the second tree from the left points to the left edge of the period after VERMONTIS. On some specimens, the top line of the "5" appears to be followed by a dash, which is probably a die defect. Compare to obverse 1.	2-B = 1785 Ryder 3
3	VERMONTIS • RES • PUBLICA • 1785 •	Landscape. Unique use of VERMONTIS. A sun ray points to the base of "P." The rightmost tree just touches the "U." Late obverse die states show a major bulge in the center of the die.	3-C = 1785 Ryder 4
4	VERMONTENSIUM. RES • PUBLICA. 1786	Landscape. Seven trees on the mountain. The fourth tree from the left is detached and floats above the mountain. The top of the leftmost tree points at the bottom right serif of the "E" in VERMONTENSIUM. The "U" in PUBLICA is misplaced and re-punched, so that a second "U" appears just below the first. Sun rays point at the tip of the bottom left serif in the "R" and at the right edge of the "E" in RES. The tip of the plowshare ends over the very left edge of "1."	4-D = 1786 Ryder 6

KB	Legend	Distinguishing Characteristics	Varieties
5	VERMONTENSIUM. RES • PUBLICA. 1786	Landscape. Nine trees on the mountain. The leftmost tree is barely visible over the mountain. Its branches are well away from the left edge of the mountain. The tree immediately to its right is tall and just touches the left downstroke of the "N." Sun rays point at the right side of the "R" and at the base of the "S" in RES. The tip of the plowshare ends over the center of "1."	5-E = 1786 Ryder 7
6	VERMONTENSIUM. RES • PUBLICA. 1786	Landscape. Nine trees on the mountain. The leftmost tree is only slightly more visible above the mountain than on obverse 5 and its branches extend to the edge of the mountain. Tops of the two leftmost trees point at the bases of "T" and "E." The "1" in the date is re-cut. The tip of the plowshare ends over the left edge of "7."	6-E = 1786 Ryder 8
-	VERMONTIS. RES PUBLICA (1785 within circle formed by legend)	Landscape. Struck. The sun rises to the viewer's left. Many, many small trees (compare to the above.) 1785 is beneath an exergue line. The exergue line joins the "C" in PUBLICA and the "M" in VERMONTIS. As on the cast version of Ryder 5, below, the point of the "V," if extended, would strike the base of the "8."	Ryder 5, Struck
-	VERMONTIS. RES • PUBLICA (1785 within circle formed by legend)	Landscape. Cast. The sun rises to the viewer's left. No exergue line. The point of the "V," if extended, would strike the bottom center of the "8." The plow beam, if extended, would strike the "O."	Ryder 5, Cast
7	AUCTORI: VERMON:	Baby Head. Unique appearance of right-facing juvenile profile and the reverse. AUC is more tightly spaced than TORI. The "A" is close to the shoulder. The base of the "U" points to the fillets. The "V" is close to the forehead. The second colon is low, close to the "N" and distant from the bust. See illustration in Chapter 10.	7-F = 1786 Ryder 9
8	VERMON: AUCTORI:	Mailed bust, facing left. Very similar to obverse 9. Main device punch shared with 1785 Connecticut head lefts. "V" is about two letter widths from bust. The "I" is only slightly low, if at all, compared to that on obverse 9.	8-G = 1786 Ryder 10
9	VERMON: AUCTORI	Mailed bust, facing left. Very similar to obverse 8. Main device punch shared with 1785 Connecticut head lefts. "V" is less than a letter width from the bust. The "I" is low and not succeeded by a colon.	9-H = 1786 Ryder 11 9-I = 1787 Ryder 15
10	VERMON• AUCTORI•	Standard Head. The "V" in VERMON is about equi-distant, about a letter width, from the bust and the fillets. The lower right corner of the "N" very nearly touches the hair. AUCTORI ends above the tip of the breast and the period after AUCTORI is about equidistant from the tip and "I." "A" is a half letter width from the forehead. A "pimple" appears on the nose, at eye level. The point of the "V," if extended would pass between the two fillets (hair ribbon ends.)	10-K = 1787 Ryder 14 10-L = 1788 Ryder 20 10-R = 1788 Ryder 21 10-Q = 1788 Ryder 22 10-O = 1788 Ryder 23 10-J = 1788 Ryder 34 10-P = 1788 Ryder 36 10-M = 1788 Ryder 37 10-N = 1788 Ryder 38

KB	Legend	Distinguishing Characteristics	Varieties
11	VERMON AUCTORI	Standard Head. The obverse bust is much closer to VERMON than AUCTORI. The "I" in AUCTORI is very distant from the breastplate and ends well above it. The "A" is also distant from the forehead. The "V" in VERMON is about a half letter width from the hair ribbons. The "N" does not touch the hair, but is close. The point of the "V," if extended, would strike the upper fillet. Compare to obverse 12.	11-K = 1787 Ryder 12
12	VERMON AUCTORI	Standard Head. The "V" in VERMON is about a letter width away from the bust and very distant from the hair ribbons (perhaps two letter widths.) The point of the "V," if extended, would pass below the lower fillet. A die crack passes across the forehead, striking the rim between "C" and "T." The "N" is slightly in the hair. The "I" in AUCTORI is in the breastplate and mostly beneath its top edge. Compare to obverse 11.	12-K = 1787 Ryder 32
13	VERMON• AUCTORI•	Standard Head. A die-crack circumscribes the bust. With the exception of the "N," which is relatively far from the "O," all letters are evenly spaced and are free of the devices. The point of the "V," if extended would pass below the lower fillet. AUCTORI ends above the tip of the mail and the period that follows it is equidistant from the tip and the "I."	13-L = 1788 Ryder 19
14	VERMON AUCTORI	Standard Head. The lower right corner of "N" just touches the head. "V" is close to the bust. Its point, if extended, would strike the lower fillet. "A" is close to the forehead. The breastplate is fully engraved, as opposed to being made up of dots, as on reverse 15.	14-S = 1788 Ryder 17
15	VERMON AUCTORI	Standard Head. The "N" in VERMON is well-separated from the head. "V" is close to the bust and its point, if extended, would strike between the fillets. "A" and "I" are relatively close to the bust and are each about the same distance from it. The breastplate is made up of dots. Other, unexplained "dots" on some Ryder-16 examples, above the head or in the field in front of the face, can resemble periods.	15-S = 1788 Ryder 16
16	VERMON+ AUCTORI+	Standard Head. "V" is close to the bust and the lower right corner of "N" just touches the hair. The point of the "V," if extended, would strike the shoulder. "A" is at the level of the eyebrow, as opposed to being at the forehead level as on most obverses. The "I" is close to the tip of the mail and the "+" following AUCTORI is well below the tip of the mail.	16-S = 1788 Ryder 24 16-U = 1788 Ryder 25 16-T = 1788 Ryder 26
17	VERMON AUCTORI	Bastard Head. Unusual bust, paired only with a worn Britannia reverse die. Refer to illustrations in Chapter 10. "N" and "A" nearly touch the head. The point of the "V," if extended, would touch the very end of the upper fillet. Both fillets are nearly vertical at their ends. Compare to obverse 18.	17-V = 1787 Ryder 13 = Vlack VT-87C

KB	Legend	Distinguishing Characteristics	Varieties
18	VERMON • AUCTORI ✸	Bastard Head. Unusual bust, resembling Machin's Mills Group III pieces. Unique use of "domed hair." That is, the hair all converges to a single point. Refer to illustrations in Chapter 10. VERMON is well away from the bust, though the period that follows it is low and close to the head. The point of the "V," if extended, would strike the very end of the lower fillet. "V" is distant from both fillets. AUCTORI ends just below the chin. "I" is very distant from the bust. Both fillets are nearly vertical at their ends. Compare to obverse 17.	18-W = 1788 Ryder 27
19	VERMON AUCTORI	Standard Head. Check for errant reverse legend: ✸ ET LIB ✸ ✸ INDE 1788. Only Ryder-18 and 35 share reverse die X. "A" is very distant from the forehead. "V," "N" and "I" are close to the bust. The bust is closer to VERMON than to AUCTORI. The point of the "V" is very close to the end of the lower fillet. A diagnostic bisecting die crack runs from 1:00 to 7:00. Compare to obverse 20.	19-X = 1788 Ryder 18
20	VERMON AUCTORI	Standard Head. Check for errant reverse legend: ✸ ET LIB ✸ ✸ INDE 1788. Only Ryder-18 and 35 share reverse die X. "A," when it can be seen, is very close to the forehead. (AUCTORI is sometimes obscured by weak striking.) "N" is close to the hair. The down-stroke of the "E" points to the upper fillet. Compared to obverse 19, the bust is closer to being equidistant from VERMON and AUCTORI.	20-X = 1788 Ryder 35
21	VERMON ✸ ✸ AUCTORI	Standard Head. The lower right corner of the "N" rests just on the hair. The "I" is close to the breastplate and parallel to it. The point of the "V," if extended would strike the lower fillet. A die break joins the "E" in VERMON and the "R" in AUCTORI, cutting across the lower neck. The first star nearly touches the hair. The "A" nearly sits on the eyebrow. Known specimens are overstruck on Irish halfpence.	21-U = 1788 Ryder 28 21-Y = 1788 Ryder 33
22	✸ VERMON ✸ ✸ AUCTORI ✸	Standard Head. The bust is closer to VERMON than to AUCTORI. The first star almost touches the shoulder's tip. The point of the "V," if extended, would strike between the fillets, but closer to the top one. The fillets are close together. The lower right corner of the "N" rests just on the hair. The "I" is distant from the breastplate. The top line of the breastplate, if extended, would strike the lower two points of the fourth star. Neither the second nor the third star touch the bust, though the second is close. A die break begins above the head and follows the line of the forehead and nose, ending at the downstroke of the "R."	22-U = 1788 Ryder 29
23	VERMON ✸ AUƆTORI	Standard Head. Very crude, buckled die. The "C" is backward. The "O" is very low and not in line with VERM. Misplaced re-cutting of "V." The lines of the mail are formed by crude scratches. Facial details are obscured by the die buckling.	23-S = 1788 Ryder 30
24	GEORGIVS• III• REX•	Standard Head. Note unusual legend. The first "G" is very near the mail. The "S" is slightly in the hair. REX ends above the breastplate. See the illustration in Chapter 10. This variety is sometimes confused with contemporary British counterfeits.	24-U = 1788 Ryder 31

KB	Legend	Distinguishing Characteristics	Varieties
25	AUCTORI CONNEC	Mule. Connecticut "small head" obverse, Miller 1.1 with Vermont reverse U. See illustrations in Chapter 10. Note unusual legend. "A" and "I" are close to the bust. CONNEC is distant from the bust.	25-U = 1788 Ryder 39
26	VERMON AUCTORI	Mule. Crude standard head with IMMUNE COLUMBIA reverse. The point of the "V" overlaps the upper fillet. MON is low and not in line with VER. AUCT is more widely spaced than ORI. The "I" is low. Always crude. See illustration in Chapter 10.	26-Z = 1785 Ryder 1
-	GEORGIVS III. REX.	Mule. Vlack's obverse 13 with Vermont reverse L. See illustrations in Chapter 10. Machin's Mills obverse, with round face and pursed lips. GEORGIVS is distant from the bust.	Vlack-13 with reverse L = 1788 Ryder 40

Reverses, by Bressett die designations:

KB	Legend	Distinguishing Characteristics	Varieties
A	STELLA . QUARTA . DECIMA •	Divine eye, wide rays with incised ends. Thin, 6-pointed stars. Long rays end squarely at the bases of "S," "E" and the second "L" in STELLA and the "Q" in QUARTA. No stars point to periods. Compare to reverses B and C.	1-A = 1785 Ryder 2
B	STELLA . QUARTA . DECIMA •	Divine eye, wide rays with incised ends. Thin, 6-pointed stars. Long rays end squarely at the base of "S" in STELLA and the second "A" in QUARTA. A star points directly at the period after QUARTA. Compare to reverses A and C. Also, see Chapter 10 illustration.	2-B = 1785 Ryder 3
C	STELLA• QUARTA • DECIMA •	Divine eye, wide rays with incised ends. Thin 6-pointed stars. Long rays do not end squarely at the bases of the "E" and second "L" in STELLA. A long ray points to each of the three periods. Compare to reverses A and B. Check for VEROMONTIS obverse 3.	3-C = 1785 Ryder 4
D	STELLA • QUARTA • DECIMA •	Divine eye, groups of lines as rays. Thin 6-pointed stars. Long rays point to the right edge of "S," the downstroke of the second "L," the downstroke of the "R" and the tip of the tail of "Q." Long rays point to either side of the "A" in STELLA and the star between the rays points directly at the "A." No stars or rays point at periods. Compare to reverse E.	4-D = 1786 Ryder 6
E	STELLA• QUARTA ˙• DECIMA •	Divine eye, groups of lines as rays. Thin 6-pointed stars. A small dot appears to the left of the period between QUARTA and DECIMA. Long rays point to the right sides of "T," the first "L" and "A" in STELLA. Long rays pass well left of the "Q," point to the right edge of "R" and just right of the center of the last "A" in QUARTA. Other long rays point to the "I" in DECIMA and directly at the period following STELLA. Compare to reverse D.	5-E = 1786 Ryder 7 6-E = 1786 Ryder 8

KB	Legend	Distinguishing Characteristics	Varieties
-	STELLA QUARTA DECIMA	Struck. Blurred Divine Eye, groups of lines as rays. Large letters. No punctuation. Long rays point to the downstroke of the "T" and the second "L" in STELLA, to the center of the "Q" and the downstroke of the "R" in QUARTA and squarely between the "A" and "S."	1785 Ryder 5, Struck
-	STELLA QUARTA DECIMA	Cast. Blurred Divine Eye, indistinct groups of lines as rays. Large "heavy" letters. No punctuation. Very thick 8-pointed stars. Overall "blurry" appearance. Rays point to locations similar to those on struck version.	1785 Ryder 5, Cast
F	INDE ⁙ ET:LIB: 1786	Seated Liberty, uniquely paired with obverse 7 (the "Baby Head.") The stalk of the branch in Liberty's hand points to the base of "E." Four wheat sheaves on shield. Wildly curving drapery in breast area. Poorly shaped legs. The globe is flat at its base. Single exergue line with all four date numerals touching it.	7-F = 1786 Ryder 9
G	INDE ⁙ ETLIB 1786	Seated Liberty, with pointed cap. Check for left facing bust as on obverses 8 and 9. The stalk of the branch in Liberty's hand ends well to the right of the base of "E" and ends on the level of the center of E's base. "D" and "E" are close to each other. Rare examples display a wheat sheaf on the shield. The left end of the exergue line is thin, as if extended by engraving a thin line, to end at the big toe of Liberty's right foot. Compare to reverses G and H.	8-G = 1786 Ryder 10
H	INDE: ⁙ ETLIB: 1786	Seated Liberty, with pointed cap. Check for left facing bust as on obverses 8 and 9. The stalk of the branch in Liberty's hand ends well to the right of the bases of "D" and "E" and on the level of the right edge of "D." "D" and "E" are widely spaced. Compare to reverses G and I.	9-H = 1786 Ryder 11
I	INDE: ⁙ E TLIB: 1787	Seated Liberty, with round hair. The stalk of the branch in Liberty's hand ends well to the right of the base of "E" and ends on the level of the left center of E's base. The top of the branch hand points to the colon after INDE. "E" and "T" are very widely spaced. The primary diagnostic is a cud that obscures all of the date, except the top halves of "8" and "7." Compare to reverses G and H.	9-I = 1786 Ryder 15
J	INDE ETLIB 1787	Seated Liberty, with round hair. Double exergue line, with lines slightly closer at left. Date numerals do not touch the exergue and the first "7" is low. The branch hand points to the right side of "D." The branch curves to the right to miss the "E" and is close to it. The "E" in ETLIB is distant from Liberty's arm, but the "B" is very close to her shield. Her staff, if extended, would just miss the "1" in the date to the left. Her feet are well to the left of the date and are above a group of odd denticles.	10-J = 1787 Ryder 34
K	INDE ETLIB 1787	Seated Liberty, with round hair. A die anomaly developed over Liberty's head. Double exergue line, with lines parallel. Date numerals do not touch the exergue and both 7's are low. The branch hand points to the right side of "D." The branch is distant from "E." The "B" is distant from the shield, which bears British crosses.	10-K = 1787 Ryder 14 11-K = 1787 Ryder 12 12-K = 1787 Ryder 32

KB	Legend	Distinguishing Characteristics	Varieties
L	INDE ETLIB 1788	Seated Liberty, with round hair. Single exergue line. Date numerals are relatively even and do not touch the exergue line. The branch hand points to the right side of "D." The branch is very close to "E." The "B" is distant from the shield, which bears British crosses. Her staff, if extended, would pass well to the left of the "1" in the date.	10-L = 1788 Ryder 20 13-L = 1788 Ryder 19 Vlack-13 with reverse L =Ryder 40
M	INDE ETLIB 1788	Seated Liberty, with round hair. Double exergue line, with lines slightly closer at right and a heavier top line. A small die break developed from the right end of the exergue lines downward. Date numerals are relatively even and only the "1" touches the lower exergue line. The branch hand points to the right side of "D." A leaf just touches the lower left corner of "E." The "B" is relatively close to the shield and is close to the exergue. The letters are evenly and widely spaced.	10-M = 1788 Ryder 37
N	INDE ETLIB 1788	Seated Liberty, with round hair. Single exergue line. The branch hand points between "D" and "E" and the branch is very near the "E." ET LIB is evenly spaced and distant from the figure. The date angles up slightly from left to right and is placed far to the right. "1" is slightly distant from"788."	10-N = 1788 Ryder 38
O	INDE ETLIB 1788	Seated Liberty, with round hair. Double exergue line, with lines much closer at right. The branch hand points at the lower left serif of "E." "1" and the first "8" touch the lower exergue line. The second "8" overlaps the lower line and touches the upper one. Some specimens show a die crack from the rim to Liberty's staff.	10-O = 1788 Ryder 23
P	INDE ETLIB 1788	Seated Liberty, with round hair. Double exergue line, with lines parallel. The branch hand points at the center of the base of "E." Only the second "8" touches the exergue line. The shield does not touch the upper exergue line. ETLIB is distant from the figure. The shield is high, with no part of it touching the exergue line.	10-P = 1788 Ryder 36
Q	INDE ETLIB 1788	Seated Liberty, with round hair. Double exergue line, with lines parallel and thick. The bottom line is shorter than the top. The top of the "7" is well below the tops of the other numerals, which touch the bottom exergue line. Parallel die breaks starts a Liberty's shin and curve up through INDE. The "L" and "I" almost touch and ETLIB is crammed together because the shield is high and angled backward. INDE, on the other hand, is widely spaced and distant from the branch hand, which points at the curve of "D."	10-Q = 1788 Ryder 22
R	INDE ETLIB 1788	Seated Liberty, with round hair. Single exergue line. The top of the "7" is slightly below the tops of the other numerals. The "1" is slightly lower than "88," but higher than the "7." A large die break starts at the globe's South Pole and curves upward, through Liberty's left knee, right thigh and the wrist of her branch hand, which points to the downstroke of the "E." INDE is closer to the figure than ETLIB. The "E" in ETLIB is distant from Liberty's arm.	10-R = 1788 Ryder 21

KB	Legend	Distinguishing Characteristics	Varieties
S	INDE ET LIB 1788	Seated Liberty, with round hair. Single exergue line. The exergue line appears to have broken between "1" and "7" and curves downward on either side. The branch hand points at the downstroke of "D." The top of the branch is just below the lower left corner of "E." ET and LIB are separated. INDE is evenly spaced.	14-S = 1788 Ryder 17 15-S = 1788 Ryder 16 16-S = 1788 Ryder 24 23-S = 1788 Ryder 30
T	INDE+ ET•LIB+ 1788	Seated Liberty, with round hair. Double exergue line, with lines apart at left and together at right. A die break joins the right side of the "E" in INDE and the top left corner of the "E" in ET, passing under Liberty's chin. The letters are evenly spaced and the figure is well centered. The branch hand points at the downstroke of the "E."	16-T = 1788 Ryder 26
U	INDE+ ET•LIB+ 1788	Seated Liberty, with round hair. Single exergue line, with 1788 not touching it. The branch hand points at the serif of the "D." The letters are evenly spaced and the figure is well centered. None of the letters is close to the figure. The "T" is missing its crossbar. See illustrations in Chapter 10.	16-U = 1788 Ryder 25 21-U = 1788 Ryder 28 22-U = 1788 Ryder 29 24-U = 1788 Ryder 31 25-U = 1788 Ryder 39
V	BRITAN NIA•	Seated Liberty, with "bubble and bun" hair. The Vlack 87C reverse from Machin's Mills Group III (See illustrations in Chapter 10.) The reverse is from a very worn die and is always very weak. Single exergue line, large date numerals. Liberty's staff, if extended, would be parallel to and to the right of the "7."	17-V = 1788 Ryder 13
W	INDE ✱ ET LIB ✱ 1788	Seated Liberty, with rounded hair and bun. Single exergue line, with no date numerals touching it. Liberty's staff, if extended, would overlap the "1." The Liberty figure is tall and thin. The branch hand points between the "E" in INDE and the star that follows it. Both INDE and ET appear on the left side of Liberty. The top of the branch points between "E" and "T" and nearly touches the "E" in ET.	18-W = 1788 Ryder 27
X	✱ ET LIB ✱ ✱ INDE 1788	Note punctuation and the errant reverse legend. "88" is higher than "17" and touches the single straight exergue line. The lower right edge of the "E" in INDE is very near the shield and INDE ends at about mid-shield. The branch hand is distant from LIB and points at the right edge of the "L." ET LIB is widely spaced. INDE is closely spaced.	19-X = 1788 Ryder 18 20-X = 1788 Ryder 35
Y	✱ INDE ✱ ✱ ETLIB 1788	Seated Liberty, with round hair. Known specimens have Irish halfpence as undertypes. Single exergue line. Both 8's touch the line, with the last "8" higher and in the line. A large die break obscures Liberty's breasts and branch hand. The extreme rarity of the variety and the scarcity of available photographs prevent further description.	21-Y = 1788 Ryder 33
Z	IMMUNE COLUMBIA 1785	Muling of a Vermont obverse with a worn Immune Columbia die. Liberty faces to the right and sits on a crate. She holds a Liberty cap-topped staff in her right hand and the scales of Justice in her left. See illustrations in Chapter 10.	26-Z = 1788 Ryder 1

INDEX AND CROSS REFERENCE

Abenaki, 296
and wampum, 39
Act of Union, 81
Adams
John, 61, 235, 361, 367, 400
and Alien and Sedition Acts, 23
committee to draft Declaration, 246
on public support of the war, 17
-Onis Treaty, 386
Samuel, 60, 235, 245
and Boston Tea Party, 15
and Sons of Liberty, 235
reaction to Stamp Act, 14
adjustment marks, 422
Admin. of Justice Act. See Intolerable Acts
Africa, African, 135, 203
and rice, 9
and slaves, 9
elephant tokens. *See* elephant tokens
exports to, 11
figures on coinage, 110, 305, 312, 317
imports from, 4
Portuguese empire, 144
agent(s)
fiscal
role of Bank of U.S., 22
sub-treasury, 397
Indian, 36
system of exchange, 11, 46, 374
agriculture, 9, 10, 46, 66
as base of British colonies, 33
associated risks, 31
British shift from, 114
Ceres, goddess of, 380
Dutch lead world in, 133
effect on dev. Of the South, 9
George I's love of, 95
symbolized, 111, 298, 301, 323, 403
Washington and G. Clinton, 284
Albany
1754 conference in, 235, 255
and Dutch settlement, 135
and wampum, 38
Church Penny, 152
Algonquin, 36, 296
Alien and Sedition Acts, 23
Allen
Ethan
raid on Ft. Ticonderoga, 60
with Ira, Vermont independence, 296
Ira, 296, 298
American
plantations tokens, 155, 200–202
Revolution, 5, 11, 19, 36, 69, 74, 141, 163, 233, 235, 243, 245, 233–54, 255, 256, 257, 271, 274, 278, 283, 284, 319, 321, 344, 372, 422, 429
and Spain's Charles III, 128
and the Great Chain, 258
and Thomas Paine, 65, 115
as a world war, 235
begins at Lexington, 16
British coinage after, 101
British factions favor Americans, 99
coin shortages after, 333
copper left over from, 306
currency restrictions as a cause of, 49
defense of personal property in, 20
depicted on R.I. ship tokens, 234
depreciation of paper currency, 49, 58
Dutch assistance in, 136
effect on small change, 240
ends at Yorktown, 17
Era coinages, 233–54
introduction, 233–34
French assistance in, 138
in the West, 75
linked to value of money, 60
nostalgia for, 371, 401, 432
personified, 361
stirrings of in 1765, 14
strategies, 16
wartime economy, 19
Amherst, Jeffrey, 98
amilas, 145
Andrew Doria, the (ship), 251
Andros, Edmund, 166
Annapolis, Maryland, 256, 267–70
Anne (Queen), 93–94, 138, 267, 463, 465, *Also see* Queen Anne's War
1704 proclamation of, 125
and coinage, 102
annealing, defined, 450
anti-
Catholic, 86, 90
counterfeiting measures
and profit margin, 263
laws, 79, 88, 104, 109, 259, 271, 285, 286, 305, 358, 373
on coins, 88, 100, 182, 189, 417
and Matthew Boulton, 101
hubbing, 431
on paper money, 51–57, 73, *Also see* counterfeits, counterfeiting
advances in, 71
Antoinette, Marie, 138, 417
apocryphal farthings, 215–18
Appalachian Mountains
and Proclamation Act of 1763, 13
gold rush in, 390
on Chalmers' shillings?, 269
archaeology, 8, 30, 79, 82, 90, 151, 154, 159, 211, 223, 240
Arkansas, 42, 210, 354, 456
and John Law, 210
Armagh (Ireland), 185
Armstrong
Thomas, Jr., and George Legg patent halfpence, 89
Thomas, Sr.
mint house of, 189
patent farthings, 89, 179, 188, 192
Arnold, Benedict
at Saratoga, 17
march on Quebec, 387
takes Ft. Ticonderoga, 60
trial of, 320
Articles of Confederation. See Confederation
Arundel Towne. *See* Annapolis, Maryland
Asia, 4, 7, 132, 203

Minor, 416
assay, assayer, 118, 119, 122, 123, 162, 275, 278, 321, 391, 409, 419, 420, 421, 443
Atlee
James Falconer, 259, 476, 478
and Confederation proposals, 339
and CT coinage, 312, 317
and imitation halfpence, 285–93, 294–95
and Immunis Columbia coppers, 259, 339–48
and Machin's Mills, 290–93
and Machin's NY proposal, 283–85
and NJ coinage(?), 322, 331
and Non Vi Virtute Vici coppers, 277–79, 346
and NY coinage proposals, 258, 259, 346
and VT coinage, 301–4
Samuel, 258, 288, 295
and Machin's Mills, 290
co-signs for William Cox, 321
life and work, 277–79
attribution guide
American imitation halfpence, 473–79
Nova Constellatio private issues, 470
Avalon, 156, 175
Aztecs, and money, 117
Bahamas, 117
halfpenny, 111–12
Bailey, John, 259
and Confederation patterns, 339
and CT coinage(?), 313, 318
and imitation halfpence, 287, 289–90, 295
and New Jersey state coinage, 330–31
and NJ coinage, 321–22
and Nova Eborac coppers, 281–82, 330
and NY coinage proposals, 258, 279–85
and Washington's sword, 279
balance of trade
between Britain and America, 10
between Spain and Asia, 7
effect on exchange system, 47
effect on paper money, 47
Baltimore, 3, 433
and Ohio Railroad, 360
First Lord, 175
Issue (Cont. Curr. notes), 65
John Chalmers in, 268
Second Lord
and Maryland colonization, 175–77
coinage of, 175–77
Idler copies, 456
Standish Barry tokens, 358, 359–60
Bank of
Amsterdam, 132
England, 22, 204
founded, 92
Maryland, 421
Massachusetts, 19
New York, 19, 258, 274
North America, 19
the U.S., 419, 440
(checks, ill.), 23
and Daniel Webster, 398
and Louisiana Purchase, 24
constitutionality challenged, 25
first charter, 22, 24
Jackson-Van Buren war with, 22, 25, 395
role in Panic of 1819, 393
second charter, 24
banks, banking, 19, 431, *Also see* individual banks
and economic panic, 72
and paper money, 70, 72
and sub-treasury system, 397
Franklin's revenue plan, 235
invented by Dutch, 132
plan for Irish, 222
state chartered, 24
unchartered, 24
Banque Royale. See Law, John, paper money
bar coppers (1785), 256, 272–73
Barbados, 167, 225
token coinage of, 110–11
Barber, Col. Francis (daughter of), 321
Barry, Standish, and tokens, 177, 358, 359–60
barter, 3, 29–42, 209, 404
as an institution, i
before European contact, 30
classification scheme. *See* commodities
in the West, 32
Maryland reverts to, 176
origins in fur trade, 33
outgrown, 33, 76
tokens supplement, 110
transition to paper, 46
with Natives, 29, 33
Bartlett, Josiah, 264
bastard heads (VT coinage), 302
Bath metal, 153
Bay Colony, 161, 166
Bayley, Simeon, 278
Beach-Grünthal hoard, 294, 295
beans, 10, 386
cocoa, as money, 117
Bechtler
Alt Christoph, 390–92
Christopher, 391
family, 359, 390–92
Karl and August, 391
beer, 224, 277, *Also see* brewer, brewing, brewery
Belcher, Jonathan, 226
Belle, the (ship), 384
Berkley, William, 175
Bermuda, 111, 156, 157–59, *Also see* Sommer Islands
penny, 112
Betts, C. Wyllys, 353
Bible, Biblical, 80, 83, 174, 429
Biddle, Nicholas, 24, 397
Bienville, Governor (Louisiana), 213
Billington, Ray Allen, 33
billon coinage, 81, 133, 142, 154, 206, 207, 208, 213
bills of
credit, 19, 32, 43, 44, 45, 46, 47, 58, 236
exchange, 10, 11, 32, 46, 47, 163
bi-metallic coinage, 88, 113, 204, 413
Birch
and 1792 cents, 413
and 1792 dismes, 412
and 1792 half dismes, 410
Robert 'Bob', 410
William Russell, 410
Birmingham, 369
and 17th century tokens, 114
and Auctori Plebis tokens, 374
and bar coppers, 272
and Confederatio decads, 340
and counterfeiting, 104, 263
and Hancock's cents, 363
and Jacob's theater tokens, 383
and Kempson's mint, 369
and Kentucky tokens, 378
and late Washington issues, 373
and Lutwyche's mint, 116

and Northwest tokens, 358, 385
and Nova Const. private coppers, 265
and Obadiah Westwood, 363
and post-1815 imports, 358
and Talbot, Allum & Lee tokens, 378
and the Wyon family, 259, 265, 294, 319, 343
and Unity States coppers, 373
Soho Mint, 101, 371, 372
standard, 283

Bishop
of London, 90
-s of Durham, 175
-s' Wars, 84
Samuel, 305–7

bit, 72, 442
American reliance on, 416, 428
defined, 129
Nova Constellatio patterns, 261, 264

black
copper, 428
doggs. *See* sols tampees
hogs, 158
ink, 53, 73, 459
ship, 122
-smith, 163, 261, 386, 409
tokens, 87, 359, 374, 386–88
wampum, 38, 40, 41

Blue Garter, Order of the. See Order of...
Board of the Treasury, 69, 350, 353
Bogata Mint, 120, 121, 122
Bolduc, Louis, 214
Bolen, John, 228, 285, 340, 456
Bolivia, 122
Bonaparte
Joseph, 129
Napoleon, 24, 129, 138, 139, 144, 430
and Louisiana Purchase, 24

bond, bonds
posted by coiners, 298, 300, 320, 321, 420
use to retire Cont. Currency, 69
used to retire debt, 21

Bonnie Prince Charlie. ***See*** **Stuart, Charles Edward**
Book of Kells, 199
Borden, Joseph, 69
Boston, 3, 5, 44, 48, 63, 161, 226, 233, 234, 235, 236, 244, 251, 379, 388, 402, 404
and distribution of wealth, 10
and MA silver coinage, 160–75
and MA state coinage, 333–39
and shipping, 10
and Sons of Liberty, 236
and specie smuggling, 8
battles around, 63
boycotts British goods, 15, 236
British troops in, 14
Dorchester Heights, 63
early history of, 161
Massacre, 237, 243
Port Bill. See Intolerable Acts
shillings, 167
small change shortages in, 215
Tea Party, 235, 243

Boucher, Jonathan, 267
Boudinot, Elias
and Nova Const. patterns, 262
as Mint Director, 424–29

Boulton
and Watt, 100, 372, 407, *Also see* Soho Mint
and Myddleton tokens, 382
planchet source for U.S. Mint, 419, 432
Matthew. *Also see* Boulton and Watt, *Also see* Watt, James, *Also see* Soho Mint, *Also see* Birmingham
and cartwheel coppers, 100–101, 115, 372
and Fugio cents, 307
die steel source for U.S. Mint, 432
on counterfeiting, 101
on production costs, 105
on value of copper coinage, 100–101
production, 115

Bourbon ruling family, 127, 128, 137, 141, 142, 235
bow and arrow, 243
Bowdoin, (Mass.) Governor James, 334
Bowers, Q. David, 250
boycott, 236
Bradford
head. *See* Connecticut, mutton head
William (of MA), 160
on wampum, 38
William (of NY), 313

Brahma (Hindu god), 244
Brasher, Ephraim
and imitation halfpence, 259, 287, 289–90
and NY coinage proposals, 258, 279–85, 281, 283
and private gold coinage, 258, 273–77
modern copies, 459
similarities to imitation halfpence, 289
similarities to Nova Eborac coppers, 283
background on, 258, 274

brass coins/tokens, 8, 88, 215, 229, 246, 340
Brazil, 144–46, ***Also see Portugal, Portuguese***
Brearly, David, 69
Breen, Walter, 159, 186, 190, 204, 206, 208, 209, 213, 215, 223, 226, 229, 246, 250, 251, 252, 278, 281, 287, 310, 330, 342, 343, 345, 363, 367, 369, 391, 410, 413, 424
Bressett, Ken, 295–304, 297, 391
brewer, brewing, brewery, 258, 277–79, 288
Brewster, William, 160, 225
bribe, bribery, 12, 99, 165, 222, 259, 306, 339, 400
Briot, Nicholas, 190
Bristol, 10, 114, 204, 216, 277, 369, 377
Britannia, 88, 102, 109, 250, 271, 286, 289, 291, 295, 300, 308, 372, 375, 381, 387, 388, 439, 477, 478
on early American coins, 87
on Roman sestertia, 87
VT variety. *See* Vermont, Repub. of, coinage

British. See individual related topics
and base metal coinage, 8
as creditors, 6
citizen's rights, 5
coin demominations, 79–82
exports, 6, 10
mercantilism, economics and policy, 3–18
policy of enumeration, 5
shipping, 10, 11

system of exchange, 11
system, and major flaw, 12
broad (gold coin), 81
broadaxe, 227
broken 'A', 312
Broome, Samuel, 306, 307, 353, 354
Brown, John, 226
Brugge, Simon Stevin van, 148, 410
Buell
Abel, 257
and CT coinage, 305–12
and early conviction, 306
and Fugio cents, 353
and NJ coinage(?), 331
and VT coinage, 301–2
leaves America, 307
surrenders CT share to son, 307
Benjamin, 317, 318
and CT coinage, 314
and Fugio cents, 352
and Machin's Mills, 353
'inherits' CT mint, 307
William
and VT coinage, 301–2
Bungtown, 259, 267, 294, 308, 317, 332, 337
Burke, Edmund, 12, 15, 60
Burr, Aaron, 319
Bushnell, Charles Ira, 174, 290, 301, 307, 331, 354, 376
Bushnell, David, 252
Butler, James. *See* Ormond, Lord
buttons, 164, 369, 370, 372, 394, 403
alternate uses of tokens, 401
as inspiration for bar coppers, 256, 272, 273
as inspiration for Nov Const. coinage, 267
English makers of, 387
used to smuggle gold, 8
cabo de barra. See cob coinage
Cabot
John, 136
Sebastian, 158
Caesar, 87, 322
Calhoun, John C., 398
Calvert
Cecil. *See* Baltimore, 2nd Lord
George. See Baltimore, 1st Lord
and Ferryland, Newfoundland, 156
camel head. See New Jersey state coinage
Camerarius, Dr. Joachim, 60
Camero, Hernando, 158
Canada, Canadian, 93, 140, 136–44, 269, 382, 384, 386–88, *Also see* place names
and Oregon, 386
and playing card money, 43, 208, 213
billon sous marques for, 213
blacksmith tokens, 386–88
British control of, 98
circulation of MA silver, 167
DK tokens, 156
early history of, 35
French coinage for, 154, 206–14
slow settlement of, 141
sols de nine deniers, 212
threat of invasion from, 297
tokens of, 102
Vexator Canadiensis tokens, 387
Cape Breton, 139, 333
Caribbean
and 1767 copper sols, 238
and end of slavery, 395
and trade with Americans, 8, 10
Dutch in, 132, 136, 251
French coins in, 213, 234
French in, 141
Carlos and Johanna, 118, 120, 127, 130, 466
silver coins, 119
Carlotto, Tony, 297
Carolina, 9, 93, Also see North and South Carolina
early history of, 203
early settlement of, 3, 82, 139
elephant tokens. *See* elephant tokens
Carroll, Charles (of Carrollton), 360
Cartier, Jacques, 139
cartwheel coppers, 101, 115, 372
Castile and Leon, 118, 119, 128
Castine hoard, 134
Catholic, Catholicism, 83, 84, 86, 90, 91, 95, 131, 137, 155, 175, 177–200, 180
and Divine Right of Kings, 162
and Maryland coinage, 175–77
Confederation, 177–200
League, 137
Cato, 283
cent
and Morris' plan, 261, 260–64
as first U.S. Mint coinage, 22
denomination created, 273
first use of denomination, 333–39
Hancock's, 357, 364
hard times tokens. *See* hard times tokens
Kentucky. *See* Kentucky cents
Talbot, Allum & Lee. *See* Talbot, Allum & Lee
U.S. large
1793 'strawberry leaf', 416
1794 'starred' reverse, 417
Birch. *See* Birch, and 1792 cents
by Gobrecht
and Kneass, transitional, 436
coronet, 436–37
by Scot
draped bust, 429
and Washington Unity States, 373
matron heads, 433, 436
Eckfeldt/Rittenhouse 1793 wreath, 415
Jefferson head, 418
liberty cap
Gardner's, 418–19
Scot's, 417–19
Wright's, 417
mintages, 437
Reich's classic head, 433
specifications, 408
use of 1767 French copper sols as, 238
Voigt's 1793 chain, 414–16
Unity Sates. *See* Washington, Unity States
Chain, chain
cents (1793), 414–16
motif/device, 63, 234, 246, 268, 271, 351, 349–55, 58–69, 461
the Great, 259, 283
Thomas Machin's. *See* Chain, The Great
Chalmers, John, 177, 256
token coinage of, 267–70
Chameau, Le (ship), 206
Champlain, Samuel de, 33, 140, 296
Chandler, Raymond, 274
Charles I, 84, 90, 84–85, 94, 113, 161, 162, 175, 177–200, 203
and Maryland colony, 175

and St. Patrick coinage, 177–200
beheaded, 85
despotism drives emigration, 161
Henrietta Maria, wife of, 84

Charles I (of Spain). See Carlos and Johanna

Charles II, 81, 85, 90, 86–90, 102, 165, 166, 175, 177–200, 188, 203, 215, 462, 465, 466, *Also see Great Restoration*
and Carolina proprietors, 203
and copper coinage, 88
and Hudson's Bay Company, 34, 140
and patent coinage, 89
and the Great Restoration, 86
comment on Mass. coinage, 170
revokes Mass. charter, 165
takes NY from the Dutch, 136

Charles II (of Spain), 123

Charles III (of Spain), 128

Charles IV (of Spain), 128

Charleston, 3, 93, 422

Cheval, Pierre, 207

Chile, 122

Chouart, Médard, 34, 140

Church of England, 91, 160

civil war
colonial, in Maryland, 175
French, 139

Civil War
English, 12, 113, 162, 175, 177–200
spurs tokens, 113
U.S., 8, 22, 25, 73, 215, 223, 242, 392, 399, 429
and demise of large cents, 436

Clark, William. *See* Lewis and Clark

Clarke, Hermann (See footnote), 165

Clay, Henry, 394, 399

Clinton, George, 283–85, 331, 346

Clinton, Henry, 251

clipping, 120, 162
and regulation, 274
effects on Spanish coinage, 124
Mass. silver coinage, 166
on planchets, defined, 448
preventative measures, 146, 168

cob coinage, 120–24, 126, 127, 130, 162

Cohen, Mendes, Hoard, 242

coin weights, 146

Colder, Cadwallader, 296

Coley, William, 278
and Vermont coinage, 297–301
NY coin proposal, 283

collar, 182, 189, 190, 293, 475
defined, 454

colonial coin, defined, 233

color printing. *See* anti-counterfeiting measures, paper

Columbian Order, 274

Columbus, Christopher, 118, 119, 139, 144, 276, 342, 345

commodity, commodities, 155
as money, 29–34, 44
classification scheme, 34
defined, 29
silver as, 48

Commonwealth
English, 6, 177–200
of Massachusetts, 155

Compagnie des Indes Occidentales, 207, 209, 210

Compaigne des Indies. *See Law, John*

Company by the Duke of York, 203

Company for Coining Coppers, 305–16

Conanicut Island, 234, 251

Conder, James, tokens, 79, 114–16, 363, 364, 374, 375, 394

confederation
Franklin's 1754 plan for, 255
the Dutch Republic, 133
the Iroqois League, 37

Confederation, 60, 75, 255–355
adoption at York, Penn., 66
and Morris monetary plan, 260–64
and Shays' Rebellion, 20
coinage proposals for, 349–55, 260–64, 259, 287, 288, 339–48
Dickinson's plan for, 255
Era American coinages, 255–355, Also *see* individual types
introduction, 255–59
Era symbolism on paper money, 66
notes backed by R. Morris, 69
weaknesses of, 19, 20, 21, 256, 318

Congress, 59, 237, 366, *Also see federal*
and a federal mint, 7, 22, 256, 261
and Confederation Era coinage proposals, 340, 341, 343
and Constitution Era coinage proposals, 366
and Continental Currency, 19, 49, 58–69, 60, 234, 245
and Continental Currency coins, 245–51
and Feuchtwanger's cents, 394
and Fugio cents, 257, 259, 349–55
and Jefferson's plan, 263
and taxes/tariffs, 22
and the 2nd U.S. Mint, 434
and the Bank of N.A., 19
and the Bank of the U.S., 22, 24
and the end of large cents, 395
and the Mint Act of 1792. *See* Mint Act of 1792
and the Mint Act of 1834. *See* Mint Act of 1834
and the Morris plan, 260–64
and the War, 17, 60, 62, 63
and Vermont, 297
considers abolishing the Mint, 418
honors Lafayette, 401
in Annapolis, 268
in Baltimore, 65
in New York, 272
in York, PA, 66

Connecticut, 48, 74, 224, 261, 452
and Higley's coppers, 153, 224–30
and New England Stuiver, 217
and wampum, 39, 41
early history of, 225
issues paper money, 44, 226
River, 135, 168, 296
shillings (fantasy), 354
state coinage, 257, 283, 300, 301
African head coppers, 305, 312
'African head' varieties, 312
and Auctori Plebis tokens, 375

- and ties to imitation halfpence, 289
- as undertypes, 327
- early issues, 308
  - head-left varieties, 309
- est. mintage, 307
- groups of (*chart*), 317
- 'Hercules head' varieties, 309
- horned bust variety, 314, 320
- laughing head, 314
- laughing head varieties, 320
- links to Machin's Mills, 311
- mutton head varieties, 313
- small head coppers, 312
- 'small head' varieties, 312
- small heads. *See* Connecticut, small heads
- the '33' die family, 312
- ties to
  - imitation halfpence, 291, 292, 293, 295
  - VT coinage, 302, 303
- ties to Machin's Mills, 314
- triple leaves varieties, 314
- triple-leaf varieties, 311

conquistadors, 117

Constable, Rucker and Company, 265

Constable, William, 265, 380

Constitution
- British, 235
- New Hampshire, 242
- of the Iroquois League, 37
- U.S.
  - and Andrew Jackson, 396
  - and Continental Currency, 69
  - and George Clinton, 283
  - and Gouverneur Morris, 260
  - and restrictions on paper money, 50
  - and state coinage, 257, 337
  - and the Bank of the U.S., 25
  - and the Nullification Crisis, 398
  - and Washington, 361
  - construction debate, 22, 25
  - ratification of, 20
  - signers on paper money, 55
  - takes effect, 354

Continental Currency
- coins, 60, 63, 64, 245–51, 259, 268, 271, 350, 354, 411, 414
  - modern copies of, 250, 456, 459
- notes, 58–69
  - Baltimore issue, 65
  - depreciation of, 59, 246
    - (*chart*), 59
  - fractional, 63
  - R. Morris underwrites, 58
  - summer 1776 issues, 64
  - types, 60
  - Yorktown issue, 66

Continental 'Dollar'. *See* Continental Currency coins

Copley, John Singleton, 161, 235, 251

copper
- alloys, U.S. Mint issues, 408
- and Bath metal, 153
- and NH coinage, 242
- believed to harbor disease, 436
- blank sources, 87
- collapse of industry in England, 189
- for Confederation decads, 263
- in Bath metal, 218
- in bi-metallic coinage, 88, 91, 156, 201, 204, 413
- in cupro-nickel coinage, 395
- in early Mexico, 117
- in pre-European barter, 30
- intrinsic value of, 100
- metallurgical properties of, 103, 450
- mines, 153, 225, 224–30
  - at Morristown, 320
  - Copper Hill. *See* Higley, Dr. Samuel, coinage of
- Panic of 1789. *See* Copper Panic of 1789
- plates for paper money, 43, 52
- poor quality, 209
- poor quality of, 'black copper', 428
- price of, 101, 105, 214, 263, 350, 412, 418
- refinement of, 286, 335, 447, *Also see Higley, Dr. Samuel*
- sheeting of, 334, 448
- sources of, 103, 179, 212, 265, 352, 411
  - federal, 350, 353
  - scrap, 335
  - Wm. Talbot, 378
  - Swedish, 179, 212

Copper Panic of 1789, 21, 257, 259, 307, 322, 353

Cortés, Hernando, 117, 118

cotton, 5, 10, 30, 51, 378, 383, 391

Council
- for New England, 161
- on Plantations, 176
- Privy, 222

counterfeits, counterfeiting, 168, 258, 305, 319, *Also see evasion coppers*, *Also see anti-counterfeiting measures*, Also see imitation halfpence, American
- and Georgivs Triumphos, 270
- and large head Non Vi Virtute Vici, 346
- and U.S. Mint coinage, 415, 418
- cast, 101, 104
- defined, 455
- effect on American economy, 263
- of Canadian tokens, 386–88
- of Conder tokens, 115
- of coppers, 8, 21, 88, 101, 102, 146
  - 1781 and 1785 halfpennies, 103
  - British-American differences, 286
  - numbers of in circ., 79, 99, 101, 109, 263
  - profitability of, 105, 286
- of CT coinage, 305, 307, 308, 312
- of French colonial coins, 214
- of MA silver coins, 168, 172, 174
- of MA state coinage, 337
- of NJ coinage, 331
- of Nova Const.coppers, 267
- of NY coinage, 281
- of paper money, 51–57
  - Abel Buell and, 306
  - Continental Currency, 59, 66, 237
    - by Wm. Smithers (alleged), 237
  - hand-engraved notes, 70
  - penalties for, 53
  - photographic, 73
- of Spanish silver coins, 125, 126, 162
- of state coinages, 257
- of VT coinage, 299
- of wampum, 41
- of Washington pieces, 372

Spanish silver, 126
spurs MA silver coinage, 162
tin, 104
versus 'evasion', 109
versus 'imitation', 105, 285
counterstamps
defined, 449
on 19th century tokens, 392, 401
on Brasher's doubloons & foreign coins, 279–85
on cob coinage, 123
on French colonial coins, 154, 206–7, 208, 213, 234, 238
counting board, 147
country money. See commodity, commodities
coureurs de bois, 3, 33
Cox and Goadsby. ***See*** **New Jersey state coinage**
Cox, Albion, 424, ***Also see*** **New Jersey state coinage**
and imitation halfpence, 288–89
and New Jersey coinage, 316–32
and U.S. Mint coinage, 420
dies, 424
in New York, 278–79
Cradock, William, 226
Craig, James, 387
credit. ***Also see debt, Also see bills of exchange,*** **Also see bills of credit**
and Albion Cox, 321
and Andrew Jackson's fiscal policy, 395, 396
and debt assumption, 21
and James Jarvis, 353
and post-war crisis, 20
and the exchange system, 9, 11, 32, 46
British/American defined, 4
by Bank of the U.S. to state banks, 24
currency favored by West, 32
Daniel Webster's stance on, 398
Dutch use of, 5, 132, 133
national, 19, 24, 58
needed for expansion, 22
paper money as a form of, 6, 45
used by Natives, 36
Cromwell, Oliver, 85–86, 90, 155, 162, 165, 170
and Maryland, 175, 176
and St. Patrick coinage, 183
plans attack on Dutch settlements, 136
takes over, 85
Crosby, Sylvester Sage, iii, 124, 158, 159, 165, 179, 181, 182, 215, 217, 226, 227, 243, 245, 250, 267, 290, 299, 301, 307, 331, 336
cross
Greek, 209
hollow, 205, 208
in CT legends, 312
in Fugio legends, 351
Jerusalem, 119, 122, 145
of Lorraine, 35, 36, 185
on Britannia's shield, 286
on Chalmers' coinage, 269
pattern of stars, 428
pistareen, 125
potent. *See* cross, Jerusalem
saltire, 205
Crown Point, 386
cud, defined, 450
Cupid and Psyche, 3, 216
Currency Act
of 1751, 45
of 1764, 13, 45, 49
currency valuations by colony, 260
Curwen, Samuel, 264, 265
cut coinage, 54, 110, 129, 166, 188
da Vinci, Leonardo, 189
Danforth, Dr. Brian J., 188–200, 223
Danish
America (Danske Amercansk), 271
orders of chivalry, 206
West Indies. *See* Danish America
David, King of Israel
and St. Patrick coinage, 177–200
Dawes, William, 8
De la Barbotiere, Captain, 158
Death's head, 54
debasement
of French coinage, 141
of Spanish coinage, 127
effect on Massachusetts, 333
illegal, 122, 123, 124, 126, 162
new plate coinage, 124
tepuzque, 117
debt, 74, 86, 246, 436, Also see credit
and
Walter Mould, 321
and 1749 Mermaid shipment, 333
and Albion Cox, 326
and barter, 29
and Native Americans, 36
and post-War crisis, 20
and Royal Flynt, 353
and Shays' Rebellion, 20
and South Sea debacle, 95
and the Bank of England, 92
and the Bank of N.A., 19
and the exchange system, 47
British, 361
from Seven Years War, 12
from wars, 12
colonial, 13, 45
consumer, 47
during the Rev. War, 49
from the Louisiana Purchase, 24
in Massachusetts, 47
in the Jackson Era, 397
national, 69, 350
assumption of, 21
taxes and tarriffs to pay, 22
owed to British merchants, 6, 11
payment options, 46
post-War, 19, 21
Spanish, 124
Spanish, and the King's Fifth, 124
to pay veterans, 69
debtors prison, 228, 321, 353
decad. See decimal monetary system
decimal
monetary system
and first U.S. Mint coinage, 411
first use by MA, 258
Jefferson's plan, 262–64
system, origins of, 148
Declaration of Independence, 55, 64, 98, 244, 246, 262, 264
and limits on paper money, 49
last surviving signer, 360
Declaratory Act of 1766, 14
deer head. See New Jersey, state coinage
Deliverance, the, 157
Democratic Party, 394, 396, 398, 399
denarius. ***See*** **penny**
denier
defined, 141
denominations

of British coins, 79–82
dentil
defined, 451
Derby, Earls of, 112, 190
d'Estaing, Comte, 251
detector notes. *See* anti-counterfeiting measures, paper
device
defined, 451
Dickeson, Dr. Montroville, 250
Dickinson, John, 69
and plan for confederation, 255
Olive Branch Petition, 60
Dickinson, Philemon, 69
die
cracks/breaks, defined, 450
defined, 449
state
terminal (defined), 451
state, defined, 450
variety (defined), 452
dime. *See* disme/dime
Dinwiddie, Gov. Robert, 97, 141
disme/dime, 126, 144
and Mint Act of 1792, 408
denomination created, 273
first coinage of, 427
Gobrecht's seated Liberty, 440
Kneass's modified capped bust, 434
origin of word, 148, 410
Reich's capped bust, 432
Scot's draped bust issues, 426, 427, 428
the 1792 patterns, 412
distilling, distillery, 11, 277, 376, 409, 411
Divine Eye
on Chalmers' coinage, 268
on Continental Currency, 66, 261
on Nova Const. patterns, 256
on private Nova Const., 267
on VT coinage, 298
on Washington success tokens, 368
Divine Right of Kings, 83, 85, 162
DK lead tokens, 156
dobra. *See* Johanne
dog dollar. *See* dollar, Dutch, Leeuwendaalder
dollar
continental (coin). *See* Continental Currency coins
continental (paper). *Also see Continental Currency notes*
depreciation of, 59
Dutch
Leeuwendaalder, 134, 135
leg dollar, 134
Rijkdaalder or rix dollar, 134
origin of word. *See* Joachimsthaler
Spanish, 8, 81
becomes world standard, 7
conversion rates, 49, 125
and Morris plan, 256, 260
in America, 201
in MA, 167, 244, 333
first minted, 118
fractional parts of, 129
milled, 8, 49, 61, 126–30
origins of, 118
pillar style, 126, 128, 333
portrait style, 128, 127–30
U.S. gold, first, 391
U.S. silver
and 1786 federal standard, 273
and Jefferson plan, 263
by Scot
draped bust, 424, 427
of 1804, 344, 427
flowing hair, 420, 421
Gobrecht's seated Liberty, 439–41
production suspended, 427
relationship to Spanish dollar, 130
dos mundos. *See* dollar, Spanish, pillar style
double De La Merique, 207
doubloon, 258, 274
Brasher. *See* Barsher, Ephraim:and private gold coinage
Spanish (defined), 121
Drake, Sir Francis, 4, 84
aids the Dutch, 131
Drapier, M.B.. *See* Swift Jonathan
drop press, 168
Droz, Jean Peter, 111, 407
and 1792 dismes patterns, 412
Drury House mint, 189
Dublin, 90, 177, 230, 250
and North America tokens, 374
and St. Patrick coinage, 177–200
city arms, 186
DuBois, Adam, 261
ducat
Danish, 271
Dutch, 135
ducaton, 134
Dudley, Benjamin
and Nova Const. patterns, 260–64
and Nova Const. private issues (?), 265
Duer, William
(official) and James Jarvis, 306
and Fugio scandal, 349–55
and Ohio land scandal, 354
duit, defined, 133
Dummer, Jeremiah, 44
dump issues, 95
Dunmore, John Murray, Earl of, 240
Dupré, Augustin, 416
Dutch, 8, 21, 86, 92, 147, 148, 154, 160, 274
and 17th cent. Amer. tokens, 215–17
and banking, 132
and credit, 133
and Edmund Andros, 166
and Rhode Island ship tokens, 251–54
and slavery, 132
Asiatic trade, 132
buy Manhattan, 132
coins in America, 131–36
competition with English, 4
engineering, 132
first to recognize U.S., 136
gold coinage, 135
golden age of, 132–34
Holland, 132
imprints on America, 136
independence from Spain, 132
mercantilism, 132
patroon system, 135
recognize American indep., 251
Republic, 132
revolutionize wampum, 38
shipbuilding, 132
Washington, the, 131, See William the Silent
West India Company, 135
dye woods, 5
eagle
denomination
and Mint Act of 1792, 408

and Mint Act of 1834, 434
capped bust style, 423
created, 273
first coining of, 422
Gobrecht's coronet head, 436
Scot's draped bust, capped, 422–23, 426
suspended, 427
Gobrecht's flying, 439
heraldic, on U.S. coins, 423, 426
John Reich's version, 430, 375–77
on Brasher's NY doubloons, 258, 273–77
on Canadian tokens, 388
on Feuchtwanger & flying eagle cents, 395
on Getz' pattern, 367
on Hancock's cents, 363–64
on hard times tokens, 392, 402
on MA state coinage, 258, 334, 333–39
on Mott tokens, 375–77
on New Yorke in America tokens, 154
on NY pattern coppers, 279–81, 283–85
on U.S. Mint issues, 407–41
on Washington Lib. & Success tokens, 369
on Washington Roman heads, 366

Eagle, H.M.S., 252

East Indies, 132

East, the, 14, 24, 32, 384, 397

Eckfeldt, Adam, 410
and early U.S. Mint issues, 409–12, 416
and Getz' pattern, 367
and William Kneass, 435
on draped bust cents, 428

Eckfeldt, Jacob, 409

Eckfeldt, John Jacob
and Nova Constellatio patterns, 261

economy
and Copper Panic of 1789, 21
and industrialization, 404
and states' rights, 19
and the Bank of the U.S., 393, *Also see Bank of the U.S.*
attempts to stabilize, 13
boom and bust nature of, 70, 390
British, shift to industrialism, 114
effect of
counterfeit coppers on, 263, 285
non-standard currency on, 260
tarriffs on, 22
French, and John Law, 209–11
Irish, 188
of Maryland, early, 176
of Massachusetts, early, 162
of New York, 274
of Virginia, 239–42
overview
of barter and frontier, 29–42
of colonial and Revolutionary, 3–18
of paper money-based, 43–69
of post-Revolutionary, 19–27
paper money as a stimulant for, 46
post-War of 1812, 398
role of middle men in, 11

ecu, 212
conversion rate, 142
defined, 141
versus Spanish dollar, 213

Ecu d'or, 142

edge
center-grained, 372
clip, defined, 448
clipping (deliberate), 166, 168
corded, 373
dating, 88, 91, 92
engrailed, 372, 373
experimental, 431
lettered, 92, 115, 182, 212, 363, 365, 369, 370, 377, 378, 379, 381, 382, 415, 417, 419, 421, 431
defined, 454
methods for applying devices, 188–200, 454
ornamented, 64, 248, 262, 264, 367, 376
plain, 262, 367, 370, 372, 374, 414
reeded, 182, 188–200, 342, 368, 369, 370, 378, 380, 412, 413, 422, 438, 439
defined, 454
vine and bars, 415, 416

Edinburgh, 61

eight [units]. *See* Nova Constellatio patterns

Eikon Basilike, 186

Elder, Thomas, 250

elephant tokens, 154, 202–6

Elephant, the (ship), 206

Elizabeth I, 79, 141
and coinage, 82
and Philip II, 4
and private tokens, 113
and Sir Humphrey Gilbert, 203
and the Dutch, 131
arms of, 84

Endecott, John, 161

England, 34, 35, Also see individual cities in, Also see British, Also see individual monarchs
Also see Parliamentary acts, 13
and mercantilism, 3–18
claims to France, 137
commercial interests seize power, 12
exports to colonies, 16
income per capita in, 9

English Commonwealth, 79, 81, 85–86, 155, 162, 165, 183, 188, 203

enumeration, principle of, 5

escudo, 274
Portuguese (defined), 145
Spanish (defined), 118

evasion coppers, 79, 109–10, 287, *Also see imitation halfpence, Also see counterfeits, counterfeiting*
and Auctori Plebis tokens, 374
and blacksmith tokens, 388
and Washington North Wales halfpence, 109, 357, 371
and William Lutwyche, 374
legends on, 109

evasive
dating
on Autori Plebis-related tokens, 375
on MA silver coinage, 170
legends
on hard times tokens, 400
on Washington Unity States coppers, 358
stories about blacksmith coppers, 387

Excelsior
coppers
New York coinage proposals
Atlee/Machin, 283–85

Bailey/Brasher, 258, 279–81, 284
ties to imitation halfpence, 289
on Brasher's gold coinage, 276
exchange system
British/American
and debt, 11, 47
and West Indian trade, 11
defined, 9, 10
in detail, 46–47
East/West, 32
exports
American, 6
and bills of exchange, 32
and the balance of trade, 47
and the exchange system, 46–47
benefits from stable market, 13
effect of 19th century tarriffs on, 398
effect of tariffs on, 22
enumeration of, 5
from the middle colonies, 10
key products, 9
MA silver coinage, 167
minor products, 10
pistareens, 125
raw copper, 103
rice and indigo, 9
South hurt most by enumeration, 13
specie, 46
to the West Indies, 10, 11
U.S. specie, 427, 434
Virginia dominance of, 240
British
American plantation tokens, 202
annual, 6
blacksmith coppers (?), 387
finished copper, 103
specie, 8, 11
and Lord Baltimore's coinage, 176
under Cromwell, 85
to America
coppers, 103
growth of, 16
to America, growth of, 10
Dutch
coinage, 134
French, 138
coinage, 206–14
Exton, Lord, 88
farthing, 204, 233, 388
and American Plantation tokens, 201
and counterfeiting, 87, 102
and MA state coinage, 334
apocryphal, 215–18
copper, first use of, 86
defined, 80
dump, under George I, 95
English/British
private tokens, 113
evasion, 109
French coins used as, 212, 214
imitation, 79, 286
jetons used as (?), 148
Matthew Boulton and, 101
musket balls used as, 29, 41
on the Mermaid, 333
patent, 79, 88–90, 113, 179, 240
Pitt tokens/medalets, 234–37
regal, 79, 86–102
St. Patrick. *See* St. Patrick coinage
standard weight of, 88
tin and plugged, 88, 92
U.S. half cents as, 437
under Queen Anne, 94
Voce Populi, 153, 230–32
federal
acceptance of state bank notes, 24
assumption of state debt, 21
backing of Cont. Currency, 68
branch mints, 390
coinage, 7, 21, 22, 255–59, 245–51, 334, 337, 407–41
contract, 306, *Also see* Confederation, coinage proposals
early use of symbols, 258
right of, 256
standards, 256, 257, 273, 281, 285, 334, 350, 391, 392
Constitution. *See* Constitution, U.S.
construction, 25
control of the West, 255
eagle, 402
government, 50, 70
inability to tax, 58
-ism, 283
and John Chalmers, 256, 269
law
and right of coinage, 390
and the Mint Act of 1792. *See* Mint Act of 1792
and the Mint Act of 1834. *See* Mint Act of 1834
and the Nullification Crisis, 398
lottery, 75
unit, 256, 260–64
conversions (*chart*), 261
Federal
-ist
Papers, 283
Party, 399
Period, 20
Reserve, 51, 67
Ferdinand VI, 128, 467
Ferdinand VII, 129, 467
Ferryland, Newfoundland, 156
Feversham, H.M.S., 134, 166
Fibonacci Sequence, 199
fire
and blacksmith coppers, 386
at the Park Theatre (NY), 383
at the U.S. Mint, 1816, 432
London, 1666, 86, 189, 190, 203
fish, fishing, 5, 10, 11, 15, 29, 34, 139
and French claims, 139
and the origins of barter, 33
beginnings of in New World, 139
colony on Cape Ann (MA), 161
Ferryland, 157
MA codfish note, 56
Fitch, John, 409
Fitzsimons, Thomas, 262
five [units]. ***See*** **Nova Constellatio patterns**
flan, defined. ***See*** **planchets, defined**
fleur de lis, 84, 206, 207, 208, 209, 211, 212, 213, 238, 274
on English coins, 137
on Georgivs Triumpho coppers, 271
flip, 224
Florida, 3
and Verazzano, 139
British demand, 1763, 141
Ft. Caroline, 1564, 139
Georgivs Triumpho coppers in, 270
plantations tokens. *See* American plantations tokens
provincial coinage, 385
returned to Spain, 1783, 128
Spanish in, 93
flour, 5, 10, 11
font variations. ***See*** **anti-counterfeiting measures, paper**

Ford (or Forde), Sir Edward, 191–97
foreign
debt, 19, 21, 24, 49, 246
incidental coinage, 77–146, 22
and jetons, 147
as a source of metal, 421
Brasher's marks on, 258
defined, 7
imitation of, 285
relative numbers of in circ., 7, 8
investment, 33
and specie drain, 427
in the Bank of the U.S., 22
Fort
Caroline, 139
Dummer, 296
Johnston (SC), 273
Necessity, 97
Orania or Orange. *See* Albany
Pitt, 36
St. Louis (Matagorda Bay), 384
Stanwix (See footnote), 37
Ticonderoga or 'Ti', 60, 63
fort, forts. *See* individual forts by name
at St. Augustine, 93
at St. Joseph, MI, 75
French, captured by British, 141
French, in the West, 97
in San Antonio, 357
on Lake Champlain, 386
fourthling. *See* farthing
France, French, 8, 202, *Also see Bonaparte, Napoleon, Also see French colonial coinages*, Also see Bourbon ruling family, Also see individual monarchs, Also see French and Indian Wars
and Caribbean holdings, 141
and early VT history, 296
and Libertas Americana medals, 416
and playing card money, 43
and silver preference, 263
attempts to take Spanish Netherlands, 91
Castorland settlement, 380
cede Lousiana to Spanish, 23
coinage denominations, 142
colonial coinages, 206–14
colonization run by private interests, 140
cycles of war and peace, 93, 97
early exploration, 139
early history of, 136–41
early southwestern exploration, 384
end of American claims, 138
end of threat in America, 141
funding of Bank of N.A., 19
hold on America solidified by trade, 33
Huguenots Settlements, 139
in America, 136–44
monetary system, 141
originate jetons, 147
paper money, 57
per capita income in, 9
playing card money, 208
Republic, 238
Revolution, 99, 138, 142, 144, 234, 238, 380
royal family ties to Spain, 123
silver shipment from, 246
squabbles prevent colonization, 137–39
symbolized on Georgivs Triumpho coppers, 271
ties to St. Patrick's coinage, 189
U.S. debt to, 21
weakened by war, 91, 93
Franklin cents. See Fugio cents
Franklin Press tokens, 379–80
Franklin, Benjamin, 15, 54, 60
advocates paper money, 48
alternatives to Stamp Act, 235
and 1754 plan for confederation, 255
and Fugio motif, 63, 245
and Libertas Americana medals, 416
and mottoes on Cont. Currency, 60
and the Libertas Americana medals, 416
anticipates Stamp Act, 14
as a printer of notes, 56
biographical information, 379–80
committee to draft Declaration, 246
Franklin and Hall, 61
on Cont. Curr. as a tax, 60
on stability of the empire, 153
pioneers
marbelized paper, 51
nature prints, 53
Frederick the Great, 97
Frederick, Prince, 96, 98
freemen
of Massachusetts, 161
of Vermont, 298
Freidus, Daniel, 228–30
French and Indian Wars, 12
1st (1689-97). *See* King William's War
2nd (1702-09). *See* Queen Anne's War
3rd (1744-48). *See* King George's War
4th (1756-63). See Seven Years War
French colonies, 136–44
coinages for, 206–14
1670 Louis XIV issues, 207
1692-1700 overstrikings, 208
1717 Perpignan issues, 209
1721-1722 copper sols, 212
1767 copper sols, 238
billion sous marques, 213
billon mousequetaires of 1709-1711, 208
coins from Le Chemeau, 212
Friends of Liberty and Trade, 233, 234–37
frontier, 24, 29, 33, 41, 141, 404
banks, 70
commercial, defined, 32
defined, 32
economy of, 29–42
life on, 32
protection of, 235
rebellion, 23
skirmishes, 6, 12, 13, 31, 36, 91, 93, 96, 384
transition from barter, 31
Fugio
cents, 21, 60, 63, 257, 259, 411, 414
and Congressional approval, 350
and CT coinage, 307
New Haven 'restrikes' of, 354, 456
scandal's effect on Mint deliberations, 407
motif
on Continental Currency coins. *See* Continental Currency coins

on Continental Currency coins. *See* Continental Currency coins
on Continental Currency notes, 60, 64, 247
Fuld, George, 272
fur, fur trade, 9, 29, 140, 209, 384
and Northwest tokens, 358, 385–86
and the New Netherlands Company, 135
and trade silver, 35
and wampum, 39
French approach v. British, 33
furs enumerated, 5
goes corporate, 34
in Oregon, 358, 385–86
makes French settlement viable, 140
starts barter with Natives, 33
Gallery Mint, 276, 354, 413, 420, 425
Galludet, Elisha
and Continental Currency coins, 245–51
and Continental Currency notes, 60
and EG initials, 248
***Garza, La (ship)*, 157**
Gaultier, Leonard. *See* St. Patrick's coinage
General Court
Connecticut, 226
Massachusetts
and MA silver coinage, 160–75
and self-government, 162
and state coinage, 333–39
establishes a mint, 164
formation of, 161
interim coinage proposals, 333
sanctions wampum, 36
George I, 94–96, 111, 153
dump issues, 95
George II, 44, 96, 98, 104, 230, 387, *Also see King George's War*
death of, 98
leads troops in battle, 96
George III, 12, 14, 79, 111, 137, 142, 148, 153, 231, 236, 241, 288, 289, 291, 295, 309, 363, 368, 387, 388
and coinage, 99
death of, 25, 99
in defense of, 98
manipulation of Parliament, 12
on Georgivs Triumpho coppers?, 256
Proclamation for Suppressing Rebellion..., 75
refuses Olive Branch Petition, 60
George IV, 102, 358, 386, 387
Georgia, 55, 270
and Dahlonega branch mint, 390, 435
Georgian architecture, 217
Georgivs Triumpho coppers, 256, 270–71
and ties to NJ coinage, 327
and ties to Nova Constellatio coppers, 267
German, 45, 86, 124, 131, 250, 382, *Also see jeton, Also see George I*
coins in America, 8, 72
immigrants
and John Law, 210
Eckfeldt family, 409
Gobrecht family, 435
John J. Astor, 385
John Reich, 376, 430
the Bechtlers, 390
to Jamestown, 148
silver, 394
Gerry, Elbridge, 247, 400
Gilbert, Sir Humphrey, 203
gilding, 241, 364
Glorious Revolution, 90, 91, 201, 231
Gloucester
County, Virginia tokens, 215–18, 217–18
Gloucester County, Virginia tokens, 154
Goadsby, Thomas, 278, Also *see* New Jersey state coinage
and Albion Cox, 319–20
and New Jersey coinage, 316–32
and New Jersey head-left varieties, 326
and the Rahway Mint, 320–21
gold, 8, 19, 22, 46, 71, 139, 147, 148, 180, 188, 375, 403, 404
coinage. Also see specie, Also see individual coins by name (e.g., Guinea, eagle, etc.)
American. Also see tri-metallic system, Also see U.S. Mint, See Bechtler, Also see Reid, Templeton, Also see Brasher, Ephraim
1786 standards, 273
Castorland demi ecu, 380
effect of California gold rush on, 409
Immune Columbia pattern, 344
in the Morris plan, 261
Massachusetts state, 334
Motts' eagle v. Reich's, 376
Washington pieces, 362, 364, 367, 373
British. *See* Chapter 5
and founding of the Smithsonian Institution, 436
during the crusades, 387
Dutch. See Chapter 7
French. See Chapter 7
aboard Le Chameau, 212
John Law associated, 154, 211
Ottoman or Arabian, 8
Portuguese. See Chapter 7
regulation of, 274
relative numbers of in circ., 8, 24
Spanish. *See* Chapter 6
and Brasher's coinage, 258
Aztec origins of, 117
depletion of reserves, 7, 427, 434
discovery of in the South, 25, 359, 390, 435
-en
age of American coinage, 444
age of private notes, 73
age of the Dutch, 132
crown. *See* St. Patrick's coinage
fleece. *See* Order of the Golden Fleece
mean. *See* Golden Mean
Libertas Americana medals, 417
Louis. *See* Louis d'or
-smith, 163, 227, 274, 334
value of, 6, 80, 240, 263, 408, 427
world production of, 7
Golden
Fleece. *See* Order of...
Mean, 199
Good Samaritan shilling, 174

Goodrich, John, 305–7
Gorges, Sir Fernando, 162
Grand
Alliance
first, 92
second, 93, 138
Committee [on coinage], 263
Dominion of New England, 203
Great
Britain. *See* Britain, British
Chain, the. *See* Chain, the Great
Commoner. See Pitt, William
Council, 37
Lakes, 30, 140
Mother of Crops, 380
Pacificator, The. *See* Clay, Henry
Pond, 283
Restoration, 86, 89, 90, 165, 183, 188, 189, 215
Seal of the U.S., 67, 258, 276, 363, 376, 425
Green
[Jonas and Anne Catharine] Print Shop, 54
Green Mountain Boys, 60
origins of, 296
Green Mountains. See Vermont
greenbacks, 73
Greene
Nathaniel, 17
Thomas, 175
Grenville, Lord, 234
and enumeration, 5
Gresham, Sir Thomas
and Gresham's Law, 6, 46
Guadeloupe, 141, 238
Guatemala, 117, 122
City Mint, 120
Guinea, 6, 80, 92, 95, 99, 100, 142, 146, 148, 189, 242, 462
Gulf of Mexico, 94
gunmoney, 79, 91, 201
Gunpowder Plot, 83
habitants, 208, 210
half
cent, 102, 273, 419
hard times tokens, 394
Massachusetts. *See* Massachusetts state coinage
U.S.
and the Mint Act of 1792, 408
by Scot
1794 liberty caps, 419
draped bust issues, 428
denomination
created, 273
reason for existence, 416
terminated, 436, 437
Gardner's 1795-1797 liberty caps, 419
Gobrecht's coronet heads, 436
Kneass' revised classic heads, 433
liberty cap
1793 head left, 416–17
design origins, 416
planchet sources, 378, 432
Reich's classic head, 432
disme/dime
and the Mint Act of 1792, 408
by Gobrecht's
seated Liberty issues, 440
by Scot
draped bust issues, 425
flowing hair issues, 422
Kneass' modified capped bust, 434
Reich's capped bust, 430
the 1792 issue, 22, 410–12
dollar, 444
and the Mint Act of 1792, 408
by Gobrecht
reeded edge, capped busts, 438–39
seated Liberty issues, 439–41
by Scot
draped bust issues, 427
flowing hair issues, 418, 422
denomination created, 273
Getz' pattern, 357, 366–68, 408
Idler copies of, 368, 456
Reich's capped bust issues, 430–31
doubloon, by Brasher. *See* Brasher, Ephraim
eagle, 430
and the Mint Act of 1792, 408
by Gobrecht
coronet head, 436
modified classic heads, 435
by Reich
capped bust, 431
capped head, 432
by Scot
draped bust, capped, 422–23
denomination created, 273
first coining of, 422
Kneass' modified classic head, 434
Reich's capped bust/head issues, 432
Scot's draped bust, capped, 426
halfpenny, 80, 146, 225, 237, 281, 308, 369, 370, Also see counterfeits, counterfeiting, *Also see copper*
1749 as American, 153
and MA state coinage, 334
Bahama, 111–12
Barbados, 110–11
contemporary value of, 259
counterfeit, 102–8
denomination created, 87
dump, 95
elephant tokens. *See* elephant tokens
evasion, 109–10, 79
Washington, North Wales as, 109
imitation. *See imitation halfpence*
importance of, 102
Irish, 79, 97, 98, 99, 375
as undertype, 232, 244
Liverpool. *See* Liverpool halfpenny
Manx, 112
Massachusetts. *See* Mass. Province Halfpenny
New Hampshire. *See* New Hampshire coinage
origins of design, 86–88
patent, 88–90
Pitt. *See* Pitt, See Pitt tokens/medalets
regal, 86–102, 79
ship. *See* Washington ship halfpenny
St. Patrick. *See* St. Patrick coinage

standard
British, 298, 335, 378
standards
Irish, 96
tokens
British/English. See Conder, James
English/British
early, 113
Virginia. *See* Virginia halfpenny
Voce Populi tokens. *See* Voce Populi
Washington
Liberty. & Security. *See* Washington Liberty & Security
North Wales. *See* Washington North Wales
Wood's coinage. *See* William Wood's coinage
Hall
and Sellers, 60, 61, 62
David, 61
Wm. & David, 62
Hamilton, Alexander, 283, 361
and Bank of New York, 258, 274
and Bank of the U.S., 22
and central government, 22
and Confederation symbolism, 341
and currency plan, 260
and debt assumption, 21
and Mint report, 407
and Morristown, NJ, 320
as a lawyer in New York, 319
interest in U.S. Mint, 410
proposes gold dollar, 391
hammered coinage
American, MA silver, 167–68
English, 80, 82–85, 88–90
at the Royal Mint, 82
French, in America, 206
process described, 449
Spanish, 117–24
cob coinage, 120–24
Lima Mint, 120
Hammersmith Iron Works, 164
Hancock, John, 235, 243, 334
and MA state coinage, 335
and smuggling, 11
Hanover ruling family. *See* individual monarchs
hapny. *See* halfpenny
Hapsburg ruling family, 122, 123, 127
hardware, defined, 290
Harmon, Reuben, Jr.
and deal with Machin's Mills, 301
and VT coinage, 297–304, 298
harp
Irish, debuts on English coinage, 84
King David's, on St. Patrick's coinage, 177–200
on Auctori Plebis mules, 375
on blacksmith tokens, 387
on Continental Currency notes, 66, 242, 461
on gunmoney, 91
on New Hampshire coinage, 242
on North American tokens, 374
on patent coinage, 88–90
on regal coinage for Ireland, 96, 97
on Virginia halfpence, 241
on Wash. North Wales halfpence, 371
on Wood's Hibernia coinage, 222–24
origins of as a symbol, 187
Harper, John
and 1792 half dismes, 410
and Getz' patterns, 366
and Jefferson head cents?, 418
Harrington, John. *See* Lord Exton
Harrison
George, 277
Richard, 277
William Henry, 320, 395, 399, 400
Harvey, Sir John, 239
Hatfield, and New Jersey state coinage?, 322, 331
Hawthorne, Nathaniel, 29, 164
and Hanna Hull story, 174
Hayne, Robert, 398
haypenny. *See* halfpenny
Heath, Sir Robert, 203
Hely-Hutchinson, John, 231
Henry IV, 141
Henry VIII, 82
Henry, Patrick, 92
Henry, Prince, the Navigator, 144
heraldry. *Also see individual types, Also see eagle, heraldic, Also see New Yorke in America tokens*
colors symbolized in, 324
desire for war or peace, 280
Hessians, 17, 65, 96
Hiawatha, 37
Hibernia, 99, 153, 220, 250, *See Ireland, Irish*
St. Patrick coinage, 177–200
Voce Populi tokens, 230–32
Wood's coinage for, 218–24
hides. See fur, fur trade
Higley
Dr. Samuel, 153, 160, 305
coinage of, 224–30
John (brother of Samuel), 226
John (father of Samuel), 225
Katherine Brewster, 225
Hilhouse, James, 305–7
proposes abolition of U.S. Mint, 424
Hingham, Massachusetts, 174
hoard, hoarding, 6, 8, 19, 49, 87, 99, 109, 113, 134, 233, 240, 295, 432
Beach-Grünthal Hoard, 294, 295
Castine Hoard, 134
Cohen Hoard, 242
Hobby Protection Act of 1973, 228, 455
Hocquart, Governor (Canada), 213
Hodder, Michael, 169, 181, 210, 245–51, 270, 276
hogge money. *See* Sommer Islands coinage
hogshead, 31
Holland, 124, 236, *Also see Dutch*
intellectual leadership by, 133
Holt, Richard, 155, 201
Holy
Grail, 197, 198
Roman Empire, 92, 99, 118, 124
Hopkins, Joseph, 305–7
Hopkinson, Francis, 261
and Confederation motif, 60, 66, 67, 262
and other currency designs, 68
as first choice for Mint Director, 408
horned bust. See Connecticut, horned bust
horse, 166, 267
on American Plantations tokens, 200–202
on Dutch riders, 134
on New Jersey state coinage, 257, 316–32
on St. Patrick's coinage, 184
power, 433
House of

Bourbon, 137, 235
Burgesses, 233
Commons, 235
Keys, 112
Money, 7
Valois, 137

Howard
Henry. *See* Maltravers, Lord
John, 378

Howe
Admiral Richard
and Rhode Island Ship tokens/medals, 251–54
Earl (John Howard), 378
General William
and Rhode Island, 251
evacuates Boston, 63
occupied by Philadelphia, 66
retakes Philadelphia, 66
William (Detroit Bookseller), 401

hub, hubbing
at the U.S. Mint, 419, 431, 437
defined, 453
on Connecticut state coinage, 311–15
on New Jersey state coinage?, 322
on Washington pieces, 370, 372

Hudson
Henry, 132, 135
River, 132, 215, 259, 277, 296
and the Great Chain, 283
-'s Bay, 94
Company, 385
and British claims to Oregon, 386
founded, 34, 140
in the 19th century, 385
use of trade beads, 42
use of trade silver, 35

Hull
and Sanderson. *See* Hull, John
John, 44, 160–75, 163, 334
and daughter, Hanna, 174
and MA silver coinage, 160–75
early life of, 163

Hume, Ivor Nöel, 8, 221, 223, 240

Hundred Years War, 137

Huron, 140

Hutchinson, Thomas, 23, 235

Idler, William, 177, 367, 456

Illinois Country, 75, 140

imitation
farthings, 286
halfpence
American, 285–95
attribution guide, 473–79
differentiating from British, 286
Group I, 288–89
Group II, 289–90, 295
Group III, 290–93
Group IV, 293–94
Group V, 294–95
groups defined, 287
introduction, 285–87
ties to CT coinage, 295
ties to Georgivs triumphos, 270
ties to NY coinage, 293
ties to VT coinage, 289, 302
British and Irish. *Also see counterfeits, counterfeiting*
counterfeits, 102–8
evasions, 109–10
MA cents
as undertypes for CT state coppers, 337
silver issues (Amer.), 286

Immune Columbia pieces, 265, 278, 342
ties to imitation halfpence, 294
ties to VT coinage, 304

Immunis Columbia pieces, 259, 340, 343, 339–48
of 1786, 342
of 1787, 278, 339
ties to NJ coinage, 345
ties to NY coinage, 284, 346

imports
to America
18th century growth of, 10, 16
and John Higley's business, 225
and John Hull's business, 166
and John Law, 210
and the exchange system, 32
and the Mott business, 375
and the Sugar Act, 13, 234
and the Townshend Acts, 14
as commodity classification, 34
blanks for U.S. Mint, 429, 432
boycott of, 15, 236
effect on NY, 236
coins intended for Ireland, 232
cost of counterfeits, 263
counterfeits, 305
early tokens, 155, 215
effect of
tariffs on, 22
War on, 20
finished copper, 103
foreign incidental coinages, 7
French coinage, 154
from the West Indies, 11
jetons, 215
St. Patrick's coinage, 178
to England/Britain
Swedish copper, 87
to Ireland
regal coppers, 223
Wood's coinage, 223
to North America
the blacksmith coppers?, 387
to Spain, 7

income, 6, 188
coining as a source of, 259, 320
effect of labor shortages on, 11
per capita, 9
regional differences in, 9

incuse, incused
'COPY' on reproductions, 455
lettering, 101, 258, 334
star on Texas jolas, 385

indented notes. *See* anti-counterfeiting measures, paper

indenture
-d servantry, 11
John Reich's, 430
documents, 74

Indian. Also see Native American, Also see French and Indian Wars
corn, 44
weed. *See* tobacco

indigo, 5, 9, 10, 13, 29, 234

industry. Also see Industry (i.e., personified)
and Hamilton's vision, 361
British, 9
copper, 189
Diderot illustration, 291
distilling, 11
jeton making, 147

regional differences in, 9
shipbuilding, 9
symbolized, 403
textile, 9
tin, 88
token making, 113, 361, 377
Industry
Liberty, as Parent of Science and, 411
on Myddleton tokens, 381
on NY Excelsior coinage, 280
inflation
and Continental Currency notes, 59, 60, 68
and supply of paper money, 48, 49
and the demise of silver pennies, 86
colonial, 47
effect on coinage values, 125, 134, 333
following Panic of 1819, 24
in Spain, 7
in the price of gold, 80
post-Revolutionary War, 20
pre-U.S. Civil War, 436
Ingle, Richard, 175
Ingram, Thomas Wells, 372
interest
and gunmoney redemption, 91
and the national debt, 21
bearing notes, 45, 48, 49, 69
bearing vouchers, 74
effect of paper money on, 48
tables, 403
Intolerable Acts, 15
Invisible College. See Royal Society
Ireland, Irish, 4, 83, 90, 250, 370
1667 petition for coinage, 189
and gunmoney, 90
and North American tokens. *See* North American token
and St. Patrick coinage, 155, *See* St. Patrick coinage
and Voce Pouli tokens. *See* Voce Populi tokens
and West Country Men, 84
Armagh, 185
arms added to English, 84
as origin of Georgivs Triumphos?, 271
effect of token coinage on, 188
effects of Commonwealth on, 188
Parliament, 231
patent coinage for, 79, 88
react to Wood's coinage, 222
regal coinage for, 79, 96, 103
Ulster, 180
Ulster Rebellion, 183
Iroquois, 140, 296
League, 36–37
under British control, 94
Irving, Washington, 136
island coinages, 110–12
Isle of
Devils, 159
Man, 79, 112, *Also see House of Keys*, *Also see Earls of Derby*
and St. Patrick coinage, 181, 190
Jackson, Andrew, 359
and Bank of the U.S., 22, 25
and Nullification Crisis, 399
Jacobites
and gunmoney, 90, 201
claims to throne, 91, 93, 95, 97, 231
origin of word (see footnote), 90
Jamaica, 270
James I, 83–84, 160
and the ascent of Parliament, 12
as Scotland's James VI, 81
charters Virg. Companies, 160
coat of arms, 83
James II, 79, 90–91
and American Plantations tokens. *See* American Plantations tokens
and gunmoney. *See* gunmoney
bi-metallic coinage, 413
sends Andros to Mass., 166
James III, 95, *Also see* Stuart, James Francis Edward
James Jarvis and Company. See Jarvis, James
James VI (of Scotland). *See* James I
Jamestown, 158
founded, 160
Irish coins found at, 84
James I and, 83
lead tokens found at, 113
Tudor coinage found at, 82
Janus (goddess), 244
Janus Copper. *See* Mass., Janus Copper
Japanese, 253
Jarvis, James, 259
and Company, 306
and Confederation coinage proposals, 344
and Congressional approval of Fugios, 350
and CT coinage, 305–12
and Fugio cents, 349–55
Jay, John, 283
Jefferson, Thomas, 92, 113, 246, 284, 361, 402, 420, 430, *Also see U.S. large cent, Jefferson head*
and Andrew Jackson's regime, 396
and Bank of the U.S., 22
and coinage design, 430
and Confederatio decads, 340
in silver, 342
and debt assumption, 21
and location of national capital, 21
and Louisiana Purchase, 23
and nail making, 30
and Nova Const. patterns, 262
and plan for coinage, 256, 260–64
and silver-centered cents, 413
and VA halfpennies, 240
interest in U.S. Mint, 410
opposes private coinage, 407
suspends coinage of specie, 427
Jenks, Joseph, 164
Jerusalem cross, 275
Jesus Christ, 85, 145, 197, 198, 199
jetons, 147–48, 215
Joachimsthaler (see footnote), 7
Joe. *See* Johanne
Johanna the Mad, 118
Johanne (Portuguese gold coin), 144, 146
Jordan, Dr. Louis, 126, 163, 202, 309
Joseph of Arimethea, 197
Kempson, Peter & Sons, 115, 369–70
Auctori Plebis tokens, 374
Conder tokens, 115
Franklin Press tokens, 379
Talbot, Allum & Lee cents, 378
Washington
Lib. & Security coppers, 357, 370
Repub. Ameri. & funeral pennies, 370
Ketland, Thomas & Sons, 363
Kilkenny Confederation. *See* Catholic Confederation
King

George's War, 44, 47, 96, 97, 153, 333
-'s Fifth, the, 118, 124
-'s House (tavern), 216
William's War, 43, 44, 91, 93, 140
Kingsland, Robert, 206
Kirke, Sir David, 156
Kleeberg, John, 154, 215, 216, 415
Knox
Henry, 63
John, 83
Sir John, 89
Krauwinckel, Hans (and family), 147, 157
Küechler, Conrad Heinrich, 101, 112, 382
La Banque Generale. See Law, John, paper money
La Louisiane. *See* Louisiana
La Plata Mint, 120
La Salle
Robert Cavalier, Sieur de, 384
Lafayette, Marquis de, 73
1824-1825 visit, 401
and Fugio cents, 306
Lancaster, Pennsylvania, 66, 247
land issues. *See* loan issues
landscape coppers. *See* Vermont landscape coppers
laughing head. See Connecticut, laughing heads
laurel (gold coin), 80
Law, John, 138, 140, 141, 154, 209–11
coinage defined, 210
paper money, 57
Lawes, William, 187
lawful money, 48, 244, 334
Le Chameau, 212, 213
lead
-based copies, 245, 250, 457
counterfeits, 101, 104
farthings, 113
pennies, 113
printing plates, 52, 53
tokens, 82, 113, 155, 215
DK, 157
New Yorke in America, 215–16
weights, as a flywheel, 291
Leddel, William, 319
leg dollar. See dollar, Dutch, leg dollar
legal tender
and colonial notes, 45
and CT coinage, 305
and St. Patrick coinage, 178
and wampum, 39
bill of credit, 50, 69
status of Spanish coins, 8, 129
Legg, George, 89
Lennox, Duke of, 89
lettered edge. *See* edge, lettered
Lewis and Clark, 31, 42, 385
Leyden
Puritans in, 160
siege of, 131–32
liberty
cap, 144, 244, 245, 342, 345, 392
Libertas Americana medal, 416
on Chalmers' coinage, 268
on Confederatio patterns, 341
origins of, 416
U.S. cents, 417
pole, 278, 281, 308, 345, 381, 439
on Immunis Columbias, 342
on Talbot, Allum & Lee cents, 378
tree
on Myddleton tokens, 381
Liberty
bare-breasted, 313
on 1776 Mass. patterns, 244
on Confederation patterns, 284
on CT state coinage, 308
on hard times tokens, 392–405
on Immune Columbias, 343
on Immunis Columbia coppers, 345
on late Washington pieces, 372
on Libertas Americana medal, 417
on Myddleton tokens, 381
on Non Vi Virtute Vici coppers, 278
on Nova Eborac coppers, 281
on NY Excelsior coppers, 280
on U.S. coins
1792 issues, 410–14
classic and capped types, 430–35
draped bust types, 422–30
flowing hair and liberty cap types, 414–22
seated and coronet types, 435–41
on U.S. large cents, 400
on Vermont coinage, 300
on Wreath cents, 415
Lima
Mint, 120, 121, 122, 274
on George II silver coinage, 97
style doubloon. *See* Brasher, Ephraim
Line of Demarcation, 144
lion dollar. See dollar, Dutch, Leeuwendaalder
livestock, 215
livre, 72, 211, 212
defined, 141
loan issues, 45, 46
Lon Don. *See* elephant tokens
London, 5, 10, 62, 90, 95, 114, 116, 166, 175, 177, 189, 202–6, 240, 250, 264, 363, 369, 370, 377, 381, 382, 383, 410, 435
arms of. *See* elephant tokens
compared to American cities, 3
elephant tokens. *See* elephant tokens
Franklin in, 61, 379
plague and fire, 1665-6, 86, 189, 190, 203
shipping industry, 10
Tower of, 81, 176, 333
long bit, 129
Long Island, and wampum, 38
Longacre, James B., 67, 409
Lord Baltimore's coinage. See Baltimore, 2nd Lord
Lord Proprietor(s)
Cecil Calvert as, 155
of Carolina, 203
Lost Colony. See Roanoke Island
Louis d'or, 142, 211
Louis XIII, 84, 137, 142, 206
Louis XIV, 86, 91, 123, 124, 137, 138, 140, 143
1670 coinage for America, 154, 207
on coinage, 207
Louis XV, 138, 154, 209, 211, 238
on coinage, 211, 212, 213
Louis XVI, 138, 368, 417
Louisiana, 72, 75, 93, 154, 136–44, 206, 209, 213, 380, 384
and John Law, 210
Purchase, 23, 24, 57
Lovelace, Francis, 154, 216

Loyalist, 36, 233, 264

Lutwyche, William
- Conder tokens, 116
- evasion coppers, 374
- Franklin Press tokens, 379
- Washington North Wales tokens, 110, 357, 371

Machin
- -'s Mills, 257, 279, 286, 289, *Also see Atlee, James, and Samuel*
  - and CT coinage, 257, 291, 292, 293, 307, 308, 311, 314, 317
    - 1788 issues, 315
    - Benjamin Buell, 353
    - small head varieties, 315
  - and Fugio cents
    - concave rays varieties, 352
    - Jarvis liquidates, 353
  - and imitation halfpence, 258
    - Group III, 287, 290–93
    - Group V, 294
    - NY muling, 289
    - ties to VT coinage, 302
  - and NJ coinage, 258, 322, 329, 331, 332
    - Mould liquidates, 321
  - and VT coinage, 257, 289, 291, 293, 297, 301–4
    - agreement, 292, 301
  - overuse of term, 287
  - partnership formed, 290–91
  - planchet sources, 304, 311
- Thomas, 277, 278, 290–93, Also *see* Machin's Mills
  - and NY coinage
    - proposals, 258, 283–85, 289, 346
    - dies, 294
  - and the Great Chain, 258
  - profits from coining, 259
- Thomas, Jr.
  - describes father's mint, 290

Madison, James, 21, 283, 350, 399, 433

malt. *See* brewer, brewing, brewery

Maltravers, Lord
- and Carolina, 203
- and patent coinage, 89

manitou, 36

maravedi, 119, 123, 466
- defined, 119

marbelized paper. *See* anti-counterfeiting measures, paper

Maris, Dr. Edward, iii, 181, 183, 271, 316–32, 345
- NJ attribution scheme, 318

mark, 264, *See* Nova Constellatio patterns
- European (see footnote), 118

Marlborough, John Churchill, Duke of, 93

Marsh, Daniel, 320

martlet, 188, 198

Martyr, Peter, 158

Mary (yacht), 181

Mary II, 92, 222, 463, *Also see* William III and Mary II
- dies of smallpox, 93

Mary, Queen of Scots, 83

Maryland, 9, 88, 134, 260, 269, 272, 361, 409, *Also see Baltimore, Also see Annapolis*
- and Dutch denominations, 49
- and right of coinage, 155, 175
- and tobacco, 155, 175
- balks on Confederation, 255
- early history of, 175
- John Chalmers' coinage. *See* Chalmers, John
- Lord Baltimore's coinage. *See* Baltimore, 2nd Lord
- Standish Barry's threepence. *See* Barry, Standish
- use of Dutch coins in, 134

Masons, Masonic, 184, 187, 198–99, 358, 360, 367, 377, 383

Massachusetts, 8, 16, 23, 56, 83, 160–75, 225, 226, 235, 243–45, 261, 281, 294, 296, 306, 333–39, 362, 398, 403, 404, 426, 433, 456
- 1749 halfpenny shipment to, 47, 153
- 1776 pattern coinage, 233, 243–45
  - modern copies of, 459
- and lead tokens, 113, 215
- and Shays' Rebellion, 20
- Bay Company, 161
- Commonwealth, 171
- early history of, 160–63
- events lead to hard coinage, 155
- first American mint, 164
- General Court, 161
  - establishes mint, 164
- Government Act. See Intolerable Acts
- Historical Society, 243, 244
- issues first paper money, 43
- Janus Copper, 244
- NE or New England coinage. *See* NE or New England coinage
- oak tree coinage. See oak tree coinage
- outlaws patent farthings, 90
- paper money reform, 47, 125, 333
- parchment small change notes, 54, 221
- petitions for coinage, 162
- pine tree coinage. *See* pine tree coinage
- Province Halfpenny, 244
- runs out of land, 296
- silver coinage, 124, 160–75
  - intrinsic value, 167
  - metal sources, 164
  - modern copies of, 174, 456, 459
  - obsessive dating of, 169
- state coinage, 71, 257, 258, 333–39
  - other proposals, 337
- use of Dutch coins in, 134
- use of lead tokens in, 155
- use of wampum, 36–42
- value of commodities in, 29
- willow tree coinage. *See* willow tree coinage

Massey, J. Earl, 179, 182

May, John, 337

Mayflower, the, 160, 225

Mazarin, Cardinal, 137

McAllister memorandom, 411

McCulloch v. Maryland, 25

McCusker, John, 46

medio, defined, 129

Meigs, Henry, 307

Melusina, Ehrenghar de, 96, 218, 222

mercantilism, 3–18
- beginnings of English, 4
- defined, 4
- Dutch, 132
- fall of British, 12
- French, 141
- legal framework for, 4
- not as successful as hoped, 12

Mermaid, the, 125, 153

Messianic lineage, 198

Messingham, Thomas, 184

Mestrelle, Eloye, 82, 189

Mexico, 119, 126, 384, 466
- City
  - Mint, 7, 118, 119, 120, 121, 126, 129
    - and gold coins, 118

money and early European contact, 117
silver production, 7
mica flecks. *See* anti-counterfeiting measures, paper
middle colonies, economy of, 10, 13
milled coinage, 152, 206, *See* any later issue
defined, 450
English/British, 82, 86–102, 462, 463, 464
French, 207
Spanish, 8, 49, 61, 86–102, 126–30, 122, 333, 466
Miller, Henry C., iii, 305–16
CT attribution scheme, 307
Millions for Defence..., 394, 400
Milton, John, 110
Mint, mint, mints. See individual mints by name, city or principal owner/operator
Act
of 1792, 22, 259
specifications, 408
of 1834, 391, 434
Brazilian, 144
early American, 7
federal, early attempts at, 260–64
federal, postponed, 264
fees for coining
in Massachusetts, 164, 167
in New Spain, 118
Grand Comittee report on, 263
New World Spaniards petition for, 117
process
for making cobs, 120
used in, 321, 447–59
Spanish domestic, 126
unidentified
and Georgivs Triumphos, 270
and Nova Const. private coppers, 265
and RI Ship tokens, 251
and St. Patrick coppers?, 188
Bungtown. *See* Bungtown
Confederation patterns/mules, 340
for Continental Currency coins, 248
for CT 'African' and 'mutton' heads, 308
for imitation halfpence, 257
Minuit, Peter, 135
mirliton, 206
Mississippi
Bubble, 57, 210
River, 93, 141, 210, 214
Missouri, 398
St. Genevieve, 214
moidores (Portuguese gold), 145
monogram, 81, 124
on bar coppers, 272
on Nova Const. private coppers, 267, 471
on Wash. funeral medals, 362
Montezuma, 117
Monticello, 240
Montreal, 44, 98, 386, 387, 388
founded, 139
Monts, Sieur de, 140
Moore
Abel Buell, 301
Samuel, 433, 434
Morris
Gouverneur
and currency plan, 256, 260–64
Robert, 256
1792 coinage bill, 366, 408
and Bank of North America, 19
and Confederatio pattern designs, 341
and Confederation patterns/mulings, 343
and currency plan, 260–64
and National Debt notes, 69
and the Castorland settlement, 380
and the search for coiners, 366
Nova Const. Private tokens, 256, 264–67
underwrites Continental Currency, 19, 58
-town
historic events at, 320
mint. *See* New Jersey state coinage
and CT state coinage, 318, 320
Mossman, Dr. Philip, 179, 246, 310
Mott
Isaac, 376
James, 320
Jordan, 376, 377
tokens, 358, 375–77
William and John, 376
Mould
-Atlee coppers. *See* imitaition halfpence, Group I
Walter, 259, 277, 278, 288, *Also see New Jersey state coinage*
and Connecticut state coinage, 320
and CT coinage, 314
and New Jersey state coinage, 316–32
in New York, 279
Moulton, William, 242
Mousequetaires, mousequetaires, 208
Mt. Vernon, 284, 411
Murray, Draper and Fairman, 71, 73
Mycall, John, 279
nails as money, 29, 30
Napoleonic Wars, 24, 139, 430
Narragansett, 38, 39
Nassau, 91
Louis of, 131
National Democrats, 399
National Republicans, 399
Native Americans, 3, 75, 139, 140, 162, 214, 215, 273
and Elias Boudinot, 429
and manitou, 36
and Northwest tokens, 385
and States' Rights, 361
and the 'Lost Colony', 82
and wampum, 36–42
and William Buell, 301
as British allies, 17, 97
attacks by, 93, 135, 139, 235, 384
barter with, 29–42
British control of, 93
British v. French view of, 33
fur trade initiates barter with, 33
in Mexico, 117, 119
in Ohio, 36
on coinage
1783 Treaty of Paris Medal, 250
Jefferson's decad design, 340
Massachusetts, 243, 258
state coinage, 333–39
NY, standing Native, 285, 289, 294, 478

Robert Morris' Confederation designs, 341
Washington portrayed as, 369
taken to Europe, 139
nature prints. *See* anti-counterfeiting measures, paper
Navigation Act
of 1651, 4
of 1660, 5
NE or New England coinage, 165, 167–68
Nelson, Dr. Phillip, 230–32
Netherlands. See Dutch
New
Amsterdam, 90, 132
Connecticut. See Vermont
England, 24, 111, 155, 162, 201, 215, Also see Mass., Conn., etc.
1630s immigration to, 161
and land speculation, 296
and wampum, 36–42
British plan to isolate, 283
coinage. *See* NE coinage
Council for, 161
economy of, 10
elephant tokens. *See* elephant tokens
Grand Dominion of, 203
hostilities in, Queen Anne's War, 93
ignored, 162
naming and early settlement of, 160
profits from shipping, 10
Restraining Act. See Intolerable Acts
silver circulating in, 46, 124
stuiver, 154, 216, 217
Wood's coinage in, 221
France. *See* France, French (in America)
Hampshire, 57, 160, 163, 226, 261, 459
claims to Vermont, 296–97
coinage, 242–43
modern copies of, 457
constitution, 242
defends against Vermont, 297
Grants, 296
ratifies Constitution, 20
Haven
'restrikes' of Fugio cents, 353, 354, 456
Jersey, 21, 45, 53, 69, 129, 134, 136, 204, 226, 247, 261, 262, 277, 305, 334, 344, 382, 424
and St. Patrick coinage, 177–200, 318, *See* St. Patrick coinage
as New Netherland, 216, *See* New Netherland
state coinage, 257, 278, 279, 316–32, 334, 452
and Bungtown, 294
as undertypes on Immunis Columbias, 339–48
camel head varieties, 323, 331
classification schema, 323
contract terms, 320
coulterless varieties, 324
Cox, Albion, 316–32
crude varieties, unknown mints, 323, 332
date-under-plow varieties. See prototype varieties, below
deer head varieties, 281, 327–28
Elizabethtown mint, 321
die varieties, 326
Goadsby, Thomas and, 316–32
head-left varieties, 326
Leddel petition, 319
mint description, 321
Morristown mint, 320
die varieties, 323, 328–30
Mould, Walter and, 288, 316–32
Ogden, Mathias and, 316–32
plaited mane varieties. See deer head varieties, above
PLURIBS varieties, 329
Rahway mint
die varieties, 320, 323, 325–27, 345
shield, 325
Rindell, Gilbert and, 321
running fox varieties, 283, 289, 322, 330–31
serpent head variety, 323, 331
Staten Island mint?, 331
ties to
Georgivs Triumphos, 271
Non Vi Virtute Vicis, 279, 346
use of Dutch coins in, 134
victories in, 65
Netherland, 39, 135
and leeuwendaalders, 134
and New Yorke in America tokens, 215
and wampum, 36–42
becomes New York and New Jersey, 216
gets Englands attention, 136
Netherlands Company, 135
Orleans, 58, 209, 399
and Louisiana Purchase, 23
branch of U.S. Mint, 436, 439, 442
ceded to Spain, 141
Spain
and Texas, 384
coinage of, 117–30
York, 5, 14, 17, 87, 136, 139, 166, 204, 225, 246, 261, 278, 296
and Continental Currency coins, 245–51
and Friends of Liberty & Trade. *See* Pitt, William, tokens
and wampum, 36–42
and Wood's coinage, 221
as New Netherland. *See* New Netherland
City, 3, 259, 278, 283, 298
and bar coppers, 272–73, 272–73
and Ephraim Brasher, 274
and the Atlees, 258, 277–79, 277
and Walter Mould, 279
Atlee's alledged mint, 279
boycotts British goods, 15, 236
Congress flees, 247
mints, 279, 312
coinage of, 215–16, 273–95
Brasher's coinage. *See* Brasher, Ephraim

Excelsior coppers. *See* Excelsior coppers
from Machin's Mills. *See Machin's Mills*
mulings, 289
New Yorke in America tokens. *See* New Yorke in America tokens
Non Vi Virtute Vici coppers, 277–79, 279
Nova Eborac coppers, 281–82
proposals, 21, 257, 258, 279, *Also see Brasher, Ephraim, Also see Bailey, John, Also see Machin, Thomas, Also see Atlee, James*
standing Native motif, 285
conflicts with New Hampshire, 242
economy of, 10
named, 90
silversmiths, 35
taken from and recaptured by the Dutch, 136
use of Dutch money/denominations in, 49, 134
Yorke in America tokens, 154, 215–16
new plate coinage (Spanish), 124–25, 333
Newbie (or Newby), Mark. *See* St. Patrick coinage
Newburgh
(ship), 291
in New York, 257, 278, 279, 288, 289, 300, 301, 308
Newgate Prison
in America, 226–28, 228, 230
in England, 381
Newman, Eric P., iii, 174, 200–202, 245–51, 265, 270, 287, 289, 349–55, 364
See footnote, 58, 351
newspaper(s)
advertise Tory counterfeits, 59
advertise Wash. funeral medals, 362
and rumored American pennies, 246
articles lament counterfeits, 102
Franklin and, 61
mention bar coppers, 272
mention Non Vi Virtute Vicis, 279
mention Nova Constellatios, 265
report 'Locofoco' story, 398
taxed under Stamp Act, 14
Newton, Sir Isaac, 409
Nicholas, Robert Carter, 233, 240
Nicholson, Francis, 267
Nicolls, Richard, 216
Noe, Sydney P., 160–75
See footnote, 165
Non Vi Virtute Vici coppers, 277–79, 346
North
Carolina, 47, 82, 203, 260, 261, 442
and Charlotte branch mint, 390, 435
and native gold, 390–92
and the Bechtlers, 390–92
U.S. Branch Mints, 390, 436
-ern Virginia, 160
Swansea, Massachusetts. *See* Bungtown
the, 21, 24, 93, 297, 424
and protectionism, 398
circulation of coppers in, 8, 21, 79, 102, 154, 394, 437
economy of, 10, 13
Northwest Ordinance, 354
Nova
Constellatio
coinage, 260–67
device on VT coppers, 298
device on Wash. success tokens, 357
origin of design, 66, 261
patterns, 248, 260–64, 459
private issues, 256, 264–67, 304
attribution guide, 470
Bungtown imitations of, 294
links to Georgivs Triumphos, 270, 271
Eborac coppers, 87, 258, 280, 281–82, 313
similarities to CT and NJ varieties, 283, 313, 330
similarities to imitation halfpence, 289
Scotia, 35, 81, 83, 134, 140, 166, 212, 387, 388
Nullification Crisis, 25, 399–400
oak
branches, 363
leaves, 216
tree coinage, 165, 170–72, 452
obverse
defined, 449
ocho de a reales. *See* piece of eight
Ogden, Mathias, 257, 259, 277
and Confederation patterns, 344
and New Jersey state coinage, 316–32
in Elizabethtown, 321
press used at U.S. Mint (footnote), 411
Ohio, 36, 73, 304, 321, 360
and William Duer, 354, 381
Company of Associates, 354
Valley, Washington's mission to, 141
Old Pretender. *See* Stuart, James Francis Edward
Olive Branch Petition, 60
Orange, 136
Fort. *See* Albany
Lake, New York, 283
William of. *See* William III
William the Silent, Prince of, 131
Order of
the Blue Garter, 127, 383
the Golden Fleece, 127
Ordinance
of 1785, 354
of 1787. *See* Northwest Ordinance
Orient. See Asia
Orléans, Duc d', 138, 209, 210
Ormond, Lord (James Butler)
and Pierre Blondeau, 188–90
and Sir Edward Ford, 192
Otis, James, 234, 243
Ottoman Empire, 8, 131
overdate, 126, 364, 425, 428, 429, 432, 433, 436
defined, 451
overplus, defined, 54
overstruck, overstriking, 208, 271, 288, 304, 321, 323, 327, 331, 345, 346, 364, 377
defined, 449
Owners Adventure (ship), 178
Paine, Thomas, 65, 115, 237

influences views on coinage, 407
palmetto coinage. *See* willow tree coinage
panic
and the Potosi Mint scandal. *See* Potosi Mint
benefits Americans, 210
general financial, 20
Panic
of 1789. *See* Copper Panic of 1789
of 1819, 24, 72, 393
of 1837, 72, 394, 397
paper. *Also see newspaper(s)*
and Charles I's terms, 85
century, the, 45
Jefferson's on coinage, 263
money, 25, 31, 32, 33, 36, 41, 43–69, 226, 242, 320, *Also see banks, banking, Also see Hall, David, Also see Franklin, Benjamin, Also see counterfeiting, Also see commodity notes, Also see bills of exchange, Also see loan issues, Also see bills of credit*
Abel Buell accused of counterfeiting, 306
advantages of, 48
and Continental Currency coins, 245–51
and Franklin's revenue proposal, 235
and Shays' Rebellion, 20, 50
and the Currency Acts, 13, 45, 49
and the Jackson regime, 396, 397
as a form of credit, 6
as war tax, 60
cancellation of, 57
colonial and confederation issues, 43–57
Continental Currency, 58–69
Crown's attitude toward, 44, 49
design similar to NY coinage, 284
early 19th century explosion in, 70–74
early uses of, 43
effect on specie circulation, 6, 46
effects of technology on, 70–74
foreign denominations on American, 8
French colonial, 57
instability of, 305
intaglio printing process, 52
Jacob Perkins' role in, 71, 362
modern copies of, 459
paper types used, 51
playing cards as, 43, 208
reform of, 47
by Massachusetts, 47, 125, 333
signatures on, 55
Spanish colonial, 58
value at end of Revolution, 58
value tied to war success, 60
William Smithers accused of counterfeiting, 237
non-money fiscal documents, 74–75
on Kentucky/starry pyramid tokens, 377
process for making, 51
-s, Robert Morris', 341
taxed under Stamp Act, 13, 234
value of John Law's regime, 210
Papers of the Continental Congress, 340
paradise metaphor, 154
Paris, 264, Also see Treaties of Paris
and Libertas Americana medals, 416
Briot and Blondeau in, 190
early history of, 137
Jefferson in, 340
Mint
and Castorland demi ecus, 380
examples, 143, 144, 207
proposed subsidiary to Boulton's mint, 307
value of trade goods in, 33
Parliament, 32, 60, 80, 89, 96, 115
and cost recovery measures, 12–16, Also see individual acts
and Cromwell, 162
and erosion of royal power, 12, 83, 84, 94, 98
and Ireland, 222
and paper money restrictions, 45, *Also see Currency Acts*
French, 138
Irish, 222, 231
reacts to counterfeiting, 104, 109
Stamp Act and Wm. Pitt, 234–37
suspended/dissolved, 84, 86, 161
views on base metal coinage, 112
Parys Mine, 371
patent
Bermuda, 158
coinage, 147
American circulation of Irish, 90, 240
for Ireland, 88–90, 113, 179, 188, 232
J.A.G. de la Garcia's, 358
John Read's proposed, 226
Wood's for Ireland and America, 218–24
Peck's machine, 388
Peter Blondeau's technology, 189
Samuel Higley's for steel-making, 226
Schenck's machine, 405
Patent
U.S. Patent Office, and Franklin's press, 380
Patience, the, 157
Patriot Boys, the, 98
pattern coinage, 22
1793 'strawberry' leaf cents as?, 415
anti-slavery tokens, 395
Boulton's cartwheel halfpence, 101
Continental Currency coins as?, 245–51
elephant tokens as?, 204
federal coinage of 1792, 410–14
for New York proposals, 257, 258, 279–81, 283–85, 346
ties to imitation halfpence, 287, 288, 289
for the Confederation, 259, 278, 279, 339–48, 426, *Also see NJ coinage, Maris reverse C, Also see Immunis Columbia, Also see Immune Columbia, Also see Confederatio decads*
ties to imitation halfppence, 294
ties to NJ coinage, 324

Fugio cents, 'American Congress', 354
Gobrecht's dollars as, 440
Lord Baltimore pennies, 175
Machin's New York proposal
as undertypes on NJ coinage, 331
Massachusetts' of 1776, 175, 233, 243–45
modern copies of, 457
New Hampshire's of 1776, 233, 242–43
New Yorke in America tokens as?, 216
Nova Constellatio issues, 248, 256, 260–64
Queen Anne coppers, 94, 102
Virginia shillings as, 100, 242
Washington pieces, 361–74, *Also see Getz, Peter, Also see Perkins, Jacob, Also see Westwood, Obadiah, Also see Perkins, Jacob, Also see Hancock, John G.*
modern copies of, 456
Wood's Rosa Americana twopence, 221, 222

Pawlette River, 298, 302

peage. *See wampum*

Peale
Charles Willson, 360, 392, 409, 438
Rembrandt, 360, 438
Titian, 439

peca (Portuguese gold), 145

Peirce, Jonathan, 337

Pennsylvania, 52, 60, 261, 409, *Also see Patterson, Robert Maskell, Also see Gobrecht, Christian, Also see U.S. Mint, Also see Patterson, Robert, Also see Dickinson, John, Also see Franklin, Benjamin, Also see Rittenhouse, David, Also see York, Also see Lancaster, Also see Philadelphia*
and elephant tokens, 204
economy of, 10
Gazette, 14, 61
silversmiths, 35
use of Dutch coins in, 134
use of foreign paper denominations, 72

penny
Barbados, 110
Bermuda, 111
Boulton's cartwheels, 101
Copper Company of Upper Canada, 382
demise of, 86
equivalence in
nails, 30
stuivers, 217
tobacco, 31
wampum, 39
evolution of, 86
Lord Baltimore, 175–77
Massachusetts
authorized (1787), 334
pine tree (fantasy), 174
State (1776). *See* Mass., State Penny
one, lawful money. *See* Mass., State Penny
origins of, 80
Theatre at New York, 382
Washington
Liberty and Security. *See* Washington, Liberty & Security
Repub. Ameri. and Funeral. *See* Washington, Repub. Ameri.
Wood's Rosa Americana, 219–22

Perkins
George C., collection, 316
Jacob
and 1792 disme patterns, 412
and 1792 Washington patterns, 362, 364
and MA state coinage, 333–39
and printing technology, 70–72
and Washington funeral medals, 362
and Washington Success tokens, 368
inventions, 70

Peru, Peruvian, 117, 122, *Also see Potosi*
as a derisive term, 124
Lima Mint, 120, 274
LIMA on British coinage, 97
silver production, 7

petition(s)
for a mint, by Spanish colonists, 117
for citizenship, by J.F. Atlee, 279
for coin standards, 147
for coinage
by Lord Ormond, 189
by Maryland, 155, 175
by Massachusetts, 162
by the colonies, 204
by Virginia, 233, 239, 240
for coinage contract
by Cox-Goadsby-Mould (NJ), 319
by Feuchtwanger, 394
by John Read, 226
by Joseph Jenks, 164
by Mould (U.S.), 341
by New Yorkers, 258, 290
by Wm. Leddel (NJ), 319
for contract extension, by Harmon (VT), 299
Olive Branch, 60
to revoke Wood's charter, by Irish, 222
to split franchise, by Cox-Goadsby-Mould (NJ), 320
Virginia's, for small change, 239

pewter coinage, 234, 246, 245–51, 251–54, 369, 463

Philadelphia, 3, 22, 66, 71, 89, 177, 233, 262, 320, 341, 367, 391
and Continental Currency coins, 247
and early 19th century tokens, 392
and Franklin's bank proposal, 235
and Hancock's cents, 363
and Kentucky tokens, 377
and mosquitoes, 419
and Pitt tokens, 236
and Wm. Russell Birch, 410
artists in. *See* Sully, Thomas, *See Peale, Titian, See West, Benjamin, See Stuart, Gilbert*
boycotts British goods, 15, 236
Congress forced to flee, 64
Congress in, 20, 60, 63, 65, 68
Franklin in, 379
Hall & Sellers in. *See* Hall & Sellers
Howe retakes, 66
John Harper's cellar mint in. *See* Harper, John, *See* Harper, John
Morris' prototypical mint in, 261
small change shortages in, 215
U.S. Mint in, 390, 407–41
use of lead tokens in, 155

Philip II, 120, 137, 139, 466
and the Dutch, 131

and the Philippines, 123
and the Spanish Armada, 4, 123, 131
seizes Portugal, 144
Philip III, 122, 123, 124, 466
Philip IV, 123, 466
Philip V, 121, 124, 125, 126, 128, 275, 467
Phoenix, the (ship), 59
photographs and drawings (in this book), iii
Phrygia, 16, 416
picayune (Also see footnote), 129
Pight, Richard, 176
Pilgrims, 83, 123, 160–62
pillar dollar. See dollar, Spanish, pillar style
pillars and waves, 122, *Also see* Brasher, Ephraim, coinage
Pillars of Hercules, 126
early use of, 119
on Brasher's Lima style doubloons, 274
on cob coinage, 122
Pinckney
Charles, 400
Thomas, 321
pine tree
coinage, 165, 166, 172–75, 452
1st issue ('large' planchet shillings), 172–73
2nd issue ('small' planchet shillings), 173–75
on 1776 Mass. State Penny, 244
on Mass. notes, 56
on New Hampshire coinage, 242
Pine, Robert Edge, 67
Pingo
Lewis, 100
Thomas, 100, 241
pirates, piracy, 4, 111, 122, 164
Barbary Coast, 394, 400
pistareen
defined, 124
Pitt, William, 12, 15, 60, 98, 430
1766 tokens, 233, 234–37
and repeal of the Stamp Act, 14
takes charge of Seven Years War, 98
plague
London, 1665, 86, 189, 190, 203
planchets, 118, 120, 166, 171, 241, 301, 302
annealing process, 450
cast, on Wood's coinage, 222
clipped, defined, 448
defined, 448
feeding devices, 305
filing to reduce weights, 422
imitation halfpence, 286
manufacturing process for, 291, 310, 448
on Blacksmith tokens, 388
oval, 272
reduced on U.S. cents, 418
small and large
Immunis Columbia coppers, 340, 345
Mass. pine tree shillings, 172–75
sources of
Connecticut state coinage, 311
for Fugio cents, 353
Machin's Mills, 304, 331, 352
Morristown (NJ) stock, 320, 323, 326
Rahway (NJ) stock, 320, 323, 326
St. Patrick coinage, 179
U.S. Mint, 414, 419, 428, 432
splitting during striking, 173
struck coins as, 267, 321, 322, 364, 367, 378, 421
thin and thick
elephant tokens, 204
Mott tokens, 376
on Mott tokens, 376
U.S. Mint
exhausts supply, 238
voids, defined, 447
plata provincial. *See* new plate
Platt, Jeremiah, 307
playing card money, 43, 208, 213
Plough, the (ship), 158
Plymouth
(or Plymoth) Colony, 38, 160
Company, 160, 161
England, 160
pocket, i
Pontgravé, Sieur du, 33, 140
Poor Fred. *See* Frederick, Prince
Popayan Mint, 120
population
1790 U.S. census, 3
slaves, 9
density on the frontier, 32
distribution of wealth, 10
French in America, 136, 140
growth and limitations on, 15
of cities, relative, 3
of John Law's settlements, 210
shifts, 70, 114, 390
Virginia's relative to U.S., 240
porcine head. *See* Connecticut, mutton head
Port Royal, 91, 93, 96, 140
portcullis coins, 81
Portugal, Portuguese, 46, 120, 124, 263
coins, 8, 11
conquered by Spain, 123
history and coins of, 144–46
poteaux en terre, 214
Potosí
Mint, 120, 127
debasement scandal, 122, 123, 155, 162
silver production, 7
pound
avoirdupois, 88
French livre v. English libra, 141
Roman, 79
Scottish, 81
Sterling. *Also see Sterling money*
equivalence in beaver pelts, 29
origins of, 79
troy, 80
press
coining, 171, 282
and 1816 U.S. Mint fire, 433
drop type. *See* drop press
mobile, 114
new U.S. Mint press, 422
rocker type. *See* rocker press
screw type. *See* screw press
slowness of U.S. Mint's, 427
steam powered, 405, 437, 443
the U.S. Mint's first, 411
printing
spread of in America, 70
used by Franklin, 379–80
pretender
to English throne, 93, 97, 153, 230–32, 231, 258
to Spanish throne, 124
price(s). Also see inflation
American domestic, 11
American goods v. British, 11

carrying charges as a percent of, 30
commodities discounted, 30
for bills of exchange, 47
instability of, 30, 46
Natives as negotiators of, 36
of beaver, in wampum, 41
of bullion, 263
of coining copper, 105
of copper, 101, 214, 263, 412, 418, *Also see Copper Panic of 1789*
paid by James Jarvis, 350
of corn, 39
of Fugio cents, 353
of Samuel Atlee's porter, 277
of silver, 79, 333
of tobacco, 31, 155, 175, 240
setting, 5
in Massachusetts, 29

princeps, 231

printing technology, 51–57
19th century advances in, 70–72
cast lead type, 52
copper
plates, 70
intaglio process, 52
nature prints, 51, 53
serial numbers, 54
two-color printing, 53
use of copper plates, 43

prison
and counterfeiting, 105, 109
and George I's queen, 95
and Mary, Queen of Scots, 83
Britannia in. *See* Georgivs Triumpho
debtors
and Albion Cox, 321
Royal Flynt and William Duer, 353
Newgate
England's, and P.P.P. Myddleton, 381
Newgate Prison
Connecticut's, 226–28
ship, and William de Saussure, 422

privateers, privateering, 4

Privy Council, 222

Proclamation Act of 1763, 13, 14

production statistics
U.S. Mint
(chart), 442

production statistics, U.S. Mint, 441

proposals
banking
Franklin's, for a central bank, 235
coinage
American Plantation tokens, 200–202
Connecticut
early, 226
state, 305–16
for the Confederation
Fugio cents, 349–55
Immunis Columbia coppers, 339–48
Morris', 260–64
various, 255–355
Massachusetts
early. *See* Jenks, Joseph
state, 333–39
New Jersey, 316–32
New York, 279–85
Vermont, 295–304
Virginia, 239–42
Washington pieces, 361–74
William Wood's, 218–24
John Harper and Jefferson cents?, 418

protectionism, 398

Protestant, 82, 83, 84, 86, 91, 131, 137, 175, 184
Reformation, 137, 160

Province Halfpenny. *See* Mass. Province Halfpenny

punch(es)
and hubbing, 308
complex, defined, 451
counterstamp
Ephraim Brasher's, 276
defined, 450, 451
device, 451
elephant tokens, 205
for early Mexico City coinage, 119
linking
state coinages and imitation halfpence, 304
Vermont coinage and imitation halfpence, 292
long term survival of, 203
Massachusetts' NE coinage, 167
on imitation halfpence, 289
on Vermont coinage, 294, 301
on Wash. Born Virginia pieces, 365
reused on early tokens, 114
U.S. cents
of 1794, 418
of 1795-1796, 418
Scot's draped busts, 428
Scot's matron heads, 433
Wright's of 1793, 417
for cutting planchets, 291, 448
letter
blunders
on Fugio cents, 351
on U.S. cents, 426
errors v. substitution, 289, 310, 344
linking
CT 'mutton heads' to Bailey's coins, 313
method in question, 277
method questioned, 322, 453
New York coinages, 280
Nova Constellatios
to Georgivs Triumphos, 267, 270, 271
to Immune Columbias, 342
St. Patrick's coinage with Briot's, 183
on Connecticut coinage, 308
U.S. cents
of 1795-1796, 429
linking
defined, 453

Puritans, 160–61

Quakers, 177, 204, *See* St. Patrick's coinage

quarter
dollar
and Mint Act of 1792, 408
by Gobrecht
seated Liberty, 440
first coinage of, 425
Kneass' modified capped bust, 434
pistareens as, 125
Reich's capped bust, 432
Scot's draped bust, 425, 427, 428
Wright's 1792 die trials, 411, 412
eagle, 423
and Mint Act of 1792, 408
by Gobrecht

coronet heads, 436
modified classic head, 435
by Scot
modified capped head, 432
first coinage of, 425
Kneass' classic head, 434
Reich's 1808 capped bust, 431
Scot's draped bust, 425–26
Quartering Act
first, 14
second. See Intolerable Acts
Quebec, 43, 91, 209
British attempts to take, 93, 98
founded, 139
silversmiths, 35
Queen Anne's War, 44, 93, 94, 124, 140
quint, 264, *See* Nova Constellatio patterns
Radisson, Pierre Esprit, 34, 140
Rahway (NJ) Mint. *See* New Jersey state coinage
Raleigh
Plantation Token, 114
Sir Walter, 31, 84, 114, 225
and Carolina, 203
Rasiere, Isaack de, 38
Read, John, 226, 305
reale
as a denomination for scrip, 72
equivalence in coffee beans, 117
legal debasement of, 127
on American Plantations tokens, 201
origins of, 118, Also see footnote, *Also see footnote*
rebus, 216, 234, 245
re-cutting, defined, 451
reeded edges, 182, 190, 342, 368, 369, 370, 378, 380, 412, 413, 423, 439, 440
regulation
of specie coins, 274, 422
-s. *See* individual governing bodies and acts
English, governing private tokens, 190
federal, and states' right to mint coins, 256
Massachusetts, on wampum, 39
Spanish
defining reales, 118
Reichenpfenniges. See jetons
Reid, Templeton, 359, 390–92, 390–92
Republican Party, 399
Restoration. *See* Great Restoration
re-valuation
of coinage, 207
of paper money, 45
Revere, Paul, 237
and 1776 Massachusetts patterns, 243–45
and copper sheeting, 448
and Joseph Callender, 334
and Pitt tokens, 233, 236
as an engraver for notes, 56
reverse, defined, 449
Rhode Island, 261, 360, 402
and wampum's origins, 38
ratification of Constitution, 50
ship tokens/medals, 234, 251–54
Ribaut, Jean, 139
rice, 5, 9, 10
Rice, Joseph, 359
Richardson, John, 297
Richelieu, Cardinal, 137
Richmond
Duke and Duchess of, 89
Virginia, 240, 242
rider
Dutch golden, 135
Dutch silver, 134
Righault and Dawson. *See* Gloucester tokens
Rijkdaalder. See dollar, Dutch, Rijkdaalder
Rindell, Gilbert. *See* NJ state coinage
Ringo, Mike, 270
rings shillings. *See Chalmers, John*
Rittenhouse, David, 443
and Nova Constellatio patterns, 261
and paper money, 56
as U.S. Mint Director, 409–22
rix dollars. *See* dollar, Dutch, rijkdaalder
roanoke (wampum). *See* wampum
Roanoke Island, 82, 203
Roberval, Siuer de, 139
Robinson, Henry R., 397
Roche (or Roach), of Dublin. *See* Voce Populi tokens
rocker press, 169, 173, 229
described, 450
Roettier (or Rotier,) James and Norbert, 204
Rogers, Woodes, 111
Rolfe, John, 30
Roma (goddess), 87
Roman
cameo, as origin for U.S. small eagle, 423
font
on Bar coppers, 272
on Nova Const. coppers, 267
goddess. *Also see Janus*, *See* Roma
head Washington pieces, 366
nose on Washington Success tokens, 368
numerals
on coins, 159, 167, 217
used in business, 147
occupation of Britain, 87
pound, 79
sestertius. *See* sestertius
use of jetons, 147
Rome, 137
and origin of
'denarius', 80
liberty cap, 416
'shilling', 80
Roosevelt, Theodore, 444
Rosa Americana coinage. *See* Wood, William
Rosicrucians, 199
Rottier, John
adapts Britannia device, 87
Royal
Africa Company, 203
Company of Adventurers, 203
Mint, 82, 110, 115, 147, 188, 189, 202, 343
Society, 198
Treasury (Spanish), 118
royalists, 85, 170, 240
Rue Port (now Rupert), Vermont, 295–304
rum, 225, 267, 301
running fox. See New Jersey state coinage
Rush, Dr. Benjamin
as father of American psychiatry (note), 425
as Mint Treasurer, 410
dispute with Elias Boudinot, 424
Russia, Russian, 42, 97, 139, 385, 386
Ryder, Hillyer (See footnote), 297
Salem, 264, 337
early settlement of, 161
witch trials, 164, 174

Samuel Atlee and Company. *See* Atlee, Samuel, life & work
Sanderson (or Saunderson), Robert, 160–75
Santiago Mint, 120
satire, satirical, 115, 222, 251, 252, 256, 271, 295, 366, 387
Saugus Iron Works. *See Hammersmith Iron Works*
Savage, Edward, 372
S-bend. See rocker press
scandal
  Fugio cents, 21, 257, 307, 407
  John Law, 140
  Potosí Mint, 122, 123, 155
Schulenburg, Ehrengharde Melusina, Gräfin von der. *See Melusina, Ehrengharde*
Scioto Company, 354
Scot, Robert, 417–36
Scotland, Scottish, 83–84, 84, 90, 95, 97, 140, 201, 383
  and the Isle of Man, 112
  coins, 81
screw press, 82, 126, 170, 173, 189, 190, 261, 265, 307, 414, 421, 422
  and Getz' patterns, 367
  description of, 449
  minting process, 291, 321
sea beasts, 186
Sea Venture, the, 157
Segovia Mint, 121
Sellers, William, 62
serial numbers. *See* anti-counterfeiting measures, paper
series
  defined, 452
serpent(s)
  head. See New Jersey state coinage
  on Chalmers' shillings, 256
  on Feuchtwanger's cents, 395
  on Libertas Americana medals, 417
  on St.Patrick coinage, 184
  Thomas Paine portrayed as, 115
sestertius, 87, 300
Settlement Act
  of 1689, 93
  of 1701, 94
Seven Years War, 12, 23, 44, 97–98, 98, 128, 138, 235, 296, 386
Sewall, Samuel, 174
Seward, William H., 400
Shakespeare, William, 382
  and Bermuda, 157
  and James I, 83
  on evasion coppers, 110, 371
Shays'[,Daniel] Rebellion, 23
  and paper money, 20, 50
shilling(s)
  Connecticut (fantasy), 354
  Connecticut coppers per, 320
  English, 79–116
  equivalents, 125, 134, 244
  Gloucester tokens as(?), 217
  gunmoney, 91
  John Chalmers', 256, 267–70
  limitation on wampum, 36
  Lord Baltimore, 175–77
  Massachusetts, 160–75, 452
  origins of, 79
  relation to sol, 141
  Scottish, 81
  Sommer Islands, 158
  state variations, 260
  Virginia, 100, 242
  wages in, 259
ship
  (s), 426, Also *see* Bahama halfpenny, Washington ship and Liverpool halfpennies, William Pitt tokens, North American tokens, etc.
    , colonies and commerce, 387
    American, 136
      navy, 63
    and the Great Chain, 283
    Astor's, (John J.), 385
    British
      navy, 43, 94, 251
    Deliverance, 157
    Dutch, 132
    early, in North America, 30, 140
    French
      Le Chameau, 206, 212
      navy, 251
    on lead tokens, 113
    Patience, 157
    Portuguese, 139
    prison, 422
    Sea Venture, 157
    ship of state metaphor, 398, 399
    Spanish
      black, 122
    the
      (La) Garza, 157
      (Le) Chameau, 206
      Andrew Doria, 251
      Belle, 384
      Elephant, 206
      H.M.S. Eagle, 252
      H.M.S. Feversham, 166
      H.M.S. Mermaid, 153, 333
      Newburgh, 291
      Owners Adventure, 178
      Phoenix, 59
      Plough, 158
      Sea Adventure. *See*
      Thomas, 240
      Turtle (submarine), 252
  -building, 9, 10
    Dutch, 132
    New England, 10
  -ping, 283, 403
    American, 166
    British, 24
    charges, 11
    Dutch, 4
    empressment of sailors, 24
    English, 4, 11
    New England, 10, 13
    Russian, 42
short bit, defined, 129
shortage(s)
  of dies, 419
  of labor, 11
  of metal for coining, 262
  of small change, 64, 99, 155
    and lead tokens, 155
    and playing card money, 208
    effect on American cities, 215
    in Massachusetts, 333
    in New Netherland, 215
    in Texas, 384
    in Virginia, 90, 233
    spurs English token industry, 112–16
  of specie
    in the colonies, 8
    in the Southeast, 390
  of U.S. coins
    late 18th century, 432
    later, 443
  of wild game, 139
Shubert Distillery, 411
silver. Also see Sterling money, Also see dollar
  alloys, 420
  and backing of paper money, 61
  and Morris' federal unit, 260
  and origins of the dollar (see footnote), 7

and paper money reform in MA, 47, 333
and redemption of gunmoney, 91
as a commodity, 48
as part of a tri-metallic system. See tri-metallic system
attempts to obtain from France, 246
coins. *See* individual coin types, *Also see individual countries*
from Machin's Mills?, 286
Congress' preference for, 263
equivalents, 45
in circulation, 8
in New England, 46
relative to gold/copper, 8
in West Indian trade, 110
-ing
on counterfeit Spanish coins, 125
on French colonial issues, 208
on hard times tokens, 400
on patent farthings, 88
on Pitt tokens, 237
on Sommer Islands coinage, 158
on VA halfpennies, 241
on Washington success tokens, 357
LA Purchase amount in (see footnote), 24
LIMA mark, 97
market price of, 79, 333
penny, 86
origins of, 80
plugs/centered, 412
pound Sterling, 79
refinement, 447
sheet, 173
shipped to Europe, 117, 427
-smith(s), 360
and trade silver, 35
Barry, Standish, 359
Bayley, Van Voorhis and Coley, 278, 283, 298
Chalmers, John, 177, 256, 268
Hull and Sanderson, 163
source of for 1792 half dismes, 410
South Seas Company, 95
Spanish. *Also see* Potosí Mint scandal
1497 standard, 118
coin content relative to U.S., 130
colonial production, 7
effect of scandals on world confidence, 122
in Massachusetts, 167
mint procedures, 118
Sterling, 9
value relative to gold, 80, 263, 427
versus
billon, 120, 208
Simitiere, Pierre Eugene du
and Higley coppers, 225
and New Jersey state seal, 323
and the Great Seal of the United States, 67
Washington engraving, 363
Simon, Thomas, 81, 86, 176
Slafter, Edmund, 297
slaves, slavery, 3, 9, 11, 267, 413
and origin of the liberty cap, 416, 430
anti-slavery movement, 395
as a devisive issue, 255
Dutch develop slave trade, 132
in Barbados, 110
numbers of in America, 9
William Pitt, on America, 235
Slingsby, Henry, 189, 190, 198
small heads. *See* Connecticut, small heads
smallpox, 82, 93
Smith, John
desires Carolina, 203
explores New England, 160
on Sommer Islands coinage, 158
Smithers, William, 233, 236
Smithson
-ian Institution, 303
James, 436, *Also see Smithsonian Institution*
Smithsonian Institution, 272, 344, 380
smugglers, smuggling, 5, 11, 112, 236
(see footnote), 8
snake(s). See serpent(s)
Snelling, Thomas, 204, 220
Society of Friends. *See* Quakers
Soho Mint, 101, 112, 371, 372, 382, 407, *Also see Boulton, Matthew*
sol, 137–39
(s) tampees, 213
1767 copper, 238
5 & 15 sols issues of 1670, 207
copper, of 1721-1722, 212
French colonial use of, 206–14
French domestic use of, 141–44
marqués, 206
origin of, 141
relative value of, 141
sou marques, 213
Solitude, 320
Somer (or Sommer)
Islands, 111
coinage, 156, 157–59, 459
Company, 206
Sons of Liberty, 14, 245
flag, 244
in New York, 236
South
Carolina, 55, 72, 139, 223, 273
agriculutural wealth of, 9
and odd monetary system, 256, 260
and the Nullification Crisis, 398, 399
Sea Company (and Bubble), 95
the
agricultural economy, 10
and population growth, 15
and Queen Anne's War, 93
and slavery, 255
and the American Revolution, 17, 252
and the War of 1812, 24
and Wood's coinage, 154
availability of Spanish silver in, 8
discovery of gold in, 25, 390
early depiction of as opposing the North, 424
economy of, 9
hit hard by enumeration, 13
opposes debt assumption, 21
role in Nullification Crisis, 398
use of privately issued gold coins in, 390
sovereign, 80
Spain, Spanish. *Also see* individual monarchs
and Florida, 141
and Louisiana, 23, 75, 141
and Portugal, 144–45
and Sir Humphrey Gilbert, 203

and St. Augustine, 93
and Texas, 384
and the Dutch, 131–36
and War of Austrian Succession, 96
and War of Jenkin's Ear, 44
Armada, 4, 82, 131
coinage of, 46, 117–30, 162, *Also see debasement*
American preference for, 425
and the Ordenanza of 1497, 118
as legal tender in U.S., 129
base metal, 8
chart, 466
cobs, 120–24
compared to Brasher's coinage, 274
earliest New World coinage, 117–20
in West Indian trade, 11
milled, 126–30
colonial gold and silver production, 7
decline of, 82, 123
early petition for New World mint, 117
effect of New World specie on, 7, 117
James II in the service of, 90
Netherlands, 132
paper money, 58
valuation of gold versus silver in, 263
Sparrow, Thomas, 268, 269
specie, 7, 241
19th century private gold, 390–92
and Gresham's Law, 6, 46
and payment of foreign debt, 21, 49
and redemption of paper money, 19, 24, 59
in MA, 44
foreign incidental
British/English/Irish. See Chapter 5
French, Dutch and Portuguese. See Chapter 7
Spanish. See Chapter 6
foreign, with Brasher counterstamp, 277
government attitude toward minting of, 94, 112, 115, 189, 421
in colonial circulation, 6, 8, 79
American. *See* Massachusetts silver, Lord Baltimore coinage, Continental Currency coins, Nova Constellatio patterns, Brasher, etc.
Dutch, 131–36
English/British, 82–102
French, 141–44
non-Hispanic, 8
Portuguese, 144–46
Spanish, 7, 117–30
regulation of weight, 274
restrictions on British export of, 11
shortage of in Southeast U.S., 390
suspension of payments
1814, 24
1837, 397
U.S. mint issued, 420–45
value relative to notes, 246
Virginia sets value of, 240
Washington's desire for gold coinage, 422
speculation
coin
and Fugio cents, 353
coins
and Wood's coinage, 223
French coppers of 1721-1722, 212
land
and John Law, 141
and Philip Parry Price, 381
in New England, 296
in Ohio, 381
Spencer, Asa, 71
splasher, 182
St.
Eustatius, 136, 251
Lawrence River, 94, 98, 139, 140
Mary's City, 175
Patrick coinage, 155, 177–200, 318
Stamp Act, 234–37
Congress, 55, 233, 235, 236
passed, 1765, 13
repealed, 14
stampees. *See* sol tampees
standards
1670 French colonial issues, 208
1767 French copper sols, 238
1776 Cont. Curr. Coins, 250
American plantations tokens, 202
bar copper, 273
Brasher's gold coinage, 277
Chalmers' coinage, 269
Connecticut state coinage, 305, 316
ecu, Le Chameau, 213
elephant tokens, 204
federal, of 1786, 273
for Jefferson's decimal coinage, 263
French colonies, Le Chemeau, 212
French copper sols of 1721-1722, 212
Georgivs Triumpho coppers, 271
Higley coppers, 229
imitation halfpence (Amer.), 286
Irish halfpenny, 96
John Law coinage, 211
John Law coppers, 211
Le Chemeau coinage, 212
Lord Baltimore's coinage, 177
Louis d'or, 211
Machin's NY proposal, 285
Mass. silver coins, 166
Mass. state coppers, 335
New York Excelsior coppers, 283
New Yorke in America tokens, 216
Nova Const. private tokens, 267
Nova Constellatio patterns, 262
Nova Eborac coppers, 283
Pitt tokens, 237
regal coppers, 88
Rhode Island ship tokens/medals, 253
Rosa Americana issues, 219
Sommer Islands coinage, 159
Spanish milled coinage, 127
St. Patrick coinage, 179
Vermont coinage, 298
Virgina halfpennies and shillings, 242
Staple Act of 1663, 5
Starbuck, Nathaniel and Sons, token, 388, 404
State Penny. *See* Mass., State Penny
states' rights, 19, 361, 399
steam
boat, 409
engine, 100, 371
powered
coining press, 404, 437, 443

coining process, 100
rolling mill, 433
steel, 410
and Joseph Jenks, 164
and Samuel Higley, 226
availability of for dies, 169, 387, 428, 432
die making technology, 308, 450
making technology, 226, 449
printing plate technology, 71
strikers, 127
Sterling
fineness, 167, 177, 241, 270
defined (See footnote), 9
money (or funds), 9, 46, 146
as backing for bills of exchange, 46
equivalent
in gold, 80
in Spanish dollars, 49, 125
in wages, 259
versus state valuations (See footnote), 6
origin of pound, 79
Stevinus. *See* Brugge, Simon Stevin van
stiver. *See* stuiver
Stone of Scone/of Destiny, 199
storehouse notes. See commodity notes
Strahan, William, 61
Straits of Gibraltar, 119, 274
striking, origin of term, 449
Stuart, 197
Charles Edward, 97, 231
Gilbert, 410, 423, 439
James Francis Edward, 93, 231
Lord Darnley, 83
ruling family, 79, 83, 86, 94, 95, 162, Also see James I, Charles I, Charles II, James II and Mary II
stuiver
defined, 133
Dutch, 131–36
equivalent
in pence, 217
in skins, 29
New England, 154, 215, 217
Stuyvesant, Peter, 215
gives up Dutch holdings in NY, 136
Sugar, sugar, 5, 9, 11, 132, 238, 267
Act of 1764, 13, 234
Sullivan, John, 251
Sun King. See Louis XIV
Swanwick, John, 261
Sweden, Swedish, 86
Carl von Linné, 40
copper, 87, 179, 212
Swift, Jonathan, 222
sword in hand (notes), 56
sword(s)
and Pitt's Stamp Act speech, 235
on coins, 91, 201, 396
Washington's
by John Bailey, 279
handed over to Congress (figuratively), 361
symbolic money surrogates, 36
Symmes, John Cleve, 320
and Symmes's Hole, 320
tariffs, 22, 398, 399, Also see tax, taxes
compromise, 399
tax issues (paper money type), 45
taxes, taxation, 5, 13, 22, 32, 69, 116, 277
amnesty for Leyden, 131
and John Law, 209
and suspected corruption, 13
and the Stamp Act, 13, 234
and the Sugar Act, 234
and the Townshend Acts, 14
Congress' inability to, 19
and state quotas, 58
Continental Currency as, 60
excise, on whiskey, 22
King's Fifth, 118
mistreatment of officials, 235
Navigation Act clears way for, 5
notes as credits against, 45
Parliament takes right from Charles I, 84
payment with
colonial notes, 44, 45
labor, 29
state notes, 24
wampum, 39
resistance to, 15
and James Otis, 234
and Wiiliam Pitt, 234–37
Taylor, Alan, 16
tea, 267, 284
and the Boston Tea Party, 15, 235
Tea Act (1773), 15
the Boston Tea Party, 243
***Tempest, The*, 157**
tepuzque, 117
terminal die state. *See* die state
Thames River, 81, 88, 202
Thirty Years War, 124, 137
Thomas, the (*ship*), 240
Thomson, Charles, 262, 264
threads, embedded. *See* anti-counterfeiting measures, paper
tin, 34, 388
alloy, 113
coinage, 88
American Plantations tokens, 200–202
copper-plugged issues, 88, 91, 92, 204
counterfeit halfpennies, 104
patent farthings (silvered), 88
Repub. Ameri. And funeral pennies, 370
Theatre at New York mule, 383
early use in Mexico, 117
farmers (mine owners), 200–202
industry, 88
metalurgical properties of, 201
pest, 201
tobacco, 5, 9, 10, 29, 30, 34, 155, 175, 267
1640s glut of, 240
1650s glut of, 175
and anti-smoking sentiment, 31
as money in Virginia, 239
beginnings, 30
Isaack de Rasiere on, 38
laws to protect, 240
-nists, 113
notes. See commodity, commodities:notes
value of, 31
warehouse receipts for, 46
token(s)
American. *See* individual types, chapters 8-11
Idler storecards, 177
lead, 155
misc. early, 215–18
as a second income for minters, 188
British, 112–16, 181, *Also see Conder, James*
makers, 371
industry emerges, 115
vie for American contracts, 265, 357, 361
merchant, 79, 89, 101
reasons for existence, 114
Canadian, 102
blacksmith, 386–88, *See* blacksmith tokens
Vexator Canadiensis, 387

communion, 152
for Barbados, 110
Irish, 190
lead, 113, 155
early, 82
Raleigh Plantation. See Raleigh Plantation token
theatre admission, 383
Tory, Tories, 17, 90
act against American currency, 59
coppers
defined, 103
term applied to American pieces, 288
evacuate New York, 277
Tower Mint, 81
and American Plantattion tokens. *See* American Plantations tokens
and Lord Baltimore's coinage, 176
and St. Patrick coppers, 183
and VA coinage, 240
Townshend Acts, 14
trade, 3, 214, 236, 361, *Also see West Indies*, *Also see* individual countries, Chapters 5-7
19th century dependence on Britain, 24
and accessibility of specie, 125, 155
and trade policy, 240, Also see individual acts, Also see Chapters 1 and 2
and wampum, 39, 162
award, 403
barter. *See* Chapter 3
beads, 41
between Virginia and Bermuda, 159
blacksmith, the, 409
coinage, 81
coining, the, 278, 290
deficit, 7, 10, 47
dispute, 44
between Canadian fur companies, 385
ducat (Dutch), 135
Dutch
monopoly on Asian, 132
superiority in, 132
support of American cause, 234
with NY natives, 215
equivalence of U.S. & Spanish dollars in, 427
free, 398
fur. *See* fur, fur trade
goods, 29–42, 117, 146, 267, 384
classification scheme, 34
defined, 30
in Oregon, 385
local, 29, 32
machinest, the, 409
monopoly
given do Henry de Monts, 140
given to Dutch West India Company, 135
Natives skilled at, 36
printing, the, 61, 379
role of
gold in, 46
land in, 74
Russian, 385
-s, 360
practiced by Templeton Reid, 391
silver, 34–36
slave, 132
tobacco. *See* tobacco
tokens. *See* tokens
used to create Native alliances, 93
transportation, 277
charges, 11, 29
industry, 10
inland, 11, 32, 33
of specie, 47, 120
trans-Atlantic, 11, 30, 212
treason, 85, 138, 162, 170, 183, 225, 237
treaty
and Oregon, 386
and war of Spanish Succession, 124
Treaty of
Ghent (1814), 24
Paris (1763), 98, 141
Paris (1783), 17, 128, 265, 271, 372, 424
medal, 250
ratification of, 268
San Ildefonso (1802), 23
Saragossa (1529), 144
Utrecht (1713), 94
tri-metallic system, 22, 246, 263, 334, 344, 364, 408
triple leaves. *See* Connecticut, triple leaves
Trott, Perient, 206
Trudgen, Gary, 165, 287, 289
True, Benjamin and Daniel, 388
Trumbull family (See footnote), 226
Tudor
ruling family, 82, 221, *Also see* individual monarchs
silver coins, 82
Turner, Frederick Jackson and the Turner Thesis, 31
Turtle, the (submarine), 252
Tyler, John, 399
type (defined), 452
Ulster
Rebellion. *See* St. Patrick's coinage
Scots, 180
undertype(s)
defined, 449
for Connecticut coppers
imitation Mass. coppers as, 337
for Getz' patterns, 367
for Immunis Columbia coppers
New Jersey coppers as, 345
for New Jersey coppers, 323
Connecticut coppers as, 327
serpent head varieties, 331
for U.S. half cents
Talbot, Allum & Lee cents as, 378
for Vermont coppers, 304
French coins as, 207
Irish
counterfeit halfpence as, 99, 232
halfpence as, 244
Nova Constellatio coppers as, 267
unite (gold coin), 80, 83
United
Colonies of New England, 162
Colonies of North America, 60, 61, 66
States
and dispute over Oregon, 386
Capital
in Annapolis, 268
in Baltimore, 65
in Lancaster, Pennsylvania, 66
in New York, 272, 274, 284
in York, Pennsylvania, 66
on the banks of the Potomac, 21
Census, 3, 9, 32

- Constitution, 69, 257, 260, *Also see Constitution*
- dollar. *Also see dollar, U.S.*
- eagle, similarity to Mott token, 376
- first recognized, 136
- Mint, ii, 7, 8, 22, 25, 56, 87, 102, 126, 152, 234, 238, 258, 259, 273, 276, 321, 354, 361, 369, 376, 395, *Also see* Chapter 12
  - and Rickett's Circus tokens, 392
  - and Talbot, Allum & Lee, 378
  - branches, 390
  - coins in circulation (chart), 443
  - faces dissolution, 425
- of North America, 60
- Patent Office, 380
- war debt, 21, 69

USA coppers. See bar coppers

Utrecht
- Psalter, 187
- Treaty of. *See* Treaty of Utrecht

Van Buren, Martin, 22
- and Jackson's war with the Bank of the U.S., 25
- fiscal policies of, 394, 396
- political jibes at, 394
- tokens honoring, 395, 400

Van Voorhis, Daniel, 278, 298, 339
- NY coin proposal, 283

variety. *See* die variety

Venus, 436
- with Psyche, 154

Verazzano, Giovanni da, 139

Vermont, Republic of, 21
- becomes a state, 297
- coinage, 257, 278, 295–304
  - and Immune Columbia muling, 304
  - and primitive imitation halfpence, 304
  - baby head coppers, 300
  - Britannia reverse, 292, 302
  - head-left coppers, 301
  - landscape coppers, 298
  - standard head coppers, 302–4
  - ties to
    - CT coinage, 302, 303
    - imitations, 302
    - Machin's Mills, 291
- encroachment on U.S., 297
- negotiates with British, 297

Verplanck, Gulian C., 400

Vexator Canadiensis, 387

vignette, defined, 53

Virgin Islands. *See* Danish West Indies

Virginia, 9, 84, 97, 134, 175, 239–42, 270
- coinage
  - 1774 shillings, 242
  - Gloucester tokens, 217–18
  - halfpence, 233, 239–42
  - petitions for, 240
  - shillings of 1774, 100
- colonial charters, 239
- Company, 83, 84, 156, 203
  - of London, 160
  - of Plymouth. See Plymouth Company
- Gloucester County, 217
- infringement on Maryland, 175
- named, 82
- patent coinage in, 90

Vlack, Robert, 203, 208, 214, 270, 285

Voce Populi tokens, 230–32, 230

Voigt (or Voight), Henry, 409, 420, 421, 430
- and 'Brirch' cents, 413
- and chain cents, 414
- and silver-centered cents, 413
- anti-Mint sentiment, 425

wages. Also see income

Walpole, Sir Robert, 95, 96, 98

wampum, 29, 36–42
- decline of, 41
- origins of use, 37

War
- Civil
  - English. See See Civil War, English
  - U.S.. See Civil War, U.S.
- First World, 250
- French and Indian. See French and Indian Wars
- Hundred Years, 137
- of 1812, 371, 385, 387, 398, 432
  - post-war protectionism, 398
- of Austrian Succession, 96, 138
- of Jenkins' Ear, 44, 96
- of Religion, 137
- of Spanish Succession, 92, 93, 124, 138
- of the Palatinate, 91
- -s
  - Bishop's, 84
  - Napoleonic. See Napoleonic Wars
- Thirty Years. *See* Thirty Years War
- with Dutch (1652-1654), 136

Washington
- Martha, 410

Washington, D.C., 24
- Jefferson and Hamilton agree on, 21

Washington, George, 17, 268
- adoration of as a unifying concept, 361
- and 1754 expedition, 97, 141
- and 1792 half dismes, 411
- and coinage resolution of 1791, 407
- and George Clinton, 283
- and Martha, 267
- and Thomas Machin, 283
- at Trenton, 65
- coinage, 361, *Also see Hancock, John G.; Perkins, Jacob; Westwood, Obadiah; Perkins, Jacob; and Getz, Peter*
  - 1792 patterns
    - American armies. *See* Washington coinage, Hancock's for Westwood, 1792 patterns
    - Perkins' involvement?, 362
  - by John Gregory Hancock, for Westwood, 357
  - confederation patterns, 340
  - Confederation patterns and mulings, 342, 339–48
  - funeral medals, 362
  - Georgivs Triumpho coppers, 256, 270–71
  - Getz' pattern half dollars, 366–68
  - Hancock's for Westwood, 363–64
    - large and small eagle cents, 363
    - Liverpool halfpence, 363
    - Roman Heads, 366
  - Kempson and Sons
    - grate tokens, 369
    - Liberty and Security, 366–68
  - Liverpool halfpence, 115

Non Vi Virtute Vici coppers, 278
North Wales halfpence, 109, 371
Standish Barry threepence, 358, 359–60
success tokens, 71, 148, 357, 368
ugly head pieces (1784), 271–72
Unity States, 358
farewell address, 23
first inauguration, 272
given commission (1775), 61
in Boston, 63
in Morristown, 320
in New York, 258, 274
Non Vi Virtute Vici coppers, 278
opposes Whiskey Rebellion, 23
satirized, 271
secures VT statehood, 297
sides with Bank of U.S., 22
signed lottery tickets, 75
supports decimal coinage, 264
sword by John Bailey, 279
views on coinage, 407
watermarks. *See* anti-counterfeiting measures, paper
Watt, James, 100, *Also see Boulton and Watt*
Watt's Printing Works, 61, 379
wealth
distribution of, 10
generation of, 9
Spanish, 7
wear, simulated, 102–8, 313, 371, 374
Wentworth, Benning, 296
West
Africa (slaves/rice), 9
Country Men, 84
Indies, 8, 9, 10, 11, 13, 79, 110, 111, 162, 201, 203, 209
and distilling industry, 11
British control of, 98
receives New England trade, 10
Spanish coins in, 125
Point, 259, 283
the, 32, 75, 97, 255
West Jersey. *See* St. Patrick's coinage
Westwood, Obadiah, 115, 407
wheat, 10, 11
Wheeler, Samuel, 261
Whig, 399
Whiskey Rebellion, 23
William
of Orange. *See* William III
the Silent, 91, 131–32
William III, 91, 138, 463
and Mary II, 81, 90, 92–93, 102, 204, 463, 465
accomplishments of, 92
College of, 92
deal with France, 124
Williams, Roger, 38
Williamsburg, 91, 217, 241
Colonial Wmsburg. Found., 241
willow tree coinage, 165, 168–70
Windsor (Connecticut), 225
Winthrop, John
founds Boston, 161
on wampum, 38
witch pieces, 166
Wither, George, 114, 187
Wolfe, James, 98
Wonka, Willy, 211
Wood, William, 153
coinage of, 87, 96, 153, 200, 218–24
Hibernia coinage, 154, 222–24
Rosa Americana coinage, 54, 154, 219–22, 223
Woodbridge, Timothy, 226
Woodward, W. Elliot, 168
wreath, 116, 212, 238, 305–16, 373, 381, 394, 395, 398, 400, 413, 416, 417, 421, 423, 428, 432, 441, 461
Brasher doubloons, 276
Chalmers tokens, 269
New Jersey state coppers (torse), 322
Nova Constellatio patterns, 262
Nova Constellatio tokens, 267, 471
Nova Eborac, 281
on Continental Currency, 61
symbolizing North and South, 424
U.S. large cents, 373, 415
Washington funeral medals, 362
Wright, Joseph, 417
1792 quarter pattern, 412
and 1792 dismes patterns, 412
Wyndham, William. *See* Lord Grenville
Wyon
family, 259, 265, 294, 343, 369, 477
and Walter Mould, 278, 288, 319, 339, 342
George, 342, 343
George III, 339
Peter George, 339, 343
Thomas, 339, 341, 343, 369, 370
Thomas Jr., 343
XYZ Affair, 400
Yale University, 273
Yeo, Richard, 241
York
Pennsylvania, 66
-town issue (Cont. Curr. notes), 66
York, James, Duke of. *See* James II
Young
Matthew, 202
Pretender. See Stuart, Charles Edward

WORKS AND FRIENDS, CITED AND CONSULTED

Works in Print:

- Adams, John. Letter to *Niles' Weekly Register*. Niles, Hezekiah, editor. Published March 7, 1818 ed. (vol. XIV, no. 2.)
- Alden, John Richard. *The American Revolution, 1775-1783*. New York, Harper and Brothers, 1954.
- *America's Smithsonian: Celebrating 150 Years*. Washington, Smithsonian Institution Press, 1996.
- Anonymous. "Brasher Doubloons Labeled $15 Coins" in *The Numismatist*, v.118, no.12, December, 2005.
- Anonymous. *The First United States Coins, Unique 1783 Nova Constellatio Pattern Coinage Set* (pamphlet.) Stacks, New York, ca.1995.
- Anton, William T., Jr. and Kesse, Bruce. *The Forgotten Coins of the North American Colonies*, Iola, Wisconsin, Krause Publications, 1992.
- Arnold, Morris S.. *Colonial Arkansas 1686-1804: A Social and Cultural History*. Fayetteville, Arkansas, University of Arkansas Press, 1991.
- Ashley, Maurice. *The Stuarts*. Edited by Fraser, Antonia. London, Cassell and Company, 2000.
- August, Richard and Sarrafian, Ed. *Thomas Machin, James Atlee and Abel Buell*. Presented to the Colonial Coin Collector's Club (C4,) in Boston, on November 7, 1997.
- Barry, John Stetson. *The History of Massachusetts, The Colonial Period.* Boston, Phillips, Sampson and Company, 1855. Also, *The Provincial Period*, 1856 and T*he Commonwealth Period*, 1857.
- Beauchamp, William M.. "Wampum and Shell Articles Used by New York Indians" in *Bulletin of the New York State Museum*, no.41, v.8. Albany, New York, April, 1901.
- Bellings, Richard. *History of the Irish Confederation and the War in Ireland. With Correspondence and Documents of the Confederation and of the Administrators of the English Government in Ireland. Contemporary Personal Statements, Memoirs, etc.*. Edited by Sir John T. Gilbert, 7 vols.. Dublin, 1882-91. (Referenced by Coonan, but not located by this author.)
- Bennett, Ross, editor. *Visiting Our Past: America's Historylands*, revised ed., Washington, National Geographic Society, 1986.
- Berry, George. *Taverns and Tokens of Pepys' London.* London, Seaby Publications, 1978.
- Billington, Ray Allen, editor. *The Frontier Thesis: Valid Interpretation of American History?* New York, Holt, Reinhart and Winston, 1966.
- Billington, Ray Allen. *Western Expansion, A History of the American Frontier*, 4th ed.. New York, Macmillan, 1974.
- Billington, Ray Allen. "Americans Spread Out" in *Visiting Our Past.* Edited by Bennett.
- Blackburn, Mark A. S., editor. *Anglo-Saxon Monetary History: Essays in Memory of Michael Dolley.* Leicester, U.K., Leicester University Press, 1986.
- Bogue, Donald J.. *The Population of the United States, Historical Trends and Future Projections.* New York, The Free Press, a division of Macmillan, Inc., 1985.
- Boorstein, Daniel, editor. *An American Primer*, copyrighted in 1966. University of Chicago. Authorized reprint by Meridian (New York,) 1995.
- Booth, Russell H., Jr.. *The Tuscarwas Valley in Indian Days 1750-1797.* Cambridge, Ohio, Gomber House Press, 1994.
- Bowers, Q. David. *The Garrett Collection, Part 3.* Los Angeles, Bowers and Ruddy Galleries, 1980.

- Bowers, Q. David. *The History United States Coinage as Illustrated by the Garrett Collection*, Los Angeles, Bowers & Ruddy Galleries, 1979.
- Bradford, William. *Of Plymouth Plantation*. Edited by Samuel Eliot Morison. New York, Alfred A. Knopf, 1996.
- Brands, H. W.. *The First American: The Life and Times of Benjamin Franklin*. New York, Anchor Books, A Division of Random House, 2000.
- Breen, Walter. *Complete Encyclopedia of U.S. and Colonial Coins*. New York, Doubleday, 1988.
- Breen, Walter. "North American Colonial Coinages Under the French Regime (1640-1763)" in *Studies on Money in Early America*. Edited by Newman and Doty.
- Breen, Walter. "Philadelphia's Original flying Disks: Early American Coppers – Blanks, Sources, identifying Marks" in *The American Numismatic Association Anthology*. Edited by Carlson and Hodder.
- Bressett, Kenneth E.. *Collectible American Coins*. Lincolnwood, Illinois, Publications International, Ltd., 1991.
- Bressett, Kenneth E.. "Vermont Copper Coinage" in *Studies on Money in Early America*. Edited by Newman and Doty.
- Brown, Craig, editor. *The Illustrated History of Canada*. Toronto, Lester & Orpen Dennys Ltd., 1987.
- Bruce, Colin R., II, senior editor. Krause, Chester L. and Mishler, Clifford. *Standard Catalog of World Coins, 17th Century*, 2nd edition. Iola, Wisconsin, Krause Publications, 1999.
- Bruce, Colin R., II, senior editor. Krause, Chester L. and Mishler, Clifford. *Standard Catalog of World Coins, 18th Century*, 2nd ed. Iola, Wisconsin, Krause Publications, 1997.
- Bruce, Colin R., II. *Standard Catalog of Mexican Coins, Paper Money, Stocks, Bonds and Medals*. Iola, Wisconsin, Krause Publications, 1981.
- Calligas, Eleni, editor. Lobel, Richard, publisher. Davidson, Mark (hammered coinage) and Hailstone, Allen (milled coinage.) *Coincraft's 1999 Standard Catalogue of English and UK Coins 1066 to Date*. London, Coincraft, 1999.
- Cantwell, Anne-Marie and Wall, Diana di Zerega. *Unearthing Gotham, The Archaeology of New York City*. New Haven, Connecticut and London, Yale University Press, 2001.
- Carlotto, Tony. *The Copper Coins of Vermont and Those Bearing the Vermont Name*. The Colonial Coin Collectors Club, printed by Bookcrafters, Chelsea, Michigan, 1998.
- Carlson, W. A. and Hodder, Michael J., editors. *The American Numismatic Association Anthology*. Published for the American Numismatic Association (Colorado Springs, Colorado,) by Bowers and Merena Galleries, Inc. (Wolfeboro, New Hampshire,) 1991.
- Carte, Thomas. *History of the Life of James, Duke of Ormonde; containing an account of the most remarkable affairs of his time, and particularly of Ireland under his government: With an appendix and a Collection of Letters*, 3 vols. (London, 1735-36.) Second ed., 6 vols. (Oxford, 1851.) Electronic edition in three volumes from TannerRitchie Publishing, Burlington, Ontario, 2005.
- Carter, Willam H.. Revised and edited by Hothem, Lar. *North American Indian Trade Silver*. Lancaster, Ohio, Hothem House, 1996.
- Charlton, James E.. *1963 Standard Catalogue of Canadian Coins, Tokens and Paper Money, 11th Edition*. Published in Toronto, by the author, and dist. in the U.S. by Whitman Publishing, 1962.
- Clain-Steffanelli, Elvira Eliza. "From the Drawing Board of a Coin-Engraver" in *The American Numismatic Association Anthology*, edited by Carlson and Hodder.
- Clarke, Hermann Frederick. *John Hull, A Builder of the Bay Colony*, Wolfeboro, New Hampshire, A.W. Pollock & Company, 1993. Originally copyrighted by Clarke in 1940 and published by The Southworth-Anthoensen Press (Portland, Maine.)

- Cohen, Roger S., Munson, Paul, Jr.. and Munde, Ray. *American Half Cents, the Little Half Sisters.* Self-published in Bethesda, Maryland, 1971. Also, Arlington, Virginia; Wigglesworth and Ghatt, 1982.
- Collot, Georges-Henri-Victor. Journey in North America, Containing a Survey of the Countries Watered by the Mississippi, Ohio, Missouri, and Other Affluing Rivers [vol. 1]. From Collot, Victor. A Journey in North America, Containing a Survey of the Countries Watered by the Mississippi, Ohio, Missouri, and Other Affluing Rivers; with Exact Observations on the Course and Soundings of These Rivers; and on the Towns, Villages, Hamlets and Farms of That Part of the New-World; Followed by Philosophical, Political, Military and Commercial Remarks and by a Projected Line of Frontiers and General Limits. Illustrated by 36 Maps, Plans, Views, and Divers Cuts. Paris, Printed for Arthus Bertrand, 1826, v.1. Online facsimile edition at www.americanjourneys.org/aj-088a/. Accessed September 28, 2003.
- Coonan, Thomas L.. *The Irish Catholic Confederacy and the Puritan Revolution.* Dublin, Clonmore and Reynolds; New York, Columbia University Press, 1954.
- Cooper, Denis R.. "The Development of Coinage Dies" (paper.) Read at the Science Museum, London, January, 10, 1996.
- Cooper, Denis R.. "The History and Development of the Coining Press" (paper.) Read at the Science Museum, London, February 12, 1975.
- Crosby, Sylvester Sage. *The Early Coins of America*, Boston, published by the author, 1875.
- Cross, W.K.. *Canadian Coins, A Charlton Standard Catalogue*, 58th ed., North York, Ontario, Charlton Press, 2004.
- Cross, W.K.. *Canadian Colonial Tokens, A Charlton Standard Catalogue*, 5th ed., North York, Ontario, Charlton Press, 2003.
- Dane, William B., editor. *The Merchant's Magazine and Commercial Review.* New York. Volume 46, January-June, 1862.
- Danforth, Dr. Brian J.. "Wood's Money: Acceptance or Rejection in Ireland" in *The C4 Newsletter*, Fall 2000, v.8, no.8.
- Danforth, Dr. Brian J.. "The St. Patrick Coinage." In two parts: "Peter Blondeau's Technology" and "Lord Ormond's National Coinage" in *The Colonial Newsletter*, December, 2002.
- De Gramont, Sanche. *Epitaph for Kings, the Long and Splendid Decline of the French Monarchy and the Coming of the Revolution*, New York, G. P. Putnam's Sons, 1967.
- De Pedro, José Montero and De Casa Mena, Marqués. T*he Spanish in New Orleans and Louisiana.* Translated by Chandler, Richard E.. Gretna, Louisiana, Pelican Publishing, 2004.
- Dickerson, Oliver M.. *The Navigation Acts and the American Revolution*, Philadelphia, University of Pennsylvania Press, 1951.
- Dolley, Michael. "The Irish Coinage, 1534-1691." Ch. XVI of *A New History of Ireland*, v.3. Edited by Moody, Martin and Byrne.
- Doty, Richard. *America's Money, America's Story, A Comprehensive Chronicle of American Numismatic History.* Iola, Wisconsin, Krause Publications, 1998.
- Doty, Richard, editor. *The Token: America's Other Money.* Proceedings no. 10 of the Coinage of the Americas Conference, held at the American Numismatic Society, October 29, 1994. New York, American Numismatic Society, 1995.
- Doty, Richard. "Making Money in Early Massachusetts" in *Money of Pre-Federal America.* Edited by Kleeberg.
- Durant, Will and Ariel. *The Story of Civilization, Part VII, The Age of Reason Begins, A History of Civilisation in the Period of Shakespeare, Bacon, Montaigne, Rembrandt, Galileo and Descarte: 1558-1648.* New York, Simon and Schuster, 1961.
- Duyckinck, Evert A.. *Portrait Gallery of Eminent Men and Women of Europe and America*, in two volumes. New York, Johnson, Wilson and Company, 1873.

- Ehrenreich, Thomas. *Railroad Extra*. Online publication of *The Baltimore American* (newspaper), July 7, 1828 issue. http://www.catskillarchive.com/rrextra/abbon.html. Accessed June 13, 2006.
- Ellis, Joseph J. *Founding Brothers, The Revolutionary Generation.* New York, Alfred A. Knopf, 2001.
- Evans, George G.. *Illustrated History of the United States Mint*, revised edition. Philadelphia, self-published, 1889.
- Ensko, Stephen G. C.. *American Silversmiths and their Marks, The Definitive (1948) Edition.* New York, reprinted by Dover Publications, Inc., undated.
- Evelyn, John. *The Diary of John Evelyn*, in two vols.. Edited by Rhys, Ernest. London, J. M. Dent and Sons, 1930. Reprint of original 1907 edition. With a prefactory note by George W. E. Russell.
- Everett, Mary Anne, editor. *Calendar of state papers, Domestic series, of the reign of Charles II, Preserved in the state paper department of Her Majesty's Public Record Office.* London, Longman, Green, Longman and Roberts, 1860 and following.
- Forbes, Esther. *Paul Revere and the World He Lived In.* Boston, Houghton Mifflin, 1942.
- Ford, Sir Edward. *Experimental Proposals how the King may have Money to Pay and Maintain his Fleets, With Ease to his People; London may be rebuilt, and all Proprietors; Money to be lent at Six per Cent. On Pawns; and the Fishing-Trade set up, which alone is able and sure to enrich us all. And all this without Altering, Straining, or Thwarting any of our Laws or Customs now in Use.* London, 1666. Printed by William Godbid. The document appears in its entirety in *The Harleian Miscellany, A Collection of Scarce, Curious and Entertaining Pamphlets and Tracts, As Well in Manuscript as in Print.* The collection was selected from the library of Edward Harley, second earl of Oxford. An edition annotated by William Oldys and Thomas Park was printed in London, in 1809, for White and Company, John Murray and John Harding.
- Ford, Worthington C., editor. *Journals of the Continental Congress, 1774-1789.* See United States Continental Congress.
- Foster, Ed. *What Makes a Family?* Presentation to the annual meeting of C4, in Boston, on November 19, 2005.
- Fraser, Antonia. *The Lives of the Kings and Queens of England.* Berkeley and Los Angeles, University of California Press, 1998.
- Freidus, Daniel. "The History and Die Varieties of the Higley Coppers." Excerpted from proceedings of the Coinage of the Americas Conference, American Numismatic Society, New York, October 29, 1994.
- Fuld, George. "Coinage Featuring George Washington" in *Coinage of the American Confederation Period.* Edited by Mossman.
- Gardner, Laurence. *Bloodline of the Holy Grail, The Hidden Lineage of Jesus Revealed.* Shaftesbury, Dorset (England,) Element Books Limited, 1996.
- *Gazette of the United States* (newspaper.) Fenno, John, editor. Philadelphia, April 16, 1791.
- Giedroyc, Richard. "Continental Dollar Retains Air of Mystery" in *Coin World.* Sidney, Ohio, Amos Press, June 8, 1992.
- Gill, John P., editor. *Journal of the Louisiana Purchase 2002 Base Line Expedition: Commemorating the First Survey of the American West.* Little Rock, Arkansas, Louisiana-Purchase Bicentennial Committee of Arkansas, 2004.
- Gillispie, Charles C.. *A Diderot Pictorial Encyclopedia of Trades and Industry, 485 Plates Selected from L'Encyclopedie of Denis Diderot*, v.1. New York, Dover Publications, 1993.
- Goodwin, Jason. *Greenback, The Almighty Dollar and the Invention of America.* New York, a John Macrae Book, Henry Holt and Company, 2003.
- Goss, John. *Blaue's, The Grand Atlas of the 17th Century World.* Published in cooperation with the Royal Geographic Society, London. New York, Barnes and Noble Books, 1997.

- Greaves, Richard L.. *Dublin's Merchant-Quaker, Anthony Sharp and the Community of Friends, 1643-1707*. Stanford, California, Stanford University Press, 1998.
- Greensword, Malachy (Mullhuland Ignatious Cobwright.) *A journey through the Monkolokian rain forests in search of the Spiney Fubbaduck*, second ed.. Self-published in the U.K., 1993.
- Hamilton, Alexander. "Report of the Secretary of the Treasury on the Subject of a Mint." Originally published in Philadelphia by William Young, in the March, 1791 (pp.189-201) and April, 1791 (pp.263-268) editions of *The Universal Asylum and Columbian Magazine*. Full text available online, the CoinFacts website at http://www.coinfacts.com/mint_history/mint_history_1781_1791/. Accessed September 5, 2006.
- Hamilton, Alexander. "The Second Report on Public Credit, December 13, 1790" in *The Works of Alexander Hamilton*. New York, G.P. Putnam's Sons, 1904, v.2. Reprinted in *American Issues* by Unger and Tomes.
- Hawke, David Freeman. *Everyday Life in Early America*. New York, Harper and Row, 1988.
- Hawthorne, Nathaniel. *The Whole History of Grandfather's Chair or True Stories from New England History, 1620-1808*. First published in Boston, 1840, by E.P. Peabody.
- Hodder, Michael J.. "The Continental Currency Coinage of 1776, A Trial Die and Metallic Emission Sequence" in *The American Numismatic Association Anthology*. Edited by Carlson and Hodder.
- Hodder, Michael J., cataloger. *The James W. Vannder Zanden Collection and Coins sold on behalf of Yale University*. Auction of June 14-15, 1995. New York, Stacks, 1995.
- Hodder, Michael J.. "Ephraim Brasher's 1786 Lima Style Doubloon" in *Money of Pre-Federal America*. Edited by Kleeberg.
- Hodder, Michael J., cataloger. *The John J. Ford Collection, Part 9*. Auction held on May 10, 2005. New York, Stacks, 2005.
- Hodder, Michael J., cataloger. *The John J. Ford Collection, Part 12*. Auction held on October 18, 2005. New York, Stacks, 2005.
- Hodder, Michael J.. "Law Resists Striking New Coinage Until Forced into Making Choices" in *Coin World*. Sidney, Ohio, Amos Press, March 27, 1995.
- Hodder, Michael J.. "Maryland Coinage Short-Lived" in *Coin World*, Sidney, Ohio, Amos Press, vol. 34, issue 1737, July 26, 1993.
- Hodder, Michael J.. "More on Benjamin Dudley, Public Copper, Constellatio Novas and Fugio Cents" in *The Colonial Newsletter*, v.34, no.2. June 1994.
- Hodder, Michael J.. "Pedigree Updates of Calvert Coinage Result of Research" in *Coin World*. Sidney, Ohio, Amos Press, vol. 34, issue 1737, July 26, 1993.
- Hodder, Michael J.. "The Case Against Thomas Goadsby" in *The Colonial Newsletter*. August 1997.
- Hodder, Michael J.. "The Gloucester County, Virginia Tokens" in *The Colonial Newsletter*, v.37, no.1, April 1997.
- Hodder, Michael J.. "Was an Automatic Planchet Feeder Used in New Haven in 1787?" in *The Colonial Newsletter*. July 1992.
- Hothem, Lar. *Indian Trade Relics, Identification and Value*. Paducah, Kentucky, Collector Books, 2003.
- Houck, Louis. Edited by Dale Van Everey. *A History of Missouri from the Earliest Explorations and Settlements Until the Admission of the State into the Union*, vols. I-III. New York, Arno Press, 1971. Originally published in 1908 by R. R. Donnelley and Sons, Chicago.
- Hume, Ivor Nöel. *A Guide to Artifacts of Colonial America*. Philadelphia, University of Pennsylvania Press. Originally published by Alfred A. Knopf, Inc., 1969.
- Hume, Ivor Nöel. *In Search of This and That, Tales from an Archaeologist's Quest*. Williamsburg, Virginia, The Colonial Williamsburg Foundation, 3rd Printing, 1998.

- Ingholt, Harald, editor. *Centennial Publication*. New York, American Numismatic Society, 1958.
- Irving, Washington. *Life of George Washington*. Illustrated Edition. In five volumes. New York, G.P. Putnam and Company, 1857 (I,) 1858 (II,) 1859 (III, IV.) Charles T. Evans and G.P. Putnam and Company, 1859 (V.)
- James, Marquis. *Andrew Jackson, Portrait of a President*. Indianapolis, The Bobbs-Merrill Company, 1937.
- James, Marquis. *The Life of Andrew Jackson*. Indianapolis, The Bobbs-Merrill Company, 1938.
- Jefferson, Thomas, ed. by Paul Leicester Ford. *The Vile Hamiltonian System*, published in *The Writings of Thomas Jefferson*, New York, G. P. Putnam's Sons, 1895, vol. 1, pp.159-166. Reprinted in American Issues by Unger and Tomes (See reference under Unger and Tomes.)
- Jenkins, Rhys. "A Chapter in the History of the Water Supply of London: and Sir Edward Ford's Patent from Cromwell" in *Transactions of the Newcomen Society*, 1928.
- Jordan, Louis. *John Hull, the Mint and the Economics of Massachusetts Coinage*, C4 Publications, The Colonial Coin Collectors Club. Distributed by University Press of New England, Hanover and London, 2002.
- Judd, J. Hewitt, M.D.. *United States Pattern, Experimental and Trial Pieces*, 4th ed., Racine Wisconsin, Western Publishing Company, Inc., 1970.
- Julian, R.W.. "The Philadelphia Mint and Coinage of 1814-1816" in *The American Numismatic Association Anthology*. Edited by Carlson and Hodder. (See reference under Carlson and Hodder.)
- Kays, Thomas A.. "When Cross Pistareens Cut Their Way Through the Tobacco Colonies" in *The Colonial Newsletter*, April 2001.
- Kleeberg, John M.. "The New Yorke in America Token" in *Money of Pre-Federal America*. Edited by Kleeberg.
- Kleeberg, John M.. "The Theatre at New York" in *The Token: America's Other Money*. Edited by Doty, Richard.
- Kleeberg, John M., editor. *Money of Pre-Federal America,* Coinage of the Americas Conference, Proceedings no. 7. Held at the American Numismatic Society, May 4, 1991. New York: American Numismatic Society, 1992.
- Kleeberg, John M.. "Shipwreck of the Faithful Steward" in *Coinage of the American Confederation Period*. Edited by Mossman.
- Kleeberg, John, "Reconstructing the Beach-Grünthal Hoard of Counterfeit Halfpence: The Montclair, New Jersey (1922) Hoard", American Journal of Numismatics, volumes 7-8, New York, American Numismatic Society, 1997.
- Krause, Chester L. and Lemke, Robert F.. Wilhite, Robert E., editor. *Standard Catalog of United States Paper Money*, 7th ed. Iola, Wisconsin; Krause Publications, 1987.
- Langguth, A.J.. *Patriots, The Men Who Started the American Revolution*. New York, Touchstone/Simon & Schuster, 1988.
- Latham, Robert and Mathews, William, editors. *The Diary of Samuel Pepys*. (See Pepys, Samuel.)
- Leyburn, James G.. *The Scotch Irish, A Social History*. Chapel Hill, North Carolina, The University of North Carolina Press, 1962.
- Liungman, Carl G.. *Dictionary of Symbols*, New York, W. W. Norton and Company, 1994. English translation of *Symboler – västerländska ideogram*. Originally published in Malmö, Sweden by Merkur International KB. Copyright 1991, Liungman.
- Lorenzo, John and Moore, Roger. "The 1787 Immunis Columbia: A Late Rahway/Elizabethtown Product?" in *The C4 Newsletter*, v.5, no.1, Spring 1997.
- Lorenzo, John. "The Horse Head Left Varieties – Why Left?" in *The C4 Newsletter*, v.7, no.3, Fall 1999.
- Lorenzo, John. "The Rhode Island Ship Medal and Matthew Boulton" in *The C4 Newsletter*, v.5, no.3, Fall 1997.

- Macaulay, Thomas Babington. *The History of England from the Accession of James II*, v.1.. New York, Harper and Brothers, 1849.
- Madigan, Thomas. *Variety Checklist and Rarity Ratings for American Colonial Issues and States Coinages*. Self-published, 1998 and following.
- Maris, Edward. *A Historic Sketch of the Coins of New Jersey*. Lawrence, Massachusetts, Quarterman Publications, 1978. Originally printed in 1881 by William K. Bellows of Philadelphia.
- Marshall, John. "McCulloch v. Maryland, 1819." Edited by Robert G. McCloskey in *An American Primer*. Edited by Boorstein.
- Martin, Joseph Plumb. *Private Yankee Doodle*. Edited by George F. Scheer. Eastern Acorn Press, 1995. Previously published by Little, Brown and Company, 1962.
- Massey, J. Earl. "Early Money Substitutes" in *Studies on Money in Early America*. Edited by Newman and Doty.
- Massey, J. Earl. *America's Money, The Story of Our Coins and Currency*. New York, Thomas Y. Crowell Company, 1968.
- McCusker, John J.. "Colonial Paper Money" in *Studies on Money in Early America*. Edited by Newman and Doty.
- Meade-Fetherstonhaugh, Margaret and Warner, Oliver. *Uppark [sic] and Its People*. London, George Allen and Unwin, Ltd., 1964.
- Meehan, Bernard. *The Book of Kells*. London, Thames and Hudson, Ltd., 1994 (reprinted 1999.)
- Miller, Henry C.. *The State Coinage of Connecticut*. Originally published by the American Numismatic Society, New York, 1920. Reprinted by Sanford J. Durst, New York, 1981.
- Miller, John C.. *Origins of the American Revolution*. Boston, Little, Brown and Company, 1943.
- Mitchelson, Joseph C.. "The Higley Coppers." Reprint from *The Numismatist* (December, 1927,) in *The American Numismatic Association Anthology*. Edited by Carlson and Hodder.
- Montgomery, David H.. *The Leading Facts of American History*, revised edition. Boston, Ginn and Company, 1910.
- Moody, T. W., Martin, F. M., and Byrne, F. J.. *A New History of Ireland, Early Modern Ireland, 1534-1691*, v.3. Oxford, Clarendon Press, 1976.
- Morris, Charles. *The Great Republic by the Great Historians*, New York, R.S. Belcher, 1901.
- Mossman, Philip L.. "A Weight Analysis of Abel Buell's Connecticut Coppers" in *Money of Pre-Federal America*. Edited by Kleeberg.
- Mossman, Philip L., editor. *Coinage of the American Confederation Period*. Proceedings no. 11 of the Coinage of the Americas Conference held at the American Numismatic Society, October 28, 1995, New York: American Numismatic Society, 1996.
- Mossman, Philip L.. *Money of the American Colonies and Confederation, A Numismatic, Economic and Historical Correlation*. New York, The American Numismatic Society, 1993.
- Mossman, Philip L.. "The Circulation of Irish Coinage in Pre-Federal America" in *The Colonial Newsletter* (ed. by Mossman) Hampton, Maine, The American Numismatic Society, v.39, no.1, serial no.110, April, 1999.
- Moulton, Gary E., editor. *Meriwether Lewis and William Clark, An American Epic of Discovery, The Lewis and Clark Journals, The Abridgement of the Definitive Nebraska Edition*. Copyrighted by the Board of Regents of the University of Nebraska, 2003.
- Nardini, Louis Raphael, Sr.. *My Historic Natchitoches, Louisiana and its Environment: A History of Natchitoches, Louisiana and the Neutral Strip area of the State of Louisiana and its Inhabitants*. Hemphill, Texas, Dogwood Press, 2004. Originally published by Nardini Publishing Company in 1963.
- Newcomb, Howard R.. *United States Copper Cents*. New York, Sanford J. Durst, 1986. This edition is a reprint of the revised edition published in 1956 by *Numismatic Review*.

- Newman, Eric P.. "A Recently Discovered Coin Solves a Vermont Numismatic Enigma" in *Centennial Publication*. Edited by Ingholt.
- Newman, Eric P.. "New Thoughts on the Nova Constellatio Private Coinage" in *Coinage of the American Confederation Period*. Edited by Mossman.
- Newman, Eric P.. *The 1776 Continental Currency Coinage and Varieties of the Fugio Cent.* New York, Sanford J. Durst, 1982. Originally published by Wayte Raymond in 1952.
- Newman, Eric P.. *The Early Paper Money of America*, 4th edition. Iola, Wisconsin, Krause Publications, 1997.
- Newman, Eric P., ed., and Doty, Richard, associate editor, *Studies on Money in Early America*, New York, The American Numismatic Society, 1976.
- Newman, Eric P.. Forward to *The Silver Coinage of Massachusetts* by Sydney P. Noe.
- Newman, Eric P.. "George Washington's Unique 1792 Pattern in Gold" in *Studies on Money in Early America*. Edited by Newman and Doty.
- Newman, Eric P.. "The James III 1/24th Real for the American Plantations" in *Museum Notes 11* (1964). As quoted by Louis Jordan, under *The American Plantations Token of 1688: Introduction.* (See online citations.)
- Newman, Eric P.. "The Secret of the Good Samaritan Shilling." Extracted in *The Silver Coinage of Massachusetts*, by Noe.
- Newman, Eric P.. "Unusual Printing Features in Early American Paper Money" in *Money of Pre-Federal America*. Edited by Kleeberg.
- *Niles' Weekly Register* (newspaper.) Niles, Hezekiah, editor. Baltimore, v.14, no.2, March 7, 1818.
- Noe, Sydney. *The Silver Coinage of Massachusetts*. Lawrence, Massachusetts, Quarterman Publications, Inc., 1973. Copyrighted by The American Numismatic Society in 1943 and 1947.
- Nuxoll, Elizabeth M.. *A Generation of Numismatic Co-operation: Findings on the Notes and Coins of the Confederation Through the Papers of Robert Morris* in *American Journal of Numismatics*, Series 9. New York, The American Numismatic Society, 1997.
- Olson, Lester C.. *Emblems of American Community in the Revolutionary Era*, Washington, DC, Smithsonian Institution Press, 1991.
- Overton, Al C.. *Early Half Dollar Varieties, 1794-1836*. Colorado Springs, Colorado, 1967.
- O'Callaghan, E.B., editor. *Documents Relative to the Colonial History of the State of New York; Procured in Holland, England and France by John Romeyn Brodhead,* v.3 (1853) and v.4 (1854.) Albany, Weed, Parsons and Company, Printers.
- Parker, Wyman W.. *Connecticut's Colonial and Continental Money*. Hartford, The American Revolution Bicentennial Commission of Connecticut, 1976.
- Pepys, Samuel. *The Diary of Samuel Pepys,* eleven vols. Edited by Latham, Robert and Mathews, William. Berkeley and Los Angeles, University of California Press, 1971.
- Pietra, Angel. "The History of the Castorland Settlement: Is the Castorland Jeton a 'Jetton de presence' or a coin?" in *The C4 Newsletter*, v.5, no.1, Spring 1997.
- Pietra, Angel. "The Mott Token Revisited" in *The C4 Newsletter*, v.6, no.3, Fall 1998.
- Pomfret, John E.. *Colonial New Jersey, A History of the American Colonies in Thirteen Volumes*. Edited by Klein, Milton M. and Cooke, Jacob E.. New York, Charles Scribner and Sons, 1973.
- Pope, Peter E. *Fish into Wine: The Newfoundland Plantation in the Seventeenth Century.* Asheville, North Carolina, The University of North Carolina Press, 2004.
- Powell, William S.. *The Proprietors of Carolina.* Raleigh, North Carolina, The Carolina Charter Tercentenary Commission, 1963. Reprinted by the State Department of Archives and History.
- *Public Statutes at Large of the United States of America, The.* By Authority of Congress. Boston, Charles C. Little and James Brown, 1845-1867, vol.1. Also available at The Library of Congress website, at http://memory.loc.gov/ammem/amlaw/lwsl.html. Accessed September 1, 2006.

- Quinn, Arthur. *A New World.* New York, Berkley Publishing Group, 1995. Originally published in Winchester, Massachusetts, by Faber and Faber, 1994.
- Randall, Willard Sterne. *Alexander Hamilton, A Life.* New York, Harper Collins Publishers, 2003.
- Reis, Rob. "Numismatics of the Conquest of Mexico" in *World Coin News.* Iola Wisconsin, Krause Publications, May 1998.
- Remini, Robert V.. *The Life of Andrew Jackson.* New York, Penguin Books, 1990.
- Rhys, Ernest, editor. (See Evelyn, John, *The Diary of John Evelyn,*) in two vols., London, J. M. Dent and Sons, 1930. Reprint of original 1907 edition. With a prefactory note by George W. E. Russell.
- Rinaldo, Tom, cataloger. *The John M. Griffee Sale of U.S. Colonial Coins, Held in Conjunction with the First Annual Convention of the Colonial Coin Collectors Club.* Presented by McCawley, Chris and Grellman, Bob on October 25, 1995, in Boston. McCawley and Grellman Auctions.
- Rinaldo, Tom, cataloger. *The Sixth Annual C-4 Convention Sale, Featuring the Albany Collection of Machins Mills Coinage.* Presented by McCawley, Chris and Grellman, Bob, in Boston on November 18, 2000. McCawley & Grellman Auctions.
- Rinaldo, Tom, cataloger. *The Eighth Annual C-4 Convention Sale featuring the Jesse Patrick Collection of Connecticut Coppers.* Presented by McCawley, Chris and Grellman, Bob, in Boston on November 16, 2002. McCawley and Grellman Auctions.
- Rinaldo, Tom. Yesteryear Coins' fixed price list. Bolinas, California, July, 1993.
- Ringo, Mike. "The Georgivs Triumpho Token" in *The Colonial Newsletter*, v.35, no.1, July 1995.
- Robertson, Alexander. *The Life of Sir Robert Moray, Soldier, Statesman and Man of Science.* London, Longmans, Green and Company, 1922.
- Ruck, Bill. "Marking the Land to Build a Nation" in *Journal of the Louisiana Purchase 2002 Base Line Expedition: Commemorating the First Survey of the American West.* Edited by Gill.
- Rulau, Russell. *Standard Catalog of U.S. Tokens 1700-1900*, Iola, Wisconsin, 1994.
- Rulau, Russell. "Pre-Civil War (1812-1861) United States Treasury Notes" in *Standard Catalog of United States Paper Money*, 7th edition. By Krause, Chester L. and Lemke, Robert F.. Edited by Wilhite, Robert E..
- Ryder, Hillyer. *The Colonial Coins of Vermont.* New York, Sanford J. Durst, 1981. Originally printed in 1920 by the American Numismatic Society. Reprinted with Slafter's *The Vermont Coinage.*
- Ryder, Hillyer. *The Copper Coins of Massachusetts.* New York, Sanford J. Durst, 1981. Originally published in 1920 by the American Numismatic Society.
- Sachs, William S.. "The Business of Colonization" in *Studies on Money in Early America.* Edited by Newman and Doty.
- Schuckers, J.W.. *A Brief Account of the Finances and Paper Money of the Revolutionary War.* New York, Sanford J. Durst, 1978. Reprint. Originally published in Philadelphia by John Campbell & Son, in 1874.
- Scott, Kenneth. *Counterfeiting in Colonial New York.* New York, The American Numismatic Society, 1953.
- Selgin, George. *A Numismatic Ramble Through Old Birmingham.* Terry College of Business, University of Georgia, Athens, GA, April 2002.
- Sellers, Charles and May, Henry. *A Synopsis of American History.* Chicago, Rand McNally and Company, 2nd ed., 1969.
- Sheldon, William H.. *Early American Cents*, New York, Harper and Brothers, 1949.
- Skalbe, James E.. "The Dating and Emission Sequence of the Oak and Pine Tree Coinage of Massachusetts Bay" in *The C4 Newsletter*, v.3, no.1, March 1995.

- Slafter, Edward. *The Vermont Coinage*. New York, Sanford J. Durst, 1981. Originally printed in 1870 in Montpelier, Vermont. Reprinted with Ryder's *The Colonial Coins of Vermont*.
- Smith, Dr. Aquilla. "On the Copper Coin Commonly Called St. Patrick's" in *Proceedings and Transactions of the Kilkenny and South-East of Ireland Archaeological Society*. Kilkenny, Ireland, Kilkenny and South-East of Ireland Archaeological Society, 1854, Part 1.
- Smith, Ellen Hart. *Charles Carroll of Carrollton*. Cambridge, Massachusetts, Harvard University Press, 1945.
- Smith, Pete. "Vermont Coppers: Coinage of an Independent Republic" in *Coinage of the American Confederation Period*. Edited by Mossman.
- Smith, Richard Norton. *Patriarch, George Washington and the New American Nation*. New York, Houghton Mifflin, 1993.
- Stabl, Alan M.. "Medals of the Comitia Americana Series in the Collections of the American Numismatic Society and Other Public Institutions" in *Coinage of the American Confederation Period*. Edited by Mossman.
- Stearns, Robert E.C.. *Wampum and Dentalium, A Study of Native American Shell Money*. Hummelstown, Pennsylvania, Tucquan Publishing, 1999. Originally published in the 1887 *Annual Report of the Board of Regents of the Smithsonian Institution* as "A Study of Primitive Money."
- Steimle, Frank. "A Tricentennial Review and Comments on 'God Preserve...' Elephant Tokens" in *The Colonial Newsletter*, v.35, no.1, April 1995.
- Stewart, Frank H.. *History of the United States Mint*. Lawrence, Massachusetts, Quarterman Publications, 1974. Originally published privately by Frank H. Stewart Electric Co., in 1924.
- Stewart, Frank H.. *Mark Newby: The First Banker in New Jersey and His Patrick Halfpence* (booklet.) Copyrighted in 1947 by Stewart and reprinted in 2001 by The Gloucester County Historical Society in Woodbury, New Jersey.
- Swoger, William. "Brasher's Gold" in *Coin World*. Sidney, Ohio, Amos Press, June 1, 1992.
- Tapié, Victor-L.. *France in the Age of Louis XIII and Richelieu*. New York, Preager Publishers, 1975.
- Taxay, Don. Rose, Joseph H. and Hazelcorn, Howard, editors. *The Comprehensive Catalogue and Encyclopedia of United States Coins*, second ed.. New York, Scott Publishing Company, 1976.
- Taxay, Don. *The U.S. Mint and Coinage, An Illustrated History from 1776 to the Present*. New York, Arco Publishing Co., second printing, 1969.
- Taylor, Alan. *American Colonies, The Settling of North America*. New York, Viking Penguin, first publication, 2001.
- Thomas, Isaiah.. *The History of Printing in America, With a Biography of Printers*, in two vols.. Reprint of second edition (1874.) New York, Burt Franklin, 1967. Originally published in 1810.
- Thorn, C. Jordan. *Handbook of American Silver and Pewter Marks*. New York, Tudor Publishing Company, 1949.
- Trudgen, Gary A.. "A Brief Look at the Life of Thomas Goadsby" in *The Colonial Newsletter*. Huntsville, Alabama, The Colonial Newsletter Foundation, v.32, no.1, February 1992.
- Trudgen, Gary A.. "Breen's 'Tory Coppers" in *The Colonial Newletter*. Huntsville, Alabama, The Colonial Newsletter Foundation, v.36, no.1, January, 1996.
- Trudgen, Gary A.. "Gilfoil's Coppers" in *The Colonial Newsletter*. Huntsville, Alabama, The Colonial Newsletter Foundation, v.27, no.2, July 1987.
- Trudgen, Gary A.. "James Atlee's Imitation British Halfpence" in *The Colonial Newsletter*. Huntsville, Alabama, The Colonial Newsletter Foundation, v.27, no.1, March 1987.
- Trudgen, Gary A.. "Samuel and James F. Atlee, Machin's Mills Partners" in *The Colonial Newsletter*. Huntsville, Alabama, The Colonial Newsletter Foundation, vol. 32, no. 3, October, 1992.
- Tuchman, Barbara W.. *The First Salute*. New York, Ballentine Books, 1998.

- Turner, Frederick Jackson. *The Significance of the Frontier in American History* in *The Frontier Thesis: Valid Interpretation of American History?* Edited by Ray Allen Billington.
- United States Continental Congress. Ford, Worthington C., editor, entries of September 5, 1774 through December 31, 1779. Fitzpatrick, John C., editor, entries of January 11, 1785 through December 31, 1786. *Journals of the Continental Congress, 1774-1789.* Washington, D.C., U.S. Government Printing Office, 1904-1937. Also available through the Library of Congress website at addresses given below. Accessed June 12, 2006, by date:
  - Vol. 2, June 17, 1775, http://memory.loc.gov/cgi-bin/query/r?ammem/hlaw:@field(DOCID+@lit(jc00238)).
  - Vol. 2, June 23, 1775, http://memory.loc.gov/cgi-bin/query/r?ammem/hlaw:@field(DOCID+@lit(jc00243)).
  - Vol. 2., July 29, 1775, http://memory.loc.gov/cgi-bin/query/r?ammem/hlaw:@field(DOCID+@lit(jc00274)).
  - Vol. 3, December 5, 1775, http://memory.loc.gov/cgi-bin/query/r?ammem/hlaw:@field(DOCID+@lit(jc00364)).
  - Vol. 28, May 13, 1785, http://memory.loc.gov/cgi-bin/query/r?ammem/hlaw:@field(DOCID+@lit(jc02895)).
  - Vol. 29, July 6, 1785, http://memory.loc.gov/cgi-bin/query/r?ammem/hlaw:@field(DOCID+@lit(jc0295)).
  - Vol. 29, August 8, 1785, http://memory.loc.gov/cgi-bin/query/r?ammem/hlaw:@field(DOCID+@lit(jc02928)).
  - Analogous entries, vols. 2-14, http://memory.loc.gov/cgi-bin/query/r?ammem/hlaw:@field(DOCID+@lit(jc0021)) through http://memory.loc.gov/cgi-bin/query/r?ammem/hlaw:@field(DOCID+@lit(jc0141)).
- Unger, Harlow Giles. *Lafayette.* Hoboken, New Jersey, John Wiley and Sons, 2002.
- Unger, Irwin and Tomes, Robert R., editors. *American Issues, A Primary Source Reader in United States History*, v.1. Upper Saddle River, New Jersey, Prentice Hall, 1999.
- Van Doren, Carl. *Benjamin Franklin*, New York, The Viking Press, 1938.
- Vlack, Robert A.. *An Illustrated Catalogue of the French Billon Coinage in the Americas.* Colonial Coin Collectors Club, 2004.
- Vlack, Robert A.. *Early American Coins.* Johnson City, New York, Windsor Research Publications, second ed., 1965.
- Vlack, Robert A.. "The Billon Coinage of North America" in *The C4 Newsletter*, v.8, no.2, Summer 2000.
- Warner, Charles Dudley. *Captain John Smith.* Electronic version, published by Outrigger Publishing, LLC, 2002. Originally published in 1881.
- Washington, George. "Farewell Address, 1796." Edited by Morris, Richard B. and reprinted in *An American Primer.* Edited by Boorstein.
- Webster, Noah. *Webster's Universal Dictionary of the English Language.* Cleveland and New York, World Publishing Company, 1940.
- West, Willis Mason and Ruth. *The Story of Man's Early Progress.* Boston, Allyn and Bacon, 1934.
- Wiencek, Henry. *The Smithsonian Guide to Historic America: Virginia and the Capital Region.* New York, Stewart, Tabori and Chang, 1989.
- Wierzba, Dennis. "A Georgivs Triumpho as the Undertype of a NJ 73-aa" in *The C4 Newsletter*, v.7, no.2, Summer 1999.
- Wierzba, Dennis. "W. WOART JUS PACIS Massachusetts Tradesman's Token" in *The Colonial Newsletter*, v.34, no.3, November 1994.
- Williams, Irving G.. "George Clinton" in *World Book Encyclopedia.* Chicago, Field Enterprises Educational Corporation, v.4, 1967.

- Willison, George F.. *Saints and Strangers, Being the Lives of the Pilgrim Fathers and their Families*. New York, Reynal and Hitchcock, 1945.
- Withers, George. *Collection of Emblems: Ancient and Modern (1635)*. Kessinger Publishing, 2004. Originally published by Withers in London.
- Wood, Anthony and Bliss, Philip. *Athenae Oxoniensis. An Exact History of all the Writers and Bishops who have had their Education in the University of Oxford. To Which are Added the Fasti, or Annals of the Said University. A New Edition, with Additions, and a Continuation by Philip Bliss*. London, printed for F. C. and J. Rivington an others, 1817, v.3.
- Wood, Gordon S.. *The American Revolution, A History*. New York, The Modern Library, 2002
- Wood, Howland. "The Canadian Blacksmith Coppers" in *The Numismatist*, v.23, April 1910. Philadelphia, various reprints.
- Yeoman, R.S.. *A Guide Book of United States Coins*. Edited by Bressett, Kenneth. Racine, Wisconsin, Western Publishing Company; 53rd edition, 2002.
- Zelinka, Jerry. "The Enigmatic Voce Populi Halfpenny of 1760" in *The Colonial Newsletter*, v.15, no.3, October, 1976.

Conversations and Correspondence, Public and Private:

- Hoover, Oliver D.. Personal email correspondence, May 3-4, 2006. Regarding St. Patrick coinage.
- Howes, Jack. Personal email correspondence, April 21, 2008. Regarding American-made imitation halfpence.
- Jordan, Louis and Williams, Ray. Presentation on the "DK Tokens" excavated at Ferryland, Newfoundland and subsequent discussion. Given at the 2006 convention of C4. Boston, December 2, 2006.
- LaSarre, Jim. As posted to the Colonial Numismatics online discussion group by Dave Wnuck on March 28, 2006. The writing comes from Sharp's "Treatise on English coins and their history...Section Of the Irish Coins." Regarding Bishop Sharp and St. Patrick coinage.
- Leone, Dr. Mark P.., Director, Archaeology in Annapolis Project. Dr. Leone is a professor of anthropology at the University of Maryland. Personal email correspondence, December 14-29, 2006.
- Lorenzo, John, series of postings to the Colonial Coins Yahoo discussion group, Digests 2454, 2472, 2474, 2475, 2485, 2487 and 2707, May 21, 2005 to October 7, 2005. Regarding St. Patrick coinage.
- Madigan, Thomas. Private discussion at the 2000 convention of C4, the Colonial Coin Collectors' Club, in Boston, Massachusetts, November 2000.
- Personal conversations at the 2006 Coinage of the America's Conference in New York, November 11, 2006. Regarding St. Patrick coinage:
    - Danforth, Dr. Brian
    - Gladfelter, David
    - Hoover, Oliver D.
    - Siboni, Roger
    - Yegparian, Vicken
- Spilman, Jim. Email to the C4 Online discussion group, Digest number 597, January 24, 2002.
- Spilman, James C.. Personal email correspondence, May 14, 2005. Regarding Continental Currency Coinage.
- Stephens, Stan. Private correspondence and telephone conversations, April through November, 2005. Regarding St. Patrick coinage.
- Waselkov, Dr. Greg. Center for Archaeological Studies at the University of South Alabama, Personal correspondence and telephone conversation, December 23, 2003. Regarding French coinage in America.

- Williams, Ray. Personal email correspondence, August 29, 2006, regarding the "WM" initials on New Jersey copper obverse, Maris 62.

Online and Other Works:

- American Numismatic Rarities, LLC. "From Our Scrapbook." http://anrcoins.com/ccArchiveMay05.aspx, May 23, 2005. Accessed November 25, 2005.
- American Numismatic Society. "Museum News" in *American Numismatic Society Newsletter*, no.72, Fall 1996. ANS website, http://www.numismatics.org/newsletter/fall96/museumnw.htm. Accessed November 27, 2006.
- Anonymous. "A Brief Account of the Rise, Progress and Present State of the Paper Currency of New England" (pamphlet.) Boston, 1749. Published at The University of Virginia website, www.people.virginia.edu/~rwm3n/webdoc4.html. Updated January 15, 2000. Accessed June 13, 2006.
- Becker, Carl. "The Eve of the Revolution, A Chronicle of the Breach with England." Ithaca, New York, 1918, Ch.4, "Defining the Issue." Published at The History Carper website, http://www.historycarper.com/resources/teotr/chap4.htm. Accessed June 13, 2006.
- Bedini, Silvio A.. "Rittenhouse, David." *American National Biography Online*, February, 2000. http://www.anb.org/articles/13/13-01396.html. Copyright American Council of Learned Societies, 2000. Published by Oxford University Press. Accessed August 30, 2006.
- Bedini, Silvio A.. "History Corner: Henry Voigt" in *Professional Surveyor Magazine*, October, 1997, v.17, no.7. http://www.profsurv.com/archive.php?issue=18&article=207. Accessed August 30, 2006.
- Belcher Foundation, The. Accessed June 11, 2006. By topic:
    - "Jonathan Belcher: Patriarch of Princeton," http://www.belcherfoundation.org/governor_jonathan_belcher.htm.
    - "November Thanksgiving Thursday: Origins of Fourth Thursday of November as Thanksgiving Day," http://www.belcherfoundation.org/thanksgiving_day.htm.
    - "The Great Seal of the United States and the Belcher Coat of Arms," http://www.belcherfoundation.org/seal.htm.
- Brock, Dr. Leslie V.. "The Colonial Currency, Prices and Exchange Rates." *Essays in History*, v.34. Edited by Ron Michener. Corcoran Dept. of History, University of Virginia, 1992, Published online at http://etext.lib.virginia.edu/journals/EH/EH34/brock34.htm. Accessed June 13, 2006.
- Bruchey, Stuart. "Banking." *The Reader's Companion to American History.* http://college.hmco.com/history/readerscomp/rcah/html/ah_007500_banking.htm. Boston, Houghton Mifflin Company. Accessed June 1, 2005.http://www.americanjourneys.org/aj-032/
- Columbia Electronic Encyclopedia, The, sixth edition. "Ohio Company of Associates." Copyright 2004, Columbia University Press, www.infoplease.com/ce6/history/a0836450.html. Accessed July 12, 2004.
- Columbia Electronic Encyclopedia, The, sixth ed.. "Simon Stevin." Copyright 2003, Columbia University Press and Wikopedia. Article "Simon Stevin," licensed under the GNU Free Documentation License, at the Answers.com website, WWW.answers.com/topic/simon-stevin. Accessed September 18, 2005.
- Columbia Electronic Encyclopedia, The, sixth ed.. "Dunlap, William." Bartlesby.Com website, www.bartlesby.com/65/du/Dunlap-W.html. Copyright 2001, Columbia University Press. Accessed June 13, 2006.
- Currency Museum of the Bank of Canada. Accessed June 11, 2006. By topic:
    - "Mexico, Gold Eight Escudos." http://collections.ic.gc.ca/bank/english/eaug80.htm.
    - "Trade Silver – The Beaver." http://collections.ic.gc.ca/bank/english/eoct73.htm.

- Dahl, Roald, writer. Stuart, Mel, director. *Willy Wonka and the Chocolate Factory* (movie.) U.S., David L. Wolper Productions, 1971.
- D'Alton, E.A.. "Giovanni Battista Rinuccini." Transcribed by Ormsbee, Nicolette. *The Catholic Encyclopedia*, v.13. Robert Appleton Company (1912.) Online edition: K. Knight (2003, 2006.) http://www.newadvent.org/cathen/13061a.htm. Accessed October 13, 2006.
- Donagan, Barbara. "Ford, Sir Edward (bap. 1605, d. 1670,)" in *Oxford Dictionary of National Biography*, ed. H. C. G. Matthew, H. C. G. and Harrison, Brian. Oxford: OUP, 2004, http://www.oxforddnb.com/view/article/9855. Accessed October 9, 2006.
- Doty, Richard. "English Merchant Tokens." Chicago Coin Club, 1986, http://www.chicagocoinclub.org/projects/PiN/emt.html. Accessed June 9, 2006.
- Erskine-Hill, Howard. "Caryll, John, Jacobite first Baron Caryll of Durford (bap. 1626, d. 1711)" in *Oxford Dictionary of National Biography*, edited. by Matthew, H. C. G. and Harrison, Brian. (Oxford: OUP, 2004), http://www.oxforddnb.com/view/article/4847. Accessed October 9, 2006.
- Forbes, Keith Archibald. *The Royal Gazette's Bermuda Online* website, www.bermuda-online.org/history. Updated June 8, 2006. Accessed June 8, 2006. By topic:
  - "Bermuda's History from 1500 to 1699, How it relates to the United States of America, United Kingdom and Canada." http://www.bermuda-online.org/france.htm.
  - "Bermuda's ties with France, Both have highest public sector costs in developed world, plus some notable events here." http://www.bermuda-online.org/france.htm.
- Forgotten NY. "the [sic] alleys of lower Manhattan." *http://www.forgotten-ny.com/Alleys/LOWER%20MANHATTAN/lower.html.* Accessed June 11, 2006. Sources cited: a.) Santé, Luc. *Low Life*, Vintage, 1992. b.) Moscow, Henry. *The Street Book*. Hagstrom, 1978. c.) Dunshee, Kenneth. *As You Pass By*. Hastings House, 1952.
- Franklin, Benjamin. "A BRIEF ACCOUNT OF THE Rise, Progress, and Present State OF THE PAPER CURRENCY OF NEW-ENGLAND. And of the Measures taken by the Massachusetts Province, for establishing a Silver Currency for the Future. Together with some PROPOSALS for rendering those Measures more effectual" (1729.) University of Virginia. www.people.virginia.edu/~rwm3n/webdoc4.html. Updated January 15, 2000. Accessed June 13, 2006.
- Fryer, S. E. and Maloney, John. "Henry Dunning Macleod (1821-1902)" in Oxford Dictionary of National Biography, Oxford University Press, http://www.oxforddnb.com/view/article/34787. Updated 2004. Accessed June 13, 2005.
- Gates, C. H.. "History [of Wampum.]" *Wampumworks*. Dunstable, Massachusetts, www.wampumworks.com. Updated January 7, 2004. Accessed July 25, 2004.
- Grassl, Gary C.. "First Germans at Jamestown." The German Heritage Society of Greater Washington, D.C.. www.serve.com/shea/germusa/jtown1a.html. Accessed September 18, 2005.
- Guth, Ron. "New York Theatre Token." *Coinfacts.com*. http://www.coinfacts.com/colonial_coins/new_york_theater_tokens/new_york_theatre_penny.htm. Accessed September 24, 2005.
- Hancks, Larry. "The Emigrant Tribes: Wyandot, Delaware and Shawnee: A Chronology." Wyandot Nation of Kansas. http://www.wyandot.org. Accessed September 24, 2005.
- Hardin, Clifford. "William Newby Family." Posted by Larry Bell in the Quaker-Roots-L Archives, January 26, 2000. RootsWeb.com, http://archiver.rootsweb.com/th/read/QUAKER-ROOTS/2000-01/0948871486. Accessed May 29, 2006.
- "Harting" in *A History of the County of Sussex: Volume 4: The Rape of Chichester (1953)*, pp. 10-21. Available online at http://www.british-history.ac.uk/report.asp?compid=41687&strquery=south%20harting. (British History Online website, Victoria County History.) Accessed: October 12, 2006.
- Henderson, H. James. "Elias Boudinot" in *American National Biography Online*, http://www.anb.org/articles/02/02-00037.html, February 2000. Accessed September 10, 2006.

- Heritage Auction Galleries. *Central States Numismatic Society Signature Auction,* auction no. 404. http://coins.heritageauctions.com/common/view_item.php?Sale_No=404&Lot_No=1860. Accessed September 3, 2006. The article refers to a study by Carl Herkowitz and Joel J. Orosz ("George Washington and America's 'Small Beginning' in Coinage: The Fabled 1792 Half Dismes" in the 2003 edition of *American Journal of Numismatics*, Second Series 15, American Numismatic Society, published 2004) and work done by Karl Moulton (to be published under the title, "Henry Voigt and Others Involved with America's Early Coinage.")
- Homren, Wayne, editor. "Washington Funeral Medal Info Found." *The E-Sylum*, vol.3, no.52, December 17, 2000. http://www.coinbooks.org/club_nbs_esylum_v03n52.html. The article describes the discovery of a newspaper advertisement by Chris Stevens. *The E-Sylum* is an online publication of the Numismatic Bibliomania Society, copyright 2000. Accessed September 18, 2006.
- Hooker, Richard. "The Iroquois League" in *Cultures in America.* Wisconsin State University. www.wsu.edu/~dee/CULAMRCA/IRLEAGUE.HTM, 1996. Updated June 6, 1999. Accessed September 24, 2005.
- Jaenen, Cornelius J. "French Expansion in North America" in *The History Teacher.* University of Ottawa, vl.34, no.2. www.historycooperative.org/journals/ht/34.2/jaenen.html. Accessed June 13, 2006.
- Jordan, Louis. *The Coins of Colonial and Early America.* University of Notre Dame, Department of Special Collections, 1997 and following. http://www.coins.nd.edu/ColCoin/ Accessed September 23, 2005 through August 1, 2006. By topic:
    - "Connecticut Coppers 1785-1788: Introduction." http://www.coins.nd.edu/ColCoin/ColCoinIntros/CT-Copper.intro.html.
    - "Irish Copper Coins: Introduction." http://www.coins.nd.edu/ColCoin/ColCoinIntros/Br-IrishCopper.intro.html.
    - "Imitation British Halfpence Associated with New York City – Introduction." http://www.coins.nd.edu/ColCoin/ColCoinIntros/NYC-Vlack.intro.html.
    - "James Falconer Atlee and Confederation Era Coppers." http://www.coins.nd.edu/ColCoin/ColCoinIntros/Atlee.intro.html.
    - "Machin's Mills Imitation British Halfpence: Introduction." http://www.coins.nd.edu/ColCoin/ColCoinIntros/Machin.intro.html.
    - "Massachusetts Bay Silver 1652-1682: General Introduction." http://www.coins.nd.edu/ColCoin/ColCoinIntros/MASilver.intro.html.
    - "Massachusetts Coppers 1787-1788: Introduction." http://www.coins.nd.edu/ColCoin/ColCoinIntros/MA-Copper.intro.html.
    - "New Jersey Coppers 1786-1790: Introduction." http://www.coins.nd.edu/ColCoin/ColCoinIntros/NJ-Copper.intro.html.
    - "Spanish Colonial Cobs. http://www.coins.nd.edu/ColCoin/ColCoinIntros/Sp-Cobs.intro.html.
    - "Spanish Silver: General Introduction." http://www.coins.nd.edu/ColCoin/ColCoinIntros/Sp-Silver.intro.html.
    - "State Patterns for Massachusetts and New Hampshire of 1776: Introduction." http://www.coins.nd.edu/ColCoin/ColCoinIntros/StatePatterns.intro.html.
    - "The American Plantations Token of 1688: Introduction." http://www.coins.nd.edu/ColCoin/ColCoinIntros/AmPlant.intro.html.
    - "The Bahamas Copper of 1806 – Introduction." http://www.coins.nd.edu/ColCoin/ColCoinIntros/Bahamas.intro.html.
    - "The Barbados Coppers 1788, 1792: Introduction." http://www.coins.nd.edu/ColCoin/ColCoinIntros/Barbados.intro.html.
    - "The Bermuda Copper of 1793: Introduction." http://www.coins.nd.edu/ColCoin/ColCoinIntros/Bermuda.intro.html

- "Willow Tree Coinage: Introduction." http://www.coins.nd.edu/ColCoin/ColCoinIntros/WillowTree.intro.html.

- Karp, Abraham J.. "From the Ends of the Earth: Judaic Treasures of the Library of Congress." Washington, D.C., Library of Congress, 1991. *The Judaic Treasures of the Library of Congress: The Antwerp Bible Illustrations.* Jewish Virtual Library. http://www.jewishvirtuallibrary.org/jsource/loc/Antwerp.html. Accessed May 10, 2006.
- Lawson, Steven M.. "Higley-Filer [genealogy.]" http://www.kinnexions.com/ancestries/higley.htm#JHigley. Accessed June 13, 2006.
- League of American Theatres and Producers. "Park Theatre." *Internet Broadway Database,* copyright 2001-2006. www.ibdb.com/venue.asp?id=1554#Park%20Theatre1799. Accessed June 11, 2006.
- McConnell, Anita. "Angier March Perkins (1799-1881)" in *Oxford Dictionary of National Biography.* Oxford University Press, http://www.oxforddnb.com/view/article/21967. Updated 2004. Accessed June 13, 2005.
- Mernick, Philip. "Jettons [sic] or Reckoning Counters." London Coin Club. www.londoncoinclub.fsnet.co.uk/jetton/jetton.htm. Accessed September 18, 2005.
- Ministry of Foreign Affairs of Denmark. "Danish Orders of Chivalry." Washington, DC, March 17, 2006. http://www.ambwashington.um.dk/en/menu/informationaboutdenmark/culture/danishnationalsymbols/the+danish+orders+of+chivalry/danishordersofchivalry.htm. Accessed June 11, 2006.
- Muñoz, Miguel L.. "A Coin Called Peso" in *Perspectives in Numismatics.* Chicago Coin Club, copyright 1986. www.chicagocoinclub.org/projects/PiN/ccp.html. Accessed September 18, 2005.
- Ohio Historical Society. "Scioto Company" in *Ohio History Central: An Online Encyclopedia of Ohio History,* 2005. http://www.ohiohistorycentral.org/entry.php?rec=982. Accessed June 11, 2006. Related links, on same site, to:
  - "French Grant." http://www.ohiohistorycentral.org/entry.php?rec=721.
  - "Manasseh Cutler." http://www.ohiohistorycentral.org/entry.php?rec=60.
  - "Ohio Company of Associates." http://www.ohiohistorycentral.org/entry.php?rec=945.
  - "William Duer." http://www.ohiohistorycentral.org/entry.php?rec=107.
  - "William Playfair." http://www.ohiohistorycentral.org/entry.php?rec=304.
- Pitt, William. Published under "William Pitt's Defense of the American Colonies." Colonial Williamsburg, http://www.history.org/Almanack/life/politics/pitt.cfm. Originally published in HTML form by Dep. Alfa-Informatica, University of Groningen under the project, *The American Revolution*, 1995. Accessed September 24, 2005.
- Public Broadcasting System (PBS.) "Inside the Corps: To Equip an Expedition." http://www.pbs.org/lewisandclark. Accessed September 24, 2005.
- Roy, Ian. "Rupert, prince and count palatine of the Rhine and duke of Cumberland (1619–1682)" in *Oxford Dictionary of National Biography*, edited by Matthew, H. C. G. and Harrison, Brian. (Oxford: OUP, 2004.) Online ed., edited by Goldman, Lawrence. May 2006. http://www.oxforddnb.com/view/article/24281. Accessed November 2, 2006.
- Rushbrook, Nigel. "William Lawes, Composer at the Court of Charles I." October 20, 2002. http://www.canterburygreenman.fsnet.co.uk/WilliamLawes.htm, October 20, 2002. Accessed May 29, 2006.
- Scott, Carole E.. "America's Colonial Period," State University of West Georgia, Richards College of Business. www.westga.edu/~cscott/history/colonial.html. Accessed October 4, 2000.
- Sedwick, Dan. "The True "First Gold Coin of the Americas," Recovered from the "Tumbaga" Wreck, Circa 1528, Off Grand Bahama Island." Published under *Anything Anywhere.*, http://www.anythinganywhere.com/commerce/coins/tumbatxt1.htm. Accessed September 24, 2005.

- "Ships of Bermuda – 1600's." RootsWeb.com. http://www.rootsweb.com/~bmuwgw/ships2.html. The site references *Memorials of the Bermudas* by J. H. Lefroy, p.740. Accessed June 13, 2006.
- Silver Institute, The. "Silver Facts: History of Silver, New World Silver (1500-1875)." Washington, D.C. www.silverinstitute.org/facts/new_world.php. Accessed June 1, 2005.
- Sullivan, Robert B.. "Benjamin Rush" in *American National Biography Online.* February 2000. http://www.anb.org/articles/15/15-00926.html, Accessed September 10, 2006.
- Sylla, Richard. "National Debt" in *The Reader's Companion to American History.* Boston, Houghton Mifflin Company. http://college.hmco.com/history/readerscomp/rcah/html/rc_063100_nationaldebt.htm. Accessed June 1, 2005.
- Talbot, Henry William, *Leinster Express* proprietor. "Historical Account of the Castle of Lea, Queen's County." Published in 1832, as a booklet by Talbot. Reprinted on the website http://www.irishmidlandsancestry.com/content/laois/community/lea_castle.htm. Published courtesy of Teddy Fennelly. Accessed September 9, 2007.
- Turner, Frederick Jackson. "The Frontier in American History" in *American Studies.* University of Virginia. http://xroads.virginia.edu. Article created by Michael W. Kidd, 1996. Modified September 30, 1997. Accessed September 24, 2005. Taken from the 1921 edition published by Henry Holt and Company, New York.
- Van Beek, Bert. "Jetons: Their Use and History." *Perspectives in Numismatics.* Chicago Coin Club, 1986. www.chicagocoinclub.org/projects/PiN/juh.html. Accessed September 18, 2005.
- Wilson, James Grant; Fiske, John; and Klos, Stanley L., editors. "Henry William De Saussure" in *Appleton's Cyclopedia of American Biography.* New York, D. Appleton and Company, 1887-1889 and 1999. Copyrighted in 2000 by StanKlos.com. http://virtualology.com/aphenrywilliamsdesaussure/. Accessed September 15, 2006.
- Wilson, James Grant; Fiske, John; and Klos, Stanley L., editors. *Appleton's Cyclopedia of American Biography*, New York, D. Appleton and Company, 1887-1889 and 1999. Copyrighted in 2000 by StanKlos.com at the website. Accessed September 15, 2006. By topic:
  - "Henry William De Saussure." http://virtualology.com/aphenrywilliamdesaussure/.
  - "Robert Patterson." http://virtualology.com/aprobertpatterson/.
- Wright, Dudley. *The Builder*, 1921. Quoted in "The first recorded initiation in England." Grand Lodge of British Columbia and Yukon. http://freemasonry.bcy.ca/texts/moray_r.html, Accessed June 11, 2006.
- *Wolverhampton's Blue Plaques.* Wolverhampton History and Heritage Society. http://www.localhistory.scit.wlv.ac.uk/plaques/LichfieldStreet.htm. Accessed August 27, 2006.

ENDNOTES

---

[1] Bogue, Donald J.. *The Population of the United States, Historical Trends and Future Projections.* New York, The Free Press, a division of Macmillan, Inc., 1985, pp. 113 and 121.
[2] Miller, John C.. *Origins of the American Revolution.* Boston, Little, Brown and Company, 1943, p.4.
[3] Miller, John C. (5.)
[4] Miller, John C. (6.)
[5] Miller, John C.(7-8). Miller quotes from "The London Magazine," v.35, 1766, p.34.
[6] Miller, John C.(9)
[7] Currency Museum of the Bank of Canada. "Mexico, Gold Eight Escudos, 1799." http://collections.ic.gc.ca/bank/english/eaug80.htm. Accessed June 11, 2006.
[8] Silver Institute, The. "Silver Facts: History of Silver, New World Silver (1500-1875)." www.silverinstitute.org/facts/new_world.php. Washington, D.C.. Accessed June 1, 2005.
[9] Taylor, Alan. *American Colonies, The Settling of North America.* New York, Viking Penguin, first publication, 2001, p.63.
[10] Taylor (63.)
[11] Hume, Ivor Nöel. *A Guide to Artifacts of Colonial America.* Philadelphia, University of Pennsylvania Press. Originally published by Alfred A. Knopf, Inc., 1969, pp.154-174.
[12] Taylor (307.)
[13] Taylor (237.)
[14] Montgomery, David H.. *The Leading Facts of American History*, revised edition. Boston, Ginn and Company, 1910, p.50.
[15] Taylor (176-177.)
[16] Taylor (176-177.)
[17] Taylor (307-308.)
[18] Wood, Gordon S.. *The American Revolution, A History.* New York, The Modern Library, 2002, p.13.
[19] Miller, John C. (8.)
[20] Taylor (310.)
[21] Wood, Gordon S. (13.)
[22] Parker, Wyman W.. *Connecticut's Colonial and Continental Money.* The American Revolution Bicentennial Commission of Connecticut, Hartford, 1976, p.7.
[23] Wood, Gordon S. (13.)
[24] Scott, Carole E.. "America's Colonial Period." State University of West Georgia, Richards College of Business, www.westga.edu/~cscott/history/colonial.html. Accessed October 4, 2000.
[25] Wood, Gordon S. (17.)
[26] Dickerson, Oliver M.. *The Navigation Acts and the American Revolution.* Philadelphia, University of Pennsylvania Press, 1951, pp. 31-62.
[27] Dickerson (21-22.)
[28] Van Doren, Carl. *Benjamin Franklin*, New York, The Viking Press, 1938, p.321.
[29] Mace, William H.. Mace's School History of the United States. Illustrated by Colby, Homer, W., Dietzler, H. W. and Fink, Denman. Portraits by Reich, Jacques. Chicago, Rand, McNally and Company, 1904, p.140.
[30] Bogue (38.)
[31] Hawke, David Freeman. *Everyday Life in Early America.* New York, Harper and Row, 1988, p.73.
[32] Taylor (45, 306-307, 425-426.)
[33] Bogue (38)
[34] Taylor (311)
[35] Bruchey, Stuart, "Banking." *The Reader's Companion to American History* website, at http://college.hmco.com/history/readerscomp/rcah/html/ah_007500_banking.htm, Boston, Houghton Mifflin Company. Accessed June 1, 2005.
[36] Randall, Willard Sterne. *Alexander Hamilton, A Life*, New York, Harper Collins Publishers, 2003, p.52.
[37] Randall (52-53)

[38] Sylla, Richard. "National Debt." *The Reader's Companion to American History.* http://college.hmco.com/history/readerscomp/rcah/html/rc_063100_nationaldebt.htm, Boston, Houghton Mifflin Company. Accessed June 1, 2005.
[39] Ellis, Joseph J. *Founding Brothers, The Revolutionary Generation.* New York, Alfred A. Knopf, 2001, pp.72-74.
[40] Sylla.
[41] Sellers, Charles and May, Henry. *A Synopsis of American History*, Chicago, Rand McNally and Company, 2nd ed., 1969, p.82.
[42] Jefferson, Thomas, "The Vile Hamiltonian System," reprinted by Unger, Irwin and Tomes, Robert R., eds. *American Issues, A Primary Source Reader in United States History*, vol. 1, Upper Saddle River, New Jersey, Prentice Hall, 1999, pp.138-140.
[43] Irving, Washington. *Life of George Washington.* Illustrated Edition. In five volumes. New York, G.P. Putnam and Company, 1857 (I,) 1858 (II,) 1859 (III, IV.) Charles T. Evans and G.P. Putnam and Company, 1859 (V.) Jefferson engraving from vol. 5, p.30.
[44] Hamilton, Alexander, "The Second Report on Public Credit, December 13, 1790," reprinted in *American Issues* by Unger and Tomes, work cited above, pp.132-134.
[45] Bruchey.
[46] Smith, Richard Norton. *Patriarch, George Washington and the New American Nation*, New York, Houghton Mifflin, 1993, pp.218-225.
[47] Washington, George. "Farewell Address, 1796." Address edited by Richard B. Morris in: Boorstein, Daniel, editor. *An American Primer*, copyrighted in 1966 by the University of Chicago. Authorized reprint by Meridian (New York,) 1995, pp.211-229.
[48] Bruchey.
[49] Marshall, John. "McCulloch v. Maryland, 1819." Edited by Robert G. McCloskey in *An American Primer.* Edited by Boorstein, as cited above, pp. 258-273.
[50] Hawthorne, Nathaniel. *The Whole History of Grandfather's Chair or True Stories from New England History, 1620-1808.* First published in Boston, 1840, by E.P. Peabody, p.23.
[51] Massey, J. Earl. "Early Money Substitutes," in *Studies on Money in Early America*, Newman, Eric P., ed., and Doty, Richard, associate editor. New York, The American Numismatic Society, 1976, p.23.
[52] Parker (7.)
[53] Massey, "Early Money Substitutes," pp.23-24.
[54] Massey, "Early Money Substitutes," p.18
[55] Hothem, Lar. *Indian Trade Relics, Identification and Value*, Paducah, Kentucky, Collector Books, 2003, p.299.
[56] Massey, "Early Money Substitutes," p.20.
[57] Hawke (23.)
[58] Public Broadcasting System (PBS.) *Inside the Corps: To Equip an Expedition*, http://www.pbs.org/lewisandclark. Accessed September 24, 2005.
[59] Turner, Frederick Jackson. "The Significance of the Frontier in American History," edited by Billington, Ray Allen in *The Frontier Thesis: Valid Interpretation of American History?* New York, Holt, Reinhart and Winston, 1966, pp.9-20.
[60] Billington, Ray Allen, *Western Expansion, A History of the American Frontier*, 4th ed.. New York, Macmillan, 1974, pp.1-11.
[61] Taylor (311.)
[62] Billington, *Western Expansion*, p.42.
[63] Billington, *Western Expansion*, p.115.
[64] Billington, *Western Expansion*, pp.111-113.
[65] Billington, *Western Expansion*, p.385.
[66] Currency Museum of the Bank of Canada. *Trade Silver – The Beaver*, http://collections.ic.gc.ca/bank/english/eoct73.htm. Accessed June 11, 2006.
[67] Hothem (195-197.)
[68] Currency Museum of the Bank of Canada, *Trade Silver – The Beaver.*
[69] Booth, Russell H., Jr.. *The Tuscarwas Valley in Indian Days 1750-1797*, Cambridge, Ohio, Gomber House Press, 1994, pp.61-62, 153-155, 183-184, 264-269, et al.
[70] Taylor (94.)
[71] Taylor (96.)
[72] From Henry Wadsworth Longfellow's *Song of Hiawatha.*

[73] Beauchamp, William M.. *Wampum and Shell Articles Used by New York Indians*, Bulletin of the New York State Museum, no. 41, volume 8, March. Albany, New York, April, 1901, pp.336-349. Also, Hooker, Richard. *The Iroquois League* at *Cultures in America* website, Wisconsin State University, www.wsu.edu/~dee/CULAMRCA/IRLEAGUE.HTM, 1996. Updated June 6, 1999. Accessed September 24, 2005.
[74] Beauchamp (340-341.)
[75] Beauchamp (340-341.)
[76] Beauchamp (336-349, et al.)
[77] Beauchamp (338.)
[78] Beauchamp (332 and following.)
[79] Stearns, Robert E.C.. *Wampum and Dentalium, A Study of Native American Shell Money*, Hummelstown, Pennsylvania; Tucquan Publishing, 1999. Originally published in the 1887 Annual Report of the Board of Regents of the Smithsonian Institution as *A Study of Primitive Money,* pp.310-311.
[80] Beauchamp (332 and following.)
[81] Beauchamp (330-331.)
[82] Bradford, William. *Of Plymouth Plantation.* Edited by Samuel Eliot Morison. New York, Alfred A. Knopf, 1996, pp.202-203.
[83] Beauchamp (355.) Beauchamp quotes William Bradford's *History of the Plymouth Plantation*, Boston, 1856, (Massachusetts Historical Society Collections. 1856. Ser.4. 3:234)
[84] Stearns (309.)
[85] Beauchamp (350-351.)
[86] Gates, C. H.. *History* [of Wampum,] *Wampumworks*. Dunstable, Massachusetts, www.wampumworks.com. Updated January 7, 2004. Accessed July 25, 2004.
[87] Stearns (310.)
[88] Taylor (194.)
[89] Crosby, Sylvester Sage. *The Early Coins of America*, Boston, published by the author, 1875, pp.26-27.
[90] Beauchamp (351.)
[91] Beauchamp (351, et al.)
[92] Stearns (304-314.)
[93] Beauchamp (354-355.)
[94] Stearns (311.)
[95] Beauchamp (351.)
[96] Stearns (311.)
[97] Stearns (309.)
[98] Mossman, Philip L.. *Money of the American Colonies and Confederation, A Numismatic, Economic and Historical Correlation*, New York, The American Numismatic Society, 1993, p.43.
[99] Beauchamp (446.)
[100] Lewis, Meriwether. As edited by Moulton, Gary E., in *Meriwether Lewis and William Clark, An American Epic of Discovery, The Lewis and Clark Journals, The Abridgement of the Definitive Nebraska Edition*, copyrighted by the Board of Regents of the University of Nebraska, 2003, p.263.
[101] Parker (10.) Others.
[102] Parker (13-14.)
[103] Van Doren, Carl (102.)
[104] Van Doren (102.) Also, Brock, Dr. Leslie V., edited by Ron Michener, *The Colonial Currency, Prices and Exchange Rates*, Essays in History, vol. 34, Corcoran Dept. of History, University of Virginia, 1992, Published online at http://etext.lib.virginia.edu/journals/EH/EH34/brock34.htm. Accessed June 13, 2006.
[105] McCusker, John J.. "Colonial Paper Money" in *Studies on Money in Early America.* Newman, Eric P., editor and Doty, Richard, associate editor. New York, The American Numismatic Society, 1976, p. 100.
[106] McCusker (94.)
[107] McCusker (95.)
[108] Fryer, S. E. and Maloney, John. *Henry Dunning Macleod (1821-1902,)* Oxford Dictionary of National Biography, Oxford University Press, http://www.oxforddnb.com/view/article/34787. Accessed June 13, 2005.
[109] Brock.
[110] McCusker (94-104)
[111] McCusker (94-104)

[112] Brock.

[113] Crosby (228.)

[114] Anonymous pamphlet. *A Brief Account of the Rise, Progress and Present State of the Paper Currency of New England*, pamphlet, Boston, 1749. Published at The University of Virginia website, www.people.virginia.edu/~rwm3n/webdoc4.html. Updated January 15, 2000. Accessed June 13, 2006.

[115] Franklin, Benjamin. *A BRIEF ACCOUNT OF THE Rise, Progress, and Present State OF THE PAPER CURRENCY OF NEW-ENGLAND. And of the Measures taken by the Massachusetts Province, for establishing a Silver Currency for the Future. Together with some PROPOSALS for rendering those Measures more effectual*, 1729, University of Virginia website, www.people.virginia.edu/~rwm3n/webdoc4.html. Updated January 15, 2000. Accessed June 13, 2006.

[116] Newman, *The Early Paper Money of America*, p.12.

[117] Newman, *The Early Paper Money of America*, p.397.

[118] Newman, *The Early Paper Money of America*, p.19.

[119] Leone, Dr. Mark P., Director, Archaeology in Annapolis Project. Dr. Leone is a professor of anthropology at the University of Maryland. Personal email correspondence, December 14-29, 2006.

[120] Newman, *The Early Paper Money of America*, pp.19-20.

[121] Newman, *The Early Paper Money of America*, pp.151-162.

[122] Newman, *The Early Paper Money of America*, pp.151-162.

[123] Parker (38.)

[124] Newman, *The Early Paper Money of America*, p.478.

[125] Newman, *The Early Paper Money of America*, p.15.

[126] Langguth, A.J.. *Patriots, The Men Who Started the American Revolution*, New York, Touchstone/Simon & Schuster, 1988, pp.265-266.

[127] Ford, Worthington C., editor, entries of September 5, 1774 through December 31, 1779. *Journals of the Continental Congress, 1774-1789.* Washington, D.C., U.S. Government Printing Office, 1904-1937. V.2, pp.95-97, June 17, 1775. Library of Congress website at http://memory.loc.gov/cgi-bin/query/r?ammem/hlaw:@field(DOCID+@lit(jc00238)). Accessed June 12, 2006.

[128] Ford. *Journals of the Continental Congress, 1774-1789,* v.2, pp.105-106, June 23, 1775. Library of Congress website at http://memory.loc.gov/cgi-bin/query/r?ammem/hlaw:@field(DOCID+@lit(jc00243)). Accessed June 12, 2006.

[129] Van Doren (123.)

[130] Thomas, Isaiah.. *The History of Printing in America, With a Biography of Printers*, in two vols., Reprint of second edition (1874.) New York, Burt Franklin, 1967. Originally published in 1810, v.1, p.246, 256, et al.

[131] Thomas, v.1, pp.235, 256, 262, et al.

[132] Ford. *Journals of the Continental Congress, 1774-1789,* v.2, pp.220-222, July 29, 1775. Library of Congress website at http://memory.loc.gov/cgi-bin/query/r?ammem/hlaw:@field(DOCID+@lit(jc00274)). Accessed June 12, 2006. (Table built from text in the referenced document.)

[133] Newman, *The Early Paper Money of America*, p.58.

[134] Newman, *The Early Paper Money of America*, p.58.

[135] Ford. *Journals of the Continental Congress, 1774-1789,* v.2, p.407, December 5, 1775. Library of Congress website at http://memory.loc.gov/cgi-bin/query/r?ammem/hlaw:@field(DOCID+@lit(jc00364)). Accessed June 12, 2006.

[136] Newman, *The Early Paper Money of America*, pp.60-61.

[137] Newman, *The Early Paper Money of America*, pp.61-62.

[138] From a ca. 1865 print in the author's collection.

[139] Newman, *The Early Paper Money of America*, p.15.

[140] Newman, *The Early Paper Money of America*, pp.15,70-73.

[141] Nuxoll, Elizabeth M.. "A Generation of Numismatic Co-operation: Findings on the Notes and Coins of the Confederation Through the Papers of Robert Morris" in *American Journal of Numismatics*, Series 9. New York, The American Numismatic Society, 1997, pp.80-85.

[142] McConnell, Anita. *Angier March Perkins (1799-1881,)* Oxford Dictionary of National Biography, Oxford University Press, http://www.oxforddnb.com/view/article/21967. Updated 2004. Accessed June 13, 2005. (Angier March Perkins was the son of Jacob Perkins.)

[143] McConnell. Also, Bowers, Q. David. *The History United States Coinage as Illustrated by the Garrett Collection*, Los Angeles, Bowers & Ruddy Galleries, 1979, pp.151-153.

[144] Crosby (363-364.)

[145] Goodwin, Jason. *Greenback, The Almighty Dollar and the Invention of America*, New York, a John Macrae Book, Henry Holt and Company, 2003, pp.135-138. Also, McConnell.
[146] a.) Goodwin (135-138.)
b.) Bowers, *The History of United States Coinage as Illustrated by the Garrett Collection*, pp.151-153.
c.) McConnell.
[147] Doty, Richard. *America's Money, America's Story, A Comprehensive Chronicle of American Numismatic History*, Iola, Wisconsin, Krause Publications, 1998, pp.94-97.
[148] Doty, *America's Money, America's Story*, pp.94-97.
[149] Rulau, Russell. "Pre-Civil War (1812-1861) United States Treasury Notes" in *Standard Catalog of United States Paper Money*, 7th edition. By Chester L. Krause and Robert F. Lemke. Edited by Robert E. Wilhite. Iola, Wisconsin, Krause Publications, 1987, pp.149-150.
[150] Rulau, "Pre-Civil War (1812-1861) United States Treasury Notes," pp.150-151.
[151] Goodwin (191.)
[152] Schuckers, J.W.. *A Brief Account of the Finances and Paper Money of the Revolutionary War*. New York, Sanford J. Durst, 1978. Reprint. Originally published in Philadelphia by John Campbell & Son, in 1874, p.20.
[153] Houck, Louis. *A History of Missouri from the Earliest Explorations and Settlements Until the Admission of the State into the Union, vols. I-III*. Edited by Dale Van Everey. New York, Arno Press, 1971, p.307. Originally published in Chicago by R. R. Donnelley and Sons, in 1908. Also, Hancks, Larry. "The Emigrant Tribes: Wyandot, Delaware and Shawnee: A Chronology." Wyandot Nation of Kansas website, http://www.wyandot.org. Accessed September 24, 2005.
[154] From *Portrait Gallery of Eminent Men and Women of Europe and America*, in two volumes. By Duyckinck, Evert A.. New York, Johnson, Wilson and Company, 1873, vol. I, opposite p.192.
[155] Webster, Noah. *Webster's Universal Dictionary of the English Language*, Cleveland and New York, World Publishing Company, 1940, p.1530.
[156] Webster (1208.)
[157] Calligas, Eleni, ed.. Lobel, Richard, pub.. Davidson, Mark (hammered coinage) and Hailstone, Allen (milled coinage.) *Coincraft's 1999 Standard Catalogue of English and UK Coins 1066 to Date*. London, Coincraft, 1999, pp.445-452.
[158] Calligas (408.)
[159] Calligas (88-89.)
[160] Hume, Ivor Nöel. *In Search of This and That, Tales from an Archaeologist's Quest*, Williamsburg, Virginia, The Colonial Williamsburg Foundation, 3rd Printing, 1998, p.97.
[161] Fraser, Antonia. *The Lives of the Kings and Queens of England*, Berkeley and Los Angeles, University of California Press, 1998, pp.219-223.
[162] Fraser, *The Lives of the Kings and Queens of England*, pp.219-223.
[163] Fraser, *The Lives of the Kings and Queens of England*, p.226.
[164] Taylor (119-120.)
[165] Fraser, *The Lives of the Kings and Queens of England*, pp.223-233.
[166] Fraser, *The Lives of the Kings and Queens of England*, p.234.
[167] Evelyn, John. *The Diary of John Evelyn*, in two vols.. Rhys, Ernest, editor. London, J. M. Dent and Sons, 1930, v.1,p.358. Reprint of original 1907 edition. With a prefactory note by George W. E. Russell. Evelyn's comment on the return of Charles II.
[168] Bressett, Kenneth E.. *Collectible American Coins*, Lincolnwood, Illinois, Publications International, Ltd., 1991, p.143.
[169] Calligas (593.)
[170] Calligas (593.)
[171] Hume, *In Search of This and That*, p.59.
[172] Hume, *A Guide to Artifacts of Colonial America*, p.156.
[173] Hume, *In Search of This and That*, pp.55-56.
[174] Calligas (401-405.) Also, Bruce, Colin R., II, senior ed.. Krause, Chester L. and Mishler, Clifford. *Standard Catalog of World Coins, 17th Century*, 2nd edition, Iola, Wisconsin, Krause Publications, 1999, p. 904.
[175] Calligas (401-405.) Also, Bruce, *Standard Catalog of World Coins, 17th Century*, p. 904.
[176] Jordan, Louis. "Irish Copper Coins: Introduction" in *The Coins of Colonial and Early America*, http://www.coins.nd.edu/ColCoin/ColCoinIntros/Br-IrishCopper.intro.html. University of Notre Dame, Department of Special Collections, 1997 and following. Accessed September 23, 2005.

[177] Hume, *In Search of This and That*, p.56. Also, Mossman, *Money of the American Colonies and Confederation*, p.107.
[178] Mossman, Philip L.. *The Circulation of Irish Coinage in Pre-Federal America* in *The Colonial Newsletter* (ed. by Mossman) Hampton, Maine, The American Numismatic Society, vol. 39, no. 1, serial no. 110, April, 1999, p.1902.
[179] Fraser, *The Lives of the Kings and Queens of England*, pp.240-246.
[180] Hume, *A Guide to Artifacts of Colonial America*, p.165
[181] Fraser, *The Lives of the Kings and Queens of England*, pp.247-253.
[182] Fraser, *The Lives of the Kings and Queens of England*, pp.247-253.
[183] Fraser, *The Lives of the Kings and Queens of England*, pp.248-153.
[184] Fraser, *The Lives of the Kings and Queens of England*, p.257.
[185] Billington, *Westward Expansion*, pp.120-122.
[186] Billington, *Westward Expansion*, pp.120-122.
[187] Fraser, *The Lives of the Kings and Queens of England*, p.258.
[188] Fraser, *The Lives of the Kings and Queens of England*, p.268.
[189] Calligas (483.) Also, Fraser, *The Lives of the Kings and Queens of England*, pp.269-271.
[190] Fraser, *The Lives of the Kings and Queens of England*, p.271.
[191] Fraser, *The Lives of the Kings and Queens of England*, pp.272-275.
[192] Fraser, *The Lives of the Kings and Queens of England*, p.275.
[193] Fraser, *The Lives of the Kings and Queens of England*, pp.272-279.
[194] Alden, John Richard. *The American Revolution, 1775-1783*, New York, Harper and Brothers, 1954, p.3.
[195] Fraser, *The Lives of the Kings and Queens of England*, pp.280-287.
[196] Calligas (546.)
[197] Calligas (575.)
[198] Hume, *In Search of This and That*, p.60.
[199] Calligas (597-598.)
[200] Calligas (583, et al.)
[201] Greensword, Malachy (Mullhuland Ignatious Cobwright.) *A journey through the Monkolokian rain forests in search of the Spiney Fubbaduck*, second ed., Self-published in the U.K., 1993, p.3.
[202] Foster, Ed. *What Makes a Family?* Presentation to the annual meeting of C4, Boston, November 19, 2005.
[203] Greensword (3-4.)
[204] Greensword (3.)
[205] Jordan, Louis. "The Barbados Coppers 1788, 1792: Introduction" in *The Coins of Colonial and Early America*, http://www.coins.nd.edu/ColCoin/ColCoinIntros/Barbados.intro.html. University of Notre Dame, Department of Special Collections, 1997 and following. Accessed September 23, 2005.
[206] Jordan, Louis. "The Bermuda Copper of 1793: Introduction" in *The Coins of Colonial and Early America*, http://www.coins.nd.edu/ColCoin/ColCoinIntros/Bermuda.intro.html. University of Notre Dame, Department of Special Collections, 1997 and following. Accessed June 2, 2007.
[207] Jordan, Louis. "The Bahamas Copper of 1806 - Introduction" in *The Coins of Colonial and Early America*, http://www.coins.nd.edu/ColCoin/ColCoinIntros/Bahamas.intro.html. University of Notre Dame, Department of Special Collections, 1997 and following. Accessed September 23, 2005.
[208] Hume, *In Search of This and That*, p.57.
[209] Crosby (114.)
[210] Hume, *A Guide to Artifacts of Colonial America*, p.155.
[211] Doty, Richard. "English Merchant Tokens." Chicago Coin Club, 1986, http://www.chicagocoinclub.org/projects/PiN/emt.html. Accessed June 9, 2006. (Supplemented with observations on shifts in the eighteenth century English population, by this author.)
[212] Bruce, Colin R., II. *Standard Catalog of Mexican Coins, Paper Money, Stocks, Bonds and Medals*, Iola, Wisconsin, Krause Publications, 1981, pp.15-20.
[213] Bruce, *Standard Catalog of Mexican Coins*, pp.19-20.
[214] Reis, Rob. "Numismatics of the Conquest of Mexico," *World Coin News*, Iola Wisconsin, Krause Publications, May 1998. Also, Sedwick, Dan. "The True 'First Gold Coin of the Americas,' Recovered from the 'Tumbaga' Wreck, Circa 1528, Off Grand Bahama Island," Anything Anywhere website, http://www.anythinganywhere.com/commerce/coins/tumbatxt1.htm. Accessed September 24, 2005.
[215] Taylor (61.)
[216] Taylor (54.)

[217] Jordan, Louis. "Spanish Silver: General Introduction" in *The Coins of Colonial and Early America*, http://www.coins.nd.edu/ColCoin/ColCoinIntros/Sp-Silver.intro.html. University of Notre Dame, Department of Special Collections, 1997 and following. Accessed September 23, 2005. Also, Bruce, *Standard Catalog of Mexican Coins*, pp.5-26.

[218] Muñoz, Miguel L.. "A Coin Called Peso" at *Perspectives in Numismatics*. Chicago Coin Club, www.chicagocoinclub.org/projects/PiN/ccp.html, copyright 1986. Accessed September 18, 2005.

[219] a.) Bruce, *Standard Catalog of Mexican Coins*, pp.21-58.
b.) Bruce, *Standard Catalogs of World Coins*, 17th Century, various.
c.) Bruce, Colin R., II, senior ed.. Krause, Chester L. and Mishler, Clifford. *Standard Catalog of World Coins. 18th Century*, 2nd ed., Iola, Wisconsin, Krause Publications, 1997, various.

[220] Mossman, *Money of the American Colonies and Confederation*, p.56. Also, Jordan, Louis. "Spanish Colonial Cobs" in *The Coins of Colonial and Early America*, http://www.coins.nd.edu/ColCoin/ColCoinIntros/Sp-Cobs.intro.html. University of Notre Dame, Department of Special Collections, 1997 and following. Accessed September 23, 2005.

[221] Durant, Will and Ariel. *The Story of Civilization, Part VII, The Age of Reason Begins, A History of Civilisation in the Period of Shakespeare, Bacon, Montaigne, Rembrandt, Galileo and Descarte: 1558-1648*. New York, Simon and Schuster, 1961, p.288.

[222] Parker (7.) Crosby (31-32) quoted Massachusetts mintmaster, John Hull, who cited counterfeiting as the chief reason for establishing a mint.

[223] Crosby (227-228.)

[224] Mossman, *Money of the American Colonies and Confederation*, p.158.

[225] Muñoz.

[226] Mossman, *Money of the American Colonies and Confederation*, p.55.

[227] Goodwin (124.)

[228] Goodwin (123.)

[229] Tuchman, Barbara W.. *The First Salute*, New York, Ballentine Books, 1998, pp.30-34.

[230] Durant and Durant (476-478) and Tuchman (25-27.)

[231] Tuchman (28-29.)

[232] Tuchman (25-27.)

[233] Durant and Durant (476-477.)

[234] West, Willis Mason and Ruth. *The Story of Man's Early Progress*, Boston, Allyn and Bacon, 1934, pp.580-581. Also, Tuchman (25-29.)

[235] Brands, H. W.. *The First American: The Life and Times of Benjamin Franklin*, New York, Anchor Books, A Division of Random House, 2000, pp.43-44.

[236] O'Callaghan, E.B., ed.. *Documents Relative to the Colonial History of the State of New York; Procured in Holland, England and France by John Romeyn Brodhead*, vols. 3 (1853) and 4 (1854.) Albany, Weed, Parsons and Company, Printers. V.4, pp.669. Letter from the Earl of Bellmont to the Lords of Trade, June 22, 1700.

[237] Mossman, *Money of the American Colonies and Confederation*, pp.53-54.

[238] Taylor (256-257.)

[239] Tuchman (5.)

[240] Jaenen, Cornelius J.. *French Expansion in North America* at *The History Teacher* website, University of Ottawa, vol. 34, no. 2, www.historycooperative.org/journals/ht/34.2/jaenen.html, par.14. Accessed June 13, 2006.

[241] Fraser, *The Lives of the Kings and Queens of England*, p.99, et al.

[242] Fraser, *The Lives of the Kings and Queens of England*, pp.123-127, et al

[243] West and West (538.) Also, Fraser, *The Lives of the Kings and Queens of England*, pp.130-133, et al.

[244] Durant and Durant (370-373.)

[245] Tapié, Victor-L.. *France in the Age of Louis XIII and Richelieu*, New York, Preager Publishers, 1975, pp.3-11, 428-438, et al.)

[246] De Gramont, Sanche. *Epitaph for Kings, the Long and Splendid Decline of the French Monarchy and the Coming of the Revolution*, New York, G. P. Putnam's Sons, 1967, pp.43-54.

[247] De Gramont (49.)

[248] De Gramont (72-74 and 141.)

[249] De Gramont (167.)

[250] Jaenen, par. 1.

[251] Billington, *Westward Expansion*, p.42.
[252] Billington, *Westward Expansion*, p.41.
[253] Jaenen, par. 2.
[254] Jaenen, par. 3.
[255] Taylor (94.)
[256] Billington, *Westward Expansion*, pp.43-47.
[257] Billington, *Westward Expansion*, pp.111-113.
[258] De Gramont (44-45.)
[259] West and West (574-577.)
[260] Cantwell, Anne-Marie and Wall, Diana di Zerega. *Unearthing Gotham, The Archeology of New York City*. New Haven, Connecticut and London, Yale University Press, 2001, pp.154-155.
[261] Durant and Durant (456-457.)
[262] Van Beek, Bert. "Jetons: Their Use and History," *Perspectives in Numismatics*, Chicago Coin Club, 1986, www.chicagocoinclub.org/projects/PiN/juh.html. Accessed September 18, 2005. Others.
[263] Mernick, Philip. *Jettons* [sic] *or Reckoning Counters*, London Coin Club, www.londoncoinclub.fsnet.co.uk/jetton/jetton.htm. Accessed September 18, 2005.
[264] Durant and Durant (484-487), et al.
[265] Grassl, Gary C.. *First Germans at Jamestown* at The German Heritage Society of Greater Washington, D.C. website, www.serve.com/shea/germusa/jtown1a.html. Accessed September 18, 2005.
[266] Grassl.
[267] Bowers, *The History of United States Coinage as Illustrated by the Garrett Collection*, p.161.
[268] Brands (335.)
[269] Kleeberg, John M.. "The New Yorke in America Token" in *Money of Pre-Federal America*, Kleeberg, John M., ed.. New York, American Numismatic Society, 1992, pp.15-57. Coinage of the Americas Conference, Proceedings no. 7. Held at the American Numismatic Society, May 4, 1991.
[270] Jordan, Louis and Williams, Ray. Presentation to the 2006 convention of C4. Boston, December 2, 2006.
[271] Pope, Peter E. *Fish into Wine: The Newfoundland Plantation in the Seventeenth Century*. Asheville, North Carolina, The University of North Carolina Press, 2004, pp.4-7, 54, et al.
[272] Pope (82-83, 132, et al.)
[273] Pope (7,87, et al.)
[274] Pope (278.)
[275] Jordan, Louis and Williams, Ray. Presentation to the 2006 convention of C4. Boston, December 2, 2006. Williams demonstrated the ease with which musket balls could be flattened with a hammer and anvil.
[276] Pope (266-267.)
[277] Forbes, Keith Archibald. *Bermuda's History from 1500 to 1699, How it relates to the United States of America, United Kingdom and Canada*, The Royal Gazette's Bermuda Online website, www.bermuda-online.org/history. Updated June 8, 2006. Accessed June 8, 2006. Also, Bowers, Q. David. *The Garrett Collection, Part 3*. Los Angeles, Bowers and Ruddy Galleries, 1980, p.10. Bowers quotes John Smith from *The General History of Virginia, New England and the Sommer Isles*.
[278] Bowers, *The Garrett Collection, Part 3*, p.10. Also, Crosby (11-24.)
[279] Forbes, Keith Archibald.
[280] Breen, Walter. *Complete Encyclopedia of U.S. and Colonial Coins*, New York, Doubleday, 1988, p.9.
[281] Vlack, Robert A.. *Early American Coins*, Johnson City, New York, Windsor Research Publications, 2nd ed., 1965, p.12.
[282] Forbes, Keith Archibald.
[283] Forbes, Keith Archibald.
[284] Forbes, Keith Archibald.
[285] Bowers, *The Garrett Collection, Part 3*, p.10.
[286] Forbes, Keith Archibald.
[287] Crosby (18.)
[288] Crosby (17-18.)
[289] This estimate is derived from Breen (*Complete Encyclopedia of U.S. and Colonial Coins*, p.10,) who knew of about fifty pieces and Hume (*In Search of This and That*, p.56,) who knew of a fifteen piece 'hoard' that surfaced after Breen's book was published. In 1875, Crosby (17-18) knew of only four examples, three shillings and one sixpence.
[290] Hume, *In Search of This and That*, p.56.

[291] Crosby (12.)
[292] Hume, *In Search of This and That*, p.56.
[293] Crosby (17-18.)
[294] Breen, *Complete Encyclopedia of U.S. and Colonial Coins*, pp.10-11.
[295] Warner, Charles Dudley. *Captain John Smith.* Electronic version published by Outrigger Publishing, LLC, 2002, p.209. Originally published by the author in New York, in 1881.
[296] Billington, *Westward Expansion*, pp.49-50.
[297] Barry, John Stetson. *The History of Massachusetts, The Colonial Period.* Boston, Phillips, Sampson and Company, 1855. pp.129, 164-165 and 174-175. Also, Billington, *Westward Expansion*, pp.69-70.
[298] Barry (181-183.)
[299] Barry (194-195.) Also, Bennett, Ross, editor. *Visiting Our Past: America's Historylands*, revised edition, Washington, National Geographic Society, 1986, pp.62-65.
[300] Billington, *Westward Expansion*, pp.70-72.
[301] Barry (318-320.)
[302] Mossman, *Money of the American Colonies and Confederation,* pp.56, 69 and 79.
[303] Jordan, Louis. *John Hull, the Mint and the Economics of Massachusetts Coinage.* C4 Publications, The Colonial Coin Collectors Club. Distributed by University Press of New England, Hanover and London, 2002, pp.1-3.
[304] Clarke, Hermann Frederick. *John Hull, A Builder of the Bay Colony*, Wolfeboro, New Hampshire, A.W. Pollock & Company, 1993, p.30. Originally copyrighted by Clarke in 1940 and published by The Southworth-Anthoensen Press (Portland, Maine).
[305] Jordan, *John Hull, The Mint and the Economics of Massachusetts Coinage*, p.129.
[306] Jordan, *John Hull, The Mint and the Economics of Massachusetts Coinage*, p.17.
[307] Jordan, *John Hull, The Mint and the Economics of Massachusetts Coinage*, p.130.
[308] Crosby (32.)
[309] Newman, Eric P.. Forward to Noe, Sydney, *The Silver Coinage of Massachusetts*. Lawrence, Massachusetts, Quarterman Publications, Inc., 1973. Copyrighted by The American Numismatic Society in 1943 and 1947, p.vii.
[310] Crosby (42.)
[311] Crosby(40.)
[312] Newman, forward to Noe's *The Silver Coinage of Massachusetts,* p.viii.
[313] Hawthorne (23.)
[314] Jordan, *John Hull, The Mint and the Economics of Massachusetts Coinage*, Chapter 8. Also, Hodder, Stack's sale of the John J. Ford Collection, Part XII, p.9.
[315] Vlack, *Early American Coins*, p.14.
[316] Newman, forward to Noe's *The Silver Coinage of Massachusetts,* p.viii.
[317] Skalbe, James E.. "The Dating and Emission Sequence of the Oak and Pine Tree Coinage of Massachusetts Bay" in *The C4 Newsletter*, Vol. 3, No. 1, March, 1995, pp.19-23.
[318] Hodder, Michael J.. Stack's auction of the John J. Ford Collection, Part XII, October 18, 2005. New York, October 15, 2005, p.9.
[319] Hodder, Stack's sale of the John J. Ford Collection, Part XII, p.9.
[320] Crosby (83-84.)
[321] Clarke (various.)
[322] Mossman, *Money of the American Colonies and Confederation,* pp.88.
[323] Breen, *Complete Encyclopedia of U.S. and Colonial Coins*, p.12.
[324] Jordan, *Hull, The Mint and the Economics of Massachusetts Coinage*, pp.68-69.
[325] Jordan, "Massachusetts Bay Silver 1652-1682" in *The Coins of Colonial and Early America*, http://www.coins.nd.edu/ColCoin/ColCoinIntros/MASilver.intro.html. University of Notre Dame, Department of Special Collections, 1997 and following. Accessed September 23, 2005.
[326] Crosby (70-71 and 79.)
[327] Jordan, Louis. "Massachusetts Bay Silver 1652-1682."
[328] Noe (6.)
[329] Crosby (36.)
[330] Crosby (42.)
[331] Noe (6.)

---

[332] Jordan, *John Hull, The Mint and the Economics of Massachusetts Coinage*, pp.86.
[333] Jordan, Louis. "Willow Tree Coinage: Introduction" in *The Coins of Colonial and Early America*, http://www.coins.nd.edu/ColCoin/ColCoinIntros/WillowTree.intro.html. University of Notre Dame, Department of Special Collections, 1997 and following. Accessed September 23, 2005.
[334] Jordan, *John Hull, The Mint and the Economics of Massachusetts Coinage*, pp.86-87. Also, Doty, "Making Money in Massachusetts," in *Money of Pre-Federal America*, ed. by Kleeberg, pp.2-14.
[335] Jordan, *Willow Tree Coinage: Introduction*. Jordan quotes Michael Hodder's letter to the C4 Newsletter, vol. 4, no. 2, p.20.
[336] Jordan, *John Hull, The Mint and the Economics of Massachusetts Coinage*, pp.26-35. Others.
[337] Breen, *Complete Encyclopedia of U.S. and Colonial Coins*, p.12.
[338] Jordan, *John Hull, The Mint and the Economics of Massachusetts Coinage*, p.89.
[339] Hodder, Stack's sale of the John J. Ford Collection, Part XII, p.45.
[340] Hawthorne (24.)
[341] Newman, "The Secret of the Good Samaritan Shilling." Extracted in Noe, p.204 and following.
[342] Crosby (74.)
[343] Hodder, "Maryland Coinage Short-Lived," p.10.
[344] Hodder, "Maryland Coinage Short-Lived," p.10.
[345] Breen, *Complete Encyclopedia of U.S. and Colonial Coins*, p.18.
[346] Breen, *Complete Encyclopedia of U.S. and Colonial Coins*, p.18.
[347] Hodder, "Maryland Coinage Short-Lived," p.10.
[348] Hodder, "Maryland Coinage Short-Lived," p.10.
[349] Bowers, Q. David. *The Garrett Collection, Part 3*, p.21.
[350] Breen, *Complete Encyclopedia of U.S. and Colonial Coins*, p.18.
[351] Breen, *Complete Encyclopedia of U.S. and Colonial Coins*, p.18.
[352] Hodder, Michael J.. "Pedigree Updates of Calvert Coinage Result of Research" *Coin World*. Sidney, Ohio, Amos Press, vol. 34, issue 1737, July 26, 1993, pp.10,12.
[353] Derived from Hodder, "Pedigree Updates of Calvert Coinage Result of Research," pp.10,12 (five pieces.) Updated with the rumored find of "between three and seven" pieces confirmed by a reliable, but presently anonymous source.
[354] Breen, *Complete Encyclopedia of U.S. and Colonial Coins*, p.19.
[355] a.) Maris, Edward. *A Historic Sketch of the Coins of New Jersey*. Lawrence, Massachusetts, Quarterman Publications, 1978. Originally printed in 1881 by William K. Bellows of Philadelphia, pp. 3-4.
b.) Stewart, Frank H.. *Mark Newby: The First Banker in New Jersey and His Patrick Halfpence* (booklet.) Copyrighted in 1947 by Stewart and reprinted in 2001 by The Gloucester County Historical Society in Woodbury, New Jersey, pp. 13-14.
c.) Breen, Walter. *Complete Encyclopedia of U.S. and Colonial Coins*, New York, Doubleday, 1988, p.34.
d.) Hardin, Clifford, editor. "William Newby Family." Posted by Larry Bell in the Quaker-Roots-L Archives, January 26, 2000. RootsWeb.com, http://archiver.rootsweb.com/th/read/QUAKER-ROOTS/2000-01/0948871486. Accessed May 29, 2006.
[356] Hardin.
[357] Tallow chandler tradition from:
a.) Maris, pp.3-4.
b.) Stewart, pp.13-14.
c.) Breen, p.34.
d.) Others.
Merchant view from personal conversations with Roger Siboni, Vicken Yegparian and David Gladfelter at the 2006 American Numismatic Society Coinage of the America's Conference, *Newby's St. Patrick Coinage*. New York, November 11, 2006.
[358] a.) From an affidavit of Thomas Sharp. Quoted by Stewart in *Mark Newby: The First Banker in New Jersey and His Patrick Halfpence,* p.14.
b.) Greaves, Richard L.. *Dublin's Merchant-Quaker, Anthony Sharp and the Community of Friends, 1643-1707*, Stanford, California, Stanford University Press, 1998, pp.97-98.
c.) Pomfret, John E.. *Colonial New Jersey, A History of the American Colonies in Thirteen Volumes*, ed. by Milton M. Klein and Jacob E. Cooke, New York, Charles Scribner and Sons, 1973, p.40.
[359] Stewart, *Mark Newby: The First Banker in New Jersey and His Patrick Halfpence*, p.10.
[360] Maris (3-4.)
[361] Stewart, *Mark Newby: The First Banker in New Jersey and His Patrick Halfpence,* p.16.

[362] Breen, *Complete Encyclopedia of U.S. and Colonial Coins*, p.34.
[363] Mossman, *Money of the American Colonies and Confederation,* p.128.
[364] Siboni, Yegparian and Gladfelter, 2006 C.O.A.C. conference, as cited.
[365] Massey, J. Earl. *America's Money, The Story of Our Coins and Currency.* New York, Thomas Y. Crowell Company, 1968, p.48.
[366] Breen, *Complete Encyclopedia of U.S. and Colonial Coins*, p.136.
[367] Mossman, *Money of the American Colonies and Confederation,* pp.126-129.
[368] Stephens, Stan. Private correspondence and telephone conversations, April through November, 2005.
[369] Mossman, *Money of the American Colonies and Confederation,* p.128.
[370] Breen, *Complete Encyclopedia of U.S. and Colonial Coins*, pp.34-36.
[371] Breen, *Complete Encyclopedia of U.S. and Colonial Coins*, pp.34-36.
[372] Mossman, 2006 C.O.A.C. conference, as cited.
[373] Leyburn, James G., *The Scotch Irish, A Social History*, Chapel Hill, The University of North Carolina Press, 1962, pp.105-125.
[374] a.) Maris, p.4.
b.) Crosby, p.136.
c.) Smith, Dr. Aquilla. "On the Copper Coin Commonly Called St. Patrick's" in *Proceedings and Transactions of the Kilkenny and South-East of Ireland Archaeological Society.* Kilkenny, Ireland, Kilkenny and South-East of Ireland Archaeological Society, 1854, Part 1, p.67.
[375] Discovered by Jim LaSarre and posted to the Colonial Numismatics online discussion group by Dave Wnuck on March 28, 2006. The writing comes from Sharp's "Treatise on English coins and their history...Section Of the Irish Coins."
[376] Smith, Dr. Aquilla, pp.67-68.
[377] With regard to Harris, Dr. Aquilla Smith is referring to *The Whole Works of Sir James Ware Concerning Ireland.* Edited by Walter Harris. Dublin, 1745.
[378] Dolley, Michael. "The Irish coinage [sic,] 1534-1691," Chapter 16 of *A New History of Ireland*, edited by T.W. Moody, F.X. Martin and F.J. Byrne, v.3, "Early Modern Ireland." Oxford, The Clarendon Press, 1976, p.417.
[379] Mossman, *Money of the American Colonies and Confederation,* p.125.
[380] Danforth, Dr. Brian J.. "Part 1: St. Patrick Coinage" and "Part 2: Lord Ormond's National Coinage." The Colonial Newsletter, serial no. 121, pp.2371-2402.
[381] Smith, Dr. Aquilla (68, 72.)
[382] Gillispie, Charles C.. *A Diderot Pictorial Encyclopedia of Trades and Industry, 485 Plates Selected from L'Encyclopedie of Denis Diderot*, v.1. New York, Dover Publications, 1993, plate 206.
[383] a.) Smith, Dr. Aquilla (68.)
b.) Crosby (136.)
c.) Maris (4.)
[384] Smith, Dr. Aquilla (69.)
[385] Maris (4.) With regard to Simon, Maris is referring to J. Simon's *An Essay Towards an Historical Account of Irish Coins, and of the Currency of Foregin (sic) Monies in Ireland With an Appendix: Containing Several Statutes, Proclamations, Patents, Acts of State, and Letters relating to the Same.* Dublin, 1749.
[386] Smith, Dr. Aquilla (69, 74.)
[387] Maris (4.) With regard to Leake, Maris is referring to Stephen Martin Leake's *Nummi Britannici Historia: or an historical account of English money, from the Conquest to the uniting of the two Kingdoms by King James I and of Great-Britain to the present time. With particular descriptions of each piece, and illustrated with cuts of the more antient. A work hitherto unattempted. Necessary for all those that would have any knowledge of this useful part of antiquity; but particularly calculated for the benefit of the curious collector of English coin.* London, W. Meadows, 1726.
[388] Crosby (136-137.)
[389] Breen, *Complete Encyclopedia of U.S. and Colonial Coins*, pp.33-37. Also, Crosby, Sylvester Sage. *The Early Coins of America.* Boston, published by the author, 1875, p.136.
[390] a.) Crosby (136-137.)
b.) D'Alton, E.A.. "Giovanni Battista Rinuccini." Transcribed by Nicolette Ormsbee. *The Catholic Encyclopedia*, vol. 13. Robert Appleton Company (1912.) Online edition: K. Knight (2003, 2006.) http://www.newadvent.org/cathen/13061a.htm. Accessed October 13, 2006.
c.) Stephens, as cited.

[391] First mutually observed during a personal conversation with Stan Stephens, April 2005.

[392] Talbot, Henry William, Leinster Express proprietor. Historical Account of the Castle of Lea, Queen's County. Published in 1832, as a booklet by Talbot. Reprinted on the website http://www.irishmidlandsancestry.com/content/laois/community/lea_castle.htm courtesy of Teddy Fennelly, former editor of the Leinster Express. Accessed September 9, 2007.

[393] Breen, *Complete Encyclopedia of U.S. and Colonial Coins*, p.34.

[394] Karp, Abraham J.. "From the Ends of the Earth: Judaic Treasures of the Library of Congress," Washington, D.C., Library of Congress, 1991. *The Judaic Treasures of the Library of Congress: The Antwerp Bible Illustrations*, at the Jewish Virtual Library website, http://www.jewishvirtuallibrary.org/jsource/loc/Antwerp.html, Accessed May 10, 2006..

[395] Hoover, Oliver D.. Personal email correspondence, May 3-4, 2006. Hoover credits Michael J. Hodder with the discovery of the similarities.

[396] Hoover, personal correspondence. Hoover credits Michael Hodder with discovery of the St. Patrick's similarities with the gold quadrupla scudo d'oro (four escudo) coin.

[397] Breen, *Complete Encyclopedia of U.S. and Colonial Coins*, pp.33-35.

[398] Hoover, as cited.

[399] Personal conversation with Dr. Brian J. Danforth, 2006 C.O.A.C., as previously cited.

[400] Withers, George. *Collection of Emblems: Ancient and Modern (1635)*, Kessinger Publishing, 2004. Originally published by Withers in London, p.65.

[401] Rushbrook, Nigel. *William Lawes, Composer at the Court of Charles I*, http://www.canterburygreenman.fsnet.co.uk/WilliamLawes.htm, October 20, 2002. Accessed May 29, 2006..

[402] Breen, *Complete Encyclopedia of U.S. and Colonial Coins*, p.35.

[403] Danforth, "The St. Patrick Coinage," pp.2371-2402.

[404] Coonan, Thomas L.. *The Irish Catholic Confederacy and the Puritan Revolution*, (Dublin: Clonmore and Reynolds and New York: Columbia University Press, 1954,) p.146.

[405] Smith, Dr. Aquilla (69.)

[406] Carte, Thomas. *History of the Life of James, Duke of Ormonde; containing an account of the most remarkable affairs of his time, and particularly of Ireland under his government: With an appendix and a Collection of Letters*, 3 vols. (London, 1735-36). Second ed., 6 vols. (Oxford, 1851). Electronic edition in three volumes from TannerRitchie Publishing, Burlington, Ontario, 2005. Coonan notes: "A main source of information for Irish affairs 1641-1649 and for the Protestant and royalist side of the Irish War. I have used both editions." In addition, *A Collection of Original Letters and Papers Concerning Affairs of England, 1641-60, found among the Duke of Ormonde's Papers*, 2 vols. (London, 1739.) Originals among the Carte Manuscripts in the Bodleian Library.

[407] The referenced work is: Bellings, Richard. *History of the Irish Confederation and the War in Ireland. With Correspondence and Documents of the Confederation and of the Administrators of the English Government in Ireland. Contemporary Personal Statements, Memoirs, etc.*. Edited by Sir John T. Gilbert, 7 vols. (Dublin, 1882-91.) Here Coonan notes, "Invaluable documentary material. It is referred to in the notes as Bellings." Elsewhere, Coonan quotes: Kavanaugh, Stanislaus, Coimisiun Laimhscribhinni na h-Eireann (Irish Manuscripts Commission), *Commentarius Rinuccinianus de Sedis Apostolicae Legatione ad Foederatos Hibernniae Catholicos per annos 1645-1649. Florentiae opus susceperunt atque absolverunt per annos 1661-1669*. Fr. Pater Richardus (Barnabus O'Farrell) Longfordensis, Fr. Pater Robertus (Daniel O'Connell,) *Desmondensis uterque e provincia Hibernica Ordinis Min.Capuccinorum*, ed., O.M.Cap., 6 vols. (Dublin, 1932-1949.) Coonan notes: "It is referred to in the notes as Com. Rin."

[408] See the *Access to Archives* website, at http://www.a2a.org.uk, Accessed June 1, 2006.

[409] Obtained through The Bodleian Library, Special Collections and Western Manuscripts. Reference: MS. Carte 60, fol. 89. November, 1664.

[410] Meade-Fetherstonhaugh, Margaret and Warner, Oliver. *Uppark [sic] and Its People*. London, George Allen and Unwin, Ltd., 1964, p.16.

[411] Donagan, Barbara. "Ford, Sir Edward (bap. 1605, d. 1670)," in *Oxford Dictionary of National Biography*, ed. H. C. G. Matthew, H. C. G. and Harrison, Brian. Oxford: OUP, 2004, http://www.oxforddnb.com/view/article/9855. Accessed October 9, 2006.

[412] "Harting" in *A History of the County of Sussex: Volume 4: The Rape of Chichester (1953)*, pp. 10-21.. At http://www.british-history.ac.uk/report.asp?compid=41687&strquery=south%20harting. (British History Online website, Victoria County History.) Accessed: October 12, 2006.

[413] "Harting." British History Online website.

[414] Donagan. Also, Erskine-Hill, Howard "Caryll, John, Jacobite first Baron Caryll of Durford (bap. 1626, d. 1711)," in *Oxford Dictionary of National Biography*, ed. by Matthew, H. C. G. and Harrison, Brian. (Oxford: OUP, 2004), http://www.oxforddnb.com/view/article/4847. Accessed October 9, 2006.

[415] Donagan. Also, Erskine-Hill.

[416] a.) Wood, Anthony and Bliss, Philip, *Athenae Oxoniensis. An Exact History of all the Writers and Bishops who have had their Education in the University of Oxford. To Which are Added the Fasti, or Annals of the Said University. A New Edition, with Additions, and a Continuation by Philip Bliss.* (London: printed for F. C. and J. Rivington an others, 1817,) vol. III, p. 906.
b.) Ford, Sir Edward. "Experimental Proposals how the King may have Money to Pay and Maintain his Fleets, With Ease to his People; London may be rebuilt, and all Proprietors; Money to be lent at Six per Cent. On Pawns; and the Fishing-Trade set up, which alone is able and sure to enrich us all. And all this without Altering, Straining, or Thwarting any of our Laws or Customs now in Use." London, 1666. Printed by William Godbid. The document appears in its entirety in *The Harleian Miscellany, A Collection of Scarce, Curious and Entertaining Pamphlets and Tracts, As Well in Manuscript as in Print.* The collection was selected from the library of Edward Harley, second earl of Oxford. An edition annotated by William Oldys and Thomas Park was printed in London, in 1809, for White and Company, John Murray and John Harding. Ford's document is included in its entirety in the Harleian Miscellany, v.4, pp.195-196.

[417] Donagan.

[418] Pepys, Samuel. *The Diary of Samuel Pepys, eleven volumes.* Edited by Latham, Robert and Mathews, William. Berkeley and Los Angeles, University of California Press, 1971. Entry of September 13, 1664.

[419] Pepys, entry of September 22, 1663.

[420] "My Lord" probably refers to the Earl of Sandwich. Mr. Coventry refers to Francis Coventry (or Coventrie.) Pepys also mentions Mr. [William] Creed.

[421] Pepys, v.4., pp.365-366.

[422] Pepys (i.e., Latham and Matthews,) footnote to the above.

[423] Roy, Ian. "Rupert, prince and count palatine of the Rhine and duke of Cumberland (1619–1682)" In *Oxford Dictionary of National Biography*, edited by Matthew, H. C. G. and Harrison, Brian. (Oxford: OUP, 2004.) Online ed., edited by Goldman, Lawrence. May 2006. http://www.oxforddnb.com/view/article/24281. Accessed November 2, 2006.

[424] Latham and Matthews, loc. cit.. Latham and Matthews reference J. R. Elder, Royal Fishery Companies, pp. 102 and 105.

[425] Everett, Mary Anne, editor. *Calendar of state papers, Domestic series, of the reign of Charles II, Preserved in the state paper department of Her Majesty's Public Record Office.* London, Longman, Green, Longman and Roberts, 1860 and following, p.439, entries of January 4, 1667.

[426] Pepys, entry of December 3, 1664.

[427] Wood, Anthony (906.) Also, Jenkins, Rhys. "A Chapter in the History of the Water Supply of London: and Sir Edward Ford's Patent from Cromwell," Transactions of the Newcomen Society, 1928.

[428] Donagan.

[429] Wood, Anthony (906.)

[430] Meade-Fetherstonhaugh and Warner (52.)

[431] Reading of Sir Edward Ford's will by the Essex Record Office, at the request of this author, March, 2006.

[432] Dahl, Roald, writer. Stuart, Mel, director. Movie: *Willy Wonka and the Chocolate Factory.* David L. Wolper Productions, 1971.

[433] Gardner, Laurence. *Bloodline of the Holy Grail, The Hidden Lineage of Jesus Revealed.* Shaftesbury, Dorset (England,) Element Books Limited, 1996, pp.1-3.

[434] Gardner (132-140.)

[435] Gardner (214-215.)

[436] Gardner (134, 160-163.)

[437] Wright, Dudley. *The Builder*, 1921. Quoted in *The first recorded initiation in England.* Grand Lodge of British Columbia and Yukon, http://freemasonry.bcy.ca/texts/moray_r.html, Accessed June 11, 2006. Quoting an entry in John Evelyn's diary, July 19, 1670: "I accompanied my worthy friend, that excellent man, Sir Robert Murray [Moray,] with Mr. Slingsby, Master of the Mint, to see the latter's seat and estate at Barrow-Green in Cambridgeshire." Also, Robertson, Alexander. *The Life of Sir Robert Moray, Soldier, Statesman and Man of Science*, London, Longmans, Green and Company, 1922, p.163, n.2.

[438] Rhys, v.1, p.375 (Evelyn with Slingsby,) pp.388,393,398 (with Ormond,) p.396 (with Moray,) et al.

---

[439] Wright, Dudley. *The Builder*, 1921. Quoted in *The first recorded initiation in England.* Grand Lodge of British Columbia and Yukon, http://freemasonry.bcy.ca/texts/moray_r.html, Accessed June 11, 2006. Quoting an entry in John Evelyn's diary, July 19, 1670: "I accompanied my worthy friend, that excellent man, Sir Robert Murray [Moray,] with Mr. Slingsby, Master of the Mint, to see the latter's seat and estate at Barrow-Green in Cambridgeshire." Also, Robertson, Alexander. *The Life of Sir Robert Moray, Soldier, Statesman and Man of Science*, London, Longmans, Green and Company, 1922, p.163, n.2.

[440] Gardner (320-322.)

[441] Meehan, Bernard. *The Book of Kells*. London, Thames and Hudson, Ltd., 1994. Reprinted 1999, pp.10-14.

[442] Meehan (138.)

[443] Meehan (68-69.)

[444] Stewart, *Mark Newby: The First Banker in New Jersey and His Patrick Halfpence,* p.11.

[445] Stewart, *Mark Newby: The First Banker in New Jersey and His Patrick Halfpence*, p.11.

[446] Lorenzo, John. series of postings to the Colonial Coins Yahoo discussion group, Digests 2454, 2472, 2474, 2475, 2485, 2487 and 2707, May 21, 2005 to October 7, 2005.

[447] Greaves, Richard L. (various.)

[448] Jordan, Louis. "The American Plantation Token of 1688: Introduction*"* in *The Coins of Colonial and Early America*, http://www.coins.nd.edu/ColCoin/ColCoinIntros/AmPlant.intro.html. University of Notre Dame, Department of Special Collections, 1997 and following. Accessed September 23, 2005.

[449] Breen, C*omplete Encyclopedia of U.S. and Colonial Coins*, p.21.

[450] Rinaldo, Tom. Yesteryear Coins fixed price list. Bolinas, California, July, 1993, item number 179.

[451] Newman, Eric P.. "The James III 1/24th Real for the American Plantations" in *Museum Notes 11* (1964,) p.324, as quoted by Louis Jordan, *The American Plantations Token of 1688: Introduction.*

[452] Jordan, "The American Plantations Token of 1688: Introduction."

[453] Jordan, "The American Plantations Token of 1688: Introduction."

[454] Hume, *In Search of This and That*, p.58.

[455] Crosby (337,) quoting Snelling who wrote in 1769 that "God Preserve..." referred to the plague.

[456] Steimle, Frank. "A Tricentennial Review and Comments on 'God Preserve...' Elephant Tokens" in *The Colonial Newsletter*, vol. 35, No.1, April, 1995, p.1483. Steimle's source was Hodder's cataloging of the Norweb III sale, by Bowers and Merena, in October, 1987.

[457] Conclusions drawn after reading Steimle (1485.)

[458] Vlack, Robert A.. *Early American Coins*, p.21.

[459] Steimle (1484.)

[460] Goss, John. *Blaue's, The Grand Atlas of the 17th Century World*, published in cooperation with the Royal Geographic Society, London. New York, Barnes and Noble Books, 1997, pp.149-150. Also, Northwestern University Library collection of African maps (Chicago.) http://hdl.library.northwestern.edu/2166.DL/inu-afrmap-4268580-recto-ah. Accessed December 31, 2007.

[461] Powell, William S.. *The Proprietors of Carolina.* Raleigh, North Carolina, The Carolina Charter Tercentenary Commission, 1963. Reprinted by the State Department of Archives and History, pp.1-3.

[462] Steimle (1484.)

[463] Breen, C*omplete Encyclopedia of U.S. and Colonial Coins*, pp.32-34.

[464] Steimle (1487.) Regarding coining petitions, Steimle quotes C.P. Nettels 1934 work, *The Money Supply of the American Colonies Before 1720*, University of Wisconsin.

[465] Crosby (337.)

[466] Calligas, Eleni, ed.. Lobel, Richard, pub.. Davidson, Mark (hammered coinage) and Hailstone, Allen (milled coinage.) *Coincraft's 1999 Standard Catalogue of English and UK Coins 1066 to Date*. London, Coincraft, 1999, p.435, et al.

[467] Breen, C*omplete Encyclopedia of U.S. and Colonial Coins*, pp.32-34.

[468] *Ships of Bermuda – 1600's,* RootsWeb.com website, http://www.rootsweb.com/~bmuwgw/ships2.html. The site references *Memorials of the Bermudas* by J. H. Lefroy, p.740. Accessed June 13, 2006. The site refers to J. H. Lefroy, *Memorials of the Bermudas*, p.740.

[469] Breen, Walter. "North American Colonial Coinages Under the French Regime (1640-1763)" in *Studies on Money in Early America.* Edited by Newman, Eric P., ed., and Doty, Richard, associate editor. New York, The American Numismatic Society, 1976, pp. 43-74.

[470] Breen, "North American Colonial Coinages Under the French Regime (1640-1763,)" p.45.

[471] Breen, *Complete Encyclopedia of U.S. and Colonial Coins*, p.43.

[472] Breen, *Complete Encyclopedia of U.S. and Colonial Coins*, p.43.

[473] Breen, *Complete Encyclopedia of U.S. and Colonial Coins*, pp.46-47.

[474] Breen, *Complete Encyclopedia of U.S. and Colonial Coins*, p.43.
[475] Breen, "North American Colonial Coinages Under the French Regime (1640-1673,)" p.52.
[476] Breen, "North American Colonial Coinages Under the French Regime (1640-1673,)" p.55.
[477] Vlack, Robert A.. "The Billon Coinage of North America" in *The C4 Newsletter*, Volume 8, Number 2. The Colonial Coin Collectors Club, Inc., Summer, 2000, pp.18-28.
[478] Taylor (384.)
[479] Vlack, "The Billon Coinage of North America," pp.18-28.
[480] Breen, "North American Colonial Coinages Under the French Regime (1640-1673,)" pp.56-57.
[481] De Gramont (87-89.)
[482] Breen, "North American Colonial Coinages Under the French Regime (1640-1673,)" p.58.
[483] Arnold, Morris S.. *Colonial Arkansas 1686-1804: A Social and Cultural History*. Fayetteville, Arkansas, University of Arkansas Press, 1991, p.9.
[484] Breen, "North American Colonial Coinages Under the French Regime (1640-1673,)" p.58.
[485] Arnold (12-17.)
[486] Arnold (12-17.)
[487] Breen, "North American Colonial Coinages Under the French Regime (1640-1673,)" p.58.
[488] Hodder, Michael J.. "Law Resists Striking New Coinage Until Forced into Making Choices" in *Coin World*. Sidney, Ohio, Amos Press, March 27, 1995, p.68.
[489] Arnold (16.)
[490] Dahl. A similar line appears in the poem, "The Microbe," by Hilaire Belloc (1870-1953.)
[491] Breen, "North American Colonial Coinages Under the French Regime (1640-1673,)" p.62.
[492] Breen, "North American Colonial Coinages Under the French Regime (1640-1673,)" p.61.
[493] Breen, "North American Colonial Coinages Under the French Regime (1640-1673,)" p.59.
[494] Breen, *Complete Encyclopedia of U.S. and Colonial Coins*, p.44.
[495] Breen, "North American Colonial Coinages Under the French Regime (1640-1673,)" pp.63-65.
[496] Vlack, "The Billon Coinage of North America," p.20.
[497] Waselkov, Dr. Greg. Center for Archaeological Studies at the University of South Alabama, Personal correspondence and telephone conversation, December 23, 2003.
[498] Breen, *Complete Encyclopedia of U.S. and Colonial Coins*, p.47.
[499] Breen, "North American Colonial Coinages Under the French Regime (1640-1673,)" p.65.
[500] Breen, "North American Colonial Coinages Under the French Regime (1640-1673,)" pp.65-68.
[501] Breen, *Complete Encyclopedia of U.S. and Colonial Coins*, p.51.
[502] Vlack, "The Billon Coinage of North America," p.22.
[503] Vlack, "The Billon Coinage of North America," p.22.
[504] a.) Vlack, "The Billon Coinage of North America," p.25.
b.) Vlack, Robert A.. *An Illustrated Catalogue of the French Billon Coinage in the Americas*. Colonial Coin Collectors Club, 2004, pp.138-141.
[505] Breen, *Complete Encyclopedia of U.S. and Colonial Coins*, p.51
[506] Vlack, "The Billon Coinage of North America," p.26
[507] a.) Breen, *Complete Encyclopedia of U.S. and Colonial Coins*, p.44.
b.) Vlack, Robert A.. *An Illustrated Catalogue of the French Billon Coinage in the Americas*, pp.138-141.
[508] Breen, *Complete Encyclopedia of U.S. and Colonial Coins*, p.40.
[509] Crosby (346.)
[510] Kleeberg, John M.. "The New Yorke in America Token" in *Money of Pre-Federal America*, ed. by Kleeberg. Coinage of the Americas Conference, Proceedings no. 7. Held at the American Numismatic Society, May 4, 1991. New York: American Numismatic Society, 1992, pp.43-49.
[511] Breen, *Complete Encyclopedia of U.S. and Colonial Coins*, p.41.
[512] Kleeberg, "The New Yorke in America Token," pp. 15-57.
[513] Montgomery (62.)
[514] Billington, *Western Expansion, A History of the American Frontier*, pp.77-78.
[515] Quinn, Arthur. *A New World*. New York, Berkley Publishing Group, 1995. Originally published in Winchester, Massachusetts, by Faber and Faber, 1994, p.227.
[516] Kleeberg, "The New Yorke in America Token," p.24.
[517] O'Callaghan, Vol. III, p.234. Letter by Sir John Werden, Secretary to the Duke of York, to Governor Andros, September 15, 1675.

[518] Kleeberg, "The New Yorke in America Token," pp.30-31.
[519] Cantwell and Wall (20-21 and 30-31.)
[520] Kleeberg, "The New Yorke in America Token," pp.43-44.
[521] Crosby (347.)
[522] Taxay, Don. Ed. by Rose, Joseph H. and Hazelcorn, Howard. *The Comprehensive Catalogue and Encyclopedia of United States Coins*, second edition. New York, Scott Publishing Company, 1976, p.37.
[523] Breen, *Complete Encyclopedia of U.S. and Colonial Coins*, p.22.
[524] Crosby (145.)
[525] Breen, *Complete Encyclopedia of U.S. and Colonial Coins*, p.27.
[526] Breen, *Complete Encyclopedia of U.S. and Colonial Coins*, p.27.
[527] Crosby (145.)
[528] Crosby (151.)
[529] Crosby (151.)
[530] Breen, *Complete Encyclopedia of U.S. and Colonial Coins*, p.23.
[531] Crosby (152-160.)
[532] Hodder, Michael J., Stack's sale of the John J. Ford Collection, Part IX. New York, Stack's, May 10,2005, pp.43-44.
[533] Crosby (160,) et al.
[534] Breen, *Complete Encyclopedia of U.S. and Colonial Coins*, p.23.
[535] Hume, *In Search of This and That*, p.58
[536] Breen, *Complete Encyclopedia of U.S. and Colonial Coins*, pp.22-23.
[537] Crosby (166.)
[538] Danforth, Dr. Brian J.. "Wood's Money: Acceptance or Rejection in Ireland" in *The C4 Newsletter*, Fall 2000, v.8, no.8, p.19.
[539] Danforth, "Wood's Money: Acceptance or Rejection in Ireland," p.18.
[540] Danforth, "Wood's Money: Acceptance or Rejection in Ireland," p.21.
[541] Breen, *Complete Encyclopedia of U.S. and Colonial Coins*, p.27.
[542] Danforth, "Wood's Money: Acceptance or Rejection in Ireland," p.24.
[543] Danforth, "Wood's Money: Acceptance or Rejection in Ireland," pp.25,30.
[544] Crosby (160-161.)
[545] *Wolverhampton's Blue Plaques.* Wolverhampton History and Heritage Society. http://www.localhistory.scit.wlv.ac.uk/plaques/LichfieldStreet.htm, Accessed August 27, 2006.
[546] Danforth, "Wood's Money: Acceptance or Rejection in Ireland," pp.25,30.
[547] Hume, *In Search of This and That*, p.58.
[548] Danforth, "Wood's Money: Acceptance or Rejection in Ireland," p.31.
[549] Freidus, Daniel. *The History and Die Varieties of the Higley Coppers*, Proceedings of the Coinage of the Americas Conference, American Numismatic Society, New York, October 29, 1994, p.2.
[550] Mitchelson, Joseph C.. "The Higley Coppers," reprint from *The Numismatist,* (December, 1927) in *The American Numismatic Association Anthology*, edited by Carlson, Carl W. A. and Hodder, Michael J.. Published for the American Numismatic Association (Colorado Springs, Colorado,) by Bowers and Merena Galleries, Inc. (Wolfeboro, New Hampshire,) 1991, p.5.
[551] Lawson, Steven M. *Higley-Filer* [genealogy,] http://www.kinnexions.com/ancestries/higley.htm#JHigley, Accessed June 13, 2006.
[552] Freidus (4.)
[553] Breen, *Complete Encyclopedia of U.S. and Colonial Coins*, p.39.
[554] Lawson.
[555] Freidus (4.)
[556] Breen, *Complete Encyclopedia of U.S. and Colonial Coins*, p.39.
[557] Freidus (4.)
[558] Breen, *Complete Encyclopedia of U.S. and Colonial Coins*, p.39.
[559] Crosby (202-207.)
[560] Crosby (206.)
[561] Breen, *Complete Encyclopedia of U.S. and Colonial Coins*, p.39.
[562] Freidus (3-4.)
[563] Freidus (10.)
[564] Freidus (7-17.)

[565] Breen, *Complete Encyclopedia of U.S. and Colonial Coins*, p.40, et al.
[566] Liungman, Carl G.. *Dictionary of Symbols*. New York, W. W. Norton and Company, 1994. English translation of *Symboler – västerländska ideogram*. Originally published in Malmö, Sweden by Merkur International KB. Copyright 1991, Liungman, pp.41-44.
[567] Breen, *Complete Encyclopedia of U.S. and Colonial Coins*, p.40.
[568] Breen, *Complete Encyclopedia of U.S. and Colonial Coins*, p.40.
[569] Kleeberg, John M.. "Shipwreck of the Faithful Steward" in *Coinage of the American Confederation Period*, edited by Mossman, Dr. Philip L.. Proceedings no. 11 of the Coinage of the Americas Conference, held at the American Numismatic Society, October 28, 1995, New York: American Numismatic Society, 1996, p.68.
[570] Breen, *Complete Encyclopedia of U.S. and Colonial Coins*, pp.36-37.
[571] John Adams's letter was published in *Niles' Weekly Register*, Niles, Hezekiah, ed.. March 7, 1818 ed. (vol. XIV, no. 2.)
[572] Langguth (49.) Also, Alden (65, 68-78, et al.)
[573] From a print in the author's collection. Believed to be from an edition of *History of the United States*, published by Samuel Walker and Company of Boston, ca. 1870.
[574] Pitt, William. Published under "William Pitt's Defense of the American Colonies." Colonial Williamsburg, http://www.history.org/Almanack/life/politics/pitt.cfm. Originally published in HTML form by Dep. Alfa-Informatica, University of Groningen under the project, *The American Revolution*, 1995. Accessed September 24, 2005. Also, Langguth (85.)
[575] Langguth (85.)
[576] Miller, John C. (7.)
[577] Becker, Carl. "The Eve of the Revolution, A Chronicle of the Breach with England." Ithaca, New York, 1918, Ch.4, "Defining the Issue." Published at The History Carper website, http://www.historycarper.com/resources/teotr/chap4.htm. Accessed June 13, 2006.
[578] Mossman, *Money of the American Colonies and Confederation*, p.144.
[579] Breen, *Complete Encyclopedia of U.S. and Colonial Coins*, p.41.
[580] Alden (67.)
[581] Langguth (552.)
[582] Vlack, Robert A.. *An Illustrated Catalogue of the French Billon Coinage in the Americas*, pp.138-141.
[583] Breen, "North American Colonial Coinages Under the French Regime (1640-1673)," pp.73-74.
[584] Breen, *Complete Encyclopedia of U.S. and Colonial Coins*, pp.57-58.
[585] Breen, *Complete Encyclopedia of U.S. and Colonial Coins*, pp.57-58.
[586] Breen, "North American Colonial Coinages Under the French Regime (1640-1673)," pp.73-74.
[587] Collot, Georges-Henri-Victor. *Journey in North America, Containing a Survey of the Countries Watered by the Mississippi, Ohio, Missouri, and Other Affluing Rivers* [vol. 1]. From Collot, Victor. *A Journey in North America, Containing a Survey of the Countries Watered by the Mississippi, Ohio, Missouri, and Other Affluing Rivers; with Exact Observations on the Course and Soundings of These Rivers; and on the Towns, Villages, Hamlets and Farms of That Part of the New-World; Followed by Philosophical, Political, Military and Commercial Remarks and by a Projected Line of Frontiers and General Limits. Illustrated by 36 Maps, Plans, Views, and Divers Cuts.* Paris: Printed for Arthus Bertrand, 1826, vol. 1, pp.i-v. ; Online facsimile edition at www.americanjourneys.org/aj-088a/. Accessed September 28, 2003. Also, introductory material by The Wisconsin Historical Society, http://www.americanjourneys.org/aj-088a/summary/index.asp.
[588] Collot. Introductory material cited above.
[589] Hume, *In Search of This and That*, p.56
[590] Doty, *America's Money America's Story*, p.27.
[591] Scott, Carole E..
[592] Hume, *In Search of This and That*, p.59
[593] Hume, *In Search of This and That*, pp.59-61.
[594] Crosby (338-339.)
[595] Hume, *In Search of This and That*, p.61.
[596] Breen, *Complete Encyclopedia of U.S. and Colonial Coins*, p.60.
[597] Breen, *Complete Encyclopedia of U.S. and Colonial Coins*, p.60.
[598] Jordan, Louis. "State Patterns for Massachusetts and New Hampshire of 1776: Introduction" in *The Coins of Colonial and Early America*, http://www.coins.nd.edu/ColCoin/ColCoinIntros/Sp-Silver.intro.html. University of Notre Dame, Department of Special Collections, 1997 and following. Accessed September 23, 2005.
[599] Breen, *Complete Encyclopedia of U.S. and Colonial Coins*, p.59.

[600] Breen, *Complete Encyclopedia of U.S. and Colonial Coins*, p.59.
[601] Crosby (304.)
[602] Crosby (304.)
[603] Crosby (304.)
[604] Crosby (304.)
[605] Newman, Eric P.. *The 1776 Continental Currency Coinage and Varieties of the Fugio Cent*, New York, Sanford J. Durst, 1982, originally published by Wayte Raymond in 1952, p.1.
[606] Newman, *The 1776 Continental Currency Coinage and Varieties of the Fugio Cent*, p.2. Also, Breen, *Complete Encyclopedia of U.S. and Colonial Coins*, p.110.
[607] Newman, *The 1776 Continental Currency Coinage and Varieties of the Fugio Cent*, p.2.
[608] Breen, *Complete Encyclopedia of U.S. and Colonial Coins*, p.110.
[609] Mossman, *Money of the American Colonies and Confederation*, pp.150,152.
[610] Taxay, *The Comprehensive Catalogue and Encyclopedia of United States Coins*, p.197.
[611] Hodder, "The Continental Currency Coinage of 1776, A Trial Die and Metallic Emission Sequence" in *The American Numismatic Association Anthology*, edited by Carlson, Carl W. A. and Hodder, Michael J.. Published for the American Numismatic Association (Colorado Springs, Colorado,) by Bowers and Merena Galleries, Inc. (Wolfeboro, New Hampshire,) 1991, p. 7
[612] Giedroyc, Richard (quoting Newman.) "Continental Dollar Retains Air of Mystery" in *Coin World*, Sidney, Ohio, Amos Press, June 8, 1992, p.10.
[613] Newman, *The 1776 Continental Currency Coinage and Varieties of the Fugio Cent*, p.3.
[614] Classification schemes taken from Hodder, "The Continental Currency Coinage of 1776, A Trial Die and Metallic Emission Sequence," pp. 17-18. Also, Newman, *The 1776 Continental Currency Coinage and Varieties of the Fugio Cent*, pp.4-5.
[615]Hodder, "The Continental Currency Coinage of 1776, A Trial Die and Metallic Emission Sequence," pp.17-18.
[616] Spilman, James C. Personal email correspondence, May 14, 2005.
[617] Breen, *Complete Encyclopedia of U.S. and Colonial Coins*, p.110 and Crosby (305-306.)
[618] Olson, Lester C.. *Emblems of American Community in the Revolutionary Era*, Washington, DC, Smithsonian Institution Press, 1991, p.139.
[619] Olson (218.)
[620] Breen, *Complete Encyclopedia of U.S. and Colonial Coins*, pp.110-111.
[621] Breen, *Complete Encyclopedia of U.S. and Colonial Coins*, pp.111-112.
[622] Mossman, *Money of the American Colonies and Confederation*, p.151.
[623] Lorenzo, John. "The Rhode Island Ship Medal and Matthew Boulton" in *The C4 Newsletter*, vol. 5, no. 3, pp. 25-37, Fall 1997, pp.25-37.
[624] Tuchman (5.)
[625] Breen, *Complete Encyclopedia of U.S. and Colonial Coins*, p.125.
[626] Breen, *Complete Encyclopedia of U.S. and Colonial Coins*, p.125.
[627] Breen, *Complete Encyclopedia of U.S. and Colonial Coins*, p.126.
[628] Alden (345-347.)
[629] Crosby (367-368.)
[630] Anonymous pamphlet, *The First United States Coins, Unique 1783 Nova Constellatio Pattern Coinage Set*, Stacks, New York, ca.1995.
[631] Nuxoll (61.)
[632] Crosby (308.)
[633] *Journals of the Continental Congress, 1774-1789*, vol. 28, pp.354-358, May 13, 1785.
[634] Crosby (307-310.) Also, Breen, *Complete Encyclopedia of U.S. and Colonial Coins*, pp.113-114.
[635] Stacks, *The First United States Coins, Unique 1783 Nova Constellatio Pattern Coinage Set.*
[636] Crosby (309-311.)
[637] Stacks, *The First United States Coins, Unique 1783 Nova Constellatio Pattern Coinage Set.* Also, Taxay, Don. *The U.S. Mint and Coinage, An Illustrated History from 1776 to the Present.* New York, Arco Publishing Co.. Second printing, 1969, p.18.
[638] Stacks, *The First United States Coins, Unique 1783 Nova Constellatio Pattern Coinage Set.*
[639] Crosby (311.)
[640] Stacks, *The First United States Coins, Unique 1783 Nova Constellatio Pattern Coinage Set.*
[641] *Journals of the Continental Congress, 1774-1789*, vol. 28, pp.354-358, May 13, 1785.
[642] *Journals of the Continental Congress, 1774-1789*, vol. 28, pp.354-358, May 13, 1785.

[643] *Journals of the Continental Congress, 1774-1789*, vol. 28, pp.354-358, May 13, 1785.
[644] *Journals of the Continental Congress, 1774-1789*, vol. 28, pp.354-358, May 13, 1785.
[645] *Journals of the Continental Congress, 1774-1789*, vol. 29, p.500, July 6, 1785.
[646] Crosby (308.)
[647] Crosby (308.)
[648] Nuxoll (67-69.) Also, Newman, Eric P., "New Thoughts on the Nova Constellatio Private Copper Coinage" in *Coinage of the American Confederation Period*, ed. by Mossman, Philip. Proceedings no. 11 of the Coinage of the Americas Conference held at the American Numismatic Society, October 28, 1995, New York: American Numismatic Society, 1996, pp.94-95 and 101.
[649] Breen, *Complete Encyclopedia of U.S. and Colonial Coins*, p.114.
[650] Nuxoll (85-86.)
[651] Newman, "New Thoughts on the Nova Constellatio Private Copper Coinage," pp.97-101.
[652] Newman, "New Thoughts on the Nova Constellatio Private Copper Coinage," pp.84-99.
[653] Hodder, Michael J.. "More on Benjamin Dudley, Public Copper, Constellatio Novas and Fugio Cents" in *The Colonial Newsletter*, vol. 34, no. 2, June, 1994, pp.1442-1450.
[654] Nuxoll (70-71.)
[655] Ringo, Mike. "The Georgivs Triumpho Token" in *The Colonial Newsletter*, v.35, no.1, July 1995, pp.1515-1520.
[656] Breen, *Complete Encyclopedia of U.S. and Colonial Coins*, pp.117-118.
[657] Wiencek, Henry. *The Smithsonian Guide to Historic America: Virginia and the Capital Region*, New York, Stewart, Tabori and Chang, 1989, pp.263-265.
[658] Breen, *Complete Encyclopedia of U.S. and Colonial Coins*, p.100.
[659] Breen, *Complete Encyclopedia of U.S. and Colonial Coins*, p.100.
[660] Breen, *Complete Encyclopedia of U.S. and Colonial Coins*, pp.18-19.
[661] Ringo, "The Georgivs Triumpho Token," pp.1515-1520.
[662] Vlack, *Early American Coins*, p.105.
[663] Wierzba, Dennis. "A Georgivs Triumpho as the Undertype of a NJ 73-aa," *The C4 Newsletter*, vol. 7, number 2, Summer, 1999, p.15. Wierzba quotes a private correspondence from Hodder on January 9, 1999,
[664] Rinaldo, Tom, cataloger. *The Eighth Annual C-4 Convention Sale featuring the Jesse Patrick Collection of Connecticut Coppers*, McCawley and Grellman Auctions, November 16, 2002, lot no. 534.
[665] Wierzba, "A Georgivs Triumpho as the Undertype of a NJ 73-aa," pp.14-20.
[666] Fuld, George. "Coinage Featuring George Washington" in *Coinage of the American Confederation Period*, p.168.
[667] Stewart, Frank H.. *History of the United States Mint*, Lawrence, Massachusetts, Quarterman Publications, 1974. Originally published privately by Frank H. Stewart Electric Co., in 1924, p. 116.
[668] Stewart, *History of the United States Mint*, p.116.
[669] *Journals of the Continental Congress, 1774-1789*, v.29, pp.503-504, August 8, 1785.
[670] Bowers, *The History of United States Coinage as Illustrated by the Garrett Collection*, p.159.
[671] Hodder, Michael J.. "The Case Against Thomas Goadsby" in *The Colonial Newsletter*, August 1997, p.1706.
[672] Bowers, *The History of United States Coinage as Illustrated by the Garrett Collection*, pp.156-159.
[673] American Numismatic Rarities, LLC. *From Our Scrapbook*, http://anrcoins.com/ccArchiveMay05.aspx, May 23, 2005. Accessed November 25, 2005.
[674] Hodder, Michael J.. "Ephraim Brasher's 1786 Lima Style Doubloon" in *Money of Pre-Federal America*, ed. by Kleeberg, pp.141-143.
[675] Hodder, "Ephraim Brasher's 1786 Lima Style Doubloon," pp.144-151.
[676] Derived from Hodder, "Ephraim Brasher's 1786 Lima Style Doubloon," pp.144-151.
[677] Trudgen, Gary A.. "Samuel and James F. Atlee, Machin's Mills Partners" in *The Colonial Newsletter*, Huntsville, Alabama, The Colonial Newsletter Foundation, v.32, no. 3, October, 1992, pp.1318-1323.
[678] Trudgen, "Samuel and James F. Atlee, Machin's Mills Partners," p.1323.
[679] Trudgen, "Samuel and James F. Atlee, Machin's Mills Partners," p.1323.
[680] This question has been raised by numerous authors, including Louis Jordan, "James Falconer Atlee and Confederation Era Coppers" in *The Coins of Colonial and Early America*, http://www.coins.nd.edu/ColCoin/ColCoinIntros/Atlee.intro.html. University of Notre Dame, Department of Special Collections, 1997 and following. Accessed September 23, 2005.
[681] *Journals of the Continental Congress, 1774-1789*, v. 29, August 18, 1785, note on page 647.

[682] Trudgen, "Samuel and James F. Atlee, Machin's Mills Partners," p.1327.
[683] Breen, *Complete Encyclopedia of U.S. and Colonial Coins*, p.93.
[684] Breen, *Complete Encyclopedia of U.S. and Colonial Coins*, p.91.
[685] Bowers, *The History of United States Coinage as Illustrated by the Garrett Collection*, p.157.
[686] Breen, *Complete Encyclopedia of U.S. and Colonial Coins*, p.94.
[687] Williams, Irving G.. "George Clinton" in *World Book Encyclopedia*, Chicago, Field Enterprises Educational Corporation, v.4, 1967, p.525.
[688] Smith, Richard Norton (29.)
[689] Jordan, Louis. "Machin's Mills Imitation British Halfpence: Introduction" in *The Coins of Colonial and Early America*, http://www.coins.nd.edu/ColCoin/ColCoinIntros/Machin.intro.html.. University of Notre Dame, Department of Special Collections, 1997 and following. Accessed September 23, 2005.
[690] a.) Trudgen, Gary A.. Several works, most notably "James Atlee's Imitation British Halfpence" in *The Colonial Newsletter,* Huntsville, Alabama, The Colonial Newsletter Foundation, v.27, no.1, March 1987, pp.966-979.
b.) Updates by Jordan, Louis, "Imitation British Halfpence Associated with New York City – Introduction" in *The Coins of Colonial and Early America*, http://www.coins.nd.edu/ColCoin/ColCoinIntros/NYC-Vlack.intro.html. University of Notre Dame, Department of Special Collections, 1997 and following. Accessed September 23, 2005.
c.) Kleeberg, John "Reconstructing the Beach-Grünthal Hoard of Counterfeit Halfpence: The Montclair, New Jersey (1922) Hoard" in *American Journal of Numismatics*, vols. 7-8, New York, American Numismatic Society, 1997, pp.187-207.
d.) Also, see Mossman, *Money of the American Colonies and Confederation*.
[691] Trudgen and others. See previous reference.
[692] Rinaldo, Tom, cataloger. *Colonial Coin Collectors Club (C4,) Sixth Annual Convention Sale, Featuring the Albany Collection of Machins Mills Coinage*. Held in Boston on November 18, 2000. McCawley & Grellman Auctions, p.17, lot no.50. The piece described is a (1771) Vlack 2-71A struck over a (1774) Vlack 8-74A.
[693] Howes, Jack. Personal email correspondence, April 21, 2008.
[694] Newman, Eric P.. "A Recently Discovered Coin Solves a Vermont Numismatic Enigma" in *Centennial Publication*, Ingholt, Harald, ed.. New York, American Numismatic Society, 1958, pp.532-533.
[695] Jordan, "Imitation British Halfpence Associated with New York City – Introduction." Jordan comments on Trudgen's findings.
[696] Crosby (193-194.)
[697] Jordan, Louis, "Machin Mills Imitation British Halfpence: Introduction" in *The Coins of Colonial and Early America*, http://www.coins.nd.edu/ColCoin/ColCoinIntros/Machin.intro.html. University of Notre Dame, Department of Special Collections, 1997 and following. Accessed September 23, 2005. Jordan reprinted Thomas Machin, Jr.'s letter to Dr. F. B. Hough. The letter was first published in 1875 by E. M. Ruttenber, in a history of Newburgh.
[698] Crosby (191.)
[699] Gillispie, plate 205.
[700] Billington, *Westward Expansion*, pp.102-103.
[701] Billington, *Westward Expansion*, pp.102-103.
[702] Carlotto, Tony, *The Copper Coins of Vermont and Those Bearing the Vermont Name*, The Colonial Coin Collectors Club, printed by Bookcrafters, Chelsea, Michigan, 1998, p.21-25.
[703] Crosby (177-178.)
[704] Crosby (178.)
[705] Crosby (179.)
[706] Breen, *Complete Encyclopedia of U.S. and Colonial Coins*, pp.61-65.
[707] Carlotto (14-15.)
[708] Crosby (181.)
[709] Crosby (183-184.)
[710] Crosby (183.)
[711] Crosby (183.)
[712] Carlotto (103-104.)
[713] Carlotto (104.)
[714] Crosby (188-189.)
[715] Crosby (192-202.)

[716] Newman, Eric P.. "A Recently Discovered Coin Solves a Vermont Numismatic Enigma" in *Centennial Publication*, Ingholt, Harald, ed.. New York, American Numismatic Society, 1958, pp.532-533.
[717] Carlotto (186-190.)
[718] Carlotto (7-8.) Crosby (189-190) included a letter written by Julian Harmon, grandson of Rueben Harmon, Jr., in 1855. Julian Harmon wrote that his grandfather went to Ohio in 1800 and there was engaged in the salt business. Carlotto's chronology is more likely correct.
[719] Miller, Henry C.. *The State Coinage of Connecticut*, Originally published by the American Numismatic Society, New York, 1920. Reprinted by Sanford J. Durst, New York, 1981, p.1.
[720] Crosby (207.)
[721] Crosby (219-220.)
[722] Crosby (222.)
[723] Hodder, Michael J.. "Was an Automatic Planchet Feeder Used in New Haven in 1787?" in *The Colonial Newsletter*, July 1992, pp.1304-1305.
[724] Crosby (220.)
[725] Jordan, Louis, "Connecticut Coppers 1785-1788: Introduction" in *The Coins of Colonial and Early America*, http://www.coins.nd.edu/ColCoin/ColCoinIntros/CT-Copper.intro.html. University of Notre Dame, Department of Special Collections, 1997 and following. Accessed September 23, 2005.
[726] Crosby (207-208 and 222.)
[727] Jordan, "Connecticut Coppers 1785-1788: Introduction."
[728] Jordan, "Connecticut Coppers 1785-1788: Introduction."
[729] Breen, *Complete Encyclopedia of U.S. and Colonial Coins*, p.146.
[730] Breen, *Complete Encyclopedia of U.S. and Colonial Coins*, p.65.
[731] Breen, *Complete Encyclopedia of U.S. and Colonial Coins*, p.147.
[732] Crosby (221-224.)
[733] Breen, as related by Jordan in *Connecticut Coppers 1785-1788: Introduction.*
[734] Crosby (210-211.)
[735] Jordan, "Connecticut Coppers 1785-1788: Introduction."
[736] Breen, as referenced by Jordan in "Connecticut Coppers 1785-1788: Introduction."
[737] Mossman, as related by Jordan in "Connecticut Coppers 1785-1788: Introduction."
[738] Jordan, "Connecticut Coppers 1785-1788: Introduction."
[739] Mossman, *Money of the American Colonies and Confederation,* pp.174-175.
[740] Mossman, as referenced in Jordan, "Connecticut Coppers 1785-1788: Introduction."
[741] Mossman, *Money of the American Colonies and Confederation,* pp.175, 203-222.
[742] Trudgen, as reported by Jordan in "Connecticut Coppers 1785-1788: Introduction."
[743] Mossman, *Money of the American Colonies and Confederation,* p.181.
[744] Rinaldo, Tom, cataloger. *The John M. Griffee Sale of U.S. Colonial Coins, Held in Conjunction with the First Annual Convention of the Colonial Coin Collectors Club.* Presented by McCawley, Chris and Grellman, Bob on October 25, 1995, in Boston. McCawley and Grellman Auctions, p.7, text for lot no.13.
[745] Trudgen, Gary A.. "A Brief Look at the Life of Thomas Goadsby" in *The Colonial Newsletter*, Huntsville, Alabama, The Colonial Newsletter Foundation, vol. 32, no. 1, February, 1992, p.1285.
[746] Hodder, Michael J.. "The Case Against Thomas Goadsby" in *The Colonial Newsletter*, August 1997, pp.1701-1714.
[747] Crosby (275-276.)
[748] Crosby (276-277.)
[749] Breen, *Complete Encyclopedia of U.S. and Colonial Coins*, p.78.
[750] Breen, *Complete Encyclopedia of U.S. and Colonial Coins*, p.78.
[751] Crosby (280.)
[752] Crosby (282.)
[753] Jordan, Louis, "New Jersey Coppers 1786-1790: Introduction" in *The Coins of Colonial and Early America*, http://www.coins.nd.edu/ColCoin/ColCoinIntros/NJ-Copper.intro.html. University of Notre Dame, Department of Special Collections, 1997 and following. Revised September 10, 2003. Accessed September 23, 2005. Also, Breen, *Complete Encyclopedia of U.S. and Colonial Coins*, pp.78.
[754] Breen, *Complete Encyclopedia of U.S. and Colonial Coins*, p.78.
[755] Breen, *Complete Encyclopedia of U.S. and Colonial Coins*, p.78.
[756] Breen, *Complete Encyclopedia of U.S. and Colonial Coins*, p.79.

[757] Crosby (286-287.)
[758] Crosby (286-287.)
[759] Jordan, "New Jersey Coppers 1786-1790: Introduction."
[760] Jordan, "New Jersey Coppers 1786-1790: Introduction."
[761] Williams, Ray. Personal email correspondence, August 29, 2006. Roger Siboni is credited with discovering the initials on obverse 62.
[762] Breen, *Complete Encyclopedia of U.S. and Colonial Coins*, pp.79,86.
[763] Crosby (283.)
[764] Crosby (282.)
[765] Madigan, Thomas. Private discussion at the 2000 convention of C4, the Colonial Coin Collectors' Club, in Boston, Massachusetts, November 2000.
[766] Crosby (225-226.)
[767] Crosby (228.)
[768] Crosby (228.) Also, Brock.
[769] Crosby (229-239.)
[770] Crosby (232.)
[771] Crosby (241.)
[772] Breen, *Complete Encyclopedia of U.S. and Colonial Coins*, p.88.
[773] Jordan, Louis, "Massachusetts Coppers 1787-1788: Introduction" in *The Coins of Colonial and Early America*, http://www.coins.nd.edu/ColCoin/ColCoinIntros/MA-Copper.intro.html. University of Notre Dame, Department of Special Collections, 1997 and following. Accessed September 23, 2005.
[774] Mossman, *Money of the American Colonies and Confederation,* p.192.
[775] Breen, *Complete Encyclopedia of U.S. and Colonial Coins*, pp.87-88.
[776] Crosby (251.)
[777] Breen, *Complete Encyclopedia of U.S. and Colonial Coins*, p.87.
[778] Crosby (261-263.)
[779] Crosby (267.)
[780] Crosby (252.)
[781] The experts are Tom Rinaldo and Mike Packard. Rinaldo and Packard as quoted in the late Thomas Madigan's self-published booklet *Variety Checklist and Rarity Ratings for American Colonial Issues and States Coinages*, as of October 1998.
[782] Crosby (264-265.)
[783] Jordan, "Massachusetts Coppers 1787-1788: Introduction."
[784] Breen, *Complete Encyclopedia of U.S. and Colonial Coins*, p.120.
[785] Nuxoll (70.)
[786] Breen, *Complete Encyclopedia of U.S. and Colonial Coins*, p.120.
[787] Crosby (315) and Breen, *Complete Encyclopedia of U.S. and Colonial Coins*, pp.120-121.
[788] Hodder, Stack's auction of June 14-15, 1995 (The James W. Vannder Zanden Collection and Coins sold on behalf of Yale University,) Page 14, lot number 18.
[789] Breen, *Complete Encyclopedia of U.S. and Colonial Coins*, p.118.
[790] Selgin, George. *A Numismatic Ramble Through Old Birmingham*, Terry College of Business, University of Georgia, Athens, GA, April 2002, pp.21-22.
[791] Breen, *Complete Encyclopedia of U.S. and Colonial Coins*, p.119.
[792] Breen, *Complete Encyclopedia of U.S. and Colonial Coins*, p.123.
[793] Lorenzo, John and Moore, Roger. "The 1787 Immunis Columbia: A Late Rahway/Elizabethtown Product?" in *The C4 Newletter*, Vol. 5, No. 1, Spring, 1997, p.43.
[794] Breen, *Complete Encyclopedia of U.S. and Colonial Coins*, p.123.
[795] Lorenzo and Moore, pp.29-52.
[796] Lorenzo and Moore, pp.29-52.
[797] Ruck, Bill. "Marking the Land to Build a Nation" in *Journal of the Louisiana Purchase 2002 Base Line Expedition: Commemorating the First Survey of the American West*, edited by John P. Gill. Little Rock, Arkansas, Louisiana-Purchase Bicentennial Committee of Arkansas, 2004, p.7.
[798] a.) Billington, Ray Allen. "Americans Spread Out" in *Visiting Our Past: America's Historylands*, revised edition, ed. by Bennett, Ross. Washington, National Geographic Society, 1986, pp.191-192.
b.) "Ohio Company of Associates" in *Columbia Electronic Encyclopedia*, 6th ed., copyright 2004, Columbia University Press, www.infoplease.com/ce6/history/a0836450.html. Accessed July 12, 2004.

c.) "Scioto Company" article in *Ohio History Central: An Online Encyclopedia of Ohio History* Ohio Historical Society., http://www.ohiohistorycentral.org/entry.php?rec=982, 2005. Accessed June 11, 2006. Related links, on same site, to:
1.) "Manasseh Cutler," http://www.ohiohistorycentral.org/entry.php?rec=60;
2.) "William Duer," http://www.ohiohistorycentral.org/entry.php?rec=107;
3.) "Ohio Company of Associates," http://www.ohiohistorycentral.org/entry.php?rec=945;
4.) "French Grant," http://www.ohiohistorycentral.org/entry.php?rec=721;
5.) "William Playfair," http://www.ohiohistorycentral.org/entry.php?rec=304.

[799] Crosby (297-298.)

[800] Crosby (297-298.)

[801] Breen, *Complete Encyclopedia of U.S. and Colonial Coins*, p.146.

[802] Crosby (299.)

[803] Breen, *Complete Encyclopedia of U.S. and Colonial Coins*, p.147.

[804] Breen, *Complete Encyclopedia of U.S. and Colonial Coins*, p.147.

[805] Breen....

[806] Madigan, *Variety Checklist and Rarity Ratings for American Colonial Issues and States Coinages.*

[807] Breen, *Complete Encyclopedia of U.S. and Colonial Coins*, p.100.

[808] Ehrenreich, Thomas. Railroad Extra website, "Baltimore & Ohio Railroad," under "Early Railroading," under "Stories, General Railroading and Civil Engineering." Online publication of *The Baltimore American* (newspaper,) July 7, 1828 issue, at http://www.catskillarchive.com/rrextra/abbon.html. Accessed June 13, 2006.

[809] Dane, William B., editor. *The Merchant's Magazine and Commercial Review*. New York. Volume 46, January-June, 1862, p.592.

[810] Smith, Ellen Hart. *Charles Carroll of Carrollton*. Cambridge, Massachusetts, Harvard University Press, 1945, p.306.

[811] Smith, Richard Norton (89-95.)

[812] Discovered by Chris Stevens and reported to the Colonial Coins Yahoo discussion forum on December 10, 2000, message no. 2559. Stevens' discovery was reported in *The E-Sylum*: Volume 3, Number 52, December 17, 2000, by the editor, Wayne Homren, Numismatic Bibliomania Society. The article is titled "Washington Funeral Medal Info Found."

[813] Breen, *Complete Encyclopedia of U.S. and Colonial Coins*, p.137.

[814] Fuld (174.)

[815] Fuld (174.)

[816] Newman, Eric P.. "George Washington's Unique 1792 Pattern in Gold" in *Studies on Money in Early America.* Newman, Eric P., ed., and Doty, Richard, assoc. ed. New York, The American Numismatic Society, 1976, pp.199-208.

[817] Fuld (192) references Newman and Breen.

[818] Fuld (198.)

[819] Breen, *Complete Encyclopedia of U.S. and Colonial Coins*, p.140.

[820] Taxay, *The Comprehensive Catalogue and Encyclopedia of United States Coins,* p.197.

[821] Taxay, *The Comprehensive Catalogue and Encyclopedia of United States Coins,* p.197.

[822] Fuld (183-184.)

[823] Breen, *Complete Encyclopedia of U.S. and Colonial Coins*, pp.152-153. Also, Fuld (184-185.)

[824] Fuld (185-189.)

[825] Fuld (189.)

[826] Selgin (13.)

[827] Breen, *Complete Encyclopedia of U.S. and Colonial Coins*, p.141.

[828] Selgin (13.)

[829] Taxay, *The Comprehensive Catalogue and Encyclopedia of United States Coins,* pp.44-45.

[830] Fuld (219-225.)

[831] Fuld (224-225)

[832] Breen, *Complete Encyclopedia of U.S. and Colonial Coins*, p.126.

[833] Breen, *Complete Encyclopedia of U.S. and Colonial Coins*, p.127-128.

[834] Crosby (335.)

[835] Pietra, Angel. "The Mott Token Revisited" in *The C4 Newsletter*, Vol. 6, No. 3, Fall, 1998, pp.25-43.

[836] Pietra, "The Mott Token Revisited," p.38.

---

[837] Pietra, "The Mott Token Revisited," pp.35-36.
[838] Breen, *Complete Encyclopedia of U.S. and Colonial Coins*, pp.101-102.
[839] Pietra, "The Mott Token Revisited," p.27.
[840] Breen, *Complete Encyclopedia of U.S. and Colonial Coins*, p.102.
[841] Breen, *Complete Encyclopedia of U.S. and Colonial Coins*, pp.128-129. Also, Taxay, *The Comprehensive Catalogue and Encyclopedia of United States Coins*, p.34.
[842] Bowers, *The History United States Coinage as Illustrated by the Garrett Collection*, pp.164-165.
[843] Cohen, Roger S., Munson, Paul, Jr.. and Munde, Ray. *American Half Cents, the Little Half Sisters*. Self-published in Bethesda, Maryland, 1971. Also, Arlington, Virginia; Wigglesworth and Ghatt, 1982. 1982 edition, p.24. Also, Breen, *Complete Encyclopedia of U.S. and Colonial Coins*, pp.163.
[844] Van Doren (53.)
[845] Van Droen (54.)
[846] Van Doren (53-55.)
[847] Breen, *Complete Encyclopedia of U.S. and Colonial Coins*, p.130.
[848] Breen, *Complete Encyclopedia of U.S. and Colonial Coins*, p.130.
[849] Breen, *Complete Encyclopedia of U.S. and Colonial Coins*, p.130.
[850] Breen, *Complete Encyclopedia of U.S. and Colonial Coins*, pp.105-106. Also, Pietra, Angel. "The History of the Castorland Settlement: Is the Castorland Jeton a 'Jetton de presence' or a coin?" in *The C4 Newsletter*, v.5, No.1, Spring, 1997, pp.15-29.
[851] Breen, *Complete Encyclopedia of U.S. and Colonial Coins*, pp.105-106.
[852] Breen, *Complete Encyclopedia of U.S. and Colonial Coins*, pp.105-106.
[853] Breen, *Complete Encyclopedia of U.S. and Colonial Coins*, pp.105-106.
[854] Breen, *Complete Encyclopedia of U.S. and Colonial Coins*, pp.105-106.
[855] Taxay, *The Comprehensive Catalogue and Encyclopedia of United States Coins*, p.37.
[856] Taxay, *The Comprehensive Catalogue and Encyclopedia of United States Coins*, p.37.
[857] Taxay, *The Comprehensive Catalogue and Encyclopedia of United States Coins*, p.37.
[858] League of American Theatres and Producers. *Internet Broadway Database*. "Park Theatre," www.ibdb.com/venue.asp?id=1554#Park%20Theatre1799, copyright 2001-2006. Accessed June 11, 2006. Also, Forgotten NY. "the [sic] alleys of lower Manhattan," *http://www.forgotten-ny.com/Alleys/LOWER%20MANHATTAN/lower.html*. Accessed June 11, 2006. Sources cited: 1.) Santé, Luc. *Low Life*, Vintage, 1992; 2.) Moscow, Henry Moscow. *The Street Book*. Hagstrom, 1978; 3.) Dunshee, Kenneth. *As You Pass By*. Hastings House, 1952.
[859] League of American Theatres and Producers and Forgotten NY websites.
[860] Columbia Electronic Encyclopedia, The. "Dunlap, William." *Bartlesby.Com* website, www.bartlesby.com/65/du/Dunlap-W.html, 6th ed., copyright 2001, Columbia University Press. Accessed June 13, 2006.
[861] Santé, Luc, *Low Life*, as quoted on the Forgotten NY website.
[862] Guth, Ron. "New York Theatre Token." Coinfacts.com website, http://www.coinfacts.com/colonial_coins/new_york_theater_tokens/new_york_theatre_penny.htm. Accessed September 24, 2005.
[863] League of American Theatres and Producers website.
[864] Kleeberg, John M.. "The Theatre at New York" in *The Token: America's Other Money*, edited by Doty, Richard G.. Proceedings no. 10 of the Coinage of the Americas Conference, held at the American Numismatic Society, October 29, 1994. New York, American Numismatic Society, 1995, pp.19-64.
[865] Billington, *Westward Expansion*, pp.358-365. Also, Nardini, Louis Raphael, Sr.. *My Historic Natchitoches, Louisiana and its Environment: A History of Natchitoches, Louisiana and the Neutral Strip area of the State of Louisiana and its Inhabitants*. Hemphill, Texas, Dogwood Press, 2004. Originally published by Nardini Publishing Company, 1963, pp.29-30, et al.
[866] Billington, *Westward Expansion*, pp.358-365.
[867] Breen, *Complete Encyclopedia of U.S. and Colonial Coins*, p.308.
[868] Breen, *Complete Encyclopedia of U.S. and Colonial Coins*, p.308.
[869] Billington, *Westward Expansion*, pp.380-383.
[870] Billington, *Westward Expansion*, pp.380-383.
[871] Bowers, *The History United States Coinage as Illustrated by the Garrett Collection*, p.165.
[872] Bowers, *The History United States Coinage as Illustrated by the Garrett Collection*, p.165.
[873] Hothem (237.)
[874] Billington, *Westward Expansion*, pp.431-452.

[875] Trudgen, Gary A.. "Gilfoil's Coppers," *The Colonial Newsletter*. Edited by Spilman, Jim. Huntsville, Alabama, The Colonial Newsletter Foundation, v.27, no.2, July 1987, pp.997-1000.

[876] Anton, William T., Jr., and Kesse, Bruce. *The Forgotten Coins of the North American Colonies*. Iola, Wisconsin, Krause Publications, 1992, p.15.

[877] Anton and Kesse (14-16.)

[878] Charlton, James E.. *1963 Standard Catalogue of Canadian Coins, Tokens and Paper Money,* 11th edition. Published in Toronto, by the author and distributed in the U.S. by Whitman Publishing, 1962, p.18.

[879] Breen, *Complete Encyclopedia of U.S. and Colonial Coins*, p.621.

[880] Breen, *Complete Encyclopedia of U.S. and Colonial Coins*, p.624. Also, Bressett, Kenneth E.. *Collectible American Coins*. Lincolnwood, Illinois, Publications International, Ltd., 1991, pp.101-102.

[881] Breen, *Complete Encyclopedia of U.S. and Colonial Coins*, p.621.

[882] Bressett, *Collectible American Coins*, p.101.

[883] Breen, *Complete Encyclopedia of U.S. and Colonial Coins*, pp.621-623.

[884] Breen, *Complete Encyclopedia of U.S. and Colonial Coins*, pp.621-623.

[885] Breen, *Complete Encyclopedia of U.S. and Colonial Coins*, p.624.

[886] Breen, *Complete Encyclopedia of U.S. and Colonial Coins*, pp.621-624.

[887] Rulau, Russell. *Standard Catalog of U.S. Tokens 1700-1900*, Iola, Wisconsin, 1994, pp.48-49.

[888] Wierzba, Dennis. "W. WOART JUS PACIS Massachusetts Tradesman's Token" in *The Colonial Newsletter*, v.34, no.3, November, 1994, p.1456. First reported by William Anton in 1987. Also, Stack's Mail Bid Sale, February 10, 1993, lot 2020. Also, Rulau, *Standard Catalog of U.S. Tokens 1700-1900*, p.25.

[889] Rulau, *Standard Catalog of United States Tokens 1700-1900*, pp.40-41.

[890] Breen, *Complete Encyclopedia of U.S. and Colonial Coins*, p.672.

[891] a.) Rulau, *Standard Catalog of United States Tokens 1700-1900*, pp.109-110.
b.) Bressett, *Collectable American Coins*, pp.98-99.
c.) Bowers, *The History of United States Coinage as Illustrated by the Garrett Collection*, pp.408-409.

[892] Rulau, *Standard Catalog of United States Tokens 1700-1900*, p.69. Rulau quotes the *Albany Argus*, October 1, 1842, as saying that liberty was threatened by "...the union of the purse and the sword in the same hands."

[893] Rulau, *Standard Catalog of United States Tokens 1700-1900*, pp.69-70 and 75.

[894] Rulau, *Standard Catalog of United States Tokens 1700-1900*, pp.69-70.

[895] Rulau, *Standard Catalog of United States Tokens 1700-1900*, pp.69-70, et al.

[896] Rulau, *Standard Catalog of United States Tokens 1700-1900*, p.80. Also, Bressett, *Collectable American Coins*, p.97. Others.

[897] James, Marquis. *The Life of Andrew Jackson*. Indianapolis, The Bobbs-Merrill Company, 1938, pp.65-66. Also, Remini, Robert V.. *The Life of Andrew Jackson,* New York, Penguin Books, 1990, p.223.

[898] James, Marquis. Andrew Jackson, *Portrait of a President*. Indianapolis, The Bobbs-Merrill Company, 1937, pp.224-226. Others.

[899] Unger, Harlow Giles. *Lafayette*. Hoboken, New Jersey, John Wiley and Sons, 2002, pp.356-358 and 379-380. Also, Rulau, *Standard Catalog of United States Tokens 1700-1900*, p.99.

[900] Rulau, *Standard Catalog of United States Tokens 1700-1900*, pp.95-96.

[901] *Public Statutes at Large of the United States of America*, First Congress, Session III, March 3, 1791, vol.1, p.225. Also, Fenno, John, ed.. *Gazette of the United States* (newspaper.) Philadelphia, April 16, 1791, back page.

[902] Hamilton, Alexander. "Report of the Secretary of the Treasury on the Subject of a Mint." Originally published in Philadelphia by William Young, in the March, 1791 (pp.189-201) and April, 1791 (pp.263-268) editions of *The Universal Asylum and Columbian Magazine*. Full text available online, the CoinFacts website at http://www.coinfacts.com/mint_history/mint_history_1781_1791/. Accessed September 5, 2006.

[903] Taxay, *The U.S. Mint and Coinage*, pp.45-47.

[904] Breen, *Complete Encyclopedia of U.S. and Colonial Coins*, p.152

[905] Taxay, Don. *The U.S. Mint and Coinage, An Illustrated History from 1776 to the Present*. New York, Arco Publishing Co.. Second printing, 1969, p.57.

[906] Taxay, *The U.S. Mint and Coinage*, pp.49-50 and 66.

[907] Nuxoll (71-72.)

[908] Bedini, Silvio A.. "Rittenhouse, David," *American National Biography Online*, February, 2000. http://www.anb.org/articles/13/13-01396.html. Copyright American Council of Learned Societies, 2000. Published by Oxford University Press. Accessed August 30, 2006.

[909] Breen, *Complete Encyclopedia of U.S. and Colonial Coins*, p.153.

---

910 Bedini, Silvio A.. "History Corner: Henry Voigt" in *Professional Surveyor Magazine*, October, 1997, v.17, no.7. Viewed online at http://www.profsurv.com/archive.php?issue=18&article=207. Accessed August 30, 2006.

911 a.) Stewart, Frank H.. *History of the United States Mint*, Lawrence, Massachusetts, Quarterman Publications, 1974. Originally published privately by Frank H. Stewart Electric Co., 1924, pp.91-92.
b.) Taxay, *The U.S. Mint and Coinage*, p.104.
c.) *The History of United States Coinage as Illustrated by the Garrett Collection*, p.192.

912 Taxay, *The U.S. Mint and Coinage*, p.96. Also, Sheldon, William H.. *Early American Cents*, New York, Harper and Brothers, 1949, pp.14-15.

913 Taxay, *The U. S. Mint and Coinage*, p.73.

914 Goodwin (125.)

915 Heritage Auction Galleries, *Central States Numismatic Society Signature Auction,* auction no. 404. Description of auction no.404, lot no.1860, at http://coins.heritageauctions.com/common/view_item.php?Sale_No=404&Lot_No=1860. Accessed September 3, 2006. The article refers to a study by Herkowitz, Carl and Orosz, Joel J. ("George Washington and America's 'Small Beginning' in Coinage: The Fabled 1792 Half Dismes," in the 2003 edition of *American Journal of Numismatics*, Second Series 15, American Numismatic Society, published 2004, pp.111-156.) and work done by Karl Moulton (to be published under the title, *Henry Voigt and Others Involved with America's Early Coinage*.) The contents of the note, which was mistakenly attributed to Dr. Jonas McClintock because it is signed "...J Mc," can be found in *Taxay, The U. S. Mint and Coinage*, p.72.

916 Orosz and Herkowitz, with input from Newman, as referenced by Heritage Auction Gallery, auction no. 404, lot 1860.

917 Breen, *Complete Encyclopedia of U.S. and Colonial Coins*, pp.153-155.

918 Bowers, *The History of United States Coinage as Illustrated by the Garrett Collection*, p.183, quoting an advertisement found by Taxay.

919 Breen, *Complete Encyclopedia of U.S. and Colonial Coins*, pp.153-155. Also, Orosz and Herkowitz, as referenced by Heritage Auction Gallery, auction no.404, lot 1860.

920 Crosby (363-364.) Also, Moulton, as referenced by Heritage Auction Gallery, auction no.404, lot 1860. See note above.

921 Breen, *Complete Encyclopedia of U.S. and Colonial Coins*, pp.153-155.

922 Moulton, as referenced by Heritage Auction Gallery, auction no.404, lot 1860. See note above.

923 Washington, as quoted by Taxay in *The U.S. Mint and Coinage*, p.73. Many others.

924 Bowers, *The History of United States Coinage*, p.182.

925 Taxay, *The U. S. Mint and Coinage*, p.71.

926 Stewart, *History of the United States Mint*, pp.22-25.

927 Sheldon (14-15.) Also, Taxay, *The U. S. Mint and Coinage*, p.72.

928 Stewart, *History of the United States Mint*, p.76.

929 Taxay, *The U. S. Mint and Coinage*, p. 71.

930 Evans, George G.. *Illustrated History of the United States Mint.* Self-published in Philadelphia, 1889, p.13.

931 Bowers, *The History of United States Coinage as Illustrated by the Garrett Collection*, p.182. Also, Judd, J. Hewitt, M.D.. *United States Pattern, Experimental and Trial Pieces*, 4th ed., Racine Wisconsin, Western Publishing Company, Inc., 1970, p.10.

932 Breen, *Complete Encyclopedia of U.S. and Colonial Coins*, pp.152-157.

933 Judd (10.)

934 Stewart, *History of the United States Mint,* p.76.

935 Judd (10.)

936 Breen, *Complete Encyclopedia of U.S. and Colonial Coins*, p.154.

937 Breen, *Complete Encyclopedia of U.S. and Colonial Coins*, pp.152-157.

938 a.) Taxay, *The U. S. Mint and Coinage*, p.104.
b.) Breen, *Complete Encyclopedia of U.S. and Colonial Coins*, p.177.
c,) Bowers, *The History of United States Coinage as Illustrated by the Garrett Collection*, p.236. Bowers gives the source as *The Argus*, published in Boston, March 25, 1793.

939 Breen, *Complete Encyclopedia of U.S. and Colonial Coins*, p.177.

940 Stewart, *History of the United States Mint*, p.106. Stewart provided the text of the letter, which was written by Carlisle Pollack to a General Williams on January 25, 1796.

941 Breen, *Complete Encyclopedia of U.S. and Colonial Coins*, p.177.

942 *Public Statutes at Large of the United States*, Second Congress, Session II, chapter 2, vol. 1, p. 299.

---

943 Breen, *Complete Encyclopedia of U.S. and Colonial Coins*, p.179.
944 Breen, *Complete Encyclopedia of U.S. and Colonial Coins*, p.179.
945 Sheldon (70-72.)
946 John Kleeberg's 1996 C.O.A.C. comments as described in American Numismatic Society Newsletter. American Numismatic Society. "Museum News" in *American Numismatic Society Newsletter*, no.72, Fall 1996. ANS website, http://www.numismatics.org/newsletter/fall96/museumnw.htm. Accessed November 27, 2006.
947 Cohen, Munson and Munde (5.)
948 Cohen, Munson and Munde (1-2.)
949 Stabl, Alan M.. "Medals of the Comitia Americana Series in the Collections of the American Numismatic Society and Other Public Institutions" *Coinage of the American Confederation Period*, edited by Mossman, Dr. Philip L.. Proceedings no. 11 of the Coinage of the Americas Conference, held at the American Numismatic Society, October 28, 1995. New York, American Numismatic Society, 1996, pp.329-332.
950 Taxay, *The U.S. Mint and Coinage*, pp.105-106.
951 Breen, *Complete Encyclopedia of U.S. and Colonial Coins*, pp.181-187.
952 Breen, *Complete Encyclopedia of U.S. and Colonial Coins*, p.186.
953 Breen, *Complete Encyclopedia of U.S. and Colonial Coins*, p.186.
954 Breen, *Complete Encyclopedia of U.S. and Colonial Coins*, p.186.
955 Stewart, *History of the United States Mint*, p.93. Also, Breen, *Complete Encyclopedia of U.S. and Colonial Coins*, pp.181-187.
956 a.) Taxay, *The U.S. Mint and Coinage*, pp.123-124.
b.) Bowers, *A History of United States Coinage as Illustrated by the Garrett Collection*, p.186.
c.) Stewart, History of the United States Mint, p.104.
957 Breen, Walter. "Philadelphia's Original flying Disks: Early American Coppers – Blanks, Sources, identifying Marks" in *The American Numismatic Association Anthology*. Carlson, W. A. and Hodder, Michael J., editors. Published for the American Numismatic Association (Colorado Springs, Colorado,) by Bowers and Merena Galleries, Inc. (Wolfeboro, New Hampshire,) 1991, pp.35-37.
958 Bowers, *A History of United States Coinage*, p.182. Also, Sheldon (12) and others.
959 Breen, *Complete Encyclopedia of U.S. and Colonial Coins*, p.423.
960 Breen, *Complete Encyclopedia of U.S. and Colonial Coins*, p.423.
961 Taxay, *The U.S. Mint and Coinage*, p.123.
962 Breen, *Complete Encyclopedia of U.S. and Colonial Coins*, p.374.
963 Stewart, *History of the United States Mint*, p.106.
964 Breen, *Complete Encyclopedia of U.S. and Colonial Coins*, p.276.
965 Breen, *Complete Encyclopedia of U.S. and Colonial Coins*, p.423.
966 Wilson, James Grant; Fiske, John; and Klos, Stanley L., editors. "Henry William De Saussure" in *Appleton's Cyclopedia of American Biography*, New York, D. Appleton and Company, 1887-1889 and 1999. Copyrighted in 2000 by StanKlos.com at the website http://virtualology.com/aphenrywilliamsdesaussure/. Accessed September 15, 2006.
967 Wilson, Fiske and Klos, "Henry William De Saussure."
968 Breen, *Complete Encyclopedia of U.S. and Colonial Coins*, p.512.
969 Breen, *Complete Encyclopedia of U.S. and Colonial Coins*, p.425.
970 Breen, *Complete Encyclopedia of U.S. and Colonial Coins*, p.425.
971 Wilson, Fiske and Klos, "Henry William De Saussure."
972 Henderson, H. James. "Elias Boudinot." *American National Biography Online*, http://www.anb.org/articles/02/02-00037.html, February 2000. Accessed September 10, 2006.
973 Breen, "Philadelphia's Original Flying Disks: Early American Coppers – Blanks, Sources, identifying Marks," p.35.
974 Cohen (24.)
975 Taxay, *The U.S. Mint and Coinage*, pp.132-134.
976 Stewart, *History of the United States Mint*, pp.63-64.
977 Taxay, *The U. S. Mint and Coinage*, pp.115-118. Also, Stewart, *History of the United States Mint*, pp.127-133.
978 Taxay, *The U. S. Mint and Coinage*, pp.115-118. Also, Stewart, *History of the United States Mint*, pp.127-133.
979 Breen, *Complete Encyclopedia of U.S. and Colonial Coins*, pp.337-338.

[980] Breen, *Complete Encyclopedia of U.S. and Colonial Coins*, pp.514-515.
[981] Breen, *Complete Encyclopedia of U.S. and Colonial Coins*, p.189.
[982] Breen, *Complete Encyclopedia of U.S. and Colonial Coins*, p.189.
[983] Breen, *Complete Encyclopedia of U.S. and Colonial Coins*, p.189.
[984] Henderson.
[985] Wilson, James Grant; Fiske, John; and Klos, Stanley L., editors. "Robert Patterson" in *Appleton's Cyclopedia of American Biography*, New York, D. Appleton and Company, 1887-1889 and 1999. Copyrighted in 2000 by StanKlos.com at the website http://virtualology.com/aprobertpatterson/. Accessed September 15, 2006.
[986] Taxay, *The U.S. Mint and Coinage*, p.107-109. Also, Breen, *Complete Encyclopedia of U.S. and Colonial Coins*, p.380.
[987] Breen, *Complete Encyclopedia of U.S. and Colonial Coins*, p.380.
[988] Breen, *Complete Encyclopedia of U.S. and Colonial Coins*, pp.518-519.
[989] Breen, *Complete Encyclopedia of U.S. and Colonial Coins*, p.518.
[990] Breen, *Complete Encyclopedia of U.S. and Colonial Coins*, p.199.
[991] Breen, *Complete Encyclopedia of U.S. and Colonial Coins*, p.200.
[992] Breen, *Complete Encyclopedia of U.S. and Colonial Coins*, p.199. Also, Bowers, *A History of United States Coinage As Illustrated by the Garrett Collection, p.*233.
[993] Robert Patterson in letters to Presidents Madison and Monroe, quoted by Bowers in *A History of United States Coinage As Illustrated by the Garrett Collection*, pp.201-203.
[994] Julian, R.W.. "The Philadelphia Mint and Coinage of 1814-1816" in *The American Numismatic Association Anthology*. Carlson, W. A. and Hodder, Michael J. editors. Published for the American Numismatic Association (Colorado Springs, Colorado,) by Bowers and Merena Galleries, Inc. (Wolfeboro, New Hampshire,) 1991, p.54.
[995] Breen, *Complete Encyclopedia of U.S. and Colonial Coins*, pp.169 and 201-203.
[996] Breen, *Complete Encyclopedia of U.S. and Colonial Coins*, pp.201-203.
[997] Taxay, *The U.S. Mint and Coinage*, pp.101-102.
[998] Bowers, *A History of United States Coinage As Illustrated by the Garrett Collection, p.236*. Also, Breen, *Complete Encyclopedia of U.S. and Colonial Coins*, pp.171-172.
[999] Bowers, *A History of United States Coinage As Illustrated by the Garrett Collection, pp.*204-209.
[1000] Breen, *Complete Encyclopedia of U.S. and Colonial Coins*, pp.490-491.
[1001] Bowers, *The History of United States Coinage*, p.209. Also, Taxay, *The U.S. Mint and Coinage*, p.109.
[1002] Wilson, Fiske and Klos, "Robert Patterson."
[1003] Bowers, *The History of United States Coinage*, pp.203-204. Also, Taxay, *The U.S. Mint and Coinage*, pp.170-171.
[1004] *America's Smithsonian: Celebrating 150 Years*, p.xiv. Also, Breen, *Complete Encyclopedia of U.S. and Colonial Coins*, p.433.
[1005] Breen, *Complete Encyclopedia of U.S. and Colonial Coins*, p.210.
[1006] Taxay, *The U.S. Mint and Coinage*, pp.166-168.
[1007] Taxay, *The U.S. Mint and Coinage*, pp.150-161.
[1008] Clain-Steffanelli, Elvira Eliza. "From the Drawing Board of a Coin-Engraver" in *The American Numismatic Association Anthology*. Carlson, W. A. and Hodder, Michael J. editors. Published for the American Numismatic Association (Colorado Springs, Colorado,) by Bowers and Merena Galleries, Inc. (Wolfeboro, New Hampshire,) 1991, pp.79-82.
[1009] Clain-Stefanelli, Elvira Eliza, pp.79-82.
[1010] a.) Breen, *Complete Encyclopedia of U.S. and Colonial Coins*, p.433.
b.) Bressett, *Collectable American Coins*, p.142.
c.) Taxay, *The U.S. Mint and Coinage*, pp.170-176.
[1011] a.) Breen, *Complete Encyclopedia of U.S. and Colonial Coins*, pp.433-436.
b.) Others, including Bressett, *Collectable American Coins*, pp.133-135 and
c.) Taxay, *The U.S. Mint and Coinage*, pp.170-176.
[1012] Stewart, *History of the United States Mint*, p.122.
[1013] Forbes, Esther. *Paul Revere and the World He Lived In*, Boston, Houghton Mifflin, 1942, pp.376-379, et al.
[1014] United States Continental Congress, *Journals of the Continental Congress, 1774-1789*, vols.2-14. Also, Newman, *Early Paper Money of America*, pp.58-69.